Guide to
Schools and Departments
of Religion and Seminaries
in the
United States and Canada

DEGREE PROGRAMS IN RELIGIOUS STUDIES

Guide to
Schools and Departments
of Religion and Seminaries
in the
United States and Canada

DEGREE PROGRAMS IN RELIGIOUS STUDIES

Compiled by
Modoc Press, Inc.

MACMILLAN PUBLISHING COMPANY
A Division of Macmillan, Inc.
New York

COLLIER MACMILLAN PUBLISHERS
London

Macmillan Publishing Company
A Division of Macmillan, Inc.
866 Third Avenue, New York, NY 10022

Collier Macmillan Canada, Inc.

Library of Congress Catalog Card Number: 86-21751

Printed in the United States of America

printing number
1   2   3   4   5   6   7   8   9   10

Library of Congress Cataloging in Publication Data

Guide to schools and departments of religion and
   seminaries in the United States and Canada.

     Includes index.
     1. Theological seminaries—United States—
Directories.   2. Theological seminaries—Canada—
Directories.   3. Bible colleges—United States—
Directories.   4. Bible colleges—Canada—Directories.
5. Religion—Study and teaching—United States—
Directories.   6. Religion—Study and teaching—
Canada—Directories.   I. Modoc Press.
BV4030.G85   1986   200'.7'1173   86-21751
ISBN 0-02-921650-8

Dedicated to the Memory
of

Reverend William Charles Burgess
1870-1944
Christian Church (Disciples of Christ)
Beattyville, Kentucky

and

Reverend Boothe Colwell Davis
1863-1942
Seventh Day Baptist
Alfred, New York

CONTENTS

ACKNOWLEDGMENT

Appreciation is extended to the institutions listed herein for their co-operation in completing questionnaires and responding to inquiries. In most cases, particularly in the general descriptions and degree program requirements, the words are their own.

INTRODUCTION

This *Guide* is intended as a source of information about postsecondary educational institutions in the United States and Canada that offer degree programs in religion or religious studies at the baccalaureate, master, post-master, and doctoral levels. Included are departments of religion and/or religious studies at four-year colleges and universities, Bible colleges, seminaries, theological schools, and schools of divinity. On rare occasion, a school is included that offers only the associate degree. Its inclusion is based upon the fact that the associate program is preliminary to a baccalaureate program in an affiliated institution. Programs leading to the associate degree in four-year institutions are presented under the "special programs" category in that institution's entry.

The study of religion may be undertaken at the undergraduate and graduate levels at many institutions of higher learning that do not have any denominational affiliation. The baccalaureate major and post-baccalaureate studies at these institutions usually focus on the broad field of religion as developed over the centuries throughout the world.

The schools of theology, seminaries, and divinity schools listed herein normally offer programs leading to the first professional degree, Master of Divinity. These programs culminate in ordination in most cases. A majority of schools in this category also offer additional degree programs at the master, post-master, and doctoral levels. The higher degrees are often for ordained clergy with pastoral experience.

Many of these schools are members of consortia or clusters, joined in cooperative efforts in both library resources and curricula, but each retaining its own distinctive character in terms of denominational emphasis. Consortia for which information was available are listed as separate entries in the *Guide*.

The majority of private, independent institutions included have a denominational affiliation and are so controlled. Others have maintained a denominational relationship but academically are ecumenical and nonsectarian. Many of these offer students the opportunity to study religion in the context of a particular denomination. In many cases, these institutions possess an ecumenical philosophy and welcome students from other denominations into their programs of study other than those preparatory to ordination. For their own denominational students, the programs normally stipulate specific courses and requirements for a degree. Many public institutions in the United States and Canada offer degree programs in religion or religious studies that are purely academic in content and approach. Those public institutions included in this volume are identified as offering such programs in the *Degrees Offered by College and Subject* volume of *The College Blue Book,* published by Macmillan Publishing Company.

For those interested in correspondence study in the field of religion, it is recommended that *The Macmillan Guide to Correspondence Study* be consulted. This *Guide* gives detailed information about such courses available from various institutions in the United States.

The information contained in this compilation was obtained by questionnaires mailed to the respective institutions and from their catalogs. A conscientious effort was made to include every school for which information was available. Insufficient information, due to the lack of a returned questionnaire and a school catalog, may have regrettably required that a school not be included.

There has been no qualitative judgment in regard to the inclusion of an institution in this *Guide,* other than its being accredited by one of the groups recognized by the Council on Postsecondary Accreditation (COPA), nor has there been any deliberate exclusion of any religious denomination. All religious bodies for which an institution exists for the training of its leaders and lay persons that could be identified and for which information could be obtained have been included. The compiler's intent is to present a truly ecumenical collection of information for those interested in any aspect of a degree program in religion, whether denominational or nonsecular in content emphasis.

ORGANIZATION OF ENTRIES

The institutions are listed alphabetically within state in the United States section, and alphabetically within province in the Canadian section. A total of 703 institutions is presented. The entries include address, telephone number, administrative officials, and a general description of the school or department of religion. A description of the parent institution is added where applicable. Other information includes campus and community environment, denominational affiliation, if any, accreditation, term system, enrollment and faculty statistics, admission requirements, costs, availability of financial aid, and housing accommodations.

The library resources of the various institutions have been emphasized when the data was available. Special collections in the field of religion and theology are detailed where possible.

The information listed for religious services and activities normally applies to the entire student body, not just to students pursuing religious studies. These are listed primarily to give the user of this *Guide* an indication of the general religious activity on the campus. The nonsectarian and public institutions may have programs of religious life, but the schools in no way become involved with the students' choices of activity. Other institutions do have required religious activity, and this is so noted where applicable.

The degree programs in religious studies are described in terms of their content and credit requirements. The descriptions do not contain listings of all the courses offered, but often list the broad groupings into which the courses fall, for example, Biblical studies, Jewish studies, Islamic studies, systematic theology, etc. Special programs for clergy, lay persons, and other interested students are also listed and briefly described.

Tuition and fees are listed only as indications of recent costs. The amounts necessary for an education continue to escalate, and all institutions reserve the right not only to increase tuition or fee rates, but also to make changes in the curriculum offered.

It is recommended that prospective students contact the institution for information regarding current costs and curriculum information. It is emphasized that the information about the institutions listed herein is given in terms of the study of religion. This may be only one facet of the institution's entire educational program and should not be considered as the only field offered. *The College Blue Book,* 20th Edition, should be consulted for information about other institutional offerings.

ACCREDITATION

Accreditation is a unique feature of American educational practice. The accrediting process involves self-study by the educational institutions and evaluation by appointed commissions comprising members from other schools. This process operates through the nationally recognized accrediting agencies and associations and certain state bodies. These agencies have adopted criteria reflecting the qualities of a sound educational program, and they have developed procedures for evaluating institutions or programs to determine whether they are operating at levels of required quality. The agencies also seek to stimulate continued educational improvement to help assure that accreditation status may serve as an authentic index of educational quality.

Institutional accreditation is granted by the following groups which are recognized by the Council on Postsecondary Accreditation (COPA), Washington, D.C. Accreditation by one or more of these groups is included, where applicable, with the entry for each institution in this *Guide*.

National Institutional Accrediting Bodies

American Association of Bible Colleges
130-F North College Street
P.O. Box 1523
Fayetteville, Arkansas 72701

Association of Theological Schools in the United States and Canada
42 East National Road
P.O. Box 130
Vandalia, Ohio 45377

Regional Institutional Accrediting Bodies

Middle States Association of Colleges and Schools
3624 Market Street
Philadelphia, Pennsylvania 19104

New England Association of Schools and Colleges
The Sanborn House
15 High Street
Winchester, Massachusetts 01890

North Central Association of Colleges and Schools
159 North Dearborn Street
Chicago, Illinois 60601

Northwest Association of Schools and Colleges
3700-B University Way, N.E.
Seattle, Washington 98105

Southern Association of Colleges and Schools
795 Peachtree Street, N.E.
Atlanta, Georgia 30365

Western Association of Schools and Colleges
c/o Mills College, Box 9990
Oakland, California 94613

UNITED STATES

ALABAMA

Southeastern Bible College
2901 Pawnee Avenue
Birmingham, AL 35256   (205) 251-2311

Administration. James A. Kallam, President; Alden A. Gannett, Chancellor; John D. Talley, Jr., Academic Dean.

General Description. Southeastern Bible College grants Master's, Bachelor's, Associate degrees, and Certificates. All four-year programs require a Bible major. The College's Graduate School offers the M.A. program for people in the ministry. Completion requires attendance for three weeks in the summer for three summers, independent studies, and a project/product.

Parent Institution. Southeastern Bible College is an independent undergraduate college with a major in Bible and Theology and vocational emphasis in Elementary Education, Christian Education, Pastoral Studies, Missions, and Nursing.

Community Environment. The College campus is situated on 14 acres in the heart of Birmingham, Alabama. The city, with a population of 301,000, is a cosmopolitan industrial center on the edge of the Appalachian Mountain Range, in the Red Mountains of Alabama. It combines many of the traditions, graces, and ways of the Old South with a forward look and modern approach to the challenges of today.

Religious Denomination. Independent (Bible Church).
Religious Emphasis. Fundamentalist.
Accreditation. American Association of Bible Colleges.
Term System. Semester; Summer Term.
Enrollment in Degree Programs in Religion 1984–85. Total 23; men 23.
Degrees in Religion Awarded 1984–85. Master of Arts 2; Men 2.
Faculty for Degree Programs in Religion. Total 8; full-time 8.
Admission Requirements. For undergraduate programs: high school graduation or equivalent (GED); religious commitment. For the Master's program: Bachelor of Arts from a Bible College or 30 hours of Bible and Theology, and two years in the ministry.

Tuition and Fees. Student Service fee $70; tuition $85 per semester hour; room $210 - $260 per semester; board $775 - $825 per semester. Graduate School tuition $60 per semester hour.
Financial Aid. VA scholarships (2nd year).
Housing. On-campus housing is available.
Library Facilities. The library contains over 30,000 volumes.

Degree Programs

The Bachelor of Arts and Bachelor of Science programs require a Bible major. The various programs available include Pastor's Program, Pre-Seminary, Missions, Bible-Missions for Nurses, Evangelism, Christian Education, Secondary Education, Church Music, and Christian Education/Church Music.

The Master of Arts programs in Pastoral Studies and Missions require the completion of 32 to 36 semester hours.

Special Programs

An Associate of Arts degree may be earned in two years and a Certificate program of one year's duration is also offered.

Spring Hill College
Theology Department
4000 Dauphin Street
Mobile, AL 36608   (205) 460-2169

Administration. Reverend Paul S. Tipton, S.J., President.

General Description. Spring Hill College considers the study of religion an integral part of its curriculum. Although the College stands in the Roman Catholic tradition, the goal of the study of religion at Spring Hill is to aid its students in nurturing their own religious experience, regardless of their particular tradition. The study of religion also aids in developing a critical appreciation of that experience by placing it in the context of human religious experience in general and the Judaeo-Christian tradition in particular. It attempts to lead the student to understand the relationship between genuine religious awakening and human freedom and development. The College provides nontraditional programs of theological studies through the Division of Lifelong Learning as well as the traditional undergraduate programs of major/minor concentration in theology, involving study beyond the courses common to all students.

Parent Institution. Spring Hill College was founded by the first bishop of Mobile and the first semester began on May 1, 1830 with an enrollment of 30 students. It is under the sponsorship of the Jesuit Fathers of the New Orleans Province of the Society of Jesus.

Community Environment. The Spring Hill College campus occupies several hundred acres of the elevation which gives its name, Spring Hill, to the surrounding residential area of Mobile, Alabama. Mobile has a population of approximately 283,000. The city has libraries, churches, theaters, hospitals, and major civic, fraternal, and veteran's organizations. It is located on a bay of the Gulf of Mexico.

Religious Denomination. Roman Catholic.

Religious Emphasis. Main Line.

Accreditation. Southern Association of Colleges and Schools.

Term System. Semester (day classes); quarter (evening and graduate classes); summer term.

Faculty for Degree Programs in Religion. Total 8.

Admission Requirements. The admissions policy at Spring Hill College is based on matriculating students who have the desire and ability to benefit from the academic program; ability must be demonstrated by high school curriculum, grades, standardized test results, rank in class, previous college work (if applicable), and recommendations.

Tuition and Fees. Tuition $2,825 (12-18 semester hours) per semester; $210 per semester hour if less than 12 semester hours; room $750 per semester; meal plans per semester $612.14 to $719.63 plus 7 percent sales tax.

Financial Aid. An entering student who is seeking financial assistance will receive an application from the Office of Admissions. It is the goal of the Financial Aid Office to make it possible for every student who is accepted for admission to complete his/her education. An offer of financial aid normally includes both grant and self-help assistance. Over 150 scholarships to both incoming and continuing students are awarded each year.

Housing. The residence facilities of the College include five residence halls. All students are under the supervision of the Dean for Students, including married and commuting students who reside off campus. All single students not residing with parents or guardians are required to live in college housing as long as residence hall space is available.

Library Facilities. The Thomas Byrne Memorial Library houses the main collection of research materials on the campus. Some specific resources are distributed among smaller departmental libraries. The library con-

tains over 150,000 volumes that serve the curricular and general needs of the college community, more than 33,000 U.S. government documents, and a collection of 14,000 microforms.

Religious Services/Activities. Campus Ministry at Spring Hill College strives to foster the spiritual and religious aspirations primarily of the students, but also of the administration, the faculty, and staff of the College. Innovative programs and projects are initiated which promote a spirit of Christian freedom and growth in spiritual, intellectual, and social life-dimensions. The various programs include Outreach Services, Baptism and Confirmation, Days of Recollection and Private/Guide Retreats, Rite of Christian Initiation of Adults, Reconciliation, Liturgy Committees, Ignatius Center Music Group, Liturgical Lectors and Servers Group, Eucharistic Ministers, Marriage Preparation, The Troubadours, International Language Outreach Program, Spanish Mass, and Eucharistic Liturgies.

Degree Programs

The Bachelor of Arts degree in Humanities with a concentration in Theology requires 12 semester hours of lower-division theology, 18 semester hours of upper-division theology, and 12 semester hours of upper-division electives. The concentration must include at least 3 hours in each of four areas: biblical, historical, moral, and systematic. The comprehensive examination, either written or oral, must be successfully completed during the final semester before graduation.

The Master of Theological Studies degree is offered in service to local and regional civic and church communities. The student may choose a general course of studies from among the five areas of scriptural studies, historical theology, systematic theology, church and ministry, and moral theology. The program is sensitive to the professional and pastoral context of the educational interests of potential degree candidates. Completion of the program requires ten graduate level courses, participation in a theological studies colloquium, and successful completion of a comprehensive examination.

Special Programs

The Toolen Institute for Parish Services provides a program of academic, spiritual, and practical formation for those interested in leadership in parish ministry. The program was initiated in 1981 to serve the need for lay ministries in the Archdiocese of Mobile. Each candidate may take one course at a time from the core curriculum. The specialized curricula of four courses follow the core courses. An integral part of the Toolen Institute's formation program is the presentation of a series of spirituality seminars. Upon satisfactory completion of the requirements, the Archdiocese certifies candidates as Ministry Leaders.

ALASKA

Alaska Bible College

Box 289
Glennallen, AK 99588   (907) 822-3201

Administration. Dr. Gene Mayhew, President.

General Description. The Alaska Bible College, owned and operated by SEND International of Alaska, an affiliate of SEND International, has no organic connection with any denomination and welcomes fellowship with Bible-believing churches of the historical, fundamental, New Testament faith.

Community Environment. The campus of Alaska Bible College is situated on 80 acres of mixed aspen and spruce timber, typical of interior Alaska, in Glenallen. Glenallen is a rural community that has developed as the crossroads between Anchorage, Fairbanks, and Valdez. Small businesses and facilities now include a post office, bank, airport, telephone and telegraph system, radio station, hospital, grocery stores, service stations, and lodges. Public services include the Public Library, Magistrate's office, State Police, and the Public Health Clinic. A pipeline maintenance pump station remains following the completion of the Alaska Pipeline through the area. There are a number of evangelical churches in the Copper River Basin that provide opportunities for worship and Christian service assignments.

Religious Denomination. Nondenominational.

Religious Emphasis. Fundamental, Evangelical.

Accreditation. American Association of Bible Colleges.

Term System. Semester.

Enrollment in Degree Programs in Religion 1984–85. Total 25; men 16, women 9.

Degrees in Religion Awarded 1984–85. Associate of Arts in Biblical Education 1; women 1. Bachelor of Arts in Biblical Education 7; men 6, women 1.

Faculty for Degree Programs in Religion. Total 11; full-time 6, part-time 5.

Admission Requirements. General application form; $10 fee; 2 references; biographical sketch; high school transcripts or equivalent; college transcripts, if applicable; ACT or SAT scores; health form.

Tuition and Fees. Tuition $50 per credit hour; room (dormitory) $750 per semester; board $750 per semester; extrasession room and board (2nd semester only) $100; books and supplies $240 per semester; student council fee $25 per semester; Christian Service fee $30 per semester; other miscellaneous fees.

Financial Aid. On-campus work is available to most students who request it; the average amount that can be earned per semester is $1,200. Grants, loans, and the Vincent J. Joy Memorial Scholarship (based upon personal character and need) are available.

Housing. Joy Hall includes men's and women's dormitories. A limited number of rental mobile homes and trailer spaces are available.

Library Facilities. The Captain Vincent J. Joy Jr. Memorial Library houses a 20,000 volume collection and is particularly strong in the Bible and theology areas; over 150 periodicals are received regularly; the library contains a wide selection of Christian Education materials and a variety of other audiovisual materials.

Religious Services/Activities. The College strives to enrich and deepen the spiritual life of its students by chapel programs, prayer groups, and encouraging private Bible reading and prayer. College chapel attendance is required. Students are expected to attend regularly scheduled services of the churches where they minister.

The College Gospel Team is an important ministry of the College. To be a member of the group presumes the willingness to travel throughout weekends during the semester and may include vacation times over Thanksgiving, Christmas, and the conclusion of the school year. Goals of the traveling groups are evangelism, church ministry, and school representation.

Degree Programs

The Bachelor of Arts programs are considered terminal. Through Biblical, Professional, and General Education studies the students are developed for entrance into church or mission related professions. Each student is a Bible major and chooses a program of study in the Pastoral, Missions, or Christian Education area.

Special Programs

The Associate of Arts Program is designed for students who may desire a Bible foundation prior to transferring to another college for specialized work or to become an effective lay witness in the working world.

A Bible Certificate program is a course of study designed for the student who has a Bachelor's degree from a liberal arts college, for the part-time student who would like an ordered curriculum and goal for his studies, for the missionary candidate who needs a Bible background, and for the student seeking a Bible base before attending a liberal arts college.

The Christian Service Ministries program is designed to complement and refine the basic skills of the students. The program also assists a student in gaining experience and skills in the area of his/her future ministry.

Alaska Pacific University
Value and Religious Service Concentration
4101 University Drive
Anchorage, AK 99508   (907) 561-1266

Administration. Dr. Glen A. Olds, President; Dr. Robert Lee, Vice President for Academic Affairs and Professor of Value and Religious Service.

General Description. The Value and Religious Service Concentration provides value orientation by offering students a rigorous academic grounding in the disciplines of philosophy, religious studies, and Biblical studies. The academic approach is balanced by the application of insights gained into other areas of study within the University through cross-disciplinary courses and to the working world through a required practicum.

Parent Institution. Alaska Pacific University, founded in the Methodist tradition in 1959, is a private, ecumenical, and nonsectarian institution. The academic program is based on the philosophy that education should be integrative, not fragmented, and should link learning with life. The focus is on the wedding of liberal learning with the world of work and career options for now and the twenty-first century.

Community Environment. The 300-acre main campus of the University is located in the center of Anchorage, a city of 200,000 people.

Religious Denomination. The United Methodist Church.

Accreditation. Northwest Association of Schools and Colleges.

Term System. Semester.

Admission Requirements. Graduation from high school or equivalent; 2.5 grade point average; SAT or ACT.

Tuition and Fees. Tuition $1,680 per semester; Campus Center fee $20; student activity fee $20; room $700-$800; board $850-$975.

Financial Aid. The major types of student aid are grants, scholarships, employment, loans, and benefit assistance.

Housing. Dormitory accommodations are available on campus.

Library Facilities. University students and faculty are served by the anchorage Higher Education Consortium Library, located within walking distance. Resources of over 330,000 bound documents, including original government documents, sheet music, nonprint media, and a special Alaska collection.

Religious Services/Activities. The Campus Ministry is a service which serves to nurture and deepen the religious faith and life of the students. Through worship services, discussion groups, special student activities, and courses, the University provides pastoral services and spiritual counseling.

Degree Programs

A student choosing Value and Religious Service as a concentration is required to complete a minimum of 30 semester hours in the concentration. The student must also complete a three semester-hour practicum which allows the student to experience a situation related to Value and Religious Studies in the working world. A Special Study Opportunity places the student in a selected Alaskan village to study the impact of Christianity on the native peoples of Alaska. The degree Bachelor of Arts is awarded.

Special Programs

The Center for Religious Studies is a developing ecumenical program which brings visiting theologians and religious leaders to Anchorage to deliver lectures and conduct workshops. The Center also sponsors an annual Summer Ecumenical Symposium for pastors and lay leaders.

ARIZONA

Grand Canyon College
Department of Religion
3300 West Camelback Road
Phoenix, AZ 85017   (602) 249-3300

Administration. Dr. D.C. Martin, Chairman, Department of Religion.

General Description. Courses in the Department of Religion are intended to give students an understanding and appreciation of the Bible, to arouse in them a desire for Christian usefulness, and to equip them for leadership in various church related activities. Many courses in the Department are designed to be beneficial to all college students. Some are courses which ministerial students should take, whether or not they expect to continue their studies in seminary.

Parent Institution. Grand Canyon College is a Christian, liberal arts college. As such, it offers Bachelor degree programs which feature academic excellence in an environment where a Christian perspective is emphasized. The first steps toward founding Grand Canyon College were taken at the annual session of the Baptist General Convention of Arizona (now the Arizona Southern Baptist Convention) in 1946. The city of Prescott was chosen as the site of the new college. The College was chartered in 1949 and began instruction with the Fall semester of that year. In 1951, the College was moved to Phoenix.

Community Environment. The College has 70 acres available for development of its campus. The original buildings were constructed in 1951. Grouped around a quadrangle landscaped with flowers and Arizona shrubs and trees, all of the buildings afford a view of the mountains surrounding the Valley of the Sun. The College is located in the northwest area of Phoenix, the capital city of Arizona. Phoenix is near the geographical center of the state and is a thriving industrial and agricultural city with a population of over 1.6 million in the metropolitan area.

Religious Denomination. Southern Baptist.

Religious Emphasis. Moderate.

Accreditation. North Central Association of Colleges and Schools.

Term System. Semester; January term; two summer terms.

Enrollment in Degree Programs in Religion 1984–85. Total 118; men 83, women 35.

Degrees in Religion Awarded 1984–85. Bachelor of Arts 70; men 47, women 23.

Faculty for Degree Programs in Religion. Total 5; full-time 3, part-time 2.

Admission Requirements. High school graduation or equivalent.

Tuition and Fees. Tuition $89 per semester hour; Center for Biblical Studies tuition $44 per semester hour; room $350-$375 per semester (double occupancy); meals $500 minimum charge.

Financial Aid. Ministerial grants and scholarships are available. The Cooperative Program of the the Arizona Baptist Convention offers grants to (1) Mission Volunteers, (2) students training for the preaching ministry, and (3) others who may qualify. A student must have made a public commitment of his call to the ministry in his local home church in which he holds membership upon entering Grand Canyon College. Arizona students must be affiliated with and be active in a local Southern Baptist Church while attending Grand Canyon College and be willing to submit a quarterly report signed by their local pastor. Out-of-state students are eligible for the grant under the same provisions described above. A student agrees to sign a promissory note stating he will repay the grant which becomes a loan if he does not continue in the preaching ministry or missions (home or foreign) at least five years following departure from college and/or seminary. The maximum grant per student is $2,000, except pastors (whose grant is 100 percent).

Housing. Students reside in campus dormitories.

Library Facilities. The Fleming Library collection contains over 120,000 books and bound periodicals. Approximately 700 magazines and journals are received currently. In 1979, the library received a donation of the now defunct Prescott College. This collection is strongest in the areas of social and behavioral sciences and literature and increased the holdings of Fleming Library by one-half.

Religious Services/Activities. The College attempts to

provide a Christian atmosphere where spiritual issues are discussed, religious experiences are encouraged, and the relevance of Christianity to our culture is explored. Activities include required attendance at chapel services, courses in Bible required for graduation, and the activities of the Baptist Student Union, Ministerial Association, and other religiously-oriented groups. Each year two special weeks of religious emphasis are held, at which time outstanding Christian leaders speak daily to the student body and hold conferences and seminars on problems and topics relevant to young Christians. The Staley Lectures are held annually.

Degree Programs

Bachelor of Arts programs with majors in Bible and Religion, and minors in Bible, Religion, and Religious Education. Required and elective courses are in the areas of Bible, New Testament Greek, Religion, and Philosophy.

Special Programs

The Department of Religion has established a Center for Biblical Studies to enlist more students in the study of Bible and religion and to render a service to the community. Under this program a person not enrolled in any other college may take up to seven hours of college work per semester, all of which must be in Bible, Greek, or Religion. These courses may be audited or taken for credit. A certificate will be awarded upon completion of 18 hours and an advanced certificate, for 30 hours.

ARKANSAS

Central Baptist College

Conway, AR 72032   (501) 329-6873

Administration. James Ray Raines, President.

General Description. Central Baptist College was founded in 1952 by the churches of the Baptist Missionary Association of Arkansas. From its inception, the College has been a junior college. When the need became apparent for a senior college in Religious Studies, such programs were inaugurated. Recently, other Bachelor degree programs (namely elementary education and missionary nursing) have been added.

Community Environment. The campus is located in central Conway, a town with a population of 20,000. It is 30 miles from Little Rock.

Religious Denomination. Baptist Missionary Association of Arkansas.

Religious Emphasis. Conservative/Evangelical.

Accreditation. American Association of Bible Colleges.

Term System. Semester.

Admission Requirements. High school graduation with a C average or better.

Tuition and Fees. Tuition $1,000 per year; room and board $1,280.

Financial Aid. Pell Grants, college work-study, Arkansas State Scholarship Program, and Guaranteed Student Loans are types of assistance available.

Housing. Men's and women's residence halls are located on campus.

Library Facilities. The J.E. Cobb Library houses over 30,000 books and additional periodicals, tapes, and microform resources.

Religious Services/Activities. Chapel-assembly is held twice weekly. The Christian Service Department gives students the opportunity to apply their faith in a practical manner.

Degree Programs

The Bachelor of Arts with a major in Bible requires a total of 127 hours of which 30 hours are in the major. Minors are available in English, History, Music, Pastoral Studies, and Religious Education. Programs with a major in Bible are also offered that lead to the Bachelor of Science degree. The Bachelor of Arts in Christian Missions requires completion of 132 hours. The Bachelor of Missionary Nursing requires a total of 141 hours. A Bachelor of Science in Church Music is offered and requires a total of 138 hours. A Bachelor of Arts in Pastoral Ministry requires a total of 130 hours.

Special Programs

The Associate of Arts is offered in similar majors as for the Bachelor's degree programs.

Harding University
Department of Bible, Religion, and Philosophy

Searcy, AR 72143   (501) 268-6161

Administration. Dr. Clifton L. Ganus, Jr., President; Dr. Allan Isom, Assistant Chairman, Department of Bible.

General Description. Baccalaureate programs are offered in the College of Arts and Sciences, and a Diploma program is available in the School of Biblical Studies. At least one course in the Department is taken by all majors each semester. In addition, majors are offered in various fields of Biblical studies. The Department seeks to equip each student with such a knowledge of the Bible that the student's life will be firmly founded on a personal Christian faith. Such a faith must include a thorough integration of Biblical truth and life experience regardless of the student's chosen field of study.

Parent Institution. Harding University is an institution of higher education composed of a College of Arts and Sciences and Schools of Business, Education, and Nursing. Graduate programs are available in Education, Accounting, and, located in Memphis, Tennessee, a Graduate School of Religion. The University is under the control of a self-perpetuating board of trustees who are members of Churches of Christ.

Community Environment. Searcy, Arkansas is a city with a population of 13,612. Founded in 1837, Searcy enjoyed a gradual growth as center of a chiefly agricultural area until the last 35 years when the location of several industries brought a favorable balance of economy and a more rapid growth than before. The city is located in east central Arkansas, about 50 miles northeast of Little Rock and 105 miles west of Memphis, Tennessee. The Harding campus occupies 200 acres east of the downtown area of Searcy.

Religious Denomination. Churches of Christ.

Religious Emphasis. Conservative and evangelical.

Accreditation. North Central Association of Colleges and Schools.

Term System. Semester; summer term.

Enrollment in Degree Programs in Religion 1984–85. Total 120; men 116, women 4.

Degrees in Religion Awarded 1984–85. Bachelor of Arts, Bible and Religion 19; men 18, women 1. Bachelor of Arts, Biblical Languages 8; men 8. Bachelor of Arts, Religious Education 1; men 1.

Faculty for Degree Programs in Religion. Total 22; full-time 16, part-time 6.

Admission Requirements. High school graduates with 15 units in academic subjects (3 in English; 9 in mathematics, science, social science, foreign language, etc.; 3 may be in other subjects); C grade average; ACT of 17 composite recommended.

Tuition and Fees. Tuition $101.50 per semester hour; registration fee $101.25 per semester. Room, board, and tuition for the year is $5,266.50; for non-boarding students, $3,247.50.

Financial Aid. Scholarships, student work, loans, and government grants are available. Application for aid should be made as follows: (1) apply for admission; (2) request forms for aid from Financial Aid Office; (3) complete ACT Family Financial Statement Form.

Housing. 10 residence halls for unmarried students and 7 married student apartments. Off-campus housing is also available for married students; single rooms range $422 to $483 per semester and apartments from $150 to $195 per month.

Library Facilities. The Beaumont Memorial Library houses 262,199 volumes of which 61,763 are on microfilm; 1,315 current periodicals; interlibrary loans available.

Religious Services/Activities. Compulsory chapel daily; Sunday morning and evening, Wednesday evening worship; frequent night devotionals; Timothy Club for Bible majors; J.O.Y. Club for Women; Annual Bible Lectureship; Uplift, a one week retreat; home and international evangelistic campaigns; Dactylology Club.

Degree Programs

Bachelor of Arts degree programs are offered in Bible and Religion, (for men) Bible and Religion (for women only), Biblical Languages, Missions, Religious Education, Youth Ministry, and Ministry (as a second major). The Bachelor of Science Degree is offered with a major in Bible and Religion.

Special Programs

The School of Biblical Studies offers a 2-year intensive program for men over 21 years of age who are not seeking a degree or graduate work.

John Brown University
Division of Biblical Studies
Siloam Springs, AR 72761   (501) 524-3131

Administration. Dr. John E. Brown, Jr., Chancellor; Dr. John E. Brown, III, President; Dr. Ralph C. Kennedy, Academic Dean; Dr. Gilbert Weaver, Chairman, Division of Biblical Studies.

General Description. The Division of Biblical Studies includes four departments: Bible, Christian Education, New Testament Greek, and Religion and Philosophy. Degree programs offered are the Bachelor of Arts and the Associate of Arts. The Division seeks to provide a curriculum and climate which will stimulate both the spiritual and intellectual development of the student. From an evangelical, nonsectarian stance there is a commitment to the Bible as the Word of God.

Parent Institution. John Brown University is an evangelical Christian college which seeks to provide Christ-centered higher education which contributes dynamically to the intellectual, spiritual, and occupational effectiveness of men and women in God-honoring living and service.

Community Environment. Located in the Benson County foothills of the beautiful Ozarks, the town of Siloam Springs, Arkansas is easily accessible from all parts of the state. The seasons are delightfully mild since Siloam Springs is far enough south to insure mild winters, and the summer nights are pleasantly cool. Northwest Arkansas is considered a very healthful location, and is noted as a summer retreat for many tourists from all sections of the United States. The campus of John Brown University includes 300 acres and 43 buildings, located in a picturesque foothill region.

Religious Denomination. Nondenominational (Christian).

Religious Emphasis. Evangelical.

Accreditation. North Central Association of Colleges and Schools.

Term System. Semester; no summer term.

Enrollment in Degree Programs in Religion 1984–85. Total 46; men 35, women 11.

Faculty for Degree Programs in Religion. Total 6; full-time 6.

Admission Requirements. Applicant must present transcript showing: (1) graduation from high school, (2) rank in graduating class, (3) the score achieved on the ACT or SAT college aptitude test, and (4) at least 15 acceptable course units. Must rank at or above the 25th percentile on ACT/SAT; high school class standing must be 30 percent or higher.

Tuition and Fees. Tuition per year $3,500; room and board $2,500; application fee $25. Room deposit $50; tuition deposit $50.

Financial Aid. Sixty percent of the student body receives some form of financial aid. Students must file ACT-FFS form or CSS-FAF form for need based aid. Some academic and merit based scholarships are available as well as loans and work-study for qualified applicants.

Housing. On-campus dormitories available for dependent students under 21 years of age; married student housing is also available on-campus.

Library Facilities. The library houses over 80,000 volumes.

Religious Services/Activities. Christian activities are a vital part of the total preparation for all students. Chapel is required twice a week. The Council to Assist in the Unity of Student Evangelism sponsors various activities that help provide practical Christian service experience.

Degree Programs

The Bachelor of Arts in Bible or Christian Education are offered. The student planning to enter a preaching or evangelistic ministry, or home or foreign missionary service, may fulfill a major in Bible as a first step in preparation. Students planning to engage in other types of Christian service, such as Christian education, youth ministry, or Christian recreation may elect to major in Christian Education.

Special Programs

The Associate of Arts degree with a major in Bible or Christian Education may also be pursued.

Ouachita Baptist University
Division of Religion and Philosophy
410 Ouachita Street
Arkadelphia, AR 71923   (501) 246-4531

Administration. Dr. Daniel R. Grant, President; Dr. Marion E. (Bud) Fray, Chairman, Division of Religion and Philosophy.

General Description. The Department of Religion of the Division of Religion and Philosophy offers courses designed for students in preparation for careers in church-related vocations and for students desiring to increase their understanding of the Christian experience and its significance for the individual and society.

Parent Institution. Ouachita Baptist University was established in 1885 by the Arkansas Baptist State Convention. The University grants the Bachelor's and Master's degrees.

Community Environment. The campus is located in Arkadelphia, a community of 10,000 people located 70 miles southwest of Little Rock and 35 miles south of Hot Springs.

Religious Denomination. Southern Baptist Convention.

Accreditation. North Central Association of Colleges and Schools.

Term System. Semester.

Faculty for Degree Programs in Religion. Total 11.

Admission Requirements. High school graduation with 15 standard units of which 3 must be in English, 2 in science or mathematics, and 1 in social science.

Tuition and Fees. Tuition $1,550 per semester; room $335; board $540; activity fee $25.

Financial Aid. Four basic types of aid are available: scholarships, grants, loans, and employment. Aid is derived from University and private sources as well as from government-funded programs. Scholastic achievement, outstanding personal qualities, demonstrated financial need, and other standards are criteria for the award of financial aid.

Housing. All unmarried students are required to reside in campus dormitories.

Library Facilities. The Riley Library houses a main book collection of over 114,000 volumes and 350,000 non-book materials. Special collections include the archives of the Arkansas Baptist State Convention.

Religious Services/Activities. Attendance at weekly chapel is required. The Baptist Student Union plans, directs, and coordinates all types of religious activities, promotes the annual Christian Focus Week, and cooperates with the Department of Student Ministries of the Southern Baptist Convention with their projects of summer missions, campus evangelism, and others.

Degree Programs

Majors leading to the Bachelor's degree are offered in Religion (Pastoral Ministry, Religious Education) and in Family Life Ministry and Church Recreation. The major consists of at least 24 hours with at least 12 hours from the junior-senior level courses.

CALIFORNIA

Ambassador College

300 West Green Street
Pasadena, CA 91129   (818) 304-6037

Administration. Herbert W. Armstrong, Chancellor and President.

General Description. Ambassador College is a privately supported, coeducational, liberal arts college founded in 1947 by Herbert W. Armstrong, President and Pastor General of the Worldwide Church of God. It is a church-related institution with Biblical and theological coursework as the main core of studies. The College grants the Associate of Arts, Associate of Science, and Bachelor of Arts degrees.

Community Environment. The 70-acre campus is located in west Pasdadena. The Ambassador Auditorium is known throughout the Los Angeles area as an outstanding performing arts center. The College has preserved some of Pasadena's most notable mansions. The Norton Simon Museum is one block from the campus and the Huntington Library, Art Gallery, and Botanical Gardens are two miles away.

Religious Denomination. Worldwide Church of God.

Term System. Semester.

Admission Requirements. High school graduation with rank in the upper half of graduating class; 16 academic units; SAT.

Tuition and Fees. Total estimated costs $4,035-$4,150 for two semesters.

Financial Aid. The College offers a variety of financial aid programs, including scholarships, grants, loans, and employment to qualified students. Most programs require demonstration of need.

Housing. Campus residences provide housing for 500 students.

Library Facilities. The College Library houses over 69,000 volumes, 17,000 microforms, and 37,000 audiovisual materials. Special collections include the Library of American Civilization, the King Leopold III slide collection, and many rare books.

Degree Programs

A major in Theology is required of all students in the Bachelor of Arts degree program. The degree requires a minimum of 128 hours; a minimum of three years' attendance is normally required.

Special Programs

The Associate of Arts degree requires a minimum 64 hours and a minimum attendance of one year at the College.

American Baptist Seminary of the West

2515 Hillegass Avenue
Berkeley, CA 94704   (415) 841-1905

Administration. Wesley H. Brown, President and Professor of Christian Ethics; William L. Malcomson, Vice President and Dean of Academic Affairs.

General Description. The American Baptist Seminary of the West believes that theological education should increase one's understanding of and commitment to evangelism and the world mission of the Church. The Master of Divinity three-year program is at the center of its task of equipping persons for continuing education including the Doctor of Ministry program. And, in cooperation with the Graduate Theological Union, the Seminary provides the context for the Master of Arts, Ph.D., and Th.D. degree programs. The American Baptist Seminary of the West is a founding and continuing member of the Graduate Theological Union, a consortium composed of nine seminaries and several affiliated centers and programs, all in the San Francisco Bay area.

Parent Institution. The purpose and commitment of the American Baptist Seminary of the West is to provide quality theological education which is both evangelical and ecumenical, which reflects the Seminary's servant and prophetic roles, and which responds to the leadership needs of the Church, and in particular to the American Baptist Churches in the U.S.A. A primary concern of such education is the encouragement of the kind of seminary life which contributes significantly toward spiritual formation. Its curriculum of study combines a strong biblical and theological base, nurtured by Baptist and free church historical roots, and balanced by an important experiential dimension.

The American Baptist Seminary of the West is the fruit of a merger between the Berkeley Baptist Divinity School and the California Baptist Theological Seminary, accomplished in 1968. The Berkeley Divinity School traces its origins to the California Baptist Educational Society, founded in 1852 by Western Baptists, for the preparation of pastors and other Christian workers. The California Baptist Theological Seminary was founded in 1944 in Los Angeles with the concern for providing preparation for ministry in the theological climate of southern California. The merger of the two seminaries was effected in order to maintain quality professional preparation for Christian ministry amid rising costs, seeking to provide the best possible educational resources.

The address of the southern California branch of the American Baptist Seminary of the West is 970 Village Oaks Drive, Covina, CA, 91724; telephone (818) 331-5337.

Community Environment. The central campus in Berkeley, California, is on beautifully landscaped grounds in the midst of the city, near the campus of the University of California, Berkeley, and the Graduate Theological Union complex. There is easy access to the entire San Francisco Bay area, as well as to the beaches and mountains. The Southwest Branch in Covina, California, is housed in the new headquarters of the American Baptist Churches of the Pacific Southwest. All students are commuters. Special arrangements have been made with the University of La Verne for the completing of undergraduate education. The Los Angeles Basin offers access to many cultural resources as well as to the beaches and mountains.

Religious Denomination. American Baptist Churches in the U.S.A.

Religious Emphasis. Evangelical, Ecumenical.

Accreditation. Association of Theological Schools in the United States and Canada.

Term System. Semester; January Intersession.

Enrollment in Degree Programs in Religion 1984–85. Total 140; Berkeley Campus 90, Covina Campus 50.

Faculty for Degree Programs in Religion. Total 11; full-time 11, numerous adjunct professors part-time .

Admission Requirements. Bachelor's degree.

Tuition and Fees. Tuition $3,200 per academic year; housing costs at Berkeley campus range from $210 to $353 per month depending upon accommodations; Doctor of Ministry total program tuition $4,000.

Financial Aid. Each student applying for financial aid is counseled regarding his/her financial needs. An aid "package" is developed on the basis of need, including grants, work-study, and loans. A small number of Presidential Scholarships are offered each year.

Housing. A limited number of studio, one- and two-bedroom apartments are available at the Berkeley campus. There is no student housing at the Southwest Branch.

Library Facilities. Students and faculty have access to the library of the Graduate Theological Union library in Berkeley, with its 500,000 holdings. There is also a small library center on campus. In the Southwest Branch there is a small library and access to the various libraries in the greater Los Angeles area.

Religious Services/Activities. There are regular chapel services, forums, and common meals at both locations. The Guidance/Support group allows for the development of close-knit communities which include faculty and local clergy as well as students. There are retreats, potlucks, and special events throughout the year. There is a strong emphasis at the Seminary on spiritual growth as a necessary part of the developing of Christian ministers. At the central campus, Partners-in-Ministry provides a support group for seminary spouses, and from time to time, various prayer groups and interest groups develop.

Degree Programs

The Master of Arts in Religion program is designed for persons who have an earned and accredited undergraduate degree or its equivalent and who wish to engage in theological education but do not intend to become ordained into the Christian ministry. The program requires that work be done in the Old and New Testaments, Church History, Theology, and Christian Ethics, that there be involvement in a Guidance/Support Group, and that electives be chosen on the basis of the particular learning goals of the student. A total of 48 semester units are required, and it is a two-year program if engaged in on a full-time basis.

The Master of Divinity degree is for those who have accredited earned undergraduate degrees and who wish to prepare for the ordained ministry. Courses are required in Old and New Testament, Hebrew, Greek, Church History, Theology, Christian Ethics, Ministry, Pastoral Care, Preaching, Worship, and Supervised Field Education, and it is also required that the person be involved in a Guidance/Support Group. Hispanic students in the Southwest Branch also take some courses with an Hispanic perspective. Baptists take Baptist History and Polity. Approximately one-third of the course work is elective and is determined by the student's learning goals. A total of 77 elective units are required, and the program is three years in length if the student is full-time.

The Doctor of Ministry program is for persons who have an accredited theological degree or its equivalent, and who have engaged in full-time professional ministry for a minimum of three years. Such persons come into the program because they wish to develop expertise in a particular area of ministry in order to renew their own ministry and to become a better resource for the life of the churches. Eight courses are required, plus a professional paper. The program is a collegial one, including lay and professional colleague committees, an advisor, and the program director.

Special Programs

Through the Graduate Theological Union, a person may enroll in the Master of Arts, Doctor of Theology, or Doctor of Philosophy programs and may affiliate with the American Baptist Seminary of the West.

American Baptist Seminary of the West - Southwest Branch

970 Village Oaks Drive
Covina, CA 91724   (818) 331-5337

General Description. See: American Baptist Seminary of the West, Berkeley, California.

Applied Theology, School of

5890 Birch Court
P.O. Box 20479
Oakland, CA 94620   (415) 652-1651

Administration. Edward B. Gillen, S.J., President; Dr. Frank B. Nieman, Academic Dean; Mary Esther Owens, O.P., Administrative Assistant, Director of Admissions.

General Description. The School of Applied Theology is an affiliate of the Graduate Theological Union of Berkeley, California. The School of Applied Theology, a graduate professional school in its second quarter-century, is committed to developing mature, experienced Christian leaders and to assisting them in becoming effective and confident in collaborative ministry. It is sponsored by the California Province of the Society of Jesus. Those moving into leadership roles in areas of spirituality, pastoral ministries, or adult religious education will experience intensive preparation for this transition, while those desiring theological and spiritual renewal in a setting of enriching dialogue among laity, religious, and clergy, will accomplish this at the School. Every student will be given many opportunities to develop the skill of "enabling" — the skill most needed by leaders in the Church today as the Church clearly enters into the era of total lay participation in the mission of the Church.

Parent Institution. The Graduate Theological Union is formed to conduct an educational institution offering instruction on the graduate theological level; to participate with theological seminaries and other institutions of higher learning in cooperative programs of study; and to grant such academic degrees as are customarily granted in universities and seminaries of learning, either in its own name only, or in conjunction with another such institution. The Graduate Theological Union is both a graduate school and a consortium of schools, as well as an agency for a variety of special programs and services. In its educational programs, the GTU draws upon the theological communities that created it and works cooperatively with the Uni-

versity of California, Berkeley. The combined full-time faculties now number approximately 135. More than 1,-400 students are enrolled in resident degree programs, including approximately 350 in GTU doctoral and M.A. studies and 1,150 in professional degree studies and in special status. In addition, more than 900 students are enrolled in continuing education programs.

Community Environment. See: Franciscan School of Theology (Berkeley).

Religious Denomination. Roman Catholic.

Religious Emphasis. Ecumenical.

Accreditation. Degrees are granted jointly with the Graduate Theological Union which is accredited by the Western Association of Schools and Colleges and the Association of Theological Schools in the United States and Canada.

Term System. Semester.

Enrollment in Degree Programs in Religion 1984–85. Total 40; men 20, women 20.

Degrees in Religion Awarded 1984–85. Master of Arts in Applied Theology 13; men 7, women 6.

Faculty for Degree Programs in Religion. Total 22; full-time 4, part-time 18.

Admission Requirements. Bachelor's degree; sufficient theological background and/or ministerial experience to do graduate-level work; three letters of recommendation; application fee of $25.

Tuition and Fees. Tuition $3,150 (includes nonrefundable $320 registration fee); library/activities fee $800.

Financial Aid. Partial scholarships for lay persons; School is approved for guaranteed student loans and Veterans benefits.

Housing. The School does not provide housing for its students, but lends assistance in selection from the options of apartments, residences maintained by sister institutions or religious orders, and rectories in the Diocese of Oakland.

Library Facilities. The Graduate Theological Union Common Library has 350,000 volumes, 150,000 microforms, slides, tapes, and video cassettes.

Religious Services/Activities. Daily liturgy; 2 Spirituality workshops; Annual Retreat; four Days of Recollection.

Degree Programs

The Master of Arts in Applied Theology degree is awarded to students who have a Bachelor's degree and one year of graduate theological studies in addition to the nine-month School of Applied Theology program. Students must also work one year in ministry and report their work in an approved in-field paper to qualify for the degree.

Special Programs

A Fall "Three-Month Sabbatical" Program is sponsored by the School for a limited number of students who are unable to be away from their ministry for a longer period of time. It runs concurrently and is integrated with the Fall semester of the graduate program. A total of 20 Continuing Education Units (CEUs) will be awarded to the participants. In an holistic approach to academic and functional theology and the development of essential ministerial skills, the participants are involved in a process that is keyed to personal spiritual renewal.

The School also sponsors Continuing Theological Education, a program of short courses to develop theological knowledge and ministerial skills.

Bethany Bible College
Division of Biblical Studies and Philosophy
800 Bethany Drive
Santa Cruz, CA 95066   (408) 438-3800

Administration. Richard B. Foth, President; Dr. Truett E. Bobo, Administrative Cabinet, Bible and Theology.

General Description. Bethany Bible College prepares students for dynamic Christian living, for ministry in the church, and for service to mankind in the Biblical perspective. The College provides the educational environment, instruction, resources, and experiences needed by its graduates for effective lay and professional ministry and church-related vocations. The College was founded in 1919 and is controlled by the Assemblies of God, Northern California-Nevada District Council, through a Board of Trustees. The College grants the Bachelor of Arts and Bachelor of Science degrees. A three-year Diploma program is offered in the areas of religious education, ministerial, and music.

Community Environment. The 40-acre campus is located on the slopes of the Santa Cruz mountains in the community of Scotts Valley, 7 miles from the resort town of Santa Cruz on Monterey Bay.

Religious Denomination. General Council of Assemblies of God.

Accreditation. Western Association of Schools and Colleges; American Association of Bible Colleges.

Term System. Semester (4-1-4 plan).

Enrollment in Degree Programs in Religion 1984–85. Total 509 (full-time equivalent).

Admission Requirements. Graduation from high school with 15 academic units; experience of Christian conversion; ACT; placement tests in Bible and English required; references.

Tuition and Fees. Tuition $3,520 per year; room and board $2,615; student fees $312.

Financial Aid. Assistance is available as scholarships, grants, loans, and employment. The College uses the Student Aid Application for California (SAAC) to determine eligibility.

Housing. Campus housing includes residence halls and a number of small apartments and annexes.

Library Facilities. The library houses over 50,000 volumes.

Religious Services/Activities. Attendance is required at daily chapel services. Students are encouraged to find a church home in the area and participate in the programs of that church. Student Ministries assists students in finding those areas of ministry for which they are best suited. Student Missions directs missionary activity throughout the year as well as the annual Missionary Convention Week.

Degree Programs

Every student who graduates with the four-year baccalaureate degree must meet the general studies requirements, the Bible and theology core requirements, and a selected major. The Bachelor of Science degree is offered with professional (ministerial) majors in the fields of Religious Education, Ministerial, and Music. The Bachelor of Arts degree is offered with the academic majors, including English, Social Science, Multiple Subjects, Music, and Psychology. The total number of units required for the degrees is 124. The Division of Biblical Studies and Philosophy offers the Ministerial major with concentrations available in Pastoral Ministries, Christian Education, Counseling, Youth Ministry, Theological Studies, and Missions/Communications. The Division of Education, Religious Education, and Psychology offers majors in Psychology, Religious Education, and Multiple Subjects. The Music major offered by the Division of Music includes concentrations in Minister of Music, Music Education, Performance, Theory/Composition, and General.

Special Programs

A three-year Diploma program is available for those students who may not choose to complete a degree. The choice of programs is restricted to Religious Education, Ministerial, and Music; the Diploma program requires a minimum of 90 units. A two-year Certificate program is offered in Pastoral Ministries and Religious Education; it requires a total of 62 units.

Biola University
Talbot Theological Seminary and School of
   Theology
13800 Biola Avenue
La Mirada, CA 90639   (213) 944-0351

Administration. Wendell G. Johnston, Th.D., Dean, Talbot Theological Seminary and School of Theology.

General Description. Talbot Theological Seminary and School of Theology was formed in the Fall of 1983 as the result of a merger between appropriate undergraduate and graduate programs of Talbot Theological Seminary. It is the purpose of Talbot to prepare for the Gospel ministry those who believe, live, and preach the great historic doctrines of the faith which have been committed to the church. Talbot offers eight advanced degree programs, each with its own distinctive purposes. Undergraduate programs leading to the Bachelor of Arts degree with majors in Biblical and Theological Studies and Christian Education are offered to undergraduate students in Biola University by the Talbot Theological Seminary and School of Theology.

Parent Institution. The purpose of Biola University, in a broad perspective, is to educate Christian men and women in order to produce graduates who are competent in their fields of study, knowledgeable in biblical studies, and earnest Christians equipped to serve the Christian community and society at large. Carrying on a tradition that dates back 78 years, Biola University now encompasses four schools: The School of Arts, Sciences and Professions; Rosemead School of Psychology; the School of Intercultural Studies and World Missions; and the Talbot Theological Seminary and School of Theology.

The history of Biola University begins with the Bible Institute founded in 1908 by Lyman Stewart and T.C. Horton. The next seven decades have witnessed tremendous growth in the development and outreach of the University. Under the leadership of Dr. Louis T. Talbot, President from 1932 to 1952, the Bible Institute program became a four-year course leading to degrees in theology, Christian education, and sacred music. The School of Missionary Medicine came into being in 1945, laying the foundation for Biola's current baccalaureate nursing program. In 1949, the Bible Institute was renamed Biola University, then moved to its present site in 1959.

Community Environment. The Biola University campus is bordered on the west by Biola Avenue and on the east by La Mirada Boulevard. It is located between the large east-west thoroughfares of Rosecrans Avenue and Imperial Highway, approximately twenty-two miles southeast of downtown Los Angeles. The campus consists of 95 acres in 30 major buildings. The Talbot Theological Seminary and School of Theology has classroom, chapel, and administrative office facilities located in Myers Hall and Feinberg Hall.

Religious Denomination. Nondenominational.

Religious Emphasis. Conservative Evangelical.

Accreditation. Western States Association of Schools and Colleges; Association of Theological Schools in the United States and Canada. Member of: American Association of Bible Colleges.

Term System. Semester; January interterm; summer term.

Enrollment in Degree Programs in Religion 1984–85. Total 893; 748 men, 145 women.

Degrees in Religion Awarded 1984–85. Bachelor of Arts 58; men 40, women 18. Master of Arts 56; men 45, women 11. Doctorate 3; men 3.

Faculty for Degree Programs in Religion. Total 60; 40 full-time, part-time 20.

Admission Requirements. Undergraduate applicants must have been graduated from an accredited high school with 16 units required; SAT or ACT; character and academic references; pastoral reference; interview recommended. Graduate programs require a Bachelor of Arts degree or its academic equivalent; other requirements vary with program.

Tuition and Fees. Undergraduate tuition $2,654 per semester; Graduate (Seminary) $1,926 per semester; room and board $2,874 per year; other fees where applicable.

Financial Aid. Biola University participates in CEEB College Scholarship Service. University scholarships, loans, and student employment available. A placement office works closely with graduate students to assist them in securing part-time internship positions in local churches. Off-campus secular employment in a wide variety of occupations can be found.

Housing. Campus living quarters are available for single men and women. All unmarried freshmen, sophomores, and juniors under 21 years of age and not living with their parents are expected to live in the residence halls if they are enrolled for ten units or more. Seniors and graduate students may live in the residence halls on a space-available basis. Talbot Seminary has no housing facilities for married students. The Biola Housing Office provides a list giving an indication of the apartment rental environment in the area.

Library Facilities. The Biola University Library is under a unified administration and serves the undergraduate and graduate levels. It houses over 170,000 volumes of books and bound journals. Special features of the library include an extensive index file of sermon outlines and illustrations, an excellent collection of bilbiographic tools and journal indexes, and a number of special collections. The principal theological journals in English are received regularly.

Religious Services/Activities. Every student is urged to set aside time, both morning and evening, for personal devotions. Undergraduate students meet daily, Monday through Friday, for a half-hour chapel service with worship and praise as the primary purpose. Each Fall, there is a Spiritual Emphasis Week. Once each semester the school observes a planned Day of Prayer and informal prayer groups meet as part of residence hall life. The Torrey Memorial Bible Conference and the Missionary Conference are high points in the development of the spiritual life of the student. Attendance is required at all of these events. The Student Missionary Union is a student organization of which every undergraduate student of Biola University is a member. A major function of this Union is to provide opportunities for students to share their faith in Christ by various means of evangelism. Also, while enrolled at Biola, a student is given the privilege of expressing his preference in Christian outreach and is expected to devote a minimum of three hours each week in his assigned area. Completion of one assignment for each semester is necessary to satisfy graduation requirements.

The Talbot Theological Seminary and School of Theology recognizes the necessity of active service in Christian work while students are pursuing their courses of study. From the time of the students' enrollment they are asked to engage in some type of approved weekly ministry. Chapel services are an integral part of the total educational experience and the corporate and individual growth of the student body. A full-time Master of Divinity student must register for field education each semester. This intensive supervised practice of the ministry is composed of three clusters of learning: supervised field experience for a minimum of 100 hours in each of two semesters; seminars with other students registered for field education internship; and individual counseling with the director of field education on specific aspects of the student's experience.

Degree Programs

The Bachelor of Arts degree at Biola University is awarded upon the completion of specified units of study. A total of 30 units of Biblical Studies and Theology must be included in the program of each student according to the American Association of Bible Colleges. Undergraduates majoring in Biblical Studies and Theology must take all of the general Bible requirements and will choose an area of emphasis (Old Testament, New Testament, Bible, Pre-Seminary). The Christian Education major is designed to prepare its graduates for professional ministries in church and parachurch agencies and to provide a foundation for graduate training. Each student is required to select a specialization in addition to the core courses (Children, Youth, Intercultural, Elementary Teacher Credential, Pre-Seminary in Christian Education, Pre-Seminary in Family Ministries, Pre-Seminary in Pastoral Ministry).

The Master of Divinity is designed as preparation for the propagation of the faith, and the effective means of its communication. Each student must select a major and satisfactorily complete the requirements of that major (Bible Exposition, Old Testament, Church History, Systematic Theology, New Testament, Practical Theology Missions, Christian Education). Two biblical languages are required (Greek and Hebrew).

The Master of Arts in Ministry includes core courses, electives, and ministry emphasis (Pastoral, Missions, and Christian Education). The program is designed for individuals who have been in ministry for a significant number of years, and have not had the opportunity to earn a baccalaureate degree. A student is enrolled tentatively in the program until 32 of the required 64 units have been completed. At the completion of 32 units, an evaluation is made regarding admission to candidacy status in the Master's program. Quality graduate-level training is provided in several essential aspects of professional ministry in order to enhance significantly the effectiveness of participating ministers. The two primary emphases of the program are Biblical and practical studies. The goal of both is improved expertise in a ministry of the Word as it relates to the daily lives of people and their eternal destiny.

The Master of Arts in Biblical Studies and the Master of Arts in Theological Studies are intensive and highly specialized programs designed for those whose calling to

Christian service is not in the area of professional ministry. The programs are comprised of 62 units each structured in common to include biblical and theological foundations in the first year, academic specialization in one of four theological disciplines in the second year, and additional elective courses.

The Master of Arts in Christian Education relates educational practice to theological principles. It is designed to meet the specific needs of the church in the light of increasing demands for persons trained in Christian education. The program is structured to include biblical and theological foundations, a core curriculum consisting of foundational courses and practical skills, vocational specialization, and additional electives.

The Master of Arts in Marriage and Family Ministries is designed to equip those in the local church for a specific ministry to families. It includes courses in biblical and theological foundations, understanding Christian education principles, ministry, and skills, and a core curriculum.

The Master of Theology prepares students for both increased effectiveness in professional pastoral ministry and further study at the Ph.D. and Th.D. level. The program is of special interest to students pursuing a teaching career. The major areas offered are in the departments of Bible exposition, missions and intercultural studies, New Testament, practical theology, semitics and Old Testment, and systematic theology.

The Doctor of Ministry is the highest professional degree for ordained persons in the parish or related ministries. It is distinct from the Th.D. or Ph.D. in that its primary emphasis is on the practice of ministry rather than on research and teaching. The program requires resident study and a dissertation action project.

The Doctor of Education is designed to provide graduates with the academic foundation, theological perspective, and skills needed to be highly competent professionals in Christian Education. The program requires a minimum of 48 units beyond the Master's degree.

Special Programs

The School of Intercultural Studies and World Missions, in addition to its undergraduate work, offers graduate work leading to the Master of Arts and the Doctor of Missiology degrees. The School was established to prepare missionary recruits from every nation with cross-cultural communication skills for international service; to provide missions the opportunity to encourage the personal and academic development of their overseas staff; and to prepare ministers and Christian education professionals for the types of cross-cultural ministries to be encountered in today's multi-ethnic and multi-national world.

The Institute of Theological Studies is a program in which graduate-level courses are offered by extension or independent study off-campus. It is a cooperative effort of the Conservative Baptist Theological Seminary, Covenant Theological Seminary, Dallas Theological Seminary, Grace Theological Seminary, Talbot Theological Seminary, Trinity Evangelical Divinity School, and Western Conservative Baptist Seminary.

Talbot Seminary began offering Master of Divinity classes at the Talbot Valley Campus in the Fall of 1977 to serve San Fernando Valley residents. Facilities for classrooms and offices are provided by the Grace Community Church of the Valley, located in Sun Valley. Administrative functions are centralized at La Mirada.

Buddhist Studies, Institute of
2717 Haste Street
Berkeley, CA 94704   (415) 849-2383

General Description. The Institute for Buddhist Studies (IBS) was founded in 1966 as a graduate school for the Buddhist ministry and for research. Founded by the Buddhist Churches of America (BCA), which is affiliated with the Honpa-Hongwanji branch of Jodo Shinshu Buddhism, the Institute grants a Master of Arts degree. In February 1985 the IBS became an affiliate of the Graduate Theological Union (GTU). The GTU is the coordinating organization for one of the most inclusive concentration of religious educational resources in the world, and this marks the first time another major world religion has joined in a consortium with religious schools from the Judeo-Christian traditions.

With this affiliation the IBS and GTU offer a joint M.A. program in Buddhist Studies. Approximately two-thirds of the courses will be taken at the IBS and the remaining courses will be taken at the GTU.

The purpose of the IBS is to make available, in English, the teachings and practices of Buddhism. Further, the IBS was formed in the belief that Buddhism must be taught and learned in the way Buddhists actually experience it: as a living and dynamic system. Its objectives are to: prepare men and women for the Jodo Shinshu Buddhist ministry; offer an M.A. degree in Buddhist studies; offer courses and seminars to all persons who seek to deepen their knowledge of Buddhism; develop instructional programs and conduct research; expand the existing library to meet the objectives of the IBS; produce academic publications; maintain a Buddhist bookstore.

Community Environment. See: Franciscan School of Theology (Berkeley) and California Institute of Integral Studies (San Francisco).

Religious Denomination. Buddhist Churches of America.

Religious Emphasis. Jodo Shinshu Buddhism.

Accreditation. California State Department of Education.

Term System. Semester.

Enrollment in Degree Programs in Religion 1984–85. Total 8; men 6, women 2.

Faculty for Degree Programs in Religion. Total 8; full-time 1, part-time 7.

Admission Requirements. Bachelor's degree from an ac-

credited institution; 3 letters of recommendation (for ministerial students, one letter should be from a member of the clergy, preferably a Jodo Shinshu minister; statement of purposes of study (2 typed double-spaced pages); Graduate Record Examination Aptitude Test scores. Prerequisites for admission include one semester of introduction to religion or world religions; one semester of introduction to Buddhism, Eastern religions, or Eastern philosophy; one year of modern college-level Japanese (ministerial students only). Students may be admitted without these prerequisites but will be required to fulfill them during the first year under a probationary status.

Tuition and Fees. $100 per unit; approximately $2,400 annual tuition for full-time students; $50 per unit for auditing.

Financial Aid. No financial assistance is currently available for the M.A. program. Financial aid in the form of work-study and federal loans is available through the Graduate Theological Union for the GTU-IBS M.A. program. Financial assistance is available from the second year, primarily in the form of tuition deferment, for the ministerial programs. Private scholarships are also available.

Housing. No campus housing.

Library Facilities. 5,000 volumes, mostly on Buddhism in English and Japanese languages.

Religious Services/Activities. Three times per week.

Degree Programs

The Master of Arts degree academic program of the Institute consists of 48 units and is a two-year course of study. The GTU-IBS M.A. program consists of 48 units and is also a two-year course of study.

The IBS M.A. track ministerial program requires, in addition to the 48 units of the IBS M.A. academic program, 18 units of functional ministerial training courses; the program is a two-to-three-year program. The GTU-IBS M.A. track ministerial program requires, in addition to the 48 units of the GTU-IBS M.A. academic program. 18 units of functional ministerial training courses. It is also a two-to-three-year program.

Special Programs

The following programs are available through the IBS Extension Division: Correspondence courses; Japan Study Program; Lay-Leader Training Program; Ministers' Continuing Education Program; Re-orientation Program (to provide preparatory training for American ministers returning from Japan); Ryukoku University Exchange Program; Summer Session; Summer Youth Program (for ages 14-19).

California Baptist College
Division of Religion
8432 Magnolia Avenue
Riverside, CA 92504   (714) 689-5771

Administration. Dr. Russell R. Tuck, President; Dr. Cecil M. Hyatt, Chairperson, Division of Religion.

General Description. California Baptist College was founded in 1950 in El Monte, California. It moved to its present campus in 1955. The College is a Christian liberal arts institution founded by Southern Baptists and grants the Bachelor of Arts, Bachelor of Science, and Bachelor of Music degrees.

Community Environment. The College is located 50 miles east of Los Angeles in Riverside. The 77-acre campus includes six main buildings.

Religious Denomination. Southern Baptist.

Accreditation. Western Association of Schools and Colleges.

Term System. Semester.

Enrollment in Degree Programs in Religion 1984–85. Total 548 (full-time equivalent).

Admission Requirements. High school graduation or equivalent; SAT or ACT; letters of recommendation; evidence of good moral character.

Tuition and Fees. Tuition $1,937 per semester; room and board $1,440; student fees $375.

Financial Aid. Financial aid "packages" from one or more of federal, state, institutional, and private sources may be granted to eligible students.

Housing. Dormitory housing is available on campus.

Library Facilities. The library houses over 105,000 volumes.

Religious Services/Activities. Chapel is held each Wednesday and is required of all students taking 7 or more units.

Degree Programs

The Division of Religion faculty seeks to assist all church-related vocational students to make the best possible preparation for their service to God, including assisting those who plan go to seminary for additional training. The requirements for a Religion major include the completion of 24 upper-division units. The Bachelor of Arts degree requires the completion of 124 units. Courses are offered in Bible (Old Testament, New Testament, Greek, and Hebrew) by the Department of Biblical Studies and in History/Theology, Ministry, and Discipleship by the Department of Religious Studies.

California Institute of Integral Studies
Philosophy and Religion Department
765 Ashbury Street
San Francisco, CA 94417   (415) 753-6100

Administration. Paul Schwartz, Philosophy and Religion Director.

General Description. The Philosophy and Religion program of the California Institute of Integral Studies (formerly California Institute of Asian Studies) promotes an historical and cultural understanding of the world's great philosophical and religious traditions. The program is structured to reflect its deep commitment to the diversity of East/West experience, honoring tradition/contemporary and orthodox/esoteric forms. This comprehensive range of courses offers students a crosscultural perspective which not only facilitates their individual growth, but makes them knowledgeable participants in the larger process of cultural evolution and expansion of human entity.

Parent Institution. The central, distinctive mission of the California Institute of Integral Studies is to provide an environment, facilities, and guidance for systematic, disciplined study and research in the integration of Eastern and Western world-views, philosophies, value-systems, psychologies, spiritual practices, and cultural traditions. The "East-West" dimension of interest is defined broadly to encompass comparative and synthesizing approaches to the understanding of all of humankind's varied cultures, and of the spiritual dimension which gives them their underlying unity. A complementary objective is the integration of the religious, mythic, and symbolic philosophies of analytic paradigms of modern science.

Community Environment. San Francisco is one of the most cosmopolitan cities in the United States. It is the financial center of the west, and an important industrial city. A great port, it serves as the terminus for trans-Pacific and coastwise steamship lines and airlines. The city is located on hills at the end of a narrow peninsula with the Pacific Ocean on one side and the San Francisco Bay on the other. The annual temperature averages 57 degrees. San Francisco is the largest landlocked bay in the world, and is the home of the beautiful Golden Gate Bridge. All modes of transportation serve the area. A large civic center includes the city hall, public library, civic auditorium, state building, federal office building, health center, opera house, and war memorial building. Job opportunities vary considerably but are available. San Francisco has 438 churches, 52 public parks, and 100 theaters. Recreational facilities are numerous for all water sports, hiking, and fishing. Mountain resort areas are approximately a three hour drive. Famous Chinatown is located here, as is the picturesque Fisherman's Wharf.

Religious Denomination. None.

Accreditation. Western Association of Schools and Colleges.

Term System. Quarter; summer term.

Enrollment in Degree Programs in Religion 1984–85. Total 38; men 20, women 18.

Degrees in Religion Awarded 1984–85. Master of Arts 1; men 1. Doctor of Philosophy 2; men 1, women 1.

Faculty for Degree Programs in Religion. Total 9; full-time 4, part-time 5.

Admission Requirements. Applications are accepted for both the M.A. and Ph.D. programs. The student must submit an application, official transcripts of undergraduate and any previous graduate study, and a statement of educational goals. An interview with the program director is required prior to full admission. Doctoral applicants are also asked to furnish a sample of previous work and two academic letters of reference.

Tuition and Fees. Tuition $135 per unit for Master's program; $175 per unit for Ph.D. program; admission application fee $35; registration fee $35; other miscellaneous fees where applicable.

Financial Aid. To participate in financial aid programs, enrollment in the Institute on at least a half-time basis (6 units) is required. Available are student loans, college work-study, Institute Work Exchange, fellowships, and scholarships.

Housing. Off-campus housing only.

Library Facilities. The library contains 28,000 titles with a growth rate of more than a thousand volumes per year. The collection is particularly strong in fields of counseling, psychology, philosophy and religion, East-West comparative studies, and various facets of an integral world view.

Degree Programs

The Master of Arts and Doctor of Philosophy programs in Philosophy and Religion prepare students for research and teaching in the fields of comparative philosophy and religion and religious studies. Because the Institute also provides complete training in psychology and counseling, mental health professionals may take advantage of the opportunity to deepen their understanding of the interrelationship between psychology and philosophy/religion. Students establish close working relationships with faculty members who can assist them in integrating all aspects of their experience at the Institute: the intellectual, the spiritual or religious, and the physical.

Special Programs

The Kern Foundation of Chicago is currently supporting Institute efforts to increase its already considerable contribution to the dissemination of understanding of Asian, East-West and theosophic teachings by augmenting Institute resources in these aspects of its curriculum. Beginning in 1978, the Kern Foundation has provided generous grants to the Institute to extend contemporary understanding of theosophic principles and relate that understanding to concepts and practices of philosophy, religion, and depth psychology.

California Lutheran College
Department of Religion
69 West Olson Road
Thousand Oaks, CA 91359   (805) 492-2411

Administration. Jerry H. Miller, President.

General Description. California Lutheran College began classes in 1961 and offers undergraduate, graduate, and continuing education programs that embody the Lutheran higher education traditions of academic excellence and a commitment to the service of God and the human community. The Department of Religion offers a major and advises in the structuring of a program for pre-theological studies. It awards the Bachelor of Arts degree.

Community Environment. The 285-acre campus is located in Thousand Oaks, one of the nation's significant industrial and research centers. It is an hour's drive from central Los Angeles and 18 miles north of the Pacific Ocean and Malibu.

Religious Denomination. American Lutheran Church and the Pacific Southwest Synod of the Lutheran Church in America.

Accreditation. Western Association of Schools and Colleges.

Term System. Semester (4-1-4 plan).

Faculty for Degree Programs in Religion. Total 5.

Admission Requirements. High school graduation with rank in the upper half of graduating class; SAT.

Tuition and Fees. Tuition $6,300 per year; student fee $130; room and board $2,600.

Financial Aid. The College has established a "Package Aid Plan" that includes scholarships, partial tuition grants, supplemental opportunity grants, PELL grants, low interest government loans, and student employment.

Housing. Dormitory accommodations are available on campus.

Library Facilities. The Pearson Library houses a book collection of more than 100,000 volumes supplemented by journals, microforms, and audiovisual software.

Religious Services/Activities. Chapel or convocation is held twice a week. Nazareth, Mission, and Open Groups are available for student participation.

Degree Programs

The major in Religion leading to the Bachelor of Arts degree requires the completion of a minimum of 33 credits of specified courses of which 21 credits must be from upper division courses. The Department also offers courses in Biblical languages (Greek and Hebrew).

California, University of - Berkeley
Religious Studies
301 Campbell Hall
Berkeley, CA 94720   (415) 642-2628

Administration. Dr. David P. Gardner, President of the University; Dr. Ira M. Heyman, Chancellor, Berkeley; Dr. Leonard V. Kuhi, Dean, College of Letters and Science.

General Description. The Religious Studies major provides opportunities for securing a broad background in the liberal arts while at the same time allowing for a focus on a thematic concern or a particular religious tradition. It views religion from a global perspective, and combines aspects of the humanities and the social sciences. The major is open to anyone concerned about the symbolic and mythic dimensions of world cultures, the valuative level of existential issues, and the ethical aspects of human societies.

Parent Institution. A publicly-supported coeducational university, this oldest and largest of the University of California campuses enrolls up to 30,000 students. Founded in 1868, the University has grown to include a distinguished faculty of over 1,900. A tradition of excellence in teaching and research has guided the University since its founding.

Community Environment. The 1,533 acres that make up the campus of UC Berkeley extend from the heart of downtown Berkeley into wooded hills that overlook the Bay and nearby San Francisco. Despite a rapid and intensive construction program, the campus retains the pleasant atmosphere of a park.

Religious Denomination. None.

Accreditation. Western Association of Schools and Colleges.

Term System. Quarter; summer term.

Admission Requirements. For information regarding admission to the University as an Undergraduate, the Office of Admissions should be contacted at: 120 Sproul Hall, UC Berkeley, Berkeley, CA 94720, (415) 642-0200.

Financial Aid. For information contact the Financial Aid Office, 250 Sproul Hall, UC Berkeley, Berkeley, CA 94720; (415) 642-6442 for last name A-K, (415) 642-6492 for last name L-Z.

Housing. The Housing Office is located at 2401 Bowditch Street, UC Berkeley, Berkeley, CA 94720, (415) 642-3642.

Library Facilities. Students have access to the University of California Library system.

Degree Programs

The Bachelor of Arts with a major in Religious Studies program requires both a general understanding of the study of religion and a particular emphasis on one specific tradition or thematic concern. The general requirement involves courses that present the methodological appro-

aches to the study of religion (such as sociology of religion, psychology of religion, history of religion) and courses that examine thematic issues and cross-cultural phenomena (such as myth, ritual, transformative experience, and comparative ethics). The religious traditions that may be included as major fields of emphasis or as supplementary courses include the Jewish, Islamic, Christian, Hindu, and Buddhist traditions, as well as the religious cultures of China, Japan, Africa, and Native American communities. Most of the courses available for the program are religion-related courses taught within such departments as history, sociology, and Near Eastern Studies. To supplement these courses the program offers a small number of courses sponsored by Religious Studies, including thematic topics of religion, and the introductory courses (one of which surveys the world's religious traditions, and the other of which introduces the study of religious phenomena thematically).

California, University of - Los Angeles
405 Hilgard Avenue
Los Angeles, CA 90024   (213) 825-5754

Administration. Charles E. Young, Chancellor.

General Description. The Study of Religion, Near Eastern Studies, and Islamic Studies are interdepartmental programs. The programs lead to the Bachelor of Arts (Study of Religion major), Bachelor of Arts in Near Eastern Studies, and the Master of Arts and Ph.D. in Islamic Studies.

Parent Institution. The University of California at Los Angeles (UCLA) is a publicly supported, coeducational university that is academically ranked among the leading universities in the United States. Its 13 schools grant the Bachelor, Master, and Doctorate as well as Teacher Certification Credentials, M.D. degree, the Juris Doctor degree, and the D.D.S. degree. The University was established in 1919.

Community Environment. The campus is located in the residential community of Westwood, five miles from Santa Monica and the Pacific Ocean and 30 minutes from the center of downtown Los Angeles to the east. The campus covers over 400 acres and contains 128 buildings.

Religious Denomination. None.

Accreditation. Western Association of Schools and Colleges.

Term System. Quarter.

Admission Requirements. Admission is based on a record of high grades in previous schoolwork and the completion of high school academic college preparatory courses; SAT or ACT.

Tuition and Fees. California residents: no tuition; fees $432 per quarter; nonresident tuition $1,272 per quarter plus fees $432; cost of housing varies.

Financial Aid. Students must demonstrate financial need. The four basic kinds of aid are grants, loans, work-study employment, and scholarships.

Housing. Many different types of housing are available. The UCLA Housing Office supplies information and current listings of available University-owned apartments and residence halls, private apartments, cooperatives, fraternities, and sororities.

Library Facilities. The University Library on the UCLA campus is one of the country's largest and most renowned academic libraries. The 24-unit system consists of the University Research Library, the College Library, 17 specialized subject libraries, and several reading rooms. Collectively they contain nearly six million volumes. Supplementing the University Library is the William Andrews Clark Memorial Library with its collection of some 80,000 volumes and 14,900 manuscripts related to English culture of the seventeenth and eighteenth centuries.

Religious Services/Activities. Many churches are located in the Westwood and neighboring Los Angeles communities.

Degree Programs

The major in the Study of Religion leading to the Bachelor's degree requires a minimum of 13 upper division courses and three related courses in foreign language. In addition, the student must select one of the following nine groups as the main area of study: Ancient Near East and Eastern Europe, Indo-European Traditions, Greece and Rome, Israel and Judaism, Christianity, Islam, South Asia, Far East, Traditional and Nonliterate Cultures.

The Master of Arts in Islamic Studies requires a minimum of nine courses, five of which must be graduate. The candidate must take no fewer than four courses on the appropriate level in the two Near Eastern languages of choice. Major fields are offered in Arabic, Persian, Turkish, history of the Near East, political science, anthropology, sociology, Islamic art, Islamic music.

An interdepartmental program offers advanced study leading to the Ph.D. degree.

California, University of - Riverside
Department of Religious Studies
Riverside, CA 92521   (714) 787-3741

Administration. Dr. June E. O'Connor, Chair, Department of Religious Studies.

General Description. The Department of Religious Studies examines the major religious traditions that have played a crucial part in the history and thought of humankind, and that continue to be of vital significance. Majoring in Religious Studies has proven to be excellent preparation for seminary for those interested in a church vocation. It provides essential background for teaching about religion in primary or secondary schools, and is appropriate preparation for graduate school in the area of religion for those interested in an academic career. The Department offers students an opportunity to engage in the study of religion in greater depth than may previously have been possible. In addition, it provides the means for developing a mature approach to life through examining the roots of religion and the various ways in which religions approach questions of meaning and fulfillment. The approach taken by the faculty is objective and nonconfessional, but at the same time empathetic in keeping with an area that has meant so much to humankind throughout history.

Parent Institution. The University of California - Riverside is a publicly supported, coeducational university which was established in 1907 as a Citrus Experiment Station to do research in the agricultural problems of the area. It now has four divisions and grants the Bachelor, Master, and Doctorate degrees.

Community Environment. Riverside, California has a population of 200,000 and is located 60 miles east of Los Angeles. The campus is located 2 miles east of downtown Riverside.

Religious Denomination. None.

Accreditation. Western Association of Schools and Colleges.

Term System. Quarter; summer term.

Enrollment in Degree Programs in Religion 1984–85. Total 12; men 9, women 3.

Degrees in Religion Awarded 1984–85. Bachelor of Arts 12; men 9, women 3.

Faculty for Degree Programs in Religion. Total 3; full-time 3.

Admission Requirements. High school graduation. A minimum of 16 units of high school work must be completed during grades 9 through 12; 15 of the 16 required units must be in academic or college-preparatory courses; 7 of the 15 must have been taken during the last 2 years of high school. Non-California residents must, in addition to the above, have a B-plus high school average, submit scores from either SAT or ACT and from 3 CEEB achievement tests.

Tuition and Fees. Per quarter: registration fee $178; education fee undergraduate $241, graduate $261; nonresident tuition $1,272. For three quarters (nine-month basis): books and supplies $330-$400, housing $3,166-$3,700.

Financial Aid. Extensive facilities are offered for assisting the students to obtain financial aid, scholarships, grants, loans, and employment.

Housing. There are two student residence halls with a total capacity of 1,200 for single students and a family housing complex with 202 two-bedroom and 66 three-bedroom houses available for married students. Fraternity and sorority students have available 244 apartments and suites. Child-care facilities as well as off-campus housing are available.

Library Facilities. The Library contains over 1 million volumes with 23,000 in the field of religion.

Degree Programs

The Bachelor of Arts degree program with a major in Religious Studies examines the religious traditions that have played a crucial part in the history and thought of humankind. Each student major is expected to take 3 lower division Religious Studies courses plus a minimum of 36 upper division units distributed as follows: (1) at least 1 course from each of the 5 areas of Eastern Religions, Origins of Western Religions, Religious Thought and Ritual, Religious Ethics, History of Western Religions; (2) one seminar course in Religious Studies or the senior thesis; (3) remaining 12 units from upper division courses in Religious Studies or related courses in other departments. For those interested in a high school teaching career, specified Religous Studies courses have been approved by the State Department of Education as satisfying the content requirement for a single subject teaching credential in social studies with an emphasis on Religious Studies.

An accelerated Master of Arts Program in Religion is available at the Claremont Graduate School for qualifying UC Riverside Religous Studies majors. The program enables those accepted to complete the M.A. in religion at the nearby school with no more than a year of study after receiving the B.A. degree at UC Riverside.

Chapman College
Department of Religion
333 North Glassell Street
Orange, CA 92666   (714) 997-6608

Administration. Dr. G.T. Smith, President; Dr. Ronald M. Huntington, Chair, Department of Religion.

General Description. Chapman College has a full undergraduate program of religious studies, with major, split majors with related departments, and minor available. The faculty backgrounds and department orientation (as well as the student body) are pluralistic and operate within a strong liberal arts context.

The founders of Chapman College had as one of their purposes the establishment of an institution where those entering church vocations could receive a broad liberal arts education as a foundation for seminary or graduate work. Over the years many outstanding leaders in the Disciples of Christ and other communions have received their basic preparation at Chapman College.

The typical pre-ministerial student should combine a broad liberal arts program with a Religion major because the essential foundations for graduate-professional studies lie in the whole range of social, intellectual, and spiritual learning that the College offers. The Department of Religion maintains a file of catalogs of major seminaries and can advise students concerning pre-seminary studies.

Parent Institution. Chapman College is named in honor of Charles C. Chapman (1853-1944), pioneer Orange County leader among members of the Christian Churches of Southern California. In 1918, California Christian College was incorporated and in 1934 the name was changed to Chapman College. The College is part of a long heritage of higher education in California related to the Christian Church (Disciples of Christ), dating back to Hesperian College, founded by members of the Christian Church in Woodland in 1861. This institution and several others later merged with California Christian College in Los Angeles. The present campus in Orange was occupied in 1954, providing the beneifts of life in a smaller community and improved plant facilities.

The College maintains ties with the Disciples of Christ which has a strong tradition of ecumenism. The study body is highly diverse, representing most religious orientations. Because nearly 20 percent of the students are international, non-Christian religions are well represented on campus.

Community Environment. The city of Orange (locally referred to as "The City") is located 32 miles southeast of Los Angeles and 94 miles north of San Diego. Its climate is mild with a very low rainfall. As the name implies, Orange lies in a vast citrus belt.

Religious Denomination. Christian Church (Disciples of Christ).

Religious Emphasis. Liberal.

Accreditation. Western Association of Schools and Colleges.

Term System. Semester with interterm (4-1-4); summer session.

Enrollment in Degree Programs in Religion 1984–85. Total 14; men 7, women 7.

Degrees in Religion Awarded 1984–85. Bachelor of Arts 3; men 1, women 2.

Faculty for Degree Programs in Religion. Total 8; full-time 6, part-time 2.

Admission Requirements. High school graduation; cumulative grade point average in all academic coursework should be at least 2.5 on a 4.0 scale; SAT or ACT scores. There are no creedal requirements for admission.

Tuition and Fees. Tuition $8,200 per year; room and board per academic year $3,180 double, $4,400 single (additional charge of $460 for interterm), apartments range from $355 to $620 per month. Additional fees where applicable.

Financial Aid. The primary purpose of the college student aid programs is to provide financial assistance to students who would be unable to attend without it. The College, however, will honor with scholarships certain students who have superior academic or performance records. All students must be admitted to Chapman College before financial aid can be offered.

In recognition of the considerable support received from the Disciples of Christ, and because Chapman desires to serve young people in the denomination in as many ways as possible, the College will recognize with a stipend a student recommended by the student's pastor, or the chief officer of the church. This stipend is not renewable unless the student can demonstrate need. Ministerial grants are available to ordained ministers whose duties are full time, to their spouses, and their children. Chapman College will match in an amount up to $500 per year, the amount of grant awarded by a student's home church. For a student preparing for a church-related vocation, the Church Matching Grant will be matched in an amount up to $700 per year. The Philosophy Scholarship for Religious Studies is awarded to students of academic excellence, personal religious commitment, and exemplary moral character who have an interest in undergraduate study of Philosophy and a commitment to pursuing graduate work in religious studies. The Zulch Scholarship is awarded with first preference given to blood relatives of the donor, and preference is given to students planning careers in Christian service.

Housing. Dormitories, college apartments for married students, and off-campus housing are available.

Library Facilities. The library of Chapman College houses 180,000 volumes with a special collection of Albert Schweitzer memorabilia. Students have formal reciprocal borrowing privileges with California State University at Fullerton.

Religious Services/Activities. Religious services are not compulsory. Protestant interdenominational services are held twice a week; Catholic Mass once a week; Jewish services of varying frequency. Optional retreats are held twice a year.

Degree Programs

The Department of Religion offers coursework leading to a Bachelor of Arts degree. The curriculum is designed to provide a liberal arts background in the contribution of religion to human civilization, a pre-professional education, and preparation for graduate work in the study of religion and related disciplines. The four emphases represented in the curriculum are Biblical Literature, World Religions, Christian History and Thought, and Applied Ministries. The Department offers a choice of two distinct emphases within the major: Emphasis I, Religion, and Emphasis, II Philosophy and Religion.

Special Programs

The Residence Education Centers of Chapman College comprise a network of over 40 military and civilian centers providing classes in a variety of locations including hospitals, prisons, factories, business establishments, and churches. Each Center offers specific degree programs to meet the particular needs of its students.

Christ College Irvine
Religion Division
1530 Concordia
Irvine, CA 92715   (714) 854-8002

Administration. Dr. D. Ray Halm, President; Dr. Shang Ik Moon, Vice President for Academic Affairs, Academic Dean.

General Description. The Religion Division of Christ College Irvine teaches its classes in the spirit of the liberal arts. The faculty teaching in this division are Evangelical Lutheran Christians. The Division has close ties with the Biblical Languages Department of the Humanities Division.

Parent Institution. Christ College Irvine is a liberal arts institution. It is dedicated to the Great Commission and emphasizes the importance of cross-cultural study, modeling of the Christian life, mission mindedness, and a commitment to excellence. The Institution is owned and operated by the Lutheran Church - Missouri Synod. It seeks to prepare Christians for enhanced service to God in the world today and tomorrow.

Community Environment. Enjoying a strategic West Coast setting 45 miles southeast of Los Angeles, Christ College Irvine is located on a rambling 63-acre plateau of hills overlooking Orange Country. The site was chosen for its wealth of opportunities for interaction with nearby educational, religious, and civic institutions.

Religious Denomination. Lutheran Church - Missouri Synod.

Religious Emphasis. Evangelical Lutheran.

Accreditation. Western Association of Schools and Colleges.

Term System. Quarter; reduced summer term.

Enrollment in Degree Programs in Religion 1984–85. Total 279; men 138, women 141. Men: 48 pre-seminary, 60 parochial teacher, 26 director of Christian education, 4 director of evangelism. Women: 1 pre-seminary, 116 parochial teacher, 22 director of Christian education, 2 parish assistant.

Degrees in Religion Awarded 1984–85. Bachelor of Arts (Pre-seminary) 11; men 11. Bachelor of Arts (Education) 16; men 5, women 11. Bachelor of Arts (Director of Christian Education) 2; men 1, women 1.

Faculty for Degree Programs in Religion. Total 28; full-time 26, part-time 2.

Admission Requirements. The applicant must be a high school graduate or have completed the equivalent of the high school level of education; must have attained a minimum cumulative grade point average of 2.00 on a 4.00 scale; completed a college preparatory program that included 3 years of English, 2 years of science, U.S. History, and 2 years of mathematics (including Algebra and Geometry). To be accepted as a regular student the applicant should have attained a total combination score of 700 on the SAT (including only the verbal and the quantitative scores), or its equivalent.

Tuition and Fees. Per quarter: tuition $1,400; room $480; activity fee $25; capital use fee $20.

Financial Aid. The College participates in many programs of financial aid for college students which have been developed nationally, within the State of California, and within the Church. Grants, loans, scholarships, and awards are available.

Housing. Unmarried students who do not live with their parents or close relatives are required to live on campus or in a designated off-campus residence.

Library Facilities. The library collection numbers approximately 56,000 volumes, 350 phonograph records, 1,300 cassette tapes, plus pamphlet files, pictures, slides, kits, filmstrip, and videotapes. The collection is strong in the area of religion and theology with an emphasis in evangelism and missions. The library of the University of California, Irvine, is available to Christ College Irvine students.

Religious Services/Activities. Chapel services are held on campus daily (except Wednesday). Other special services are held regularly. Students have many evening devotions and Bible studies organized on campus. The College encourages area church attendance and worship and endorses congregational participation. The Campus Chaplain is responsible for the spiritual life of the campus.

Degree Programs

The Bachelor of Arts degree programs leading to preparation for full-time Church vocations and secular occupations are offered. These programs include: Pre-Seminary Pastoral Program, Teacher Education Program, Director of Christian Education Program, Director of Evangelism Program, Social Works Program, and a Liberal Arts Program. Each program of study consists of three component parts: (1) General Education, (2) Professional Sequence, and (3) Major-Minor. The curriculum may be adjusted and revised to meet specific needs of students.

Special Programs

The Associate of Arts degree program is offered in General Studies and Pre-Professional (Pre-Deaconsess).

Credit and noncredit courses are available through the Continuing Education Program and they may be applied toward a degree. In-service education for teachers, DCE's, pastors, church officers, and congregation members are regularly offered.

The Colloquy Program qualifies teachers who have not had religion courses which they need to be considered eligible for listing as Lutheran teachers on the official roster of the Lutheran Church-Missouri Synod.

Christian Heritage College
Department of Ministerial Training
2100 Greenfield Drive
El Cajon, CA 92021   (619) 440-3043

Administration. Dr. David Jeremiah, President.

General Description. The Department of Ministerial Training gives general education in Biblical studies as well as preparatory studies for professional service in pastoral work, missionary work including missionary aviation, and teaching in secondary educational settings.

Parent Institution. Christian Heritage College was opened in the Fall of 1970 under the sponsorship of Scott Memorial Baptist Church in San Diego. The first graduates were awarded degrees in June of 1973. Classes met in the building of the Church in San Diego for the first three years. The present campus was acquired and is now shared by the College, Christian High School, and Scott Memorial Baptist Church (El Cajon).

The beautifully landscaped thirty-acre complex has ten buildings. In addition to the church and classroom buildings, facilities include a modern dining hall, air-conditioned dormitories, a large library, chapel, music room, student lounges, and indoor recreation areas. Outdoor facilities include tennis, basketball, and volleyball courts; soccer, football, and baseball fields; and an olympic-size swimming pool.

Community Environment. The campus is situated in the foothills approximately two miles from the center of El Cajon, a suburb of San Diego, giving access to nearby air, rail, and bus terminals. Greenfield Drive connects the College with Interstate 8, one mile to the north. El Cajon's moderate winter climate makes outdoor activities a year-round possibility. The location of the College affords short travel distances to nearby mountain, desert, and beach resort areas. Freeways put any point in the San Diego vacationland within 45 minutes of the campus. San Diego's many cultural, entertainment, and research centers afford Christian Heritage College students excellent opportunities to participate in a wide variety of educational, recreational, and cultural activities.

Religious Denomination. Baptist.

Religious Emphasis. Fundamentalist.

Accreditation. Western Association of Schools and Colleges; Transnational Association of Christian Schools.

Term System. Modular ("Single-Subject-in-Sequence" academic calendar). This type of calendar is a unique approach to scheduling classes which derives its name from the fact that students take one course at a time "in sequence" instead of taking from four to seven courses concurrently. The 15-week semester is divided into five short terms, or modules, each of which lasts three weeks. Summer term.

Enrollment in Degree Programs in Religion 1984–85. Total 40; men 30, women 10.

Degrees in Religion Awarded 1984–85. Bachelor of Arts

17; men 13, women 4.

Faculty for Degree Programs in Religion. Total 11; full-time 3, part-time 8.

Admission Requirements. Graduation from a standard high school or the equivalent; satisfactory SAT score.

Tuition and Fees. Tuition $1,840 per semester; part-time $155 per unit; student activities fee $45 per semester; room $450 per semester; board for dormitory students $665 per semester. Additional fees where applicable.

Financial Aid. A broad spectrum of student-aid programs is available including scholarships, grants, student-loan funds, and student work opportunities.

Housing. On-campus residence hall facilities are available for more than 200 single students. These facilities include two- and three-student rooms with lounges and laundry equipment located nearby. Single rooms are provided on a space-available basis.

Library Facilities. The library consists of more than 61,000 volumes. Periodicals number over 750 in the main collection and more than 150 in the Institute for Creation Research collection. Students have access to more than two million volumes in university and college libraries in the San Diego area.

Religious Services/Activities. All degree-seeking, full-time students are required to complete a Christian Service (Sunday School teaching, special education, bus ministry, rest homes, Turning Point Television) each semester. A Christian Service is selected by the student, must be part of a local church ministry, and involve approximately three hours a week or about 45 hours a semester. Chapel is required of all students, whether full-time or part-time when they are in either a morning or afternoon module. One week during the spring semester is devoted to morning and evening sessions with outstanding Bible expositors. These sessions are required for all full-time students. All degree-seeking students are required to complete successfully an evangelism program. Evangelism classes meet an hour a week, and students are expected to invest about three hours a week in field work in addition to other assignments.

Degree Programs

The Bachelor of Arts in Biblical Studies is designed to provide preparation toward seminary entrance, while including certain additional training focused on foundational Bible knowledge, speaking skills, and practical Christian experiences through an intern program. Objectives for Pastoral and Christian School Teacher Training focus on providing learning experiences that encourage in the student effective use of the Bible in personal life and public ministry, and provide the student with a basic mastery of all the major doctrines of the Word of God that will enable him to construct a defensible system of truth for use as both an apologetic and a polemic. Training in General Missions is designed to foster Biblical knowledge, evangelism, and techniques for organizing a local church, and to provide an understanding of languages, cultural

variations, and religious differences.

The Bachelor of Science in Missionary Aviation Maintenance has been designed to enable students to go to the mission fields as maintenance personnel, as well as being church organizers and being able to carry out other specific missionary duties.

The Bachelor of Science in Missionary Aviation is designed to help the student earn the FAA private and commercial licenses with the instrument and multi-engine ratings, along with the airframe and powerplant mechanic's rating.

Church Divinity School of the Pacific
2451 Ridge Road
Berkeley, CA 94709   (415) 848-3282

Administration. William S. Pregnall, President.

General Description. The Church Divinity School of the Pacific is the official seminary of the Province of the Pacific of the Episcopal Church. It was founded in 1893 and is open to men and women preparing for the ministry and for other forms of church work. It is a participating member of the Graduate Theological Union. *See:* Graduate Theological Union.

Community Environment. The School is located one block north of the North Gate of the University of California in Berkeley, one of the nation's leading educational centers for scholarship and research.

Religious Denomination. Episcopal Church (Province of the Pacific).

Accreditation. Western Association of Schools and Colleges; Association of Theological Schools in the United States and Canada.

Term System. Semester.

Enrollment in Degree Programs in Religion 1984–85. Total 91.

Admission Requirements. Bachelor of Arts degree from an accredited college or university; Graduate Record Examination.

Tuition and Fees. Tuition $3,700 per academic year; housing $816; board $2,520.

Financial Aid. The School follows the policies of the Association of Theological Schools in making grants-in-aid to students on the basis of need.

Housing. Residence hall accommodations are available on campus. A limited amount of housing is available for married students.

Library Facilities. Students have access to the combined libraries of member institutions of the Graduate Theological Union and the University of California.

Religious Services/Activities. Each weekday, Morning Prayer and Evening Prayer, and Holy Eucharist are read or sung in the chapel. Each Thursday evening, the entire community gathers for Eucharist. Quiet days and class retreats are planned.

Degree Programs

The Master of Divinity degree prepares men and women for professional ministry, whether lay or ordained. Both academic study and practical pastoral experience are emphasized. In the first two years, students establish a firm grounding in Bible, church history, ethics, and theology. As the Old and New Testament are studied, students are taught sufficient Hebrew and Greek to use exegetical tools. Elective courses in the senior year provide time to develop special interests such as counseling, liturgics, or biblical studies.

The Master of Theological Studies is a two year program providing academic grounding in theological disciplines for persons who do not plan an ordained ministry. The degree requires sixteen 4-unit courses from the areas of Bible, Theology, Church History, and Thesis/Project.

The Master of Arts degree is granted jointly by the School and the Graduate Theological Union. It prepares people to teach religion at elementary through junior college levels or to undertake Doctoral studies. Joint Doctoral degree programs are also available.

Claremont Graduate School
Department of Religion
900 North College Avenue
Claremont, CA 91711   (714) 621-8000

Administration. Dr. John H. Hick, Danforth Professor of Religion, Chairman of the Department of Religion.

General Description. The graduate study of Religion is a joint program with the School of Theology at Claremont and the Institute for Antiquity and Christianity whose staffs participate in teaching and supervision and research.

Parent Institution. The Claremont Graduate School, founded in 1925, is a private college devoted to study beyond the bachelor's degree. The School has over 70 faculty members. In addition, it draws upon the faculties of the five undergraduate Claremont Colleges and two other affiliated institutions.

Community Environment. Claremont is located 35 miles east of Los Angeles. It has a population of 21,500.

Religious Denomination. Nondenominational.

Accreditation. Western Association of Schools and Colleges.

Term System. Semester.

Faculty for Degree Programs in Religion. Total 30.

Admission Requirements. Bachelor's degree from recognized institution; excellent undergraduate record; letters of recommendation; GRE.

Tuition and Fees. Tuition $3,975 per semester; continuous registration fee $220 per semester; doctoral study fee $420 per semester; institutional services fee $50 per semester; graduate housing $185-$470 per month depending upon accommodations.

Financial Aid. Merit fellowships, teaching and research assistantships, associateships, institutional loans, state and federal aid are among the types of assistance available.

Housing. Graduate apartments are available (usually a waiting list).

Library Facilities. The library resources of the The Claremont Colleges total over 1,200,000 volumes. The central Honnold Library has extensive holdings of journals and receives more than 4,800 periodicals and 2,800 other serials. There are numerous special collections. The McCutchan Collection has assembled many rare books on American hymnology.

Religious Services/Activities. Three college chaplains serve the total academic community. Activities at McAlister Center for Religious Activities are ecumenical and voluntary.

Degree Programs

The faculty in Religion offers graduate programs leading to the Master of Arts and Doctor of Philosophy degrees in the following areas: Philosophy of Religion and Theology, including Theological Ethics; Old Testament; and New Testament.

Claremont, School of Theology at
1325 North College Avenue
Claremont, CA 91711   (714) 626-3521

Administration. Dr. Richard W. Cain, President; Dr. Joseph C. Hough, Jr., Dean.

General Description. The School of Theology at Claremont is a seminary of the United Methodist Church. Its primary purpose is to provide education for students who are preparing to enter the variety of ministries of the church and church-related institutions. The basic degree granted is the Master of Divinity. Also offered are the degrees Doctor of Ministry, the professional Doctor of Ministry (In Service), the Master of Arts, and the Doctor of Philosophy. The Master of Arts degree is available for students who wish to study religion or who wish to pursue theological studies independently of ordination or preparation for the ministry; its fields of specialization are Religion, Theological Studies, Religious Education, and Religion and the Arts. The Doctor of Philosophy degree (Ph.D.) is offered in Theology and Personality, with emphasis in either Counseling or Education. In addition to its own Ph.D. programs, the School jointly provides the Ph.D. programs in Biblical Studies, Theology, Ethics, and Church History in cooperation with the Claremont Graduate School. The Claremont Graduate School is one of the Claremont Colleges, and the School of Theology is an affiliate of that university complex.

Community Environment. Situated at the foot of the San Gabriel Mountains, the School of Theology is surrounded by natural beauty. Bordering it on the north and east is the Rancho Santa Ana Botanic Garden, a display of trees and plants native to the area. Within an hour's drive are the Pacific beaches, Palm Springs and the desert resorts, and the ski slopes of Mt. Baldy, the latter rising over 10,000 feet. The Los Angeles centers of commerce and culture provide a working laboratory of today's complex culture. Among the churches of the area the Gospel is proclaimed in 17 languages.

Religious Denomination. United Methodist Church; the School also has specific affiliate relationships with the Christian Church (Disciples of Christ) and the Episcopal Church.

Religious Emphasis. Main-line Protestant.

Accreditation. Western Association of Schools and Colleges; Association of Theological Schools in the United States and Canada.

Term System. Semester; summer term.

Enrollment in Degree Programs in Religion 1984–85. Total 351; men 213, women 138.

Degrees in Religion Awarded 1984–85. Master of Arts 10; men 5, women 5. Master of Divinity 50; men 27, women 23. Doctor of Ministry 27; men 17, women 10.

Faculty for Degree Programs in Religion. Total 60; full-time 18, part-time 42.

Admission Requirements. Admission requirements to the Master's degrees are a Bachelor of Arts degree or Bachelor of Science degree from an accredited university, with a minimum grade point average of 2.5, and a minimum Graduate Record Examination score of 1000. For the Ph.D. program, A Master of Divinity degree must have been completed in an accredited school, with a grade point average of 3.5 and a minimum Graduate Record Examination score of 1100.

Tuition and Fees. Tuition for Master of Arts and Master of Divinity $2,300 (16 semester units), for Ph.D. $3,680 (16 semester units); room/apartment $105 to $400 per month.

Financial Aid. Aid is administered on the basis of the principles of the Association of Theological Schools. This is done by needs assessment, and the School attempts to meet all financial need with the combined use of student work stipends, guaranteed student loans, and outright grants for tuition. The maximum grant is full tuition.

Housing. The School has housing for both single and married students on campus. The Housing Office assists students in finding off-campus housing when desired or needed.

Library Facilities. The School of Theology Library contains over 123,000 volumes. There is a notable collection of rare books. Of special interest to United Methodists is a group of original Wesley letters and publications. Students have access to the Honold Library in Claremont as well as the holdings of the Southern California Western Theological Library Association members.

Religious Services/Activities. Ecumenical worship and eucharistic services are held once each week. There are annual community retreats and annual faculty retreats.

Degree Programs

The Master of Divinity degree is the basic professional degree offered at the School. Students wishing to qualify for this degree must complete satisfactorily all of the basic studies required and elective advanced studies. In addition, each student must complete a summer or semester of supervised field studies at Claremont. An additional 8 units of credit is given for the field studies requirement. The total units required for graduation are 104. The completion of the program will normally require three full years of study plus one summer of internship. The Basic Studies component of the curriculum includes Basic Aspects of the Study of the Old Testament; Early Christianity: History and Literature; Backgrounds of Contemporary Theology; Christian Thinking About Moral Decisions; History of the Church: Images of Christ to 1650; The Global Context of Ministry; Denominational Studies; and two semesters of an integrative course entitled Foundations of the Arts of Ministry. The Advanced Studies components include Old Testament, New Testament, Theology, Church History, and Ethics.

The School of Theology offers four programs leading to the Master of Arts degree in Religion, Theological Studies, Religious Education, and Religion and the Arts. Each program consists of 60 units of required course work.

The Doctor of Ministry program enables students to continue in advanced studies and to do some specialization in areas of the curriculum that are of particular interest to them. To receive the degree, students must successfully complete the requirements for the Master of Divinity degree and take an additional 32 units.

The Doctor of Philosophy degree program is designed to prepare students for teaching in colleges or theological schools, and for professional leadership in the church and society. The School offers the degree in Theology and Personality with emphasis in either Counseling or Education.

Special Programs

Courses in Continuing Education are taught by the School of Theology faculty members in a number of Western communities. In recent years, classes have been conducted in such cities as Portland, Seattle, Phoenix, Tucson, and Honolulu. Special summer programs are offered in Claremont and the Pacific Northwest.

Dominican School of Philosophy and Theology
2401 Ridge Road
Berkeley, CA 94709   (415) 849-2030

Administration. Antoninus Wall, O.P., President.

General Description. The Dominican School began over 130 years ago with the arrival of six Spanish novices in Monterey, California, to enter the new Novitiate of Saint

Dominic. The novitiate/school moved in 1854 to the seaport town of Benicia on the northern part of the San Francisco Bay. Nearly 80 years later the traditional attraction of the Dominican Order to major university centers led to the final move of the School from Benicia to the Oaklnd/Berkeley area in 1932, in order to be near the University of California. In 1964, the school entered the Graduate Theological Union, a consortium of theological schools, establishing a faculty residence in Berkeley. In 1978, the name was changed from Saint Albert's College to its present name. *See:* Graduate Theological Union.

Parent Institution. The School was established to proved students, both men and women, with training in philosophy, theology, and other related sciences that enable them to carry out the works of ministry in preaching, teaching, and pastoral care. The School emphasizes the systematic learning inspired by its own philosophical and theological tradition which stems from St. Thomas Aquinas.

Community Environment. The campus of 5½ acres is in Berkeley, near the campus of the University of California.

Religious Denomination. Roman Catholic.

Religious Emphasis. Dominican.

Accreditation. Western Association of Schools and Colleges; Association of Theological Schools in the United States and Canada.

Term System. Quarter.

Enrollment in Degree Programs in Religion 1984–85. Total 78.

Admission Requirements. Bachelor's degree from an accredited college or university with 2.0 grade point average.

Tuition and Fees. Tuition $2,800 per year.

Library Facilities. Students have access to the library holdings of the member schools of the Graduate Theological Union and the University of California.

Degree Programs

The program, which for Dominican students consists of six years, is divided into two departments. The Department of Philosophy covers two years of upper division work leading to a Bachelor of Arts in Philosophy with optional pursuit of a Master of Arts degree for qualified students. The Department of Theology consists of four years and offers the academic degree of Master of Arts, Master of Theological Studies, and the professional Master of Divinity in Theology.

Franciscan School of Theology
1712 Euclid Avenue
Berkeley, CA 94709   (415) 848-5232

Administration. Xavier J. Harris, O.F.M., President.

General Description. The Franciscan School of Theology seeks to provide a theological education that is intellectually solid and pastorally sound. Through a variety of programs the Franciscan School prepares students for the manifold ministries of the contemporary Church - whether for the ordained or the non-ordained; for men or women; for students pursuing the Master of Divinity degree required of candidates for ordination or the Master of Theological Studies degree designed for other pastoral ministries - all receive a theological education imbued with the Franciscan charisms of practicality and simplicity.

The Franciscan School of Theology has its origins in the very history of California. The conversion of the Indian tribes of California was committed to the apostolic colleges of San Fernando in Mexico City; of Our Lady of Guadalupe in Zacatecas, Mexico; and of Santa Cruz in Queretaro, Mexico. A total of 127 Franciscan missionaries worked in California between 1769 and 1833. Under the the Presidency of Fray Fermin Francisco de Lasuen, Mission Santa Barbara was founded on December 4, 1786. This mission, like the other twenty missions of California, served as an integral part of the Spanish program for Christianization of the California Indians. Part of the mission program was educational, and at Mission Santa Barbara a school was established for the manual arts, instrumental and vocal music, and religious formation.

Out of this rudimentary educational operation, Mission Santa Barbara was chartered as an apostolic college in 1854. This lasted until 1885. As an apostolic college, it provided a training course for missionaries. From 1869 to 1877 Mission Santa Barbara was also a college for lay men with boarding and day students. Mission Santa Barbara remained the center for theological studies and continued to operate as a theological seminary until 1968 when the theology school was transferred to Berkeley, California as a participating school in the Graduate Theological Union.

Parent Institution. The Franciscan School of Theology is a participating school of The Graduate Theological Union which has become, since its founding in 1962, the major theological center in the western United States. Its faculty is drawn largely from the combined faculties of the nine participating schools. The variety of religious traditions represented in the Union makes it a uniquely diversified ecumenical center, one of the most inclusive in the world. Its library constitutes one of the largest theological collections in the nation. See also: Graduate Theological Union.

Community Environment. The city of Berkeley, with a population of 110,000, lies directly opposite the Golden Gate Bridge, with a magnificent view over the Bay and the city of San Francisco. Berkeley, known as "The Athens of the West," has a long tradition of political activism, varied architecture, and lively repertory theater. Its business and political leadership reflects the city's great ethnic diversity. Students benefit from Berkeley's extraordinary array of civic institutions, cafes, bookstores, handicrafts, and music. Berkeley has many churches, libraries, and art centers. The Tilden Regional Park has facilities for outdoor recreational activities. All forms of transportation are available. The climate is mild.

Across the Bay is San Francisco, one of the world's great cities, with a thriving financial center, distinctive neighborhoods, museums, and the very best in the performing arts.

Religious Denomination. Roman Catholic.

Religious Emphasis. Contemporary-Centrist.

Accreditation. Western Association of Schools and Colleges; Association of Theological Schools. Member of: National Catholic Educational Association.

Term System. Semester; no summer term.

Enrollment in Degree Programs in Religion 1984–85. Total 149; 79 men, 70 women.

Degrees in Religion Awarded 1984–85. Master of Divinity 13; men 11, women 2. Master of Arts 2; women 2. Master of Theological Studies 16; men 7, women 9. Ph.D. 1; men 1.

Faculty for Degree Programs in Religion. Total 18; full-time 11, part-time 7.

Admission Requirements. Transcripts of previous Bachelor program; three letters of academic reference; statement of purpose; nonrefundable application fee $20.

Tuition and Fees. Tuition $1,400 per semester; graduation fee $25.

Financial Aid. Limited Grants in Aid available.

Housing. Housing facilities are not available to students who have not been accepted into the formation program for the Franciscan Order. However, the Dean will assist non-Franciscan students in acquiring housing in the adjacent are, if this be needed.

Library Facilities. The Graduate Theological Union Library represents the merger of the libraries of member schools and is the most visible expression of the ecumenical cooperation that has been established. It is located at 2400 Ridge Road in Berkeley. The current holdings of the Library include more than 350,000 books and journals and 150,000 items in microform, slides, tapes, photo records and video cassettes. This composite collection has not only the breadth to support the full range of theological programs, but also has remarkable depth in many areas of religious and theological studies. These include the specialized collections brought by the member schools. Students receive a library card which entitles them to use the library facilities of the University of California at Berkeley, which contains over 6,300,000 volumes and 101,000 current periodicals and serials.

Religious Services/Activities. Daily Liturgy of Hours and Eucharist; occasional retreats.

Degree Programs

The Master of Divinity degree requires a 3.0 average in all courses, 96 units, and four-year residency. The program leads to a professional degree which testifies to proficiency in those sciences and skills necessary for ordination to the priesthood in the Catholic Church. As a graduate degree program it is concerned with the academic and professional side of the training for ordination and of itself does not indicate that a recipient of the degree is qualified

in all areas for ordination, since there are the areas of spirituality, emotional maturity, religious commitment, and the ecclesia call, which are not covered by the degree itself.

The Master of Theological Studies requires a 3.0 average in all courses, 36 semester units including a project, and two-year residency. The program seeks to develop the general theological understanding which Roman Catholic laypeople, teachers, permanent diaconate candidates, members of religious their spiritual and pastoral activity.

A Master of Arts program is available through the Graduate Theological Union and requires a 3.0 average in all courses, 14 three-unit courses, language requirement, thesis, and oral defense. See also: Graduate Theological Union.

Special Programs

To provide for pastoral preparation for a ministry with the Spanish-speaking, the Franciscan School of Theology has entered into a formal agreement with the Mexican American Cultural Center in San Antonio, Texas. Students at the Franciscan School of Theology may engage in either the summer programs in San Antonio or the Pastoral Program for Seminarians from the first of January to the end of July.

Both the Franciscan School of Theology and the Graduate Theological Union offer a wide range of continuing education resources. The Continuing Education Program is meant for anyone who already has obtained at least a first theological degree and who wishes to do advanced studies but without pursuing a further degree.

Fuller Theological Seminary
135 North Oakland Avenue
Pasadena, CA 91101   (818) 449-1745

Administration. David A. Hubbard, President.

General Description. Fuller Theological Seminary, embracing the Schools of Theology, Psychology, and World Mission, is an evangelical, multidenominational, international, and multiethnic community dedicated to the preparation of men and women for the manifold ministries of Christ and his Church. It was founded in 1947 and was named after Henry Fuller, a devout Christian layman who actively supported many Christian causes in the United States and overseas. The first classes were held in the building of the Lake Avenue Congregational Church of Pasadena. The Seminary moved to its present location in 1953. The Seminary has programs of study leading to a variety of professional and academic degrees.

Community Environment. The campus of 6 acres is located in Pasadena, California, a city with a population of 125,000. It is at the foot of the San Gabriel Mountains and nine miles from downtown Los Angeles.

Religious Denomination. Nondenominational.

Accreditation. Western Association of Schools and Colleges; Association of Theological Schools in the United States and Canada.

Term System. Quarter.

Enrollment in Degree Programs in Religion 1984–85. Total 1,320 (full-time equivalent).

Faculty for Degree Programs in Religion. Total 82.

Admission Requirements. Baccalaureate degree from an accredited institution.

Tuition and Fees. Tuition $84.25 per unit; School of Psychology $6,756 per year; student activities fee $20 per quarter; housing $100-$360 per month; food service $345-$512 per quarter.

Financial Aid. Through employment, long- and short-term loans, and grants, the Seminary seeks to alleviate financial need.

Housing. Dormitory rooms, studio apartments, and 1- and 2-bedroom apartments are available.

Library Facilities. The McAlister Library houses over 141,000 volumes.

Religious Services/Activities. The Seminary has committed itself to the principle that the spiritual development of every student is a matter of prime importance in theological education. To foster and implement this awareness, the Spiritual Life Committee has an office and a program of spiritual formation. Chapel services are held three days per week. There is a retreat program, a small-group program, and prayer and fellowship groups.

Degree Programs

The School of Theology offers programs leading to the degrees Master of Divinity, Master of Arts, Doctor of Ministry, Master of Theology, and Doctor of Philosophy (Ph.D.). It is possible to develop an area of concentration within the overall curriculum for the degree. Concentrations include Christian Formation and Discipleship, Cross-Cultural Studies, Family Pastoral Care and Counseling, Youth Ministries, Marriage and Family Ministries, and Semitic Languages and Literature.

The School of World Mission offers degrees to pre-field missionaries in Cross-Cultural Studies and missiology degrees to missionaries and church and mission leaders who have had at least three years of field experience in cross-cultural Christian ministry. It grants the Master of Arts, Master of Theology in Missiology, and the Doctor of Missiology degrees. The curriculum consists of a combination of coursework, reading, and directed study tailored to fit an individual's requirements.

The Graduate School of Psychology prepares men and women as clinical psychologists, coupling Christian understanding with refined clinical and research skills. The School grants the Doctor of Philosophy (Ph.D.) degree in Clinical Psychology.

Golden Gate Baptist Theological Seminary
Strawberry Point
Mill Valley, CA 94941   (415) 388-8080

Administration. Dr. Franklin D. Pollard, President; Dr. Robert L. Cate, Dean of Academic Affairs.

General Description. The Golden Gate Baptist Theological Seminary prepares Christian leaders for ministry throughout the world. Founded in 1944, the school is an official seminary of the Southern Baptist Convention and is supported through tithes, offerings, and other gifts. The Seminary strives to accomplish its purposes through both curricular and extra-curricular programs. The primary concern of the curriculum is to provide graduate, professional theological education but the Seminary also offers some diploma- and certificate-level training. The curriculum is organized into five main areas of study: Christian Sources and Origins, Christian Life and Thought, Christian Proclamation and Ministry, Christian Education and Administration, and Ministry of Church Music.

Community Environment. San Francisco is across the Bay and the location has made the site of the Seminary unique among seminaries in the world. It is here that cultural, educational, and cosmopolitan resources have created an unusual and rich environment for the school. The campus has fifty-four buildings on a 148-acre campus. The campus site was once considered for the United Nations complex now based in New York. The Seminary is located just five miles north of the Golden Gate Bridge and the surrounding hills give the campus its peaceful park-like setting.

Religious Denomination. Southern Baptist.

Religious Emphasis. Conservative.

Accreditation. Western Association of Schools and Colleges; Association of Theological Schools in the United States and Canada; National Association of Schools of Music.

Term System. Semester; summer term.

Enrollment in Degree Programs in Religion 1984–85. Total 865; men 628; women 237.

Degrees in Religion Awarded 1984–85. Master of Religious Education 14; men 10, women 4. Master of Christian Ministries 8; men 4, women 4. Master of Divinity 66; men 60, women 6. Doctor of Ministries 12; men 12. Certificate/Diploma 8; men 8.

Faculty for Degree Programs in Religion. Total 64; full-time 23, part-time 41.

Admission Requirements. The Seminary accepts as students men and women seeking to prepare for Christian ministries and who are properly recommended by their churches. Applicants must submit transcripts of all college work. Some programs require a baccalaureate degree.

Tuition and Fees. Matriculation fee $300 per semester (additional instruction fee of $450 for non-Baptist students); Doctor of Philosophy matriculation fee $420 per semester (additional instruction fee of $560 for non-Baptist students); Doctor of Ministry degree program is operated on a single-fee basis of $2,400 for the two-year course; additional fees where applicable; Housing charges range from $115 to $395 depending upon accommodations.

Financial Aid. Various scholarships and awards are available. The Cooperative Program of the Southern Baptist Convention provides tuition for Baptist students. Opportunities for campus employment exist and there are many opportunities for service in the churches and missions of the San Francisco Bay area. Secular employment in the various communities of Marin County is also possible.

Housing. The Seminary seeks to provide the best possible student housing at rates well below the average rate in the community. Dormitories for single students, studio apartments, and two- and three-bedroom duplex and triplex units are available. To be eligible for Seminary-provided housing, one must be a full-time student carrying a minimum of 12 hours per semester and 30 hours per year.

Library Facilities. The Seminary Library has holdings of over 100,000 volumes, an additional 5,000 audio- and video-tape recordings, and subscriptions to 725 periodicals. In addition, students have access to the libraries of the Graduate Theological Union in Berkeley with holdings of over 500,000 volumes.

Religious Services/Activities. Worship is fundamental in life and work at the Seminary. The faculty and students gather regularly for a period of devotion. The missionary enterprise is at the heart of all activities. One week during the year is given to World Mission Week, at which time speakers from various denomination agencies, churches, and the mission fields present the challenge of missions to the student body. The Golden Gate Mission Conference, a student-faculty sponsored program for college and college-age youth climaxes World Mission Week.

The Religious Education Club meets periodically for study and fellowship. It serves as host to the Western Religious Education Association each year. The Church Music Workshop is an annual feature for students and ministers of music. The Seminary Revival is held biennially to enhance the spiritual growth of students, faculty, and administration. The Seminary Women's Fellowship meets monthly and is an organization for the wives of students, faculty, staff, and for women employed by or enrolled in the Seminary. Lecture-Dialogues, the H.I. Hester Lectureship on Preaching, and the Derward W. Deere Lectures bring distinguished scholars to the campus.

Degree Programs

The Master of Divinity is the basic theological degree offered by the Seminary. A total of 89 hours is required and the program consists of a core curriculum and restricted and free electives. The program's objectives are designed to stimulate the student to establish an adequate foundation for the beginning of ministry and for the life-long process of learning and experiencing.

The Master of Divinity with a major in Religious Edu-

cation equips students with competencies needed to become pastors, missionaries, teachers, campus ministers, and ministers of outreach and visitation. The program blends courses in religious education with those in the biblical and theological disciplines, and assures a broader dimension of preparation for ministry. Total hours required vary depending upon area of emphasis.

The Master of Religious Education is the foundational, professional degree for one preparing for ministry in religious education. Its objectives seek to encourage the student to develop skills for the performance of ministry, and to continue pursuit of activities of professional and personal enrichment necessary for an effective ministry in religious education. A total of 66 hours is required for the degree.

The Master of Church Music is designed to equip the individual to meet the changing needs of the church music ministry. The only major in this degree program is Ministry of Music. A total of 58 hours is required for the degree.

The Master of Church Music and Master of Religious Education (2 degrees) is a full three-year program which prepares students to serve capably in both music and religious education. A total of 99 hours is required for the degree.

The Doctor of Ministry requires the completion of 17 to 19 hours of advanced seminary work beyond the Master of Divinity (or the equivalent), plus a ministry project. The program consists of seminars, supervised ministry practice, and a field project to be conducted in conjunction with the student's ministry.

The Doctor of Philosophy (Ph.D.) is designed to provide training at the highest academic level for students of exceptional ability and promise. It is currently offered in the Biblical field, with an emphasis in either the Old Testament or New Testament. The program requires the completion of 40 hours of advanced study credits beyond the Master of Divinity degree (or its equivalent), plus a dissertation.

Special Programs

Associate of Divinity, Associate of Religious Education, and Associate of Church Music degree programs have been designed for students over thirty years of age, without a college degree, but with a high school diploma or its equivalent. Such programs represent a two-year course of study.

The Diploma in Theology and the Diploma in Religious Education are offered in selected off-campus centers. The Diploma in Christian Ministries program has been designed and approved by Golden Gate Seminary and the Language Missions Department of the Home Missions Board to provide basic knowledge and skills to ethnic pastors and church leaders in the language of the group. The program is limited to those with an ethnic background who may not have a college degree; students must be at least 18 years old. The work is offered in an off-campus setting known as an Ethnic Leadership Development Center. The program requires twenty-four hours of study in twelve two-hour courses. It can be completed in approximately two years.

Graduate Theological Union
2465 Le Conte Avenue
Berkeley, CA 94709   (415) 841-9811

Administration. Michael Blecker, O.S.B., President; Claude Welch, Dean; Elizabeth K. Over, Associate Dean for Student Services.

General Description. The Graduate Theological Union (GTU) emerged out of the concerns of Roman Catholics, Protestants, and Jews for cooperative educational experiences of the highest quality. The constituent members fulfill their primary goal of excellence in theological education in an ecumenical community of interdependence where a free exchange of ideas takes place in an atmosphere of openness, sensitivity, and mutual respect; where a concern for common issues - in the church, the synagogue, and society as a whole - will foster a new understanding wherein the common and the unique will combine to enrich the lives and work of those who participate in the shared experience.

GTU is both a graduate school and a consortium of schools, as well as an agency for a variety of special programs and services. In its educational programs, the GTU draws upon the theological communities that created it and works cooperatively with the University of California, Berkeley. Structurally, the GTU is a distinct entity, governed by an independent Board of Trustees which includes members nominated by the participating seminaries. Participating members are: American Baptist Seminary of the West; Church Divinity School of the Pacific; Dominican School of Philosophy and Theology; Franciscan School of Theology; Jesuit School of Theology at Berkeley; Pacific Lutheran Theological Seminary; Pacific School of Religion; San Francisco Theological Seminary; Starr King School for the Ministry (See separate entries for each).

For the Master of Arts, Doctor of Philosophy, and Doctor of Theology programs administered by the GTU, faculty members of the schools constitute a single graduate faculty. Professional programs and degrees (e.g., Master of Divinity, Master of Theology, Master of Sacred Theology, and Doctor of Ministry) are the province of each of the participating seminaries in the GTU. The resources needed for these programs are developed in concert through the instrumentality of the GTU; however, the requirements for the degrees are set by the faculties of the schools.

Community Environment. The GTU is located in Berkeley in an area adjacent to the north gate of the University of California. Berkeley is located across the bay from San Francisco. The Bay Area is noted for its wealth of special institutions and centers of study and its wide sociological and cultural diversity.

Religious Denomination. Independent.

Accreditation. Western States Association of Schools and Colleges; Association of Theological Schools in the United States and Canada.

Term System. Semester; January intersession; no summer term.

Enrollment in Degree Programs in Religion 1984–85. Total 344; men 191, women 153.

Degrees in Religion Awarded 1984–85. Master of Arts 16; men 7, women 9. Master of Arts in Applied Theology 14; men 7, women 7. Doctor of Philosophy/Doctor of Theology 17; men 13, women 4.

Faculty for Degree Programs in Religion. The Graduate Theological Union draws on the combined faculties of the member schools which number approximately 100 full-time persons.

Admission Requirements. Bachelor of Arts from an accredited college or university; three letters of recommendation (academic); GRE (Aptitude only); for Ph.D./Th.D. previous work on the graduate level in theological/religious studies.

Tuition and Fees. Tuition, Master of Arts program $1,-600 per semester; thesis fee $50; Ph.D./Th.D. programs $3,200 per semester; dissertation fee $100; food and housing $5,060 single (12 month period); books and supplies $336.

Financial Aid. Substantial funds for doctoral student scholarships are made available through contributions from the participating seminaries, the Atholl McBean Scholarship Endowment Fund, the GTU Guild Scholarship fund, and from general GTU resources.

Housing. No student housing.

Library Facilities. The GTU Library was created in 1969 to replace the bibliographic center, GTU's first cooperative library effort. The Library represents the full merger of the libraries of the member schools and is the most visible expression of the ecumenical cooperation that has been established. The pooling of resources enables the Library to meet the needs of the full range of academic programs at the GTU, to avoid unnecessary duplication of material, and to develop the potential as a research library of national significance with materials for specialized study in major areas of teaching, as well as in significant minor religious movements. The current holdings include more than 350,000 books and journals and 150,-000 items in microform, slides, tapes, photo records, and video cassettes.

Degree Programs

The Master of Arts program is designed for those who plan to continue toward the doctoral degree but do not yet possess the expertise necessary to enter upon a doctoral program; for those who desire a terminal degree which will equip them to teach religion at the elementary, secondary, or junior college level; those who wish to engage in counseling or community service work; others who have a primary professional competence in a field other than religion who may wish to develop a basic competence in the area of theological studies; and individuals whose only intent is to pursue a personal, avocational interest in religious studies. Two years of residence are required. Students take a program of courses with special emphasis in one of the fields of religious study: Bible; Historical Study; Systematic and Philosophical Theology; Theology and Education; Religion/Theology and the Arts (including Proclamation and Worship); History and Phenomenology of Religions; Jewish Studies.

The Doctor of Philosophy programs focus on theological studies in the context of university disciplines. Accordingly, a substantial portion of the work for the Ph.D. will be taken in a university, normally in the Graduate Division of the University of California, Berkeley. The Doctor of Theology programs focus on specifically formulated courses of theological study in the context of the entire theological spectrum. Hence, work in relevant areas of the total theological curriculum naturally belongs to the Th.D. program. Doctoral studies are administered through broad area groupings: Biblical Studies; Historical Studies; Systematic and Philosophical Theology and Philosophy of Religion; Religion and Society; Religion and the Personality Sciences; Religion and Education; Religion/Theology and the Arts; The History and Phenomenology of Religions; Inter-Area Studies; Judaic Studies.

Hebrew Union College - Jewish Institute of Religion, Los Angeles

3077 University Avenue
Los Angeles, CA 90007   (213) 749-3424

Administration. Dr. Alfred Gottschalk, Rabbi, President (Office in Cincinnati). In Los Angeles: Dr. Uri D. Herscher, Rabbi, Executive Vice President, Dean; Gerald B. Bubis, Director, School of Jewish Communal Service; Dr. Stanley F. Chyet, Rabbi, Director, School of Graduate Studies; Dr. David H. Ellenson, Rabbi, Director, School of Judaic Studies; Sara Lee, Director, School of Education; Dr. Michael A. Signer, Rabbi, Director, Outreach Programs.

General Description. The Los Angeles School of the Hebrew Union College - Jewish Institute of Religion is a coeducational institution offering programs which train future religious leaders, scholars, educators, and communal workers according to the highest academic and professional standards. Its School of Rabbinic Studies, Edgar F. Magnin School of Graduate Studies, Rhea Hirsch School of Education, Jerome H. Loucheim School of Judaic Studies, School of Jewish Communal Service, and Department of Sacred Music provide undergraduate and graduate courses of study leading to the Bachelor, Master, and Doctorate degrees.

Parent Institution. Hebrew Union College - Jewish Institute of Religion is the institution of higher learning in

American Reform Judaism. It is dedicated to the study of Judaism and related areas in the spirit of free inquiry. Nothing in the Jewish or general past or present is alien to its interest. Sensitive to the challenge imposed by a world of change, it believes that Jewish ideas and values, along with the contributions of other religions and civilizations, are meaningful to the building of the future. The Los Angeles School and its sister institutions in Cincinnati, New York City, and Jerusalem comprise the 4-campus complex of Hebrew Union College - Jewish Institute of Religion. It is under the patronage of Reform Judaism's Union of American Hebrew Congregations.

Hebrew Union College was founded in 1875 in Cincinnati, the first institution of Jewish Higher learning in America. Its founder was Rabbi Isaac Mayer Wise, the architect of American Reform Judaism, who had established the Union of American Hebrew Congregations two years earlier. In 1922, Rabbi Stephen S. Wise established the Jewish Institute of Religion in New York. The similar operation of the two schools led to their merger in 1950. A third center was opened in Los Angeles in 1954, and a fourth branch was established in Jerusalem, Israel, in 1963. *See also:* entries in Ohio and New York.

Hebrew Union College is affiliated with the University of Cincinnati, the Greater Cincinnati Consortium of Colleges and Universities, the University of Southern California, Washington University in St. Louis, New York University, the University of Pittsburgh, and the Hebrew University in Jerusalem. These associations provide variously for cross-registration privileges, the use of libraries and other facilities, joint course offerings, and cooperative degrees.

Community Environment. The Los Angeles School occupies a 5-acre site in the center of the city, adjacent to the University of Southern California. Most facilities are housed in a large, 2-wing building. The Hebrew Union College Skirball Museum is one of the foremost Jewish museums in the world. Its approximately 14,000 objects, comprising artifacts of biblical archaelogoy, Jewish ceremonial art, and fine arts, reflect 4,000 years of Jewish history, culture, and art. A new Cultural Center for American Jewish life is currently in the planning stage, to be located on a recently-acquired 15-acre site.

Religious Denomination. Jewish.

Religious Emphasis. Reform.

Accreditation. North Central Association of Colleges and Schools; Middle States Association of Colleges and Secondary Schools; Western Association of Schools and Colleges.

Term System. Semester; summer term.

Enrollment in Degree Programs in Religion 1984–85. Total 68; men 29, women 39.

Degrees in Religion Awarded 1984–85. Master of Arts in Jewish Education 9; men 3, women 6. Master of Arts in Jewish Communal Service 25; men 7, women 18. Master of Hebrew Letters 11; men 8, women 3.

Faculty for Degree Programs in Religion. Total 30; full-

time 17, part-time 13.

Admission Requirements. Bachelor's degree from an accredited college or university or its equivalent; Graduate Record Examination; interview with Admissions Committee; psychological testing.

Tuition and Fees. Tuition $5,100; part-time student $210 per unit.

Financial Aid. Whenever possible, financial aid is awarded as a combination of scholarship assistance and an interest-free loan. In cases of demonstrated need, financial aid is available for tuition, fees, and living expenses.

Housing. None available.

Library Facilities. The Frances-Henry Library contains more than 70,000 volumes. The library also houses the Joseph H. Rosenberg Branch of the American Jewish Archives and a branch of the American Jewish Periodical Center.

Religious Services/Activities. Synagogue services are held weekly.

Degree Programs

The Bachelor of Science in Judaic Studies is offered by the Jerome H. Louchheim School of Judaic Studies. It requires a total of 120 units: 52 units in Judaic Studies which shall include 14 units in Hebrew language and literature, and 38 units of upper division Judaic Studies courses; plus 68 units in liberal arts from an accredited college or university. The program must be completed in six years, of which two must be in residence consecutively. The Bachelor of Arts with a major in Religion and a specialty in Jewish Studies requires a total of 128 units which shall include 20 units in upper division Judaic Studies offered by Hebrew Union College. This degree is offered by the University of Southern California in cooperation with the College.

The Rabbinic School offers a five-year program leading to the Master of Arts degree and ordination. Students admitted to the rabbinic program are required to spend their first academic year in Israel. Upon the completion of the first year of study in Jerusalem, students return to the Los Angeles School for the second- and third-year rabbinic courses, leading to the master of Arts degree, after which students transfer either to Cincinnati or New York for their final two years of study. An additional one-year program (not counted toward the normal five-year rabbinic course) is available to rabbinic students who wish to specialize in Jewish education.

A Master of Arts in Judaic Studies is offered by the Edgar F. Magnin School of Graduate Studies to candidates holding a Bachelor of Science in Judaic Studies or its equivalent. The degree is conferred upon successful completion of a minimum of 36 units of study, at least 20 of which must be in residence. An acceptable thesis or successful completion of mastery examinations is required of all candidates. Other Master of Arts programs include Jewish Education, Jewish Communal Service and Jewish Education, double Master of Arts in Jewish Communal

Service and Social Work, double Master of Arts in Jewish Communal Service and Master of Science in Gerontology, and double Master of Arts in Jewish Communal Service and Public Administration.

The Doctor of Hebrew Letters degree is available from the Edgar F. Magnin School of Graduate Studies only to rabbinic graduates of Hebrew Union College on the basis of the Master of Arts degree that they have earned and the two years of post-M.A. residency required for ordination. A candidate must propose, in consultation with three members of the faculty, a program of study which includes one major and two minor areas chosen from the following: Bible and Non-Canonical Literature; Medieval Biblical Exegesis; Talmud and Rabbinic Literature; Midrashic and Homiletic Literature; Rabbinic Backgrounds of the New Testament; Jewish History; Hebrew Literature; Jewish Philosophy and Ethics; Jewish Theology; Jewish Liturgy; Contemporary Jewish Studies; Human Relations; and Jewish Religious Education (minor field only). Either the major or both minors must utilize Hebrew texts.

The Doctor of Hebrew Studies is also offered by the Edgar F. Magnin School of Graduate Studies and is open to qualified candidates who are not alumni of the College. Sixty credit hours beyond the bachelor's degree or its equivalent are required.

A program in which a candidate may pursue studies leading to the Ph.D. degree at the University of Southern California in cooperation with the Magnin School of Hebrew Union College is offered. This degree program, under the aegis of the School of Religion at the University of Southern California, is in the field of social ethics with a concentration in Judaic Studies.

The Doctor of Philosophy degree in Jewish Education is offered by the Rhea Hirsch School of Education. In selected areas, the school provides undergraduate courses for practicing teachers and educators. Preparation for a degree in education includes courses offered in other programs at the College and at the University of Southern California.

Special Programs

Special courses are offered for synagogue professionals, organists, and choir directors dealing with the various literatures and background of synagogue music. The program is supplemented by courses in education and Judaic Studies, plus in-service training.

Jesuit School of Theology at Berkeley
1735 LeRoy Avenue
Berkeley, CA 94709   (415) 841-8804

Administration. Lyndon J. Farwell, S.J., President; T. Howland Sanks, S.J., Academic Dean; Lorna Wallace McKeown, Assistant to the Dean.

General Description. The Jesuit School of Theology at Berkeley is both a professional theological school and a pontifical faculty of theology whose primary mission is the theological, professional, and personal preparation of candidates, especially Jesuits, for ordination to the priesthood in the Catholic Church. The academic and professional dimension of this preparation for ordination is provided by the Master of Divinity program, extended by the Master of Sacred Theology and Master of Theology for the sake of specialization. As a pontifical faculty, the two-year Licentiate in Sacred Theology is offered.

The Jesuit School of Theology was established in 1934 with the name Alma College and was located at Los Gatos, California until 1969. It was founded to serve the needs of the two Jesuit Provinces of the West, California and Oregon. In 1969, the decision was reached to relocate the school in Berkeley in close proximity to the Graduate Theological Union, its member schools, and the University of California. The name of the theologate was changed to its present name in that year. In 1971, upon receiving independent accreditation by the Western Association of Colleges and Schools, a long history of affiliation with the University of Santa Clara as its School of Divinity was ended. In 1972, the School was selected to be one of three national theological centers operated by the Society of Jesus in the United States.

Community Environment. Housed in several buildings in a residential neighborhood and within a radius of one block of each other, the school is situated two blocks north of the University of California at Berkeley on a direct line with the famous Campanile. The offices of the Graduate Theological Union and the Flora Lamson Hewlett Common Library are located one and one-half blocks west.

Religious Denomination. Roman Catholic.

Accreditation. Western States Association of Schools and Colleges; Association of Theological Schools in the United States and Canada.

Term System. Semester; no summer term.

Enrollment in Degree Programs in Religion 1984–85. Total 211; men 152, women 59.

Degrees in Religion Awarded 1984–85. Master of Divinity 30; men 26, women 4. Master of Theology 2; men 1, women 1. Master of Sacred Theology 12; men 9, women 3. Licentiate in Sacred Theology 6; men 4, women 2.

Faculty for Degree Programs in Religion. Total 28; full-time 23, part-time 5.

Admission Requirements. All students must have a bachelor's degree or its equivalent; programs have varying other requirements.

Tuition and Fees. Tuition per semester $1,800 full-time (12 semester credits), part-time $150 per credit; (Master of Arts program $1,500 full-time, part-time $150 per credit); Institute of Spirituality and Worship fee $400 per semester; other miscellaneous fees.

Financial Aid. Most students in need of aid rely upon the Guaranteed Student Loan Program, available from individual banks, to finance their education. The School has a very limited amount of financial aid available.

Housing. The Jesuit Community of the School provides living accommodations for members of the Society of Jesus; limited housing available for other students.

Library Facilities. The School is a participating member of the Graduate Theological Union common library, with its more than 500,000 holdings in theology. See: *Graduate Theological Union,* Berkeley, California.

Religious Services/Activities. Within the context of the academic program, students are encouraged to seek out other resources in preparation for pastoral ministry to the world. An important dimension of that preparation consists of theological reflection upon contemporary human concerns, a contemplative reflection requiring time, disciplined training, communal experience, study dialogue and prayer. In further service of growth in this process, the School actively promotes opportunities for spiritual direction, retreats, and daily liturgical worship.

Degree Programs

The Master of Arts is two-year program leading to an academic degree in theology. The School participates in this joint Master of Arts program of the Graduate Theological Union. See: *Graduate Theological Union,* Berkeley, California.

The Master of Theology and Master of Sacred Theology degrees are each one-year programs in advanced theological study beyond the Master of Divinity degree, and are available in almost any area of specialized interest. The focus of the Master of Theology is toward the communication of the Christian Gospel; the focus of the Master of Sacred Theology is toward a deeper personal knowledge and scholarly advancement in some particular area of the theological disciplines.

The Licentiate in Sacred Theology is a two-year program in advanced theological study beyond the three-year Bachelor of Sacred Theology degree. It is the second cycle in the program of ecclesiastical degrees and requires an area of specialization beyond the general theological formation of the first cycle.

Special Programs

The resources available through the School for continuing education in theology or theological renewal are considerable. The ecumenical, urban, and university context of the Seminary offers unique opportunities for persons who wish to broaden their theological backgrounds and/or sharpen pastoral skills. A Certificate in Theological Studies can be earned in either of the following programs.

The Institute for Spirituality and Worship is designed for men and women who have been engaged in active ministry. Within the context of general theological renewal, students focus on areas such as liturgical leadership, spiritual renewal in religious life, formation, and prayer apostolates.

The Special Student program is designed for persons whose primary objective is an unstructured "sabbatical" year or time for general theological renewal. It is also for persons who are not certain that they want to enroll in a formal degree program, but do want to undertake some graduate theological study. Applicants must have a bachelor's degree.

Judaism, University of
Graduate School of Judaica
15600 Mulholland Drive
Los Angeles, CA 90077   (213) 879-4114

Administration. David A. Lieber, President; Elliot N. Dorff, Provost, Dean of Graduate Studies.

General Description. The University of Judaism offers Bachelor and Master's degrees in Jewish Studies, but its specific program for those interested in the rabbinate is in the rubric of the Graduate School of Judaica. That program is a two year, post-baccalaureate curriculum in intensive studies of Hebrew, Bible, Talmud, and Midrash with some work in Jewish law and philosophy. Students interested in the rabbinate continue their studies at the branch of the Jewish Theological Seminary of America in Jerusalem for one year and then complete their work at the Jewish Theological Seminary itself in New York. The entire rabbinic program normally takes six years, the first two of which may be taken at the University of Judaism in Los Angeles.

Parent Institution. The Jewish Theological Seminary of America in New York offers undergraduate and graduate programs in Judaica in addition to its programs for training Jewish cantors, educators, and rabbis. It is the only seminary specifically designed to train professionals for the Conservative Movement in Judaism, although its strictly academic programs are open to anyone regardless of religion, race, sex, or creed.

Community Environment. The campus is located in the Santa Monica Mountains, a chain of low peaks which extend from the Pacific Ocean to mid-Los Angeles. It is near the campus of UCLA in Westwood. Los Angeles is a major metropolitan center with a semi-arid climate. There are many fine museums and libraries in the city, a music center, and entertainment attractions. Los Angeles is situated in southern California, approximately 150 miles north of the U.S./Mexican border. It is the second most populous city in the U.S.

Religious Denomination. Jewish.

Religious Emphasis. Conservative.

Accreditation. Western Association of Schools and Colleges.

Term System. Semester.

Enrollment in Degree Programs in Religion 1984–85. Total 28; men 14, women 14.

Degrees in Religion Awarded 1984–85. Bachelor of Literature 4; men 4. Master of Arts 3; men 2, women 1.

Faculty for Degree Programs in Religion. Total 45; full-time 22, part-time 23.

Admission Requirements. Bachelor of Arts from an accredited college or university with a 3.0 GPA minimum.

Transcipt of all college work, scores on the Graduate Record Examination, $25 nonrefundable application fee. Students deficient in Hebrew language skills may be required to enroll in the intensive Hebrew language course in the University's Summer Institute preceding enrollment.

Tuition and Fees. $140 per unit with a maximum of $2,100 per semester; $20 registration fee per semester; room and board $3,350 per school year; married student housing (furnished 1 bedroom apartment) $575 per month.

Financial Aid. Guaranteed Student Loans, tuition waivers, and tuition deferments available.

Housing. Dormitory rooms are available for single students; furnished apartments for married students.

Library Facilities. The Ostrow Library houses 170,000 volumes and 500 periodicals. A Documentaiton Center contains topically arranged files of more than 600,000 clippings, brochures, and other sources of information covering aspects of contemporary Jewish life throughout the world. The Clejan Educational Resources Center maintains teaching material with state-of-the art audiovisual and computer equipment.

Religious Services/Activities. Daily morning service (conservative) and Friday evening services.

Degree Programs

Bachelor of Literature degree program students will be placed into courses appropriate to their previous studies in Judaica. Courses include Pentateuch with Rashi, Former Prophets, Introduction to Critical Study of the Bible, Introduction to Classical Jewish Commentaries; Survey of Latter Prophets; Survey of Hagiographa.

The Master of Arts in Jewish Studies is granted to students who complete a total of 30 credits selected from Bible, Contemporary Jewish Life, Jewish History, Hebrew Literature, Jewish Philosophy, and Rabbinic Literature. Students may choose to concentrate in one or two of these areas.

The Master of Arts in Rabbinic Literature requires 18 credits in courses in the Talmud plus 12 credits chosen from at least 2 of the the areas of Midrash, Codes, and Rabbinic Literature (Survey of Mishnah). Examinations are required: an oral examination in fifty folio pages, of Talmud, chosen from consecutive sections of not more than three tractates; an assigned passage in the Talmud, which the candidate must explain after a brief period of preparation; a written departmental examination on the social and historical background of rabbinic literature. Candidates for the degree of Master of Arts must pass a Hebrew language proficiency examination to demonstrate competency in modern Hebrew; candidates may also be asked to demonstrate a reading comprehension in one or more foreign languages other than Hebrew, depending on their area of specialization.

L.I.F.E. Bible College
1100 Glendale Boulevard
Los Angeles, CA 90026   (213) 413-1234

Administration. Rev. Jack E. Hamilton, President.

General Description. L.I.F.E. Bible College was so named from the initials representing Lighthouse of International Foursquare Evangelism. The College was founded in 1923 by Aimee Semple McPherson. It began as a training institute for ministers and missionaries. Today it continues to instruct men and women in the personal and Biblical tools needed for ministry leadership. The College's program concentrates on understanding the Bible in its historical setting and context, its doctrine and theology, and on the development of thinking, writing, and speaking skills to communicate these teachings.

Community Environment. The College is located in downtown Los Angeles. The main building is adjacent to the Angelus Temple.

Religious Denomination. International Church of the Foursquare Gospel.

Accreditation. American Association of Bible Colleges.

Term System. Quarter.

Enrollment in Degree Programs in Religion 1984–85. Total 453.

Admission Requirements. High school graduation; non-high school graduates accepted only if they pass an aptitude test; evidence of an approved Christian character; should have received or be seeking baptism; entrance examination.

Tuition and Fees. Tuition $730 per quarter; residence fee $225 per month; Associated Student Body fee $50 per quarter.

Financial Aid. The College is approved for participation in the federally funded Pell Grant program which provides financial aid to students who have not already obtained an undergraduate degree. The College does not participate in the Student Loan Program.

Housing. All single students 21 years of age and under are required to live in the residence halls on campus.

Library Facilities. The library contains over 18,000 volumes.

Religious Services/Activities. Student Ministry is an integral part of the program at the College. It is based on a "hands on" approach—of being a doer and a worker of the Word.

Degree Programs

The core of the curriculum requires every student to spend a minimum of 52 hours in Bible Study. Another 24 hours are given to the study of doctrine to provide a strong base for the development of effective ministry. In addition to these courses, the core curriculum includes many ministry-orientation subjects such as Spiritual Gifts and Ministry, Relational Ministry, and Theology of Ministry.

To qualify for the Bachelor of Arts degree, a student must earn a minimum of 180 quarter units with a selection of one of the following five areas of specialization for a concentration of 30 hours of study: Pastoral; Cross-Cultural; Christian Education; Music; General Church.

The Bachelor of Theology program is available only to students who have already completed an accredited undergraduate degree in a field other than Bible. The student enrolling for this two-year degree will not fulfill a minor requirement, but will specialize in the field of study related to his vocational goals.

The Standard Ministerial program will equip a student for general church leadership, including the role of pastor, in a three-year period. The program provides a firm foundation of basic studies and qualifies a student to receive a Four-Square Ministerial License. All units earned in this program can be transferred toward the Bachelor of Arts degree.

Special Programs

The Associate of Arts degree program is provided for those persons who desire a strong foundation in Bible training, but plan to pursue a different major at another college or university, or who already have vocational skills in another field.

Los Angeles Baptist College
21726 West Placerita Canyon Road
Newhall, CA 91322   (805) 259-3540

Administration. Dr. John R. Dunkin, President.

General Description. Los Angeles Baptist College was founded in 1927 to meet the need for a fundamental Baptist school on the West Coast. The College serves fundamental Baptist churches and others of a similar doctrinal position providing a Christian liberal arts education under the evangelical and Baptist auspices. The College grants the Bachelor and Associate degrees and a Diploma in Bible.

Community Environment. The 35-acre campus is located in Newhall, a community 32 miles northwest of Los Angeles.

Religious Denomination. General Association of Regular Baptist Churches.

Religious Emphasis. Evangelical.

Accreditation. Western Association of Schools and Colleges.

Term System. Semester.

Admission Requirements. High school graduation with a grade point average of 2.00; 15 required units (English 3, mathematics 2, science 1, history 1, electives 8.

Tuition and Fees. Tuition $1,800 per semester; room and board $1,265.

Financial Aid. In addition to its own funds, the College participates in both federal and state financial aid programs.

Housing. Single students who do not live in their own homes in the vicinity are required to live in the school dormitories.

Library Facilities. The Powell Library contains approximately 40,000 volumes.

Religious Services/Activities. Various programs such as chapel periods, Days of Prayer, Bible Conferences, and Missionary Conferences are regularly scheduled.

Degree Programs

The Department of Biblical Studies stresses the understanding and interpretation of Biblical literature, from both the English version and the original languages. The Department provides guidance for the effective preparation of ministers, teachers, missionaries, church leaders, and other ministering personnel. Majors leading to the Bachelor's degree are offered in Bible with options in Pre-Theological, Biblical Languages, Biblical Ministries, Christian Education, and Youth Ministry. The degree requires a total of 120 semester hours of prescribed courses in general education and the major field.

Special Programs

The Associate of Arts programs in Biblical Studies and Christian Education are terminal degrees. They offer a basic preparation of courses in general education and Biblical studies as a foundation for further study and for service in the churches. A minimum of 62 semester units of credit are required.

A Diploma in Bible is offered as a one-year concentration of courses in Biblical Studies.

Loyola Marymount University
Department of Theology

Loyola Boulevard at West 80th Street
Los Angeles, CA 90045   (213) 642-2700

Administration. Dr. James N. Loughran, S.J., President; Dr. Anthony B. Brzoska, S.J., Dean, College of Liberal Arts; Dr. John R. Connolly, Chair, Department of Theology.

General Description. The Department of Theology functions principally as a center of Christian thought dedicated to the exposition and development of theoretical and practical aspects especially of the Catholic tradition. It offers two types of courses: (1) The focus is on theological questions as they have been developed within the tradition of Catholic Christianity; (2) The focus is on religious experience and belief as a universal phenomenon operative in human history and culture. The degrees Bachelor of Arts in Theology and Master of Arts in Religious Education are granted.

Parent Institution. Loyola Marymount University emphasises education in the humanities, social sciences, law, science, engineering, business adminstration, education, communicative arts, performing arts, and fine arts. The University strives toward its goals within the context of an institutional commitment to Christianity and the Catholic

tradition. The divisions of the University are: Colleges of Liberal Arts, Fine and Communicative Arts, Business Adminstration, Science and Engineering, the Graduate Division, and the School of Law.

Community Environment. All colleges and divisions of the University except the School of Law are located on the Westchester campus, a 130-acre mesa overlooking the Pacific Ocean about ten miles west of downtown Los Angeles.

Religious Denomination. Roman Catholic.

Accreditation. Western Association of Schools and Colleges.

Term System. Semester; summer term.

Admission Requirements. High school graduation with 16 units including 4 English, 2 foreign language, 3 math, 1 science, 3 social science, 3 academic electives; SAT or ACT; recommendation of high school official.

Tuition and Fees. Tuition per year $6,625; associated fees $35; rooms $1,522-$1,664 in residence halls, $1,932-$2,010 in apartments; board $1,506 (20 meal per week plan).

Financial Aid. Scholarships, grants, loans, and employment opportunities are available. Sixty-four percent of the student body receives some financial aid.

Housing. Housing facilities include self-contained apartments, 168 of which accommodate 1,684 students.

Library Facilities. The main campus library contains 242,000 volumes.

Religious Services/Activities. Besides the large number and variety of daily and weekend Eucharistic Liturgies, the Campus Ministry Center provides a number of weekend retreats off campus, personal and religious counseling or spiritual direction, and a wide variety of student programs.

Degree Programs

The Bachelor of Arts degree in Theology requires 4 pre-major courses in Theology with a C (2.0) average plus 24 semester hours in upper division Theology courses, including 1 course in Scripture, 2 in Systematics, 1 in Morality, and a prescribed Seminar. An average of C (2.0) in the major courses is required.

The Master of Arts degree in Religious Education is a professional preparation for the Ministries of the World, especially catechesis, evangelism, sacramental celebration, and the teaching of theology and scripture. There are five areas of study: theology, scripture, sacraments and liturgy, moral catechesis, and ministry; these include 36 credits of course work plus a Practicum (a specialized project in ministry) and an oral comprehensive examination.

Special Programs

The Graduate Certificate in Religious Education signifies preparation for ministry beyond that ordinarily achieved in undergraduate study or diocesan certification programs. The candidate completes the same 18 credit requirements as for the Master of Arts degree but does not take the comprehensive examination or prepare the thesis.

A Lay-Ministry minor requires 18 semester hours in Theology with at least 15 in upper division courses. At least one course each is required from Scripture, Morality, Systematics, Personal Growth and Spirituality, and Pastoral Aspects of Ministry. This is at the baccalaureate level.

Mennonite Brethren Biblical Seminary
4824 East Butler Avenue
Fresno, CA 93727   (209) 251-8628

Administration. Dr. Elmer A. Martens, President.

General Description. Training for leadership in the church has been important for Mennonite Brethren since the founding of the denomination in Russia in 1860. The denomination maintained several colleges in the United States beginning in 1908. In 1955, the Seminary in Fresno was founded with the first classes offered at the Pacific Bible Institute (now Fresno Pacific College). The Seminary is an evangelical, Anabaptist educational institution of the Mennonite Brethren Churches of North America. The curriculum is organized into three divisions: Biblical Studies, Theological/Historical Studies, and Practical Studies. The Master of Arts and Master of Divinity degrees are awarded as well as a Certificate in Christian Studies.

Community Environment. The campus is located three miles from downtown Fresno, a city of over 250,000 and the largest city between Los Angeles and San Francisco. The campus is a former estate.

Religious Denomination. Mennonite Brethren Church of North America.

Religious Emphasis. Evangelical; Anabaptist.

Accreditation. Western Association of Schools and Colleges; Association of Theological Schools in the United States and Canada.

Term System. Semester.

Admission Requirements. Bachelor of Arts degree or equivalent from an accredited university or college.

Tuition and Fees. Tuition $105 per unit.

Financial Aid. Mennonite Brethren students receive a bursary of 25 percent of tuition.

Housing. Apartments in Mission Memorial Court may rented for $210 per month.

Library Facilities. The Hiebert Library, operated jointly with Fresno Pacific College, contains over 72,000 volumes. The Center for Mennonite Brethren Studies is a part of the library. The records of the Mennonite Brethren Church and its history are preserved there.

Religious Services/Activities. Chapel is held each Tuesday and Friday throughout the academic year. A Spiritual Emphasis week is held in the fall semester. Convocations, retreats, and field trips are scheduled.

Degree Programs

The Master of Divinity degree offers four program options: Pastoral Ministries, Christian Education, World Mission, and Pastoral Counseling. It requires 96 semester units, 53 of which are taken in a core program and 43 units in the program option selected.

The Master of Arts degree has three program options: Old Testament, New Testament, and Theology. It requires 64 semester units, 32 of which are taken in a core program and 32 units in the option chosen.

Special Programs

A Certificate in Christian Studies is designed to provide graduate level courses in religion for personal enrichment and to equip men and women for a more effective lay ministry. The one-year program includes courses from each area of the Seminary curriculum.

Mount St. Mary's College
Graduate Program in Religious Studies
10 Chester Place
Los Angeles, CA 90007   (213) 746-0450

Administration. Dr. Marie Alexis Navarro, I.H.M., Director, Graduate Program in Religious Studies.

General Description. The Graduate Programs in Religious Studies are designed to serve not only professionals in the field of religious education, but also those desirous of advancing to doctoral work in religious studies. The programs reflect a commitment to Catholic scholarship within the broader range of ecumenical Christian thought in the fields of Scripture, systematics, and ethics. Included in the program are courses in applied spiritual theology, leadership in religious education, pastoral ministry, and hispanic ministry. It is projected that the diverse programs will in the near future be coordinated within a school of religious studies and ministry.

Parent Institution. Mount St. Mary's College is a Catholic college whose programs are designed to serve both undergraduate and graduate students in pursuit of studies ranging from traditional liberal arts studies to individually designed programs. The undergraduate program serves women students, while the graduate programs are open to both men and women. Both levels of education enhance the student's awareness of an everchanging context within which the values of the individual must operate. It is in this latter context of a dynamic society that the College best serves the needs of our time.

Community Environment. Mount St. Mary's College is located on two campuses in the city of Los Angeles. The Doheny Campus at Chester Place, near the intersection of the Harbor and Santa Monica Freeways is located on property formerly owned by Edward L. Doheny and his wife, the Countess Estelle Doheny. The two city blocks of Victorian residences in their setting of exotic trees and flowers have been converted to educational purposes. These buildings have been supplemented by an auditorium, lecture rooms, and laboratories, and provide facilities for two-year, career-oriented associate degree programs, graduate degree programs, and California Credential programs.

The Chalon Campus is an impressive multi-level complex of buildings and gardens on a thousand-foot-high ridge overlooking UCLA and Westwood Village. The architecture is white Spanish colonial, with arched walkways connecting many of the buildings. The Chapel occupies the central position on campus with wide stone stairways approaching it on two sides. The address of the Chalon campus is 12002 Chalon Road, Los Angeles, CA 90049; telephone (213) 476-2237.

Religious Denomination. Roman Catholic.

Religious Emphasis. Ecumenical Roman Catholic Christian.

Accreditation. Western Association of Schools and Colleges.

Term System. Semester; 6-week summer term.

Enrollment in Degree Programs in Religion 1984–85. Total 36; men 11, women 25.

Degrees in Religion Awarded 1984–85. Master of Arts in Religious Studies 4; men 1, women 3.

Faculty for Degree Programs in Religion. Total 9; full-time 2, part-time 7.

Admission Requirements. Bachelor's degree from an accredited institution; evaluation of academic background; interview with program adviser; meet other general requirements of the Graduate Division.

Tuition and Fees. $155 per unit (ordinarily 30 units); graduation fee $75.

Financial Aid. All financial aid at the College is administered in accordance with established national principles. The financial aid programs available include scholarships/grants/awards; loans; and employment. Tuition discount is available to full-time teachers in Catholic schools.

Housing. No housing available except during summer session.

Library Facilities. The Charles Willard Coe Memorial Library, located on the Chalon Campus, is the principal library of the College. It houses the majority of library materials for both campuses and also houses the Instructional Media Center. The Doheny Campus Library houses the Mayer Grant Special Education collection. Current holdings for both campuses is over 130,000 volumes, including bound periodicals, and there are subscriptions to over 600 periodicals.

Religious Services/Activities. Many activities are coordinated by the Campus Ministry.

Degree Programs

The Master of Arts degree in Religious Studies is designed to serve not only professionals in the field of religious education, but also those desirous of advancing to doctoral work in religious studies. The program reflects a commitment to the pursuit of Catholic scholarship within the broader range of ecumenical Christian thought in the fields of Scripture, systematics, and ethics. The 30-unit M.S. program is basically a summer program; however, courses and credit/non-credit workshops are offered during the Fall and Spring semesters of the academic year. The Master of Arts in Applied Spiritual Theology is designed for the professional, personal, and faith development of persons who have been involved in and will continue to participate actively in ministry within the Catholic church. An applicant is required to complete a 12-hour, non-credit introductory survey of contemporary Catholic teaching before admission to the program.

Special Programs

A Certificate as Director of Religious Education is awarded upon completion of a program designed for persons who are already experienced in a supervisorial capacity in the field of religious education. It is granted upon successful completion of 12 units of selected graduate course work.

Continuing education courses for Pastoral/Catechetical Ministry are also offered by the College.

Pacific Christian College
2500 East Nutwood Avenue
Fullerton, CA 92631   (714) 879-3901

Administration. Knofel L. Staton, President.

General Description. Pacific Christian College began in 1928 as Pacific Bible Seminary. The first classes were held in the building of the Alvarado Church of Christ in Los Angeles. In 1930, the Seminary was moved to Long Beach, where it conducted classes in the building of the First Christian Church. In 1962, the present name was adopted and in 1973 the move to Fullerton was accomplished.

Parent Institution. The College is a privately supported, coeducational institution affiliated with the Christian Churches and Churches of Christ. It offers the Associate of Arts and the Bachelor of Arts degrees. The Graduate School of Church Dynamics awards the Master of Arts degree.

Community Environment. The 11-acre campus is located in the northern Orange Country community of Fullerton, 35 miles southeast of downtown Los Angeles. It is adjacent to the campus of California State University - Fullerton.

Religious Denomination. Christian Churches and Churches of Christ.

Accreditation. Western Association of Schools and Colleges; American Association of Bible Colleges.

Term System. Semester (4-1-4 plan).

Enrollment in Degree Programs in Religion 1984–85. Total 414.

Admission Requirements. High school graduation or

equivalent; 15 academic units; SAT.

Tuition and Fees. Tuition $1,415 per semester; room and board $1,930; student fees $300.

Financial Aid. Assistance is available in the form of federal and state programs as well as Pacific Christian College scholarships, awards, and employment.

Housing. Dormitory housing is available on campus for 400 students.

Library Facilities. The Hurst Memorial Library houses approximately 45,000 volumes. The adjacent California State University Library, with over 600,000 volumes, is also available to Pacific Christian College students.

Religious Services/Activities. A student's first year at the College is expected to be characterized by active Christian service and participation in an area congregation.

Degree Programs

Every graduate from the College is considered to hold a major in Biblical Studies. The Bachelor of Arts degree requires the completion of 40 units in Biblical Studies, 40 units in General Studies, and 40 units of Major Studies. Majors are offered in the following fields: Church Growth (Preaching, Christian Education, Missions, Youth Ministry, Children's Ministry, Diversified Ministry); Church Music; Education (Diversified General Studies - K-6 Teaching); Management and Business Administration; Social Science (Child Development, Psychology, General Social Science, Social Work); and Contract Majors (Communication, History, Philosophy, Occupational Missions).

The Graduate School of Church Dynamics offers a 36 semester unit program leading to the Master of Arts degree. There is a core requirement of 24 semester units and an elective emphasis requiring 12 semester units.

Special Programs

The Associate of Arts is awarded for completion of two-year programs in Early Childhood Education, General Studies, Specialized Studies, and Cross-Cultural Missions.

A Certificate of Achievement is awarded for the completion of an 18 semester unit program by students who qualify for graduate studies at the Graduate School of Church Dynamics.

Pacific Lutheran Theological Seminary
2770 Marin Avenue
Berkeley, CA 94708   (415) 524-5264

Administration. Dr. Walter M. Stuhr, President.

General Description. Pacific Lutheran Theological Seminary as an institution offers preparation for the first-professional degree in theology which also qualifies persons for ordained ministry in the Lutheran Church. Degree and non-degree programs for persons not planning on ordained ministry, as well as post-Master of Divinity pro-

grams are offered. Through its membership in the Graduate Theological Union, Master and Doctoral programs in theology and religion are offered. The Seminary serves as a resource center for the ministry of reaching out with the Gospel to all people in every situation. In fulfilling this mission, the Seminary's primary goal is training women and men for professional leadership in the church.

The Seminary was founded by the California and Pacific Synods of the United Lutheran Church in America, which later became part of the present Lutheran Church in America. The Seminary's roots also go back to a Lutheran seminary which operated in the Pacific Northwest until 1932. Trust funds from the Seattle facilities helped with the purchase of the Berkeley campus. Over the years, faculty and students from all major Lutheran church bodies have been involved in the Seminary. In 1985, the Association of Evangelical Lutheran Churches, the American Lutheran Church, and the Lutheran Church in America - the three bodies that will unite in 1988 - established joint ownership of the Seminary. In this way, the Seminary serves as a model for theological education in the new Lutheran Church.

Parent Institution. The Seminary is a participating school of the Graduate Theological Union which has become, since its founding in 1962, the major theological center in the western United States. Its faculty is drawn largely from the combined faculties of the nine participating schools. The variety of religious traditions represented in the union makes it a uniquely diversified ecumenical center, one of the most inclusive in the world. Its library constitutes one of the largest theological collections in the nation. See also: Graduate Theological Union.

Community Environment. The city of Berkeley, with a population of 110,000, lies directly opposite the Golden Gate Bridge, with a magnificent view over the Bay and the city of San Francisco. Berkeley, known as "The Athens of the West," has a long tradition of political activism, varied architecture, and lively repertory theater. Its business and political leadership reflects the city's great ethnic diversity. Students benefit from Berkeley's extraordinary array of civic institutions, cafes, bookstores, handicrafts, and music. Berkeley has many churches, libraries, and art centers. The Tilden Regional Park has facilities for outdoor recreational activities. All forms of transportation are available. The climate is mild.

Across the Bay is San Francisco, one of the world's great cities, with a thriving financial center, distinctive neighborhoods, museums, and the very best in the performing arts.

Pacific Lutheran Theological Seminary is situated on the crest of the Berkeley Hills, about two miles north of the Graduate Theological Union Library and the University of California. The eight-acre campus overlooks San Francisco Bay to the west and Tilden Regional Park to the east. Two Spanish-style mansions, a classroom and office building, a dormitory, and the Chapel of the Cross are located in beautiful wooded surroundings.

Religious Denomination. Lutheran Church in America; The American Lutheran Church; Association of Evangelical Lutheran Churches.

Accreditation. Western Association of Schools and Colleges; Association of Theological Schools in the United States and Canada.

Term System. Semester; intersession (January); summer term.

Enrollment in Degree Programs in Religion 1984–85. Total 136; men 93, women 43.

Degrees in Religion Awarded 1984–85. Master of Divinity 21; men 12, women 9. Master of Arts in Theology 1; women 1. Master of Arts 1; women 1. Doctor of Ministry 4; men 4.

Faculty for Degree Programs in Religion. Total 24; full-time 15, part-time 9.

Admission Requirements. BA degree or its equivalent from an accredited college or university with a minimum of 2.0 grade point average; scores of the Graduate Record Examination report (general test plus test in area of major, if available); letters of reference; physical examination report; autobiography; nonrefundable application fee of $25. Prospective students should have the ability to work with the Hebrew and Greek text (it is expected that students enrolling in the Master of Divinity program will have completed the equivalent of one year of classical or Koine Greek at the college level); admission to the Seminary is a judgment, primarily on the basis of the application documents, that the applicant is adequately prepared, personally and academically, to undertake the Master of Divinity program.

Tuition and Fees. Tuition $2,150 to $3,000 per year, depending upon program; unclassified students $270 per course. Other fees vary. Dormitory $450 per semester single, $285 double; apartment rent $175-$200 per month. Dinner (cooperative plan) $160 to $265 per semester.

Financial Aid. Several forms of financial aid are available to students, depending on their personal financial situation and resources. These include grants from the Seminary ($400 maximum); loans; Guaranteed Student Loans from independent financial lenders. A Financial Aid Brochure is available from the Financial Aid Coordinator.

Housing. In order to make the most equitable distribution of available Seminary-owned housing, the Seminary has adopted a policy of prioritized consideration for dormitory rooms and for apartments. The Seminary seeks to satisfy the most pressing housing needs by rental of available rooms and units.

Library Facilities. The Graduate Theological Union Library represents the merger of the libraries of member schools and is the most visible expression of the ecumenical cooperation that has been established. It is located at 2400 Ridge Road in Berkeley. The current holdings of the Library include more than 350,000 books and journals and 150,000 items in microform, slides, tapes, photo records and video cassettes. This composite collection has not only the breadth to support the full range of theological programs, but also has remarkable depth in many areas of religious and theological studies. These include the specialized collections brought by the member schools. There is also a special collection documenting the new religious movements that have sprung up in American since 1965, which attracts international scholars who are beginning to produce the first body of secondary literature on the subject. Close cooperation with the University of California, Berkeley, and Stanford University gives students access to nationally recognized collections. Similar cooperative arrangements have been developed with the Golden Gate Baptist Theological Seminary in Mill Valley and the Mennonite Biblical Seminary in Fresno.

Religious Services/Activities. The Center for Multi-Cultural Ministry provides library resources, consultation, and programs for the churches. Facilities are available for congregational and church body retreats and conferences.

Degree Programs

The Master of Divinity requires a minimum of twenty-four 3-unit courses, the Integrative Growth sequence and Teaching Parish, a Cross-Cultural Experience, a one-quarter full-time Clinical Pastoral Education experience, and a nine- or twelve-month full-time Internship. Twelve prescribed courses are taken at the Seminary. Eleven area electives and one free elective may be taken from offerings by other member schools of the Graduate Theological Union as well as those of the Seminary. Area electives are taken in Bible (one each in Old and New Testament), church history, systematic theology, pastoral care, homiletics, education, leadership, ethics, and cross-cultural studies or world religions. The Teaching Parish constitutes the field dimension of the first two years of the curriculum. Students are related to selected parishes in the First Year and continue in the same parish through the Second Year.

The Master of Arts in Theology is designed for both those persons preparing for professional service in the Church without ordination, and those persons desiring study in theological disciplines but not necessarily preparing for professional service in the Church. The curriculum is essentially the same as that for the first two years of the Master of Divinity program, except that the Teaching Parish requirement and courses specifically related to pastoral competence can be replaced by electives.

The Master of Theology affords an opportunity for men and women who have received the Master of Divinity degree or its equivalent to pursue advanced theological studies. The program is especially recommended for pastors who seek additional competence in one of the foundational disciplines. To be considered for admission to the program a student should hold the Master of Divinity degree or its equivalent from an accredited theological school. The candidate must successfully complete eight semester courses of 3-units each at the graduate level with grades of B or better.

The program leading to the Doctor of Ministry engages pastors and congregations in a shared experience of mutual growth that uses normal congregational activities as the primary learning resource. The aim of the program is that its graduates gain increased ability to inspire, evoke, and empower the exercise of authentic and faithful ministry by all members of their congregations through their various vocations. Participants are expected to complete a minimum of 19 semester units of instruction in graduate level theological courses with a minimum grade of B; completion of the Congregation Ministry Project; participation in eight quarterly collegium (Seminar in Ministry) meetings; completion of twelve additional units by enrollment in the Graduate Theological Union Cooperative Summer Session; completion of a Project Report.

Special Programs

Each summer the Seminary joins with other seminaries of the Graduate Theological Union in sponsorship of a Cooperative Summer Session which brings major theologians to laypersons and pastors who gather in Berkeley from throughout the western United States and beyond.

Seminary involvement in Continuing Theological Education has been enlarged and enriched through relationships with the Center for Theological Study located at California Lutheran College, Thousand Oaks, California, and with the Lutheran Institute for Theological Education at Pacific Lutheran University, Tacoma, Washington. These two centers sponsor extension credit and non-credit courses for clergy and laity in local areas throughout the region served by Pacific Lutheran Theological Seminary.

Pastors in Residence is a program providing the opportunity for a parish pastor to spend seven days on the Seminary campus engaged in whatever activity seems most helpful: individual reading, study, and meditation; conferences; attending classes and seminars.

During the academic year, lectures and discussions are held at the Seminary dealing with a variety of subjects of interest and assistance to pastors in the practice of ministry.

Pacific School of Religion
1798 Scenic Avenue
Berkeley, CA 94709　　　　　　　　(415) 848-0528

Administration. Dr. Neeley D. McCarter, President; Dr. Barbara Brown Zikmund, Dean; Alan A. Schut, Director of Admissions.

General Description. Pacific School of Religion (PSR) is an independent, interdenominational seminary affiliated with the Graduate Theological Union, Berkeley, a consortium of ten Protestant, Roman Catholic, and Buddhist seminaries, and the University of California, Berkeley. See also Graduate Theological Union.

Community Environment. Pacific School of Religion is located on a beautiful promontory overlooking San Fran-

cisco Bay and across the street from the University of California, Berkeley. Although it is in the midst of the cultural diversity of the Bay Area, the campus enjoys a peaceful, well-landscaped environment. See also Franciscan School of Theology (Berkeley) and California Institute of Integral Studies (San Francisco).

Religious Denomination. Nondenominational, with close links to the United Church of Christ, the Disciples of Christ, and the United Methodist Church.

Religious Emphasis. Ecumenical and pluralistic.

Accreditation. Western Association of Schools and Colleges; Association of Theological Schools in the U.S. and Canada.

Term System. Semester; summer term.

Enrollment in Degree Programs in Religion 1984–85. Total 237; men 119, women 118.

Degrees in Religion Awarded 1984–85. Master of Divinity 43; men 28, women 15. Master of Arts 7; men 2, women 5. Certificate of Theological Studies 5; men 2, women 3. Certificate of Special Studies 2; men 2. Certificate in Advanced Professional Studies 2; men 2. Doctor of Ministry 5; men 4, women 1.

Faculty for Degree Programs in Religion. Total 51; full-time 13, part-time 38.

Admission Requirements. Applicants must possess a baccalaureate degree or its equivalent from an accredited institution. Master of Divinity degree and certificate program applicants should possess at least a B average in undergraduate work; Master of Arts applicants should possess at least a B plus average. The Graduate Record Examination (aptitude only) is required under certain circumstances as described in the catalog. A TOEFL score of 550 is required of all international applicants.

Tuition and Fees. Tuition $3,600 per year; fees $33 per year; room and board $2,216; married student housing $3,564.

Financial Aid. Financial aid is provided on the basis of need as determined by the financial aid application. Financial aid packages usually include partial tuition grants and college work study supplemented by National Direct Students Loans, Guaranteed Student Loans, California Loans to Assists Students, and various denominational loan programs.

Housing. The School provides a total of 62 single student dormitory spaces and 67 married student housing apartments. The School is happy to accommodate pets. All housing is on campus or within one block of the campus.

Library Facilities. The Graduate Theological Union Common Library is across the street from the Pacific School of Religion. It contains 352,000 volumes. Students also have access to the collections of both the University of California at Berkeley and Stanford University.

Religious Services/Activities. Chapel services are held regularly on Tuesday and Thursday mornings; vesper services are held every Monday afternoon. One formal retreat is planned each semester and the community sponsors various prayer groups, bible study groups, and support groups. Worship services at the School are ecumenical.

Degree Programs

The Master of Divinity degree fulfills the basic academic and professional requirements for ordination in most major Protestant denominations. It is designed to develop proficiencies for Christian ministry. The degree requires a minimum of three years of theological study totaling 72 semester units.

The Master of Arts degree is an academically-oriented program of study preparing persons form forms of lay ministry in non-ecclesiastical agencies and institutions through such vocations as counseling and teaching. It can also be combined with the Master of Divinity degree for more intensive specialization within the broad preparation for ministry. It requires a minimum of 2 years of theological study totaling 48 semester units.

A joint M.Div./M.A. program requires 4 years and 96 semester units, with basic expectations being met concurrently for both degrees. If the M.Div. is held from another seminary, the full 48 semester units are required for the M.A. degree.

The School is involved in two types of doctoral degree programs: a very small and basically residential Doctor of Ministry program for mature religious professionals who have the Master of Divinity degree or its equivalent, and a larger Doctor of Philosophy and Doctor of Theology program in cooperation with the Graduate Theological Union.

Special Programs

The Pacific School of Religion offers, in cooperation with other Graduate Theological Union schools, a full summer session of workshops and courses. The School sponsors separately the annual Pastoral Conference and Earl Lectures in late January and an annual Lay Leaders' Conference in October. An annual Racial/Ethnic Leadership Conference is also sponsored in cooperation with other Graduate Theological Union schools.

Four Certificate programs are also offered. I. The Certificate of Theological Studies (C.T.S.) is designed: (1) to aid in the clarification of one's personal faith journey, (2) to allow experimentation in theological education while determining a vocational direction, (3) to serve those seeking a grounding in disciplined theological study before entering their chosen vocation. A minimum of 24 semester units is needed to complete the C.T.S. II. The Certificate of Special Studies (C.S.S.) is awarded to a regularly admitted international student who has been in residence for a minimum of 2 regular semesters, has earned at least 9 semester units of work each semester, and has maintained a grade point average of C (2.0). III. The Certificate in Ministry Studies (C.M.S.) is offered for pastors or lay preachers over age 32 who are serving ethnic minority churches. The emphasis is on learning ways to integrate

theological disciplines with the practice of ministry for others in ethnic churches. Twelve semester credits are needed to complete the program. IV. The Certificate of Advanced Professional Studies (C.A.P.S.) is awarded to a regularly admitted student who has the M.Div. degree or its equivalent, has completed an additional 18 semester units of work at PSR, and has maintained a grade point average of C (2.0).

Patten College
College of Christian Ministries
2433 Coolidge Avenue
Oakland, CA 94601   (415) 533-8300

Administration. Dr. Priscilla C. Patten, President; Dr. Bebe H. Patten, Founder-Chancellor; Dr. Rebecca Patten, Academic Dean.

General Description. Patten College is a coeducational college of Christian ministries offering programs leading to the Associate of Arts and Bachelor of Arts degrees. The College strives to be a doorway to discovery, challenge, commitment, and service. At Patten all students complete a core of liberal arts courses and a major in Biblical Studies. In addition, students may select concentrations and courses to meet their personal and professional goals in the areas of General, Biblical, and Professional Studies. One of the major aims of the college is to provide each student a balanced Christian education in an environment that is conducive to social, intellectual, and spiritual growth.

Community Environment. The Oakland Bay area is one of the most beautiful and culturally varied educational centers in the United States. A great variety of recreational, athletic, cultural, and religious activities of interest to students is within a few minutes of the Patten campus. San Francisco is 20 minutes away via the Bay Bridge. Lake Merritt, a 155-acre body of salt water surrounded by beautiful Lakeside Park, is a short distance from the campus. The East Bay Regional Park System contains 26,000 acres of semi-wild recreation areas. The 5-acre campus is centrally located in the Fruitvale-Coolidge Avenue residential district. A park-like atmosphere has been achieved by a landscape design that includes flowers, foliage, lawns, tall elms, palms, olives, and several other varieties of trees.

Religious Denomination. Interdenominational.

Religious Emphasis. Evangelical.

Accreditation. Western Association of Schools and Colleges.

Term System. Semester.

Enrollment in Degree Programs in Religion 1984–85. Total 189; men 79, women 110.

Degrees in Religion Awarded 1984–85. Bachelor of Arts in: Biblical Studies 7; men 6, women 1. Pre-Seminary 2; men 2. Ministerial 2; men 2.

Faculty for Degree Programs in Religion. Total 23; full-time 9, part-time 14.

Admission Requirements. Candidates for admission to the B.A. degree program should present the equivalent of 16 academic units from an approved high school; candidates 18 years of age or older who have not graduated from high school may register for the A.A. degree and be admitted on probation; candidates for admission to the Certified Christian Worker program need to meet only the qualifications that will enable them to succeed in the program.

Tuition and Fees. Tuition 12-16 units $1,206 per semester; more than 16 units $70 per unit; Certified Christian Workers Program per class tuition $77; room and board per school year $2,417; all students with 6 or more units are charged a fee of $50 each semester.

Financial Aid. By distributing funds according to need, Patten's financial aid program makes it possible for many students, regardless of their financial circumstances, to continue their education. The amount of financial aid awarded is generally a combination of scholarship, grant, loan, and employment.

Housing. Single students are encouraged to live in the college dormitories or secure other housing that is approved by the director of housing.

Library Facilities. The College library houses a steadily expanding collection of approximately 20,000 books, 195 religious and secular journals, 2 daily papers, a vertical file, and an audiovisual department.

Religious Services/Activities. Students are encouraged to give time to prayer and Bible reading. The prayer chapel is open daily and students may join the prayer groups that are held on campus three times daily. Daily chapel services are led by students, faculty members, and outstanding leaders from many backgrounds. Students are required to attend chapel regularly. Students are expected to be active members of a church while enrolled at Patten.

In order to help students achieve their potential in Christian leadership, the College has developed a Christian Service program, designed to involve them in practical ministry. Beginning with the sophomore year, each student must complete one-half unit in Christian Service activity per semester. This is done by visiting churches, conducting services, calling on the sick in hospitals or convalescent homes, working with needy children, sharing Christ with prisoners, or serving in some other capacity.

Degree Programs

The Bachelor of Arts degree program requires the completion of 130 semester units which include prescribed courses in general studies, biblical and theological studies, professional studies, and concentration in one of four areas: Ministerial Studies (pastoral), Christian Education, Sacred Music, and Liberal Studies (other options are Pre-Seminary Studies and Electives). The Pre-Seminary Studies option is designed to meet the needs of students whose denominations require a degree beyond the B.A. as the entering level for careers in evangelism, teaching, or pastoral work.

Special Programs

The College provides a course of study for students who desire a two-year college program. Candidates who complete 63 units may receive the Associate of Arts degree. The program includes courses from the divisions of General, Biblical, and Professional Studies.

The Certified Christian Worker Program consists of sixty units of course work including a required core of five courses to meet the Evangelical Teacher Training Association (E.T.T.A.) requirements and an additional fifteen elective courses drawn from the Biblical and Professional Studies divisions. The E.T.T.A. Silver Seal Advanced Certificate is awarded upon completion of the program.

Pepperdine University
Seaver College, Religion Division
24255 Pacific Coast Highway
Malibu, CA 90265   (213) 456-4351

Administration. Dr. David Davenport, President; Dr. Charles B. Runnels, Chancellor; Dr. John F. Wilson, Dean, Seaver College and Professor of Religion.

General Description. The Religion Division is dedicated to study that combines academic excellence and personal commitment to Jesus Christ. The intent is to introduce the major to a broad spectrum of religious thought with a particular focus upon the Bible. The Division is designed to prepare students to be ministers, missionaries, education and youth directors, for church leadership, for teaching, for benevolent ministries, for writing ministries, for counseling ministries, and for other types of Christian services. Two degrees are offered by the Division: Bachelor of Arts in Religion and Master of Arts in Religion.

Parent Institution. Pepperdine University is an independent, medium-sized university enrolling approximately 6,000 students in 4 colleges and schools. Seaver College and the School of Law are located on the University's 830-acre campus overlooking the Pacific Ocean at Malibu, California. The Graduate School of Education and Psychology and the School of Business and Management are based at the Pepperdine University Plaza building, 3415 Sepulveda Boulevard, Los Angeles. Courses are taught at this location and at other Educational Centers in southern California.

Community Environment. Picturesquely located where the Santa Monica Mountains reach the Pacific Ocean, the Seaver College campus enjoys a commanding view of both. The winding seashore, the rugged beauty of Malibu Canyon, and the clean ocean air enhance the towering campus location. The moderate climate permits year-round outdoor recreation. Malibu lies in Los Angeles County, less than an hour from downtown Los Angeles and the Los Angeles International Airport. As a world center for trade, recreation, culture, industry, and education, Los Angeles offers students the advantages of a vast metropolitan area.

Religious Denomination. Churches of Christ.

Accreditation. Western Association of Schools and Colleges.

Term System. Trimester; 3rd trimester is the summer term.

Enrollment in Degree Programs in Religion 1984–85. Total 60; men 40, women 20 (estimates).

Degrees in Religion Awarded 1984–85. Bachelor of Arts; Master of Arts.

Faculty for Degree Programs in Religion. Total 17; full-time 7, part-time 10.

Admission Requirements. The Admissions Committee examines the student's current academic record to determine and evaluate the grade point average, the number and kinds of classes taken, the trends in the grades, and scores from the SAT or ACT. A personal interview is highly recommended. Admission to the Graduate Program in Religion requires a baccalaureate degree from an accredited college or university with a major in religious studies.

Tuition and Fees. Tuition $295 per unit; room and board (double occupancy) $1,960 per trimester in dormitory, $2,120 in apartment; board only $830 per trimester.

Financial Aid. The University awards financial aid on the basis of verified financial need. Financial aid programs include loans, grants, college work-study, state financial aid, academic scholarships, special achievement awards, missions scholarships, restricted awards, and emergency student loans.

Housing. There is on-campus housing for approximately 1,500 unmarried students. Apartments with kitchen facilities are available on campus for a limited number of upper division students.

Library Facilities. The Payson Library on the Malibu campus houses over 250,000 volumes and maintains a Religion Collection of 25,000 volumes. The University Educational Center libraries together maintain a collection of 102,000 volumes. These off-campus libraries are available to all students.

Religious Services/Activities. The student who attends Pepperdine's Seaver College in Malibu should be aware of the emphasis placed on spiritual development. Both academic and extracurricular activities are affected by this emphasis. Undergraduate students are required to attend a weekly convocation and are encouraged to attend the voluntary daily chapel. The University Church, which meets on campus, provides a spiritual program directed toward the University community. An Annual Religion Majors' Dinner is held as well as a Missions Practicum with workshops and internships.

Degree Programs

The Bachelor of Arts in Religion is designed to prepare students to be ministers, missionaries, education and youth directors, for church leadership, for teaching, for benevolent ministries, for writing ministries, for counseling ministries, and for other types of Christian services.

The Master of Arts in Religion program offers the possibility of concentration in the areas of Scripture, History of Christianity, Christian Thought and Ethics, Ministry, or Missions. Graduate study in religion is designed to aid students in their preparation as ministers, as missionaries, and as teachers of religion. It is also the design of this program to aid in the development of those tools necessary to scholarly contributions in research and writing. A significant number of Seaver College graduates, on the basis of the master's degree in religion, proceed to other institutions where they work toward terminal degrees.

Special Programs

An off-campus Master of Arts program in Religion is offered in the Western states at strategic locations and taught by Pepperdine Religion faculty who journey to these sites.

The Staley Lectures and William Green Lectures are offered annually.

Pomona College
Department of Religion
Claremont, CA 93257   (209) 781-3130

Administration. Professor J. William Whedbee, Chair, Department of Religion.

General Description. The concentration in Religion offered by the Department of Religion is designed to address the broad goals of a liberal arts education in the humanities and to introduce students to historical-critical and comparative methodologies. While recognizing the importance and legitimacy of personal involvement in the study of religion, the Department does not represent or advocate any particular religion as normative. Courses offered by the Department are in the areas of introductory courses, the Literature and History of Religion, Religion and Culture, interdisciplinary courses, and Guided Reading. Courses are also available from Claremont McKenna College, Pitzer College, and Scripps College.

Parent Institution. Pomona College was incorporated in 1887 by a group of early settlers who wanted to see in Southern California a "Christian College of the New England type." Instruction began in 1888 in the city of Pomona. A few months later, the College moved to Claremont but the name had become so definitely fixed to the institution that it was retained. As a member of The Claremont Colleges, Pomona College is part of a unique arrangement in American higher education—five autonomous undergraduate colleges and a graduate school on adjacent campuses. The Colleges jointly support certain central facilities, open their courses to one another's students, and cooperate in sponsoring a number of special academic and extracurricular programs.

Community Environment. The campus is in Claremont, a city of 21,500 residents. It is 35 miles east of Los Angeles. The College occupies a campus of 130 acres.

Religious Denomination. Nondenominational.

Accreditation. Western Association of Schools and Colleges.

Term System. Semester.

Faculty for Degree Programs in Religion. Total 4.

Admission Requirements. High school graduation from an accredited school with superior academic grades and outstanding personal qualifications; SAT or ACT; 3 achievement tests recommended.

Tuition and Fees. Tuition $4,700 per semester; health and counseling fee $80; Associated Student dues $50; other fees $200; room and board $1,950 per semester.

Financial Aid. The College has an extensive financial aid program. It usually consists of a combination of grants, loans, and term-time earnings. Various scholarships are also available.

Housing. The College maintains several coeducational residence halls with separate living areas for men and women students within some buildings.

Library Facilities. Honold Library is the central library serving the students and faculty of the Claremont Colleges. The resources total over 1,200,000 volumes.

Religious Services/Activities. The McAlister Center for Religious Activities provides offices for the College Chaplain and is the center for religious activities at the Claremont Colleges.

Degree Programs

The concentration in Religion leading to the Bachelor of Arts degree requires the completion of Theories of Religion; The Oriental Heritage I: Sacred Traditions of India; The Oriental Heritage II: Sacred Traditions of China and Japan; and The Oriental Heritage III: Medieval India, Hindu, and Muslim; plus two additional religion courses. A Senior Seminar and thesis are required of all senior concentrators.

St. John's Seminary
5012 East Seminary Road
Camarillo, CA 93010   (805) 482-2755

Administration. Very Rev. Charles E. Miller, C.M., Rector; Rev. Newman C. Eberhardt, C.M., Vice Rector; Rev. John C. Kesterson, Academic Dean.

General Description. The purpose of St. John's Seminary is to prepare men to become priests in the Roman Catholic Church. In the Seminary's understanding, a priest may be described as a disciple called to be a builder of community through the ministry of the sacraments, especially of the Eucharist, and of the Word. The Seminary is primarily dedicated to forming priests for the diocesan priesthood in parochial ministry within the southwestern part of the United States. It is committed to the principle of integrating all aspects of priestly formation. St. John's Seminary is engaged with Hebrew Union College of Los Angeles and with the University of Judaism in a faculty exchange program intended to promote mutual understanding and insight into Jewish and Christian traditions. St. John's grants the Master of Divinity and Master of Arts degrees.

Community Environment. St. John's Seminary is located on a 150-acre campus 2 miles east of the city of Camarillo, California, and 60 miles northwest of Los Angeles. Camarillo is in a rural, suburban area, with churches of all denominations, and 4 hospitals within a 10-mile radius. The Point Mugu State Park is nearby as are Pacific Ocean beaches and county parks.

Religious Denomination. Roman Catholic.

Accreditation. Western Association of Schools and Colleges; Association of Theological Schools in the United States and Canada.

Term System. Semester.

Enrollment in Degree Programs in Religion 1984–85. Total 100; men 100.

Degrees in Religion Awarded 1984–85. Master of Divinity 20; men 20. Master of Arts 2; men 2.

Faculty for Degree Programs in Religion. Total 23; full-time 15, part-time 8.

Admission Requirements. Bachelor's degree or its equivalent; satisfactory proof of religious status and moral qualifications.

Tuition and Fees. Tuition $2,900; part-time students not in residence $90 per semester hour of credit.

Financial Aid. Applications forms for Guaranteed Student Loans and Fellowship Grants are available from the Business Office.

Housing. All resident students reside in Seminary housing.

Library Facilities. The Edward Laurence Doheny Memorial Library has over 123,000 volumes (jointly with nearby St. John's College) readily available for scholarly pursuits. The volumes that comprise the rare book library number over 10,000: English and American first editions, manuscript books dating from the ninth century, early printed books, Californiana, private press books, children's literature, book illustrators, fine bindings, books with fore-edge paintings, a First Volume Gutenberg Bible, other rare Bible editions, and reference books pertaining to all of the fine art and book categories in the Collection. There are also four thousand rare manuscripts and letters of historical and literary figures.

Religious Services/Activities. The Field Education Program is an integral part of the formation of candidates for the priesthood. During their years in the Seminary, all students are required to dedicate a specified amount of time to supervised pastoral apostolic works. Daily Mass, morning and evening prayer, monthly days of recollection, yearly retreat, and regular spiritual conferences are held.

Degree Programs

The Master of Divinity is a professional degree. The program has for its purpose the preparation of students for an effective ministry in the Church. The program normally requires a minimum of four academic years of full-time work or the equivalent. The degree requirements include academic studies in Biblical Studies, Canon Law, Church History, Homiletics, Moral Theology, Liturgical Studies, Dogmatic Theology, Pastoral Theology, Spiritual Theology, and electives. Twelve hours in Spanish are also required.

The Master of Arts is an academic degree and is the usual form of recognition that a student has achieved excellence in theological studies and has acquired skill in an area of specific research as manifested in the successful completion of a thesis. The program offers to qualified students the opportunity to pursue advanced courses in Religion, while providing for a minor field of concentration at the option of the student in Church History, and to obtain training in research.

Special Programs

The Candidacy Program is designed primarily for students who have earned their B.A. degree from an accredited college other than a seminary college and who do not have sufficient background in theological programs. Emphasis is placed on Christian personal formation. All aspects are coordinated by the director of the program in cooperation with the other officers of the Seminary.

St. John's Seminary College
Program of Theology and Religious Studies
5118 East Seminary Road
Camarillo, CA 93010   (805) 482-4697

Administration. Most Rev. Donald W. Montrose, D.D., President, Rector; The Rev. Roy A. Persich, C.M., Vice President, Vice Rector, Academic Dean.

General Description. Presently the program in Religion is a requirement for all students — 16 units in a four-year period. The solitary major presently is in Philosophy. A major in Humanities is being added in the 1987-88 school year, with a secondary concentration possible in Theology and Religious Studies. The program concentrates upon spiritual, disciplinary, apostolic, and academic formation.

Parent Institution. St. John's is a free-standing seminary college that emphasizes the liberal arts and has a curriculum that leads to the degree Bachelor of Arts in Philosophy. The overall purpose of St. John's is to prepare men for the Catholic priesthood. Completing the program in the seminary college, the student can continue his education and formation in a seminary theologate. This seminary college is a feeder for St. John's Seminary, a school of theology preparing its students for ordination.

Community Environment. St. John's Seminary College is located on a 150-acre campus 2 miles east of the city of Camarillo, California, and 60 miles northwest of Los Angeles. Camarillo is in a rural, suburban area, with churches of all denominations, and 4 hospitals within a 10 mile radius. The Point Mugu State Park is nearby as are Pacific Ocean beaches and county parks.

Religious Denomination. Roman Catholic.

Accreditation. Western Association of Schools and Colleges.

Term System. Semester.

Enrollment in Degree Programs in Religion 1984–85. Total 91; men 91.

Degrees in Religion Awarded 1984–85. Bachelor of Arts in Philosophy 15; men 15. These figures are for the 1985-86 school year.

Faculty for Degree Programs in Religion. Total 5; full-time 2, part-time 3.

Admission Requirements. High school graduation; SAT score; letters of recommendation; psychological testing as required by the sponsoring diocese or religious community.

Tuition and Fees. Tuition $2,900 per year.

Housing. All full-time students reside in dormitories.

Library Facilities. The Carrie Estelle Doheny Memorial Library houses a basic collection of 49,000 volumes.

Religious Services/Activities. Daily morning and evening prayer and Mass; monthly Days of Recollection; annual five day retreat; special retreats and prayer days for classes and groups scheduled periodically. The Formational Program includes spiritual formation, disciplinary formation, and apostolic formation. The program is under the general direction of the Director of Apostolic Formation. A full-time assistant director supervises the students' involvement in these activities and acts as liaison between the Seminary and the field directors of the cooperating apostolic programs.

Degree Programs

The Bachelor of Arts with a major in Philosophy is awarded upon completion of all requirements. The major in Philosophy requires 28 semester hours. Courses in Theology and Religious Studies and in Religious Education are also required as part of the program. A total of 128 semester hours is required for the degree.

St. Patrick's Seminary
320 Middlefield Road
Menlo Park, CA 94025   (415) 325-5621

Administration. Rev. Howard P. Bleichner, S.S., President-Rector; Rev. Lawrence B. Terrien, S.S., Vice-Rector, Academic Dean.

General Description. St. Patrick's Seminary trains men to be priests in the Roman Catholic Church. This work of preparation for priestly ministry is carried out under the authority of the Archbishop of San Francisco with the assistance of priests from the Society of St. Sulpice in accord with the directives of the Second Vatican Council, the Sacred Congregation of Education, and the Program of Priestly Formation of the National Conference of Catholic Bishops. Degrees offered are Master of Divinity and Master of Arts in Theology.

Community Environment. Menlo Park is a residential community 30 miles south of San Francisco and 20 miles north of San Jose. The climate is moderate. There are buses and trains to the area, and the San Francisco International Airport is 16 miles to the north.

Religious Denomination. Roman Catholic.

Accreditation. Western Association of Schools and Colleges; Association of Theological Schools in the United States and Canada.

Term System. Semester; no summer term.

Enrollment in Degree Programs in Religion 1984–85. Total 96; men 96.

Degrees in Religion Awarded 1984–85. Master of Divinity 13; men 13. Master of Arts in Theology 1; men 1.

Faculty for Degree Programs in Religion. Total 31; full-time 9, part-time 22.

Admission Requirements. Master of Divinity: Bachelor's degree; 18 hours of Philosophy; GRE scores; official acceptance by diocese or religious order. Master of Arts in Theology: Bachelor of Arts in Religious Studies; 3.0 or better grade point average; comprehensive overview of the history of philosophy.

Tuition and Fees. Tuition $2,125 per year; room and board $2,000 per year; non-resident students $125 per credit.

Financial Aid. Guaranteed Student Loans, state graduate fellowships, and Veterans Benefits are among the resources available.

Housing. Students must live on campus in dormitories.

Library Facilities. The library houses 62,425 volumes. It also maintains the complete collection of Archbishop Alemany, first Bishop of San Francisco.

Religious Services/Activities. Roman Catholic daily Mass; daily afternoon prayer service; annual retreat; six days of recollection.

Degree Programs

The Master of Divinity degree is earned by successful completion of the regular academic and pastoral curriculum requiring 120 semester units in coursework and field education. The student must earn a passing grade in all required courses, achieve an overall 2.0 grade point average, and successfully pass comprehensive examinations in Sacred Scripture, dogmatic theology, and moral theology.

The Master of Arts in Theology is designed for those who plan to go on to further graduate studies in theology or who desire a terminal degree which will assist them in various educationally based ministries (e.g., teaching, religious education programs, campus ministry, etc.). The

student must obtain a minimum of 30 semester units in Scripture Studies, Systematic Theology, and Moral Theology. A 3.0 grade point average must be maintained and a thesis is required.

Special Programs

A Bachelor of Arts in Theology program for older students is a special academic and formational program designed especially for applicants for the Catholic priestly ministry who are 30 years of age or older and who have had little or no previous college background.

San Diego, University of
Religious Studies Department
Alcala Park
San Diego, CA 92110   (619) 260-4784

Administration. Dr. Author E. Hughes, President; Sr. Sally Furay, R.S.C.J., Ph.D., Vice President and Provost; Dr. C. Joseph Pusateri, Dean, College of Arts and Sciences; Dr. Norbert J. Rigali, Chair, Religious Studies Department; Dr. Ronald A. Pachence, Chair, Graduate Program in Practical Theology.

General Description. The Department of Religious Studies assists students in developing a mature and critical understanding of the Christian faith and exploring the subsequent responsibilities which flow from that experience. While the theological emphasis is Roman Catholic, the curriculum is ecumenical and cross-cultural in scope. A major in Religious Studies leading to the Bachelor of Arts degree is offered by the Department.

The Graduate Program in Practical Theology is part of the College of Arts and Sciences and is housed in the Institute for Christian Ministries. It is designed for students who wish to investigate issues which emerge when Christian tradition confronts the perspectives and problems of contemporary life. Specifically, the discipline of Practical Theology explores ways in which one can be faithful both to the demands of Biblical religion and to the challenges of participation in pluralistic society. The Master of Arts in Practical Theology is awarded.

Parent Institution. The University of San Diego is an independent, Roman Catholic institution. It is independent in that ultimate responsibility for the governance of the University lies in its own Board of Trustees. It is Catholic by virtue of its commitment to the examination of the Catholic tradition as the basis of a continuing search for meaning in contemporary life. The University is a community of scholars. It shares with all institutions of higher education the search for truth and the pursuit of academic excellence. Students of all races, creeds, and cultural backgrounds are welcome to join the intellectual quest. The University includes the College of Arts and Sciences, the Muriel Hahn School of Nursing, the Business School, the School of Law, and the School of Education.

Community Environment. The city of San Diego lies along and around one of the world's ten most beautiful protected natural harbors, and has a very special "sea-washed and air-conditioned climate." The city is a manufacturing and shipping center, with its main industies being fishing, fish packing, and the construction of aircraft parts, missiles, and boats. With a population of 800,000, San Diego has 19 miles of Pacific Ocean shores with beautiful beaches. The greater metropolitan area is home to 1,700,000 people.

Religious Denomination. Roman Catholic.

Religious Emphasis. Post-Vatican II Catholic.

Accreditation. Western Association of Schools and Colleges.

Term System. Semester; summer term.

Enrollment in Degree Programs in Religion 1984–85. Total (graduate) 62; men 16, women 46.

Degrees in Religion Awarded 1984–85. Master of Religious Education 11; men 3, women 8. Master of Arts in Religious Education 4; men 1, women 3.

Faculty for Degree Programs in Religion. Total 11; full-time 2, part-time 9.

Admission Requirements. Undergraduate: High school graduation; SAT score; academic recommendation from high school faculty; personal essay. Graduate: A bachelor's degree from an accredited college or university with a minimum of 12 undergraduate credits in religion; an undergraduate G.P.A of at least 3.0 on a 4.0 scale.

Tuition and Fees. Tuition $235 per unit; application fee $25; Associated Students fee $30 (12 units or more), $15 (7-11 units), $5 (3-6 units); Graduate Student Association fees $15 (1-6 units), $25 (7 units or more); deposit fees $50; comprehensive examination fee $10 (each exam); room and board for undergraduate students $1,300 to $2,250 per semester depending on accommodations and/or meal plan.

Financial Aid. A financial aid package is designed to meet the financial needs of each individual student. Each package may consist of monies from one or more programs and may range from $200 to $11,000 depending on established need and/or merit. USD offers financial assistance programs for graduate students including assistantships, graduate fellowships, California State fellowships, guaranteed student loans, work-study, national direct student loans, and USD graduate grants. Students in the Practical Theology program may inquire at the Financial Aid office concerning the Spain family endowment.

Housing. Resident living accommodations are available on campus, currently housing about 1,350 students. Rooms are available in traditional dormitory style, suite living buildings, and apartment units. Limited housing is available for graduate students.

Library Facilities. The Helen K. and James S. Copley Library houses over 250,000 books and bound periodicals. More than one thousand current periodical and serial titles are received, as well as newspapers, pamphlets, government documents, and microform materials.

Religious Services/Activities. A Campus Ministry team consisting of 2 priests, 1 sister, and 1 lay woman has been established, including a minister whose role is to serve the graduate student community. Services include daily masses, retreats, counseling, and social outreach.

Degree Programs

The Department of Religious Studies offers a major in Religious Studies leading to the Bachelor of Arts degree. The requirements of the major include courses in the History of Religion (alternate, Christianity and Other Faith Traditions); Jesus in Christian Tradition; Christian Worship; Community Called Church; Biblical Studies; and nine upper division elective units.

The Master of Arts in Practical Theology program offers professional training which enhances the student's ability to assume an active role in ecclesial communities. Three areas of emphasis are available: religious education, parish ministry, spirituality and social justice. In conjunction with an advisor, each student designs a curriculum which integrates various theoretical perspectives with the student's academic and professional needs. The program requires thirty units of coursework, three units of supervised field experience/research, and comprehensive examinations.

Special Programs

Non-degree programs of the Institute for Christian Ministries include mini-courses, conferences, and workshops for the public.

San Francisco Theological Seminary
2 Kensington Road
San Anselmo, CA 94960   (415) 453-2280

Administration. Dr. J. Randolph Taylor, President; Dr. Donald P. Buteyn, Dean; Dr. Walter T. Davis, Jr., Director of Advanced Pastoral Studies.

General Description. San Francisco Theological Seminary, an institution of the Presbyterian Church (U.S.A.), has as its central purpose to assist in equipping the whole church for its ministry. It is evangelical, ecumenical, and reformed in its self understanding. The Seminary offers 6 accredited master and doctorate degree programs for clergy and laity, as well as a variety of non-degree, short-term conferences and seminars both on campus and by extension. The degree programs are: Master of Divinity, Master of Arts in Values, Master of Arts, Doctor of Ministry, Doctor of Theology, Doctor of Philosophy. In 1985 the Seminary decided to replace the Doctor of the Science of Theology (STD) degree with some form of post-doctoral studies yet to be determined. The policies and practices of the Seminary secure its life as an academic community and as a spiritual community for all those who seek enrichment from the school of the church. The Seminary is a founding member of the Graduate Theological Union in

Berkeley, California.

Community Environment. San Francisco Theological Seminary is located on 21 acres overlooking Ross Valley, 15 miles north of the Golden Gate Bridge, in San Anselmo, Marin County, California. Several of its buildings are styled after stone castles, and the location is called Seminary Hill. The San Francisco Bay Area is highly diverse, taking its character and climate from the great San Francisco Bay which it surrounds. A basic asset of the area is the region's social and economic variety. Around the shores of the Bay, within easy distance of San Anselmo, is almost every type of social situation — a microcosm of contemporary American society.

Religious Denomination. Presbyterian Church (U.S.A.).

Religious Emphasis. Reformed.

Accreditation. Western Association of Schools and Colleges; Association of Theological Schools in the United States and Canada.

Term System. Semester; January Inter-Session; summer term for the Doctor of Ministry program.

Enrollment in Degree Programs in Religion 1984–85. Total 1,010. By Program: Master of Divinity 210; Doctor of Ministry 515; Master of Arts in Values 195; Master of Arts 5; Doctor of Theology 4; Doctor of Philosophy (Ph.D.) 21; Doctor of the Science of Theology (STD) 60. The Master of Divinity program is made up of 50 percent women.

Degrees in Religion Awarded 1984–85. Master of Arts 2; men 1, women 1. Master of Arts in Value 11; women 11. Master of Divinity 53; men 23, women 30. Doctor of Ministry 53; men 51, women 2. Doctor of the Science of Theology 3; men 3.

Faculty for Degree Programs in Religion. Total 25; full-time 17, part-time 8 (teaching administrators). There are also visiting lecturers, instructors, and adjunct faculty.

Admission Requirements. The Seminary is open to qualified students of all Christian traditions. Every student must possess the degree of Bachelor of Arts or its equivalent, based upon four years of work beyond secondary education, in a college or university approved by one of the regional accrediting bodies. Priority in admission will be given to applicants who have achieved an average grade of B or better in appropriate baccalaureate or pre-M.Div. subjects.

Tuition and Fees. Tuition $3,600 per year or $150 per unit; Seminary housing $990 to $2,700 for the nine-month academic year.

Financial Aid. The Seminary provides substantial financial aid for Master of Divinity candidates. Unclassified students are not eligible for financial aid. The total amount of financial aid in any case does not exceed the amount of student need. In order to qualify for financial aid, a student is expected to provide a minimum income of $500 from summer savings and $1,800 from earnings during the academic year.

Housing. Seminary apartments are available for rent both on the San Anselmo campus and in Berkeley amidst the other seminaries of the Graduate Theological Union.

Library Facilities. The library on the San Anselmo campus is a branch of the Flora Lamson Hewlett Library of the Graduate Theological Union. It contains 97,681 volumes and 316 periodical subscriptions.

Religious Services/Activities. Chapel services for the Seminary community are held three times weekly and on special occasions. Numerous prayer groups meet on campus and the Seminary has a Center for Christian Spiritual Disciplines which offers seminars, courses, workshops, and retreats for degree and non-degree candidates.

Degree Programs

The Master of Divinity degree is the basic professional degree program of the Seminary. It is designed for those who wish to prepare themselves for some form of ordained ministry in the church. Its primary purpose is the preparation of persons for the tasks of pastoral ministry in the context of the local congregation. A total of 76 units of credit is required for the degree and distributed among Biblical Disciplines, Historical and Systematic Disciplines, and Social and Behavioral Disciplines. A field/experience internship and electives are also required.

The Master of Arts in Values program intends to enable students to sharpen skills and insight into the value orientations upon which human action is based. The major goal of the curriculum is to enable the student to develop a critical understanding of human values which can be brought to bear upon decisions in the situations in which he/she lives and works. Forty-two semester units are required for completion of the degree. The program is conducted off-campus in the students' communities and on a schedule that enables participants to continue with their current jobs and avocations. Academic work is done in learning groups of ten to fifteen students.

The Master of Arts degree is a preliminary to the doctoral degree, a terminal degree for teaching lower division levels, a theological preparation for counseling or community service, and an advancement in a personal avocational interest in religious studies.

The Doctor of Philosophy program focuses on theological studies in the context of university disciplines. The Doctor of Theology programs focus on theological studies in the context of the entire theological spectrum. Applicants for the Doctor of Theology degree are expected to have a distinguished record in the completion of their first professional degree, the Master of Divinity or its equivalent.

The Doctor of Ministry basic curriculum is the same for all students, but the design is arranged into four different options to meet the diverse situations of a variety of clergy. The basic design comprises three major components common to all options: the collegium group, the summer term, and the dissertation/project. In addition, Option A (for local groups) includes two professional seminars; Options B (for persons without a local group) and C (for persons from overseas) require an 8-unit in-parish project; and

Option D (in-residence program for clergy on sabbatical) provides a year's residence with course offerings from the Graduate Theological Union. The program requires a minimum of two years and a maximum of five years of part-time study, research, and writing.

Special Programs

The Seminary's educational programs allow pastors and lay people to participate in educational experiences in their own locale. The programs are sponsored by the Seminary and often conducted by Seminary professors. In partnership with several governing bodies of the Presbyterian Church, the Seminary operates five Extension Centers including one on the San Anselmo campus. The others are in Los Angeles, Phoenix, Portland, and Seattle. Each Center provides conferences, seminars, and group meetings.

San Francisco, University of
Department of Theology and Religious Studies
Ignatian Heights, Campion Hall D-3
San Francisco, CA 94117   (415) 666-6601

Administration. Joseph F. Eagan, S.J., Chairperson, Department of Theology and Religious Studies.

General Description. The University of San Francisco offers both Bachelor of Arts and Master of Arts degrees in Theology. During their years of study at the University, students are familiarized with the Roman Catholic tradition as it has been expressed and formulated through history so that the theological enterprise may proceed within the context of the community of faith. In the spirit of the ecumenical interest, every effort is made to provide in-depth courses in the full Judaeo-Christian tradition, in comparative religion, and in religion and society. Students and faculty reflect scientifically on the faith of the community and articulate this faith in relation to the contemporary human condition, thus becoming more fully aware of their roles in today's world. They are also invited to join in celebrating their community in worship and social concern.

The Department of Theology and Religious Studies, in collaboration with faculty of other disciplines, offers courses which explore such topics as sociological exegesis, the sociology and psychology of religion, theological dimensions of personal and social ethics, of ecology and literature, theology as autobiography, and theological critique of film.

Parent Institution. The University of San Francisco is a Catholic and Jesuit university. It is a private university, incorporated under the laws of the State of California. It admits students of any race, religion, sex, color, handicap, national and ethnic origin, to all the rights, privileges, programs, and activities generally accorded or made avail-

able to students at the school. The University currently enrolls 3,300 undergraduate students, half of whom live on campus. Total enrollment is approximately 6,500 students. Over 70 different majors are offered in USF's 6 academic colleges and professional schools. Student-faculty ratio is 17 to 1.

Community Environment. See: California Institute of Integral Studies (San Francisco).

Religious Denomination. Roman Catholic.

Accreditation. Western Association of Schools and Colleges.

Term System. Semester; summer term.

Enrollment in Degree Programs in Religion 1984–85. Graduate total 15; men 4, women 11. Undergraduate total 25; men 8, women 17.

Degrees in Religion Awarded 1984–85. Master of Arts in Theology 7; men 3, women 4. Bachelor of Arts in Theology/Religious Studies 6; men 2, women 4.

Faculty for Degree Programs in Religion. Total 13; full-time 5, part-time 4, half-time 4.

Admission Requirements. The University seeks students who are sincerely interested in pursuing a well-rounded education. The admission process is selective, and each application is reviewed individually. To enhance the quality and diversity of its student body, the University encourages men and women of all races, nationalities, and religious beliefs to appply. Eligibility is based on the high school grade point average, completion of a minimum of 15 academic units, a personal recommendation, and satisfactory test scores. All applicants are required to take the SAT or ACT tests.

Tuition and Fees. Tuition $6,450 per school year; room and board $3,490 for the academic year; books, fees, travel, and other expenses about $1,800 per year.

Financial Aid. A wide variety of scholarships, grants, loans, and work-study programs are available. Applicants should submit a Student Aid Application for California to the appropriate office of the College Scholarship Service; the University will also accept the Finanaical Aid Form for students from out of state.

Housing. The University provides comfortable room and board facilities for 1,400 men and women residents. Off-campus housing information is not available and there are no on-campus facilities for married students.

Library Facilities. The library houses more than 500,-000 volumes with about 41,000 volumes in the area of theology; 12,000 volumes are in special collections.

Religious Services/Activities. The Department of Theology and Religious Studies has its identity in an active and cohesive community of faculty and students who join together not only in academic study but also in social life and liturgical celebration. Graduate and undergraduate students form their own department organization, the Theology Students Community, which promotes intellectual, spiritual, and social activities with the Department.

Degree Programs

The Bachelor of Arts degree with a major in Theology and Religious Studies leads to a number of professional skills and employment opportunities: the teaching of religion in primary or secondary schools, youth and campus ministry, religious radio and TV programming, social service work under religious sponsorship, graduate study leading to college teaching or other advanced positions, pre-professional training in business, the medical sciences, law, etc. Special preparation for these professional applications of theological study can be arranged either within the major or double major programs.

The Bachelor of Arts degree with a major in Psychology and Religion is administered through the Psychology Department in conjunction with the Theology/Religious Studies Department. The program is designed for those students with an interest in psychology in a pastoral context and who currently do not intend to advance further in the field of psychology.

The Master of Arts in Theology curriculum is built around the five basic areas of the Text, the Founder, the Tradition, the Religious Experience, and the Mores. Students must have completed 18 units of undergraduate work in Theology as well as other undergraduate courses in philosophy.

The Master of Arts degree in Applied Spirituality is offered during summers only. The aim of the program is personal spiritual renewal and growth for the sake of mission in the contemporary church. It seeks to develop spiritual leaders who effectively integrate three elements of ecclesial service: prayer, serious study of Christian theology, and pastoral ministry.

The Master of Arts in Religious Education program is offered by the Office of Pastoral Ministries and is designed to provide theological knowledge and competency in the educational process and to meet the continuing educational needs of people professionally involved in a variety of teaching ministries within the Church. The curriculum focuses on the career objectives of each student indicated in a personally written statement of goals.

The Master of Arts in Pastoral Ministry program is planned to provide professionally involved men and women with both theological knowledge and competency in the various ministerial activities of the Christian churches at both the parish and diocesan levels. The program is offered by the Office of Pastoral Ministries.

The Master in Pastoral Theology degree program is offered jointly by the Office of Religious Education and Pastoral Ministry and the Department of Theology and Religious Studies. The program is planned for people who wish to enrich their background in Theology on a graduate level without professional involvement in either Religious Education or Pastoral Ministries. It may be earned either on-campus or-off campus.

Special Programs

There are 20-unit programs of study designed to provide a balanced integration of Theology and practical application to meet the continuing needs and interests of people involved in all forms of ministry within the Church. Each program focuses on the career objectives of the student and is designed to allow students to select courses from a broad range of related areas. Certificates may be earned on the undergraduate, graduate, and post-graduate levels, in on-campus or off-campus programs.

San Jose Bible College
790 South 12th Street
San Jose, CA 95112   (408) 293-9058

Administration. Bryce Jessup, President; Michael Bowman, Vice President of Academic Affairs.

General Description. San Jose Bible College is a nondenominational Evangelical Christian college training students for ministry. Degrees are offered in Bible, Pastoral Ministry, Youth Ministry, Missions, Christian Education, and Music. The educational programs include approximately an equal mix of general education, Bible, and ministry. There is an emphasis on practical skills in each major area, so that every four-year graduate is required to do an intensive internship program, thereby making practical and usable some of the more theoretical classroom work. Because the College is small, there exists an authentic spirit of family or community on campus, yet the academic climate is demanding. In addition to the Bachelor of Arts and the Bachelor of Science degrees the College offers a 2-year Associate of Arts degree, a 2-year Certificate of Christian Arts, and a 1-year Bible certificate.

Community Environment. The present campus of San Jose Bible College was established in 1951 on 7½ acres at Twelfth and Virginia Streets in San Jose, California. San Jose is a major metropolitan city of 700,000, with a small town charm and hospitality. It is only 40 minutes from San Francisco with Fisherman's Wharf, Golden Gate Park, and Pier 39. The beach is within a forty-minute drive, water skiing is available at several areas in the city itself, and snow skiing is but a few hours away.

Religious Denomination. Nondenominational (Christian).

Religious Emphasis. Evangelical.

Accreditation. American Association of Bible Colleges.

Term System. Quarter; no summer term.

Enrollment in Degree Programs in Religion 1984–85. Total 176; men 92, women 84.

Degrees in Religion Awarded 1984–85. Bachelor of Arts 8; men 8. Bachelor of Science 14; men 9, women 5.

Faculty for Degree Programs in Religion. Total 28; full-time 7, part-time 21.

Admission Requirements. High school diploma or equivalent; minister's letter of recommendation; personal letter of purpose; health form; SAT or ACT recommended but not required.

Tuition and Fees. Tuition $80 per quarter unit; fees $75 per quarter; room and board $700 per quarter.

Financial Aid. Pell, SEOG, GSL, VA, Cal Grant A and B, CLAS; 50 percent discount to children of full-time ministers and missionaries; College-administered scholarships and tuition discounts.

Housing. Men's and women's dormitories on campus; limited married students' housing in school-owned homes.

Library Facilities. The library contains a collection of 28,877 volumes with extensive holdings in Bible exegesis and in Restoration history.

Religious Services/Activities. Chapel services are held three times each week. Planned devotions and prayer in each dorm are held. Under the direction of the student-led outreach committee, students serve in a wide variety of activities.

Degree Programs

The Bachelor of Arts and Bachelor of Science degrees are offered by the College. A total of 192 quarter hours is required. Basic requirements include 44 hours in Bible, 25 hours in Doctrine and Ministry, and 65 hours in general education. The remaining credit hours are dependent upon the students goals. The Bachelor of Arts in Bible and Theology may be pursued with a minor in Christian Education, Missions, or Pastoral Ministry. The Bachelor of Science in Bible and Theology may be pursued with a minor in Christian Education, Early Childhood Education, Music Ministry, Pastoral Ministry, or Youth Ministry.

Special Programs

A two-year degree program leading toward the Associate of Arts degree is intended either for the student who may transfer to a liberal arts college or for one who wants a well-rounded education that balances Bible, ministry, and education.

Certificate Program in Christian Arts is a two-year terminal program designed to provide the graduate with a basic Biblical knowledge and some specific practical skills to serve as a volunteer worker in the church.

A Cross-Cultural Bible Institute is held in the evenings for ethnic students. Courses are taught in Korean, Spanish, Cambodian, as well as English.

The Logos School of the Bible offers evening classes off-site both for credit and adult education.

Summer study tours send missions majors overseas for internships during the summer.

Santa Clara, University of
Department of Religious Studies
Santa Clara, CA 95053   (408) 554-4547

Administration. James W. Reites, S.J., Chair, Department of Religious Studies; Sr. Anne Marie Mongoven, O.P., Director, Graduate Program.

General Description. The Religious Studies Department fulfills a twofold function: to offer courses as part of the University's core curriculum and to offer a major area of undergraduate study for those who wish to concentrate in the study of religion. The Department offers a wide range of courses, with a special emphasis on the Catholic tradition. This emphasis, however, is not exclusive, and the Department is ecumenical in its faculty and in its approach to the study of religion.

The graduate program was initiated in the Fall of 1983. It offers the following degrees: Master of Arts in Catechetics, Master of Arts in Pastoral Liturgy, Master of Arts in Spirituality. The program offers a well-defined educational schema with five required theology courses as foundational to each area of specialization. Although the curriculum has other specific requirements, it is flexible and sensitive to the needs and goals of individual students, offering opportunity for some personal curriculum design and development.

Parent Institution. The University of Santa Clara, founded in 1851, bears the distinction of being the oldest college - public or private - in the state of California. It is also the only college built on the site of one of the original twenty-one California missions - Mission Clara de Asis. The beautiful campus reflects its mission heritage in its architecture, and promotes a pleasant feeling of community among the faculty, staff, and students.

The University is a Jesuit school with a proud heritage of excellence in teaching. Throughout its long history, Santa Clara has reflected an abiding concern for the individual student. The University regards academic discipline which is explicitly concerned with a critical understanding of the religious question as a central moment in the student's liberal education. Santa Clara is a comprehensive University with Schools of Law, Engineering, and Business, as well as the College of Arts and Sciences.

Community Environment. The city of Santa Clara is 46 miles from San Francisco near the southern tip of the Bay in an area rich in opportunities for learning. The campus is situated in the midst of one of the nation's greatest concentrations of high-technology industry and professional and scientific activity. The cultural and entertainment centers of San Francisco, Berkeley, Oakland, and Marin County are within one-hour's travel by bus, train, or car. Santa Clara has a moderate Mediterranean climate.

Religious Denomination. Roman Catholic.

Accreditation. Western Association of Schools and Colleges. Member of: Association of Jesuit Colleges and Universities.

Term System. The Santa Clara Plan is designed to encourage in-depth study by limiting the number of courses a student takes at any one time. The academic year (September to June) is divided into three 11-week terms. The eleventh week is devoted to examinations. Freshmen and sophomores normally take four 4-unit courses each term, while juniors and seniors ordinarily take three 5-unit courses per term. A six-week summer session is offered.

Enrollment in Degree Programs in Religion 1984–85. Total 125.

Degrees in Religion Awarded 1984–85. BA in Religious Studies 9; men 4, women 5. First graduate degrees to be awarded in 1986.

Faculty for Degree Programs in Religion. Total 23; full-time 17, part-time 6. Visiting faculty of 5 during summer session.

Admission Requirements. Nonrefundable application fee $25; recommendation from high school counselor; high school transcript; SAT score. Applicants for the Graduate program must have completed a baccalaureate degree from an accredited college or university and have sufficient background in contemporary theology and Scripture. Ministerial experience may fulfill the requirement for background studies in theology and Scripture.

Tuition and Fees. Undergraduate tuition $2,037 per quarter; room and board $1,101 per quarter; other fees where applicable. Graduate tuition $127 per quarter unit.

Financial Aid. The University of Santa Clara maintains a broadly-based program of scholarships, loans, grants, and part-time employment. Administered by the Office of Financial Aid, these resources help bridge the gap between the cost of education and what parents can reasonably contribute. More complete information is available in the Student Financial Services bulletin, *Putting It Together.* Partial scholarships for students in the Graduate Program of 25 percent tuition, on the basis of need, may be available to those involved in church ministry.

Housing. The University maintains 11 residence halls and three apartment complexes accommodating about 2,000 undergraduate students. On-campus housing for graduate students is not available during the academic year; apartments available for summer students.

Library Facilities. The Michel Orradre Library, with 110,000 square feet of space, has over 410,000 books and periodicals and 360,000 microforms. It is an official depository for both California and U.S. government documents, numbering some 214,000. The Library has an open shelf plan and is open seven days a week for a total of 106 hours.

Religious Services/Activities. The Campus Ministry staff at Santa Clara reflects the reality of the Church today - a group of lay women and men, women religious and clergy, who encourage all members of the University community to deepen their Christian commitment to the "service of faith, of which the promotion of justice is an absolute requirement." To attain this end, Campus Ministry offers to the University community a variety of weekend and overnight experiences, from silent retreats to discussion and reflection sessions. Campus Ministry also sponsors guest speakers, workshops, and service opportunities in the community. It is responsible for the coordination and preparation of Eucharistic Celebrations in the Mission Church.

Degree Programs

In addition to the University's Bachelor of Arts requirements in general education for all students, the following are specific for students completing the B.A. major in Religious Studies: Philosophy, Foreign or Classical Language, History of Western Civilization, Fine Arts, Scripture, Systematic Theology, Cross-Cultural Religious Studies, senior research paper, and Biblical Languages (Koine Greek and Biblical Hebrew).

The Master of Arts in Catechetics, the Master of Arts in Pastoral Liturgy, and the Master of Arts in Spirituality are offered by the Religious Studies Department. For the MA degree, 52 quarter units of course work and comprehensive examinations are required. The Master of Arts in Catechetics may be earned during the academic year and/or in the summer session. The Master of Arts in Pastoral Liturgy and the Master of Arts in Spirituality are summer session programs.

Southern California, University of
School of Religion
University Park
Los Angeles, CA 90007   (213) 743-2311

Administration. Dr. James H. Zumberge, President; Dr. Donald E. Miller, Director, School of Religion.

General Description. The School of Religion offers courses in all of the major areas of religious studies: Bible and ancient near eastern religion; theology and philosophy of religion; ethics; world religions; and historical, literary, and scientific studies of religion. Courses are designed to facilitate the appreciation and critical evaluation of all religious traditions in the light of past and present scholarship. There are also a number of special programs and offerings: the Religion Honors Program, the Bioethics University Certificate Program; and the opportunity to take courses at Hebrew Union College and receive regular USC course credit. Students have the option to take an occasional course at Hebrew Union College, or they may declare a Judaic Studies major in religion.

Parent Institution. The University of Southern California was established in 1880. It is a nonsectarian, coeducational institution enrolling over 28,000 students. Degree programs are offered in more than 150 fields. Eighteen of the University's schools are professional schools. The center of the University's undergraduate education is the liberal arts college, the College of Letters, Arts, and Sciences, of which the School of Religion is a part.

Community Environment. The main campus is located

near downtown Los Angeles in the area known as University Park. The Coliseum, site of the 1984 Summer Olympics, is nearby.

Religious Denomination. None.

Accreditation. Western Association of Schools and Colleges.

Term System. Semester.

Faculty for Degree Programs in Religion. Total 14.

Admission Requirements. Graduation from high school or equivalent; minimum of 12 academic units; SAT or ACT.

Tuition and Fees. Tuition $4,743 per semester; room and board $2,000; fees $100.

Financial Aid. Scholarships based on academic achievement, financial assistance based on need; loans to parents, and other forms of tuition financing are available.

Housing. Nearly 6,000 students live in University housing. A variety of accommodations is available.

Library Facilities. The University Libraries include the general library and 14 departmental libraries housing over 2 million bound volumes and numerous periodicals, pamphlets, microforms, and audiovisual materials.

Degree Programs

The major in Religion leading to the Bachelor of Arts degree requires at least 6 but not more than 8 upper division courses, with at least one course in three areas of religious studies: (1) Bible and ancient near easter religion, (2) theology and philosophy of religion; (3) ethics; (4) world religions, and (5) historical, literary, and scientific studies of religion.

A Bachelor of Arts in Religion with a specialty in Judaic Studies is offered in cooperation with the Hebrew Union College Jewish Institute of Religion. Students must meet all undergraduate requirements of the University, completing 128 units, 16 of the last 32 units being USC courses. The Student takes 20 units of courses offered by the Hebrew Union College and 12 units in the USC School of Religion.

Starr King School for the Ministry
2441 Le Conte Avenue
Berkeley, CA 94709   (415) 845-6232

Administration. Gordon B. McKeeman, President.

General Description. Starr King School for the Ministry is a privately supported coeducational graduate theological school. It is the Pacific Coast Educational Center for the Unitarian Universalist Association. Most graduates of Starr King enter the Unitarian Universalist ministry. A growing number explore and enter alternative forms of religious leadership in counseling, education, the arts, chaplaincies, or experimental gatherings and organizations.

Parent Institution. The School is a member of the Graduate Theological Union and shares its resources with member schools. It is named after Thomas Starr King, the Civil War-time minister of First Unitarian Church in San Francisco. Classes at the School were first held in 1904. *See:* Graduate Theological Union.

Community Environment. The campus is located in the midst of a university and seminary environment in Berkeley, two blocks from the University of California campus.

Religious Denomination. Unitarian Universalist Association.

Accreditation. Association of Theological Schools in the United States and Canada.

Term System. Semester.

Enrollment in Degree Programs in Religion 1984–85. Total 52; men 28, women 24.

Admission Requirements. Admission is highly selective.

Tuition and Fees. Tuition $2,750 per year.

Financial Aid. Limited financial assistance is provided.

Housing. No housing is provided.

Library Facilities. The School shares the joint library facilities of the Graduate Theological Union and has access to over 400,000 volumes.

Degree Programs

See: Graduate Theological Union, Berkeley, California.

Talbot Theological Seminary and School of Theology
13800 Biola Avenue
La Mirada, CA 90639   (213) 944-0351

General Description. See: Biola University, La Mirada, California.

Thomas Aquinas College
10000 North Ojai Road
Santa Paula, CA 93060   (805) 525-4417

Administration. Dr. Ronald P. McArthur, President.

General Description. Founded in 1971, Thomas Aquinas College is an independent Roman Catholic institution controlled solely by its Board of Governors. The College has the blessing and approbation of His Emminence Timothy Cardinal Manning, Archbishop of Los Angeles. All classes are seminars and tutorials. The four-year program requires reading and discussion of Great Books: the greatest writings in mathematics, science, literature, history, theology, and philosophy. Because Thomas Aquinas College is explicitly a Roman Catholic college, Sacred Scripture and the *magisterium* of the Church are understood to be the most important sources of enlightenment. The College grants the Bachelor of Arts degree.

Community Environment. The campus is located in a rural setting, 60 miles from Los Angeles and 45 miles from Santa Barbara. It lies between Santa Paula and Ojai, and east of Ventura. The 130-acre campus is bordered on three sides by the Los Padres National Forest.

Religious Denomination. Roman Catholic.

Accreditation. Western Association of Schools and Colleges.

Term System. Semester.

Admission Requirements. High school graduation or GED; ACT or SAT.

Tuition and Fees. Tuition $5,795; room and board $2,935.

Financial Aid. Students requesting financial aid are to submit either the Financial Aid Form (FAF) of the College Scholarship Service or the Family Financial Statement (FFS) of the American College Testing Program.

Housing. Men's and women's dormitories are available on campus.

Library Facilities. The library houses over 22,000 volumes.

Religious Services/Activities. Religious exercises are not required of students. Masses are offered daily in the College chapel and no classes are scheduled at those times so that all may attend. Twenty-four hour exposition and adoration of the Blessed Sacrament are part of the monthly First Friday observance. The Rosary and Compline are said daily and confessions are scheduled twice weekly. Discussions of the works of Cardinal Newman and other spiritual writers are held in the College president's home on Sunday evenings. A Legion of Mary chapter is active on campus.

Degree Programs

The curriculum leading to the Bachelor of Arts degree is a four-year program of seminar and tutorials: Language Tutorial (two-years); Logic Tutorial (one year), Mathematics Tutorial (four years); Music Tutorial (one year); Philosophy Tutorial (three years); Theology Tutorial (four years); Laboratory (four years), Seminar (four years); and Readings (by year and course). Compositions and a Senior Thesis are an integral part of the curriculum.

West Coast Christian College
6901 North Maple Avenue
Fresno, CA 93710   (209) 299-7201

Administration. Dr. Hubert P. Black, President.

General Description. The purpose of the College is to provide an environment and an opportunity for the study of the Scriptures, Church Doctrines, and Arts and Sciences. The College is committed to the pursuit of truth, in the belief that it is a Christian obligation to study, to learn, and to understand. It offers approved courses and programs of instruction for the training of ministers, Christian educators, and Christian lay workers by including general studies, selected vocational programs, and concurrent enrollment with California State University, Fresno. The College grants the Associate in Arts degree and the Bachelor's degree.

Parent Institution. West Coast Christian College was founded in Pasadena in 1949 and moved to Fresno in 1950. It is affiliated with The Church of God.

Community Environment. The 21-acre campus is located in the heart of the San Joaquin Valley in the northeastern part of the city of Fresno.

Religious Denomination. The Church of God (Cleveland, Tennessee).

Accreditation. Western Association of Schools and Colleges.

Term System. Semester.

Admission Requirements. High school graduation or equivalent; ACT.

Tuition and Fees. Tuition $1,080 per semester; room and board $999-$1,498; student activity fee $30.

Financial Aid. Financial aid at the College is intended to assist qualified students in meeting normal expenses. Every student must have at least a 2.0 grade point average to be qualified to receive financial assistance.

Housing. Dormitory accommodations are available for 120 women and 120 men.

Library Facilities. The library contains over 26,000 volumes.

Religious Services/Activities. The entire campus community meets for worship and sharing three mornings each week in chapel. Student attendance is required at chapel services, convocations, and assembly programs. Students are also required to attend Sunday School, morning worship, and Sunday evening services at a local church. Regular devotional services of the student clubs and dormitories, private worship, prayer before each class, and participation in various religious clubs and musical groups provide additional opportunities for spiritual enrichment and practical Christian service.

Degree Programs

The Bachelor of Arts degree requires the completion of 130 semester hours. A concentration of studies totalling not less than 30 semester hours in one academic discipline constitutes a major. All graduates are considered to hold a major in Bible in addition to any other major they may have earned. The Bachelor of Arts degree may be awarded in Bible, Christian Ministries, Christian Education, Elementary Teacher Education for Christian Schools, Inter-Cultural Ministries, or Music. Minors are available in Business, Christian Education, English, Evangelism and Missions, Music, Pastoral Studies, Psychology, and Social Sciences.

Special Programs

The Associate of Arts degree requires the completion of a minimum of 64 semester hours including all required courses. The degree is awarded in Bible, Business, General Studies, or Music.

Westmont College
Religious Studies Department
955 La Paz Road
Santa Barbara, CA 93108   (805) 969-5051

Administration. Dr. David K. Winter, President; Dr. Thomas F. Andrews, Vice President and Academic Dean; Dr. Curtis Whiteman, Chairman, Religious Studies Department.

General Description. Westmont College has committed itself to a belief in the Scriptures as inspired and authoritative. Because of the importance of Biblical and theological study for meeting the goals of the college, the Department of Religious Studies performs a significant task. It administers a program of required courses in Bible, theology, and theological history that provides a balanced perspective for all students, regardless of their major. Equipped with a solid base from which they may grow as intelligent Christians, students are then better prepared to take upper division courses. The Religious Studies major is the most rigorous program in the college. The faculty members in the department have earned Ph.D.'s from some of the world's most prestigious institutions. The faculty is active in scholarship and in the lives of their students.

Parent Institution. Westmont College is a private, liberal arts, Evangelical Christian college. Over 80 percent of the faculty have earned doctorates and many of the programs are designed to accommodate the needs of pre-professional students. Along with this attention to academic rigor is an emphasis on the spiritual growth of the individual student. The small size of the student body (1,200 students), the attractive faculty-student ratio (1:17), and the concern for individual growth on the part of the entire campus community all contribute to this distinction.

Community Environment. Santa Barbara is a county seat and the largest city between Los Angeles and San Francisco. It is known as the "Riviera of the Pacific." The city lies at the foot of the Santa Ynez Mountains facing the Pacific Ocean. The climate is moderate with temperature varying only 7 degrees in summer and winter. All modes of transportation serve the area. Santa Barbara offers many cultural activities.

Religious Denomination. Nondenominational, primarily Protestant.

Religious Emphasis. Evangelical.

Accreditation. Western Association of Schools and Colleges. Member of: Independent Colleges of Southern California; Association of Independent California Colleges and Universities; Christian College Consortium.

Term System. Semester; 4-6 weeks summer term (May).

Enrollment in Degree Programs in Religion 1984–85. Total 100; men 50, women 50.

Degrees in Religion Awarded 1984–85. Bachelor of Arts in Religious Studies 37; men 20, women 17.

Faculty for Degree Programs in Religion. Total 6; full-time 6.

Admission Requirements. High school B average and acceptable SAT or ACT scores; assessment of personal areas covered by the application form such as activities, leadership, motivation, and quality of written response.

Tuition and Fees. $6,454 per year plus $3,220 room and board.

Financial Aid. Considerable aid available through grants, loans, and work-study; college and national loan programs; college and state scholarships; some awards for merit and leadership during sophomore-senior years.

Housing. Primarily dormitories; some off-campus housing. Students are given the opportunity to find their own accommodations off-campus.

Library Facilities. 125,000 volumes. Library has access to the University of California library system.

Religious Services/Activities. Weekly opportunities for service off-campus in church and social service organizations; tri-weekly chapel services and numerous Bible study and prayer/worship groups on campus.

Degree Programs

In the Bachelor of Arts program, students are permitted to tailor the major to suit an interest in Greek, Urban Ministries, Mission, or Christian Education. Beyond the core of four courses, the student selects seven upper division semester courses, four from distribution areas (Old Testament, New Testament, Systematic Theology, and Theological History) and three electives. Students are encouraged to double-major with Philosophy, English, Sociology, Psychology, or some other complementary discipline.

Special Programs

Students in the Urban Ministries track of the major spend one semester working and studying in San Francisco. The college has a dual-credit arrangement with the Institute for Holy Land Studies in Jerusalem. Internships are available for combined study and field work. Students are also encouraged to develop one-on-one tutorials with individual professors and to design their own majors according to individual interests.

Whittier College
Department of Religion
1306 East Philadelphia
Whittier, CA 90608   (213) 693-0771

Administration. Eugene S. Mills, President.

General Description. The Department of Religion within the Division of Humanities offers the major in Religion. Students planning to enter ministry, religious education, or the teaching of religion at the college and university levels are provided with a wide and carefully selected set of pre-professional courses.

Parent Institution. Whittier College, named for the poet

John Greenleaf Whittier, was founded in 1887 by members of the Society of Friends. The College ended its formal ties with the Society in the 1940s. It is a privately supported, coeducational liberal arts college controlled by an independent and self-perpetuating board of trustees, one-third of whom are members of the Society of Friends. Throughout its history, the College has been committed to high quality, innovative education and to a Quaker concern for the individual, particularly as a member of a community.

Community Environment. The campus of 120 acres is located at the foot of the Puente Hills in the city of Whittier, 18 miles southeast of Los Angeles.

Religious Denomination. Nonsectarian. (Religious Society of Friends heritage).

Accreditation. Western Association of Schools and Colleges.

Term System. Semester (4-1-4 plan).

Admission Requirements. High school graduation; ACT or SAT.

Tuition and Fees. Tuition $8,000 per year; room $1,600-$2,143; meal plans $1,330-$1,530; student body fees $36; student health fee $70.

Financial Aid. The College provides extensive financial aid to worthy students in the form of grants, scholarships, loans, and jobs.

Housing. Dormitories and apartment-style or small housing are available on campus.

Library Facilities. The Bonnie Bell Wardman Library has collections totaling over 200,000 volumes. Special collections include The John Greenleaf Whittier Collection; The Clifford and Susan Johnson Library of Quaker Literature which is the most complete collection of its kind in the West; The Jessamyn West Collection; and a collection of published materials on Richard M. Nixon, including some campaign memorabilia.

Religious Services/Activities. The College Chaplain encourages growth in religious experience and coordinates activities.

Degree Programs

Through inquiry into the ways in which religious beliefs, symbols, and practices function, the Department of Religion aims to assist students in the development of their own self-understanding and to cultivate an understanding and appreciation of other peoples. The major requires a minimum of 36 credits, 18 of which must be at the upper division level. Courses are grouped into the following: Experiential; Introductory and Survey; Sacred Stories, Texts, and Scriptures; Judeo-Christian Religions; Asian, African, and Aboriginal Religions; Religion and Culture; Themes in the Study of Religion; Methods in the Study of Religion; and Seminar for Majors and Directed Study. The Bachelor of Arts requires a total of 120 semester hours.

COLORADO

Belleview College
Belleview Bible Seminary
3455 West 83rd Avenue
Westminster, CO 80030   (303) 427-5461

Administration. Dr. Robert B. Dallenbach, President; Dr. Donald J. Wolfram, Dean.

General Description. The Belleview Bible Seminary is a small, theologically conservative Bible seminary preparing both men and women for the ordained ministry, missions, radio ministry, and lay ministry.

Parent Institution. Belleview College is a small four-year liberal arts college with emphasis on quality education in a context of Christian community. It is maintained and controlled by the Board of Trustees of the Pillar of Fire, Incorporated, of Colorado. The courses are determined in accordance with modern educational standards by the Committee on Education and the faculty.

Community Environment. The College is located four miles north of the city limits of Denver, near the intersection of Federal Boulevard and the Denver-Boulder Freeway. Together with the associated schools, Belleview Bible Seminary and Belleview Preparatory Schools, this is the western center of higher education in the development of a nation-wide educational system in the Pillar of Fire Church. There is a total of 19 buildings on more than six hundred acres.

Religious Denomination. Pillar of Fire.

Religious Emphasis. Holiness (theologically conservative).

Term System. Semester.

Enrollment in Degree Programs in Religion 1984–85. Total 20; men 10, women 10.

Faculty for Degree Programs in Religion. Total 10; part-time 10.

Admission Requirements. Candidates for admission may be admitted either by Certificate (high school graduation) or by examination (GED). High school graduates should present an official transcript showing satisfactory completion of 16 acceptable units of work.

Tuition and Fees. Tuition $60 per semester hour for collegiate degrees; boarding students may pay the combined charges for tuition, room, and partial board of $3,000; tuition for seminary certificate students $30 per semester hour; fees approximately $20 per year; books and supplies additional. Summer session fee for tuition, room and partial board (six weeks) is $575.

Financial Aid. Eligible veterans may receive VA benefits; some work-study is available. Full-time workers in Pillar of Fire Church or Belleview Schools are entitled to tuition reduction or waiver.

Housing. Dormitory accommodations available; some on-campus housing for married students. Apartment housing in the area is plentiful.

Library Facilities. The library houses 20,000 volumes with a special collection of Pillar of Fire Church history.

Religious Services/Activities. Sunday School; Sunday services (morning and evening); midweek testimony service; early chapel (Tuesday and Thursday); weekly prayer meeting and Bible study. Most services are broadcast over radio station KPOF, a full-service non-commercial 24-hour AM Christian radio station located on campus.

Degree Programs

The Bachelor of Arts/Bachelor of Science degree program with a major/minor in Religion requires the completion of a minimum of 124 credit hours. The Bachelor of Theology degree program is a five-year program and requires the completion of a minimum of 156 credit hours of which 71 credit hours must be in the required Bible and Religion courses.

Special Programs

The Associate of Arts degree is conferred on students who have completed a minimum of 62 credits, including several required courses. Two-year and four-year seminary certificates (available concurrently with or separately from the above collegiate degrees) are awarded upon completion of the required courses.

Colorado Christian College

180 South Garrison
Lakewood, CO 80226   (303) 238-5386

Administration. Joe L. Wall, President; L. David Beckman, Chancellor.

General Description. Colorado Christian College seeks to prepare students for careers of Christian service in the church and in the world. To accomplish its purpose, the College offers accredited undergraduate programs in church-related professions such as youth ministries and church planting, and in professions such as administration and communication. The arts and sciences are examined from a Christian perspective, and students learn to integrate Christian principles with other disciplines.

The College is the fusion of Rockmont College and Western Bible College; Rockmont was founded in 1914 and Western Bible in 1948. In 1985, the two institutions joined forces to become Colorado Christian College.

Community Environment. The College operates two unique facilities. The Lakewood Campus, located in the southwest Denver suburbs, provides a quiet setting for central offices, classrooms, library, music building, chapel, student union, and 74 apartments. The Foothills Campus and Conference Center, located 20 minutes away in the foothills of the Rocky Mountains, provides 50 acres for conferences, the KWBI radio station, soccer field, and 12 additional apartments.

Religious Denomination. Interdenominational.

Religious Emphasis. Evangelical Christian.

Accreditation. North Central Association of Colleges and Schools; American Association of Bible Colleges. Christian school certification with the Association of Christian Schools International.

Term System. Semester; summer session.

Faculty for Degree Programs in Religion. Total 5; full-time 4, part-time 1.

Admission Requirements. SAT or ACT; high school or college transcripts; three personal references; TOEFL required for international students.

Tuition and Fees. Costs per semester: tuition $2,000; fees $225; room $565; board $275.

Financial Aid. A wide variety of grants, scholarships, and loans are available. Some are based on financial need; some on academic standing or special abilities: Pell Grants, College Work-Study, Supplementary Educational Opportunity Grants (SEOG), Federal Guaranteed Student Loan Program, National Direct Student Loan Program, Parent Loans for Undergraduate Students, Colorado Student Incentive Grants.

Housing. On-campus, fully-furnished apartments available for single and married students; assistance for locating off-campus housing.

Library Facilities. The library houses over 50,000 volumes and subscribes to 380 periodicals including Christian magazines and theological journals. There is a special collection of 500 hymnals.

Religious Services/Activities. Chapel attendance required twice per week; optional chapel service held one evening per week; local church affiliation required; discipleship groups meet once per week; Day of Prayer once per semester; Spiritual Life retreat in fall required.

Degree Programs

The Bachelor of Arts degree provides a specialized major and a full range of studies in the arts and humanities, natural and social sciences, and Bible and ministry. The degree is designed to equip students for effective service in selected professions and to prepare them for additional study at the graduate level. The degree requires a minimum of 128 semester hours, including 30 semester hours of biblical and theological studies and approximately 30 semester hours in a selected major. Some of the majors available include Biblical Studies, Church Music, Contemporary Christian Music, Pastoral Studies (Pre-Seminary and Professional), Special Ministries (Christian Education, Church Administration, or Juvenile Delinquency), World Missions (Cross-Cultural or Church Planting and Growth), and Youth Ministries (Church and Parachurch Ministries or Outdoor Christian Ministries).

Denver Baptist Bible College and Theological Seminary

1200 Miramonte Street
Broomfield, CO 80020   (303) 469-1984

Administration. Dr. William R. Fusco, President; Dr. Charles A. Hauser, Jr., Vice President; Dr. Earl M. Bohnett, Academic Dean; Dr. Ralph G. Turk, Dean, Theological Seminary.

General Description. The Denver Baptist Bible College and Theological Seminary is a professional school whose primary purpose is to provide Bible-centered, doctrinally-sound, evangelically-fervent, church-related training. The academic program offers students, whatever their particular interest or vocation, a broad foundation in the arts, sciences, and theological studies. The College offers academic training for specific ministries in church-related vocations at the Diploma, Associate, and Bachelor levels. The Seminary trains Christian leaders to be Bible expositors, providing thorough training on the graduate level.

Community Environment. The College is located in Broomfield, Colorado, a beautiful northern suburb in metropolitan Denver. The Administration Building houses the administrative, development, and business offices, the chapel, dining room and kitchen, the bookstore, and the music and speech classrooms. Denver, the mile-high city, is located at the foothills of the spectacular Rocky Mountains. A mild, sunny, semiarid climate with moderate temperatures and low humidity presents a desirable setting for comfortable living.

Religious Denomination. Baptist.

Religious Emphasis. Fundamentalist.

Accreditation. American Association of Bible Colleges (Candidate).

Term System. Semester; summer term.

Enrollment in Degree Programs in Religion 1984–85. Total 141; men 86, women 55.

Degrees in Religion Awarded 1984–85. Diploma 1; women 1. Associate of Arts 7; men 3, women 4. Bachelor of Arts 16; men 10, women 6. Master of Arts 5; men 4, women 1. Master of Divinity 2; men 2. Master of Theology 1; men 1.

Faculty for Degree Programs in Religion. Total 16; full-time 5, part-time 11.

Admission Requirements. Each applicant must testify that he/she has personally trusted Jesus Christ as Savior from sin. Personal references must also be received. Graduation from high school or its equivalent is required.

Tuition and Fees. $85 per credit hour; resident fee per semester $1,260; student services and activity fee $80 for 12 hours or more, $55 for 6-11 hours, $30 for 1-5 hours; housing for single students $1,260 per semester.

Financial Aid. Denver Baptist Bible College offers a number of scholarship: Valedictorian award is one-half the tuition for four semesters; Salutatorian award is one-fourth tuition for four semester; upper ten percent of high school graduating class award is 15 percent of tuition for four semesters; full-time student family grant is one-half tuition for wife and one-fourth for children; full-time Christian workers grant is one-fourth tuition each semester. Veterans assistance is also available.

Housing. Living accommodations for single students available. Information for married students describing housing in the area is available upon request.

Library Facilities. The library contains over 20,000 volumes and over 216 periodicals. There are special collections of 35mm slides, cassette and reel-to-reel tapes, maps, overhead transparencies, records, filmstrips, missions agencies file, and college and seminary files.

Religious Services/Activities. Chapel is held every school day; various retreats are scheduled throughout the school year to promote Christian growth.

Degree Programs

The Bachelor of Arts degree is awarded upon satisfactorily completing a minimum of 132 credit hours to include all the requirements as stated in each of the major programs. The College offers professional majors in Elementary Teacher Education, General Ministries, Pastoral Ministries, Women's Ministries, and a nonprofessional major in Theological Studies. Professional minors are offered in Church Education, Church Music, and Missiology. Seniors may enrich their studies by developing skills in research and analysis for college credit in areas not structured as part of the regular curriculum. A Field Ministries program provides supervised on-the-job training in order that students might put into practice that which they have been taught in the classroom.

The Master of Arts one-year program is designed for the Bible college graduate or the Christian liberal arts Bible major graduate. It is designed to give a broader preparation for Christian service. The areas of concentration are Old Testament (emphasis on Hebrew), New Testament (emphasis on Greek), Bible Exposition, Systematic Theology, and Practical Theology.

The Master of Arts two-year program is designed to give the liberal arts college graduate a basic Biblical education background. This may be for one anticipating a church-related vocation other than ministerial (pastoral, youth evangelism, missions) or for one planning for a life of service in conjunction with a non-church-related vocation.

The Master of Theology program is designed to give professional and research training for the Christian ministry, with the opportunity for in-depth study in one of the theological disciplines. It is especially recommended for those interested in a ministry primarily in teaching in a school of higher Christian education. This four-year theological degree program is also recommended as a thorough discipline in preparation for pastoral, missionary, or similar ministries.

Special Programs

The Associate of Arts degree in Biblical Education may be awarded upon satisfactory completion of a minimum of 64 credit hours including all specific requirements of the program.

A Selective Studies program enables persons to apply for selective studies without entering a specific degree program.

A Certificate of Theological Studies program is designed for men called into the ministry at a more mature age, who have not earned a baccalaureate degree, and for whom it is impractical to take time for both college and seminary.

Denver Conservative Baptist Seminary
P.O. Box 10,000
Denver, CO 80210   (303) 761-2482

Administration. Dr. Haddon W. Robinson, President; Dr. Ralph R. Covell, Academic Dean.

General Description. A summary of the mission of Denver Conservative Baptist Seminary declares that it is an evangelical seminary in the Baptist tradition and in fellowship with the Conservative Baptist Association of America, that it trains leaders, professional and lay, to serve in and through local churches. Ministry to, through, by, and for the local church in its culture serves as the integrating point for the school's curriculum.

Education at Denver Seminary centers in the Bible. The faculty is committed to Baptist distinctives and the great doctrines of the Protestant faith. While this understanding of the Scriptures is presented in the classroom, the Seminary's approach to education is not uncritical indoctrination. The Seminary declares that every effort is made to teach in a context of integrity, open-mindedness, and intellectual vigor. It explains that at Denver Seminary one will not find unanchored liberalism — freedom to think without commitment. Nor will one find an encrusted dogmatism — commitment without freedom to think.

Community Environment. The Seminary occupies 8 buildings, all located on its 12-acre campus in southeast metropolitan Denver, Colorado. Denver, the Mile High City, was founded on the site of a small Indian village at the confluence of Cherry Creek and the South Platte River. Originally a trade center for the 1859 gold-rush mountain mining camps, the town, at 5,280 feet above sea level, enjoys a mild, sunny, semi-arid climate with moderate temperatures and low humidity. Thrusting upward west of the city are more than 50 peaks rising over 14,000 feet into the sky.

Religious Denomination. Conservative Baptist Association of America.

Religious Emphasis. Evangelical.

Accreditation. North Central Association of Colleges and Schools; Association of Theological Schools in the United States and Canada.

Term System. Quarter; summer term.

Enrollment in Degree Programs in Religion 1984–85. Total 544; men 448, women 96.

Degrees in Religion Awarded 1984–85. Master of Divinity 43; men 41, women 1. Master of Arts 41; men 29, women 12; Doctor of Ministry 3; men 3.

Faculty for Degree Programs in Religion. Total 25; full-time 13, part-time 12.

Admission Requirements. Bachelor's degree from a recognized undergraduate institution; GRE combined scores of 1000; church endorsement; 5 references; health certificate.

Tuition and Fees. $85 per quarter hour up to $1,020 per quarter; general fee $5.50 per quarter hour up to $41 per quarter; on-campus housing $235-$260 per month.

Financial Aid. Scholarships, loans, and awards are available.

Housing. The Seminary has a limited number of housing units on campus for married and single student use. Rent is charged on a monthly basis.

Library Facilities. The Vernon Grounds Learning Center houses over 80,000 volumes. A separate area houses the Vernon Grounds Collection of 20,000 volumes.

Religious Services/Activities. Chapel is held three times per week. Two days each year are devoted entirely to prayer and mediation. The Seminary sponsors a conference each year with a central thrust toward the development of the spiritual life.

Degree Programs

The Master of Divinity degree program is designed primarily to prepare persons for church ministries requiring ordination. As the standard theological degree program, its scope is sufficiently broad to equip students for varied church or mission vocations. The heart of the program is the core curriculum of required courses, selected because they are demanded by the very nature of the ministerial task.

The Master of Arts programs are intended for students who plan to engage in some specific form of Christian service which may require a different type of training from the professional Master of Divinity degree. By intensively studying some limited area of specialization, the student will be equipped to serve in one of the varied capacities needed by the Christian community.

The Doctor of Ministry program is planned to lead to competence beyond the Master of Divinity in the following areas: theological and biblical dimensions of ministry; pastoral, ethical, and communicative dimensions of ministry; and educative and management dimensions of ministry. The two tracks in the program are the Pastoral Track and the Missionary Track.

Iliff School of Theology
2201 South University Boulevard
Denver, CO 80210   (303) 744-1287

Administration. Dr. Donald E. Messner, President; Dr. Delwin Brown, Interim Vice President and Dean of Academic Affairs.

General Description. The Iliff School of Theology is a graduate theological school of the United Methodist Church. Iliff cooperates in education programs with the University of Denver but is a separate institution from the University. The primary purpose of the School is to prepare persons for Christian ministry, with an accent on the local parish. Complimentary to this objective are its commitments to continuing education outreach, Master of Arts in Religion, and the Ph.D. degree, the latter offered jointly by Iliff and the University of Denver.

Community Environment. Iliff's 8-acre campus contains 6 buildings in a beautiful, park-like setting. It is located in the University Park area of Denver, Colorado, adjoining the campus of the University of Denver. Close in proximity is St. Thomas Seminary (Roman Catholic). Cross-registration in both of these schools is available. The city of Denver (the "Mile High City") has a climate which draws an expanding population to the city and is ideal for study as well as for recreation. The Rocky Mountains west of the city, with Pikes Peak to the south and Longs Peak to the north, offer recreational facilities which appeal each year to a large number of tourists from all parts of the country.

Religious Denomination. United Methodist.

Religious Emphasis. The Iliff School of Theology is dedicated to an open search for truth with strong emphasis on Biblical studies and academic freedom.

Accreditation. North Central Association of Colleges and Schools; Association of Theological Schools in the United States and Canada.

Term System. Quarter; summer term.

Enrollment in Degree Programs in Religion 1984–85. Total 342; men 178, women 164.

Degrees in Religion Awarded 1984–85. Master of Arts in Religion 9; men 3, women 6. Master of Divinity 47; men 30, women 17. Doctor of Ministry 9; men 9. Doctor of Theology 1; women 1.

Faculty for Degree Programs in Religion. Total 25; full-time 21, part-time 4.

Admission Requirements. Baccalaureate degree from an accredited college; admission based on several factors: grade point average, personal references, statement of purpose in seeking admission to The Iliff School of Theology.

Tuition and Fees. Tuition $150 per quarter hour for Master of Divinity, Master of Arts, and non-degree students; $210 per quarter hour for Doctoral students; graduate fee Master's students $10; graduate fee Doctor of Philosophy students $200; annual registration fee for all doctoral students $210.

Financial Aid. Scholarhips, grants-in-aid, work-study, and student assistantships available on a limited basis.

Housing. Students must be enrolled for 8 quarter hours or more to be eligible for seminary housing. Apartments range in size from buffet at $198 per month to two-bedroom at $242 per month; utilities are included in the rent.

Library Facilities. The Ira J. Taylor Library was erected in 1955 and offers substantial resources for theological study and research. The collection is the primary resource for theological materials for the nine-state Rocky Mountain regions. It presently houses over 131,000 books, pamphlets, microforms, and other non-print resources. The archives of the American Academy of Religion, the Society of Biblical Literature, the Rocky Mountain Conference of The United Methodist Church, and The Iliff School of Theology are housed in the library.

Religious Services/Activities. Regular chapel services are held twice weekly under the leadership of a student Community Worship Committee. Various lectures are held throughout the academic year. *The Iliff Review* is published three times a year and is an independent journal of religious studies designed to be of significance for the parish minister as well as the specialized scholar.

Degree Programs

The Master of Divinity degree program provides professional theological education for qualified college graduates. Training in knowledge and skills, and personal development for the practice of ministry characterize the program. The curriculum includes four divisions (Biblical and Historical Interpretation; Philosophy, Theology, and Ethics; Persons, Society, and Culture; The Church and Its Ministries) and field education. At least 120 quarter credit hours with a cumulative grade point average of 2.0 or better are required for the degree.

The Master of Arts in Religion degree program provides graduate studies in religion for persons not seeking ordination. Theoretical and functional studies which vary to meet particular educational or vocational objectives

characterize the program. The curriculum includes four divisions (Biblical and Historical Interpretation; Philosophy, Theology, and Ethics; Persons, Society, and Culture; The Church and Its Ministries) and field education. At least 80 quarter credit hours with a cumulative grade point average of 2.00 or better are required for the degree.

The Doctor of Philosophy in Religious and Theological Studies is a joint program of The Iliff School of Theology and The University of Denver. The program is designed to prepare persons for independent inquiry, criticism, and research in religion and theology. The curriculum is structured in four areas of specialization: American Religion and Culture, Biblical Interpretation, Religion and Psychological Studies, Theology and Philosophy of Religion. Special features of the program include doctoral colloquia, interdisciplinary team teaching, research seminars, independent study, special lectures and events, and access to doctoral level study in other areas of the University and affiliate institutions.

Special Programs

The Iliff Week of Graduate Lectures and the Rocky Mountain Pastors' School is a weeklong event offering lectures by outstanding theologians, workshops, and public forums.

Summer school includes courses for academic credit or Continuing Education Units; evening courses are being opened for special auditors in an enrichment program.

Travel seminars and travel abroad is available for academic or continuing education credit; study in Israel in cooperation with Education Opportunities, Inc.; other programs offered on a yearly basis.

Naropa Institute
Buddhist Studies Department
2130 Arapahoe Avenue
Boulder, CO 80302   (303) 444-0202

Administration. Barbara Dilley, Chancellor; Ruth Astor, Assistant to the Chancellor; William McKeever, Vice Chancellor.

General Description. In the Buddhist Studies program, Naropa Institute presents Buddhism as a living tradition in its many dimensions, both historical and doctrinal. Included is the study of root texts, commentaries and the oral tradition of Buddhist masters, and study and practice of meditation.

Parent Institution. Naropa Institute, founded in 1974 by Chogyam Trungpa, Rinpoche, has developed an approach to education that joins intellect and intuition. This approach is based on appreciation of the disciplines of both East and West, with special influence from the Tibetan Buddhist tradition. Training in contemplative and meditative disciplines is available to interested students. The Buddhist tradition articulates three primary principles which, when taken together, provide a guidline for integrated educational development: discipline, meditation, and intellect. It is through the skillful balance of all three principles or practices that the training of a fully educated person can take place.

The Institute offers 2 options of study: (1) Continuing Education study, and (2) Degree and Certificate study. The Institute is a college of arts and humanities with programs of study at the Certificate, Bachelor, and Master's levels. B.A. programs are currently offered for students who have completed, or are close to completing, the first two years of undergraduate study. Continuing education is available on an open admissions basis.

Religious Denomination. Tibetan Buddhist.

Accreditation. North Central Association of Colleges and Schools (Candidate).

Term System. Quarter; summer programs.

Enrollment in Degree Programs in Religion 1984–85. Total 18; men 12, women 6.

Degrees in Religion Awarded 1984–85. Certificate, Bachelor, Master.

Faculty for Degree Programs in Religion. Total 6; full-time 3, part-time 3.

Admission Requirements. Entrance requirements vary for each program offered. A standard application packet, to be completed by all applicants to undergraduate and graduate programs, includes main application form, personal statement of interest, three letters of recommendation, official college transcripts, photograph, and $20 application fee.

Tuition and Fees. Tuition $80 per credit hour; $45 per credit if registering on a non-credit basis; Continuing Education students are required to pay a $5 application fee each quarter of attendance; $5 Student Activities fee is charged each quarter for students taking from 4 to 6 credit hours of classes, $10 fee for those taking over 6 credit hours of classes.

Financial Aid. Students accepted into a Naropa Program (B.A., M.A., or Certificate) may qualify for financial aid. Aid in the form of Pell Grant, Supplemental Education Opportunity Grant, National Direct Student Loan, College Work-Study, Naropa Work-Study, Guaranteed Student Loan, and Naropa Institute Scholarships are available.

Housing. Except during Summer courses, Naropa Institute does not provide housing. Most students are able to find permanent housing within a week of their arrival in Boulder, with the help of the Naropa Housing Directory and local papers. To rent a room in a house or apartment, students may expect to pay from $150 to $250 per month; a private studio apartment or one-bedroom apartment begins at $300 per month.

Library Facilities. The Naropa Institute Library has a specialized 20,000 volume collection carefully selected to support the educational programs of the school. Strengths of the collection include the holdings in psychology, Buddhist studies, and contemporary American poetry. The Institute's collection of Tibetan and Sanskrit texts is one of the finest in North America. The library has on tape many events of educational and cultural significance held at the Institute throughout its eleven-year history. Naropa Institute students have access to the two million volume Norlin Library of the University of Colorado, a short walk from the Institute's campus.

Religious Services/Activities. All students, faculty, and staff at the Institute are encouraged to practice a traditional contemplative discipline. Such practices are designed to provide a method of self-inquiry, and later, of harmonization of the mental, emotional, and physical resources of a person's life. Daily meditation sessions, as well as more intensive programs and seminars, are offered. Other traditional contemplative disciplines available either directly through the Institute or through affiliated groups are: T'ai-Chi Ch'uan, Akido, Kyudo (zen archery), Ikebana (flower arranging), and Bugaku (classical Japanese Imperial Court dance). The Shambhaia Training program, founded by Chogyam Trungpa, Rinpoche is a series of weekend intensives consisting of meditation instruction, individual interviews, group discussions, and talks focused on the path of the warrior. Warriorship is training to be brave and gentle and learning to meet the challenge of living without aggression and fear.

Degree Programs

The Institute's Bachelor of Arts programs are "upper divisional," i.e., the last two years of undergraduate study are offered. Majors are offered in Book Arts, Buddhist and Western Psychology, Buddhist Studies, Dance/Movement Studies, Dance/Dance Therapy, Music, Psychology of Health and Healing, Writing and Poetics, and Interdisciplinary Studies.

The Master of Arts in Buddhist and Western Psychology is a 2¼ year training program in clinical psychotherapy which consists of three quarters of academic coursework, a one quarter group meditation intensive and study of Buddhist psychology ("Maitri Program"), and a 9-month, supervised clinical internship. The program is designed specifically to train psychotherapists.

The Master of Arts in Dance Therapy is a 2-year program designed to qualify students as professional registered dance therapists. It has been developed to meet the standards of education and training outlined by the American Dance Therapy Association. The program involves intensive study in the theory and practice of dance therapy, movement observation and diagnosis, psychology, and related subjects. Included in the program are a 400-hour fieldwork placement and a 700-hour internship in a mental health setting. The internship provides supervision by a registered dance therapist. A final thesis is required.

Special Programs

Certificate Programs are specifically designed to provide focused study for students of diverse educational backgrounds: students on Junior Year study programs, college graduates, and high school graduates. The programs are comprised of 45 credit hours of which at least 27 hours must be in the student's area of concentration.

The Institute's Continuing Education study option permits students who wish to study without working towards an Institute degree or certificate to do so on a space-available basis.

Nazarene Bible College
111 Chapman Drive
Colorado Springs, CO 80916   (303) 596-5110

Administration. Rev. Jerry D. Lambert, President; Lawrence E. Jantz, Registrar and Director of Applied Church Ministries.

General Description. Nazarene Bible College is an institution of the Church of the Nazarene. Its role is determined by the church through its official representatives. It is directly regulated by a Board of Trustees elected by the General Assembly of the church. The College opened in September 1967 in facilities provided by the First Church of the Nazarene in Colorado Springs. The new campus, with three uniquely designed buildings, was dedicated in October 1968.

The College was founded for the specific purpose of training men and women for Christian ministries in the Church of the Nazarene. Consequently, the program gives high priority to spiritual values and to the development of Christian insight and commitment on the part of its students.

Community Environment. Colorado Springs is a city of 325,000 situated on the eastern slopes of the Rocky Mountains. The city is headquarters for several Christian organizations, such as Navigators, Young Life, International Students Ministries, Compassion and Christian Book Sellers. Eleven Nazarene churches, including a Spanish-speaking church, serve the people of this area and provide opportunities for Christian service. The 62-acre campus is located on the hill northeast of the intersection of Academy and Fountain Boulevards.

Religious Denomination. Church of the Nazarene.

Religious Emphasis. Wesleyan-Arminian.

Accreditation. American Association of Bible Colleges.

Term System. Quarter; two 4-week summer terms.

Enrollment in Degree Programs in Religion 1984–85. Total 248; men 234, women 14.

Degrees in Religion Awarded 1984–85. Associate in Biblical Studies 42; men 40, women 2.

Faculty for Degree Programs in Religion. Total 15; full-time 11, part-time 4.

Admission Requirements. High school diploma or equivalent; written testimony of Christian experience and reasons for wanting to attend Nazarene Bible College; two letters of recommendation.

Tuition and Fees. $30 per quarter hour; registration $7.50 per quarter; student activity fee $17; other fees where applicable.

Financial Aid. Federal aid programs, scholarships, grants and local employment are available.

Housing. The College does not provide dormitories or on-campus housing for students.

Library Facilities. The library contains over 35,000 volumes and houses the Wesleyan Collection.

Religious Services/Activities. Two chapel services are held each week for day students and two each week night for the night students. Outstanding church leaders are secured to preach or lecture on some phases of Christian life one week each quarter. The Mission in Action Club and the Christian Education Fellowship provide opportunities for students to learn more about the worldwide outreach and inter-staff operations of the church. Other campus activities enhance the spiritual life and contribute to the maturity of the students. There are opportunities for student preaching, applied Christian ministries, participation in church and community life and guidance of local pastors.

Degree Programs

The Associate of Arts degree in Biblical Studies is conferred upon successful completion of the three-year prescribed program. This program fulfills the minimum educational requirements leading to ordination in the Church of the Nazarene. One hundred forty-seven quarter hours of credit must be earned.

The Associate of Arts degree in Christian Education is a three-year program which includes biblical-theological studies, but with a specific emphasis on Christian education ministry. It fulfills the educational requirements leading toward commission as a minister of education in the Chruch of the Nazarene, with considerable work beyond the minimum.

The Associate of Arts degree in Christian Music is a three-year program which includes certain biblical-theological studies, but which stresses both theoretical and applied music studies as a preparation for ministry in church music. It fulfills and exceeds the educational requirements leading toward the Minister of Music or Song Evangelist commission in the Church of the Nazarene.

Special Programs

The Diploma in Lay Ministries Program may be completed within three quarters, or a longer period of time is acceptable. A stated intention to graduate is not required for entrance into the program which is intended for lay people. It equips students for lay service in the local church through the enrichment and development of personal skills. All courses are optional, selected under the guidance of an academic advisor.

Regis College
Department of Religious Studies
West 50th Avenue and Lowell Boulevard
Denver, CO 80221   (303) 458-3504

Administration. Rev. David M. Clarke, S.J., President; Rev. Michael J. Sheeran, Vice President for Academic Affairs; Dr. Thomas A. Duggan, Director, Division of Philosophy and Religious Studies; Dr. Lester L. Bundy, Chairman, Religious Studies.

General Description. The Program of Religious Studies functions within the Department of Religious Studies, a part of the overall college program. In addition to providing a major and a minor in Religious Studies, the Department provides the courses for the core requirements in Religious Studies for all students. The Bachelor of Arts in Religious Studies is granted.

Parent Institution. Regis College is an institution in the Catholic and Jesuit tradition committed to educating for balanced personal and social growth, as well as specific expertise and the well rounded knowledge for adapting to new situations.

Community Environment. Regis College is located in Denver, Colorado, the youngest of the great American cities and the financial, industrial, professional, and cultural center of the vast Rocky Mountain region. Denver's metropolitan area has a population of over one million persons. The city is the political capital of Colorado and is known as the "Mile High City," situated 5,280 feet above sea level, a few miles east of the Rockies. Denver is served by a network of air, highway, and rail routes which make it easily accessible from any part of the nation.

Religious Denomination. Roman Catholic.

Religious Emphasis. Jesuit.

Accreditation. North Central Association of Colleges and Schools.

Term System. Semester; summer term.

Enrollment in Degree Programs in Religion 1984–85. Total 27; men 12, women 15.

Degrees in Religion Awarded 1984–85. Bachelor of Arts in Religious Studies 12; men 5, women 7.

Faculty for Degree Programs in Religion. Total 13; full-time 5, part-time 8.

Admission Requirements. High school graduation with a minimum of 15 academic units completed between grades 9-12; letters of recommendation; interviews are encouraged and in some instances may be required; ACT or SAT scores.

Tuition and Fees. Tuition $2,380 per semester or $177 per credit hour; health fee $35; student activity fee $30; nonrefundable admission fee with all applications $20.

Financial Aid. All financial aid awards are made through the use of the American College Testing Family Financial Statement. College work-study programs are also available and awarded in the same manner.

Housing. Single and double occupancy housing is available in three of Regis's coed dorms. All unmarried, non-metropolitan Denver freshmen and sophomores must reside on campus.

Library Facilities. The library contains over 66,000 volumes. Books from the Religious Studies special collection are available with permission to all students.

Religious Services/Activities. Weekend and daily mass; several retreats for men or women are scheduled throughout the academic year.

Degree Programs

The Bachelor of Arts in Religious Studies requires at least 12 upper divisional hours in Religious Studies beyond the 9-hour Core Studies requirement. Other core requirements include English Composition, Economic Systems, Literature/Humanities, Philosophy, Social Sciences, Mathematics/Natural Science, and Foreign Language. A minor must also be selected, and at least 128 semester hours completed for graduation.

Special Programs

RECEP III is a program equivalent to the Religious Studies program and is packaged for adults who want to expand their philosophy and religious studies in the context of adult learning and development. RECEP III also offers two certificate programs for the adult learner.

St. Thomas Seminary
1300 South Steele Street
Denver, CO 80210   (303) 722-4687

Administration. Rev. John E. Rybolt, C.M., Rector-President.

General Description. St. Thomas Seminary is a liberal arts and theological institution for men. It is operated by the Vincentian Fathers for the Roman Catholic Church. The programs of the Seminary College and the School of Theology are designed specifically to prepare young men for Catholic priesthood.

Community Environment. The 60-acre campus is located in southeast Denver.

Religious Denomination. Roman Catholic.

Accreditation. North Central Association of Colleges and Schools; Association of Theological Schools in the United States and Canada.

Term System. Quarter.

Enrollment in Degree Programs in Religion 1984–85. Total 78 (Seminary College); 88 (School of Theology).

Faculty for Degree Programs in Religion. Total 40; full-time 28, part-time 12.

Admission Requirements. Seminary College: Graduation from high school; C average; 15 academic units. School of Theology: Bachelor's degree with 12 semester hours (18 quarter hours) of philosophy and 12 hours of religion.

Tuition and Fees. Seminary College: Tuition $1,125;

room and board $1,425; student fees $200. School of Theology tuition $1,425.

Housing. Campus housing is available for 250 men.

Library Facilities. The Seminary Library contains over 86,000 volumes.

Degree Programs

The Seminary College grants the Bachelor's degree. The School of Theology offers programs leading to the Master of Arts degree (academic) and the Master of Theology degree (professional).

CONNECTICUT

Albertus Magnus College
Department of Religious Studies
700 Prospect Street
New Haven, CT 06511   (203) 773-8550

Administration. Sr. Julia McNamara, O.P., President; Dr. Anthony Fasano, Chairman, Department of Religious Studies.

General Description. The program within the Department of Religious Studies examines the fundamental values and ultimate meaning within a religious perspective. As a college of Roman Catholic tradition, Albertus Magnus emphasizes this religious heritage in its academic offerings but also offers courses which present other religious and humanistic systems as well. Although the College does not offer a major in religious studies, students who wish to study religion in greater depth may elect humanities or general studies as a major. Religious studies, then, would be a component of these majors.

Parent Institution. Albertus Magnus College is a Catholic liberal arts, residential college for women, the oldest institution of its kind in New England. It was founded in 1925 by the Dominican Sisters of St. Mary of the Springs.

Community Environment. The 45-acre campus is located in Prospect Hill on the outskirts of New Haven.

Religious Denomination. Roman Catholic.

Accreditation. New England Association of Schools and Colleges.

Term System. Semester.

Admission Requirements. Graduation from an accredited high school; 16 academic units; SAT or ACT.

Tuition and Fees. Tuition $5,990 per year; room and board $3,340 per year; student activity fee $50 per semester.

Financial Aid. Assistance for meeting the cost of a private education is available in the form of scholarships, grants, loans, and employment. Awards are generally based on student need.

Housing. The College operates houses on campus for resident students.

Library Facilities. The library and media center are located in Rosary Hall. It contains over 96,000 volumes, 400 periodicals, and numerous microforms and sound recordings.

Religious Services/Activities. A chapel for Sunday liturgies is located in Reynolds Hall. A smaller oratory, Catherine Chapel, is used for daily liturgy and private prayer.

Degree Programs

The scheme of courses in the Department of Religious Studies is designed to provide introductory, basic, and advanced investigation into religious experience.

Berkeley Divinity School
363 Ronan Street
New Haven, CT 06520

Administration. Dr. James E. Annand, President and Dean of Berkely Divinity School.

General Description. Since 1971, Berkeley Divinity School, an Episcopal seminary, has been affiliated with Yale University Divinity School. Berkeley Divinity School retains its identity through its continuing Board of Trustees, its Dean, and the Berkeley Center where its offices are located. The Center is one block down the hill from the main Divinity School buildings and houses a chapel, classrooms, and staff offices. Episcopal students come under the care of the Dean of Berkeley Divinity School for spiritual formation and counseling, but are not differentiated from other students. As a result of the affiliation, there is one integrated student body and faculty.

The Berkeley Divinity School was founded by Bishop John Williams, and opened its doors on May 3, 1854, in Middletown, Connecticut. It was named after George Berkeley, Bishop of Cloyne, Ireland. The School was moved to New Haven in 1928 in order to fulfill its function more adequately by being in touch with the resources of an urban center and a great university, a purpose fulfilled by the affiliation of 1971.

Parent Institution. See: Yale University.

Hartford Seminary
77 Sherman Street
Hartford, CT 06105   (203) 232-4451

Administration. Dr. Michael R. Rion, President; Dr. William McKinney, Director of Educational Programs.

General Description. Hartford Seminary serves diverse constituents around the world through a distinctive blend of programs arising from the interaction of research, teaching, and consultation. Major programmatic emphases include degree programs (Doctor of Ministry, Master of Arts, and Black Ministries Certificate), continuing theological education for laity and clergy, social and religious research, Islamic Studies, expertise on contemporary Christian-Muslim relations through research, teaching, and consultation, and public policy. Founded in 1834, Hartford Seminary continues its heritage of innovation and responsiveness, seeking to strengthen the integrity and vitality of Christian ministry and vocation in their many forms.

Community Environment. Hartford Seminary's award-winning building located in Hartford's West End affirms the commitment to the city. It also gives visual expression to the Seminary's bold and imaginative programs. The building houses the chapel, meeting room, offices, and Education Resource Center. Hartford, the capital of the state, is a major manufacturing city and port of entry. Community and cultural facilities include over 200 churches and many cultural opportunities.

Religious Denomination. Nondenominational (Christian).

Accreditation. New England Association of Schools and Colleges; Association of Theological Schools in the United States and Canada.

Term System. Semester; summer term.

Enrollment in Degree Programs in Religion 1984–85. Total 118; men 86, women 32.

Degrees in Religion Awarded 1984–85. Master of Arts 4; men 3, women 1. Doctor of Ministry 3; men 3.

Faculty for Degree Programs in Religion. Total 20; full-time 10, part-time 10.

Admission Requirements. Master of Arts: Bachelor's degree from an accredited college or university. Doctor of Ministry: Master of Divinity degree from an accredited institution and three years' experience in ministry.

Tuition and Fees. Tuition $125 per credit hour.

Financial Aid. Limited financial assistance is available.

Housing. The Seminary has no residential facilities for students enrolled in degree programs. Housing is available for the summer session.

Library Facilities. The library consists of approximately 70,000 volumes of which 1,200 are illustrated Arabic manuscripts dating from the ninth to the nineteenth century. Also maintained is the A.C. Thompson Collection of 19th century missiological materials. A collection of papers of early New England theologians is also housed here.

Religious Services/Activities. Weekly chapel.

Degree Programs

The Master of Arts in Religious Studies is designed for those who want to develop or increase their theoretical and practical skills for Christian ministry, or for students wishing to concentrate in Islamic Studies and Christian-Muslim relations. The program provides the opportunity to interrelate the different branches of the study of religion through courses in scripture, the historical and pastoral disciplines, theology, spirituality, and social and cultural environments. The degree requires the completion of 42 credits.

The Doctor of Ministry program is aimed at increasing the competence and effectiveness of professional ministry while remaining in a ministry setting. Special attention is given to relating program offerings to parish settings. The degree requires the completion of 36 credits.

Special Programs

The Black Ministries Certificate Program is a one-year introduction to theological study for clergy and laity.

The Assistants in Christian Education Program is a one-year program for church educators co-sponsored with the Connecticut Conference of the United Church of Christ.

The Seminary also offers Certificate program opportunities for persons interested in Islamic Studies and Christian-Muslim relations.

Holy Apostles College
33 Prospect Hill Road
Cromwell, CT 06416   (203) 635-5311

Administration. V. Rev. Leo J. Ovian, M.Ss.A., President-Rector.

General Description. Holy Apostles College is committed to guiding adults through self-development in the Christian liberal arts traditions. Persons of all ages, interests, and backgrounds are encouraged to reach increasingly higher plateaus of knowledge and deeper insights into their own value judgments and spirituality. The College is sponsored and administered by the Missionaries of the Holy Apostles, a Roman Catholic Society of Apostolic Life whose purpose is to provide priests and religious leaders. The College offers full-time instruction both in the College Division and in the Seminary Division.

Parent Institution. The College traces its origin to Holy Apostles Seminary, founded in 1956 by Very Reverend Eusebe M. Menard, O.F.M., a Canadian priest who saw the need to provide American adults inclined toward the Catholic priesthood with an education and seminary environment suited to their age and background. The Seminary Division of Holy Apostles College continues Father Menard's work for adult vocations.

Community Environment. The campus occupies more than 30 acres set in the scenic and rustic surroundings overlooking the Connecticut River in the town of Crom-well, 13 miles south of Hartford.

Religious Denomination. Roman Catholic.

Accreditation. New England Association of Schools and Colleges.

Term System. Semester.

Enrollment in Degree Programs in Religion 1984–85. Total 171.

Faculty for Degree Programs in Religion. Total 24.

Admission Requirements. High school graduation or equivalent; 15 academic units; personal interview.

Tuition and Fees. Tuition $1,300 per semester; room and board $1,225; personality/aptitude testing fee (if taken at Holy Apostles) $175.

Financial Aid. The College has a Director of Financial Aid to guide students who may need financial assistance.

Housing. Residential accommodations are available on campus for men only.

Library Facilities. The Seminary Library contains over 50,000 volumes.

Religious Services/Activities. Religious exercises are a regular part of campus life. Catholic students attend Mass and the Liturgy of the Hours each day. Confessions are heard by appointment or by request. All seminarians are required to have a personal spiritual director. A structured priestly formation program is provided.

Degree Programs

Several programs of preparation for the priesthood are available at Holy Apostles College. These programs take into consideration the educational backgrounds and life experiences of candidates admitted to the seminary. Each program conforms to the standards set by the National Conference of Catholic Bishops for priestly formation.

The Bachelor of Arts is granted by the College Division in religious studies, philosophy, the social sciences and the humanities.

The Master of Divinity Program is an academic degree attesting to the recipient's competency for exercising priestly ministry from a background of dogmatic, moral, ascetical and pastoral theology, Sacred Scripture, canon law, liturgy, homiletics, and Church History.

The Master of Arts Degree in Theology is a graduate degree which attests to the holder's special competence in a specific area of theology, Biblical studies, or Church history. An Integrated Program is offered for students who have not taken philosophy.

Special Programs

The Associate of Arts in Religious Studies may be pursued in the College Division.

Sacred Heart University
Department of Religious Studies
Bridgeport, CT 06606   (203) 371-7900

Administration. Dr. Thomas P. Melady, President; Dr. Walter E. Brooks, Chairperson, Department of Religious Studies.

General Description. The Religious Studies Department offers a program that invites the student to enter into a process of reflection on his/her own experience at the deepest level. From this standpoint the student is encouraged to investigate a broad range of religious expressions representative of the human attempt to come to terms with questions of ultimate significance. Specific courses in the program examine the various symbols and myths, rituals and creeds, events and institutions that illuminate the religious imagination and understanding. In addition, the student is encouraged to investigate the cultural interaction between religion and both the natural sciences and the arts. Methodologically and topically diverse, the program is unified by its commitment to the task of exploring the basic religious beliefs and insights that render human life and experience meaningful. The Department offers courses leading to the Bachelor of Arts and the Master of Arts in Religious Studies.

Parent Institution. Sacred Heart University was founded in 1963 by the Most Reverend Walter W. Curtis, Bishop of Bridgeport. He visualized an institution of higher learning, rooted in the Catholic intellectual heritage and reflecting the ecumenical thrust of post-Vatican II. The University has been unique since its inception in that it has always been staffed and administered primarily by lay people who reflect in their diversity the ecumenical vision of its founder. The University offers programs in liberal arts, teacher education, and secretarial studies.

Community Environment. The University is located off the Merritt Parkway between Bridgeport and Fairfield, only 20 minutes from the Yale University campus in New Haven and one hour from New York City.

Religious Denomination. Roman Catholic.

Accreditation. New England Association of Schools and Colleges.

Term System. Semester.

Admission Requirements. High school graduation or equivalent; 16 academic units; SAT; GRE required for graduate program.

Tuition and Fees. Tuition $2,250 per semester; student activity fee $25.

Financial Aid. Financial aid programs are based on the student's academic potential, character, citizenship, and demonstrated financial need.

Housing. The Counseling Center of the University maintains a file of available housing in the area.

Library Facilities. The library houses over 135,000 volumes and 900 periodical titles.

Religious Services/Activities. Students of all faiths are welcome at the University. The Campus Ministry reflects this ecumenical vision through its interfaith representation. A priest of the diocese, a representative from the Sisters of Notre Dame, a pastor from the local Baptist congregation, and a rabbi from a local Jewish congregation are assigned as chaplains to assist students in their search for understanding and commitment.

Degree Programs

The major in Religion leading to the Bachelor of Arts degree requires the completion of 30 credits including Introduction to the Study of Religion and nine Religious Studies electives selected in consultation with a Religious Studies advisor.

The Master of Arts in Religious Studies degree is designed to suit the needs of a wide variety of students; it includes preparation for doctoral work in religion, a career in religious education, or personal enrichment. The student selects a field of concentration.

St. Alphonsus College
1762 Mapleton Avenue
Suffield, CT 06078   (203) 668-7393

Administration. V. Rev. Patrick McGarrity, C.SS.R., President.

General Description. St. Alphonsus College is a privately supported theological seminary college whose purpose is to provide an integral college education for young men who want to be priests of the Congregation of the Most Holy Redeemer. It was founded in in 1963. As a seminary, it follows standards set for it by the Holy See and by the Hierarchy of the United States, especially in its *Program of Priestly Formation.* The College is a religious house, or community, where members usually known as "Redemptorists" live together in a common endeavor of study, prayer, work, and recreation.

Community Environment. The College is situated on the northeast border of the town of Suffield. It lies 17 miles north of Hartford, Connecticut and 7 miles south of Springfield, Massachusetts.

Religious Denomination. Roman Catholic.

Religious Emphasis. Congregation of the Most Holy Redeemer.

Accreditation. New England Association of Schools and Colleges.

Term System. Trimester.

Enrollment in Degree Programs in Religion 1984–85. Total 52.

Faculty for Degree Programs in Religion. Total 19; full-time 8, part-time 11.

Admission Requirements. Graduation from high school or equivalent; SAT or ACT.

Tuition and Fees. Tuition $900 per term; room and board $600 per term; library fee $30 per year; services $120 per year.

Financial Aid. Financial aid is available through the Pell Grant program; state scholarship programs, the Associate Redemptorist Student Aid Fund, the Saint Alphonsus Grant-in-Aid program, and Veteran's Benefits.

Housing. Students reside in College facilities.

Library Facilities. The library houses over 32,000 volumes.

Religious Services/Activities. The apostolic program at the College is planned around three elements: preparation for apostolic work, the accomplishment of it, and reflection on the experience.

Degree Programs

The Bachelor of Arts degree is awarded to the student who has maintained a quality point level of 2.0 and obtained a minimum of 128 hours of credit. Degree requirements include those in the various branches of the humanities which the College considers necessary for the Bachelor of Arts with a major in Philosophy and those in the special branches which many seminaries consider necessary pre-requirements for entrance into their graduate programs.

St. Basil College
195 Glenbrook Road
Stamford, CT 06902   (203) 324-4578

Administration. Monsignor Peter Skrincosky, Rector-President.

General Description. St. Basil College is a center of learning and formation. As a College Seminary, it aims to help the student mature as a liberally educated person, committed to Christ and to the service of people. The academic program of the College corresponds to the goals of a four-year liberal arts college. It gives the student an awareness of traditional and contemporary thought in the the liberal arts, based on a philosophical and pre-theological core curriculum. It focuses on man's place in history and world cultures.

Parent Institution. The College was founded in 1939 by the Most Reverend Constantine Bohachevsky, S.T.D., then Bishop of the Ukrainian Catholic Diocese of America. It was intended primarily as a minor seminary for prospective priests of the Byzantine-Ukrainian Rite and, as such, was the first college of its kind in the country. It seeks to fulfill the needs of young Ukrainian Catholic men who desire, besides a greater knowlege of their ethnicity and their religious heritage, the intellectual development necessary to serve the spiritual and cultural needs of their people.

Community Environment. The College is located in the city of Stamford, at the intersection of Glenbrook Road and Hope Street.

Religious Denomination. Ukrainian Catholic.

Term System. Semester.

Admission Requirements. High school graduation with completion of 16 academic units; SAT or ACT.

Tuition and Fees. Tuition $2,500 per semester; room and board $1,500 per semester.

Financial Aid. The College is eligible to participate in federal programs of student assistance (PELL grants, guaranteed student loans, PLUS), and has scholarships available.

Housing. Dormitory accommodations are available for all students.

Library Facilities. The library houses over 19,000 volumes with a major concentration in philosophy and religion. Special collections include those on Eastern Catholicism and Ukrainian studies. The Ukrainian Museum is located on the college grounds and is the only artistic and cultural center of its kind in the United States.

Religious Services/Activities. The Spiritual Director has the role of implementing the formation of the Christian community of the Seminary. By his conferences given to students and especially by his individual direction, he encourages spiritual formation. It is his responsibility to provide the unity of direction necessary for the priestly life through the integration of study, apostolic activity, and prayer.

Degree Programs

St. Basil College offers a four-year liberal arts program of study leading to the degree of Bachelor of Arts. The degree requires a major in Philosophy and a total of 120 semester hours.

St. Thomas Seminary
College Formation Program
467 Bloomfield Avenue
Bloomfield, CT 06002   (203) 242-5573

General Description. St. Thomas Seminary is not a degree-granting institution. Its students are matriculated at area colleges and universities. The Seminary offers baccalaureate-level courses in Religious Studies, Philosophy, and Latin, which are credit bearing and which are accepted for transfer to the students' host institutions toward their undergraduate degrees. A major objective of the Seminary is to offer undergraduate studies to young men interested in exploring and preparing for their futures as Roman Catholic priests.

Parent Institution. St. Thomas Seminary comes under the auspices of the Roman Catholic Diocese of Hartford.

Community Environment. The campus has three buildings on 167 acres in Bloomfield, Connecticut. Bloomfield adjoins West Hartford. Many cultural and recreational facilities are available in the greater Hartford area. Hartford, the capital of the state, is a major manufacturing city and port of entry. There are over 200 churches of most denominations.

Religious Denomination. Roman Catholic.
Religious Emphasis. Mainstream Roman Catholic.
Accreditation. State of Connecticut.

Term System. Semester; no summer term.
Faculty for Degree Programs in Religion. Total 3; full-time 1, part-time 2.

Admission Requirements. Young men on the undergraduate level interested in exploring and preparing for a future as a Roman Catholic priest.

Tuition and Fees. Tuition and fees as stated by the college or university at which the student is matriculated; room and board at the Seminary $1,500 to $2,000.

Financial Aid. As offered by the college or university at which the student is matriculated. The Seminary also provides some financial aid when needed.

Housing. Dormitory accommodations are available.

Library Facilities. The Seminary library houses over 50,000 volumes.

Religious Services/Activities. Roman Catholic daily Masses and prayer service; annual retreat; a day of recollection each semester.

Special Programs

No degree programs are offered. Courses offered in Religious Studies are: Introduction to Roman Catholicism, Introduction to Christian Religious Thought, Christian Spirituality, Christian Morality, and Mission and Ministry.

Trinity College
Department of Religion
Summit Street
Hartford, CT 06106   (203) 527-3151

Administration. Dr. John A. Gettier, Chairman, Department of Religion.

General Description. The Religion Department is made up of the equivalent of 5 2/3 people who cover Hebrew language and Bible, New Testament, history of religious thought in the West, philosophy of religion, Judaica, Islam, Asian religions, African religions, and anthropolgy of religion. (New Testament Greek is offered by the Classics Department.) Some majors graduate to follow a career or to pursue further studies in religion. Most, however, are pointing toward careers in law, medicine, or business. The major is geared to provide undergraduates with a sound and comprehensive liberal arts major without reference to any religious persuasion or profession. All teaching faculty in the Department have their doctorates from exemplary graduate schools (Brown, Yale, Pennsylvania, Temple, Union Theological Seminary in New York).

Parent Institution. Trinity College is an undergraduate, liberal arts, coeducational, college with about 1,700 students and a faculty of 140. The curriculum has 26 majors of which Religion is one (and is distinct from Philosophy). The College has no denominational affiliation, there are no academic or non-academic religious requirements, and religion is taught in an objective, academic manner as any other subject or field.

Community Environment. Bounded on the west by an escarpment and on the east by gently sloping fields, the campus site had been known in the 18th century as Gallows Hill. Influenced by the architecture of the Oxford and Cambridge colleges, Trinity's designers created four enclosed quadrangles extending north and south from a massive Gothic chapel. Generally viewed as the earliest example of "collegiate Gothic" in the United States, these buildings exerted an important influence on academic architecture for several decades. Together with the imposing Gothic chapel completed in 1932, they are a constant reminder of the medieval origins of collegiate institutions.

Religious Denomination. None.

Accreditation. New England Association of Schools and Colleges.

Term System. Semester; no summer term for religious studies.

Enrollment in Degree Programs in Religion 1984–85. Total 43; men 24, women 19.

Degrees in Religion Awarded 1984–85. Bachelor of Arts 15; men 11, women 4.

Faculty for Degree Programs in Religion. Total 5 2/3; full-time 5, part-time 1.

Admission Requirements. Diploma from and certification by an accredited secondary school for the following subjects: English (4 years), foreign language (2 years), algebra (2 years), plane geometry (1 year), history (1 year), laboratory science (1 year). The SAT and the Achievement Test in English Composition are required. Any student in good standing at the College is accepted as a major in the Religion Department.

Tuition and Fees. Tuition $8,620; fees including room and board $3,700.

Financial Aid. Financial aid is available in the form of loans, bursary employment, and direct grants. Awards are made on the basis of financial need, intellectual promise, character, and leadership.

Housing. Ninety per center of the students live in campus housing.

Library Facilities. The library houses approximately 700,000 volumes covering all undergraduate fields.

Religious Services/Activities. All denominations are represented on campus. Non-academic activities are conducted by various clubs, i.e., Hillel, Newman, etc. In addition the College chapel sponsors many events and holds weekly services.

Degree Programs

The Bachelor of Arts in Religion requires the accumulation of 36 course credits in Religion with a C- or better in ten courses. One course in each of three religious traditions is required as well as one course in each of the four methodological areas (scriptural and textual analysis, historical development of religious thought and institutions, philosophical evaluation of beliefs and concepts, ethical and cultural expressions of religion). The major must also participate in the general examination program.

Yale Divinity School
Yale University
409 Prospect Street
New Haven, CT 06510   (203) 436-2494

Administration. Dr. Angelo Bartlett Giamatti, President; Dr. William Crittenden Brainard, Provost; Dr. Leander Earl Keck, Dean, Yale Divinity School; Dr. James E. Annand, Associate Dean of Yale Divinity School, and President and Dean of Berkeley Divinity School; Dr. H. Frei, Chairman, Department of Religious Studies of the Graduate School.

General Description. Yale University Divinity School is a graduate professional school whose primary purpose is to educate men and women for the Christian ministry. It also provides a theological education for persons who expect to be engaged in professions such as education, social work, or in community agencies. The Divinity School is interdenominational and completely nonsectarian. The faculty is drawn from the major Christian traditions, and the students represent from 30 to 40 denominations and groups. Instruction is provided in the history, doctrines, and polity of all the major church bodies.

The Divinity School offers programs of study leading to the degrees Master of Divinity (M.Div.), Master of Arts in Religion (M.A.R.), and Master of Sacred Theology (S.T.M.). Programs for the degree Doctor of Philosophy (Ph.D.) are offered by the Department of Religious Studies in the Graduate School.

In 1973 the Institute of Sacred Music was founded. It is linked to both the School of Music and the Divinity School.

Since 1971, Berkeley Divinity School, an Episcopal seminary, has been affiliated with Yale Divinity School. *See:* Berkeley Divinity School.

Parent Institution. Training for the Christian ministry was a main purpose in the founding of Yale College in 1701. As expressed in its original charter it was to be a school "wherein Youth may be instructed in the Arts and Sciences who through the blessing of Almighty God may be fitted for Publick employment both in Church and Civil State." That purpose has always been recognized at Yale, and the history of the University is one of increasing development in the facilities for training religious service. Today Yale University consists of Yale College, the Graduate School, the School of Medicine, the Law School, the School of Arts, the School of Music, the School of Forestry and Environmental Studies, the School of Architecture, the School of Nursing, the School of Drama, the School of Organization and Management, and the Divinity School.

Community Environment. The Divinity School is housed principally in the Sterling Divinity Quadrangle which includes a chapel, classroom building, administration building, library buildings, refectory, common room, the Institute of Sacred Music building, 8 dormitories, and

2 guest lodges.

Religious Denomination. Nondenominational (Christian).

Religious Emphasis. Liberal - reformed.

Accreditation. New England Association of Schools and Colleges; Association of Theological Schools in the United States and Canada.

Term System. Semester; no summer school.

Enrollment in Degree Programs in Religion 1984–85. Includes Berkeley Divinity School: Total 423; men 233, women 190. Enrollment by programs: Master of Divinity 310; men 159, women 151. Master of Arts in Religion 77; men 36, women 41. Master of Sacred Theology 36; men 29, women 7.

Degrees in Religion Awarded 1984–85. Includes Berkeley Divinity School: Master of Divinity 82; men 41, women 41. Master of Arts in Religion 33; men 19, women 14. Master of Sacred Theology 16; men 14, women 2.

Faculty for Degree Programs in Religion. Includes Berkeley Divinity School: Total 42; full-time 35, part-time 7.

Admission Requirements. Students must be graduates of colleges or universities of recognized standing. Admission is selective, based on academic standing and ability, personal qualifications, vocational goals, and evidence of intention to carry through a program of study.

Tuition and Fees. Tuition $7,350 for full-time students; other expenses (hospitalization fee, rent, meals, books, clothing, travel, incidentals) are estimated to be $6,725.

Financial Aid. Limited resources are available for grants-in-aid and loans. These resources are allocated according to need. The school provides assistance in meeting financial obligations by helping students and spouses find employment and by helping students solicit aid from outside sources.

Housing. Sterling Divinity Quadrangle provides on-campus housing for single students. A total of eight dormitories are available, and board is obtained at the refectory. Three apartment complexes house married students; apartments vary in size; child-care facilities are available. Information and referrals are available for students wishing to live off campus.

Library Facilities. The Yale University Library consists of a central collection, the Sterling Memorial Library, seven school libraries, and forty-seven departmental and college libraries, containing in all over 8 million volumes. The Divinity Library was established in 1932 through the consolidation of the Day Historical Library of Foreign Missions, the Trowbridge Reference Library, and the Richard Sheldon Sneath Memorial Library of Religious Education. It currently houses over 350,000 volumes.

Religious Services/Activities. Daily worship is held in Marquand Chapel (Monday through Friday). St. Luke's Chapel at the Berkeley Center and the Prayer Chapel are also used on a regular basis for worship. Denominational services supplement the worship life at the Divinity School.

Degree Programs

The Master of Divinity degree certifies completion of a program of theological studies designed primarily, although not exclusively, to prepare the candidate for ordination to the Christian ministry. The requirements reflect the intention of the School to provide an education that is theologically informed, professionally competent, academically rigorous, and oriented to the life of the church. The minimum requirement for the degree is the successful completion of seventy-two semester hours, normally within three years. Two years of resident work must be completed, one of which must be the final year.

The Master of Arts in Religion degree certifies either completion of a comprehensive program of study in preparation for one of the many forms of lay ministry or service, or completion of one of the concentrated programs of advanced study. The minimum requirement for the degree is the successful completion of two academic years of study with a total schedule of at least forty-eight semester hours. If necessary a program may be expanded, but all requirements must be completed within three years. Students must normally complete at least three semesters of work in the Divinity School. A student must spend the final semester of the degree program in residence. Concentrated program are in Bible, History of Christianity, Theology, Ethics, Liturgics, Religion and the Arts, Music and Worship.

The Master of Sacred Theology degree program is for graduates of theological schools of recognized standing who have obtained the B.D. or M.Div. degree. The work for this degree is to be regarded as a fourth year of preparation for the Christian ministry. It may be used for a a specialized form of Christian service such as a college or university ministry; the chaplaincy in industry, institutions, and the armed services; the urban or inner-city ministry; ecumenical leadership; the directing of continuing education; home missions; foreign missions; and ministry to the elderly. The program may also be used as a year of specialized work in one of the theological disciplines as preparation for doctoral studies. A candidate for the degree must complete the equivalent of at least twenty-four semester hours of graduate study in the Divinity School beyond the B.D. or M.Div. degree, including a major seminary paper or other acceptable project in the major field of study. The work for the degree may be taken in one year, or distributed over two, three, or four years; it must be completed within four years after matriculation.

In conjunction with the Yale University Graduate School a student may complete work for the degrees Master of Arts, Master of Philosophy, and Doctor of Philosophy (Ph.D.). The Graduate School grants these degrees. The fields of study are Buddhism, ethics, history of ancient Christianity, history of Christianity, Islamic religion, Judaica, New Testament, Old Testament, philosophy of religion, and theology.

Special Programs

Each Fall the Divinity School offers continuing education seminars.

Yale University
Department of Religious Studies
New Haven, CT 06520   (203) 436-4771

Administration. Dr. A. Bartlett Giamatti, President; Dr. Hans Frei, Chairman, Department of Religious Studies.

General Description. The Department of Religious Studies offers courses that concentrate on given historical religions, both Western and Eastern, both ancient and modern, and on recurrent doctrinal, philosophical, and social issues, which often cut across traditions. A variety of methods is employed in these historical and systematic inquiries. Students are free to choose among diverse introductory and advance offerings, in order to gain initial exposure to an area of interest or to acquire specialized competence in a particular subject.

Parent Institution. Yale University was founded in 1701 and was the first university in the United States to award the Ph.D. degree. The University is composed of 12 schools and colleges and it grants the Bachelor, Master, and Doctoral degrees. Programs in Religious Studies are offered by Yale College and the Graduate School. The Yale Divinity School offers graduate study leading to the first professional degree. *See also:* Yale Divinity School.

Community Environment. The campus is located in New Haven, ninety minutes from New York City and three hours from Boston.

Religious Denomination. Nondenominational.

Accreditation. New England Association of Schools and Colleges.

Term System. Semester.

Admission Requirements. Graduation from high school or equivalent in upper half of class; 16 academic units including English 4, mathematics 3, laboratory science 2, social studies 2, foreign language 2; SAT.

Tuition and Fees. Inclusive fee for resident undergraduates $15,020.

Financial Aid. Yale University provides a number of programs which are designed to assist families in financing the cost of a Yale education. Various means, such as tuition payment plans, parent and student loan programs, term-time employment, and scholarship funds are available.

Housing. Living accommodations are provided on campus for over 5,000 students.

Library Facilities. The University libraries have collections totaling over 8,440,000 volumes.

Degree Programs

A number of different approaches to the study of religion are represented in the Department: the history and scriptures of specific religions; theology; ethics; philosophy of religion; psychology of religion; and sociology of religion. Each student majoring in Religious Studies normally concentrates in one of these. The Department offers two programs that a student may elect, either the standard major or religious studies combined with another subject. Both programs require a core of courses in religious studies and a Senior essay. The core requirement is four term courses: one course in theology, ethics, or philosophy of religion; one course in psychology of religion, sociology of religion, or anthropological study of religion; and two courses in historical or textual study, one in each of two major religions (Buddhism, Christianity, Hinduism, Islam, Judaism).

DISTRICT OF COLUMBIA

American University
Department of Philosophy and Religion
Massachusetts and Nebraska Avenues, N.W.
Washington, DC 20016   (202) 885-1000

Administration. Dr. Richard Berendzen, President; Charles S.J. White, Chair, Department of Philosophy and Religion.

General Description. The study of religion deals with the literature, history, theology, theories, and practices associated with the world's major religious traditions. Courses are offered in Judaism, Christianity, and Islam, as well as substantial offerings in non-Western religions such as Hinduism and Buddhism. Opportunities are provided for studying the effects of religious traditions on contemporary society and the interplay of modern religious, scientific, and cultural movements. The Bachelor of Arts and Master of Arts in Religious Studies are offered. The Department has a special sharing arrangement with Old Dominion University for the Department's doctoral program.

Parent Institution. Chartered in 1891 and incorporated by Act of Congress in 1893, the University was founded as a Methodist-related graduate school of history and public affairs. Today it offers a wide range of graduate and undergraduate degree programs and nondegree study through its five divisions.

Community Environment. The 78-acre campus sits on the hill where Massachusetts and Nebraska Avenues meet in Washington, D.C.

Religious Denomination. The United Methodist Church.

Accreditation. Middle States Association of Colleges and Schools.

Term System. Semester.

Admission Requirements. Graduation from high school with rank in the upper 50 percent of class; 16 academic units; SAT or ACT.

Tuition and Fees. Tuition $3,800 per semester (1984-85); room $852-$1,371; board $284-$691.

Financial Aid. The University has an extensive program of scholarships, loans, and grants.

Housing. Dormitory accommodations for undergraduate men and women are available for 2,600 students.

Library Facilities. The University Library contains over 440,000 volumes and more than 425,000 microforms. Over 2,500 periodicals are received each year.

Religious Services/Activities. The Abraham S. Kay Spiritual Life Center serves the University community as a place of worship, celebration, meditation, outreach, study, and sharing the life of faith.

Degree Programs

The Bachelor of Arts in Religion requires a total of 120 semester hours with 39 semester hours in the Department.

The Master of Arts in Religious Studies requires at least 30 semester hours of approved graduate work, including 6 hours of Master's Thesis Seminar.

Catholic University of America
School of Religious Studies
Washington, DC 20064   (202) 635-5684

Administration. Rev. William Cenkner, O.P., S.T.L., Ph.D., Dean.

General Description. From its foundation, The Catholic University of America has given academic priority to religious studies and related disciplines. First structured as the School of Sacred Sciences, the academic programs in these fields gave rise in succession to the School of Canon Law (1923), a Seminary Department (1931), the Department of Religion (1932), and later a division into distinct Schools of Sacred Theology and Philosophy (1937). After extensive study of programs and structures, the Academic Senate approved the establishment of a new School of Religious Studies and made this recommendation to the Board of Trustees, which in turn, established the new school, effective in 1973.

The School of Religious Studies includes five departments: Biblical Studies, Canon Law, Church History, Religion and Religious Education, and Theology. The Department of Church History draws upon existing university programs in the Departments of History (School of Arts and Sciences) and Theology; the Department of Biblical Studies offers a program of advanced studies in biblical exegesis. The Program in Liturgical Studies is interdepartmental, drawing upon offerings in canon law, theology, and religion and religious education.

Parent Institution. Meeting in the Second Plenary Council of Baltimore in 1866, the Roman Catholic bishops of the United States expressed their desire to have under Catholic auspices a university in which "all the letters and sciences, both sacred and profane, could be taught." During the Third Plenary Council of Baltimore in 1884, they proposed to use a gift from Miss Mary Gwendoline Caldwell of Newport, Rhode Island, to establish a school of theology from which a complete university might develop. Pope Leo XIII formally approved the project of a national university on April 10, 1887 (commemorated annually as Founders Day). Although originally the university had been conceived to be for graduate instruction and research exclusively, it began to offer undergraduate courses within a few years after its establishment.

Community Environment. The campus is located in the northeast quadrant of Washington with a main entrance at Michigan Avenue and Fourth Street, N.E. The city of Washington, the capital of the United States, is located on the Potomac River between Maryland and Virginia. It is a beautiful and historic city of tree-shaded streets and impressive buildings. All major forms of transportation are available. The Metro, a subway system, serves all sections of the city.

Religious Denomination. Roman Catholic.

Accreditation. Middle States Association of Colleges and Schools; Association of Theological Schools in the United States and Canada.

Term System. Semester; summer term.

Enrollment in Degree Programs in Religion 1984–85. Total 1,042; men 829; women 213.

Degrees in Religion Awarded 1984–85. Doctor of Philosophy 14; men 8, women 6. Doctor of Ministry 12; men 10, women 2. Doctorate in Canon Law 3; men 2, women 1. Licentiate in Canon Law 21; men 15, women 6. Doctorate in Sacred Theology 1; men 1. Licentiate in Sacred Theology 10; men 8, women 2. Master in Religious Education 4; men 1, women 3. Master of Arts 24; men 14, women 10. Master of Divinity 24; men 24. Bachelor of Sacred Theology 5; men 5.

Faculty for Degree Programs in Religion. Total 77; full-time 53; part-time 24.

Admission Requirements. Undergraduate admission requires high school graduation; SAT. Graduate admission is based on decision by the academic dean; applicants for graduate study will be expected to have earned a Bachelor's degree from an appropriately accredited institution, and their records should indicate that they are prepared to pursue advanced study and research in the field or fields in which they intend to specialize; two or more letters of recommendation (officials or faculty members).

Tuition and Fees. Full-time tuition per semester $3,600; part-time $276 per credit hour; board fees range from $758 to $865 per semester; room fees vary from $945 to $1,420 per semester.

Financial Aid. The University offers a wide variety of scholarships, grants, loans, and work appointments to new and continuing students. For graduate students, there are teaching and research assistantships, tuition remission for Seminarians, fellowships, Divinity Burses, and other sources of financial aid.

Housing. The University maintains ten residence halls. There is special housing for graduate students, married students, religious women, and priests.

Library Facilities. The main library facilities of the university are located in the John K. Mullen of Denver Memorial Library. The collection includes more than one million volumes housed in seven subject divisions in Mullen Library and in six school and departmental libraries on campus. In addition, the student has conveniently available the library resources of the Washington area. These include not only the Library of Congress but many specialized public and private collections in the area, such as the Dumbarton Oaks collection, the Folger Shakespeare Library, the National Archives, the National Library of Medicine, and the libraries of the Washington Theological Consortium.

Religious Services/Activities. Campus ministry is the official pastoral presence of the Roman Catholic Church at the University. It is exercised through the presence of all the ministers to the members of the university community, through liturgy and common prayer, through activities of social concern, and through retreats, counseling, educational events, and social activities.

Degree Programs

Department of Biblical Studies. The Master of Arts and Doctor of Philosophy degrees offered by the Department are designed to provide men and women with the training necessary for effective teaching, research, and publication in the biblical field. The main emphasis is placed on control of biblical languages and exegesis. The student will also be directed to advanced work in theological areas related to critical study of the Bible.

Department of Canon Law. The Licentiate in Canon Law is a two-year post-graduate program designed to help the student become acquainted with the whole *corpus* of Church law, understand it in terms of its theological, philosophical, and historical background, and learn the method and practice of scientific research.

The Doctorate in Canon Law is the advanced degree offered by the Department.

Department of Church History. The Master of Arts and Doctor of Philosophy degrees offered by the Department focus on the Catholic Church from the first century to the twentieth. They emphasize the internal life of the Church (the history of its doctrine, discipline, policy, worship, spirituality, and piety), its expansion through missionary work, and its charitable and educational activities. The program also includes the Church's relationship with secular society and civil government, the collective influences of its members in the intellectual, cultural, social, and political spheres, their attitudes toward their contemporary situations, and the effects of different environments on its growth and decay.

Department of Religion and Religious Education. The Bachelor of Arts degree aims to introduce the student to the question of the meaning and value of religion for human life by an academic study of modern interpretations of religion, of the Catholic doctrinal and theological tradition, and of the relationship between religion and other dimensions of life.

The Master of Arts program offers a choice of three orientations, determined by which of the proseminars one selects: Religion Study, History of Catechetics, or Introduction to the Study of Spirituality.

A Master of Religious Education, also offered by the Department, is a professional program especially designed for practitioners in religious education and catechetics.

At the Doctor of Philosophy level, the Department aims to promote understanding of the interaction between religion and culture. There are five areas of specialization: Catholic theological tradition, biblical literature, spirituality, religion and culture, and religious education/catechetics.

A Liturgical Studies program leading to the Master of Arts degree is administered by the Department of Religion and Religious Education. This program is interdisciplinary in character and provides a study of liturgical tradition and current reforms. A specialization in Liturgical Studies at the Doctoral level is offered in conjunction with other Departments.

Department of Theology. The Master of Arts offered by the Department is the basic advanced degree in general Roman Catholic theology. It is intended and designed to introduce the student to the mastery of knowledge, creative scholarship, and research in the science of theology.

The Master of Divinity is a first professional degree; the purpose of the program is to foster basic theological understanding and to develop initial pastoral competence on the part of students preparing themselves for ministry.

The Doctor of Ministry degree is a professional doctorate which signifies that its recipient is prepared for competent and effective ministry. The primary focus of the program is on the practice of ministry. Biblical, historical, and theological understanding are integrated with supervised field experience to develop effective ministerial leadership in the contemporary world.

The Doctor of Philosophy degree marks high achievement in preparation for creative scholarship and research. The program is designed to prepare a graduate student to make significant contributions to knowledge.

Special Programs

The Department of Canon Law and the Department of Theology have pontifical or ecclesiastical faculties. By virtue of accreditation by the Holy See, programs leading to degrees in theology and canon law are recognized as having canonical effects. Such programs satisfy both the norms established by the Holy See and the University requirements. The Bachelor of Sacred Theology, Licentiate in Sacred Theology, Doctor of Sacred Theology, Licentiate in Canon Law, and Doctorate in Canon Law are offered as Pontifical Degree Programs.

The Pastoral Center is a division of the Department of Theology and offers the student an opportunity to develop an integrated program which brings a pastoral dimension to studies in theology and related fields and to formal spiritual development. Through the Doctor of Ministry degree, the program of continuing education in pastoral ministry, and various individualized programs, the Pastoral Center is able to train seminarians, priests, Protestant clergy, members of religious communities, and laity for the many ministries expected in the Church today.

The Theological College of the University offers diocesan students preparing for the priesthood programs of theological instruction and professional pastoral training. The direction of Theological College has been entrusted to the Sulpician Fathers, a group of diocesan priests whose apostolate for three hundred years has been preparation of men for priestly service. Students are sent to the College by bishops throughout the United States.

The Catholic University of America was one of the founding member institutions of the Washington Theological Consortium in 1967. Since its incorporation in 1971, the consortium has worked actively to coordinate programs of theological education among and for its member institutions: Cluster of Independent Theological Schools, Howard University Divinity School, Episcopal Theological Seminary, Washington Theological Union, Wesley Theological Seminary, and Lutheran Theological Seminary (at Gettysburg).

Cluster of Independent Theological Schools c/o De Sales School of Theology
721 Lawrence Street, N.E.
Washington, DC 20017

General Description. The Cluster of Independent Theological Schools is an interdependent theological enterprise of three religious communities: the Oblates of Mary Immaculate (Oblate College), the Oblates of St. Francis de Sales (De Sales School of Theology), and the Dominican Fathers (Dominican House of Studies). Each school takes charge of that part of the curriculum it views as closely connected with the communication of its spirit, while it shares with the others those courses and programs common to the theological education for priesthood and other ministries.

The purpose of the Cluster is threefold: (1) It enables the three religious communities to offer an integrated pastoral, academic, and spiritual program for the formation of their members; (2) It enriches the theological education of all the members of these religious communities by sharing traditions and ideals and by personal acquaintances. The basic elements of the training program for priestly formation are taught by professors from three religious traditions. Exposure to these different traditions is of value to the student, enriching knowledge and broadening vision; (3) It creates a framework for new joint programs.

The three schools have set forth the following goals to be accomplished through the process of clustering: (1) To develop pastoral agents who will be enabled to serve in the ministry of leadership in the contemporary Church; (2) To create an approach to theological reflection and ministerial preparation that interrelates the Church's traditions of the study of academic theology, of spirituality, and of commitment to mission in the Church; (3) To respond to the desire among the laity for deeper ongoing Christian formation and the development of skills for fuller ecclesiastical participation in the life of the Church; (4) To respond to the desire among the clergy for ongoing theological, ministerial, and spiritual growth.

The Cluster is a constituent member of the Washington Theological Consortium.

Religious Denomination. Roman Catholic.

Accreditation. Middle States Association of Colleges and Schools; Association of Theological Schools in the United States and Canada.

Term System. Semester.

Faculty for Degree Programs in Religion. Total 35; full-time 25, part-time 10.

De Sales School of Theology
721 Lawrence Street, N.E.
Washington, DC 20017   (202) 269-9412

Administration. Very Rev. William J. Ruhl, O.S.F.S., President; Rev. Lewis S. Fiorelli, O.S.F.S., Academic Dean.

General Description. The De Sales School of Theology is conducted under the auspices of the Oblate of St. Francis de Sales. It was founded in 1949 "to foster a more careful integration of the academic, pastoral and spiritual components of the Oblate priesthood." It views its challenges as: (1) the development of programs that would provide Oblate students with the necessary academic credentials, (2) the admission of candidates for the priesthood from other religious communities and dioceses, (3) the preparation of lay persons with an adequate background and foundations for assumption of ministries in the Church, and (4) the updating and renewal of clergy, religious, and laypersons. The School grants the degrees Master of Divinity and Master of Arts in Theology.

De Sales is a member of the Cluster of Independent Theological Schools, with the Dominican Fathers of the Dominican House of Studies and the Oblates of Mary Immaculate of Oblate College. Each school assumes responsibility for that part of the curriculum which it views as essential to the transmission of its spirit, while those courses and programs which belong to the area of common theological education for ministry are shared mutually by the 3 schools. The Cluster is, in turn, a member of the Washington Theological Consortium, composed of 3 Roman Catholic and 4 Protestant theological schools who share their resources by open cross registration and complete library availability.

Community Environment. The De Sales School of Theology is situated adjacent to the Catholic University of America in Washington, D.C. It is within walking distance of the Dominican House of Studies and Oblate College.

Religious Denomination. Roman Catholic.

Religious Emphasis. Roman Catholic Spiritual Theology.

Accreditation. Middle States Association of Colleges and Schools; Association of Theological Schools in the United States and Canada.

Term System. Semester.

Enrollment in Degree Programs in Religion 1984–85. Total 29; men 22, women 1, special students 6 women.

Degrees in Religion Awarded 1984–85. Master of Arts 2; men 2.

Faculty for Degree Programs in Religion. Total 11; full-time 6, part-time 5.

Admission Requirements. Bachelor's degree or equivalent from an accredited college or university; satisfactory grades in at least 18 credit hours of philosophy which must include two courses in History of Philosophy and one course each in Metaphysics, Theodicy, Philosophy of Man, Epistemology, and Ethics; adequate proof of a reading knowledge of Latin.

Tuition and Fees. Tuition full-time $1,250 per semester; part-time $125 per credit hour.

Library Facilities. The De Sales School of Theology has entered into a merger with Oblate College with reference to the housing of mongraphs. The combined collection numbers approximately 55,000 volumes. De Sales has retained the most complete and up-to-date collection of materials on Salesian spirituality in the United States. De Sales has also entered into a cooperative library arrangement concerning periodicals. The Cluster Periodical Center is located within the Library of the Dominican House of Studies. In addition, students have access to the fifteen libraries of the member institutions of the Washington Theological Consortium.

Religious Services/Activities. Students of the Cluster gather for religious events at the beginning, during, and at the end of the school year.

Degree Programs

The Master of Divinity degree program is designed as the first professional degree that prepares a student, particulary an Oblate of St. Francis de Sales, for pastoral ministry and/or ordination in the Roman Catholic Church. The program is composed of thirty-nine courses divided over the following subject areas: Sacred Scripture, Doctrinal Theology, Sacraments and Worship, Moral Theology, Pastoral Theology, Church History, and Spiritual Theology. Twenty-six credits are required in the pastoral area covering the fields of canon law, preaching (basic and advanced), a skill course, a liturgical practicum, and four semesters of supervised ministry: circle of praxis. A written comprehensive examination of an integrative pastoral nature is also required.

The Master of Arts in Theology program leads to an academic degree designed to prepare students desiring to be teachers of theology with a solid theological foundation and to offer such students the credentials for the assumption of competitive administrative positions in the schools in which they might serve. It is also designed to prepare those students who desire to pursue doctoral work in theology with the necessary theological competence. The student is offered the option of choosing a concentration in general Roman Catholic studies or a more specific area of Roman Catholic Theology.

Special Programs

A Salesian/Spiritual Out-Reach Program offers courses to religious and laity in the Washington, D.C. metropolitan area. Courses are taught off-campus at the Georgetown Visitation Academy.

Dominican House of Studies

487 Michigan Avenue N.E.
Washington, DC 20017　　　　(202) 529-5300

Administration. Rev. Mark Heath, O.P., President.

General Description. The Dominican House of Studies offers a full post-graduate program in Roman Catholic theology. Included in the curriculum are studies in Sacred Scripture, Systematic and Moral Theology, Church History, and Canon Law. Further, a program of supervised ministry is available. The main goal of the program is to prepare men for the Roman Catholic priesthood, especially members of the Dominican Order. The school is open to men from other religious communities or dioceses as well as lay men and women who seek one of the two degrees available, or simply wish to enrich themselves in certain areas of sacred studies. The Dominican House of Studies is a member of the Cluster of Independent Theological Schools as well as a charter member of the Washington Theological Consortium whose offices are located at the Dominican House. The school offers two general degree programs. One is the first professional degree for

religious ministry: Master of Divinity. The second is an advanced or post-Master of Divinity degree, the Licentiate in Sacred Theology.

Community Environment. The Dominican House of Studies is housed in a Roman Catholic Dominican priory which is located in the vicinity of Catholic University of America. It is in northeast Washington, a short distance from unlimited educational, research, artistic, cultural, and political resources.

Religious Denomination. Roman Catholic.

Accreditation. Middle States Association of Colleges and Schools; Association of Theological Schools in the United States and Canada.

Term System. Semester.

Enrollment in Degree Programs in Religion 1984–85. Total 38; men 38.

Degrees in Religion Awarded 1984–85. Master of Divinity/Bachelor of Sacred Theology 7; men 7. Licentiate in Sacred Theology 5; men 5.

Faculty for Degree Programs in Religion. Total 9; full-time 9.

Admission Requirements. Bachelor's degree from an accredited college, ordinarily in such liberal arts as English, history, natural sciences, and languages; cumulative grade point average of at least 3.0 on a 4.0 scale; completion of 18 hours in philosophy, particularly the history of philosophy and systematic philosophy.

Tuition and Fees. Tuition $1,250 per semester; part-time $100 per credit hour; registration fee $25; application fee $15; graduation fee $35.

Housing. Dominican students are housed on campus.

Library Facilities. The library contains 56,720 volumes with special collections in Thomistic Studies, Dominican History, and Catholic Doctrine (rare books).

Religious Services/Activities. Liturgy of the Word and Eucharist (Mass) and the Liturgy of the Hours (Prayer) are held daily. There is also an annual retreat.

Degree Programs

The Master of Divinity degree program conforms in its detail to the standards for this degree of the Association of Theological Schools and the program requirements of the Roman Catholic Bishops' *Plan for Priestly Formation.* The Dominican House of Studies is authorized by the Holy See to grant the Bachelor in Sacred Theology, according to the provisions of the Constitution *Sapientia Christiana* and its own Statutes. The requirements for the Master of Divinity and the Bachelor in Sacred Theology are identical. Students must successfully complete six semesters of prescribed courses; have a reading knowledge of scholastic Latin and a basic knowledge of Biblical Greek (certified by a written examination); and successfully complete a two-part comprehensive examination, one oral, and the other written, on a selected set of topics.

Special Programs

The Dominican House of Studies also offers ancillary programs in training for ministry. Special in-course training for deacons is offered. The faculty offers special programs in preparation for installation into the Ministries of Lector and Acolyte and for ordination to the Diaconate and Priesthood. This program consists of study, lectures, seminars, and practical experiences.

George Washington University
Washington, DC 20052   (202) 676-6040

Administration. Dr. Lloyd H. Elliott, President.

General Description. The Department of Religion in the Columbian College of Arts and Sciences offers a program leading to the Bachelor of Arts with a major in Religion. The Graduate School of Arts and Sciences offers the Master of Arts in Religion, Religious Education, Religion and Medical Care, and History of Religions - Hinduism. The Doctor of Philosophy in American Religious History is offered in cooperation with the Department of History.

Parent Institution. The George Washington University had its beginning in 1821 as The Columbian College in the District of Columbia. The name of the institution was changed in 1873 to Columbian University and in 1904 to its present name. The University includes nine colleges, schools, and divisions.

Community Environment. The University is located in downtown Washington, between Pennsylvania Avenue and 19th, F, and 24th Streets. In immediately adjacent areas are the White House, the Corcoran Gallery of Art, the Department of State, and the John F. Kennedy Center for the Performing Arts.

Religious Denomination. Nondenominational.

Accreditation. Middle States Association of Colleges and Schools.

Term System. Semester.

Admission Requirements. High school graduation in top 40 percent of class; 15 academic units; SAT. Graduate School: Baccalaureate degree from an accredited college or university.

Tuition and Fees. Tuition $3,675 per semester; room and board $4,300.

Financial Aid. Undergraduate aid consists of two basic types: awards for academic achievement without reference to financial circumstances (honors scholarships) and scholarships, grants, loans, and employment based upon demonstrated financial need. The program of financial assistance for graduate students includes assistantships, fellowships, traineeships, graduate scholarships, research appointments, part-time employment, and loans.

Housing. Dormitory accommodations are available for 2,500 undergraduates.

Library Facilities. The library collections, totaling over 1,390,000 volumes, are housed in the Melvin Gelman Library, the National Law Center, and the School of Medicine and Health Sciences.

Religious Services/Activities. Catholic, Jewish, and Protestant bodies sponsor various groups and form a link between the University and the religious community. Religious services and special observances are also provided for the University community.

Degree Programs

The major in Religion leading to the Bachelor of Arts degree requires 30 semester hours, including at least 21 hours of upper-level courses. Twelve of these hours must be chosen from one of the following religious traditions: Christianity, Hinduism, Islam, and Judaism. The program must also include Theories in the Study of Religion and at least one course in each of the following areas: Hebrew Scriptures, New Testament, Eastern Religions, and Western Religions.

In addition to the general requirements of the Graduate School of Arts and Sciences, The Master of Arts in Religion degree requires 24 semester hours of required courses and a Comprehensive Examination. The Master of Arts in Religious Education degree requires completion of 24 semester hours exclusive of the thesis. The Master of Arts in the field of Religion and Medical Care program of study consists of 36 semester hours of approved coursework with or without a thesis. The Master of Arts in the field of History of Religions - Hinduism requires 24 hours of coursework exclusive of thesis, including a sequence of four courses in the literature of the Hindu tradition and one course in method in history of religions. The Master's Comprehensive Examination is required of all students and will cover specified fields.

Georgetown University
Department of Theology
37th and O Streets, N.W.
Washington, DC 20057   (202) 625-0100

Administration. Rev. Timothy S. Healy, S.J., President; Dr. Royden B. Davis, S.J., Dean, The College of Arts and Sciences; William C. McFadden, S.J., V.M., Chairman, Department of Theology.

General Description. Students majoring in Theology follow one of three paths that include (1) Christian Theology: a concentration providing a grounding in the sacred writings, history, and systematic elaboration of the Christian faith; (2) Biblical Studies: a concentration designed for students who wish to study extensively the books of the Bible, the traditions contained therein, as well as the methodology for uncovering their meaning; and (3) Religious Studies: a concentration for students wishing to organize a major around a particular problem or theme in which religious thought or values are of predominant interest. The Bachelor of Arts degree is granted.

Parent Institution. Georgetown University was founded

in 1789 by the first Catholic bishop of the United States. Due to the location in what was to become the District of Columbia, Georgetown's charter of incorporation was granted by the United States Congress. The University is composed of five undergraduate schools and four graduate and professional schools with programs leading to the Bachelor's, Master's, and Doctorate degrees.

Community Environment. The 110-acre campus is situated on the heights above the Potomac River, near the Key Bridge.

Religious Denomination. Roman Catholic.

Accreditation. Middle States Association of Colleges and Schools.

Term System. Semester.

Faculty for Degree Programs in Religion. Total 29.

Admission Requirements. High school graduation; 16 academic units; SAT or ACT.

Tuition and Fees. Tuition $4,650 per semester; part-time $310 per credit; room $2,005-$2,275 per academic year; apartment $3,245 (per person, 12-month lease).

Financial Aid. Most students meet their needs through a financial aid package consisting of some combination of grants, loans, and employment.

Housing. Dormitories and apartments are available on campus.

Library Facilities. The Lauinger Memorial Library contains over 1,112,000 volumes.

Degree Programs

The major in Theology leading to the Bachelor of Arts degree follows one of three paths as described above. In addition, it is recommended that students majoring in Theology fulfill the general education requirements by taking the courses The Problem of God and Introduction to Biblical Literature. Students interested in graduate school are advised to take German and/or French and/or Latin. Students preparing for graduate work in Biblical Studies are encouraged to take Greek and/or Biblical Hebrew. The Senior Seminar is required of all majors. A minimum of 120 semester hours is required for the Bachelor of Arts degree.

Howard University
The Divinity School
1240 Randolph Street, N.E.
Washington, DC 20017   (202) 636-6100

Administration. Dr. James E. Cheek, President; Dr. Lawrence N. Jones, Dean, The Divinity School.

General Description. The Divinity School (formerly the School of Religion) emphasizes (1) the preparation of professional religious leaders for service in educational or religious institutions and service in the urban, underserved, poor Black communities; (2) an international cross-cultural inquiry into human values; and (3) further graduate study primarily in the cultural and religious heritage of Afro-Americans. The School offers programs of study leading to the Master of Arts in Religious Studies, Master of Divinity, and Doctor of Ministry degrees.

Parent Institution. Howard University was authorized by a charter of the 39th Congress in 1867. Traditionally, Howard University has maintained the largest gathering of Black scholars in the world. The University administers 17 schools and colleges.

Community Environment. The Divinity School is located in northeast Washington in a combination dormitory-dining-teaching and conference center. The facility was dedicated in the winter of 1980.

Religious Denomination. Nondenominational.

Accreditation. Middle States Association of Colleges and Schools; Association of Theological Schools in the United States and Canada.

Term System. Semester.

Faculty for Degree Programs in Religion. Total 18.

Admission Requirements. Baccalaureate degree from an accredited college or university; biographical statement; letter from church official; letters of recommendation; admission is through the Office of Graduate Admissions of Howard University.

Tuition and Fees. Tuition $2,700 per year; university fee $75 per semester; student activities fee $32.50 per semester; Divinity School housing $521-$622.

Financial Aid. The Divinity School operates several scholarships, fellowships, assistantships, grants, and awards. They are provided usually on the basis of outstanding scholarship, with many provided on the basis of outstanding scholarship and financial need.

Housing. The Divinity School has housing with single/double accommodations.

Library Facilities. The University Libraries system includes the general library and eight branches in three divisions. The Divinity branch is within the Humanities and Social Sciences division.

Degree Programs

The Master of Arts in Religious Studies degree is designed for persons interested in teaching (e.g., secondary or community college level), in continuing studies in religion and theology, or in preparation for advanced theological education. The program is interdisciplinary, providing a maximum of flexibility in program planning for one of the following areas: Biblical Studies, Historical Studies, Theological Studies, Ethics and Society, Religion and Personality, History of Religions, and Religious Education. The program normally requires a minimum of 48 credit hours, thesis, a "B" average or higher.

The Master of Divinity degree is designed to prepare persons for the ministry of the church, both as pastors and in related fields including chaplaincies, Christian education, and staff positions within denominations. The degree is the basic professional degree for clergy. The program requires the completion of a minimum of 90 credit hours of classroom work with a C average or higher. Courses are required in areas of concentration including Biblical Studies; Ethics, Society, and Culture; Historical Studies; Ministry; and Theological Studies.

The Doctor of Ministry program is designed for people who wish to engage in an advanced level of preparation for ministerial practice. Its primary goal is the integration of theological and anthropological understandings in the context of responsible engagement of ministry. All candidates are expected to be engaged in some acceptable form of ministerial practice. Candidates for the degree are required to complete a minimum of 30 credit hours at the B level or higher approved by the Doctoral Committee. Students must also satisfactorily participate in a two-semester doctoral colloquy.

Special Programs

The School's Urban Institute for Religious Studies offers a nondegree certificate program for clergy and lay persons serving an urban inner-city constituency who seek to strengthen their basic ministerial skills and theological understandings.

Oblate College
391 Michigan Avenue, N.E.
Washington, DC 20017   (202) 529-6544

Administration. Francis Hassett, O.M.I., Chancellor; J. Chester Schwab, O.M.I., President, Donald Dietz, O.M.I., Academic Dean.

General Description. Oblate College was founded in Washington, D.C. in 1916 by the Eastern Province of the Oblates of Mary Immaculate. It is located in the northeast section of the city across the street from the Catholic University of America and the National Shrine of the Immaculate Conception. The mission of the school is the formation and training of future ministers, especially priests, as apostles in the mission of the church. Since opening in Washington, D.C. over 75 years ago Oblate College has educated more than 600 priests. Its graduates have served in Africa, Latin America, Asia, Oceania, as well as in Canada and the United States.

Community Environment. See: Catholic University of America.

Religious Denomination. Roman Catholic.

Accreditation. Middle States Association of Colleges and Schools; Association of Theological Schools in the United States and Canada.

Term System. Semester; no summer term.

Enrollment in Degree Programs in Religion 1984–85. Total 41; men 39, women 2.

Degrees in Religion Awarded 1984–85. Master of Arts 4; men 4. Master of Divinity 6; men 6.

Faculty for Degree Programs in Religion. Total 10; full-time 7, part-time 3.

Admission Requirements. Bachelor of Arts degree; 14 credits in Philosophy; letter of recommendation; personal interview.

Tuition and Fees. Tuition $1,250 per semester; fees $75 per semester.

Financial Aid. Students must make application for financial aid.

Housing. Limited housing for priesthood candidates.

Library Facilities. In 1983, De Sales School of Theology and Oblate College merged their libraries and formed the Oblates' Theology Library. It contains more than 60,000 volumes. The fifteen libraries of the member institutions of the Washington Theological Consortium are open for use by the students and faculty. The combined collections total over 900,000 volumes.

Religious Services/Activities. Roman Catholic services are held on a limited basis.

Degree Programs

The Master of Arts in Theology program aims to help people develop within a mission perspective their theological abilities for ministry in the Catholic community through a deepened understanding of the church's theological tradition: sacred scriptures, the church fathers and doctors, official ecclesial documents. The program requires forty-eight theology credits, twenty-four of which are specified.

The Master of Divinity degree program aims to help prepare ministers for people following Jesus today in the Catholic community and way. It emphasizes pastoral action and thought both theological and philosophical. The program requires seventy-six theology credits, thirty of which are specified. In addition to the courses, a qualifying project is needed.

Special Programs

The Bachelor of Arts in Philosophy degree is possible for students entering the 5-year program who do not have an undergraduate degree. The degree can be obtained at the end of two years (normally 60 liberal arts credits).

Trinity College
Department of Theology
125 Michigan Avenue, N.E.
Washington, DC 20017   (202) 939-5000

Administration. Dr. Donna M. Jurick, President.

General Description. Because Trinity is a Catholic College, theology is essential to its identity and curriculum. The Department's main purpose is to provide students with an intellectual appreciation of the Christian tradition and way of life. Courses have been constructed to introduce students to the major methodologies and areas of the discipline and to theological responses to the most significant contemporary questions. In addition to developing the ability for critical thinking and effective expression within the theological discipline, the Department is also concerned with acquainting students both with the interrelatedness of theology and the other liberal arts and with the role of faith commitment in the achievement of a meaningful life for the individual and society. The major in Theology leads to the Bachelor of Arts degree.

Parent Institution. Trinity College is the oldest Catholic women's college founded as such in the United States. It was established in 1897 by the Sisters of Notre Dame de Namur, a religious community founded by Julie Billiart in early nineteenth-century France. As a Catholic college, Trinity is committed to providing Catholic students with the opportunity to continue their spiritual growth and to develop a sound intellectual support for their faith.

Community Environment. The 34-acre campus is located on Michigan Avenue, 2½ miles north of the United States Capitol building.

Religious Denomination. Roman Catholic.

Accreditation. Middle States Association of Colleges and Schools.

Term System. Semester.

Admission Requirements. Graduation from high school with completion of 16 academic units; SAT or ACT.

Tuition and Fees. Tuition $6,825 per year; room and board $4,325; matriculation fee $25; student activity fee $100.

Financial Aid. Except for a small number of limited scholarships given solely on the basis of academic merit, financial aid is awarded according to financial need.

Housing. Dormitory accommodations are available on campus.

Library Facilities. The Sister Helen Sheehan Library houses a collection of approximately 160,000 volumes on open shelves. The Rare Book Room houses a collection which includes incunabula, fine bindings, and first editions.

Religious Services/Activities. Programs sponsored by Campus Ministry include justice education, community service, volunteer experiences in Appalachia, womens' programs, liturgy and prayer, peer ministry, counseling, and retreats.

Degree Programs

The major in Theology requires 36 credits. No specific distribution of courses is required but consultation with the Department in planning one's program is essential. The Bachelor of Arts degree requires the completion of a minimum of 128 semester hours.

Special Programs

The College offers a program to prepare lay women volunteers of the Archdiocese of Washington for the kinds of parish work which require background in theology and scripture. The program is called Education for Parish Service and involves two days a week for two academic years, leading to a Certificate for Parish Service.

The Department offers professional certificate programs in Pastoral Ministry and Educational Ministry. These programs utilize the lectures given for the Educa-

tion for Parish Service program but also require related seminars.

Washington Theological Consortium
487 Michigan Avenue, North East
Washington, DC 20017   (202) 832-2675

Administration. Reverend Daniel F. Martensen, Ph.D., Director; Eileen R. Griffin, Administrative Assistant.

General Description. The Washington Theological Consortium is an association of theological schools in the Washington area. The Consortium is intended to make possible greater cooperation on an ecumenical basis in theological education, and to take advantage of the resources of the Washington metropolitan area in preparing men and women for ministry. Students in any member school of the Consortium are permitted to take courses for credit in any other member school. In addition, there are opportunities for exchanges of faculty for particular courses and for participation in Consortium seminars led by a faculty team representing two or more member schools.

Most of the members of the Consortium have adopted an academic policy by which each student is required to elect at least one course "in another tradition" or in a Consortium seminar during his or her academic career. Recognizing that a chief obstacle to the implementation of the requirement is the geographical dispersion of the schools, an attempt has been made to offer "exchange" courses on only one day of the week, especially Thursday, "Consortium Day." Over 200 courses are offered in this once-a-week format. In addition, each school has agreed to offer at least one course a semester on the campus of another school, with which it is paired that semester. Open cross registration in over 350 other courses offered each semester is maintained.

The Washington Institute of Ecumenics was founded by action of the Board of Trustees of the Washington Theological Consortium to promote the unity of the Church and the unity of humankind by encouraging and facilitating research and study in the field of ecumenics. In carrying out its work, the Institute serves the ecumenical goals of Christian world communions, national church bodies, ecumenical organizations, and theological schools. It works cooperatively wherever possible. The Institute is affiliated with the Washington Theological consortium and offers courses for its members.

Members of the Consortium are: Catholic University of America, School of Religious Studies; The Cluster of Independent Theological Schools (De Sales School of Theology; Dominican House of Studies; Oblate College); Protestant Episcopal Theological Seminary in Virginia; Howard University Divinity School; Washington Theological Union (Augustinian College; Capuchin College; Holy Name College; Holy Trinity Mission; Whitefriars Hall); Wesley Theological Seminary; Lutheran Theological Seminary at Gettysburg; St. Paul's College (Associate).

Wesley Theological Seminary
4500 Massachusetts Avenue, N.W.
Washington, DC 20016   (202) 885-8600

Administration. Dr. G. Douglas Lewis, President; Dr. Marjorie Suchocki, Dean.

General Description. Wesley Theological Seminary is a free-standing (as distinct from those seminaries which are divisions of a larger university), graduate, professional school dedicated to the preparation of men and women for ordained and lay forms of ministry. A seminary of the United Methodist Church and a member of the Washington Theological Consortium, Wesley Seminary is committed to a form of theological education both loyal to its denominational heritage and supportive of the ecumenical movement toward a united church. The Seminary offers the degrees Master of Divinity, Master of Religious Education, Master of Theological Studies, and Doctor of Ministry. Through its Center for the Arts and Religion, Lay Resource Center, and Institute of Urban Ministry, it reaches into and creatively serves the Washington, D.C. community. Its National Capital Semester for Seminarians provides students from seminaries around the world an opportunity to experience at first-hand the political realities of our nation.

Community Environment. See: Catholic University of America.

Religious Denomination. United Methodist.

Accreditation. Middle States Association of Colleges and Schools; Association of Theological Schools in the United States and Canada.

Term System. Semester; summer term.

Enrollment in Degree Programs in Religion 1984–85. Total 412; men 225, women 187.

Degrees in Religion Awarded 1984–85. Master of Divinity 54; men 38, women 16. Master of Religious Education 5; men 1, women 4. Master of Theological Studies 11; men 7, women 4. Doctor of Ministry 12; men 9, women 3.

Faculty for Degree Programs in Religion. Total 36; full-time 24, part-time 12.

Admission Requirements. For Master's degree programs, applicants must hold the Bachelor of Arts or equivalent from a regionally accredited college or university, and must present recommendation from appropriate denominational official. Undergraduate grade average must be at least 2.70 on a 4.00 scale. Doctor of Ministry applicants must hold a Master of Divinity degree from an ATS-accredited seminary, and must be at least two years post-Master of Divinity.

Tuition and Fees. Master's: $132 per semester hour; Doctor of Ministry: $135 per semester hour; dormitory rates range from $440 (double occupancy) to $590 (sin-

gle); apartment rental ranges from $215 to $300.

Financial Aid. Available on demonstrated need to students in the Master of Divinity and Master of Religious Education degree programs.

Housing. Dormitory accommodations for unmarried students; 42 apartments available for married students. Many students have housing provided by the church they serve while in seminary.

Library Facilities. The Library has a collection of 110,000 volumes and subscriptions to more than 500 periodicals, in addition to study space and research facilities. It also houses special collections of Methodistica and Wesleyana.

Religious Services/Activities. Chapel services are held regularly on Tuesday and Friday mornings. One spiritual life retreat is held yearly in the Spring.

Degree Programs

The Master of Divinity degree prepares persons for the practice of Christian ministry. Most candidates for this degree seek to become qualified for ordination, and the degree is designed in part to meet the basic ordination requirements of most Christian denominations. Students must successfully complete 90 semester hours of course work in the regular curriculum, including a senior thesis and supervised field education.

The Master of Religious Education degree serves primarily to prepare for professional service in the church persons who wish their emphasis in ministry to be education. Within this broad framework, possibilities for particular emphases exist: Parish Educational Ministries, Diaconal Ministry, and Mission Service. Students must successfully complete 60 semester hours of course work.

The Master of Theological Studies degree is offered as a means of pursuing one or more of the following goals: developing the general understanding which all persons need as the religious basis for their life and work, and which equips them for effective participation in the life and mission of the church; providing a background in the theological disciplines as a basis for further graduate study; offering multidisciplinary education for persons entering or engaged in other professions who wish to pursue those professions from the enlarged perspectives of a religious community. The degree requires sixty hours of course work, a thesis, and an oral examination.

The Doctor of Ministry program is designed for persons who are committed to pastoral ministry rather than for prospective teachers in higher education. It is for ministers of demonstrated ability, and proposes to enhance their effectiveness by means of an advanced-level curriculum which integrates the experiences of ministry with the academic resources of the Seminary. The program is of three years duration, with opportunity for specialization after the first year of study. The program requires successful completion of 30 semester hours of course work plus a project/thesis.

Special Programs

The National Capital Semester for Seminarians is available to students who have completed one year of a degree program in any ATS-accredited seminary. The Lay Resource Center offers noncredit courses for lay persons.

FLORIDA

Baptist Bible Institute

1306 College Drive
Graceville, FL 32440   (904) 263-3261

Administration. Joseph P. DuBose, Jr., President; Walter D. Draughon, Jr., Dean.

General Description. Baptist Bible Institute, founded in 1943, is affiliated with the Southern Baptist Convention, and offers four- and three-year theological programs as follows: Bachelors of Theology, Religious Education, Music, Ministry, and Ministry with Religious Education/Music; and Diplomas of Theology, Religious Education, Music Ministry, and Ministry with Religious Education/Music. The purpose of the Institute is to train adults to serve the pastoral, educational, music, evangelistic, youth, and mission ministries; to offer theological studies worthy of recognition of educational and Christian leaders; and to establish its students in Christian doctrines and to train them to represent these doctrines.

Community Environment. The campus of Baptist Bible Institute is located in Graceville, Florida, near the junction of the Alabama, Florida, and Georgia state lines. Graceville is 20 miles south of Dothan, Alabama; 23 miles northwest of Marianna, Florida, and 60 miles directly north of Panama City, Florida. With a population of approximately 3,000, Graceville is a thriving trade center characterized by a progressive community spirit, a considerable measure of culture and refinement, and well-developed community institutions.

Religious Denomination. Southern Baptist.

Religious Emphasis. Conservative.

Accreditation. Southern Association of Colleges and Schools.

Term System. Semester; 2 summer sessions.

Enrollment in Degree Programs in Religion 1984–85. Total 333; men 277, women 56. (Statistics as of fall 1984.)

Degrees in Religion Awarded 1984–85. Bachelor of Ministry in Biblical Studies 54; men 54. Bachelor of Ministry in Religious Education 9; men 3, women 6. Bachelor of Ministry in Church Music 8; men 4, women 4.

Faculty for Degree Programs in Religion. Total 26; full-time 13, part-time 13.

Admission Requirements. High school diploma or equivalent (non-high school graduates are admitted to a special program which leads to passing the high school equivalency examination and the development of academic skills to handle college work). Student must be 20 years of age.

Tuition and Fees. Tuition $30 per semester hour; fees $37 (registration, student activities, library, car registration, post office box. Non-Baptists tuition is $60 per semester hour; men's dormitory $2.75 per person per day; apartments for families $75 to $130 per month; mobile home space rental $25 per month; limited apartments for single women $60 to $90 per month.

Financial Aid. Programs available include Pell Grant, Supplemental Educational Opportunity Grant, College Work-Study, Guaranteed Student Loan, Parent Loans for Undergraduate Students, Florida Student Assistance Grant, Florida Academic Scholars Program, private loans, Veterans Assistance, outside-funded scholarships, Vocational Rehabilitative Assistance, and Institute funded loans and scholarships.

Housing. Housing available on-campus for student families and singles supplemented by Institute-owned mobile homes, housing in Graceville and nearby towns, pastoriums furnished by churches served, and trailer space rented by the Institute to student mobile home owners.

Library Facilities. The Ida J. McMillan Library book collection contains 46,372 volumes. Currently 332 journals are received by the Library. A substantial collection of associational minutes and state convention annuals is maintained in addition to Southern Baptist Convention annuals. Current pamphlets and other general information are maintained in vertical files.

Religious Services/Activities. Chapel services are held four days per week. Student clubs meeting once per month include Theology Club, Christian Social Ministries Club, Religious Education Club, Music Guild, and Baptist Women/Baptist Young Women. Annual occasions include Spiritual Life Week and Denominational Awareness Conference.

Degree Programs

The Bachelor of Theology degree requires the completion of 130 semester hours including a general education core, specialized core, and electives. The Bachelor of Religious Education also requires 130 semester hours with a specialized core concentration in Religious Education and Psychology, a theological core, general education core, and electives. The Bachelor of Music Ministry degree requires 130 semester hours with a specialized core concentration of an applied major/applied minor or applied major/conducting minor or conducting major/applied minor plus the theological core, general education core, and electives. The Bachelor of Ministry degree with Religious Education/Music requires 130 semester hours with a specialized core concentration in Religious Education and Music, the theological core, general education core, and electives.

Special Programs

Diploma program in Theology, Religious Education, Music Ministry, and Ministry with Religious/Education/Music are also available. Each program requires the completion of 98 semester hours.

Bethune-Cookman College
Area of Religion and Philosophy
640 Second Avenue
Daytona Beach, FL 32015   (905) 255-1401

Administration. Dr. Oswald P. Bronson, President; Dr. Cleo S. Higgins, Vice President for Academic Affairs, Dean of Faculty.

General Description. The Area of Religion and Philosophy of Bethune-Cookman College offers the Bachelor of Arts degree in Religion and Philosophy combined, with a greater interest on religion. Courses are offered in Bible, religions of the world, philosophy of religion, and contemporary religious concerns. In philosophy, courses are offered in the history of philosophy and ethics. This major is designed for students who wish to enter the ministry directly or continue their theological training in seminary. The major in religious education is designed for students who wish to qualify as full-time religious workers such as directors of church schools, directors of youth work, and other religious programs.

Parent Institution. Bethune-Cookman College is a four-year, liberal arts college with emphasis on career preparation. It is owned by the Board of Higher Education of the United Methodist Church. It is a historically Black college which was founded in 1904 as a normal school for girls by Mary McLeod Bethune. Today 28 different majors are offered. The mission of the College is to serve in the Christian tradition the educational and self-developmental needs of its students who reflect the demographic, socio-economic, and educational diversity found in the

state of Florida. However, there are students from over 30 states and several foreign countries. There is a strong emphasis on scientific research in the science division.

Community Environment. Daytona Beach is a resort area located on the Atlantic Ocean, with a subtropical climate. All modes of transportation serve the area. The community facilities include 2 libraries, 2 museums, many churches, 1 hospital, and the usual major civic organizations. Part-time employment opportunities are limited. Recreational activities include all the water sports, stock car racing, and archery. Beach drivers almost outnumber swimmers. Special events include the Antique Car Meet and car racing known as Speed Weeks.

Religious Denomination. United Methodist.

Religious Emphasis. Orthodox/Liberal.

Accreditation. Southern Association of Colleges and Schools.

Term System. Semester; summer term.

Enrollment in Degree Programs in Religion 1984–85. Total 14; men 13, women 1.

Degrees in Religion Awarded 1984–85. Bachelor of Arts in Religion and Philosophy 3; men 3.

Faculty for Degree Programs in Religion. Total 4; full-time 3, part-time 1.

Admission Requirements. High school diploma with a C average; recommendations from minister, principal, and others.

Tuition and Fees. $6,000 per year, includes dormitory housing.

Financial Aid. Available to all who qualify for Basic Education Opportunity Grants, State aid; work-study, and academic scholarships. The latter are for those scoring 3.5 or higher on a 4 point average in high school and college.

Housing. Dormitory housing is provided for both men and women. A cafeteria is available on campus capable of providing meals for all who wish them. No dormitories are available for married students.

Library Facilities. The Carl Southwick Swisher Library houses over 117,000 volumes. There is a Special Negro Selections containing books on the history, sociology, religion, etc. of the Negroes in Africa and America.

Religious Services/Activities. Religious services are the vespers each Sunday evening, general campus worship on Monday once a month, and a Religious Life Fellowships which meets twice a month to plan and carry out religious activities and projects. The Fellowship is interdenominational.

Degree Programs

The Bachelor of Arts in Religion and Philosophy and the Bachelor of Arts in Religious Education are offered. See General Description above.

Special Programs

A Ministers' Institute is conducted once each May or June for one week for adult continuing education for ministers in Florida. It is open to all denominations.

The College has five satellite programs in cities in Florida, with religion courses offered in all of them.

Clearwater Christian College
Division of Biblical Studies
3400 Gulf-to-Bay Boulevard
Clearwater, FL 33519   (813) 726-1153

Administration. Dr. Arthur E. Steele, President.

General Description. The Division of Biblical Studies offers majors in Bible, Biblical Literature, and English Bible. Each of these majors is designed to equip an individual with a thorough knowledge of God's Word and various related subjects including Ancient and Church History, Philosophy, Theology, Comparative Religions, and Cults.

Parent Institution. The purpose of Clearwater Christian College as an undergraduate institution is to assist in the academic and spiritual development of the personal character of students by providing a quality education in the arts and sciences, using an integrated understanding of the Bible to make judgments and establish priorities in the world around us. The first classes were held in 1966. The College grants the Associate of Science degree in two major areas of study and also in twelve major areas of study leading to the Bachelor of Arts and Bachelor of Science degrees.

Community Environment. The 50-acre campus is situated on Tampa Bay which is the eastern boundary of the city of Clearwater. The city is located halfway down the Florida peninsula on the Gulf of Mexico.

Religious Denomination. Nondenominational.

Religious Emphasis. Fundamentalist.

Accreditation. Southern Association of Colleges and Schools.

Term System. Semester.

Enrollment in Degree Programs in Religion 1984–85. Total 702.

Faculty for Degree Programs in Religion. Total 23.

Admission Requirements. High school graduation or equivalent; SAT or ACT.

Tuition and Fees. Tuition $1,100 per semester; room and board $1,200.

Financial Aid. The College makes available several federal, state, and college-funded financial aid programs to assist the needy Christian student.

Housing. Accommodations for students are provided on campus in separate men's and women's residence halls.

Library Facilities. The library houses over 40,000 volumes and receives 160 periodicals.

Religious Services/Activities. Students are required to attend and support one of the fundamental, Bible-believing churches in the area. Midweek prayer service is conducted on Wednesday evenings throughout the school year. Chapel services are held daily.

Degree Programs

The majors in Bible, Biblical Literature, and English Bible leading to the Bachelor degree require the completion of specified courses. The major in Bible requires two years of Greek and includes an emphasis on studies in the English Bible. The major is designed as preparation for seminary studies but has value as a terminal degree for some ministries. The major in Biblical Literature requires three years of Greek Studies with the third year composed of text studies in New Testament books. One semester of Elementary Hebrew is required and an optional second semester is offered. This program serves the student who desires a greater proficiency in New Testament Greek on the undergraduate level. The Biblical Literature major is also offered for pre-seminary preparation.

Florida Beacon Bible College
6900 142nd Avenue, North
Largo, FL 33541   (813) 531-4498

Administration. Dr. David E. Okerstrom, President.

General Description. Florida Beacon Bible College exists for the primary purpose of training Christian ministers and Christian workers who will witness and preach Jesus Christ to this generation. The College places the major emphasis of all programs upon the Bible and the preparation of the Christian worker. All degrees conferred by the College major are in Bible Theology. The curriculum is designed around the Core Program which lays the Biblical foundation for further study in specialized concentrations.

Parent Institution. The College traces its origins to 1947 when classes were started in the educational quarters of Faith Temple. The school was then known as St. Petersburg Bible Institute. In 1963, classes began on the new campus in Largo.

Community Environment. The 12-acre campus is located in Largo, near Clearwater, equidistant between Tampa and St. Petersburg. It is in the heart of Pinellas County, easily accessible by major highways.

Religious Denomination. Nondenominational.

Accreditation. Southern Accrediting Association of Bible Institutes and Bible Colleges.

Term System. Semester.

Faculty for Degree Programs in Religion. Total 16.

Admission Requirements. High school graduation or GED.

Tuition and Fees. Total approximate cost per school year $2,320.

Financial Aid. Financial aid is available as scholarships, federal and state aid, and student employment. The area surrounding the College has numerous opportunities for ministry.

Housing. Living accommodations are provided on campus for unmarried men and women.

Library Facilities. The Joel O. Stephens Library contains over 8,000 volumes.

Religious Services/Activities. The chapel and prayer and praise services are an important part of the College's program and students are required to attend. Students are expected to attend all regular Sunday services at the local campus assembly and to actively participate in the Church's ministries.

Degree Programs

The Core Program is the foundation upon which all degree programs are built. It is a comprehensive study of the Scriptures, Bible literature, doctrine, and other selected courses needed for advanced study in the specialized fields. Areas of concentration are offered in Bible Theology, Missions, Biblical Counseling, and Tele-Communications. The Bible Theology concentration is a pre-seminary or pastoral program. The Bachelor of Arts degree is awarded upon completion of all requirements and a total of 120 semester hours.

Special Programs

The School of Ministry is a one-year Certificate program conducted in the evening for working professional and nonprofessional believers desiring to establish ministry or seeking an indepth study of the Scriptures, and the working of the Holy Spirit.

Miami Christian College
2300 N.W. 135th Street
Miami, FL 33167   (305) 685-7431

Administration. Dr. George S. Pearson, President.

General Description. The mission of Miami Christian College is the educational development of its students through a balanced program of Biblical studies and general education. The program of the College is designed to give undergraduate studies leading to the associate and baccalaureate degrees in a variety of subject areas, but emphasizing the training for Christian service careers.

Parent Institution. The College was founded in 1949 as the Miami Bible Institute by Dr. Willis S. Garrett who recognized the need for a fundamental Bible school in the Miami Area. It became Miami Bible College in 1962 with the inauguration of a fourth year of study and the offering of a Bachelor of Arts degree in Biblical Education. While Miami Christian College is committed to a system of beliefs relative to the Christian faith, the school is not affiliated with any church or denominational group. The institution has served evangelical Protestants of many denominations since its founding.

Community Environment. The new campus of 16 acres was acquired in 1966 and has four buildings and an adjacent apartment complex. It is 20 minutes by car from downtown Miami and 30 minutes from Fort Lauderdale. The immediate area offers a wide variety of recreation and cultural experiences from water sports to opera.

Religious Denomination. Nondenominational (Christian).

Religious Emphasis. Evangelical.

Accreditation. Southern Association of Colleges and Schools (Candidate); American Association of Bible Colleges.

Term System. Semester.

Enrollment in Degree Programs in Religion 1984–85. Total 322; full-time 133, part-time 189.

Admission Requirements. Graduation from a recognized high school; upper half of graduating class.

Tuition and Fees. Tuition $1,550 per year; room $380 per semester; board $745 per semester.

Financial Aid. Those who lack adequate financial resources may receive assistance through scholarships, grants, loans, and employment.

Housing. All residence space is on campus or approved by the College.

Library Facilities. The library in Alice Hall contains over 31,000 volumes and a considerable number of audiovisual materials.

Religious Services/Activities. Daily chapel programs are required of all students. One day each semester is given entirely to prayer sessions, devotional thought, singing, and testimonies. These days of prayer supplement the regular weekly prayer meetings and dormitory prayers meetings. Four weeks are set aside each year for special lectureships. There is a Spiritual Emphasis Week, Missions Week, and the Staley Lectures.

Degree Programs

The Bachelor of Arts degree requires a minimum of 130 semester hours. The Core Curriculum is composed of four sets: Bible, Theology, Church Ministries/Missions, and General Education. Each student completes a major in Biblical Studies when the Core Curriculum is completed. A student may complete a major or a minor in another area. These include Biblical Languages; Biblical Studies (Biblical Studies with Pre-Seminary Program, Bible Education); Christian Service; Church Ministries (Church Education, Specialized Youth Leadership, Pastoral Ministries emphases); Communications; Education; General Education; Missions; Music (Music/Church Ministries, Music Education); Physical Education; and Psychology and Counseling.

Special Programs

In cooperation with Florida International University, the College offers the Associate in Arts degree.

A One-Year Bible Certificate Program requires the completion of 30 semester hours, including specified courses.

New College
Humanities Division
5700 North Tamiami Trail
Sarasota, FL 33580   (813) 355-7671

Administration. Dr. John Lott Brown, President of the University of South Florida; Dr. Gregory M. St. L. O'Brien, Provost of the University; Dr. Robert R. Benedetti, Provost of New College; Dr. James G. Moseley, Chairman, Division of Humanities, New College.

General Description. At New College, Religion is an area of concentration (major) in the Division of Humanities. Since religion is an aspect of human life, several disciplinary perspectives are required for investigating the nature and role of religion in various areas of life. At New College the study of Religion involves at least the following: conceptual approaches (theology, ethics, philosophy), psychological approaches, sociological approaches, textual interpretation, and historical interpretation. The perspectives are employed to analyze religious phenomena in both western and non-western traditions.

Parent Institution. The philosophy of New College is both old and new. It took its name from an Oxford College, and its style of education brings together the English tutorial system and the German seminar. With the great universities of the past, it shares a commitment to the liberal arts and sciences and to the student's participation in his/her own education.

In 1960, with assistance from the national Congregational and Christian Church, local civic leaders created the framework for a small liberal arts college entitled New College. The College grew, and in 1974 became affiliated with the University of South Florida which maintains its Sarasota Branch on the New College campus.

Community Environment. Surrounding New College are two thriving communities, Sarasota and Bradenton, which attract people from all parts of the nation and the world. Visitors are drawn to the area by its pleasant weather, its location on the Gulf of Mexico, and its cultural life.

Religious Denomination. Nondenominational.

Accreditation. Southern Association of College and Schools.

Term System. Semester; no summer term.

Enrollment in Degree Programs in Religion 1984–85. Total 10; men 5, women 5.

Degrees in Religion Awarded 1984–85. Bachelor of Arts 4; men 2, women 2.

Faculty for Degree Programs in Religion. Total 3; full-time 2, part-time 1.

Admission Requirements. The candidacy of each applicant for admission is assessed on an individual basis, without reference to any quota, cut-off points, or formulas. The Admissions Office asks for a number of items in support of the application: two academic recommendations; high school transcripts; SAT or ACT scores; and personal interview.

Tuition and Fees. Tuition 1st semester resident $591.20, nonresident $1,611.20; health fee $16 per semester; housing semester I $630; semester II (includes interterm) $810.

Financial Aid. In general, financial aid refers to grants, loans, and work programs that are distributed to students on the basis of financial need. Scholarships and other merit based awards are generally handled through the Admissions Office for new students, and through the Office of Assistant Provost for continuing students.

Housing. Residence halls at New College differ from those at most colleges in that all rooms have private entrances. Students are assigned two to a room with a private bath, carpeting, and limited maid service. New students are required to live in residence halls on campus. The residency is optional thereafter.

Library Facilities. The campus Library houses over 160,000 volumes and more than 20,000 microforms.

Religious Services/Activities. The Ecumenical Board for Campus Ministry, supported by the efforts and funding of thirty-two local churches and denominational groups, provides a Campus Minister for New College, as well as for students in the University Program and the nearby Ringling School of Art and Design. The Campus Minister is an integral part of the campus counseling services and participates as a member of the Student Affairs Staff. Activities, in addition to pastoral counseling, have included special films, guest speakers, Bible study, ecumenical retreats, and traditional pastoral programs.

Degree Programs

The Bachelor of Arts with a major in Religion program involves an investigation of the role of religion in various areas of life and requires an interdisciplinary perspective. It entails textual and historical interpretation and employs these perspectives to analyze phenomena in both Western and non-Western traditions. A majoring student must take an introductory course in religion as well as in the Bible and must become versed in the history of Western theology, and also do work in a non-Western religious tradition. The student must do advanced coursework, tutorials, or an independent study project in one conceptual area (theology, ethics, philosophy).

Rollins College
Department of Philosophy and Religion
Winter Park, FL 32789   (305) 646-2139

Administration. Dr. Thaddeus Seymour, President; Dr. Daniel DeNicola, Vice President for Academic Affairs, Provost, and Dean of the Faculty; Dr. Sara Ann Ketchum, Head, Department of Philosophy and Religion.

General Description. A major in Religious Studies requires work in 3 religious traditions in some depth in addition to comparative studies. A minor requires study of 2 religious traditions as well as comparative studies.

The curriculum emphasizes primary sacred texts, and the capstone to study is a thesis for the major and an independent study project for the minor.

Parent Institution. Rollins College is a 4-year accredited liberal arts college offering the A.B. degree. Language offerings include Greek, Hebrew, and Latin.

Community Environment. Rollins College is located in Winter Park, Florida, an attractive residential community adjacent to the city of Orlando. Fifty miles from the Atlantic Ocean and 70 miles from the Gulf of Mexico, the 65-acre campus is bounded by Lake Virginia to the east and south. A traditional Spanish-Mediterranean architecture characterizes the College's facilities.

Religious Denomination. Nondenominational.

Religious Emphasis. Interfaith and interdenominational.

Accreditation. Southern Association of Colleges and Schools.

Term System. Four-one-four; summer term in the Division of Continuing Education.

Faculty for Degree Programs in Religion. Total 4; full-time 2, part-time 2.

Admission Requirements. Rollins seeks students who have pursued a demanding high school curriculum in preparation for college entrance. The minimum requirements for admission include the following courses: four years of English, two years of history or social studies, two years of a laboratory science, and three years of mathematics, including Algebra I, Geometry, and Algebra II; two years of a foreign language are also strongly recommended.

Tuition and Fees. Comprehensive fee $9,976 which includes tuition, room, board, and fees.

Financial Aid. Available upon evaluation of financial aid form. Funds are provided by the College as well as federal and state sources. Student aid consists of scholarships, grants, loans, and employment.

Housing. Most Rollins students live in one of the twenty residence halls on campus.

Library Facilities. The Rollins Library houses 216,119 volumes. There are over 18,000 volumes in special collections: Whitman Collection, Jessie B. Rittenhouse Poetry Collection, Benjamin Franklin Collection, Constance Fennimore Woolson Collection, Nehrling Collection (botany), Mead Collection (botany), Florida Collection, Hispanic Collection, and Government Documents.

Religious Services/Activities. The nurture of the religious life in the Rollins community is the mission of Knowles Memorial Chapel and the United Campus Ministries, the work of both being coordinated by the Dean of the Chapel. The character and programs of the Chapel are interdenominational, seeking both to serve and support persons in a variety of faith-traditions and to emphasize conviction and commitments they share with one another. Jewish candlelighting, Roman Catholic mass, and Protestant interdenominational services are held weekly. Spiritual growth groups, retreat weekends, and other programs

are held seasonally.

Degree Programs

The Bachelor of Arts with a major in Philosophy/Religion is conferred upon the successful completion of required and elective courses. The major deals with the basic principles and concepts and provides a broad, integrated, and analytical grasp of the liberal arts. Students at Rollins may also minor in Philosophy/Religion or Religion.

Special Programs

The Division of Continuing Education offers eight courses in Religion including Hebrew.

St. John Vianney College Seminary
2900 South West 87th Avenue
Miami, FL 33165   (305) 223-4561

Administration. Rev. Robert N. Lynch, Rector/President; Rev. Barnard Kirlin, Vice-Rector; Rev. Stephen P. Trzecieski, C.M., Director of Pre-Theology.

General Description. St. John Vianney College Seminary is a four-year college of basic liberal arts, with a major in Philosophy. It is bilingual, multicultural, with all programs offered in both Spanish and English. Its primary goal is to provide an undergraduate education preparatory for those students whose stated objective in life is to serve the Catholic Church in the Priesthood. It also assumes responsibility for the spiritual and intellectual formation of these seminarians within an Anglo-Hispanic setting. It is also committed to establishing ancillary education services for the lay ministries.

Community Environment. St. John Vianney College Seminary is located in metropolitan Dade County, Florida, only minutes from the international city of Miami. With a metropolitan area population of several million people, Miami sits at the threshold of all of Latin America and the Caribbean. Economically, Miami is very much tied to the progress of peoples throughout the Caribbean and South America.

Religious Denomination. Roman Catholic.

Accreditation. Southern Association of Colleges and Schools.

Term System. Semester.

Admission Requirements. Minimum of high school graduation; SAT; personal interview; recommendations; referral by the Bishop of the student's Diocese.

Tuition and Fees. Tuition, room and board $4,750; fees $100.

Financial Aid. Pell Grant, Supplemental Educationaal Opportunity Grant, Guaranteed Student Loan, Florida Student Assistance Grant, Knights of Columbus Seminarian Loans, Parents Loans for Undergraduate Students, Diocesan Assistance.

Housing. All housing is on campus.

Library Facilities. The library houses 44,321 volumes

and subscribes to 161 periodicals. There is a Philosophical Collection in Spanish as well as in English.

Religious Services/Activities. Roman Catholic services at daily chapel; weekends of recollection four times yearly; yearly retreats; and numerous other opportunities. Spiritual direction is provided on an individual basis for all students.

Degree Programs

The undergraduate program leads to a baccalaureate degree in Philosophy and requires a total of 128 hours of which 38 hours are in philosophy. Each student must acquire as much proficiency in his alternate language (Spanish/English) as possible.

Special Programs

A one-year special program in pre-theology is provided for students who have completed their baccalaureate degrees in a non-seminary college or university. The year's study provides immersion in philosophy and some religious instruction.

St. Leo College
Division of Philosophy and Theology
Box 2158
St. Leo, FL 33574   (904) 588-8288

Administration. L. Tyson Anderson, Ph.D., Chairman, Division of Philosophy and Theology.

General Description. The Division of Philosophy and Theology at St. Leo College offers a Bachelor of Arts degree with a concentration in Religious Education or Religious Studies. The degree in Religious Education is a state of Florida approved teacher education program and the student completing this program will be certified on the secondary level. The degree in Religious Studies is designed as a preparation for graduate study in Theology. Graduates in this area also become Directors of Religious Education for a parish. Other graduates enter major seminaries in preparation for the priesthood.

Parent Institution. St. Leo College is a Catholic, liberal arts college. It was founded in 1956 as a junior college and adopted a four-year program in 1963. The campus is situated on 150 acres of rolling hill country near Lake Jovita.

Community Environment. The city of St. Leo is located 35 miles northeast of Tampa and 5 miles from Dade City. The area has a semi-tropical climate.

Religious Denomination. Roman Catholic.

Accreditation. Southern Association of Colleges and Schools.

Term System. Semester; 3 summer sessions.

Enrollment in Degree Programs in Religion 1984–85. Total 9; men 6, women 3.

Degrees in Religion Awarded 1984–85. Bachelor of Arts in Religious Education 2; women 2. Bachelor of Arts in Religious Studies 2; men 2.

Faculty for Degree Programs in Religion. Total 9; full-time 5, part-time 4.

Admission Requirements. High school diploma or equivalent.

Tuition and Fees. $4,740 per year; fees (including dormitory fee) $1,270 per year.

Financial Aid. There are a number of scholarships specifically for Religious Education/Religious Studies concentrators: honor scholarships $1,000 per year; Intercommunity Forum Scholarship; Father George Paulson Theology Endowment Fund of various amounts; Religious Education/Religious Studies Scholarship Fund of various amounts.

Housing. Dormitory facilities available.

Library Facilities. The library houses over 85,000 volumes.

Religious Services/Activities. Chaplain's office; daily liturgy; daily monastic prayers.

Degree Programs

The Bachelor of Arts degree program with a Religious Education concentration requires 45 credits in basic studies, 13 in foundation courses, 27 in professional education courses, 30 in theology courses, plus electives and physical education, for a total of 124 credits. The concentration in Religious Studies requires 45 credits in basic studies, 15 in the theology core, 15 in theology electives, plus 45 in electives and 4 in physical education for a total of 124 credits.

Special Programs

St. Leo College offers an external degree program in Religious Studies through Educational Services. This program may also serve as preparation for the Permanent Diaconate as well as various lay ministries.

St. Vincent de Paul Regional Seminary
School of Theology
10701 South Military Trail
P.O. Box 460
Boynton Beach, FL 33436   (305) 732-4424

Administration. Very Rev. Felipe Estevez, President/Rector; Rev. Thomas Foudy, Vice Rector; Rev. James Murtagh, Academic Dean.

General Description. The primary purpose of St. Vincent de Paul Regional Seminary is to provide a spiritual, intellectual, and cultural program designed to educate and train candidates for the Roman Catholic Priesthood. Its geographical position justifies its two-fold orientation to offer bilingual, multicultural programs in a professional school of theology. St. Vincent's is 800 miles from the nearest major Catholic seminary to the west and more than 1,000 miles south from the nearest northern major Catholic seminary. It looks out to the Bahamas off the east coast, and, standing at the gateway to Latin America, overlooks the Caribbean off the southeast coast. It also serves as a center for continuing education of the clergy, religious, and laity. Thus, qualified non-seminarian students may enroll in the theological courses and may seek the appropriate degrees.

Community Environment. The 160-acre campus of St. Vincent de Paul is located 4 miles from the city of Boynton Beach, Florida, convenient to the Delray Beach exit of the Sunshine State Parkway, the Boynton Beach exit of Interstate 95, and the Palm Beach International Airport. The Seminary complex, which is relatively new, consists of 9 buildings in a modern Spanish-mission style. The degrees Master of Divinity, Master of Arts, and Master of Theology are granted.

Religious Denomination. Roman Catholic.

Accreditation. Southern Association of Colleges and Schools; Association of Theological Schools in the United States and Canada (Associate Member).

Term System. Semester.

Enrollment in Degree Programs in Religion 1984–85. Total 103; men 90, women 13.

Degrees in Religion Awarded 1984–85. Master of Arts 11; men 10, women 1. Master of Divinity 5; men 5.

Faculty for Degree Programs in Religion. Total 20; full-time 17, part-time 3.

Admission Requirements. Bachelor's degree from an accredited college or university or the equivalent of that level of educational achievement; minimum 18 hours in Philosophy and 12 hours of Religious Studies or its equivalent.

Tuition and Fees. $2,625 per semester.

Financial Aid. Federal government student loans; Veterans Administration.

Housing. The students' residence and wings house one hundred fifty seminarians.

Library Facilities. The Seminary library contains over 60,000 volumes.

Religious Services/Activities. The spiritual formation program is designed in accord with the *Vatican II Decree on Priestly Formation, No. 8.*

Degree Programs

The first professional degree program offered in the School of Theology is a three-year course of studies leading to the degree of Master of Divinity. The goals and objectives of the program are to provide an education for the Christian ministry that will integrate the traditional academic and theological disciplines with a field education in the skills of pastoral ministry to the end that the student will have acquired special professional competency and identity in the pastoral ministry. The degree requirements include the completion of 82 semester hours of theological and related studies of which 5 semester hours are in field education seminars and 2 semester hours in a comprehensive seminar. A minimum of 2.0 grade point average is required in all Biblical and theological courses taken. A written comprehensive examination is given in Biblical and theological studies plus an oral comprehensive examination in all areas studied in the program.

The Master of Arts degree offers a graduate program of theology designed to meet particular needs and specialized areas. The program seeks to serve the individual needs of students who wish to be accredited teachers of theology in academic institutions and parochial programs of religious education. It is available to Sisters, Deacons, and all those involved in lay ministry, as well as those who seek to deepen and enrich their own theological understanding of the areas offered. Three areas of concentration are offered: Biblical Studies, Systematic Theology, and Moral/Spiritual Theology. The degree requires 24 credit hours in an area of concentration, 18 hours from the other two areas divided as equally as possible, 6 credit hours in two comprehensive seminars in area of concentration, cumulative grade point average of 3.0 on a 4.0 scale, and a comprehensive examination in the area of concentration.

GEORGIA

Atlanta Christian College

2605 Ben Hill Road
East Point, GA 30344   (404) 761-8861

Administration. Dr. James C. Donovan, President.

General Description. Atlanta Christian College provides for men and women college-level education in the areas of general, Biblical, and practical studies. It is affiliated with the Christian Churches and Churches of Christ. The educational program of the College is in harmony with the faith and practice of these churches. Most of the financial support for the College comes from congregations and individuals who belong to this fellowship. While the majority of students also come from this fellowship, the student body includes people who are members of other churches. Founded in 1928, The College grants the Bachelor of Arts and Bachelor of Science degrees.

Community Environment. The campus is located in the suburban area of East Point, Georgia, 7 miles from downtown Atlanta.

Religious Denomination. Christian Churches and Churches of Christ.

Accreditation. American Association of Bible Colleges.

Term System. Semester.

Enrollment in Degree Programs in Religion 1984–85. Total 164; full-time 125, part-time 39.

Faculty for Degree Programs in Religion. Total 16.

Admission Requirements. High school diploma or its equivalent; SAT or ACT; evidence of genuine Christian faith.

Tuition and Fees. Tuition: $1,560 per year; room and board $1,600; fees $170.

Financial Aid. The College makes numerous financial aid programs available to students. An eligible student may be involved in one or more of these programs.

Housing. All single students are required to live in college housing.

Library Facilities. The John A. Burns Memorial Library houses over 43,000 bound volumes besides tracts, magazines, and more than 12,000 microforms.

Religious Services/Activities. The College family worships together twice a week in chapel. Students meet week-

ly for prayer and singing. Small-group gatherings in dormitories provide an opportunity for sharing needs together. While the entire program of education is service-oriented, specific involvement in Christian service is required of all full-time students.

Degree Programs

All students are required to complete the appropriate core curriculum, a major in Bible, and a minor in their chosen field(s) of practical education. Practical fields of study are Christian Ministries, Christian Education, Music, and Missions. Most of the degree programs are terminal in nature and designed to prepare the student for a life of service in a church-related field. All programs are designed to give students a knowledge of the Bible and theology. The Bachelor of Arts degree and the Bachelor of Science degree require a minimum of 128 to 130 semester hours.

Atlanta Theological Association
c/o Columbia Theological Seminary

Box 520
Decatur, GA 30031

General Description. The Atlanta Theological Association develops and coordinates the educational programs and resources of its member institutions which include approximately 800 students, 85 faculty, and a combined total of 600,000 volumes in the individual libraries. Among significant and promising cooperative endeavors are cross registration, sharing of faculty, library, and lectureship resources, interseminary courses, and experimental programs in various academic disciplines and professional specializations. Also available through the Association are the Georgia Association of Pastoral Care and the Urban Training Organization of Atlanta. Members of the Atlanta Theological Association are Candler School of Theology, Columbia Theological Seminary, Erskine Theological Seminary, and Interdenominational Theological Center. The members cooperate in awarding the degrees of Doctor of Sacred Theology and Doctor of

Ministry (In-Ministry).

Beulah Heights Bible College
892-906 Berne Street, S.E.
P.O. Box 18145
Atlanta, GA 30316   (404) 627-2681

Administration. Dr. Richard E. Edwards, President; Dr. James B. Keiller, Vice President and Dean.

General Description. Beulah Heights Bible College's purpose is to provide its students with the best in Biblical education in order to provide a quality training for young men and women for the Christian ministry. It was founded in 1918 by the Reverend Paul T. Barth, his wife, Dr. Hattie M. Barth, and her mother, Elizabeth A. Sexton as the Beulah Heights Bible Institute. The school has expanded through the years and in 1962, at a meeting of the General Conference of the International Pentecostal Assemblies, it was decided to change the name of the Institute to Beulah Heights College, Seminary, and Institute, thus establishing a four-year Bible College with the hopes of a graduate school in future years. It was the interest of the conference to establish a school of higher education where quality Christian Education could be achieved as well as spiritual training. The present name was adopted in 1972.

Community Environment. Atlanta, capital of Georgia, is the commercial, industrial, and financial giant of the southeast. It is located in the foothills of the Blue Ridge Mountains. Atlanta's moderate climate permits year-round golf, fishing, and outdoor living. All major forms of public transportation are available. The city is the cultural center of the south with her symphony, art center, and theaters. It is a major manufacturing and business center; excellent part-time employment opportunities are available.

Religious Denomination. International Pentecostal Church of Christ.

Religious Emphasis. Evangelical; Pentecostal.

Accreditation. Southern Accrediting Association of Bible Colleges.

Term System. Semester; summer term.

Enrollment in Degree Programs in Religion 1984-85. Total 114; men 79, women 35.

Degrees in Religion Awarded 1984-85. Bachelor of Arts in Biblical Education 8; men 6, women 2.

Faculty for Degree Programs in Religion. Total 8; full-time 5, part-time 3.

Admission Requirements. High school diploma or GED.

Tuition and Fees. Tuition $40 per semester hour; fees $15 per semester; room and board $700 per semester; cafeteria surcharge $50.

Financial Aid. Limited number of work-study scholarships and needy-student grants.

Housing. Single student dormitories; limited number of married student apartments on campus.

Library Facilities. The College library houses 16,883 volumes on open shelving.

Religious Services/Activities. Chapel is held three times per week. The Student Missionary Fellowship is an organization composed of the entire student body whose leaders keep the students informed of the needs of the mission fields throughout the world in order to promote missionary giving and to produce missionary minded men and women. The Christian Service Department provides a unique opportunity for students to develop Christian Leadership and Spiritual Ministry.

Degree Programs

The Bachelor of Arts in Biblical Education program requires the completion of 130 semester hours including the required general education core, the Biblical Education core (Bible, Old and New Testaments; General; Church History; Theology), and the Professional Education core of 29 semester hours.

Brewton-Parker College
Division of Christianity
College Avenue
Mount Vernon, GA 30445   (912) 583-2241

Administration. Scott Nash, Chairman, Division of Christianity.

General Description. The Division of Christianity consists of one Junior College program, the Associate of Arts in Christianity, and one Senior College program, the Bachelor of Ministry. The college provides a basic liberal arts core of study for all students along with an introduction into a major field of study.

Parent Institution. Brewton-Parker College is a coeducational Southern Baptist institution owned by the Georgia Baptist Convention. Primarily a junior college offering the Associate of Arts and the Associate of Science degrees, Brewton-Parker has in recent years also enabled students to earn a four-year bachelor's degree through an arrangement with Tift College, another Georgia Baptist institution. The Bachelor of Ministry degree is the only four-year degree offered by Brewton-Parker. The Associate in Divinity degree is no longer offered.

Community Environment. The College is located on a 137-acre campus. College buildings include residence halls, student center, library, and air-conditioned classrooms. Recreational facilities include a 5-acre lake, a fully equipped gymnasium, and lighted tennis courts. The campus is located partly in Aiely and partly in Mount Vernon, the county seat of Montgomery County. The two towns have a combined population of 2,000. The area has mild winters with adequate rainfall to support a variety of agricultural and forest products.

Religious Denomination. Southern Baptist.

Religious Emphasis. Enlightened Conservative.

Accreditation. Southern Association of Colleges and Schools.

Term System. Quarter; summer term.

Enrollment in Degree Programs in Religion 1984–85. Total 56; men 50, women 6.

Degrees in Religion Awarded 1984–85. Bachelor of Ministry 22; men 21, women 1. Associate in Divinity 6; men 5, women 1. Associate of Arts in Christianity 7; men 5, women 2.

Faculty for Degree Programs in Religion. Total 10; full-time 6, part-time 4.

Admission Requirements. Open admissions for Associate programs. The Bachelor of Ministry program requires an Associate degree or equivalent number of hours in prescribed areas prior to acceptance.

Tuition and Fees. $49 per credit hour; lab sciences require a $15 fee; room and board approximately $1,600 per year.

Financial Aid. Students are eleigible for federally-funded programs based on need, for Georgia State Equalization Grants, and for other special program grants. Christianity students may receive Georgia Baptist Foundation scholarships, Church Leadership scholarships, Ministerial Aid grants, and Bachelor of Ministry grants.

Housing. On-campus housing is available for single male and female students. Campus personnel assist in securing local housing for other students.

Library Facilities. The Brewton-Parker library houses 32,000 volumes. Special funds have been provided for the library for the Bachelor of Ministry program.

Religious Services/Activities. The College offers Baptist Student Union programs, Ministerial Association programs, weekly chapel, and quarterly Ministerial seminars on selected topics. Local Baptist Association meetings are held on campus. Chapel attendance is required.

Degree Programs

The Bachelor of Ministry degree program is offered through a cooperative agreement with Tift College. Students major in Pastoral Ministry, Music Ministry, Education Ministry, or Recreation Ministry.

Special Programs

The Associate of Arts in Christianity (the Associate in Divinity is no longer offered) is a two-year program designed for students intending to transfer to a senior college or university program. The requirements include the completion of a core curriculum plus special courses in the Division of Christianity.

Brewton-Parker College conducts off-campus centers throughout south Georgia and in area correctional institutions through which persons may obtain the Associate in Arts degree. The Bachelor of Ministry program conducts quarterly seminars for area ministers. The Crawley Institute is a summer program designed to assist area ministers and laity, especially in the Black churches, in acquiring basic communication and ministry skills.

Carver Bible Institute and College
437 Nelson Street, S.W.
Atlanta, GA 30313   (404) 524-0291

Administration. Dr. William Hungerpiller, President.

General Description. Carver Bible Institute was founded under a deep sense of need for such a school. At the time of World War II many had been wanting a Bible-believing school for the training of Negro Christians in the South. In 1942, Talmage and Grace Payne came home from China after 16 years of service with the China Inland Mission. The Paynes opened Carver Bible Institute in the fall of 1943 with 14 students. After 5 short years the newly-built Institute buildings were packed to capacity.

In the history of the Bible institute movement there has been a gradual upgrading of standards. Carver began as an evening school but 3 months later added a day school program. In 1964 it added a Bible college curriculum leading to the Bachelor of Arts degree in Bible. This is in addition to the 3-year institute rather than a replacement of it. An Associate of Arts degree has been designed for those students desiring studies in the Bible before pursuing another vocation. The Institute also grants the degree Bachelor of Theology, a five-year program, and the Certificate for those who do not find it possible to pursue a full-time course of study.

Community Environment. In 1952 the original Haynes Street buildings did not provide sufficient classroom space for the growing school, and so the Nelson Street campus was purchased and has become the main campus of Carver Bible Institute. In 1965 additional property was acquired; the total expanded facilities now include 14 buildings. A literature publishing business is connected with the Institute.

Religious Denomination. Nondenominational.

Religious Emphasis. Fundamentalist.

Accreditation. Southern Accrediting Association of Bible Institutes and Bible Colleges.

Term System. Semester; summer term.

Enrollment in Degree Programs in Religion 1984–85. Total 60; men 42, women 18.

Degrees in Religion Awarded 1984–85. Bachelor of Arts in Bible 3; men 3. Bachelor of Bible Education 3; men 3.

Faculty for Degree Programs in Religion. Total 14; full-time 6, part-time 8.

Admission Requirements. A candidate must be born again and be a high school graduate or equivalent.

Tuition and Fees. Tuition $1,360 per term; miscellaneous fees $197; room and board $2,074.

Financial Aid. A limited number of Work Scholarships and Tuition Scholarships are available.

Housing. Dormitories are available on campus for single students. There is some on-campus housing for married couples.

Library Facilities. The library contains approximately 12,000 volumes and has a tape library, Bible School materials, and periodicals.

Religious Services/Activities. Campus activities include the Christian Life Conference in the fall semester; Missionary Conference in the spring semester; and Youth Conference in the spring semester. There is an active Student Foreign Missions Fellowship chapter. Christian service is required weekly from each college student.

Degree Programs

Carver Bible College offers a five-year course leading to a Bachelor of Theology degree. A total of 160 semester hours of college work is required plus a thesis. Students who have earned two years of liberal arts credits in an approved college may earn the Bachelor of Theology degree at Carver by completing a total of 160 semester hours credit, including the credits from the liberal arts college, plus the thesis. Students who hold a Bachelor's degree from an approved college may also matriculate. A minimum of 30 semester hours in Bible study and 10 semester hours in Theology must be included in the total semester hour requirements of 160 hours for the degree. The thesis is also required.

The Bachelor of Arts degree in Bible requires a minimum of 130 semester hours with 30 semester hours in Bible study, 12 semester hours in theology, 9 semester hours in English, 6 semester hours in social studies, and 3 semester hours in education. All students must pass an oral and/or written exam given by the faculty in Bible, theology, and Christian living. The Bachelor of Bible Education is awarded when students elect the non-language curriculum.

Special Programs

The Associate of Arts course is a two-year full-time college course designed to give a solid Biblical foundation to those who will be working in another field. It meets approximately 17 hours a week for two years or may be completed in night school within three years. The total requirements for the course include a minimum of 65 semester hours with a minimum of 20 hours in Bible, 6 hours in theology, 3 hours in English, and 3 hours in social studies. All students must pass an oral and/or written examination.

The Bible Institute Course is a three-year, full-time course designed to give the high quality training necessary for pastoral and missionary ministries. The total requirements are 90 semester hours with a minimum of 30 semester hours in Bible study, 12 semester hours in Bible doctrine or systematic theology, and 6 semester hours in English. All students must pass an oral and/or written examination.

Columbia Theological Seminary
701 Columbia Drive
Box 520
Decatur, GA 30031   (404) 378-8821

Administration. Dr. J. Davidson Phillips, President; Dr. Oscar J. Hussel, Dean of Faculty.

General Description. Columbia Theological Seminary is an instrument of the Presbyterian Church (U.S.A.), and as such its programs are formed in relation to the mission of the Church. It is owned by the Synods of Florida, Mid-South, and Southwest, and is controlled by a Board of Dirtectors. The Seminary is a graduate professional school engaged in preparing men and women for Church leadership. Three basic commitments have marked and continue to mark Columbia Seminary's program: (1) Biblical Authority, (2) Doctrinal Fidelity, (3) Ecclesiastical Loyalty. The Seminary awards the degrees Master of Arts in Youth Ministry, Master of Divinity, Master of Arts in Theological Studies, Master of Theology, Doctor of Ministry, and Doctor of Sacred Theology.

Community Environment. The campus of the Columbia Theological Seminary contains 9 buildings on 60 acres. Decatur, Georgia, the home of the Seminary, is 6 miles from downtown Atlanta, and easily accessible to Columbia students. Atlanta offers numerous opportunities for personal contact with a variety of cultures for study. Decatur is 2 hours away from the mountains and 5 hours away from the Georgia coastline.

Religious Denomination. Presbyterian Church (U.S.A.).

Religious Emphasis. Reformed.

Accreditation. Southern Association of Colleges and Schools; Association of Theological Schools in the United States and Canada.

Term System. Four-one-four; summer term.

Enrollment in Degree Programs in Religion 1984–85. Total 422; men 343, women 79.

Degrees in Religion Awarded 1984–85. Master of Arts 2; men 1, women 1. Master of Divinity 30; men 25, women 5. Master of Theology 10; men 10. Doctor of Ministry 30; men 27, women 3. Doctor of Sacred Theology 1; men 1.

Faculty for Degree Programs in Religion. Total full-time 26; does not include visiting instructors or adjunct professors in supervised ministry.

Admission Requirements. Baccalaureate degree from an accredited college or university; GRE; endorsement of home church; interview required following submission of application.

Tuition and Fees. Tuition $100 per credit; room $400 per term; supervised ministry fees vary.

Financial Aid. Financial assistance is available to first professional degree students, and a limited number of graduate students based upon need.

Housing. Dormitory housing is available for unmarried students. Suites of two rooms with private bath are available for married students without children. One-, two-, and three-bedroom unfurnished apartments are available for married students with children.

Library Facilities. The library contains approximately 90,000 volumes.

Religious Services/Activities. Prayer before classes; chapel every class day; weekend retreats throughout the year.

Degree Programs

The Master of Divinity degree and the Doctor of Ministry degree are complementary programs. At the time of entering, seminary students are admitted to the first professional degree program which means either a three component program leading to the Master of Divinity degree or a four component program leading to the Doctor of Ministry degree. The first two components of both degrees involve a common program. Students pursuing the Master of Divinity degree move to a third component. Students qualifying for the Doctor of Ministry degree proceed to two further components, the first of which includes a twelve-month period of supervised ministry in an approved setting. The final, on-campus component involves, in addition to academic work, a series of seminars enabling the student to reflect on his or her period of supervised ministry and to complete a written dissertation.

The Master of Arts in Theological Studies provides systematic study of the Christian faith for people who are not preparing for ordination to professional ministry. It is designed for students who want to broaden and deepen their understanding of the faith so that they can be more knowledgeable and effective Christians as lay people in the Church and in their lay vocations, and for others who are preparing for further academic work in a theological discipline. The five areas of specialization available include Old Testament, New Testament, Church History, Theology, and Ethics.

The Master of Arts in Youth Ministry program equips persons for competent leadership in ministry with youth. The program is meant for persons who are not considering ordination but who want a broad background in theological studies with strong emphasis on the theory and practice of ministry with youth in congregational, camp, and para-parochial settings.

The Master of Theology degree is offered with specialization in pastoral counseling, pastoral supervision, Biblical studies, historical-doctrinal studies, and pastoral studies.

The Doctor of Ministry degree program is offered for the working minister and was established by the schools participating in the Atlanta Theological Association. The program has been designed to continue the education of persons for their practice of ministry in the church and in related institutional settings.

The Doctor of Sacred Theology in Pastoral Counseling is also offered through the Atlanta Theological Association. The program concentrates upon the counseling, guidance, and consultation aspects of the minister's professional function.

Special Programs

A summer travel seminar is sponsored by the Seminary and consists of a three-week study trip to Israel, Jordan, and Greece.

Emmanuel College
School of Christian Ministries
Spring Street
P.O. Box 129
Franklin Springs, GA 30639   (404) 245-9226

Administration. Dr. David R. Hopkins, President; G. Earl Beatty, Academic Dean, School of Christian Ministries.

General Description. The Emmanuel College School of Christian Ministries is a coeducational professional school sponsored by the Pentecostal Holiness Church. It exists for students who wish to receive quality education in the context of historical holiness and pentecostalism and the evangelical Christian faith as they prepare for Christian ministry and service. The School of Christian Ministries offers five terminal professional programs: a three-year diploma, and a Bachelor of Arts or Bachelor of Science in Christian Education or Pastoral Ministries. Emmanuel College offers the Associate of Arts in Religion and in Religion - Church Music.

Parent Institution. Emmanuel College began operation in 1919 under the name of Franklin Springs Institute. During its first years, the institution offered the first eleven grades of school and a Biblical Department for prospective ministers. In 1939, the name of the institution was changed to Emmanuel College.

Community Environment. The foothills of the Blue Ridge Mountains provide a picturesque setting for the campus. Currently there are resident halls for men and women, an administration-classroom building, a gymnasium, a Student Center, music hall, chapel, and a learning resources center which houses the library. Franklin Springs is located in northeast Georgia approximately 100 miles from Atlanta.

Religious Denomination. Pentecostal Holiness Church.
Religious Emphasis. Charismatic; Conservative.
Accreditation. Southern Association of Colleges and Schools; American Association of Bible Colleges.
Term System. Quarter (Fall, Winter, Spring); no summer term.
Enrollment in Degree Programs in Religion 1984–85. Total 35; men 24, women 11.
Degrees in Religion Awarded 1984–85. Bachelor of Arts in Religion 10; men 8, women 2. Bachelor of Science in Religion 6; men 3, women 3.
Faculty for Degree Programs in Religion. Total 5; full-

time 4, part-time 1.

Admission Requirements. For the School of Christian Ministries, the Associate of Arts or equivalent; all records, SAT or ACT scores, and transcripts of work taken in any college must be sent to the Admissions Office; medical form; applicants must give evidence of a Christian conversion experience and a sincere desire to seek and experience the truths of God's Word; must be committed to the will of God and preferably to Christian service.

Tuition and Fees. Tuition $2,235 per year; room and board $1,893 per year.

Financial Aid. Grants, scholarships, loans, and campus work-study programs are available.

Housing. There are four residence halls for single students and apartment facilities and mobile units for married students and their families.

Library Facilities. The Shaw-Leslie Learning Resources Center, constructed in 1981, contains holdings of 31,000 volumes, 220 periodical subscriptions, and over 3,000 microforms. In addition, the Audiovisual Department contains a wide variety of materials such as films, tape and disc recordings, music scores, and art slides.

Religious Services/Activities. Each quarter begins with a special revival or religious emphasis. The King Memorial Lectures are held every October. Every year in February, a Christian Education Emphasis is held on campus in memory of Mrs. Irene S. Todd (1879-1972). This emphasis offers workshops and seminars which provide intensive training and preparation in various aspects of Christian service education. The Staley Distinguished Christian Scholar Lecture Program is held during the Spring quarter. Chapel services are held twice a week and are mandatory. All resident students are required to attend midweek and Sunday services at the Franklin Springs Pentecostal Holiness Church. Weekly prayer meetings are held in each of the residence halls. Each student is also given a weekly Christian Service ministry.

Degree Programs

The Bachelor of Arts or the Bachelor of Science in Religion with a major in Christian Education are awarded upon the completion of 195 quarter hours in a specified curriculum in the School of Christian Ministries. The program prepares students to become Christian Education directors, leaders, and workers in the church. The program is based upon the Associate degree foundation as offered at Emmanuel College. A major in Bible and Theology is also available through the Pastoral Ministries curriculum. This program prepares the student to become a competent pastor or evangelist and is regarded as terminal, i.e., the graduates are ready to enter these ministries upon graduation.

Special Programs

The Associate of Arts degrees in Religion and Religion - Church Music in the junior college (Emmanuel College) provide the general education courses basic to the four-year Bible college program described above.

The Emmanuel College School of Christian Ministries holds active membership in the Evangelical Teacher Training Association, Wheaton, Illinois, and is qualified to offer the Silver Seal Advanced Teachers Certificate in teacher training in the local church. A student pursuing a degree in Christian Education can meet requirements for the Certificate or the Christian Education Diploma as he/she meets the other requirements for graduation.

Emory University
Candler School of Theology
1380 South Oxford Road, N.E.
Atlanta, GA 30322   (404) 329-6123

Administration. Dr. James T. Laney, President; Dr. Jim L. Waits, Dean, Candler School of Theology.

General Description. The Candler School of Theology is one of 13 official seminaries of the United Methodist Church. It is a professional school of Emory University. The school was founded in 1914 and became a part of Emory University in 1915. The School offers programs leading to the Master of Divinity, Master of Theological Studies, Doctor of Ministry, and Doctor of Sacred Theology. Continuing education is also provided for clergy, church professionals, and lay persons.

Parent Institution. Emory University is a private, co-educational university affiliated with the United Methodist Church. It awards over 2,000 undergraduate and graduate degrees annually.

Community Environment. The 550-acre campus is located 6 miles northeast of downtown Atlanta.

Religious Denomination. United Methodist Church.

Accreditation. Southern Association of Colleges and Schools; Association of Theological Schools in the United States and Canada.

Term System. Semester.

Enrollment in Degree Programs in Religion 1984–85. Total 699.

Faculty for Degree Programs in Religion. Total 53; full-time 42; adjunct 8; visiting 3.

Admission Requirements. Bachelor of Arts, Bachelor of Science, or equivalent degree from a regionally accredited college or university.

Tuition and Fees. Tuition $2,490 per semester; part-time academic work $208 per semester hour; apartment rental $200-$250 per month.

Financial Aid. Scholarships and grants-in-aid based on need are offered.

Housing. There are approximately 200 campus apartment units for married and single graduate and professional students.

Library Facilities. The Pitts Theological Library represents one of the finest theological collections in North America. It contains over 394,000 volumes, 35,000 microform units, approximately 4,500 manuscript pieces, and several thousand Methodist conference journals and reports. The primary strength of the library is in the traditional disciplines of Biblical literature, theology, and church history, as well as in Third World Studies. Special collections include the Beck Collection of Lutherana, the Warrington/Paine/Pratt Hymnology Collection, and Wesleyana. Students have full access to the Emory University libraries.

Degree Programs

The curriculum of the School is grouped into four broad areas: The Bible, History and Interpretation of Christianity, Christianity and Culture, and Church and Ministry.

The Master of Divinity program is designed for persons preparing for service in the parish or other forms of ministry. It is structured so as to be completed in three years of full-time study. It requires the minimum of 6 full-time semesters with at least 80 semester hours.

The Master of Theological Studies is a nonordination course of study that focuses on the academic exploration of theology. It is intended for persons who want to engage in some aspect of teaching and research. The program's focus is on historical and constructive issues of religious and theological reflection in all fields. The degree requires a minimum of 4 semesters with at least 51 hours of credit. A Colloquy on Theological Studies and a major research paper or thesis are also required.

The Doctor of Ministry degree is offered in two programs: (1) In-Course for students currently enrolled in the School and who have completed two years of professional studies and (2) In-Career, a continuing education degree for persons who have completed their basic theological training. The programs require a Doctor of Ministry core seminar, one or more clinical experiences, academic coursework, and a doctoral project.

The Doctor of Sacred Theology in Pastoral Counseling is designed to prepare persons for the specialized ministry of pastoral counseling.

Interdenominational Theological Center
671 Beckwith Street, S.W.
Atlanta, GA 30314   (404) 522-1772

Administration. Dr. James Hutton Costen, President.

General Description. The Interdenominational Theological Center is an ecumenical professional graduate school of theology. It was chartered in 1958 through the mutual efforts of four schools of theology. The constituent seminaries of the Center are Gammon Theological Seminary (United Methodist), Charles H. Mason Theological Seminary (Church of God in Christ), Morehouse School of Religion (Baptist), Phillips School of Theology (Christian Methodist Episcopal), Johnson C. Smith Theological Seminary (Presbyterian Church U.S.A.), and Turner Theological Seminary (African Methodist Episcopal). The Center is under the direction of a forty-member Board of Trustees. Twenty-eight of these trustees come from the six participating schools; the remaining twelve are members-at-large chosen without regard to denominational affiliation. The Trustees employ the faculty and administration, set the policies, and manage the physical and financial resources of the Center.

The Interdenominational Theological Center has maintained continuously that its primary mission is to provide quality theological education for the predominantly Black Christian churches. The Center endeavors to promote the advancement of theological education through excellence in teaching, research, and service to the predominantly Black church, and an environment in which each student can participate in those learning experiences essential for effective Christian ministry. The Center accepts a responsibility to educate persons for pastoral and other ministries in the Black Christian churches and the world at large. Applications are invited from those prospects who represent the constituent denominations in the Center, persons of African descent, and other persons regardless of race, sex, religion, nationality, or ethnic origin.

Community Environment. The Center is located in Atlanta, Georgia and is part of the Atlanta University Center.

Religious Denomination. Interdenominational.

Accreditation. Southern Association of Colleges and Schools; Association of Theological Schools in the United States and Canada.

Term System. Semester; summer term.

Enrollment in Degree Programs in Religion 1984–85. Total 326; men 265, women 61.

Degrees in Religion Awarded 1984–85. Doctor of Ministry 1; men 1. Master of Divinity 61; men 52, women 9. Master of Religious Education 5; men 1, women 4 (this degree is no longer awarded; it has been replaced with the Master of Arts in Religion).

Faculty for Degree Programs in Religion. Total 36; full-time 26, part-time 10.

Admission Requirements. Bachelor of Arts degree or its equivalent from an accredited college or university; official transcript of all college, university, or seminary records; certificate from a major official of the applicant's denomination (e.g., bishop, president, or registrar of annual conference presbytery, association, or pastor) indicating that the applicant is an acceptable candidate for service in the denomination and that admission to the Center is approved; GRE General Test Scores.

Tuition and Fees. Costs per semester: tuition $875 (constituent), $1,250 (nonconstituent); board $500; room single $800, double $400; housing $562 to $703 depending upon accommodations; registration fee $10; library fee $5.

Financial Aid. Guaranteed student loans, national direct student loans, college work-study, and institutional aid represent the financial aid available.

Housing. Dormitory accommodations as well as efficiency housing and trailers are available.

Library Facilities. The Robert W. Woodruff Library is

a result of a merger of the Center's own library and the libraries of the Atlanta University Center. It houses approximately 581,000 volumes.

Religious Services/Activities. Services of worship, which are held regularly throughout the school year, are planned and directed by a joint Faculty-Student Committee. These services provide for the deepening and enriching of the devotional life of students and faculty, and for participation in the conduct of public worship. The Student Christian League is the representative body of the Center's community of students. It is responsible for directing a wide variety of seminarian activities.

Degree Programs

The Master of Divinity degree is designed to integrate theological studies and the work of ministry so that theory and practice, academy and parish become complementary components of the educational process. Of the 90 semester credits required for graduation, 63 are distributed among four areas of the curriculum, and constitute a core. In addition, each student is required to elect an area of concentration among the five fields of the curriculum.

The Master of Arts in Religion with a concentration in Christian Education requires 60 semester credits. It is designed for but not limited to lay persons who wish to participate in the church's work and simultaneously pursue other careers, informed by religious commitment, or for church staff workers.

The Master of Arts in Religion with a concentration in Church Music is designed with an awareness of the urgent need for church musicians who have a broad understanding of music ministry. The goal of the program is to meet the needs of persons who seek deeper theological, biblical, and liturgical understanding in the theory and practice of church music.

The Doctor of Ministry Degree program is offered to qualified men and women currently engaged in ministry through the Atlanta Theological Association. The In-Career program is designed to continue the education of persons for their practice of ministry in the church and in related institutional settings. The program rests on a base of general theological preparation and moves toward an area of concentration that permits the student to explore the conjunction of theory, experience, and professional intentions in ministry.

The Doctor of Sacred Theology degree in Pastoral Counseling is offered through the Atlanta Theological Association by the Candler School of Theology, the Columbia Theological Seminary, and the Interdenominational Theological Center. The Atlanta Theological Association has responsibility for approving admissions to the program, establishing curriculum offerings, and certifying candidates for awarding of degrees. The purpose of the degree is to prepare persons for the specialized ministry of pastoral counseling at a doctoral level of competence. The degree is intended for those whose interest in pastoral counseling is primarily professional and theological.

Special Programs

Black Women in Church and Society is a program of the Center which seeks to enhance the participation and function of women in the church and society by focusing on church structures and seminary/theological education, using education and re-education as tools for constructive and positive change. The four components of the program are Dialogue, Seminar, Mid-Year Institute, and Research/Resource Center.

A Continuing Education program offers a variety of life-long learning experiences.

Mercer University
The Roberts Department of Christianity
1400 Coleman Avenue
Macon, GA 31207   (912) 744-2755

Administration. Walter Byron Shurden, Chair, The Roberts Department of Christianity.

General Description. The Roberts Department of Christianity functions as an instructional Department in the College of Liberal Arts. The department offers collegiate training to men and women who intend to enter specific Christian service; furnishes formal instruction in religious subjects which should form a serious part of the work of every student in a Christian college; and emphasizes in the entire college program those values for which Mercer University, as a Christian institution, stands.

The courses available in the Department should also have special appeal to lay workers who seek better preparation for effective and intelligent service in the local church.

Parent Institution. Mercer University first opened its doors as Mercer Institute in 1833 at Penfield, Georgia. The University is named for Jesse Mercer (1769-1841), an eminent Georgian, a distinguished Baptist clergyman, and a principal organizer of the Georgia Baptist Convention. In 1871, the University was moved from Penfield to Macon.

The College of Liberal Arts is the oldest and largest of the University's schools and represents the heart of its traditions. Located on a beautiful 130-acre tract in the city of Macon, the college buildings present a striking combination of tradition and progress. The administrative offices of the University are located on this campus in one of the most notable architectural monuments of the city. The College of Liberal Arts currently serves about 2,000 students, 55 percent of whom reside in campus housing. The College offers a full array of baccalaureate programs in the humanities, fine arts, social sciences, and sciences. It offers Master's degrees in liberal studies and education.

Community Environment. The city of Macon is situated on the Ocmulgee River, six miles from the geographical center of the state. Macon is a picturesque blend of Old

South culture and New South progress. Many industries are located here. Tobesofkee Lake, two miles away, has facilities for boating, camping, and fishing.

Religious Denomination. Southern Baptist.

Accreditation. Southern Association of Colleges and Schools. Member of: Association of Southern Baptist Colleges and Schools.

Term System. Quarter; summer term.

Faculty for Degree Programs in Religion. Total 11; full-time 8, part-time 3.

Admission Requirements. High school diploma with 16 units overall, of which 13 must be academic units. The College desires to select students who will be successful and who can best profit from the Mercer education program. Credentials essential to the Committee on Admissions are (1) application with $10 nonrefundable fee; (2) a complete high school record showing rank in class; (3) a recommendation from the guidance counselor; (4) scores on the SAT or ACT; (5) a complete listing of extracurricular activities including work.

Tuition and Fees. Tuition $1,788 per quarter; commuter tuition $1,395 per quarter; room rent and health fees $389 per quarter; meal ticket (required of all resident students): 7-day ticket per quarter $482, 5-day ticket (Monday through Friday, available to Juniors and Seniors) $460 per quarter.

Financial Aid. Mercer University student loan and undergraduate scholarship funds are administered in conjunction with a nationally-established policy and philosophy of financial aid for education. All applications for student financial aid must be received by the Financial Aid Office prior to May 1 for consideration for the following academic year.

Housing. All students under 21 years of age, with certain exceptions, are required to live on the campus. The residence halls at Mercer provide opportunities for students to become a part of a community and to create and encounter a variety of educational, cultural, and recreational experiences.

Library Facilities. The Eugene W. Stetson Memorial Library contains 46,000 square feet of floor space and more than 170,000 cataloged volumes. There is space for 400 readers and the building contains study carrels for students and faculty, a conference room, audiovisual facilities, microform materials, and a special collections room which contains the Mercer and Georgia Baptist Convention archives, in addition to other archival materials. The Library collection also includes 12,000 volumes which once comprised the Mercer Theological Library. Probably the most notable collection is the library of the late Dr. Albert H. Newman, containing several hundred volumes of Baptist history and theology, as well as books of general interest.

Religious Services/Activities. A commitment to the provision of worship opportunities and other religious activities for significant spiritual growth is an integral part of the past and present of Mercer University. Campus religious activities are provided through University Ministries by the Senior Minister to the University, Dr. C. Welton Gaddy. Various campus religious organizations include the Baptist Student Union, Campus Baptist Young Women, College Life Bible Study, Jewish Student Organization, Lutheran Student Organization, Mercer Ministerial Association, Newman Club, Presbyterian Student Organization, Wesley Foundation, Episcopal Student Fellowship.

A worship service for all students, faculty, staff, and administration is held in Newton Sanctuary each Thursday morning under the direction of the Senior Minister to the University. The Chapel Choir, a voluntary organization, provides music leadership for the University Chapel Services.

Degree Programs

The Bachelor of Arts degree program with a major in Christianity consists of a minimum of 40 quarter hours in courses offered in the areas of Biblical Studies, Christian History, Christian Ethics, and Christian Thought.

Shorter College
Department of Religion and Philosophy
Shorter Avenue
Rome, GA 30161   (404) 291-1863

Administration. Robert G. Gardner, Department Head.

General Description. The Department of Religion and Philosophy of Shorter College offers a program for undergraduate majors leading to the Bachelor of Arts degree.

Parent Institution. Shorter College is a four-year liberal arts college and is a member institution of the Georgia Baptist Convention. There are no denomination requirements for enrollment. There are students of virtually every major Protestant denomination as well as students of Roman Catholic, Jewish, and other religious affiliations. At Shorter College, students are prepared for an inevitably changing world through their life-oriented liberal arts program. The Shorter campus on "The Hill" abounds in tradition. Resisting an urge to become starkly modern a few years ago, the College completely remodeled and fully modernized all of her stately buildings. Five additional buildings have been constructed in recent years. The College sponsors a wide range of events including faculty, alumni, and student music recitals, speech festivals and recitals, drama and opera productions, and art exhibits. In the city of Rome and on other college campuses nearby there are additional opportunities to participate in or attend cultural, social, and athletic events.

Community Environment. From its location in the Appalachian foothills, Shorter is ideally situated to make it possible for students to pursue a wide variety of extracurricular interests. Just 90 minutes to the south is Atlanta with her museums, art center, symphony, ballet, theatre, professional athletics, and dozens of other attractions. The city of Rome has a population of 50,000 and is the site of three colleges.

Religious Denomination. Southern Baptist.

Accreditation. Southern Association of Colleges and Schools.

Term System. Semester; summer term.

Enrollment in Degree Programs in Religion 1984–85. Total 18; men 14, women 4.

Degrees in Religion Awarded 1984–85. Bachelor of Arts 3; men 3.

Faculty for Degree Programs in Religion. Total 2; full-time 2.

Admission Requirements. Nonrefundable application fee $15; high school transcript; SAT or ACT; certificate or statement by high school principal or counselor or by the Dean of Students from any college previously attended; health certificate. In determining admissions, consideration is given to the compatibility of the student's purpose and interests with the basic philosophy of the college as a Christian liberal arts institution.

Tuition and Fees. For two semesters, tuition $3,640; basic room and board $2,240; student activity fee $60; other fees may apply.

Financial Aid. Financial aid available; it is divided into three categories of institutional aid, state aid, and federal aid. Students are required to complete an application for Financial Aid as well as the Financial Aid Form from the College Scholarship Service in order to determine their eligibility in the programs.

Housing. All students are required to live in college dormitories and to take meals in the college dining hall, unless married, living with parents, 23 years of age, or having received written authorization by the Dean of Student Affairs.

Library Facilities. The Livingston Library, a gift of the Roy Livingston family, has a collection of over 100,000 books, 1,175 periodical titles, 1,800 microfilm materials, 5,000 musical recordings, 6,250 musical scores, and a diverse and growing collection of films, slides, video tapes, and cassettes. There are conference rooms, projection rooms, a graphics preparation room, typewriters, music listening facilities, and computer terminals.

Religious Services/Activities. The Shorter Christian Association (SCA) presents religious and current-interest programs. An attempt is made to help each student find a religious activity suited to his interests and abilities. The SCA sponsors vesper services, Religious Focus Week, and other special projects to encourage Christian thought and action on the campus. The Baptist Student Union sponsors activities designed to nurture and develop spiritual life and are open to all students. The Wright-Meredith Club is composed of students who are volunteers for professional Christian service. Students of all faiths are encouraged to participate in the life of the church of their choice in the Rome area.

Degree Programs

For the Bachelor of Arts degree with a major in Religion and Philosophy, concentration may be in either Religion or Philosophy with supporting courses from the other. Course offerings in Religion are mainly in the Biblical and historical fields. Course offerings in Philosophy are mainly in the historical, ethical, and metaphysical areas. A Religion and Philosophy departmental major consists of 42 semester hours credit of which 24 credits shall be taken in the department in courses at the junior-senior level as advised by the department, 12 semester hours in related departments, and the remaining six hours in either. Candidates for a degree must have earned a minimum of 126 semester hours with 252 quality points.

Wesleyan College
4760 Forsyth Road
Macon, GA 31297   (912) 477-0115

Administration. Dr. Robert K. Ackerman, President.

General Description. The Bachelor of Arts program in Religion is based mainly on the Judeo-Christian tradition. It seeks to acquaint the student with the major religious systems, particularly Western Christianity, with man's spiritual and moral heritage, and with the more important problems in religion. The program is also a foundation for further theological study. The major in Religious Education is an expansion of the general religion program and is geared primarily to church-related employment. An internship program, often done in a local church setting, is required to assist the student in gaining basic understanding of a specific vocation in religion.

Parent Institution. Wesleyan College is a four-year women's residential college conferring degrees in the liberal and fine arts. It was founded in 1836 and is affiliated with The United Methodist Church.

Community Environment. The College is located on a 240-acre wooded campus in residential Macon, a city of 130,000 in the mid-Georgia area.

Religious Denomination. The United Methodist Church.

Accreditation. Southern Association of Colleges and Schools.

Term System. Semester.

Admission Requirements. High school graduation; rank in upper half of graduating class; 16 academic units; SAT or ACT.

Tuition and Fees. Tuition $4,350 per year; room and board $2,700; student activities fee $150.

Financial Aid. Wesleyan College awards scholarships along with financial aid from federal, state, and local funds including grants, loans, and campus employment.

Housing. Dormitory accommodations are available for 600 women.

Library Facilities. The Lucy Lester Willet Memorial

Library contains over 117,000 volumes and subscribes to 480 periodicals.

Religious Services/Activities. The Council of Religious Concerns of the Student Government Association serves as coordinator for religious organizations and activities on the campus.

Degree Programs

The major in Religion leading to the Bachelor of Arts degree requires a minimum of 27 semester hours of prescribed and elective courses. The major in Religious Education consists of a minimum of 30 semester hours in religion and philosophy.

HAWAII

Brigham Young University - Hawaii Campus
55-220 Kulanui Avenue
Laie, HI 96762   (808) 293-3211

Administration. Dr. J. Elliot Cameron, President.

General Description. Brigham Young University - Hawaii Campus has since its inception sought to provide opportunity for students to grow and progress spiritually through classroom religious instruction. Many courses in religion are available to the undergraduate student. No degree is offered in Religious Studies. The intent of religious instruction at the University is to permit the student to study religion simultaneously with regular study of other academic disciplines. One religion class must be taken during each semester of full-time registration in residence until the total requirement of 14 hours is completed.

Parent Institution. Brigham Young University - Hawaii Campus (formerly the Church College of Hawaii) is a church-related, four-year, coeducational institution. It was established in 1955 and is controlled by The Church of Jesus Christ of Latter-day Saints. A university education is provided in an atmosphere consistent with the ideals and principles of the Church. The University offers the degrees Bachelor of Arts, Bachelor of Science, Bachelor of Social Work, Associate of Arts, and Associate of Science.

Community Environment. The 60-acre campus is located in Laie on the windward shore of Oahu, 38 miles from Honolulu.

Religious Denomination. The Church of Jesus Christ of Latter-day Saints.

Accreditation. Western Association of Schools and Colleges.

Term System. Semester.

Admission Requirements. High school graduation with rank in upper half of graduating class; ACT.

Tuition and Fees. Tuition LDS students $600 per semester; non-LDS $900 per semester; room and board $980.

Financial Aid. The Financial Aid office assists students in various types of aid programs.

Housing. University housing includes room and board residence halls for single men and women, and married student apartments.

Library Facilities. The Joseph F. Smith Library and the Ralph E. Woolley Media Center contain collections of over 125,000 volumes, 1,000 current periodicals, 445,000 microform holdings, and other non-print materials. Special collections include Pacific Islands, Children's, and Mormonism.

Religious Services/Activities. Devotional assemblies are usually held on Friday mornings. These assemblies enable students to hear messages of inspirational power from carefully chosen Church leaders, including General Authorities of The Church of Jesus Christ of Latter-day Saints. The Church is organized into a number of wards under the leadership of two BYU-Hawaii Stakes. Each ward has a membership of approximately 200. The wards are organized to provide students the maximum opportunity for active participation in programs of the Church. All single LDS students living away from home become members in one of the BYU-HC wards.

Degree Programs

Students in the baccalaureate program must take one religion class each semester of full-time registration in residence until the total requirement of 14 hours is complete. The Bachelor's degree requires a total of 133 semester hours.

Chaminade University of Honolulu
Department of Religious Studies
3140 Waialae Avenue
Honolulu, HI 96816   (808) 735-4735

Administration. Rev. Raymond A. Roesch, S.M., President.

General Description. The express purpose of the Department of Religious Studies is to assist the student to develop a mature and critical understanding of the Christian Faith and the structures for expressing that Faith in our world. The theological view is Roman Catholic and ecumenical and cross cultural in scope.

Parent Institution. Chaminade University of Honolulu, an independent, coeducational institution founded by the Society of Mary in 1955, is the only Roman Catholic university in Hawaii. As an academic institution, Chaminade's first priority is dedicated teaching which best serves its students. Academic programs are offered in liberal arts, preprofessional training, teacher education, and business administration.

Community Environment. The 72-acre campus is located in the St. Louis Heights section of Honolulu, about two miles from the Waikiki area and three miles from downtown.

Religious Denomination. Roman Catholic.

Accreditation. Western Association of Schools and Colleges.

Term System. Semester.

Admission Requirements. Graduation from high school with a C average; 15 academic units; SAT or ACT.

Tuition and Fees. Tuition $1,900 per semester; library fee $15; student activities fee $20; student government $35; room $525-$750; board $779-$864.

Financial Aid. Financial assistance to students is available as scholarships, grants, work opportunities, and loans.

Housing. Dormitory accommodations area available on campus for 126 women and 106 men.

Library Facilities. The library contains over 55,000 volumes and receives 550 periodicals.

Religious Services/Activities. The Campus Ministry program includes opportunities for a full liturgical and sacramental life, meditation and other prayer forms, and spiritual counseling.

Degree Programs

The Bachelor of Arts or Bachelor of General Studies degree programs with a major in Religious Studies require the completion of a general education core in addition to pre-major and major requirements. The major requires 24 semester hours of upper division Religion courses.

Hawaii, University of - Manoa
Department of Religion
Sakamaki Hall, Room A 311
2530 Dole Street
Honolulu, HI 96822   (808) 948-8299

Administration. Dr. Marvin J. Anderson, Chancellor, U. of H., Manoa; Richard H. Kosaki, Vice President for Academic Affairs; Rex A. Wade, Acting Dean, College of Arts and Sciences.

General Description. The Department of Religion is part of the Faculty of Arts and Humanities which in turn is within the College of Arts and Sciences. The degrees Bachelor of Arts and Master of Arts are awarded with a major in religion.

Parent Institution. The University of Hawaii is a multi-campus system of post-secondary educational institutions serving the state of Hawaii. The University of Hawaii at Manoa (UHM), on the island of Oahu, is the major comprehensive research campus with more than 20,000 students and is commonly referred to as UH-Manoa or the Manoa Campus. It is the founding campus of the system, and began in 1907 as a land-grant college of agriculture and mechanic arts known as the College of Hawaii. Today, UHM is a multi-dimensional university operation conducting education, research, and public service programs for the state, the nation, and the world community. Throughout its history, UHM has emphasized studies related to the distinctive geographical and cultural setting of Hawaii.

The state's multi-racial culture and close ties to Asia create a favorable environment for the study of various aspects of diverse cultural systems. Currently more than 200 of the University's activities have an international dimension.

The University offers course work leading to bachelor's degrees in 89 fields of study, master's in 77, doctorates in 41, first-professional degrees in law and medicine, and a number of certificates.

Community Environment. The University of Hawaii at Manoa is located on some 300 acres of land in Manoa Valley, a residential section close to the heart of metropolitan Honolulu, the state capital. Easy access to the center of the commercial, cultural, and political life of Hawaii is an extra benefit for students.

Religious Denomination. None.

Accreditation. Western Association of Schools and Colleges.

Term System. Semester; summer term.

Enrollment in Degree Programs in Religion 1984–85. Total 33; men 21, women 12.

Degrees in Religion Awarded 1984–85. Bachelor of Arts in Religion 9; men 5, women 4. Master of Arts in Asian Religions 5; men 4, women 1.

Faculty for Degree Programs in Religion. Total 9; full-time 8, part-time 1.

Admission Requirements. UHM admits applicants who demonstrate ability to benefit from and contribute to one of its educational programs. The number of nonresident students is limited. Individual academic programs may have special admissions policies and procedures. Consult the colleges and schools for specific information. Applicants must first be admitted into UHM before consideration for admission into the various programs,

Tuition and Fees. Tuition full-time undergraduate resident $470 per semester, nonresident $1,685; part-time undergraduate resident $40 per credit hour, nonresident $141 per credit hour; full-time graduate resident $555 per semester, nonresident $2,010; part-time graduate resident $47 per credit hour, nonresident $168 per credit hour; Campus Center fee per semester $12 (9 or more credit hours) or $7 (8 or fewer credit hours); other miscellaneous fees; housing (residence halls) $444 to $656 depending upon accommodations (most are shared doubles).

Financial Aid. UHM requires the College Scholarship Services (CSS) form to develop a composite financial aid student file to determine eligibility for most student assistance programs. Deadline for submission of the form is March 1. Late applications will be accepted until funds are depleted.

Housing. There are on-campus residential facilities for 3,100 single students. Most of these assignments go to State of Hawaii residents since priority is given to them. A limited number of one-bedroom apartments are available to married students who are Hawaii residents.

Library Facilities. University of Hawaii Libraries provide extensive library resources and information services. The libraries comprise the largest collection of research materials in the state, with approximately 5 million items, including 35,000 currently received serial titles, mostly in open stacks. Information services include reference and research paper consultation, computerized information retrieval, and instruction in library use.

Degree Programs

The Bachelor of Arts degree with a major in Religion requires the completion of the general requirements for a degree including 27 semester hours at the non-introductory-level or above, including at least 9 hours in upper division. There are required courses in the major field and students must plan a sequence in one subfield to the advanced seminar level; if an Asian sequence is chosen, at least one course in the Western tradition must be taken, and vice versa.

The Master of Arts program in Religion with a specialization in Asian Religions requires students to hold a bachelor's degree from an accredited U.S. college or university or its equivalent from a recognized foreign institution of higher learning. The degree requires a minimum of 30 credits (12 credits must be in graduate-level core courses or above, exclusive of research methods courses). A thesis or written examinations are required, depending upon whether Plan A or Plan B options are followed.

ILLINOIS

Association of Chicago Theological Schools
c/o St. Mary of the Lake Seminary
Route 176
Mundelein, IL 60060

General Description. The Association of Chicago Theological Schools is an ecumenical association of twelve Protestant and Catholic seminaries formed in 1984 from two clusters of Seminaries in the Chicago metropolitan area (the Chicago Theological Institute and the Chicago Cluster of Theological Schools). The Association is intended to be the chief avenue of cooperation among its member institutions, particularly in the areas of student cross-registration, library access and acquisitions, interchange among faculty members in the various disciplines of theological education, and communications between the schools. Students from the member schools have library checkout privileges at the other member schools. In addition, a daily courier service between the libraries makes quick circulation through inter-library loan possible. The schools also offer a joint catalog listing all courses, faculty, staff, and other pertinent information.

Five of the schools are located on Chicago's south side, in Hyde Park: Catholic Theological Union (Roman Catholic), Chicago Theological Seminary (United Church of Christ), Lutheran School of Theology (Lutheran), Meadville/Lombard Theological School (Unitarian Universalist), and McCormick Theological Seminary (Presbyterian). Two schools are in the western suburbs: Bethany Theological Seminary (Church of the Brethren) and Northern Baptist Theological Seminary (Baptist). The remaining five schools are in the northern metropolitan area: St. Mary of the Lake Seminary (Roman Catholic), Seabury-Western Theological Seminary (Episcopal), Garrett-Evangelical Theological Seminary (United Methodist), Trinity Evangelical Divinity School (Evangelical Free Church of America), and North Park Theological Seminary (Evangelical Covenant).

Together, the schools within the Association of Chicago Theological Schools offer an enormously rich network of resources for theological education, making it one of the very few such centers of theological education in the world. Available to the approximately 3,500 students enrolled at its member schools is a faculty of some 300, over 1,000 courses offered annually, and library collections of over 1.2 million volumes and nearly 5,000 currently received periodical subscriptions. Several of the schools have well-stocked theological bookstores. Most important, the Association makes it possible for students and faculty to pursue their work, study, and reflection in interaction with people from many different cultural and theological traditions.

Augustana College
Department of Religion
7th Avenue and 38th Street
Rock Island, IL 61201   (309) 794-7000

Administration. Arnold G. Levin, Professor of Religion.

General Description. The Department of Religion offers the Bachelor of Arts degree with a major in Religion. Students may take one of two tracks: (1) a pre-professional track normally taken by students who plan to attend a seminary or divinity school and (2) a liberal arts track which offers in-depth study in Bible, Church History, Christian Ethics, History of Religions, and Theology.

Parent Institution. Augustana College traces its origin to the Old World universities of Uppsala and Lund in Sweden, founded in 1477 and 1668, respectively. Graduates of these ancient European seats of learning founded Augustana College in 1860 on the near north side of Chicago to provide leaders for the new churches being organized by Swedish immigrants and to educate the youth of these new communities. The College moved from Chicago to Paxton, Illinois in 1863, and finally to Rock Island in 1875. The Theological Seminary separated from the College in 1948 and in 1967 returned to the Chicago area.

The College has always stood in close relationship to the church - first the Augustana Lutheran Church, and since 1962, the Lutheran Church in America. The name Augustana derives from the origin of the Lutheran

Church. The Latin name for the Augsburg Confession, the Reformation document drawn up in 1530, is *Confessio Augustana*. The College's commitment to the liberal arts is expressed in its general graduation requirements. Each student is asked to study in a broad range of fields, including writing and literature, foreign language, speech, fine arts, philosophy, religion, social science, natural science, and physical education.

Community Environment. Augustana is located on rolling hillsides of the Mississippi River valley. Scenic walkways connect twenty-five buildings situated on 100 acres of landscaped campus away from the busy urban community of Rock Island. The city is one of several in the thriving industrial complex known as the Quad-Cities. The other municipalities are Moline and East Moline, Illinois, and directly across the river, Davenport and Bettendorf, Iowa. Rock Island is almost midway between Chicago, 162 miles to the east, and Des Moines, 176 miles to the west.

Religious Denomination. Lutheran Church in America.
Religious Emphasis. Liberal.
Accreditation. North Central Association of Colleges and Schools.
Term System. Quarter; summer term.
Faculty for Degree Programs in Religion. Total 6, full-time 6.
Admission Requirements. Preference in admission will be shown to those who evidence superior ability to do college work as demonstrated by the high school record, and ACT or SAT scores; personal interviews and campus visits are encouraged; satisfactory health report.
Tuition and Fees. $2,054 per quarter; room and board $856 per quarter; student fee $15; other fees where applicable.
Financial Aid. Most financial aid is awarded based on financial need and is available in the form of grants, loans, and scholarships.
Housing. All full-time students not living at home are required to live in College residence halls unless permission to live elsewhere is granted by the Office of Student Services or the Student Personnel Committee.
Library Facilities. The Denkmann Memorial Library houses 272,000 catalogued items. It is growing at the rate of 6,000 items per year and receives more than 1,400 current periodicals. A rare book collection, including first editions of Milton and Spenser as well as hundreds of volumes of Mississippiana, is displayed in a special room. The Swenson Swedish immigration Research Center, established in 1981, is a major research and resource facility devoted to the study of all aspects of Swedish immigration to the United States.
Religious Services/Activities. As a college of the Lutheran Church in America, Augustana embodies a concern for Christian faith and its values as well as for learning and its uses. Augustana Campus Ministry seeks to embody this friendship between faith and learning through a variety of programs: three regular weekly services of worship,

study programs, volunteer service projects (including chapters of Amnesty International and Bread for the World), fellowship activities, and pastoral counseling. The College provides two full-time campus pastors, a Lutheran pastor, and a Roman Catholic priest. Campus Crusade for Christ and the Fellowship of Christian Athletes meet regularly on the campus.

Degree Programs

The Bachelor of Arts degree program with a major in Religion requires the completion of 36 credits in the major field including at least one course from each of the five departmental areas (Bible, Church History, Christian Ethics, History of Religions, Theology) and at least three courses from one of the areas. A pre-professional major in Religion may also be pursued.

Bethany Theological Seminary
Butterfield and Meyers Roads
Oak Brook, IL 60521   (312) 620-2200

Administration. Dr. Warren F. Groff, President; Dr. Graydon F. Snyder, Dean; Dr. Donald E. Miller, Director of Graduate Studies.

General Description. As the only seminary for the Church of the Brethren, Bethany fills an important position of leadership within the denomination. Its primary commitment is to prepare loving, faithful, and skilled servants of Jesus Christ, for all the ministries of the church and society. While its principal affiliation through the years has been with the denomination, Bethany is ecumenical in spirit and has always welcomed all qualified students. From its earliest days, the themes of modern biblical scholarship, openness to social science and secular disciplines, and practical involvement in ministry have been present. The Seminary grants the degrees Master of Arts in Theology, Master of Divinity, and Doctor of Ministry. Bethany and 6 other theological schools of the Hyde Park, Oak Brook, and Lemont areas form the Chicago Cluster of Theological Schools, with a student body of 1,500 and a faculty of over 200. The Cluster provides a common curriculum open to all enrolled students, and also provides access to the graduate division of Spertus College of Judaica.

Community Environment. The Seminary's 60-acre campus at the intersection of Meyers and Butterfield Roads is 18 miles west of downtown Chicago. Construction of the 11 buildings was completed in 1963. Campus and buildings are contemporary in style and functional in use.
Religious Denomination. Church of the Brethren.
Religious Emphasis. Anabaptist, Free Church.
Accreditation. North Central Association of Colleges and Schools; Association of Theological Schools in the United States and Canada.
Term System. Quarter; no summer term.
Enrollment in Degree Programs in Religion 1984–85.

Total 138; men 86, women 52.

Degrees in Religion Awarded 1984–85. Master of Divinity 18; men 12, women 6. Master of Arts in Theology 12, men 6, women 6. Doctor of Ministry 4; men 4.

Faculty for Degree Programs in Religion. Total 21; full-time 10, part-time 11.

Admission Requirements. Bachelor's degree from an accredited college or university; satisfactory grade average in undergraduate courses; adequate preseminary foundation.

Tuition and Fees. Tuition Master level $80 per hour; Doctor of Ministry program $4,000; graduation fee $15; intern fee $240; room/apartment $1,278 to $4,815 per year.

Financial Aid. Aid is generally administered on the basis of demonstrated need. Two merit scholarships are available to outstanding first-year students. Aid sources include Bethany scholarships, grants, loans, and federal assistance.

Housing. Sufficient on-campus housing facilities are available to students, single or married (dormitory, apartments).

Library Facilities. The Seminary Library serves both Bethany Theological Seminary and Northern Baptist Theological Seminary. The collection includes over 137,000 books, bound periodicals, and pamphlets. Special collections include the Biblical Archaeology collection of A.T. Olmstead and the extensive English Bible collection of Ora I. Huston. Affiliations with other schools in the greater Chicago area provide access to over 1.2 million volumes and 5,000 periodicals.

Religious Services/Activities. Bi-weekly chapel services; choir; weekly all-campus common meal; campus-wide spiritual retreats; prayer groups.

Degree Programs

The Master of Divinity curriculum offers training in specific area of professional service for those preparing for a church vocation and ordination. A student must complete satisfactorily three years of work or 108 quarter hours of credit. Students participate in a Colloquium in Ministry and Mission and complete requirements in the areas of The Biblical Foundations of the Church; The Life and Faith of the Church in Relation to Culture; and the Ministries of the Church.

The Master of Arts in Theology is designed for persons who desire a broad theological education as part of the ministry they share with other members of the faith community and as a religious base for their life work. The degree requires two years of work or 72 quarter hours. Distribution requirements include the Colloquium in Ministry and Mission; Biblical foundations of the Church; Life and Faith of the Church in Relation to Culture; and the Ministries of the Church. A Senior Field examination is required.

The Doctor of Ministry is an in-ministry program (requiring a minimum of three years full-time experience beyond the first-professional degree). A total of 36 quarter hours are required. The program involves an orientation session, two summer sessions, learning units, field consulation, project, as well as the required credits.

Special Programs

The Centers for Reformation and Free Church Studies, Jewish-Christian Studies, and Theology and the Human Sciences offer programs leading to a Doctor of Theology degree and prepare the student for teaching in college, university, seminary, or for research. Bethany Theological Seminary participates in the programs of these three Centers.

The Seminary also offers Advanced Pastoral Training Seminars as well as the Bethany Extension Schools for local church leaders.

Catholic Theological Union
5401 South Cornell
Chicago, IL 60615   (312) 324-8000

Administration. John Linnan, C.S.V., President; Robert Schreiter, C.PP.S., Vice President and Dean.

General Description. Catholic Theological Union at Chicago is a school of ministry in the Roman Catholic tradition, begun in 1968 by a number of religious communities of men who combined resources in order to educate more creatively for priesthood. Today that founding vision embraces preparation for many forms of public ministry in the Church from ordained priesthood to lay ministries. The school accepts qualified men and women who show vocational commitment and seek graduate ministerial education. It grants the degrees Master of Divinity, Master of Arts in Theology, and Master of Theological Studies.

The community life of the school reveals the influence of the religious institutes which founded and sponsor the school. Thus inclusion, mutuality, and participation mark the ecclesiastical context of the entire educational program. Within this context students live, grow, and experience formation in faith and ministry. It also provides the impetus for the school's strong emphasis on mission, justice, and the cross-cultural dynamics of ministry in the modern world and in a global church. Membership in the Chicago Cluster of Theological Schools and cooperation with the Divinity School of the University of Chicago offer opportunities for ecumenical participation in the preparation for ministry and for academic research in theology.

Community Environment. Catholic Theological Union is located in Hyde Park on Chicago's south side. This is a cosmopolitan, stably integrated community, with a strong sense of identity. Within walking distance are shopping centers, theatres, restaurants, churches, parks, the Lake Michigan beaches, and the Museum of Science and Industry. Downtown Chicago is 15 minutes away by car or rapid transit. More importantly, the Union is close to the Divinity School of the University of Chicago and to several schools of theology in the area. From its earliest days, Chicago has been a major cosmopolitan center, with its many neighborhoods representing a wide variety of racial and ethnic groups, as well as a broad spectrum of cultural and religious traditions.

Religious Denomination. Catholic.

Religious Emphasis. Progressive.

Accreditation. North Central Association of Colleges and Secondary Schools; Association of Theological Schools in the United States and Canada.

Term System. Quarter; no summer term.

Enrollment in Degree Programs in Religion 1984–85. Total 260; men 216, women 44.

Degrees in Religion Awarded 1984–85. Master of Divinity 42; men 40, women 2. Master of Theological Studies 12; men 4, women 8. Master of Arts in Theology 9; men 5, women 4.

Faculty for Degree Programs in Religion. Total 50; full-time 35, part-time 15.

Admission Requirements. Bachelor's degree or its equivalent from an approved college or university; official college transcripts; letters of recommendation.

Tuition and Fees. Tuition $135 per credit hour; thesis/project direction fee $405; activity fee $5 per course; matriculation fee $30; housing rental $1,776 to $2,880 (September 15 to June 15) depending upon accommodations; food service contract fall quarter $670, winter quarter $620, spring quarter $570.

Financial Aid. Because the theological education of the majority of students at CTU is financed in full from funds of the particpating communities, resources for financial aid are limited.

Housing. Participating communities at CTU generally provide housing for their own students. A limited amount of housing for independent students is available.

Library Facilities. The CTU Library contains 100,000 volumes and currently receives over 540 periodicals. In addition to the general theological holdings, the library has special collections in mission studies, history of religions, and homiletics. The Chicago Cluster of Theological Schools' libraries are available to CTU students.

Religious Services/Activities. The participating communities of CTU generally provide services in the area of counseling and spiritual direction for their own students. For students who are not members of participating communities, referral for counseling and spiritual direction is available through the office of the Dean of Students. Each of the participating communities celebrates daily liturgies. In addition, CTU sponsors regular liturgies for the entire school.

Degree Programs

The Master of Divinity degree is a graduate professional program. It combines theological education, guided ministerial experience, and structures for integrative reflection. As the first professional degree for candidates for ordained ministry, its aim is generalist in nature, while allowing for some specialization within its broad framework. The program seeks to implement faithfully the guidelines of the 1981 *Program of Priestly Formation* of the National Conference of Catholic Bishops.

The Master of Arts in Theology is designed to provide the theological background for those who wish: to prepare for entrance into a doctoral program in theology; to teach religion at a secondary or college level; to develop a basic competence in the area of theological studies although their principal specialization lies elsewhere.

The Master of Theological Studies aims to provide the students with a general theological understanding as a context within which they will also develop selected pastoral skills and competencies. Building upon previous ministerial experience, the program provides (1) education in the foundational areas of theological disciplines; (2) a focus for developing selected pastoral skills; and (3) an integration of these skills within the framework of a general theological understanding. The program is intended for persons who have had some ministerial experience and who wish to prepare for new ministries or to enhance their effectiveness in their current ministries.

Special Programs

The Hispanic Ministries Program provides theological education through courses which are historically, culturally, and religiously grounded in the Hispanic context and experience. It supports these efforts with additional educational opportunities such as seminars, workshops, community dialogue, and other special events.

The Certificate in Pastoral Study program provides an opportunity to develop a course of study either to enhance one's effectiveness in one's current ministry or to prepare for another ministry. It is especially designed as a program for continuing education.

Other continuing education programs are available, as well as the Biblical Sprirituality Program, the National Capital Semester Program for Seminarians, United Nations and World Faiths Program, Louvain Study Program, and the Israel Study Program.

Chicago Cluster of Theological Schools
Jesuit House
5554 South Woodlawn Avenue
Chicago, IL 60637   (312) 493-6637

Administration. Dr. David J. Bowman, S.J., Cluster Coordinator.

General Description. The Chicago Cluster of Theological Schools is an ecumenical association of one Roman Catholic and six Protestant seminaries. Its stated purpose has been to facilitate and coordinate education for ministry which would be of the highest quality, broadly ecumenical, and fiscally efficient. Two of the seven member schools are located on contiguous campuses in west suburban Oak Brook and Lombard. Five schools are grouped closely together on the south side of Chicago adjacent to the University of Chicago, with which they maintain relationships on various levels: bi-registration, a coordinated M.Div./Ph.D. program, faculty interaction, library, and physical education facilities.

The Cluster's diverse and extensive networks of resources for theological education are unparalleled in the Midwest and are among the most outstanding in North America. The almost 1,500 Cluster students have access to resources such as those represented by its large and diverse faculty; over 500 courses annually; library collections of over 900,000 volumes and about 3,000 currently received periodicals; and contemporary electronic media equipment, including portable and studio video capabilities.

Related resources available to the Cluster include the Urban Academy, the Spertus College of Judaica, and five other Chicago-area theological schools (comprising the Chicago Theological Institute). Cluster students may draw on these together with the vast resources of numerous institutions of higher learning and innumerable organizations and agencies of a religious, humanitarian, cultural, and scientific character in Chicago and its suburbs.

The Cluster member seminaries are: Bethany Theological Seminary; Catholic Theological Union; Chicago Theological Seminary; Lutheran School of Theology at Chicago; McCormick Theological Seminary; Meadville/Lombard Theological School; Northern Baptist Theological Seminary.

The Chicago Cluster of Theological Schools enjoys a cordial and fruitful working relationship with the Chicago Theological Institute, a consortium of five theological schools located in the northern metropolitan area. By common agreement, students enjoy tuition-free cross-registration privileges in all other member schools. Members of the Institute are: Garrett-Evangelical Theological Seminary; North Park Theological Seminary; Seabury-Western Theological Seminary; St. Mary of the Lake Seminary; Trinity Evangelical Divinity School.

The Cluster itself does not offer courses nor grant degrees. Application for study within the Cluster is made to the individual member schools. The seven Cluster schools offer a variety of academic and professional degrees at the Master and Doctoral levels, and programs of continuing education for clergy and laity.

Community Environment. The study of theology at the Cluster is exciting not simply because of the exceptional gifts of students and faculty, but also because of the environment created by one of America's major metropolitan centers and the University of Chicago. The city, with its rich social, religious, and ethnic diversity is a learning laboratory, valuable and challenging for those who learn to minister by ministering.

Chicago Theological Institute
c/o North Park Theological Seminary
3225 West Foster Avenue
Chicago, IL 60625

General Description. The Chicago Theological Institute is a cooperative venture among five theological seminaries in the northern part of the Chicago area. These seminaries are: North Park Theological Seminary (Evangelical Covenant Church), Garrett-Evangelical Theological Seminary (United Methodist), Seabury-Western Theological Seminary (Episcopal), Trinity Evangelical Divinity School (Evangelical Free Church), and St. Mary of the Lake Seminary (Roman Catholic). Its purpose is to study means of strengthening theological education among its member schools, to facilitate cooperation among theological seminaries on the north side of Chicago, and to coordinate when appropriate the resources of these schools for theological education and research.

Full-time students in these schools may take classes at any of the other schools at no additional charge up to one class per term. Each fall, one day is given over to a joint educational experience. A topic of discussion is chosen and the students and faculty join in dialogue. Each year the Institute offers a joint seminar which includes faculty representatives from each seminary. The ecumenical dialogue growing out of these experiences is broadening and enriching for all involved.

Chicago Theological Seminary
5757 South University Avenue
Chicago, IL 60637   (312) 752-5757

Administration. Dr. Kenneth B. Smith, President; Dr. Yoshio Fukuyama, Academic Dean.

General Description. At each point in its history, Chicago Theological Seminary has been an energetic and enthusiastic pioneer in theological education, always willing to risk being vulnerable in thought and deed. The Seminary's constant purpose is "to render service to a living Lord and to a church which is his body; that is, service not only for *Christ,* but through the *church."* Chicago Theological Seminary (CTS) was created and nurtured by the Congregational Churches. The cultural and theological ethos of those churches, which viewed themselves as standing on the cutting edge of prophetic insight into the Gospel message for each generation provided a congenial home for the CTS pioneering spirit and innovation. The Seminary grants the degrees Master of Arts, Master of Divinity, Master of Theology, Doctor of Ministry, and Doctor of Philosophy.

The Chicago Theological Seminary is one of twelve theological schools in the Chicago metropolitan area that make up the Association of Chicago Theological Schools (ATS). This ecumenical organization provides students with enormous resources for theological studies. Students may also take advantage of the vast resources of nearby University of Chicago.

Community Environment. The Chicago metropolitan area is a unique environment for the education of ministers and other human services professionals with its variety of ethnic groups, its many community organizations, medical facilities, churches, and cultural institutions. Chicago's 15 seminaries make it the largest center for theological education in North America.

Religious Denomination. United Church of Christ.

Religious Emphasis. Liberal.

Accreditation. North Central Association of Colleges and Schools; Association of Theological Schools in the United States and Canada.

Term System. Quarter; no summer term.

Enrollment in Degree Programs in Religion 1984–85. Total 166; men 88, women 78.

Degrees in Religion Awarded 1984–85. Master of Divinity 21; men 10, women 11. Master of Arts in Religion 2, men 2. Master of Theology 3; men 3. Doctor of Ministry 10; men 9, women 1.

Faculty for Degree Programs in Religion. Total 25; full-time 13, part-time 12.

Admission Requirements. Bachelor of Arts degree or its equivalent with a good record from an accredited college or university; personal qualification showing promise of usefulness in a vocation or field of service for which a program of theological study provides appropriate preparation; those applying for the Doctor of Ministry must in addition be graduates of accredited seminaries or divinity schools and possess an M.Div. or B.D. degree and have three years experience in ministry.

Tuition and Fees. Master's programs $390 per course, Ph.D. per course $475; Doctor of Ministry tuition for degree $4,200; general service fee $15; single room $505 per quarter; apartments $905-$1,065 per quarter.

Financial Aid. All full-time students in the first professional degree program may apply for grant assistance on the basis of financial need. Loans and student employment available. A number of special fellowships are also available.

Housing. All Seminary student housing is located in or adjacent to the main Seminary building.

Library Facilities. The Hammond Library is a working theological collection of over 97,000 volumes of books, pamphlets, and bound periodicals. The collection is strong in the classical theological subject areas of Bible, Church History, and Theology.

Religious Services/Activities. Weekly worship; social issues forums; religious forums; yearly retreat.

Degree Programs

The Master of Divinity program is the basic degree program at the Seminary. It requires that students demonstrate competency and creativity: (1) in both interpreting and communicating the meaning of Christian history, faith, and heritage; (2) in relating Christian faith and belief to contemporary issues and problems in the church and the world; and (3) in enabling the personal and social transformation of individuals, organizations, and systems. The curriculum for this degree requires courses in which the student demonstrates knowledge of the Christian Heritage; Theology, Ethics, and Contemporary Culture; and Christian Ministries.

The Master of Arts degree is designed to provide for the educational needs of persons wishing to study the Christian faith without the intention of ordination.

The Master of Theology degree is a flexible one-year post M.Div. program of study suitable for international students.

The Doctor of Ministry is an advanced professional degree, presupposing a first professional degree, designed to prepare men and women for responsible leadership in a wide variety of groups. The program of study includes seven regular academic courses. All students include in their individualized programs of study the following common professional requirements: a two-week group process and research design intensive; three professional consultations on the professional paper proposal prior to the candidacy exam; the candidacy examination; the professional paper seminar; and a successful oral defense of the professional paper.

Special Programs

The Center for Theology and the Human Sciences and the Center for Jewish-Christian Studies offer programs leading to the Doctor of Philosophy degree and require a minimum of two academic years of residence.

Chicago, University of
Humanities Collegiate Division
116 East 59th Street
Chicago, IL 60637   (312) 962-8650

Administration. Jonathan Z. Smith, Director of Undergraduate Studies.

General Description. The aims of the program in Religion and the Humanities are: (1) the understanding of religion as one of man's primary responses to and expressions of the human condition and (2) an appreciation of the difficulties inherent in undertaking a critical, disciplined study of religion. The area requirements, consisting of problem-oriented courses, imply that there is an intellectual tradition of the study of religion that must be mastered. All students in the program are required to take one quarter course in each of the four areas of basic problems in the study of religion, basic strategies in the interpretation of religion, basic issues in the self-interpretation of religion, and religious literature and expression.

Parent Institution. The University of Chicago is a private institution enrolling over 8,000 students. A diversity of generous donors, including the American Baptist Education Society, Marshall Field, and John D. Rockefeller, made the creation of the University possible in 1891.

Community Environment. The campus has over 130 buildings covering 170 acres on both sides of the Midway Plaisance. Chicago is the third largest city in the nation with a metropolitan area extending along the southern end of Lake Michigan. The campus is located in a residential neighborhood along the lake shore, fifteen minutes away from the central downtown area.

Religious Denomination. Nondenominational.

Accreditation. North Central Association of Colleges and Schools.

Term System. Quarter.

Admission Requirements. Graduation from an accredited high school; SAT or ACT; personal interview recommended.

Tuition and Fees. Tuition $8,670 per year; room and board $4,100; student fees $282.

Financial Aid. Financial aid packages are provided to those demonstrating financial need and generally consist of gift, loan, and/or term time work.

Housing. Residential halls on or near the campus are available.

Library Facilities. The University of Chicago Library houses over 4,750,000 volumes.

Degree Programs

The program in Religion and Humanities leading to the Bachelor of Arts degree requires the completion of one quarter course in each of four areas (see above). Students must also take one Western and one non-Western civilizational sequence in order to gain appreciation for the problems of interpreting religion within a wider historical and cultural setting. After completing the four area requirements, students select at least five courses from the wide range of College and graduate courses regularly offered on some aspect of religion. Some of these may be independent study. At least three of these courses must represent concentration in either a particular religious tradition or in a set of problems in the study of religion.

Chicago, University of, Divinity School
1025-35 East 58th Street
Chicago, IL 60637   (312) 962-8217

Administration. Franklin I. Gamwell, Dean of the Divinity School; Richard A. Rosengarten, Assistant to the Dean.

General Description. As the predecessor of the University and its oldest professional school, the Divinity School promotes systematic research and inquiry into the manifold dimensions of religion. While the School is mindful of its origins in the Morgan Park Seminary of the Baptist Theological Union, chartered in 1865, it has consistently drawn its faculty and student body from among the various Christian traditions as well as from the other major religions of the world.

Parent Institution. The University of Chicago is a private, coeducational institution, founded in 1891 by John D. Rockefeller on the south side of Chicago. Since that time, the University has established itself as a pioneer in higher education. Under the leadership of its first President, William Rainey Harper, the University made a number of innovations now considered commonplace in American colleges and universities: the four-quarter system; extension courses and programs in the liberal arts for adults; the junior college concept; equal opportunities for women in education; and an emphasis on broad humanistic studies for undergraduates. Such achievements have been fostered by Chicago in an atmosphere of independent, free inquiry responsive to the needs of communities lying outside the University itself.

Community Environment. The Divinity School is located in Swift Hall near the center of the main Quadrangles of the University of Chicago campus. The campus can be reached from downtown Chicago (commonly referred to as the Loop) by commuter train, bus, and by car.

Religious Denomination. Nondenominational.

Accreditation. North Central Association of Colleges and Schools; Association of Theological Schools in the United States and Canada.

Term System. Quarter; no summer term.

Degrees in Religion Awarded 1984–85. Master of Arts. Master of Arts in Religious Studies.

Faculty for Degree Programs in Religion. Total 40; full-time 29, part-time 11.

Admission Requirements. Transcripts; GRE aptitude scores; four letters of evaluation; an essay on intellectual development and academic/professional objectives. Persons applying directly for doctoral studies must submit all of the above plus a second essay on the proposed area of study in light of University resources.

Tuition and Fees. Costs per year: tuition $9,825; health service $126; student activities $30; medical insurance $306 (when comparable coverage is unavailable).

Financial Aid. Financial aid in the forms of scholarships, fellowships, and loans is awarded on the basis of need and academic promise. All applicants for financial aid must submit a Graduate and Professional School Financial Aid Service form.

Housing. The University of Chicago provides campus housing for both single and married students who request it. These include both dormitory and neighborhood apartments. Off-campus housing in the forms of walk-ups, high-rise buildings, and homes is also available. Housing costs are variable depending upon accommodations.

Library Facilities. The University of Chicago has over 5 million books in its library system; about 3 million of these volumes are housed in the Joseph Regenstein Library. Library resources bearing on religion are conservatively estimated at over 600,000 volumes. Special collections include the Grant Collection of English Bibles; the American Bible Union and Hengstenberg Collections of Early Theology and Biblical Criticism; the Goodspeed

Collection of New Testament Manuscripts with four Latin, six Armenian, and three Syriac pieces; and the Ludwig Rosenberger Collection of Judaica.

Religious Services/Activities. Sunday morning services of worship are held throughout the academic year in Rockefeller Memorial Chapel. Special services are scheduled for the major seasons of the church year. The Chapel is open daily for private meditation and prayer. In addition, Episcopal, Jewish, and Roman Catholic groups have houses near the Quadrangles, and a wide diversity of Christian, Jewish, and other religious groups in the neighborhood welcome students.

Degree Programs

The Master of Arts program in Religious Studies serves students who seek a general introduction to the contemporary study of religion, or who wish to update credentials in religious studies. It is a terminal degree. Students are introduced to the broad areas of study in religion by focusing on four spheres of inquiry: Religious Models; Religious Texts; Religions of the World; and Religions of the West.

The Master of Divinity program is the foundational program for students without previous graduate degrees who wish to pursue the Ph.D. in the Divinity School. This program of study is particularly designed to prepare students for traditional, well-defined ministerial professions as well as new and emerging forms of ministry.

The Doctor of Ministry program provides an opportunity for a specialized program of advanced studies to students who already hold the Master of Divinity degree.

The Doctor of Philosophy program prepares students for scholarship, teaching, and research in the area of religion and for the profession of ministry. Students preparing for careers in ministry are strongly encouraged to apply for admission to the special, year-long program in "Certification in Ministerial Studies for Ph.D. Students" (see *Special Programs* below).

Special Programs

The Certification in Ministerial Studies program is intended for students whose ultimate educational and professional goals require scholarly attainment in one of the fields of religious studies and who desire as well the professional educational qualifications for religious leadership. The program includes requirements in field education, arts of ministry, and major papers in theology, ecclesiology, and a problem in ministry. A sequence is pursued during one full year of a student's Ph.D. program, normally at the Research or Advanced Residence stage.

De Paul University
Department of Religious Studies
25 East Jackson Boulevard
Chicago, IL 60604   (312) 341-8300

Administration. E. Bruce Vawter, C.M., S.S.D., Chairman, Department of Religious Studies.

General Description. The Department of Religious Studies offers a critical approach to religion in a pluralistic perspective. Students are encouraged to explore diverse religions, world-views, and value systems, to clarify their own beliefs and values, and to develop the power to make critical and informed judgments. The Department offers two major concentrations: (1) Academic is offered students who wish to do religious study with emphasis on research or who desire greater personal or academic enrichment; and (2) Professional, offered in cooperation with the School of Education and intended for those contemplating a career in teaching religion.

An interdisciplinary program in Jewish Studies has been developed in cooperation with the Spertus College of Judaica.

Parent Institution. De Paul University is one of the ten largest Catholic universities in the world. It was founded in 1898 by Vincentian Fathers. De Paul offers baccalaureate and graduate degrees.

Community Environment. The Loop campus is located in downtown Chicago, the third largest city in the U.S. The Lincoln Park Campus is located at 2323 North Seminary Avenue. A broad spectrum of activities is offered by the city's cultural and recreational facilities.

Religious Denomination. Roman Catholic.

Accreditation. North Central Association of Colleges and Schools.

Term System. Quarter.

Admission Requirements. High school graduation from an accredited school; SAT or ACT; GRE required for graduate school.

Tuition and Fees. Tuition $116 per quarter hour; student life fee $15 per term; room and board $2,717-$3,398 per academic year.

Financial Aid. Scholarships, grants, loans, and employment constitute the types of aid available.

Housing. Most students reside at home; three residence halls and off-campus housing are available.

Library Facilities. The Lincoln Park Campus Library collection includes over 215,000 volumes.

Degree Programs

In addition to the 12 quarter hours required in Common Studies, all students are required to complete 16 courses distributed through 4 divisions as part of their Bachelor of Arts in Religious Studies degree. Academic or Professional concentrations have specific departmental requirements.

Elmhurst College
Department of Theology and Religion
190 Prospect
Elmhurst, IL 60126   (312) 279-4100

Administration. Dr. Ivan E. Frick, President; Dr. John E. Bohnert, Dean of the College; Dr. Armin H. Limper, Chairperson, Department of Theology and Religion.

General Description. The Department of Theology and Religion views theology as the disciplined study of the faith and life of a religious community. The focus of its work is on probing the relationships between Christian faith and the contemporary world of learning and living. The Department provides courses for undergraduate general fulfillment requirements plus the major and minor in Theology, the major in Christian Education, and pre-seminary education.

Parent Institution. Founded in 1871, Elmhurst College is one of the largest independent liberal arts colleges in Illinois, enrolling 2,000 day and 1,500 evening students. It stands in the tradition of American liberal arts colleges dedicated to the preparation of people for leadership and responsible service to society. This dedication is evident in the College's concern for religious faith and moral values. While the College takes pride in its origin in one Protestant tradition (United Church of Christ), it advocates an ecumenical perspective and celebrates the strong representation among students and faculty from Protestant, Roman Catholic, and Jewish traditions.

Community Environment. Located 16 miles west of Chicago's famous Loop and surrounded by suburbs, the College maintains, on 35 acres, excellent instructional facilities and a beautiful campus established as a national arboretum.

Religious Denomination. United Church of Christ.

Accreditation. North Central Association of Colleges and Schools.

Term System. Four-one-four; summer term.

Enrollment in Degree Programs in Religion 1984–85. Total 5.

Degrees in Religion Awarded 1984–85. Total 1.

Faculty for Degree Programs in Religion. Total 13; full-time 3, part-time 10.

Admission Requirements. Applicants must be graduated, or candidates for graduation, from a fully-accredited secondary school, and must present a minimum of sixteen academic units. Applicants must submit results from the ACT or the SAT. Test results are evaluated as part of the student's overall level of preparation for Elmhurst College work; minimum composite scores recommended are 18 on the ACT or 850 on the SAT.

Tuition and Fees. Tuition residents $3,325 per term; nonresidents $2,245 per term; interterm $572.

Financial Aid. The College administers a wide variety of institutional, state and federal financial aid programs, including scholarships, grants, loans, and student employment opportunities. Most financial aid is awarded to those students demonstrating financial need.

Housing. Students live in residence halls on campus.

Library Facilities. The A.C. Buehler Library houses a book collection of over 170,000 volumes plus large collections of pamphlets, annual reports, and curriculum materials for student teachers. It subscribes to over 800 periodicals.

Religious Services/Activities. Chapel is held two times a week. Campus Ministry plans student retreats, lectures, and discussions.

Degree Programs

The Bachelor of Arts program of the Theology and Religion department offers majors in Theology and Christian Education. The major in Theology requires a minimum of two courses from each of the sections: Bible, Theology and Doctrine, and Faith and Culture. The major in Christian Education emphasizes the liberal arts, theology, psychology, and communication. Some majors are able to include a second major, e.g., public education or church music. The department and College Chaplain assist students in planning individualized academic programs to prepare for seminary or graduate school in religious studies.

Garrett-Evangelical Theological Seminary
2121 Sheridan Road
Evanston, IL 60201   (312) 866-3900

Administration. Dr. Richard D. Tholin, Dean.

General Description. Garrett-Evangelical Theological Seminary is a graduate school of religion established and supported by the United Methodist Church which trains persons for professional ministries in the Church through the Master of Divinity, Master of Christian Education, and Doctor of Ministry degrees. It provides theological studies for laypersons through the Master of Theological Studies degree and a diploma program, and, through a joint Doctor of Philosophy (Ph.D.) program with Northwestern University, prepares persons for teaching and research in the field of religion.

The Seminary gives special emphasis to the training of black ministers for service to both black and white congregations, to the creation of openness and receptivity for women in the professional ministry, and to the cause of peace and world community.

Parent Institution. Garrett-Evangelical Theological Seminary is an independent institution located on the campus of Northwestern University.

Community Environment. Northwestern University's campus covers a mile along the shoreline of Lake Michigan and is bordered on three sides by the suburban city of Evanston. Evanston adjoins the northern limits of the city of Chicago and is 12 miles from the center of the city. It offers the advantages of a quiet, modern community close to a great thriving city.

Religious Denomination. United Methodist.

Accreditation. North Central Association of Colleges and Schools; Association of Theological Schools in the United States and Canada.

Term System. Quarter, summer term.

Enrollment in Degree Programs in Religion 1984–85. Total 353; men 178, women 175.

Degrees in Religion Awarded 1984–85. Master of Divinity 81; men 39, women 42. Master of Theological Studies 6; men 6. Master of Christian Education 9; women 9. Doctor of Ministry 1; men 1.

Admission Requirements. Graduation from an accredited college or university; grade point average of 2.5 on a 4.0 scale; recommendations; proficiency in English language. Some waivers and provisional admission possible in special circumstances. Transfers: satisfactory certification of credits earned; evidence of good standing; honorable dismissal. International students: qualification for graduate work; passing score on TOEFL.

Tuition and Fees. Tuition: Master of Divinity, Master of Christian Education, Master of Theological Studies $1,-200 per quarter; Doctor of Ministry $2,000 per year; Ph.D. (in conjunction with Northwestern University) $3,-234 per quarter. Matriculation fee $15; graduation fee $40; Northwestern University health service $60 per quarter; assessment services $20; other fees and deposits for particular programs and services. Meal plan Monday through Friday $455 per quarter.

Financial Aid. Need-based grants up to full tuition; academic scholarships up to full tuition, room, and board; ethnic minority scholarships; doctoral fellowships. Assistance in securing United Methodist and other denominational and designated scholarships. Employment opportunities including college work-study program and field education.

Housing. Single, double, and suite dormitory rooms ($320-$515 per quarter); efficiency, 1- and 2-bedroom apartments, furnished and unfurnished, for single or married students $250-$370 per month.

Library Facilities. The United Library combines the holdings of the Seminary and Seabury-Western Seminary for a total of 259,000 volumes. Special collections include works in 19th Century American denominationalism, pietism, patristics, Biblical studies, Christian art and archaeology, church history, Christian education (especially Protestant, 19th and 20th centuries), black theological studies, women's studies, Methodistica, Anglicana; manuscripts, journals, and letters of early Methodist leaders; Bibles.

Religious Services/Activities. Chapel services are held twice weekly; weekly communion and vespers; some special services.

Degree Programs

The Master of Divinity program is designed to lead students to an articulate personal theology of ministry through coursework, evaluation, and field work. Thirty-one units are required including Introduction to Ministry; Field Education; 3 Foundational courses; and 2 elective courses each in Biblical Interpretation and History of Christianity; 4 Foundational courses and 2 elective courses in Theology and Ethics; 2 Foundational courses in Preaching; 1 in Pastoral Psychology, 1 in Christian Education, 1 in Administration and Evangelism; and 2 elective courses among these five. The program requires 3 years for completion.

The Master of Theological Studies is a 2-year postbaccalaureate program for introduction and specialization in theology. It requires 18 units with specialization in one area of Bible and History, Theology and Ethics, or Theory and Practice of Worship plus a thesis or project.

The Master of Christian Education is a 2-year postbaccalaureate program with course requirements similar to the Master of Divinity program but with emphasis in Christian Education.

The Doctor of Ministry degree is a competency-based, contextually-oriented, collegially-focused program to facilitate career development. It requires 2½ to 5 years with on-campus seminars, directed correspondence study, and supervised practice in place of ministry. The Doctor of Philosophy, granted by Northwestern University in cooperation with the Seminary, offers specialization in Ancient Israel and Early Christianity, History of Modern Christianity, Religion in Society and Personality, or Contemporary Christian Thought.

Special Programs

A Certificate in Theological Studies is an 11-course program for lay persons. Continuing Education and Summer School are also available.

Hebrew Theological College/Jewish University of America

7135 North Carpenter Road
Skokie, IL 60077   (312) 267-9800

General Description. The Hebrew Theological College/Jewish University of America was founded to advance the principles of Orthodox Judaism, to ordain rabbis and spiritual leaders for the synagogue, and to train school administrators, teachers, youth leaders, and personnel to serve the needs of the Jewish community. Students are given thorough training in Talmud, Jewish Law, Hebrew Language and Literature, Bible and Commentaries, Jewish History and Philospohy. At the same time, students may pursue courses in the liberal arts and sciences on campus, thus preparing themselves for effective leadership in contemporary society, especially in the rabbinate, the chaplaincy, Jewish education, youth leadership, and Jewish community service. Degrees granted in addition to Ordination are Bachelor of Hebrew Literature, Master of Hebrew Literature, Master of Religious Education, Master of Pastoral Counseling, Doctor of Pastoral Counseling, and Doctor of Hebrew Literature.

Parent Institution. The privately-supported College/University is composed of a Liberal Arts College, Rabbinic College, Division of Advanced Hebrew Studies, Teachers Institute, Graduate School, and Talmudic Research Institute.

Community Environment. The College was established in 1922 and moved to a 16-acre campus in Skokie, Illinois, in 1958. The main building houses the dining hall, auditorium, book store, computer center, administrative offices, classrooms, laboratories, library, and residence hall. To the south of the main building is the synagogue. A suburb of Chicago and adjacent to Evanston, Skokie (population 69,000) has all the usual community facilities.

Religious Denomination. Jewish.

Religious Emphasis. Orthodox.

Accreditation. Approved by the Illinois State Department of Instruction, U.S. Office of Education.

Term System. Semester.

Enrollment in Degree Programs in Religion 1984–85. Total 99; men 17, women 82.

Degrees in Religion Awarded 1984–85. Ordination 5; men 5. Bachelor of Hebrew Literature 4; men 3, women 1. Master of Hebrew Literature 1; women 1. Master of Religious Education 1; men 1. Master of Pastoral Counseling 2; men 2. Doctor of Pastoral Counseling 2; men 2. Doctor of Hebrew Literature 2; men 2.

Admission Requirements. An applicant must be a graduate of an accredited high school and at the same time have completed high school Hebrew studies or pass examinations that show equivalent knowledge. The student must be able to interpret particular selections of the Talmud without the aid of an instructor; he must be well versed in the Scriptures and basic commentaries, must have an excellent knowledge of the Hebrew language, and must be familiar with the sections of the Shulchan Arukh (The Code of Law) that pertains to personal conduct.

Tuition and Fees. Tuition for Rabbinic Department and Division of Advanced Hebrew Studies $1,900; Jewish Studies Program $1,900; Afternoon Rabbinic Program (per semester) $450; School of Liberal Arts and Sciences $40 per semester hour; Graduate School $125 per semester hour.

Financial Aid. Pell Grants, National Direct Student Loans, Supplementary Educational Opportunity Grants, Guaranteed Student Loans, College Work-Study, and School Scholarships are available.

Housing. Dormitory rooms are available as well as apartments for married students.

Library Facilities. The library contains over 63,000 volumes with a special collection in Judaica.

Religious Services/Activities. Orthodox Jewish services are held daily.

Degree Programs

The requirements for the baccalaureate degrees are 120 semester hours for the Bachelor Hebrew Literature and 120 semester hours for the Bachelor of Religious Education. The Master's degrees in Hebrew Literature, Religous Education, and Pastoral Counseling require the completion of 20 courses plus a thesis. The Doctor of Hebrew Literature, Doctor of Religious Education, and the Doctor of Pastoral Counseling each require the completion of 40 courses plus a thesis.

Special Programs

The Hebrew Teacher Certificate program is offered.

Illinois Benedictine College
Department of Religious Studies
5700 College Road
Lisle, IL 60532   (312) 960-1500

Administration. Dr. Richard C. Becker, President; Dr. Thomas A. Byrnes, Head, Department of Religious Studies.

General Description. The Department of Religious Studies undertakes to offer general instruction in the history and theology of Christianity and other major religions, to foster interdisciplinary studies exploring the relationship of religion to other fields of study, and to prepare students for advanced study, teaching, or other careers in the field of religion. The major in Religious Studies leads to the Bachelor of Arts degree.

Parent Institution. Illinois Benedictine College was founded by the Benedictine monks of St. Procopius Abbey in 1887. It is a privately supported, coeducational Roman Catholic college of liberal arts and sciences.

Community Environment. The 108-acre campus is located in Lisle a suburban city located in the greater Chicago area, 26 miles from the downtown Loop. It is situated between the towns of Lisle and Naperville.

Religious Denomination. Roman Catholic.

Accreditation. North Central Association of Colleges and Schools.

Term System. Semester.

Faculty for Degree Programs in Religion. Total 3.

Admission Requirements. High school graduation or GED; minimum of 16 academic units; ACT or SAT.

Tuition and Fees. Tuition $5,286 per year; room and board $2,790-$2,840 per year.

Financial Aid. Financial aid is administered on the basis of need.

Housing. Dormitory accommodations are available on campus for 650 students.

Library Facilities. The Theodore F. Lownik Library houses over 125,000 volumes.

Religious Services/Activities. Roman Catholic and Benedictine by nature, the campus community realizes its commonality and dignity not only in work but also in prayer. The center of the community's life is the liturgical worship. The Eucharist is celebrated daily and on weekends. Other liturgical gatherings are Advent/Lenten Reconciliation services; liturgical planning committees; and reading/singing groups at Masses. The Campus Ministry is directed by a staff of Benedictines, a diocesan priest, and a team of students who may also be comprised of interns as peer ministers.

Degree Programs

In addition to the college requirements, students majoring in Religious Studies must complete a minimum of 36 hours in the field with a grade of C or better. These must include Introduction to the Bible, Jesus Christ in Christian Theology, The Church in Christian Theology, five courses at the intermediate level, and three courses at the upper level. Of the other courses completed by Religious Studies degree candidates, at least 60 hours are recommended in the humanities, education, psychology, and sociology. Majors are advised to give high priority among their electives to courses in history, languages, and philosophy.

Illinois, University of - Urbana-Champaign Program in Religious Studies
3014 Foreign Languages Building
707 South Mathews
Urbana, IL 61801   (217) 333-0473

Administration. Dr. Stanley O. Ikenberry, President; Dr. William F. Prokasy, Dean, College of Liberal Arts and Sciences; Dr. Nina Baym, Director, School of Humanities.

General Description. The Program in Religious Studies of the University of Illinois, Urbana-Champaign is an interdisciplinary unit within the School of Humanities, in the College of Liberal Arts and Sciences. The unit offers a large number of courses, primarily on the undergraduate level, in the major traditions of the world, the texts and languages of these religious traditions, and the philosophy, sociology, and anthropology of religion. The area of studies designated as Religion and Culture is designed for students seeking a broad liberal arts education with a focus in religious studies. The following designated areas of study are for students thinking about graduate work in one of the traditional areas of religious studies: Philosophy of Religion, Western Religion, Asian Religions, Biblical Studies, and Judaica. The degree Bachelor of Arts in Religious Studies is offered.

Parent Institution. The University of Illinois, Urbana-Champaign is one of the distinguished universities in America. While particularly strong in the sciences, the University contains units within the School of Humanities which rank among the best in the country. The University

offers a full range of graduate and undergraduate degrees, as well as some professional training and certification.

Community Environment. The University of Illinois' oldest and largest campus is located in the adjoining cities of Champaign and Urbana. The surrounding countryside is prairie and includes some of the finest farmland in the world. Champaign and Urbana have a combined population of about 100,000 and can easily be reached by air, rail, and bus. The city is 2½ hours from Chicago. The University is a residential campus of 180 major buildings on 705 acres.

Religious Denomination. None.

Accreditation. North Central Association of Colleges and Schools.

Term System. Semester; summer term.

Enrollment in Degree Programs in Religion 1984–85. Total 12; men 5, women 7.

Degrees in Religion Awarded 1984–85. Bachelor of Arts 2; men 1, women 1.

Faculty for Degree Programs in Religion. Total 8; full-time 6, part-time 2.

Admission Requirements. Admission of beginning freshmen applicants will be based on the completion of specific high school subjects and on a combination of high school percentile rank and admission test score. Those approved for admission must have at least a on-in-two (50 percent) chance of achieving a 3.0 (C) average for one or more terms of the first academic year on campus. Applicants are required to submit either ACT or SAT scores.

Tuition and Fees. Tuition for Illinois resident freshmen and sophomores $1,112 per semester; nonresidents $2,360; for resident juniors and seniors $1,231 per semester; nonresident juniors and seniors $2,717.

Financial Aid. For information write: Student Financial Aid Office, 420 Fred H. Turner Student Services Building, 610 East John Street, Champaign, IL 61820.

Housing. The University provides a full range of housing options. In addition, a number of the religious foundations on campus provide housing and a number of small religious groups also provide cooperative housing plans.

Library Facilities. The library houses over 6 million bound volumes within a total collection of nearly 10.5 million items.

Religious Services/Activities. Virtually all of the religious denominations found in the U.S. are represented on campus and provide worship, living, and education opportunities to interested students.

Degree Programs

The Bachelor of Arts in Religious Studies requires a minimum of 24 hours in the major. The areas of specialization offered include Religion and Culture, Philosophy of Religion, Western Religion, Asian Religions, Biblical Studies, and Judaica. The area of Religion and Culture is designed for students seeking a broad liberal arts education with a focus in religious studies. Persons thinking of the ministry or rabbinate are encouraged to consider this area. The last five areas are designed especially for students thinking about graduate work in one of the traditional areas of religious studies.

Lewis University
Religious Studies Department
Lewis University
Romeoville, IL 60441   (815) 838-0500

Administration. Br. David Delahanty, FSC, President; Br. Eugene Lappin, FSC, Vice President for Academic Affairs; Br. Raphael Mascari, FSC, Dean, College of Arts and Sciences.

General Description. The Religious Studies Department offers a major program that studies the religious dimension of individuals in their contemporary and historical expressions. The Department offers a variety of courses that may be taken to satisfy the general education requirements of the University.

Parent Institution. Lewis University is a small, private, independent, coeducational university. It is Catholic in tradition and character, and is under the leadership of the Christian Brothers. The University is open to students of all ages, regardless of race, religion, or sex, and welcomes students with a wide range of personal and career interests. The University offers its students programs in liberal learning, professional education, and technical training, with services adapted to the needs of its diverse student population. As part of its service to the community, and in addition to its undergraduate programs, Lewis offers graduate programs of high social relevance in education, social justice, business, and nursing.

Community Environment. Lewis University occupies 125 acres of a 670-acre development located 35 miles southwest of Chicago and 6 miles north of Joliet, Illinois. The Lewis-Lockport Airport is adjacent to the main campus and Lewis offers aviation maintenance management courses.

Religious Denomination. Roman Catholic.

Accreditation. North Central Association of Colleges and Schools.

Term System. Semester; summer term.

Enrollment in Degree Programs in Religion 1984–85. Total 1; women 1.

Faculty for Degree Programs in Religion. Total 7; full-time 4, part-time 3.

Admission Requirements. Applicants should be graduated from an approved high school with academic rank in the upper two-thirds of the graduating class and a minimum grade of C or an average of 77 percent; the student should have accumulated 15 high school units; three of those units must in English, the remaining 12 units in college preparatory courses; ACT or SAT; physical record on file in the University Health Center.

Tuition and Fees. Undergraduate tuition $162 per credit hour; graduate tuition $164 to $191 depending upon program; undergraduate activity fee $40 per semester; other fees where applicable; room $515 to $630 per semester; board $607.50 to $757.50 per semester.

Financial Aid. The Office of Financial Aid sponsors programs by which the University, in cooperation with federal, state, and private agencies, assists students in meeting the cost of higher education; to be eligible for programs, students must apply for admission to Lewis University and obtain and complete the Financial Aid Form (FAF) of the College Scholarship Service in accordance with state and federal policies.

Housing. Students may live on-campus if they wish; there are no special provisions for married students.

Library Facilities. The library houses over 150,000 volumes.

Religious Services/Activities. Campus Ministry is charged with the responsibility of furthering spiritual development on campus and invites all students to participate in those activities which facilitate the revelation of God in their lives. Daily Mass, Sunday Liturgy, Bible study, monthly retreats, and weekly prayer groups are some of the activities available.

Degree Programs

The Religious Studies Department offers a major program leading to the Bachelor of Arts degree that studies the religious dimension of individuals in their contemporary and historical expressions. Particular attention is given to the Christian tradition. A Religious Studies major must complete at least 36 hours in Religious Studies.

Lincoln Christian College and Seminary
100 Campus View Drive
Lincoln, IL 62656   (217) 732-3168

Administration. Dr. Charles McNeely, President; Dr. Gary Weedman, Academic Dean, College; Dr. Wayne E. Shaw, Academic Dean, Seminary.

General Description. Lincoln Christian College and Seminary is composed of a Bible college and a seminary sharing the same campus. There are many administrative services in common, such as business office, registrar, library, maintenance, and housing. However, there are separate academic deans, faculties, and classroom facilities. Undergraduate majors include Preaching, Youth Ministry, Christian Education, Day Care, Teacher Education, Business Administration, Sacred Music, World Mission, Church Growth, and Deaf Ministry. Examples of some Graduate majors are Preaching, Old Testament, New Testament, Church History, Theology, Philosophy, Christian Education, Pastoral Care and Counseling, World Mission, Church Growth, Linguistics and Bible Translation. Graduate degrees are Master of Divinity, Master of Arts, Master of Religious Education.

Community Environment. Lincoln Christian College's campus of 227 acres is located in the city of Lincoln,

Illinois (population 17,582). The city was founded in 1852, the only one of 24 similarly-named cities of the United States which was named for Abraham Lincoln before he became famous. He assisted in planning the city and performed law work necessary for its incorporation. Lincoln christened the town with the juice of a watermelon when the first lots were sold in 1853. The city of Lincoln is midway between Chicago and St. Louis on the main line of the Alton route of the GM & O Railroad. Churches of many denominations are located here.

Religious Denomination. Independent Christian Churches and Churches of Christ.

Religious Emphasis. Fundamentalist.

Accreditation. The College: American Association of Bible Colleges; The Seminary: Associate Member of the Association of Theological Schools in the United States and Canada.

Term System. Semester; summer term.

Enrollment in Degree Programs in Religion 1984–85. Total 535; men 360, women 175.

Degrees in Religion Awarded 1984–85. Bachelor of Arts 35; men 25, women 10. Master of Arts 8; men 8. Master of Divinity 10; men 10. Master of Religious Education 2; men 1, women 1.

Faculty for Degree Programs in Religion. Total 55; full-time 33, part-time 22.

Admission Requirements. College applicants must have high school diploma or GED; character references; transcripts from all previous schools; medical report. Seminary applicants must have a degree from an accredited college.

Tuition and Fees. College $95 per semester hour plus $40 per semester in mandatory fees; Seminary $70 per semester hour plus $55 per semester in mandatory fees; housing $370 to $555 per semester depending upon accommodations; board $465 or $575 depending upon meal plan; other fees where applicable.

Financial Aid. College: Church membership grants; state and federal grants; privately-funded scholarships; merit scholarships; loans; employment. Seminary: Privately-funded scholarships; loans; employment.

Housing. Dormitories are available for all unmarried students; separate dormitory floor for Seminary men; one-, two-, and three-bedroom apartments for married students.

Library Facilities. The Jessie C. Eury Library provides over 74,000 bound and microtext volumes and subscribes to 450 journals annually. In addition, the Library Media Center has a collection of some 7,000 records, 6,500 cassettes (lectures and sermons), 2,500 slides (mostly of the Holy Land), and over 1,400 filmstrips. The Rare Book Room contains an additional 800 volumes of Greek and Hebrew manuscripts and early Restoration Movement journals and documents. In conjunction with Enos E. Dowling's collection of 2,000 rare hymn books (800 of which are directly related to the Restoration Movement), it comprises one of the finest rare book accumulations in

the brotherhood.

Religious Services/Activities. The College has 3 chapel services per week, numerous prayer meetings, devotional programs, and musical programs. Chapel attendance is required of all students enrolled for seven or more semester hours of credit. Because each undergraduate degree program is designed to prepare a student for a specific Christian ministry, in-the-field service in the area of the student's major is a prerequisite for graduation. Early each spring all full-time students participate in a school sponsored week of evangelism and service.

There is a special chapel service once a week in the Seminary plus special seminars and lectureships each semester.

Degree Programs

The Bachelor of Arts degree requires completion of 128 semester hours with majors offered in various areas. The Christian Ministries major is designed to provide the ministerial students with a core of courses which will enable them to perfect the practical work necessary for the effective performance of the duties required of the Christian minister. Students may follow the Preaching Ministry or the Youth Ministry programs. There are majors in Christian Education, Church and Family Life Education (with a special Day Care Center Ministry program), Deaf Ministry, Teacher Education (in conjunction with Sangamon State University and Illinois State University), World Mission and Church Growth, Linguistics and Bible Translation, Christian Secretary (with special programs combined with Christian Education, Church and Family Life Education, and Youth Ministry), and Church Music. A Bachelor of Sacred Music degree program is also offered and requires completion of 164 semester hours.

The Master of Arts degree has a minimum requirement of 50 semester hours beyond the Bachelor's degree. The program of study must be approved each semester by the major professor assigned to the student and involves 18 hours in a major, 12 hours of core courses in at least three different departments other than the major, Biblical Languages, and Orientation to Seminary Studies.

The Master of Divinity Degree is offered for those desiring further preparation in the various fields of study for their chosen work. The degree requires the completion of 90 semester hours.

The Master of Religious Education requires 60 semester hours beyond the Bachelor's degree. It requires 25 hours in the major, 27 hours of core courses, 6 hours of Biblical Languages/Electives, and 2 hours of Orientation to Seminary Studies.

Special Programs

The Christian Workers' Certificate program is designed for those who want Bible college training for service in the local church but who feel that they cannot spend the time necessary to earn a full degree. Upon completion of the requirements for any of the programs, the student will be presented with a Certificate bearing the College seal.

Lutheran School of Theology at Chicago
1100 East 55th Street
Chicago, IL 60615   (312) 667-3500

Administration. Dr. William E. Lesher, President; Dr. Franklin Sherman, Dean of Faculty.

General Description. The Lutheran School of Theology at Chicago came into existence in 1962 as the result of the merging of four Lutheran seminaries: Augustana Theological Seminary (founded 1860), Grand View Seminary (1886), Chicago Lutheran Theological Seminary (1891), Suomi Theological Seminary (1896). In 1967, Central Lutheran Theological Seminary of Fremont, Nebraska joined the group. The most recent addition, Christ Seminary - Seminex of Chicago brings the addition of 9 faculty to the former number of 19. The Lutheran School of Theology at Chicago is now supported by nine synods of the Lutheran Church in America. Its basic degree program is the Master of Divinity. The Master of Arts, Master of Theology, Doctor of Theology, and Doctor of Ministry degrees are also granted. The School is a member of the Chicago Cluster of Theological Schools. *See:* Chicago Cluster of Theological Schools.

Community Environment. The School occupies a 2½-square block area at the north edge of the University of Chicago campus in the Hyde Park section of the city.

Religious Denomination. Lutheran Church in America.

Accreditation. North Central Association of Colleges and Schools; Association of Theological Schools in the United States and Canada.

Term System. Quarter.

Enrollment in Degree Programs in Religion 1984–85. Total 297 (full-time equivalent).

Faculty for Degree Programs in Religion. Total 28.

Admission Requirements. Baccalaureate degree or equivalent from an accredited college or university.

Tuition and Fees. Lutheran students tuition (Master of Divinity, Master of Arts) $1,575-$1,800 per year; all others $2,370-$2,700. Master of Theology, Doctor of Theology, Doctor of Ministry $2,370 per year.

Financial Aid. Financial assistance, usually in the form of grants-in-aid, is awarded primarily on the basis of need. The School also provides a number of merit grants, awarded to first-year students on the basis of their academic record and general performance in college.

Housing. Rental rates for School-owned apartments are determined by the size of the apartment and whether it is furnished or unfurnished.

Library Facilities. The library contains over 375,000 volumes.

Religious Services/Activities. Worship services are held each school day and the Eucharist is celebrated each week. Students are urged to develop a discipline of personal Bible study and prayer; the School encourages the development of spiritual growth groups for this purpose.

Degree Programs

The Master of Divinity degree is normally of four years duration. The first two years are devoted to gaining knowledge in Biblical, historical, and theological studies and in the practice of ministry and Old Testament. The Old Testament is begun in the first semester; the New Testament in the second. The program requires a total of 33 courses: Foundational-level work in Christian Tradition (14), Teaching Parish (5), Senior Seminar (2), and Electives (12) or Thesis (8). Further requirements include: Awareness Workshop, Clinical Pastoral Education, Workshop on Ministry (Preparation for Internship), Internship, Mission Requirement (course or project), Workshop on Educational Minstry, and Cross-Cultural Requirement.

The Master of Arts degree is a two-year program and may be taken in either a "General" or "Specialized" form, the latter directed to the field of Educational Ministry. In both programs, the student will normally take 3 courses per term in the fall and winter quarters of the first year, and 4 courses per term thereafter.

The Master of Theology degree is offered in Biblical Studies, Historical Studies, Theological Studies, Church and Society, and World Missions.

The Doctor of Theology degree is offered in the fields of Biblical Studies, Historical Studies, and Theological Studies. A minimum of two years of coursework (18 courses beyond the Master of Divinity or equivalent) is required for the doctorate.

The Doctor of Ministry is a professional degree representing the achievement of excellence in a study program in parish ministry. Requirements of the program include satisfactory completion (at "B" level or above) of a series of components totaling no less than the equivalent of 15 courses; demonstrated advanced competence in pastoral performance and theological reflection; and a comprehensive examination. It is designed to be accomplished over a three to four year period while engaged in parish ministry.

Special Programs

The School provides several programs of lay theological education which are intended to relate Biblical faith to the ministry of lay people in family, congregational, and vocational contexts. Lay persons with an appropriate academic background may also take regular curricular courses as Special Students.

McCormick Theological Seminary
5555 South Woodlawn Avenue
Chicago, IL 60637   (312) 241-7800

Administration. Dr. Jack L. Stotts, President; Dr. Lewis S. Mudge, Dean.

General Description. McCormick is a seminary which trains men and women for Christian ministry. Holding membership in the Chicago Cluster of Theological Schools and associated with the University of Chicago, it is an integral part of one of the world's great centers of theological education and research. It is an autonomous institution, with an ecumenical student body and related to the Presbyterian Church (U.S.A.) through its general assembly. Offering a curriculum of graduate professional education, the Seminary grants the degrees Master of Arts in Theological Studies, Master of Divinity, Doctor of Ministry, and Certificate in Theological Studies.

Community Environment. McCormick Theological Seminary is located in the city of Chicago, Illinois. The immediate neighborhood, an integrated community known as Hyde Park, is also the home of four other seminaries and the University of Chicago. The green trees and lawns, the stone and brick of academic buildings, apartment houses, shops and homes, form the setting of this vigorous community.

Religious Denomination. Presbyterian Church (U.S.A.).

Religious Emphasis. Reformed.

Accreditation. North Central Association of Colleges and Schools; Association of Theological Schools in the United States and Canada.

Term System. Quarter; summer term for D. Min. students only.

Enrollment in Degree Programs in Religion 1984–85. Total 551; men 429, women 122.

Degrees in Religion Awarded 1984–85. Master of Arts in Theological Studies 5; men 3, women 2. Master of Divinity 58; men 30, women 28. Doctor of Ministry 95; men 88, women 7. Diploma 2; men 2.

Faculty for Degree Programs in Religion. Total 24; full-time 17, part-time 7.

Admission Requirements. Bachelor of Arts or its academic equivalent; readiness and aptitude for study at graduate level; ordinarily it is expected that students will present an above average academic achievement of 3.0.

Tuition and Fees. Tuition $3,920; housing $337 to $440 per month.

Financial Aid. Aid is available for full-time degree candidates at the Master's level in the form of grants, loans, employment opportunities, college work-study, fellowships, scholarships, and awards.

Housing. The Seminary owns 2 apartment houses and rents space from nearby Lutheran School of Theology.

Library Facilities. The library houses over 365,000 volumes, 104,000 microforms, and 1,200 current periodicals. McCormick's library dates from 1829, when the earliest portions of its collection were founded as part of Lane Theological Seminary. Under the leadership of its first librarian, Charles Evans, later to become one of America's greatest bibliographers, and successor librarians, McCormick has contributed a number of initiatives nationally to theological library development.

Religious Services/Activities. Community worship is held each Monday at noon.

Degree Programs

The Master of Arts in Theological Studies offers a flexible program of eighteen courses that can be completed in two years of full-time study. The degree is offered in two forms: (1) concentration in a particular field (Bible, Church History, Theology, or a particular area of Ministry); (2) general theological studies.

The Master of Divinity program is distinguished by its focus on preparation for ordained ministry in the Church. A total of 27 full courses or their equivalent is required. The degree must be completed within six years of matriculation.

the Doctor of Ministry program is offered for pastors and other church professionals. There are three tracks available to students: Parish Revitalization, Church Executive Development, and Pastoral Care. The program consists of a minimum of nine units beyond the Master of Divinity plus the thesis in the practice of ministry. It is normally completed in three to four years.

The Master of Divinity and Doctor of Philosophy is a coordinated program offered in cooperation with the Divinity School of the University of Chicago. It is designed for students with marked academic talent and leads to a McCormick Seminary Master of Divinity degree and a Ph.D. from the University of Chicago.

Special Programs

The Certificate in Theological Studies is designed for students with a Bachelor's degree (1) who will be engaged as lay persons in the nonprofessional life of the church, or (2) who wish to correlate theological study with university studies leading to a graduate degree in another professional field. The requirements of the Certificate are a total of nine full courses and a research project.

The Diploma of the Seminary, whose content is the same as that of the degree of Master of Divinity, is offered to students in the Hispanic Ministries Program who do not hold a Bachelor's degree.

Meadville/Lombard Theological School
5701 South Woodlawn Avenue
Chicago, IL 60637   (312) 753-3195

Administration. Gene Reeves, Dean and Chief Executive; Neil H. Shadle, Dean of Students.

General Description. Meadville/Lombard Theological School is a graduate professional school offering programs of study for preparation for professional religious leadership. Master of Divinity and Doctor of Ministry degrees are awarded. The School is adjacent to and affiliated with the University of Chicago, where Meadville/Lombard students are full enrolled, take much of their course work in the Divinity School, and often earn Master's degrees en route to a Meadville degree. Meadville/Lombard is a founding member of the Association of Chicago Theological Schools, making the faculty, courses, library resources, and other benefits of 11 other schools available to its students. Through participation in The Urban Academy of Chicago, the School offers unusual opportunities and resources for training in urban and public issue-oriented ministry. In addition, international relations and global concerns are emphasized, and students from other regions of the world are usually enrolled at Meadville/Lombard.

The central purpose of Meadville/Lombard is preparation for ministry, primarily for ministry within the societies of the Unitarian Universalist Association, though some of its graduates pursue other careers. Courses, seminars, tutorials, clinical pastoral education, internships, field education, special lectures and workshops, worship services, and interaction with a wide variety of ministers, scholars, lay leaders, and other students, provide those at Meadville/Lombard with rich opportunities to prepare for ministry in the liberal religious tradition, to learn of its roots and promises, to participate in its present life, and to work creatively for its transformation and greater effectiveness.

Community Environment. The School is located at the corner of 57th Street and Woodlawn Avenue in the Hyde Park section of Chicago. It is adjacent to the University of Chicago. The center of the city of Chicago can be reached in 15 minutes by automobile, by the Illinois Central Railroad, or by CTA bus or train.

Religious Denomination. Unitarian Universalist Association.

Religious Emphasis. Liberal.

Accreditation. Association of Theological Schools in the United States and Canada.

Term System. Quarter; no summer term.

Enrollment in Degree Programs in Religion 1984–85. Total 35; men 26, women 9.

Degrees in Religion Awarded 1984–85. Master of Divinity 4; men 2, women 2. Doctor of Ministry 4; men 4.

Faculty for Degree Programs in Religion. Total 13; full-time 4, part-time 9.

Admission Requirements. Academic records of graduation from accredited college; Graduate Record Examination; personal statement; letters of recommendation.

Tuition and Fees. Tuition $6,300 per year; fees $711 per year.

Financial Aid. There are several sources of financial aid for students, including school scholarship funds, denominational funds, and bank loans.

Housing. Some housing for single students is available. Married student housing is available at the University of Chicago. Housing for both single and married students is available at neighboring theological schools.

Library Facilities. Meadville/Lombard's own library includes nearly 100,000 volumes and 120 currently received periodicals. In addition, the Regenstein Library of the University of Chicago is one block away and students have access to the several libraries of the Association of Chicago Theological Schools. The archives include special collections of papers of important Unitarian and Universalist ministers, including William Ellery Channing, Jenkin Lloyd Jones, A. Powell Davies, Vincent B. Silliman, Charles Lyttle, Clinton Lee Scott, and Jack Mendelsohn.

Religious Services/Activities. Vesper Services are held every Friday evening. Other special services are held occasionally. There are many churches in the neighborhood.

Degree Programs

The Master of Divinity program is designed to meet minimal requirements for a career in professional ministry. The basic requirement for the degree is a minimum of thirty courses or course equivalents in Ministerial Practice, Meadville/Lombard core courses, and Area Requirements. The program can be completed in ten quarters of full-time study, including a quarter in an approved pastoral education program and six quarters in an approved program of concurrent Field Education.

The Doctor of Ministry Program is designed for those who desire to pursue an advanced professional program for ministry by including within their work a concentration on a particular area of ministry or study. The degree may be completed in four years of full-time study, but often takes longer. A thesis is required.

Special Programs

A variety of continuing education programs are sponsored by the School, including an annual Winter Institute in Madison, Wisconsin.

Millikin University
Religion Department
1184 West Main Street
Decatur, IL 62522   (217) 424-6277

Administration. Dr. Roger Miller, President; Dr. C. Richard Decker, Provost/Vice President; Gerald A. Redford, Dean, College of Arts and Sciences; Dr. William G. Bodamer, Chair, Department of Religion.

General Description. The Religion Department of Millikin University seeks to teach religion from a textual, historical, and philosophical perspective. It seeks to be in touch with modern movements in religion and therefore introduces students to the current behavioral approach. The classical and modern are held in tension and cooperation to allow the students to pursue religious studies at more advanced and deeper levels in seminaries or graduate schools. The Department awards the degree Bachelor of Arts in Religion.

Parent Institution. Through its varied curricula, Millikin University provides opportunities for acquiring professional competence. It strives to develop a sense of ethical responsibility within the framework of Judeo-Christian convictions and perspectives. Through a program of study common to the four schools of the University (College of Arts and Sciences, College of Fine Arts, School of Nursing, Tabor School of Business and Engineering) Millikin seeks to bring each student to a critical assessment of him/herself and of his/her relationship to society, the physical universe, and God. Recognizing man's need for religious faith, the University places the quest for wholeness within the framework of Judeo-Christian perspectives.

Community Environment. Millikin University is located in Decatur, Illinois, a city of more than 90,000. This growing city is in the heart of central Illinois, 130 miles northeast of St. Louis, 180 miles southwest of Chicago, and 150 miles west of Indianapolis. The Millikin 40-acre campus is located near one of Decatur's most attractive residential areas.

Religious Denomination. Presbyterian Church (U.S.A.).

Religious Emphasis. Reformed.

Accreditation. North Central Association of Colleges and Schools.

Term System. Semester; summer term.

Enrollment in Degree Programs in Religion 1984–85. Total 4; men 4.

Degrees in Religion Awarded 1984–85. Bachelor of Arts 1; men 1.

Faculty for Degree Programs in Religion. Total 2; full-time 2.

Admission Requirements. In general, freshman candidates who present an above average secondary school record and satisfactory scores on either the SAT or ACT are considered scholastically acceptable.

Tuition and Fees. $8,000.

Financial Aid. The Financial Aid Program of Millikin University is designed to provide financial assistance to students who, without such aid, would be unable to attend. Additional awards are also made in recognition of character, academic achievement, and the need of the University for the particular talents or ability of the applicant.

Housing. Dormitory facilities and some off-campus housing are available.

Library Facilities. The Staley Library collection numbers approximately 154,000 volumes.

Religious Services/Activities. There are a variety of student religious organizations on campus including Brothers and Sisters in Christ, Campus Christian Fellowship, Fellowship of Christian Athletes, and denominational groups such as Baptist Students, Christian Science Students, and Newman Club. Weekly chapel is held and attendance is optional.

Degree Programs

The major in Religion leading to the Bachelor of Arts degree consists of 27 to 36 credits and provides basic coverage of both Christian and non-Christian studies. The Religion Department offers independent study and honors work to qualified students in their sophomore, junior, and senior years. Qualified students may also pursue any regu-

lar course in the department as directed study.

Special Programs

The Malone Fellow Program in Continuing Education is offered whereby a minister comes to the campus for a week to work with a faculty mentor on a proposed project.

Moody Bible Institute
820 North La Salle Drive
Chicago, IL 60610   (312) 329-4000

Administration. George Sweeting, President; Donald E. Hescott, Executive Vice President and Chief Operating Officer; Kenneth G. Hanna, Vice President and Dean of Education; Howard A. Whaley, Academic Dean; Thomas S. Baurain, Director, Moody Evening School; Jay C. Fernlund, Director, Correspondence School.

General Description. The Moody Bible Institute operates through a Day School, an Evening School, and a Correspondence School. It offers only the Bible major, but features emphases in: Bible-Theology; Bible-Theology, Greek; Bible-Theology, Hebrew; Christian Education; Evangelism; Pastoral Studies; Pastoral Studies-Christian Education; Missions; International Ministries; American Intercultural; Jewish and Modern Israel Studies; Missionary-Aviation Technology; Sacred Music-Church Music; Christian Education-Music; Communications.

Moody Bible Institute is a 100-year old school founded by D.L. Moody to train lay men and women to assist pastors in Sunday School-Evangelism in the local church. The school has grown to include 13 city blocks of campus in downtown Chicago, with 1,400 students, 700 employees, radio stations, the Moody Press, and the Moody Monthly. All students are required to do practical Christian work assignments each semester. The Institute offers a three-year diploma and a four-year Bachelor of Arts degree. The Advanced Studies Program for college graduates leads to a Certificate of Completion; it is for those whose undergraduate work is deficient in meeting Bible and theology requirements established by missionary boards. A member of the Evangelical Teacher Training Association, the Institute offers the Standard Training course, for which the teacher's diploma is awarded.

Since 1903 Moody Evening School has served the nation's churches by providing their members with training in the Bible and related subjects. It is conducted through three regions: Midwest (Chicago area, Michigan, Indiana, Wisconsin, and Illinois), Mideast (Ohio), and southeast (Florida). Each location has a master curriculum cycle designed to enable the student to achieve an academic credential.

Community Environment. The Institute's campus consists of 11 buildings in 13 city blocks of downtown Chicago, Illinois. *See:* North Park College and Theological Seminary for information about Chicago.

Religious Denomination. Nondenominational (Protestant).

Religious Emphasis. Fundamental - Evangelical.

Accreditation. American Association of Bible Colleges.

Term System. Semester.

Enrollment in Degree Programs in Religion 1984–85. Total 1,400.

Degrees in Religion Awarded 1984–85. Bachelor of Arts 86; men 63, women 23. Diploma 222; men 129, women 93.

Faculty for Degree Programs in Religion. Total 95; full-time 85, part-time 10.

Admission Requirements. High school graduation or equivalent; ACT; good Christian character; membership in an evangelical Protestant church and acceptance of the Institute's doctrinal statement.

Tuition and Fees. Moody Bible Institute Day School students pay no tuition. Room and board $1,675 to $1,495 per semester; student benefit fee for resident student $118 per semester, nonresident student $163 per semester.

Financial Aid. Because of its tuition-free policy, the Institute has chosen not to register for the various student financial aid programs available through federal and state agencies. Scholarships and grants are available.

Housing. Full-time students live on campus in residence halls.

Library Facilities. The Institute Library contains 107,-173 volumes. Students also have access to the collections of a large number of theological libraries in the Chicago area through interlibrary loan. The library houses the Moodyana and historical collection.

Religious Services/Activities. Chapel is held daily and attendance is required. There are many prayer meetings and meetings with a missions focus.

Degree Programs

Students enrolled in the Bachelor of Arts degree program must complete 130 semester hours. The academic requirements are in three groups: general education (46 hours), general professional (57 hours), and departmental major (24 hours), plus a required elective (3 hours), to make up the total of 130 hours. There is also a Christian Ministries core (21 hours) included in the required total hours. Majors are offered in Bible-Theology, Christian Education, Evangelism, Pastoral Studies, International Ministries, American Intercultural Ministries, Jewish and Modern Israel Studies, Missionary Aviation Technology, Church Music, Christian Education-Music, and Communications. Requirements for the B.A. degree with a major in Church Music or in Christian Education-Music and the B.S. degree with a major in Missionary Aviation Technology vary from the above in terms of credit hours required and length of time for completion.

Special Programs

Three-year programs of study require the completion of 98 semester hours of academic work plus Orientation. A Diploma of the Institute is awarded.

An extensive correspondence program is available from the Institute. For a detailed summation of courses offered, see *The Macmillan Guide to Correspondence Study,* Second Edition.

North Park College and Theological Seminary
North Park Theological Seminary
3225 West Foster Avenue
Chicago, IL 60625   (312) 794-5250

Administration. Dr. William R. Hausman, President; Dr. Robert K. Johnston, Vice President and Dean of the Seminary.

General Description. North Park Seminary, founded in 1891, is a professional school designed to equip men and women for the ministry. The Seminary is a community of faculty, staff, and students gathered not only for the purpose of theological study, but for reflection, fellowship, and the deepening of spiritual life. It sees itself as a servant of the Church of Jesus Christ, and particularly, of the Evangelical Covenant Church, its sponsoring denomination. The School is rooted in the pietistic renewal of the Swedish Lutheran Church, and nourished by the evangelical revival movement of this country. Central to that heritage is the dual emphasis on a new life of Christ and the Bible as the authoritative word of God.

Academic studies are organized into four major fields: biblical, historical, theological, and ministry. Three major programs of study are offered: Master of Divinity, Master of Arts in Religious Education, and Master of Arts in Theological Studies. The Seminary is a member of the Association of Chicago Theological Schools, a consortium of 12 Protestant and Catholic seminaries formed for the purpose of inter-institutional cooperation on all levels, especially in student cross-registration, library access and acquisitions, and interchange among faculty members.

Parent Institution. North Park College and Theological Seminary are under one "umbrella," but in many ways operate as separate institutions.

Community Environment. The diversity of life found in Chicago makes the city a classroom in itself. Chicago has always attracted a broad spectrum of people who represent varied ethnic, cultural, and religious traditions. In addition, Chicago offers vast cultural opportunities. It is the home of some of the world's leading museums and cultural centers. The best in music, art, theater, and sports is available the year around. Chicago has an uncommon amount of scenic beauty as well. The shoreline of Lake Michigan is a breath-taking sight. Hundreds of parks and forest preserves dot the city, giving it a greenness which is rare in large cities.

Religious Denomination. Evangelical Covenant Church.

Religious Emphasis. Evangelical.

Accreditation. North Central Association of Colleges

and Schools; Association of Theological Schools in the United States and Canada.

Term System. Quarter; summer term.

Enrollment in Degree Programs in Religion 1984–85. Total 165; men 135, women 30.

Degrees in Religion Awarded 1984–85. Master of Divinity 27; men 24, women 3. Master of Arts in Theological Studies 1; men 1. Master of Arts in Religious Education 3; men 2, women 1.

Faculty for Degree Programs in Religion. Total 28; full-time 12, part-time 16.

Admission Requirements. College degree with 2.5 grade point average from an accredited institution; testing for new students (Meyers/Briggs Test; Nelson-Denny Reading Test; Biblical Proficiency Test); satisfactory personal references.

Tuition and Fees. Tuition $1,015 per quarter; summer school tuition $253; activities fee $30; health and counseling fee $45 per term; housing $200 to $450 per month.

Financial Aid. Grant-in-aid program, scholarships, and student loan fund are available for financial aid.

Housing. Efficiency, family apartments, family bungalow, and single housing are available at the Seminary.

Library Facilities. The Mellander Library is a collection of materials in the field of religion and related subjects. The collection contains over 66,700 volumes as well as microforms and audiovisual materials. It currently subscribes to 330 journals. The Covenant Archives and Historical Library has approximately 5,000 books. In addition there are over 800 volumes of bound periodicals, about 750 reels of microfilm of which about half are records of local churches founded before 1930. Official correspondence, minutes and reports from various departments of the Evangelical Covenant Church, manuscripts, diaries, and personal records as well as 4,000 photographs have been indexed, copied, and filed for retrieval. Much of the material written before 1925 is in Swedish. The primary purpose of the Archives is to preserve and make available records of the Evangelical Covenant Church, but the holdings also include literature in the fields of Swedish history, Swedish Americana and other denominations of Swedish origin. Among its treasures is a copy of the Gustav Vasa Swedish Bible published in 1541. The Swedish-American Historical Society and Archives, a unique collection of Swedish Americana is also located here.

Religious Services/Activities. The religious life of the community is directed by the devotional life committee composed of both students and faculty. This group plans the worship life of the community as it is represented in the three weekly chapel services, special community services of Holy Communion, cottage prayer meetings, and other programs of spiritual care.

Degree Programs

The Master of Divinity degree is primarily designed to train persons for the parish ministry. It is a professional degree, preparing the student for some form of ministry — pastoral, chaplaincy, campus ministry, etc. — following a core curriculum and field education. The degree program also offers three other options: Specialized Ministries, Religious Education Focus, and Participation in the Seminary Consortium for Urban Pastoral Education.

The Master of Arts in Religious Education degree has as its purpose the equipping of persons for competent leadership in Christian education ministries in Covenant churches. It is designed in response to church needs and concerns that the denominational school should prepare persons for ministry in the area of Christian education. The program requires core courses in the Biblical, Historical, and Theological areas.

The Master of Arts in Theological Studies is a two-year academic program intended for lay persons who desire graduate study in Bible, theology, church history, and Christian mission, but who do not anticipate professional ministries such as the pastorate or Christian education. A person entering the program may choose either of two routes: (1) 90 quarter hours of study plus a comprehensive examination; (2) 81 quarter hours of study plus 9 hours of research and a thesis. In addition, each student will select an area of concentration.

Special Programs

The Seminary also offers Orientation Studies for Covenant Ordination, world missions courses, theological studies for the laity, and clinical pastoral education. It is a participating member of the Seminary Consortium for Urban Pastoral Education (SCUPE).

Northern Baptist Theological Seminary
660 East Butterfield Road
Lombard, IL 60148   (312) 620-2100

Administration. Dr. William R. Myers, President; Dr. David M. Scholer, Dean.

General Description. The ten basic commitments of Northern Baptist Theological Seminary are: (1) Biblical theology, (2) wholeness of the person, (3) growth in faith, (4) ministry to persons, (5) evangelical fervor, (6) social concern, (7) vocational diversity and skill, (8) excellence in scholarship, (9) integrity, and (10) spirit of cooperation. The Seminary awards the degrees Master of Divinity, Master of Arts in Christian Education, Master of Arts in Theological Studies, and Doctor of Ministry.

The Seminary is a member of the Chicago Cluster of Theological Schools, an ecumenical association of one Catholic and six Protestant seminaries. The seven member schools pool their resources to provide broadly ecumenical education for ministry which is of the highest quality. Along with the other Cluster schools, Northern also has beneficial relations with the Chicago Theological Institute, a consortium of five other theological schools.

Community Environment. The campus of Northern

Baptist Theological Seminary is located on 40 acres of rolling hills just 30 minutes from Chicago's Loop. Chicago is the ideal center for theological education. There are more seminaries in the Chicago area than in any other city in the United States or Canada — some 13. The greater Chicago area provides the widest variety of resources and settings for theological education from urban ghetto to world church. Major industrial, social, ecclesiastical, cultural, and other institutions are headquartered in the Chicago area. The opportunity to learn from, interact with, and serve these institutions is limitless.

Religious Denomination. American Baptist Churches in the U.S.A.

Religious Emphasis. Evangelical.

Accreditation. North Central Association of Colleges and Schools; Association of Theological Schools in the United States and Canada.

Term System. Quarter; no summer term.

Enrollment in Degree Programs in Religion 1984–85. Total 230; men 179, women 51.

Degrees in Religion Awarded 1984–85. Master of Arts in Theological Studies 11; men 8, women 3. Master of Arts in Christian Education 3; men 2, women 1. Master of Divinity 23; men 20, women 3. Doctor of Ministry 5; men 5.

Admission Requirements. Bachelor's degree or equivalent.

Tuition and Fees. Tuition $75-$95 per quarter hour, depending on number of hours; activity and service fee $20 per quarter.

Financial Aid. Assistance is provided for those students who may not otherwise be able to afford preparation for ministry. It is limited to: master's degree candidates; 9 hour minimum registration per quarter; demonstration of financial need. Average grant is $1,615 per year.

Housing. Apartments are available for rent (studio to three-bedroom).

Library Facilities. The library houses over 130,000 volumes and subscribes to 640 periodicals.

Religious Services/Activities. Chapel is held twice weekly and special convocations and lectureships are scheduled throughout the year.

Degree Programs

The Master of Divinity is the normal professional degree program, designed to prepare persons for ordained Christian ministry (such as pastoral, missionary, chaplaincy, and related ministry functions). The general aim of the program is to develop readiness for ministry in the areas of academic competence, ministry skills, personal qualities, social aptitudes, and religious maturity. Requirements of the degree include satisfactory completion of 120 quarter hours (including 12 hours of field education), which is normally a minimum of three years of full-time work. Each student must complete three Readiness for Ministry Assessments.

The Master of Arts degree in Christian Education pro-

gram prepares men and women for service as directors of Christian education, youth ministers, or as teachers in church-related institutions. Requirements for the degree include the satisfactory completion of 75 quarter hours and a comprehensive examination.

The Master of Arts in Theological Studies is a two-year degree program designed for college graduates whose vocational goals are best served by some theological education without the full preparation for the professional ministry. The program requires the completion of 75 quarter hours of study. Thirty-nine of these required hours must be taken in the major divisions of the curriculum (Biblical History and Thought, Christian History and Thought, and Ministries of the Church).

The Doctor of Ministry is an "in-ministry" post-Master of Divinity professional degree program featuring a collegial style of learning and engagement in ministry. It is designed for persons engaged in a wide variety of ministries. The curriculum is composed of six primary components: core courses, foundation courses, functional seminars in specialized areas, In-Ministry Units, external courses, and the final Project. A total of 36 quarter hours is required for the degree.

Special Programs

The Hispanic Tracks of the Master Programs provide theological education at the seminary level to Hispanics and non-Hispanics who serve or will serve in the Christian ministry among the Hispanic communities of this country and abroad.

Olivet Nazarene College
Division of Religion and Philosophy
Kankakee, IL 60901   (815) 939-5264

Administration. J. Ottis Sayes, Chairman, Division of Religion and Philosophy; Gary W. Streit, Chairman, Division of Graduate Studies.

General Description. The Division of Religion and Philosophy includes the Departments of Biblical Literature, Philosophy, Christian Education, and Theology. Practical as well as theoretical in scope, this Division has certain immediate objectives which relate the specific aims of its departments to the general objectives of the College. Among these are the following: (1) to acquaint the student with the religious, cultural, and scriptural heritage of the Christian faith that he may be led to self-realization through a full commitment to Christ; (2) to help the student to arrive at the world view in harmony with both reason and revelation; (3) to help the student gain a sense of responsibility for evangelism and to apply Christian principles to the socioeconomic and cultural problems of our day; (4) to prepare lay ministerial students for a life of Christian service in the church and community; and (5) to prepare students for further graduate studies in their chosen fields. Associate, Bachelor, and Master's degrees (from the Division of Graduate Studies) are awarded.

Parent Institution. Olivet Nazarene College is affiliated with the Church of the Nazarene, serving those who share her values and priorities. It seeks to communicate effectively the historical and cultural heritage and to provide opportunity for liberal arts education in a Christian academic community.

In 1907, a group of devout people in Georgetown, Illinois, who desired a distinctly Christian atmosphere for the education of their children, started an elementary school. A year later, the group purchased several acres of land three miles south of the original location, and enlarged the school to include a secondary level of education. This community became known as Olivet, Illinois, and was later to share its name with the school located there. In 1909, the school added a college of liberal arts and became known as Illinois Holiness University. The present name was adopted in November 1939.

Community Environment. The campus of the College consists of 160 acres of contiguous land. The principal buildings are arranged on about 50 acres, the remainder serving as playing fields, parking, and sites for future development. The College is situated in the village of Bourbonnais north of Kankakee, sixty miles south of Chicago.

Religious Denomination. Church of the Nazarene.

Religious Emphasis. Conservative, Evangelistic, Wesleyan Holiness.

Accreditation. North Central Association of Colleges and Schools. Member of: Christian College Coalition.

Term System. Semester; summer term.

Enrollment in Degree Programs in Religion 1984–85. Total 261; men 208, women 53.

Degrees in Religion Awarded 1984–85. Master of Arts 5; men 5. Master of Church Management 3, men 3. Bachelor of Arts 24; men 20, women 4. Bachelor of Science 12; men 5, women 7. Bachelor of Theology 4; men 4. Associate of Arts 27; men 14, women 13.

Faculty for Degree Programs in Religion. Total 12; full-time 8, part-time 4.

Admission Requirements. Undergraduate requirements include high school graduation or GED; 15 units with average grade of C; upper¾ of class; two certificates of recommendation; ACT. Graduate requirements include a Bachelor's degree from an accredited college or university; grade point average of 2.5; moral character consistent with attendance at a Christian college.

Tuition and Fees. Tuition $1,996 per semester; room and board (average) $1,137 per semester; registration fee $10; general fee $65 per semester; other fees where applicable.

Financial Aid. A comprehensive financial aid program includes scholarships, grants, loans, and employment opportunities.

Housing. On-campus residence halls are available.

Library Facilities. The Benner Library and Learning Resource Center houses over 137,000 volumes, plus 55,000 other items. It receives 800 periodicals.

Religious Services/Activities. The Chapel/Convocation programs are normally held Tuesday, Wednesday, and Thursday mornings in Chalfant Auditorium from 9:35 to 10:15. During revival time and other special occasions, convocation chapel is also held on Monday and Friday and last about one hour. All resident students are required to attend all services.

The Spiritual Life Organization assumes responsibility for two on-campus programs: Campus Ministries, which meets informally for Christian worship and fellowship, and Sunrise, which is designed to maintain a missionary emphasis among the students and provide fellowship for students preparing for the mission field. The Prayer Band meets each Tuesday and Thursday evening and provides a time for students to minister to students through the Word of God, song, and testimony. Spiritual Life also directs three off-campus ministries which include Life-Song Ministries, Disciples in Drama, and Evangels.

Degree Programs

The Bachelor of Arts with Religion major requires 39 hours of specified and supporting courses.

The Bachelor of Theology degree has the same requirements as the Bachelor of Arts with Religion major, except for the language requirement. Students may select six hours of courses in International Relations, Foreign Culture, Ethnic or Cross-cultural Interaction instead of the 10 hours of language.

Bachelor of Arts or Bachelor of Science with Christian Education Major are programs which provide training to individuals who feel called to this type of work. A combination major (B.A. or B.S.) in Christian Education and Church Music may also be pursued.

The Master of Arts in Religion requires the completion of core courses, additional departmental offerings, and 1 course selected from World Literature, World Mission, Holy Land Tour, or Philosophic Systems of the World. The program's objective is to train students for service in the various ministries of the church.

Special Programs

An Associate of Arts degree program with specialization in Practical Ministries is offered in a cooperative arrangement between Olivet Nazarene College and the Salvation Army School for Officer's Training in Chicago. The degree is awarded upon the completion of a minimum of 64 semester hours of credit plus fulfillment of other requirements.

The Institute for Church Management is a continuing education program intended to provide training in church management for pastors with experience in the pastoral ministry. Three week-long seminars a year are offered on campus in September, January, and May in which the pastors have concentrated studies with a variety of expert speakers. The week will include fifty hours of classes and discussion groups. The minister may earn either a certificate of credit, or fulfill requirements for the Master of

Church Management degree.

For those persons who have felt their call to the ministry later in life and who are not able to take the full degree program, Olivet Nazarene College offers the Ministerial Certificate Program. There are no formal academic requirements for admission to this program, but students must complete an orientation program before registering for courses. Credits earned in the program may not be counted toward a degree program. The Certificate is awarded upon satisfactory completion of the 86-87 hours of work specified.

Principia College
Humanities Department
Elsah, IL 62028   (618) 374-2131

Administration. Dr. Elaine R. Follis, Chairman.

General Description. Principia offers a Bachelor of Arts with a major in Religion and Philosophy, and three minors: Religion, Biblical Studies, and Philosophy. The Religion and Philosophy Department is part of the the Humanities Field (an academic division) that includes faculty in History, Religion, Philosophy, and Writing.

Parent Institution. Principia College is a small, private, coeducational, residential, liberal arts college for Christian Scientists. It is not formally affiliated with the Christian Science Church. It offers 25 Bachelor of Arts majors and 6 Bachelor of Science majors. Principia seeks to serve the cause of Christian Science by (1) developing in students thinking skills and (2) qualities of Christian character (mainly through on-campus academics, but also through athletics, student life, and off-campus programs), and (3) leading all students to master the basic principles, concepts, and skills in major fields of human knowledge.

The College historically traces its beginnings to a school established in 1897 by Mary Kimball Morgan. As other Christian Scientists learned of Mrs. Morgan's informal school and its goals, they asked if she would teach their children. The school grew and in 1906 Principia graduated its first high school class. In 1912, a junior college was added (one of the first in the nation). In 1934, Principia's new four-year liberal arts college at Elsah graduated its first class. Principia's purpose, policies, and history are found in *Education at the Principia*, and *The Sowing*, by Edwin S. Leonard, Jr.

Community Environment. The College rests on a four mile stretch of bluffs overlooking the Mississippi River and covers approximately 3,000 acres. Much of the acreage is protected as a National Wildlife Preserve. Elsah is situated 12 miles from Alton and 40 miles from St. Louis.

Religious Denomination. Christian Science.

Accreditation. North Central Association of Colleges and Schools.

Term System. Quarter; short summer session.

Enrollment in Degree Programs in Religion 1984–85. Total 7; men 2, women 5.

Degrees in Religion Awarded 1984–85. Bachelor of Arts 4; men 2, women 2.

Faculty for Degree Programs in Religion. Total 6; full-time 3, part-time 3.

Admission Requirements. High school graduates who are Christian Scientists with a successful high school background of 15 to 16 solid, college preparatory courses; participation in extracurricular activities; and an active, sincere interest in growing as a Christian Scientist, are eligible for admission.

Tuition and Fees. Tuition $7,128 per academic year; room and board $3,744 per academic year.

Financial Aid. Financial aid is available on the basis of need and is awarded after acceptance for enrollment. Financial aid may include a combination of grants, loans, and/or work programs.

Housing. Housing is provided on campus in 14 different student dormitory houses. Limited housing is available on and off campus for married students.

Library Facilities. The library maintains a collection of 148,000 books and 1,000 periodicals. It is a partial depository for United States Government documents. The Treasure Room houses a valuable collection of rare books. A national computerized system gives students access to collections throughout the country.

Religious Services/Activities. Sunday and Tuesday Christian Science services are held during the quarter by the Christian Science Organization on campus. It also sponsors a Sunday evening hymn sing. The annual Zion Bible Lecture brings to the campus a scholar of international reputation. Speakers have included Bernhard Anderson, Howard Kee, Paul Hansen, and David Noel Freedman.

Degree Programs

The Bachelor of Arts with a major in Religion and Philosophy offers students the opportunity to investigate and analyze concepts basic to their own and other faiths. A study of biblical languages and literature, modern religious traditions of the East and West, and the history of Judaeo-Christian tradition contributes to general education in the liberal arts, and it cultivates sensitivity to human needs and their satisfaction through spiritual means. Minors are available in both Religion and Biblical Studies.

Special Programs

Adults come to the Principia campus for 2 two-week Summer Sessions and 2 two-week Autumn Sessions, during which at least four courses in Biblical Literature and History are offered. During the Summer Session, there is also a course in New Testament Greek.

Travel-study programs are planned on occasion for students (10 weeks) and for adults (3 weeks). Countries visited have included Israel, Greece, Egypt, and Turkey.

St. Mary of the Lake Seminary
Route 176
Mundelein, IL 60060   (312) 566-6401

Administration. Very Rev. Gerald F. Kicanas, President-Rector; Rev. John F. Canary, Vice-Rector; Rev. John G. Lodge, Academic Dean.

General Description. St. Mary of the Lake Seminary has its roots in a charter granted by the state of Illinois over 130 years ago. As a seminary and school of theology it prepares candidates academically, formationally, and spiritually for the Roman Catholic priesthood. As an ecclesiastical faculty of theology, the Seminary is empowered to confer the Baccalaureate, Licentiate, and Doctoral degrees in Sacred Theology. Additionally, the Seminary regularly offers the Master of Divinity degree to priesthood candidates and the Doctor of Ministry degree to any qualified candidate. St. Mary of the Lake is a member of the Association of Chicago Theological Schools, a consortium of 12 Protestant and Catholic seminaries formed for the purpose of inter-institutional cooperation on all levels, especially in student cross-registration, library access and acquisitions, and interchange among faculty members.

Community Environment. The campus of St. Mary of the Lake Seminary is located in Mundelein, Illinois, 40 miles northwest of downtown Chicago. The 14 major buildings comprising the physical plant are situated at the west end of the campus overlooking a lake.

Religious Denomination. Roman Catholic.

Accreditation. Association of Theological Schools in the United States and Canada.

Term System. Quarter; no summer term.

Enrollment in Degree Programs in Religion 1984–85. Total 199; men 180, women 19.

Degrees in Religion Awarded 1984–85. Bachelor in Sacred Theology 6; men 6. Master of Divinity 20; men 20. Licentiate in Sacred Theology 1; men 1. Doctor of Ministry 3; men 2, women 1.

Faculty for Degree Programs in Religion. Total 36; full-time 22, part-time 14.

Admission Requirements. Bachelor's degree from an accredited college or university; 18 credit hours of undergraduate philosophy courses including: an introduction to philosophical question and methodology, a course in the medieval period, a course in the modern or contemporary period, and at least 12 credit hours in religious studies.

Tuition and Fees. Tuition $1,010 per quarter (in residence); board $670 per quarter; room $375 per quarter; general fee $25; non-resident tuition $140 per credit hour; retreat fee (off-campus) $85.

Financial Aid. Guaranteed Student Loan; Work Program.

Housing. Each student has a private room with individual study, shower, and toilet facilities.

Library Facilities. The Feehan Memorial Library houses over 140,000 volumes. It is especially strong in its sections covering philosophy, patristic studies, theology, and church history, with a view to supporting research work in these fields. The library maintains subscriptions to over 400 periodical publications. It participates in inter-library loan programs with theological and general libraries in the Chicago area. Students thereby have access to nearly one million volumes in a variety of disciplines.

Degree Programs

The Master of Divinity curriculum is designed as a four-year program of academic study and field work. The student entering his first year will spend eleven quarters taking courses on campus, one quarter working on-site in a pastoral internship off-campus, and one summer (after Third Year) in a program of Clinical Pastoral Education or some other approved internship program.

The Doctor of Ministry program is sponsored conjointly by the St. Mary of the Lake Seminary and the Archdiocesan Center for Pastoral Ministry. The goal of the program is to develop the ministerial skill of theological reflection in and through projects concerned with ministering to ministers. The program interrelates three elements: project centeredness, formal input, and resource supervision. This interrelating takes place primarily within the peer group of candidates.

The Doctorate in Sacred Theology requires the completion of at least two years of study with at least one year devoted full-time to research. During the first year in the program, candidates must successfully complete a minimum of three seminars. Upon the completion of the course work (at least nine credit hours), the student becomes a candidate for the doctorate.

Special Programs

The programs of study for the Baccalaureate and Licentiate in Sacred Theology are being revised according to observations of the Sacred Congregation for Catholic Education about the recently rewritten Statutes of the Faculty of St. Mary of the Lake Seminary, and in terms of the rearrangement of the basic, required courses that are part of the Seminary's Master of Divinity program. Contact the Seminary for the revised details.

Seabury-Western Theological Seminary
2122 Sheridan Road
Evanston, IL 60201   (312) 328-9300

Administration. Very Rev. Mark S. Sisk, Dean and President; Rev. William P. Haugaard, Associate Dean for Academic Affairs.

General Description. Seabury-Western Theological Seminary is an accredited seminary of the Episcopal Church. It exists to provide theologically informed leadership for the Church, through the priestly and other ministries, of both ordained and lay men and women. It seeks to maintain the historic Anglican balance, at once Catholic and evangelical, evangelistic and scholarly spiritual, yet socially aware. The Seminary confers the following degrees and diplomas: Master of Divinity, Master of Arts in Special Ministries, Master of Theological Studies, Licentiate in Theology, and Certificates of Study. Seabury-Western is a member of the Association of Chicago Theological Schools, a consortium of 12 Protestant and Catholic seminaries formed for the purpose of inter-institutional cooperation on all levels, especially in student cross-registration, library access and acquisitions, and interchange among faculty members.

Community Environment. Evanston with its lovely old homes and wide, tree-lined streets, is an ideal setting for scholarly study. Situated on Northwestern University's main campus and across the street from Garrett-Evangelical Theological Seminary, Seabury-Western is in a milieu that is spiritually, educationally, and culturally alive. With a racially and economically diverse population of 74,000, Evanston is the 8th largest city in the state. Chicago, the nation's third largest city, is only 30 minutes away by car or public transportation.

Religious Denomination. Episcopal.

Religious Emphasis. Anglican.

Accreditation. North Central Association of Colleges and Schools; Association of Theological Schools in the United States and Canada.

Term System. Quarter; no summer term.

Enrollment in Degree Programs in Religion 1984–85. Total 63; men 44, women 19.

Degrees in Religion Awarded 1984–85. Master of Divinity 29; men 19, women 10.

Faculty for Degree Programs in Religion. Total 15; full-time 11, part-time 4.

Admission Requirements. Normally a Bachelor's degree; aptitude portion of the Graduate Record Examination; on-campus interview; approval of Bishop or other ecclesiastical authority.

Tuition and Fees. Tuition $4,300 for 3 quarters; health fee $358; student body fee $50; single student residence $1,159; married student apartments $260 to $460 per month; refectory meal plan $1,400.

Financial Aid. Funds are administered solely on the basis of need according to the guidelines of the Association of Theological Schools. Students file a Graduate and Professional Schools Financial Aid Service application to determine need. Financial aid packages include outright grants and the approval to apply for work-study jobs.

Housing. Dormitory rooms for single students and on-campus apartments for married students are available; limited number of nearby off-campus apartments.

Library Facilities. The United Library of Garrett-Evangelical and Seabury-Western is located on both campuses of the seminaries. The collections, which number around 250,000 volumes, have strengths in Bible, Patristics, Anglicana, Methodistica, Liturgics, and nineteenth-century American Protestantism. Seabury-Western's special collections include the Hibbard Library of ancient Near Eastern material and the Hale Rare Book Collection with

exemplars of the early prayer books. Located at Garrett-Evangelical are the Wesleyana Collection and the Keen Bible Collection of English editions of the Bible. Garrett-Evangelical also has a collection of curriculum materials housed in the Religious Education Curriculum Laboratory.

Religious Services/Activities. Daily Episcopal chapel services, morning and evening prayer, and Holy Eucharist are celebrated in the Chapel of St. John the Divine. All liturgies authorized by the Episcopal Church are used on a rotating basis, and a variety of liturgical styles are used. There are informal prayer and fellowship groups on campus.

Degree Programs

The Master of Divinity degree program is designed to proved the first level of professional competence for students seeking ordination or some other form of professional ministry. A flexible core curriculum has been developed which provides the essentials common for all who are called to professional ordained ministry and allows each student, in close consultation with an advisor, to shape a program that will build upon knowledge and skills brought to seminary and accommodate particular interests which suggest directions of future ministry.

The Master of Arts in Special Ministries is a two-year program designed to prepare for special ministries men and women not seeking ordination to the priesthood. Its curriculum is a blend of academic and professional elements providing instruction and experience to promote the development of effective leadership for Church and society.

The Master of Theological Studies is a two-year program which is specifically designed (1) for persons who wish to develop an increased theological knowledge as a basis for their life and work; (2) to provide a broad background in theological disciplines with a particular focus in one discipline; or (3) to offer multi-disciplinary education for those in or preparing for other professions who wish to combine that vocation with the perspective of a theological understanding.

Special Programs

Students not holding a baccalaureate degree or its equivalent who fulfill all requirements for the Master of Divinity degree will be awarded the diploma of Licentiate in Theology.

Students following a one- or two-year course of study prepared in consultation with the Seminary, their Bishops, and/or Commissions on Ministry will be awarded an appropriate Certificate of Study.

Southern Illinois University
Religious Studies Department
Carbondale, IL 62901   (618) 453-3067

Administration. Dr. Albert Somit, President; John C. Guyon, Vice President for Academic Affairs and Research.

General Description. The Religious Studies Department is conceived with the purpose of studying religion critically, comparatively, and scientifically. It offers a full range of courses designed to provide students with the intellectual background and tools required for a critical understanding of the forms and traditions of religion that have appeared in human culture.

Parent Institution. Southern Illinois University was originally chartered as a normal school. Now it includes the Schools of Agriculture, Technical Careers, Law, and Medicine, and the Colleges of Business and Administration, Communications and Fine Arts, Education, Engineering and Technology, Human Resources, Liberal Arts, and Science.

Community Environment. Southern Illinois University is located in Carbondale, Illinois. The city is the economic center of southern Illinois and is only hours away from Chicago, St. Louis, and Memphis. The University sits among rolling hills, farmlands, and orchards just 60 miles above the confluence of the Mississippi and Ohio Rivers. Two state parks (that are geological relics of the Great Glacier), four large lakes, and the spectacular 240,000-acre Shawnee National Forest are close at hand. The Mid-South climate is ideal for year-around outdoor activities.

Religious Denomination. None.

Accreditation. North Central Association of Colleges and Schools.

Term System. Semester.

Enrollment in Degree Programs in Religion 1984–85. Total 9; men 6, women 3.

Degrees in Religion Awarded 1984–85. Bachelor of Arts 3; men 2, women 1.

Faculty for Degree Programs in Religion. Total 5; full-time 2, part-time 3.

Admission Requirements. High school graduates who (1) have an entrance examination score at the fiftieth percentile or higher or (2) have an entrance examination score in the thirty-third percentile or higher and rank in the upper half of their graduating classes based on class rank are eligible for admission to any semester.

Tuition and Fees. Tuition 12 or more more semester hours $447; student center fee $29; student activity fee $855; student recreation fund fee $24; athletic fee $30; Student-to-Student grant program fee $2.25; medical fee $60; revenue bond fee $52.80; room and board costs vary.

Financial Aid. The Office of Student Work and Financial Assistance aids students in seeking monetary assistance for financing their postsecondary education. A package of financial aid is prepared for those students who qualify. The package may include scholarships, grants, work, and loans.

Housing. The University offers a variety of living experiences through the on-campus residence halls for single students. Both furnished and unfurnished apartments are available for married students.

Library Facilities. The Morris Library houses 1,666,000 printed volumes, more than 1,960,000 microtext units, and over 14,900 current serials. The library is one of the largest open-shelf, subject-division academic libraries in the United States.

Degree Programs

The Bachelor of Arts with a major in Religious Studies requires the completion of 24 credits in the major, distributed as follows: 9 hours or three courses on specific religious traditions; 9 hours or three courses on religious themes or issues; and 10 hours of electives, 6 of which (with the Department's approval) may come from other departments such as English, History, Anthropology, Philosophy, or Psychology.

Spertus College of Judaica
618 South Michigan Avenue
Chicago, IL 60605   (312) 922-9012

Administration. Dr. Howard A. Sulkin, President; Dr. Byron L. Sherwin, Vice President for Academic Affairs; Dr. Nathaniel Stampfer, Director of the Holland Graduate Program in Jewish Education.

General Description. Spertus College is the largest non-theological, secular institution of higher Jewish learning in the midwest. It is a liberal arts institution specializing in Judaic Studies. It offers undergraduate and graduate degrees in Jewish studies, Jewish education, Jewish communal service, and human services administration. Spertus also serves as the common department of Judaic Studies for several local colleges and universities including two (University of Illinois at Chicago and Northeastern Illinois University) with which it has cooperative agreements offering reciprocal courses and credits. In addition, Spertus also has cooperative programs with Roosevelt University, DePaul University, Mundelein College, and the Chicago Cluster of Theological Schools.

Community Environment. The Spertus College of Judaica, housed in the Ratner Center, is just south of the Chicago Loop area, one mile east of the University of Illinois at Chicago, and one block south of Roosevelt University. Within a 2-mile radius are the Chicago Cultural Center, the Art Institute, Orchestra Hall (home of the Chicago Symphony Orchestra), as well as the downtown campuses of De Paul, Loyola, and Northwestern Universities. The College faces Grant Park and the famed Lake Michigan lakefront. Chicago, Illinois, the third largest city in the nation, has a population of 3,740,000, and consists of a metropolitan area extending along the southern end of Lake Michigan. It is a leading industrial, medical, educational, and cultural center.

Religious Denomination. Jewish.

Accreditation. North Central Association of Colleges and Schools.

Term System. Quarter; summer term.

Enrollment in Degree Programs in Religion 1984–85. Total 176.

Degrees in Religion Awarded 1984–85. Bachelor of Arts in Judaic Studies 3; men 1, women 2. Bachelor of Judaic Studies 2; men 1, women 1. Master of Arts in Jewish Education 5; men 1, women 4. Master of Arts in Jewish Studies 2; women 2. Master of Arts in Jewish Communal Service 2; women 2.

Faculty for Degree Programs in Religion. Total 22; full-time 8, part-time 14.

Admission Requirements. Bachelor's degree: graduation from high school; transcript; interview. Master's degree: Bachelor's degree from accredited institution; transcripts; letters of recommendation; interview.

Tuition and Fees. Tuition $2,880 per year; estimated books and personal expenses $1,500 per year.

Financial Aid. Scholarships and grants, loans, and College-Work Study Program are available.

Housing. No student housing.

Library Facilities. The Norman Asher and Helen Asher Library is one of the largest circulating libraries of Judaica in the Midwest. Its resources of 75,000 volumes include extensive collections in Judaica and Hebraica; a distinguished rare book collection; Israeli publications; the Badona Spertus Library of Art in Judaica; and the Chicago Jewish Archives, which hold the archives of the Jewish Federation of Metropolitan Chicago. The Library has developed the Levin microfilm and microfiche collection of Jewish newspapers and journals.

Degree Programs

All Bachelor of Arts students are required to complete 180 quarter hours of course work. Of these, 90 hours are in Judaic Studies, and 90 in general studies. The 90 quarter hours in Judaic Studies include 24 hours in Hebrew language and 66 hours in Judaica.

The Bachelor of Judaic Studies program is offered mainly to individuals who already possess a bachelor's degree in a field other than Jewish Studies. The requirements for the degree are 78 quarter credit hours with 24 hours in Hebrew, 30 hours in Jewish Studies, and 24 hours of elective credit.

The Master of Arts in Jewish Education has the objective of training individuals in the competencies necessary to work in and administer Jewish schools of all types. The main areas of concentration are Teaching and Curriculum Development and School Administration. Other possible options, individually arranged, are Special Education, Early Childhood Education, and Adult Education.

The Master of Arts in Jewish Communal Service is a professional degree program designed to train individuals as administrators and managers in Jewish social service

agencies. The curriculum components are professional core courses in Jewish Communal Studies; graduate level courses in Judaica; and field work experience in a Jewish agency.

The Master of Arts in Jewish Studies is a program in which students may select major and minor areas of concentration from the following: Bible, Hebrew Literature, Jewish History, Jewish Thought, and Rabbinic Literature.

The Master of Science in Human Services Administration is a one-year evening program offered to individuals already working in the field who are seeking positions on a managerial level. The basic goal of the program is to provide the requisite skills for administrative and managerial positions in hospitals, social service agencies, and other institutions involved in the helping professions.

Special Programs

The School of Social Work of Loyola University of Chicago and Spertus College have developed a parallel degree program for persons who intend to direct practice in Jewish communal agencies. It leads to a Master of Arts in Jewish Communal Service and a Master of Social Work.

The Joseph M. Levine Program of Extension Studies offers courses in suburban areas of Chicago. The courses are designed mainly for adults who wish to develop an awareness and appreciation of Jewish culture, thought, and history.

Trinity Christian College
Theology Department
6601 West College Drive
Palos Heights, IL 60426   (312) 597-3000

Administration. Dr. Kenneth B. Bootsma, President; Dr. Burton J. Rozema, Vice President of Academic and Student Affairs; Dr. Douglas M. Eckardt, Chairman, Theology Department.

General Description. The Theology Program at Trinity Christian College is characterized by an emphasis on Biblical studies. Students who pursue this program take courses which deal with questions regarding the nature and history of the Scriptures, the key Biblical ideas which are significant for a Christian perspective in other academic areas, and how to study the Bible. This approach incorporates elements of historical and systematic theology in the course work.

The Pre-Seminary program prepares the student to meet the entrance requirements of the seminary of one's choice. Most seminaries require a strong liberal arts education and knowledge of Greek as well as a modern foreign language. Most seminaries discourage majoring in theology at the undergraduate level; they prefer this at the seminary level. Trinity provides the appropriate major programs.

The senior year of both the Theology major and the

Pre-Seminary Program features participation in the field technology course. Here the student receives practical experience in applying academic knowledge and personal skills. Trinity Theology students serve churches in various capacities; they also study and evaluate churches of different faiths. The application of Biblical insight to contemporary issues is a major objective of this program.

Parent Institution. Trinity Christian College's educational plan has been developed to offer what the college believes to be the "best of all worlds" in education: a solid core program designed to enable all students to develop a Christian perspective on the world and life; a major in the liberal arts enabling the student to deal academically with the past, with schools of thought, relationships, cultural dimensions, and forms of communication. It also permits preparatory studies for the professions. The goal of Trinity Christian College is to graduate students who will bring Christian influence into whatever area of life they have been called. The degrees Bachelor of Arts and Bachelor of Science are awarded.

Community Environment. Trinity Christian College is located in Palos Heights, Illinois, a residential area 25 miles from downtown Chicago. The campus was formerly a country club. It is comprised of 8 buildings on 50 wooded acres.

Religious Denomination. Trinity Christian College is governed by a society of administrators from the Christian Reformed Church and the Reformed Church in America.

Religious Emphasis. Reformed.

Accreditation. North Central Association of Colleges and Schools.

Term System. Semester; no summer term.

Faculty for Degree Programs in Religion. Total 5; full-time 1, part-time 4.

Admission Requirements. High school transcript showing a minimum of 16 units of credit; grade point average of 2.0 or more on a 4.0 scale; average or above average grades in English and Mathematics; college prep courses including 3 or 4 years of English; 3 years in either math, science, or social studies; 2 two-year sequences in either a foreign language, math, science, or social studies; ACT or SAT.

Tuition and Fees. Tuition $2,545 per semester (12-18 hours); $175 per semester hour (less than 12 hours or more than 18); room $980 per year; board (meal ticket) $1,310 per year.

Financial Aid. National Direct Student Loan, Pell Grant, Supplementary Educational Opportunity Grant, federal and state loans, state scholarships, merit recognition, institutional-sponsored programs, and scholarship endowments.

Housing. Residence halls and apartments are available; no married student housing.

Library Facilities. The library contains over 50,000 volumes, 19,000 microfiche, and 300 periodical subscriptions. There is a Dutch Heritage Collection.

Religious Services/Activities. Chapel is held three times

per week and attendance is optional.

Degree Programs

The Bachelor of Arts degree with a major in Theology requires the completion of 125 credit hours. The major consists of a minimum of 27 semester hours of theology credit, plus a recommended one-year study of Greek. The major must include 2 core courses in Biblical Foundations, 3 Biblical literature courses, 3 upper division courses, field technology experience or a seminar.

A Pre-Seminary program is designed with flexibility to allow students to meet the entrance requirements of the seminary of their choice.

Trinity Evangelical Divinity School
2045 Half Day Road
Deerfield, IL 60015   (312) 945-8800

Administration. Dr. Kenneth M. Meyer, President; Dr. Warren S. Benson, Vice President of Academic Administration; Dr. Walter C. Kaiser, Academic Dean and Vice President of Education.

General Description. Trinity Evangelical Divinity School is a graduate-level institution that has as its purpose the training of leaders in church-related positions and the training of teachers in various academic areas. The School offers a variety of master- and doctorate-level programs in numerous areas of specialization. The School has more than 60 regular and visiting faculty, the majority of whom hold earned doctorates from recognized universities and theological schools in the United States and abroad. These scholars, among the finest in the evangelical community, are committed to the preparation of men and women for significant roles as Christian leaders in the church and community. With over 1,000 students from many different denominational and academic backgrounds, Trinity Evangelical Divinity School is one of the ten largest theological schools in the world. Degrees offered include Master of Arts (in: Old Testament, New Testament, Biblical Archaeology, Church History, Christian Thought, Philosophy of Religion, Counseling Psychology, Mission and Evangelism, Christian Education), Master of Religious Education, Master of Divinity, Master of Theology, Doctor of Ministry, Doctor of Missiology, and Doctor of Education. Also offered is the Certificate in Biblical Studies.

Community Environment. The School is located on a wooded 30-acre campus about 6 miles from the shores of Lake Michigan and 25 miles from the Chicago Loop area, in Deerfield, Illinois, population 20,000.

Religious Denomination. Evangelical Free Church of America.

Religious Emphasis. Evangelical.

Accreditation. North Central Association of Colleges and Schools; Association of Theological Schools in the United States and Canada.

Term System. Quarter; summer term.

Enrollment in Degree Programs in Religion 1984–85. Total 818; men 695, women 123.

Degrees in Religion Awarded 1984–85. Master of Arts 43; men 26, women 17. Master of Religious Education 4; men 4. Master of Divinity 124; men 120, women 4. Master of Theology 15; men 15. Doctor of Ministry 16; men 16. Doctor of Missiology 18; men 18. Doctor of Education 1; men 1. Certificate in Biblical Studies 13; men 7, women 6.

Faculty for Degree Programs in Religion. Total 61; full-time 43, part-time 18.

Admission Requirements. Bachelor of Arts degree or its equivalent. Other requirements vary by degree program.

Tuition and Fees. Tuition $143 per quarter hour; fees $23 per quarter (full-time), $9 per quarter (part-time); dormitory $320-$360 per quarter, apartments for married students $220-$380 per quarter.

Financial Aid. College Work-Study Program, National Direct Student Loan; limited grant aid available.

Housing. Dormitories are available for single students; on-campus apartments for married students.

Library Facilities. The library contains 116,000 volumes plus microforms; over 1,000 current periodicals are received.

Religious Services/Activities. Chapel services are held weekly.

Degree Programs

The Master of Divinity degree is designed to equip students for professional ministry (pastor, missionary, counseling, social work, Christian education, campus evangelism, youth ministry, etc.) and may also serve as the basis for further graduate study in preparation for research and/or teaching in some Biblically- or theologically-related discipline. A minimum of 136 quarter hours is required with a minimum cumulative grade point average of 2.0 Courses from the following divisions are prescribed: Old Testament, New Testament, Church History and the History of Christian Thought, Mission and Evangelism, Philosophy of Religion, Christian Education, Pastoral Counseling and Psychology, and Practical Theology.

The Master of Arts programs offered require intensive study in a limited area of specialization and are intended primarily for Christian workers, missionaries on furlough, teachers in Christian or public schools, teachers in Bible institutes and Bible colleges, and students planning to pursue doctoral-level graduate study. Normally, the Master of Arts programs will required a minimum of two full-time academic years or their equivalent in achievement. These programs are not designed to substitute for the professional programs in terms of an adequate preparation for the professional ministry. The programs offered include Old Testament, New Testament, Biblical Archaeology, Church History, Christian Thought, Philosophy of Religion, Mission and Evangelism, and Christian Education. The School also offers Master of Theology programs.

The Doctor of Education program trains specialists in the field of Christian Education for church and institutional ministry. Emphasis within the program is in three areas of specialization: Family life ministry, local church Christian education administration, and teaching Christian education.

The Doctor of Ministry program is a program of intensive seminar work (at least 32 quarter hours) and a project (4 quarter hours).

The Doctor of Missiology program is designed for people who are actively involved in some phase of missionary service, missionaries on furlough, mission executives, professors of mission, Third World church leaders, and evangelists in cross-cultural ministries.

Special Programs

Extensive summer school courses are offered on a three-week basis and Independent Study courses are available for off-campus study.

INDIANA

Anderson School of Theology
Anderson College
Anderson, IN 46012   (317) 649-9071

Administration. Robert A. Nicholson, President.

General Description. Anderson College was established in 1917 as Anderson Bible Training School. Through the years the College has evolved and expanded to meet the increasing responsibilities and opportunities of Christian higher education. In 1950, a graduate division of Anderson College was established for the advanced professional preparation of ministerial students and is known as the Anderson School of Theology. It is a recognized seminary of the Church of God.

Community Environment. The School of Theology building is located on the campus of Anderson College. The city of Anderson has a population of over 70,000 and is 35 miles northeast of Indianapolis, Indiana.

Religious Denomination. Church of God.

Accreditation. North Central Association of Colleges and Schools; Association of Theological Schools in the United States and Canada.

Term System. Semester.

Admission Requirements. Baccalaureate degree from an accredited college or university.

Tuition and Fees. Tuition $1,130 per semester.

Financial Aid. Sources of student aid include scholarships, tuition grants, and loans. Most seminary students meet a portion of their seminary expenses through part-time employment in church or other work.

Housing. The School maintains a current listing of available housing for graduate students. Apartments for married students are available on and off campus.

Library Facilities. The Byrd Memorial Library of the School of Theology houses over 58,000 volumes. The adjacent Wilson Library of Anderson College houses an additional 138,000 volumes. The Church of God Archives are maintained as a special collection. The Warner Memorial Historical Collection is a considerable resource for ministers and scholars who wish to do research in the heritage of the Church of God.

Religious Services/Activities. The Chapel and Spiritual Life Committee plans and maintains oversight of chapel programming and other events.

Degree Programs

The three-year Master of Divinity degree is the standard professional preparation for persons entering the Christian ministry. It involves significant exposure in Biblical, theological, historical, and church ministry studies with a variety of supervised field education experiences. The degree requires the completion of a minimum of 90 graduate-level semester hours.

The purpose of the Master of Religious Education degree is to facilitate professional competence in Christian Education. It is professional in preparation and practical in orientation. Parish and field experiences are made integral to the classroom experience. The program requires completion of a minimum of 60 graduate-level semester hours.

The Master of Arts in Religion is a two-year program intended for persons seeking to begin preparation for an academic career or for those wishing to develop an area of specialization. The program is flexible in order to serve relevantly the needs of a diverse constituency. The degree requires at least 45 semester hours of coursework.

Special Programs

The Theological Studies Certificate is a special program of graduate studies for lay persons, selected international students, spouses of degree candidates, and other special students. A minimum of 24 semester hours is required.

Bethel College
Division of Religion and Philosophy
1001 West McKinley Avenue
Mishawaka, IN 46545   (219) 259-8511

Administration. Dr. James A. Bennett, President; Dr. Gerald G. Winkleman, Vice President for Academic Affairs; Dr. Edward L. Oke, Chairperson, Division of Religion and Philosophy and Director of Graduate Studies.

General Description. The Division of Religion and Philosophy seeks to prepare students for ministry in the church as pastors, missionaries, Christian educators, youth workers, and specialists in Biblical interpretation from a Wesleyan Arminian perspective. The goals are that a student shall possess (1) knowledge of Biblical truth and its relation to faith and practice, (2) knowledge of the Christian ministries and their operation as a response to the teachings of Christ, (3) knowledge of major philosophies, religious systems, and theological concepts, and (4) skill in the use of inductive and exegetical methods of Biblical study. The degrees Master of Ministries, Bachelor of Arts in Biblical Literature, Christian Ministries, and Philosophy, and Associate of Arts in Biblical Studies are awarded.

Parent Institution. Bethel College is a private, Christian, coeducational, liberal arts college that offers bachelor and two-year associate degrees as well as the Master of Christian Ministries degree. Bethel College provides a Christian environment in which to grow intellectually, spiritually, and socially. Bethel is dedicated to quality education. Because of the low student-faculty ratio, students receive the special individualized attention that might not be available at larger institutions.

Community Environment. Bethel College is located on a wooded 60-acre campus in the heart of the Mishawaka/South Bend, Indiana community. The location provides both the intimacy of a small-campus atmosphere and opportunities for off-campus employment, entertainment, and educational experiences in the immediate major metropolitan area.

Religious Denomination. Missionary Church.

Religious Emphasis. Evangelical.

Accreditation. North Central Association of Colleges and Schools.

Term System. Semester.

Enrollment in Degree Programs in Religion 1984–85. Total 550; men 187, women 363.

Degrees in Religion Awarded 1984–85. Bachelor of Arts 61; men 31, women 30. Master of Ministry 2; men 2. Associate of Arts 14; men 3, women 11.

Faculty for Degree Programs in Religion. Total 5; full-time 5.

Admission Requirements. Admission is determined on an individual basis. High school records, SAT or ACT scores, leadership ability, and character are considered. It is recommended, but not required, that high school courses include 4 units of English and 2 units each of mathematics, laboratory science, foreign language, and social studies.

Tuition and Fees. Tuition $145 per semester hour; health insurance $28 per semester; student fee (full-time) $60; housing $1,080 to $1,170; married student housing $200 per month.

Financial Aid. Pell Grant, Supplemental Education Opportunity Grant, National Direct Student Loan, College Work-Study, State Student Assistance Commission of Indiana, Guaranteed Student Loan, Plus Loan Program, Admission with Distinction Scholarship, Achievement Grants, Valedictorian and Salutorian Scholarships, Divisional Assistantship Program, Leadership Grant, Minister Tuition Reduction Grant, Sibling Tuition Reduction Grant, Missionary Church Minister and Missionary Award, Athletic Grants.

Housing. Residences for both single and married students are available.

Library Facilities. The library contains over 58,000 volumes and houses the Bowen Archives and the Missionary Church Historical Collection.

Religious Services/Activities. Chapel is held 3 times per week. There is a College Church as well as adjacent churches of many denominations.

Degree Programs

The Christian Ministries major leading to the Bachelor of Arts degree requires 73 semester hours in Biblical studies, ministerial studies, and ministerial practice in the four areas of Christian education, missions, pastoral ministry, or youth ministry.

The Master of Ministries degree is a professional degree for ministers and church workers. Generally one and one-half years of full-time study beyond the baccalaureate degree are required. A total of 34 semester hours with at least a 2.5 grade point average is required as well as a position paper and a residence requirement for the last 19 hours. A major in Christian Ministries requires 34 semester hours of courses including electives from the three areas of Church and Ministry, History and Theology, and Biblical Studies.

Special Programs

The Associate of Arts degree program is also available from the Department.

Butler University
Department of Philosophy and Religious Studies
4600 Sunset Avenue
Indianapolis, IN 46208   (317) 283-8000

Administration. W. Malcolm Clark, Head, Department of Philosophy and Religious Studies.

General Description. The Department of Philosophy and Religious Studies is one of fifteen departments in the College of Liberal Arts and Sciences of Butler University. The primary goal of the Department is to provide a Bachelor of Arts major in Philosophy and/or Religious Studies and to provide courses in those areas for non-majors. The Department cooperates with Christian Theological Seminary, located immediately adjacent to Butler University, in offering a Master of Arts in Religious Studies. For this degree, half of the course work is taken at each institution and the degree is conferred by Butler University.

Parent Institution. Butler University is a private, coeducational, nonsectarian university. Founded in 1855, Butler offers undergraduate and graduate programs. Each major program is grounded on a strong program of liberal education through the core curriculum of the University College. The University has 3,861 full and part-time, graduate and undergraduate students, and 170 full-time faculty.

Community Environment. The University is located on a scenic 254-acre campus in a residential area approximately seven miles from the heart of Indianapolis. Excellent transportation, cultural, recreational, and shopping facilities are readily available as are churches, public and parochial schools, and museums.

Religious Denomination. None.

Accreditation. North Central Association of Colleges and Schools.

Term System. Semester; summer term.

Degrees in Religion Awarded 1984–85. Bachelor of Arts in Philosophy/Religion 5; men 2, women 3. Master of Arts in Religious Studies 6; men 1, women 5; Master of Arts in Personality Theory and Religion 10; men 1, women 9 (program is being phased out).

Faculty for Degree Programs in Religion. Total 7; full-time 3; part-time 4.

Admission Requirements. Undergraduate: high school graduation; transcript; SAT or ACT. Graduate: evidence supporting likelihood of applicant to meet the standards of the Graduate Division (undergraduate grades; scores on standardized tests).

Tuition and Fees. Costs per semester: Tuition full-time $3,170, part-time $265 per credit hour (day) or $80 per credit hour (evening); board (20 meals a week) $1,360; with single room and 20 meals per week $1,650.

Financial Aid. The University offers a variety of financial assistance programs based on the demonstration of academic excellence, performance, or financial need. This assistance may be in the form of federal and state assistance, scholarships or grants from the University, loans, and campus employment.

Housing. Male and female dormitories; living accommodations for undergraduates also are available in fraternity and sorority houses.

Library Facilities. The Irwin Library houses approximately 200,000 volumes. Students may also use the library of nearby Christian Theological Seminary.

Religious Services/Activities. Cooperative campus ministry; YWCA/YMCA; some specific denominational groups (e.g., Catholic Newman Center, Southern Baptist, Lutheran); Intervarsity and Campus Crusade.

Degree Programs

The Bachelor of Arts program in Religious Studies serves those students who desire (1) a knowledge of various concerns and expressions of religion throughout history and in different cultures; (2) a more detailed knowledge of the Judaeo-Christian tradition; (3) a suitable background for graduate study in religion as a preparation for research and teaching; (4) a pre-professional background prior to graduate work at a theological seminary or rabbinical or other religious professional school leading to a professional career in religious work. There is a common core of courses to be taken by all majors.

The Master of Arts in Religious Studies is offered in cooperation with the Christian Theological Seminary. The program is designed to enable students to explore personal interests or vocational options, to acquire a background for teaching at the secondary level, and/or to attain a foundation for further programs. Candidates may choose on of the following three programs in Religious Studies: General Master of Arts, Specialty Master of Arts, or Cross-Disciplinary Master of Arts. The University and the Seminary will collaborate in the program with a major in the University and a minor in the Seminary.

Christian Theological Seminary
1000 West 42nd Street
Indianapolis, IN 46208   (317) 924-1331

Administration. Dr. Thomas J. Liggitt, President; Dr. Richard D.N. Dickinson, Jr., Vice President and Dean.

General Description. Christian Theological Seminary is an ecumenically-oriented graduate school for preparing men and women for the ministries of the church. It offers college graduates several academic programs, varying in length from one to three years of full-time study, which are designed to help students develop competence in various forms of religious leadership and to offer the opportunity for advanced studies in religion. Two basic programs form the center of the Seminary's academic life. Both the Master of Divinity and the Master of Arts (with specialization), are designed for women and men preparing for ministries in the church and in church institutions. The Master of Sacred Theology and the Doctor of Ministry degrees are advanced professional degrees, intended for persons whose basic theological studies have been completed and whose ministerial standing is established. One degree is offered jointly with Butler University, Indianapolis: the Master of Arts in Religious Studies.

Community Environment. The Seminary now occupies facilities of three buildings on a 30-acre campus. One leading art critic has described them as the most distinguished and exciting complex of buildings ever erected in Indiana. Indianapolis is the capital city, located in the exact center of the state, enjoying a fine climate. All modes of transportation are available. Excellent city facilities include the library with 21 branches, churches of all denominations, and 17 hospitals.

Religious Denomination. Christian Church (Disciples of Christ).

Religious Emphasis. Ecumenical.

Accreditation. North Central Association of Colleges and Schools; Association of Theological Schools in the

United States and Canada.

Term System. Semester; summer term.

Enrollment in Degree Programs in Religion 1984–85. Total 390; men 203, women 187.

Degrees in Religion Awarded 1984–85. Master of Arts with specialization in Communication 4; men 3, women 1. Master of Arts with specialization in Counseling 2; men 1, women 1. Master of Divinity 23; men 13, women 10. Master of Sacred Theology 8; men 8. Master of Arts (with Butler University) 11; men 2, women 9. Doctor of Ministry 11; men 9, women 2.

Faculty for Degree Programs in Religion. Total 26; full-time 15, part-time 11.

Admission Requirements. Bachelor of Arts degree or its equivalent; letters of introduction and appraisal on forms supplied by the seminary; standardized tests when recommended by the admissions committee; statement of purpose for seminary study.

Tuition and Fees. Tuition $125 per hour; application fee $15 (applicable to first semester's tuition); transient dormitory $5 per night; apartment rental $180 per month plus utilities; meals appoximately $6 to $12 per day.

Financial Aid. Grants and scholarships, employment, and loans constitute the financial aid resources for students.

Housing. Transient dormitory and apartments are available.

Library Facilities. The library houses 108,318 volumes with a special Heritage Collection of Disciples of Christ Literature.

Religious Services/Activities. Worship services are held 3 times per week. The annual Indiana Pastors Conference is held on the campus.

Degree Programs

The Master of Divinity is a comprehensive program of studies that meets educational requirements leading to ordination and leadership in the church's life and mission. It is built upon a pattern of required courses that assure breadth as well as depth. A large number of field electives provide the framework for disciplined choice as students develop responsibility for their preparation to be ministers. The basic requirement for the degree is the completion of 90 semester hours of work in approved courses with a cumulative grade point average of at least 2.0.

The Seminary offers several programs of study that lead to the Master of Arts degree. The Master of Arts with specialization is offered in the fields of Christian Education, Church Music, Communication, Community Ministries, and Pastoral Care and Counseling.

The Master of Sacred Theology is an advanced professional degree intended for persons whose basic theological studies have been completed and whose ministerial standing is established. It requires 30 to 36 hours of work.

The Doctor of Ministry program is designed for experienced ministers interested in a systematic program of theological study and advanced professional work, orga-

nized to advance their competence as leaders of religious organizations. The general program concentrates on parish ministry and general ministries in the church. The program in pastoral care and counseling focuses on specialized counseling ministries, either in the congregation or other settings.

Special Programs

A Master of Arts in Religious Studies is offered in cooperation with Butler University. The emphasis is upon Bible, Church History, Theology, Ethics, or Religion and Culture.

Programs in Clinical Pastoral Education are offered in conjunction with accredited training centers in Indiana. The basic and advanced level courses are designed for students preparing for either the parish or specialized ministries, and for ministers desiring continuing education.

Concordia Theological Seminary
6600 North Clinton Street
Fort Wayne, IN 46825   (219) 482-9611

Administration. Dr. Robert D. Preus, President; Dr. G. Waldemar Degner, Chairman, Exegetical Theology; Dr. Eugene F. Klug, Chairman, Systematic Theology; Dr. Heino O. Kadai, Chairman, Historical Theology; Dr. Gerhard Aho, Chairman, Pastoral Ministry and Director of Graduate Studies.

General Description. Concordia Theological Seminary is an institution of the Lutheran Church-Missouri Synod headquartered in St. Louis, Missouri. The major purpose of the Seminary is to prepare students for the pastoral office for the Lutheran Church-Missouri Synod. Degrees awarded are Master of Divinity, Master of Arts in Religion, Master of Sacred Theology, and Doctor of Ministry. The Master of Divinity program is intended to lead directly to ordination into the ministerium of the Church. A formal Hispanic Ministries program at the Master of Divinity level is offered.

Community Environment. Concordia Theological Seminary is located in Fort Wayne, the second largest city in Indiana, with a population of 172,000. It is an industrial center in the heart of northeastern Indiana'a agricultural region. The campus comprises 191 acres of gently rolling land bordered by the St. Joseph River and a wooded area of 25 acres.

When Eero Saarinen designed the buidings and grounds of the Seminary, he drew his inspiration from the Lutheran Church itself. The village-like plan of the campus reflects the Christian brotherhood in which the seminarians live and work. Through the simple, geometric lines of the buildings and the soaring angles of the chapel, the architect suggests both the strength of their faith and the exhilaration of their calling. To complement the architectural beauty of the campus, Concordia has incorporated works of art into the everyday life of the Seminary. Each building is graced with creations of artists who celebrate the theme *Te Deum Laudamus*.

Religious Denomination. Lutheran Church-Missouri Synod.

Religious Emphasis. Orthodox.

Accreditation. North Central Association of Colleges and Schools; Association of Theological Schools in the United States and Canada.

Term System. Quarter; summer term.

Enrollment in Degree Programs in Religion 1984–85. Total 530; men 529, women 1.

Faculty for Degree Programs in Religion. Total 41; full-time 35, part-time 5.

Admission Requirements. Master of Divinity and Master of Arts in Religion programs: Bachelor's degree with a 2.25 grade point average and 12 hours of Greek language. Master of Divinity requires one year membership in a congregation of the Lutheran Church-Missouri Synod. Master of Sacred Theology and Doctor of Ministry require a Master of Divinity or equivalent; the Doctor of Ministry also requires three years of parish experience.

Tuition and Fees. Tuition $90 per quarter hour; various fees $70 per quarter; room and board $840 per quarter.

Financial Aid. Assistance is available only for men preparing for the pastoral office in the Lutheran Church-Missouri Synod.

Housing. Dormitory accommodations are available and low cost housing can be found in Fort Wayne.

Library Facilities. The library houses over 118,000 volumes. A special collection includes various volumes from the period of Lutheran Orthodoxy.

Religious Services/Activities. Daily chapel services; Saturday Family Vespers; regular series of Choral Vespers incorporating choirs and chamber orchestra.

Degree Programs

The Master of Divinity degree program is intended to lead directly to ordination into the ministerium of The Lutheran Church-Missouri Synod. Requirements for the degree include core hours in Exegetical Theology, Systematic Theology, Historical Theology, and Pastoral Ministry; field education; vicarage; areas of concentration electives; thesis hours; and additional electives for a total of 155 quarter hours.

The Master of Sacred Theology degree program is designed to provide qualified graduates of an accredited seminary the opportunity to engage in scholarly work and research in theology on an advanced level. The program not only provides qualified individuals the opportunity to earn an advanced degree in theology, but also offers training for theological leadership in the church with respect to teaching and research. A minimum of 36 quarter hours is required plus a thesis and a reading knowledge of at least one Biblical language.

The Master of Arts in Religion program is designed for the student who seeks to achieve a level of professional competence in theology, but does not wish to pursue the

full program as required for the Master of Divinity degree. A minimum of 90 quarter hours is required.

The Doctor of Ministry is designed for pastors of unusual promise and demonstrated ability who have served at least three years in the public ministry of the church. The program combines classroom and field-oriented learning and in a variety of ways integrates Biblical-theological knowledge and insights with ministerial disciplines and pastoral skills. The program is carried out in a context of ministry. A total of 51 quarter hours is required and must be completed within 5 years. A project/dissertation is also required.

Special Programs

Programs available include an extension program with courses offered across the country and Canada; an Irvine, California extension for the Doctor of Ministry degree; Hispanic missions; deaf work, and cross-cultural mission work.

Earlham School of Religion
609 National Road West
Richmond, IN 47374   (317) 962-6561

Administration. DeWitt C. Baldwin, Jr., President.

General Description. The purpose of Earlham School of Religion is to be a seeking, caring, seminary community after the manner of Friends. Its main function is to prepare men and women for ministry. The School of Religion was opened on an experimental basis by Earlham College in the autumn of 1960. After a two-year period during which only the M.A. in Religion was offered, the Board of Trustees authorized the expansion of the program to include a three-year Bachelor of Divinity degree. Eventually the Bachelor program was eliminated by upgrading it to Master's status. The title of this degree has been changed to Master of Ministry. Since 1963, Earlham School of Religion has operated with its own dean and faculty with a separate operating budget.

The Earlham School of Religion is related to the Religious Society of Friends and is committed to a historic view of Quakerism grounded in Christian faith and life. The Quaker movement, from its inception in the seventeenth century, has had the vision of a universal ministry in which every Christian, of whatever occupation, is involved. The objective of the School is to train and equip individuals who accept the responsibility of encouraging and training their fellow Christians by serving as pastors and meeting secretaries, teachers and counselors, campus and retreat center ministers, and mission and service workers at home and abroad. It is the philosophy of the School that such persons not be set apart by special status, nor should they be though of as "the minister." It is believed that every member of the church is a minister in his/her own life. The School holds that the New Testament concept of ministry places emphasis on *calling* and *function* rather than *position* and *status,* and that this is also in keeping with the historic Quaker understanding of ministry.

Parent Institution. The presence of the School of Religion in close association with Earlham College brings it in touch with many currents of contemporary intellectual life. Earlham College was founded by Friends in 1847 and is known nationally for its high academic standards. These same standards characterize the Earlham School of Religion.

Community Environment. The School of Religion is located on the northeast corner of the Earlham College campus. The Jenkins House and the Robert Barclay Center are the main components of the School. College facilities other than those specifically occupied by the School are available to students of the School of Religion. The School is located in Richmond, Indiana on the southwest side of the city. Richmond has a population of 43,000 and is approximately 40 miles west of Dayton, Ohio.

Religious Denomination. Religious Society of Friends.

Accreditation. North Central Association of Colleges and Schools; Association of Theological Schools.

Term System. Trimester; summer term.

Enrollment in Degree Programs in Religion 1984–85. Total 72; men 32, women 40.

Degrees in Religion Awarded 1984–85. Master of Ministry 3; men 3. Master of Divinity 6; men 2, women 4. Master of Arts 4; men 1, women 3.

Faculty for Degree Programs in Religion. Total 7; full-time 7.

Admission Requirements. Any student who has a Bachelor of Arts or Science degree or its equivalent from an accredited institution and whose personal and vocational objectives are compatible with the goals of the School may apply for admission.

Tuition and Fees. Three courses per term are the normal load for a full-time student. Tuition for 3 courses $735, 2 courses $550, 1 course $365; room $300 to $330 per term; apartment housing for married students $170 to $225 per month.

Financial Aid. The financial aid program of the School of Religion reflects the definitions, principles, guidelines, and procedures developed by the Association of Theological Schools. Factors considered in granting aid include need, leadership potential, and academic ability. Aid available through grants, loans, and employment.

Housing. Rooms for single students are located upstairs in the Robert Barclay Center. All-electric apartments with basic household furnishings are available for married couples.

Library Facilities. Library resources include all the books, periodicals, and multi-media holdings of Lilly Library at Earlham College. This collection totals more than 290,000 volumes, 1,300 periodicals, and 15 foreign and domestic papers. The Kelson Religion section of Lilly Library contains a collection of 34,000 volumes on religion belonging to Earlham School of Religion and the Religion Department of Earlham College. There are approximately 120 subscriptions to religious periodicals relating to theological studies. A Quaker Collection totaling 10,000 volumes serves the particular interest of Friends. The Lilly Library has assigned a staff member trained for theological library work in a liaison relationship with the School of Religion.

Religious Services/Activities. Worship experiences are both planned and spontaneous. Daily All-School worship is held Tuesday through Friday under the direction of the Ministry and Counsel Committee. Students are involved also in various forms of community service. One of the unique features of Earlham School of Religion is the sharing of a Common Meal each Tuesday. The purpose of this event is to deepen and enrich the fellowship of the School community on both spiritual and intellectual levels. The All-College Meeting for Worship is held each Sunday. Other campus activities in which students of the School of Religion can participate include Young Friends Group, Meetinghouse Cabinet, prison visitation, and visitation to Friends meetings and churches.

Degree Programs

The Master of Arts degree program is an academic program for specially qualified students who enter with a college religion major or substantial previous studies in religion. The program is primarily intended for students who wish either to pursue a terminal degree with a view to secondary level teaching in Quaker or other parochial schools, or to continue toward a doctoral program in religious studies.

The Master of Ministry degree (equivalent to the Master of Divinity degree) is a three-year program designed to equip graduates for a variety of ministries, including pastoral ministry, Friends Meeting secretary, counseling, religious education, campus ministry, retreat-renewal center ministry, and social ministry.

A Doctor of Ministry degree is offered cooperatively by the consortium of theological seminaries participating in the Consortium for Higher Education Religious Studies (CHERS). Participating seminaries include: the Earlham School of Religion; Mount St. Mary Theological Seminary in Cincinnati, Ohio; Payne Theological Seminary at Wilberforce University in Zenia, Ohio; Department of Theological Studies at the University of Dayton, Ohio; and the United Theological Seminary in Dayton. Prerequisite for this program is a Master of Divinity degree or its equivalent. Students register for the program through United Theological Seminary in Dayton, Ohio.

Special Programs

Seminaries of the Historic Peace Churches (Brethren, Friends, Mennonite) cooperate in offering courses for persons whose degree emphasis is peace studies or social ministry. Students with this interest may take work on the campus of at least one of the other two seminaries, Bethany Theological Seminary in Chicago and Associated Mennonite Biblical Seminaries in Elkhart, Indiana.

Yokefellow Institute is an ecumenical church renewal center serving to train the general membership of congregations for leadership in the church and to provide pastors with opportunities for increasing leadership skills. The Institute programs offer laboratory experience for School of Religion students interested in renewal or retreat center ministry.

The Quaker Hill Conference Center is operated by Friends and provides opportunities for participation in conferences, retreats, seminars, and workshops.

Fort Wayne Bible College
Biblical Studies Division
1025 West Rudisill Boulevard
Fort Wayne, IN 46807   (219) 456-2111

Administration. Dr. Harvey R. Bostrom, President; Richard P. Dugan, Vice President for Academic Affairs.

General Description. The Division of Biblical Studies offers courses in the following areas: General Biblical, Old Testament, Biblical Languages (Greek, Hebrew), New Testament, and Theology. In addition to the professional major, a Biblical Studies Divisional major is required of all undergraduate students.

The Division of Professional Studies offers specialized education and training. All baccalaureate-seeking students select a major from one of the following: Christian Counseling, Christian Education, Christian Ministries Management, Music, Pastoral Ministries, Teacher Education, or World Mission. Graduates may enter their chosen professions immediately or after further study in graduate programs.

Parent Institution. Founded in 1904, Fort Wayne Bible College is an evangelical Christian institution of higher education teaching and serving in the Bible college tradition. Through the integration of Biblical, general, and professional studies, as well as cocurricular experiences, the College provides foundational preparation for life and ministry through the Church in its world mission. The College is one of the denominational colleges of the Missionary Church, Inc. The student body is interdenominational.

Community Environment. Fort Wayne, Indiana is the hub of the great north central industrial and agricultural area of the United States. The city has a population of 178,000 and is the gateway to the northern Indiana lake region. The city has 147 churches.

Religious Denomination. Missionary Church.

Religious Emphasis. Evangelical.

Accreditation. North Central Association of Colleges and Schools; American Association of Bible Colleges.

Term System. Semester; post session.

Enrollment in Degree Programs in Religion 1984–85. Total 400.

Degrees in Religion Awarded 1984–85. Bachelor of Arts

15; men 9, women 6. Bachelor of Science 27; men 23, women 4.

Faculty for Degree Programs in Religion. Total 4; full-time 4.

Admission Requirements. Applicant must state clearly in writing his/her conversion experience and the Biblical basis of faith in Jesus Christ; high school graduation or equivalent; rank in the upper three fifths of the high school class and have the minimum equivalent of 2.0 grade point average on a 4.0 scale; receive a positive evaluation of background, character, and abilities; ACT or SAT.

Tuition and Fees. General service fee $80 per semester; tuition $1,950 per semester; room (double occupancy) $470; and board (3 meals option) $725 per semester.

Financial Aid. Scholarships, awards, grants, and loans are available. All students are eligible to apply for financial aid. A college work/study program is also available.

Housing. Three dormitories are available for single students plus a limited number of apartments for married students.

Library Facilities. The library contains over 51,000 volumes.

Religious Services/Activities. All students taking eight or more credit hours are expected to attend Sunday service (morning and evening; Chapel on Monday, Tuesday, Thursday and Friday (10:00-10:35 AM); Thirty Minutes on Wednesday (10:00-10:35 AM); all services of the Fall and Spring Spiritual Emphasis; Spiritual Emphasis Morning once a month (8:30-11:30 AM). All four-year degree programs require a minimum of six semesters of Christian service projects with a definite requirement in the senior year.

Degree Programs

The Bachelor of Science degree with a major in Christian Counseling is granted upon the satisfactory completion of 128 designated hours of academic credit. Courses are distributed among Biblical Studies, General Studies, Professional Studies, and free electives.

The Bachelor of Science degree with a major in Christian Education prepares Christian leaders to teach and administer the educational programs of the local church. It further trains students as educators, facilitators, creative leaders, and role models of Biblical philosophy and methodology for the church and related ministries. The degree is granted upon the satisfactory completion of 128 designated hours of academic credit.

The Bachelor of Science degree with a major in Christian Ministries prepares people who will serve in the managerial, financial, and secretarial positions in churches and church-related organizations. It requires the satisfactory completion of 128 designated hours of academic credit.

The Bachelor of Science degree with a major in Music exposes all students to aesthetic musical expression, train students whose chosen vocations will utilize musical skills, and prepare musicians who are committed to Christ to minister through music in the church and church-related agencies, the school, and the community. Students may choose an area of concentration from the following: church music; music education; composition; and performance in voice, piano, organ, orchestral, and other instruments. A total of 128 designated hours of academic credit is required for the degree.

The Bachelor of Music degree with a major in Performance or Composition is a 154-hour, five-year program. The concentration of hours in music offers graduates of this program greater development of their musical skills and experiences to minister in the church and church-related agencies and the community through performance, teaching privately, and, after graduate study, teaching on the college level.

The Bachelor of Science degree with a major in Pastoral Ministries is designed for those anticipating pastoral ministry following graduation. It is granted upon the satisfactory completion of 128 designated hours of academic credit.

The Bachelor of Science degree with a major in Elementary Education is granted upon the satisfactory completion of 145 designated hours of academic credit.

The Bachelor of Arts degree with a major in Pastoral Ministries is designed for those anticipating seminary training following graduation. It has a 14-hour Greek language requirement and the degree is granted upon the satisfactory completion of 128 designated hours of academic credit.

The objectives of the programs for the Bachelor of Science or Bachelor of Arts in World Mission are to produce graduates who can cope with, learn to thrive on, and be effective in cross-cultural ministry. Both degree programs required the completion of 128 designated hours of academic work. The Bachelor of Arts program has a 14 hour Greek language requirement.

Special Programs

An Associate of Arts degree is designed especially for those who desire the distinctive type of education offered by a Bible college but who may be uncertain of their vocational goals, expect to pursue a major not offered at Fort Wayne Bible College, or wish to terminate their college experience with a two-year program. A total of 64 hours is required for the degree.

Several options are available to the student wishing to combine missions training at Fort Wayne Bible College with medical training at another institution.

Graduates of other institutions who would like a one-year concentration in such areas as Biblical studies and missions may design a special program in consultation with the Registrar or appropriate program director.

The Christian Worker's Certificate Program is designed for those who are able to enroll for a year only of residence work, who can take only a few courses in residence at the college and wish to complete the remaining requirements by correspondence, or who wish to take all of their work

by correspondence. The program involves a total of 33 semester hours.

Goshen Biblical Seminary (Associated Mennonite Biblical Seminaries)
3003 Benham Avenue
Elkhart, IN 46517   (219) 295-3726

Administration. Dr. Marlin E. Miller, President; Richard A. Kauffman, Administrative Vice President.

General Description. Goshen Biblical Seminary is a graduate ministerial training school of the General Conference Mennonite Church. The Seminary is operated by authorization of this Conference under the supervision of a Board of Trustees.

In the academic year 1958-59 Goshen Biblical Seminary (then on the campus of Goshen College, Goshen, Indiana) and Mennonite Biblical Seminary (then located in Chicago) entered a cooperative relationship known under the name Associated Mennonite Biblical Seminaries. By action of their respective boards of control a plan of academic cooperation was set up, designed to provide substantial advantages for both seminaries, while retaining the organizational and financial independence of each. The Associated Mennonite Biblical Seminaries provide an integrated program under the direction of a unified faculty. Degrees offered include the Master of Divinity and the Master of Arts in Peace Studies. A One Year Theology Curriculum (culminating in the Certificate of Theological Studies) for persons with the B.A. degree is designed individually according to the student's respective goals. The Certificate of Theology for mature persons serving in the pastoral ministry represents a 5-year program of study designed without the normal liberal arts foundation.

Parent Institution. The General Conference Mennonite Church consists of 64,000 members with central offices located at 722 Main Street, Newton, Kansas. Its 320 member churches are located in the United States and Canada. The Conference receives regular reports from the Seminary, and through its budget provides 3/5 of the annual operating costs.

Community Environment. Approximately 5 miles south of the Michigan-Indiana border, Elkhart, Indiana is only 10 miles from the city of South Bend and Notre Dame University. Facilities in South Bend include the Morris Civic Auditorium and the new Century Center for professional drama as well as concerts by the South Bend Symphony and the South Bend Art Association where classes and workshops are conducted daily in the auditorium.

Religious Denomination. General Conference Mennonite Church.

Religious Emphasis. Evangelical with peace emphasis.

Accreditation. North Central Association of Colleges and Schools; Association of Theological Schools in the United States and Canada.

Term System. Semester/Interim/Semester (4-1-4); no

summer term.

Enrollment in Degree Programs in Religion 1984–85. Total 91; men 64, women 27.

Degrees in Religion Awarded 1984–85. Master of Divinity 20; men 13, women 7. Master of Arts (Peace Studies) 3; men 2, women 1. Certificate in Theological Studies 1; women 1.

Faculty for Degree Programs in Religion. Total 15; full-time 9, part-time 6.

Admission Requirements. A statement with regard to the candidate's Christian faith convictions; participation in the full scope of the community in addition to the regular curricular requirements; graduation from a liberal arts course of an accredited college (some exceptions may be made by special Curriculum Committee action).

Tuition and Fees. Tuition $2,280 per year; student activity fee $24; matriculation fee $20; housing $87 to $285 per month; boarding club meals $110 per month.

Financial Aid. Resources for financial aid are available from special funds and are based on the student's need. Aid assistance consists of scholarships, loans, tuition and living expense grants, and employment.

Housing. Both on- and off-campus housing is available for single and married students.

Library Facilities. The library comprises 98,000 volumes and receives 313 periodicals and journals by subscription and another 226 by gift or otherwise. A collection of research materials in Mennonite and Anabaptist history, especially with reference to the General Conference Mennonite Church is maintained at Elkhart. Another special collection is the Gerald Studer Bible Collection. The Mennonite Historical Library is housed in a special section of the Harold and Wilma Good Library at Goshen College. Archives of the Mennonite Church are housed in the Newcomer Center in Elkhart.

Religious Services/Activities. Chapel is held three times weekly. A weekly forum, regular weekly prayer services, and up to four retreats for spiritual formation are also held.

Degree Programs

The purpose of the Master of Divinity curriculum is to equip candidates for effective participation in the various ministries of the church at home and around the world. There are six different curricular designs through which students prepare for particular ministries. These focus on pastoral ministry, Christian education, overseas ministries, pastoral counseling, church planting and evangelism, and academic ministries. In addition to three courses in the biblical languages, each design requires six courses from each department.

The purpose of the Master of Arts in Peace Studies is to provide the environment for a deepening understanding of and commitment to the biblical vision of peace and justice and its embodiment in the world. While not designed for a specific profession, the program prepares students for peace and justice ministries from congregational

to world-wide levels. Completion of the course will normally require two full academic years.

Special Programs

A One-Year Theology Curriculum has the dual purpose of equipping lay people for stronger participation in the life of the church, and of serving those going on in graduate or professional training who wish a better understanding of the Christian faith and the church's ministry in the world, as well as of the Mennonite commitment in faith and work.

A Certificate in Theology Curriculum is designed for mature persons of about 30 years of age or older who have not completed a college degree program, who are involved in leadership responsibilities in their home congregations, or if not presently involved have had a significant responsibility in the past which would indicate that they will profit from an educational experience for future leadership.

Other special programs at the Seminary include Black and Hispanic Leadership Training, Ministers in Vicinity Program, and Conference-Based Theological Education.

Grace College
Division of Religion and Philosophy
Department of Biblical Studies
200 Seminary Drive
Winona Lake, IN 46950   (219) 923-3651

Administration. Dr. Homer A. Kent, Jr., President; Dr. Ronald E. Manahan, Chairman, Division of Religion and Philosophy.

General Description. The Department of Biblical Studies seeks to fulfill two functions. As a part of the general education program, it seeks to provide for all students an understanding of the Word of God and of the Christian faith as a basis on which they may intelligently formulate their own convictions and Christian philosophy. For those students who choose to major in the field, the Department also seeks to provide a comprehensive knowledge of the Bible and related fields in preparation for advanced theological training and for positions of lay leadership in the local church. Programs offered in the Department are the Bachelor of Arts degree with a major in Biblical studies, the minor in Biblical studies, and the two-year Associate in Biblical studies.

Parent Institution. Grace College is an evangelical Christian institution of arts and sciences offering a variety of programs leading to the Bachelor of Arts and the Bachelor of Science degrees. It is the only undergraduate institution affiliated with the Fellowship of Grace Brethren Churches. The College was founded in 1948. The Grace Theological Seminary is located on the campus. *See also:* Grace Theological Seminary.

Community Environment. The 150-acre campus is located in the town of Winona Lake, near Warsaw, Indiana. The area is centrally located between Detroit, Indianapolis, and Chicago. Fort Wayne is 40 miles to the east and South Bend is 50 miles north.

Religious Denomination. Fellowship of Grace Brethren Churches.

Religious Emphasis. Evangelically conservative.

Accreditation. North Central Association of Colleges and Schools.

Term System. Semester.

Faculty for Degree Programs in Religion. Total 7.

Admission Requirements. Graduation from high school with rank in upper half of graduating class; ACT or SAT.

Tuition and Fees. Tuition $3,782 per year; room and board $1,460; fees $346.

Financial Aid. Financial aid falls into two basic categories: gift aid (grants and scholarships) and self-help (work or loan). Combinations of both are packaged for qualified students and are need-based.

Housing. Dormitory accommodations are available on campus.

Library Facilities. The combined Libraries of Grace College and Grace Theological Seminary total over 110,-000 volumes.

Religious Services/Activities. Daily chapel services and assemblies involving the entire student body are conducted throughout the academic year. Prayer meetings are organized and led by students and are regularly held in dormitories, during breakfast meetings, and in missionary prayer bands. Highlighting each year are the spiritual emphasis and missionary conference weeks.

Degree Programs

The requirement for a major in Biblical Studies is 42 hours in the field. A teaching major in Biblical Studies has the same requirement. The Bachelor's degree requires a total of 124 semester hours. A minor in Missions is also available through the Department. Students who plan to prepare for graduate study in Grace Theological Seminary are strongly encouraged to pursue a liberal arts program leading to a Bachelor of Arts degree. The Biblical Studies, Greek, and Biblical Language majors are highly recommended for seminary preparation. Other appropriate majors are English, history, behavioral science, or speech.

Special Programs

For those not committed to a four-year degree program, an Associate degree of two years' length is available in Biblical studies and consists of a total of 30 hours in Bible and the balance in general education.

Grace Theological Seminary
200 Seminary Drive
Winona Lake, IN 46590   (219) 372-5100

Administration. Dr. Homer A. Kent, Jr., President.
General Description. Grace Theological Seminary is a

graduate school of theology established for the education of leaders for various ministries in the Fellowship of Grace Brethren Churches and other evangelical Christian groups. The Seminary offers programs leading to the Master of Divinity, Master of Theology, and Master of Arts degrees.

Parent Institution. The Seminary had its beginning in 1937. It has the advantage of sharing a campus with Grace College, a four-year liberal arts college with a strong Christian emphasis. It was under the sponsorship of Grace Seminary that Grace College came into existence in 1948. *See also:* Grace College.

Community Environment. The Seminary shares a 150-acre campus with Grace College and is located in Winona Lake in north-central Indiana. The city is known all over the world as the home of one of the nation's best known Bible conferences. The interdenominational Bible conference, which is owned and operated by Grace Schools Corporation, provides a year-round program with special emphasis on the conferences held during the summer months. Winona Lake was once the home of evangelist Billy Sunday.

Religious Denomination. Fellowship of Grace Brethren Churches.

Religious Emphasis. Evangelically conservative.

Accreditation. North Central Association of Colleges and Schools.

Term System. Semester.

Enrollment in Degree Programs in Religion 1984–85. Total 264 (full-time equivalent).

Admission Requirements. Baccalaureate degree from an accredited college or university. Master of Theology program requires previous seminary training.

Tuition and Fees. Tuition $1,600 per semester; registration, library, and student activity fees $82.

Financial Aid. A limited number of scholarships and loan programs are available.

Housing. The Seminary owns a limited number of housing units; off-campus housing is also available.

Library Facilities. The Betty Zimmer Morgan Library houses the collections of both Grace College and the Seminary. The holdings total more than 110,000 volumes and over 35,000 microforms. It receives more than 850 periodicals. Included in the Seminary collection is a slide archive of Holy Land pictures, a Middle East map collection, and a cassette library. Students are within driving distance of a number of other major theological libraries.

Religious Services/Activities. A student-faculty retreat, Grace Bible Conference, World Missions Fellowship, and the Seminary Women's Fellowship are among the activities available for participation.

Degree Programs

The Master of Divinity program provides the basic curriculum in graduate theological study for a ministry of the Word. It is a three-year program requiring 98 semester hours of credit, including a thesis.

The Master of Theology program offers majors in Theology, Old Testament, New Testament, and Missions and requires four years of seminary study, including a thesis. For those who already have the Master of Divinity degree, the program requires a minimum of 28 hours of advanced graduate studies, including a thesis. It requires at least one full year of residence, except that the Missions major requires missionary experience and may be completed in summer sessions.

The Master of Arts in Biblical Counseling requires a minimum of 48 hours of graduate work and may be completed in a little more than one calendar year (usually 13 months). The Master of Arts in Christian School Administration requires a minimum of 30 hours of graduate study (or 32 hours without a thesis), and may be completed in three summers. The Master of Arts in Missions requires a minimum of 30 hours of graduate work (or 32 hours without a thesis), at least two years of successful missionary experience, and may be completed in two summers (ordinarily within an extended furlough).

Special Programs

The Diploma in Theology is awarded upon completion of a reduced three-year curriculum. This program is open to those whose circumstances make the acquisition of a full seminary education impractical, but whose unusual ability and devotion warrant special consideration.

The Certificate in Biblical Studies is awarded upon completion of a one-year curriculum, with emphasis upon theology and English Bible, but also with opportunity for pursuit of other special interests.

Indiana Central University
Philosophy and Religion Department
1400 East Hanna Avenue
Indianapolis, IN 46227   (317) 788-3368

Administration. Dr. Herbert Cassel, Chairman of the Philosophy and Religion Department.

General Description. The Philosophy and Religion Department offers courses that correlate with other parts of the curriculum. The courses in religion enable students to examine their own religious heritage as well as that of others. Attention is given to pre-theological education for students planning careers in Christian ministry.

Parent Institution. Indiana Central is in its ninth decade of Christian higher education. Founded as a coeducational liberal arts institution, it was incorporated on October 7, 1902. Academic studies began on September 26, 1905. The University is one of three United Methodist Church institutions of higher learning in Indiana, the others being DePauw University and the University of Evansville.

Community Environment. The University is located on the southeast side of Indianapolis at Hanna and Otterbein Avenues in the part of the city known as University Heights. It is served by the Indianapolis Metro bus system

and is fifteen minutes from the heart of the city. The physical plant of the University is located on an attractively landscaped campus of 60 acres. The campus has excellent recreational areas for track, football, baseball, softball, soccer, and tennis. A wooded park and picnic area add to the attractiveness of the campus.

Religious Denomination. United Methodist.

Religious Emphasis. Mainline Traditional.

Accreditation. North Central Association of Colleges and Schools. Member of: University Senate of the United Methodist Church.

Term System. Semester; summer term.

Enrollment in Degree Programs in Religion 1984–85. Total 8; men 5, women 3.

Degrees in Religion Awarded 1984–85. Bachelor of Arts 2; men 1, women 1.

Faculty for Degree Programs in Religion. Total 8; full-time 3, part-time 5.

Admission Requirements. Applicant must rank in upper half of high school class; SAT or ACT; must have at least twelve preparatory high school units.

Tuition and Fees. Commuter students $4,930 per school year; campus resident students $7,190 per school year (includes room and board); an additional $103 per credit hour is charged for all hours in excess of 16 each semester; University apartments for married students range from $125 to $145 per month.

Financial Aid. Federal, state, and university funds are available; some for academic excellence apart from need but primarily available for students in financial need. The University awards grants to dependent children of United Methodist ministers upon application and qualification. A number of United Methodist loans and scholarships are also available.

Housing. There are four residence halls for single students and apartments for married students.

Library Facilities. The Krannert Memorial Library provides space for nearly 200,000 volumes. In addition to the main reading room, the library includes a listening room, typing rooms, conference rooms, and private study carrels.

Religious Services/Activities. Convocation is an integral feature of the liberal arts program at the University and attendance is required. The Christian Life Committee is a student organization that plans and organizes activities related to the expression of one's Christian faith, including retreats, workshops, Bible studies, mid-week and chapel services, and Christian Awareness Week each semester.

Degree Programs

The Bachelor of Arts with a major in Religion requires the completion of a course in world religions plus 24 additional hours in religion of which four courses are specified. The Department offers a sequence of four courses in the Judaic-Christian tradition providing a historical overview from the beginnings of Israel to the present day. The first two form the foundation in Biblical studies to which is added an advanced course in interpretation and a three-semester sequence in Greek. A separate course deals with the other living religions of the world. The remaining courses deal with topics of religious significance for thoughtful persons today.

Marian College
Theology/Philosophy Department
3200 Cold Spring Road
Indianapolis, IN 46222   (317) 929-0274

Administration. Dr. Louis C. Gatto, President; Sr. Margaretta Black, O.S.F., Dean of Academic Affairs.

General Description. The Theology/Philosophy Department of Marian College offers Bachelor of Arts degrees in both Theology and Religious Education, as well as an Associate of Arts degree in Religious Education. For degrees in Religious Education, the Department works in conjunction with the Education and Psychology Departments to provide students with the background necessary for teaching and/or administration in the field of Religion.

Parent Institution. Marian College is an independent, Catholic educational liberal arts college, established to provide post-secondary education for both resident and non-resident students. The college aims to offer opportunities for a cultural and professional education devised to develop group responsibility as well as intellectual, social, and religious leadership. The principle purpose of Marian College is to provide its students with the opportunity for a liberal education by means of a well-balanced education, supplemented by training in those specific fields of learning which will satisfy the student's choice for vocational preparation.

Community Environment. The campus of Marian College consists of 28 buildings on 114 acres in Indianapolis, Indiana. Indianapolis is the capital city, located in the exact center of the state. Excellent city facilities include a library with 21 branches, museum, 17 hospitals, and churches of all denominations.

Religious Denomination. Roman Catholic.

Accreditation. North Central Association of Colleges and Secondary Schools.

Term System. Semester; summer term.

Enrollment in Degree Programs in Religion 1984–85. Total 8; men 3, women 5.

Degrees in Religion Awarded 1984–85. Bachelor of Arts in Theology 2; men 1, women 1.

Faculty for Degree Programs in Religion. Total 4; full-time 2, part-time 2.

Admission Requirements. Applicants must be graduates of a high school of recognized standing, and their high school program should fulfill requirements in 16 acceptable units. The units to be presented are: 3 in English; 1 in laboratory science; 2 in mathematics; 2 in the same foreign language (strongly recommended). Factors considered are high school rank, curriculum studied, and academic po-

tential as reflected by the SAT and/or ACT.

Tuition and Fees. Tuition per semester $2,065; application fee $15; room and board $1,053 to $1,283 per semester depending on meal plan selected.

Financial Aid. The types of financial aid offered fall into two broad categories: gift aid in the form of scholarships and grants and aid by which the student helps himself/herself. This "self-help" aid consists of loans and part-time employment. Usually a combination of these aid resources is offered.

Housing. Dormitory housing with single or double occupancy is available. There is limited apartment housing on campus for married students.

Library Facilities. The Mother Theresa Hackelmeier Memorial Library houses over 109,000 volumes.

Religious Services/Activities. Daily Roman Catholic liturgy opportunities; retreats once each semester; penance services two or three times per year; informal prayer groups; Bible study; social action programs/opportunities.

Degree Programs

The major in Theology leading to the Bachelor of Arts degree requires 30 hours in specified courses. The major in Religious Education leading to the Bachelor of Arts degree requires 40 hours in specified courses and electives, plus professional education requirements.

Special Programs

The Associate of Arts in Religious Education requires the completion of specified general education courses plus 22 to 24 hours.

Marion College
Department of Religion/Philosophy
4201 South Washington Street
Marion, IN 46953   (317) 674-6901

Administration. Dr. James P. Hill, Jr., President; Dr. William R. Klinger, Academic Dean; R. Duane Thompson, Chairperson, Department of Religion/Philosophy, Director of Ministerial Education.

General Description. The Department of Religion/Philosophy offers the Bachelor of Science and Bachelor of Arts degrees in Biblical Literature, Christian Education, Christian Ministries, and Religion/Philosophy; and the Associate of Arts in Christian Education. The Department also offers a graduate program with emphasis upon the Weslyan tradition and outlook.

Parent Institution. Marion College is a Christian, liberal arts, coeducational college related to the Wesleyan Church, and began serving students in 1920. In its search for truth within the framework of Christian faith and philosophy, Marion College recognizes the varied needs of each student in arriving at satisfactory personal fulfillment, professional competence, and spiritual satisfaction.

Marion College addresses itself to these needs through several programs, disciplines, and degree routes.

Community Environment. Marion College is situated on a 60-acre campus in Marion, Indiana, an industrial city in a farming and fruit raising region. Marion is 70 miles northeast of Indianapolis and 50 miles southwest of Ft. Wayne, in Grant County. Mississinewa Lake and Salamonie Reservoir and Dam are nearby, providing facilities for many outdoor sports. The city has facilities for tennis, swimming, and picnics.

Religious Denomination. Wesleyan Church.

Religious Emphasis. Evangelical.

Accreditation. North Central Association of Colleges and Schools.

Term System. Semester.

Enrollment in Degree Programs in Religion 1984–85. Total 28; men 27, women 1.

Degrees in Religion Awarded 1984–85. Master of Arts 4; men 3, women 1.

Faculty for Degree Programs in Religion. Total 9; part-time 9.

Admission Requirements. Undergraduate: High school transcript; test scores (SAT or ACT); autobiography; recommendations. Graduate: Baccalaureate degree from accredited college; 2.5 grade point average on 4.0 scale; 40 hours in the undergraduate major (12 Biblical, 9 Doctrinal, 7 Historical, 12 Practical).

Tuition and Fees. Tuition (12-15 credit hours) $2,400 per semester; student activity fee $82 per semester; other fees where applicable; room $458 per semester; board $700 per semester (20 meals per week).

Financial Aid. Students qualify for financial aid by virtue of their need, academic performance, major area of study, or church affiliation. Forms of aid include scholarships, grants, loans, and work programs.

Housing. All single freshmen, sophomore, and junior students under 23 years of age and not living with parents, enrolled for seven hours or more, are expected to live in college supervised housing; off-campus housing for married students.

Library Facilities. The library contains 110,817 volumes and houses a Wesleyana Collection of 1,437 items.

Religious Services/Activities. College chapel is held each Monday, Wednesday, and Friday and attendance is required. At the beginning of each semester, a week is set aside for spiritual emphasis. There are also small group Bible studies and prayer meetings in all dorms and outside housing. The College provides many opportunities for students to be involved in areas of service through Christian Service Teams, College Choir and Chapel Singers, Student Missions Outreach, Voluntary Service Outreach, and the Student Ministerial Association.

Degree Programs

The Bachelor of Arts and Bachelor of Science degrees with majors in Biblical Literature, Christian Education, Christian Ministries, and Religion/Philosophy are of-fered. The major in Christian Ministries is the degree which contains the fullest set of courses designed to prepare young persons for the ministry of the Church. This degree is the only degree offered which meets certification requirements for ordination in the Wesleyan Church; moreover, it is the primary degree taken by students of other denominations seeking ordination. The Religion/Philosophy major is for students anticipating seminary or an advanced degree. The Christian Education major is for those interested in lay Christian service in the Sunday School, youth work, missionary service, children's ministry, Christian recreational and retreat ministries, and daycare programs. A minor in Missions and Christian Education is available.

The Master of Arts degree with a major in Ministerial Education is offered by the Department of Graduate Studies of Marion College. The program permits study in the major area of Biblical, Doctrinal, Historical, and Practical concerns. A total of 30 credit hours is required for the degree including a thesis/practicum/project and electives.

Special Programs

Special programs and features include the Associate of Arts in Christian Education, the ETTA Diploma, and Study Abroad. The ETTA program provides qualified graduating students with a Standard Teaching Diploma granted by the Evangelical Teacher Training Association (ETTA). It gives international recognition as a qualified teacher in Christian Education leadership courses. Marion College is affiliated with The American Institute of Holy Land Studies in Jerusalem, Israel. Junior year students can study for a full year or semester in the areas of Bible, Archaeology, History, Geography, and/or Hebrew Language and Literature in the Holy Land.

Mennonite Biblical Seminary
(Associated Mennonite Biblical Seminaries)
3003 Benham Avenue
Elkhart, IN 46517   (219) 295-3726

Administration. Dr. Henry Poettcker, President; J. Herbert Fretz, Coordinator of Church and Seminary Relations.

General Description. Mennonite Biblical Seminary is a graduate ministerial training school of the General Conference Mennonite Church. The Seminary is operated by authorization of this Conference under the supervision of a Board of Trustees.

In the academic year 1958-59 Mennonite Biblical Seminary (until then located in Chicago) and Goshen Biblical Seminary (then on the campus of Goshen College, Goshen, Indiana) entered a cooperative relationship known under the name Associated Mennonite Biblical Seminaries. By action of their respective boards of control a plan of academic cooperation was set up, designed to provide substantial advantages for both seminaries, while retaining the organizational and financial independence of each. The Associated Mennonite Biblical Seminaries provide an integrated program under the direction of a unified faculty. Degrees offered include the Master of Divinity and the Master of Arts in Peace Studies. A One Year Theology Curriculum (culminating in the Certificate in Theological Studies) for persons with the B.A. degree is designed individually according to the student's respective goals. The Certificate of Theology for mature persons serving in the pastoral ministry represents a 5-year program of study designed without the normal liberal arts foundation.

Parent Institution. The General Conference Mennonite Church consists of 64,000 members with central offices located at 722 Main Street, Newton, Kansas. Its 320 member churches are located in the United States and Canada. The Conference receives regular reports from the Seminary, and through its budget provides 3/5 of the annual operating costs.

Community Environment. Approximately 5 miles south of the Michigan-Indiana border, Elkhart, Indiana is only 10 miles from the city of South Bend and Notre Dame University. Facilities in South Bend include the Morris Civic Auditorium and the new Century Center for professional drama as well as concerts by the South Bend Symphony and the South Bend Art Association where classes and workshops are conducted daily in the auditorium.

Religious Denomination. General Conference Mennonite Church.

Religious Emphasis. Evangelical with peace emphasis.

Accreditation. North Central Association of Colleges and Schools; Association of Theological Schools in the United States and Canada.

Term System. Semester/Interterm/Semester (4-1-4); no summer term.

Enrollment in Degree Programs in Religion 1984–85. Total 91; men 64, women 27.

Degrees in Religion Awarded 1984–85. Master of Divinity 20; men 13, women 7. Master of Arts (Peace Studies) 3; men 2, women 1. Certificate in Theological Studies 1; women 1.

Faculty for Degree Programs in Religion. Total 15; full-time 9, part-time 6.

Admission Requirements. A statement with regard to the candidate's Christian faith convictions; participation in the full scope of the community in addition to the regular curricular requirements; graduation from a liberal arts course of an accredited college (some exceptions may be made by special Curriculum Committee action).

Tuition and Fees. Tuition $2,280 per year; student activity fee $24; matriculation fee $20; housing $87 to $285 per month; boarding club meals $110 per month.

Financial Aid. Resources for financial aid are available from special funds and are based on the student's need. Aid assistance consists of scholarships, loans, tuition and living expense grants, and employment.

Housing. Both on- and off-campus housing is available for single and married students.

Library Facilities. The library comprises 98,000 volumes and receives 313 periodicals and journals by subscription and another 226 by gift or otherwise. A collection of research materials in Mennonite and Anabaptist history, especially with reference to the General Conference Mennonite Church is maintained at Elkhart. Another special collection is the Gerald Studer Bible Collection. The Mennonite Historical Library is housed in a special section of the Harold and Wilma Good Library at Goshen College. Archives of the Mennonite Church are housed in the Newcomer Center in Elkhart.

Religious Services/Activities. Chapel is held three times weekly. A weekly forum, regular weekly prayer services, and up to four retreats for spiritual formation are also held.

Degree Programs

The purpose of the Master of Divinity curriculum is to equip candidates for effective participation in the various ministries of the church at home and around the world. There are six different curricular designs through which students prepare for particular ministries. These focus on pastoral ministry, Christian education, overseas ministries, pastoral counseling, church planting and evangelism, and academic ministries. In addition to three courses in the biblical languages, each design requires six courses from each department.

The purpose of the Master of Arts in Peace Studies is to provide the environment for a deepening understanding of and commitment to the biblical vision of peace and justice and its embodiment in the world. While not designed for a specific profession, the program prepares students for peace and justice ministries from congregational to world-wide levels. Completion of the course will normally require two full academic years.

Special Programs

A One-Year Theology Curriculum has the dual purpose of equipping lay people for stronger participation in the life of the church, and of serving those going on in graduate or professional training who wish a better understanding of the Christian faith and the church's ministry in the world, as well as of the Mennonite commitment in faith and work.

A Certificate in Theology Curriculum is designed for mature persons of about 30 years of age or older who have not completed a college degree program, who are involved in leadership responsibilities in their home congregations, or if not presently involved have had a significant responsibility in the past which would indicate that they will profit from an educational experience for future leadership.

Other special programs at the Seminary include Black and Hispanic Leadership Training, Ministers in Vicinity Program, and Conference-Based Theological Education.

Notre Dame, University of
Department of Theology
327 O'Shaughnessy Hall

Notre Dame, IN 46556   (219) 239-7811

Administration. Rev. Theodore M. Hesburgh, C.S.C., President of the University; Dr. Timothy O'Meara, Provost; Dr. Robert E. Gordon, Vice President for Advanced Studies (Graduate School); Richard P. McBrien, Chairman, Department of Theology; James F. White, Director of Graduate Studies, Department of Theology.

General Description. Within the Department of Theology the following graduate programs are offered: Master of Arts, Master of Divinity, and Doctor of Philosophy. There are required Theology courses for undergraduates, and there is a Major in Theology at the baccalaureate level.

The Institute for Pastoral and Social Ministry at Notre Dame was established in 1976 to further pastoral and social ministry in the American Church and to coordinate special programs which come under this general heading. The programs are: Notre Dame Study of Catholic Parish Life; Notre Dame Center for Pastoral Liturgy; Notre Dame Institute for Clergy Education; Program for Church Leaders; Center for Social Concerns; Retreats International. Also on the Notre Dame campus are the Center for the Philosophy of Religion and the Center for the Study of American Catholicism.

Moreau Seminary, located on the Notre Dame campus and under the supervision of the Holy Cross Fathers, is the formation community for all seminarians. Moreau Seminary welcomes any seminarian, diocesan or religious, provided he is properly registered by the Graduate School of the University for the Department of Theology, sponsored by a diocese or a religious community, and in compliance with the admission requirements of the Seminary.

Parent Institution. The University of Notre Dame was founded in 1842 by a priest of the Congregation of Holy Cross, a French missionary order, and is located just north of South Bend, Indiana. Chartered by the State of Indiana in 1844, the University was governed by the Holy Cross Fathers until 1967 when governance was transferred to a predominantly lay Board of Trustees. Graduate programs of the University have always been open to women, and Notre Dame has admitted undergraduate women since 1972. Enrollment at Notre Dame in the fall of 1984 was: undergraduate, 7,507; graduate, 1,235; professional, 789.

Community Environment. The campus of Notre Dame has 95 buildings on 1,250 acres. Its twin lakes and wooded areas provide a setting of natural beauty. The city of Notre Dame, a part of South Bend, Indiana, is located on the St. Joseph River just off the Indiana Toll Road, near Lake Michigan. All forms of major transportation are available. City facilities include the Morris Civic Auditorium and the New Century Center for professional drama as well as concerts by the South Bend Symphony. The South Bend

Art Association conducts classes and workshops daily in the auditorium.

Religious Denomination. Roman Catholic.

Religious Emphasis. Liberal.

Accreditation. North Central Association of Colleges and Schools; Association of Theological Schools in the United States and Canada.

Term System. Semester; Master of Arts is available in the Summer Session.

Enrollment in Degree Programs in Religion 1984–85. Total 150; men 110, women 40.

Degrees in Religion Awarded 1984–85. Master of Arts 39; men 19, women 20. Master of Divinity 42; men 36, women 6. Doctor of Philosophy 69; men 55, women 14.

Faculty for Degree Programs in Religion. Total 44; full-time 40, part-time 4.

Admission Requirements. Master of Arts: Bachelor of Arts with major in theology (religious studies) or equivalent; Graduate Record Examination; one foreign language for research option. Master of Divinity: Bachelor of Arts; GRE scores of at least 500 in both verbal and quantitative; three recommendations; 18 hours in philosophy; evidence of mature personality and commitment to Christian faith. Doctor of Philosophy: Bachelor of Arts; Master of Divinity, Master of Arts in Theology, or equivalent; GRE scores of at least 600 each; facility in some languages required.

Tuition and Fees. Tuition $7,650 per year plus fees; housing $510 to $625 per semester.

Financial Aid. Financial aid is available for Ph.D. and Master of Divinity students in the form of Fellowships and Graduate Assistantships.

Housing. Moreau Seminary houses candidates for priesthood. There is some housing in dorms. Off-campus housing for women and married students.

Library Facilities. The University library system consists of eight libraries which house most of the books, journals, manuscripts, and other nonbook library materials available on the campus. Currently, the collections contain more than 1,500,000 volumes, 765,000 microform units, and 8,500 recordings to support the teaching and research programs.

Religious Services/Activities. Regular religious services in the campus chapel are Roman Catholic. There are churches of all denominations in close proximity to the campus.

Degree Programs

The Master of Arts in Theology program is designed to provide graduate-level training in theology through one of several areas of study within the department. It offers a well-defined and flexible educational program which allows for a diversity of goals of individual students. It seeks to prepare individuals for further graduate study in theology or related disciplines; serves those requiring a basis for high school teaching, especially in Roman Catholic schools; serves those interested in preparing for new areas of ministry, e.g., liturgical leadership, religious education, justice education, campus ministry; serves those seeking continuing education and theological updating; and serves those desiring an opportunity to reflect on their ministry and freshen their grasp of current theological fields.

The Master of Divinity is a a professional degree. It is designed to prepare students for learned and effective ministry in today's Church. The program of studies normally extends over six semesters and encompasses 72 hours. Courses required are in the areas of Biblical Studies, Historical Studies, Systematic Theology, Christian Ethics, Liturgy, Field Education, Ministerial Skills, and electives.

The Doctor of Philosophy program provides advanced study in theology through specialization in one of three areas within the department: Christianity and Judaism in Antiquity, Liturgical Studies, and Theological Inquiry. The graduate program is open to all qualified students regardless of religious affiliation. The doctoral program requires 72 credit hours and lasts a minimum of four years.

St. Mary's College
Department of Religious Studies
Notre Dame, IN 46556   (219) 284-4000

Administration. Dr. William A. Hickey, Acting President; Dr. Keith J. Egan, Chairman, Department of Religious Studies.

General Description. The Department of Religious Studies offers a major in Religious Studies as well as supplying the required six semester hours of Religious Studies necessary for graduation for every student. The courses in Religious Studies endeavor to nuture interest in persons as religious beings. Christianity and the Roman Catholic religion are the focal points for this study. Besides indicating the religious dimensions in life, the courses also endeavor to cultivate skills necessary to the study of religion. The Department of Religious Studies is coordinate with the Theology Department of the University of Notre Dame. The Bachelor of Arts in Religious Studies is awarded by St. Mary's College.

Parent Institution. St. Mary's College is a Catholic liberal arts college for women. While fostering an academic climate in which individual needs are identified and where diverse talents are both challenged and channeled, the College seeks to create a learning community where the Christian tradition both of the past and present may be appreciated.

Community Environment. St. Mary's College is on 275 acres of landscaped campus along the St. Joseph River in Notre Dame, Indiana. Nearby is the University of Notre Dame.

Religious Denomination. Roman Catholic.

Accreditation. North Central Association of Colleges and Schools.

Term System. Semester.

Admission Requirements. High school graduate with 16 academic units; two personal recommendations; SAT or ACT; 3 College Board Achievement Tests.

Tuition and Fees. Tuition per semester $3,270; part-time $250 per semester hour; room and board $1,225-$1,780; comprehensive fee $119.

Financial Aid. The primary purpose of financial aid is to provide assistance to students who otherwise would be unable to pursue their education. Requirements are proving financial need and maintaining a 3.4 cumulative grade point average. Many types of scholarships, grants, and loans are available.

Housing. Residence facilities include space for approximately 1,600 students.

Library Facilities. The Cushwa-Leighton Library, in a new 77,000 square foot building, has seating for 540 and a capacity for 250,000 volumes. The library also includes an A/V center and a Rare Book Room containing among other treasures a Dante collection.

Religious Services/Activities. Services provided by the Campus Ministry include availability of the sacraments, including daily celebration of the Eucharist, weekend retreats, days of reflection, special prayer and liturgical services, small prayer and scripture study groups, pre-marriage programs, various support groups, training for peer ministry, spiritual direction, and counseling.

Degree Programs

The major in Religious Studies leading to the Bachelor of Arts degree is offered jointly by the St. Mary's Department of Religious Studies and the Theology Department of University of Notre Dame. The major consists of 24 credit hours beyond the introductory course. At least one course must be taken in each of the following areas: Scriptures, historical theology, theological method, and systematic theology. In addition, the student chooses a coherent combination of courses at the junior or senior level in areas such as Scriptures, systematic theology, spirituality, or religious education.

St. Meinrad School of Theology
Saint Meinrad, IN 47577   (812) 357-6525

Administration. Rev. Daniel Buechlein, O.S.B., President-Rector; Catherine C. Etienne, Registrar.

General Description. The tradition of educating priests was begun at St. Meinrad in 1857. The School of Theology aims to provide its students with opportunities to develop in themselves those strengths of mind and spirit which are the indispensable basis of effective ministry as Roman Catholic priests. The Master of Divinity program is a four-year professional degree program offered for men preparing for the priesthood.

Parent Institution. The St. Meinrad School of Theology is operated by the Benedictine Monks of St. Meinrad Archabbey. Unlike an undergraduate institution, the School of Theology is a professional school, and the curriculum and life-style are shaped by the needs of pastoral ministry.

Community Environment. The School is located on a 350-acre campus in rural Harrison Township of Spencer County, approximately 50 miles from Evansville, Indiana. The St. Meinrad Archabbey is one of seven archabbeys in the world.

Religious Denomination. Roman Catholic.

Accreditation. North Central Association of Colleges and Schools; Association of Theological Schools in the United States and Canada.

Term System. Trimester; summer term.

Enrollment in Degree Programs in Religion 1984–85. Total Master of Divinity 146; men 146. Master of Theological Studies and Master of Religious Education summer enrollment 54; men 18, women 36.

Degrees in Religion Awarded 1984–85. Master of Divinity 38; men 38. Master of Theological Studies 18; men 7, women 11. Master of Religious Education 9; men 3, women 6.

Faculty for Degree Programs in Religion. Total 29; full-time 9; part-time 20.

Admission Requirements. Bachelor's degree with 18 semester hours of philosophy and 12 semester hours of theology.

Tuition and Fees. Tuition $3,152 per year; board and lodging $1,663 per semester; retreat fee $126; various other fees.

Financial Aid. Each year the School of Theology awards three competitive scholarships to first year students who possess outstanding qualities of intellectual ability and Christian leadership. A Work-Study Program provides part-time jobs to theology students who need financial aid and who must earn a part of their educational expenses. Such employment is usually awarded in conjunction with other financial aid programs as part of a package.

Housing. Students are housed in either Sherwood Hall or Conley Hall.

Library Facilities. The library houses 130,000 volumes of books and journals in open stacks.

Religious Services/Activities. Roman Catholic Mass daily. The Oratory Chapel and the Emmaus Prayer Center provide space for a variety of personal prayer experiences. Students participate in evening prayer in small groups throughout the School of Theology. Four times during the school year, the Spiritual Life program offers a day of recollection for the entire theology community. The Sacrament of Reconciliation is celebrated by the Community several times each year. The retreat policy of the School of Theology is an annual six-day directed retreat for each student. The Towards Jerusalem program is devoted exclusively to the prayer life of the disciple. Presentations are offered on the nature of prayer and the art of praying.

Degree Programs

The Master of Divinity program encourages academic excellence, intellectual integrity, and personal appropriation of the insights of theology. It is awarded for completion of four years of graduate professional theological studies. The program is in two phases, each phase of two-years duration (four semesters). Phase One is entitled The Church in Christ and Phase Two is entitled Sacrament of Humanity's Unity and Its Union with God. The program requires the completion of 116 semester hours, four interterms, and 15 practicum units. Completion of eight semesters as a full-time student is also required and a student must complete the program with a C (2.00) cumulative grade point average.

The Master of Religious Education degree program is offered during the summer session. This program is viewed as the formation of a Christian educator who will be able to deal effectively with the complexities of communicating the faith in the contemporary world. Two options are available: (1) Option A is designed for those students who have a graduate or undergraduate degree in Education or hold a state teaching certificate; (2) Option B is tailored to meet the needs of those students who do not have an education major or hold teacher certification. The student must complete a total of forty-eight semester hours of work at the C (2.00) level.

The Master of Theological Studies program has been designed for those who wish to further their understanding of the nature and work of ministry, the contemporary situations in which ministry is done, and the resources of the Christian tradition. The summer program provides courses in a forty-eight hour general curriculum. It must be completed by the end of the tenth summer session from the time of first enrollment.

Special Programs

In cooperation with the Mexican American Cultural Center in San Antonio, Texas, the School of Theology offers a specialized program in Ministry with the Hispanic-American. Upon approval from their Bishops and the administration of the School of Theology, the students who take part in this program spend the second semester and summer of the second year in San Antonio.

A cooperative Master of Arts Degree Program with Indiana University permits students to earn a Master of Arts in Religion from Indiana University. The Department of Religious Studies of Indiana University accepts eight hours of graduate credit from the School of Theology toward the Master's degree. Students who qualify for this program spend the first semester of their second year in residence at Indiana University.

Taylor University
Department of Religion, Philosophy, and
Biblical Languages
Upland, IN 46989   (317) 998-5148

Administration. Dr. Greg O. Lehman, President; Dr. Richard J. Stanislaw, Vice President for Academic Affairs; Dr. Herbert Nygren, Head, Department of Religion, Philosophy, and Biblical Languages.

General Description. The Department of Religion, Philosophy, and Biblical Languages offers the Bachelor of Arts and Bachelor of Science degrees with a choice of four majors: Biblical Literature, Religious Studies, Christian Education, and Philosophy of Religion. Also available are the Certificate of Religious Studies and the Certificate in Missions.

Parent Institution. Taylor University is an independent, interdenominational Christian liberal arts college. As a Christian institution, Taylor recognizes that all truth has its source in God. The students' quest for truth begins with this conviction and relates to all aspects of the liberal arts setting including the fine arts, humanities, social and behavioral sciences, and the natural sciences.

Community Environment. The campus of Taylor University consist of approximately 250 acres, located on the south side of the town of Upland, Indiana. The main campus is developed on 170 acres and contains major campus buildings and recreational and athletic fields. An additional 80 acres adjacent to the main campus is for future campus development. Upland (population 3,700) has all the advantages of quiet, country life with the nearby cities for activities. It is located 14 miles southeast of Marion and 23 miles north of Muncie. The community has churches of many denominations as well as health services and hospitals.

Religious Denomination. Nondenominational.

Religious Emphasis. Evangelical Protestant.

Accreditation. North Central Association of Colleges and Schools.

Term System. Semester; January interterm; summer term.

Enrollment in Degree Programs in Religion 1984–85. Total 78; men 40, women 38.

Degrees in Religion Awarded 1984–85. Bachelor of Arts 18; men 12, women 6.

Faculty for Degree Programs in Religion. Total 7; full-time 7.

Admission Requirements. Graduation in the upper half of secondary school class; satisfactory aptitude test scores; high school transcript.

Tuition and Fees. Tuition $5,981; room and board $2,224.

Financial Aid. Loans, grants, and work-study programs are available to students who have completed the Financial Aid Forms and are judged to have need.

Housing. Approximately 1,200 college-supervised spaces are available on campus. Off-campus housing owned by the College is available for married students. Other private housing (unless family) must be approved by the College.

Library Facilities. The library contains over 134,000 volumes and houses the University Archives.

Religious Services/Activities. Chapel services are held three times weekly; Sunday morning Worship service; planned retreats by campus director of Student Ministries.

Degree Programs

All Bachelor degree students complete approximately 50 hours in general education courses. B.A. students must have second year level of proficiency in another language; B.S. students must have a cognate in education and systems analysis. The Department of Religion, Philosophy, and Biblical Languages offers four majors: Biblical Literature, Religious Studies, Christian Education, and Philosophy of Religion. The major requires a minimum of 40 hours with specified requirements within the concentration.

Special Programs

A Certificate in Religious Studies is available to students in any major program who complete courses totaling at least 15 religion credit hours beyond the general education requirements. A Certificate in Missions is available to students in any major program as well as to students majoring in religion and philosophy.

Valparaiso University
Department of Theology
Lembke Hall
Valparaiso, IN 46383   (219) 464-5201

Administration. Edgar P. Senne, Chair, Department of Theology.

General Description. The Department of Theology provides programs of study and advising services for students who wish to prepare for professional careers in the church: (1) programs of study in preparation for Deaconess Ministry that are structured by the Department in cooperation with the Lutheran Deaconess Association; (2) programs for preparation for seminary studies individually tailored to the needs and interests of the student; and (3) programs for students interested in service as Directors of Christian Education or Youth Workers. Completion of the requirements of the College of Arts and Sciences with a major in Theology leads to the Bachelor of Arts degree. The Theology component of the general education requirement at Valparaiso University is three courses of three credit hours each. These courses are taken from each of three levels.

Parent Institution. Begun by Methodists in 1859 as an institution pioneering in coeducation, the Valparaiso Male and Female College was forced by the reverses of the Civil

War to close its doors in 1871. It was revived in 1873 as the Northern Indiana Normal School and renamed Valparaiso College in 1900 and Valparaiso University in 1907. The University was purchased in 1925 by the Lutheran University Association, beginning the modern phase of the University's history.

Community Environment. The spacious campus of 310 acres contains more than seventy academic and residential buildings. The campus is located in the small city of Valparaiso, attractively situated in a rural setting at the edge of the busy industrial district of northwest Indiana. The city of Chicago with its vast cultural resources is an hour's drive from the campus.

Religious Denomination. Lutheran Church - Missouri Synod.

Religious Emphasis. Classical Ecumenical Lutheranism.

Accreditation. North Central Association of Colleges and Schools. Member of: Lutheran Education Association.

Term System. Semester; summer term.

Enrollment in Degree Programs in Religion 1984–85. Total 37; men 10, women 27.

Degrees in Religion Awarded 1984–85. Bachelor of Arts 15; men 1, women 14.

Faculty for Degree Programs in Religion. Total 20; full-time 10, part-time 10.

Admission Requirements. Graduation from an approved secondary school or equivalent; SAT or ACT.

Tuition and Fees. Tuition $2,865 per semester; general fee $100 per semester; room and board $1,165 per semester.

Financial Aid. Awards, scholarships, loan funds, and rehabilitation grants are available. Campus employment is also possible.

Housing. The majority of students live in one of nine university residence halls or in one of eleven fraternity houses located on or near the campus.

Library Facilities. The Henry F. Moellering Memorial Library houses a collection of approximately 240,000 bound volumes, 88,000 microforms, and 1,300 current periodicals.

Religious Services/Activities. Students and faculty participate with the University Pastor and University Associate Pastor in preparing a rich range of services. In addition to holding services on Sunday and throughout the week at various times, the University has designated a specific time (10:10 AM) for Morning Prayer Monday through Friday when members of the community may come together for meditation, prayer, and praise. Attendance is voluntary. Students chair chapel ministry groups of worship, social concerns, international concerns, evangelism, and hospitality.

Degree Programs

A Bachelor of Arts program is offered for students to prepare themselves for seminary entrance. The pre-semi-

nary program meets all the standards of the Association of Theological Schools for undergraduate education, as well as the entrance requirement of all Lutheran and other Protestant seminaries. Upon graduation from this program, students are usually accepted into the seminaries not only of the Lutheran Church - Missouri Synod, but also of other Protestant bodies and in graduate divinity schools throughout the United States. The program includes studies in the arts and humanities, theology, biblical languages, and in areas of the student's own special interest.

The Bachelor of Arts degree with a major in Theology can be pursued in a program of courses including Theology, Biblical Studies, History of the Church, Contemporary Religion and Practice, and History of Religions.

Special Programs

The University and the Lutheran Deaconess Association cooperate in the education of women for service in Deaconess Ministry.

IOWA

Central College
Department of Philosophy and Religion
812 University Street
Pella, IA 50219   (515) 628-5213

Administration. David E. Timmer, Chair, Department of Philosophy and Religion.

General Description. Central College has educated students for the Christian ministry since its very beginning in the 1850s. In 1981, the College initiated a more formalized approach to Pre-Ministerial Studies. The program is designed to help students clarify their understanding of the ministry as a profession and to explore the various directions such a profession might take. The College has deliberately chosen not to establish a pre-ministerial major, but to encourage students to select an existing departmental major which requires demonstration of intellectual curiosity, comprehension of subject matter, ability to think analytically, and above average communication skills. Majors in Philosophy and Religion are also offered.

Parent Institution. The College is a private, four-year, liberal arts institution affiliated with the Reformed Church in America. Total enrollment is approximately 1,500, with 1,300 at the home campus and 200 in the International Studies Program.

Community Environment. The campus is situated on 77 acres with 31 major buildings. It is located in the city of Pella, Iowa which has a population of 8,700 and is one hour southeast of Des Moines on Highway 163.

Religious Denomination. Reformed Church in America.

Religious Emphasis. Reformed/Ecumenical.

Accreditation. North Central Association of Colleges and Schools.

Term System. Trimester.

Enrollment in Degree Programs in Religion 1984–85. Total 2; men 2.

Faculty for Degree Programs in Religion. Total 3; full-time 3.

Admission Requirements. Graduation from an accredited high school or equivalent; rank in the upper half of high school graduating class; ACT or SAT.

Tuition and Fees. Costs per term: Tuition $1,977; board $438; room $354; activity fee $37.

Financial Aid. More than 85 percent of the student body received financial assistance totaling nearly $8 million in 1984-85. Financial assistance is awarded on a yearly basis. Pre-ministerial scholarships are available.

Housing. On-campus residence halls for single students. The general rule is two persons to a room.

Library Facilities. The Geisler Learning Resource Center houses 130,000 volumes. It has subscriptions to 850 periodicals and numerous items in microform. The third floor archives house documents relating to the early history of Pella and to the Dutch in Iowa and America.

Religious Services/Activities. Retreats, church services, and chapel services are sponsored by the Campus Ministries.

Degree Programs

The Bachelor of Arts with a Religion major requires, in addition to the general education requirements, 45 quarter hours of courses chosen from the Religion Track. Central's pre-ministerial program assumes basic courses in Religion and Philosophy and a heavy concentration of courses in the humanities. A special pre-ministry adviser, normally the College Chaplain, works with the students on selection of courses and with the choice of seminary, as well as assisting in the application process.

Special Programs

An Associate in Church Work program is designed for students who wish to prepare for careers in church work, short of entering the ministry. They spend three years at Central in a liberal arts program leading to a major in Religion. The program is a cooperative 3-and-1 program with Western Theological Seminary in Holland, Michigan. The final year is on the Seminary campus where courses in Christian education, theology, Bible, counseling, and religious communications are available.

Divine Word College

Epworth, IA 52045　　　　　　　(319) 876-3353

Administration. Rev. John J. Donaghey, S.V.D., President.

General Description. The Divine Word College is a four-year college of liberal arts and is an integral part of the training program of the Divine Word Missionaries in their world-wide mission and work for the welfare of mankind. The College is also open to receive men preparing for the Diocesan Priesthood or for other Religious Orders. The Divine Word Missionaries were founded by Rev. Arnold Janssen of Steyl, Holland, in 1875. At present they number some 5,000 members scattered throughout the world. The College awards the degrees Bachelor of Arts and Bachelor of Science.

Community Environment. The 35-acre campus includes two buildings in rural Epworth, Iowa, 15 miles west of Dubuque and 10 miles east of Dyersville.

Religious Denomination. Roman Catholic.

Accreditation. North Central Association of Colleges and Schools.

Term System. Semester.

Enrollment in Degree Programs in Religion 1984–85. Total 90; men 90.

Faculty for Degree Programs in Religion. Total 25; full-time 15, part-time 10.

Admission Requirements. High school graduation or equivalent; 16 academic units; SAT or ACT.

Tuition and Fees. Tuition and fees $3,500 per year; room, board, and laundry $1,200.

Financial Aid. Divine Word College Scholarships, Presidential Scholarships, state and federal aid programs are available.

Housing. The College has dormitory accommodations for 125 students.

Library Facilities. The library contains more than 84,-000 volumes. The library annex contains over 7,300 bound periodicals, a microform collection, and over 5,300 records and cassettes.

Religious Services/Activities. The College provides an environment for the students to grow in their religious missionary vocation by proposing the members of the Epworth religious community, with whom the students live closely, as examples of missionary life. The college also challenges such growth in the students by expecting them to live out the life-style of Divine Word Missionaries.

Degree Programs

The College, as required by the diversified activities of the Society, seeks to promote the harmonious development of the physical, psychosocial, intellectual, and value endowments of the students as maturing persons. The Liberal Arts program is designed to guide the students in the acquisition of information, attitudes, and skills in traditional and contemporary subject matter areas. It strives to provide opportunity for the student to develop habits of creative and critical thinking coupled with facility in effective communication. This is viewed as immediately preparatory to professional diversification into such specialized career areas as the priesthood, education, counseling, and social action. Degrees may be obtained in four fields of concentration: Philosophy, English, Sociology, and General Science. All students must take the Basic Program of courses that includes Theology, Philosophy, English Composition, Speech, and History. The Bachelor of Arts and the Bachelor of Science degrees are awarded.

Dubuque, University of
Theological Seminary

2050 University Avenue

Dubuque, IA 52001　　　　　　(319) 589-3112

Administration. Dr. Walter F. Peterson, President; Dr. Arlo D. Duba, Dean, Theological Seminary.

General Description. The University of Dubuque Theological Seminary is one of ten theological seminaries operated under the authority of the General Assembly of the Presbyterian Church (U.S.A.). It was founded in the mid-19th century to serve German-speaking populations of the upper midwest and continues to have as its primary task the preparation of men and women for Christian ministry. As an integral part of the University, it maintains close relations with the undergraduate College of Liberal Arts. As a partner in the Schools of Theology in Dubuque, it enjoys a close consortium relationship with Wartburg Seminary of the American Lutheran Church. The Seminary is a graduate professional school and grants, through the University of Dubuque, the Master of Arts in Religion, the Master of Divinity, and the Doctor of Ministry degrees.

Parent Institution. The University of Dubuque was founded in 1852. The present University grew out of a number of different schools and educational institutions (German Presbyterian Theological Seminary of the Northwest, the Dubuque Academy, Dubuque College, Dubuque Academy of Music, and a university high school). The overall structure became the University of Dubuque in the 1920s.

Community Environment. The Seminary is situated on the 56-acre campus of the University of Dubuque. The many parks of the city of Dubuque are available to students, as are the recreational facilities of the Mississippi River and the adjacent hills.

Religious Denomination. Presbyterian Church (U.S.A.).

Accreditation. North Central Association of Schools and Colleges; Association of Theological Schools in the United States and Canada.

Term System. Semester (4-1-4 plan).

Admission Requirements. Baccalaureate degree from an accredited college or university or its equivalent.

Tuition and Fees. Tuition $1,575 per semester; board $950 per year; room $1,000 per year; student fee $50 per year. Doctor of Ministry tuition $3,700 for the program; major project fee $275; continuation fee (beyond three and one-half years) per six months $300; graduation fee $75.

Financial Aid. Financial assistance is available on the basis of need and in the form of scholarships, grants, loans, and Seminary employment.

Housing. Housing for single students is in small residential groups in individual houses on the campus. Married students have housing in the Potterveld apartments, adjacent to the campus.

Library Facilities. The Library of the Schools of Theology in Dubuque is composed of the libraries of this Seminary and Wartburg Theological Seminary. Although it is considered one library, it is housed in two buildings: The Reu Memorial Library in Fritschel Hall on the Wartburg Campus, and the Ficke-Laird Library and the Couchman Memorial Library on the University of Dubuque campus. The total library resources include over 150,000 volumes of print and nonprint materials, 900 reels of microfilm, and 1,000 units of microfiche. Lutheran materials will be found on the Wartburg campus, and Reformed and Methodist tradition materials are on the University of Dubuque campus. Both are strong in Biblical studies. The collection of materials on philosophy, medical ethics, and other religions is particularly extensive on the Dubuque campus. Religion and literature, music, and nonprint materials are particularly strong at Wartburg.

Religious Services/Activities. The Seminary community gathers for worship each Monday through Friday. The corporate worship life is under the supervision of the Worship Council. A prayer service is held each day. Student prayer and study groups are encouraged.

Degree Programs

The Master of Arts in Religion program is designed to equip men and women for lay and ordained specialized ministries in the church. The program requires 54 credit hours in the three divisions of the Seminary: Biblical Studies, Historical-Theological Studies, and Ministry Studies.

The Master of Divinity requires a minimum of 84 credit hours from the three divisions of the curriculum. A minimum of 12 credit hours is required in the Supervised Practice of Ministry. Specific denominational requirements must also be met.

The Doctor of Ministry degree is intended for persons who, in addition to having completed their basic theological education, have shown outstanding service of at least three years in the professional ministry. The degree is offered by the Schools of Theology in Dubuque (STD), a joint program of the Wartburg Theological Seminary and the University of Dubuque Theological Seminary. The program is professional, theological, and personal. It requires a minimum of 36 semester hours including a Doctor of Ministry core of 12 hours, graduate courses of 18 hours, and a major project/disquisition. The program is designed for the integration of theology and practice in general ministry. In addition, two other majors are offered: Town and Rural Ministry, and Worship.

Faith Baptist Bible College and Theological Seminary
1900 N.W. Fourth Street
Ankeny, IA 50021   (515) 964-0601

Administration. Dr. Gordon L. Shipp, President; Dr. George G. Houghton, Academic Vice President; Dr. Robert G. Delnay, Dean of the Seminary.

General Description. Faith Baptist Theological Seminary believes that the high goal of a seminary is to train leaders who are Bible expositors, and so it sees as its goal the training of leaders for Christian service. It views each of the Seminary's programs as a means to help its students to be capable teachers. Degrees granted are: Master of Divinity; Master of Arts in either Biblical Studies, Pastoral Studies, or Theological Studies. The Master of Divinity program is designed to prepare pastors and missionaries for service. Every student in the Bible College is a religion major with a second major in an area of specialization.

Community Environment. The city of Ankeny, Iowa (population 15,429) is 5 miles north of the capital city of Des Moines and its recreation centers, theaters, and competitive sports. Two of the main industries are manufacturing of farming equipment and retail products. Community facilities of Ankeny include a library, churches, city parks, and public golf course.

Religious Denomination. General Association of Regular Baptist Churches.

Religious Emphasis. Fundamentalist.

Accreditation. American Association of Bible Colleges.

Term System. Semester.

Enrollment in Degree Programs in Religion 1984–85. Total 295; men 143, women 152.

Degrees in Religion Awarded 1984–85. Bachelor of Arts 10; men 10. Bachelor of Science 53; men 29, women 24. Master of Arts 1; men 1. Associate of Arts 24; men 6, women 18. One-year Certificate 2; men 1, women 1.

Faculty for Degree Programs in Religion. Total 24; full-time 15, part-time 9.

Admission Requirements. Bachelor's degree from an approved college with evidence of potential for work on the graduate level. At the discretion of the faculty, the applicant may be required to complete deficiencies in the undergraduate division; completion of all applications and submission of the required application credentials; proven Christian character and established purpose of ministry; agreement with the doctrinal standards of Faith Baptist Theological Seminary.

Tuition and Fees. Tuition $1,550 per semester (14-18 hours), $120 per credit (1-11 hours); room $410 per semester.

Financial Aid. Available.

Housing. Dormitories are provided for men and women on campus and there are close-in apartments for married students provided by the school.

Library Facilities. The library houses 39,151 volumes.

Religious Services/Activities. Numerous religious functions and services are held.

Degree Programs

The Bachelor of Science or Bachelor of Arts in Biblical Studies are offered with emphasis in Pastoral Training, Christian School, Missions, Assistant Pastor/Youth, Sacred Music, Christian Education, and Basic Bible. All students major in Bible.

The Master of Arts in Biblical Studies is designed for teachers, missionaries, and church workers who have been in service and desire a year of spiritual and mental refreshing. It is also for students from colleges and universities who want Bible training without having to undertake a whole undergraduate program.

The Master of Arts in Pastoral Studies was established to offer graduate work in a Bible college framework for graduates of accredited Bible colleges. The purpose of the program is to build upon the education of those who have already taken a college major in Bible and/or theology. Such a program assumes a program in pastoral theology and related Biblical subjects and stresses the importance of the application of material gained on the undergraduate level.

The Master of Divinity degree program is the standard seminary program for preparing individuals to serve as pastors, missionaries, teachers, and leaders in other areas of vocational ministry.

Special Programs

A one-year certificate program is also offered and extension programs are scheduled periodically on needed subjects.

Iowa Wesleyan College
Department of Religion and Philosophy
Mount Pleasant, IA 52641   (319) 385-8021

Administration. Dr. Thomas W. Clayton, Acting President; Dr. George E. LaMore, Jr., Coordinator for the Religion and Philosophy Program.

General Description. The Department of Religion and Philosophy offers a major intended to be one of the broadest possible exposures to the liberal arts—a study of the influential commitments, values, beliefs, and ideas that have directed the story of mankind. In order to present the human experience in its widest dimensions, numerous other academic disciplines are consulted frequently in the form of dual-discipline courses. Students contemplating church careers are equipped by a major in this program for graduate education in theological seminaries and a wide range of preprofessional programs and a variety of careers which involve the understanding of persons, the capability of making sense in variable work circum-

stances, and a capacity for lifetime learning in order to keep up to date and flexible in the changeable, vocational world of the future.

Parent Institution. Iowa Wesleyan College was founded in 1842. It is a four-year liberal arts college affiliated with The United Methodist Church.

Community Environment. The 60-acre campus is located in the community of Mount Pleasant, Iowa, at the intersection of U.S. Highways 218 and 34.

Religious Denomination. The United Methodist Church.

Accreditation. North Central Association of Colleges and Schools.

Term System. Semester (4-1-4 plan).

Admission Requirements. High school graduation or equivalent; 15 academic units; SAT or ACT.

Tuition and Fees. Tuition $2,650 per semester; room $500-$600; board $635.

Financial Aid. Full-time students preparing for the ministry or other church-related work may borrow $500. This loan will be cancelled by two years of seminary attendance or full-time church-related work completed within five years of graduation. Scholarships, loans, and campus employment are available and are awarded on the basis of need, academic achievement, character, and promise.

Housing. Housing accommodations are available for 280 women and 350 men.

Library Facilities. The J. Raymond Chadwick Library houses over 82,000 volumes.

Religious Services/Activities. The College Chaplain provides a direct and ready access to personal and spiritual counseling for the students and maintains general oversight, coordination, and direction of the on-campus religious activities. Numerous religious leaders, groups, and programs are brought to the campus each year in conjunction with the weekly Cultural and Theological Encounter program. Regular voluntary chapel services are observed on the campus. Campus Vesper Services are held weekly. A Week of Religious Emphasis is celebrated each spring.

Degree Programs

The Religion-Philosophy major requires 40 hours including prescribed courses; the Religion major requires 30 hours including specified courses. Both majors lead to the Bachelor of Arts degree.

Luther College
Department of Religion and Philosophy
Decorah, IA 52101   (319) 387-2000

Administration. Dr. H. George Anderson, President; Dr. A. Thomas Kraabel, Vice President and Dean of the College; Dr. Wilfred Bunge, Department Head, Department of Religion and Philosophy.

General Description. Although the work of the Department of Religion and Philosophy is focused primarily on the development of educated people, it takes care to prepare interested and qualified students for careers in areas where theological and philosophical training is of fundamental importance, especially teaching, law, the ministry, social services, and health-related professions.

Parent Institution. Luther College is a four-year liberal arts institution affiliated with the American Lutheran Church. The College is proud of a diverse and capable student body, a modern physical plant, and a well-qualified and dedicated staff. As a liberal arts college of the Church, Luther College seeks to attract and retain a distinctive faculty committed to undergraduate education in a Christian context.

Community Environment. Luther College is located in Decorah, Iowa, population 8,068. Situated in the hills of northeast Iowa, the town is in a rural setting with trout and bass streams, riding trails, a ski run, and other opportunities for outdoor activities. It is 65-75 miles from La Crosse, Wisconsin, Rochester, Minnesota, and Waterloo, Iowa. It is 120-150 miles from Madison, Wisconsin, Minneapolis, Minnesota, and Iowa City, Iowa.

Religious Denomination. American Lutheran Church.

Accreditation. North Central Association of Colleges and Schools.

Term System. Four-one-four system includes the January Term; there is a summer term.

Enrollment in Degree Programs in Religion 1984–85. Total 21; men 12, women 9.

Degrees in Religion Awarded 1984–85. Bachelor of Arts 11; men 6, women 5.

Faculty for Degree Programs in Religion. Total 12; full-time 7, part-time 5.

Admission Requirements. Normally top half of high school graduating class; ACT median composite of 25.

Tuition and Fees. Comprehensive fee (includes tuition, general fees, facilities fees, room, board, subscription to student publications, admission to college supported athletic and forensic events, some concerts and lectures) $8,600; commuter comprehensive fee $6,465.

Financial Aid. Luther's financial assistance program includes scholarships, grants, loans, and part-time work on campus.

Housing. All students are required to live in college-owned housing unless married or commuting from their parents' homes.

Library Facilities. Preus Library contains more than 260,000 volumes and a manuscript library of which 443 collections containing 27,000 items have been fully cataloged. The library also has Norwegian language newspapers and a collection containing Norwegian immigration historical archives.

Religious Services/Activities. There are Lutheran and Roman Catholic worship services regularly under auspices of a campus student congregation. Numerous groups, formal and informal, are organized for discussion of religious issues and fellowship.

Degree Programs

The Bachelor of Arts degree with a major in Religion requires a minimum 24 hours in the Department of Religion with at least one course in each of the following areas: historical theology, Biblical studies, theology, ethics, non-Christian religions. A senior seminar for two credit hours in which attention will be given to research in the field of religious studies is also required. One course in philosophy and a minimum of two semesters of a foreign language, ancient or modern, must also be taken.

Mount Mercy College
Religious Studies Department
1330 Elmhurst Drive N.E.
Cedar Rapids, IA 52402   (319) 363-8213

Administration. Dr. Thomas R. Feld, President; Jean F. Sweat, Vice President for Academic Affairs.

General Description. The required course in religious studies at Mount Mercy College introduces the student to the major role of religion in the development of human culture. Advanced courses emphasize areas of Christian theology which are considered fundamental for those who might wish to pursue postgraduate studies or to engage in church-related careers. Religious study majors find employment as teachers of religion, directors of religious education programs, or as pastoral ministers of various kinds, such as youth ministers, liturgical ministers, and general pastoral associates.

Parent Institution. Mount Mercy College is a coeducational, four-year, Bachelor of Arts degree-granting institution. It functions under the auspices of the Sisters of Mercy who founded the College in 1928. In the past 10 years the College has doubled its enrollment and has close ties with the Cedar Rapids community. Mount Mercy has been selected as one of the top 10 small independent colleges in the nation for its outstanding programs for the nontraditional continuing education student.

Community Environment. Mount Mercy College is situated on a 51-acre campus northeast of the business section of Cedar Rapids, Iowa. Cedar Rapids is a metropolitan city located in an area of rich agricultural production in east-central Iowa. Community facilities include over 100 churches, symphony orchestra, library, and hospital. The city has over 59 city parks which offer a variety of recreational activities.

Religious Denomination. Roman Catholic.

Accreditation. North Central Association of Colleges and Schools.

Term System. Semester, plus January Interim (4-1-4 system).

Enrollment in Degree Programs in Religion 1984–85. Total 9; men 4, women 5.

Degrees in Religion Awarded 1984–85. Bachelor of Arts 1; men 1.

Faculty for Degree Programs in Religion. Total 5; full-time 2, part-time 3.

Admission Requirements. Graduation from an accredited high school with 16 high school units or have successfully completed the GED exams; ACT, PSAT, or SAT scores.

Tuition and Fees. Tuition $4,900 per year; housing $775 to $1,215 depending upon accommodations; board $1,300 per year; other fees where applicable.

Financial Aid. The financial aid program is designed to meet the full range of needs. There are four basic sources of aid: scholarships, grants, loans, and employment.

Housing. Dormitories and apartments are available.

Library Facilities. The Lundy Library gives students access to print and non-print media, either at the College or through search and loan programs conducted by professional librarians.

Religious Services/Activities. Campus Ministry provides a variety of services, programs, and activities, many reflecting the Roman Catholic roots of Mount mercy, but others designed to be of help to Christians of all denominations. Attendance at religious functions is not required at Mount Mercy, and the religious beliefs of all students are respected.

Degree Programs

The Bachelor of Arts degree program in Religious Studies offers three possible tracks: General Religious Studies, Catechetics, and Pastoral Ministry. The latter two specialties utilize courses from other disciplines to give the student adequate career training in the respective areas and provide students with practicum experience in community settings.

Open Bible College
2633 Fleur Drive
Des Moines, IA 50321   (515) 283-0476

Administration. Dr. Dennis M. Schmidt, President.

General Description. Open Bible College is the official conference college of the Central Division of the Open Bible Standard Churches, Inc. It was founded in 1930 as the Midwest Preparatory Bible School of L.I.F.E. of Des Moines. The current name was adopted in 1953. The College has as its purpose the training for Christian ministry and the preparation for effective lay service to Christ.

Community Environment. The 10-acre campus is located in Des Moines, one of the leading insurance and publishing centers in the midwestern United States.

Religious Denomination. Open Bible Standard Churches, Inc.

Accreditation. American Association of Bible Colleges.

Term System. Semester (4-1-4 plan).

Enrollment in Degree Programs in Religion 1984–85. Total 81.

Admission Requirements. High school graduation or GED; ACT.

Tuition and Fees. Tuition $1,200 per semester; library fee $40; room and board $1,325.

Financial Aid. Scholarshps, grants, and other forms of financial aid are available to eligible students. A 25 percent tuition grant is given to all licensed and/or ordained Open Bible Standard ministers and their dependents. This also applies to Open Bible Standard missionaries and their dependents.

Housing. All students, except those living with parents or guardians within commuting distance of the College, must reside in the school residence halls. Married students may rent apartments on campus.

Library Facilities. The Carrie Hardle Memorial Library houses over 19,500 volumes. Also accessible to students is the Edith Hofer Children's File containing valuable material for those training for Christian education ministries.

Religious Services/Activities. Every student is encourage to maintain systematic private devotions. Regularly scheduled activities include Chapel (twice weekly), a World Evangelism Conference, and a Spiritual Life Week. Students enrolled for 7 or more hours are required to participate in a Christian service activity either in their home church or in some other college-approved service activity.

Degree Programs

The College offers terminal professional programs leading to the Bachelor of Arts in Pastoral Ministries, the Bachelor of Religious Education, the Bachelor of Sacred Music, and the Bachelor of Science in Missions. The curriculum is divided into three divisions: General Education, Biblical Education, and Professional Education. All baccalaureate programs require 38 hours in General Education, 53 hours of Biblical Education, and 38 hours of Professional Education.

St. Ambrose College
Theology Department
518 West Locust
Davenport, IA 52803   (319) 383-8804

Administration. Dr. William J. Bakrow, President; Rev. Edmond J. Dunn, Chairperson, Theology Department.

General Description. The Theology Department of St. Ambrose College is part of the Philosophy/Theology Division within the College. It offers courses in Systematic, Moral, Biblical, and Historical Theology, in addition to Pastoral Theology courses leading to a Ministry Concentration. The Department participates in an interdisciplinary minor in Peace and Justice.

Parent Institution. St. Ambrose College is a private, coeducational Catholic college offering four-year undergraduate programs and a master's program in business administration. The College promotes a religious environment and has an established commitment to the liberal arts with pre-professional and career preparation. Founded in 1882, St. Ambrose is rich in tradition and strong in stature.

Community Environment. St. Ambrose College is located in Davenport, Iowa (population 100,400) which is on the north bank of the Mississippi River. It has an average temperature of 57 degrees. Community facilities include 91 churches, hotels, hospitals, four radio stations, three TV stations, public library, and 27 city parks.

Religious Denomination. Roman Catholic.

Religious Emphasis. Contemporary Roman Catholic with an ecumenical perspective.

Accreditation. North Central Association of Colleges and Universities.

Term System. Semester.

Enrollment in Degree Programs in Religion 1984–85. Total 13; men 7, women 6.

Faculty for Degree Programs in Religion. Total 11; full-time 5, part-time 6.

Admission Requirements. Graduation from an accredited high school with a cumulative grade point average of 2.50 or above on a 4.00 scale; applicants with high school averages between 2.00 and 2.49 are eligible for admission as freshmen if they have an ACT composite score of 18 or higher or an SAT total score of 779 or above.

Tuition and Fees. Tuition $185 per credit hour; room $365 to $640 depending on accommodations selected; board $560 to $635 per semester depending on meal plan.

Financial Aid. Information and applications for financial aid, scholarships, loans, college employment, grants, work-study, and cooperative programs can be obtained through the College Financial Aid Office.

Housing. Dormitories with varying accommodations are available on campus.

Library Facilities. The McMullen Library and Learning Center contains over 125,000 volumes and offers an environment for independent study, coordinated learning, reference direction, and discussion groups.

Religious Services/Activities. St. Ambrose offers a religious environment emphasizing the values, attitudes, and goals of the Catholic heritage. The Campus Ministry Program offers religious and personal counseling. Regular Masses are offered daily during the academic year in Christ the King Chapel on campus. In addition, the College Seminary Department provides daily prayer and retreat opportunities.

Degree Programs

The major in Theology leading to the Bachelor of Arts degree requires 30 semester credits of Theology including specified courses in Philosophy-Theology, one course in moral Theology, and one course in systematic Theology. It is recommended that the major include two courses in the History of Philosophy and the course in Metaphysics. Pastoral Theology courses are also offered leading to a Ministry Concentration.

Wartburg Theological Seminary
333 Wartburg Place
Dubuque, IA 52001   (319) 589-0200

Administration. Julius Bodensieck, President; Sally Fuller, Registrar.

General Description. Wartburg Theological Seminary is one of three theological schools owned and operated by The American Lutheran Church to prepare candidates for lay and ordained ministry. The roots of the Seminary go back to the missionary efforts of Wilhelm Loehe in Neuendetteslau, Bavaria. Pastors sent out from his seminary founded an educational institution in Saginaw, Michigan in 1852. The following year the school was moved to Dubuque, and in 1854 seminary education was begun. Four years later, adverse economic conditions forced a move to St. Sebald in Clayton County, Iowa, where the name Wartburg was first chosen. In 1875 expansion necessitated a move to Mendota, Illinois where the Seminary remained until 1889 when it was returned to Dubuque.

Several seminaries have merged with Wartburg over the years. In 1930, Luther Seminary in St. Paul was moved to the Wartburg campus. In 1956, Trinity Theological Seminary (United Evangelical Lutheran Church) in Blair, Nebraska was moved to Dubuque and officially merged with Wartburg at the formation of The American Lutheran Church in 1960.

The Seminary awards the Master of Divinity, the Master of Arts, and the Master of Sacred Theology degrees. The Doctor of Ministry degree is awarded through a cooperative program of The Schools of Theology in Dubuque, a program that is ecumenical in scope while remaining faithful to the schools' individual traditions.

Community Environment. The present campus of some thirty acres is situated on the brow of a lofty ridge in southwest Dubuque, commanding a view in all directions of the rugged hill country surrounding the city. Dubuque is located on the central eastern border of Iowa at the junction of Iowa, Wisconsin, and Illinois along the Mississippi River. It is the oldest city in Iowa and has a population of 63,000.

Religious Denomination. The American Lutheran Church.

Accreditation. North Central Association of Colleges and Schools; Association of Theological Schools in the United States and Canada. Member of: Association for Clinical Pastoral Education.

Term System. Semester (4-1-4); summer term.

Enrollment in Degree Programs in Religion 1984–85. Total 222; men 159, women 63.

Degrees in Religion Awarded 1984–85. Master of Arts 12; men 5, women 7. Master of Divinity 43; men 34, women 9. Master of Sacred Theology 6; men 5, women 1. Doctor of Ministry 2; men 2.

Faculty for Degree Programs in Religion. Total 19; full-time 12, part-time 7.

Admission Requirements. The academic requirement

for admission to the Master's programs is the Bachelor of Arts degree or its equivalent. Normally this degree will be from a regionally accredited college or university. It is important that students who plan to study theology bring a broad background in liberal arts as well as knowledge of some specific areas in depth. For the Doctor of Ministry degree, the candidate must be in full-time ministry, be commissioned or ordained for the ministry, and have been in the ministry for a minimum of three years; the student must also have received the Master of Divinity degree or its equivalent.

Tuition and Fees. Tuition $1,800 per academic year; fees average around $40 per year; board and room $765 per semester, $185 for interim term.

Financial Aid. Limited financial assistance in the form of grants-in-aid and loans is available for full-time needy students at the discretion of the student-faculty Financial Aid Committee.

Housing. Dormitory rooms for single students; the Seminary has 60 houses and apartments for married students, about half of which are reserved for couples with children.

Library Facilities. The Reu Memorial Library houses 87,200 volumes. The Library has a rare book collection of Lutheran materials. The Library operates under a unified management with the Ficke-Laird Library and the Couchman Memorial Library on the University of Dubuque campus. This arrangement is under the Library of the Schools of Theology in Dubuque (Wartburg Theological Seminary and the University of Dubuque Theological Seminary). There is daily courier service between the two schools.

Religious Services/Activities. Many students are involved in service activities of various kinds in Dubuque, either in local churches and institutions or through Project Concern and United Way. Worship services are conducted at nursing homes on a voluntary basis, visitation programs are conducted in behalf of the elderly and homebound, and some students participate in a "big-brother, big-sister" program. Under the leadership of the dean of the chapel, a daily service of worship in conducted with the Eucharist celebrated each Wednesday. Well-known theologians are invited each year to Wartburg.

Degree Programs

The Master of Divinity program is divided into three divisions: Biblical Studies, History and Theology, and Ministry. The program normally requires a minimum of three full years of academic study plus one year of internship with a supervising pastor in a parish or related ministry. Normally the internship comes between the middler and senior years. Graduates of the seminary who are members of The American Lutheran Church are certified for Call by the faculty through a process of evaluation during the fall semester of the student's senior year. Evaluation for certification involves personal qualities and theological orientation that equip one for effective minis-

try in the Lutheran Church.

The Master of Arts degree is designed for those who wish to integrate the study of theology with their present discipline (e.g., education, music, counseling, administration, communications) and who have professional goals for service in church or society; those who wish to enhance their skills for ministry in a way best served by this degree program; and those who are interested in theological study at the seminary level for personal growth as they continue as laity in a variety of vocations.

The Master of Sacred Theology is a post-Master of Divinity degree intended primarily for pastors who are interested in more extensive theological study in one or more areas of the seminary curriculum. It can provide a "refresher" program for the parish pastor, as well as enhancing one's professional standing through the attainment of a graduate degree. The degree requires a total of 18 semester hours of class work (exclusive of thesis) and is a degree that persons involved in ministry will find reasonably attainable through part-time and summer course work.

The Doctor of Ministry is a joint program with the Schools of Theology in Dubuque. It offers to men and women already in the practice of ministry a program of professional and personal growth by providing a means to develop further the attitudes, skills, knowledge, and maturity essential for an advanced level of competency.

Special Programs

A limited number of students can meet part of the Seminary requirements by studying at Wartburg's House of Studies in Denver, Colorado. This program offers an opportunity for studying theology in an urban context and for integrating theological reflection with the practice of ministry.

Since 1975 Wartburg Seminary has maintained the Hispanic Ministry Program in Austin, Texas. This program provides an opportunity for Hispanic students to prepare for the ordained ministry under the Alternate Routes to Ordained Service program of The American Lutheran Church. The basic Master of Divinity program is adhered to, with flexibility exercised in regard to language requirements and the one-year internship requirement.

The Seminary participates in the National Capital Semester for Seminarians, a program sponsored each spring semester by Wesley Theological Seminary in Washington, D.C.

Wartburg Seminary participates in the archaeological dig at Tell el-Hesi in the Negev, Israel. Students receive basic training in archaeological field methods and read and hear lectures on ancient and modern Middle East history and culture. The role of archaeology is investigated as a research tool of the historian, biblical scholar, and anthropologist.

KANSAS

Central Baptist Theological Seminary

Seminary Heights
31st and Minnesota
Kansas City, KS 66102   (913) 241-0723

Administration. Dr. William F. Keucher, President.

General Description. Affiliated with the American Baptist Churches in the U.S.A., the Seminary exists as a professional school to equip the student with the knowledge and skills needed for effective ministry. It was founded in 1901 as a divinity school to train leaders for Christian service throughout the world.

Community Environment. The 24-acre campus is located in Seminary Heights. This location offers a view of the metropolitan community that is linked to the two states of Kansas and Missouri.

Religious Denomination. American Baptist Churches in the U.S.A.

Accreditation. North Central Association of Colleges and Schools; Association of Theological Schools in the United States and Canada.

Term System. Semester (4-1-4 plan).

Faculty for Degree Programs in Religion. Total 14; full-time 7, part-time 7.

Admission Requirements. Bachelor's degree or equivalent from an accredited college or university; membership with an organized church or a recognized fellowship of Christians; approval of purpose by student's local church; recommendations.

Tuition and Fees. Tuition $65 per semester hour; housing $95-$183 per month, depending on accommodations selected.

Financial Aid. The Seminary has a program of merit scholarships, work grants, grants-in-aid, and loans for students who need financial assistance.

Housing. Campus housing for both single and married students is available.

Library Facilities. The library contains over 57,000 volumes. The Seminary's location near three other theological seminaries gives students access to library resources of over 200,000 volumes.

Religious Services/Activities. Spiritual Formation is a central goal of the Seminary community. Added to the daily disciplines and devotion embraced by individuals, voluntary chapel, prayer fellowships, and service projects are built into the curriculum, into field education, and extracurricular activities.

Degree Programs

The Master of Divinity degree program includes study in the major fields of Old and New Testaments, History and Mission of the Church, Christian Theology and Philosophy of Religion, and Pastoral Theology. The program is on a three-year basis. Each student, at the completion of the junior year (30 semester hours) will choose a major for concentration in the area of interest beyond the core curriculum. The majors offered are in Biblical Interpretation, History and Mission of the Church, Religious Education, Theology, and Pastoral Theology. The major will constitute a part of the 25 semester hours of electives allowed in the 90 semester hours required for graduation.

The Master of Arts in Religious Studies curriculum is to enhance the ministry of qualified professional persons who are not seeking ordination but who want to serve in the varied ministries of the church. The fields studied include Old and New Testaments, History and Mission of the Church, World Religions, Christian Theology, Religious Education, and Pastoral Theology. The degree requires 48 semester hours to be completed, normally within two years.

Special Programs

The Diploma in Theological Studies program is designed to offer quality theological studies to a limited number of mature ministers who have not as yet been able to complete formal theological education.

Friends Bible College

607 North Kingman
Box 288
Haviland, KS 67059   (316) 862-5252

Administration. Norman V. Bridges, President; Dr. Bruce A. Hicks, Academic Dean.

General Description. The purpose of Friends Bible College is to prepare students for effective Christian life, service, and leadership. The College grants the Bachelor of Arts in Religion and the Bachelor of Science in Religion degrees.

Community Environment. Haviland, Iowa, home of Friends Bible College, is a small town in a rural area. Haviland provides a friendly, supportive atmosphere, especially welcoming to young families.

Religious Denomination. Friends.

Religious Emphasis. Evangelical.

Accreditation. American Association of Bible Colleges.

Term System. Semester; miniterm in May.

Enrollment in Degree Programs in Religion 1984–85. Total 92; men 42, women 50.

Degrees in Religion Awarded 1984–85. Bachelor of Arts in Religion 7; men 6, women 1. Bachelor of Science in Religion 4; men 2, women 2.

Faculty for Degree Programs in Religion. Total 12; full-time 8, part-time 4.

Admission Requirements. High school graduation or equivalent; references; transcripts; ACT scores.

Tuition and Fees. Tuition $2,000; room and board $1,-600; student fees $200.

Financial Aid. Scholarships, grants, loans, and employment are available.

Housing. Dormitory accommodations are available for single students; apartments and houses for rent to married students.

Library Facilities. The library contains 28,653 volumes.

Religious Services/Activities. Chapel is held for one half hour each week day. Drama, music ensembles, and Gospel Teams are offered for student participation.

Degree Programs

The Bachelor of Science in Religion and the Bachelor of Arts in Religion are offered. Each student must have a Bible major. Besides this major the following concentrations are offered: Pastoral Ministry, Christian Ministry, Christian Education, Christian Missions, Church Music, Business Administration, and Elementary Education.

Friends University
Division of Religion and Philosophy

2100 University
Wichita, KS 67213   (316) 261-5871

Administration. Dr. Richard Felix, President; Dr. Harper L. Cole, Executive Vice President and Academic Dean;

General Description. The Division of Religion and Philosophy is 1 of 7 academic divisions within the undergraduate college. Within the framework of a liberal arts education, divisional expertise and concerns provide a solid foundation of pre-professional preparation for professional and volunteer Christian service. The Religion curriculum is designed to lead students to understand and appreciate the content of the Bible as the divinely inspired source book of Christian faith and to grapple with both the Christian heritage and contemporary religious issues. The degrees Bachelor of Arts with a major in Religion and Philosophy and Bachelor of Christian Studies (a post-baccalaureate program) are offered.

Parent Institution. Friends University is a church-related, privately-supported Christian college, free and independent from control by political agencies. The school was founded in 1898 and is operated by a Board of Trustees. The school is coeducational and is thoroughly committed to the Quaker belief in the worth, dignity, and equality of each person in the sight of God. The school subscribes to the principle of equal opportunity for all students. A campus atmosphere is sought that is conducive to the development of religious aspirations and wholesome living. About 900 students and 45 faculty members comprise the institution.

Community Environment. Friends University exists on a modern campus of 54 acres, offering up-to-date facilities for all the academic, social, and spiritual needs of the students. The city of Wichita has grown from a frontier "cowtown" to a modern industrial city, now known as the "Air Capital of the World."

Religious Denomination. Society of Friends (Quaker).

Religious Emphasis. Conservative.

Accreditation. North Central Association of Colleges and Schools.

Term System. Semester; summer term.

Enrollment in Degree Programs in Religion 1984–85. Total 40; men 30, women 10.

Degrees in Religion Awarded 1984–85. Bachelor of Arts 10; men 7, women 3.

Faculty for Degree Programs in Religion. Total 5; full-time 5.

Admission Requirements. High school graduation with 2.0 grade point average or higher; ACT or SAT.

Tuition and Fees. Tuition $139 per credit hour; student fees $2.50 per credit hour; room and board $1,000 per semester. Annual costs cards are available from the Admissions Office and the Financial Aid Office.

Financial Aid. Ministerial scholarship, privately funded scholarships, plus various forms of federal assistance are available.

Housing. Dormitory accommodations are available for single students. A 12-unit apartment building and a few small houses are available for rent by married students.

Library Facilities. The Edmund Stanley Library collection totals over 89,000 volumes and more than 400 periodicals are received regularly. Special collections include the Quaker Collection, the Education Curriculum laboratory, and the Music Collection.

Religious Services/Activities. Several nearby churches are attended by students and there are numerous student-led Bible study groups. Chaplaincy services are provided by Quaker pastors in the area. There is an active organization of Religion students.

Degree Programs

The Bachelor of Arts degree is offered with a major in Religion and Philosophy. The major requires at least 49 semester hours within the Division of Religion and Philosophy and may emphasize Christian Ministry, Biblical Studies, Philosophy and Theology, or a Diversified Track (general preparation). Each emphasis has additional requirements in Christian Heritage, Philosophy, Bible, and Divisional electives.

The Bachelor of Christian Studies is designed principally to serve those who desire to augment their previous college education with serious study of religion. It may appeal particulary to those who wish to prepare for more effective Christian service as lay workers. The degree offers an opportunity both for serious training and for recognition of work accomplished in order to give greater competency and acceptance.

Special Programs

The Associate of Arts degree may also be earned in the Division of Religion and Philosophy.

The University also sponsors Annual Seminars for Ministers for which continuing education credit is awarded. FRONTIERS is an annual 6-week lay institute for religious growth. Free tuition for persons 65 years or older is offered in regular college classes.

Kansas Wesleyan College
Religion Department
100 East Claflin
Salina, KS 67401   (913) 827-5541

Administration. Dr. Marshall Stanton, Interim President; John Khanjian, Associate Professor, Religious Studies.

General Description. The Religion Department has a dual role in the life of the school: it assists in the Liberal Studies program by providing courses in Biblical Heritage and Philosophy and by offering three degree programs in Christian Education, Religion, and Pre-Ministry. The strength of the programs lies in the Biblical emphasis which is seen as the foundation for work in the church, seminary, or graduate school. The Department is oriented toward exploring and understanding the Christian Faith and its relevance to people, culture, and the world.

Parent Institution. Kansas Wesleyan is a liberal arts college affiliated with the Kansas West Conference of the United Methodist Church. The institution was founded in 1886.

Community Environment. The campus is situated on a 30-acre campus in the city of Salina which is located in the central part of the state.

Religious Denomination. United Methodist Church.

Religious Emphasis. Reformed.

Accreditation. North Central Association of Colleges and Schools.

Term System. Semester; two 4-week summer sessions.

Enrollment in Degree Programs in Religion 1984–85. Total 15; men 11, women 4.

Degrees in Religion Awarded 1984–85. Bachelor of Arts in Religion 2; men 1, women 1. Bachelor of Arts in Christian Education 1; men 1.

Faculty for Degree Programs in Religion. Total 3; full-time 1, part-time 2.

Admission Requirements. Graduation from an accredited high school or equivalent; grade point average of 2.0 (normally); ACT scores.

Tuition and Fees. Per semester: tuition $2,038.50 for 15 semester hours; fees $250; room $505; board $744.50.

Financial Aid. Kansas Wesleyan has an innovative financial aid program which makes it possible for nearly everyone to attend the school; students must file appropriate forms.

Housing. Dormitories and apartments are available on campus for all students.

Library Facilities. The library houses 70,000 volumes.

Religious Services/Activities. There are weekly chapel services and attendance is optional; weekly fellowship and study for religious majors; Annual Retreat for the Religion Department.

Degree Programs

The Bachelor of Arts program of the Religion Department is designed to explore the Christian Faith and its relevance to contemporary persons and culture. The Department offers courses which study the Bible in its historical and theological context, which investigate the traditions of Christian thought in the light of contemporary culture, and which introduce philosophy in order to aid the student to reflect critically upon his/her value priorities and attempt to develop a consistent personal theology. The degree programs can be designed to prepare students for career programs in a local church such as the Ordained ministry, the Diaconate ministry, Christian Education, Youth work, Mission work, and counseling. The study done in this department can also prepare students for graduate study in religion or related fields such as theological school education.

Marymount College of Kansas
Department of Religious Studies
P.O. Box 5050

Salina, KS 67401 (913) 825-2101

Administration. Dr. Dan C. Johnson, President; Dr. William J. Medland, Academic Dean and Dean of the Faculty; Dr. Robert Schimoler, Chairperson, Division of Humanities; Sr. Catherine Michaud, C.S.J., M.A., Chairperson, Department of Religious Studies.

General Description. The Department of Religious Studies, through a series of basic educational courses and electives provides opportunities for students (1) to develop an appreciation for the spiritual and historical riches of religious traditions with particular emphasis on Christianity; (2) to develop a greater sensitivity and responsiveness to the religious dimensions of every genuinely human experience; (3) to develop meaningful methods and concepts for coming to terms with their own religious roots and possibilities; (4) to develop a social consciousness and concern for justice; (5) to study the Roman Catholic tradition; (6) to graduate with a major in religious studies which prepares one for leadership in parish and pastoral work. The Bachelor of Arts degree with a major in Religious Studies is pastoral and theological in nature, designed to prepare individuals for full-time parish and pastoral work.

Parent Institution. Marymount College is a Catholic, undergraduate college for men and women, located in Salina, Kansas; it is owned and sponsored by the Diocese of Salina, Kansas. It is a community of learners which seeks as its primary aim the quest for knowledge in a faith context and the development of the critical intellect to its highest potential. Marymount was the first 4-year liberal arts college for women in Kansas. It became coeducational in 1968.

Community Environment. The Marymount Campus consist of 28 acres situated at the northwest corner of East Iron and Marymount Road in Salina, Kansas. At the intersection of Interstates 70, 135W, and US 81, Marymount is easily accessible by air and bus. Salina, situated in the central part of the state, is the fifth largest city in Kansas. The wheat that supplies Salina's large flour mill and grain storage tanks comes from one of the greatest hard wheat belts in the world.

Religious Denomination. Roman Catholic.

Accreditation. North Central Association of Colleges and Schools.

Term System. Semester; summer term.

Enrollment in Degree Programs in Religion 1984–85. Total 9; men 4, women 5.

Degrees in Religion Awarded 1984–85. Bachelor of Arts 4; men 3, women 1.

Faculty for Degree Programs in Religion. Total 2; full-time 2.

Admission Requirements. Official high school transcript or GED; ACT or SAT.

Tuition and Fees. Tuition $4,200 per year; room and board $2,400; board only $1,150.

Financial Aid. Marymount College participates in the College Scholarship Service of the College Entrance Examination Board and the Financial Aid Services of the American College Testing Program. Loans, grants, scholarships, and college work-study are available.

Housing. All students are expected to reside on campus.

Library Facilities. The Marymount College Library houses a collection of approximately 70,000 volumes.

Religious Services/Activities. The College provides numerous opportunities for each student to deepen his/her life experience. It offers the availability and counseling of a Chaplain in the Office of Campus Ministry, a wide choice of books for spiritual reading, encounter-retreats and workshops for Christian living, and the availability of the daily Eucharistic Celebration of the Mass on campus.

Degree Programs

The Bachelor of Arts degree with a major in Religious Studies is pastoral and theological in nature and is designed to prepare individuals for full-time parish and pastoral work. The College also offers the degree with a major in Music with an emphasis in Religious Studies. This degree provides the student an understanding of the theological and cultural principles of Catholic worship and the ability to plan and facilitate quality liturgical celebrations.

Mid-America Nazarene College
Division of Religion and Philosophy
2030 College Way

P.O. Box 1776

Olathe, KS 66061 (913) 782-3750

Administration. Dr. R. Curtis Smith, President; Dr. Richard L. Spindle, Chairman, Division of Religion and Philosophy.

General Description. The Division of Religion and Philosophy offers courses in Biblical Language, Biblical Literature, Christian Education, Church History, Missions, Philosophy, Practical Theology, Theology, and Urban Ministries. The majors in Religion and Christian Education lead to the Bachelor's degree.

Parent Institution. Mid-America Nazarene College, founded in 1966 by the General Assembly of the Church of the Nazarene, is a private, holiness college in the Wesleyan tradition. It is a coeducational, career-oriented undergraduate college of liberal arts sponsored and supported by the North Central Region of the International Church of the Nazarene.

Community Environment. The 103-acre campus is located in Olathe, a city 19 miles southwest of downtown Kansas City.

Religious Denomination. Church of the Nazarene.

Accreditation. North Central Association of Colleges and Schools.

Term System. Semester (4-1-4 plan).

Faculty for Degree Programs in Religion. Total 7.

Admission Requirements. Graduation from high school or equivalent; 15 academic units; SAT or ACT.

Tuition and Fees. Tuition $105 per semester hour; room $1,208 per year; board $1,218 per year; general fee $220 per year.

Financial Aid. The majority of financial aid is awarded based on a student's financial need.

Housing. Dormitory accommodations are available on campus for 420 men and 428 women.

Library Facilities. The Mabee Library contains over 80,000 volumes, 19,000 in microfilm and the balance in bound volumes. It subscribes to 350 periodicals.

Religious Services/Activities. Chapel services are held two days a week. Students are urged to attend Sunday and mid-week services.

Degree Programs

The majors in Religion and Christian Education require a total of 126 credits overall, including 36 credit hours of Religion core courses and 27 hours of Religion or Education specialization. A comprehensive examination is also a requirement. The object of the comprehensive is (1) to serve as an integrating examination in helping the student pull together the various aspects of the curriculum, (2) to evaluate the student's expertise in the major area of concentration, and (3) to give an indication of the effectiveness of classroom instruction.

Students in the Pre-Seminary program pursue a major in any academic area, following their interests and sense of calling. Students desiring to meet ordination requirements in the Church of the Nazarene are urged to select a major in Religion as well as to fulfill provisions as stated by the denomination. Graduates from Nazarene Bible Colleges throughout the world with an Associate in Biblical Studies may graduate with a minimum of 30 hours and receive the Bachelor of Arts degree in Religion, provided all requirements are met.

Tabor College
Department of Biblical and Religious Studies
400 South Jefferson

Hillsboro, KS 67063   (316) 947-3121

Administration. Vernon Janzen, President.

General Description. The Department of Biblical and Religious Studies is one of seven in the Humanities Division of Tabor College. The Department offers a pre-seminary curriculum, a co-major in biblical and religious studies, a contemporary church ministries major, and an Associate of Arts degree program in Christian studies.

Parent Institution. Tabor College was founded in 1908 by the Mennonite Brethren and Krimmer Mennonite Churches of North America. Tabor is owned and operated by the Tabor Senate whose members are selected from Mennonite Brethren Churches, and its doctrinal foundation is derived from the Mennonite Brethren Confession of Faith. The College offers liberal arts and professional/career education in a Christian context, consistent with what Mennonite Brethren understand to be biblical, to help persons achieve their highest potential as servants of Christ and His Church, ministering to the needs of all people.

Community Environment. The campus consists of eighteen buildings located on a twenty-six acre tract in the southeast part of Hillsboro. The town has a population of 3,000 and sits in a prosperous wheat and dairy area approximately fifty miles north of Wichita. Besides Tabor College, the town has a hospital, homes for the aged, a municipal park with a public swimming pool and golf course. Numerous educational and cultural opportunities are available in communities within a one-hour drive of Hillsboro.

Religious Denomination. Mennonite Brethren Church.

Religious Emphasis. Evangelical and Anabaptist.

Accreditation. North Central Association of Colleges and Schools. Member of: Council of Mennonite Colleges; Christian College Coalition.

Term System. Semester; January interterm; summer term.

Enrollment in Degree Programs in Religion 1984–85. Total 11; men 9, women 2.

Degrees in Religion Awarded 1984–85. Bachelor of Arts in Biblical/Religious Studies 3; men 3. Bachelor of Arts in Contemporary Church Ministries 1; men 1.

Faculty for Degree Programs in Religion. Total 2; part-time 2.

Admission Requirements. Open door policy. Each student is asked to respond to questions about his/her lifestyle and faith on the application for admission; references; school transcripts.

Tuition and Fees. Tuition $3,990 per year; room and board $2,190 per year; other fees $120.

Financial Aid. Tabor College is committed to the ideal of providing education to qualified students, regardless of their financial means. Financial aid is offered to students with need through scholarships, grants, loans, and employment. Students are encouraged to seek financial assistance from their church congregations. Churches may provide a grant in the name of students to be applied on account. The College will match that grant up to $250 per semester as financial aid.

Housing. The College provides convenient and comfortable housing on campus for residential students. There are five dormitories for men and three for women.

Library Facilities. The Tabor College Library, built in 1957, houses a collection of 64,000 books, 450 current journal subscriptions, and more than 5,600 bound volumes of periodicals, and the Mennonite Brethren Heritage Collection. Additional library materials are available through the Associated Colleges of Central Kansas, providing access to more than 350,000 volumes from their combined book collections. Materials are also available through the statewide Kansas Library System.

Religious Services/Activities. Convocations are planned by the Student Development Office and include liberal arts and community building activities of various kinds. Speakers, concerts, Bible conference lectures, mission lectures, touring groups, and films are all a part of the total convocations program. Convocations are scheduled each semester during the day and occasionally at night. Fifteen convocations per semester are required of all students.

Worship services are held weekly, usually on Thursday. While worship is voluntary and no records of attendance are kept, worship is an important part of life at Tabor College.

The Campus Ministries Council directs and coordinates the efforts of student ministries. The council consists of an elected executive and one member of each of the following outreach ministries: Logopedics, Intercollegiate Peace Fellowship, Youth Conference, Jail Ministries, Prayer Breakfast, Women's Prayer and Share, Bible Study/Core Groups, Tabor Fellowship, and the Scroll. The Fellowship of Christian Athletes is open to all students interested in athletics.

Degree Programs

The Bachelor of Arts with a concentration in Biblical and Religious Studies requires 24 hours beyond the basic requirements for Humanities division majors.

The Bachelor of Arts degree program with a co-major in Biblical and Religious studies is offered for students who wish to major in Biblical and Religious Studies in addition to completing another major, e.g., Social Science, Natural Science, Social Work, etc. This program consists of 24 hours of Biblical and Religious Studies above the general education requirements on the model of the Humanities/Biblical and Religious Studies concentration.

The Bachelor of Arts with a major in Contemporary Church Ministries requires 38 hours of studies in Biblical and Religious Studies courses and Church Ministries courses. In addition, each student selects a concentration as a support program (Human Services, Music, Recreation, Education, or Cross-Cultural Services).

Special Programs

The Associate of Arts in Christian Studies requires a total of 66 hours including basic courses, electives in Biblical exposition, general electives, and general education requirements.

Students anticipating further studies in a seminary are usually advised to choose a broad base of liberal arts subjects rather than to concentrate on Bible studies in the undergraduate program. Also, in addition to a full year of elementary Greek language studies, seminaries generally advise students to include important supportive courses for ministering: Philosophy, History, Counseling, Mar-

riage and the Family, World Religions, and courses that deal with people-helping skills.

Tabor College is one of approximately 70 members of the Christian College Coalition (CCC). By virtue of this membership, Tabor students are eligible to participate in the CCC sponsored American Studies Program in Washington, D.C. This semester-long program combines intensive study of public policy issues with internship experiences in the offices of government officials or various national organizations. Students live in community with Christians from varied backgrounds and regions, with an emphasis on integrating faith, learning, and living into all aspects of life.

KENTUCKY

Asbury Theological Seminary

204 North Lexington Avenue
Wilmore, KY 40390   (606) 858-3581

Administration. Dr. Melvin E. Dieter, Vice President and Provost.

General Description. Asbury Theological Seminary exists to prepare men and women who are called by God for effective Christian ministries. This preparation takes place in a multi-denominational community whose faculty and students embrace Christian, biblical, Wesleyan-Arminian, and evangelical beliefs. The Seminary community is committed to the experience, nurture, and practice of personal and social holiness as defined by Scripture and Wesleyan theology.

The Seminary was officially opened in the fall of 1923. From 1923 to 1931, the Seminary was an integral part of Asbury College but became a separate educational unit in 1931. In 1939, the Seminary moved to its present campus and since 1931 has been an independent administrative unit.

The Seminary is an interdenominational graduate school of theology. Members of 10 Protestant denominations serve on the faculty and the student body represents 40 denominations. The Seminary is approved by the University Senate of the United Methodist Church for the preparation of ministers for that denomination.

Community Environment. The Seminary is situated on 30 acres in Wilmore, a small rural residential town about 16 miles south of Lexington, one mile from U.S. Route 68, and four miles west of Route 27. Lexington is served by USAir, Air Kentucky, Tennessee Air, Delta Airlines, and by the Greyhound Bus Company.

Religious Denomination. Interdenominational.

Religious Emphasis. Wesleyan-Evangelical.

Accreditation. Southern Association of Colleges and Schools; Association of Theological Schools in the United States and Canada.

Term System. Semester (4-1-4); January interterm; 3 summer sessions.

Enrollment in Degree Programs in Religion 1984–85. Total 751; men 648, women 103.

Degrees in Religion Awarded 1984–85. Doctor of Ministry 4; men 4. Master of Arts in Religion 34; men 17, women 17. Master of Divinity 171; men 158, women 13. Master of Theology 9; men 9.

Faculty for Degree Programs in Religion. Total 57; full-time 44; part-time 13.

Admission Requirements. Official transcripts of all undergraduate and graduate credits; recent photograph; GRE score on the general aptitude section.

Tuition and Fees. Tuition $130 per credit hour; various fees where applicable; approximate total cost for an average single boarding student enrolled for 14 hours per semester (excluding health insurance) is $2,931 per semester and $695 for the January interterm.

Financial Aid. The Seminary provides a variety of financial aid to assist students with limited resources in meeting their educational expenses. The Office of Student Financial Aid administers the scholarship-grant, student loan, and other student employment programs under the policies set by the Committee on Financial Aid.

Housing. The Seminary presently maintains dormitory accommodations for approximately 190 single students. Housing for married students includes both furnished and unfurnished duplexes/apartments.

Library Facilities. The B.L.Fisher Library contains a collection of over 135,000 volumes and receives 600 periodical titles regularly. Specific emphasis has been placed on securing an extensive research collection in the area of Biblical Studies. In harmony with the Wesleyan emphasis in the Seminary's program, a constant effort is also made to strengthen holdings in the areas of Wesleyana, Methodistica, and holiness movements.

Religious Services/Activities. Chapel services are held three times weekly. The Seminary Wednesday Evening Vespers is sponsored by the student body. The Days of Holiness Emphasis and Dedication is an annual event for the entire Seminary.

The Christian Service Brotherhood is designed to encourage, coordinate, and give direction to the efforts of students who desire to participate in a form of Christian service while in seminary. World Outreach maintains a missionary emphasis with regular meetings.

Lectures are given throughout the academic year by outstanding leaders in theology. An annual ministers' conference is held at the Seminary with the objective "to emphasize the content of the Christian message and the deepening of the spiritual life, and to face fearlessly the contemporary religious and theological issues."

Degree Programs

The Master of Divinity program consists of a 90-semester-hour program of study designed primarily as preparation for the parish ministry. Flexibility has been built into the program for a wide variety of areas of concentration.

The Master of Arts in Religion is offered in the following areas: Christian Education, Christian Education major and Church Music minor; Church Music major and Christian Education minor; Christian Education major and Evangelism minor; Christian Education major and Missions minor; Biblical Literature; Theology; World Mission and Evangelism; Philosophy of Religion.

The Doctor of Ministry program is designed to provide pastors with the opportunity for specialized advanced degree work which will equip them with a significantly high level of competence in certain aspects of any of the three basic forms of ministry: prophetic, priestly, and "kingly" (leadership, stewardship, or management). There are three tracks of possible concentration: Evangelism/World Mission, Spiritual Formation, Leadership and Care.

Special Programs

The E. Stanley Jones School of World Mission and Evangelism functions both as the Division of Mission and Evangelism for the Seminary's Master of Divinity and Master of Arts programs and as a post-Master of Divinity graduate school in world mission and evangelism, offering programs leading to the Doctor of Ministry and Master of Theology.

Cumberland College
Department of Religion and Biblical
Languages
Williamsburg, KY 40769   (606) 549-2200

Administration. Dr. James H. Taylor, President; Dr. Joseph E. Early, Academic Dean; Dr. G. Willard Reeves, Chairman, Department of Religion and Biblical Languages.

General Description. The Department of Religion and Biblical Languages of Cumberland College places emphasis upon Greek and Hebrew as preparation for further theological study. There is a two-fold approach to Christian ministry: church ministry and missions ministry; and a two-emphasis approach to religious studies: Biblical studies and religious education. The Department makes available to students preparing to serve in church-related vocations the foundation courses needed for effective work. The degrees Bachelor of Arts and Bachelor of

Science are awarded. The College also awards the Bachelor of Music in Church Music.

Parent Institution. Cumberland College is a 4-year, liberal arts, coeducational college of the Kentucky mountains, serving a geographical area of southeastern Kentucky, northeastern Tennessee, Ohio (especially southern), and contiguous states. The College is affiliated with the Kentucky Baptist Convention, and has an enrollment of more than 2,000 students. Sports programs include basketball, football, baseball, tennis, golf. The largest department is Business.

Community Environment. Williamsburg, Kentucky, the location of Cumberland College, is in the southern part of the mountains of eastern Kentucky. It is on the Louisville and Nashville Railroad, about 200 miles south of Cincinnati, an equal distance from Louisville, and about 80 miles north of Knoxville. The business section of the city lies in a small valley of the Cumberland River; the College and main residence section are situated in the surrounding hills. Cumberland's main campus is on 3 hills which divide it into 3 distinct parts and afford a magnificent view of the surrounding area.

Religious Denomination. Southern Baptist.

Religious Emphasis. Moderate, conservative.

Accreditation. Southern Association of Colleges and Schools.

Term System. Semester; 2 summer terms.

Faculty for Degree Programs in Religion. Total 7; full-time 4, part-time 3 adjunct.

Admission Requirements. The College will seriously consider the application of any student without regard to race, creed, color, age, or sex. Preliminary acceptance is based upon evidence that the applicant possesses the qualities needed for satisfactory achievement in terms of character, academic preparation, purpose, personality, and health. This evidence is obtained from the Application for Admission, ACT student profile, and high school transcript.

Tuition and Fees. Tuition $2,780; room and board $1,776.

Financial Aid. Assistance is available through the Financial Aid Office.

Housing. Dormitories are available for men and women; no married student housing.

Library Facilities. The Norma Jeanne Perkins Hagan Library houses a collection of over 155,000 volumes.

Religious Services/Activities. The College has an active Baptist Student Union. Its unit organizations of the Baptist Young Women, the Ministerial Association, and the Missions Fellowship, function cooperatively. The organization of other Christian denominational groups is encouraged.

Degree Programs

The Bachelor of Arts degree is offered with either a Biblical Studies or Religious Education emphasis. The major requires completion of 30 semester hours in the

Department of Religion plus 4 courses in foreign language (same language). The Bachelor of Science degree can also be obtained in either emphasis. This major requires 21 semester hours in sociology, psychology, and philosophy plus the 30 semester hours in religion. Both degrees require a total of 128 semester hours. A Bachelor of Music in Church Music may also be pursued.

Special Programs

The Ministerial Training Program provides instruction and practical experiences in church-related activities. The program is open to ministerial students, regardless of college major, and is required of a student who applies for the ministerial scholarship.

An Associate degree in Church Secretarial Administration is offered by the College.

Georgetown College
Department of Religion
College Street
Georgetown, KY 40324   (502) 863-8124

Administration. Dr. W. Morgan Patterson, President; Dr. Joe O. Lewis, Vice President for Academic Affairs; Dr. Alan W. Gragg, Chairman, Department of Religion.

General Description. The Department of Religion offers a strong major in Religion with emphasis on the centrality of the Bible and the Christian faith. The courses give the student a thorough introduction to both Old and New Testaments as well as Biblical interpretation. Ministerial preparation for further seminary study correlates classroom instruction with "on-site" training. Instruction from committed Christian professors provides a strong basis for student involvement in on-campus religious organizations as well as service in the local churches. An emphasis on individual instruction and class scheduling helps ministerial preparation become a "learning contract" between the student and an assigned person, church, or organization. The Bachelor of Arts in Religion is awarded.

Parent Institution. Georgetown College is a coeducational liberal arts college providing students with a climate for achievement within a Christian context. Now approaching its 155th year, the College has been known as a community of rich tradition, high ideals, and academic excellence. The relationships between students, faculty, and administration are personal, and the community is dedicated to discovering ways in which Christian men and women may serve most effectively in contemporary society. Georgetown College, historically related to the Kentucky Baptist Convention, exists for the purpose of maintaining an institution of higher learning under Christian influences.

Community Environment. Georgetown College is located in the heart of the Bluegrass at Georgetown, Kentucky. It is 12 miles from Lexington, 70 miles from Louisville, and 68 miles from Cincinnati. The campus is situated on

52 gently rolling acres, blending colonial red brick buildings with the beauty of the Kentucky Bluegrass. There are 3 antebellum buildings as well as 8 other more modern structures.

Religious Denomination. Southern Baptist.

Religious Emphasis. Evangelical.

Accreditation. Southern Association of Colleges and Schools.

Term System. Semester; 2 summer terms.

Enrollment in Degree Programs in Religion 1984–85. Total 18; men 14, women 4.

Degrees in Religion Awarded 1984–85. Bachelor of Arts in Religion 2; men 1, women 1.

Faculty for Degree Programs in Religion. Total 5; full-time 3, part-time 2.

Admission Requirements. High school graduation with "C" or better in academic subjects.

Tuition and Fees. Tuition in-state $3,978; out-of-state $4,078; student articulation fee $25; other fees may apply for individual courses.

Financial Aid. Awarded on basis of need.

Housing. All full-time single students are required to live in campus housing. Some married housing is available on campus.

Library Facilities. The Cooke Memorial Library contains over 105,000 volumes of which 25,000 are bound periodicals. Special collections include the Thompson Collection of Biblical Literature, the Spears Collection of American Literature, and the Smith Law Library.

Religious Services/Activities. Six religious cocurricular services are held per semester plus special services and retreats. The Campus Ministry Council is an interdenominational group whose student representatives are chosen by the Campus Minister. This council helps in the planning and presentation of campus-wide worship convocations and Christian programs at special seasons of the church year. The Baptist Student Union and the Fellowship of Christian Athletes also provide for various student activities.

Degree Programs

The major in Religion leading to the Bachelor of Arts degree requires 33 semester hours of including courses in New Testament, Old Testament, Indian Religious Philosophies or Eastern Religious Philosophies, Advanced Topics in New Testament Interpretation or Old Testament Interpretation, Seminar, and 12 additional hours in the Religion Department.

Kentucky Christian College
College and Landsdowne
Grayson, KY 41143   (606) 474-6613

Administration. L. Palmer Young, President.

General Description. Kentucky Christian College is a privately supported college offering programs for the preparation of young men and women who plan to enter Christian vocations. Included are those who will serve as ministers, missionaries, evangelists, Christian teachers, church secretaries, church musicians, and religious education directors. The college awards the Bachelor's degree.

Parent Institution. The College was founded in in 1919 by members of the Christian Churches and Churches of Christ.

Community Environment. The campus is located in Grayson, in the Appalachian foothills of eastern Kentucky. Ashland, Kentucky and Huntington, West Virginia, both industrial and business centers, are approximately a half-hour's drive from the Grayson campus.

Religious Denomination. Christian Churches and Churches of Christ.

Accreditation. American Association of Bible Colleges.

Term System. Semester.

Admission Requirements. High school graduation; limited number of non-high school graduates over the age of 21 may be admitted; ACT required.

Tuition and Fees. Tuition $49 per semester hour; library fee $60; student programs and health fee $65; room $410 per semester; board $570; married student housing $775-$870 per semester.

Financial Aid. The College has a substantial program of financial aid for students on a need basis. Scholarships are available.

Housing. Dormitories and married student housing are available.

Library Facilities. The Library-Media Center houses more than 83,000 volumes, curriculum and mission labs, and an audiovisual lab. The Archives Center for Literature of the Restoration Movement is located in the Center.

Religious Services/Activities. Prayer Circles for men and women in the dormitories, a weekly Prayer Meeting on Wednesday, daily devotional periods, and Chapel Services two days each week are offered. Chapel attendance is required.

Degree Programs

The Bachelor of Arts programs are designed to prepare the student for a career in some specialized area of Christian service and as a preparatory program for graduate study, especially in the areas of Bible and Theology. Two years of language are required for this degree. The Bachelor of Science degree is designed to prepare the student for a career of specialized services such as Christian Education, Evangelism, Missions, Psychology, and Church Music. There is no language requirement.

The Bachelor of Theology curriculum is designed to provide the prospective Christian worker with additional undergraduate preparation. Its purpose is to provide a degree for the student who intends a specialized ministry upon graduation and to prepare more thoroughly those students who do not plan to enter graduate studies in religion and theology. This program requires at least 28

semester hours beyond the completion of the Bachelor of Arts requirement of 132 semester hours.

Kentucky Wesleyan College
Department of Religion and Philosophy
3000 Frederica Street
Owensboro, KY 42301   (502) 926-3111

Administration. Luther W. White, III, President; Dr. Edward Beavin, Chairperson, Department of Religion and Philosophy.

General Description. The Department of Religion and Philosophy offers both a major and a minor in Christian Religion and Philosophy. The major leads to the Bachelor of Arts degree.

Parent Institution. Kentucky Wesleyan College is a liberal arts learning community with a Christian perspective. It is affiliated with The United Methodist Church and was founded in 1860. The Civil War delayed the opening of the institution until 1866. The College offers liberal arts programs and grants the Bachelor's degree. Over 900 students are enrolled annually.

Community Environment. The 70-acre campus is located in the southern part of Owensboro, the largest city in western Kentucky. The city is 110 miles west of Louisville and 48 miles east of Evansville, Indiana.

Religious Denomination. The United Methodist Church.

Accreditation. Southern Association of Colleges and Schools.

Term System. Semester.

Admission Requirements. Graduation from an accredited high school or equivalent; rank in upper three quarters of graduating class; SAT or ACT.

Tuition and Fees. Tuition $1,840 per semester; room $445-$570; board $530-$620; activity fee $50.

Financial Aid. The College offers an extensive program of financial assistance to those students who qualify for one or more of the various programs. Students with demonstrated financial need may qualify for grants, low-interest loans, and on-campus work-study. The College also has other scholarships, grants, and tuition remissions available without regard to need.

Housing. Students live in four residence halls. All students dine together in the Presidents' Hall.

Library Facilities. The Library Learning Center houses more than 170,000 books, periodicals, government documents, and audiovisual materials. The Heritage Room houses materials for the Kentucky United Methodist Heritage Center as well as a Kentuckiana Collection.

Religious Services/Activities. Chapel is held each Thursday morning. Holy Communion is usually celebrated on the fourth Tuesday of each month. The services include both traditional and modern forms of worship, reflecting the variety of backgrounds within the Wesleyan community. The College Chaplain who leads the worship also serves as a full-time pastor to the faculty, students, and staff.

Degree Programs

The major in Christian Religion and Philosophy leading to the Bachelor of Arts degree requires a minimum of 42 semester hours, including 18 semester hours of Bible, 12 semester hours of philosophy, and 12 semester hours of departmentally approved related subjects; or 18 semester hours of philosophy, 12 semesters of Bible, and 12 semester hours of departmentally approved subjects.

Lexington Baptist College
147-151 Walton Avenue
Lexington, KY 40508   (606) 252-1130

Administration. Ross L. Range, D.D., President.

General Description. Lexington Baptist College is a Bible college and thus holds a distinctive educational philosophy which maintains that a thorough knowledge of the Bible as the Word of God must be the first step in the educational process. The disciplines of the liberal arts and sciences are then studied and understood in their proper perspective with the truth of God's Word as the integrating core of all human knowledge. The College also believes that a balanced knowledge of the Bible is necessary and fundamental to all Christian work as well as for personal spiritual growth and development. A Bible core of 30 hours is required of all Bachelor's graduates, as well as a strong general education requirement.

Parent Institution. The College was officially organized in 1950 under the name of Ashland Avenue Baptist Bible Training School - the name indicating its connection to the Ashland Avenue Baptist Church. The Pastor of the Ashland Avenue Baptist Church is designated as the president of the College and chairman of the Board of Trustees to the College. The Board of Trustees are chosen from members of the Ashland Avenue Baptist Church and others of like faith and order.

Community Environment. Lexington Baptist College is located in Lexington, Kentucky, a thriving city and Kentucky's eastern metropolis. Besides the many cultural opportunities, Lexington is also an educational center serving as home to several colleges. Nearby are many scenic and historical points of interest: Shakertown at Pleasant Hill, Fort Harrod in Harrodsburg, Constitutional Square in Danville, the homes of Henry Clay and John Hunt Morgan in Lexington, My Old Kentucky Home at Bardstown, Abraham Lincoln's birthplace near Hodgenville, Cumberland Falls, Mammoth Cave, Natural Bridge, and the Red River Gorge.

Religious Denomination. Baptist.

Religious Emphasis. Conservative.

Accreditation. Licensed by the Kentucky Council on Higher Education. Member of: Association of Christian Schools International; Association of Christian Service Personnel.

Term System. Semester; summer session.

Enrollment in Degree Programs in Religion 1984–85. Total 55; men 40, women 15.

Degrees in Religion Awarded 1984–85. Bachelor of Arts 6; men 5, women 1. Associate of Arts 2; men 1, women 1.

Faculty for Degree Programs in Religion. Total 16; full-time 5, part-time 11.

Admission Requirements. High school graduation; ACT (entering Freshmen only); four recommendations, one of which must be from the applicant's pastor, and three general recommendations.

Tuition and Fees. Tuition $25 per semester hour ($300 for 12-16 hours); application fee $15; registration/library fees $25.

Financial Aid. Most of the students of the school find it necessary to seek employment to supplement other sources of income. The College assists students in finding employment.

Housing. The College does not maintain a dormitory but will provide information to help students find off-campus housing.

Library Facilities. The College library contains over 15,000 volumes. The library is constantly growing as friends contribute both books and funds for the purchase of new works and audiovisual equipment. Other libraries available for research in the immediate area are the M.I. King Library at the University of Kentucky, the library at the Lexington Theological Seminary, and the Lexington Public Library.

Religious Services/Activities. A chapel service for all students is a part of the program. At these services students have the opportunity of hearing outstanding speakers, faculty members, and fellow students. All students are expected to attend every chapel service when on campus.

Because the purpose of Lexington Baptist College is to train students for local church-related service, it is imperative that a program of practical work experience be an integral part of all programs. A bridge between the academic and the practical is established through a comprehensive program of Christian Service which emphasizes service for God's glory. Students fulfill their Christian Service assignments in local churches on a regular basis and in behalf of the College in its outreach ministries. This practical training prepares students for full-time, vocational ministries after graduation.

Degree Programs

The Baccalaureate program consists of 128 credit hours at the Bachelor level with a required general education core of courses and a declared area of concentration. The College has four major areas of professional studies emphasis: Ministerial program (Bachelor of Arts in Bible), Missions program (Bachelor of Arts in Missions), Christian Education program (Bachelor of Arts in Christian Education), and Church Music program (Bachelor of

Arts in Sacred Music).

The Advanced Study programs provide the student an opportunity to do more in-depth, intensive study through a fifth year. There are two major areas of concentration: the Bachelor of Theology program and the Bachelor of Religious Education program.

Special Programs

The Associate of Arts in Bible degree provides a two-year program of study for those who desire to obtain a basic understanding of the Bible and related subjects. It has a basic Bible/Theology core curriculum.

Lexington Theological Seminary
631 South Limestone
Lexington, KY 40508   (606) 252-0361

Administration. Wayne H. Bell, President; William O. Paulsell, Dean.

General Description. Lexington Theological Seminary offers an environment in which students may pursue the personal growth, academic development, and professional training essential to preparation for Christian ministry. It provides individual attention in small classes, extensive library holdings, a sensitive faculty, a warm community spirit, and employment opportunities in churches. The Seminary is ecumenical in its approach. The denomination variety of faculty and students encourages an exchange of viewpoints derived from the different traditions. This convergence of ideas is stimulating and helps students clarify and develop their own faith. The faculty are committed to teaching, scholarship, and ministry. A number of them are authorities in their fields. All of them are counselors to students and seek to be role models for ministry.

The Seminary is the pioneer institution of the Christian Church (Disciples of Christ) located within the Bluegrass region of Kentucky where much of the Disciples' early history occurred. The Seminary dates its founding from 1865 when it was The College of the Bible, one of several colleges in Kentucky University. Another of these colleges was the College of Agriculture and Mechanical Arts, which separated from the mother institution in 1878 and through a series of name changes emerged as the present University of Kentucky. The College of the Bible occupied buildings on the campus of Transylvania University until 1950, when it moved to its present location. The Seminary acquired its own charter in 1878. At its centennial in 1965, The College of the Bible took the name of Lexington Theological Seminary. Thus three institutions of higher education in Lexington are of the same background: Transylvania University, the University of Kentucky, and Lexington Theological Seminary. Transylvania and Lexington Seminary are members of the Division of Higher Education of the Christian Church (Disciples of Christ).

Community Environment. The campus of the Seminary is situated on five and one-half acres. The city of Lexington has a population of approximately 210,000 and offers a pleasant combination of historically important architecture and progressive business development. The city is set within a countryside that is world famous for the beauty of the rolling green pastures of its horse farms accented by white plank fences. Among the leading area locations are the Kentucky Horse Park, several historic state parks, Statesmen Henry Clay's home Ashland, Mary Todd Lincoln's home, the Red River Gorge, the restored Shaker Village at Pleasant Hill, student industries and crafts at Berea College, and historic Cane Ridge Meeting House near Paris.

Religious Denomination. Christian Church (Disciples of Christ).

Religious Emphasis. Open.

Accreditation. Southern Association of Colleges and Schools; Association of Theological Schools.

Term System. Semester; interterm; summer session.

Enrollment in Degree Programs in Religion 1984–85. Total 207; men 150, women 57.

Degrees in Religion Awarded 1984–85. Master of Arts 4; men 1, women 3. Master of Divinity 15; men 10, women 5. Doctor of Ministry 10; men 10.

Faculty for Degree Programs in Religion. Total 13; full-time 9, part-time 4.

Admission Requirements. Applicants must have a B.A. degree or its equivalent from an accredited college; students with at least a B average are given preference. Applicants for the Master of Divinity program who seek ordination need to have the character attributes that would indicate probable success in ministry.

Tuition and Fees. Tuition $100 per semester hour; student fee $5 each semester; miscellaneous fees where applicable; dormitory accommodations range from $63 to $180 monthly.

Financial Aid. Scholarships and Grants-in-Aid are available. The Presidential Associates Award of $50 per semester hour is applied for at registration (all who apply receive it). Up to four scholarships are available for entering Disciple students each year under Theodore P. Beasley Scholarships. They are awarded on the basis of demonstrated leadership ability and promise for effective ministry (the scholarship includes the Presidential Associates Award). Entrance Grants, Entrance Scholarships, Honors Entrance Scholarships, Scholastic Awards, Fellowships, and other named scholarships from individual churches for various amounts are available.

Housing. The Seminary provides approximately 60 apartments and rooms in four buildings to accommodate students.

Library Facilities. The Bosworth Memorial Library has approximately 100,000 volumes and regularly receives over 1,000 periodicals, including all the Disciples of Christ publications and the major religious journals of the world. An additional two million volumes are available at the

University of Kentucky Library across the street from the Seminary. The Seminary has a library-sharing agreement with the four other members of the Theological Association of Mid-America, with books and periodicals numbering over one-half million. This cooperation provides a coordinated list of more than 2,300 periodicals currently received and a union list of more than 6,000 periodicals. **See also:** Asbury Theological Seminary (KY), Louisville Presbyterian Theological Seminary (KY), Saint Meinrad School of Theology (IN), and Southern Baptist Theological Seminary (KY).

Religious Services/Activities. The Seminary community assembles every class day for worship, convocation, or fellowship. A variety of speakers from off campus, as well as faculty and students, contribute to these programs.

Degree Programs

The Master of Divinity is a professional degree designed to help men and women prepare for service in the Christian ministry. The degree is normally completed in three years. The curriculum includes Foundations for Ministry; Bible; History and Interpretation of Christianity; Personality, Culture, and Religion; and Communications and Leadership.

The Master of Arts is a program for lay people wishing to do serious theological study on the graduate level. It introduces students to the main theological disciplines, provides opportunity for some specialization, and requires a research paper specifically designed for the Master of Arts program. The program is not intended for persons desiring ordination.

The Doctor of Ministry is a professional degree designed to help ministers improve their skills and religious understandings. Students must have a Master of Divinity or its equivalent from an accredited school and normally three years in full-time ministry. The 36 semester hours may be completed on either a full- or part-time basis. Scores from the Miller Analogies Test must be submitted as part of the admission procedure. The Doctor of Ministry student selects one of four tracks: The Minister as Pastor; The Minister as Pastoral Counselor; The Minister as Preacher; The Minister as Theologian. Each of the tracks has specific requirements.

Special Programs

A Seminary student or graduate may apply to the Graduate School of Ecumenical Studies in Geneva, Switzerland, for a scholarship for one semester of study at that institution.

Advanced work in Clinical Pastoral Education is available at the University of Kentucky's A.B. Chandler Medical Center. This works leads to greater expertise in counseling and may qualify as credit toward certification as a chaplain by the Association for Clinical Pastoral Education.

A double-competence program in ministry and social work allows students to earn the Master of Divinity degree from the Seminary and the Master of Social Work degree from the University of Kentucky in less time than it would take to earn the degrees separately.

Louisville Presbyterian Theological Seminary
1044 Alta Vista Road
Louisville, KY 40205   (502) 895-3411

Administration. Dr. John M. Mulder, President; Dr. Louis B. Weeks, Dean of the Seminary.

General Description. Louisville Presbyterian Theological Seminary has been established by the church and assigned the task of preparation of men and women for gospel ministry, for preparation of professionals who will exercise double competency in such areas as theology, law, and social work, and for preparation of chaplains for service such as in hospitals and prisons. As an institution related uniquely to the two major Presbyterian bodies in the nation, the Seminary has a particular responsibility to preserve the values of the Presbyterian tradition. It is a freestanding seminary. Degrees granted are: Master of Divinity, Master of Arts in Religion, and Doctor of Ministry.

Community Environment. The Louisville, Kentucky metropolitan area, with a population of 912,000, provides opportunities for students to work in hospitals, campus ministries, social agencies, prisons, and inner city churches. Students may also gain experience in the town and country churches of rural Kentucky and southern Indiana.

Religious Denomination. Presbyterian Church (U.S.A.).

Religious Emphasis. Reformed, Ecumenical.

Accreditation. Southern Association of Colleges and Schools; Association of Theological Schools in the United States and Canada.

Term System. Four-one-four; summer term.

Enrollment in Degree Programs in Religion 1984–85. Total 190; men 116, women 74.

Degrees in Religion Awarded 1984–85. Master of Arts 3; men 1, women 2. Master of Divinity 58; men 39, women 19. Doctor of Ministry 11; men 10, women 1.

Faculty for Degree Programs in Religion. Total 40; full-time 16, part-time 24.

Admission Requirements. For Master of Divinity: Bachelor's degree from accredited undergraduate institution; promise for ministry; vocational aspirations consonant with program. For Master of Arts in Religion: Bachelor's degree; good grades. For Doctor of Ministry: Master of Divinity degree; admission on basis of B or better average in seminary and three years service in ministry; seriousness in undertaking the program.

Tuition and Fees. Tuition $105 per credit hour; intern fee $315 per year; special composition class $50; special student fee $25.

Financial Aid. Available for Master of Divinity students according to need. Also available are 4-6 Presidential scholarships per year, $4,000 each for a first year of study. Special assistance is available for minorities, especially Presbyterians studying for gospel ministry.

Housing. Sufficient dormitory, efficiency, one-bedroom, two-bedroom, and three-bedroom apartments on campus for most Master of Divinity students.

Library Facilities. The library houses over 100,000 volumes. Special collections are in support of disciplines within theological education, especially those of concentration in areas of specialization in the Doctor of Ministry program.

Religious Services/Activities. Chapel; spiritual development groups; classes focusing on spirituality; courses in history and Bible giving attention to spiritual growth.

Degree Programs

The master of Divinity program is a three-year program (81 hours) in which about two-thirds of the study consist of required and required elective courses. Students may take field education in several settings, especially in settings appropriate to the ministry anticipated.

The Master of Arts in Religion requires 54 hours of study (approximately two years) and may be focused particularly in Bible or religious thought.

The Doctor of Ministry consists of 27 hours of academic course work, and a Doctor of Ministry project for nine hours' credit.

Special Programs

One-week workshops for ministers and other continuing education programs for clergy are offered. Also offered through the Louisville Lay Institute of Theology under seminary leadership are courses for Bible teachers, church officers, and church leaders in various aspects of life.

Mid-Continent Baptist Bible College
Route 2
Mayfield, KY 42066   (502) 247-8521

Administration. Raymond Lawrence, President; Dr. Larry Salmon, Dean.

General Description. Mid-Continent Baptist Bible College is a coeducational institution with programs leading to either the Bachelor of Arts or Bachelor of Religious Education degrees. It specializes in undergraduate teaching and provides, within a Christian context, an atmosphere which encourages student achievement. It is a Baptist school and all trustees, administrative officers, faculty, and staff are members of Southern Baptist Churches. The primary purpose of the College is to provide education, training, and preparation for pastors and other workers for service in Baptist Churches and institutions. The College has the additional purpose of providing various educational services to the community. The College seeks to achieve its goals through general educational courses, intensive theological courses, practical in-service

guidance courses, conferences, workshops, and seminars.

The College was established in 1949 and moved to its own campus in 1950 as the West Kentucky Baptist Bible Institute. In 1957, the Institute was moved to Mayfield and the present name adopted.

Community Environment. Mayfield, Kentucky is located about thirty miles from the confluence of the Ohio and Mississippi Rivers. This location is not far from the population center of the Untied States. Excellent educational, medical, and social services are available. The College is situated on North Fifteenth Street.

Religious Denomination. Southern Baptist.

Religious Emphasis. Conservative.

Accreditation. Southern Association of Colleges and Schools.

Term System. Semester; two summer sessions.

Enrollment in Degree Programs in Religion 1984–85. Total 88; men 76, women 12.

Degrees in Religion Awarded 1984–85. Bachelor of Arts 3; men 3. Bachelor of Religious Education 2; men 2.

Faculty for Degree Programs in Religion. Total 7; full-time 5, part-time 2.

Admission Requirements. High school graduation or GED; personal interview recommended.

Tuition and Fees. Tuition $33 per semester hour; application fee $5; registration fee $20; other miscellaneous fees.

Financial Aid. Student Aid Funds available and are based on need.

Housing. Men's dormitory available.

Library Facilities. The library contains over 30,000 volumes, the bulk of which are directly related to course offerings.

Religious Services/Activities. The College endeavors to help provide an atmosphere that is conducive to the development of the student's spiritual life. Worship is encouraged. Faculty and students attend the scheduled chapel services. School activities always defer to local church services in such a way as not to interfere with the participation of the student. Bible conferences are scheduled under the auspices of the Alumni Association and the Church Relations Advisory Council. Commencement is a celebrative service of worship.

Degree Programs

The Bachelor of Arts and the Bachelor of Religious Education programs both require Bible as the only area of concentration. Candidates for the Bachelor of Religious Education degree must complete four courses (12 semester hours) in Religious Education.

Special Programs

By arrangement with Western Baptist Hospital in Paducah, Kentucky, courses in pastoral Clinical Education are offered.

By arrangement with the Kentucky State Penitentiary, Eddyville, Kentucky, a supervised program in corrections counseling is offered at the prison to qualified students, and classes for inmates are also offered in the prison chapel.

Advanced Mid-Continent students may do supervised work at the J.U. Kevil Mental Health-Mental Retardation Center and the Shedd Academy which leads to credit in the field of Education.

Southern Baptist Theological Seminary
2825 Lexington Road
Louisville, KY 40280   (502) 897-4011

Administration. Dr. Roy L. Honeycutt, President.

General Description. The Seminary offers programs of professional and graduate theological education designed to equip men and women for Christian ministries in local churches and other settings for which advanced theological training is desirable. The Seminary was founded in 1859 in Greenville, South Carolina and relocated to Louisville in 1877. The Seminary currently has four schools: Theology, Church Music, Christian Education, and Church Social Work. The degree programs are divided into the professional or Master's level programs entered on the basis of a college degree and the graduate or Doctor's level programs entered on the basis of a seminary professional degree.

Community Environment. The campus is situated in a residential area within a short distance of downtown Louisville, Kentucky.

Religious Denomination. Southern Baptist Convention.

Accreditation. Southern Association of Colleges and Schools; Association of Theological Schools in the United States and Canada.

Term System. Semester (4-1-4 plan).

Admission Requirements. Baccalaureate degree from an accredited college or university; applicants over 30 years of age with high school graduation or equivalent may be admitted to the diploma program.

Tuition and Fees. No tuition. Registration fee $300 per semester; dormitory room $80-$115 per month; apartment $135-$270 per month.

Financial Aid. Since its inception in 1859, the Seminary has charged no tuition. A substantial portion of the instructional costs of educating its students is borne by the Southern Baptist Convention through the denomination's Cooperative Program of financial distribution. Student fees help to defray the costs of certain academic and student services.

Housing. Men's and women's residence halls and apartments for married students are available on campus.

Library Facilities. The James P. Boyce Centennial Library is named for the Seminary's first president. It contains over 626,000 items, including books, periodicals, pamphlets, manuscripts, microfilms, films, filmstrips, slides, cassettes, tape and disc recordings, and anthems. Over 285,000 of these items are fully-catalogued bound

volumes. The Billy Graham Collection of materials relating to the crusades of the evangelist are housed in a special display and research room.

Religious Services/Activities. Chapel services are conducted three days a week during the school year. Every member of the Seminary community is expected to participate in Tuesday chapel, and all are urged to attend Wednesday and Friday worship services.

Degree Programs

The Master of Divinity degree is offered with eleven specializations in the School of Theology to train pastors and teachers, missionaries, pastoral care and counseling ministers, evangelists, campus ministers, denominational staff persons, Christian social ministers, ministers to ethnic groups, ministers in communications, urban church ministers, and family ministers.

The Master of Divinity in Christian Education is offered through the School of Christian Education.

The Master of Church Music degree trains persons for music ministries and is offered through the School of Church Music.

The Master of Arts degree program prepares persons for ministries in education and is offered through the School of Christian Education.

The Master of Social Work degree which trains persons in the area of Christian Social ministries is offered through the Carver School of Church Social Work.

The School of Theology offers the Master of Theology degree.

The Seminary offers through the School of Theology the Doctor of Ministry and Doctor of Philosophy degrees. The Doctor of Musical Arts and the Doctor of Education degrees are offered through the Schools of Church Music and Christian Education respectively.

Special Programs

A program of Professional Studies equips qualified students for the practice of effective Christian ministry. The Diploma in Theology is granted.

Spalding University
Programs In Religious Studies - Humanities Department
851 South Fourth Street
Louisville, KY 40203   (502) 585-9911

Administration. Dr. Eileen M. Egan, President; Dr. Edward Griffen Smith, Director of Graduate Study and Dean of the College; Dr. M. Janice Murphy, Chairperson, Department of Humanities.

General Description. The Religious Studies Programs are integrated into the overall endeavors of the Humanities Department. The students are brought into contact with religion as part of the broad spectrum of human experiences and enterprises which are personally or culturally enriching. At the undergraduate level the programs firstly assist the major or minor in Religious Studies as a basis for later personal or career objectives. The Master of Arts degree has a strong academic component but is flexible enough to be used for professional certification and various areas of church-related work. The Bachelor of Arts in Religious Studies and the Master of Arts in Religious Studies are granted.

Parent Institution. The mission of Spalding University is to offer undergraduate and graduate education of high quality in the liberal arts and sciences and in selected professional areas of study. As an urban, independent institution in the Catholic tradition for students of all traditions, Spalding concerns itself with the personal development of each student as an individual and as a member of society. The purpose of Spalding University derives from and continues in the purposes of its pioneer founders, the Sisters of Charity of Nazareth. Stated in contemporary terms, that purpose is the preparation of self-directed, value-oriented, liberally-educated, and professionally-competent women and men. Students at Spalding University represent a broad range of ages and come from various academic, social, economic, and national beckgrounds. Their interaction with a well-prepared and experienced faculty is marked by mutual concerns in a climate where learning is valued.

Community Environment. The Spalding University campus is located between the main business section of the city of Louisville, Kentucky, and "Old Louisville," a neighborhood of elegant Victorian mansions, which in the latter half of the 19th century were the center of gracious living. The University is a participant in a major effort to preserve and restore the rich architectural heritage of the Central Area. The campus is within walking distance of most of the cultural offerings of Louisville, a moderately large American city.

Religious Denomination. Roman Catholic.

Religious Emphasis. Moderate.

Accreditation. Southern Association of Colleges and Schools.

Term System. Semester; summer term.

Enrollment in Degree Programs in Religion 1984–85. Total 44; men 13, women 31.

Degrees in Religion Awarded 1984–85. Bachelor of Arts in Religious Studies 1; men 1. Master of Arts in Religious Studies 4; men 2, women 2.

Faculty for Degree Programs in Religion. Total 5; full-time 2, part-time 3.

Admission Requirements. For the undergraduate major: completion of at least 30 semester hours of college credit with a minimum standing of 2.0 in religious studies; for the Master's degree: Bachelor's degree, 18 undergraduate hours in religious studies or related areas.

Tuition and Fees. Undergraduate tuition $1,950 per semester or $122 per credit hour; graduate tuition $132 per credit hour; application fee $15; general fee $3 per credit hour; graduation fee $50.

Financial Aid. For undergraduates, there are multiple scholarships, grants, loans and work opportunities. For graduates, National Direct Student Loans and the Professional Educators Incentive Program are available.

Housing. Dormitory accommodations are available for single students.

Library Facilities. The library contains over 120,000 volumes.

Religious Services/Activities. Daily Roman Catholic Mass; annual interdenominational retreat.

Degree Programs

The Bachelor of Arts degree with a major in Religious Studies requires the completion of the general education requirements plus thirty semester hours in Religious Studies, eighteen of which must be in upper division courses.

The Master's degree in Religious Studies is offered and applicants should have completed at least eighteen semester hours in Religious Studies or related subjects at the undergraduate level. In some cases, approved by the coordinator and the Dean, certain noncredit experiences may satisfy a portion of these prerequisites.

Transylvania University
Religion Program, Humanities Division
300 North Broadway
Lexington, KY 40508   (606) 233-8235

Administration. Dr. G. Philip Points, Religion Program Director.

General Description. The Religion Program offers courses ranging from the biblical and historical to the theological and philosophical study of religion, as well as non-Western and comparative religions. In seeking to provide for the study of religion within a liberal arts curriculum, there are two main concerns: (1) understanding religion within society and culture, including the role of religious institutions and visions in structuring societies, both maintaining and changing human values; and (2) personal development in religious faith and commitment.

Parent Institution. Transylvania University is a liberal arts institution offering 23 majors. Chartered in 1780, the University has been affiliated with the Christian Church (Disciples of Christ) since 1865. With approximately 850 undergraduates, the student/faculty ratio is 13 to 1. Along with its commitment to the philosophy that a liberal education is the only education that can have lasting value in a complex and rapidly changing society, the University recognizes also the value of career-oriented and preprofessional programs.

Community Environment. The campus is located on the north side of the city of Lexington, within a few blocks of downtown. Immediately surrounding the campus is a historical district, highlighted by Gratz Park with its ring of restored homes.

Religious Denomination. Christian Church (Disciples of Christ).

Accreditation. Southern Association of Colleges and Schools.

Term System. Semester (4-1-4); summer term.

Enrollment in Degree Programs in Religion 1984–85. Total 1; men 1.

Degrees in Religion Awarded 1984–85. Bachelor of Arts 1; men 1.

Faculty for Degree Programs in Religion. Total 2; full-time 1, part-time 1.

Admission Requirements. High school graduation; SAT or ACT.

Tuition and Fees. Per academic year: tuition $5,995; general fee $250; room and board $2,695.

Financial Aid. Both merit- and need-based awards in the form of scholarships, grants, loans, and work-study (campus employment). Among the numerous University scholarships and grants are the Thomas Jefferson Scholarships awarded each year to 25 exceptionally well qualified prospective freshmen, National Merit Scholarships, and numerous scholarships for students intending to enter the ministry.

Housing. Dormitory rooms for single students; no provision for married students on campus.

Library Facilities. The Frances Carrick Thomas Library houses the undergraduate library of 115,000 volumes. There is also a Rare Book Room, the Old Medical Library, and a special collection of Kentucky memorabilia.

Religious Services/Activities. Approximately 6 interdenominational services are held during the academic year. Religion, Learning and Living: A Campus Forum was established to discuss major questions of religious faith and to attempt to understand them constructively. A few specialized religious groups have their own objectives.

Degree Programs

The Bachelor of Arts with a major in Religion requires the completion of all general requirements plus 10 courses in Religion. A preministerial program is under the guidance of the Religion Program Director.

LOUISIANA

Centenary College of Louisiana
Department of Religion
2911 Centenary Boulevard
Shreveport, LA 71134   (318) 869-5131

Administration. Donald A. Webb, President.

General Description. The Department of Religion offers a major in Religious Studies and Christian Education. Its Church Careers program prepares men and women for vocations as skilled church professionals. Students are prepared for work in Christian education, sacred music, youth work, children's work, church social work, certain areas of religious communications, program coordination, and church administration, as well as for seminary and graduate study.

Parent Institution. Established in 1825 as the College of Louisiana in Jackson, the school merged in 1848 with Centenary College which had been founded in 1842 by the Methodist Church in Clinton, Mississippi. The College relocated to Shreveport in 1908. It is a four-year liberal arts college approved by the University Senate of The United Methodist Church. It enrolls 1,500 students and offers the Bachelor and Master's degrees.

Community Environment. The College campus of 65 acres is located two miles south of downtown Shreveport, the second largest city in Louisiana. The city is in the northwestern part of the state.

Religious Denomination. The United Methodist Church.

Accreditation. Southern Association of Colleges and Schools.

Term System. Semester (4-1-4 plan).

Faculty for Degree Programs in Religion. Total 6.

Admission Requirements. Graduation from an accredited high school with rank in upper 50 percent of graduating class; SAT or ACT required.

Tuition and Fees. Tuition $2,000 per semester; student fee $60; room $545-$745; board $620-$720.

Financial Aid. Most assistance is awarded on the basis of need. Scholarships, grants, loans, and work are available.

Housing. Men's and women's dormitory facilities are available on campus.

Library Facilities. The John F. Magale Memorial Library houses over 153,000 volumes.

Religious Services/Activities. The Methodist Student Movement is the organized ministry of the United Methodist Church to the campus.

Degree Programs

The Department of Religion attempts to lead students in serious philosophical and theological consideration of the question of humanity's origin, destiny, meaning, and purpose. The basic assumption of the courses is that these questions are best dealt with in the Jewish-Christian history and writings. The major in Religion leading to the Bachelor of Arts degree requires 30 semester hours in Religion courses including prescribed and supported courses. The major in Christian Education leading to the Bachelor of Arts requires 15 semester hours in Religion courses, 15 in Christian education courses, 6 in electives, and supporting courses in psychology, Sociology, Philosophy, and English. A Pre-Theological Curriculum is also offered in consultation with the Department.

The Church Careers Program requires the satisfactory completion of an approved major, all degree requirements, and the requirements of the Program. Students interested should contact the Director of the Church Careers Program.

Loyola University - New Orleans
Department of Religious Studies
6363 St. Charles Avenue
New Orleans, LA 70118   (504) 865-3943

Administration. Dr. James C. Carter, S.J., President; Dr. John F. Christman, Director, Graduate Programs; Dr. Robert A. Ludwig, Director, Department of Religious Education and Pastoral Studies; Dr. Vernon Gregson, Chairman, Department of Religious Studies.

General Description. The Department of Religious Studies offers undergraduate and graduate programs. The

Master of Arts program in Religious Studies aims at providing a solid and well-rounded theological foundation. Therefore, the emphasis is on theological content rather than pedagogical methodology.

The function of Religious Education and Pastoral Studies is provided by the Institute for Ministry. The Institute, along with its students, faculty, and staff, forms a learning community gathered to enhance the quality of pastoral ministry in the Church. The Institute serves as an educational resource for professionals and paraprofessionals engaged in, or preparing for, ministry and religious education, as well as laity who want to address themselves intentionally to their ministry in the world. The Master's degrees (Master of Religious Education and Master of Pastoral Studies) and certificate programs address themselves to such an integration.

Parent Institution. Loyola University - New Orleans is a Catholic institution that revolves around the Jesuit tradition of contributing to the liberal education of the whole person. It is a liberal arts university with Schools of Arts and Sciences, Music, Law, Business, City College, and Graduate Programs. Loyola is the largest Catholic university south of St. Louis in an area extending from Arizona to Florida.

Community Environment. The campus of Loyola University is located in a residential area of New Orleans, Louisiana known as the University Section. Fronting on tree-lined St. Charles Avenue where streetcars are the mode of public transportation, Loyola's main campus faces Audubon Park directly across the avenue. The 19-acre location is a collection of beautiful Tudor-Gothic buildings and modern architecture. Two blocks farther up St. Charles Avenue is the recently acquired four-acre Broadway Campus.

Religious Denomination. Roman Catholic.

Religious Emphasis. Ecumenical; Vatican II.

Accreditation. Southern Association of Colleges and Schools.

Term System. Semester; summer term.

Enrollment in Degree Programs in Religion 1984–85. Total 30; men 10, women 20.

Degrees in Religion Awarded 1984–85. Bachelor of Arts 6; men 3, women 3. Master of Arts 6; men 2, women 4.

Faculty for Degree Programs in Religion. Total 20; full-time 10, part-time 10.

Admission Requirements. Undergraduate: Accredited high school graduation or equivalent; ACT or SAT. Graduate: Bachelor's degree or equivalent; overall undergraduate grade average of 2.5 or better; appropriate background.

Tuition and Fees. Undergraduate tuition $4,390 per year; room and board $2,900; student fees $76. Graduate tuition $182 per credit hour; Loyola will give a 20 percent discount to laity, religious, and clergy who are engaged in full-time ministry, either educational or pastoral; Loyola will give an additional 20 percent matching discount to those whose employers will pay 20 percent of the tuition.

Financial Aid. Scholarships, loans, and work-study are available.

Housing. On-campus residence halls; board is voluntary and paid separately.

Library Facilities. The Loyola library consists of the Main Library and specialized libraries in music and audiovisual materials. Holdings include more than 317,620 volumes, 1,631 periodicals and journal subscriptions. Noteworthy among the special collections are the rare holdings of Spanish and French colonial archival documents on microfilm.

Religious Services/Activities. Campus Ministry strives for the complete integration of Catholic and Jesuit spirituality within the entire university community.

Degree Programs

The Bachelor of Arts degree with a major in Religious Studies is offered by Department of Religious Studies.

The Master of Arts in Religious Studies program provides a solid and well-rounded foundation in religious studies. It cultivates in the student a knowledge of and a sensitivity to scripture, an understanding of the historical development of western theology, an insight into the relationship of religion to culture, an interdisciplinary mentality, and an ecumenical awareness. Each student must take one course in each of the foundational areas: biblical study, history of Christian thought, systematic theology, and ethics. Areas of concentration are available in biblical studies, historical-systematic theology, and ethics. A student must take 12 hours of credit in one of these areas.

The Institute of Ministry at Loyola University also offers the degrees of Master in Religious Education and Master in Pastoral Studies.

Special Programs

A Certificate in Pastoral Studies or Religious Education is awarded to persons who have completed a total of 18 hours of graduate study at Loyola's Institute for Ministry in a concentrated area of ministerial studies. Program requirements must be completed within four summers.

New Orleans Baptist Theological Seminary
3939 Gentilly Boulevard
New Orleans, LA 70126   (504) 282-4455

Administration. Dr. Landrum P. Leavell II, President; Dr. Joe H. Cothen, Vice President for Academic Affairs; Dr. Jerry L. Breazeale, Director of the School of Christian Training.

General Description. The New Orleans Baptist Theological Seminary is one of six graduate schools operated by the Southern Baptist Convention. It is organized into five academic divisions: Biblical Studies, Church Music, Church History and Theology, Pastoral Ministries, and Religious Education. The Seminary grants the degrees Master of Divinity, Master of Religious Education, Master of Church Music, Doctor of Theology, Doctor of Musical Arts, Doctor of Ministry, and Doctor of Education (R.E.). The institution also has an undergraduate professional program at the Associate level offering an Associate of Divinity degree with concentrations in Religious Education Ministries, Church Music Ministries, and Pastoral Ministries. New Orleans Seminary has extension centers in San Juan, Puerto Rico; Miami, Florida; Marietta, Georgia; Birmingham, Alabama; Shreveport, Louisiana. The Seminary's purpose is to provide quality education in theology, religious education, and church music, primarily at the graduate level, but also at the undergraduate level. The program of instruction is Biblical in orientation and relevant in application.

Community Environment. The 81-acre campus has 112 buildings, most of which are of French Colonial architecture. The 1.2 million people in New Orleans are engaged in running this business, banking, judicial, and cultural capital. Understandably, many students find the city to be as much a place of learning and intellectual challenge as the classroom. New Orleans is one of the largest seaports in the United States and, as such, a marketing center for cotton, oil, salt, sulphur, natural gas, agriculture, and forest products.

Religious Denomination. Southern Baptist Convention.

Religious Emphasis. Conservative.

Accreditation. Southern Association of Colleges and Schools; Association of Theological Schools in the United States and Canada.

Term System. Semester (two 8-week terms per semester); summer term.

Enrollment in Degree Programs in Religion 1984–85. Total 2,704; men 2,325, women 379.

Degrees in Religion Awarded 1984–85. Associate of Divinity 53; men 52, women 1. Master of Divinity 166; men 152, women 14; Master of Religious Education 75; men 53, women 22. Master of Church Music 16; men 13, women 3. Doctor of Education 3; men 2, women 1. Doctor of Ministry 13; men 13. Doctor of Musical Arts 2; men 1, women 1. Doctor of Theology 9; men 9.

Faculty for Degree Programs in Religion. Total 89; full-time 49, part-time 40.

Admission Requirements. Statement of conversion and call; approval from the local church of which the individual is a member; degree from an accredited college or university; four positive individual references.

Tuition and Fees. No tuition; fees $340 per semester for Southern Baptist students and $640 per semester for non-Southern Baptist students.

Financial Aid. Aid other than the tuition support is available only to Southern Baptist students and comes primarily in the form of moneys adequate to cover fees and books based on need and credible work.

Housing. One women's dormitory; four men's dormitories; 480 student apartments available.

Library Facilities. The John T. Christian Library collection consists of more than 220,000 items, including over 165,000 bound volumes plus periodicals, annuals and minutes, microfilm, vertical file materials, manuscripts, and a rare book collection. The library is a depository for Baptist materials and contains specialized book collections, manuscripts, and memorabilia from outstanding church leaders. The library houses the 5,000 volumes of the personal library of Dr. Robert G. Lee, an outstanding pulpit orator. The J.D. Grey Missionary Home houses the library of Dr. J.D. Grey. A specialized collection of music materials has been developed and housed in the library. It includes 9,000 books, reference works, and bound periodicals; 9,500 scores; 1,500 hymnals and psalters; 3,000 recordings; and several thousand anthems and larger classical works. The Edmond D. Keith collection of 5,000 books, hymnals, and scores is a special feature of this collection.

Religious Services/Activities. Chapel is held three times per week with ten special lecture programs held on an annual basis and approximately 25 continuing education type workshops and/or seminars.

Degree Programs

The curriculum of the Master of Divinity degree requires 88 hours and includes courses in Basic Studies; Core Courses (Biblical Archaeology, Old Testament Exegetical Studies, New Testament Exegesis, Preaching, Church History, Ethics, Systematic Theology, Pastoral Work, Advanced Field Education); and Elective Courses. The degree program offers the student the opportunity to major in Religious Education.

The Master of Church Music degree is a graduate professional degree for those who plan to serve in the music ministry of churches and denominational agencies or institutions, or who plan to serve as missionaries. The course requirements are designed to help the student develop a maximum level of proficiency in performance, a comprehensive knowledge of church music, including music theory, music history, music education, and an understanding of the theological context of church music. The program requires the completion of 56 semester hours in specified courses.

The Doctor of Ministry Degree is a professional degree which is patterned to provide qualifed students the opportunity to achieve a high level of excellence in the practice of ministry. The degree is built upon the prerequisite of the Master of Divinity degree or equivalent theological preparation, high intellectual achievment and professional capability, and three years of substantial experience in ministry. The program constitutes approximately two additional calendar years beyond the Master of Divinity degree consisting of a combination of seminars, an intensive period of supervised ministry under competent guidance, and a field project with a written report. A total of 28 semester hours is required.

The Doctor of Musical Arts degree prepares students of exceptional ability for leadership and teaching in church music. The program emphasizes a high level of performance and research. A total of 48 semester hours is required.

The Doctor of Education degree program blends clinical research with the traditional research methods. It combines the professional and research approaches, bringing biblical principles to focus upon practical applications and present problems. The program is designed to prepare students for a variety of tasks, such as teaching, counseling, denominational positions, local church leadership, and missionary service. Vocational requirements include two calendar years of professional-quality ministry. Residence requirements include a total of 58 hours. Seminar examinations and a dissertation are also major requirements for the degree.

The Doctor of Theology degree is a research degree involving graduate study in the areas of Bible, theology, history of Christianity, and related studies. The program is designed to prepare qualified students for teaching in colleges, universities, and seminaries, for holding administrative positions, for working in the boards, agencies, and commissions of the Southern Baptist Convention, and for providing a specialized pastoral leadership. The program involves a minimum of two years of study beyond the first graduate professional degree in theology, comprised of seminars, supervised reading, and qualifying and comprehensive examinations, followed by the writing of a dissertation.

Special Programs

The Seminary offers through its School of Christian Training the Associate of Divinity degree in the areas of Pastoral Ministry, Religious Education Ministry, and Church Music Ministry.

Notre Dame Seminary
2901 South Carrollton Avenue
New Orleans, LA 70118   (504) 866-7426

Administration. The Very Rev. Msgr. John C. Favalora, President-Rector; The Rev. William S. Swann, Academic Dean.

General Description. Notre Dame Seminary has as its primary purpose the education and formation of candidates for the priesthood and pastoral ministry in the Roman Catholic Church. To this end it offers students preparing for the priesthood the degrees Master of Divinity or Master of Arts in Theological Studies, or, under certain circumstances, both of these degrees. Moreover, as a graduate school of theology, it welcomes into all its degree programs a variety of non-seminarian applicants: clergy, religious, and lay people of all faiths. Historically and geographically, Notre Dame Seminary has sought and continues to seek to serve the Province of New Orleans and the Gulf South in general, catering to the general theological needs and the special ministerial problems of this area.

Community Environment. Notre Dame Seminary is located in the Carrollton section in the heart of New Orleans, Louisiana. New Orleans, "The Crescent City," is the center of commerce and industry in the South with an exciting and fascinating past which can be relived daily in its enchanting "French Quarter." New Orleans offers numerous opportunities for entertainment, cultural activities, exhibits, and fine restaurants. The city enjoys a comfortable climate year-round.

Religious Denomination. Roman Catholic.

Accreditation. Southern Association of Colleges and Schools; Association of Theological Schools in the United States and Canada.

Term System. Semester; no summer term.

Enrollment in Degree Programs in Religion 1984–85. Total 124; men 117, women 7.

Degrees in Religion Awarded 1984–85. Master of Divinity 12; men 12.

Faculty for Degree Programs in Religion. Total 21; full-time 11, part-time 10.

Admission Requirements. Bachelor of Arts or Ph.B. from an accredited college or university; undergraduate courses in philosophy; Graduate Record Examination.

Tuition and Fees. Tuition $1,513 per semester; room and board $1,650 per semester; registration fee $50.

Financial Aid. Students at the Seminary may be eligible for financial aid to help them meet demonstrated needs. College Work-Study, short-term student loans, Veterans Benefits are among the resources available.

Housing. Housing is available for students pursuing ordination to the priesthood (men only).

Library Facilities. The library maintains a book collection of over 80,000 volumes, including bound periodicals.

Religious Services/Activities. The Seminary is committed to the task of helping candidates for the ministerial priesthood attain a degree of maturity commensurate with the needs and responsibilities of ministry now and in the future. The Seminary faculty and administration regard the student's growth in faith and response in service as primary for the development of the contemporary priest. The Seminary offers spiritual direction, psychological counseling, consultation with a class advisor, class formation groups, community living and prayer, celebration of the Sacred Liturgy, and days of recollection and retreats.

Degree Programs

The Master of Arts in Theological Studies program is open to qualified students — clerical, religious, and lay. The student is required to take a foundational program in the four areas of: Sacred Scripture, Systematic Theology, Historical Theology, and Moral Theology. Additionally, 24 credit hours must be taken from upper level courses including 12 credit hours in one area of concentration; a thesis is required.

The Master of Divinity program requires the completion of foundational courses which are prerequisite to the program. These courses constitute the Pre-Theology Year for students whose undergraduate studies were deficient in philosophy. They embrace the requirements of the U.S. Bishops *Program of Priestly Formation.* A First Theology year includes further propaedeutic courses required by the same *Program.* The Upper-Level courses include a two-year theology cycle (for Second and Third Theology) and annually-repeated courses. Comprehensive examinations are required and an overall grade of at least C must be maintained.

Special Programs

The Graduate School of Theology offers afternoon and evening classes for clergy and laity as part of a program in continuing education. Courses in the following areas are offered: Sacred Scripture, Historical Theology, Liturgical Theology, Moral Theology, Systematic Theology, Canon Law, Homiletics, and Pastoral Education.

St. Joseph Seminary College
St. Benedict, LA 70457   (504) 892-1800

Administration. Very Rev. Pius C. Latigue, O.S.B., President-Rector; Thomas A. Siegrist, O.S.B., Director of Admissions, Registrar.

General Description. St. Joseph Seminary College was founded in 1891 at Gessen, near Ponchatoula, Louisiana, as St. Joseph Minor Seminary of the Archdiocese of New Orleans. Over the years the Seminary enrollment grew and during the 1950s construction of the new St. Joseph Seminary was planned and implemented. In 1964, the High School Department was phased out. Major Departments of Psychology and Religion were added in 1973 to those of History, Literature, and Philosophy. The Seminary operates under an expanded Board of Trustees comprised of Bishops, priests, and laymen. The College now endeavors to serve the entire Ecclesiastical Province of New Orleans as well as other interested dioceses. The Seminary is conducted by the Ecclesiastical Province of New Orleans and the Benedictine Monks of St. Joseph Abbey.

The purpose of St. Joseph Seminary College is to provide academic and personal formation for aspirants to the Roman Catholic priesthood. Commensurate with its resources, the Seminary also provides continuing Christian education opportunities for other adults.

Community Environment. The Seminary College is situated upon a fifteen-acre campus in the midst of the piney woods of the Ozone belt. Surrounding the Seminary, and available at all times to the students, is a twelve-hundred acre tract of rich forest land. A small river, the Bogue Falaya, deriving its name from the Choctaw Indians who once inhabited the site, borders on the western side of the campus. Located one mile off Louisiana Highway 25, four miles north of Covington, the Seminary is only fifty minutes from downtown New Orleans and slightly over an hour from Baton Rouge. Both Greyhound and Continen-

tal Trailways bus lines serve the area and taxi service is available from Covington.

Religious Denomination. Roman Catholic.

Accreditation. Southern Association of Colleges and Schools.

Term System. Semester.

Enrollment in Degree Programs in Religion 1984–85. Total 16; men 16.

Degrees in Religion Awarded 1984–85. Bachelor of Arts in Religion 4; men 4.

Faculty for Degree Programs in Religion. Total 6; part-time 6.

Admission Requirements. Medical examination report completed by a physician; letter of sponsorship from the Diocesan Vocation Director or religious superior; transcript of academic work previously completed; evidence of graduating from an approved secondary school; proof of ability to follow the curriculum of the Seminary.

Tuition and Fees. Charges per semester for full-time students: tuition $1,250; room $600; board $800.

Financial Aid. Financial aid is available.

Housing. Full-time students must live on campus in the dormitories provided.

Library Facilities. The Rouquette Library accommodates an expanding collection of books (70,000 in 1982).

Religious Services/Activities. The primary purpose of the Pastoral Formation Program at the Seminary is to provide the college seminarian with an opportunity to minister in the parochial setting. In this process of ministering the student is exposed to a variety of pastoral experiences in order to familiarize him with various facets of ministry. The program presently employs a creative ministry model which consists of prayer and preparation before the pastoral experience, the experience itself, and a follow-up evaluation of the experience under careful supervision. Presently, the Program is involved in Ministry to the Aged, Parish Liturgical Ministry, Youth Retreat Work, Catechetics, and on a limited basis, Ministry to the Orphaned and Handicapped.

Degree Programs

The Bachelor of Arts is awarded to students who fulfill the general minimum requirements. Course work is specified and 130 semester hours are required for the degree. The Seminary College considers it urgent for the seminarian to join religious, cultural, and apostolic programs and opportunities as offered to students in the rich and vital liturgical tradition of the Benedictines. These aspects are spiritual formation, intellectual formation, social formation, cultural formation, and apostolic formation.

MAINE

Bangor Theological Seminary

300 Union Street
Bangor, ME 04401   (207) 942-6781

Administration. Dr. Walter R. Dickhaut, Dean of the Seminary.

General Description. Bangor Theological Seminary offers a 3-year Master of Divinity program. In addition, it is unique in its creation of the "Bangor Plan" which is an educational program providing the opportunity for students without an undergraduate degree to pursue a theological studies program.

The Seminary is one of the five oldest institutions for preparing ministers in the United States. It was established by the Society for Theological Education, founded in Portland in 1811 and incorporated in 1812. The Seminary, founded by Congregationalists, is closely related to the United Church of Christ, and courses in history, doctrine, and polity are approved by the University Senate of the United Methodist Church. Its emphasis is ecumenical and there are representatives from most of the major religious denominations in the Seminary's faculty and student body.

Community Environment. The campus of ten acres is situated on a hill overlooking the Penobscot River and the city of Bangor, Maine's third largest city. Serviced by bus and an international airport, Bangor is the commercial and cultural center of eastern Maine. The Seminary campus consists of many buildings of 19th century origin and is listed in the National Register of Historic Places. The home of the Seminary President, once the home of Hannibal Hamlin (Abraham Lincoln's first Vice President), is also an historic landmark.

Religious Denomination. Closely related to the United Church of Christ and open to all denominations.

Religious Emphasis. Ecumenical.

Accreditation. New England Association of Schools and Colleges; Association of Theological Schools in the United States and Canada.

Term System. Semester; January intensive term; no summer session.

Enrollment in Degree Programs in Religion 1984–85.
Total 130; men 84, women 46.

Degrees in Religion Awarded 1984–85. Master of Divinity 18; men 9, women 9. Diploma 3; men 2, women 1.

Faculty for Degree Programs in Religion. Total 14; full-time 9, part-time 5.

Admission Requirements. Students with high school equivalent and little or no college may be admitted under the "Bangor Plan." Students wishing to be admitted directly into the Theological Studies program must have a Bachelor's degree from an accredited college or university.

Tuition and Fees. $350 per course; audited courses are free provided the student is registered for a minimum of 4 courses during the semester, otherwise, $75 per audited course; registration fee $20; Student Association dues $15; room and board will vary according to arrangement requested, but average $990 per year for dormitory housing and $1,335 per year for board.

Financial Aid. Various scholarships, grants, loans, and work opportunities are available through application to the Financial Aid Office.

Housing. Dormitory rooms are available for students without families. On-campus apartments are available for single and married students (with or without families). A Housing Committee is available to assist students in locating housing on or off campus.

Library Facilities. The Moulton Library houses over 75,000 volumes of books and periodicals, primarily covering the fields of religion and philosophy. It is the largest collection of its kind in northern New England.

Religious Services/Activities. Morning prayers are held each Monday, Tuesday, Thursday, and Friday and on the first and third Wednesday of the month. Chapel services are held each Tuesday and Thursday. Communion service is held on the second and fourth Wednesday and first and third Thursday of the month. Other special services are arranged.

Degree Programs

The Master of Divinity has two paths toward attaining the degree. The first path is the traditional three-year Master of Divinity degree program of theological studies.

The second path, the "Bangor Plan," provides an opportunity for second-career persons, with a partial or no college education, to prepare for the ministry in a setting in which their maturity is an asset and they are welcome among their peers. Aspirants in this program may prepare for full-time ministry through a combination of Liberal Arts Studies and Theological Studies over a four to seven year period. The curriculum in Theological Studies, required of both paths, is designed to combine a solid core of required basic theological courses with as much flexibility and enrichment of the student's program as is possible within the normal three-year time span. The core of required courses is distributed over the four areas of Biblical Studies, Historical Studies, Theology and Christian Ethics, and Pastoral Studies. In addition, the student will take the equivalent of ten elective courses to complete the 30 courses required.

Special Programs

Under the "Bangor Plan," the Seminary provides a two-year course of study in the liberal arts and sciences for those persons who have a partial or no formal college education. The curriculum is designed to prepare the student for the regular theological work of the Seminary as described above. A total of 20 courses is required to complete the Liberal Arts Studies curriculum and qualify for Junior standing in the Theological Studies program. Under this plan students are required to have completed 60 hours of prescribed Liberal Studies work which they may do at the Seminary. Upon successful completion of these 60 hours and the 3-year Theological Studies program, they receive a Diploma from the Seminary which may be converted to a Master of Divinity upon completion of their undergraduate degree within seven years from obtaining their Diploma. This program has been particularly attractive to persons making a mid-life career change.

Theological Education for Laity is a practical program of 48 credits designed to equip and enable women and men to become more competent and effective in their places of Christian ministry, and leads to a Master's degree or Certificate in Professional Studies. This program is offered in association with the New York Theological Seminary. The program is run on a workshop/seminar basis with both individual and group projects. The sessions take place on two weekends each month during the academic year and on five consecutive days during the summer. Upon satisfactory completion of the course requirements, the Master of Professional Studies degree will be awarded to those holding a baccalaureate degree. A Certificate of Professional Studies will be awarded to those who have not yet attained a baccalaureate degree.

Bowdoin College
Department of Religion
Massachusetts Hall
Brunswick, ME 04011   (207) 725-8731

Administration. Dr. Arthur LeRoy Greason, President; Dr. Robert Carl Wilhelm, Dean of the College; Dr. Burke O. Long, Chairman, Department of Religion.

General Description. The primary and central purpose of the religion major is to provide means for the study of the distinctive subject matter of religion in a liberal arts context. Methods employed in other liberal arts and sciences are also used in the study of religion. The Department offers the Bachelor of Arts degree with a liberal arts major in Comparative Religions. Students may specialize in religions of ancient near Eastern origin, South and East Asian religions, or religious thought and philosophy.

Parent Institution. Bowdoin is a coeducational liberal arts undergraduate institution founded in 1793 offering the Bachelor of Arts degree. It began its active educational life with 8 students and enrolled only men. In 1970, the College voted to enroll women undergraduates.

Community Environment. Bowdoin College is located on 110 acres in 41 buildings. Brunswick, Maine is within brief driving distance of several fine beaches and summer resort areas; skiing is available in the winter. Portland, Maine, the state's largest city, is 26 miles away. Portland is at the head of beautiful Casco Bay, on a peninsula, with a fine harbor.

Religious Denomination. None.

Accreditation. New England Association of Schools and Colleges.

Term System. Semester.

Enrollment in Degree Programs in Religion 1984–85. Total 17; men 10, women 7.

Degrees in Religion Awarded 1984–85. Bachelor of Arts 17; men 10, women 7.

Faculty for Degree Programs in Religion. Total 3; full-time 3.

Admission Requirements. Bowdoin is particularly interested in the superior student who seeks out and has excelled in a demanding college preparatory curriculum. Particular emphasis is placed on academic performance in the junior and senior years of secondary school.

Tuition and Fees. Tuition $4,990 per semester; room $792.50 to $1,090 per semester; student activities fee $90 per year; health insurance $112 per year.

Financial Aid. Scholarship grants, loans, and student employment are the principal sources of aid for Bowdoin students who need help in meeting the expenses of their education. The College asks candidates for financial aid to file information through the College Scholarship Service.

Housing. Dormitories and apartments are available on campus.

Library Facilities. The Nathaniel Hawthorne-Henry Wadsworth Longfellow Library has a total collection of more than 600,000 volumes.

Religious Services/Activities. The variety of student organizations, Christian and Jewish, carry out different religious activities during the year. Bowdoin has no official religious posture, nor does Bowdoin provide clergy on its staff. The College is open to clergy of all denominations to work with students.

Degree Programs

The major in Religion leading to a Bachelor of Arts degree consists of at least eight courses in religion approved by the department. The course Introduction to the Study of Religion must be taken not later than the sophomore year. Each major must take at least one course from each of the following three groups: Religions of South or East Asian Origin; Religions of Near Eastern Origin; and Religious Thought.

Special Programs

The Intercollegiate Sri Lanka Educational Program is a fall semester study program in Sri Lanka to facilitate a rigorous and authentic intellectual and cultural experience for mature, motivated students with a demonstrated interest in South Asian studies, especially religion.

MARYLAND

Baltimore Hebrew College
School of Undergraduate Studies
Peggy Meyerhoff Pearlstone School of
  Graduate Studies
5800 Park Heights Avenue
Baltimore, MD 21215   (301) 466-7900

Administration. Dr. Leivy Smolar, President; Dr. Samuel Iwry, Dean; Dr. Robert O. Freedman, Dean, School of Graduate Studies.

General Description. The School of Undergraduate Studies offers the Bachelor of Arts in Jewish Studies and the Bachelor of Hebrew Literature, National Teacher's License. It also sponsors a Graduate Seminar in Israel, participates in the work of the Baltimore Institute for Jewish Communal Service together with the School of Social Work and Community Planning of the University of Maryland and the Associated Jewish Charities and Welfare Fund of Baltimore, and is a co-sponsor with Towson State University of the Baltimore Center for Jewish Education.

The Peggy Meyerhoff Pearlstone School of Graduate Studies offers programs leading to the degrees Master of Arts and Doctor of Philosophy (Ph.D.) in Jewish Studies.

Parent Institution. Baltimore Hebrew College is a unique institution in this country. Its philosophy of education is deliberately eclectic and students are exposed to competing, interrelating, and challenging attitudes toward the development of Jewish civilization. Every field of research and teaching in Judaica is represented on the faculty. The mission of the College is to effect a creative interaction between the emerging values in democratic, pluralistic, scientific, 20th-century America and the historic insights and tested ideals of Judaism. Baltimore Hebrew College also has an arrangement to exchange faculty and students (for credit courses) with Goucher College and Johns Hopkins University.

Community Environment. Baltimore is the home of many outstanding colleges. It is Maryland's greatest economic center and is an important port, industrial area, and educational center. Nearby Chesapeake Bay is the scene of all major water sports as well as fishing. The city is known as the City of Shrines and Monuments.

Religious Denomination. Jewish.

Accreditation. Middle States Association of Colleges and Schools.

Term System. Semester.

Enrollment in Degree Programs in Religion 1984–85. Full-time 130; part-time 61.

Faculty for Degree Programs in Religion. Total 20.

Admission Requirements. Undergraduate level: graduation from an accredited high school; SAT scores; three letters of recommendation (two from academic sources); personal interview. Graduate level: Bachelor's degree from an accredited college or university; three letters of recommendation (two from academic sources; Graduate Record Examination Aptitude Test (optional).

Tuition and Fees. Tuition $850.

Financial Aid. Approximately 50 percent of the recent freshman class received some form of financial aid.

Library Facilities. The Joseph Meyerhoff Library is the central resource in the Baltimore area for research in Judaica. The collection contains some 40,000 volumes. All aspects of Jewish life and history are covered, including Ancient Near Eastern History, Biblical Literature, Rabbinics, Jewish Languages and Literature, Jewish Philosophy and Mysticism, Medieval and Modern Jewish History, Sociology of Jewish Life, Modern Middle Eastern Affairs, State of Israel, and International Relations. The Library contains over 600 rare books, which date from the sixteenth to the eighteenth centuries. Included are texts of the Bible, Biblical and Talmudic commentaries and supercommentaries, and law codes and collections. Many of these volumes were rescued from the rubble of European synagogues by the United States Army after World War II and later distributed among several important Judaica libraries in the United States.

Religious Services/Activities. The Herman and Rosa Lebovitz Cohen Auditorium is the central assembly hall of the College. Thousands of people representing the entire range of Jewish organizational life and their own interests attend lectures, seminars, and other cultural activities held throughout the academic year.

Degree Programs

The Bachelor of Arts in Jewish Studies program is devoted to the study of the varied aspects of Jewish civilization. The Bachelor of Hebrew Literature is the most intensive program offered at the College in Hebrew literary and historical sources. Successful completion of the program entitles students to receive the Temporary Hebrew Teacher's License issued by the National Board of License.

The Master of Arts in Jewish Studies program trains students in both classical and contemporary Jewish Studies. Each student takes four core courses: Introduction to Biblical Literature and Civilization, The Talmud and Its Era, Medieval Jewish History, and Modern Jewish History. The student then chooses a major from one of the five fields offered by the College: Biblical Literature; Rabbinic Literature; Hebrew Literature; Jewish Philosophy; and Jewish History. A student must complete thirty credits of coursework.

The Doctor of Philosophy in Jewish Studies program trains scholars in Biblical and Early Post-Biblical Jewish History and Literature and Modern Jewish History and Literature. A student must complete sixty credits of coursework.

Capital Bible Seminary
6511 Princess Garden Parkway
Lanham, MD 20706   (301) 552-1400

Administration. Dr. Harry E. Fletcher, President; Dr. Homer Heater, Jr., Dean.

General Description. Capital Bible Seminary was founded in 1958 and is the graduate division of Washington Bible College. The Seminary grants the Master of Divinity degree, the Master of Theology degree, and the Master of Arts degree.

Parent Institution. See: Washington Bible College, Lanham, Maryland.

Columbia Union College
7600 Flower Avenue
Takoma Park, MD 20012   (301) 270-9200

Administration. William Loveless, President.

General Description. Columbia Union College is a co-educatonal college offering degree programs in liberal arts, sciences, and some professional fields. The College is owned and operated by the Seventh-day Adventist Church. The Bachelor of Arts degree with majors in Religion and Theology is offered.

Community Environment. The 19-acre campus is located in Takoma Park, Maryland, a suburban area near Washington, D.C. The campus adjoins the grounds of Washington Adventist Hospital.

Religious Denomination. Seventh-day Adventist.
Accreditation. Middle States Association of Colleges and Schools.
Term System. Semester.
Faculty for Degree Programs in Religion. Total 6.
Admission Requirements. High school graduation from an accredited school or equivalent; ACT.
Tuition and Fees. Tuition $4,536 per year; room and board $2,390; student fees $174.
Financial Aid. Through scholarships, grants, loans, and part-time employment, the Office of Student Finance assists the student in financing much of the college costs.
Housing. Men's and women's dormitories are available on campus.
Library Facilities. The Theofield G. Weis Library contains over 110,000 volumes, bound periodicals, and pamphlets.
Religious Services/Activities. Chapel is held once each week and there are Friday evening Vespers, College Sabbath School, and church services. A Week of Religious Emphasis is held each fall and spring.

Degree Programs

The Religion major is a preparation for the teaching ministry, at either the secondary or college level. It requires the completion of 33 hours of required courses in Religion and 6 hours in required cognates. The program leads to the Bachelor of Arts degree which requires a total of 128 semester hours.

The Theology major is designed for persons planning to enter the gospel ministry as pastor, evangelist, Bible worker and its allied professions, or to fulfill pre-seminary requirements. The program requires the completion of 33 hours in specified Theology courses and 37 hours in required cognates. It leads to the Bachelor of Arts degree.

Students interested in teaching religion in the secondary school may earn a major in Religion and complete a minor in Secondary Education.

Eastern Christian College
2410 Cresswell Road
P.O. Box 629
Bel Air, MD 21014   (301) 734-7727

General Description. Eastern Christian College offers programs designed to provide training for those who plan to become local ministers, missionaries, directors of Christian education, church secretaries, and ministers of music. The College awards a one-year Certificate in Biblical Studies and a four-year Bachelor of Arts in Biblical Studies degree.

Community Environment. The College is located in 7 buildings on a 44-acre campus in Bel Air, Maryland. Bel Air is a suburban community on the John F. Kennedy Memorial Highway. The community provides a library and churches of many denominations. The Susquehanna

River and state parks provide facilities for water sports.

Religious Denomination. Christian Churches and Churches of Christ.

Accreditation. Maryland State Board.

Term System. Semester.

Enrollment in Degree Programs in Religion 1984–85. Total 57; men 27, women 30.

Degrees in Religion Awarded 1984–85. Bachelor of Arts 5; men 4, women 1. Certificate 2; men 2.

Admission Requirements. High school diploma or GED.

Tuition and Fees. Tuition $40 per credit hour; room and board $1,490; student fees $120.

Financial Aid. Federal and state aid are available.

Housing. Dormitories are available on campus for men and women; limited married student housing.

Library Facilities. The library houses over 17,000 volumes.

Degree Programs

The Bachelor of Arts in Biblical Studies program includes a balance of general studies and professional studies, and requires the completion of 131 semester hours. Practical Ministries/Specialized Studies Options include Christian Ministry, Youth Ministry, Christian Education, Urban Ministry, Early Childhood Education, and Music Ministry. A sequence of courses leading to the degree is offered in conjunction with Harford Community College.

Special Programs

A one-year Certificate Program is also offered by the College.

Hood College
Department of Philosophy and Religion
Frederick, MD 21701   (301) 663-3131

Administration. Martha E. Church, President.

General Description. The Department of Philosophy and Religion offers the major in both of these fields. Interdisciplinary-interdepartmental programs in Church Music and Youth Work/Religious Education are also offered.

Parent Institution. Hood College is dedicated to giving women the opportunity to grow intellectually and personally as they prepare for careers. Founded in 1893 by the United Church of Christ as a liberal arts college for women, Hood continues its commitment to quality education for women. The College offers programs leading to the degrees Bachelor of Arts and Bachelor of Science and enrolls both full-time and part-time students.

Community Environment. The campus of 100 acres is located near downtown Frederick, 45 miles west of Baltimore.

Religious Denomination. United Church of Christ.

Accreditation. Middle States Association of Colleges and Schools.

Term System. Semester.

Admission Requirements. High school graduation or equivalent; ACT or SAT.

Tuition and Fees. Tuition $6,790 per year; room and board $3,530; student fees $100.

Financial Aid. Assistance is based on need.

Housing. There are five large residence halls and several smaller residences on campus.

Library Facilities. The Joseph Henry Apple Library contains over 138,000 volumes.

Religious Services/Activities. The Catholic Campus Ministry and the Hood Christian Fellowship are sponsor activities.

Degree Programs

The Department of Religion and Philosophy offers three majors: Religion, Philosophy, and a combined major in the two fields. All of the majors allow a great flexibility in the selection of courses. The Religion major acquaints students with the world's major religious traditions and helps them develop a critical understanding of the issue involved in the academic study of religion. A minimum of 24 credits and a maximum of 60 credits in Religion in prescribed and elective courses is required for the major.

An interdepartmental major, directed by the Department of Music, prepares students for professional positions within the church as choir director, organist, director of youth, and religious education specialist. Majors have the unusual opportunity of studying campanology on Maryland's largest carillon. Those interested in youth work should consult the chairpersons of the Departments of Physical Education, Recreation and Leisure Studies, and of Religion and Philosophy for recommended courses. A minimum of 51-60 credits in music, religion, psychology, sociology, education, recreation, and physical education is required for the programs in Church Music and Youth Work/Religious Education.

Loyola College
Department of Theology
4501 North Charles Street
Baltimore, MD 21210   (301) 323-1010

Administration. Rev. Joseph A. Sellinger, S.J., President.

General Description. The Department of Theology offers a major in Theology as well as a Pre-Ministerial Program. This latter provides support for students engaged in undergraduate preparation for the Catholic priesthood under the auspices of a bishop or religious community, for those considering the call to priesthood, and for women and men contemplating entrance into religious life.

Parent Institution. Loyola College, established in 1852, is ninth according to date-of-origin among the 28 American Jesuit collegiate foundations. It is under the aegis of the Society Jesus in collaboration with the Sisters of

Mercy.

Community Environment. The College campus of 65 acres is located in the northern suburbs of Baltimore.

Religious Denomination. Roman Catholic.

Accreditation. Middle States Association of Colleges and Schools.

Term System. Semester (4-1-4 plan).

Faculty for Degree Programs in Religion. Total 14.

Admission Requirements. Graduation from an accredited high school with rank in the upper fifty percent of graduating class; SAT.

Tuition and Fees. Tuition $2,937 per semester; activities and services fee $80; room $1,650 per nine-month year; board $1,630 per nine-month year.

Financial Aid. Scholarships, grants, loans, and work programs are available.

Housing. Dormitory accommodations and apartment buildings are available.

Library Facilities. The Loyola-Notre Dame Library contains over 225,000 volumes.

Religious Services/Activities. Campus Ministries serves the spiritual needs of the Loyola Community. Students are welcome to participate in liturgies as planners, Eucharistic Ministers, readers, and ushers. Mass is scheduled daily.

Degree Programs

The Theology Department will assist all students to confront reflectively and to pursue intellectually their own religious beliefs from the perspective of the Judaeo-Christian tradition. All theology courses manifest an academic approach in a spirit of ecumenical awareness. The major leading to the Bachelor of Arts degree is offered.

Mount Saint Mary's College
Department of Theology
Emmitsburg, MD 21727   (301) 447-6122

Administration. Robert J. Wickenheiser, President.

General Description. Mount Saint Mary's College is the oldest independent Catholic college in the United States, founded in 1808 by the Reverend John DuBois, a French emigre priest. The College is committed to undergraduate education in the liberal arts, to seminary education, and to graduate education in theology and business within a small, coeducational community. It is Catholic in the contemporary ecumenical spirit of Vatican II.

Community Environment. The 1300-acre campus is twelve miles south of the famed Civil War battlefield at Gettysburg, Pennsylvania and within easy commuting distance of Washington, D.C. to the south and Baltimore to the east,

Religious Denomination. Roman Catholic.

Accreditation. Middle States Association of Colleges and Schools.

Term System. Semester.

Admission Requirements. Graduation from an accredited high school with rank in the upper half of graduating class; SAT.

Tuition and Fees. Tuition and fees $5,650 per year; room $1,475; board $1,475.

Financial Aid. The College offers scholarships, grants, loans, student employment, and special payment plans.

Housing. The college has residential accommodations for 1,235 students.

Library Facilities. The Phillips Library has a book collection of more than 126,000 volumes and receives 568 journals. There are also special collections of Marylandia, early Catholic Americana, and rare books.

Religious Services/Activities. While the liturgical life of the campus begins in the eucharistic celebrations at the Chapel of the Immaculate Conception, there are other times and places where the Mass is celebrated to best meet the needs of students and faculty. The Sacrament of Reconciliation is offered on a regularly scheduled basis. The Campus Ministry Office, with the chaplain and campus priests, offers spiritual direction.

Degree Programs

Courses offered in the Department of Theology aim to promote a reflective exploration of the religious dimension of human experience, the sources and historical development of the Christian and in particular the Roman Catholic tradition, the major themes in the Christian understanding of the relation between God and human beings, and the relations among Christianity, other religions, and contemporary secular culture. Two courses are required as part of the core curriculum of the college. Students who major in theology are required to complete a minimum of 30 units in the Department.

The Concentration in Religious Education aims to help prepare a student to teach religion on the elementary or secondary level. It requires 15 credits in theology and 9 credits in education, and may be taken together with a major in theology or a major in another subject. This concentration provides academic credits needed for Professional Catechist Certification in the Archidiocese of Baltimore.

Mount Saint Mary's Seminary has trained priests since the early 19th Century. It is known as "the Cradle of Bishops." Undergraduate students of Mount Saint Mary's College may register for courses offered at the Seminary.

Notre Dame of Maryland, College of
Religious Studies Department
4701 North Charles Street
Baltimore, MD 21210   (301) 435-0100

Administration. Sr. M. Francis Regis Carton, Chairperson, Religious Studies Department.

General Description. The College of Notre Dame of Maryland was founded in 1873 by the Sisters of Notre Dame. It is built on a commitment to the education of women—women of all ages, religious beliefs, and ethnic backgrounds. The College offers a liberal arts curriculum. The Religious Studies Department offers a major leading to the Bachelor of Arts degree.

Community Environment. The campus of 58 acres is located in the northern suburbs of Baltimore, fifteen minutes from the nationally known Inner Harbor area and forty-five minutes from Washington, D.C.

Religious Denomination. Roman Catholic.

Accreditation. Middle States Association of Colleges and Schools.

Term System. Semester (4-1-4 plan).

Faculty for Degree Programs in Religion. Total 4.

Admission Requirements. Graduation from high school in the upper half of the graduating class; SAT.

Tuition and Fees. Tuition $2,750 per semester; room and board $1,650.

Financial Aid. Assistance consists of scholarships, grants, loans, and paid employment.

Housing. Two residence halls on located on the campus.

Library Facilities. The Loyola-Notre Dame Library houses over 215,000 volumes.

Religious Services/Activities. The Campus Ministry Team, composed of students and faculty, provides opportunities for small-group liturgies, campus-wide celebrations on festive days, retreats, group prayer and discussions, counseling and spiritual direction, and social outreach activities.

Degree Programs

The Religious Studies Department endeavors to introduce and prove the religious dimension of the human experience in general and in its various facets. The Department offers courses for the general education requirement of two courses as well as a concentration and a minor. The concentration requires the completion of 9 courses (17 credits) plus 5 elective courses (15 credits) from the offerings of the Department. The concentration leads to the Bachelor of Arts degree.

St. Mary's Seminary and University
5400 Roland Avenue
Baltimore, MD 21210   (301) 323-3200

Administration. Dr. Robert F. Leavitt, President-Rector; Dr. Thomas J. Donaghy, Academic Dean, School of Theology.

General Description. St. Mary's Seminary and University was founded in Baltimore in 1791 to meet the need for an educated and committed clergy for the then emerging Catholic Church in America. Owned and operated by the Society of Saint Sulpice, the essential purpose of St. Mary's through the years has been and continues to be the spiritual, intellectual, and pastoral preparation of candidates for priesthood from dioceses across the nation.

In addition to being the first Roman Catholic seminary in the United States, St. Mary's is distinctive in two other respects. First, it is a civil university, having been granted the right to confer degrees in 1804 and having been granted a university charter by an act of the Maryland General Assembly in 1839. Second, by title, rights, and privileges granted in 1822 by Pope Pius VII, St. Mary's is one of six schools in the United States with a canonically recognized Ecclesiastical Faculty. Therefore, St. Mary's awards both civil degrees by the authority of the State of Maryland and canonical degrees by the authority of the Holy See.

The School of Theology offers to both resident seminarians and non-resident day students professional academic programs. The various curricula have as their focus preparation for priesthood in the Roman Catholic Church. The Master of Divinity, Master of Sacred Theology, Master of Arts in Theology, Baccalaureate in Sacred Theology, and Licentiate in Sacred Theology degrees are offered.

Community Environment. St. Mary's is comprised of 4 buildings located on 90 acres in the city of Baltimore, Maryland. Baltimore is the home of many outstanding colleges. It is Maryland's greatest economic center and is an important port, industrial area, and educational center. The city is known as the City of Shrines and Monuments.

Religious Denomination. Roman Catholic.

Accreditation. Middle States Association of Colleges and Schools; Association of Theological Schools in the United States and Canada.

Term System. Semester.

Enrollment in Degree Programs in Religion 1984–85. Total 136; men 133, women 3.

Degrees in Religion Awarded 1984–85. Bachelor of Arts 7; men 7. Master of Arts 10; men 10. Master of Sacred Theology 4; men 4. Master of Divinity 24; men 24. Doctor of Ministry 21: men 17, women 4.

Faculty for Degree Programs in Religion. Total 18; full-time 14, part-time 4.

Admission Requirements. Bachelor of Arts degree; Graduate Record Examination; sponsorship by a Roman Catholic Bishop.

Tuition and Fees. Tuition and formation $3,770; room and board $2,830. Non-Seminarians tuition $100 per credit hour.

Housing. Seminarians reside on campus.

Library Facilities. The Library traces its roots back to 1791 when the priests of the Society of St. Sulpice founded the institution. These men had brought with them from Paris a collection of theology books to support their educational efforts in the new world. The book collection now numbers over 90,000 volumes. Subjects include theology, philosophy, church history, sacraments, liturgy, canon law, pastoral works, and scripture.

Religious Services/Activities. The Seminary is fundamentally a formational community marked by the sharing of faith, prayer, study, and living together. Daily Eucharist, morning and evening prayer, monthly days of prayer, and annual retreats are held.

Degree Programs

The Baccalaureate in Sacred Theology (S.T.B.) is the first level canonical degree. Through this program the student is offered an organic exposition of the whole of Catholic doctrine together with an introduction to scientific theological methodology.

The Licentiate in Sacred Theology is a two-year program of advanced theological studies beyond the first cycle of general theological studies which is undertaken in the S.T.B. program. The licentiate program includes both a specialization in Biblical studies or theological studies (systematic theology or moral theology) and a major research paper.

The Master of Divinity degree is designed to provide the knowledge and skills needed to begin the practice of priestly ministry. The requirements include completion of 196 semester credits and a comprehensive examination.

The Master of Sacred Theology is a post-Master of Divinity degree. It offers the student a more extensive exposure to the content and methods of biblical and theological studies, and the opportunity for fuller mastery of the resources of those disciplines. The degree requires the completion of twenty-four semester hours, a reading knowledge of one modern and one ancient language, a thesis.

The Master of Arts in Theology is open only to seminarians who have completed St. Mary's Bachelor of Arts in Theology. Seminarians who have completed the B.A./M.A. track of studies fulfill all academic requirements for ordination. The M.A. requirements include completion of 46 semester credits and a comprehensive examination.

The Doctor of Ministry program is offered for men and women involved in full-time pastoral ministry. The program brings the educational process to places where persons are engaged in ministerial work. Groups of twelve to twenty within a geographical area reasonably close to one another work together for three years. The program is ecumenical by design.

Special Programs

St. Mary's Seminary offers two programs for older individuals preparing to enter a theologate: A Bachelor of Arts/Master of Arts sequence (see above) for students 23 years of age and older and a year of philosophy and religious studies for college graduates lacking the prerequisites for the graduate-professional study of theology.

Washington Bible College
The Bible College and The Capital Bible
Seminary

6511 Princess Garden Parkway
Lanham, MD 20706   (301) 552-1400

Administration. Dr. Harry E. Fletcher, President; Dr. Homer Heater, Jr., Dean, Graduate School, Capital Bible Seminary; James S. Schuppe, Dean, Undergraduate School, Washington Bible College.

General Description. Washington Bible College is an independent, evangelical, fundamental school with one- to seven-year programs to train lay and professional leaders in Christian ministries: pastoral, missionary, music, Christian education, and elementary education. Undergraduate programs are offered by the College; graduate programs, by the Seminary. The undergraduate programs of the Washington Bible College are the Certificate in Biblical Studies, the Diploma in Biblical Studies, and the Bachelor of Arts Degree. The graduate programs of the Capital Bible Seminary are the Biblical Studies Certificate, the Master of Divinity Degree, the Master of Theology Degree, and the Master of Arts Degree.

Community Environment. The campus of Washington Bible College/Capital Bible Seminary is located in Lanham, Maryland, within a 30-minute drive of the U.S. Capitol Building and within one mile of the main highways leading to Baltimore and Annapolis. As one of the prominent capitals of western civilization, Washington, D.C. provides the student with unusual opportunities for broadening one's knowledge of national and world affairs. Culturally, there are many events and attractions unique to the city of Washington. In addition to being the nation's capital, Washington provides the usual advantages of any large city.

Religious Denomination. Nondenominational.

Religious Emphasis. Evangelical and Fundamental.

Accreditation. American Association of Bible Colleges.

Term System. Semester (undergraduate); quarter (graduate); summer term.

Enrollment in Degree Programs in Religion 1984–85. Total 731; men 466, women 265.

Degrees in Religion Awarded 1984–85. Bachelor of Arts 66; men 48, women 18. Master of Arts 2; men 1, women 1. Master of Divinity 14; men 14. Master of Theology 5; men 5.

Faculty for Degree Programs in Religion. Total 48; full-time 28, part-time 20.

Admission Requirements. Undergraduate: High school graduation, C average; approved Christian character. Graduate: Bachelor's degree; approved Christian character; agreement with doctrinal statement.

Tuition and Fees. Undergraduate tuition $97 per semester hour; fees $110 per semester; dormitory $520 per semester. Graduate: Tuition $872 per quarter; fees $15 per quarter.

Financial Aid. Pell Grant, Guaranteed Student Loans, SEOG, VA, College Work-Study, and institutional grants and scholarships are available.

Housing. Men's and women's dormitories are available on campus as well as efficiency apartments for married students without children.

Library Facilities. The library contains 41,629 volumes as well as a variety of audiovisual materials and periodicals. Special files on such topics as Christian education publishers and mission boards are also maintained. A satellite Christian Service Library is maintained.

Religious Services/Activities. Daily chapel services; times of prayer are held regularly. The Christian Service Department assists students in various forms of practical Christian work and directs them to a specific Christian service activity in which they will gain experience in actual life situations. There are many opportunities for students to assume pastoral and preaching assignments, teach Sunday school, lead boys' and girls' church groups, and minister to youth and adults in area local churches.

Degree Programs

The Bachelor of Arts degree is structured around one major, Bible. Every student has a Biblical Education core of over 60 semester hours. To this core is added a General Education core and an additional 33 Professional Education courses from one of the minors chosen by the student according to his/her vocational interest. A total of 128 semester hours is required for the degree.

The Master of Arts degree program is designed to give concentrated biblical training to teachers, missionaries, experienced pastors, and other professionals. The program may be completed in two years, or one year if prerequisites have been met.

The Master of Divinity program prepares the student for pastoral ministry, missions, chaplaincy, and other church related vocations. The program is the basic program of the Seminary and may be completed in three years, or two years if prerequisities have been met.

The Master of Theology program is designed to provide research and enrichment opportunities for those who have completed the Master of Divinity program. Its purpose is to prepare teachers for Bible colleges as well as to enhance the preparation for the pastoral ministry. This program may be completed in one year by those who have completed a Master of Divinity program at Capital Bible Seminary or any other seminary whose doctrinal position and academic requirements are equivalent to Capital's.

Special Programs

The Biblical Studies Certificate program is a one-year non-degree course of study offered to those with college or professional degrees who are planning to go into the mission field but have no formal Bible preparation.

Primary and Intermediate Certificates are awarded upon completion of specified courses in the Adult Education Program. This program is designed particularly for person who find it necessary to work full-time and find it impossible to meet the demands of the Collegiate program.

Washington Theological Union
9001 New Hampshire Avenue
Silver Spring, MD 20903   (301) 439-0551

Administration. Very Rev. Vincent Cushing, O.F.M., President; Rev. James A. Coriden, Academic Dean; Rev. John F. Welsh, O. Carm., Chairman, Pastoral Studies Department.

General Description. Washington Theological Union began in 1968 when several Catholic theology schools in the Washington area found that they had common concerns, goals, and ideals. The seminaries, sponsored by diverse religious communities, decided to pool their resources and function as one school; these were Augustinian College, Capuchin College, Holy Name College, Holy Trinity Mission, and Whitefriars Hall. The Union is now one of the largest fully-accredited Roman Catholic schools of theology in the country, and educates the students of approximately 30 religious communities of men and women in addition to many lay students. It is a ministerial school; it prepares men and women for a variety of positions of service, witness, mission, and leadership in the Church. Most of the students are candidates for the ordained priestly ministry, but others are preparing for non-ordained ministries — a wide diversity of teaching, caring, and organizational roles in the Christian community. The Union grants the degrees Master of Divinity, Master of Arts in Theology, and Master of Theological Studies.

Washington Theological Union is a member of the Washington Theological Consortium.

Religious Denomination. Roman Catholic.

Accreditation. Middle States Association of Colleges and Schools; Association of Theological Schools in the United States and Canada.

Term System. Semester (four-one-four plan).

Enrollment in Degree Programs in Religion 1984–85. Total 279; full-time 175, part time 104.

Faculty for Degree Programs in Religion. Total 45; full-time 27, part-time 18.

Admission Requirements. Bachelor's degree from an accredited college with at least 90 hours in liberal arts studies; a cumulative GPA of 2.5 on a 4.0 scale; 18 credits in philosophy; GRE.

Tuition and Fees. Tuition $1,755 per year; $10 application fee.

Library Facilities. The library contains 126,000 volumes, with approximately 65,000 unique titles, and 355 periodicals.

Degree Programs

Master of Divinity, Master of Arts in Theology, and Master of Theological Studies.

MASSACHUSETTS

Amherst College
Department of Religion
Amherst, MA 01002   (413) 542-2181

Administration. Dr. Peter R. Pouncy, President; Dr. Richard D. Fink, Dean of the Faculty; Dr. David W. Wills, Chair, Department of Religion.

General Description. The Department of Religion presents the study of religion as a diversified and multi-faceted discipline which involves the study of both specific religious traditions and the general nature of religion as a phenomenon of human life. It includes cultures of both East and West, ancient as well as modern, in an inquiry that involves a variety of textual, historical, phenomenological, social, scientific, theological, and philosophical methodologies. The degree Bachelor of Arts with a major in Religion is offered.

Parent Institution. Amherst College, a private, liberal arts college, was founded in 1821 as an independent, nonsectarian institution for men. It is now coeducational and offers courses leading to the Bachelor of Arts degree. The College participates in a 5-college cooperative program including interchange course registration with Mount Holyoke College, Smith College, Hampshire College, and the University of Massachusetts.

Community Environment. Located on the eastern edge of the Connecticut Valley, the city of Amherst was the home of well-known American poets Emily Dickinson, Robert Frost, and Eugene Field, as well as author Ray Stannard Baker (David Grayson). Recreation is provided at Mt. Sugarloaf and Mt. Tom Reservation nearby.

Religious Denomination. None.

Accreditation. New England Association of Schools and Colleges.

Term System. Semester; no summer term.

Enrollment in Degree Programs in Religion 1984–85. Total 21; men 11, women 10.

Degrees in Religion Awarded 1984–85. Bachelor of Arts 5; men 3, women 2.

Faculty for Degree Programs in Religion. Total 6; full-time 5, part-time 1.

Admission Requirements. Grades, standardized test scores, essays, recommendations, independent work, the quality of the individual's secondary school program and achievements outside the classroom are among the factors used to evaluate the student for admission.

Tuition and Fees. Comprehensive fee (tuition, room, board) $13,400 per academic year; student activities fee $116; residential governance fee $32; campus programs fee $43; student health insurance (optional) $140.

Financial Aid. The College grants financial aid only in cases of demonstrated financial need.

Housing. Dormitory and house rooms are available.

Library Facilities. The library contains 613,102 volumes, 18,202 microforms, and subscribes to 1,823 periodicals.

Religious Services/Activities. Weekly Protestant, Catholic, and Jewish services are held.

Degree Programs

The Bachelor of Arts in Religion requires a degree of mastery in three areas of the major field as a whole. First, students will be expected to gain a close knowledge of a particular religious tradition, including both its ancient and modern forms, in its Scriptural, ritual, reflective, and institutional dimensions. Second, all majors will be expected to gain a more general knowledge of some other religious tradition quite different from that on which they are concentrating. Third, all majors will be expected to gain a general knowledge of the theoretical and methodological resources pertinent to the study of religion in all its forms.

Special Programs

The Luce Seminar includes the course "Fundamentalism in Comparative Perspective" and the Mellon Seminar, "On Understanding the Art of Other Cultures."

Andover Newton Theological School
210 Herrick Road
Newton Centre, MA 02159   (617) 964-1100

Administration. George Peck, President; Orlando E. Costas, Dean.

197

General Description. Andover Newton Theological School is a professional graduate school dedicated to the education of men and women who will speak for the Christian faith, lead the Church in its institutions, and inspire the people of God in all walks of life. While open to those with other unclear commitments and vocational goals, the programs of the School are designed to develop a learned ministry called to Christian discipleship, skilled in personal and group relations, and convenanted to promote a just and righteous human community.

Founded in 1807, Andover Newton is the oldest Protestant school of Theology in the United States and Canada. The origin of the school can be traced back to Phillips Academy, which was established in 1778 in Andover, Massachusetts. After a century at Andover as the Andover Theological Seminary and a transitional period in Cambridge, the Seminary became affiliated in 1931 with the Newton Theological Institution in Newton Centre to form Andover Newton Theological School. The Newton Theological Institution grew out of a meeeting of Baptist ministers and laymen gathered in the First Baptist Church in Boston in 1825. One of the oldest Baptist seminaries in America, Newton has pioneered throughout its history. Soon after 1890, it was one of the first seminaries to admit women, and it was among the first denominational institutions to effect an affiliation with a seminary of another denomination.

Andover Newton is a founding member of the Boston Theological Institute, an ecumenical association of nine theological schools in the Boston area. The library resources and facilities of the nine institutions are available to students enrolled in any of the participating schools.

Community Environment. Andover Newton is located on a hill-top expanse of 45 green and wooded acres in Newton Centre. The serenity of the campus provides the retreat necessary for contemplation and serious study, while its proximity to Boston allows students ample opportunity for urban ministry experience.

Religious Denomination. Interdenominational with historic ties to United Church of Christ and American Baptist Churches in the U.S.A.

Religious Emphasis. Classical foundations of Christianity.

Accreditation. New England Association of Schools and Colleges; Association of Theological Schools in the United States and Canada.

Term System. Semester; summer term for Clinical Pastoral Education only.

Enrollment in Degree Programs in Religion 1984–85. Total 406; men 217, women 189.

Degrees in Religion Awarded 1984–85. Master of Arts 2; women 2. Master of Divinity 53; men 17, women 36. Master of Sacred Theology 1; women 1. Doctor of Ministry 16; men 13, women 3.

Faculty for Degree Programs in Religion. Total 63; full-time 17, part-time 46.

Admission Requirements. Bachelor of Arts or equiva-

lent for Master of Arts and Master of Divinity programs; Master of Divinity or equivalent for the Master of Sacred Theology and Doctor of Ministry programs.

Tuition and Fees. $143 per credit hour for full-time Master of Arts or Master of Divinity; all other programs $153 per credit hour; student fee $40 per semester; acceptance fee $45; registration fee $35; room and board $2,374 per year; married student apartments $185 per month.

Financial Aid. Scholarships, work-study, and field education placements available.

Housing. Single student dormitories and married student apartments are available on campus. Overnight rooms are available for commuting students.

Library Facilities. The 180,000 volume library is housed both at the Franklin Trask Library on-campus and at the Andover-Harvard Theological Library in Cambridge. Special collections include the American Board of Commissioners for Foreign Missions Bible Collection; Jonathan Edwards manuscripts; Backus Historical Society library; published and unpublished works in analytical psychology; and religious education curriculum.

Religious Services/Activities. Daily chapel; specific additional denominational services; denominational student groups meet regularly. Prayer groups, choir, and denominational retreats are also available for participation.

Degree Programs

The Master of Divinity program seeks to prepare students for ordination in the major Protestant denominations. As early as possible in the seminary course of study, a student should become acquainted with denominational requirements and should contact the appropriate denominational official in order to begin the process which leads to ordination. The program requires a minimum of three years (six semesters) of study with the satisfactory completion of 90 course credits, a cumulative average of 2.0 (C), and one year of supervised field education.

The Master of Arts degree is offered only in the departments of Old Testament, New Testament, Church History, Missiology, Religion and Society, and Theology. It is open to prospective college teachers as pre-doctoral study, to ecumenical scholars from abroad, to writers and editors, and to other college graduates who seek foundational courses in theological studies but who plan careers in fields other than parish ministry. The course requires a minimum of two years (four semesters) of resident study on a graduate level and the preparation and defense of a thesis of approximately one hundred pages. No field work is required.

The Master of Sacred Theology is intended either as a continuing education degree for those who wish to pursue a terminal, advanced academic degree or to prepare for specialized doctoral studies. The requirements for the degree include a minimum of two semesters (25 course credits) of full-time resident graduate study with a minimum cumulative average of 3.0 (B). An extended research paper of publishable quality in the student's major field is also required.

The Doctor of Ministry program is a post Master of Divinity course of study designed for those ministers who are qualified to pursue advanced professional study and practice of ministry. The focus of the degree is on such professional roles as preaching, counseling, chaplaincy, administration, education, supervision, field education, and other areas pertaining to the practice of ministry. Candidates should be prepared to spend a minimum of one academic year and one summer to complete the requirements.

Special Programs

Men and women engaged in full-time professional service to the Church may register without tuition charge as auditors for not more than two courses a semester provided that permission has been obtained from the instructors concerned.

The Center for the Ministry of the Laity is an innovative campus-based research center that is developing new strategies and techniques for empowering the ministry of lay people in their work places.

Atlantic Union College
Religion Department
South Lancaster, MA 01561   (617) 365-4561

Administration. Lawrence T. Geraty, President.

General Description. Atlantic Union College is a four-year coeducational liberal arts professional institution. Although established by the Seventh-day Adventist Church primarily to serve the needs of its constitutents in Bermuda and the northeastern part of the U.S., it welcomes applications from Adventist students all over the world and non-Adventist students who desire a campus atmosphere consciously structured on Christian principles. The College is operated by the Atlantic Union Conference of Seventh-day Adventists. The Religion Department has the dual function of serving the general student in the areas of spiritual development and introduction to theological studies from the Adventist perspective.

Community Environment. The 314-acre campus is located in the town of South Lancaster in central Massachusetts.

Religious Denomination. Seventh-day Adventist (Atlantic Union Conference).

Accreditation. New England Association of Schools and Colleges.

Term System. Semester.

Admission Requirements. High school graduation or equivalent; ACT.

Tuition and Fees. Tuition $196 per semester hour; room $606 per semester; board $30 per week (minimum).

Financial Aid. Aid is based on need. Federal and state programs, loan funds, and college-based scholarships are types of assistance available.

Housing. Students reside on campus in residence halls.

Library Facilities. The G. Eric Jones Library contains 110,900 books, 6,311 microforms, and subscribes to 642 journals.

Religious Services/Activities. Chapel/Convocation is held twice weekly. The fall Week of Prayer emphasizes a specific theme; the spring Week of Prayer is planned and presented by students. Friday Vespers, Sabbath Worship (Saturday), and residence hall worship are held.

Degree Programs

The Bachelor of Arts in Religion degree provides a general education in the field of religion and the curriculum may serve as preparation for graduate work. A second curriculum offers preparation for the teaching of religion on the elementary or secondary level in the Adventist school system. All majors are required to attend the Departmental Forums. The Bachelor's degree requires a total of 128 hours.

The Bachelor of Arts in Theology degree fulfills pre-seminary requirements and is preparation for the pastoral ministry and allied professions such as hospital chaplaincy and public evangelism. Three tracks are available: Track I is for those who take only theology as a major; Track II is designed for those who desire a second major for enrichment or to broaden their employment options; Track III (Hispanic Emphasis) is for those who desire to serve in a bilingual ministry. Courses in Theology are grouped into the areas of Biblical Studies, Theological Studies, Historical and Apologetical Studies, and Applied Theology.

Berkshire Christian College
Division of Christian Ministries
200 Stockbridge Road
Lenox, MA 01240   (413) 637-0538

Administration. Dr. Lloyd M. Richardson, President.

General Description. Berkshire Christian College traces its roots to year 1897, when classes were held in a rented room in Boston, Massachusetts as concerned people of the Advent Christian Church began to fulfill their original charge, "in the east, a training school for Gospel workers." In 1902, the school incorporated as the Boston Bible School and over the next several years the school strengthened its educational commitment by assembling a competent and scholarly faculty and by expanding its curriculum and educational resources. In 1943, the Commonwealth of Massachusetts granted the right to confer the degree Bachelor of Arts in Theology. In 1959, the College moved to the Berkshire hills of western Massachusetts and settled on an estate in the town of Lenox.

The College is an evangelical school and requires faculty and administration to be fully committed in belief to an evangelical position, and in practice, to an evangelical life style. The college endorses the doctrinal statement of the American Association of Bible Colleges as expressing the evangelical faith the College seeks to advance. The College's distinctive purpose places it in the mainstream of Bible college education in America. It is the third oldest Bible college in the United States.

Community Environment. The College is located in the Berkshire hills of western Massachusetts. The entire area is rich with historical and cultural significance and provides ample opportunity for year-round recreational activity. The campus is located in the southern section of the community of Lenox and encompasses 64 acres of lawn, garden, and woodland, including private frontage on what is known as Lily Pond. Formerly a large private estate, the campus was purchased in 1957 and the move to Lenox was accomplished at the beginning of the 1958-59 academic year.

Religious Denomination. Advent Christian.

Religious Emphasis. Evangelical.

Accreditation. American Association of Bible Colleges.

Term System. Modular system (9 modules per academic year); summer term.

Enrollment in Degree Programs in Religion 1984–85. Total 65; men 35, women 30.

Faculty for Degree Programs in Religion. Total 7; full-time 7.

Admission Requirements. High school graduation; transcripts; autobiography; 2 references; SAT or ACT.

Tuition and Fees. Application fee (applied toward tuition) $50; tuition $5,100 per academic year; room and board $2,680 per year.

Financial Aid. External and internal financial aid available. Full tuition waiver for those in missions and pastoral programs.

Housing. Dormitories and married student housing available.

Library Facilities. The Dr. Linden J. Carter Library contains over 45,000 volumes. The holdings have been developed to support the curricula with strong collections in Bible, theology, and religious vocational fields. Subscriptions and back files are maintained for over 450 selected periodicals. The Special Collection Room contains the Adventist historical collection. This is an outstanding library of literature, photographs, and other materials relating to the origin and growth of Adventism. In addition to the publications of the Advent Christian denomination, it is rich in Millerite publications, many of which came from the editorial library of the *Advent Herald.* These include complete issues of *The Midnight Cry* and *The Signs of the Times - Advent Herald,* the chief organs of the movement. Publications of the several Adventist denominations are collected, including files on the local churches and conferences of the Advent Christian denomination.

Religious Services/Activities. Students are afforded ample opportunities for practical firsthand experience in various types of Christian work under the auspices of the Christian Service Department and also through student organizations and individual student and faculty con-

tracts.

As the campus organization concerned with promoting interest in world missions and future missionary service, the Student Mission Fellowship offers an organized program of fellowship and information both on campus and in ministry to churches. Two highlights of its annual efforts are the Spring and Summer Missionary Programs, the latter assisting in the financing and placing of Berkshire students in missionary service outside the United States. The Student Mission Fellowship is affiliated with Inter-Varsity Christian Fellowship and sends a delegation to sessions of the Inter-Varsity Missionary Convention at Urbana, Illinois.

Degree Programs

The Bachelor of Arts in Theology is offered by the College and all Berkshire graduates are "Bible majors." In addition to the Bible and theology courses and the general interdisciplinary core courses, each student may take courses in an area of concentration in order to prepare for a specific career area. These areas of career preparation are offered in two general categories: the Division of Christian Education and the Division of Christian Discipleship. Each area of concentration has a basic core of Divisional courses and a set of Specialization courses.

Boston College
College of Arts and Sciences
Commonwealth Avenue
Chestnut Hill, MA 02167   (617) 552-8000

Administration. V. Rev. J. Donald Monan, S.J., President.

General Description. The College of Arts and Sciences is the oldest and largest of the four undergraduate schools at Boston College. The Department of Theology offers courses for the required core curriculum as well as the major in an area of concentration. The Bachelor's and Master's degrees are awarded.

Parent Institution. Boston College is one of 28 Jesuit colleges and universities in the United States. The main campus at Chestnut Hill is six miles from the center of Boston in an area known as University Heights. The Heights is a three-level campus of more than 160 acres punctuated by 80 buildings including some examples of the finest in English collegiate gothic architecture. The Newton campus is a 40-acre tract located one and a half miles from the main campus.

Community Environment. Boston is the historic capital of Massachusetts.

Religious Denomination. Roman Catholic.

Accreditation. New England Association of Schools and Colleges.

Term System. Semester.

Admission Requirements. High school graduation from an accredited school with rank in the upper ten percent of graduating class; SAT and three achievement tests required.

Tuition and Fees. Tuition $8,200 per year; health service fee $140; room $970-$1,200 per semester; board $975 per semester.

Financial Aid. Various types of financial aid are available.

Housing. The College offers a variety of accommodations for undergraduate students in dormitories.

Library Facilities. The Thomas P. O'Neill, Jr. Library, named for the Speaker of the House of Representatives and a 1936 graduate, houses over 700,000 volumes. The Bapst Library houses the most-used library, the Rare Books and Special Collections Department, and the University Archives.

Religious Services/Activities. Religious organizations on campus include Campus Crusade for Christ, Hillel, Student Ministry, and Charismatic Prayer Community.

Degree Programs

The Department of Theology grants the Bachelor and Master degrees in Religion.

Boston Theological Institute
Congregational Church
Garden Street
Cambridge, MA 02138

General Description. The Boston Theological Institute is an interfaith consortium of nine theological schools in and around Boston, providing opportunities for a sharing of facilities and programs and for working in cooperative ecumenical projects. Major lectureships and interdisciplinary conferences are open to the other member schools' students. The Institute includes 250 full- and part-time faculty, some 900 courses each year, and combined library holdings of nearly two million volumes. Such a major resource enhances the theological education, the ministerial training, and the ecumenical understanding of all who participate in the Institute's many courses, programs, and activities.

Students of member institutions may cross-register for courses in any of the other Institute schools. Students also have the full use of all of the libraries of the member schools, and there are some joint programs in field education and other pastoral training projects. To facilitate cross-registration, a yearly catalog listing all the courses of the nine member schools is published in September.

Member schools are: Andover Newton Theological School; Boston College, Department of Theology (includes the Institute of Religious Education and Pastoral Ministry); Boston University School of Theology; Episcopal Divinity School; Gordon-Conwell Theological Seminary; Harvard Divinity School; Holy Cross Greek Orthodox School of Theology; St. John's Seminary; Weston School of Theology.

Boston University
School of Theology
121 Bay State Road
Boston, MA 02215   (617) 353-2000

Administration. Dr. John R. Silber, President; Dr. Richard D. Nesmith, Dean, School of Theology.

General Description. Boston University's School of Theology is a graduate professional school. Its life and thought interpenetrate the life and thought of Boston University's other Schools and Colleges as well as the Christian Church and its historic and contemporary expressions. From its origin as the first school of Boston University, the School of Theology has been related to Methodism. Today, it maintains that tie while also supporting strong ecumenical commitments in both faculty and student body. The School of Theology offers the first professional and second-level professional degrees.

Parent Institution. Boston University originated in 1839 when a group of lay and ministerial delegates of the Methodist Episcopal Church began a school for the improvement of theological training. By 1874, programs in law, music, oratory, liberal arts, medicine, and a graduate school of all sciences were offered. Today, students in the nonsectarian University have available to them the rich resources of 16 Schools and Colleges.

Community Environment. The School of Theology stands at the heart of the Charles River campus in Boston, the historic capital of Massachusetts.

Religious Denomination. The United Methodist Church.

Accreditation. New England Association of Schools and Colleges; Association of Theological Schools in the United States and Canada.

Term System. Semester.

Admission Requirements. Graduation from an accredited college or university; doctoral programs require a Master of Divinity or equivalent from an accredited seminary with a 3.0 grade point average.

Tuition and Fees. Tuition $2,250 per semester; student union fee $80 per year; Theological Student Association fee $10 per year; housing $2,290-$2,630 per academic year.

Financial Aid. The amount of financial assistance granted is based on student need. All students in degree programs, with the exception of Doctor of Ministry, are eligible to apply for financial assistance.

Housing. A coed residence hall on Bay State Road accommodates thirty graduate students. Theology students have first priority. Married student apartments are also available in various apartment buildings nearby.

Library Facilities. The School of Theology Library is an independent unit of the Boston University library system. The library collections number over 120,000 volumes with more than 950 serial subscriptions. The library houses several noteworthy special collections: the Metcalf-Nutter

Hymnal Collection, the New England Methodist Historical Society and Historical Repository of the Southern New England Conference UMC, the Massachusetts Bible Society Library, the Kimball Bible Collection, and the Percy Woodward Collection of Oriental Religious Art. The newest collection is the Organ Library, which includes the manuscripts, notations, and recordings of E. Power Biggs. All members of the theology community have full access to the extensive Boston University library system.

Degree Programs

The Master of Divinity program requires a minimum of six semesters of full-time study for a total of 96 semester credits. Students must complete six Common Elements courses, a theology requirement, and an Integrative Major. The Integrative Major combines one or more of the disciplines within Biblical and Historical Studies; Philosophy, Theology and Ethics; Religion, Culture, and Personality; and Ministry in Church and Society. The Integrative Major is divided into two parts: the Concentration and Ministry Formation.

The Master of Theological Studies normally requires a minimum of 4 semesters of full-time study for a total of 64 semester credits. The student must complete 6 Common Elements courses and an academic major. The Master of Theological Studies in Diaconal Ministry is also offered. It includes majors such as Evangelism, Communications, Education, and Administration.

The Master of Sacred Music requires successful completion of 60 credits including 20 semester credits in theology and 20 semester credits in music.

The Master of Sacred Theology is a second-level graduate professional degree for those who wish to pursue a year of more advanced coursework focusing on a particular discipline. It requires eight semester courses or 32 credits with a major in a discipline.

The Doctor of Ministry degree program has the goal of enabling the professional minister to set new learning objectives for ministry, to find appropriate resources and experiences for reaching those objectives, and to discover creative ways to use these resources. Candidates must complete a minimum of ten semester courses or 40 credits. A Doctoral Project Thesis and comprehensive examination are required.

The Doctor of Theology degree program is offered to students wishing to enhance their knowledge and ministerial competence in certain advanced areas of theology and ministry. The program involves an interdisciplinary major based on practical theology and one of the other disciplines of the School. The program requires a minimum of 12 courses or 48 credits.

Dual degree programs are also offered in Theology and Ministry, Theology and Music Ministry, and Theology and Social Work.

Brandeis University
Lown School of Near Eastern and Judaic Studies
415 South Street
Waltham, MA 02254   (617) 647-2878

Administration. Marvin Fox, Director, Lown School.

General Description. The Department of Near Eastern and Judaic Studies is the primary teaching and research unit in the Lown School. In this Department the University has assembled distinguished scholars who offer a broad curriculum. The School encompasses and intensive teaching and research program in all the main areas of Judaic studies, the Ancient Near East, and the Modern Middle East. In addition, the Lown School has programs which prepare students for Jewish communal service and programs of research in areas of direct concern to the American Jewish community.

Parent Institution. Brandeis University is a private nonsectarian university established in 1948 by members of the American Jewish Congregations. It is named for the late Justice of the Supreme Court, Louis Brandeis.

Community Environment. The University is located ten miles west of Boston on the Charles River.

Religious Denomination. Nondenominational.

Accreditation. New England Association of Schools and Colleges.

Term System. Semester.

Faculty for Degree Programs in Religion. Total 27.

Admission Requirements. Accredited high school graduation with high rank in class; completion of 16 units including 4 English, 3 mathematics, 1 science, 3 foreign language, 1 social studies; SAT or ACT; three achievement tests.

Tuition and Fees. Tuition and fees $10,445 per year; room $2,035; board $2,350.

Financial Aid. The University maintains a substantial aid program consisting of grants, loans, and jobs.

Housing. Eighty percent of the student body lives in residence halls.

Library Facilities. The John Goldfarb Library and the Gerstenzang Library have total collections of over 729,-000 volumes.

Religious Services/Activities. Religious activities and related programs are centered in the Three Chapels Association and are conducted by the student religious organizations: B'nai B'rith Hillel Foundation, the Bethlehem Chapel Community, and the Harlan Chapel Christian Community.

Degree Programs

The Judaic Studies program is designed to give students a broad education in Judaic Studies as well as a specialized and thorough training in at least one specific field. Students work in close cooperation with the faculty in developing a plan of study designed to meet the special interests and needs of each individual. Studies offered are in Biblical Studies; Talmud and Rabbinic Literature; Jewish Philosophy and Thought; Jewish History; Hebrew Literature; and Contemporary Jewish Studies. The Islamic and Middle Eastern Studies program is also offered. The Bachelor's degree requires the completion of a total of 32 semester courses (including the area of concentration) and to be in residence four academic years. A four-year Bachelor of Arts - Master of Arts program is designed to enable exceptional or gifted undergraduates to earn two degrees during their period of study at Brandeis.

Eastern Nazarene College
Division of Religion and Philosophy
23 East Elm Avenue
Wollaston, MA 02170   (617) 773-6350

Administration. Henry W. Spaulding, II, Chairman, Division of Religion and Philosophy.

General Description. The Department of Religion of the Division of Religion and Philosophy seeks to serve a diverse group: (1) those persons who are preparing for full-time Christian ministry, (2) reflective laypersons who seek to understand their faith more fully, and (3) Eastern Nazarene College students who take required courses for a basic liberal arts degree.

Parent Institution. Eastern Nazarene College is a liberal arts college of the Church of the Nazarene. The College has more than a half century of dedication to Christian values in an increasingly secular society. The majority of its graduates enter their vocations with a sense of service to God and their fellow human beings.

Community Environment. The College is located in historic Quincy, Massachusetts, a suburb of Boston on the South Shore. The campus of fifteen acres is within two blocks of Wollaston Beach which edges an inlet of Boston Harbor. The Blue Hills are within a few miles, so that fauna and flora of both ocean and forest are available for study in their natural habitat.

Religious Denomination. Church of the Nazarene.

Religious Emphasis. Evangelical Wesleyan.

Accreditation. New England Association of Schools and Colleges.

Term System. Semester; 3 summer terms (1 graduate).

Enrollment in Degree Programs in Religion 1984–85. Total 90; men 60, women 30.

Degrees in Religion Awarded 1984–85. Bachelor of Arts 20; men 17, women 3. Master of Arts 9; men 9.

Faculty for Degree Programs in Religion. Total 5; full-time 4, part-time 1.

Admission Requirements. High school graduation; recommendations; SAT results.

Tuition and Fees. Costs per semester: Tuition $2,053; student fee $141; room and board $1,350.

Financial Aid. Scholarships, loan funds, and part-time employment represent the financial aid program of the College.

Housing. Dormitories for single students and apartments for married students are available on campus.

Library Facilities. The Nease Library contains more than 100,000 volumes and 470 periodicals are received regularly.

Religious Services/Activities. As a Christian college, Eastern Nazarene gives first place in its co-curricular program to spiritual values and to the development of Christian insight and commitment on the part of its students. This goal is achieved through regular chapel services, weeks of special religious emphasis, and the regular ministry of the Wollaston Church of the Nazarene. Opportunities are provided under the coordination of Christian Life and Service for students to engage actively in programs of service in the local church and nearby churches and through the organized efforts of the Evangelistic Association, the World Student Outreach Society, the Student Ministerial Association, Students in Action, the Student National Education Association, and the Circle K Club.

Degree Programs

The Bachelor of Arts candidate may choose from among three tracks: Pre-Seminary/Graduate School; Ordination; Christian Education. A total of 130 semester hours is required for graduation, including all of the core curriculum. A major in Church Music/Youth Ministries is offered jointly by the Music and Religion Departments and requires a balance of course requirements in both areas.

The Master of Arts in Religion is offered through the Department of Religion. It is designed to prepare the student for various phases of the Christian ministry and foreign missions. The aim of the curriculum is to encourage Biblical understanding, theological competence, social awareness, and practical adaptability.

The Master of Arts in Pastoral Counseling is directed to both the pre-seminary and post-seminary graduates who feel the need to develop an understanding of the major presenting problems of the parish and to develop an awareness of pastoral counseling models and methods. Emphasis is given to preparing chaplains, counselors, ministers, lay persons, and associates for the many facets of care and counseling ministry.

Emmanuel College
Theological Studies Department
400 The Fenway
Boston, MA 02115   (617) 277-9340

Administration. Rev. Richard J. Beauchesne, Ph.D., Chair, Theological Studies Department.

General Description. Theological Studies at Emmanuel College take into consideration the momentous problems related to our life today in order to discover creative and liberating ways of dealing with these issues in light of scripture, religious traditions, and contemporary theological reflection. Special consideration is given to the Catholic tradition.

Parent Institution. Founded in 1919 by the Sisters of Notre Dame de Namur, Emmanuel college is New England's first Catholic college for women. The College combines the liberal arts curriculum with the religious and ethical perspectives of Catholicism.

Community Environment. The campus is comprised of nine buildings located on 17 acres in the heart of Boston, the historic capital of Massachusetts.

Religious Denomination. Roman Catholic.

Accreditation. New England Association of Schools and Colleges.

Term System. Semester system.

Faculty for Degree Programs in Religion. Total 12.

Admission Requirements. Graduation from an accredited high school with rank in upper half of graduating class; SAT or ACT required; 2 achievement tests recommended.

Tuition and Fees. Tuition $2,960 per year; room and board $1,575; student fees $150.

Financial Aid. The College tries, insofar as funds permit, to meet each student's financial need usually through a combination of scholarships, grants, loans, and part-time work opportunities.

Housing. Emmanuel College encourages on-campus living for its students.

Library Facilities. The Cardinal Cushing Library contains over 117,000 volumes and subscribes to 490 periodicals.

Religious Services/Activities. Campus Ministry seeks to provide a place for students to integrate their lives on campus with reflection, prayer, discussion groups, service activities, retreats, and liturgical celebration.

Degree Programs

For students who wish to acquire a major in Theological Studies leading to the Bachelor of Arts degree, the Department offers four possibilities: (1) a major specifically related to Liberal Arts; (2) a major specifically related to the discipline of Theology for ministry and/or graduate studies; (3) an interdepartmental major; and (4) a double major in conjunction with one other department. Courses offered fall into the following areas: Foundational, Religious Traditions, Judaeo-Christian Scripture, Ethical, Historical, Topical, Interdisciplinary, Methodological, Christological, Ecclesiological, and Special Offerings.

Educational and Pastoral Ministry programs are offered including the Master of Arts programs in Clinical Pastoral Counseling (at least 45 graduate credits), Pastoral Counseling (at least 36 graduate credits), and Educational and Pastoral Ministry (at least 30 graduate credits).

Special Programs

The Women's Theological Center offers a one-year program of theological education for women engaged in ministries for social change.

Certificate programs in Pastoral Counseling and Educational and Pastoral Ministry are also available.

Episcopal Divinity School
90 Brattle Street
Cambridge, MA 02138   (617) 868-3450

Administration. Bishop Otis Charles, Dean.

General Description. The Episcopal Divinity School came into being in 1974 through the merger of the Philadelphia Divinity School and the Episcopal Theological School, both over 100 years old. The union emerged from a conviction that responsible stewardship of the resources for theological education called for imaginative and courageous realignment. Access to the resources and stimuli of a great urban university center, with particular reference to Harvard University and the Boston Theological Institute, was a major factor in the decision to locate the combined school on the Cambridge campus. The curricular tradition of the two preceding schools has continued. The majority of students are candidates for ordination in the Episcopal Church.

The Episcopal Divinity School enjoys close working relationships with a number of educational institutions where not only the sharing of facilities and resources are possible, but also student and faculty exchanges can be arranged. Among these institutions are Harvard University, the Weston School of Theology, and the Boston Theological Institute.

Community Environment. The School is located within a five minute walk of Harvard University and Harvard Square. The center of Boston can be reached within eight minutes by subway.

Religious Denomination. The Episcopal Church.

Accreditation. New England Association of Schools and Colleges; Association of Theological Schools in the United States and Canada.

Term System. Semester.

Admission Requirements. Bachelor's degree or equivalent; GRE. Admission is not limited to Episcopalians but is open to members of other Christian denominations.

Tuition and Fees. Tuition $5,600 per year; room $1,050, board $1,375; infirmary and health insurance $600.

Financial Aid. The School has limited funds available for grants-in-aid from restricted endowment funds and annual gifts from friends, churches, and graduates.

Housing. School housing accommodations include dormitory rooms and apartments.

Library Facilities. The libraries of the Episcopal Divinity School and Weston School of Theology form a single operation under a common staff. Together they provide nearly 250,000 volumes, including over 1,000 periodical titles. The history of English Christianity is especially well served, since the two institutions enrich the whole collection from both Anglican and Catholic perspectives. Special attention is given to maintaining an outstanding reference collection, particularly in bibliography and ecclesiastical documentation. Some 4,000 volumes pertaining to Islam and the Arab world comprise a special Weston collection.

Religious Services/Activities. Morning prayer begins each school day. A daily Eucharist is celebrated alternately at noon or in the late afternoon. One Eucharist a week is designated as a time for the whole school to gather for a corporate communion, and one a month seeks to incorporate student families into the School's liturgical life.

Degree Programs

The Master of Arts Program provides an opportunity for selected qualified persons to pursue theological studies in the context of a witnessing community. It is designed to serve those who wish to develop general theological understanding as the basis for work outside the institutional church. The program requires four semesters of work in residence, completion of the Curriculum Conference and Tutorial, and Certification of General and Special Competence. A concentration in Human Services Ministry is offered.

The Master of Divinity program prepares persons for ordained and non-ordained ministries within the Christian church by seeking to engage each student with the Christian message, the Christian heritage, and the challenge of Christian ministry in today's world. The program requires a minimum of six semesters' work in residence; completion of the Curriculum Conference, Program Conference, and Tutorial; completion of at least two projects; Certification of General and Special Competence.

The Doctor of Ministry program is designed for persons actively engaged in ministry who are able to identify their particular interests and needs for intellectual and professional development, to create a plan of study, and to take responsibility for their own learning. It requires a minimum of two semesters of work, participation in a Colloquium/Integrative Seminar, participation when not in residence in a tutorial arrangement with a faculty member, completion of a project/thesis which represents a substantial inquiry into the theological and practical dimensions of some aspect of ministry related to the student's goals and program, and Certification by the Faculty Degrees Committee.

Special Programs

The School offers non-degree programs and continuing education for clergy and lay persons.

Gordon College
255 Grapevine Road
Wenham, MA 01984   (617) 927-2300

Administration. Richard F. Gross, President.

General Description. In the fall of 1984, the boards of trustees of Gordon College and Barrington College of Rhode Island voted in favor of combining the resources of the two institutions, effective September 1985. Both colleges were born out of the evangelical Christian tradition, Gordon in 1889 and Barrington in 1900. Gordon College is a four-year interdenominational, Christian liberal arts college. As a member of both the Christian College Consortium and the Christian College Coalition, Gordon College proves a number of educational opportunities beyond its own campus in cooperation with selected Christian colleges from coast to coast.

Community Environment. The 1,000-acre campus is located in Wenham on historic Cape Ann, 26 miles northeast of Boston.

Religious Denomination. Nondenominational.

Accreditation. New England Association of Schools and Colleges.

Term System. Quarter.

Faculty for Degree Programs in Religion. Total 8; full-time 5, part-time 3.

Admission Requirements. Graduation from an accredited high school; ACT or SAT.

Tuition and Fees. Tuition $2,210 per quarter; room $560; board $351; comprehensive fee $112.

Financial Aid. Assistance is made to eligible students in the form of scholarships, grants, loans, and campus employment opportunities.

Housing. A diversity of student housing is available on campus.

Library Facilities. The Winn Learning Resources Center houses a collection of over 215,000 items. Students have access to the Goddard Library of nearby Gordon-Conwell Seminary.

Degree Programs

The Biblical and Theological major is designed to prepare students for admission to seminary and various ministries of teaching the Word. For others it provides the basic foundation in Biblical education needed for various church vocations and ministries both at home and around the world. Others are encouraged to make the Bible their major emphasis in a broad liberal arts education. The major requires the completion of 15 courses in the department. Eight of these are specified as Bible, a senior seminar, and a theology core course. Of the remaining seven Bible electives, two are from theology. All majors must complete a three-course sequence in a foreign language. Either Greek or Hebrew is strongly recommended. The major in Youth Ministries is to prepare students to work effectively with young people in churches, para-church organizations, and other social agencies engaged in youth work. The concentration in Biblical Languages requires five courses in Greek, three in Hebrew, a senior seminar, and the writing of at least three exegesis papers in conjunction with department offerings. A Bible Teaching concentration is also offered in conjunction with the Division of Education.

Gordon-Conwell Theological Seminary
130 Essex Street
South Hamilton, MA 01982 (617) 468-7111

Administration. Dr. Robert E. Cooley, President; Dr. Robert E. Fillinger, Director of Admissions and Registration.

General Description. Gordon-Conwell Theological Seminary has its roots in two institutions which have provided evangelical leadership for the Christian Church in a variety of ministries. Conwell School of Theology was founded in 1884 by Russell Conwell, a Baptist minister known for his famous sermon and book, *Acres of Diamonds.* The Conwell School later developed into Temple University in Philadelphia. Gordon Divinity School was established in 1889 in the Boston area by a group of ministers who had a deep concern for missions abroad and New England urban centers. Upon the death of Rev. A.J. Gordon, prominent Baptist minister and founding leader, the institution was given his name. In 1969 these two schools united.

The purpose of Gordon-Conwell is to equip persons for leadership in many forms of ministry. It has a commitment to the urban scene, to the needs of minority groups, and to the poor of the world.

Community Environment. Situated on Boston's North Shore, the Seminary is ideally located to take advantage of the rich opportunities afforded those studying in New England. The campus occupies 123 acres.

Religious Denomination. Nondenominational.

Religious Emphasis. Evangelical.

Accreditation. Association of Theological Schools in the United States and Canada.

Term System. Semester; January and May sessions; summer term.

Enrollment in Degree Programs in Religion 1984–85. Total 675; men 562, women 113.

Degrees in Religion Awarded 1984–85. Master of Religious Education 18; men 9, women 9. Master of Arts in Theological Studies 51; men 37, women 14. Master of Divinity 110; men 103, women 7. Doctor of Ministry 1; men 1.

Faculty for Degree Programs in Religion. Total 42; full-time 35, part-time 7.

Admission Requirements. Ordinarily college and university graduates with a grade point average lower than 2.5 on a 4.0 scale are non considered for the Master of Divinity and Master of Religious Education. Students with a grade point average of 2.5-2.7 may be admitted on academic probation. Master of Arts in Theological Studies applicants must have a grade point avergage of at least 3.0. Enrollment is open to qualified students who, without distinction of race, sex, handicap, or denomination, desire to undertake serious theological study and who show promise of success in such an endeavor. Applicants for the Doctor of Ministry degree must have completed the Master of Divinity or equivalent and must be presently in-

volved in ministry, having completed at least 5 years of active ministry experience.

Tuition and Fees. Tuition from $535 for one course to $2,530 for six courses; fees from $140 to $210 plus matriculation deposit of $50. For the Doctor of Ministry degree, tuition costs include 4 courses at $300 each, 4 seminars at $150 each, and 4 projects at $350 each; other fees total approximately $1,375. Housing $365 to $495 per semester; married student housing from $165 to $285 per month plus utility charge from $40 to $90; flexible board plan.

Financial Aid. A variety of scholarships (need and merit based), loans, and other programs such as College Work-Study are available to qualified students.

Housing. Single student dormitories and units for married students are available on campus.

Library Facilities. The Burton L. Goddard Library houses 110,000 books and bound periodicals. The core strength of the collection is in Biblical and theological studies and other classic disciplines of theological study. Special emphases in recent years have been given to extending the collection in missiology, Christian social ethics, pastoral psychology and counseling, and preaching/communications arts. The Rare Book Room houses an important collection of Bibles which belonged previously to Roger Babson and the Open Church Foundation. Two other special collections are the 2,000 Assyro-Babylonian volumes from the personal library of the late Samuel A.B. Mercer and the Edward Payson Vining Collection of rare Bibles, manuscripts, and linguistic studies. These are maintained at nearby Gordon College.

Religious Services/Activities. Student prayer meetings and small group studies are developed according to needs and interests and are fostered by the counsel of the Dean of Students and faculty friends. Chapel services are led by faculty, students, and visiting speakers. Formal convocations and special lecture series are held periodically.

Degree Programs

The Master of Divinity degree is designed primarily for those who expect to enter the formal ministry: either the pastorate or in organizations associated with the work of the local church. It is a flexible program and allows for special emphasis in the areas of evangelism, missions, urban studies, counseling, Christian education, and allied interests. The concern of the program is to educate men and women to promote the building of the Church, the growth of individual Christians, and the sharing of the gospel with all people in accord with the Biblical mandate. A strong interest in the total implications of the gospel for society pervades the program. Concentrations in the following tracks are offered: Church Educational Ministry, Urban Year in Boston, World Missions, and Youth Ministries.

The Master of Religious Education program equips students for competent ministry in the educational work of the Church. The program enables students to (1) formulate a Biblical philosophy of education, (2) understand the basic principles of the teaching-learning situation, and (3) develop the specific competencies which are necessary for teaching, organizing, and administering programs, and for effective leadership in a variety of situations. The concern of the program is that students will not simply assimilate information but that they will know how to communicate the information effectively, persuasively, and sensitively. Students may follow the Generalist Program in Christian Education, an Individualized Program in Christian Education, or the Urban Educational Ministry Program.

The Master of Arts in Theological Studies degree is a two-year program with considerable flexibility, designed to provide graduate theological education rather than preparation for the ordained ministry, or for a church or professional position involving specialized skills. Each student's curriculum is arranged in consultation with an advisor. No courses are required but each is chosen on the basis of the student's vocational objective.

The Doctor of Ministry is designed for persons already successfully engaged in ministry. The candidate for the degree will be seeking assistance in developing to the fullest extent his or her function in parish, parachurch, or missionary service. This will be accomplished through an integration of active ministry, academic endeavor, and disciplined reflection with the Doctor of Ministry faculty.

Special Programs

The Center for Urban Ministerial Education was established in Roxbury, Massachusetts in 1976. The Center's chief objective has been to help equip urban pastors and church leaders for more effective ministry and outreach in the community. In keeping with the Seminary's heritage, purpose, objectives, and concerns, it seeks to serve the Black and Hispanic communities of Boston and surrounding cities. The curriculum has been organized to provide students with access to the very best Biblical, theological, and ministerial training that the Seminary has to offer and to provide courses and instructors that reflect a commitment to Black and Hispanic church ministry and community leadership training. The Master of Religious Education degree program is offered through the Center.

Harvard Divinity School
Harvard University
45 Francis Avenue
Cambridge, MA 02138   (617) 495-5761

Administration. Dr. Derek Bok, President of Harvard Divinity School; Dr. George W. MacRae, S.J., Acting Dean of the Divinity School.

General Description. While Harvard Divinity School is a part of Harvard University and also a part of the Boston Theological Institute (a consortium of theological schools) and shares the resources that these larger bodies have to offer, it remains a relatively small graduate school with its

own sense of community, fostered by accessible faculty and administration. The student body is very diverse, in religious affiliation, in age, and in experience. The campus, located in a quiet part of Cambridge, includes the Center for the Study of World Religions, both a residential building and an administrative center for the History of Religions Department.

The curriculum of the Divinity School is designed to address the challenges that confront religious communities when commitment is considered in a global context. Because it aspires to embody theological education in in this sense, the curriculum directs attention not only to required subject areas but also to the methods, sensitivities, and competencies that are indispensible to leadership in contemporary religious life and thought. The curriculum is organized into three areas: Scripture and Interpretation, Christianity and Culture, and Religions of the World. The School offers the following degree programs: Master of Divinity, Master of Theological Studies, Master of Theology, Doctor of Theology, and related programs for advanced degrees.

Parent Institution. Harvard University, private and nonsectarian, was established in 1636 by the General Court of the Colony of Massachusetts Bay and was opened for instruction in 1638. The University is coeducational in 13 of its divisions with the exception of Harvard College which admits men only to its undergraduate curriculum. Radcliffe College is a women's undergraduate college closely associated with the University and offers a liberal arts curriculum taught by the Harvard Faculty of Arts and Sciences.

Community Environment. Settled in 1630, Cambridge, Massachusetts has been the home of such famous writers as Henry Wadsworth Longfellow, James Russell Lowell, and Oliver Wendell Holmes. The city has many historical places of interest as well as museums. It is a suburb of Boston, three miles away. Known as the "University City," Cambridge is served by the Boston Metropolitan Transit System and railroads.

Religious Denomination. Nondenominational.

Religious Emphasis. Liberal.

Accreditation. New England Association of Schools and Colleges; Association of Theological Schools in the United States and Canada.

Term System. Semester; summer: Language Program only.

Enrollment in Degree Programs in Religion 1984–85. Total 443; men 226, women 217.

Degrees in Religion Awarded 1984–85. Master of Theological Studies 57; men 28, women 29. Master of Divinity 49; men 24, women 25. Master of Theology 10; men 9, women 1. Doctor of Theology 6; men 5, women 1.

Faculty for Degree Programs in Religion. Total 63; full-time 30, part-time 33.

Admission Requirements. Master of Theological Studies and Master of Divinity programs: Bachelor's degree; submission of application with official transcripts, letters of recommendation; statement of purpose. Master of Theology and Doctor of Theology programs: the above plus the Master of Divinity degree.

Tuition and Fees. Master of Divinity, Master of Theological Studies, Master of Theology: $6,640 per year; Doctor of Theology: $10,236 for first 2 years, $2,326 for second two years, $626 per year thereafter for students in Boston area, $250 for students outside the area; health service fee $325; Blue Cross/Blue Shield $330; housing $1,945.

Financial Aid. Based on need; awards are composed of grants, loans, and work-study.

Housing. Two dormitories are available for single students. Harvard housing and outside apartment listings are also available for married or single students.

Library Facilities. The Andover-Harvard Theological Library of Harvard Divinity School is one of the finest theological libraries in the country. The 370,000-volume collection is international in scope and constitutes the University's research collection for Protestant and Biblical studies. The resources are particularly rich in the areas of 17th and 18th century Continental European Protestantism, early New England theology, the liberal movement in American theology, the free church tradition, and biblical studies. Special collections include the Paul Tillich Archive, the archives of the American Unitarian Association and the Universalist Church of America, and the Hungarian Protestant collection.

Religious Services/Activities. Community worship service is held weekly; eucharist weekly; various denominations have their own services at the school on a regular basis.

Degree Programs

The Master of Divinity program prepares women and men for a learned ministry through the critical appropriation of Christian traditions, the understanding of a religiously and ideologically plural world, and the development of the sensitivities and capacities necessary for effective practice of ministry. The program is designed to encourage integration of study in the three curricular areas; of historical, comparative, and normative methods; and of theoretical and practical dimensions of theological education.

The two-year Master of Theological Studies degree program allows candidates to study a variety of theological disciplines, and provides an opportunity to specialize in a field of interest. The degree program is flexible and can be adapted easily to the special needs and interests of its students to satisfy a variety of objectives. It may be considered as preparatory to entering a doctoral program in some related discipline, or as a means to approach another discipline or profession from a religious perspective. The degree is a means through which a student may pursue questions of personal religious concern or gain a better knowledge of religious tradition.

The Master of Theology degree program affords an opportunity for students who have received the Master of Divinity degree or its equivalent to pursue advanced theological studies for one year. The program is especially recommended for students who seek to gain additional competence for the ministry beyond that provided by the Master of Divinity degree. It is equally appropriate for those who, after some years in the ministry, wish to return to a theological institution to clarify their thinking or to prepare themselves for new tasks. The student should concentrate study primarily in one of the following areas: Scripture and Interpretation, Christianity and Culture, Religions of the World.

The Doctor of Theology degree program emphasizes the study of the institutions, languages, and religious literatures that have shaped the Jewish, the Christian, and the Western humanistic traditions in their histories and in their encounters with other cultures and religions in past and present. This study is conducted with special attention to the concerns of the Christian theological tradition. The student specializes in one of the fields of Christian theological scholarship such as: Old Testament; Hellenistic Judaism and Intertestamental Literature; New Testament and Christian Origins; Theology of the Bible; History of Christianity; Theology (Historical and Systematic); Christian Ethics; Comparative Religion; Religion and Society.

Special Programs

The Women's Studies in Religion Program, established in 1980, serves as an international center for research and teaching. It is the only major center nationally that is designed to explore women's distinctive religious experience and perspectives in their cultural and racial diversity, and to examine male-centeredness and sexism in religious traditions of the world. The Program encourages and guides the development of women's studies in religion in order to help transform the study of religion so it more adequately reflects the study of human experience.

Lay persons and clergy of all faiths may participate in the Theological Opportunities Program which was organized to make the School's resources for the study of religion available to a wider audience in the greater Boston community. Each fall and spring, the Program offers a series of Thursday morning lectures providing theological perspectives on topics of current interest.

Harvard University
Faculty of Arts and Sciences
Committee on the Study of Religion
Cambridge, MA 02138   (617) 495-1551

Administration. Dr. Derek Bok, President; Dr. A. Michael Spence, Dean of the Faculty of Arts and Sciences; Dr. Wei-ming Tu, Chairman, Committee on the Study of Religion.

General Description. The Faculty of Arts and Sciences has immediate charge of Harvard College, the Graduate

School of Arts and Sciences, Special Students, the Summer School of Arts and Sciences and Education, and University Extension. It is also responsible for educational policy, and for the instruction of students at Radcliffe College.

Courses in Religion are offered by the Committee on the Study of Religion and by various departments. The Committee is responsible for the program of concentration for undergraduates in the Comparative Study of Religion and for the program of studies leading to the Ph.D. in the Study of Religion. Undergraduate concentrators may, with the approval of the Head Tutor, take courses offered by other departments and by the Divinity School for credit toward concentration requirements. Candidates for higher degrees should consult other departments and the Divinity School for information relevant to their programs.

Courses in Religion are offered under the following groupings: General—Comparative and Methodological; Ancient Near Eastern and Israelite; Judaic; Greek, Hellenistic, and Roman; Iranian and Central Asian; Christian; Modern Western; Islamic; Hindu; Buddhist; Chinese and Japanese; African and Other.

Parent Institution. Harvard University, private and nonsectarian,was established in1636 by the General Court of the Colony of Massachusetts Bay and was opened for instruction in 1638. The University is coeducational in 13 of its divisions with the exception of Harvard College which admits men only to its undergraduate curriculum. Radcliffe College is a women's undergraduate college closely associated with the University and offers a liberal arts curriculum taught by the Harvard Faculty of Arts and Sciences.

Community Environment. Settled in 1630, Cambridge, Massachusetts has been the home of such famous writers as Henry Wadsworth Longfellow, James Russell Lowell, and Oliver Wendell Holmes. The city has many historical places of interest as well as museums. It is a suburb of Boston, three miles away. Known as the "University City," Cambridge is served by the Boston Metropolitan Transit System and railroads.

Religious Denomination. Nondenominational.

Religious Emphasis. Liberal.

Accreditation. New England Association of Schools and Colleges.

Term System. Semester.

Admission Requirements. Applicants to undergraduate programs must be high school graduates with high scholastic abilities; SAT and three Achievement Tests; admission is extremely competitive and selective; high school 18 units including 4 English, 4 math, 3 lab science, 3 foreign language, 3 social studies, 1 fine arts.

Tuition and Fees. Tuition $9,800 per year, board and room $3,560; student fees $740. Fees for graduate courses vary.

Financial Aid. Financial aid is available and is based on need.

Library Facilities. The libraries include approximately 11 million volumes and 3 million microforms.

Hebrew College
43 Hawes Street
Brookline, MA 02146   (617) 232-8710

Administration. Dr. Eli Grad, President and Dean of Faculty; Dr. Michael Libenson, Associate Dean.

General Description. Hebrew College is a nonsectarian, coeducational institution of Judaic studies serving the needs of serious students and persons wishing to familiarize themselves with the rich Judaic heritage. The College offers undergraduate and graduate degree programs with concentrations in all Judaic disciplines: Hebrew language and literature, the Bible, Rabbinic literature, Jewish history, Jewish thought, and contemporary Jewish studies. Hebrew College offers an intimate student-faculty ratio with ready accessibility to renowned scholars in all areas of Judaic studies. Degrees granted are: Bachelor of Jewish Education, Bachelor of Hebrew Literature, Master of Jewish Education, and Master of Arts in Judaic Studies. A Teacher's Diploma is also awarded. Hebrew College is a constituent agency of the Combined Jewish Philanthropies.

Community Environment. Hebrew College occupies 2 buildings in Brookline, Massachusetts, a sizeable suburb of Boston. The area has public libraries, Antique Auto Museum, hospitals, and excellent shopping facilities. President John F. Kennedy was born here.

Religious Denomination. Jewish.

Accreditation. New England Association of Schools and Colleges.

Term System. Semester.

Faculty for Degree Programs in Religion. Total 35.

Admission Requirements. Undergraduate admission is based on secondary school records and recommendations along with scores achieved on scholastic aptitude tests and college board examinations, or suitable equivalents. Graduate admission is based on degrees earned at accredited institutions and recommendations.

Tuition and Fees. Tuition $1,500 per academic year; part-time tuition $95 per semester credit; registration fee $10; graduation fee $25.

Financial Aid. Applications for grants and/or loans are processed on the basis of demonstrated financial need.

Library Facilities. The Jacob and Rose Grossman Library and the Lawrence Jay and Anne Cable Rubenstein Library, together, constitute a nationally acclaimed facility of 85,000 volumes of Hebraica and Judaica. The Hebrew College Libraries belong to the Fenway Library Consortium which consists of eleven academic libraries and the library of the Museum of Fine Arts. The consortium has over 1 million volumes.

Religious Services/Activities. A continuing program of lectures and lecture series brings to the College community outstanding scholars who present elements of wisdom from the accumulated experience of the Jewish heritage.

Degree Programs

The Bachelor of Jewish Education is awarded to students who comply with the requirements for a Teacher's Diploma and who have also completed no less than 60 semester credits in general academic subjects, meeting specific distribution requirements at a college of recognized standing. The Bachelor of Hebrew Literature is awarded to students who have completed 104 semester credits (including the specific requirements in an area of concentration other than education, and in the various subject areas as prescribed by the faculty), and who have also completed no less than 60 semester credits in general academic subjects, meeting specific distribution requirements at a college of recognized standing. Courses of instruction are offered in the following areas of concentration: Bible, Hebrew Language, Hebrew Literature, Jewish History, Talmud and Midrash, Jewish Education, Jewish Thought and Philosophy, and Contemporary Jewish Studies. Degree candidates are required to be proficient in understanding, reading, speaking, and writing Hebrew.

The Master of Arts in Judaic Studies and the Master of Jewish Education are offered through the Graduate Division. Concentration may be based on either a subject area or in an interdisciplinary manner on a historical period, a genre of literature, or another acceptable unifying academic principle approved by the Faculty Committee. The Master's degree requires 30 credits in graduate studies of which at least 20 must be in the candidate's chosen area of concentration.

Special Programs

A Teacher's Diploma is awarded upon successful completion of the required 104 semester credits, including no less than 18 semester credits in Jewish education, student teaching, and the various subject areas as prescribed by the faculty.

Merrimack College
Department of Religious Studies
Turnpike Street
North Andover, MA 01845   (617) 683-7111

Administration. Dr. John E. Deegan, O.S.A., President; Dr. Francis E. Griggs, Jr., Vice President for Academic Affairs and Dean of the College; Rabbi Samuel J. Fox, Ph.D., Chairman, Department of Religious Studies.

General Description. The study of religion at Merrimack College is not designed to elicit particular confessional commitments from the student body. The academic study of religion transcends rather than supplants individual confessional commitments. The program for a major in Religious Studies is, therefore, designed to promote an understanding and intellectual grasp of religion as an important human concern and an influential force in history. The Ministry concentration of the Religious Studies major is designed to develop an integrated grasp of theological theory and practical skills in Christian ministry. The Bachelor of Arts in Religious Studies is offered.

Parent Institution. Merrimack College is a small, comprehensive, modern Catholic center of higher learning, reflecting in its policies the teaching traditions of the founding Order of St. Augustine. The College has Divisions of Arts and Sciences (Humanities, Social Sciences, and Science and Engineering), Business Administration, and Continuing Education. Because liberal arts constitutes a primary commitment, programs in all divisions carry a core of Humanities and Social Sciences intended to provide a broad framework within which a degree of specialization will fit. The College places high value on philosophy and theology which are incorporated into the program for every student.

Community Environment. Located in the towns of Andover and North Andover, Merrimack College is 25 miles north of Boston and a mile south of the city of Lawrence in the Merrimack River Valley. Many worlds converge upon this area: a Yankee world of white meeting houses and colonial mansions; a world of immigrant heritage from which workers came to staff the mills of a once flourishing woolen capital; and a newer world of high technology industries and fine suburban homes.

Religious Denomination. Roman Catholic.

Religious Emphasis. Liberal.

Accreditation. New England Association of Schools and Colleges.

Term System. Semester.

Enrollment in Degree Programs in Religion 1984–85. Total 7; men 4, women 3.

Degrees in Religion Awarded 1984–85. Bachelor of Arts in Religious Studies 3; men 3.

Faculty for Degree Programs in Religion. Total 7; full-time 7.

Admission Requirements. Graduation from an approved secondary school with specific entrance units applicable to the academic major to be pursued; test results of SAT or ACT; recommendation from a teacher or guidance counselor.

Tuition and Fees. Tuition $3,100 per term; room and board $1,750 per term.

Financial Aid. The College offers a variety of scholarships, loans, grants, and employment opportunties.

Housing. Dormitories, townhouses, and off-campus facilities are available.

Library Facilities. The McQuade Library houses a collection of 90,000 volumes and 900 periodicals.

Religious Services/Activities. Campus Ministry is responsible for the spiritual life of the campus. The campus community gathers daily for Eucharist; each Sunday is a special eucharistic liturgy. The Merrimack Out-Reach Experience offers retreat weekends every semester. Liturgical planning and music are also given emphasis in serving the community.

Degree Programs

The Bachelor of Arts with a major in Religious Studies requires the completion of ten courses in Religious Studies (two of which fulfill the institutional requirements) plus three cognate courses. The areas which must be covered are: Biblical Studies, Systematics, Ecclesial Studies, History of Religions, Religious Studies Electives, and Cognates. The Young Adult Ministry concentration of the Religious Studies major is designed to develop an integrated grasp of theological theory and practical skills in Christian ministry. Students in this concentration should have a foundational knowledge of the basic human dynamics, structures, and dysfunctions of social groups and processes. Twelve courses in Religious Studies (two of which fulfill the institutional requirements) plus three cognate courses are required for a major in Young Adult Ministry. The areas which must be covered are: Biblical Studies, Systematics, Ecclesial Studies, History of Religions, Ministry Studies, Religious Studies Electives, and Cognates.

Special Programs

The Division of Continuing Education offers night courses, summer programs, and coordinates day courses for adult students.

St. Hyacinth College and Seminary

66 School Street
Granby, MA 01033   (413) 467-7191

Administration. Rev. Alexander Cymerman, OFM Conv., Chief Executive Officer; Rev. Linus DeSantis, OFM Conv., Registrar.

General Description. St. Hyacinth College and Seminary is a Franciscan institution of higher learning which seeks to prepare its students, both religious and lay, to assume roles of leadership and service in the Church, society, and the Franciscan community.

The Conventual Franciscan Friars of the St. Anthony of Padua Province sought to establish a seminary on the 525 acres of land upon which St. Hyacinth College and Seminary is now located. In 1926, the cornerstone was laid and the institution was named and placed under the patronage of St. Hyacinth. A Philosophical-Theological program was established and continued until 1943 when the program was transferred to Ellicott City, Maryland. In 1957, the Scholastic Commission of the St. Anthony Province decided to consolidate all college studies at St. Hyacinth Seminary and in 1958, St. Hyacinth College and Seminary was granted its charter. In 1961, the St. Anthony of Padua Province and the Immaculate Province of Conventual Franciscan Friars decided to consolidate their seminary systems. Accordingly, St. Hyacinth's became the college department of the system, and St. Anthony-on-Hudson became the professional graduate-theology department.

Community Environment. St. Hyacinth's is located in the town of Granby, County of Hampshire, Massachusetts, north of Holyoke and Springfield on Route 202. It is accessible by automobile via the Massachusetts Turnpike and Interstates 91 and 291. The Amtrak system supplies train service to Springfield.

Religious Denomination. Roman Catholic.

Accreditation. New England Association of Schools and Colleges.

Term System. Semester; summer session (when scheduled).

Enrollment in Degree Programs in Religion 1984–85. Bachelor of Arts.

Faculty for Degree Programs in Religion. Total 40.

Admission Requirements. Diploma from recognized secondary institution; C average in courses of college preparatory curriculum.

Tuition and Fees. Tuition $100 per credit hour; room and board $1,500 per semester; fees where applicable.

Financial Aid. Financial aid program includes Pell Grants, Gilbert Matching Scholarship Grants; Guaranteed Student Loan Program.

Housing. On campus housing provided only for those students pursuing a religious vocation to priesthood and brotherhood.

Library Facilities. The Kolbe Memorial Library houses 100,000 volumes. The major composition of the Library's collections is in the fields of Philosophy and Theology. Special features of the holdings include a collection of Franciscan works, collections of Polish materials and pre-1800 volumes. There is a growing collection of books, articles, and memorabilia devoted to St. Maximilian Kolbe, the Franciscan saint martyred at Auschwitz in 1940 and canonized by Pope John Paul II in 1983.

Religious Services/Activities. Full formation program of liturgical and paraliturgical programs of personal and communal spiritual enrichment.

Degree Programs

The Bachelor of Arts degree with a major in Philosophy requires the completion of 120 credit hours. This includes certain core requirements in the behavioral and natural sciences, mathematics, and oral and written communication, as well as literature, history, and theology; 30 credit hours in the Philosophy major; and 18 hours in a minor, an area of concentration other than Philosophy.

St. John's Seminary College

197 Foster Street
Brighton, MA 02135   (617) 254-2610

Administration. Most Rev. Alfred C. Hughes, Rector and President; Rev. Thomas J. Daly, Vice Rector; Rev. Frederick J. Murphy, Dean of the College.

General Description. St. John's Seminary College prepares students from the Archdiocese of Boston, and from other dioceses sponsored by the local bishop, for eventual entry into a school of theology. The major focus of study is philosophy and the liberal arts. There is an extensive program of spiritual formation of the seminarians.

Parent Institution. St. John's Seminary prepares Catholic men for ordination to the Roman Catholic priesthood. It accepts students from its own seminary college, and from other colleges. Seminarians must be sponsored by their own bishop.

Community Environment. The campus of St. John's Seminary College is located on Commonwealth Avenue in Brighton, a suburb of Boston. The eastern portion of the campus, bounded by Foster Street, is the site of St. Clement's Hall which serves the College. The School of Theology is located on the west side of the campus, bounded by Lake Street.

Religious Denomination. Roman Catholic.

Accreditation. New England Association of Schools and Colleges; Association of Theological Schools in the United States and Canada.

Term System. Semester; no summer term.

Enrollment in Degree Programs in Religion 1984–85. Total 79; men 79.

Admission Requirements. Letters of recommendation; academic and psychological testing program; interviews with faculty; high school/college transcripts.

Tuition and Fees. Tuition $1,050 per semester; room and board $1,050 per semester.

Financial Aid. Seminary scholarships, Pell Grant, College Work-Study Program; state scholarships.

Housing. All students reside in the Seminary during the school year.

Library Facilities. The Seminary Library includes more than 120,000 volumes. The collection has been assembled in the light of the Seminary curricula of both the College of Liberal Arts and the School of Theology.

Religious Services/Activities. The common spiritual life of the seminary centers on the daily offering of the Eucharist and morning and evening prayer. Retreats are held periodically to provide an opportunity for sustained prayer and reflection on the Christian life and ministry. Days of Recollection, Bible, and Penitential services offer the student the richness of Christian liturgical experience.

Degree Programs

The Bachelor of Arts degree program provides the student with the intellectual discipline and cultural background which will prepare him for the program of studies in the School of Theology and for future service in the community. While all students major in Philosophy, a number of elective courses are open to them.

Special Programs

The Seminary also offers an Apostolic Works Program (community outreach) of 5 hours per week. There are also programs in Spiritual Development.

Swedenborg School of Religion
48 Sargent Street
Newton, MA 02158   (617) 244-0504

General Description. The General Convention of the New Jerusalem maintains the School of Religion to prepare a trained and consecrated ministry. It was founded in 1866 and was incorporated as the New Church Theological School in 1881. The School is not a degree-granting institution.

Community Environment. The School is comprised of three buildings and is located in Newton, a Boston suburban area.

Religious Denomination. Swedenborgian (The New Jerusalem).

Term System. Semester.

Enrollment in Degree Programs in Religion 1984–85. Total 11; men 5, women 6.

Admission Requirements. Bachelor of Arts degree or equivalent.

Tuition and Fees. Tuition $1,200 per year; housing $450; married students housing $900.

Financial Aid. Assistance from an Augmentation Fund is available.

Housing. Living accommodations are available for single students and families.

Library Facilities. The library contains 32,700 volumes.

Tufts University
Department of Religion
Medford, MA 02155   (617) 381-3170

Administration. Professor Howard E. Hunter, Chairman, Department of Religion.

General Description. The Department of Religion concerns itself with the various expressions of religion encountered in human experience. It offers the student the opportunity to investigate the field of religion in both its functional and theoretical aspects. Courses are designed to give a broad cultural appreciation of the subject in accordance with the principles of a liberal education.

Parent Institution. Tufts University was founded by members of the Universalist denomination in 1850 and was then known as the Tufts Institution of Learning. While it has long since become a nonsectarian institution, it remains true to a tradition of a liberal education. The University offers both undergraduate and graduate degree programs in many disciplines.

Community Environment. The University is located in Medford, five miles northwest of Boston.

Religious Denomination. Nondenominational.

Accreditation. New England Association of Schools and Colleges.

Term System. Semester.

Admission Requirements. All candidates are evaluated individually on the basis of credentials submitted for admission. Most applicants have graduated from high school in the top 15 percent of their class. SAT and three achievement tests required.

Tuition and Fees. Tuition $9,280 per year; room and board $4,280; student fees $76.

Financial Aid. Tufts University students are eligible for a full range of financial aid in the form of university, state, and federal scholarships, long-term loans, and college work-study.

Housing. Dormitory accommodations are available on campus.

Library Facilities. The Nils Yngve Wessell Library is located on the Medford campus. The resources of the University libraries include more than a million and a half books, microforms, slides, pamphlets, and government publications.

Degree Programs

The major in Religion leading to the Bachelor of Arts degree requires the completion of eight courses, four of which must be chosen as one each from the four groups of courses offered: Philosophy and Theology; Literature and Culture; Western Religions (Judaism, Christianity, Islam); and Eastern Religions. Additional courses are also offered by the Department.

Weston School of Theology
3 Phillips Place
Cambridge, MA 02138   (617) 492-1960

Administration. Dr. Edward M. O'Flaherty, S.J., President; Dr. Richard J. Clifford, S.J., Dean.

General Description. The central mission of Weston School of Theology is the preparation of approved candidates for the Catholic priesthood. Related to and in part constitutive of that central mission are professional education of laity and religious for ministry in the Catholic Church; continuing and advanced education for those already engaged in these ministries; theological research and publication; ecumenical cooperation in education for ministry; and theological enrichment for others to the extent compatible with ministerial education.

Weston exists to provide such theological and ministerial preparation for the priesthood for members of the Society of Jesus. The School is one of two national theological centers sponsored by the American Assistancy of the Society of Jesus. It also provides such an education for the priesthood for several other religious orders of men who regularly send their candidates to Weston. Weston is one of the founding and continuing members of the Boston Theological Institute, a consortium of 7 theological seminaries exchanging facilities and students.

Community Environment. Weston is located in one of

the most historic parts of the country. Much of America's colonial and revolutionary past began here. In all seasons, particularly in the autumn and in the spring, New England has great natural charm and a mellow beauty. The Atlantic Ocean and the Berkshire, White, and Green Mountains are within easy driving distance.

Religious Denomination. Roman Catholic.

Accreditation. Association of Theological Schools in the United States and Canada.

Term System. Semester; no summer term.

Enrollment in Degree Programs in Religion 1984–85. Total 137; men 102, women 35.

Degrees in Religion Awarded 1984–85. Master of Theological Studies 13; men 7, women 6. Master of Divinity 26; men 21, women 5. Master of Theology 10; men 10.

Faculty for Degree Programs in Religion. Total 27; full-time 13, part-time 14.

Admission Requirements. All applicants seeking admission as full-time degree seeking students must submit an application form, three letters of recommendation, and a personal statement; transcripts of college and graduate school records; Graduate Record Examination or Miller Analogies Test scores. The individual programs also have admission requirements.

Tuition and Fees. Tuition $4,100 per year; registration fee $25 per semester; graduation fee $50; part-time tuition $550 per course.

Financial Aid. Resources for financial aid at the disposition of the School are limited and students are urged to explore all other possible sources. Any aid from the School is limited to some tuition remission.

Housing. Weston does not provide housing. A Housing Coordinator assists students in finding housing.

Library Facilities. The libraries of Weston School of Theology and the Episcopal Divinity School form a single operation under a common staff. Together they provide over 220,000 volumes, including over 800 periodical titles. The history of English Christianity is especially well served, since the two institutions enrich the whole collection from both Catholic and Anglican perspectives. Continental European theology is a particular strength of the Weston Library. Some 4,000 volumes pertaining to Islam and the Arab world comprise another special Weston collection.

Religious Services/Activities. There is a noon-time liturgy each day in the Chapel of the Holy Spirit and one day each week in St. John's Chapel. Other services are organized appropriate to the liturgical season.

Degree Programs

The Master of Theological Studies degree program provides students with general theological knowledge through the study of the various dimensions of theology, while also permitting them to concentrate in one of five areas: Bible, Church History, Historical-Systematic Theology, Moral Theology, Spirituality. A two-year program, it serves as the first graduate degree in theology. As a disciplined course of study in Catholic theology, the program is designed for those planning to teach religion in secondary schools, for experienced church ministers preparing for a second career or desiring to deepen their knowledge of theology, for individuals considering further graduate work on the doctoral level, for those desiring to relate religion and their professional work in other areas, and for others seeking to deepen their knowledge of theology. The program is not designed to prepare individuals for priesthood or pastoral ministry.

The Master of Divinity degree program provides the foundational training necessary for leadership in ecclesial ministry. It is designed to assist both those preparing for the Catholic priesthood and those seeking to serve in the other public ministries of the Church. The program stresses disciplined theological study, a superior command of the documents of the Christian tradition and the official teachings of the Church, and an understanding of the meaning, development, and relevance of Christian revelation in church and world.

The Master of Theology is a one-year post-Master of Divinity program designed to enable students to achieve a mastery of resources in a specific area. Two program options are offered. Option A involves a specialization in one of the theological disciplines. Concentrations are available in Biblical Studies, Historical-Systematic Technology, Moral Theology, and Spirituality. Option B focuses on an advanced understanding and competence in a particular form of church ministry. This option leads to specialization in a particular area of ministry through a combination of course work and field-based learning. Possible areas of specialization include ministry in educational contexts; social ministry; spirituality and spiritual direction.

The Licentiate in Sacred Theology degree program is to assist students, who have a general knowledge of theology and of scientific methodology, to study one area of theology in depth and to acquire skill in research methods. The Licentiate is the degree of the second cycle conferred by the Ecclesiastical Faculty of Weston and is a two-year program.

Special Programs

Weston Fellows - A Sabbatical Program is available for those who desire to update their theological and ministerial competence or who wish to acquire new skills. It is a non-degree program, either a full year or semester in length. Priests, religious women and brothers, lay men and lay women who have engaged in ministry for some years may make use of Weston's resources and become part of the Weston community of faith, learning, and worship.

The Minister-in-the-Vicinity Program makes it possible for those engaged in full-time professional ministry in a church setting within the Archdiocese of Boston to audit one course each semester, paying only the special registration fee of $50.

Wheaton College
Department of Religion
Norton, MA 02766   (617) 746-2356

Administration. Dr. Alice Frey Emerson, President; Dr. Hannah F. Goldberg, Provost and Academic Vice President; Andronike Janus, Dean of Wheaton College; Dr. Charles Conrad Forman, Chair, Department of Religion.

General Description. The Department of Religion offers a major in Religion. Also, majors in Religion and Philosophy, and Religion and History are offered jointly with the respective departments. The Department also offers a Dual Degree Program with Andover Newton Theological School which prepares students for careers in Religion. The program permits the completion of requirements for the Bachelor of Arts degree from Wheaton and the degree Master of Arts in Religion from Andover Newton in five years.

Parent Institution. Founded in 1834, Wheaton has grown and changed during its first century and a half, but its central mission remains the same: to educate women of promise for successful lives in an increasingly complex and challenging world. At the heart of the curriculum is an historic commitment to the liberal arts. The academic programs offer a rich blend of the traditional and the contemporary.

Community Environment. Wheaton's 300-acre campus is located in Norton, Massachusetts, 45 minutes from Boston and 20 minutes from Providence, Rhode Island. It contains more than 50 buildings. It has access to railroad and bus services. Community services facilities, recreational and cultural pursuits are available in the neighboring cities.

Religious Denomination. None.

Accreditation. New England Association of Schools and Colleges.

Term System. Semester; no summer term.

Degrees in Religion Awarded 1984–85. Bachelor of Arts 2; women 2.

Faculty for Degree Programs in Religion. Total 3; full-time 2, part-time 1.

Admission Requirements. Although Wheaton does not rigidly prescribe entrance requirements, the College strongly recommends the following high school curriculum: four years of English with emphasis on composition skills, three or four years of mathematics, three or four years of one or two foreign languages, three years of social studies, and two or three years of laboratory science. Candidates must submit scores on SAT or ACT. A personal interview is strongly recommended.

Tuition and Fees. Tuition $9,950; residence fee $1,945; student activities fee $90; automobile registration fee $40 per year.

Financial Aid. Awarded in three basic forms: grants and scholarships, loans, and student employment.

Housing. Residence halls are located on-campus.

Library Facilities. The Madeleine Clark Wallace Library currently holds more than 251,000 volumes and 1,200 periodical titles.

Degree Programs

The Bachelor of Arts with a major in Religion (10 semester courses) includes a semester course in each of the following areas: Old Testament, New Testament, Post-Biblical History of the Jewish or Christian Tradition. There are other required courses and a Senior Major Proficiency Evaluation. The major in Religion and Philosophy, and Religion and History are offered jointly with the Departments of Philosophy and History respectively. The Departments of Religion and Classics have drawn up guidelines for an interdepartmental major in Ancient Studies. Minor concentrations are available in Religion, Bible, World Religions, Judaic Studies, Hebrew, and Christian Thought and History.

For information regarding Dual Degree Programs (A.B./M.A.) with Andover Newton Theological School, contact the Chair of the Religion Department, Wheaton College.

MICHIGAN

Adrian College
Department of Philosophy and Religion
110 South Madison Street

Adrian, MI 49221   (517) 265-5161

Administration. Dr. Donald S. Stanton, President; Dr. James F. Traer, Vice President and Dean for Academic Affairs; Dr. Fritz Detwiler, Chair, Department of Philosophy and Religion.

General Description. Adrian College's Department of Philosophy and Religion offers majors in philosophy, religion, and philosophy/religion. Faculty specializations are in the areas of religion and literature, Bible, church history, American religion, Native American religions, patristics, and philosophical theology. As an integral part of Adrian College's emphasis on liberal arts education the Department encourages majors to develop an academic program emphasizing breadth in the humanities and provides students throughout the college an opportunity to think philosophically and religiously. The Department also offers students preparation for seminary.

Parent Institution. Adrian College is a private liberal arts college. Its mission is to maintain a personalized learning environment that stimulates individual growth and academic excellence. Founded by Methodists and chartered in in 1859, the College remains actively affiliated with The United Methodist Church. The College's commitment to pluralism reflects the social concerns of Christianity in general and the tradition of John Wesley in particular.

Community Environment. Adrian College is located in Adrian, Michigan, the county seat of Lenawee County in the southeastern part of the state. Adrian is a city of 22,000 people situated in the center of an agricultural, industrial, and recreational area. Nearby freeways provide easy access to the metropolitan areas of Detroit, Toledo, Chicago, Cleveland, and Pittsburgh. The campus is modern for a college celebrating its 125th anniversary in 1984. All but a few of the buildings were constructed in the last 25 years, but the ivy-covered 19th century walls of Downs Hall recall the College's long educational tradition.

Religious Denomination. The United Methodist Church.

Religious Emphasis. Liberal.

Accreditation. North Central Association of Colleges and Schools.

Term System. Quarter; summer term.

Enrollment in Degree Programs in Religion 1984–85. Total 5; men 4, women 1.

Degrees in Religion Awarded 1984–85. Bachelor of Arts 4; men 2, women 2.

Faculty for Degree Programs in Religion. Total 4; full-time 3, part-time 1.

Admission Requirements. Applicants should present at least 15 units of secondary school preparation, including three units of English, two units of mathematics, and remaining units in social sciences, laboratory sciences, and foreign languages. Students should maintain at least a 2.5 average in a college preparatory course of study and perform satisfactorily on either the ACT or SAT test.

Tuition and Fees. Tuition $5,522; comprehensive fee $254; room $806; board $1,216.

Financial Aid. Financial aid is secured through application. The Velma Knight Fund has been established specifically to aid pre-seminary or pre-professional students in religion. Scholarships from this fund are granted in addition to other aid available from the college.

Housing. Most resident students live in dormitories although off-campus housing is permitted for upperclass students.

Library Facilities. The library has holdings of 127,367 volumes of which 8,500 are in religion and philosophy. Special collections include the Swift Collection (books in Christianity) and the William A. Rush Collection.

Religious Services/Activities. Weekly chapel/convocation is optional; Major Cole (society of pre-seminary students), Newman Catholic Center (weekly Masses); Concerned Jewish Students; Religious Concerns Committee.

Degree Programs

Students majoring in Religion leading to the Bachelor of Arts degree complete a minimum of 27 hours of credit in Religion with at least one course in each of five major areas: Biblical, Historical, Theological, Ethical, and World Religions. A total of 124 hours is needed for graduation. Students majoring in Philosophy-Religion must complete a minimum of 27 semester hours of credit, including 12 hours in Religion and 12 hours in Philosophy.

Special Programs

An Associate of Arts degree in Religion is also offered by the Department as well as programs in continuing education for United Methodist pastors.

Albion College
Department of Religious Studies
Albion, MI 49224   (517) 629-5511

Administration. Dr. Frank S. Frick, Chairman, Department of Religious Studies.

General Description. The Department of Religious Studies offers courses that are intellectually stimulating and personally challenging in order to help students think critically about the meaning of life, and to explore the importance of religion for the individual and society. Conscious of Albion's religious heritage, attention is given to the fundamental importance of the Judeo-Christian tradition in the development of our Western cultural and intellectual life.

Parent Institution. The College was founded in 1835 as the Spring Arbor Seminary of the Methodist Church. The present name was adopted in 1861. Albion is a four-year liberal arts college, privately supported and related to The United Methodist Church. It has an enrollment of 1,600 students and awards the Associate and Bachelor degrees.

Community Environment. The campus of 90-acres is located in the town of Albion in south central Michigan. It is 90 miles west of Detroit and 175 miles east of Chicago.

Religious Denomination. United Methodist Church.

Accreditation. North Central Association of Colleges and Schools.

Term System. Semester.

Faculty for Degree Programs in Religion. Total 4.

Admission Requirements. Graduation from an accredited high school with 15 units; SAT or ACT.

Tuition and Fees. Tuition, fees, room and board (comprehensive fee) $9,792 per year.

Financial Aid. Loans, scholarships, and work opportunities are available.

Housing. Student residence halls are available on campus. Housing for married students is available in the College-operated Burns Street apartments.

Library Facilities. The Mudd Learning Center/Stockwell Memorial Library complex houses a 250,000-volume general collection.

Religious Services/Activities. The setting for student

ministry is ecumenical in nature. The College chaplain is a United Methodist minister and is responsible for coordinating religious activities on campus.

Degree Programs

The major in Religious Studies leading to the Bachelor of Arts degree requires a minimum of eight units in Religious Studies or designated cognate courses. The major must include one unit from each of the following six groups: Comparative Religions, Biblical Studies, Christian Theology, Ethics, Religion and Imaginative Literature, Religion and Psychology.

Alma College
Department of Religious Studies
614 West Superior Street
Alma, MI 48801   (517) 463-7139

Administration. Oscar E. Remick, President.

General Description. Alma College is a private liberal arts college founded by the Presbyterian Church of Michigan in 1886. It grants the degrees Bachelor of Arts, Bachelor of Science, Bachelor of Fine Arts, and Bachelor of Music. Major areas of concentration are offered by 21 departments in addition to teacher certification in elementary and secondary education. The Department of Religious Studies offers a major in the field.

Community Environment. The College is located in Alma at the center of Michigan's lower peninsula. The 83-acre campus has 24 buildings.

Religious Denomination. Presbyterian Church (U.S.A.).

Accreditation. North Central Association of Colleges and Schools.

Term System. Semester (4-1-4 plan).

Admission Requirements. Graduation from an accredited high school; SAT or ACT.

Tuition and Fees. Tuition $6,910 per year; room $1,236; board $1,560.

Financial Aid. Assistance is available through Alma College scholarships, State of Michigan scholarships and grants, federal grants and loans, and/or student loans.

Housing. Students who are not living with parents must reside in college residence halls.

Library Facilities. The library houses over 145,000 volumes.

Religious Services/Activities. The Chapel Affairs Committee coordinates all religious activities on campus.

Degree Programs

The study of religion includes exploration of the nature and meaning of the religious dimensions of human experience, study of the major traditions which remember and transmit religious experience and expressions, encouragement of an inquisitive, analytical, and open approach to multiple religious perspectives, and exploration of the value frameworks in various religious perspectives to help clarify students' own values. The major leading to the Bachelor of Arts degree requires 36 credits in Religious Studies. The degree requires a total of 136 semester hours.

Andrews University
Seventh-day Adventist Theological Seminary
Berrien Springs, MI 49104   (616) 471-3536

Administration. Dr. W. Richard Lesher, President; Dr. Richard W. Schwarz, Vice President for Academic Administration; Dr. Gerhard F. Hasel, Dean, S.D.A. Theological Seminary.

General Description. The Seventh-day Adventist Theological Seminary has the task of training candidates for effective leadership in ministry and teaching for the Seventh-day Adventist Church. This task is grounded in the Biblical, historical, and theological witness of Christianity at large and particularly as understood within the context of the Seventh-day Adventist Church. The Seminary grants the degrees Master of Divinity, Master of Arts in Pastoral Ministry, Master of Theology, Doctor of Ministry, Doctor of Philosophy, and Doctor of Theology. The Master of Arts degree (Joint Program in Religion) is offered by the School of Graduate Studies but utilizes the facilities of the Seminary.

Parent Institution. Andrews University is a Seventh-day Adventist institution of higher education. It was established to provide a high quality education in the arts and sciences and in vocational pre-professional education for the youth of the Adventist church. High priority is given to maintaining a campus environment favorable for the spiritual, intellectual, social, and physical development of students. The University consists of six schools: College of Arts and Sciences, College of Technology, School of Graduate Studies, School of Business, School of Education, Seventh-day Adventist Theological Seminary.

Community Environment. The University campus of approximately 1,600 acres provides a spacious setting for the development of a modern university. There are now 23 instructional buildings, 3 large residence halls, and 5 apartment complexes. In addition, 12 industrial and plant-service buildings house auxiliary enterprises.

Religious Denomination. Seventh-day Adventist Church.

Religious Emphasis. Evangelical.

Accreditation. North Central Association of Colleges and Schools; Association of Theological Schools in the United States and Canada.

Term System. Quarter; summer term.

Enrollment in Degree Programs in Religion 1984–85. Total 450; men 440, women 10. (These figures are for the 1985-1986 school year.)

Degrees in Religion Awarded 1984–85. Master of Divinity 105. Doctor of Ministry 6. Doctor of Philosophy 4. Doctor of Theology 1. (These figures are for the year 1983.)

Faculty for Degree Programs in Religion. Total 48; full-time 32, part-time 16.

Admission Requirements. Baccalaureate degree or its equivalent from an accredited senior college.

Tuition and Fees. Master of Divinity $365 per quarter; Master of Arts $138 per credit; Doctoral program $175 per credit; room and board $837 to $1,004 per quarter.

Financial Aid. Awards and financial assistance vary according to the student's need and the availability of funds.

Housing. Dormitories and married student apartments are available.

Library Facilities. The James White Library collection contains over 1 million volumes. The Seminary Library has its own reference collection of over 112,000 volumes and receives 788 periodicals. Strengths in the Seminary Library are in the various areas of Biblical studies, both monographs and periodicals. An attempt is made to collect exhaustively materials having to do with the Biblical books of Daniel and Revelation and the subject of the Sabbath. A Seventh-day Adventist Archive and Research Center is a department of the James White Library. It holds material on the history and development of the Advent Movement and the Seventh-day Adventist Church since 1844. Also housed are the Advent Source and Conditionalist Faith Collections made up of several thousand items dealing with the origins of Adventists and history of the doctrine of conditional immortality.

Religious Services/Activities. The Campus Ministry of the University emphasizes personal religion and makes provision for students to participate in pursuits which nurture spiritual growth. Seminary students and faculty worship together regularly in chapel. All students are required to attend at least one chapel service per week, as well as the weekend worship services.

Degree Programs

The Master of Divinity program is the basic preparation for the Adventist ministry. It is recommended as the basic training for the Adventist ministry by the General Conference of Seventh-day Adventists and the North American Division. It is a three-year professional program in nine quarters with at least 129-135 credits. The cognitive components involve instruction and coursework by the six departments of the Seminary in Old and New Testament, Theological and Ethical, Church Historical, and Mission as well as Church and Ministry Studies. The Master of Theology program provides an opportunity for one year of specialized academic study beyond the Master of Divinity degree.

The Master of Arts in Pastoral Ministry degree is a professional program that provides opportunity for mature persons in ministry, who have served at least twelve years (or are normally thirty-five years of age or older), and whose ministerial functions make it impossible to study at the Seminary for extended periods of time, to engage in a study program consisting of 72 credits of professional training leading to a six-quarter degree. The curriculum consists of studies in the areas of Biblical Studies, Theology, Church and Ministry, Church History, Mission, and electives.

The Doctor of Ministry is a professional degree for persons who are qualified to pursue advanced professional study and practice of ministry. In keeping with the understanding of the ministry in the Seventh-day Adventist Church, this program is designed specifically to augment competencies for pastoral-evangelistic ministry.

The Doctor of Philosophy in Religion degree has as its primary purpose the providing of teacher-scholars for church-operated colleges and seminaries around the world. The program is designed to train individuals to be able to do original and responsible research, to be equipped with skills and methods appropriate to genuine scholarship, to be proficient in applying sound and valid principles of biblical interpretation and historical research, and to be effective in the classroom. The degree program is offered in the areas of New Testament Studies, Old Testament Studies, Theological Studies, and Adventist Studies.

The primary purpose of advanced studies leading to the Doctor of Theology degree is to help provide teacher-scholars in the fields of Biblical and Theolgocial Studies for the Seventh-day Adventist Church. The program is offered in two fields of study: Biblical Studies with concentrations in Languages and Literature, Archaeology and History, and Exegesis and Theology; Theological Studies with concentrations in Historical Theology and Systematic Theology. A minimum of two academic years of formal courses or not less than six quarters of full-time study (12 credits per quarter) is required of each student.

Aquinas College
Department of Religious Studies
1607 Robinson Road, S.E.
Grand Rapids, MI 49506   (616) 459-8281

Administration. Norbert J. Hruby, President.

General Description. Aquinas College was founded by the Dominican Sisters of Grand Rapids in 1886. It became the first Catholic college to become coeducational in 1931. The College offers a choice of more than 40 majors and grants the Associate, Bachelor, and Master's degrees. A major in Religious Studies leading to the Bachelor of Arts degree is offered by the Department of Religious Studies.

Community Environment. The campus of 70 acres is located in the city of Grand Rapids, 60 miles northwest of Lansing, the state capital.

Religious Denomination. Roman Catholic.

Accreditation. North Central Association of Colleges and Schools.

Term System. Semester.

Admission Requirements. Graduation from an accredited high school with completion of 15 units; ACT or SAT required.

Tuition and Fees. Tuition $2,800 per semester; room and board $2,436 per year.

Financial Aid. Financial aid in the form of federal and state assistance, loans, scholarships, and college work-study is available.

Housing. Students reside in residence halls.

Library Facilities. The library contains over 110,000 volumes.

Religious Services/Activities. The Campus Ministry Team serves the entire Aquinas community. Masses and other liturgical services are celebrated regularly in the Pastoral Center.

Degree Programs

A major in Religious Studies requires a minimum of 36 semester hours including prescribed courses plus at least one course in each of the areas of Sacred Scripture, Christian Morality, and Liturgy. The Department offers a minor in Religious Studies, Liturgy, and Religious Education as well as cognates in Liturgical Music, Pastoral Ministry, and Religious Education. The Bachelor's degree requires the completion of a total of 124 semester hours.

Calvin Theological Seminary
3233 Burton Street, S.E.
Grand Rapids, MI 49506   (616) 957-6034

Administration. Dr. James A. DeJong, President; Harold Dekker, Academic Dean.

General Description. Calvin Theological Seminary is an institution of the Christian Reformed Church in North America for the scholarly study of the Reformed faith and for the education of persons in and for Christ's ministry. The Seminary's primary task is to educate persons for ordained ministry. To achieve this, the Seminary brings together committed students, an excellent faculty, and a contemporary program. The Seminary strives for high standards in theological excellence and professional competence. It does so in the spirit of its motto, inherited from John Calvin and preserved in its official seal: "My heart I offer to you, Lord, promptly and sincerely."

In addition to its graduate-level degree programs and several special program offerings, the Seminary presents continuing education workshops. Some of these are scheduled in response to specific requests of local or regional church bodies; others are promoted by the Seminary, to which pastors and church education leaders are invited.

Community Environment. Calvin Seminary is located on Burton Street near the East Beltline (M37) in southeast Grand Rapids, Michigan. The Seminary shares with Calvin College the aesthetically pleasing 165-acre Knollcrest campus of trees, lawns, and architecturally unified buildings. The city of Grand Rapids provides a growing cultural base for the area's six colleges. It has a lively interest in the arts, as evidenced by an active symphony orchestra, civic theater, ballet association, and art museum.

Religious Denomination. Christian Reformed Church in North America.

Religious Emphasis. Reformed.

Accreditation. Association of Theological Schools in the United States and Canada.

Term System. Quarter.

Enrollment in Degree Programs in Religion 1984–85. Total 238; men 224, women 14. These figures are for the 1985-86 school year.

Degrees in Religion Awarded 1984–85. Master of Theology 6; men 5, women 1. Master of Divinity 27; men 27. Master of Church Education 3; men 2, women 1. Master of Theological Studies 1; women 1. Special Program for Ministerial Candidacy 5; men 5.

Faculty for Degree Programs in Religion. Total 25; full-time 17, part-time 8. Support staff 4.

Admission Requirements. Completed application form accompanied by an autobiography, a recent photograph, and application fee of $10; certificate of good health; transcripts of all academic work beyond high school; recommendation from the governing body of the church in which the applicant holds membership; recommendation from the department of the applicant's major area of study; two communication evaluations: one for English and one for speech; interview with members of the admissions and standards committee. Any person who possesses an undergraduate theological degree from an accredited seminary, has a good academic record, and desires to take seminary graduate courses for continuing education is eligible for admission to graduate studies. Admission to candidacy for the Master of Theology degree is a separate step and involves additional requirements.

Tuition and Fees. Tuition $56 per credit hour.

Financial Aid. Financial aid resources include Classical Aid (for students who are members of the Christian Reformed Church and who are preparing for the ministry in that denomination), Specialized Funds, Public Funds, and Seminary Administered Programs.

Housing. Seminary on-campus housing is available to full-time married and single international and Canadian students on a first-come basis. Assistance is offered in finding off-campus housing.

Library Facilities. The Calvin Library has a collection of 360,000 books and bound periodicals. Of special interest to theological students and researchers are the religious periodical catalog, the sermon index, the adjacent Meeter Center, and several special collections. Among the latter are the Calvin Research Collection, the Calvin Rare Book Collection, and the Colonial Origins Collection which consists of manuscripts, papers, documents, records, and archives of Christian Reformed leaders, congregations, and organizations.

Religious Services/Activities. Worship in the seminary chapel is an integral part of seminary life. Faculty members, students, and guests lead in songs, prayers, and brief meditations on Scripture. Classroom activities are supplemented with frequent lectures and presentations.

Degree Programs

The Master of Divinity program is designed primarily for persons wishing to prepare themselves for the ordained ministry. The program seeks to integrate a classical theological curriculum with supervised field education in contemporary ministry. Normally a student will complete the program in four academic years. A total of 136 quarter hours is required.

The Master of Church Education is a program designed for persons wishing to prepare themselves for assuming positions of leadership in the church, particularly in its educational ministry. Normally it is a two-year program, combining background theological studies with a concentration of study and field experience in church education. A total of 86 quarter hours is required.

The Master of Ministry is a Native American theological education program designed to equip leaders for Native American churches. This is an alternate program for the mature Native American student seeking ordination. The Master of Ministry is a two-year program which integrates classical theological studies with supervised field education within the Native American culture and cross-culturally. A total of 86 quarter hours is required.

The Master of Theological Studies is a program designed for persons who do not seek ordination but desire theological education in support of various vocational objectives. Normally it is a two-year program and requires a student to concentrate in the area of Biblical or Theological Studies. A total of 94 quarter hours is required.

The Master of Theology degree is generally considered to be a post-Master of Divinity degree. The fields of specialization are Old Testament, New Testament, Church History, Systematic Theology, Philosophical and Moral Theology, Pastoral Theology, and Missiology. A special program in Pastoral Care and Counseling is also offered.

Special Programs

Other programs include Special Program for Ministerial Candidacy, Seminary Consortium for Urban Pastoral Education, Consortium for Pastoral Counseling Training, Clinical Pastoral Education, and Continuing Education Workshops.

Central Michigan University
Department of Religion
Moore Hall 422
Mt. Pleasant, MI 48859   (517) 774-3793

Administration. Arthur E. Ellis, Interim President; Dr. John E. Cantelon, Provost; Dr. William W. Reader, Chairperson, Department of Religion.

General Description. The Department of Religion has seven faculty members each with a specific area of expertise (Asian Religions, Islam, Christianity, Religion in

America, Bible, Ethics, and Society) and in any given semester has about 700 students enrolled in its classes. The Department offers both a major and a minor in Religion. The Religion Department is not sanctioned to, nor does it attempt to, prepare students for careers in religious work. Rather, it presents religion as an academic discipline, providing the opportunity to explore different systems of belief along with ethical and aesthetic values prominent in different cultures. The Department contributes considerably to the general education program of the University.

Parent Institution. Central Michigan University was founded in 1892 and presently is a medium-sized state supported institution with about 14,400 undergraduate and 1,500 graduate students. Its size, location, academic reputation, and competitive fees make it a popular choice among the state's college-bound high school students. It offers a wide range of Bachelor and Master degrees. The common base for all degree programs is a liberal education: one-quarter of the credits earned toward the Bachelor degree must fulfill general education requirements.

Community Environment. The University is located at the southern boundary of Mount Pleasant, Michigan, a city of 23,660, accessible from nearby U.S. and state highways. Campus beauty is cultivated in the belief that the quality of the physical surroundings affects the quality of learning. Mount Pleasant is located in the approximate center of the state. Ten lakes nearby offer excellent recreational facilities. There is an Indian reservation four miles east of the city.

Religious Denomination. None.

Accreditation. North Central Association of Colleges and Schools.

Term System. Semester; summer terms of 3, 6, and 12 weeks.

Degrees in Religion Awarded 1984–85. Bachelor of Science 9; men 4, women 5. Bachelor of Arts 2; men 2.

Faculty for Degree Programs in Religion. Total 8; full-time 7, part-time 1.

Admission Requirements. High school diploma or equivalent; transfer from community college or other college/university.

Tuition and Fees. Tuition state residents $47 per credit hour, non-residents $120 per credit hour; room and board (20 meals per week) $2,350 per year; single student and family housing apartments range from $235 to $247 per month.

Financial Aid. The University in conjunction with federal and state governments and private and civic organizations offers a variety of scholarship, grant, loan, and employment opportunities.

Housing. Residence halls and family housing apartments are available.

Library Facilities. The Park Library houses 750,000 volumes. The Clarke Historical Library located on the fourth floor has 60,000 books, periodicals, and extensive collections of manuscripts, maps, newspapers, and photographs relating to the history of Michigan and the Great Lakes area.

Religious Services/Activities. The University sponsors no religious activities, but a variety of local congregations serve the student body. There are also several self-organized student groups with religious orientation.

Degree Programs

The major in religion leading to the Bachelor of Arts or Bachelor of Science degrees is recommended for students planning graduate study in religion, theology, and related fields. Recommended minors include history, English, philosophy, foreign languages, anthropology, sociology, and psychology. Students majoring in religion are encouraged to include the study of a foreign language, ancient or modern; for an interest in Biblical studies, Greek, German, and French; for an interest in theology or the history of religions, German, French, Greek, and Latin. The major in religion consists of at least 30 hours, including specified components.

Concordia College
4090 Geddes Road
Ann Arbor, MI 48105   (313) 665-3691

Administration. Alan Harre, President.

General Description. Concordia College is a four-year coeducational college established and operated by the Lutheran Church-Missouri Synod. It is part of the fifteen-school system of colleges of the Synod. It offers a liberal arts curriculum to provide preprofessional training for students preparing to enter the service of the church. The College awards the Associate and Bachelor degrees.

Community Environment. The 234-acre campus is located in Ann Arbor, two miles east of the University of Michigan North Campus. It is situated on the former Earhart estate.

Religious Denomination. Lutheran Church-Missouri Synod.

Accreditation. North Central Association of Colleges and Schools.

Term System. Quarter.

Admission Requirements. High school graduation; ACT required.

Tuition and Fees. Tuition $3,448 per year; dormitory service fee $990; meal service $1,658; synodical tuition/deposit $100; student union fee $50.

Financial Aid. Various forms of financial assistance are available.

Housing. Sixteen student residences, each housing 32 students, are available on campus. Married students reside off campus.

Library Facilities. The library houses over 100,000 volumes.

Religious Services/Activities. The Spiritual Life Committee has a varied program of service opportunities.

Chapel and worship services are held in the Chapel of the Holy Trinity.

Degree Programs

In addition to a General Liberal Arts program, the College offers a Pre-Ministerial Program which provides the student with the traditional training preferred as the route to a seminary of The Lutheran Church-Missouri Synod. A Teacher Education Program prepares men and women for teaching positions in Lutheran elementary and secondary schools. These programs lead to the Bachelor's degree and the Lutheran Teacher Diploma. A Parish Assistant program is offered leading to the Bachelor of Arts degree. Students must meet all the requirements of the Bachelor of Arts in the General Liberal Arts Program, but with significant coursework in Religious Studies plus nine hours in Theology.

Detroit, University of
College of Liberal Arts
Department of Religious Studies
4001 West McNichols Road
Detroit, MI 48221   (313) 927-1000

Administration. Rev. Robert A. Mitchell, S.J., President; Dr. John O. Dwyer, Dean, College of Liberal Arts; Fr. Justin Kelly, S.J., Chairperson, Department of Religious Studies.

General Description. The Religious Studies Department of the University of Detroit offers courses leading to the Bachelor's and Master's degrees. The University's Religious Identity Statement affirms that the need for ultimate meaning is the most basic human need. The programs offered by the Department are designed to help the student become aware of some of the myriad ways humans have sought to fulfill that need and expressed their religious longings. The University, because of its roots in the Catholic tradition, places special emphasis on that tradition, while offering students a broad acquaintance with other traditions, Christian and non-Christian. The Department provides the courses necessary for students to fulfill their Religion requirements; all students must take a 3-credit course, and Liberal Arts students must take an additional 3-credit course. For majors in Religious Studies, the degree Bachelor of Arts is awarded.

The Department also offers graduate programs in Religious Studies. The programs have been developed to meet the need of advanced theological education in the Detroit area. The Master of Arts in Religious Studies is awarded. The Department also participates in an interdisciplinary program leading to the Master of Arts in Humanities, and in special Master's programs with other institutions. The University is a member of the Ecumenical Theological Center.

Parent Institution. The University of Detroit describes itself as an urban, Catholic university in the Jesuit tradition, offering a value-oriented education. Its member colleges include Liberal Arts, Business, Architecture, Engineering, Law, Education and Human Services, and Dentistry. Its population is quite diverse ethnically, racially, and religiously. It currently serves about 6,000 full-time and part-time students. The University has a Core Curriculum for all undergraduates requiring some 56 credit hours in liberal arts subjects, including six in Religious Studies.

Community Environment. University of Detroit students are taught on four campuses, three located within the city of Detroit and a fourth at Colombiere Center in Clarkston, Michigan. The McNichols or Main Campus is the heart of the University, situated on 70 acres in a northwest Detroit residential area. The undergraduate schools and colleges and their affiliated graduate programs can be found there, as well as six student resident halls and the Jesuit residence. The newly-renovated Renaissance Campus, located across from the Renaissance Center in downtown Detroit, houses the University's School of Law and Evening College of Business and Administration. It is also the site of the Kresge Law Library. Nearby is the University's School of Dentistry. The University's Clarkston Campus at Colombiere Center is attended by undergraduate students enrolled in a combined liberal arts and business curriculum.

Religious Denomination. Roman Catholic.

Accreditation. North Central Association of Colleges and Schools.

Term System. Semester; summer term.

Enrollment in Degree Programs in Religion 1984–85. Total 30; men 16, women 14. (These are approximate figures, representing the Master of Arts degree.)

Degrees in Religion Awarded 1984–85. Master of Arts 8; men 4, women 4.

Faculty for Degree Programs in Religion. Total 10-11; full-time 6-7, part-time 4.

Admission Requirements. To become a Religious Studies major on the undergraduate level, the student must normally have completed his/her freshman year with a grade point average of 2.5 or above. To be accepted into the Master's program, an applicant must normally have taken 30 hours of undergraduate work in religious studies, philosophy, or related humanities with a grade of B or above, and have met the general Graduate School requirement of a 3.0 average.

Tuition and Fees. $200 per credit hour; $20 applications fee.

Financial Aid. No assistantships or fellowships are available. Seminarians and religious are granted reductions in tuition fees. For further financial aid, consult the University's Graduate and Undergraduate Bulletins and the Financial Aid Office.

Housing. Seven residence halls house up to 1,000 students. Single and semi-private rooms are available as well as married housing.

Library Facilities. There are five libraries in the University system which has more than 500,000 volumes, 3,000 leading literary, scientific and professional journals, and a collection of over 75,000 U.S. Federal and State government documents.

Religious Services/Activities. Mass is celebrated several times daily and Sundays in the University chapel; retreats are available 3 or 4 times a year; other services and activities are available through Campus Ministry.

Degree Programs

The Master of Arts in Religious Studies is offered under three plans. Plan A requires 24 credit hours of coursework, comprehensives, and a Master's thesis. Plan B requires 30 credit hours of coursework, two research papers, three written comprehensive examinations, one oral comprehensive. Eighteen course hours must be taken in one of the areas of concentration: Eastern Religious Traditions, Western Religious Traditions, or Contemporary Society and Religious Thought. Plan C permits students to combine 24 hours of Religious Studies with 12 hours in a related field (Education, History, Philosophy, Psychology, and Sociology). This plan requires 36 hours of coursework. In addition to the above programs, special Master's degree programs are offered in conjunction with St. John's Provincial Seminary and St. Cyril and Methodius Seminary. The Religious Studies Department also participates in an interdisciplinary program leading to the Master of Arts in Humanities.

Ecumenical Theological Center
8425 West McNichols
Detroit, MI 48221   (313) 862-8000

General Description. The Ecumenical Theological Center was founded in 1980. It is an association of schools, religious denominations, and other institutions that develop and enhance the educational resources supporting Christian ministry regionally, and that foster ecumenical awareness, cooperation, and service. Services available include basic biblical and theological education for clergy and laity (non-degree and degree programs); a locally based Doctor of Ministry program; seminars and courses in mission and ministry; regional on-site workshops in response to specific needs; programs and resources for direct use in local churches; resources for Black and other ethnic groups; cooperative programming with denominations; experiential program design through cooperation among member institutions; and institutional and individual membership.

Affiliated institutions include: Association for Clinical Pastoral Education (Southeastern Michigan Cluster); Disciples of Christ, Christian Church (Michigan Region); Institute for Advanced Pastoral Studies; Marygrove College; Psychological Studies and Consultation Program; St. John's Provincial Seminary (consulting relationship); School for Ministry; Whitaker School of Theology (Episcopal Diocese of Michigan); United Methodist Church (Detroit Annual Conference); and the University of Detroit.

Grand Rapids Baptist College
Division of Bible, Religion, and Ministries
1001 East Beltline, N.E.
Grand Rapids, MI 49505   (616) 949-5300

Administration. Dr. Charles U. Wagner, President; Dr. W. Wilbert Welch, Chancellor.

General Description. The Division of Bible, Religion, and Ministries offers three degrees: Bachelor of Arts (B.A.), Bachelor of Religious Education (B.R.E.), and Associate in Religious Education (A.R.E.). The B.A. degree offers a major in Religion, and the B.R.E. offers majors in Bible, Christian Education, Missions, Pastoral Studies, and Missionary Flight.

Parent Institution. Grand Rapids Baptist College is a four-year college of liberal arts and sciences, an approved agency of the General Association of Regular Baptist Churches. It shares a campus with Grand Rapids Baptist Seminary.

Community Environment. The College occupies a beautiful 100-acre campus, which it shares with the Grand Rapids Baptist Seminary, located 4 miles from downtown Grand Rapids. See also: Calvin Theological Seminary for information about the city of Grand Rapids.

Religious Denomination. Independent Baptist (General Association of Regular Baptist Churches).

Religious Emphasis. Conservative.

Accreditation. North Central Association of Colleges and Schools.

Term System. Semester.

Enrollment in Degree Programs in Religion 1984–85. Total 224; men 194, women 30.

Faculty for Degree Programs in Religion. Total 15; full-time 7, part-time 8. (Includes the Seminary.)

Admission Requirements. All applicants must give a clear testimony of salvation and commitment to Jesus Christ. An applicant must be a high school graduate with a high school grade average of C or better and is required to take the ACT assessment.

Tuition and Fees. Tuition $1,655 (14-17 aggregate semester hours); room and board $1,233 per semester (21 meal plan); fees $125.

Financial Aid. Gift Aid Programs, federal and state financial aid, and campus employment are available.

Housing. Dormitories and apartments are available on campus. Off-campus housing is also possible.

Library Facilities. The library houses 71,579 volumes.

Religious Services/Activities. Attendance at daily chapel services is required. All students carrying seven hours or more (excluding first semester) are required to be involved in a student ministries assignment each semester. Students may choose to serve in local area churches or in community activities.

Degree Programs

The major in Religion leading to the Bachelor of Arts degree introduces the student both to Biblical faith and to religous phenomena in other cultures and thought patterns. It is preparatory for further graduate theological study and the teaching of religion and Bible on an elementary and secondary level. The major in Ministry concentrates on the attitudes, philosophy, and skills for the specific ministry vocation one is planning (Christian Education, Missions, Pastoral Studies) along with a significant concentration in Biblical and theological studies. The Bible major is for those anticipating a ministry of the Word of God. Its primary aim is to bring the student to a comprehensive understanding of the Bible as a whole and to a reasonable competency in independent Bible study and to develop skill in the communication and defense of the Gospel.

The Bachelor of Religious Education degree is designed particularly for students choosing to enter ministry as Christian education directors, missionaries, or pastors. The degree may be elected by pre-seminarians, by the paraprofessionally oriented who envision subsequent training, and by those who for reasons of age or previous experience should seek a professional degree. A Missionary Flight program is also offered.

Special Programs

The Associate Degree in Religious Education is offered through the Division of Bible, Religion, and Ministries.

A Bible Certificate Program is a one-year program designed primarily for the lay person in the church, or for the student who desires a foundation study of the Bible prior to pursuing professional and/or vocational goals.

The Special Studies Institute is a one-year program for the college graduate or one who has an equivalency in experience. It is especially designed for the person who does not wish to pursue professional training for a formal ministry but wishes to gain more knowledge in Bible and doctrine as preparation for a lay ministry. It is also for the college graduate who lacks the background for seminary level training.

Grand Rapids Baptist Seminary
1001 East Beltline, N.E.
Grand Rapids, MI 49505   (616) 949-5300

Administration. Dr. Charles U. Wagner, President; Dr. W. Wilbert Welch, Chancellor; James M. Grier, Academic Dean.

General Description. Grand Rapids Baptist Seminary is a Graduate Center of World Missions and Church Ministries providing a dynamic setting for learning. The Seminary grew out of the pre-seminary program of the Grand Rapids Baptist College founded in 1941 as an evening Bible school in the city's Wealthy Street Baptist Church. Today the Seminary and College share a new 132-acre campus 4 miles from downtown Grand Rapids, and operate under the same board of trustees and president. The Seminary enjoys separate facilities and is administered by its own administrative office and faculty.

The program "Impact Ministries," a unique contractual agreement with many churches offers the student the opportunity to engage in supervised activity in evangelism, teaching, and administration. The Seminary awards the degrees Master of Divinity, Master of Religious Education, and Master of Theology.

Community Environment. The city of Grand Rapids is a fine locale for a seminary. A quiet, sprawling city with a metropolitan population of over 400,000, it has been called "the city of churches" and "the center of orthodoxy." One hundred thirty fundamental churches within 50 miles of the Seminary offer many opportunities for Christian service and fellowship. See also: Calvin Theological Seminary for information about Grand Rapids.

Religious Denomination. Independent Baptist (General Association of Regular Baptist Churches).

Religious Emphasis. Conservative.

Accreditation. North Central Association of Colleges and Schools.

Term System. Semester.

Enrollment in Degree Programs in Religion 1984–85. Total 224; men 194, women 30.

Degrees in Religion Awarded 1984–85. Master of Theology 1; men 1. Master of Divinity 21; men 21. Master of Religious Education 29; men 25, women 4.

Faculty for Degree Programs in Religion. Total 15; full-time 7, part-time 8.

Admission Requirements. The Seminary accepts applicants of all races and ethnic groups who give evidence of the new birth, possess the necessary gifts for the ministry, have earned a B.A. degree or its equivalent from a recognized college or university, and adhere to a doctrinal statement which is required for admittance, degree candidacy, and for graduation. In addition to the application, the applicant must submit a $10 nonrefundable fee, official transcripts from all colleges attended, and references. Applicants for the Master of Religious Education, Master of Divinity, and Master of Theology degrees should have a minimum college grade point average of 2.5; applicants for the Master of Theology degree should have a "B" average in his/her Master of Divinity work.

Financial Aid. Financial aid for seminarians is available through grants, loans, and opportunities for employment. Contact the Financial Aid Office.

Housing. A limited number of moderately priced one and two bedroom unfurnished apartments are available. Rooms are available for single students on a double occupancy basis with the provision of board at the dining commons.

Library Facilities. The Seminary Resources Center houses the teaching-learning equipment and 20,000 of the select volumes needed for graduate research in biblical studies, theology, missions, education, and church related ministries. It is a branch of the main Miller Library of Grand Rapids Baptist College and provides access to the Miller collection and through computer service is linked to the libraries of the major universities in the midwest.

Religious Services/Activities. Daily chapel services, periodic retreats, area church participation.

Degree Programs

The Master of Religious Education is a two-year, 62-credit-hour program designed for those who wish to engage in supportive ministries. A minimum 2.5 grade point average; 40 hours of core curriculum; 17 hours of ministries; 5 hours of electives.

The Master of Religious Education In-Service Program is a one-year program designed for persons who have had a minimum of 5 years of successful pastoral ministry. It is a 32-hour program built around concentrations in Bible, Theology, and a chosen area of service. A minimum 3.0 grade point average is required with 32 hours in residence.

The Master of Divinity is recommended for pastors, missionaries, and Christian Education workers whose primary task will be ministry. The program consists of 95 hours which emphasize the study and interpretation of the Scriptures in the original languages, and the development of competency in preaching and teaching the Word of God. A minimum 2.5 grade point average, 67 hours of core curriculum, 20 hours of ministries, and 8 hours of electives. Five years from date of matriculation are allowed to complete all degree requirements.

The Master of Theology degree is a 30-hour, graduate theological degree built upon the the Master of Divinity degree. It is offered on a very limited basis each year as an independent research degree; the development of mastery and competency in the major field is the primary purpose of this degree.

Special Programs

The program "Impact Ministries" is described in General Description, above.

Great Lakes Bible College

6211 West Willow

Lansing, MI 48917   (517) 321-0242

Administration. Curtis D. Lloyd, President.

General Description. Great Lakes Bible College functions primarily as a college specializing in the preparation of young men and women for Christian vocations, including the preaching ministry, ministries of music, of youth programming, associate ministries, missions, and numerous others. The college curriculum consists of a solid block of liberal arts and religious studies. Graduating stu-

dents must complete a major or minor in Biblical studies. Additionally, co-operative programs with Michigan State University and Davenport Business College offer opportunities to choose from a vast selection of areas of specialization such as history, English, pre-law, business, and other professional fields. Degrees from the College presently include the Associate of Religious Education and the Bachelor of Religious Education. They may be terminal or preparatory to graduate studies.

Community Environment. Great Lakes Bible College's trustees and administration planned and developed the 50-acre campus which opened in 1972. It retains all the advantages of a state capital city (Lansing) without a limitation on future growth. Lansing is well known for its automotive-connected industries. Over two-thirds of its products are gas engines, auto parts, drop forgings, and castings.

Religious Denomination. Christian Churches and Churches of Christ.

Accreditation. American Association of Bible Colleges.

Term System. Quarter; no summer term.

Enrollment in Degree Programs in Religion 1984–85. Total 149; men 96, women 53.

Degrees in Religion Awarded 1984–85. Bachelor of Religious Education 12; men 6, women 6. Associate of Religious Education 2; men 1, women 1.

Faculty for Degree Programs in Religion. Total 13; full-time 11, part-time 2.

Admission Requirements. High school graduation; 3 character references; college transcript where applicable.

Tuition and Fees. Tuition $2,100; registration $30; library fee $60; activity fee $75; insurance $73.50; room $750 to $855; married student's apartment $235 to $265 per month; meals $1,350.

Financial Aid. Pell Grant, Supplemental Educational Opportunity Grant, College Work-Study, academic and music scholarships, and supporting church scholarships are among the types of financial aid available.

Housing. Dormitory accommodations for women, men's apartments, and married student's apartments are available.

Library Facilities. The library contains 28,723 volumes.

Religious Services/Activities. Chapel service is held twice each week and a lecture series is scheduled each term.

Degree Programs

The Bachelor of Religious Education degree requires the completion of 192 quarter hours.

Special Programs

The Associate of Religious Education degree requires the completion of 96 quarter hours.

An Adult Continuing Education program offers off-campus classes in local churches.

Hillsdale College

33 East College Street
Hillsdale, MI 49242   (517) 437-7341

Administration. George C. Roche, III, President.

General Description. Hillsdale College was founded in 1844 in Spring Arbor, Michigan under the name of Michigan Central College by a group of Free Will Baptists. The present name was adopted in 1863. In 1870 a full theological course leading to the degree of Doctor of Divinity was established. This existed for 45 years when it was supplanted by the present Department of Philosophy and Religion.

Parent Institution. The College is a private, liberal arts college granting the baccalureate degree. It enrolls slightly over 1,000 students.

Community Environment. The 175-acre campus is located in Hillsdale, 90 miles west of Detroit and 200 miles east of Chicago.

Religious Denomination. Nondenominational.

Accreditation. North Central Association of Colleges and Schools.

Term System. Semester.

Admission Requirements. High school graduation from an accredited school; SAT or ACT.

Tuition and Fees. Tuition $5,800 per year; room $1,200; board $1,630.

Financial Aid. Financial aid is available in many forms. Aids based on need are made on a first-come basis.

Housing. All students reside in college residence halls.

Library Facilities. The Carr Memorial Library houses over 110,000 volumes. It maintains the Varnum T. Hull Collection of Rare Bibles, dating from 1591 to the early 1900s.

Degree Programs

The courses in Religion offered by the Department of Philosophy and Religion are designed to ground the student in the history, philosophy, theology, and ethics of the Judaeo-Christian tradition and to expose him/her to non-Christian religious thought. Ultimately, the courses aim to provide the intellectual tools necessary to study, interpret, and critically evaluate religious beliefs, and then to integrate these both intellectually and personally. The major in Religion requires a minimum of 33 semester hours with no more than 6 hours in philosophy. An oral comprehensive examination is required during the senior year. The Bachelor of Arts degree requires a total of 124 semester hours.

Hope College
Department of Religion

Lubbers Hall, Hope College
Holland, MI 49423   (616) 392-5111

Administration. Dr. Gordon J. Van Wylen, President; Dr. Elton J. Bruins, Dean for Arts and Humanities; Dr. Dennis N. Voskuil, Chairperson, Department of Religion.

General Description. The Department of Religion is part of the Humanities Division presenting an area of study and research that students preparing for various professions may choose as the focus of their liberal arts education. The department is divided into five areas of academic investigation: Biblical studies, historical studies, world religions, and religion in culture. While each student majoring in religion is required to enroll in advanced level courses in each of the five areas, most religion majors concentrate in one area and develop, thereby, a considerable expertise. Many students have found the religion major an excellent way of focusing their liberal arts education at Hope College.

Students majoring in religion participate in a wide variety of academic and service activities which include: assisting professors with research programs; enrolling in the Philadelphia or Chicago Urban Semester to investigate alternative ministries in an urban setting; leading youth groups, both denominational and nondenominational, in area churches and performing community services.

Parent Institution. Hope College is a distinguished and distinctive liberal arts, four-year undergraduate college affiliated with the Reformed Church in America. The curriculum offers courses in 36 major fields leading to the Bachelor of Arts, Bachelor of Science, Bachelor of Music, and Bachelor of Science in Nursing degrees.

Community Environment. The 25-acre campus of Hope College, located near the shores of Lake Michigan, is approximately 150 miles north of Chicago and 150 miles west of Detroit. Facilities include an 85-acre biological field station. Settled by the Dutch in 1847, the city of Holland, Michigan still has many of the characteristics of a Dutch town. This is the tulip center of America. Located on Lake Macatawa and Lake Michigan, the area is surrounded by large fruit-growing and farming areas and is also an industrial and resort town.

Religious Denomination. Reformed Church in America.

Religious Emphasis. Reformed.

Accreditation. North Central Association of Colleges and Schools.

Term System. Semester; also May Term, June Term, Summer Term.

Enrollment in Degree Programs in Religion 1984–85. Total 30; men 18, women 12.

Degrees in Religion Awarded 1984–85. Bachelor of Arts in Religion 14; men 8, women 6.

Faculty for Degree Programs in Religion. Total 9; full-time 7, part-time 2.

Admission Requirements. High school graduation from a program including four years of English, two years of mathematics; two years of foreign language, two years of social science, and one year of a laboratory science as well as five other academic courses; SAT or ACT (ACT preferred).

Tuition and Fees. Tuition (12 to 16 credit hours) $3,122 per semester; board (21 meals per week) $805; room $580 per semester; activity fee $18 per semester.

Financial Aid. Hope College provides financial assistance to students on the basis of both financial need and academic achievement. A Religion Scholarship and Endowment Fund is administered by the Religion Department for the awarding of scholarships, teaching fellowships, and Biblical research grants to superior students contemplating church vocations.

Housing. Fifteen residence halls and 23 cottages (houses on or near the campus) provide housing for students.

Library Facilities. The Van Zoeren Library and its two branches include more than 190,000 volumes, 1,150 current periodical subscriptions, 1,200 cassette tapes, and over 25,000 reels and cards of microtext material. Students also have access to the Herrick Public Library and the Beardslee Library of Western Theological Seminary.

Religious Services/Activities. The Chaplain and his staff serve as the primary focus of the College's religious programming and give leadership to the Ministry of Christ's People, organized by students. The Ministry of Christ's People provides leadership and opportunities for Christian service in four broad areas: worship, social ministries, evangelism, and personal and interpersonal Christian growth. Sunday worship services are held in Dimnent Memorial Chapel and chapel services are held on Monday, Wednesday, and Friday plus special days on the Christian calendar.

Degree Programs

The major in Religion leading to a Bachelor of Arts degree requires 27-30 semester hours of courses elected from the five disciplines: Biblical Studies, Historical Studies, Theological Studies, Studies in World Religions, and Studies of Religion in Culture. Options for religion majors include seminars or individual research, and in consultation with the department chairperson, the opportunity to fulfill selected required courses through a tutorial reading program. For students interested in pursuing careers in Christian education and youth work in the local church, the religion major-church worker program is available. It consists of the regular religion major course of study to which particular courses for skill development are added.

Institute for Advanced Pastoral Studies
8425 West McNichols Road
Detroit, MI 48207   (313) 862-8000

Administration. Dr. John Biersdorf, Director; Matthew Ripley-Moffit, Administrator and Registrar.

General Description. The oldest of its kind in the nation, founded in 1957, the Institute for Advanced Pastoral Studies pioneered and continues to innovate in the field of continuing theological education. It is broadly ecumenical in outreach, serving churches and religious leaders of all denominations. Throughout its history the Institute has had the single aim of continuing education for excellence in ministry. It is a worshiping, teaching/learning research community. Its commitment is carried out through the following principles: (1) Prayer is a metaphor for understanding, being in, and doing ministry. The liturgical celebration of the church community, personal faith and prayer discipline, and the specific actions of caring and mission form a coherent whole called ministry. Theological education is prayer, deepening faith and love and knowledge of God. (2) The focus of the educational process is the whole person in community. Educating the whole person in community means that every person has gifts to bring in a collegial process where all teach and all learn together. (3) Continuing education is a life-long process of professional and personal development. Learning how to learn in ministry frees one to ask fundamental questions and make penetrating new discoveries about the theory and practice of ministry.

Parent Institution. The Institute is a member institution of the Ecumenical Theological Center, a consortium of 10 schools, denominations, and other institutions seeking to develop and enhance the educational resources that support Judeo-Christian ministry within Michigan and the surrounding region. While serving generally the degree and non-degree continuing theological education and institutional enrichment needs of the constituency, the Center intends in addition to be specifically responsive to those committed to ethnic ministries and to those throughout the territory desiring on-site learning opportunities. See: Ecumenical Theological Center, Detroit, Michigan.

Community Environment. At the turn of the 20th century, Detroit was a quiet, tree-shaded community brewing beer and producing comfortable carriages and comforting stoves. The serenity was broken by Henry Ford's creation, a vehicle "propelled by power generated from within itself." Today, it is the greatest automobile-manufacturing city in the world. Definitely an industrial city, Detroit also has a new civic center complex on the riverfront, an excellent park system, and numerous museums and galleries.

Religious Denomination. Nondenominational.

Religious Emphasis. Ecumenical.

Accreditation. Licensed by the Michigan State Board of Education to offer the Doctor of Ministry degree.

Term System. Year: September to August; no summer term.

Enrollment in Degree Programs in Religion 1984–85. Total 71; men 63, women 8.

Degrees in Religion Awarded 1984–85. Doctor of Ministry 3; men 3.

Faculty for Degree Programs in Religion. Total 15; fulltime 5, part-time 10.

Admission Requirements. Master of Divinity or equivalent; experience in the practice of ministry; official approval by the board of the ministry setting; completion of application procedure.

Tuition and Fees. Fees per candidate to be paid as each component is contracted for: (1) Admission $300; (2) Introductory Seminar $135 (tuition only); (3) Ecumenical Theological Center membership $25 yearly; (4) Colleague Group $300 each year with Faculty Consultant; (5) Seminars and Miniprojects $1,650 ($225 tuition and $50 miniproject supervision x 6); (6) Project Dissertation $525 (Research Seminar $225, Contents Specialist $300).

Financial Aid. If financial assistance beyond that available from local, state, and national headquarters of each denomination is required, contact the Administrator of the Institute.

Housing. Dormitory housing available during program components.

Library Facilities. The Institute has its own special collection and an interlibrary loan agreement with three other local libraries: the graduate theological collections at St. John's Provincial Seminary in Plymouth, the University of Detroit, and Marygrove College.

Degree Programs

The Doctor of Ministry program is designed on the conviction that education for ministry should grow out of worship, prayer, and meditation practice. It is a continuing education program aimed at excellence in ministry. Offering educational structures and resources for life long intentional professional development, the curriculum is continually built out of the actual life and mission of the church. Every aspect of the program is meant to be directly relevant to the ministries of participants. The major components of the program, in addition to admission requirements, are the colleague group, the ministry setting, area seminars, mini-projects, and the project dissertation. A total of 44 credits is required. The program is jointly owned by the Ecumenical Theological Center and the Institute for Advanced Pastoral Studies, and is governed by a joint committee composed of representatives of the two institutions.

Special Programs

Twenty to thirty 5-day intensive continuing education seminars are offered each year. These seminars are organized around four dimensions of emphasis: Worship, Prayer, and Meditation Practice; Spiritual Care and Counseling; Congregational Renewal; Social Transformation. While a given seminar will focus on one or another of these dimensions, all four dimensions will be addressed in each seminar.

Kalamazoo College
1200 Academy Street
Kalamazoo, MI 49007   (616) 383-8411

Administration. David W. Breneman, President.

General Description. Kalamazoo College was founded as the Michigan and Huron Institute in 1833 by Thomas W. Merrill, a Baptist missionary from New England, and a Michigan pioneer named Caleb Eldred. It was the first institution of higher learning in Michigan. It became Kalamazoo College in 1855. The College offers a liberal arts curriculum and grants the Bachelor's degree.

Community Environment. The campus of nearly 60 acres is located in a quiet residential area of Kalamazoo, a city of 200,000.

Religious Denomination. American Baptist Church.

Accreditation. North Central Association of Colleges and Schools.

Term System. Quarter.

Admission Requirements. High school graduation in top 25 percent of graduating class; ACT or SAT.

Tuition and Fees. Tuition $2,245 per semester; resident fee $907.

Financial Aid. The College participates in the College Scholarship Service of the College Board. Grants are the most important feature of the financial aid program.

Housing. Six residence halls are available on campus.

Library Facilities. The Upjohn Library houses over 250,000 volumes.

Religious Services/Activities. The College actively cultivates its historic connection with the American Baptist Church. A weekly service chapel service is held and religious organizations on campus are initiated by students.

Degree Programs

Courses in Religion are grouped in three divisions: History of Religions, Biblical Literature, and Religious Thought in the Christian Tradition. All courses count toward a major, and majors must undertake some study in each area. A minimum of eight units plus two units earned in the Senior Individualized Project are required as well as four units in each of two cognate areas. One cognate must be selected from philosophy, English, history, or sociology. The Bachelor of Arts degree requires the completion of 36 units.

Marygrove College
Graduate Studies, Pastoral Ministry
8425 West McNichols
Detroit, MI 48224   (313) 862-8000

Administration. Dr. John E. Shay, Jr., President; Dr. Doreen A. Poupard, Academic Dean; Rev./Dr. Anthony

R. Kosnik, Director of Pastoral Ministry.

General Description. Marygrove's Pastoral Ministry Program responds to one of the greatest needs in the Church today — a formation program specifically designed for the non-ordained pastoral minister. This program, rooted in the Roman Catholic tradition, is open to members of all Christian communities. Participants may work toward a Master of Arts degree in Pastoral Ministry or participate in a non-degree program.

Parent Institution. Marygrove College is an independent, Catholic, coeducational college which accepts the challenge of service through its goals: to promote competence — the ability to understand and participate in the promise of our world today; to foster compassion — an awareness of human worth and dignity; to encourage commitment — the will to act upon one's beliefs and to make just use of one's abilities. The Graduate Program is designed primarily for evening students during the fall and winter terms; it grants the degrees Master of Arts in Pastoral Ministry and Master of Education.

Community Environment. The Marygrove community enjoys the best of both academic worlds: it is located on the enclosed campus of 68 wooded acres in northwest Detroit, Michigan, and is easily accessible from all parts of the city and outlying suburbs. The cultural and social opportunities of Marygrove's location are considerable: theatre, symphony, ballet, opera, Detroit Institute of Arts, and four major universities within 15 to 40 minutes of the campus.

Religious Denomination. Roman Catholic.

Accreditation. North Central Association of Colleges and Schools.

Term System. Semester; summer term.

Degrees in Religion Awarded 1984–85. Master of Arts in Pastoral Ministry 84; men 14, women 70.

Faculty for Degree Programs in Religion. Total 61; full-time 61. Many local and nationally-known educators and administrators are adjunct faculty members for the Graduate Division during the regular terms and in particular for the summer sessions.

Admission Requirements. For admission to the Graduate Division a student must have earned: (1) an undergraduate degree or its equivalent; (2) a minimum grade point average of 3.0 (B) in all graduate and undergraduate work. An initial interview with the Director of the Pastoral Ministry Program will serve to evaluate the candidate's necessary readiness for this degree program. Achievement in these areas will be reviewed: (1) formal study in Scripture, Theology, and Liberal Arts; (2) non-credit experiential learning in ministry.

Tuition and Fees. Application fee (nonrefundable) $15; graduate tuition $146 per credit; semiprivate room and 5-day meal plan $1,115/semester; private room and 5-day meal plan $1,450/semester.

Financial Aid. By distributing funds accoring to need, Marygrove's financial aid program makes it possible for the greatest number of students to continue their educa-

tion. An independent, objective, nationally-recognized method developed by the College Scholarship Service is used to analyze the financial circumstances of parents and students before each student's awards are determined by Marygrove's Financial Aid officers. There are Federal, State, and Marygrove aid packages.

Housing. During the regular school year most graduate students commute from homes and workplaces in the city and suburbs. During the summer, many come from longer distances and reside on campus. The College provides on-campus residence for men and women; the living areas are divided into suites, generally accommodating 2 students each.

Library Facilities. The College library has an outstanding collection of books and periodicals, as well as excellent research facilities.

Degree Programs

The Master of Arts in Pastoral Ministry degree is a 36 semester credit hour program. It combines a learning program of required core seminars, elective coursework, a supervised internship, and final project. The core seminars establish a solid base in the essential component areas of scripture, theology, spirituality, and pastoral/professional skills formation. The elective coursework gives support to the particular learning and ministerial needs of the candidate. The supervised internship and final project, ususally 3-4 semester credit hours, provide learning experiences which integrate scholarship and ministerial life. The degree may be completed within 2 or 3 years by combining the academic year and summer terms; or within a 5 to 6 year summer program.

Special Programs

Students who seek graduate study enrichment opportunities, but do not wish to matriculate into a degree program, may register for most Pastoral Ministry Courses by way of Post-Master's or Special Student Status admissions.

Mercy College of Detroit
8200 West Outer Drive
Detroit, MI 48219   (313) 592-6030

Administration. Sr. Maureen A. Fay, R.S.M., President.

General Description. Mercy College of Detroit is a private liberal arts college affiliated with the Roman Catholic Church and conducted by the Religious Sisters of Mercy. Both undergraduate Bachelor's and graduate degrees are awarded in a variety of disciplines.

Community Environment. The campus of 4 acres is located in northwest Detroit.

Religious Denomination. Roman Catholic.

Accreditation. North Central Association of Colleges and Schools.

Term System. Semester.

Admission Requirements. High school graduation or the equivalent; ACT score of 16 required.

Tuition and Fees. Tuition $1,944 per semester; room $425-$800; meal plan $325.

Housing. On-campus housing is available for approximately 300 students.

Library Facilities. The library houses over 125,000 volumes and 700 periodicals.

Religious Services/Activities. Campus Ministry finds its expression in four general areas: Worship, Evangelization, Community Building, and Service. Opportunities are proved for daily worship, small group prayer, retreats, and direct service to those in need.

Degree Programs

The program in Religion is designed to provide students with the opportunity to study contemporary religious issues and to understand these issues in the context of religious traditions and current American religious and philosophical discussion. Courses are available in the areas of Scriptural Studies, Christian Theology: Systematic and Historical, Ethics, and Cross-Disciplinary Studies.

Michigan Christian College
800 West Avon Road
Rochester, MI 48063   (313) 651-5800

Administration. Milton Fletcher, President.

General Description. Michigan Christian College was founded in 1959 and began offered the Bachelor of Religious Education degree program in 1978. The College is a private, coeducational college supported by the Churches of Christ. It awards the Associate in Arts/Sciences, the Associate in Applied Science, and the Bachelor of Religious Education.

Community Environment. The 91-acre campus has ten major buildings. It is located in Rochester, the northernmost suburb of Detroit.

Religious Denomination. Churches of Christ.

Accreditation. North Central Association of Colleges and Schools.

Term System. Semester.

Admission Requirements. High school graduation or equivalent; ACT.

Tuition and Fees. Tuition $1,286 per semester; room $357; board $751; general fee $84.

Financial Aid. Scholarships, grants, loans, and part-time employment constitute the financial assistance available.

Housing. Students are required to live in college residence halls unless married or living with relatives.

Library Facilities. The Muirhead Library has a collection of over 40,000 volumes.

Religious Services/Activities. Chapel attendance is required each academic day. Devotionals, Bible lectureship, Mission Emphasis, and His Wordsmen are other activities

available for participation.

Degree Programs

The Bachelor of Religious Education degree is designed with three majors: Biblical Studies, Biblical Studies Composite, and Christian Ministry. All majors focus on the mission of building the church in areas like the Midwest. The degree requires a total of 128 semester hours.

Michigan State University
Department of Religious Studies
East Lansing, MI 48824   (517) 353-2930

Administration. Dr. Cecil Mackey, President; Dr. Clarence L. Winder, Provost and Vice President for Academic Affairs; Dr. Alan M. Hollingsworth, Dean, College of Arts and Letters; Dr. Robert T. Anderson, Chairperson, Department of Religious Studies.

General Description. The Department of Religious Studies provides a liberal arts and academic program focused on the description and analysis of religious phenomenon in world religions.

Parent Institution. Michigan State University is a pioneer land-grant institution which offers the Bachelor, Master, Specialist, and Doctorate degrees, and professional degrees in Medicine, Osteopathy, and Veterinary Medicine.

Community Environment. The 2,010-acre campus has a familiar landmark in Beaumont Tower, which stands on the site of the first building where agriculture was taught as a science on a university campus. The University is located in a metropolitan area adjacent to Lansing, the state capital of Michigan. East Lansing has 4 hospitals and churches of all denominations.

Religious Denomination. None.

Accreditation. North Central Association of Colleges and Schools.

Term System. Quarter; summer term.

Enrollment in Degree Programs in Religion 1984–85. Total 17; men 8, women 9.

Degrees in Religion Awarded 1984–85. Bachelor of Arts in Religious Studies 8; men 6, women 2.

Faculty for Degree Programs in Religion. Total 6; full-time 6.

Admission Requirements. Accredited high school graduation with completion of 16 units including 4 English; SAT or ACT.

Tuition and Fees. Tuition lower division $634 per quarter, upper division $702 per quarter.

Financial Aid. The University has a program of financial aid offering scholarships, loans, and part-time work.

Housing. Dormitories and apartments are available on campus.

Library Facilities. The University library houses over 3 million volumes. Special collections include Samaritan Manuscripts and an Asian collection.

Degree Programs

A major in Religious Studies leading to the Bachelor of Arts degree requires a minimum of 45 quarter hour credits in accordance with an established minimum distribution. Course offerings include Exploring Religion, Western Religions, Eastern Religions, Old Testament, New Testament, Writings of St. Paul, Development of Christian Thought, Modern Judaism, and Islam.

Special Programs

A teaching minor is available through the Department and requires 30 credits distributed between Eastern and Western Religions.

Olivet College
Main Street
Olivet, MI 49076   (616) 749-7635

Administration. Dr. Donald A. Morris, President.

General Description. Olivet College is a four-year liberal arts institution affiliated with the Congregational Christian Churches and the United Church of Christ. It is coeducational and under private control. The College awards the Bachelor's degree. The academic emphasis is on the liberal arts with special attention to career planning and work experiences during the undergraduate program. The College was founded in 1844.

Community Environment. The campus is located in the town of Olivet in south central Michigan, 30 miles south of Lansing and 125 miles west of Detroit.

Religious Denomination. Congregational Christian Churches and the United Church of Christ.

Accreditation. North Central Association of Colleges and Schools.

Term System. Semester.

Admission Requirements. High school graduation with rank in the upper 50 percent of the graduating class; ACT or SAT.

Tuition and Fees. Tuition $5,080 per year; room $1,100-$1,160; board $1,230-$1,250; activity fee $40.

Financial Aid. Olivet participates in the College Scholarship Service. Aid from federal and state programs is offered on the basis of demonstrated need and will take the form of scholarships, grants, loans, and work.

Housing. There are three housing options open to students: residence halls, society housing, and married student apartments.

Library Facilities. The library collections contain over 75,000 books and periodicals.

Degree Programs

The Religion and Philosophy program epitomizes Olivet's heritage as a value-conscious, church-related college. Many of the courses offered are designed to be available to a wide range of the student body so that this field can be accessible to all students. Requirements for the major are under review and prospective majors should consult the Department Chairman.

An interdisciplinary program in Religious Education prepares students for careers related to the church such as director of Christian education, or after appropriate postgraduate training, the ministry. The major requires 38-43 semester hours.

Reformed Bible College
1869 Robinson Road, SE
Grand Rapids, MI 49506   (616) 458-0404

Administration. Dr. Dick L. Van Halsema, President; Connie J. Scheurwater, Registrar.

General Description. Reformed Bible College provides biblical, general, and professional studies for Christian students. It trains missionaries, lay evangelists, youth leaders, and effective members of Christ's church.

The College was founded by a group of pastors and laymen in 1939 to provide biblical and theological training for students interested in working in mission, evangelism, and church education. The College began as a three-year institute. In 1970 it became a four-year Bible college and awarded its first Bachelor of Religious Education degrees in 1971.

The College operates under the jurisdiction of a Board of Trustees and confesses the doctrines set forth in the Apostles' Creed and the Nicene Creed. The College also subscribes to the tenets of the Reformed or Calvinistic faith as they are incorporated in the Heidelberg Catechism, the Belgic Confession, and the Canons of Dort, documents that reflect the teaching of the Protestant Reformation.

Community Environment. The College is located on the grounds of a former estate in a residential section of southeast Grand Rapids. The city has a population of approximately 250,000 in a metropolitan area of half a million people. Grand Rapids is served by United, Republic, Northwest Orient, Piedmont, USAir, and Freedom airlines plus several bus lines. Michigan's modern interstate highways crisscross the area, making it possible to drive to Grand Rapids from Detroit in two and a half hours and from Chicago in three and a half hours.

Religious Denomination. Nondenominational.

Religious Emphasis. Reformed.

Accreditation. American Association of Bible Colleges.

Term System. Semester; Spring term (May).

Enrollment in Degree Programs in Religion 1984–85. Total 223; men 132, women 91.

Degrees in Religion Awarded 1984–85. Bachelor of Religious Education 36; men 28, women 8. Associate in Religious Education 10; men 5, women 5. Associate of Arts 8; men 3, women 5.

Faculty for Degree Programs in Religion. Total 21; full-time 17, part-time 4.

Admission Requirements. High school graduation or equivalent.

Tuition and Fees. Tuition and fees $3,370 for the academic year; housing $2,300 per academic year.

Financial Aid. The College offers a program of financial assistance for worthy students who are able to demonstrate financial need.

Housing. One residence hall for 64 students; 4 houses for approximately 10 students each; three married students apartments.

Library Facilities. The library has 40,000 volumes, receives over 200 periodicals, and has a large collection of pamphlets and audiovisual materials. The area of concentration has been in Bible and Theology.

Religious Services/Activities. Devotions in residence halls and daily chapel services are held. Students participate in chapel by presiding, giving messages, and by providing music. The Fall Semester Retreat is held on campus under Administration sponsorship. It is held in conjunction with the Fall Bible Conference. The Winter Semester Retreat is held on or off campus under Student Council sponsorship.

Degree Programs

The Bachelor of Religious Education degree is designed as the basic educational preparation for Christians anticipating service in evangelism, missions, Christian education, or similar ministries. It consists of a minimum of 129 semester hours with specific requirements. Major areas of concentration are Christian Education and Evangelism/Missions.

Special Programs

The Associate in Religious Education degree program is a two-year course of study designed for the student who desires a Bible college supplement to technical or professional training in preparation for some form of Christian service and for students who wish a two-year course of specialized Biblical studies. A minimum of 69 semester hours is required for the degree.

The Associate of Arts degree program provides a solid foundation in Biblical studies and liberal arts core requirements for those who plan to continue undergraduate studies at another institution.

Sacred Heart Seminary College
2701 West Chicago Boulevard
Detroit, MI 48206   (313) 868-2700

Administration. Very Reverend F. Gerald Martin, Director; Paul W. Guenther, Registrar.

General Description. Sacred Heart Seminary College has as its primary goal the education of potential candidates for the diocesan priesthood at the college level. The Seminary is committed to the liberal education of the human person and offers a Bachelor of Arts degree with majors in English, History, Interdisciplinary Studies, and Philosophy. As additional goals, the Seminary also offers an Associate of Arts in Ministry degree, a Pastoral Ministry Certificate, and studies for the Permanent Diaconate. Sacred Heart Seminary prepares potential priesthood candidates for entry into the Provincial Graduate School of Theology. Other students are prepared for either ordination to the Permanent Diaconate or for various lay ministries in the Archdiocese.

The Seminary was established in September 1919 by the Most Reverend Michael J. Gallagher, Bishop of the Diocese of Detroit, to train young men for the Priesthood; temporary quarters were found on Martin Place in Detroit. In 1924 the Seminary was moved to its present location.

Community Environment. The Seminary has a twenty-acre campus located within five miles of downtown Detroit. It is bounded on the north by Chicago Boulevard, on the east by Linwood, on the south by Joy Road, and on the west by Lawton Avenue. The Seminary buildings are of English Tudor-Gothic architecture.

Religious Denomination. Roman Catholic.

Accreditation. North Central Association of Colleges and Schools. Endorsed by the National Council of Catholic Bishops.

Term System. Semester; summer term.

Enrollment in Degree Programs in Religion 1984–85. Total full-time 43, part-time 200; men full-time 42, part-time 120; women full-time 1, part-time 80. The part-time students are enrolled in non-degree programs.

Faculty for Degree Programs in Religion. Total 25; full-time 7, part-time 18.

Admission Requirements. Degree programs require high school diploma with 2.5 grade point average on a 4.0 system or a GED score of 50 or over; satisfactory ACT or SAT score; minimum high school involvement in a college preparatory program; letter of recommendation from the candidate's pastor or another community leader. Other programs require a high school diploma or equivalency.

Tuition and Fees. Costs per year: full-time tuition $2,-600; fees $185; room and board (formation candidates only) $1,750. Part-time tuition $125 per credit hour; special programs $65 per credit hour.

Financial Aid. Guaranteed Student Loans, College Work-study, Seminary Employment Program, Pell Grant, SEOG, Michigan Tuition Grants, Michigan Scholarship Grants, Knights of Columbus Loan Program, and Sacred Heart Seminary Scholarship Aid constitute the various forms of financial aid available.

Housing. Potential priesthood candidates reside at the Seminary.

Library Facilities. The Leo J. Ward Memorial Library contains approximately 60,000 volumes. The Canfield Special Collections Room is where the Rare Book Collection, Michigan Historical Collection, and Cardinal Mooney Collection are kept. The Archives Room contains the Seminary Archives and there is a modest collection of pedagogic materials in the Faculty Room.

Religious Services/Activities. Roman Catholic Morning and Evening Prayer and Eucharist daily; Sacraments of Reconciliation periodically; three retreats annually; days of Prayer and Recollection scheduled periodically.

Degree Programs

The Bachelor of Arts degree requires the completion of a minimum of 128 semester hours of credit representing four years of work. Distribution of this work must include one major of 30 semester hours and one minor course of at least 15 semester hours in addition to the Theology minor required of all students. Candidates may major in Philosophy, English, History, or Interdisciplinary Studies.

Special Programs

The Associate of Arts Degree in Ministry was established to fill the need for a liberal arts/vocational degree in a two-year format in the area of Christian ministry. This degree is designed not as an end in itself, but rather to give the student the basic tools upon which he/she can build by seeking another more advanced degree or at least to be able to make effective use of less formal learning experiences.

A Certificate in Pastoral Ministry is granted by the Archdiocese of Detroit through the Department of Formation. The Office of Pastoral Ministries is specifically charged to assess all candidates through the discernment of skills and competencies in a portfolio that the potential candidate gathers. A wide range of basic skills and a number of theological reflection seminars and retreats are offered and required for certification. The courses are administered by the Academic Dean for Evening Programs.

The Permanent Diaconate requires certification as a Pastoral Minister before candidacy in Diaconal Studies can begin. The curriculum of study has been approved by the Archdiocese of Detroit and conforms to the Program of Diaconal Formation approved by the National Conferences of Catholic Bishops. Ordination as a Permanent Deacon requires completion of the course of studies and a there is a series of canonical requirements that must be met. The Diaconal Courses are administered by the Academic Dean for Evening Programs.

St. John's Provincial Seminary
44011 Five Mile Road
Plymouth, MI 48170   (313) 453-6200

Administration. Very Rev. Robert H. Byrne, S.T.L., Rector/President; Rev. William F. Meyers, S.T.L., Academic Dean/Registrar.

General Description. In continuity with its original purpose, St. John's Provincial Seminary prepares candidates for the Roman Catholic priesthood. In light of today's vision and needs, the Seminary also offers professional training to men and women beginning or continuing their preparation for other Christian ministries. From the very beginning the direction of the Seminary was entrusted to priests of the Society of St. Sulpice who have a long association with the history of Michigan and the United States. In 1971 the Seminary was reorganized and entrusted to the direction of diocesan priests of the Province of Detroit.

To prepare people for leadership of various ministries of the Church, St. John's offers two degree programs: (1) Master of Divinity, designed for the professional preparation of candidates for the Catholic priesthood and other pastoral ministries; (2) Master of Theological Studies which offers a general theological education for men and women in diverse ministries or in preparation for other forms of higher education.

Community Environment. St. John's Provincial Seminary is located 20 miles northwest of Detroit and 15 miles northeast of Ann Arbor, in Plymouth Township. Once farmland, the area is now considered a prosperous residential suburb of Detroit. It is well served by state and interstate highway systems which give access to downtown Detroit in 35 minutes, and to downtown Ann Arbor and the University of Michigan in 25 minutes. St. John's campus is located on a rolling 179 acres with orchards and woods. The cultural and intellectual life of Detroit and Ann Arbor offers a rich variety of opportunities.

Religious Denomination. Roman Catholic.

Accreditation. North Central Association of Colleges and Schools; Association of Theological Schools in the United States and Canada.

Term System. Semester; summer term.

Enrollment in Degree Programs in Religion 1984–85. Total 117; men 73, women 44.

Degrees in Religion Awarded 1984–85. Master of Divinity 21; men 19, women 2. Master of Theological Studies 15; men 7, women 8.

Faculty for Degree Programs in Religion. Total 27; full-time 15, part-time 12.

Admission Requirements. Master of Divinity: Bachelor's degree from an accredited institution; 18 semester hours in philosophy, 12 in religion, and 6 in introduction to psychology and sociology; minimum of two courses in either a classical or modern language. Roman Catholic seminarians: recommendation by a Diocese; interviews. All other applicants: Bachelor's degree from an accredited institution; 9 semester hours in philosophy, 12 in religion, 6 in introductory psychology and sociology.

Tuition and Fees. Tuition $70 per credit hour; activities fee $15; graduation fee $25; recording fee $15.

Financial Aid. A tuition grant program is available for Roman Catholic residents of Michigan with a commitment to ministry. A statement of financial need must be submitted and other requirements fulfilled.

Housing. On-campus living is open to any full-time student. Study rooms are available for commuter students for $20 per term.

Library Facilities. The Seminary library houses over 58,000 volumes including 10,500 bound periodicals in French, English, German, Portuguese, Spanish, Hebrew, and Italian. The Gabriel Richard Room houses special materials on the early Church in Michigan, including several hundred volumes from the personal library of the pioneer missionary, Michigan educator and legislator, Father Gabriel Richard, S.S., and the Seminary's collection of rare books and fine printings.

Religious Services/Activities. Daily celebration of the Eucharist; morning prayer; periodic celebration of Reconciliation and occasional prayer vigils. A priesthood formation program and a ministerial formation program are required of all Master of Divinity candidates.

Degree Programs

The Master of Divinity degree requirements include 102 credits distributed among the core curriculum cognate courses, and field education; a cumulative grade point average of 2.5; and successful completion of Integrating Seminary. All applicants for the degree must go through the process of psychological/academic/formational screening. If accepted, all applicants must participate fully in the curriculum, including ministerial formation. Field education is also an integral part of the curriculum.

The Master of Theological Studies degree is designed primarily to meet academic needs. The program prepares a student for either advanced study in a related discipline or professional field, or supports the student's undergraduate preparation. Core courses required include Foundations of Theology, Fundamental Moral Theology, Introduction to the Old Testament, Synoptics, Sacraments of Initiation, Christology, and Ecclesiology. Candidates may follow the specialization or generalist options. A comprehensive examination is required.

Special Programs

The Seminary offers continuing education courses in scripture, Biblical languages, and theology.

St. Mary's College
Commerce and Indian Trail Roads
Orchard Lake, MI 48033   (313) 682-1885

Administration. Reverend Leonard F. Chrobot, President.

General Description. For over one hundred years, St. Mary's College has dedicated itself to the ideal of integrating Catholic faith and Polish tradition within the context of an American identity. In origin, the idea of a Polish Seminary emerged in the late 1870s as a response of the Polish American community to its experience of massive immigration, its needs for pastoral care, and its requirement of a native clergy sensitive to its particular ethnic concerns. In 1885, the idea became a reality and today it has been broadened to include both lay and clerical students, both men and women, both residents and commuters.

The College is an independent, coeducational Catholic liberal arts college. In cooperation with SS. Cyril and Methodius Seminary, the College conducts a Program of Priestly Formation for men called to the ordained ministry. Through its Religious Education program, it provides training from catechists, parish religious education coordinators, and other pastoral ministers. The College also features a major program in Polish Studies as well as the major liberal arts disciplines.

Community Environment. The campus is located in Orchard Lake, four miles west of Pontiac in southeastern Michigan. The College maintains the Polish Cultural Center and a museum containing outstanding works of Polish art.

Religious Denomination. Roman Catholic.

Accreditation. Semester.

Term System. North Central Association of Colleges and Schools.

Admission Requirements. High school graduation with rank in upper 50 percent of class; ACT.

Tuition and Fees. Tuition $1,275 per semester; room $450-$650; board $750; student fees $50.

Financial Aid. Financial assistance in various forms is available.

Housing. Dormitory space is available on campus.

Library Facilities. The Alumni Memorial Library has a book collection of over 60,000 volumes; it adds about 2,000 titles annually. The holdings include specialized collections in theology, philosophy, and Polish language and culture.

Religious Services/Activities. The Christian Service Commission is open to all students and sponsors Christian service activities for the entire college.

Degree Programs

The priestly formation program is conducted with the cooperation and guidance of SS. Cyril and Methodius Seminary. Seminarians discerning a vocation to the priesthood are offered an opportunity to experience community living, spiritual direction, growth in prayer, personal formation, and the academic foundation requisite for entering priesthood formation at the theologate level.

The major in Religious Education leading to the Bachelor's degree requires 36 credit hours. A major in Theology requires 30 credit hours.

Special Programs

An Associate of Arts in Religious Education and a Religious Education Certificate are also offered by the Department of Religious Education.

Siena Heights College
1247 East Siena Heights Drive
Adrian, MI 49221 (517) 263-0731

Administration. Cathleen Real, President.

General Description. Siena Heights College was founded in 1919 by the Adrian Dominican Congregation as a Catholic liberal arts college. It was originally a college for women who intended to become teachers and in the late 1960s became coeducational. Programs are offered leading to the Associate, Bachelor, and Master's degrees.

Community Environment. The campus of 140 acres is located sixty miles from Detroit in southeast Michigan.

Religious Denomination. Roman Catholic.

Accreditation. North Central Association of Colleges and Schools.

Term System. Semester.

Admission Requirements. High school graduation from an accredited school; ACT or SAT.

Tuition and Fees. Tuition $146 per semester hour; room and board $1,200-$1,500 per semester.

Financial Aid. Aid packages are awarded after the student has been admitted and submitted the financial aid application.

Housing. Residence halls are available on campus.

Library Facilities. The library houses over 92,000 volumes.

Religious Services/Activities. The Campus Ministry is responsible for the schedule of religious events on campus.

Degree Programs

The Bachelor of Arts degree with a major in Religious Studies requires the completion of 120 semester hours.

Spring Arbor College
Division of Philosophy and Religion
106 East Main Street
Spring Arbor, MI 49283 (517) 750-1200

Administration. Dr. Kenneth H. Coffman, President; Dr. R. Wayne Clugston, Vice President for Academic Affairs and Dean of the Faculty; Dr. Charles N. Dillman, Chairman, Division of Philosophy/Religion.

General Description. The Division of Philosophy/Religion is engaged in four major activities: (1) Pre-seminary theological education, with a strong emphasis on integration with Liberal Arts and Christian social action; (2) Christian vocational (professional) training, through the Contemporary Ministries major; (3) Philosophy Major; (4) Service of providing Bible courses and other Religion courses to students of other Divisions.

Parent Institution. Spring Arbor College is a Christian liberal arts college offering a baccalaureate degree with over 20 majors. The religious stance of the College and its faculty is evangelical and in the Wesleyan tradition.

Community Environment. Spring Arbor College is located in a rural setting, not far from population centers and major academic centers in southern Michigan. It is near the city of Jackson, Michigan, an important industrial city manufacturing mostly automobile and airplane parts and supplies. The county has numerous lakes and parks. Cultural activities include a symphony orchestra, music, dance, and theater groups.

Religious Denomination. Free Methodist.

Religious Emphasis. Evangelical, Wesleyan tradition.

Accreditation. North Central Association of Colleges and Schools.

Term System. Semester; January Interim; summer term.

Enrollment in Degree Programs in Religion 1984–85. Total 45; men 31, women 14.

Degrees in Religion Awarded 1984–85. Bachelor of Arts 8; men 5, women 3.

Faculty for Degree Programs in Religion. Total 7; full-time 4, part-time 3.

Admission Requirements. The college accepts applications from all persons without regard to race, color, creed, national origin, sex, age, or handicap. Applications are accepted from all persons who provide evidence of potential academic success at the college level and who will contribute to the Christian ideals of Spring Arbor College. An ACT composite score of 18 and a grade point average of 2.6 are recommended.

Tuition and Fees. Tuition $5,290 per year (includes Interim); room and board $2,208 per year; books, travel, and personal expenses $1,185 per year.

Financial Aid. Assistance may be received from the federal and state governments, as well as from college funds, in the form of grants, scholarships, loans, and employment.

Housing. Men's and women's dormitories, apartments for married students, and private apartments in the vicinity are available.

Library Facilities. The Hugh A. White Library includes over 81,686 catalogued items. In addition, 344 periodicals are available for faculty and student use. The library has special strength in Jewish Studies and Biblical Studies.

Religious Services/Activities. The College sponsors a Philosophy-Religion Forum annually as well as a Study-Tour to Israel in alternate years. It also participates at the annual meeting of the Wesleyan Theological Society. There are several enrichment programs that are cognizant of and addressed to Christian Perspective themes. These include convocations, Lecture Series, Spiritual Emphasis Series, and required chapel attendance.

Degree Programs

Academic majors in Philosophy-Religion leading to the Bachelor of Arts degree are offered in the areas of Contemporary Ministries, Philosophy, and Philosophy-Religion. The religion curriculum has several distinct objectives. General courses acquaint the student with Biblical literature, Christian theology, and the history of

Christianity. In keeping with the academic values of the college, the religion major provides a good foundation for graduate or seminary studies. It also exemplifies the mission of the college by its emphasis on the development of practical skills and perspectives for pastoral or missionary services, Christian education, and other ministries. The major requires a minimum of 36 hours from the division with specified courses.

The contemporary ministries major is designed to (1) cultivate a broad perspective on Christian life as ministry; (2) introduce the student to an expanding variety of special ministries in the church and society; (3) provide significant preparation for service in one of several vocational areas; (4) help the student assess what further education might be needed for effective service in the chosen area of ministry. Significant emphasis is placed upon the meaningful integration of academic and experiential learning. The program leads to a Bachelor of Arts degree.

The Supporting Church Ministries Program, also leading to a Bachelor of Arts degree, is designed to prepare the student to serve in a supporting role in the local church by providing preparation in Church Music, Christian Education, and Youth Ministry, as well as in Philosophy and Religion. Those interested in full-time music ministry may pursue the Sacred Music Major program offered by the Music department.

Special Programs

A special 20-hour Christian Discipleship Certificate Program is offered.

Western Michigan University
Department of Religion
Kalamazoo, MI 49008   (616) 383-1626

Administration. Dr. Dieter H. Haenicke, President; Dr. Philip Denefeld, Vice President, Academic Affairs; Dr. A. Bruce Clarke, Dean, College of Arts and Sciences; Dr. E. Thomas Lawson, Chairman, Department of Religion.

General Description. The Department of Religion offers a Bachelor of Arts in Religion and a minor in the teaching of the study of religion leading to teacher certification. The major and minor are designed as preparation for graduate study in religion, for teaching of the academic study of religion in the public schools, and for a vocation associated with religion.

Parent Institution. Western Michigan University is a state university with approximately 20,000 students, offering undergraduate and graduate degrees.

Community Environment. The University is located midway between Chicago and Detroit. The East Campus consists of 70 acres of which 15 acres are devoted to physical education and recreation. The West Campus of more than 400 acres is the location of current and anticipated expansion. At one time a gathering place for the Potawatomie Indians, Kalamazoo, Michigan received its name from the Indian word meaning "place where the water boils." Today the city is an important paper-manufacturing center, with an annual production of over three million tons.

Religious Denomination. None.

Accreditation. North Central Association of Colleges and Schools.

Term System. Semester.

Degrees in Religion Awarded 1984–85. Bachelor of Arts 9; men 5, women 4.

Faculty for Degree Programs in Religion. Total 9; full-time 9.

Admission Requirements. High school graduation; ACT.

Tuition and Fees. Tutition lower division $46.25 per credit hour, upper division $50.75 per credit hour; health maintenance fee (more than 7 credit hours) $36 per semester; room and board $1,253 for fall semester and $1,323 for winter semester.

Financial Aid. Student Financial Aid and Scholarships administers the Michigan Competitive Scholarship and University scholarship programs, and the Pell Grant, Supplemental Educational Opportunity Grant, College Work-Study, long-term loan, and short-term loan programs.

Housing. Residence halls and on-campus apartments are available. All students are permitted to live in housing of their own choosing.

Library Facilities. The main collection is housed in the Dwight B. Waldo Library. The total collection numbers over two million bibliographic items including books, bound periodicals, music scores, recordings, maps, documents, and materials in microform.

Religious Services/Activities. The University endorses no particular faith or religious tradition, but it welcomes and facilitates the presence of many religious organizations. A broad spectrum of religious opportunities including traditional, contemporary, and experimental worship, individual and small group Bible studies, workshops and retreats, study-travel experiences, social concerns, religious drama, and action groups is available to interested students.

Degree Programs

A major in Religion leading to the Bachelor of Arts degree consists of a minimum of 28 hours chosen from courses in the topics of Introductory Studies, Historical Studies, Comparative Studies in Religion, Methodological Studies in Religion, and Constructive Studies in Religion. Many of the courses in the department are approved for General Education, and students can extend their general education to include knowledge of religious thought and practice and to relate their knowledge of religion to their knowledge derived from other disciplines in the University.

Western Theological Seminary

86 East 12th Street
Holland, MI 49423   (616) 392-8555

Administration. I. John Hesselink, President.

General Description. In 1866, nineteen years after the arrival of Albertus C. Van Raalte and his orthodox pietist seceders from the state church of the Netherlands, the Reformed Church was petitioned for theological education by seven members of Hope College. Thus, the roots of Western Theological Seminary were established. For more than a century of service, Western has continued emphasis upon an understanding of the Biblical languages as a solid foundation for the interpretation of the Scriptures, together with a thorough study of both systematic and historical theology.

The Seminary is an educational institution of the Reformed Church in America. It has as its primary purpose the training of men and women for the diverse forms of Christian ministry in today's world. The Seminary offers four degree programs: Master of Divinity, Master of Religious Education, Master of Theology, and Doctor of Ministry.

Community Environment. The Seminary is located in Holland, Michigan, a city settled by the Dutch in 1847. The city is famous as the "Tulip Center of America."

Religious Denomination. Reformed Church in America.

Accreditation. North Central Association of Colleges and Schools; Association of Theological Schools in the United States and Canada.

Term System. Quarter.

Admission Requirements. Bachelor's degree from an accredited college or university with a balanced liberal arts program.

Tuition and Fees. Tuition $50 per credit hour; Doctor of Ministry program $3,600 for the three year program.

Financial Aid. Financial aid is available and based upon need. Work scholarships and loans can be arranged.

Housing. The Seminary owns thirteen houses comprising twenty-two apartments that are available to students. Students are responsible for making their own housing arrangements.

Library Facilities. The John Walter Beardslee Library includes more than 85,000 books, and files of over 800 periodicals, 500 of which are current subscriptions. A large collection of photographic slides depicts archaeology, church history, and church art and architecture. The Kolkman Memorial Archives preserves letters and papers which document the history of the Reformed Church in American and the Seminary, as well as the lives and labors of men and women influential in the mission and ministry of the church.

Religious Services/Activities. Emphasis is placed on the practice of prayer. Chapel services are held each morning and special preaching services are conducted from time to time for the benifit of the entire community.

Degree Programs

The Master of Divinity program has a requirement of 144 term hours. The curriculum is structured so as to enable each student to lay a foundation in theological education by studying required courses, building on that foundation by choosing additional courses in each major area, and developing depth in at least one aspect of theological education by completing an individual concentration.

The Master of Religious Education program has a requirement of 90 term hours. The In-Ministry track is for students already engaged in a ministry setting. The three-year program requires a one-week intensive seminar in August and a one-day each week residency. The program includes Biblical and theological foundations, equipping for shared ministry instruction, the development of ministerial units, and shared praxis discussions of work in the ministerial setting. A two-year residency track is also offered.

The Master of Theology degree is offered only to students from outside North America.

The Doctor of Ministry program is designed to assist persons in ministry to enhance and integrate Biblical-theological knowledge with ministerial disciplines and pastoral skills. The program is self-designed with two learning units and one elective in each of two years and an in-ministry project in the third year.

William Tyndale College
Department of Bible/Theology

35700 West Twelve Mile Road
Farmington Hills, MI 48018   (313) 553-7200

Administration. Dr. William A. Shoemaker, President; Dr. Herbert Cocking, Vice President for Academic Affairs; Paul E. Wilson, Chairman, Department of Bible/Theology; Matthew Parker, Director, Urban Ministry Program.

General Description. The Department of Bible/Theology offers studies in the areas of Biblical literature, theology, ministry, biblical languages, and church history. The Department's Biblical Literature program has a twofold purpose. First, it helps prepare the student to integrate Christian values into life and vocation. Second, it serves as an adequate foundation for graduate studies in Bible and Theology. It provides a base for pastoral work in a local church or other ministerial work such as missions, the chaplaincy, inner-city missions, evangelism, and Christian education ministries. It is the program to build on for graduate work leading into the pastoral ministry or the teaching ministry on the Bible college and seminary level. The Department's Pastoral Studies Specialization program is designed for those who wish to move immediately into the pastorate following graduation and are not planning to go on to seminary. Degrees offered are the

Bachelor of Religious Education in Biblical Literature or in Pastoral Studies; the Bachelor of Theology in Theology; the one-year Certificate in Basic Biblical Studies.

Parent Institution. William Tyndale College is a four-year institution offering programs in Biblical studies, liberal arts, and ministry. Bachelor and Associate degrees and Certificates are awarded. Its historical roots extend back to the Detroit Bible Institute of 1925, and its current curriculum includes majors in psychology, music, communication arts, cross-cultural student education, aviation, youth ministry, interdisciplinary studies, missions, and urban studies. Formerly known as Detroit Bible College, the school adopted the present name in 1981.

Community Environment. William Tyndale College is located on a 28-acre campus in Farmington Hills, Michigan, easily accessible from major expressways. The city is a growing suburban community in Oakland County, not far from Detroit. The campus is within a short drive of lakes and parks, museums, sports centers, evangelical churches and Christian organizations, the Detroit River front, and the border of Canada. This mix of rural, urban, suburban, and international communities near the campus provides an assortment of off-campus activity for students.

Religious Denomination. Nondenominational.

Religious Emphasis. Evangelical Protestant.

Accreditation. American Association of Bible Colleges.

Term System. Semester; summer term.

Faculty for Degree Programs in Religion. Total 10; full-time 4, part-time 6.

Admission Requirements. High school graduation; ACT; commendable Christian character; acceptable references.

Tuition and Fees. Tuition $2,656 per year; room and board $2,420 per year.

Financial Aid. All programs qualify for federal financial aid. Some programs are eligible for State of Michigan aid.

Housing. Dormitories are available for single students; apartments are available in the local community for married students.

Library Facilities. The library contains over 55,000 volumes.

Religious Services/Activities. Daily chapel services; Day of Prayer each semester; Spiritual Life Conference for one week of each semester; Student Ministries; Missions Conference for one week each year.

Degree Programs

The Bachelor of Religious Education degree is a four-year program and may be earned in the following areas: Biblical Literature, Communications, Cross-Cultural and Ethnic Studies, Education, Interdisciplinary Studies, Music, Pastoral Studies, and Psychology. The educational core consists of 30 hours in Biblical and theological subjects (every student "majors" in Bible). Foundational studies include 11 hours in courses that introduce the student to critical issues related to self, others, and the world community. Liberal Arts courses, or general educa-

tion courses, with a minimum of 42 hours are also required. The departmental major requires 42 semester hours for a total of 125 hours.

The Bachelor of Music degree is a four-year program and the student can major in Performance (Voice, Keyboard, or Orchestra Instrument) or Composition.

The Bachelor of Theology degree is a five-year course of study that combines 60 hours of general education earned at a regionally accredited institution with 89 hours of Biblical and theological education earned at William Tyndale College.

Special Programs

A Certificate in Basic Biblical Studies is a one-year non-degree program in Bible that includes 30 semester hours of required work in Bible, theology, and related fields.

Noncredit continuing education courses are available on campus and at 8 extension centers in southeastern Michigan.

MINNESOTA

Augsburg College
Department of Religion
731 21st Avenue, South
Minneapolis, MN 55454   (612) 330-1212

Administration. Charles S. Anderson, President.

General Description. The primary orientation of the Department of Religion is to provide a series of courses which will enable students to become better acquainted with the content and character of the Christian faith and enable them to reflect theologically on their own religious commitment. A major in the Department leads to the Bachelor of Arts degree.

Parent Institution. Augsburg College is a four-year liberal arts college of The American Lutheran Church. It was founded in 1869, the first seminary founded by Norwegian Lutherans in America and named after the confession of faith presented by Lutherans in Augsburg, Germany, in 1530. The College offers programs in a variety of disciplines leading to the Bachelor's degree.

Community Environment. The campus of 18 acres is located near the Minneapolis Loop and the University of Minneapolis.

Religious Denomination. The American Lutheran Church.

Accreditation. North Central Association of Colleges and Schools.

Term System. Semester.

Faculty for Degree Programs in Religion. Total 5.

Admission Requirements. High school graduation or equivalent; PSAT, ACT, or SAT.

Tuition and Fees. Tuition $5,560 per year; room $1,210; board $1,180.

Financial Aid. In addition to aid administered by the College, students are urged to investigate the possibility of scholarships, grants, and loans that might be available in their own communities.

Housing. Student housing is available in dormitories on campus.

Library Facilities. The George Sverdrup Library houses over 139,000 volumes. Students have access to over 5 million volumes through the Twin Cities private college consortium and Minitex.

Religious Services/Activities. Chapel is held three days each week. Students gather on Wednesday night for Holy Communion. Bible studies, fellowship groups, Gospel teams, retreats, and conferences are scheduled.

Degree Programs

The Bachelor degree major in Religion requires the completion of 8 courses in the Department. A Major in Church Staff Work requires 9 courses in the Department with specified courses in other departments leading to Augsburg certification. A program for Christian Day School Teachers is available through the Department of Education. In addition to the teacher education licensure program, 5 courses in Religion are required. This program prepares students who are interested in teaching in Christian Day Schools, particularly those of the American Lutheran Church, although participation is not limited to such schools.

Bethel College
Biblical and Theological Studies
3900 Bethel Drive
St. Paul, MN 55112   (612) 638-6400

Administration. Dr. George K. Brushaber, President; Dr. Dwight Jessup, Vice President and Dean; Robert G. Duffett, Dean of Christian Faith and Life.

General Description. The Department of Biblical and Theological Studies has four primary objectives: (1) to assist liberal arts students in fulfilling their graduation requirements of three courses in Biblical and theological studies; (2) to prepare students for seminary or other graduate studies in the fields related to theology; (3) to provide Biblical and theological background for other ministries which students may enter without a graduate degree; (4) to enrich the life and ministry of the Church by equipping educated lay persons with the tools for life-long Bible study.

Parent Institution. Bethel College is a 4-year Christian

liberal arts college which is owned and operated by the Baptist General Conference to provide Christ-centered higher education as a part of its teaching ministry. The student body is comprised of students from 29 countries and 41 states with over 35 religious denominations represented. Enrollment is approximately 1,800. The College shares the campus with The Bethel Theological Seminary.

Community Environment. Bethel College's campus consists of 214 acres of rolling, wooded terrain surrounding a spring-fed lake. The Twin Cities — Minneapolis-St. Paul — are located approximately 10 minutes away and provide an abundant array of cultural and recreational activities.

Religious Denomination. Baptist General Conference.

Religious Emphasis. Conservative.

Accreditation. North Central Association of Colleges and Schools.

Term System. Semester.

Enrollment in Degree Programs in Religion 1984–85. Total 99; men 62, women 37.

Degrees in Religion Awarded 1984–85. Bachelor of Arts in Biblical and Theological Studies 15; men 11, women 4.

Faculty for Degree Programs in Religion. Total 8; full-time 5, part-time 3.

Admission Requirements. Prospective students should submit an admissions application; take the SAT, ACT, or PSAT/NMSQT; have their high school academic records (or other college records) sent to Bethel; and see that reference forms are complete. Students must rank in the upper half of their graduating class, show evidence of personal commitment to Jesus Christ, and agree to live within Bethel's lifestyle practices. Students will be notified by letter of their acceptance status. Early application by January 1, if possible, is advantageous concerning financial aid awards.

Tuition and Fees. Tuition $5,990; room rental $1,485; food plans $865 to $1,175.

Financial Aid. Scholarships are awarded for academic achievement or participation in sports, music, debate, theater, and art. Grants are provided by churches and matched by Bethel. Loans are available on an interest-free basis until after college. Job opportunities are provided on campus and in the Twin Cities.

Housing. Freshmen and sophomores live in residences on campus; campus townhouses provided for smaller clusters of students. Off-campus apartments are available to juniors and seniors.

Library Facilities. The library houses over 115,000 volumes. Students have access to over 1 million volumes in the Minneapolis-St. Paul area.

Religious Services/Activities. Daily chapel; integration of faith with learning; Bible study groups and Christian service involvement. In addition to many group experiences which stimulate Christian growth, Bethel provides an intensive one-on-one discipleship program under the leadership of its Campus Pastor, beginning initially through student leaders in the campus residences and

spreading individually among the entire student body. The goal for all Bethel graduates is that they will be equipped to make a positive Christian impact in the world through their lives and vocations.

Degree Programs

The Bachelor of Arts with a major in Biblical and Theological Studies involves the historical foundations and doctrines of the Christian faith from the Old and New Testaments and provides the context in which this faith can be examined, strengthened, and applied to a variety of situations and opportunities. The student has opportunity to understand the teachings of the most significant world religions and is encouraged to learn one or more of the languages in which the Christian Scriptures were written.

Bethel Theological Seminary
3949 Bethel Drive
St. Paul, MN 55112   (612) 638-6288

Administration. Dr. George K. Brushaber, President; Dr. Gordon G. Johnson, Vice President and Dean, Theological Seminary.

General Description. Bethel Theological Seminary seeks to graduate men and women of spiritual maturity and broad sympathies whose perspectives of service embrace the world. This sense of world mission is consistent with the objectives of the Baptist General Conference, the denomination which supports the Seminary. The program is designed around objectives which are functional, pedagogical, and religious. The Seminary offers the degrees Master of Arts in Christian Education, Master of Arts in Theological Studies, Master of Divinity, Master of Theology, and Doctor of Ministry. It also offers Certificates in Theological Studies and Lay Ministry. The Seminary shares a campus with Bethel College.

Community Environment. See: Bethel College.

Religious Denomination. Baptist General Conference.

Religious Emphasis. Evangelical.

Accreditation. North Central Association of Colleges and Schools; Association of Theological Schools in the United States and Canada.

Term System. Quarter; summer term.

Enrollment in Degree Programs in Religion 1984–85. Total 489; men 407, women 82.

Degrees in Religion Awarded 1984–85. Master of Arts in Theological Studies 19; men 16, women 3. Master of Arts in Christian Education 4; men 4. Master of Divinity 46; men 43, women 3. Master of Theology 5; men 5. Doctor of Ministry 2; men 2.

Faculty for Degree Programs in Religion. Total 59; full-time 25, part-time 34.

Admission Requirements. Bachelor of Arts or Bachelor of Science degree.

Tuition and Fees. Tuition $3,180 full-time; testing fee $90; activity fee $10.50; room $110-$305 per month depending upon accommodations.

Financial Aid. Grants, scholarships, loans, employment; honor program for outstanding students.

Housing. Apartment housing available.

Library Facilities. 115,000 volumes.

Religious Services/Activities. Daily chapel; annual retreats.

Degree Programs

The Master of Arts in Theological Studies is a two-year academic program offered by the Seminary. Also available are the two-year professional Master of Arts in Christian Education degree, the three-year Master of Divinity professional program, the one-year post-graduate academic Master of Theology degree program, and the post-graduate professional Doctor of Ministry degree.

Special Programs

The Seminary has an extension campus in San Diego, California which is fully accredited and offers the same programs. The Seminary also offers a special program in Youth, Missions, and Urban Ministry.

Carleton College
Department of Religion
Northfield, MN 55057   (507) 663-4000.

Administration. Robert H. Edwards, President.

General Description. The Department of Religion offers the major in Religion, studied as a significant expression of human culture in the past and present. For those planning a career in teaching or ministry, courses serve as an introduction to a graduate or professional field of study.

Parent Institution. Carleton College was founded by the Minnesota Conference of Congregational Churches under the name of Northfield College in 1866. The present name was adopted in 1871. During its formative years, the College received significant support and direction from the Congregational churches. Although it is now autonomous and nonsectrian, the College respects these historical ties and gives continuing recognition to them through membership in the council for Higher Education of the United Church of Christ. The College offers a four-year liberal arts education leading to the Bachelor's degree.

Community Environment. The campus of 90 acres is located in Northfield, 40 miles south of Minneapolis/St. Paul, Minnesota.

Religious Denomination. Congregational Church.

Accreditation. North Central Association of Colleges and Schools.

Term System. 3-3 plan (three 10-week-long terms).

Faculty for Degree Programs in Religion. Total 9.

Admission Requirements. High school graduation or equivalent with rank in the upper 20 percent; ACT or SAT.

Tuition and Fees. Tuition and fees $8,460 per year;

room and board $2,440.

Financial Aid. Various types of aid are available, including scholarships, grants, loans, and campus employment.

Housing. Dormitory facilities accommodate over 1,600 students.

Library Facilities. The library houses over 360,000 volumes.

Degree Programs

The Bachelor degree major in Religion requires 60 credits in the Department distributed among prescribed courses. The historical traditions of the major religions are examined as well as theoretical and existential problems and issues which religion poses to men and women individually and in communities. The program of study leads to the Bachelor of Arts degree which requires a total of 210 credits. Students may petition for a special major in Jewish Studies, or take a concentrated program within a major in Religion.

Concordia College
Religion Department
901 South 8th Street
Moorhead, MN 56560   (218) 299-3334

Administration. Dr. Paul J. Dovre, President; Dr. James L. Haney, Jr., Chairperson, Religion Department.

General Description. The Religion Department provides the students' core requirement of two religion courses, and offers a major and minor in Religion.

Parent Institution. Concordia College is a liberal arts college of the American Lutheran Church. It grants the Bachelor of Arts and Bachelor of Music degrees. The 1984-85 enrollment was 2,464.

Community Environment. The Concordia College campus, located on 120 acres in the heartland of residential Moorhead, Minnesota, is both beautiful and functional. The city of Moorhead is separated from Fargo, North Dakota by the Red River of the North. Together they constitute a metropolitan-area population of 130,000. The two cities offer the convenience of small town living with the many advantages of the big city. The Minneapolis-St. Paul area is 250 miles southeast; Winnipeg, Manitoba is 250 miles to the north. Rich farmland, beautiful lake country, and pine forests are just minutes away.

Religious Denomination. American Lutheran Church.

Religious Emphasis. Reformed.

Accreditation. North Central Association of Colleges and Schools.

Term System. Semester; 2 summer terms: May and June.

Enrollment in Degree Programs in Religion 1984–85. Total 58.

Degrees in Religion Awarded 1984–85. Bachelor of Arts in Religion 9; men 9. Bachelor of Arts with a Religion minor 13; men 13.

Faculty for Degree Programs in Religion. Total 11; full-time 9, part-time 2.

Admission Requirements. High school graduation; admission test scores (SAT, PCT, PSAT); three recommendations.

Tuition and Fees. Tuition per academic year $5,950; room $850; board $1,110; student fee $50.

Financial Aid. 192 scholarships are available plus grants and federal and state aid.

Housing. Residence halls and one apartment building for single students; no married student housing on campus, but a list of apartments is maintained by the Office of Student Affairs.

Library Facilities. The Carl B. Ylvisaker Library holds over 265,000 volumes plus newspapers, magazines, tapes, and videotapes. Rare and valuable books such as early pioneer memoirs from the days of the first Red River Valley settlements are maintained.

Religious Services/Activities. Chapel services are held Monday through Friday. Many religious organizations are available for student participation.

Degree Programs

The Bachelor of Arts degree with a major in Religion requires the completion of nine courses. The selection of courses is governed by the following: (1) four of the five areas of Bible, Church History, History of Religions, Theology, and Ethics must be represented by at least one course; (2) no more than three of the religion core courses may be counted toward the major; (3) five courses must be selected from among the advanced courses and additional courses; and (4) The Research Seminar must be among the five courses selected from the advanced courses and additional courses, and should be taken during the senior year.

Special Programs

The Adults Continuing at Concordia (ACCORD) program is for those students aged 23 and over who want to take classes at the college level in order to earn a degree, make a career change, or just experience personal enrichment.

An ecumenical center for church and community, CHARIS is a program at Concordia that provides various forms of continuing theological education in Fargo-Moorhead and throughout the Upper Midwest. These offerings include graduate courses, lay academics, conferences, and workshops.

Concordia College - St. Paul
Division of Religion
Oswald Hoffman School of Christian
  Outreach
Hamline and Marshall Avenue
St. Paul, MN 55104   (612) 641-8229

Administration. Milton L. Rudnick, Acting President; Robert A. Kolb, Chairman, Division of Religion.

General Description. The Division of Religion of Concordia College offers Bachelor of Arts programs for pre-seminary students and for those seeking to become directors of Christian education, directors of evangelism, directors of parish music, and Lutheran parish school teachers, in conjunction with other divisions of the College. The Oswald Hoffman School of Christian Outreach cooperates with the Division of Religion in providing curricular and co-curricular programs for students and professional workers in the church, as well as lay people, in evangelism and missions.

Parent Institution. Concordia College - St. Paul, a 4-year liberal arts college with a variety of Bachelor of Arts programs, is owned and operated by the Lutheran Church - Missouri Synod. In addition to its programs in religion, it offers programs in business and a number of areas in the liberal arts and sciences.

Community Environment. Located in the middle of the "Twin Cities" metropolitan area, Concordia College is situated in the Midway district of St. Paul, Minnesota, immediately south of Interstate 94, which joins the business loops of St. Paul and Minneapolis. The 26-acre campus includes buildings which are conveniently located with many of them interconnected.

Religious Denomination. Lutheran Church - Missouri Synod.

Religious Emphasis. Confessional Lutheran.

Accreditation. North Central Association of Colleges and Schools.

Term System. Quarter; summer term.

Degrees in Religion Awarded 1984–85. Bachelor of Arts in: Church Teacher 35; men 7, women 28. Pre-Seminary 24; men 24; Director of Christian Education 12; men 8, women 4. Director of Evangelism 4; men 3, women 1. Director of Parish Music 1; men 1. Bible Translation 1; women 1.

Faculty for Degree Programs in Religion. Total 10; full-time 10.

Admission Requirements. Applicants must have graduated from high school or earned an equivalent certificate by passing the General Education Development Tests (GED).

Tuition and Fees. Tuition $4,575; residence hall and food service $1,980.

Financial Aid. Available in the form of grants, loans, scholarships, and campus employment.

Housing. Residence halls are available for single students and some apartments are provided for married students and their families.

Library Facilities. The Buenger Memorial Library contains 97,651 volumes (including curriculum materials).

Religious Services/Activities. Daily chapel services. Student Spiritual Life Committee sponsors various opportunities for study and service on and off campus.

Degree Programs

The Bachelor of Arts degree programs at Concordia College include the Director of Christian Education curriculum (also available with a Teacher Education combination curriculum), the Director of Evangelism curriculum, the Director of Parish Music Curriculum, and a Liberal Education program with a major in Religion. Students in the Liberal Education program include pre-seminary students. Students may choose a major (of which Religion can be selected) and two minors among which are the areas of Biblical Languages, Biblical Studies, Christian Thought, Church History, and Church Music.

Special Programs

The Associate in Arts degree is offered and includes a requirement of 7-8 credits in Religion.

The School of Adult Learning was introduced on campus in the fall of 1985 to serve qualified nontraditional students who have had two or more years of previous college experience.

Crosier Seminary Junior College
Onamia, MN 56359   (612) 532-3103

Administration. Rev. Eugene D. Plaisted, Rector; Rev. Tom O'Brien, Academic Dean.

General Description. Crosier Seminary Junior College offers the first two years of a liberal arts curriculum for young men investigating the priesthood of the Roman Catholic Church. The students participate in a program of investigation of the priesthood as well as completing the academic requirements for an Associate of Arts in the Humanities degree. Founded in 1922, the Seminary is connected with Crosier Monastery, and is conducted by the Canons Regular of the Holy Cross.

Community Environment. The Seminary is located on 35 acres in Onamia, Minnesota, and is housed in a single unit which follows the 16-century Flemish Rennaisance architecture of the original monastery. Onamia is near Mille Lacs Lake, one of the largest and most beautiful lakes in Minnesota with about 150 miles of shoreline. It is 50 miles northwest of St. Cloud, Minnesota (population 40,000).

Religious Denomination. Roman Catholic.

Religious Emphasis. Main-stream Catholic tradition.

Accreditation. North Central Association of Colleges and Schools.

Term System. Semester; no summer term.

Enrollment in Degree Programs in Religion 1984–85. Total 25; men 25.

Degrees in Religion Awarded 1984–85. Associate of Arts in the Humanities 7; men 7.

Admission Requirements. High school graduation; PSAT, SAT, or ACT; recommendations; interest in priesthood as personal possibility.

Tuition and Fees. $4,200 per year.

Financial Aid. Assistance is available. Contact the Financial Aid Office for procedure.

Housing. On-campus dormitory.

Library Facilities. The library houses over 25,000 volumes.

Religious Services/Activities. Daily celebration of the Eucharist and evening prayer required.

Degree Programs

The Associate of Arts degree is awarded upon completion of a minimum of 20 courses distributed through four Divisions of Instruction: Humanities, Natural Science and Mathematics, Social and Behavioral Science, Philosophy and Theology. Because of the directives of the American Catholic Bishops regarding proficiency in the ecclesiastical languages, all students are required to take courses in Latin and Greek.

Dr. Martin Luther College
New Ulm, MN 56073   (507) 354-8221

Administration. Rev. Lloyd O. Huebner, President.

General Description. Dr. Martin Luther College, now owned and operated by the Wisconsin Evangelical Synod, was founded in 1884 by the Evangelical Lutheran Synod of Minnesota and other states. The College offers a four-year curriculum in elementary teacher education, culminating in a Bachelor of Science in Education and enabling graduates with full synodical certification to teach in the schools of the Wisconsin Evangelical Lutheran Synod.

Community Environment. The campus of 50 acres is located in New Ulm, a rural area 100 miles southwest of Minneapolis/St. Paul, Minnesota.

Religious Denomination. Wisconsin Evangelical Lutheran Synod.

Accreditation. North Central Association of Colleges and Schools.

Term System. Semester.

Admission Requirements. High school graduation or equivalent; ACT.

Tuition and Fees. Tuition $805 per semester; room and board $810; student fees $258.

Financial Aid. Aid is available in the form of scholarships, grants-in-aid, loans, and employment.

Housing. Residence halls are available on campus.

Library Facilities. The Library houses more than 108,000 items, including books and non-print material.

Religious Services/Activities. Students attend divine services at St. John's or St. Paul's Lutheran churches. Chapel services are held each school day in the Academic Center auditorium.

Degree Programs

Because the College offers only a program of education to prepare elementary teachers for the public ministry of the Wisconsin Evangelical Lutheran Synod, a student must pursue the prescribed teacher education program. The Bachelor of Science degree in Education requires the completion of 138-139 credits.

Gustavus Adolphus College
Department of Religion
St. Peter, MN 56082   (507) 931-8000

Administration. Dr. John S. Kendall, President; Dr. David C. Johnson, Dean of the College; Dr. Conrad Hyers, Chair, Department of Religion.

General Description. The program of the Department of Religion is designed to meet the needs of all students for a better understanding of religion as a basic aspect of human experience, of the Christian heritage and its contemporary expressions, and of the methods appropriate to the study of religion. The curriculum is organized under 4 areas of concentration: Biblical Studies, Christian Thought, Religion and Culture, and History of Religions. The Department also supplies the Religion course requirement of all students. The degree Bachelor of Arts is awarded.

Parent Institution. Gustavus Adolphus College is a four-year liberal arts institution, residential in character, supported by the Lutheran Church in America. It was founded in 1876 by Swedish Lutheran immigrants, and preserves both its Swedish and Lutheran traditions while being open to students and faculty of other traditions.

Community Environment. Gustavus Adolphus College overlooks the town of St. Peter, Minnesota and the Minnesota River Valley from its position on the west bank. There are grassy malls and tall shade trees among the buildings and on the hillside. St. Peter is a community of 8,900 about 65 miles southwest of Minneapolis and St. Paul and 12 miles north of Mankato (population 40,000), along the Minnesota River. Surrounded by rich farmland and wooded areas, Mankato is an historic city with parks, businesses, and fine old homes.

Religious Denomination. Lutheran Church in America.

Religious Emphasis. Liberal.

Accreditation. North Central Association of Colleges and Schools.

Term System. Four-one-four semester system; summer term.

Enrollment in Degree Programs in Religion 1984–85. Total 32; men 16, women 16.

Degrees in Religion Awarded 1984–85. Bachelor of Arts

13; men 6, women 7.

Faculty for Degree Programs in Religion. Total 8; full-time 6, part-time 2.

Admission Requirements. High school graduation or equivalent; SAT or ACT scores.

Tuition and Fees. Tuition $6,500; room and board $2,-700.

Financial Aid. Federal, state, and institutional aid are available.

Housing. Most students reside on campus.

Library Facilities. The library contains over 200,000 volumes and houses the Archives of Minnesota Synod-Lutheran Church in America, the Scandinavia Library, and a federal government document collection.

Religious Services/Activities. Daily chapel; religious organizations (Lutheran Youth Organization, Fellowship of Christian Athletes, Campus Crusade, Chapel Worship Committee, Youth Outreach).

Degree Programs

The major in Religion leading to the Bachelor of Arts degree requires 7 courses selected in consultation with an advisor plus the senior thesis seminar. Each of the four departmental areas (Biblical Studies, Christian Thought, Religion and Culture, and History of Religions) must be represented in the courses chosen.

Hamline University
Department of Religion
1536 Hewitt Avenue
St. Paul, MN 55104   (612) 641-2207

Administration. Charles J. Graham, President.

General Description. The Department of Religion offers courses designed to provide the student with a better understanding of his/her own and other faiths; an appreciation of the role of religion in history, in culture, and in personal life; and criteria for evaluating various religious perspectives. The Department offers two majors: a standard departmental major and a major with a Jewish studies focus. The Bachelor degree is awarded.

Parent Institution. Hamline University is the oldest institution of higher learning in Minnesota. It was chartered in 1854 by the legislative assembly of the Territory of Minnesota. The University is a coeducational, private, independent institution affiliated with the United Methodist Church. It grants the Bachelor, Master, and Juris Doctor degrees.

Community Environment. The campus of 37 acres is located in the Midway district of St. Paul, almost equidistant from the downtown business areas of St. Paul and Minneapolis.

Religious Denomination. United Methodist Church.

Accreditation. North Central Association of Colleges and Schools.

Term System. Semester (4-1-4 plan).

Faculty for Degree Programs in Religion. Total 6.

Admission Requirements. Graduation from an accredited high school or equivalent; rank in upper fifty percent of graduating class; SAT, ACT, or PSAT.

Tuition and Fees. Tuition $6,910 per year; room and board $2,680; student fees $150.

Financial Aid. Assistance is granted on the basis of the student's estimated financial need.

Housing. Dormitories plus fraternity and sorority houses supply living accommodations on campus.

Library Facilities. The Bush Memorial Library houses over 175,000 volumes.

Religious Services/Activities. Special convocations and other programs are held in the Hamline United Methodist Church adjacent to the campus.

Degree Programs

The standard Religion major requires a minimum of nine courses. Students are urged to seek both breadth and depth in their religious studies: the former through acquaintance with the Biblical, historical, philosophical-ethical and non-Western offerings of the Department, the latter by developing a focus of concentration within one of them. Students planning on a church-related vocation should take at least four religion courses if they choose not to major in religion.

The Religion major with a Jewish studies focus prepares students for careers or graduate study in a variety of fields. A major consists of a minimum of nine course credits. The Bachelor's degree requires completion of 35 course credits.

Luther Northwestern Theological Seminary
2481 Como Avenue
St. Paul, MN 55108   (612) 641-3456

Administration. Lloyd Svendsbye, President; Carol E. Baker, Registrar.

General Description. Luther Northwestern Theological Seminary provides theological education to those who are preparing for service as pastors, missionaries, teachers, and for other forms of lay or ordained ministry. Theological resources are also provided for the continuing education of laity and clergy.

The Seminary, through a series of mergers covering more than a half century, represents the consolidation into one seminary of what at one time were six separate institutions. The Seminary traces its origin to the "Chicago Lutheran Divinity School," begun in Chicago in 1920 following action taken by the English Evangelical Lutheran Synod of the Northwest, a synod of the United Lutheran Church in America. In 1921 the Seminary moved to Fargo, North Dakota and the folowing year to Minneapolis. From 1921 to 1982, its name was Northwestern Lutheran Seminary. Located in north Minneapolis from 1922 to 1940, and in the former Pillsbury mansion in

south Minneapolis for the next 27 years, it moved to the campus of Luther Theological Seminary in 1967. Luther and Northwestern Seminaries functionally unifed in 1976. The current single seminary was established in 1982 as Luther Northwestern Theological Seminary.

Community Environment. The campus is located on more than 40 acres of rolling and wooded land in the residential neighborhood of St. Anthony Park. Situated between the two metropolitan campuses of the University of Minnesota, the Seminary is neighbor to a dozen other colleges and professional schools. The Twin Cities of Minneapolis/St. Paul abound in cultural advantages of every kind. Great art galleries, theaters for the performing arts, notable musical organizations, both choral and instrumental, parks, lakes, and professional sports are found here.

Religious Denomination. The American Lutheran Church and The Lutheran Church in America.

Accreditation. North Central Association of Colleges and Schools; Association of Theological Schools in the United States and Canada.

Term System. Quarter; summer term.

Enrollment in Degree Programs in Religion 1984–85. Total 834; men 593, women 241.

Degrees in Religion Awarded 1984–85. Master of Arts. Master of Divinity. Master of Theology. Doctor of Ministry.

Faculty for Degree Programs in Religion. Total 62; full-time 62.

Admission Requirements. For Master of Divinity and Master of Arts degrees: Bachelor degree; 4 semesters or 6 quarters of college Greek (not required for M.A. unless majoring in New Testament); 6 semester hours or 9 quarter hours of Philosophy; GRE general test scores; transcripts; four references; medical statement signed by a physician; autobiography. For the Master of Theology and Doctor of Ministry degrees: Master of Divinity degree with grade point average of at least 3.0 on a 4.0 scale. For Doctor of Ministry degree: a minimum of 3 years in some form of professional ministry after receipt of Master of Divinity degree; personal statement; 3 letters of reference.

Tuition and Fees. Costs per year: tuition full-time $1,-800, part-time $62.50 per quarter hour; service fee full-time $105, part-time $25; Student Body fee $8; dormitory housing $741 to $999 depending upon accommodations; apartments for married students $155 to $310 (efficiency to three-bedroom); board plans from $1,080 to $1,260 per 9-month basis.

Financial Aid. The Seminary operates on the premise that all students worthy of admission or presently in good standing are eligible for financial assistance if they show evidence of financial need. Part-time employment opportunities are available both on and off campus.

Housing. Residence halls and apartment complexes are on a space-available basis.

Library Facilities. The Seminary library houses 200,000 volumes and more than 700 periodical titles are received regularly. The library has an extensive collection of 17th and 18th century Lutheran theology. The Carl Doving Hymnology Collection of about 1,000 volumes contains hymnbooks of most religious denominations in many European and non-European languages. Also of special interest is the Jacob Tanner Catechism Collection, which contains the translations of Luther's Small Catechism into 160 languages and dialects. The Rare Book Room is the repository of over 2,500 rare books. Among these are 13th century French Bible manuscripts, leaves from medieval Books of Hours, three Syriac manuscripts from the 16th and 17th centuries, and a 1478 imprint from the press of Peter Bartua & Sons in Venice. Among the Room's features are the special stained glass windows which depict the printing logos of six prominent early Reformation printers.

Religious Services/Activities. The Luther Northwestern community gathers daily to express in prayer, praise, and thanksgiving its shared faith. Both the ancient forms of liturgy and modern expresssions of worship are utilized. Holy Communion is celebrated weekly. A full-time Campus Pastor serves the seminary community in the areas of counseling, worship, and spiritual formation.

Degree Programs

The Master of Divinity program is a four-year course, three years in residence and one year in internship, and is designed primarily to prepare students for the parish ministry. The classic disciplines of biblical, historical, doctrinal, and pastoral theology furnish the core of the curriculum, supplemented by a wide selection of elective courses.

The Master of Arts program is designed for persons who are engaged, or plan to be engaged, in various lay ministries in the church (e.g., parish assistants, parish education directors, youth workers, parish administrators, etc.) and other lay persons who have interest in the study of theology. This is a two-year program which offers majors in the departments of Old Testament, New Testament, Church History, Systematic Theology, Pastoral Theology and Ministry, and in the area of Youth Ministry.

The Master of Theology is a one-year full-time residence program beyond the Master of Divinity degree which aims to develop in the candidate a high degree of informed, critical, theological awareness in the chosen field of study. The candidate must choose to specialize in one of the following fields: Biblical Studies, Church History, Systematic Theology, Missions and World Religions, Pastoral Theology and Ministry, and Pastoral Care (which includes programs in clinical pastoral theology and Ministry in Pastoral Care and Social Change).

The Doctor of Ministry is the highest professional degree for ordained persons in the parish or related ministries. With a primary emphasis upon the practice of ministry, the course of study aims at equipping persons in the integration of theological disciplines; development of their own programs of continuing study; skill in dealing with peers; and the establishment of the ministries of lay persons. The minimum time for completion of the program is two years; the maximum time is five years.

Special Programs

There are numerous offerings, including continuing education, off-campus programs, evening courses for lay persons, cross-cultural studies, and overseas studies and seminars.

Lutheran Brethren Schools
Junior Bible College and Seminary
West Vernon Avenue
Fergus Falls, MN 56537   (218) 729-3375

Administration. Omar N. Gjerness, President; Donald W. Brue, Vice President and Chairman, Department of Practical Theology, Education, and Psychology; Harold E. Hosch, Chairman, Department of Biblical Languages and Exposition.

General Description. The Lutheran Brethren Schools constitute The Junior Bible College and the Seminary, on the same campus. The Junior Bible College grants the Associate in Arts degree. The Seminary grants the Master of Arts in Religion and the Master of Divinity degrees. There is a special program of training for the ministry designed for students who because of age or other considerations desire to enter the ministry but have not had the preparation of a bachelor's degree. This special program grants a diploma. The Lutheran Brethren Schools are an educational institution of the Church of the Lutheran Brethren of America. This church body is low-church, Lutheran, Evangelical, Evangelistic, and Pietistic.

Community Environment. One of the largest shipping points in the midwest for dairy products and poultry, Fergus Falls, population 12,449, also has the largest cooperative creamery in the region. There are 1,000 lakes in the area which are from 10 to 60 minutes away by car.

Religious Denomination. Lutheran.

Religious Emphasis. Evangelical-Conservative.

Term System. Semester; no summer term.

Faculty for Degree Programs in Religion. Total 15; full-time 6, part-time 9.

Admission Requirements. High school diploma for Junior College; Bachelor's degree for Master of Arts and Master of Divinity Programs.

Tuition and Fees. Tuition $1,100; room rent $320; board $530; activity fee $20; registration fee $25; student body fee $12 (all per semester).

Financial Aid. Scholarships available upon application; usually given during the course of the school year.

Housing. Campus housing; most married students live off-campus. Assistance is available in finding housing.

Library Facilities. The Broen Media Center houses the Bible College and Seminary library of over 15,000 volumes.

Religious Services/Activities. Church located on campus; Prayer Day observed once each semester; chapel attendance is required daily. Assignments are given in church-related activity. There are occasional field trips to hear guest speakers and there are occasional guest lectureships on campus.

Degree Programs

The Master of Divinity degree (Pastor's degree) is granted to Seminary students upon the completion of the 3-year program. Requirements include 14 credits of New Testament Greek and Greek Exegesis; 98 credits in Seminary courses meeting all the departmental course requirements; minimum of 2 and maximum of 4 credits in practical experience, a senior project, and 6 semester credits in Homiletics and Advanced preaching. The Master of Arts in Religion degree is a non-pastoral 2-year degree program. Requirements include a minimum of 8 credits in each of the five theological disciplines of Old Testament, New Testament, Systematic Theology, Historical Theology, and Practical Theology; 64 credits in Seminary courses with at least 40 credits in theological courses; minimum of 3 and maximum of 6 credits in practical experience; and a senior project.

Special Programs

Seminary students who are deficient in the College prerequisites but who are accepted for Seminary status, or students who may not meet the requirements for the Master of Divinity degree, will be granted a Diploma upon completion of the required 98 credits with a grade point of not less than 2.0.

The Associate of Arts degree is granted by the Bible College upon completion of the prescribed courses of study as outlined in the curriculum with a minimum total of 64 credits of work and a grade point average of not less than 2.0.

A correspondence course on cassette is available in Systematic Theology.

Macalester College
Department of Religion
1600 Grand Avenue
St. Paul, MN 55105   (612) 696-6357

Administration. Dr. Robert M. Gavin, Jr., President.

General Description. The Department of Religion offers courses that focus on the study of Christianity in both its historical and contemporary expressions, as well as a major in non-Christian religious thought. The program of studies aims not only at students whose academic specialization or vocational choice is related to religion, but also at supporting a student's total curriculum by courses that can help unlock the religious dimensions encountered in other disciplines.

Parent Institution. Macalester College was founded in 1873 with the support of the Presbyterian Church. The Church-College ties are still strong and meaningful today. From the beginning, Macalester's leaders decided that the College should be nonsectarian in its instruction and attitudes. It is a four-year liberal arts institution offering programs leading to the Bachelor's degree.

Community Environment. The campus of 44 acres is located in Macalester Park, a residential section nearly equidistant from the downtown areas of St. Paul and Minneapolis.

Religious Denomination. Presbyterian Church (U.S.A.).

Accreditation. North Central Association of Colleges and Schools.

Term System. Semester (4-1-4 plan).

Admission Requirements. Graduation from an accredited high school; ACT or SAT.

Tuition and Fees. Tuition $7,520 per year; room and board $2,600; student activity fee $75.

Financial Aid. The financial aid program is open to all full-time students. A student may receive Macalester aid up to eight semesters assuming all criteria are met.

Housing. Dormitory accommodations are available on campus.

Library Facilities. The Weyerhaeuser Library and Olin Science Library have collections totaling over 292,000 volumes.

Religious Services/Activities. The Weyerhaeuser Memorial Chapel serves as a campus center for worship each Sunday of the school year. The Macalester Jewish Cultural Organization/Hebrew House sponsors special Jewish religious programs. The Muslim Student Center also sponsors services and programs. The full-time College Chaplain is an ordained Presbyterian minister.

Degree Programs

The Bachelor degree major concentration in Religious Studies consists of eight courses in religion, two courses in history, philosophy, or English. A "senior dialogue" with members of the Department is required for all majors. This dialogue represents a sharing of views on questions of mutual interest rather than an oral examination. Three foundation courses are required for the major. The core concentration in Religious Studies consists of 12 courses directly related to a particular problem or theme, six of which shall be in the Department. A "senior dialogue" is also required of all cores.

Minnesota Bible College
920 Mayowood Road S.W.
Rochester, MN 55902   (507) 288-4563

Administration. Bruce E. Miller, President.

General Description. Minnesota Bible College is a four-year institution that educates persons for leadership in church-related ministries. The College relocated to Rochester in 1971 from Minneapolis where it was first established in 1913. Bachelor of Arts programs include majors in Pastoral Ministry, Christian Education, and Music. The Associate of Arts program can be completed in two years. It is designed to prepare students for specialized study for church vocations by providing a foundational core of Biblical studies along with general education in the arts and sciences. Cooperative degree programs are available through regionally-accredited colleges in nursing, elementary education, and secondary education.

Community Environment. The College is located on 43 acres in six buildings. The Mayo Clinic founded by Drs. William and Charles Mayo has made Rochester (population 60,000) world famous. The transient population is estimated at 8,000 to 10,000 at any one time. Visitors are estimated at 550,000 annually. Community cultural activities abound.

Religious Denomination. Christian Churches and Churches of Christ.

Accreditation. American Association of Bible Colleges.

Term System. Quarter; no summer term.

Enrollment in Degree Programs in Religion 1984–85. Total 21; men 16, women 5 (upper division students only).

Degrees in Religion Awarded 1984–85. Bachelor of Arts 10; men 9, women 1. Bachelor of Science 4; men 3, women 1.

Faculty for Degree Programs in Religion. Total 13; full-time 10, part-time 3.

Admission Requirements. A high school diploma is normally required, however, under certain circumstances a GED is acceptable. ACT scores are required. Evidence of good character and appreciation and acceptance of the purposes and ideals of Minnesota Bible College (as stated in promotional materials) is also required. A short essay stating educational goals and reasons for choosing Minnesota Bible College along with the $10 application fee should accompany the Application for Admission form.

Tuition and Fees. Tuition $2,250 per year; room $990 per year; miscellaneous fees are minimal; board is not provided; estimated costs of textbooks $350 to $400 per year.

Financial Aid. The following types are available: Pell Grant, Minnesota State Scholarship and Grants, Minnesota Guaranteed Student Loan, Minnesota College Work-Study. The College requires the completion of the Family Financial Statement (FFS) offered through the American College Testing program. Information on the FFS is used to apply for several of the aforementioned scholarships and/or grants.

Housing. Townhouse units for all full-time single students are available; married student housing is available as one bedroom efficiency apartments.

Library Facilities. The library houses over 23,000 volumes plus periodicals, microfiche, and audiovisual materials.

Religious Services/Activities. Chapel services are held twice a week with attendance required for full-time students seeking a degree. Special emphasis is given to mis-

sions in the fall and to various other areas in specially held week-long activities.

Degree Programs

All Bachelor programs require an additional 2 years after receiving the Associate of Arts degree (98 credit hours), a "General Ministry" program. The core curriculum of the Upper Division is intended to satisfy the need for a broad understanding and foundation for a church leadership vocation. It includes 40 credit hours in Religion and Bible, 4 in the Arts and Sciences, 8 in Christian Education, and 4 in Music and Christian Ministries. Majors leading the Bachelor of Arts degree include Preaching Ministry, Christian Education, and Music and require a minimum of 40 quarter hours. A Bachelor of Science program is designed for students who wish to pursue Biblical studies at an upper division level but without a view to professional leadership in the church. A Major in Bible Theology and at least one minor from any department for a total of 96 quarter hours is required.

North Central Bible College
910 Elliot Avenue South
Minneapolis, MN 55404   (612) 332-3491

Administration. Dr. Don Argue, President.

General Description. North Central Bible College received its first students in 1930 under the name of North Central Bible Institute and offered a three-year program with a general Bible curriculum. The College became a four-year institution in 1955 and the name was adopted in 1957. The purpose of the College is to educate students for ministry and to proved a special environment for higher education and spiritual development. It grants a Diploma and the Associate and Bachelor degrees. The College is owned and supported by the Minnesota District Council of the Assemblies of God.

Community Environment. The College is located in the heart of the metropolitan area of downtown Minneapolis.

Religious Denomination. Assemblies of God.

Accreditation. American Association of Bible Colleges.

Term System. Semester.

Enrollment in Degree Programs in Religion 1984–85. Total 524; men 302, women 222.

Faculty for Degree Programs in Religion. Total 35; full-time 22, part-time 13.

Admission Requirements. Graduation from an accredited high school or GED; ACT.

Tuition and Fees. Tuition $98 per credit hour; dormitory housing $550-$605 per semester; apartment complex $240-$380 per month; general fee $145.

Financial Aid. Assistance is granted on the basis of the student's estimated financial need.

Housing. Dormitory rooms and apartments are available on campus.

Library Facilities. The T.J. Jones Memorial Library

contains over 21,000 volumes.

Religious Services/Activities. Chapel services are held daily. The College Ministries Office directs various activities including musical gospel teams, evangelism, local church ministry, and the student missions organization.

Degree Programs

The College offers a four-year program leading to a Bachelor of Arts or Bachelor of Science degree. Majors are offered in Pastoral Studies, Pastoral Studies (Deaf), Christian Education, Elementary Education, Cross Cultural Ministries, Deaf Culture Ministries, Sacred Music, and Behavioral Science. The Bachelor's degree requires the completion of 126 credits.

Special Programs

The Associate of Arts degree requires the completion of 62 credits, the Diploma requires 96 credits, and 30 credits are required for the One-Year Bible Certificate.

Northwestern College
Division of Bible and Ministries
3003 North Snelling
St. Paul, MN 55113   (612) 636-4840

Administration. Dr. Donald O. Erickson, President; Dr. William B. Bernsten, Chancellor; Dwight W. Gunberg, Dean of Faculty.

General Description. The Bible and Ministries Division of Northwestern College seeks to provide a Biblical Arts curriculum which will assist every Christian person to achieve a practical and purposeful knowledge and understanding of the Word of God, prophetic truth, effective Bible study methods, doctrine, philosophical problems, and missionary and personal witness responsibilities as related to the Christian life. Every College degree program requires one year of Bible. The Division awards the Bachelor of Arts degree in Biblical Studies, Christian Education, Ministries, Pastoral Studies, or Youth Ministries; the Bachelor of Science in Christian Education or Youth Ministries. Also available are Certificates in Biblical Arts and in Biblical Arts and Vocational Studies.

Parent Institution. Northwestern College is a Christian institute of the Bible, Arts, Sciences, and Vocational Education. It states that it is a "Faith Affirming, Christian College, standing unapologetically for the Christian faith, and is intent upon the presentation of the whole realm of truth, with a view toward rational integration of major fields of learning in the context of Biblical revelation." The College strives to promote the development of truly Christian values in character and deportment.

Community Environment. After 60 years in the heart of Minneapolis, Northwestern College is now in a suburban setting on the shores of two lakes — Lake Johanna and Little Lake Johanna — only minutes from downtown Minneapolis or St. Paul. The 95-acre campus is divided between the cities of Roseville and Arden Hills, and includes 7 major buildings, athletic fields, and recreation areas, including woodlands, hiking paths, and beaches. The campus is superbly suited for exciting and meaningful collegiate life for students.

Religious Denomination. Nondenominational.

Religious Emphasis. Conservative Evangelical.

Accreditation. North Central Association of Colleges and Schools.

Term System. Quarter; summer term.

Enrollment in Degree Programs in Religion 1984–85. Total 138; men 96, women 42.

Degrees in Religion Awarded 1984–85. Bachelor of Arts in Ministries 16; men 12, women 4. Bachelor of Arts in Pastoral Studies 3; men 3. Bachelor of Arts/Bachelor of Science in Christian Education 17; men 8, women 9. Bachelor of Arts/Bachelor of Science in Youth Ministries 10; men 6, women 4.

Faculty for Degree Programs in Religion. Total 9; full-time 9.

Admission Requirements. Autobiographical essay; reference forms; high school transcript; ACT, SAT, or PSAT scores (for counseling and guidance).

Tuition and Fees. Tuition $1,800; board $325-$350; room $400.

Financial Aid. Financial assistance is available in a variety of forms: time-payment plan, loans, scholarships, grants-in-aid, and work-study programs.

Housing. Northwestern requires that anyone not living at home shall live in a college residence except for the few instances where approval is given for other housing arrangements.

Library Facilities. The Riley Memorial Library contains 67,800 volumes; other resources include 400 currently received periodical titles.

Religious Services/Activities. Attendance is required at regular daily chapel services. The Director of Christian Ministries assists students in finding churches where they may fellowship and serve.

Degree Programs

The Bachelor of Arts degree is awarded to students completing the requirements with majors in Biblical Studies, Ministries, and Pastoral Studies. The Bachelor of Arts degree or the Bachelor of Science degree is awarded upon the completion of all requirements with majors in Christian Education, Youth Ministries.

Special Programs

The Associate in Arts and Bible program is designed to prepare the graduate for transfer to an upper degree program at Northwestern or at another institution. The degree is granted upon completion of 94 credits as specified by the Division.

The Certificate in Biblical Arts provides tools for continuing Bible study and for effective Christian witness. It is of value to professional men and women going to the mission field and needing such a concentrated study of the Bible. It is granted upon completion of 45 credits as specified by the Division.

St. Benedict, College of
Department of Theology
College Avenue South
St. Joseph, MN 56374   (612) 363-5308

Administration. Sr. Emmanuel Renner, O.S.B., President.

General Description. The Department of Theology emphasizes information, appreciation, and critical evaluation of religious experience and expression. While the tradition of the Department is mainly Roman Catholic, its offerings include studies in other Christian traditions, in Jewish life and thought, and in world religions. The Bachelor of Arts degree is granted.

Parent Institution. The College of St. Benedict is a Catholic liberal arts college founded by and for women. It is also engaged in a full-time cooperative academic exchange with nearby St. John's University for men in Collegeville.

Community Environment. The campus of 700 acres is located in St. Joseph, 75 miles from Minneapolis/St. Paul, Minnesota.

Religious Denomination. Roman Catholic.

Accreditation. North Central Association of Colleges and Schools.

Term System. Semester (4-1-4 plan).

Admission Requirements. High school graduation from an approved high school or equivalent.

Tuition and Fees. Tuition $5,140 per year; part-time tuition $190 per credit hour; room $1,100-$1,395; board $950 (minimum).

Financial Aid. The Committee on Scholarships and Financial Aid at the College reviews applications for assistance in terms of need, academic ability, participation in extracurricular activities, and character.

Housing. Dormitory accommodations are available on campus.

Library Facilities. The library is a joint library with St. John's University four miles away. The combined resources total over 410,000 volumes.

Religious Services/Activities. Campus Ministry offers a variety of experiences that challenge students to participate and discover the implications of Gospel living. Retreats, Bible studies, daily Mass, and Sunday Eucharist are regularly scheduled.

Degree Programs

Three concentrations are available for majors in the Department of Theology: Theology (40 credits), Religious Education (36 credits), and Pastoral Ministry (36 credits). Courses are offered in the areas of Scripture, Systematic: Doctrine/Moral, History/Historical Theology, Liturgical Studies, Religious Education, and Pastoral Theology/

Ministry. The Bachelor of Arts degree is awarded and requires a total of 120 semester hours.

St. Catherine, College of
Department of Theology
2004 Randolph Avenue
St. Paul, MN 55105   (612) 690-6017

Administration. Dr. Anita Pampusch, Acting President; Dr. Michael Murphy, Acting Academic Dean; Dr. Joan Timmerman, Director, Master of Arts Program in Theology.

General Description. The Department's Master of Arts program is unique in that it offers advanced theological education as an *academic* — not ministry-related — program for men and women who are not preparing for ordained ministry. It offers an environment supportive of women's equality and leadership. It is a compact, specifically-focused program concentrating on the study of Christian classics. Students in the M.A. program also have the opportunity to acquire the College's certification in Pastoral Ministry by completing certain additional requirements. Those who combine these programs gain a professional theological foundation with pastoral credentials, experience, and skills — with guidance to integrate these areas of study.

Parent Institution. Founded in 1905 as a Catholic liberal arts college for women, The College of St. Catherine continues to adhere to this mission in its undergraduate program. Sponsored by the Sisters of St. Joseph of Carondolet, the College offers over 30 major fields of study in liberal arts and professional disciplines. The College's reputation as an institution of academic rigor and strength goes back to its founding. In 1937 it became the first Catholic college or university to be awarded a chapter of Phi Beta Kappa. The College offers students of all faiths the experience of a believing community. It creates an atmosphere supportive of religious values and provides opportunities for worship.

Community Environment. Located on 110 acres in residential St. Paul, Minnesota, the College is convenient to the heart of 2 major metropolitan areas. It is very accessible to public transportation.

Religious Denomination. Roman Catholic.

Religious Emphasis. Moderate.

Accreditation. North Central Association of Colleges and Schools.

Term System. Semester (B.A., M.A., Certificate); Trimester (B.A., Certificate, Weekend College); summer term.

Degrees in Religion Awarded 1984–85. Bachelor of Arts in Theology 9; women 9. Master of Arts in Theology 5; women 5. Certificate in Pastoral Ministry 20; men 2, women 18.

Faculty for Degree Programs in Religion. Total 14; full-time 10, part-time 4.

Admission Requirements. Undergraduate: admission to College; $15 application fee; official high school transcript; results of ACT, SAT, or PSAT; student must petition to major after completing 3 theology courses (grade point average of at least 3.0 in theology courses strongly recommended); written essay. Master's program: Bachelor's degree from accredited institution; 3 letters of recommendation; scores of Miller Analogies Test; $15 application fee.

Tuition and Fees. $735 per 4-credit course ($187.50 per credit); activity fee $5; room $720 per semester; board $562 per semester.

Financial Aid. M.A. students are eligible for a GSL of up to $5,000 per year if they are taking at least 2 courses per semester. There is also a ½ tuition scholarship program administered through the Theology department for qualified students. Varying amounts of financial assistance to undergraduate students who demonstrate financial aid is also available.

Housing. Residence halls and college-owned apartment buildings are available.

Library Facilities. The library houses over 227,368 volumes and subscribes to over 1,000 periodicals and newspapers. It also maintains the Women's Collection.

Religious Services/Activities. Campus Ministry programs are open to all college community members and include spiritual direction and retreats, vocational exploration, and formation in ministry. Sunday and weekday Eucharist are celebrated; morning and evening prayer are also offered.

Degree Programs

The Bachelor of Arts with a major in Theology requires the completion of required general education courses plus ten theology courses.

The Master of Arts in Theology requires the completion of nine courses with a minimum of C; an overall grade point average of 3.0; successful completion of oral and written comprehensive examinations after successful completion of coursework and demonstration of reading ability in one of the following languages: Hebrew, Latin, Greek, French, German, Spanish, or Italian; the nine courses include three courses each in Historical, Scriptural, and Systematic Theology.

Special Programs

The Certificate in Pastoral Ministry program prepares individuals to take professional positions in church ministries such as parish administration, religious education, youth ministry, adult formation, crisis counseling, hospital pastoral ministry, and spiritual guidance. It consists of six courses in Theology including two pastoral theology courses and a nine-month supervised internship. It can be earned through the regular day-school program or in the Weekend College.

A Summer Institute of Christian Spirituality and Ministry is offered each year for those actively involved in ministry and for individuals who wish to deepen their understanding and practice in Christian Spirituality.

St. John's University
School of Theology
Collegeville, MN 56321   (612) 363-2100

Administration. Dr. Daniel Rush Finn, Dean; Sister Elise Saggau, O.S.F., Assistant Dean for Students.

General Description. St. John's School of Theology is dedicated to the preparation of ministers for the Church. It provides theological education to young men preparing for the Catholic priesthood and residing at the local diocesan seminary. It also serves women and men who are preparing for a wide range of services in the Church. In addition to academic formation, it provides for the ongoing spiritual and personal growth of its students through a variety of services and opportunities. It places a strong emphasis on a community atmosphere and draws deeply on the Benedictine tradition which is the context for the School's life.

Parent Institution. The University was founded by the Benedictines in 1857 and is committed to the liberal and professional education of men. It cooperates with the nearby College of St. Benedict, a 4-year women's liberal arts college, to provide a strong education for both men and women.

Community Environment. The campus is located in a beautiful rural area of woods and lakes, just 10 miles from St. Cloud, Minnesota, the site of a large state university. It is 80 miles from the metropolitan center of Minneapolis/St. Paul.

Religious Denomination. Roman Catholic.

Accreditation. North Central Association of Colleges and Schools; Association of Theological Schools in the United States and Canada.

Term System. Semester; January term; summer term.

Enrollment in Degree Programs in Religion 1984–85. Total 133; men 96, women 37.

Degrees in Religion Awarded 1984–85. Master of Divinity 16; men 15, women 1. Master of Arts in Theology 15; men 6, women 9. Master of Arts in Liturgical Studies 3; men 2, women 1. Master of Arts in Religious Education 6; men 3, women 3.

Faculty for Degree Programs in Religion. Total 26; full-time 3; part-time 23.

Admission Requirements. Bachelor's degree; 12 undergraduate credits in theology; 12 undergraduate credits in philosophy (18 for the Master of Divinity degree); GRE.

Tuition and Fees. Tuition $2,710 per semester; January term $675; activity fee $27.50; application fee $10; registration fee (new student) $10; housing single $710 per semester (January term $180), apartment per semester $1,400 (January term $350).

Financial Aid. Available in the form of scholarships, work-study, guaranteed student loans. Awarded on basis of need and academic ability.

Housing. Two residence buildings on campus; off-campus housing available in nearby small towns.

Library Facilities. The Alcuin Library holds 400,000 volumes, approximately 40 percent of which are theological, and receives 1,700 periodicals. In the field of liturgy, update cards are processed regularly for the liturgical index produced by the Abbey of Mont-Cesar in Belgium. Rare monographic series support the collection in biblical studies and patristic theology. Adjacent to the Alcuin Library is the Hill Monastic Manuscript Library. It houses the world's largest collection of microfilmed medieval manuscripts.

Religious Services/Activities. Daily morning and evening prayer and Eucharistic celebration in both the monastery and the seminary; monthly School of Theology Eucharistic celebration; annual retreat available to each student; spiritual directors available on an on-going basis.

Degree Programs

The Master of Divinity program is designed for students who are preparing for ministry in the Church. Historically, the program was designed for ordained ministry, but in keeping with the expanding role of ministry in the church the program is open to all qualified men and women who seek intense preparation for ministry. The program is built around a 4-year program of required courses and supervised pastoral ministry. When endorsed by the Diocese, a seminarian may plan a full year of parish internship following the second year of this program. All seminarians pursue a semester of course work in the Holy Land. The degree program is ordinarily followed by an internship for priesthood candidates in their home diocese under the aegis of the candidate's bishop or religious superior.

The Master of Theological Studies is a program designed for men and women already in active ministry but who wish to deepen and broaden the foundation for their work. It provides both a broad academic background in theology as well as carefully planned courses in pastoral theology and ministry. The degree is shaped to enable the student to integrate theological reflection and ministerial activity. Four semesters (48 credit hours) are required to complete the degree.

The Master of Arts in Theology program allows the student to choose to concentrate in one of six areas: Church History, Liturgy, Monastic Studies, Scripture, Spirituality, or Systematic Theology. Through a study of the sources and methods of theological investigation and through an examination of the contributions of both the tradition and contemporary scholarship, the student develops a critical, historically rooted approach to theology.

The Master of Arts in Liturgical Studies familiarizes students with the sources of development of the Christian liturgical tradition, with the nature of ritual process and with the problems of culture and liturgy. The program presumes a solid background in theology and scripture on the part of the student.

The Master of Arts in Religious Education is designed to provide the foundation for persons planning ministries in Christian education. It introduces the student to the major theological and social scientific elements that form the basis of religious education today.

Special Programs

The Pre-Theology Program has been specifically designed for a candidate for the priesthood who has completed a college degree but does not have the required academic background for graduate theological studies. While living in the seminary and participating in the formational life of that community, the pre-theology student, in consultation with an advisor, spends one or two semesters, depending on need, pursuing prerequisite undergraduate studies.

The Jerusalem Studies Program is an opportunity for students to encounter in Israel the earth upon which the events of Scripture took place. This program is offered in fall, spring, and summer.

A Monastic Studies Program for a Master of Arts in Theology or for special non-degree study is offered for persons with special affinity for the monastic way of life.

St. Mary's College
Winona, MN 55987   (507) 452-4430

Administration. Brother Louis DeThomasis, F.S.C., President.

General Description. Saint Mary's College is a Catholic liberal arts college founded in 1912 and administered by the Christian Brothers since 1933. The College offers bachelor's and master's degree programs. The Department of Theology offers programs directed toward various ministries in the Church and for advanced study.

Community Environment. The campus of 350 acres is located in Winona, 125 miles southeast of Minneapolis/St. Paul, Minnesota.

Religious Denomination. Roman Catholic.

Accreditation. North Central Association of Colleges and Schools.

Term System. Semester.

Admission Requirements. Graduation from an accredited high school or equivalent with completion of 16 academic units; ACT or SAT.

Tuition and Fees. Tuition $5,200; room and board $2,270; student fees $50.

Financial Aid. Various types of assistance are available to qualified students.

Housing. Dormitory facilities for men and women are available.

Library Facilities. The Fitzgerald Library houses over 160,000 volumes.

Religious Services/Activities. The members of the Campus Ministry team encourage the development of Christian community on campus. Sacraments and student-centered campus liturgy are offered. Prayer groups, days of meditation, and retreats are regularly scheduled.

Degree Programs

All Theology majors must complete the core curriculum and courses prescribed for either the Theology major, Youth Ministry concentration, or Religious Education major. The core curriculum includes courses in Christian Morality Today, Introduction to the Old and New Testaments, the Man Jesus, Sacraments and Community, Shaping of Catholicism, and History of Catholic Thought. The Bachelor degree is awarded.

St. Olaf College
Department of Religion
Northfield, MN 55057   (507) 663-2222

Administration. Dr. Harlan F. Foss, President; Dr. Keith O. Anderson, Vice President and Dean of the College; Dr. Harold H. Ditmanson, Chair, Department of Religion.

General Description. The Department of Religion supplies the core requirement for all students of three courses in Religion. Its objective is to present the distinctive development and content of Christian theology in varieties of courses dealing with Biblical, doctrinal, historical, and ethical fields, including religions of non-Western cultures and the relation of Christian thought to other academic disciplines. The major in Religion may embrace an area of emphasis in traditional fields such as Biblical studies, theology, history of Christianity, history of religions, and ethical studies, or in dialogical fields such as religion and literature, or religion and art. The degree Bachelor of Arts is awarded.

Parent Institution. St. Olaf College is a liberal arts college of The American Lutheran Church. It is coeducational and open to all qualified students. St. Olaf aims to offer an education that prepares for self-understanding, vocational usefulness, and responsible citizenship. It believes that indispensible to this program is encounter with the Christian Gospel which can lead to a mature faith in God. The College takes the position that men and women are called by God to faith and service. Accordingly, it provides the opportunity for worship and seeks to graduate students who are morally sensitive and theologically literate.

Community Environment. The 300-acre campus of St. Olaf College is located 40 miles south of Minneapolis and St. Paul in Northfield, Minnesota. With a population of 13,000, Northfield is the home of many fine dairy farms and several major industries which contribute to the prosperity of the community.

Religious Denomination. The American Lutheran Church.

Accreditation. North Central Association of Colleges and Schools.

Term System. Four-one-four semester system; 2 summer terms.

Enrollment in Degree Programs in Religion 1984–85. Total 187; men 116, women 71.

Degrees in Religion Awarded 1984–85. Bachelor of Arts in Religion 49; men 35, women 14.

Faculty for Degree Programs in Religion. Total 17; full-time 15, part-time 2.

Admission Requirements. Graduation from an accredited high school or equivalent, including at least 3 units of English and 2 units of mathematics; satisfactory scores on the SAT or ACT; recommendations of pastor and high school principal, counselor, or teacher.

Tuition and Fees. Comprehensive fee $9,450 per year.

Financial Aid. Types of aid include scholarships, grants, National Direct Student Loan Program, Guaranteed Student Loans, Supplemental Educational Opportunity Loans, Parent Loan for Undergraduate Students, and student work-study.

Housing. All full-time students are housed in twelve residence halls. The College maintains off-campus houses which are available for upperclass student housing. College housing for married students is not available.

Library Facilities. The Rolvaag Memorial Library contains over 350,000 volumes. Special collections include manuscript and book collections of the Norwegian-American Historical Association. The Kierkegaard Library, one of the major research libraries in the world for the study of the thought of Soren Kierkegaard is housed in Holland Hall.

Religious Services/Activities. Daily chapel services; Student Congregation; various volunteer and community service opportunities.

Degree Programs

The major in Religion leading to a Bachelor of Arts degree usually emphasizes breadth and includes a freshman course and one course each in Biblical Studies, History of Christianity, History of Religions, and Theological Studies. A Religion major may also emphasize depth as well as breadth by means of a contract which expands the major to include an area of emphasis and includes a seminar or independent research in Religion. A minimum of 6 courses is required for the major.

St. Paul Bible College
Bible College, MN 55375   (612) 446-1411

Administration. Dr. L. John Eagen, President; Dr. Gene H. Hovee, Academic Dean.

General Description. The primary mission and goal of St. Paul Bible College is to prepare men and women for church-related ministries for the Church in general and for The Christian and Missionary Alliance in particular. For these programs the Bachelor degree is offered. A secondary mission of the College is to provide one- and two-year foundational general education and Biblical programs at a Certificate and/or Associate degree level for students wishing to pursue other vocations.

St. Paul Bible College is the midwestern regional college of The Christian and Missionary Alliance, an extensive missionary denomination with headquarters at Nyack, New York. The Alliance was organized in 1887 and now numbers over 1,900 churches in North America, supporting both home and overseas missions. Nearly 10,000 national workers serve with over 1,000 Alliance missionaries in 51 countries.

Community Environment. St. Paul Bible College is located just 9 miles west of the western Minneapolis, Minnesota suburbs. It enjoys the quiet beauty of a rural setting while providing easy access to the metropolitan Twin Cities. The rolling hills and lakeside setting offer a serenity well suited for academic endeavor. The beauty of the Minnesota seasons enhances the location.

Religious Denomination. The Christian and Missionary Alliance.

Accreditation. North Central Association of Colleges and Schools; American Association of Bible Colleges.

Term System. Semester; summer term of two 4-week sessions.

Enrollment in Degree Programs in Religion 1984–85. Total 412.

Degrees in Religion Awarded 1984–85. Bachelor of Arts in: Bible and Theology 9; men 8, women 1. Christian Education 8; men 4, women 4. History 16; men 14, women 2. Missiology 16; men 9, women 7. Communications 8; men 1, women 7. Bachelor of Science in: Teacher Education 39; men 6, women 33. Family and Child Development 1; women 1. Bachelor of Religious Education 2; women 2. Bachelor of Music Education 1; women 1.

Faculty for Degree Programs in Religion. Total 16; full-time 12, part-time 4.

Admission Requirements. Official high school transcripts including class rank; ACT, SAT, or PSAT results; recent photograph; current health examination form; autobiography and personal testimony form; pastoral and character references.

Tuition and Fees. Tuition full-time $112 per credit hour, part-time (less than 12 hours) $125 per credit hour; single room $650 per semester; double room $500 per semester; board $750 per semester. The College guarantees that as long as a student maintains full-time status (12 or more semester hours), the credit hour tuition will never rise; continuous, full-time enrollment is required; attendance at summer sessions is not required to maintain continuous enrollment.

Financial Aid. Grants, college work-study, and loans are available for eligible applicants.

Housing. All single students not living at home or with immediate relatives reside in residence halls. Some apartments are available on campus for married students. All single students participate in the College Food Service program provided in the College dining room.

Library Facilities. The library collection includes 76,241 volumes plus periodicals and microform titles.

Religious Services/Activities. Activities include Missionary Cabinet, chapel, prayer bands, missionary meetings, Staley Christian Scholarship Lectureship, Deeper Life Week, Missionary Conference, and student ministries.

Degree Programs

The Bachelor of Arts degree is offered with majors in Bible and Theology, Christian Education, Communications, History, History/Social Science, Secondary Education, Missiology, Music, and Pastoral Ministries.

The Bachelor of Science degree is offered with majors in Church Music and Ministries, Elementary Education, Family and Child Development, Prekindergarten Education. A Bachelor of Science degree in Missions with a major in Missionary Nursing is also offered. A Bachelor of Science in Church Music may also be pursued.

A Bachelor of Music Education and a Bachelor of Religious Education with a major in Christian Education are other programs available. In the baccalaureate degree programs (except Bible and Theology and Pastoral Ministries majors) the student earns an additional major in Bible and Theology. In addition, minors are offered by every academic department.

Special Programs

Associate of Arts in Bible, Associate of Arts, and Associate of Science degrees are two-year programs available at the College.

One-year certificate programs in Bible and Christian Education are designed for those who desire to increase their effectiveness in Christian lay ministry and wish an intensive year of Bible and ministry training before entering their planned vocations.

The diploma of the Evangelical Teacher Training Association may be pursued at the College.

St. Paul Seminary
2260 Summit Avenue
St. Paul, MN 55105   (612) 698-0323

Administration. Rev. Charles L. Froehle, President; Mr. Victor Klimoski, Dean of Students.

General Description. A Roman Catholic institution owned by the Archdioceses of St. Paul and Minneapolis, Minnesota, The St. Paul Seminary is an institution for the education of men for the Roman Catholic priesthood, and for educating lay people for ministry in the Church. The Master of Divinity and Master of Arts in Theology degrees are offered.

Community Environment. St. Paul Seminary is situated on 40 acres of property bordering on the Mississippi River. The city of St. Paul, with a population of over 300,000, is the capital of Minnesota. It is a major transportation and industrial center of the midwest.

Religious Denomination. Roman Catholic.

Accreditation. North Central Association of Colleges and Schools; Association of Theological Schools in the United States and Canada.

Term System. Four-one-four (semester).

Enrollment in Degree Programs in Religion 1984–85. Total 98; men 93, women 5.

Degrees in Religion Awarded 1984–85. Master of Divinity 11; men 11. Master of Arts in Theology 3; men 3.

Faculty for Degree Programs in Religion. Total 21; full-time 19, part-time 2.

Admission Requirements. Bachelor's degree from an accredited college or university with a grade point average of C (2.0) or better, with liberal arts coursework in history, literature, the arts, and the social and natural sciences; sufficient undergraduate study in theology and philosophy; Graduate Record Examination; introductory understanding of ecclesiastical Latin sufficient to translate Latin tests with the aid of a dictionary and grammar (for M.Div.); two letters of recommendation.

Tuition and Fees. $2,260 per semester.

Financial Aid. Students are eligible for Federal and State Guaranteed Loan Programs, the College Work-Study Program, and the Institutional Work Program. Limited scholarship opportunities and partial tuition grants are available.

Housing. Priesthood students live in dormitories on campus.

Religious Activities. The major on-going activities of the Seminary are governed by three committees which exercise delegated authority: Religious Practices, Curriculum, and Campus Life. There are numerous formal and informal opportunities throughout the year at which faculty, students, and staff can gather to enjoy camaraderie and increase the sense of community endeavor.

Library Facilities. The John Ireland Memorial Library serves the spiritual, intellectual, and pastoral formation needs of students and faculty. It houses approximately 67,000 volumes and 425 periodical titles.

Degree Programs

The Master of Divinity degree is an intense program with a pastoral ministry orientation, requiring the equivalent of three years of full-time study. It seeks to develop a deeper appreciation of the importance of faith and its application for Christian living and theological understanding, to establish a pastoral context for theological study, to foster understanding of the critical relationship between spiritual growth and academic and pastoral development, and to prepare candidates for pastoral ministry in accord with the norms and discipline of the Roman Catholic Church.

The Master of Arts in Theology is a two-year academic degree providing specialization in one of the major areas of theology: scripture, sacramental theology, moral theology, dogmatic theology, or church history. The goals of the program are for the candidate to become proficient at thorough research in a chosen area of theological specialization, to focus research efforts in a clear articulation of the insights gained, and to attain a highly informed and critical theological understanding by means of appropriate sources of theology.

St. Scholastica, College of
Department of Religious Studies
1200 Kenwood Avenue
Duluth, MN 55811   (218) 723-6000

Administration. Daniel H. Pilon, President.

General Description. The Department of Religious Studies provides opportunities to gain a critical appreciation for the riches of religious traditions. This is accomplished through the study of sacred writings, symbols, and rituals; historical development, and central faith convictions. The Bachelor degree is awarded.

Parent Institution. The College of St. Scholastica is the only coeducational, independent college in northeastern Minnesota. It was founded in 1906 and is affiliated with the Benedictine Sisters of Duluth.

Community Environment. The campus of 160 acres is located near the center of Duluth, the gateway to the sea for mid-America on Lake Superior.

Religious Denomination. Roman Catholic.

Accreditation. North Central Association of Colleges and Schools.

Term System. Quarter.

Admission Requirements. Graduation from an accredited high school or equivalent; ACT or SAT.

Tuition and Fees. Tuition $4,977 per year; room $957-$1,128; board $1,449; activity fee $90; health service fee $36.

Financial Aid. Aid can be awarded in the form of scholarships, grants, loans, or employment. Most students receive a combination of the pertinent forms in a financial aid package.

Housing. Dormitory facilities are available on campus.

Library Facilities. The Library contains over 93,000 volumes and subscribes to 620 current periodicals.

Religious Services/Activities. Sunday worship services for both Catholics and Protestants are held on campus. Retreats, workshops, Bible studies, and prayer groups are available to all.

Degree Programs

The Department of Religious Studies prepares a student for careers in the following areas offering majors in: Youth Ministry, a field for full-time work with the adolescent through young adulthood; Religious Education, administering and/or teaching in Catholic or Protestant religious education programs; and Religious Studies, advanced study in graduate schools or seminaries. The course offerings are divided into the areas of Quest for Meaning, Biblical Literature, Christian Development in History, Value Response in Society, and Major World Religions. The various programs lead to the Bachelor's degree.

St. Thomas, College of
Graduate Programs in Pastoral Studies

2115 Summit Avenue
P.O. Box 5010
St. Paul, MN 55105   (612) 647-5715

Administration. Rev. Terrence J. Murphy, President; Dr. Charles J. Keffer, Provost; Dr. John G. Nemo, Dean of the College; Rev. Thomas J. Conroy, Chair, Department of Theology; Gene A. Scapanski, Dean/Director, Center for Religious Education.

General Description. Focusing on personal growth, faith development, and competencies for ministry, the Graduate Programs in Pastoral Studies of the College's Center for Religious Education offer a balance of quality academic preparation, a pastorally sensitive faculty, and a community setting in which individuals may choose to specialize in one of 9 different areas of church history. The Master of Arts in Pastoral Studies is offered.

Parent Institution. The College of St. Thomas is a private, coeducational, Catholic, liberal arts college located in St. Paul, Minnesota. The College awards the B.A., M.A., M.B.A., M.B.C., and Ed.S. degrees. It is an academic community committed to the total development of the student through a liberal arts education in the Catholic tradition and through a high degree of personal attention in a spiritually and intellectually stimulating campus environment. This education seeks to develop culturally aware individuals who combine career competency with a sense of moral responsibility.

Community Environment. The College of St. Thomas is located on historic Summit Avenue in St. Paul, Minnesota. The 50-acre wooded campus is situated in a quiet residential area midway between downtown St. Paul and downtown Minneapolis. This location gives the student all the advantages of a small-college atmosphere in the heart of a large metropolis. The Mississippi River is just a short walk away, and there are several parks in the area which are excellent for ice-skating in the winter and outdoor activities in the spring and fall.

Religious Denomination. Roman Catholic.

Religious Emphasis. Roman Catholic Sacramental Theology.

Accreditation. North Central Association of Colleges and Schools.

Term System. Semester.

Enrollment in Degree Programs in Religion 1984–85. Total 156; men 34, women 122.

Degrees in Religion Awarded 1984–85. Master of Arts in Pastoral Studies 3; women 3.

Faculty for Degree Programs in Religion. Total 30; full-time 3, part-time 27.

Admission Requirements. Bachelor of Arts degree from an accredited institution with a B average; 18 credits in religious studies; 3 credits in developmental psychology, 3 credits in social sciences or education; Graduate Record Examination or Miller Analogy Test; 3 letters of recommendation.

Tuition and Fees. Tuition $155 per credit hour; audit fee $40 per credit hour; matriculation fee $15; graduation fee $40.

Financial Aid. Financial aid is available based on need. Applications are available at the Graduate Programs in Pastoral Studies Office.

Housing. On campus housing is available to graduate students during summer sessions only. Contact the Housing Office for further information.

Library Facilities. The O'Shaugnessy Library houses over 190,000 volumes. The holdings include subscriptions to 1,500 periodicals in the area of Religious Studies/ Theology and in excess of 15,000 volumes in the same areas.

Religious Services/Activities. The Office of Campus Ministry of the College has a staff of professional ministers and offers daily liturgies, prayer services, and annual weekend retreats as well as spiritual counseling and direction. Both Catholic and Protestant services are offered.

Degree Programs

The Master of Arts degree is offered in the Graduate Program in Pastoral Studies. The degree requires the completion of a total of 36 credits of which 18 are in core courses, 9 in process courses, and 9 credits in the area of focus. The student may focus in the areas of Adult Educator, Religious Education Coordinator, Liturgist, Youth Minister, Religion Teacher/Department Chairperson, Pastoral Care Minister, Social Justice Minister, or Parish Administrator.

Special Programs

The Center for Religious Education of the College is a resource center for religious education and pastoral ministers. Since its beginning in 1975, the Center has offered lectures, short courses, workshops, and institutes for more than 30,000 people. The Center's services include: Clinical Pastoral Education, noncredit short courses for adults, training programs for parish councils, religion teachers, youth ministers, and clergy institutes.

United Theological Seminary of the Twin Cities

3000 Fifth Street, N.W.
New Brighton, MN 55112   (612) 633-4311

Administration. Howard M. Mills, President; Clyde J. Steckel, Academic Vice President.

General Description. United Theological Seminary offers three degree programs: Master of Divinity, Master of Arts in Religious Education, and Doctor of Ministry. The latter is offered in cooperation with the Minnesota Consortium of Theological Schools. The Seminary was founded in 1960 as a merger of the Mission House School of Theology of Plymouth, Wisconsin, and the Yankton School of Theology of Yankton, South Dakota. Mission House represented the Evangelical and Reformed traditions in the United Church of Christ and Yankton represented the German Congregational tradition. The merger of the two schools not only expressed the spirit of union which had led to the formation of the United Church of Christ in 1957, but also was in response to the need expressed by leaders in the United Methodist, United Presbyterian, Episcopal, and Roman Catholic leaders in Minnesota for an ecumenical center of theological studies in the Twin Cities of Minneapolis/St. Paul. By its charter, United Theological Seminary is a constitutionally independent and interdenominational institution, while continuing to serve the United Church of Christ as one of its closely related seminaries.

Community Environment. The Seminary is located in the suburb of New Brighton in the metropolitan area of Minneapolis/St. Paul. Classes began at a newly acquired and developed campus in the fall of 1962.

Religious Denomination. Affiliated with the United Church of Christ with an ecumenical stance.

Religious Emphasis. Liberal.

Accreditation. North Central Association of Colleges and Schools; Association of Theological Schools in the United States and Canada.

Term System. Semester (4-1-4); summer session.

Enrollment in Degree Programs in Religion 1984–85. Total 266; men 115, women 151.

Degrees in Religion Awarded 1984–85. Master of Divinity 40; men 17, women 23; Master of Arts in Religious Studies 7; men 1, women 6. Doctor of Ministry 4; men 4.

Faculty for Degree Programs in Religion. Total 22; full-time 17, part-time 5.

Admission Requirements. Undergraduate degree; letters of recommendation; statement of purpose (for M.A. in Religious Studies); autobiography (for Master of Divinity); take such tests as may be designated by Admissions Committee.

Tuition and Fees. Costs per year: tuition $3,500 ($350 per course if registration is less than full load); miscellaneous fees about $50; unfurnished apartment housing $225 per month.

Financial Aid. Financial aid available includes merit grants (based on undergraduate grade point average); need grants, and loans.

Housing. Limited housing on campus.

Library Facilities. The Seminary maintains a collection of 58,000 volumes geared to its curriculum. Resources of the Consortium of Minnesota Theological Schools are available to students.

Religious Services/Activities. The Annual Spring Convocation provides an opportunity for pastors, laity, and students to hear from and discuss with leading figures issues in the church and society. The Convocation includes lectures, workshops, worship, and special alumni/ae events. There is a Fall Student/Faculty Retreat; student- and faculty-led chapel services 4 times per week; bi-weekly Forums.

Degree Programs

The Master of Divinity degree is designed to equip women and men of various backgrounds and life situations for professional service in the churches and in other forms of Christian ministry. The program of studies seeks to assist seminarians with their search for theological understanding of persons and the world in terms of biblical faith. Academic course work, including disciplined study and research, and direct involvement with contemporary life in urban and rural areas, political and social arenas, corporate and ecclesiastical structures are both essential to the integration of theory and practice and the integration of faith, tradition, and modern experience upon which the degree is based. The program of studies finds expression in three basic areas: Christianity and Culture, Interpreting the Christian Heritage, and the Church's Ministry.

The Master of Arts in Religious Studies has two purposes: to offer students the opportunity to pursue the academic study of religion and to provide theological education for lay people. The degree requires the completion of 18 courses (2-year full-time equivalent), four of which may be earned by writing a thesis and successful completion of written and oral comprehensive examinations.

The Doctor of Ministry is offered in cooperation with the Minnesota Consortium of Theological Schools. The primary emphasis is on learning in the practice of professional ministry (rather than on academic research only). The course of study includes on-campus and on-site research, study, and writing.

Special Programs

The Program in Religion and the Arts is designed to explore the relationship of religion to the visual, literary, and performing arts. This area of concentration is not in itself a degree program, but is open to candidates in all three degree programs, students from Consortium schools, and special students from the larger community.

In cooperation with a number of institutions across the country, Native American students can earn the Master of Divinity Degree or certification for ministry in the Native American community. The program allows Native American church leaders to pursue their theological education by combining residential study at United Theological Seminary and other schools, with workshops, summer sessions, and theological education by extension study.

The Parallel Reading Program is a Continuing Education program providing resources and structured study for individuals and groups. The topics range from biblical interpretation to issues of administration in the local church, from Christian symbols of creation to Love. There are three levels of participation: directed reading, individual self-study, and guided group study.

Belhaven College
Department of Christian Ministries
1500 Peachtree Street
Jackson, MS 39206   (601) 968-5940

Administration. Verne R. Kennedy, President.

General Description. The Department of Christian Ministries offers a major designed to prepare students for graduate study in a seminary, a graduate school of missions, counseling, or church ministries; or to prepare students for specialized forms of church or parachurch ministries.

Parent Institution. Bellhaven College, an institution of the Presbyterian Church, is a coeducational, four-year liberal arts college. It was founded in 1883 and operated as a college for women until 1954 when it became coeducational. The College grants the Bachelor degree.

Community Environment. The 42-acre campus is near the heart of Jackson, the capital and largest city in Mississippi.

Religious Denomination. Presbyterian Church (U.S.A.).

Accreditation. Southern Association of Colleges and Schools.

Term System. Semester.

Admission Requirements. Graduation from an accredited high school or GED; ACT or SAT.

Tuition and Fees. Tuition and fees $2,035 per semester; room $365; board $550.

Financial Aid. Through a program of scholarships, grants, loans, and campus employment, the College provides a comprehensive plan to assist students who establish a definite financial need.

Housing. There are five dormitories for resident students.

Library Facilities. The Warren A. Hood Library has holdings of over 66,000 volumes.

Religious Services/Activities. Chapel is held every Tuesday and attendance is required.

Degree Programs

The Department of Christian Ministries offers concentrated preparation in social ministries, congregational ministries, international ministries, counseling ministries, and recreational ministries. The major requires courses in Christian Ministries, Bible, completion of a foreign language (Greek required for the congregational ministries), and the area of concentration.

Blue Mountain College
Biblical and Associated Studies
Blue Mountain, MS 38610   (610) 685-4771

Administration. Dr. James L. Travis, Chairman, Department of Bible.

General Description. The Department of Bible offers a broadly-based, Bible-centered, intellectual and practical preparation for meeting the spiritual dimension in life. The thrust of studies offered is to provide educational experiences which would equip the major to be adequately prepared to enter either a graduate school in Christian ministry or to begin an immediate ministry in a church-related vocation. A Seminary Extension Center is maintained on the campus. The Department offers the degrees Bachelor of Arts and Bachelor of Science.

Parent Institution. Blue Mountain College was founded in 1873. It is owned by the Mississippi Baptist Convention and is a senior college for women with a coordinated academic program for men preparing for church-related vocations.

Community Environment. The campus is located in the rural community of Blue Mountain, 70 miles from Memphis, Tennessee.

Religious Denomination. Mississipi Baptist Convention.

Accreditation. Southern Association of Colleges and Schools.

Term System. Semester.

Faculty for Degree Programs in Religion. Total 3.

Admission Requirements. Graduation from an accredited high school or equivalent.

Tuition and Fees. Tuition $1,050 per semester; matriculation fee $107; student activity fee $23; room and meals $855 (average).

Financial Aid. A wide range of assistance is made available in the form of scholarships, grants, loans, and work programs.

Housing. There are three dormitories at the College.

Library Facilities. The library houses over 50,000 volumes and subscribes to 210 periodicals.

Religious Services/Activities. All students are required to attend Chapel services three times per week. The Baptist Student Union coordinates other activities on campus.

Degree Programs

A student majoring in Bible must complete at least 30 semester hours of specified and elective courses. Ministerial students at the College are required to major in Bible. The program leads to the Bachelor of Arts degree. The Church-Related Vocation Program is interdepartmental in scope and is designed for students who are preparing for a church-related vocation. The major may earn either the Bachelor of Arts or the Bachelor of Science degree. Primary fields of concentration may be earned in Bible, Business Administration, Music, and Religious Education.

Jackson College of Ministries
1555 Beasley Road
Jackson, MS 39206   (601) 981-1611

Administration. Thomas L. Craft, President; David K. Bernard, Assistant Vice President.

General Description. Jackson College of Ministries exists to train men and women for Christian leadership and service. It offers specialized training in the areas of Theology, Missions, Music, and Christian Education, and is committed to academic excellence, personal development, diversity of interest, faculty competence, and worldwide perspective.

Shortly after the merger of the Pentecostal Church Incorporated and the Pentecostal Assemblies of Jesus Christ in 1945, the Pentecostal Bible Institute opened in Tupelo, Mississippi. In 1975, the Institute moved to Jackson and the present name was adopted.

Community Environment. The 26-acre campus is located in the northern part of Jackson, the capital city of Mississippi. A city rich in historical significance and heritage, Jackson is now a thriving modern city with a population of over 350,000. The city of Jackson is situated on the banks of the Pearl River and is 40 miles east of the Mississippi River and 100 miles west of the Alabama state line.

Religious Denomination. United Pentecostal Church International.

Religious Emphasis. Oneness Pentecostal.

Accreditation. Approved by the Board of Education, United Pentecostal Church International.

Term System. Semester; no summer term.

Enrollment in Degree Programs in Religion 1984–85. Total 328; men 179, women 149.

Degrees in Religion Awarded 1984–85. Bachelor of Theology 15; men 13, women 2. Bachelor of Arts 13; men 5, women 8.

Faculty for Degree Programs in Religion. Total 20; full-time 11, part-time 9.

Admission Requirements. High school graduation or GED; pastoral recommendation.

Tuition and Fees. Tuition $675 per semester; fees and books average $250 per semester; room and board $63 per week.

Financial Aid. The Youth Division of the United Pentecostal Church makes available an annual scholarship of $1,500 for an outstanding student applying to the College. Partial or full tuition scholarships are available from time to time based on academics, need, involvement, spirituality, and pastoral recommendation.

Housing. On-campus housing is available for single students.

Library Facilities. The library has an extensive collection of sermon tapes as well as 5,000 books, periodicals, filmstrips, and clippings.

Religious Services/Activities. Chapel is held three times weekly and attendance is mandatory. The First Pentecostal Church of Jackson is the official church home of the student body. All students must attend and participate in regular worship services and the stewardship program. Campus ministries include the United Ministerial Association, Prayer and Bible Conference, Mission Conference, National Music Ministry Conference, student teaching, evangelism trips, Outreach in Jackson, and overseas missions tours.

Degree Programs

The Bachelor of Theology degree with majors in Theology and Missions requires the completion of a core curriculum and a required curriculum from the School of Theology. Each student is exposed to a strong Biblical foundation of courses which provides not only facts, but life-long tools of study. Elective hours allow the student to shape his own preparation for ministry.

The Bachelor of Arts degree with a major in Music includes a variety of areas: competence as a musical performer and conductor, basic instruction in Biblical studies, and Christian education, commitment to ministry among individuals, and the nurture of administrative leadership qualities. The major in Christian Education prepares men and women for teaching and administrative positions in Christian schools and in all Christian education programs of the local church. It provides the necessary theological and educational tools to teach the Christian message, as well as offering student participation in a wide variety of teaching situations. The Religious Studies major is designed for those seeking a solid Bible college education, but may not necessarily plan to work full-time as a preacher, missionary, music director, or teacher.

Special Programs

The Summer Institute of Theology offers a two-week course for preachers.

Millsaps College
Preparation for Ministry Program
Department of Religion
1700 North State Street
Jackson, MS 39210   (601) 354-5201

Administration. Dr. Lee H. Reiff, Chairman, Department of Religion.

General Description. Millsaps College has enjoyed a tradition of close involvement with students from all denominations and faiths—particularly from The United Methodist Church—whose vocational goals or interests were a form of professional ministry. The Preparation for Ministry Program is designed to offer a wide variety of experiences for persons who have decided on or would like to explore some form of Christian ministry as a personal vocation. The Program provides a basic link between the College and the conference/diocese/presbytery or other structure to which a student is responsible. In the case of United Methodists, the Program is a supplement to the candidacy program. The Program is also a clearinghouse for student employment in various capacities in congregations or church agencies.

The Department of Religion offers a major in the field leading to the Bachelor of Arts degree.

Parent Institution. The College was founded in 1890 and is supported by the United Methodist Church. The 1,300-member student body represents about 35 states and several foreign countries. Students come from 25 different religious denominations.

Community Environment. The 100-acre campus with 15 buildings is located in Jackson, the capital of Mississippi.

Religious Denomination. United Methodist Church.

Accreditation. Southern Association of Colleges and Schools.

Term System. Semester.

Admission Requirements. High school graduation or equivalent; ACT or SAT.

Tuition and Fees. Tuition $2,700 per semester; student association fee $37.50; activity fee $50; room $575-$650; board $580.

Financial Aid. Millsaps College grants scholarships and financial aid to students on the basis of academic excellence and financial need.

Housing. Dormitory rooms are available on campus.

Library Facilities. The Millsaps-Wilson Library has more than 150,000 volumes. The library maintains the Mississippi Methodist Archives.

Religious Services/Activities. The religious life at Millsaps centers around the churches of the city of Jackson and the religious life program coordinated through the Campus Ministry.

Degree Programs

The major in Religion leading to the Bachelor of Arts degree requires a minimum of 25 hours in Religion beyond those used to meet core requirements for graduation. Courses required include Introduction to the Old Testament, Introduction to the New Testament, Ways of Being Religious, History of Christianity, and a Seminar. The degree requires a total of 124 semester hours.

Mississippi College
Department of Religion and Philosophy
College Station
P.O. Box 4086
Clinton, MS 39058   (601) 924-5131

Administration. Dr. A.J. Glaze, Head, Department of Religion and Philosophy.

General Description. The Department of Religion and Philosophy offers studies in the areas of Bible, Religion, Religious Education, Philosophy, and New Testament Greek. Recognizing its close affiliation with the Mississippi Baptist Convention, the Department proposes to make a significant contribution to the intellectual and spiritual development of students at Mississippi College. It seeks to give them a deep appreciation for and understanding of the values of Christian faith, to encourage their commitment to Christian ideals, and to aid them in the implementation of these values and ideals. The Department offers a major in Religion and minors in Bible, Religious Education, and Philosophy.

Parent Institution. Mississippi College is a coeducational institution of liberal arts and professional studies, owned and operated by the Mississippi Baptist Convention. It is the largest private college in the state. More than 2,000 students are enrolled for undergraduate studies and more than 1,000 students are enrolled in the Graduate School.

Community Environment. The 180-acre campus is located in Clinton, a suburban community five miles west of Jackson, the state capital.

Religious Denomination. Mississippi Baptist Convention.

Accreditation. Southern Association of Colleges and Schools.

Term System. Semester.

Admission Requirements. High school graduation or equivalent; ACT.

Tuition and Fees. Tuition, fees, room, board $5,200 per year.

Financial Aid. Scholarships, loans, grants, and work-study are available. Aid is also available for ministerial students.

Housing. There are four residence halls for women and three for men.

Library Facilities. The Leland Speed Library has a book collection of over 205,000 volumes. The minutes and other materials of the Mississippi Historical Commission are serviced and maintained in a special section of the library.

Religious Services/Activities. Chapel services are held two days per week. The Baptist Student Union coordinates religious activities.

Degree Programs

Students preparing for church-related vocations are urged to major or minor in the Department of Religion and Philosophy. The major in Religion requires 36 semester hours of prescribed courses and all requirements for the Bachelor of Arts degree. Students who plan to enroll in one of the Southern Baptist seminaries for studies leading to the basic theological degree are encouraged to pursue a comprehensive liberal arts education. Electives in the fields of communication, computer sciences, and business are recommended.

Reformed Theological Seminary

5422 Clinton Boulevard
Jackson, MS 39209   (601) 922-4988

Administration. Dr. Luther G. Whitlock, Jr., President; Dr. Richard G. Watson, Academic Dean; Dr. Norman E. Harper, Dean, Graduate School of Education.

General Description. The Reformed Theological Seminary provides professional education on the graduate level in order to prepare men and women for Christian service in all branches of evangelical Christianity, especially the Presbyterian and reformed family. The program of the Seminary is characterized by Biblical fidelity, confessional integrity, and academic excellence. The Seminary grants the degrees Master of Divinity, Master of Christian Education, Master of Arts, and Doctor of Ministry.

Community Environment. Reformed Theological Seminary is located in a residential section of Jackson, the state capital of Mississippi. Jackson is a modern, thriving city with an estimated metropolitan area population of 325,-000. In addition to the normal cultural advantages that a city this size offers, opportunities for higher education are also available. Close by are Belhaven College, Millsaps College, Mississippi College, Tougaloo College, and Jackson State University, as well as branches of all the large state universities at the Universities Center, and the University of Mississippi Medical School. Area lakes, countryside, and parks afford excellent camping, fishing, hunting, and water sports.

Religious Denomination. Presbyterian.

Religious Emphasis. Reformed.

Accreditation. Southern Association of Colleges and Schools; Association of Theological Schools in the United States and Canada.

Term System. Semester; summer term.

Enrollment in Degree Programs in Religion 1984–85. Total 243; men 204, women 39.

Degrees in Religion Awarded 1984–85. Master of Arts 12; men 9, women 3. Master of Divinity 42; men 42. Master of Christian Education 10; men 8, women 2. Doctor of Ministry 10; men 10.

Faculty for Degree Programs in Religion. Total 14; full-time 13, part-time 1.

Admission Requirements. Bachelor's degree; statement of Christian faith; statement of reasons for wishing to pursue a particular degree; transcripts of all previous academic work; recent photograph; personal interview may be required.

Tuition and Fees. Tuition $1,000 per semester (13 to 18 semester hours); dormitory rent $70 per month; campus apartments $180-$200 per month; total cost for three-year Doctor of Ministry program $3,075.

Financial Aid. A limited amount of financial aid is available to full-time Seminary students.

Housing. Housing is available for single students in Seminary-owned and supervised quarters. A limited number of seminary apartment units are also available.

Library Facilities. The library collection consists of approximately 55,000 volumes, 625 periodicals, and 15,000 units of microfilm. The Blackburn Memorial Library houses the former personal library of John C. Blackburn of Cayce, South Carolina and represents his private collection of Presbyterian books and periodicals.

Religious Services/Activities. A chapel service is conducted daily and all regular students are expected to attend.

Degree Programs

The Master of Divinity degree is designed to provide a complete and balanced preparation for the Gospel ministry or other forms of Christian service. Completion of the course ordinarily requires three academic years and two summers. Approved Christian service during the two summers that precede graduation must be accomplished.

The Master of Christian Education degree program requires candidates for the degree to have successfully completed 15 semester hours in Christian Education.

The Master of Arts program is designed for persons who seek to serve in the supportive ministry of the church, but who do not desire ordination to the professional ministry. It provides concentrated study in a field or discipline on the background of a general understanding of theology and biblical studies. Specializations in the following areas are offered: Christian Studies; Old Testament/New Testament; Marriage and Family Counseling; and Missiology.

The Doctor of Ministry equips the candidate for a higher level of competence in the practice of ministry than can normally be expected from a recipient of the Master of Divinity degree. The program is built upon the biblical, theological, and professional foundations of the Master of Divinity degree. The program is designed to be flexible enough to meet individual needs while seeking to encourage increased competence in the classical and functional disciplines already taken in pre-professional courses required for professional ministry.

Special Programs

The Graduate School of Education offers a graduate program of professional education that equips teachers and administrators at the elementary and secondary levels to relate a Christian world and life view to educational theory and practice in our contemporary society. The Master of Education degree is offered.

Southeastern Baptist College
4229 Highway 15 North
Laurel, MS 39440   (601) 426-6346

Administration. A. Marion Wilson, President.

General Description. The Baptist Missionary Association of Mississippi adopted a resolution to establish the college in 1948 with the purpose of offering educational services on the junior college level and as a Bible training center. Classes began in the facilities of Parkview Baptist Church in Laurel. A new campus was occupied in 1955. The College now offers a full four-year program leading to the Bachelor degree. The objectives of the College are to (1) train Christian workers to serve local churches, Baptist Missionary Association interest, and the interest of Christianity, and (2) to provide pre-seminary training for students who plan to pursue advanced degrees.

Community Environment. The 20-acre campus is located in the city of Laurel which has a population of 35,000. Laurel is in south central Mississippi, 80 miles southeast of the capital city of Jackson.

Religious Denomination. Baptist Missionary Association of Mississippi.

Accreditation. American Association of Bible Colleges (Candidate).

Term System. Semester.

Admission Requirements. Graduation from an accredited high school or equivalent.

Tuition and Fees. Tuition $600 per semester; room $250; board $350.

Financial Aid. Several financial aid programs are available to students.

Housing. Men's and women's residence halls are available on campus.

Library Facilities. The A.R. Reddin Memorial Library houses over 17,000 volumes.

Religious Services/Activities. The Association of Baptist Students sponsors campus activities including discipleship training, devotional life, campus revival, and fellowship. All students are required to attend chapel. The Ministerial Alliance participates in worship services.

Degree Programs

The Division of Biblical Studies offers programs with a Bible major leading to the degrees Associate of Arts (66 hours), Bachelor of Arts (126 hours), and Bachelor of Science (66 hours). Courses offered include introductory Bible, Old Testament, New Testament, Biblical languages, theology, and philosophy.

The Division of Professional Studies includes the subject areas of Pastoral Training, Christian Education, Missions, and Sacred Music. The Division offers the degrees Associate of Arts in Sacred Music (76 hours), Bachelor of Sacred Music (137 hours), Bachelor of Science - Pastoral Training (129 hours), and Bachelor of Christian Education (129 hours).

Special Programs

The Division of General and Continuing Education offers programs in Bible and Bible-related courses during the daytime and evening and by independent study. The Certificate of Christian Leadership, Diploma of Christian Leadership, and Diploma in Bible are awarded.

Wesley College
P.O. Box 70
Florence, MS 39073   (601) 845-2265

Administration. Dr. Frances R. Allen, Academic Dean; Roman Miller, Director, Biblical and Pastoral Studies.

General Description. Wesley College was founded by the Congregational Methodist Church to provide educational opportunities within the framework of a Bible college guided by a Christ-centered educational philosophy, offering baccalaureate programs of Biblical and professional studies revolving around a general education core curriculum. Bachelor of Arts programs are classified as preparatory for graduate study; Bachelor of Science programs are considered to be terminal. Majors in either B.A. or B.S. are: Biblical Literature, Christian Education, Christian Ministries, Church Music, and Pastoral Studies.

Community Environment. Wesley College occupies a beautiful 40-acre campus situated one-half mile east of U.S. Highway 49 South, 12 miles south of Jackson, Mississippi, in Florence. Jackson is a rapidly growing city with a population of over 300,000 people. Known as the "crossroads of the South," Jackson is the political, cultural, industrial, educational, and business capital of Mississippi. The proximity of the campus to Jackson provides ample opportunity for employment, in addition to the other advantages one might find in a larger city. The city of Florence has a population of 1,100.

Religious Denomination. Congregational Methodist.

Religious Emphasis. Wesleyan-Arminian.

Accreditation. American Association of Bible Colleges.

Term System. Semester; no summer term.

Enrollment in Degree Programs in Religion 1984–85.

Total 32; men 20, women 12.

Degrees in Religion Awarded 1984–85. BA/BS in Pastoral Studies 3; men 3. BA/BS in Christian Education 4; women 4.

Faculty for Degree Programs in Religion. Total 3; full-time 2, part-time 1.

Admission Requirements. High school graduate or GED; ACT score of 14 or SAT of 700; be a Christian; evidence sympathetic appreciation for the standards and spirit of the College; moral character in harmony with its purposes; emotional and physical health adequate for the demands of college life.

Tuition and Fees. $1,600 per year including fees; room and board $1,850 per year.

Financial Aid. Pell Grant, SEOG, College Work-Study, institutional grants, and scholarships available.

Housing. Dormitory housing plus mobile homes (two- and three-bedroom).

Library Facilities. The library houses over 22,000 volumes.

Religious Services/Activities. Chapel twice weekly; church attendance required; week-long revival at the beginning of each semester. Missionary speakers at chapel for one month each year; mission trip to Mexico each year; evangelistic teams to churches frequently.

Degree Programs

The Bachelor of Science program requires the completion of 128 semester hours including a total of 30 hours in Bible. The program may include a minor area selected with the approval of the major professor in that area and the academic dean, or a minor in Christian Education, Christian Missions, Music, or Pastoral Studies. A Bachelor of Arts in Biblical Literature with a minor in Pastoral Studies may also be pursued. The Division of Professional Studies offers programs which introduce the student to academic disciplines not pursued in the programs of the Biblical and General Education divisions described above. Programs leading to the Bachelor of Science degree include Christian Education, Christian Ministries (Bible, Christian Education, Music), Religious Education with emphasis on Missions, and Church Music. A Pastoral Studies program within the Division leads to the Bachelor of Arts in Pastoral Studies.

William Carey College
Department of Biblical Studies and Church Vocations
Tuscan Avenue
Hattiesburg, MS 39401   (601) 544-2053

Administration. Dr. J. Ralph Noonkester, President; Dr. E. Milton Wheeler, Academic Vice President and Dean of Arts and Sciences; Dr. William M. Clawson, Chairman, Department of Biblical Studies and Church Vocations.

General Description. Since William Carey College is sponsored and supported by Mississippi Baptists, the Department of Biblical Studies and Church Vocations plays an essential role in upholding the Baptist ideal that the Bible is the only role of doctrine and authority for Christian living. In order to help students in their interpretation of life, to acquaint them with their spiritual heritage, and to enrich their appreciation of Christianity, the Department is built on a foundation of studies of the Old and New Testaments. These courses develop an understanding of Biblical principles which can be applied to daily living. The Department offers the Bachelor of Arts in: Biblical Studies, Church History and Missions, Philosophy and Biblical Studies, and Church Vocations.

Parent Institution. William Carey College's stated purpose is to engage faculty, staff, and students in an educational process which stimulates intellectual, spiritual, and cultural development and which prepares students to assume or augment career and professional responsibilities within the Baptist denomination and within society as a whole. The College has two branch campuses, one in New Orleans for its School of Nursing, and one in Gulfport, Mississippi. The College is organized into 4 schools and 2 divisions: the Schools of Arts and Sciences, Business Administration, Music, and Nursing; the Graduate Division and Division of Continuing Education.

Community Environment. The main campus of William Carey College, founded in 1906, is in Hattiesburg, Mississippi. On 65 acres, the campus faces a beautiful evergreen forest on the south side of the city. Thanks to its similar proximity to Jackson, Meridian, New Orleans, and Mobile, Hattiesburg is known as the Hub City. With a population of 50,000, it is served by numerous transportation facilities.

Religious Denomination. Southern Baptist.

Religious Emphasis. Conservative.

Accreditation. Southern Association of Colleges and Schools.

Term System. Semester; summer session is composed of two 5-week terms.

Enrollment in Degree Programs in Religion 1984–85. Total 54; men 52, women 2.

Degrees in Religion Awarded 1984–85. Bachelor of Arts 10; men 10.

Faculty for Degree Programs in Religion. Total 6; full-time 4, part-time 2.

Admission Requirements. Graduation from accredited secondary school (rank in third or fourth quartile); SAT or ACT.

Tuition and Fees. Tuition $89 per semester hour; room $300-$675 per semester; board $650 per semester.

Financial Aid. Grants, loans, scholarships, and college work-study available. The Mississippi Baptist Convention allocates a certain percent of its budget to aid students preparing for the ministry.

Housing. All unmarried students are required to live in

one of the campus residence halls and to board in the college cafeteria.

Library Facilities. The I.E. Rouse Library houses approximately 110,000 items including books, bound periodicals, music scores, microtexts, phonodiscs, and other library materials. The Clarence Dickinson Collection is centered around church music and contains 5,600 items. The Otis Seal Ministerial Library forms another special collection of more than 2,000 items that assist ministerial students in the preparation of sermons.

Religious Services/Activities. The Baptist Student Union sponsors Fall Retreat, noon day services twice a week, nursing home visitations, summer missions, and backyard Bible studies. The Ministerial Association holds a student-led revival and meets twice a month; visits nursing homes; students serve in churches and lead in services. The Staley Lectures are held once per year.

Degree Programs

The Bachelor of Arts degree is offered by the Department of Biblical Studies and Church Vocations with majors in the following areas: (1) Biblical Studies, primarily for those interested in pastoral ministery; (2) Church Vocations, primarily for those interested in the educational ministry; (3) Missions and Church History, primarily for those in preparing for missionary service; and (4) Biblical Studies and Philosophy, primarily for those interested in understanding the Bible and the application of Christianity from a philosophical viewpoint. Each major requires the student to take a complete year (6 semester hours) of Old Testament, a study that covers the entire Old Testament and a complete year (6 semester hours) of New Testament; a course in Biblical Backgrounds; one in principles of interpretation; one in world religions; and if Southern Baptist, a course in Baptist Work that treats the work of Southern Baptists. Then the student will take courses which will emphasize his major field. In this way, upon completing his degree, the student will be equipped to work in a church with confidence or continue his preparation in one of the seminaries without difficulty.

Special Programs

Each semester a Bible course is offered on the local television station and on the Southern Baptist Convention network.

MISSOURI

Aquinas Institute of Theology
3642 Lindell Boulevard
St. Louis, MO 63108   (314) 658-3882

Administration. Dr. John F. Taylor, O.P., President; Dr. Benjamin J. Russell, O.P., Vice President and Academic Dean.

General Description. Aquinas Institute is a graduate school of theology in the tradition of the Roman Catholic Dominican Religious Order. Its purpose is to advance theological understanding and to educate men and women for service to the Church and to society in various Christian ministries. Aquinas Institute offers programs with professional and research emphasis. The programs with a more professional orientation are the degrees Master of Arts in Pastoral Studies (M.A.P.S.) and the Master of Divinity (M.Div.). The Master of Arts in Theology (M.A.) degree is oriented more towards research.

Community Environment. Aquinas Institute's location on the campus of St. Louis University, St. Louis, Missouri, and its relationship with the University give it all of the advantages of a school many times its size. There are many cultural, entertainment, and educational activities available on the attractive St. Louis University campus. The city of St. Louis itself also offers many attractions. Only a few blocks away are Powell Hall, home of the St. Louis Symphony, Fox Theater, featuring traveling theatrical companies, an outstanding botanical garden, a fine art museum, and one of the country's best zoological parks. There are many opportunities for students to be engaged in ministry during their studies, not only at the University itself, but at various other places in the city.

Religious Denomination. Roman Catholic.

Religious Emphasis. Contemporary.

Accreditation. North Central Association of Colleges and Schools; Association of Theological Schools in the United States and Canada.

Term System. Semester.

Enrollment in Degree Programs in Religion 1984–85. Total 85; men 59, women 26.

Degrees in Religion Awarded 1984–85. Master of Arts in Pastoral Studies 14; men 1, women 13. Master of Divinity 4; men 4. Master of Arts in Theology 2; men 2.

Faculty for Degree Programs in Religion. Total 20; full-time 13, part-time 7.

Admission Requirements. Bachelor of Arts; some philosophy and theology at undergraduate level; Graduate Record Examination.

Tuition and Fees. Tuition $2,150 per semester (10 hours or more); semester hour $225; matriculation fee $20; student fee $30; graduation fee $20.

Financial Aid. Loan programs include NDSL, GSLP, and PLUS. A College Work-Study program and the Mahoney Scholarship for Catholic lay persons are also available.

Housing. Off-campus housing is available.

Library Facilities. The library houses over 33,000 volumes.

Religious Services/Activities. Roman Catholic Liturgies twice weekly; days of recollection.

Degree Programs

The Master of Arts in Pastoral Studies degree is a two-year program offering an opportunity for graduate-level theological education and the development of professional skills for ministry in a variety of pastoral settings. Through coursework, integrative seminars, supervised practice of ministry, and other learning experiences, the program seeks to integrate theology and the practice of ministry with the development of a personal pastoral identity. A student chooses one of four possible concentrations: Liturgical Ministry, Pastoral Care, Preaching, or Religious Formation.

The Master of Arts in Theology program is designed to prepare men and women for teaching on the secondary and college levels. A student chooses one of two possible concentrations: Systematic Theology or the Thought of Thomas Aquinas. The teaching and research tradition of the Dominican Order and the synthesis of Thomas Aquinas are the bases for the focuses of these programs.

The Master of Divinity degree offers men and women the opportunity to obtain a general theological education in the Roman Catholic tradition and to develop various professional skills for ministry within the Church. Such ministry can take many forms depending upon the needs of persons served, the social and cultural settings, and the particular requirements of specialized forms of ministry. In addition to courses in scripture, history, theology, and the various aspects of ministry, the program provides opportunities for developing ministerial competence through field education projects, supervised clinical training, and other kinds of contextual learning.

Special Programs

Continuing education courses are offered by the Institute as well as sabbatical programs tailored to individual needs.

Assemblies of God Theological Seminary
1445 Boonville Avenue
Springfield, MO 65802   (417) 862-3344

Administration. Dr. Thomas F. Zimmerman, President; Dr. James D. Brown, Executive Vice President; Dr. H. Glynn Hall, Academic Dean.

General Description. The Assemblies of God Theological Seminary is a nonprofit institution affiliated with the Assemblies of God which provides graduate level theological training for ministers/church leaders of the Assemblies of God and others who are sympathetic to and in harmony with the objectives of the Seminary. Academically, the Seminary consists of the Departments of Bible and Theology, Practical Theology, and Missions. It provides advanced work for those interested in pastoral, missionary, evangelistic, and chaplaincy ministries as well as teaching ministries in Bible colleges at home and abroad. The Seminary grants the Master of Divinity degree and 7 distinct Master of Arts degrees in: Biblical Literature, Biblical Languages, Bible/Missions, Christian Education, Pastoral Counseling, Intercultural Ministries, and Missiology. The Master of Arts in Biblical Literature may be acquired entirely through the extension program.

Community Environment. The Assemblies of God Theological Seminary occupies the top floors of the International Distribution Center of the General Council of the Assemblies of God in Springfield, Missouri. It includes administrative offices, a chapel, conference rooms, lounge areas, and classrooms. The facilities can accommodate a student body of more than 400. Because the Seminary is located within the Assemblies of God International Headquarters, students have ample opportunities to become familiar with the operation and resources of the church they are preparing to serve. The city of Springfield offers students a resource they will find in few seminary towns — a large community of committed Pentacostal Christians. More than 18 Assemblies of God congregations are located in and around Springfield, offering students rich opportunities for family worship, fellowship, and practicum experiences.

Religious Denomination. Assemblies of God.

Religious Emphasis. Pentecostal.

Accreditation. North Central Association of Colleges and Schools; Associate member of Association of Theological Schools in the United States and Canada.

Term System. Semester; summer term.

Enrollment in Degree Programs in Religion 1984–85. Total 248; men 213, women 35.

Degrees in Religion Awarded 1984–85. Master of Divinity 26; men 25, women 1. Master of Arts 50; men 37, women 13.

Faculty for Degree Programs in Religion. Total 27; full-time 10, part-time 17.

Admission Requirements. Baccalaureate degree or equivalent from an acceptable four-year college with a minimum grade point average of 2.5 on a 4.0 system; basic knowledge of Bible and theology, including 6 hours of Systematic Theology; at least one course in introduction to philosophy, introduction to psychology, and the social sciences.

Tuition and Fees. Tuition $115 per hour; basic semester fee $6 per hour.

Financial Aid. National Direct Student Loans, Guaranteed Student Loans, College Work-Study Program, and a Loan Program are available.

Housing. The Seminary does not provide housing. However, there is a surfeit of housing in the area providing apartments and houses for rent or sale.

Library Facilities. The Cordas C. Burnett Library has holdings of 46,000 bound volumes, 34,000 microfiche, 2,700 microfilm reels, 2,000 cassettes, and 860 periodicals.

Religious Services/Activities. Chapel is held Tuesday through Friday.

Degree Programs

The Bible and Theology Department offers programs leading to the Master of Arts in Biblical Literature and the Master of Arts in Biblical Languages. An interdisciplinary degree, designated Master of Arts in Bible/Missions is also offered. All three programs required 36 hours of credit.

The Practical Theology Department offers three degree programs: the Master of Arts in Christian Education (36 hours of credit), the Master of Arts in Pastoral Counseling (42 hours of credit), and the Master of Divinity (72 hours of credit). The Master of Divinity program has a variety of concentrations within it as options from which the student may choose.

The Missions Department offers pre-field and mid-career missionaries training for cross-cultural ministry. It offers the following degrees: Master of Arts in Missiology and Master of Arts in Intercultural Ministries. An interdisciplinary degree desginated as a Master of Arts in Bible/Missions is also offered.

Special Programs

The degree of Master of Arts in Biblical Literature may be completed entirely through extension and continuing education programs. One-week sessions are held off-campus during which the student may earn 2-4 hours credit. Pre-session and post-session work is required. The student attends 9 sessions of 4 hours each to earn the 36-hour Master of Arts degree.

Avila College
Department of Religious Studies
11901 Wornall Road
Kansas City, MO 64145   (816) 942-8400

Administration. Sr. Olive Louise Dallavis, President.

General Description. Avila College, sponsored by the Sisters of St. Joseph of Carondelet, is an academic community dedicated to education in the liberal arts and the professional areas. It was chartered in 1916 as the first private college for women in Kansas City and was known as the College of St. Teresa. Avila became a four-year college in 1940 and adopted the present name in 1963 on the move to a new suburban campus. The College became coeducational in 1969. The Department of Religious Studies offers a major leading to the Bachelor of Arts degree.

Community Environment. The 50-acre campus is located Kansas City, a major railroad center at the confluence of the Kansas and Missouri Rivers. Many cultural activities are available throughout the metropolitan area.

Religious Denomination. Roman Catholic.

Accreditation. North Central Association of Colleges and Schools.

Term System. Semester.

Admission Requirements. Graduation from an accredited high school or equivalent; rank in upper 50 percent of graduating class; ACT or SAT.

Tuition and Fees. Tuition $2,250 per semester; student center and activity fee $40; room and board $1,050-$1,250.

Financial Aid. The College provides assistance to qualified students on the basis of both need and merit.

Housing. Residential facilities consist of two modern and air-conditioned residence halls.

Library Facilities. The library houses over 74,000 volumes.

Religious Services/Activities. Through the Campus Ministry, services are offered for all members of the community regardless of religious preference. Liturgical celebrations, music, volunteer services, and retreats are offered for student participation.

Degree Programs

The Department of Religious Studies offers a major requiring 27 hours in Religious Studies to be chosen with the approval of the major advisor. Students majoring in Religious Studies will be expected to take at least three one-hour courses with a practical orientation by the Center for Pastoral Life and Ministry.

Special Programs

A Lay-Ministry Program is planned and is to be offered jointly by Avila College and the Center for Pastoral Life and Ministry. The program is to be ecumenical, recognizing the unique features of each Christian tradition and stressing those features that all Christian communities hold in common. A Certificate in Christian Ministry will be awarded. All courses are planned for weekends.

Baptist Bible College
628 East Kearney
Springfield, MO 65803   (417) 869-9811

Administration. Dr. A.V. Henderson, President; Dr. Parker Dailey, Vice President; Dr. W.E. Dowell, Chancellor; Dr. James Sewell, Director, Biblical Studies.

General Description. Baptist Bible College's purpose is to be a training center for prospective preachers, missionaries, and other Christian workers. The College was established as an integral part of the Baptist Bible Fellowship which is comprised of over 3,500 churches in the United States and over 200 missionary families on the foreign field. It is currently owned and operated by the Fellowship. Degrees offered are Bachelor of Arts (in Pastoral Studies, Missions, Music); Bachelor of Science (in Pastoral Studies, Missions, Church Education, Elementary Education, Secondary Education, Secretarial Administration, Music Education); Associate of Arts (in Secretarial Skills).

Community Environment. Baptist Bible College is located on a campus of over 38 acres in the northern section of Springfield, Missouri. Springfield, called the "Queen City of the Ozarks," is a thriving community of more than 200,000 residents. The city was originally chosen as the site of the College because of its strategic location in the center of the nation. Within a 200-mile radius of Springfield are located St. Louis, Kansas City, Tulsa, and Little Rock. The Springfield area contains a large number of Fellowship churches which allow students to participate in a local church. The strength and ministry of the churches serve as a model for prospective Christian workers enrolled in the College.

Religious Denomination. Baptist.

Religious Emphasis. Fundamentalist.

Accreditation. American Association of Bible Colleges.

Term System. Semester; summer term.

Enrollment in Degree Programs in Religion 1984–85. Total 808.

Degrees in Religion Awarded 1984–85. Bachelor of Science in Bible 50; men 50. Bachelor of Science in Church Education 35; men 11, women 24.

Faculty for Degree Programs in Religion. Total 56; full-time 37, part-time 19.

Admission Requirements. High school transcript; medical report; statement of salvation, Pastor's recommendation; college transcript (if applicable); $50 application fee.

Tuition and Fees. Tuition for Bible-related majors $495 (12-18 hours); Education-related majors $595 (12-18 hours); $25 per credit hour for 1-11 hours of any major; comprehensive fee for Bible $140, Education $200; room and board $985.

Financial Aid. Pell Grant, Veterans Administration benefits, Guaranteed Student Loan Program.

Housing. Dormitories are available for single students. Married student housing is available (efficiencies $135 per month, one-bedroom apartments $145 per month).

Library Facilities. The library contains 35,973 volumes.

Religious Services/Activities. Chapel services; Wives Fellowship; Mission Prayer Band; Student Publications; Christian Drama Club; Christian Service.

Degree Programs

A Bachelor of Arts degree is offered in Pastoral Studies, Missions, and Music. The Bachelor of Science degree is offered in Pastoral Studies, Missions, Church Education, Elementary Education, Secretarial Administration, and Music Education.

Special Programs

The Associate of Arts is offered in Secretarial Skills, Word Processing, English, and History.

The Correspondence School offers refresher pastoral courses and Bible courses designed for layworkers. An extension program offers the fourth year Bachelor's program on cassette tape.

Calvary Bible College
Division of Biblical Education
Kansas City, MO 64147   (816) 322-0110

Administration. Leslie Madison, President.

General Description. Calvary Bible College was established to provide an environment for the personal, spiritual, and academic growth of young men and women who are preparing for Christian Ministries. It was founded in 1932 under the name of the Kansas City Bible Institute and in 1961 merged with the Midwest Bible and Missionary Institute to form Calvary Bible College. The College offers various major fields of Biblical study leading to the Associate, Bachelor, and Master's degrees.

Community Environment. The campus of 80 acres in located near Belton, Missouri, 20 miles south of downtown Kansas City.

Religious Denomination. Nondenominational.

Accreditation. American Association of Bible Colleges.

Term System. Semester (4-4-1-1 plan).

Faculty for Degree Programs in Religion. Total 34.

Admission Requirements. Graduation from an accredited high school or equivalent; rank in upper half of graduating class; ACT.

Tuition and Fees. Tuition $70 per semester hour; room

$390 per semester; board $690.

Financial Aid. The Financial Assistance Officer will assist students in obtaining need-based aid.

Housing. Men's and women's dormitory accommodations are available.

Library Facilities. The Kroeker Library is a 45,000-volume resource center with approximately 60 percent of the collection in Theology.

Religious Services/Activities. Attendance at chapel service is required. Students are expected to attend one of the many fundamental, Bible-believing churches in the Kansas City area. During the fall semester, a Missions Emphasis week is scheduled.

Degree Programs

The Division of Biblical Education offers a program in Biblical studies leading to the degrees Associate of Arts, the Bachelor of Arts, the Bachelor of Science, and the Master of Arts. The Division includes the Department of English Bible, Department of Theology, and Department of Biblical Languages. The Division of Vocational Education offers programs through its various departments: Pastoral Studies, Missions, Education, Physical Education, Music, Christian Aviation, and Christian Communications. Each program has varying course completion requirements.

The Master of Arts program emphasizes Biblical Languages. An individual with an undergraduate degree from a Bible college can earn the degree with a minimum of 32 credit hours.

The Master of Science is designed as a two-year program. The emphasis of the minor is toward Christian camping administration and is to be taken in the first year of graduate training on site at Camp Forest Springs in Westboro, Wisconsin.

Special Programs

The Associate of Arts degree in Biblical Studies and a One-Year Bible Certificate program are offered by the Division of Biblical Education.

Cardinal Glennon College
5200 Glennon Drive
St. Louis, MO 63119   (314) 644-0266

Administration. Patrick V. Harrity, President.

General Description. Cardinal Glennon College is a liberal arts college for young men who wish to prepare for the Roman Catholic Priesthood in the Archdiocese of St. Louis. It was established in 1898. The College is owned and operated by the Archdiocese of St. Louis and is administered by members of the Congregation of the Mission (Vincentians).

Community Environment. The College is located in the city of Shrewsbury which borders on the southwest limits of St. Louis, Missouri.

Religious Denomination. Roman Catholic.

Accreditation. North Central Association of Colleges and Schools.

Term System. Semester.

Enrollment in Degree Programs in Religion 1984–85. Total 98.

Admission Requirements. The College admits only students desirous of studying for the Priesthood who are sponsored by their Ordinary (local Bishop or Provincial Superior).

Tuition and Fees. Tuition, room, and board $2,500 per semester; part-time tuition $135 per semester hour.

Financial Aid. The Archdiocese of St. Louis gives financial aid to its students to the extent of 50 percent of charges for room, board, and tuition.

Housing. All full-time diocesan students are required to board at the College.

Library Facilities. The library contains over 72,000 volumes.

Religious Services/Activities. Because the College is a Seminary, it strives, besides offering the academic program, to provide an environment suitable to the vocational objectives of its students. Religious exercises include a daily regimen centered around prayer, a manual work program, and a program of social action in service to the larger community.

Degree Programs

The instructional program is designed to give the student a general education with emphasis on the humanities, concentrating in philosophy, and to prepare him for future specialization, especially for theology. A major concentration is offered in philosophy. The Bachelor of Arts degree is awarded upon completion of the four-year program of 128 semester hours.

Central Bible College
3000 North Grant
Springfield, MO 65803   (417) 833-2551

Administration. Rev. H. Maurice Lednicky, President; Dr. Elmer E. Kirsch, Dean.

General Description. The primary purpose of Central Bible College is to offer intensive instruction in God's Word so that by the time of graduation students will have a thorough understanding of the Bible. In its curricular offerings the College is not attempting to compete with secular schools. Its primary emphasis is upon the Bible with strong emphasis given to such other disciplines as are deemed necessary for a proper approach to the Bible and to its relation to life. With its curricular offerings constructed on the foundations of Biblical Theism, its comprehensive goal is to prepare men and women for leadership in the Church. Central Bible College grants the Bachelor of Arts degree, a Diploma for completion of a three year course, and the Associate of Arts degree for

completion of a two year course. The College is owned and controlled by the General Council of the Assemblies of God, Springfield, Missouri.

Community Environment. Central Bible College is located in Springfield, Missouri, near the summit of the Ozark Mountain plateau, on a scenic 108-acre campus. The south half of the campus is shaded by an oak grove which furnishes a beautiful natural setting. Springfield is a thriving industrial and business center, with an area population of approximately 200,000. The rolling tree-covered countryside is well known for its dairying and animal husbandry, and abounds with springs, parks, and lakes. The college campus is situated on the north border of the city.

Religious Denomination. Assemblies of God.

Religious Emphasis. Evangelical.

Accreditation. American Association of Bible Colleges.

Term System. Semester; 3 summer sessions.

Enrollment in Degree Programs in Religion 1984–85. Total 900; men 550, women 350.

Degrees in Religion Awarded 1984–85. Associate of Arts 15; men 7, women 8. Bachelor of Arts 171; men 102, women 69.

Faculty for Degree Programs in Religion. Total 59; full-time 33, part-time 26.

Admission Requirements. High school graduation in upper 60 percent of graduating class or special consideration; ACT or SAT scores; personal references.

Tuition and Fees. Tuition $69 per semester credit hour; general fee $120; room and board $1,090 to $1,120.

Financial Aid. Institutional grants, loans, and scholarships; National Direct Student Loans; Guaranteed Student Loans; PLUS; work-study.

Housing. Dormitories for single men and women; apartments and homes for married students; mobile home park.

Library Facilities. The library houses over 143,000 volumes and receives approximately 670 periodicals. The Meyer Pearlman Collection is maintained.

Religious Services/Activities. Daily chapel; Campus Missions Fellowship weekly under student direction; practical ministry by students in a variety of areas; student internships for upperclassmen both at home and overseas; Missions Convention; lectureships.

Degree Programs

The Bachelor of Arts degree in Bible is offered by the Division of Biblical Education and requires completion of 126 semester hours including 30 in Bible, 15 in Theology, 23 in Pastoral Ministries, and 43 in General Education. A pre-seminary concentration is also offered as well as major emphasis in Pastoral Ministries/Youth Ministries Minor, Pastoral Ministries/Deaf Ministries Concentration, Pastoral Ministries Concentration, and Pastoral Ministries/ Youth Ministries Concentration. The Division of Church Ministries offers the Bachelor of Arts degree in Missions which requires 126 semester hours including 21 hours in Bible, 15 in Theology, 19 in Pastoral Ministries, 29 in

Missions, and 40 in General Education.

Special Programs

An Associate of Arts degree in Bible is offered and requires the completion of 64 semester hours.

Diploma programs are offered in Bible and Missions which require completion of 95 semester hours.

Central Methodist College
Department of Philosophy and Religion
Fayette, MO 65248   (816) 248-3391

Administration. Joe A. Howell, President.

General Description. Central Methodist College began classes in 1857. It is a four-year undergraduate college of the United Methodist Church. Its mission is to provide opportunities for undergraduate students to achieve a liberal and relevant education, including the liberal arts, combined with vocational preparation enriched by a clear consciousness of Christian values. The Department of Philosophy and Religion offers majors in both fields leading to the Bachelor of Arts degree.

Community Environment. The College is located in Fayette (population 3,500), midway between St. Louis and Kansas City.

Religious Denomination. United Methodist Church.

Accreditation. North Central Association of Colleges and Schools.

Term System. Semester (4-1-4 plan).

Admission Requirements. Graduation from an accredited high school or equivalent; ACT.

Tuition and Fees. Tuition $4,640 per year; room and board $2,260; student fees $50.

Financial Aid. Scholarships, grants and benefits, employment, federal aid programs, and church-sponsored scholarships are available.

Housing. Men's and women's dormitories are available on campus. Some living accommodations for married students are also available.

Library Facilities. The College Library contains over 100,000 volumes. It is the official depository of the missouri West conference of the United Methodist Church Commission on Archives and History.

Religious Services/Activities. The Religious Life Committee coordinates the activities of the campus Christian groups and plans special events and programs. Chapel services are held every Tuesday morning.

Degree Programs

The major in Religion is designed for persons planning upon entering the Christian ministry, Christian education, or other church-related vocations, or for persons who wish to have a thorough understanding of Christian thought and life. The major requires 30 hours in religion. An emphasis in Christian Education can be combined with Religion, Music, and Elementary Education. The

Bachelor's degree requires the completion of a total of 124 semester hours of credit.

Conception Seminary College
Department of Religion
Conception, MO 64433   (816) 944-2218

Administration. Rt. Rev. Jerome Hanus, O.S.B., Chancellor.

General Description. The Department of Religion offers a Bachelor's degree with a major in Religion. This program consists of a required core sequence of courses acquainting and introducing the student to the principal areas of theological study/reflection and providing the necessary background for entrance into a graduate level program. A sequence of elective courses develops selected areas of religion/theology.

Conception Seminary College is a liberal arts, four-year college specializing in the work of helping men discern their vocation to ministry and prepare for ministry as Roman Catholic priests. The history of the College, especially in its early years, is closely identified with that of Conception Abbey. Conception's founder and first abbot, the Rev. Frowin Conrad, was commissioned at the Swiss abbey of Engelberg to establish the American monastery and translate the true Benedictine spirit to new fields of endeavor in America. When the "New Engleberg Abbey of the Immaculate Conception" was first incorporated under Missouri law in 1882, its charter included the set purpose of "conducting schools: a college and a seminary; fostering and promoting intellectual science and arts, and of encouraging agricultural and other useful industries." In 1886, the first college building was erected and in 1891, New Engelberg Abbey and College were reincorporated under the title Conception Abbey and Conception College with authority to grant degrees. The name of the College was changed to Conception Seminary in 1942, the word "Immaculate" was added in 1958, and in 1972 the name was modified to Conception Seminary College to reflect a new determination and a clearer focus.

Community Environment. The Seminary buildings, mostly of red brick construction, were erected and remodeled at various times during the period from 1901 to 1966. They are situated on a 30-acre campus, part of a 640-acre tract belonging also to the farm, orchards, and workshops of the Abbey and to the Printery House of Conception Abbey. The Abbey Basilica of the Immaculate Conception, consecrated in 1891 and raised to the rank of a minor basilica by Pope Piux XII in 1941, is the main liturgical center for celebrations involving the entire Abbey and Seminary community.

Religious Denomination. Roman Catholic.

Accreditation. North Central Association of Colleges and Schools.

Term System. Semester; no summer term.

Enrollment in Degree Programs in Religion 1984–85.

Total 114.

Degrees in Religion Awarded 1984–85. Bachelor of Arts 6; men 6.

Faculty for Degree Programs in Religion. Total 5; full-time 5.

Admission Requirements. High school graduation or the equivalent; 16 credits in college preparatory work; rank at graduation above the lowest quartile (for schools large enough for this distinction to be significant); ACT scores above 14 (composite).

Tuition and Fees. Tuition $2,520 per year; general activity fee $90; board $1,660 per year; room $860 per year.

Financial Aid. Government programs, church programs, institutional grants, scholarships, work-study, and other financial aid programs available (parish, Knights of Columbus, etc.)

Housing. All full-time seminary students are required to live on campus.

Library Facilities. The library occupies two entire floors of St. Joseph's Hall. Its resources include 109,000 books and bound periodicals, a special rare book collection, and a significant audiovisual collection of records and tapes. There are special collections on Religion-Theology, Philosophy, Monastic History, Spirituality, and Biography. The rare book collection of approximately 1,700 volumes includes incunabula through the 1700s concentrated in religion-related areas.

Religious Services/Activities. Daily Mass; daily praying of Morning Prayer and Evening Prayer (in common); two annual retreats, monthly day of recollection; weekly religious conferences; individual meeting with individual spiritual director (every other week).

Degree Programs

The Bachelor of Arts program with area of concentration in Religion is made up of courses which deal primarily with the foundation of the Christian religious community, the individual believer's place in the worshiping life of that community, and his role in its outward mission to the world of the secular. All students, regardless of area of concentration, must be enrolled in a core religion course each semester of residence and regardless of previous credit.

Special Programs

By means of the Patrick Cummins Chair of Theology, the Seminary brings speakers of recognized competence and professional standing to the Seminary for participation in symposia or colloquia centering on theological themes, individual speakers for lectures or series of lectures on theological topics, or for special theological workshops.

The Seminary has instituted a Pre-Theology Program of priestly formation for the college graduate and older student. To enter this program, the student must have the sponsorship of either a diocese or religious order.

Concordia Seminary
801 DeMun Avenue
St. Louis, MO 63105   (314) 721-5934

Administration. Karl L. Barth, President.

General Description. Concordia Seminary was founded in 1839 by a group of emigrants from Germany. It is owned and operated by the Lutheran Church-Missouri Synod. The Seminary prepares young men for ordination as parish pastors, chaplains, and mission workers.

Community Environment. The campus occupies 72 acres in Clayton, a suburban area of St. Louis, Missouri.

Religious Denomination. Lutheran Church-Missouri Synod.

Accreditation. North Central Association of Colleges and Schools; Association of Theological Schools in the United States and Canada.

Term System. Quarter.

Faculty for Degree Programs in Religion. Total 47.

Admission Requirements. Bachelor's degree or equivalent; Graduate Record Examination.

Tuition and Fees. Tuition $65 per quarter hour (Seminary); $80 per quarter hour plus fees (School of Graduate Studies); activity fee $25 per quarter; room $710-$840 per quarter.

Financial Aid. Aid is available in the form of employment and campus-based aid.

Housing. Living accommodations are available in dormitories and apartments.

Library Facilities. The book collection of the library numbers over 165,000 volumes.

Religious Services/Activities. The Pastoral Staff of the President has the primary responsibility for policies concerning campus worship and the spiritual life of the entire community.

Degree Programs

The Master of Arts in Religion degree requires completion of at least 48 quarter hours of advanced work. Majors are available in Exegetical Theology, Systematic Theology, Historical Theology, and Practical Theology.

The Master of Sacred Theology degree requires the completion of a minimum of 36 quarter hours with a major in one of the four areas.

The Doctor of Theology program is designed to enable the candidate to achieve mastery in the field of specialization. It requires 48 quarter hours of work beyond the Master of Divinity and must be earned in a major field. Work is in the areas of Exegetical Theology, Systematic Theology with an emphasis on Lutheran Theology, and Historical Theology with an emphasis on the period from the Lutheran Reformation to the present.

Covenant Theological Seminary

12330 Conway Road
St. Louis, MO 63141   (314) 434-4044

Administration. Dr. Paul E. Kooistra, President; Dr. David C. Jones, Vice President for Academic Affairs; Dr. Robert G. Rayburn, Director of D.Min. Studies.

General Description. Covenant Theological Seminary is a professional school of higher learning, owned and operated by the Presbyterian Church in America, which has as its chief purpose the provision of a program of studies and training for those called to the ministry. It serves the needs of the sponsoring denomination for an educated ministry, but it welcomes evangelical students from other denominations as well. The Seminary has programs leading to the following degrees: Master of Divinity, Master of Arts, Master of Theology, and Doctor of Ministry. In addition, there are Graduate Certificate programs in Biblical and Theological Studies, and Missions Studies.

Community Environment. The Seminary campus is located slightly west of St. Louis, Missouri on a 20-acre tract of land that includes wooded areas and spacious lawns. The township of Creve Coeur, within the bounds of which the Seminary campus lies, is less than half an hour from the cultural, recreational, and educational advantages of the entire metropolitan St. Louis area.

Religious Denomination. Presbyterian Church in America.

Religious Emphasis. Reformed, Conservative, and Evangelical.

Accreditation. North Central Association of Colleges and Schools; Association of Theological Schools in the United States and Canada.

Term System. Semester; summer term.

Enrollment in Degree Programs in Religion 1984–85. Total 131; men 125, women 6.

Degrees in Religion Awarded 1984–85. Master of Divinity 101; men 101. Master of Arts 12; men 10, women 2. Master of Theology 6; men 6. Doctor of Ministry 11; men 11. Graduate Certificate 12; men 8, women 4.

Faculty for Degree Programs in Religion. Total 17; full-time 12, part-time 5.

Admission Requirements. Bachelor of Arts degree or equivalent; transcripts; references.

Tuition and Fees. Tuition $100 per credit hour (10 hours or less), $90 per credit hour (12 hours or more), maximum $1,440 per semester; application fee $15; entering testing fee $40; library, activity, and car registration fees $35 per semester.

Financial Aid. Grants, loans, and work-study jobs are available. Additional financial aid available to men under care of the Presbyterian Church in America Presbyteries.

Housing. Single men's dormitory is available on campus; assistance is rendered in locating suitable off-campus housing for married students and families.

Library Facilities. The library houses over 48,000 volumes including the 1,000 volume Ian Tait Puritan and Rare Book Collection. Students have access to the libraries of five other theological schools in the St. Louis area.

Religious Services/Activities. A time set aside for corporate worship is part of the daily schedule at the Seminary. On one day each semester classes are suspended and the time is given to worship and prayer.

Degree Programs

The Master of Divinity degree is the standard degree for ordination to the professional ministry in the Presbyterian Church in America. The curriculum can be completed in three years. A total of 102 hours is required provided that a prerequisite of 6 hours of Beginning Greek has been fulfilled. A four-year schedule is also available.

The Master of Arts program is offered in Exegetical Theology and Historical Theology. Each program requires the completion of 60 hours in specified courses and electives.

The Master of Theology is offered as a specialized program, which normally includes a thesis, and prepares the advanced student for a ministry of teaching and research. It is offered in each of the five academic disciplines at the Seminary: Old Testament, New Testament, Systematic Theology, Church History, and Practical Theology. The Master of Theology in Biblical and Pastoral Theology is designed as a fourth-year sequel to the Master of Divinity degree. This program aims at a high degree of integration of Biblical studies and practical ministry. A total of 30 graduate credit units are required.

The Doctor of Ministry program is designed both in content and schedule to meet the needs of the active parish pastor. Its goal is to enable the minister better to draw upon Biblical, historical, and theological resources for ministry and to attain a higher degree of professional competence in the practice of ministry. In particular, the four core courses are designed to deepen the student's understanding and to sharpen his ministerial skills in four major areas of pastoral leadership: worship, preaching, counseling, and congregational life. The degree is awarded upon completion of 30 credit units plus a project and dissertation.

Special Programs

The Graduate Certificate of Biblical and Theological Studies requires the completion of 30 units of credit which may be applied to one of the Seminary's degree programs. Admission is open to those who hold the Bachelor of Arts degree or its equivalent.

Drury College
Department of Philosophy and Religion

900 North Benton Avenue
Springfield, MO 65802   (417) 865-8731

Administration. John E. Moore, Jr., President.
General Description. Drury College is affiliated with the

United Church of Christ (formerly the Congregational Church) and the Christian Church (Disciples of Christ). It was founded by Congregationalists in 1873 and was called Springfield College. The Drury School of Religion, established in 1909, was maintained by the Christian Church (Disciples of Christ) until Drury College became formally affiliated with this denomination. It continues to exist as a separate entity, affiliated with Drury, to assist the College in the implementation of its church relationship.

Community Environment. The 43-acre campus has 20 buildings in the city of Springfield, a city of 145,000 located on a plateau in the Missouri Ozarks.

Religious Denomination. United Church of Christ; Christian Church (Disciples of Christ).

Accreditation. North Central Association of Colleges and Schools.

Term System. Semester (4-1-4 plan).

Admission Requirements. Graduation from an accredited high school or equivalent; ACT or SAT.

Tuition and Fees. Tuition $2,350 per semester; room $865-$1,045; board $1,150.

Financial Aid. The College has an extensive scholarship and award program designed to acknowledge academic excellence, leadership, or other special abilities. Grants, loans, and college-work study are also available.

Housing. Dormitories and fraternity houses are available on campus.

Library Facilities. The Walker Library houses over 95,000 volumes.

Religious Services/Activities. Chapel services are conducted under the direction of the college chaplain. The chaplain is responsible for college worship, coordinates religious groups on campus, and counsels with students.

Degree Programs

The Department of Philosophy and Religion offers a major in either field consisting of 24 credit hours, at least 12 of which must be upper division courses, plus a senior seminar or a course in independent research. The major leads to the Bachelor of Arts degree (124 semester hours).

Eden Theological Seminary
475 East Lockwood
St. Louis, MO 63119   (314) 961-3627

Administration. Malcolm L. Warford, President.

General Description. The goal of Eden Theological Seminary is to provide outstanding professional leadership for the ministry of the Church and to equip persons to engage in a lifelong career of faithful, informed theological study. Eden's teaching-learning enterprise seeks to nurture and develop persons who are both exceptional practitioners of contemporary forms of professional ministry and mature, functioning persons of faith. Students from seventeen different denominations are engaged in theolog-

ical education at Eden. The Seminary remains committed to its evergrowing vision of sending forth faithful and effective leaders for church and society. The Seminary counts among its distinguished graduates Reinhold and H. Richard Niebuhr, as well as other leading twentieth-century theologians, pastors, and church administrators.

Eden Theological Seminary was established in the summer of 1850 at Marthasville, Missouri, as a training school for ministers by the Church Society of the West (der Kirchenverein des Westens). The Seminary was founded to educate pastors for German Evangelical churches on the American frontier. In 1883, the Seminary moved to Wellston, Missouri, on the outskirts of St. Louis, where it acquired its present name, Eden, inspired by the railroad station that served the seminary. In 1924, another relocation brought the Seminary to its present location in Webster Groves. In 1934, Eden Seminary completed a merger with Central Theological Seminary and Oakwood Institute of Cincinnati, Ohio, which was one of the first fruits of the formation of the Evangelical and Reformed Church. Conversations held at the Eden campus gave rise to the movement which resulted in the formation of the United Church of Christ. Dr. Samuel D. Press represented the Evangelical and Reformed traditions; the Reverend Truman Douglass, pastor of a St. Louis Congregational Church, represented the congregational Christian traditions. The two merged to become the United Church of Christ in 1957.

Community Environment. The Eden campus is located on twenty acres of wooded land in Webster Groves, Missouri, an older suburban community on the edge of the St. Louis city limits. Its four main buildings form a quadrangle with the head being the gothic tower over the chapel. The base of the quadrangle is the Library with its major architectural support in the form of trees - symbolically suggesting knowledge.

Religious Denomination. United Church of Christ.

Religious Emphasis. Liberal.

Accreditation. North Central Association of Colleges and Schools; Association of Theological Schools in the United States and Canada.

Term System. Semester; summer term (June).

Enrollment in Degree Programs in Religion 1984–85. Total 211; men 132, women 79.

Degrees in Religion Awarded 1984–85. Doctor of Ministry 22; men 11, women 11. Master of Arts 1; women 1. Master of Divinity 29; men 17, women 12. Certificate 1; men 1.

Faculty for Degree Programs in Religion. Total 15; full-time 11; part-time 4.

Admission Requirements. Bachelor's degree from an accredited college or university; grade point average of at least 2.7 on a 4.0 scale; letters of reference; an autobiographical statement; pre-admission interview.

Tuition and Fees. Tuition $100 per credit hour; room per semester double $374, single $660; miscellaneous fees.

Financial Aid. Financial aid is available in the form of

tuition grants, field education remuneration, work study, off-campus employment, loans, summer employment, and scholarships.

Housing. Furnished rooms are available in Schultz Hall for single students. One, two, and three bedroom unfurnished apartments are available for married students.

Library Facilities. Eden Seminary and Webster University share a common library built by the Seminary in 1968. The combined collections of Eden and Webster total more than 177,000 volumes, over 800 French, German, and American journals, and a constantly growing collection of audiovisual materials. The Archives of the Evangelical Synod of North America, known more familiarly as the Eden Archives, are located on the lower level of the Eden-Webster Library. The Eden Archives collect, maintain, and make available to researchers historical books and manuscripts relating to the parent denomination of Eden Seminary, the Evangelical Synod, and its successors in the Evangelical and Reformed Church and the United Church of Christ. The collection emphasizes records relating to churches, ministers, the Seminary, denominational agencies, and missions.

Religious Services/Activities. The worship of God is held daily throughout the school year. The thirty minute service is intentionally placed in the middle of the morning class schedule to suggest its centrality to the whole educational process. On Friday, the Eucharist is celebrated within a full liturgy of Word and Sacrament. Annually, in the week following Easter, the Seminary hosts a three-day convocation for pastors and laypersons. Eden faculty are joined by scholars from around the country to lecture on a significant theme. A week in June is devoted to one or two intensive workshops on worship and related topics such as music and preaching. Pastors, church musicians, and laypersons may enroll for one or both workshops.

Degree Programs

The Master of Divinity is a professional degree designed to equip women and men for the Church's ministry. The degree is normally the educational prerequisite for ordination, and prepares persons to function as ordained leaders in the Church's ministry and mission. The program combines the critical study of theology with the continual practice of ministry.

The Master of Arts program is designed for those who wish to study the biblical, theological, and historical foundations of the Christian religion. It is a degree which centers on the study of theology with no attention given to the practice of ministry.

The Doctor of Ministry is an advanced professional degree designed for ordained men and women. It provides an opportunity for continued theological study in a focused and disciplined manner. The program enhances the leadership of the Church through critical dialogue and reflection. The Seminary intends, through this program, to challenge persons to participate in the continuing reformation of the Church's ministry and mission. The pro-

gram has been structured with flexibility to meet individual needs.

The Doctor of Ministry in Pastoral Counseling program enables students to receive didactic and clinical training in pastoral counseling through the Care and Counseling agency while engaging in the academic and professional program of Eden's Doctor of Ministry program. Care and Counseling is a fully accredited counseling and training center which offers a complete certificate program in Pastoral Counseling. Growing out of rich relationships with the psychoanalytic community in St. Louis, the program incorporates recent developments from dynamic ego psychology and systems theory. The heart of the program is supervised clinical work in which intensive long term pastoral psychotherapeutic modalities and brief and supportive modalities of pastoral care are stressed.

Special Programs

Students who do not hold an undergraduate degree may apply to the Seminary's Certificate Program. Through this program, the Seminary recognizes the life experience of exceptional second career students as a prerequisite for theological studies. Upon completion of the Master of Divinity graduation requirements, a certificate student receives a Certificate of the Seminary. Persons who receive the Certificate and who complete an undergraduate degree program within 5 years can have the Certificate converted to a Master of Divinity degree.

Evangel College
Biblical Studies and Philosophy Department
1111 North Glenstone Avenue
Springfield, MO 65802   (417) 865-2811

Administration. Dr. Robert H. Spence, President; Dr. Zenas J. Bicket, Academic Dean; Twila Edwards, Chairperson, Department of Biblical Studies and Philosophy.

General Description. The Department of Biblical Studies and Philosophy offers a major in Biblical Studies designed to prepare students for either graduate school or seminary. In addition to this function, the Department also serves the entire student body in that all students are required to take a 16-credit sequence in Biblical Studies as part of their general education total.

Parent Institution. Evangel College, a coeducational senior college of arts and sciences owned by the General Council of the Assemblies of God, opened in September, 1955. The College confers four baccalaureate degrees: Bachelor of Arts, Bachelor of Business Administration, Bachelor of Music Education, and Bachelor of Science. A student may earn an Associate of Arts degree under an approved two-year program.

Community Environment. The College is located on a 66-acre campus in Springfield, Missouri, in the heart of the scenic Ozarks. The northwest edge of the campus borders on an attractive city park. Located on a plateau in the mountains, Springfield (population 145,000) is noted as a dairy center. Some of the industries located here are General Electric, Minnesota Mining and Manufacturing, Zenith, the Gospel Publishing Company, and Kraft Foods.

Religious Denomination. Assemblies of God.

Religious Emphasis. Evangelical, Pentecostal.

Accreditation. North Central Association of Colleges and Schools.

Term System. Semester; summer term.

Enrollment in Degree Programs in Religion 1984–85. Total 154.

Degrees in Religion Awarded 1984–85. Bachelor of Arts 34; men 30, women 4.

Faculty for Degree Programs in Religion. Total 11; full-time 7, part-time 4.

Admission Requirements. High school diploma or equivalent; ACT; good moral character; a confession of Christian faith; sympathy with the doctrinal beliefs of the Assemblies of God; a willingness to abide by the Student Handbook; medical history.

Tuition and Fees. Tuition $1,595 per semester; fee $35; room and board $1,150 per semester.

Financial Aid. Pell Grant; SEOG; NDSL; GSL; PLUS; Work-Study; Academic Achievement Award; Valedictorian Scholarship; Academic Department Scholarships; Evangel-in-Aid Scholarships; ROTC Scholarships; Endowment Scholarships; Private Scholarships.

Housing. Over 75 percent of students live in residence halls. Apartments and mobile homes are available on campus for married students.

Library Facilities. The library houses a collection of over 110,000 volumes.

Religious Services/Activities. Daily attendance in chapel is required of all students. SCOPE is a campus organization that provides opportunities for Christian witness on the campus, in the community, and on other college campuses. Traveling teams minister in churches, and students assist with foreign and home missions during the summer months.

Degree Programs

The Bachelor of Arts degree with a major in Biblical Studies is designed to prepare students for either graduate school or seminary. The program consists of the 16-hour general education Biblical Studies sequence, plus and additional 21 hours, which are specified by the Department. The many varied forms of Christian service and the resulting varying needs of individual students make it desirable to develop individual programs and combinations of programs. Concentrations or minors from outside the Biblical Studies and Philosophy Department may be included in interdisciplinary programs which can be justified by the needs of the student. One such program, managed by the Department, is an interdisciplinary pre-missions major, designed to prepare students to enter a graduate missions program, such as that sponsored by the Assemblies of God

Graduate School.

Special Programs

An Associate of Arts program may be earned in communication skills (Christian communications, church communications) as well as other areas. The program requires the completion of general education and other specific requirements.

Kenrick Seminary
St. Louis Roman Catholic Theological Seminary
7800 Kenrick Road
St. Louis, MO 63119   (314) 961-4320

Administration. Rev. James A. Fischer, C.M., President/Rector; Rev. John P. Heil, Academic Dean.

General Description. Kenrick Seminary is a graduate school of theology belonging to the Archdiocese of St. Louis. It prepares men for their roles as priests in the Archdiocese and is open to all priesthood candidates of other dioceses and religious congregations. Kenrick Seminary also accepts students who are interested in taking individual courses offered in the curriculum. The Seminary is served by a diversified faculty consisting of the Vincentian Fathers, Archdiocesan priests in residence, other priests from the Archdiocese, order priests, sisters, and lay professors, as well as faculty members from neighboring institutions.

The "St. Louis Roman Catholic Theological Seminary" was originally incorporated under the laws of the State of Missouri in 1869. The name Kenrick Seminary, taken in memory of Peter Richard Kenrick, the first Archbishop of St. Louis, and by which the Seminary is more popularly known, dates from the year 1893.

Community Environment. The present Kenrick Seminary, located in the village of Shrewsbury, near the southwest city limits of St. Louis, opened in 1915. The Seminary building, English Collegiate Gothic in design, was built during the years 1912-1915. The chapel, Gothic in style, is the focal point of the Seminary. The decoration of the chapel, carried on over many years, is noteworthy for the hand-carved oak woodwork, and black and white marble floor. Eighteen art-glass windows depict themes of priesthood from the Old and New Testaments.

Religious Denomination. Roman Catholic.

Accreditation. North Central Association of Colleges and Schools; Association of Theological Schools in the United States and Canada.

Term System. Semester.

Degrees in Religion Awarded 1984–85. Master of Divinity 6; men 6. Master of Arts 2; men 2.

Faculty for Degree Programs in Religion. Total 27; full-time 18; adjunct 9.

Admission Requirements. Bachelor of Arts from an accredited college; basic philosophy courses; transcript from all colleges and seminaries attended; Graduate Record Examination results.

Tuition and Fees. Tuition $1,500 per semester full-time; part-time up to 9 hours, $140 per credit; activity fee $40 per year; room and board $1,000 per semester.

Housing. There are 13 faculty suites and 160 student rooms located on the upper floors of the Kenrick Seminary building.

Library Facilities. The Charles L. Souvay Memorial Library is the product of the fusion of two principal collections: the St. Louis Archdiocesan collection, or St. John's Library, assembled by Bishop Rosati and by Archbishop Kenrick and given to the Seminary at its foundation in 1893, and the St. Catherine Library Association collection, originally placed at St. Vincent's College, Cape Girardeau, Missouri, where diocesan students for the priesthood received their education prior to 1893. The library has holdings of more than 70,000 books, bound periodicals, theses or major papers, and rare books. The library subscribes to about 350 periodicals. The holdings of the library reflect the curriculum in the predominance of monographs, periodicals, and audiovisual materials in the Sacred Sciences supporting the courses of study pursued at the Seminary.

The 1,800 rare and special books range from a 1495 Bible, the earliest of the Bibles in the collection, to some area histories of the Church in the United States, a number of diocesan synods before 1930, yearbooks of the Archdiocese of St. Louis, and most of the works of the two Archbishops Kenrick, Peter Richard of St. Louis, and Francis Patrick of Philadelphia.

The library has a collection of the writings of Thomas Merton. In addition to his books, there is a 22-volume set compiled by Father Thomas J. Nelson, C.M., an alumnus of Kenrick, which consists of the writings of Merton found in periodical literature, poetry, pamphlets, and books with contributions, including some unpublished manuscripts. The library also has a set of cuneiform tablets given principally to Father Souvay, whose name now graces the library.

Religious Services/Activities. The goals of the Spiritual Formation Program are drawn from the *Decree on Priestly Formation, No. 8* of the Vatican Council II and from the *Program of Priestly Formation* of the National Conference of Catholic Bishops. In summary, these goals are to instruct, guide, facilitate, and encourage the growth of each seminarian's union with God the Father through his Son, Jesus Christ, in the Holy Spirit. Each day, and several times during the day, the Kenrick student is expected to pray. The celebration of the Eucharist is the central action in the life of each member of the community and of the community as a whole. Each day is sanctified by the communal celebration of morning and evening prayers. A period is set aside in the daily schedule for private meditation. In connection with the Formation Program, a spiritual conference is scheduled approximately every two weeks.

In harmony with the liturgical seasons, the community gathers informally for other forms of prayer experience (penance services, Marian Devotions, Benediction, shared prayer, etc.). Each student makes a week-long annual retreat which offers the quiet, reflective atmosphere needed for a prolonged experience of prayer. The Spiritual Formation Program progresses through the four years, each subsequent year building upon the previous one.

The Field Education program of Kenrick Seminary aims at training a seminarian to become a priest who is a professional minister of the Roman Catholic Church. The program is designed to aid the student to reflect upon the situations in which he finds himself and to see how he represents the work of God. This is accomplished through a three-fold process: Experience, Supervision, and Theological Reflection.

Degree Programs

The Master of Divinity is a professional degree oriented to ministry; the completion of the degree is presumed by the Seminary. All students are initially enrolled in this program which requires completion of certain courses deemed necessary for a basic foundation in theological thought and ministerial practice.

The Master of Arts in Theology is a suitable preparation for one whose work will focus on research or on teaching - whether at elementary, secondary, college, or graduate level. It is more restricted in scope than the Master of Divinity degree and requires greater academic proficiency. Areas of concentration are Systematic Theology, Scripture, Pastoral Theology, or Church History.

Special Programs

The Seminary offers a special two-semester program called the Pre-Theology Philosophy Program. It is designed for priesthood students who have a bachelor's degree but do not have sufficient undergraduate credits (18 hours) in philosophy. The program provides them with the opportunity to fulfill this requirement.

Midwestern Baptist Theological Seminary
5001 North Oak Street Trafficway
Kansas City, MO 64118   (816) 453-4600

Administration. Milton Ferguson, President; N. Larry Baker, Academic Dean.

General Description. The Midwestern Baptist Theological Seminary exists to provide theological education, with the Bible at the center of the curriculum, for God-called men and women. The Seminary was established by Southern Baptists in 1957. It is one of six Southern Baptist seminaries. Midwestern offers five degrees with specializations possible through use of elective options: Doctor of Ministry, Master of Divinity, Master of Religious Education, Associate of Divinity, Associate of Religious Education. Concentration in Church Music Education is available to Master and Associate candidates.

Parent Institution. An institution of the Southern Baptist Convention, the Seminary is guided by a board of trustees, elected by the Convention in its annual sessions. There are 36,740 churches related to the Southern Baptist Convention with a membership of 14,349,657. The Convention has an Executive Committee and 20 national agencies: four boards, six seminaries, seven commissions, a foundation, and two associated organizations. The Convention exists in order to help the churches to lead people to God through Jesus Christ. The seminary derives the majority of its financial support from the Southern Baptist Cooperative Program.

Community Environment. The Midwestern campus covers 200 acres of wooded and rolling meadows in Kansas City North, 10 minutes from downtown Kansas City. The Seminary is strategically located in proximity to major transportation networks. The campus consists of three main areas - an administrative complex, faculty/classroom complex, and student housing. The three major buildings surround a grassy courtyard/fountain area from which the Seminary symbol, a 50-foot spire, rises toward the sky. The spire has come to symbolize the Christian ministry of the school and serves as a reminder to the faculty, students, and staff that their mission is to reach upward for strength to spread the Christian message.

Religious Denomination. Southern Baptist.

Accreditation. North Central Association of Colleges and Schools; Association of Theological Schools in the United States and Canada.

Term System. 10 four-week terms per year; primary matriculation in August, February, and June; classes offered in four- and eight-week modules.

Enrollment in Degree Programs in Religion 1984–85. Total 568; men 441, women 127.

Degrees in Religion Awarded 1984–85. Associate of Religious Education 2; men 2. Associate of Divinity 7; men 7. Master of Religious Education 22; men 16, women 6. Master of Divinity 59; men 57, women 2. Doctor of Ministry 10; men 9, women 1.

Faculty for Degree Programs in Religion. Total 22; full-time 22. Faculty assisted by 20 to 30 guest professors each year.

Admission Requirements. Bachelor of Arts or Bachelor of Science or its equivalent. The Seminary adheres to the Association of Theological Schools standards which limit the number of students that can be accepted from non-accredited schools. Candidates for the Doctor of Ministry degree must have, in addition to the B.A. or B.S., an accredited Master of Divinity degree or its equivalent. Applicants for Associate degree programs must show proof of age (over 30) and submit evidence of having earned a high school diploma or GED.

Tuition and Fees. Tuition $90 per four-week term (average); residence hall double occupancy $77.50 per month,

single occupancy $135 per month; married student housing $205 - $300 per month.

Financial Aid. Financial assistance is generally possible through scholarships, guaranteed student loans and/or small emergency loans.

Housing. On-campus housing for single students is available in the Residence Hall and for married students and their families in Seminary apartments and modular houses.

Library Facilities. The Seminary Library houses a collection of nearly 80,000 fully cataloged volumes in addition to a large body of general and denominational periodicals and other serial materials.

Religious Services/Activities. The students, faculty, and staff gather regularly for both formal and informal worship. Chapel services are held at least twice each week in the Seminary auditorium. These services offer a variety of community worship experiences, from the traditional church service to dialogues to dramatic or musical presentations. The Seminary sponsors four World Missions Days a year and each winter sponsors a three-day student mission conference, inviting college students from the surrounding states to the Seminary campus for a series of worship services, seminars, lectures, musical specials, and fellowship.

The Seminary encourages student service in a ministry setting and assists interested students to secure the ministry positions. Midwestern students also have the opportunity to participate in several intern programs sponsored by various departments of both state and national convention agencies. The three major programs offered involve Christian social ministries, pioneer field mission work, and student ministry internships.

Degree Programs

The Master of Divinity degree is directed toward preparing students for pastoral ministry in the church. It is recommended as preparation for forms of ministry beyond the congregation; it is foundational to participation in graduate degree programs. The programs include courses which the student may elect as a career specialty or as academic preparation for a future graduate specialty.

The Master of Religious Education degree is directed toward preparing the student for educational ministry in the church. It is also recommended as preparation for forms of ministry beyond the congregation and is foundational to participation in graduate degree programs, although entrance into some graduate programs may require additional studies.

The Doctor of Ministry degree is a post-master's program. It is an extended, intensive graduate course of study and supervision directed toward preparing the student for ministering in church, denominational, and other ministry settings. The focus of the degree is competence in ministry. The degree program is designed to prepare students to undertake the total ministry of the church. Candidates must be grounded in the biblical, historical, and theological heritage of the Christian faith.

Special Programs

The Associate of Religious Education and the Associate of Divinity degree programs provide theological training for individuals who have not completed a B.A. or B.S. degree or the equivalent and are thereby ineligible for the regular Master's level work.

The Seminary offers a special educational program for persons who are interested in furthering their own biblical and theological knowledge but who are not seeking a specific theological degree. This program, the School of Christian Training, welcomes those interested persons who simply wish to take a course once in a while, but one which also offers comprehensive and encompassing study. In addition, the School of Christian Training offers a formal three-year program which is a more regulated approach to study and leads the student to a certificate of graduation.

Missouri Baptist College
Religion Department
12542 Conway Road
Saint Louis, MO 63130   (314) 434-1115

Administration. Arlene R. Dykstra, Academic Dean; Dennis L. Sansom, Chairman of the Humanities Division.

General Description. The Religion Department attempts to educate the student in the field of religious studies. This education is shaped by the liberal arts tradition of openness, the quest for truth, and the Baptist tradition of evangelical Christianity. The program also prepares students for professional schools for the ministry.

Parent Institution. Missouri Baptist College, chartered in 1963, is an evangelical Christian, four-year liberal arts college. In 1966, the Missouri Baptist Convention approved the consolidation of Hannibal-LaGrange and Missouri Baptist Colleges as one college with two campuses, to be known as Missouri Baptist College, Hannibal-La-Grange campus, and St. Louis campus. Inititally offering a two-year program until the Fall of 1971, the College then became a three-year program, followed by a four-year program in 1972.

Community Environment. The College is located on an 84-acre tract in Creve Coeur, a suburb of St. Louis.

Religious Denomination. Southern Baptist.

Religious Emphasis. Conservative.

Accreditation. North Central Association of Colleges and Schools.

Term System. Semester; 3-week May term; 2 5-week summer terms.

Enrollment in Degree Programs in Religion 1984-85. Total 36; men 26, women 10.

Degrees in Religion Awarded 1984-85. Bachelor of Arts 7; men 5, women 2.

Faculty for Degree Programs in Religion. Total 3; full-

time 2, part-time 1.

Admission Requirements. High school graduation.

Tuition and Fees. Tuition full-time $1,475 per semester; part-time (fewer than 12 hours) $100 per hour; other fees where applicable; room and meals $950 per semester.

Financial Aid. Grants, loans, scholarships, and work-study programs available.

Housing. A facility for men and another for women were completed in 1980. Because of the major highways adjacent to the campus, students can easily commute from their homes or quarters found in the surrounding communities.

Library Facilities. The library has holdings of approximately 98,700 volumes and 400 periodical titles. There is also a curriculum library for church leadership, containing current publications of the Southern Baptist Convention.

Religious Services/Activities. Mandatory chapel programs are planned to provide the students, faculty, and staff with a period devoted to spiritual improvement. Chapel programs include preaching services, hymn-sings, films, group discussions, musical performances, drama, and a variety of other experiences. Periodic convocation programs are planned to provide a period devoted to overall personal improvement. Distinguished visitors are invited for these programs. Christian Focus Week is held during the Fall semester and Missions Week during the Spring semester.

Degree Programs

The Bachelor of Arts in Religion provides the beginning stages of the professional training for the ministry, preparing students for graduate school or seminary training. The courses are presented from the evangelical perspective.

The Bachelor of Arts in Religious Education includes courses in Religious Education, Church Administration, and Internship as well as other electives.

Special Programs

The Associate of Arts in Religion requires a total of 64 semester hours with a concentration in Theology.

The W.L. Muncy, Jr. Certificate Program in Biblical Studies and Christian Service is provided as a service to churches in the St. Louis area. Courses are offered at night, usually meeting once a week, in five-week terms. A student may often schedule two courses during a term. The cost is $35 per course for credit.

Missouri, University of - Columbia
Department of Religious Studies
416 General Classroom Building
Columbia, MO 65211   (314) 882-4769

Administration. Dr. James C. Olson, President, University of Missouri; Dr. Barbara S. Uehling, Chancellor, U.M. - Columbia; Dr. Ronald R. Brown, Provost, U.M.

- Columbia; Dr. Milton Glick, Dean, College of Arts and Science.

General Description. Founded in 1981, the Department of Religious Studies at the University of Missouri - Columbia is dedicated to the teaching of the major types of religion (Eastern, Western, tribal) in a state university. It teaches religions through the same types of communication which the religions themselves use, i.e., sound, sight, action, narrative. The regular faculty members teach Bible, History of Christianity, Asian Religions, and Afro-American Religions. The adjunct faculty members teach Judaism, New Testament, Religion and Literature, and Religion and Psychology. The degree Bachelor of Arts in Religious Studies is granted.

Parent Institution. The University of Missouri is a land-grant institution with four campuses: St. Louis, Kansas City, Rolla, and Columbia. The Columbia campus is the oldest, being founded in 1839, and the largest, with approximately 24,000 students. The University at Columbia is a research and teaching facility with undergraduate and graduate colleges. The Department of Religious Studies is housed in the College of Arts and Science.

Community Environment. The city of Columbia, Missouri is located midway between Kansas City and St. Louis. The economy of the area is based on higher education, medicine, manufacturing, and the insurance industry. The city offers numerous educational and medical facilities. The Lake of the Ozarks recreation area is within a 2-hour drive and provides opportunities for many outdoor sports.

Religious Denomination. None.

Accreditation. North Central Association of Colleges and Schools.

Term System. Semester; no summer term.

Faculty for Degree Programs in Religion. Total 9; full-time 5, part-time 4.

Admission Requirements. Admission to the freshman class is determined by a combination of the applicant's high school class rank and ACT, SAT, or SCAT test score.

Tuition and Fees. Tuition $728 for Missouri students, $1,379 for out-of-state students; housing $1,865 per academic year.

Financial Aid. The University assists approximately 12,000 eligible students from low and medium income families, whose personal and family resources do not meet the minimum cost of an education. Information is supplied in the brochure *All About Financial Aid at UMC,* available from the Financial Aids Office.

Housing. Students are not required to live in residence halls.

Library Facilities. The Ellis Library houses over 2 million volumes. The Religion collection contains approximately 40,000 volumes.

Degree Programs

The Bachelor of Arts degree in Religious Studies requires the completion of 120 semester hours of credit with an overall average of C. The major requires Introduction to Religion, Ways of Understanding Religion, plus 18 hours of other Religious Studies courses and 8 hours of related courses.

Nazarene Theological Seminary
1700 East Meyer Boulevard
Kansas City, MO 64131   (816) 333-6254

Administration. Dr. Terrell C. Saunders, President; Dr. Chester O. Galloway, Dean of the Faculty.

General Description. Educationally, Nazarene Theological Seminary is a post-baccalaureate professional community practicing and equipping for practice in Christian ministries. Organizationally, it is an integral part of the international Church of the Nazarene and is mandated by the denomination as its graduate-professional school for ministry. Theologically, the Seminary adheres to the Wesleyan tradition, especially in its commitment to the doctrine and experience of complete sanctification. Professionally, the Seminary is committed to academic, theological conversation with the broader world of Christian scholarship for explanation, exploration, and mutual edification. Practically, the Seminary's academic disciplines, professional experiences, and devotional exercises are designed to contribute to the spiritual formation of each member of the seminary community.

While the Seminary's principal academic focus is the course of studies leading to the Master of Divinity degree, it does give careful attention to three other degree programs: the Master of Religious Education, the Master of Arts in Missiology, and the Doctor of Ministry.

Community Environment. Nazarene Theological Seminary is located on 10½ acres in Kansas City, Missouri. Kansas City is a thriving midwestern metropolitan area with a population of over 1 million. Kansas City is a city of churches and gives abundant opportunity for observation and experience in relation to the whole field of modern church life. The Church of the Nazarene has more then 30 congregations in the greater Kansas City area where seminary students may worship and work in various fields of Christian service. To Nazarenes the world around, Kansas City means "International Center." Here are all the general offices of the denomination and the Nazarene Publishing House, which ranks among the finest of religious publishing companies.

Religious Denomination. Church of the Nazarene.

Religious Emphasis. Evangelical.

Accreditation. Association of Theological Schools in the United States and Canada.

Term System. Semester; summer term.

Enrollment in Degree Programs in Religion 1984–85.

Total 415; men 365, women 50.

Faculty for Degree Programs in Religion. Total 29; full-time 20, part-time 9.

Admission Requirements. Graduation from an accredited four-year college or university with stipulated undergraduate foundation courses for graduate study in religion; references.

Tuition and Fees. Tuition $50 per semester credit hour; fees $45.50.

Financial Aid. Some scholarsips and grants-in-aid are available.

Housing. Off-campus housing only.

Library Facilities. The library contains over 70,000 volumes. A special collection of Wesleyana Methodistic Material is maintained. The library resources are supplemented by those of other Protestant seminaries through the formation of the Kansas City Theological Library Association.

Religious Services/Activities. Chapel is held three times weekly.

Degree Programs

The Master of Divinity program requires 65 hours of prescribed courses and 28 hours of electives. Normally a minimum of three years is required to complete the program. The student is required to take an hour and one-half, short answer, written examination on the content of the entire Bible. The examination must be taken by the end of the student's middler year. An oral examination is required at the beginning of the senior year. The Master of Divinity in Religious Education requires the completion of 72 hours of prescribed courses and 21 hours of electives. The Master of Divinity in Missiology requires the completion of 76 prescribed courses and 17 hours of electives.

The Master of Religious Education is a competency-based degree. The program is structured to insure the development of basic competencies, competencies of essential ministry, and competencies in the practice of ministry. Two years are normally required for the completion of the degree. A candidate must complete a total of 64 semester hours of which the final year's work, or 30 hours, must be taken in residence.

The Master of Arts in Missiology is a program of maximum flexibility for missionary preparation and missions specialization. The overall design of the program is to equip persons for servant-leadership ministries in transcultural contexts. Of the 62 course hours required, 46 are prescribed and the remaining hours are free electives.

The Doctor of Ministry degree is the highest professional degree offered for persons actively engaged in ministry. The purpose of the program is to equip one for a higher level of competence in the practice of ministry than that achieved in the foundational work of the Master of Divinity degree. A minimum of two years is required to complete the degree. A two-hour oral examination will be held following the completion of all studies and the submission

of the final ministry project.

Ozarks, School of the
Philosophy and Religion Department
Point Lookout, MO 65726   (417) 334-6411

Administration. Dr. Stephen G. Jennings, President; Dr. Howell W. Keeter, Chancellor; Dr. James A. Zabel, Dean of the Faculty; Courtney Furman, Chair, Philosophy and Religion Department.

General Description. The curriculum of the Philosophy and Religion Department examines life's major questions, particularly as posed by the Bibical tradition. Majors in this area often enter some form of church vocation and/or pursue graduate studies. Minors may also be interested in a church vocation, or may use the minor to help them gain a more integrated outlook on their profession, their world, and their lives. The Department also provides the required Religion core courses for every student.

Parent Institution. The School of the Ozarks is a 4-year, private liberal arts college, founded in 1906. Today it exists for the purpose of providing the advantages of a liberal arts education in a Christian environment especially for those who are worthy but are without sufficient financial means. It grants the Bachelor of Arts and the Bachelor of Science degrees. A feature of the college that makes it truly unique is the Work Program, an arrangement whereby students work 20 hours per week and three 40-hour work weeks per year at a variety of campus jobs to pay for their college education.

Community Environment. The 930-acre campus of the School of the Ozarks is located in Point Lookout, Missouri, 40 miles south of Springfield, near Branson and Hollister. Point Lookout is in a rural area where bus service is available and air service is little more than 30 minutes away.

Religious Denomination. United Presbyterian.

Religious Emphasis. Reformed.

Accreditation. North Central Association of Colleges and Schools.

Term System. Semester; summer term.

Faculty for Degree Programs in Religion. Total 3; full-time 3.

Admission Requirements. High school graduation; two recommendations (preferably from school personnel); ACT; Federal Student Aid Results (Pell Grant).

Tuition and Fees. Tuition for dormitory students is paid by a scholarship for the amount of their tuition; off-campus students not participating in the College work program are charged $65 per semester hour.

Financial Aid. All students receive financial aid. (Each student works a total of 960 hours per year.)

Housing. Housing is available to 80 percent of the students.

Library Facilities. The library contains 100,000 volumes, over 600 periodicals, 3,000 reels of microfilm, and other audiovisual materials.

Religious Services/Activities. Students can be expected to be exposed to Christian teaching and activities. Students are at liberty to participate in religious activities of their own choosing off campus, but only in addition to campus programs. Participation in the chapel services and in various other campus religious activities is considered a part of their duties, responsibilities, and privileges. The Sunday Chapel services are primarily designed to enhance the spiritual enrichment of the student. Convocations are held for a variety of purposes. Each spring, a Christian Emphasis series of lectures, including the Thomas F. Staley Distinguished Christian Scholar Lecture, is featured by the College.

Degree Programs

The Bachelor of Arts degree with a major in Philosophy and Religion requires, in addition to the College's general education requirements, specific courses of which a minimum of 27 hours (15 upper division) must be in the Department. The major should include at least three Philosophy courses and at least three Religion courses. Prospective seminary students are advised to ascertain whether an Introduction to New Testament Greek is a prerequisite for their Seminary studies.

Park College
Graduate School of Religion
The Auditorium
P.O. Box 1059
Independence, MO 64051   (816) 833-1000

Administration. Wesley B. Spillman, Commissioner of Minsterial Education.

General Description. The graduate program in Religion is designed to meet the needs of a variety of students. For those persons wanting a broad and stimulating exposure to a variety of religious issues and topics, the concentration in religious studies allows a maximum freedom to design a program that speaks to their particular interests. The other concentration, religious leadership, is directed primarily at persons currently or potentially involved in significant leadership responsibilities in churches or other religious organizations. The concentration in religious leadership is designed primarily, though not exclusively, for clergy and lay leaders of the Reorganized Church of Jesus Christ of Latter Day Saints. This option examines traditions and doctrines unique to that organization and provides skill development opportunities for a variety of church leadership responsibilities. Both concentrations include classes covering a broad overview of Biblical, historical, and theological issues common to all Christian denominations. The balance of the programs in each concentration can be arranged to support the particular needs of any specific denomination.

Parent Institution. Park College is a liberal arts college with two graduate programs (Religion, Public Affairs) and several unique undergraduate programs including a school for community affairs in Kansas City, Missouri, numerous residence centers on military bases, and a special baccalaureate "portfolio" program for nontraditional education. The College was founded in 1875 and is affiliated with the Reorganized Church of Jesus Christ of Latter Day Saints, headquartered in Independence, Missouri.

Community Environment. The main 800-acre campus of Park College is situated in the suburb of Parkville and includes 21 buildings. It is in the Kansas City metropolitan area of Missouri on the state's western border. Independence is located about 10 miles to the east of Kansas City.

Religious Denomination. Reorganized Church of Jesus Christ of Latter Day Saints.

Religious Emphasis. Moderate.

Accreditation. North Central Association of Colleges and Schools.

Term System. Semester; 3-week terms in May and August.

Enrollment in Degree Programs in Religion 1984–85. Total 12; men 10, women 2.

Degrees in Religion Awarded 1984–85. Master of Arts 13; men 13.

Faculty for Degree Programs in Religion. Total 10; full-time 3, part-time 7.

Admission Requirements. Baccalaureate degree; no less than 2.5 grade point average on a 4.0 scale in last 60 semester hours of work; three letters of recommendation from persons who can attest to applicant's ability to do graduate work; satisfactory completion of the Miller Analogies Test during first full semester.

Tuition and Fees. Tuition $130 per credit hour; $25 application fee.

Financial Aid. Scholarships, guaranteed student loans, and tuition grants for qualifying persons in religious leadership concentration.

Housing. Dormitories for both singles and married students on main campus. Off-campus housing readily available in Independence, Missouri near site of classes.

Library Facilities. The primary bibliographical resource for the Graduate School of Religion is the Library and Archives of the Reorganized Church of Latter Day Saints, located in the Auditorium in Independence, Missouri. These resources include 5,800 volumes in religion. Resources of the Carnegie Library on the Park College campus are also available. There are 4,700 volumes in religion and philosophy in that collection.

Religious Services/Activities. Twice a week religious services in numerous local congregations; special seminars and guest speakers available periodically throughout the year.

Degree Programs

The Master of Arts in Religion requires the completion of no less than 36 semester hours of approved course work; completion of the specified requirements for a concentration in Religious Leadership or in Religious Studies; overall grade point average of at least 3.0; passing proficiency examinations in written and oral presentation; and passing of a Comprehensive Examination over the full course of the graduate program. The Religious Leadership option includes Temple School courses as applicable to the Reorganized Church of Latter Day Saints.

St. Louis Christian College
1360 Grandview Drive
Florissant, MO 63033   (314) 837-6777

Administration. Thomas W. McGee, President; Earl R. Beaty, Academic Dean.

General Description. St. Louis Christian College subscribes to a faith and manner of life that is Christ-centered and Bible-based. St. Louis Christian College is supported on a voluntary basis by congregations and concerned Christians who consider the work of the College meritorious and contributory to the achievement of their own Christian objectives. The services of the College are offered without respect to such support. St. Louis Christian College labors in behalf of the undenominational fellowship of Christian Churches and Churches of Christ. The affiliation is fraternal, not connectional. The College is autonomous.

The College was founded in 1957 out of a common concern of three St. Louis ministers (Luther Perrine, Hubert Burris, and Vernon Newland) for a need for a "center of evangelism" in the St. Louis area. The College offers 2-year and 4-year programs leading to the Bachelor of Arts and the Associate of Arts degrees. A 5-year program leading to the Bachelor of Theology degree is also offered.

Community Environment. The campus encompasses a 27-acre tract of land fifteen miles from downtown St. Louis in the suburb of Florissant. Interstate 270 is two blocks from the campus. An impressive amount of cultural and recreational opportunities are available in the city of St. Louis.

Religious Denomination. Nondenominational. Fraternal affiliation with the Christian Churches and Churches of Christ.

Accreditation. American Association of Bible Colleges.

Term System. Semester; no summer term.

Enrollment in Degree Programs in Religion 1984–85. Total 126; men 74, women 52.

Degrees in Religion Awarded 1984–85. Bachelor of Arts. Bachelor of Theology. Bachelor of Science. Associate of Arts.

Faculty for Degree Programs in Religion. Total 17; full-time 15, part-time 2.

Admission Requirements. High school graduation.

Tuition and Fees. Tuition $65 per semester hour; various miscellaneous fees; housing two students per room $350 per semester if paid in advance, or $25 weekly; apartment for married students $210 to $235 per month.

Financial Aid. Financial assistance through the college to those who qualify is available in the form of several Federal aid programs, as well as a limited amount of institutional aid.

Housing. Students may reside in supervised dormitories; apartments are available for married students.

Library Facilities. The library has holdings of 43,245 volumes. A special collection of Bible materials covers the Old and New Testaments, Biblical Theology, Church History, and the Restoration Movement of the 19th century.

Religious Services/Activities. Chapel service is held Tuesday through Friday. All students are expected to be engaged in some specific Christian service at least one hour per week. All students are expected to attend Bible School and Lord's Day worship services and to participate in midweek prayer and Bible Study services. Regularly scheduled dormitory devotions are provided to complement personal devotions. Classes are recessed one week each Spring for extensive evangelistic endeavors. Faith Promise Rallies are held one week per semester to emphasize missions.

Degree Programs

The Bachelor of Arts in Ministry degree is designed to equip students for the ministry of the Word. A Bible major is supplemented with courses in ministry, doctrine, and general education. Proficiency in Biblical Greek is required.

The Bachelor of Arts in World Missions and Evangelism is designed to equip students for missionary service. Majors in Bible and missions are supplemented with general education, doctrine, and practical ministry courses. Proficiency in a foreign language or Greek is required.

The Bachelor of Science in Christian Education is designed to equip students for an effective Christian education or youth ministry. Majors in Bible and Christian Education are supplemented with general education, doctrine, and practical ministries courses.

The Bachelor of Science degree in Church Music is designed to prepare students for a ministry in church music. Majors in Bible and Church Music are supplemented with general education and doctrine courses. A recital is required of all Church Music majors.

The Bachelor of Theology degree is an advanced study program beyond the Bachelor of Arts. An emphasis on bible, doctrine, and Biblical Hebrew are part of the program. A research paper is required for graduation.

Special Programs

The Associate of Ministry degree program is for mature students with a background in Christian service. Bible, doctrine, and ministerial courses are designed to equip students for the work of Christian ministry.

The Associate of Secretarial Science degree is designed to equip students in secretarial and office skills for use specifically in church related ministries. Bible, doctrine, and secretarial courses prepare the student for this specialized ministry.

The Associate of Arts in General Studies degree program provides foundational courses in general education and biblical studies to prepare students for tentmaking ministries.

The one-year Christian Service Certificate is for students who anticipate attending Bible College for only one year. The program is built on a heavy Biblical emphasis.

St. Louis University
Department of Theological Studies
3634 Lindell Boulevard
St. Louis, MO 63108   (314) 658-2881

Administration. Dr. Thomas R. Fitzgerald, S.J., President; Dr. Paul C. Reinert, S.J., Chancellor; Dr. John H. Gray, S.J., Academic Vice President; Dr. R. O'Tool, S. J., Chairperson, Department of Theological Studies.

General Description. The Department of Theological Studies is a part of the College of Arts and Sciences, with its Graduate Programs being answerable to the Graduate School. The faculty of the Department consists of 8 Jesuits, 2 diocesan priests, 2 Montfort Missionaries, 1 Franciscan, 6 laymen (3 of them non-Catholic), and 3 religious sisters. The emphasis is Roman Catholic/Jesuit, but definitely not in a confessional bent. Students choosing the Ph.D. program in Historical Theology are, on an average, at least 50 percent non-Catholic. Degrees granted by the Department are as follows: Bachelor of Arts in Theological Studies, Master of Arts in Religious Studies, Master of Arts in Historical Theology, Doctor of Philsophy (Ph.D.) in Historical Theology. Also offered is the Certificate in Corporate Ministry.

Parent Institution. St. Louis University has been a part of the city of St. Louis, Missouri since 1818. It is a private university under Roman Catholic/Jesuit auspices. In addition to the campus which houses the Department of Theological Studies, there is a Medical campus which is well-renowned, and Parks College (Cahokia, IL) for aeronautics study. The total enrollment on the main campus is close to 10,000, with about 6,000 of these being on the undergraduate level.

Community Environment. The 171-acre campus of St. Louis University is located in the heart of the city of St. Louis, Missouri. St. Louis is one of the great industrial centers of the nation and a leading world market. The city is also an important transportation center of Missouri and central United States.

Religious Denomination. Roman Catholic.

Religious Emphasis. Roman Catholic/Jesuit emphasis, but not in a confessional bent.

Accreditation. North Central Association of Colleges and Schools.

Term System. Semester; summer term.

Enrollment in Degree Programs in Religion 1984–85. Total 133; men 74, women 59.

Degrees in Religion Awarded 1984–85. Bachelor of Arts in Theology 8; men 4, women 4. Master of Arts in Religious Studies 16; 4 men, 12 women. Ph.D. in Historical Theology 1; men 1. (M.A. in Spirituality 1; men 1. This program is no longer available.)

Faculty for Degree Programs in Religion. Total 22; full-time 20, part-time 2.

Admission Requirements. For first-time freshmen, SAT or ACT scores. For Master of Arts: GRE scores; accredited Bachelor of Arts; all transcripts; letters of recommendation; a combination of at least 24 hours of theology and philosophy (together) on the undergraduate level. For Ph.D.: The same as M.A. with these additions: Bachelor of Arts must be in theology or its equivalent; must have 12 hours in undergraduate philosophy and 9 hours of Western Civilization.

Tuition and Fees. Tuition $225 per credit hour; registration fee $20; room $893 to $1,295 per term; board $756 to $870 per term.

Financial Aid. Veteran's and Social Security Assistance, College Work-Study Program, Guaranteed Student Loans, National Direct Student Loans, scholarships, grants, and teaching assistantships are available.

Housing. On-campus dormitories; Religious Houses for Women. Some availability of housing for clergy and religious brothers.

Library Facilities. The combined holdings of the libraries total over 1.5 million volumes. The Divinity Library contains over 130,000 books. The Vatican Film Library holds 35 million pages of Vatican manuscripts.

Religious Services/Activities. On campus is the St. Francis Xavier (College) Church, staffed by the Society of Jesus, Missouri Province, with six Masses daily. Also, a Campus Ministry organization arranges for Masses in the dorms as well as special retreats, social issues lectures, and other activities.

Degree Programs

The Bachelor of Arts in Theology requires a total of 120 hours with a minimum of 33 hours in Theology and 17 hours in related fields.

The Master of Arts in Religious Studies offers specialization in the following areas: Spirtuality, Religious Education, Pastoral Ministry, Moral Life and Counseling, Scripture, Systematic Theology, and Interdisciplinary Plans. The program requires a total of 30 hours with 15 of these in the area of specialization.

The Master of Arts in Historical Theology requires a total of 30 hours, as well as competency in one foreign language and a scholarly essay.

The Doctor of Philosophy in Historical Theology requires a total of 60 hours as well as competency in two foreign languages and a dissertation.

Special Programs

The Corporate Ministry Certificate program provides an experience of renewal in ministry for laity, priests, and religious by integrating a solid grounding in theology with ministerial experience. The program is a certified, nine-month (September-May), thirty-two hour, graduate pastoral leadership program.

St. Paul School of Theology

5123 Truman Road
Kansas City, MO 64127   (816) 483-6676

Administration. William K. McElvaney, President.

General Description. Saint Paul School of Theology is a graduate, professional school of the United Methodist Church. It was chartered in 1958 and the emphasis has been upon pastoral ministry. The School is a theological community rooted in the Wesleyan heritage. The Master of Divinity and the Doctor of Ministry degrees are awarded.

Community Environment. The School is located on the east side of Kansas City, one of the country's largest railroad centers. The city is at the confluence of the Kansas and Missouri Rivers.

Religious Denomination. United Methodist Church.

Accreditation. North Central Association of Colleges and Schools; American Association of Theological Schools in the United States and Canada.

Term System. Quarter.

Faculty for Degree Programs in Religion. Total 33.

Admission Requirements. Bachelor's degree or equivalent from an accredited college or university with a grade point average of 2.5 on a 4.0 scale.

Tuition and Fees. Tuition $3,625 per year; housing $63-$303 per month.

Financial Aid. Aid is provided on the basis of demonstrated financial need.

Housing. Housing is available in dormitories and apartments.

Library Facilities. The Dana Dawson Library contains over 62,000 volumes and subscribes to 340 periodicals.

Religious Services/Activities. The community gathers twice each week for community worship. The Common Meal is served each noon, Tuesday through Friday.

Degree Programs

The Master of Divinity degree requires three academic years of full-time study and the completion of a minimum of 126 quarter hours. The curriculum is three-phased: Foundational, Functional, and Focus. Each Phase has a specified program. The Focus Phase may be within one of the areas of specialization: Christian Education, Gerontology, or Parish Development.

The Doctor of Ministry is an advanced professional

degree designed for those who desire an academic program that deepens and broadens their practice of ministry. Incorporating a method of personalized learning, the doctoral program is focused upon the practice of ministry. Five options are offered: General Practice of Ministry, Ministry in Aging, Pastoral Care and Counseling, Christian Education, and Ethics and Social Changes.

Southwest Baptist University
Redford School of Theology and Church
Vocations

1601 South Springfield
Bolivar, MO 65613   (417) 326-5281

Administration. Dr. James L. Sells, Chancellor; Dr. Charles L. Chaney, President; Dr. Bill Little, Vice President for Academic Affairs; Dr. Don Baker, Acting Dean, Redford School of Theology and Church Vocations.

General Description. The Redford School of Theology and Church Vocations offers majors and minors through the Departments of Bible and Biblical Languages, Christian Ministries, Religious Education, and Theology and Church History. A minor is offered in Philosophy. There are also interdisciplinary and interdepartmental majors, minors, and special programs. These programs are at the baccalaureate level.

Parent Institution. Southwest Baptist University is a 4-year liberal arts, coeducational university. It is an educational agency of the Missouri Baptist Convention. The University offers study in over 50 fields with majors in 36 areas and minors in 40 areas. Academically, the University is divided into the School of Arts and Sciences, School of Business, School of Education and Social Sciences, Casebolt School of Music and Fine Arts, and Redford School of Theology and Church Vocations.

Community Environment. Southwest Baptist University is located in Bolivar, Missouri, the county seat of Polk County, a city of approximately 6,000, and 28 miles north of Springfield. The original Stufflebam Campus is 4 blocks southwest of the public square and 1 block north of the new Shoffner Campus. The 2 campuses include 39 buildings and 123 acres, with additional buildings planned for the new campus. A statue of Simon Bolivar, presented to the city by Venezuela in 1948, evidences "the good will and friendship between the liberty-loving peoples of two nations."

Religious Denomination. Southern Baptist.

Religious Emphasis. Conservative — a strong emphasis on the Bible.

Accreditation. North Central Association of Colleges and Schools.

Term System. Semester; January term; summer term.

Enrollment in Degree Programs in Religion 1984–85. Total 65; men 51, women 14.

Degrees in Religion Awarded 1984–85. Bachelor of Arts

in: Religious Studies 45; men 39, women 6. Theological Studies 2; men 2. Religious Education 4; men 2, women 2. Bible 1; men 1. Christian Ministries 1; men 1. Bachelor of Science in: Religious Education 8; men 3, women 5. Church Secretarial Science 1; women 1. Bachelor of Music in Church Music 2; men 2.

Faculty for Degree Programs in Religion. Total 15; full-time 8, part-time 7.

Admission Requirements. Graduation from an accredited or approved high school with rank in the upper ½ of the class or a cumulative grade average of C or M (2.0) in solid subjects. Students not fulfilling this requirement may be conditionally accepted after a personal interview with the Director of Admissions.

Tuition and Fees. Tuition $1,840; part-time student (fewer than 12 hours) $153.50 per hour; auditing students $76.75 per hour; enrollment deposit $75; room and board $775 per semester.

Financial Aid. Scholarships, loans, grants, and college work-study are available.

Housing. Regularly enrolled students (unmarried under 23 years of age) are generally required to live in University residence halls unless they live with their parents. Some off-campus housing is available; no provisions for married students.

Library Facilities. The Estep Library houses over 108,000 books and periodicals. Special collections include the Butler Baptist Heritage Collection, SBC Collection, Library of American Civilization Collection, and the Dr. Earl R. Allen Library.

Religious Services/Activities. Bible studies; supply preaching; interim work; Discipleship retreats; Associational Meeting speakers; revivals. Chapel is held Monday and Wednesday; students enrolled in 12 or more hours are generally required to attend three-fourths of the Chapel services in a semester.

Degree Programs

The Bachelor of Arts with a major in Bible is offered by the Department of Bible and Biblical Languages. The Department of Christian Ministries offers programs leading to the Bachelor of Arts with a major in Christian Ministries. Emphasis can be in Preaching and Pastoral Ministry, Evangelism, or Lay Ministry. The Department of Religious Education offers programs leading to either the Bachelor of Arts or Bachelor of Science with a major in Religious Education. The Department of Theology and Church History offers programs leading to the Bachelor of Arts degree with a major in Theological Studies. Emphasis can be in Missions and Church Growth or Christian Doctrine.

Special Programs

The Redford School of Theology also offers a two-year Diploma in Theology and a three-year Advanced Diploma in Theology. This program is for ministers and laymen who cannot pursue a regular college degree but still wish to gain proficiency in practical religious studies.

The School of Extended Studies offers classes at various off-campus locations as the need arises. Current extended classroom centers are located in Dexter, Joplin, and Springfield, Missouri; Chicago, Illinois; and Denver, Colorado.

Correspondence courses are also available from the University.

Tarkio College
Tarkio, MO 64491   (816) 736-4131

Administration. Roy McIntosh, President.

General Description. Tarkio College is a privately supported liberal arts college. It was founded in 1883 by a group of businessmen and farmers in the Tarkio Valley who were graduates of church-related, liberal arts colleges. After one year, it became affiliated with the Presbyterian Church and through the years the relationship has remained active and strong. The College offers programs of study in many categories and grants the Bachelor's degree.

Community Environment. The campus occupies 65 acres in Tarkio, a busy northwestern Missouri trade center. It is 75 miles south of Omaha and Council Bluffs and 120 miles north of Kansas City.

Religious Denomination. Presbyterian Church (U.S.A.).

Accreditation. North Central Association of Colleges and Schools.

Term System. Semester (4-1-4 plan).

Admission Requirements. High school graduation or equivalent; rank in upper 50 percent of graduating class.

Tuition and Fees. Tuition $4,500 per year; room and board $2,800; student fees $70.

Financial Aid. Assistance is available to all qualified students.

Housing. Students not residing with their parents are required to live in the college residence halls.

Library Facilities. The Thompson Library-Learning Center contains 65,000 volumes.

Degree Programs

The major in Religion leading to the Bachelor of Arts degree requires the completion of 30 semester hours in specified and elective courses. The degree requires a total of 128 semester hours.

Westminster College
7th and Westminster Avenue
Fulton, MO 65251   (314) 642-3361

Administration. J. Harvey Saunders, President.

General Description. Fulton College was founded in 1851 by Missouri Presbyterians and was adopted in 1853 by the Missouri Synod which gave it the Presbyterian name "Westminster." The union with the Presbyterian Church remained until 1969 when Westminster College and the Church agreed to sever legal ties. In 1984, the College and the Synod of Mid-America of the Presbyterian Church (U.S.A.) approved a covenant which recognizes that the College and the Church remain independent entities but affirms a historic and continuing relationship of mutual concern and support.

The College is a coeducational liberal arts college and grants the Bachelor's degree.

Community Environment. The campus grounds cover 55 acres in Fulton, a community of 13,000 people located 100 miles west of St. Louis.

Religious Denomination. Nondenominational, but continues its relationship with the Presbyterian Church (U.S.A.).

Accreditation. North Central Association of Colleges and Schools.

Term System. Semester (5-4-1 plan).

Admission Requirements. High school graduation from an accredited high school or equivalent; SAT or ACT.

Tuition and Fees. Tuition $5,200 per year; room and board $2,500; student activity fee $100.

Financial Aid. Grants, loans, work, and scholarships are available to qualified students.

Housing. Dormitories and fraternity houses are available on campus.

Library Facilities. The Reeves Memorial Library at Westminster and the William H. Dulany Memorial Library at William Woods College have combined collections of 150,000 books.

Degree Programs

The courses in the Department of Religion are designed to provide students with an opportunity to understand their own religious heritage and to know and appreciate faiths other than their own. Religion is examined as a living part of its larger cultural setting, not as an isolated phenomenon. The approach to the subject matter is descriptive and historical. The major in Religion leading to the Bachelor of Arts degree requires completion of a minimum of 27 hours in the Department. The degree requires a total of 122 semester hours.

MONTANA

Carroll College
Borromeo Pre-Seminary Program
Helena, MT 59625   (406) 442-3450

Administration. Dr. Francis J. Kerins, President; Sr. Mary Sarah Fasenmyer, Vice President for Academic Affairs; Dr. William M. Thompson, Chairman, Department of Theology; Dr. Thomas M. O'Donnell, Director, Borromeo Pre-Seminary Program.

General Description. The Borromeo Pre-Seminary Program is a college-level residential program for students preparing for Catholic theological seminary. Following in a tradition which has long been an important part of Carroll College, the men in the program explore different aspects of the priestly life through discussion, spiritual direction, apostolic work, and in the liturgy. Through this exploration the men of the program strive to discern the path of their calling and to develop a community of support and understanding. Students follow a baccalaureate program at Carroll which will prepare them for seminary academic requirements.

The Department of Religion offers the Bachelor of Arts in Theology and the Bachelor of Arts in Religious Education.

Parent Institution. Carroll College is a Catholic, diocesan college of liberal arts and science in the ecumenical tradition of the Second Vatican Council. The College grants the Bachelor of Arts and the Associate of Arts degrees.

Community Environment. The College's geographic setting is a major asset in the pursuit of its goals. Montana's colorful capital city, Helena, is the hub of the Big Sky Country. Sixty-five percent of the state's population is within 120 miles. Yellowstone and Glacier National Parks are just hours away. Helena and the surrounding region afford a broad range of educational, cultural, and service opportunities, enabling many Carroll departments to offer their students internship or cooperative employment experiences, blending theory with practice. Carroll's striking hilltop campus was once contemplated as the site for the state capitol and is named Capitol Hill. Its 63 acres comprise a major attraction and a substantial resource for the Helena community.

Religious Denomination. Roman Catholic.

Religious Emphasis. In the tradition of the Second Vatican Council.

Accreditation. Northwest Association of Schools and Colleges.

Term System. Semester; summer term.

Admission Requirements. High school graduation; ACT, SAT, or PSAT scores.

Tuition and Fees. Tuition $1,770 per semester; part-time $118 per semester hour; room $403 to $484 per semester; board $733 to $769 per semester.

Financial Aid. Federal grants, state loan program, scholarships, and college work-study are available.

Housing. All unmarried freshman students who do not live with their parents are required to reside in College residence halls unless permission is secured from the Dean of Students to reside off-campus.

Library Facilities. The library collection includes 93,000 volumes.

Religious Services/Activities. The role of ministry to students is fulfilled by the campus pastoral team. The team leads the college prayer life, the Eucharist, and other sacramental celebrations. It is also available for counseling and guiding those who seek advice.

Degree Programs

The Bachelor of Arts in Theology and the Bachelor of Arts in Religious Education are offered by the Department of Theology. Five basic courses (Biblical Studies, Christian Thought, Systematic Theology, Moral Theology, and Religious Education) are designed to give the student an overall view of the field of Theology. Students in the major programs are required to take the introductory courses required for their areas of concentration and are encouraged to complete the basic courses before taking the specialized courses.

Special Programs

The Borromeo Pre-Seminary Program is a group of men within the Carroll College community exploring the priestly call. They explore different aspects of the priestly life through discussion, spiritual direction, apostolic work, and in the liturgy. Although no single major is specified by the college for the Pre-Seminary Program, the student should recognize that graduate schools of theology and seminaries require students to have a background in philosophy and adequate preparation in Latin.

Rocky Mountain College
1511 Poly Drive
Billings, MT 59102   (406) 657-1000

Administration. Bruce T. Alton, President.

General Description. The primary mission of Rocky Mountain College is to provide a quality liberal arts education with a value-centered, Christian orientation around which students can develop and test their philosophy of life. The College is Montana's oldest college. It was founded in 1878; two institutions, Intermountain Union College and Billings Polytechnic, subsequently merged in 1947 to form Rocky Mountain College. It is a private, four-year liberal arts college and is affiliated with the United Methodist Church, the United Church of Christ, and the Presbyterian Church, U.S.A.

Community Environment. The 60-acre campus is located in the northwest residential section of Billings, a city with large oil and sugar refineries, meat-packing plants, and live-stock yards.

Religious Denomination. United Methodist Church; United Church of Christ; Presbyterian Church, U.S.A.

Accreditation. Northwest Association of Schools and Colleges.

Term System. Semester.

Admission Requirements. High school graduation from an accredited school; ACT.

Tuition and Fees. Tuition $1,687 per semester; room $405; board $679.

Financial Aid. Grants and scholarships, loans, and work opportunity are the types of aid available.

Housing. Men's and women's residence halls are available on campus.

Library Facilities. The Paul M. Adams Memorial Library houses a main book collection of over 65,000 volumes.

Religious Services/Activities. A variety of Christian fellowships and events are available. Frequent chapel services, study groups, prayer fellowships, weekend retreats, and special programs are scheduled.

Degree Programs

The Department of Christian Thought seeks to promote reflection about the Christian faith in the human search for meaning in life. The Department seeks to help Christian students attain an articulate faith attuned to the contemporary world. To non-Chrisitan and uncommitted students, the Department aims to give a fair presentation of the Christian alternative for their reflection. A pre-

theological studies program can be developed in consultation with the Department. The major in Christian Thought includes a minimum of 24 hours. It leads to the Bachelor of Arts degree which requires a total of 124 semester hours.

NEBRASKA

Dana College

Blair, NE 68008   (402) 426-4101

Administration. Elwin Falwell, Interim President.

General Description. The roots of Dana College are in Trinity Seminary and the United Evangelical Lutheran Church. In 1884, Danish Lutheran pioneers of that Church established Trinity for the purpose of training men for the parish ministry. In 1956, the merger with the Evangelical Lutheran Church and the American Lutheran Church became more definite and it was decided to move Trinity to the campus of Wartburg Seminary in Dubuque, Iowa. Following the merger of the three Church bodies, Dana College assumed its place as one of eleven senior colleges of the new American Lutheran Church. It is one of two educational institutions in America to be founded by Danish people. The College grants the Bachelor's degree in a variety of curricular offerings.

Community Environment. The campus of 250 acres is located west of the city of Blair, 25 miles north of Omaha.

Religious Denomination. American Lutheran Church.

Accreditation. North Central Association of Colleges and Schools.

Term System. Semester (4-1-4 plan).

Admission Requirements. High school graduation or equivalent; SAT or ACT required.

Tuition and Fees. Tuition $2,250 per semester; room $390; board $585; general fee $110.

Financial Aid. The College maintains an extensive program of financial aid through the use of various scholarships, grants, loans, and campus employment opportunities.

Housing. Dormitories are available on campus.

Library Facilities. The library houses over 111,000 volumes.

Religious Services/Activities. Chapel Convocation is held on Monday, Wednesday, and Friday mornings. Attendance is encouraged and expected. The Dana campus congregation, Ekklesia Koinonias, sponsors various educational, fellowship, and service opportunities.

Degree Programs

The Religion Program is constructed especially for students planning to continue their studies in a theological seminary or graduate school of religion, or who intend to seek employment in a church-related vocation. The major in Religion leading to the Bachelor of Arts degree requires 30 hours. The Church Staff Associates Program is designed to equip students to serve as lay professionals in congregations of the church. A major in religion is required in combination with a supporting program of courses to be constructed by each student in accordance with specific occupational interests under the direction of the Director of the Program and a faculty member representing a supporting area chosen by the student.

Doane College
Philosophy - Religion Department

Crete, NE 68333   (402) 826-2161

Administration. Dr. Paul J. Bock, Professor of Religion.

General Description. In addition to offering a liberal arts program with a major in Philosophy-Religion, Doane College has a pre-professional program which prepares students for careers in Christian ministry. Students interested in religious education or missionary work can also prepare by taking specific courses in religion, philosophy, literature, history, social studies, music, and drama.

Parent Institution. Doane College was incorporated in 1872 as a non-profit institution by an independent self-perpetuating board of trustees. The impetus for its development came from the Congregational Church, the pioneer in higher education in Nebraska, which founded a college at Vontenelle near Omaha in 1858. Doane College has maintained its relationship with the Church, which, through merger, is now the United Church of Christ. It is the representative institution for the Nebraska, Rocky Mountain, and Kansas-Oklahoma conferences of the United Church of Christ.

Community Environment. Crete is located 25 miles southwest of Lincoln, Nebraska. The community has a population of 5,000. The 360-acre campus includes 19 buildings.

Religious Denomination. United Church of Christ.

Religious Emphasis. Liberal.

Accreditation. North Central Association of Colleges and Schools.

Term System. Semester; January interterm; summer term.

Enrollment in Degree Programs in Religion 1984–85. Total 7; men 4, women 3.

Degrees in Religion Awarded 1984–85. Bachelor of Arts 4; men 2, women 2.

Faculty for Degree Programs in Religion. Total 3; full-time 2, part-time 1.

Admission Requirements. Graduation from a recognized secondary school program or GED; satisfactory completion of a secondary school program that would prepare the student to study within Doane's liberal arts curriculum; SAT or ACT.

Tuition and Fees. Tuition $2,575 per semester (includes fees); board and room $1,000 per semester; tuition per credit for less than 12 credits or more than 17 credits $163; part-time fees $25 to $122.50 depending upon number of credit hours.

Financial Aid. Doane College's financial aid programs are awarded to a student based upon his/her qualifications and/or financial need. Aid based upon the family's financial need must be renewed each year.

Housing. Doane is a residential college and all unmarried full-time students are expected to live and board on campus. The residence halls provide a variety of accommodations.

Library Facilities. The library contains 152,000 volumes. Each student is expected to develop competence in the use of the library.

Religious Services/Activities. Doane College affirms historical connections with the United Church of Christ and joins in fellowship and service with other United Church of Christ colleges in the United States. Students are encouraged to realize their spiritual growth through participation in campus religious organizations, through involvement with Doane faculty and staff, and through religious worship in any of the Crete churches.

Degree Programs

The Bachelor of Arts with a major in Philosophy-Religion consists of, in addition to the general education and other requirements for a degree, ten courses distributed between philosophy and religion, including certain courses at the appropriate level. A senior thesis is required. Each major is required to take part in the Department's monthly colloquia in philosophy and religion.

Grace College of the Bible
1515 South 10th Street
Omaha, NE 68108   (402) 449-2843

Administration. Warren Bathke, President; Donald J. Tschetter, Vice President of Education.

General Description. Grace College of the Bible has as its purpose to prepare men and women for professional and lay church-related ministries. It is a conservative, interdenominational college offering associate and baccalaureate degrees. In addition to the Bible major included in all programs, students may major in Pastoral Ministries, World Missions, Church Education, Elementary Education, Music, and Radio Communications. Students may also combine vocational-technical training with Bible education. Programs offered: Certificate (one year) in Basic Bible, Post-University, Missions/Bible. Associate degrees in Bible-Vocational-Technical, Bible-General Education, Bible-Professional Education. Bachelor of Arts in Pastoral Ministries, Pre-Seminary, Missions, Christian Education. Bachelor of Science in Bible-Vocational-Technical, Pastoral Ministries, Missions, Nursing, Christian Education, Christian Education-Music, Christian Camping, Pre-School Ministries, Christian Elementary Education, Vocational-Technical-Christian Education or Missions, Church Music, Radio Communications.

Community Environment. Grace College of the Bible is comprised of 27 buildings on 7.6 acres in Omaha, Nebraska. Omaha is in a period of rapid renewal through publicly and privately supported programs. Metropolitan Omaha has a population of over one-half million people and serves as a communication and cultural center for the Plains States.

Religious Denomination. Nondenominational.

Religious Emphasis. Conservative.

Accreditation. American Association of Bible Colleges.

Term System. Semester.

Enrollment in Degree Programs in Religion 1984–85. Total 272; men 149, women 123.

Degrees in Religion Awarded 1984–85. Bachelor of Arts 11; men 11. Bachelor of Science 28; men 28. Associate degree 11; men 11.

Faculty for Degree Programs in Religion. Total 30; full-time 22, part-time 8.

Admission Requirements. High school graduation in top half of class; Christian character.

Tuition and Fees. $1,560 per semester; room and board $1,050 per semester.

Financial Aid. Scholarships, loans, and other forms of aid are available.

Housing. All single students, except those living in their own homes within commuting distance, must reside in College residence halls and take their meals in the College dining hall. The College has a number of furnished and unfurnished apartments for married students.

Library Facilities. The library houses over 54,000

volumes plus cassettes, filmstrips, microfiche, and recordings. It receives 270 magazines and periodicals.

Religious Services/Activities. Prayer meetings, missionary prayer groups, days of prayer, and daily chapel are some of the opportunities for spiritual growth and development. A Fall Bible Conference and a Missionary Conference are annual highlights.

Degree Programs

The Bachelor's degree programs consist of a Bible major, general education, and professional studies. The curriculum is organized into the Departments of Bible and Theology, Pastoral Ministries and Evangelism, World Missions, Christian Education, Music, Radio Communications, and General Education.

Special Programs

The Associate in Bible and Christian Ministries degree is designed for students who plan to return to their home communities and become involved in the varied opportunities of the local church. The degree requires the completion of 57 hours in Biblical subjects, 20 hours in general education subjects, 15 hours in professional electives, and 3 hours in free electives for a total of 95 hours. The degree requires 3 years to complete.

A Basic Bible Program of one year is offered as well as a Post-University Program of one year of intensive Bible study. A one year certificate program in Missions/Bible is also offered.

Midland Lutheran College
Department of Philosophy/Religion
720 East Ninth Street
Fremont, NE 68025   (402) 721-5480

Administration. Carl L. Hansen, President.

General Description. Founded in 1883, Midland Lutheran College is the product of college and church mergers. It is affiliated with the Nebraska and Rocky Mountain Synods of the Lutheran Church in America. The College offers 12 Associate of Arts concentration areas, 19 Bachelor of Arts majors, and 31 preprofessional fields of study.

Community Environment. The College is located in Fremont, Nebraska, a community of 25,000 approximately 30 miles northwest of Omaha and 50 miles north of Lincoln. The campus of 15 buildings occupies 22 acres.

Religious Denomination. The Lutheran Church in America.

Accreditation. North Central Association of Colleges and Schools.

Term System. Semester (4-1-4 plan).

Admission Requirements. Graduation from an accredited high school or equivalent; 15 academic units; ACT.

Tuition and Fees. Tuition $5,000 per year; room $375 per term; board $725 per term.

Financial Aid. Aid is provided in the form of scholar-

ships, grants, loans, and part-time work on campus.

Housing. Dormitory facilities are available on campus.

Library Facilities. The library contains over 106,000 volumes.

Religious Services/Activities. Chapel is held every Tuesday and Thursday.

Degree Programs

The Department of Philosophy/Religion offers a major in the field leading to the Bachelor of Arts degree. A total of 128 semester hours is required for the degree. In addition to pre-seminary training, several programs of study in church vocations are available. These programs are designed to meet the academic portion of the certification requirements of the Lutheran Church in America for lay professionals. The program in Church Business Administrator requires the student to major in Business Administration and minor in Philosophy/Religion. The Organist-Choirmaster program requires a major in Music and a minor in Philosophy/Religion.

Nebraska Christian College
1800 Syracuse Avenue
Norfolk, NE 68701   (402) 371-5960

Administration. Harold B. Milliken, President; Loren T. Swedburg, Academic Dean.

General Description. Nebraska Christian College is a four-year Bible college offering two-year, four-year, and five-year degrees leading to church-related careers. These include Minister, Youth Minister, Music Minister, Christian Education Minister, Christian School Teacher. It is the primary purpose of the College to educate Christians for leadership ministries, both in the church and to the world, who believe in and are supportive of the principles of the New Testament church.

Community Environment. Norfolk, Nebraska, home of Nebraska Christian College, is located in the northeastern sector of the state, 80 miles southwest of Sioux City. It is predominantly a retail community, serving north central and northern Nebraska. The College's location is enhanced by the presence of many churches located within reasonable driving distance, and which are of such a size as to provide week-end ministries for students.

Religious Denomination. Christian Churches and Churches of Christ.

Religious Emphasis. Evangelical.

Accreditation. Candidate, American Association of Bible Colleges.

Term System. Semester.

Enrollment in Degree Programs in Religion 1984–85. Total 156; men 88, women 68.

Degrees in Religion Awarded 1984–85. Bachelor of Arts 3; men 3. Bachelor of Science 10; men 8, women 2. Associate of Arts 17; men 6, women 11.

Faculty for Degree Programs in Religion. Total 13; full-

time 5, part-time 5.

Admission Requirements. High school diploma or GED; ACT.

Tuition and Fees. Tuition $1,280; room and board $1,650; student fees $120.

Financial Aid. Institutional scholarships, Pell Grants, Guaranteed Student Loans, Supplemental Educational Opportunity Grants, and College Work-Study are among the types of aid available.

Housing. Almost all students are housed on campus in dormitories or apartments.

Library Facilities. The library contains over 24,000 volumes.

Religious Services/Activities. Chapel is held on a regular basis and attendance is required. There is a Spiritual Emphasis week and a College Spring Convention. A Church Leadership Seminar is held each fall.

Degree Programs

The Bachelor of Arts and the Bachelor of Science degree programs require 130 hours of which 35 to 40 hours are in the Biblical major plus a practical ministry major (pastoral ministry, youth ministry, Christian Education, Church Music, Elementary Education).

The Bachelor of Theology degree is a 5-year program designed with a major concentration in Bible-Theology and Christian Education, plus wide studies in the field of general education. The degree requires completion 158 semester hours.

Special Programs

The Associate of Arts requires the completion of 64 semester hours of which 20 hours are in Bible and Theology and 21 hours in Christian Education. This degree can also be earned with emphasis in working with the deaf.

Nebraska Wesleyan University
Religion Department
50th and St. Paul
Lincoln, NE 68504   (402) 465-2300

Administration. Dr. John R. White, Jr., President; Dr. Paul H. Laursen, Provost; Dr. Louis DeGrazia, Head, Department of Religion.

General Description. A department of the Division of Humanities, the Religion Department offers a major in religion leading to the Bachelor of Arts degree.

Parent Institution. Nebraska Wesleyan University is an academic community dedicated to intellectual and personal growth within the context of a liberal arts education and in an environment of Christian concern. The University was established by the United Methodist Church and actively maintains its relationship with the church.

Community Environment. The 44-acre campus of Nebraska Wesleyan University is located in suburban northeast Lincoln, Nebraska, and contains 33 buildings.

Lincoln is the capital of Nebraska, and lies in the southeastern part of the state in a vast agricultural region where irrigation is an important factor.

Religious Denomination. The United Methodist Church.

Religious Emphasis. Liberal.

Accreditation. North Central Association of Colleges and Schools.

Term System. Semester.

Enrollment in Degree Programs in Religion 1984–85. Total 7; men 5, women 2.

Degrees in Religion Awarded 1984–85. Bachelor of Arts 4; men 4.

Faculty for Degree Programs in Religion. Total 5; full-time 2, part-time 3.

Admission Requirements. High school graduation.

Tuition and Fees. Tuition $5,055.50; housing $2,200 per year.

Financial Aid. Assistance is available and is based on need and merit.

Housing. Dormitories are available on campus.

Library Facilities. The library contains over 300,000 volumes.

Religious Services/Activities. Chapel is held once a week and other religious activities are available.

Degree Programs

The major in Religion leading to a Bachelor of Arts degree requires 30 hours in Religion including the basic courses in Bible, Church History, and Theology.

Special Programs

The Wesleyan Institute of Lifelong Learning (WILL) offers evening programs. Courses available include regular offerings in Religion.

Union College
3800 South 48th Street
Lincoln, NE 68506   (402) 488-2331

Administration. Benjamin R. Wygal, President.

General Description. Founded in 1891, Union College is an independent, four-year coeducational college of liberal arts and sciences, owned and operated by the Seventh-day Adventist Church. The College offers programs leading to the associate and baccalaureate degrees.

Community Environment. The 22-acre campus is located in a suburb of Lincoln, a city in southeastern Nebraska in a vast agricultural area.

Religious Denomination. Seventh-day Adventist.

Accreditation. North Central Association of Colleges and Schools.

Term System. Semester.

Admission Requirements. Graduation from an accredited high school or the equivalent.

Tuition and Fees. Tuition $5,800 per year; room $513

per semester; board $450 (average) per semester.

Financial Aid. The College has a program of financial aid which is a comprehensive package. It includes federal grants and loans and work-study.

Housing. Living accommodations are available on campus.

Library Facilities. The library houses over 114,000 volumes.

Religious Services/Activities. The College requires attendance at a specified number of religious services each week. Chapel and convocation are held weekly. Daily worships are conducted in residence halls Sunday through Friday.

Degree Programs

The major leading to the Bachelor of Arts in Theology requires the completion of 35 semester hours in the Department plus contextual requirements of 26 semester hours. A major in Youth Ministry requires 35 semester hours in the Department plus 23 hours of contextual requirements. The Bachelor of Arts in Religious Education is offered with a teaching major in Religion. A total of 32-37 hours is required in the major.

NEW HAMPSHIRE

St. Anselm College
Department of Theology
Manchester, NH 03102   (603) 669-1030

Administration. Rt. Rev. Joseph J. Gerry, O.S.B., Chancellor; Br. Joachim W. Froehlich, O.S.B., President; Rev. Peter J. Guerin, O.S.B., Dean of the College; Dr. James McGhee, Chairperson, Department of Theology.

General Description. In St. Anselm College the study of Theology occupies an essential position in the core curriculum. Each student must complete three courses in Theology as a requirement for the baccalaureate degree. The task of Christian Theology is to express meaningfully the revelation of Jesus, and to examine the faith of the Christian community in its historical and contemporary context. Furthermore, Theology is concerned with the practical implications of living a life of faith, particularly in its moral, spiritual, and liturgical aspects.

Parent Institution. St. Anselm College is a Catholic liberal arts college in the Benedictine tradition. Its purpose is to offer its students access to an educational process which will encourage them to lead lives that are both creative and generous. As a Catholic, Benedictine institution, Saint Anselm observes and promotes Christian standards of value and conduct. The College accepts and retains students on the condition that they observe these standards. The Bachelor of Arts degree is awarded.

Community Environment. St. Anselm College is located just outside the city of Manchester, New Hampshire, about 50 miles north of Boston, and may be reached easily by bus, automobile, or by air.

Religious Denomination. Roman Catholic.

Accreditation. New England Association of Schools and Colleges.

Term System. Semester; summer term.

Degrees in Religion Awarded 1984–85. Bachelor of Arts 4; men 4.

Faculty for Degree Programs in Religion. Total 11; full-time 9, part-time 2.

Admission Requirements. High school graduation with 16 acceptable units of secondary school coursework, or its equivalent; SAT scores.

Tuition and Fees. Tuition $3,050 per semester; residence fees $1,110 to $1,600 per semester.

Financial Aid. Scholarships, grants, loans, and work-study are available.

Housing. Dormitory accommodations and some off-campus housing; no provision for married students.

Library Facilities. The Joseph H. Geisel Library houses 160,000 volumes. Included in this collection are basic theological works.

Religious Services/Activities. A Benedictine monastery is located on campus. The Abbey Church is the liturgical center of the College. Monastic services are held several times daily (liturgy of the hours, Mass) and there are seasonal programs during the Advent and Lenten seasons. The Campus Ministry provides spiritual direction and counseling, retreats and evenings of reflection, and participation in programs of social justice.

Degree Programs

Students majoring in Theology for the Bachelor of Arts degree are required to complete ten courses in theology. These include Biblical Theology, The Early Church, and one course in contemporary theology, two courses in systematic theology, one course in ethics, one course in the history of religions, and three electives, one of which must be a seminar. Also, one ancient language and one modern language on the intermediate level are required. Majors are required to complete successfully the written and oral comprehensive examinations.

NEW JERSEY

Drew University
Theological School
36 Madison Avenue
Madison, NJ 07940   (201) 377-3000

Administration. Dr. Paul Hardin, President; Thomas W. Ogletree, Dean, Theological School.

General Description. Drew University was a seminary before it became a university. The School was founded in 1866 by the General Conference of the Methodist Episcopal Church to prepare persons for service in Christian ministries. Subsequently, the Drew trustees in 1928 established a College of Liberal Arts and a Graduate School, transforming the seminary into a university-related theological school. The Theological School has retained its commitment to ministerial preparation, particularly of candidates for ordination in the United Methodist Church.

Parent Institution. Drew University is comprised of The Theological School, the College of Liberal Arts, and the Graduate School. Programs of study lead to the Bachelor, Master, and Doctorate degrees. The Department of Religion offers a major in the field. Pre-theological preparation for seminary is also offered.

Community Environment. The Seminary is located in Madison, a suburban community in New Jersey, 27 miles from New York City.

Religious Denomination. The United Methodist Church.

Accreditation. Middle States Association of Colleges and Schools; Association of Theological Schools in the United States and Canada.

Term System. Semester.

Admission Requirements. Bachelor's degree or its equivalent from an accredited college or university.

Tuition and Fees. Tuition $2,236 per semester; room and board $1,402-$1,456; fees $183.

Financial Aid. With the exception of Tipple Scholars and Faculty Scholars, financial aid is distributed on the basis of need.

Housing. Graduate and Theological students are housed in three apartment complexes, a traditional residence hall, and in a number of houses.

Library Facilities. The resources of the Drew University Library contain nearly a half-million volumes. The theological collection of more than 250,000 volumes is one of a relatively small number of especially strong collections in North America and contains books and manuscripts of high value for scholarship research. Resources are exceptional in Biblical scholarship, patristics, Reformation, and nineteenth century American theology.

Religious Services/Activities. The community gathers for worship each morning in Craig Chapel. Holy Communion is celebrated weekly using a variety of liturgical traditions. Campus groups sponsor early morning worship and vespers. Prayer and faith-sharing groups form each year in different housing units.

Degree Programs

The Theological School offers four degree programs, three directed to ministerial practice and the fourth to studies pursued independently of particular vocational goals. The Master of Divinity is the basic three-year program providing preparation for ordained ministry. The Master of Sacred Theology and the Doctor of Ministry are advanced programs which presuppose the Master of Divinity degree. The Master of Sacred Theology degree is a one-year program for those who wish further study in one or more of the theological disciplines. The Master of Theological Studies is a flexible, two-year program for those who desire theological study for a range of diverse purposes: personal enrichment or service as diaconal ministers, lay leaders, and theologically informed practitioners of other vocations.

The Doctor of Ministry is a two-year, half-time "in-ministry" program for ordained, practicing ministers. It is offered each year to four or five regional groups in various locations selected on the basis of student interest and institutional feasibility.

Immaculate Conception Seminary
School of Theology and Pastoral Ministry of
   Seton Hall University
400 South Orange Avenue
South Orange, NJ 07079   (201) 761-9575

Administration. Rev. Monsignor John J. Petillo, Chancellor; Rev. Monsignor Edward J. Ciuba, Rector/Dean; Rev. Francis A. DeDomenico, Associate Dean; Rev. Joseph P. Masiello, Vice Rector.

General Description. Immaculate Conception Seminary is the Graduate School of Theology and Pastoral Ministry of Seton Hall University. It offers degree programs for men and women studying for the various ministries of the Church and, in particular, for men studying for the Roman Catholic priesthood. It grants the degrees Master of Arts in Pastoral Ministry, Master of Arts in Theology, and Master of Divinity in Pastoral Ministry.

Parent Institution. See: Seton Hall University.

Community Environment. See: Seton Hall University.

Religious Denomination. Roman Catholic.

Accreditation. Middle States Association of Colleges and Schools; Association of Theological Schools in the United States and Canada.

Term System. Semester; summer term.

Enrollment in Degree Programs in Religion 1984–85. Total 158; men 107, women 51 (figures for fall 1985).

Degrees in Religion Awarded 1984–85. Master of Arts in Pastoral Ministry 4; men 1, women 3. Master of Arts in Theology 6; men 2, women 4. Master of Divinity in Pastoral Ministry 65; men 59, women 6.

Faculty for Degree Programs in Religion. Total 28; full-time 14, part-time 14.

Admission Requirements. Bachelor of Arts degree in the humanities or its equivalent from an accredited college or university.

Tuition and Fees. Tuition $1,500 per semester; student fee $50; room and board $1,700 (Newark $1,150).

Financial Aid. Available for Newark seminarians only.

Housing. Housing is available for seminarians.

Library Facilities. The School of Theology and Pastoral Ministry Library is part of the Seton Hall University Library system. It constitutes, in effect, the University's research collection for theological, biblical, and pastoral studies. The collection is particularly rich in the area of liturgy and Bible studies and numbers over 58,000 titles and 400 periodicals.

Religious Services/Activities. Formation program for seminary candidates for priesthood; spiritual direction available for non-ordination students; Masses are celebrated daily in the Immaculate Conception Chapel.

Degree Programs

The Master of Divinity in Pastoral Ministry requires 72 hours of coursework (48 hours in Biblical, historical, ethical, and doctrinal studies; 24 hours in pastoral ministry).

Candidates seeking ordination to the priesthood are to be guided in their choice of courses by the directives of the Program of Priestly Formation.

The Master of Arts in Pastoral Ministry requires 48 credit hours of academic study in Foundational Areas (30 credit hours), Pastoral Electives (12 credit hours), and Field Education Placements (6 credit hours). Each student is required to develop a program of spiritual formation with the guidance and approval of the director of lay ministry candidates.

The Master of Arts in Theology requires the completion of 36 credits in coursework of which 21 credits must be in the area of concentration/specialization (Biblical Studies, Systematic Theology, Moral Theology) and 15 credits in the two other areas of concentration.

New Brunswick Theological Seminary
17 Seminary Place
New Brunswick, NJ 08901   (201) 247-5241

Administration. Dr. Robert A. White, President; Dr. Paul R. Fries, Academic Dean; Benjamin Alicea, Dean of Evening Theological Education Program.

General Description. Founded in New York in 1784 as the first graduate school of theological education in the United States, the New Brunswick Theological Seminary was established to train ministers for the Reformed Church in America. It was moved to New Brunswick, New Jersey in 1810. The development of the present campus, adjacent to that of Rutgers University, was begun in 1856. The Seminary today has an ecumenical student body which represents a dozen different Christian denominations. The Seminary is enriched with the diversity provided through the large number of students from various racial and ethnic backgrounds. In addition to its daytime programs, New Brunswick offers evening classes on its campus, and an extension program in New York City for those unable to attend daytime classes.

The purpose of New Brunswick Seminary is to train servants of the church for specialized ministries through which the people of God are equipped for work in his service, the body of Christ is built up, and the Word of God is spoken and lived obediently in the world.

The Seminary has the advantage of proximity of Rutgers University, and many of the facilities of Rutgers are available to Seminary students, including classroom instruction.

Community Environment. The main campus of New Brunswick Theological Seminary occupies a dozen buildings scattered over an 8-acre tract overlooking the Nielson Campus of Rutgers University. The main building, Zwimmer Hall, was dedicated in 1967. It is centered around a chapel of contemporary design and complemented by a variety of educational facilities. The location of the main campus suits it remarkably for its tasks. Fifty minutes by train, bus, or turnpike from Times Square, New York

City, on the north, and one hour from Philadelphia on the south, New Brunswick lies at the hub of a network of institutions.

The New York City campus location in Jamaica, Queens, is also convenient. Located in the heart of the business district, it is easily accessible by public transportation or automobile. With a suite of classrooms and offices in the newly renovated First Reformed Church, the Seminary can meet the needs of students from Brooklyn, Queens, and Long Island.

Religious Denomination. Reformed Church in America.

Accreditation. Association of Theological Schools in the United States and Canada.

Term System. Semester; summer term.

Enrollment in Degree Programs in Religion 1984–85. Total 143; men 97, women 46.

Degrees in Religion Awarded 1984–85. Master of Arts 5; men 3, women 2. Master of Divinity 14; men 13, women 1. (Students completing both degrees are listed only once.)

Faculty for Degree Programs in Religion. Total 11; full-time 7, part-time 4.

Admission Requirements. An undergraduate degree from an accredited institution or its equivalent is a prerequisite for admission (the Master of Theology in Pastoral Care and Counseling requires a Master of Divinity or its equivalent); grade point average of 2.5 on a 4.0 scale; requirements for various programs vary.

Tuition and Fees. Tuition for Reformed Church members $110 per credit hour; others $121 per credit hour; matriculation fee $100; registration fee $25 per semester; student activities fee $25 per year; housing single $1,210 per year, double $1,065 per year; married student apartments range from $262 to $410 per month.

Financial Aid. Limited financial aid is available to deserving and academically progressing students with preference given to Reformed Church students.

Housing. One large residence for married students; two smaller residences for single students.

Library Facilities. The Gardner Sage Library contains 138,686 volumes. The Leiby Collection (Dutch-American colonial and New Jersey history) and other 17th and 18th century works (especially theology, Greek and Roman classics, including Hellenistic literature) are housed here. The archival holdings of the Reformed Church in America provide a unique resource for the study of its history and doctrine.

Religious Services/Activities. During the academic year chapel services are held four mornings a week and each evening that classes meet. Special evening services are held in the Chapel, including Fall and Spring Convocations and senior-led worship. Time is allowed in the weekly schedule for colloquies which enrich extracurricular life at the Seminary. The Society of Inquiry is the student organization which plans for various religious and social events.

Degree Programs

The Master of Divinity degree is designed to prepare students for a wide range of Christian ministry, including service in the parish, missions, and other varied forms of church vocation. Instruction is distributed through three departments: the Biblical Department with studies in both Old and New Testaments; the Theological Department with studies in the historical, conceptual, and moral resources of the church; and the Practical Department, which integrates resources from the behavioral sciences with the skills needed for Christian ministry.

The Master of Arts in Theology degree is designed to offer an advanced program in theological studies in conjunction with graduate study at Rutgers University or some other graduate institution. The program is an appropriate foundation for doctoral studies or for vocations in which a graduate academic degree is desirable.

The Master of Arts in Theology and Church Music is designed for students preparing to be professional church musicians and is offered in cooperation with the Graduate Music Faculty of Rutgers University. The degree requires the completion of 60 hours of credit, 27 at the Seminary in Biblical, theological, historical, and liturgical subjects and 27 at Rutgers in music history, theory and composition and performance. A reading knowledge of German, French, Italian, or Latin must be demonstrated through examination. A thesis, composition, or a performance equivalent, for 6 hours' credit, must be completed.

The Master of Arts in Theology in Pastoral Care and Counseling is designed for parish and institutional clergy and other qualified religious professionals who wish to strengthen their counseling ministry.

Special Programs

Combined Degree Programs in conjunction with Rutgers University and a Doctor of Ministry degree program in conjunction with Princeton Theological Seminary are also available.

Northeastern Bible College
12 Oak Lane
Essex Fells, NJ 07021   (201) 226-1074

Administration. Dr. Robert W. Benton, President; Dr. Charles W. Anderson, Chancellor; James Bjornstad, Academic Dean.

General Description. The purpose of Northeastern Bible College is to provide higher education within the context of Christian values. It emphasizes high academic standards, practical application, and spiritual development. Within this framework, the College provides curricula leading to the degrees Bachelor of Arts in Biblical Literature, Bachelor of Sacred Music, and a 5-year Bachelor of Theology. Also awarded are a 2-year Associate of Religious Arts degree and a 1-year Biblical diploma.

Community Environment. Northeastern Bible College is located in Essex Fells, New Jersey, directly west of New York City and can be reached via I-80 and I-280 by automobile, and by adequate public transportation facilities including bus, railway, and air. The campus is within minutes of the Newark International Airport.

Religious Denomination. Nondenominational.

Religious Emphasis. Conservative Evangelical.

Accreditation. Middle States Association of Colleges and Schools; American Association of Bible Schools.

Term System. Semester.

Enrollment in Degree Programs in Religion 1984–85. Total 266; men 165, women 101.

Faculty for Degree Programs in Religion. Total 23; full-time 15, part-time 8.

Admission Requirements. Applicants must have a high school diploma or its equivalent. Each student is assessed according to academic background, moral character, personal testimony for the Lord Jesus Christ, and desire to study the Scriptures. SAT or ACT scores are required of all recent high school graduates (international students excepted).

Tuition and Fees. Tuition $4,000; required fees $220; room and board $2,500; music lessons and laboratory fees are additional.

Financial Aid. Northeastern participates in all of the grant, employment, and loan programs of the federal government except NDSL. Most awards are based on need. New Jersey residents are eligible to apply for state grants, while students from other states should determine if their home states offer portable grants to New Jersey college attendees. Job opportunities are available both on and off campus. Scholarships offered are not need-based. To apply for aid, students should file the Financial Aid Form with the College Scholarship Service.

Housing. Dormitory rooms are available for single students. Apartments for married students are limited; off-campus housing is available.

Library Facilities. The library contains 45,756 volumes with a special Edward N. Cleaveland Jewish collection of 4,000 volumes.

Religious Services/Activities. Daily chapel; annual Spiritual Life Conference and Missions Conference.

Degree Programs

A Bachelor of Arts in Biblical Literature is offered in the following four- and five-year programs: Christian Education, Counseling, Elementary Education, Missions and Evangelism, Music Education, and Pastoral Ministries. Upon completion of a four-year program in Music, a Bachelor of Sacred Music degree is awarded. A five-year program in Theology offers a Bachelor of Theology degree.

Special Programs

Northeastern has a two-year program resulting in an Associate in Religious Arts degree and a one-year program leading to a Diploma in Bible Studies.

Princeton Theological Seminary
CN 821
Princeton, NJ 08542   (609) 921-8300

Administration. Dr. Thomas W. Gillespie, President; Dr. Conrad H. Massa, Dean of the Seminary; Dr. James N. Lapsley, Jr., Academic Dean.

General Description. Princeton Theological Seminary was established in 1812 by the Presbyterian Church to prepare men and women for ministry in the Christian church and in society. It is a graduate institution which offers five degree programs at the Master and Doctorate levels. Although committed to the Reformed theological tradition which is its heritage, the Seminary accepts qualified students of many denominations and is committed to an ecumenical outreach around the world. Through its academic departments — church history, Biblical studies, theology, and practical theology — it seeks to strengthen the spiritual life of its students and to confront them with probing questions about faith and life in today's world.

A Field Education Program is an integral part of the theological curriculum. Students under the supervision of pastors and specialists work at a variety of assignments in selected churches and institutions in the interest of developing (1) a habit of working in the context of disciplined theological reflection, (2) a growing understanding of the church and its ministry, (3) a life style congruent with the gospel, (4) sound ways of relating to different persons, and (5) competencies which are professional in the sense of including mastery of skills with knowledge of the theoretical bases of each. Assignments are available in churches and institutions of every type in an area that includes two huge metropolitan centers, smaller cities and towns, and rural neighborhoods.

The School of Christian Education provides graduate professional training of religious educators in a two-year program leading to the degree Master of Arts.

Degrees awarded by Princeton Theological Seminary are: Master of Divinity (the basic professional degree in ministry), Master of Arts in Christian Education, Master of Arts in Theological Studies, Master of Theology, Doctor of Ministry, and Doctor of Philosophy (Ph.D.).

Community Environment. The Seminary's campus of more than 20 buildings occupies 30 acres in the center of Princeton, New Jersey. Princeton is an academic, research, and residential community midway between New York and Philadelphia. Already on the map in colonial times, history was made here during the Revolution with George Washington and the Battle of Princeton. Woodrow Wilson proceeded from the University to the White House, and Albert Einstein strolled back and forth from his home on Mercer Street, just below the Seminary, to his office at the Institute for Advanced Study. Princeton is a small town but rich in educational and cultural resources, with libraries, museums, churches, theaters, concerts, athletic events, and a continuous program of lectures on the arts and sciences open to both town and gown.

Religious Denomination. Presbyterian Church (U.S.A.).

Religious Emphasis. Reformed.

Accreditation. Middle States Association of Colleges and Schools; Association of Theological Schools in the United States and Canada.

Term System. Semester; summer term.

Enrollment in Degree Programs in Religion 1984–85. Total 859; men 608, women 251.

Degrees in Religion Awarded 1984–85. Master of Divinity 151; men 99, women 52. Master of Arts 22; men 8, women 14. Master of Theology 64; men 56, women 8. Doctor of Ministry 8, men 6, women 2. Doctor of Philosophy (Ph.D.) 16; men 14, women 2.

Faculty for Degree Programs in Religion. Total 70; full-time 46, part-time 24.

Admission Requirements. For basic professional degree in ministry (Master of Divinity): college or university degree and transcript; 60 undergraduate hours in the liberal arts; letter of endorsement from church governing body; 3 letters of reference.

Tuition and Fees. Tuition $3,000; comprehensive fee $255; application fee $25; graduation fee $15; room and board $2,555.

Financial Aid. Assistance is granted on the basis of demonstrated need.

Housing. On-campus dormitories are available for single students; apartments available both on campus and in off-campus Seminary-owned apartments for married students.

Library Facilities. The The Robert E. Speer Library houses over 376,000 volumes. Special collections include The Louis F. Benson Collection of Hymnology (over 10,000 volumes); The Grosart Library of Puritan and Nonconformist Theology (over 5,000 volumes); The Sprague Collection, a large collection of early American theological pamphlets; Agnew Baptist Collection (2,000 volumes); and a collection of 3,000 pamphlets on the controversy regarding the proper form of baptism.

Religious Services/Activities. There is a full-time pastor to the Seminary community; student deacons in each dormitory; daily worship services; student-led Bible study and prayer groups.

Degree Programs

The Master of Divinity degree is designed to prepare students for the parish ministry, for graduate study in theology and related disciplines, for various types of chaplaincy, for mission work at home and abroad, and for other forms of church vocation. The curriculum is planned to provide the maximum of flexibility and independence consonant with a broad theolgical foundation. Instruction is organized under four academic departments: Biblical Studies, History, Theology, and Practical Theology. The program requires 78 credit hours of aca-

demic work distributed over 6 semesters of full-time resident study; a program of Senior studies in some area of the curriculum, and the completion of an approved program of field education.

The program of study leading to the degree of Master of Arts in Christian Education is designed as preparation for service in various professional capacities, particularly that of Director of Christian Education or Religious Education Coordinator in the parish. The program requires 52 credit hours distributed over 4 semester of study, a professional examination over the basic material in Christian Education and in the other areas of the Seminary program, and the completion of an approved program of field education. The Master of Arts in Theological Studies is a program designed to provide graduate education for persons currently engaged professionally in the teaching ministry of the church or for persons who have an attested expectation of such engagement. In most instances, the candidate will distribute courses over 2 or 3 related areas. The program focuses in the classical disciplines of theological inquiry where attention can be directed to theoretical foundations, basic methodology, historical perspectives, and contemporary trends. Satisfactory completion of 24 credit hours is required.

The Master of Theology degree is designed for students who wish to improve or deepen their preparation for the ministry beyond the level reached by their Master of Divinity course, or who desire to acquire a preparation for specialized ministries of the church. Courses are ordinarily taken in the area of the department in which the candidate is specializing. The program requires the completion of 24 credit hours.

The Doctor of Ministry degree is designed for men and women who wish to pursue, at an advanced level, education for ministerial practice. The program is oriented to the integration of theological and behavioral understandings in the context of continuing responsible engagement in service. The candidate is expected to be engaged in a recognized form of full-time ministerial practice for the duration of the program. The degree requires the satisfactory completion of two terms of workshop experience, individualized preparation for the qualifying examination and its satisfactory completion, and a thesis project in some area associated with the practice of ministry.

The Doctor of Philosophy program is designed to prepare men and women for independent scholarship in various dimensions of the study of religion and for teaching in colleges and theological seminaries. Work is offered in five areas: Biblical Studies, History and Ecumenics, Theology, Religion and Society, and Practical Theology.

Special Programs

The Program for Asian-American Theology and Ministry provides training for bilingual and bicultural leadership for second-generation Asian-American immigrant churches.

the Institute of Theology is a 10-day seminar held in

July of each year for clergy and laity from across the country and abroad.

The Center of Continuing Education offers over 65 on-campus and 4 off-campus seminars annually. Courses in Biblical Greek and Hebrew are offered during Summer School and the Summer Language Program.

Rabbinical College of America
226 Sussex Avenue
Morristown, NJ 07960   (201) 267-9404

Administration. Rabbi M. Herson, President.

General Description. The Rabbinical College of America, a affiliate of the worldwide Lubavitch movement, was founded in 1956. The new campus in Morris Township was occupied in 1971. The College seeks to develop scholars thoroughly trained in all aspects of advanced Jewish scholarship. It prepares students for positions as rabbis, teachers, and communal leaders, as well as for responsible, conscientious, and intelligent lay membership in the community. The College provides opportunities for original research and intensive advanced study and encourages the publication of the results of such research. It is concerned as well with transmitting the ethical, philosophical, and spiritual teachings and values of Judaism, particularly the unique philosophy of Chabad-Lubavitch Chassidism. The College awards the Bachelor of Religious Studies requiring a total of 120 credits.

Community Environment. The 15-acre campus is one mile from the city of Morristown.

Religious Denomination. Jewish.

Religious Emphasis. Lubavitch Chassidism.

Accreditation. Association of Advanced Rabbinical and Talmudic Schools.

Term System. Semester.

Enrollment in Degree Programs in Religion 1984–85. Total 230.

Admission Requirements. High school diploma or its equivalent. For the Advanced Talmudic Option, the student must have a Talmudic High School graduation or equivalent; competence in the entire Pentateuch and commentaries; completion of at least 150 folio pages of the Talmud; and competence in the laws and customs in the Code of Jewish Law and personal commitment to their observance.

Tuition and Fees. Tuition $3,450 per year; room $1,150; board $1,750.

Financial Aid. The three most accessible sources of aid are the six federally-sponsored student aid programs, the State of New Jersey Tuition Aid Grant program, and the school's own scholarship program.

Housing. Living accommodations are provided on campus.

Library Facilities. The Talmudic Library includes all the basic tools for scholarship and research. It contains numerous editions of the Bible, the Talmud, Codes, Re-sponsa literature, ethical and philosophical works, expositions on Jewish Liturgy, Hebrew language texts and a complete collection of Chabad works. For supplementary research into commentaries not usually incorporated into the volume of Talmud, the library provides an extensive array of ancient, medieval and modern classics, as well as a fine selection of responsa works for further study.

Religious Services/Activities. There is a uniform daily schedule of activities for all students in the New Direction Program. The schedule embraces the academic activities of the students as well as such activities as prayer and meals.

Degree Programs

The Bachelor of Religious Studies program (New Direction Program) aims for the acquisition of a significant amount of broad-ranging knowledge and an array of analytical tools and skills. Thus the graduating student is equipped with the background and skills necessary to pursue a lifetime of Talmudic study. He will have acquired an extensive education in Talmud, Codes, Bible, and Philosophy. In addition, a student will have amassed considerable background in the Hebrew, Yiddish, and Aramaic languages, and in Jewish history. Courses are offered in the various departments of Talmud, Codes, Liturgy, and Hebrew Language and Grammar.

The Bachelor of Religious Studies, Advanced Talmud Option is designed for young men with a secondary education in Jewish Studies. The core of the academic program lies in the area of Talmudic studies. A great portion of the curriculum consists of the analysis of selected tracates of the Talmud which are studied for both in-depth comprehension and broad-ranging scholarship.

Rutgers, The State University
Department of Religion
Faculty of Arts and Sciences
New Brunswick, NJ 08903   (201) 932-3770

Administration. Mahlon H. Smith, Chairperson, Department of Religion.

General Description. The Department of Religion offers a major leading to the Bachelor of Arts degree.

Parent Institution. Rutgers consists of 10 day-time undergraduate colleges on various campuses in Camden, Newark, and New Brunswick.

Community Environment. New Brunswick is located on the Raritan River, 30 miles southwest of New York City.

Religious Denomination. None.

Accreditation. Middle States Association of Colleges and Schools.

Term System. Semester system; three summer terms.

Faculty for Degree Programs in Religion. Total 9.

Admission Requirements. Graduation from an accredited high school; SAT required.

Tuition and Fees. Tuition in-state $1,520 per year; out-of-state $3,040; room and board $2,498; student fees $347.

Financial Aid. Financial aid is awarded on a first-come, first-served basis to admitted students, depending upon the availability of funds and according to the student's financial need as determined by federal and state guidelines.

Housing. Residence halls and apartments are available throughout the campus area.

Library Facilities. The Rutgers University Libraries have holdings of more than three million volumes. Each campus of the University has its own library and students may use any library in the system.

Religious Services/Activities. The Student Affairs Office within the Office of the Provost provides information for students of all religions, backgrounds, and affiliations regarding local houses of worship. Many faiths are represented through student organizations on the various campuses of the University. Nonsectarian services of worship, preaching, and music are provided by the University each Sunday morning in Kirkpatrick and Voorhees chapels, and on Sunday evenings the New Hope Church meets in Tillett Hall on the Kilmer campus.

Degree Programs

The Bachelor of Arts major requires a minimum of 36 credits in the field. To qualify for honors in religion, a student must have a cumulative grade point average of 3.0 or better and an average of 3.4 or better in the major.

St. Peter's College
Department of Theology
2641 Kennedy Boulevard
Jersey City, NJ 07306   (201) 333-4400

Administration. John M. Buckley, S.J., Chairman, Department of Theology.

General Description. The Department of Theology at St. Peter's College offers an undergraduate major in Theology leading to the Bachelor of Arts degree.

Parent Institution. St. Peter's College, New Jersey's Jesuit college, was founded in 1872 as an independent liberal arts college. One of 28 colleges and universities in the United States sponsored by the Society of Jesus, the College has become Alma Mater to more than 18,680 graduates and has met the educational needs of many other students. St. Peter's College began as a men's college. It became fully coeducational in 1966.

Community Environment. The 9-acre main campus of St. Peter's College has long been a landmark on Kennedy Boulevard in Jersey City. The College's atmosphere, architecture, and activity reflect a dynamic, vital, urban institution offering important intellectual resources to the community. The New York City skyline, visible from Jersey City, is a constant reminder of the College's proximity to a major cultural center.

Religious Denomination. Roman Catholic.

Religious Emphasis. Mainline.

Accreditation. Middle States Association of Colleges and Schools.

Term System. Semester; summer session.

Enrollment in Degree Programs in Religion 1984–85. Total 8; men 3, women 5.

Degrees in Religion Awarded 1984–85. Bachelor of Arts 2; men 1, women 1.

Faculty for Degree Programs in Religion. Total 11; full-time 8, part-time 3.

Admission Requirements. High school diploma or its equivalent; completion of 16 units of high school academic courses; satisfactory SAT score.

Tuition and Fees. Tuition $150 per credit.

Financial Aid. Financial assistance to eligible students is available in the form of grants, loans, and employment opportunities.

Housing. Minimal on-campus housing.

Library Facilities. The Theresa and Edward O'Toole Library houses a collection of approximately 230,000 volumes and offers extensive services and research facilities to the College community.

Religious Services/Activities. The Office of Campus Ministry sponsors numerous programs throughout the year. Optional worship services are held.

Degree Programs

The Bachelor of Arts with a major in Theology requires the completion of 66 credits in the core curriculum plus 63 credits in electives and courses in Methods and Sources of Theology; The Church: A Contemporary Study; The Theology of Grace; The Jewish Bible; and Survey of the New Testament.

Seton Hall University
Department of Religious Studies
400 South Orange Avenue
South Orange, NJ 07079   (201) 761-9480

Administration. Reverend Monsignor John J. Petillo, Chancellor; Dr. Charles R. Dees, Jr., Vice Chancellor for University Affairs; Rev. Richard M. Nardone, Chairman, Department of Religious Studies.

General Description. The Department of Religious Studies offers a program of study leading to the degree Bachelor of Arts. The Department seeks to give students an understanding of Christian theology and the phenomenon of Religion in its various manifestations. Man's religious quest is investigated in relation to other areas of life, particularly human relationships, social interaction, and political realities. Since 1984 the graduate program has been provided by Immaculate Conception Seminary / Graduate School of Theology and Pastoral Ministry (see separate entry).

Parent Institution. Seton Hall University was founded in 1856 as the first diocesan college in the United States and established as a university in 1950. It continues to operate under the auspices of the Roman Catholic Archdiocese of Newark. The University is composed of 6 schools: College of Arts and Sciences, W. Paul Stillman School of Business, School of Education, College of Nursing, and University College, all on the South Orange Campus, and the School of Law in Newark.

Community Environment. The main campus is on 58 acres in the Village of South Orange, population approximately 17,000. It is only 14 miles from New York City, a short trip by bus, train, or car to the cultural events and entertainment of one of the world's most exciting cities.

Religious Denomination. Roman Catholic.

Accreditation. Middle States Association of Colleges and Schools.

Term System. Semester; summer term.

Enrollment in Degree Programs in Religion 1984–85. Total undergraduates 16; men 10, women 6.

Degrees in Religion Awarded 1984–85. Bachelor of Arts 4; men 3, women 1.

Faculty for Degree Programs in Religion. Total undergraduate programs 17; full-time 10, part-time 7.

Admission Requirements. The minimum academic requirement for admission is satisfactory completion of a college preparatory course of study in an accredited secondary school with credit for 16 acceptable units. Applicants should submit a completed application with $25 fee, official copy of high school transcript, and SAT or ACT scores.

Tuition and Fees. Tuition $172 per credit (certain religious receive 50 percent discount and seminarians and teachers in Catholic schools a 25 percent discount); University fee per semester $125; vehicle registration $25 per year; lodging $871 to $1,034 per semester; board $523 to $584 per semester.

Financial Aid. The University maintains and administers programs of financial aid funded by the University, federal and state governments, various industries and foundations. Financial aid may be in the form of a scholarship, grant, loan, employment opportunity, or a combination of these.

Housing. On-campus housing is available.

Library Facilities. The McLaughlin Library houses over 360,000 volumes. A separate Seminary Library contains 58,000 volumes.

Religious Services/Activities. Immaculate Conception Chapel is open every day for private devotions, and there is an additional chapel in Boland Hall for student use. Masses are scheduled every day at convenient hours and confessions are heard every day. An active campus ministry team works to involve students in a Christian experience. Among the campus ministry programs are retreats, days of reflection, and prayer groups.

Degree Programs

The Bachelor of Arts degree with a major in Religion must meet the standards and requirements of the College of Arts and Sciences and complete a minimum of 36 credits in religious studies. The Department of Religious Studies offers eight basic groups of courses: Fundamental and Special Questions of Ethics; Questions of Religious Belief; Questions of Ecumenism; World Religion; Biblical Studies; The History of Christianity; Basic Theological Themes of the Catholic Christian Tradition; Religion and Social Sciences.

Special Programs

The Interim Youth Minister Program was established in 1979 to help the Church in the development of comprehensive youth ministries. The Interim Program acts as a catalyst for the growth of local youth ministries by placing qualified, trained, and faith-filled young adults in positions of full-time ministry with youth. For young adults who want to serve the Church and test out a possible career in lay ministry, Interim provides formation, support, and a two-year supervised internship experience in actual ministry with youth.

Upsala College
Prospect Street
East Orange, NJ 07019   (201) 266-7191

Administration. Dr. Rodney O. Felder, President.

General Description. Upsala College is a privately supported, coeducational liberal arts college affiliated with the Lutheran Church in America. As a church-related college, Upsala takes pride in its religious heritage and considers its affiliation with the Lutheran Church a source of strength. The College promotes the study of the Judeo-Christian tradition, its history, its literature, and its ethical norms, and it encourages critical inquiry into the traditions and values of a pluralistic society. Upsala was founded in 1893 by Lutherans of Swedish descent living in the eastern United States. The College grants the Bachelor's degree and offers the major in Religion, a pre-seminary program, and a program in Judaic Studies conducted in cooperation with the Midrasha/Jewish Education Association of Metropolitan New Jersey.

Community Environment. The campus of 45 acres is located in a residential section of East Orange, 15 miles from New York City.

Religious Denomination. The Lutheran Church in America.

Accreditation. Middle States Association of Colleges and Schools.

Term System. Semester (4-1-4 plan).

Admission Requirements. Graduation from an accredited high school with rank in the upper half of graduating class; ACT or SAT.

Tuition and Fees. Tuition $2,839 per semester; room and board $1,360-$1,600; student fees $100.

Financial Aid. Scholarships, grants, on-campus employment, and low-interest loans are types of aid available.

Housing. Dormitory accommodations are available for 750 students.

Library Facilities. The library houses over 150,000 volumes.

Religious Services/Activities. Weekly worship services are offered regularly under the direction of the Chaplain of the College. The campus spiritual life includes Bible study, discussion groups, and social events.

Degree Programs

A major in Religion consists of a minimum of seven courses, including Foundations of Judaic Thought and Foundations of Christian Thought. Religion majors are required to demonstrate a competence in a foreign language at the intermediate level and take one course involving a non-Western culture.

The concentration in Judaic Studies consists of a minimum of five courses, at least one of which must be in the area of Hebrew Bible.

A preprofessional Pre-Seminary Program is offered for those students contemplating graduate study and church-related vocations.

NEW MEXICO

Eastern New Mexico University
Department of Religion
Box 2005
Portales, NM 88130   (505) 356-4252

Administration. Dr. Robert L. Matheny, President; Dr. Bill D. Engman, Vice President, Academic Affairs; Dr. Thurman Elder, Acting Dean, College of Liberal Arts and Sciences; Dr. Glenn W. McCoy, Chairperson, Department of Religion.

General Description. The academic program of religion is maintained through the cooperative interests of Baptist Churches, the Christian Church, the Church of Christ, the Methodist Church, and the Roman Catholic Church. The program is organized with the needs of several types of students in mind: (1) any student, a non-major in religion, wishing to develop religious insight and understanding as part of his/her cultural background; (2) the prospective religious worker not planning to pursue graduate theological study but desiring to major in religion during his/her undergraduate work; (3) the prospective religious worker planning to attend a graduate school of religion. The degrees Bachelor of Arts, Bachelor of Science, and Master of Arts in Religion are awarded.

Parent Institution. Eastern New Mexico University is a comprehensive multi-campus state university with a wide variety of undergraduate and graduate programs in the liberal arts and sciences, education, business, fine arts, and selected vocational/technical areas. The University is committed to providing quality education through small classes, close student-faculty relationships, and research and scholarly endeavor. The current enrollment is 3,800 on the main campus and 3,600 on the branch campuses.

Community Environment. The Eastern New Mexico University campus of more than 400 acres is located in Portales, New Mexico, on the eastern side of the state. Portales, the county seat of Roosevelt county, has an elevation of 4,000 feet and a population of about 10,000. The climate is considered one of the best in the United States.

Religious Denomination. None.

Accreditation. North Central Association of Colleges and Schools.

Term System. Semester.

Enrollment in Degree Programs in Religion 1984–85. Total 42; men 31, women 11.

Degrees in Religion Awarded 1984–85. Bachelor of Arts 2; men 2. Bachelor of Science 8; men 7, women 1.

Faculty for Degree Programs in Religion. Total 7; full-time 6, part-time 1.

Admission Requirements. Undergraduate: Graduation from an accredited high school with units required by the North Central Association and/or by the State Department of Education; non-high school graduates may be admitted under certain conditons. Graduate: Baccalaureate degree from an accredited college or university; graduates of a non-accredited institution may apply for special permission to matriculate.

Tuition and Fees. Tuition resident $371.40, nonresident $1,149 per semester; fewer than 12 hours or more than 18 hours resident $39.95 per credit, nonresident $95.75; dormitory room $380 per semester (double occupancy); married student housing $145-$195 per month.

Financial Aid. Grants include Pell, Supplemental Educational Opportunity, and New Mexico Student Incentive. Both Guaranteed Loans and National Direct Student Loans are available. Scholarships are also available. Graduate students should contact the Director of Student Financial Aids for information on monies available.

Housing. Undergraduates may live in dormitories; family and graduate housing are available.

Library Facilities. The Golden Library houses over 270,000 volumes covering all areas of study. The holdings in religious subjects number 10,500. A special collection covers Religion in the Southwest.

Religious Services/Activities. Denominations represented in the teaching program have frequent off-campus retreats and conferences. All denominations join together for an annual Faith-in-Life emphasis.

Degree Programs

The Master of Arts in Religion may be earned with either the thesis or non-thesis plan. All candidates must take a written and/or oral field examination which includes five of the following fields: Old Testament, New Testament, Church History, World's Religions, Languages, Canon and Archaeology, Philosophy, and Religious Thought. The exam is to be taken before the student has completed 12 hours of graduate work. Its purpose is to aid in planning the course of study for the student. For students following the thesis plan, a minimum of 18 credits plus 6 thesis credits must be earned in the area of religion. A minimum of 30 credits in graduate coursework is required for the degree. For those following the non-thesis plan, a minimum of 24 credits must be earned in religion. A minimum of 32 hours of graduate coursework is required for the degree.

The Bachelor of Arts and Bachelor of Science degrees with a major in Religion are offered with a wide variety of courses in archaeology, Bible, church history, Greek, Hebrew, homiletics, philosophy of religion, religious education, sociology of religion, psychology of religion, and world's religions. In addition to the general requirements for the baccalaureate degree, the major must complete required courses in Religion (27 credits) and 18 credits in Religion electives.

Special Programs

Weekend workshops are offered each semester and summer educational tours are conducted which concentrate upon religious subject matter.

NEW YORK

Barnard College
Department of Religion
Milbank Hall 219
3009 Broadway
New York, NY 10027   (212) 280-2597

Administration. Dr. Ellen V. Futter, President of Barnard College and Dean in the University; Dr. Charles S. Olton, Vice President for Academic Affairs and Dean of the Faculty.

General Description. The program in religion offered by Barnard College and Columbia College offers a unique context for the interdisciplinary study with faculty with areas of expertise (philosophy of religion, sociology and anthropology of religion, history of Eastern and Western religious traditions, comparative religion) providing the student with a clear picture of the range of specialization available. Moreover, the large Columbia University community provides training in a broad spectrum of disciplines related to the study of religion: the social sciences, humanities, arts, and the professions. Barnard and Columbia Colleges also offer intensive training in the languages of the major religious traditions of the world, e.g., Arabic, Chinese, Greek, Hebrew, Japanese, Latin, Persian, Sanskrit, Tibetan. Students are encouraged to use the resources of the Jewish Theological Seminary of America and Union Theological Seminary.

Parent Institution. Barnard College is a selective liberal arts college for women, affiliated with Columbia University and integrally related to New York City. Barnard is committed to the fundamental values of the liberal arts and sciences, and the curriculum reflects that commitment. The cultural and social resources of New York and the intellectual resources of Columbia University are as important a part of an undergraduate education at Barnard as the commitment to learning and scholarship that is everywhere apparent in the College environment. Barnard College was among the pioneers in the late 19th century crusade to make higher education available to young women. Today Barnard has a faculty of over 225 and an enrollment of 2,200.

Columbia University traces its history to 1754 when a group of New York citizens was granted a charter by George II for the founding of King's College, dedicated to instruction in "the Learned Languages and the Liberal Arts and Sciences."

Community Environment. Barnard's campus occupies 4 acres of land adjacent to Columbia University, in upper Manhattan, New York City. There are 11 buildings which include dormitories for 1,500 students. New York City, the largest city in the nation, is also its business, entertainment, and industrial capital. This teeming city is considered the greatest center of higher education in the country, and claims the largest library outside the Library of Congress. Its intellectual and cultural opportunities are limitless and virtually impossible to duplicate anywhere. New York Harbor's mile-wide entrance clears more than 26,000 vessels a year which handle 40 percent of the entire foreign trade of the United States.

Religious Denomination. None.

Religious Emphasis. Diverse.

Accreditation. Middle States Association of Colleges and Schools.

Term System. Semester.

Enrollment in Degree Programs in Religion 1984–85. Total 16; women 16.

Degrees in Religion Awarded 1984–85. Bachelor of Arts in Religion 12; women 12.

Faculty for Degree Programs in Religion. Total 9; full-time 5, part-time 4.

Admission Requirements. Proven academic strength and potential for further intellectual growth; high school records; recommendations; SAT and three Achievement tests; consideration given for special abilities and interests. Each applicant is considered in terms of her individual qualities of mind and spirit and her potential for successfully completing four years of study at Barnard.

Tuition and Fees. Tuition $10,112; comprehensive fee $434; housing $2,786 to $3,120; board (19 meals per week) $1,944.

Financial Aid. Grants, loans, and opportunities for part-time employment; participation in federal programs: Pell Grant, the Supplemental Educational Opportunity

Grant program, the National Direct Student Loan program, the Parents Loan for Undergraduate Students, and College Work-Study program; New York State Higher Education Opportunity program.

Housing. Traditional dormitories, suite arrangements, apartments in College-owned buildings adjacent to campus. Spaces available in cooperative exchange with Columbia College for coeducational arrangements; off-campus apartments; independent housing in campus vicinity.

Library Facilities. The Wollman Library has a main collection of more than 155,000 volumes. Special collections include the Barnard Archives; the personal library of Nobel Prize-winning Gabriela Mistral; the Overbury Collection of 3,300 books and manuscripts by and about American women authors; and a strong collection in women's studies, supplemented by the Women's Center resource collection.

Degree Programs

The Bachelor of Arts with a major in Religion requires the satisfactory completion of 120 points of academic work and two terms of physical education; students must fulfill the applicable general education requirements. The major requires completion of 10 courses. At the levels of the introductory and traditional courses, students are expected to gain exposure to both Eastern and Western religions. The majors' colloquium, to be taken in the senior year, and 3 additional points in seminars, colloquia, or guided reading are also required. Majors are required to prepare a senior essay or project in consultation with a member of the department. It is strongly recommended that majors, especially those considering graduate work in religion, pursue the study of the language of one religious tradition (e.g., Arabic, Chinese, Greek, Hebrew, Latin, Sanskrit, etc.) in addition to fulfilling the College language requirement.

Bexley Hall
Colgate Rochester Divinity School
1100 South Goodman Street
Rochester, NY 14620   (716) 271-1320

Administration. Dr. William H. Petersen, Dean.

General Description. Bexley Hall, founded in 1824, united its educational forces in 1968-69 with the Colgate Rochester Divinity School. In 1970 Crozer Theological Seminary joined them and together with the University of Rochester and St. Bernard's Institute, students study together with their Protestant and Catholic counterparts in class and library. The combined divinity schools form the nucleus of an ecumenical center for theological studies. *See:* Colgate Rochester Divinity School.

Canisius College
Religious Studies Department
2001 Main Street
Buffalo, NY 14208   (716) 883-7000

Administration. Rev. James M. Demske, S.J., President; Rev. Benjamin Fiore, S.J., Chairman, Department of Religious Studies.

General Description. The aims of the Department of Religious Studies are: (1) to help develop an inquiring mind in matters of religious import; (2) to provide the student with the methodological tools, both scientific and theological, for the academic study of religion; (3) to aid students to appreciate the religious viewpoints and values within their own communities and in the broader community of mankind. To these ends the Department presents in its courses a scientific and theological study and appreciation of the unique approaches of Roman Catholicism, other confessional Christian churches, Jewish religious thought, and other religions. A major in Religious Studies provides for those who wish to study religion in greater depth.

Parent Institution. Canisius College is a mid-sized largely undergraduate institution, emphasizing liberal arts but with fully-accredited undergraduate and graduate business schools, in the Roman Catholic and Jesuit tradition.

Community Environment. The Canisius College campus of 18 acres is located close to the hub of the city of Buffalo, New York, but convenient to the suburban areas as well. Buffalo (population 463,000) is the second largest city in New York, ranked eleventh as a manufacturing city within the nation, and forms a link to Canada by the Peace Bridge. Buffalo is also a leading inland port.

Religious Denomination. Roman Catholic.

Religious Emphasis. Jesuit.

Accreditation. Middle States Association of Colleges and Schools.

Term System. Semester; summer term.

Degrees in Religion Awarded 1984–85. Bachelor of Arts 4; men 2, women 2.

Faculty for Degree Programs in Religion. Total 18; full-time 11, part-time 7.

Admission Requirements. Secondary school program of studies including 16 units of credit in academic subjects.

Tuition and Fees. Tuition $2,700 per semester (12-15 credit hours), $135 per credit hour for part-time non-matriculating students; board $465 to $715 depending upon meal plan; room $700 to $950; student government tax $20 full-time, $8 part-time; college fee $60 full-time, $4 per credit hour part-time.

Financial Aid. The Office of Student Financial Aid suggests and provides financial assistance in a variety of ways to qualified students who, without aid, would be unable to attend Canisius.

Housing. Student dormitories are available.

Library Facilities. The library collection numbers over

260,000 volumes.

Religious Services/Activities. Daily Eucharist service (Roman Catholic); frequent prayer services and Bible studies (nondenominational Christian); retreats each semester.

Degree Programs

The Bachelor of Arts degree with a major in Religious Studies provides for those who wish to study religion in greater depth. This major program offers courses in five different areas: World Religions, Judeo-Christian Origins, History of Christianity, Christianity in the Modern World, and Systematic Theology.

Special Programs

The Youth Ministry Certificate Program is designed primarily for people seeking to gain specialized knowledge and skills in Youth Ministry. As designed, this program is tailored to the needs of parish youth ministers, coodinators of religious education, school youth ministers and chaplains, high school religion teachers, and prospectve youth ministers. The program is designed so that participants may choose to enroll in the entire program, or select only those courses in which they are most interested.

Cathedral College of the Immaculate Conception
7200 Douglaston Parkway
Douglaston, NY 11362   (718) 631-4600

Administration. Reverend Monsignor James P. Grace, S.T.L., President; Reverend Martin T. Geraghty, S.T.L., Academic Dean.

General Description. Cathedral College of the Immaculate Conception is a liberal arts college for the education of young men for the Catholic Priesthood. This program extends over a period of twelve years, four of which are on the secondary school level, four on the college level, and four on the level of a professional school of theology. The function of the College is to provide the student with the solid training in the liberal arts and sciences required for an educated, mature candidate for graduate theological studies.

In 1914, the Diocese of Brooklyn established its minor seminary under the title Cathedral College of the Immaculate Conception. The first wing of the permanent building of the minor seminary was opened at Washington and Atlantic Avenues in Brooklyn in 1915. In 1926, the ground work for a major seminary was laid by the establishment of the Institute of Philosophy at Huntington, New York. This institution continued to exist as a house of philosophical studies until 1930 when the newly erected Seminary of the Immaculate Conception was completed and opened at Huntington. The traditional six-year arrangement for each division of seminary education, major and minor, continued until 1967. In that year, the entire

operation was divided into three distinct phases of four years each, one for high school, one for college, and one for theological studies. The college program of Cathedral was established as an independent unit offering a complete course of study in the liberal arts on a single campus at Douglaston Parkway, Douglaston, New York. The College is the only institution in the metropolitan area which provides the specialized college portion of the educational program in preparation for the priesthood.

Community Environment. The 28-acre campus of Cathedral College is located midway between the Long Island Expressway and the Grand Central Parkway near the northern shore of Long Island. It is situated in the New York City borough of Queens.

Religious Denomination. Roman Catholic.

Accreditation. Middle States Association of Colleges and Schools.

Term System. Semester; no summer term.

Enrollment in Degree Programs in Religion 1984–85. Total 112; men 112.

Faculty for Degree Programs in Religion. Total 41.

Admission Requirements. Admission to the College is limited to candidates who are sincerely interested in the diocesan priesthood; candidates are accepted from the graduating class of the high school department of the preparatory seminary on recommendation of the high school faculty; applications are accepted on the basis of scholastic ability, conduct, character, and general suitability.

Tuition and Fees. Tuition $3,600 per year; fees $200 per year; room and board $2,000 per year.

Financial Aid. Students are eligible for the New York State Regents Scholarship and Tuition Assistance Program. The College participates in the Federal Student Financial Aid Programs.

Housing. Students reside in campus dormitory facilities.

Library Facilities. The library contains approximately 75,000 volumes, 375 periodicals, and a microform and sound recording collection.

Religious Services/Activities. The college has a complete seminary formation program. Candidates to the priesthood will be called upon to begin preparation for every aspect and function of that sacred office designed for the sanctification and salvation of the human family.

Degree Programs

The Bachelor of Arts curriculum is in three parts: credits prescribed for all students, credits within the student's major, and elective credits. A total of 132 credits is required for the degree. In a program formulated by the student in consultation with his faculty advisors, a choice will be made, preferably by the end of the sophomore year, of one of the following areas of concentration: Philosophy, English, or Psychology.

Christ the King Seminary
Graduate School of Theology

711 Knox Road

P.O. Box 607

East Aurora, NY 14052   (716) 652-8900

Administration. Rev. Kevin E. Mackin, O.F.M., President-Rector; Rev. Paul J.E. Burkhard, Director of Formation/Vice Rector; Sr. Kathleen L. Uhler, Academic Dean.

General Description. Christ the King Seminary is a professional and graduate school of theology whose goals are: (1) primarily to educate and prepare candidates for the priesthood in the Roman Catholic Church, (2) to offer graduate programs in theological studies to men and women who wish to pursue an advanced degree and/or prepare for special ministries, (3) to contribute to the religious enrichment of groups and individuals within the western New York area through the sharing of professional resources, (4) to carry on the educational and theological tradition of the Franciscan Order. The Seminary offers three programs of study: one professional, leading to the degree of Master of Divinity; and two academic, leading to the degrees of Master of Arts in Theology, and Master of Arts in Pastoral Ministry.

Community Environment. Christ the King Seminary is set on 132 acres of landscaped open spaces and native woodlands, near the Village of East Aurora, New York, a small distinctive community known for its symphony orchestra, art galleries, historical and science museums, centers of higher learning, theater district, banking center, ethnic heritage, and sporting clubs. The Seminary is easily accessible by way of the New York State Thruway and the Route 400 Expressway. It is within 30 minutes of the Greater Buffalo International Airport and within convenient travel time of area ski resorts and retreat facilities.

Religious Denomination. Roman Catholic.

Accreditation. Middle States Association of Colleges and Schools; Association of Theological Schools in the United States and Canada.

Term System. Semester.

Enrollment in Degree Programs in Religion 1984–85. Total 140; men 102, women 38. There are 84 seminarians and 56 commuter students.

Degrees in Religion Awarded 1984–85. Master of Divinity (seminarians) 18; men 18. Master of Divinity (commuter students) 3; men 2, women 1. Master of Arts in Pastoral Ministry 2; women 2.

Faculty for Degree Programs in Religion. Total 31; full-time 18, part-time 13.

Admission Requirements. Admission to the Master of Divinity and the Master of Arts programs is open to students preparing for ordination, male and female religious and laity, and clergy engaged in on-going formation. Admission depends on academic background and personal qualifications for entering upon studies for pastoral minis-try or theology.

Tuition and Fees. Tuition $1,450 per semester; room $650 per semester; board $1,100 per semester; fees $50 semester; student activity fee $40 per year; parking fee $10 per year; optional Blue Cross/Blue Shield $250 per year; part-time students $110 per credit hour.

Financial Aid. Types of aid include student loans and scholarships.

Housing. On-campus residence halls are available.

Library Facilities. The library collection numbers 100,-000 volumes. Although primarily a research collection for theology and related areas, the collection contains standard works in other disciplines, especially in philosophy. The Library houses the Monsignor James Bray Collection of 750 volumes dealing with the history of the Niagara Frontier and French Canada.

Religious Services/Activities. The main chapel is central to the campus and at the heart of the Seminary's life. In addition to the main chapel, each residence hall has its own chapel for daily use.

Degree Programs

The Master of Divinity program offers a first professional degree for ministry that seeks to integrate the traditional academic and theological disciplines with a pastoral education in the skills of ministry. Each seminarian is admitted to the program under the sponsorship of a diocese. The program's goals are to educate and prepare candidates for priesthood in the Roman Catholic Church and to develop within the Christian person a competency and identity in pastoral ministry. The requirements include courses in Sacred Scripture; Dogmatic/Sacramental/Liturgical Theology; Moral/Spiritual Theology; Historical Studies; Pastoral Studies; Canon Law; Theological Field Education; and free electives. A Master of Divinity program for commuters is also offered.

The Master of Arts in Theology program offers a first graduate degree in academic theology. This degree has a primary thrust toward theological understanding and secondary thrust toward professional practice. Normally the program requires two full-time academic years. The goals of the program are to provide the theological background to enable students to teach religion at the secondary or college level; to develop a basic competence in the area of theological studies; and to provide a deep, religious basis for life, work, and ministries.

The Master of Arts in Pastoral Ministry program provides a general theological education along with the development of ministerial skills in an area of specialization through supervised internships. Foundational and pastoral theology courses complement the student's ministry and reflection seminars relate theology and ministry. The areas of specialization include Pastoral Associate; Director/Coordinator of Religious Education; Evangelization and the Catechumenate; Spiritual Director; Director/Coordinator, Justice and Peace Ministries; Hospital Chaplaincy; Prison Chaplaincy; Coordinator of Youth

Ministry; Sacramental Preparation.

Special Programs

A Master of Divinity Degree for Priests Program permits any ordained priest to acquire a fully accredited degree. It is because of the priest's basic theological education and pastoral experience that this option has been made available. The program consists of courses, projects, theological updating, and pastoral reflection.

Colgate Rochester Divinity School
1100 South Goodman Street
Rochester, NY 14620   (716) 271-1320

Administration. Dr. Larry L. Greenfield, President; Dr. Leonard I. Sweet, Provost; Dr. William H. Petersen, Dean of Bexley Hall; Dr. Kenneth L. Smith, Dean of Crozer Theological Seminary.

General Description. Colgate Rochester Divinity School is a privately-supported, coeducational, graduate theological seminary. It was established in 1817 and with Bexley Hall, founded in 1824, united their educational forces in 1968-69 and were joined by Crozer Theological Seminary in 1970. Together with the University of Rochester, with which Colgate Rochester is affiliated, and St. Bernard's Institute, students study together with their Protestant and Catholic counterparts in class and library. The combined divinity schools form the nucleus of an ecumenical center for theological studies.

The primary mission of the combined schools is the preparation of persons for the ministries of all churches committed to Jesus Christ. It continues its historic commitment to the preparation of leaders for the American Baptist Churches and the Episcopal Church. The schools foster an educational program which builds upon the richness of diverse racial, ethnic, and cultural groups, including men and women who together constitute the total Church.

The Divinity School is a member of the Rochester Area Colleges, a consortium of private and public institutions that encourages and enables institutional cooperation as well as resource and program sharing. Membership also includes Rochester Institute of Technology, Baptist-related Keuka College, Episcopal-related Hobart and William Smith Colleges, St. John Fischer College, Nazareth College, Alfred University, the State University campuses of Brockport and Geneseo, Empire State College, Roberts Wesleyan College, and the University of Rochester.

Ecclesiastically the school maintains its historic relationships with the American Baptist Churches in the U.S.A. and the Protestant Episcopal Church. Actual student enrollment includes Baptist and Episcopal students as well as members of the Presbyterian, United Methodist, Roman Catholic, United Church of Christ, and Congregational communions, to name but a few of the more than 20 denominational affiliations maintained by the student body.

Degrees offered are Master of Divinity, Master of Arts, and Doctor of Ministry. In addition, the School offers other academic programs which serve to provide educational resources for clergy and laity of the churches and the wider public.

Community Environment. Rochester, New York and the surrounding suburbs and villages constitute a population of three quarters of a million people, creating the ambience of a progressive yet manageable metropolis, including an impressive array of cultural activities. Just as the campus provides an environment conducive to creating a cohesive unit, the city's urban agenda demands that the seminary students reach out and deal with the realities that confront society and the Church throughout the nation. The Seminary's campus covers 24 acres atop a hill that dominates the skyline at the southern edge of the city of Rochester.

Religious Denomination. American Baptist Churches in the U.S.A. and the Protestant Episcopal Church.

Religious Emphasis. Interdenominational.

Accreditation. Association of Theological Schools in the United States and Canada.

Term System. Semester.

Faculty for Degree Programs in Religion. Total 34; full-time 21, part-time 13 visiting and adjunct faculty. In addition, St. Bernard's faculty 3 full-time, 7 part-time.

Admission Requirements. Graduation from an accredited college with a minimum cumulative grade point average of 2.5; physical and emotional health, maturity of character and purpose; religious commitment appropriate to the applicant's vocational objectives. Applicants to the Doctor of Ministry program must hold the Master of Divinity degree.

Tuition and Fees. Tuition full-time $1,850 per semester; matriculation fee $20; student activities fee $6; graduation fee $65; boarding fee $615; student health fee (full-time students, standard coverage) $188; dormitory room $630.

Financial Aid. The Student Financial Aid program of the School is designed to provide assistance to students in meeting the gap between projected income and expenses. The School extends financial assistance in the form of grants, loans, scholarships, and employment.

Housing. Dormitory housing and apartments are available on campus.

Library Facilities. The library resources gathered on the Divinity School campus are in excess of 325,000 volumes representing a variety of Christian traditions and a broad spectrum of theological interests. The Ambrose Swasey Collections number 205,000 volumes to which are added the 45,000 volumes of the St. Bernard's Institute and the 75,000 volumes of the American Baptist Historical Society.

Religious Services/Activities. All-School Worship takes place Monday through Thursday of each week. Other worship and meditational opportunities are available to members of the community throughout the day, including

Morning Prayer, Evensong, and lectionary studies. The Worship and Spiritual Life Committee of the School's Senate coordinates and plans the worship life of the school.

Degree Programs

The Master of Divinity program is designed to prepare persons for leadership and the ministries of the church. It is a three-year course of study and requires the completion of 24 courses (96 units). The curriculum incorporates principles of course balance among the four academic divisions (Biblical Studies, Historical Studies, Theological Studies, and Ministry Studies), freedom of electives, independent study, and specialization.

The Master of Arts program is designed for persons interested in educational enrichment through studies in religion at the Master's level within the context of a theological school, but who do not intend to be ordained to the ministry. The curriculum is a two-year period of study and requires the successful completion of 16 courses (64 units). All candidates must submit a thesis or project (which counts for two course credits toward the required 16) and pass an oral or written examination.

The Doctor of Ministry program is designed to enable the candidate to undertake study and training in an area of specialization related to the professional practice of ministry. Candidates undertake a minimum of one year of study (twelve months) which may be extended over a period not to exceed four years from the date of matriculation. All candidates must also take part in a Doctor of Ministry colloquium which is interdivisional and interdisciplinary. Programs of study include an individualized program and a Family Ministries program. A minimum of 8 courses (32 units) is required.

Special Programs

An Alternate Education Program is designed specifically to serve practicing Black and Hispanic clergy who have had little opportunity for undergraduate or graduate theological education. Emphasis is placed on institutional administration, counseling, educational programming, and community organization.

Colgate University
Department of Philosophy and Religion
Hamilton, NY 13346   (315) 824-1000

Administration. Jerome Balmuth, Chairman of the Department of Philosophy and Religion.

General Description. Courses offered by the Department of Philosophy and Religion are methodological, historical and literary, and include others dealing systematically with ethical, theological, and philosophical issues and their relation to every day problems. The concentration programs provide work in the history and methods of philosophical and theological inquiry as the preparation

for all of the professions as well as for graduate study in philosophy, intellectual history, and theology.

Parent Institution. Colgate University is a privately supported coeducational liberal arts college founded in 1819 by the Baptist Education Society. Originally the institution admitted only students preparing for the ministry. In 1928, the theological seminary merged with its Rochester counterpart to form the Colgate Rochester Divinity School and Colgate became an independent college of the liberal arts.

Community Environment. The 1400-acre campus is in Hamilton, a city with a population of 2,000. It lies 30 miles south of Utica and 38 miles southeast of Syracuse, New York.

Religious Denomination. Nondenominational.

Accreditation. Middle States Association of Colleges and Schools.

Term System. Semester (4-1-4 plan).

Faculty for Degree Programs in Religion. Total 19.

Admission Requirements. Graduation from an accredited high school with rank in the upper 20 percent; SAT or ACT; three achievement tests required.

Tuition and Fees. Tuition $9,700 per year; student activities fee $90; room $1,720; board $1,770.

Financial Aid. Scholarships, work opportunities, and loan funds are available to students, selected on the basis of academic qualifications, total performance, and character.

Housing. University residence halls are available on campus.

Library Facilities. The Colgate University Libraries have holdings of over 390,000 volumes.

Religious Services/Activities. The University Chaplain serves as adviser to the student religious organizations and is in charge of the services of the University Church. Activities of the Colgate Jewish Union, the Roman Catholic Community at Colgate (Newman), the University Church, as well as the churches of Hamilton are available to all students.

Degree Programs

The Department of Philosophy and Religion offers three concentration programs: Philosophy, Religion, and a combined program in Philosophy and Religion. The requirements for the concentration in Religion are eight courses in religion including: Introduction to Religion, one course selected from those dealing with the Hebrew Scriptures/Old Testament or New Testament, and one course dealing with a religious tradition that is neither Jewish nor Christian; at least one seminar normally taken in the senior year. The Bachelor degree is awarded.

Columbia University
Department of Religion
617 Kent Hall
116th Street and Amsterdam Avenue
New York, NY 10027   (212) 280-3218

Administration. Professor Robert Somerville, Chair, Department of Religion.

General Description. The Graduate Program in Religion at Columbia University is a cooperative program between the Department of Religion and Union Theological Seminary for the study of the history, the literature, the theory, and the functions of religion in its various forms within different societies and cultures. A distinctive feature of this program is the opportunity for students not only to gain advanced training in specific fields of religious studies, but also to acquire a basic knowledge of the world's major religious traditions and of the principal methods and theories employed in the study of religion. Such knowledge is useful as preparation for teaching courses of broad scope and as a background for the study of more limited areas employing selected methods. In addition to their work in special fields students must complete three written general examinations covering (1) theory and methods for the study of religion, (2) major Eastern and (3) major Western religious traditions.

Parent Institution. Founded by the vestrymen of Trinity Church after receiving a royal charter in 1754 from George II, Columbia University is now definitely "Ivy League" but is unique among those institutions by being located in the City of New York.

Community Environment. The campus of Columbia University, designed by McKim, Mead, and White, is in the Morningside Heights neighborhood of Manhattan, in the Upper West Side. Nearby are the Union Theological Seminary and the Jewish Theological Seminary. The real campus can truly be said to be the entire City and there is a wealth of cultural opportunities available to students who study here.

Religious Denomination. None.

Accreditation. Middle States Association of Colleges and Schools.

Term System. Semester.

Enrollment in Degree Programs in Religion 1984–85. Total 68; men 37, women 31.

Faculty for Degree Programs in Religion. Total 27; full-time 16, part-time 11.

Admission Requirements. The student must hold a bachelor's degree with a record that indicates capacity for graduate work of high quality. Preparation should include a reading knowledge of French or German and such additional language study as may be required for work in the proposed area of specialization. There should be extensive work in the liberal arts, including history, literature, and philosophy, as well as in the social sciences if the proposed area of concentration is a social-scientific approach to the study of religion.

Tuition and Fees. Residence Unit $5,140; Half Residence Unit (three or fewer courses) $2,785; Quarter Residence Unit for designated part-time M.A. programs only (two or fewer courses) $1,608; Extended Residence $1,430 per term; matriculation and facilities $430 per term; on-campus housing ranges from $1,910 to $3,360 depending on accommodations.

Financial Aid. A comprehensive program is offered including fellowships and assistantships.

Housing. The University provides limited housing for men and women. An Off-Campus Registry helps students to find rooms or apartments in rental properties not owned or operated by Columbia University.

Library Facilities. The library resources at Columbia, consisting of more than 5,375,000 volumes, 2,956,000 microform pieces, and 20 million manuscript pieces, are organized into a system of libraries designed to serve the instructional and research needs of the University. In addition to the libraries of Columbia University, Union Theological Seminary, and the Jewish Theological Seminary of America, there are numerous collections of books and manuscripts in the archives of the several church headquarters in the city, in the library of the New York Historical Society, and in the New York Public Library.

Religious Services/Activities. Frequent religious services are held both on and off campus.

Degree Programs

The Master of Arts degree in Religion is a program of study to be arranged individually with a faculty adviser who is designated by the departmental Director of Graduate Studies. Courses in the following categories are available: History and Theory of Religion (General); Asian Religions (Indian and Tibetan, Chinese, Japanese, Comparative Asian); Western Religions (Ancient Near Eastern, Iranian, Greco-Roman, Armenian; Judaism; Christianity; Islam; Comparative Western); Culture, Society, and Religion (Philosophy of Religion, Anthropology of Religion, Religion and Society, Issues in Religion and Culture); Guided Reading and Research.

The Master of Philosophy degree is planned in consultation with a faculty adviser in the student's field of specialization. Courses available include the categories listed above. Students are required to take the Colloquium on Comparative Religion and are encouraged to take the colloquium in their second or third year.

The Doctor of Philosophy degree requires the completion of the Master of Philosophy degree, an oral examination on a research proposal for a dissertation, and the writing and defense of a dissertation.

Concordia College

171 White Plains Road
Bronxville, NY 10708   (914) 337-9300

Administration. Ralph C. Schultz, President.

General Description. Concordia College is a four-year, coeducational liberal arts college sponsored by The Lutheran Church-Missouri Synod. It was founded in 1881. The College is dedicated to serving both the laity and the professional church worker. The Associate and the Bachelor's degree are awarded.

Community Environment. The 30-acre campus is located in Bronxville, 15 miles north of New York City.

Religious Denomination. The Lutheran Church-Missouri Synod.

Accreditation. Middle States Association of Colleges and Schools.

Term System. Semester.

Admission Requirements. Graduation from an accredited high school or equivalent; SAT or ACT.

Tuition and Fees. Tuition $3,955 per year; dining hall fee $1,685; room $1,260; facilities use $560; student services fee $210; capital use fee $60.

Financial Aid. The total amount of aid will vary according to individual circumstances but the cumulative amount allocated for Lutheran Church-Missouri Synod membership and curriculum grants and merit scholarships will not exceed the cost of tuition.

Housing. All students whose homes or legal residences are not within a reasonable commuting distance live in college residence halls.

Library Facilities. The Scheele Memorial Library contains over 40,000 volumes.

Religious Services/Activities. The tenets of the Christian faith and the teachings of the Lutheran Church are the foundation and guiding principles for campus activities.

Degree Programs

The Division of History, Religion, and Languages offers the major in the Judeo-Christian Heritage (Religious Studies) leading to the Bachelor of Arts degree. It requires the completion of 30 credits in the major field. A four-year pre-seminary program requires the fulfillment of the basic curriculum requirements for the Bachelor of Arts majors and the pre-seminary concentration.

The Division of Literature and Music offers a Bachelor of Arts degree program with a major in Church Music.

Crozer Theological Seminary
Colgate Rochester Divinity School

1100 South Goodman Street
Rochester, NY 14620   (716) 271-1320

Administration. Dr. Kenneth L. Smith, Dean.

General Description. Crozer Theological Seminary joined with the Colgate Rochester Divinity School in

1970. Together with the University of Rochester, Bexley Hall, and St. Bernard's Institute, students study together with their Protestant and Catholic counterparts in class and library. The combined divinity schools form the nucleus of an ecumenical center for theological studies. *See:* Colgate Rochester Divinity School.

Dominican College

10 Western Highway
Orangeburg, NY 10962   (914) 357-7800

Administration. Sr. Mary Eileen O'Brien, President.

General Description. Dominican College is an independent four-year liberal arts college for men and women. It was chartered in 1952 as a three-year college offering a teacher preparation program for women religious. In 1957 the College was opened to lay students. The College grants the Bachelor degree. The Humanities Concentration is designed to build on the general education curriculum, providing direction and focus for students interested in pursuing a broad-based study of the humanities. A joint concentration in Philosophy and Religion is offered.

Community Environment. The campus is located in Rockland County, 17 miles north of New York City and 3 miles north of Bergen County, New Jersey.

Religious Denomination. Roman Catholic.

Accreditation. Middle States Association of Colleges and Schools.

Term System. Semester.

Admission Requirements. Graduation from an accredited high school with 16 academic units; SAT.

Tuition and Fees. Tuition $3,150 per year; room and board $2,800; student fees $170.

Financial Aid. Various types of assistance are available.

Housing. Dominican's Residence Center is located 1½ miles south of the campus on Western Highway.

Library Facilities. The library contains over 85,000 volumes.

Religious Services/Activities. The Director of Campus Ministry plans activities on campus such as liturgies, seders, retreats, lectures, discussions, and other religious experiences.

Degree Programs

Religious Studies offers an academic, ecumenical approach to the significant religious experience of the principal religious traditions of mankind in order to introduce the undergradaute to the content and methods in the fields of religion and theology. This is accomplished by presenting in the courses the outstanding events, explanations, and values of major religious faiths as they have been proposed by great authors and founders and as they have interacted with changing cultures. A joint specialization in Philosophy and Religion is available in the Humanities concentration.

Fordham University
Graduate School of Religion and Religious
   Education
Bronx, NY 10458   (212) 579-2539

Administration. Rev. Vincent M. Novak, S.J., Dean.

General Description. In cooperation with all denominations, the Graduate School of Religion seeks to serve religion's and religious education's research needs. While it is thus committed to help chart future directions, it also confronts the contemporary problems of church communities. Students of all religious backgrounds are welcome, whether as matriculated degree students or as visiting non-matriculates from other institutions. Candidates for degrees come from all over the United States and Canada, and from many foreign countries.

Parent Institution. Fordham is a University in the Jesuit tradition. It is governed by a self-perpetuating, independent Board of Trustees under a charter granted in 1846 by the New York State Legislature. For more than a century and a quarter, Fordham University has served American society by offering instruction in the liberal arts and selected professional areas, on both the undergraduate and graduate levels. What distinguishes Fordham from other universities is the complex of academic specialties and traditions, which is the result of its heritage and its growth in New York City.

Community Environment. The Rose Hill Campus of Fordham University is located in the Bronx, one of five boroughs in the city of New York, just north of the island of Manhattan. The Lincoln Center Campus is located in mid-Manhattan.

Religious Denomination. Fordham University was established under Roman Catholic auspices.

Accreditation. Middle States Association of Colleges and Schools. Member of: Association of American Colleges; Association of Jesuit Colleges and Universities.

Term System. Semester; 2 summer sessions.

Enrollment in Degree Programs in Religion 1984–85. Total 154; men 36, women 118.

Degrees in Religion Awarded 1984–85. Master of Arts 31; men 7, women 24. Master of Science 12; men 3, women 9. Professional Diploma 7; women 7.

Faculty for Degree Programs in Religion. Total 12; full-time 8, part-time 4.

Admission Requirements. Bachelor's degree and a total of 20 credits in theology and philosophy or their equivalent.

Tuition and Fees. Tuition $205 per credit.

Financial Aid. The University provides a generous number of work scholarships, both full and partial, according to need. Preference is given to full-time students in the Master of Arts program and those serving underprivileged communities. Several graduate assistantships with stipend are available; also outside funding for full tuition in return for service upon completion of degree at Catholic centers

in American rural areas.

Housing. Off-campus housing (apartment building with single and double rooms) reserved exclusively for degree candidates in the School.

Library Facilities. The combined libraries of the University contain over 1,200,000 bound volumes and more than 4,800 periodicals and serials. In addition to the University libraries, graduate students may use the New York Public Library System and many of the 750 special libraries in the New York metropolitan area.

Religious Services/Activities. Regular and frequent availability of religious services, especially Roman Catholic.

Degree Programs

The Master of Arts program offers core areas of concentration in Parish/Pastoral Ministry and Church Leadership; Spirituality and Spiritual/Direction; Children's Education and Family Ministry; Adolescent Religious Development; Ministry with Adults; Generalist. Candidates for the degree must complete 36 credits of course work. As a major requirement, candidates must produce a serious research work exploring a significant theological-pastoral theme.

The Master of Science program offers core concentration in the same areas as above. Candidates must complete 36 credits of course work. No major research papers are required, but all individual course requirements must be fulfilled as well as a major project of significant value.

Special Programs

The Professional Diploma in Religion/Religious Education is intended to provide advanced training beyond the Master's level. It would serve leadership personnel in the work of religion and religious education in the churches' schools and parishes, as well as in other forms and aspects of pastoral ministry. Of the thirty credits required for this advanced diploma, eighteen must be taken within the Graduate School of Religion and Religious Education, with the option of six from outside institutions or as many as twelve from other departments and schools of Fordham University.

The Graduate School of Religion and Religious Education collaborates with the Graduate School of Education in the latter School's Ph.D. program in Administration and Supervision designed to train church and school leaders for administrative responsibilities.

General Theological Seminary
175 Ninth Avenue
New York, NY 10011   (212) 243-2150

Administration. The Very Rev. James C. Fenhagen, Dean; The Rev. Boyce M. Bennett, Jr., Sub-Dean for Academic Affairs.

General Description. This privately-supported, coeducational graduate theological seminary was established in 1817 and was the first institution in the Anglican Communion devoted exclusively to theological education. The basic degree program featured at General Theological Seminary is the Master of Divinity which prepares the student for ordination in the Episcopal Church. The curriculum for this degree is designed to enable the Seminary to make effective use of field placements and specialized studies, and to deal with the issues and methodologies constantly coming to the fore in the modern world, while at the same time maintaining the Seminary's historic commitment to a rigorous grounding in the foundations of the Christian tradition. Also offered are the degrees Master of Arts, Master of Arts in Spiritual Direction, Master of Sacred Theology, Master of Sacred Theology in Spiritual Direction, and Doctor of Theology.

The Seminary, together with the Department of Urban Affairs at Hunter College, City University of New York, offers two joint degrees in Urban Studies: the Master of Sacred Theology/Master of Science in Urban Studies and the Master of Divinity/Master of Science in Urban Studies.

Community Environment. General Theological Seminary is located in the heart of Manhattan, New York City, in Chelsea Square. The buildings include a chapel, a library, administrative offices, classrooms, and housing for faculty and students. New York City, the largest city in the nation, is also its business, entertainment, and industrial capital. This teeming city is considered the greatest center of higher education in the country, and claims the largest library outside the Library of Congress.

Religious Denomination. Episcopal.

Religious Emphasis. Diverse Eucharistic.

Accreditation. Middle States Association of Colleges and Schools; Association of Theological Schools in the United States and Canada.

Term System. Semester.

Enrollment in Degree Programs in Religion 1984–85. Total 123; men 75, women 48.

Degrees in Religion Awarded 1984–85. Master of Divinity 32; men 23, women 9. Master of Sacred Theology 11; men 10, women 1. Doctor of Theology 1; women 1.

Faculty for Degree Programs in Religion. Total 26; full-time 18, part-time 8.

Admission Requirements. Baccalaureate degree; GRE; recommendation from diocese helpful.

Tuition and Fees. Tuition $5,800 per year; room/apartment $150 to $565 per month; board $1,250 to $1,500.

Financial Aid. Assistance is need-based.

Housing. Housing is normally available on campus for all students and families.

Library Facilities. The library houses over 200,000 volumes with special collections of Bibles, prayerbooks, and liturgical documents.

Religious Services/Activities. Daily Offices and Eucharists; retreats are held annually.

Degree Programs

The basic program of the Seminary is a three-year course leading to the degree of Master of Divinity. It is designed to equip students for leadership in the Christian ministry, particularly for ordination in the Episcopal Church. The Integrative Foundations Curriculum consists of a series of required basic (foundation) courses and a broad distribution of electives. A minimum of 74 hours of credit with an average of not less than C minus is required for graduation.

The Master of Arts program is offered to a limited number of lay persons who are interested in the study of theology but who do not seek training for ordination. The program offers the student a solid foundation in Biblical Studies, Church History and Theology, combined with an opportunity to explore in some depth one of these areas or to develop an emphasis in Liturgical Studies, Christian Spirituality, or Anglican Studies. A minimum of 40 hours of credit is required, 21 of which are in Foundations courses. The Master of Arts in Spiritual Direction is a first theological degree especially designed for lay-people and the program allows for certain specializations of which Spiritual Direction is one. The program requires successful completion of 40 units of credit including the required foundation courses.

The Master of Sacred Theology program is designed to enable qualified candidates to attain special competence in some particular area of theological study or in some aspect of the practice of ministry. The program is pursued with a focus on research and with concentration on a special area or field of theological study; or it may be pursued as a professional study with a focus on some aspect of the practice of ministry. The fields or areas of study include Bible (Old and New Testament), Church History, Theology (both historical and systematic), Liturgical Studies, Ascetical and Moral Theology, Christian Ethics, and Anglican Studies.

The Master of Sacred Theology in Spiritual Direction is also offered. The academic emphasis is on subjects related to spirituality and spiritual direction, especially as they have been understood and interpreted within the Anglican tradition.

The degree Master of Sacred Theology/Master of Science in Urban Studies and the degree Master of Divinity/Master of Science in Urban Studies are joint degrees offered in conjunction with Hunter College. The overall goal of the program is to enable the theological student to deal critically and imaginatively with the urban environment by providing skills and competence aimed at equipping the student for participation in changing and shaping parts of that environment as his/her ministry.

The Doctor of Theology program is designed to prepare men and women for careers of leadership in theological teaching, research and inquiry, whether in institutions of higher learning or in positions of pastoral responsibility in the church. The degree may be pursued in the following fields of study: History of the English Church, History of the Episcopal Church in the USA, Liturgical Studies, New Testament, Moral and Ascetical Theology, Anglican Theology. The candidate must complete 12 units of doctoral study, pass comprehensive examinations in the areas of concentration, and submit and successfully defend a thesis.

Hartwick College
Department of Philosophy and Religion
Oneonta, NY 13820   (607) 432-4200

Administration. Dr. Philip S. Wilder, Jr., President; Dr. Bryant L. Cureton, Vice President and Dean of the College; Dr. Robert E. Mansbach, Chair, Department of Philosophy and Religion.

General Description. The Department of Philosophy and Religion has 6 majors (5 in philosophy, 1 in religion at present). There are several minors in the philosophy of religion. Although the number of religion majors fluctuates between one and five, the courses offered are well attended; many non-majors take religion courses.

Parent Institution. Hartwick College was founded in 1797 under the will of John Christopher Hartwick, a Lutheran missionary who ministered to the Indians of the Susquehanna Valley region. The College became a four-year coeducational liberal arts college under its present charter in 1928. Students now may select courses from 30 areas offered by 19 departments. The Bachelor of Arts and Bachelor of Science degrees are awarded.

Community Environment. Oneonta, New York is a city of about 17,500 people in the northwestern foothills of the Catskill Mountains. It is on Interstate 88, about 75 miles from Albany and 60 miles from Binghamton. The College is located on Oyaron Hill and commands an impressive view of the city and some 20 miles of the Susquehanna Valley. There are 17 buildings on the 375-acre campus, as well as several recreational areas, athletic fields, and tennis courts.

Religious Denomination. Nondenominational.

Accreditation. Middle States Association of Colleges and Schools.

Term System. Semester; January Term.

Degrees in Religion Awarded 1984–85. Bachelor of Arts 1; women 1.

Faculty for Degree Programs in Religion. Total 5; full-time 5.

Admission Requirements. The framework of recommended courses of secondary school study for applicants includes 4 units of English, 2 units of modern or classical language, 3 units of mathematics, 2 units of science, and 2 units in history. A prospective student's course of study and demonstrated achievement are the primary focus in the selection process. This information is supplemented qualitatively by the results of the SAT or ACT, required of all candidates for admission. Applicants are encouraged

to supplement the formal application with any additional materials which will reflect special talents and interests. An interview in the Office of Admissions, while not required, is strongly recommended.

Tuition and Fees. Tuition $7,975 per academic year; room $1,300; board $1,625; student activity fee $75.

Financial Aid. Financial assistance is of two types: need based financial aid and non-need based financial aid. Grants, loans, scholarships, and work-study programs are available.

Housing. A variety of different residence situations are provided.

Library Facilities. The College Library contains 188,000 volumes and extensive microfilm holdings. It subscribes to more than 950 periodicals. Special collections include the North American Indian Collection, the Winston Churchill collection of first editions of his works, the John Burroughs Collection, the James Fenimore Cooper collection of first editions written by and about him, and the personal library of John Christopher Hartwick.

Religious Services/Activities. The religious life at Hartwick College is planned to provide an environment in which students may develop as individuals and as social beings with knowledge of and concern for their fellows. The Oneonta Campus Ministry Committee, a group of full-time and part-time campus ministers representing various denominations in the Oneonta area, conducts special seminars, weekend retreats, and discussion groups on the campus. On-campus worship services are conducted weekly in the Shineman Chapel by the Roman Catholic Collegiate Community and the Hartwick Ecumenical Protestant Community. Jewish High Holy Days services are conducted on campus by the Congregation of Oneonta's Temple Beth-El.

Degree Programs

The Bachelor of Arts degree with a major in Religion requires, in addition to the general requirements, nine courses in religion, including one term of individual study. A student who desires to major in religion must work out a program of studies with an advisor in the department. The religion curriculum covers three general areas: (1) the history and thought of the Judeo-Christian tradition; (2) the religious traditions of the non-Western world; and (3) contemporary religious expression.

Hebrew Union College - Jewish Institute of Religion, New York
One West 4th Street
New York, NY 10012   (212) 674-5300

Administration. Dr. Alfred Gottschalk, Rabbi, President (Office in Cincinnati). In New York: Dr. Paul M. Steinberg, Rabbi, Dean; Dr. Lawrence W. Raphael, Rabbi, Associate Dean; Dr. Lawrence A. Hoffman, Rabbi, Director, School of Sacred Music; Kerry M. Olitzky, Rabbi, Director, School of Education.

General Description. The Rabbinic School: The Rabbinic School offers a 5-year program of full-time graduate study leading to the Master of Arts degree and ordination. Students admitted to the rabbinic program are required to spend their first academic year in Israel. Upon completion of the first year of study in Jerusalem, students return to one of the 3 American campuses (New York, Los Angeles, Cincinnati) to which they were assigned upon admission. The Los Angeles School offers only the 2nd and 3rd years of the rabbinic program; students transfer to either Cincinnati or New York for their final 2 years of study. The second through fifth year program is divided between required and elective courses in various areas of specialization. The student's selection of electives and rabbinic thesis topic determines the area of specialization.

Graduate Programs offer doctoral and master's degrees. The doctoral programs lead through advanced and specialized studies to advanced scholarship in Judaic and cognate subjects. New York offers the Doctor of Hebrew Letters.

The School of Sacred Music in New York trains cantors and synagogue music directors; it awards the degree Master of Sacred Music. The School emphasizes intensive training for the position of cantor. On completion of the 4-year curriculum, a student is invested and commissioned as a cantor and receives a diploma as cantor and the degree. The School of Sacred Music has established a Cantor Certification Program to establish standards among cantors. The Board on Cantor Certification periodically reviews applicants for cantor certification.

The School of Education in New York offers a program leading to the degree Master of Arts with specialization in religious education. Adult courses on a graduate level are offered leading to the Judaic Studies Certificate. The School also sponsors and supervises an extensive outreach program offering accredited courses at host congregations throughout the greater New York area.

Parent Institution. Hebrew Union College - Jewish Institute of Religion is the institution of higher learning in American Reform Judaism. It is dedicated to the study of Judaism and related areas in the spirit of free inquiry. Nothing in the Jewish or general past or present is alien to its interest. Sensitive to the challenge imposed by a world of change, it believes that Jewish ideas and values, along with the contribution of other religions and civilizations are meaningful to the building of the future. The New York school and its sister institutions in Cincinnati, Jerusalem, and Los Angeles comprise the 4-campus complex of Hebrew Union College - Jewish Institute of Religion. It is under the patronage of Reform Judaism's Union of American Hebrew Congregations.

Hebrew Union College was founded in 1875 in Cincinnati, the first institution of Jewish higher learning in America. Its founder was Rabbi Isaac Mayer Wise, the architect of American Reform Judaism, who had established the Union of American Hebrew Congregations two

years earlier. In 1922, Rabbi Stephen S. Wise established the Jewish Institute of Religion in New York. The similar operation of the two schools led to their merger in 1950. A third center was opened in Los Angeles in 1954, and a fourth branch was established in Jerusalem, Israel, in 1963. (See also under entries in Cincinnati and Los Angeles.)

Hebrew Union College is affiliated with the University of Cincinnati, the Greater Cincinnati Consortium of Colleges and Universities, the University of Southern California, Washington University in St. Louis, New York University, the University of Pittsburgh, and the Hebrew University in Jerusalem. These associations provide variously for cross-registration privileges, the use of libraries and other facilities, joint course offerings, and cooperative degrees.

Community Environment. The New York campus (Brookdale Center) is situated on West Fourth Street, New York City, adjacent to New York University in Greenwich Village. It contains the Minnie Petrie Synagogue, the Backman Conference Center, the Rudin-Davidson Lounge, the Joseph Exhibition Room, the Petrie Great Hall, the Klau Library, the Jack A. Goldfarb Administrative Center, and the Rabbi Bernard Heller Educational Center. Also included at the New York School are the Talve Music Center, the Obermayer Educational Resource Center, the Chaim and Rivka Heller Center for American Jewish Archives and Periodicals, the Esther A. and Joseph Klingenstein Rare Book Room, the Karpus Music Listening Area, the Sisterhood Reading Room, and the Bieber Lounge.

Religious Denomination. Jewish.

Religious Emphasis. Reform.

Accreditation. Middle States Association of Colleges and Schools; North Central Association of Colleges and Schools; Western Association of Schools and Colleges.

Term System. Semester; special summer programs.

Enrollment in Degree Programs in Religion 1984–85. Total 346; men 190, women 156.

Degrees in Religion Awarded 1984–85. Doctor of Philosophy (Ph.D.) 5; men 5. Doctor of Hebrew Literature 2; men 2. Master of Arts in Hebrew Literature 40; men 27, women 13. Master of Sacred Music and Investiture as a Cantor 13; men 5, women 8. Invested as Rabbis 32; men 20, women 12. Master of Arts in Jewish Communal Service 23; men 7, women 16. Master of Arts in Education 9; men 3, women 6.

Faculty for Degree Programs in Religion. Total 150; full-time 70, part-time 80.

Admission Requirements. Bachelor of Arts degree or its equivalent from an accredited university or college; Graduate Record Examination; interview with the admissions committee; psychological testing.

Tuition and Fees. Tuition $5,100.

Financial Aid. Whenever possible, financial aid is awarded as a combination of scholarship assistance and interest-free loan. More than 50 percent of all full-time students receive financial aid.

Housing. Students are assisted in finding appropriate housing in the private sector.

Library Facilities. The Klau Library contains more than 115,000 volumes. Its collection of modern Hebrew literature is especially rich. The library also houses a branch of the microfilm collections of the American Jewish Archives and of the American Jewish Periodical Center. The library and other cultural and educational facilities of New York University are also available to students and faculty.

Religious Services/Activities. Regular religious services, conducted by students and/or faculty, are held in the Minnie Petrie Synagogue.

Degree Programs

The Rabbinic School offers a five-year program leading to the Master of Arts degree and ordination. Students admitted to the rabbinic program are required to spend their first academic year in Israel. Upon the completion of the first year of study in Jerusalem, students return to Cincinnati to commence the four-year program which is divided between a required core program and elective courses in various areas of specialization. The student's selection of electives and rabbinic thesis topic determines the area of specialization. During the first two years, a student takes a total of 22 courses. Upon earning credit for the 22 courses, the student is awarded the Master of Arts in Hebrew Letters. A total of 40 course units is necessary to complete the credit requirements for ordination. Each student must serve for at least one year as the student-rabbi of a congregation or its approved equivalent. Rabbinic students are responsible for a morning sermon presentation during the regularly scheduled religious services.

The Master of Sacred Music degree requires completion of a four-year program. Areas of study include conducting, synagogue prayer modes and harmonization of traditional melodies, *Nusah* and *Chazanut,* cantillation, bibliography of synagogue choral literature, and synagogue practicum and cantorial ceremonials.

The School of Education offers a graduate program leading to the Master of Arts with specialization in Religious Education. Programs of study are planned to meet the individual needs and interests of the students. Thirty-two credits are required as well as supervised field work.

Special Programs

Adult courses on a graduate level are offered leading to the Judaic Studies Certificate. The School of Education also sponsors and supervises an extensive outreach program offering accredited courses at host congregations throughout the greater New York area.

In cooperation with the Emanu-El Midtown YM-YWHA, older adults have an opportunity to study Judaica in courses led by members of the faculty and qualified graduate students. An additional part of the program, "Sunday Afternoon at the College," offers a series of lectures and concerts.

Houghton College
Division of Religion and Philosophy
Houghton, NY 14744   (716) 567-2211

Administration. Dr. Daniel R. Chamberlain, President; Dr. Frederick D. Shannon, Vice President and Dean of the College; Dr. Carl Schultz, Chairman, Division of Religion and Philosophy.

General Description. Religious studies are an integral part of the liberal arts curriculum at Houghton College. All students are required to take 10 hours of religion courses. Majors are offered in Bible, Religion, Philosophy, and Christian Education. A ministerial curriculum is available as well as several preseminary curricula which combine the liberal arts and religious studies.

Parent Institution. Houghton College may well be described as a small college which cherishes its private tradition, its church relationship, its rural location, its independence, and its distinctive mission. According to research which used the College and University Environment Scales (CUES), the College emphasizes scholarship and the pursuit of knowledge more so than do many colleges and universities. Also, there is a strong sense of community among the students and others who comprise the college family, and the College is characterized by a strong climate of propriety. Houghton traces its existence to 1883, when it was founded as a seminary (high school) by the Wesleyan Methodist Church of America (now the Wesleyan Church). It now offers 800 different courses in 32 major fields. The Associate and Bachelor degrees are granted.

Community Environment. Houghton is a small rural community in southwestern New York State, 65 miles southeast of Buffalo and 60 miles south of Rochester. It is near Letchworth State Park which affords good fishing, hunting, and skiing.

Religious Denomination. Wesleyan Church.

Religious Emphasis. Evangelical/Wesleyan.

Accreditation. Middle States Association of Colleges and Schools.

Term System. Semester; summer term.

Enrollment in Degree Programs in Religion 1984–85. Total 72; men 52, women 20.

Degrees in Religion Awarded 1984–85. Associate in Applied Science 4; men 2, women 2. Bachelor of Arts 16; men 9, women 7. Bachelor of Science 13; men 10, women 3.

Faculty for Degree Programs in Religion. Total 11; full-time 11.

Admission Requirements. Applicants for admission to Houghton must submit a completed application, a pastor's recommendation, high school transcript, and SAT or ACT scores.

Tuition and Fees. Tuition $5,150; fees $245; housing averages $950 per year.

Financial Aid. Students receive financial aid from federal, state, and college sources. Houghton offers a loan/grant program specifically for students planning on going into full-time Christian service.

Housing. The College has two men's dorms and two women's dorms in addition to a wide variety of off-campus housing opportunities. Married students live off-campus.

Library Facilities. The library contains approximately 160,000 volumes and subscribes to 633 journals. There is a special collection of Wesleyan documents, writings, and literature in the College library.

Religious Services/Activities. The Houghton Wesleyan Church holds Sunday morning and evening services in the College chapel during the school year. In addition, there are class prayer meetings, dorm and floor Bible studies, class retreats, a week-long missions conference, as well as a Christian Life Emphasis Week to begin each semester. Chapel is required of all students and meets Tuesday through Friday.

Degree Programs

The ministerial curriculum that leads to the Bachelor of Science degree is a four-year terminal course designed to prepare students for going directly into ministerial service. The curriculum is so structured that by class courses and independent studies all academic requirements for ministerial ordination in The Wesleyan Church can be fullfilled.

The comprehensive major in religion leading to the Bachelor of Arts degree consists of 39 hours in Bible and related departments. This program is provided for those who want a liberal arts degree with a maximum of Biblical and theological studies. A major concentration in Bible or in Christian Education is offered for those expecting to become missionaries, directors of Christian Education, or leaders in para-church ministries.

Special Programs

The Associate in Applied Science degree program is a two-year Christian Ministries curriculum that provides a Bible-centered preparation for Christian service in the church or the mission field.

Immaculate Conception, Seminary of the
West Neck Road
Huntington, NY 11743   (516) 423-0483

Administration. Msgr. John J. Strynkowski, Rector/President.

General Description. The Seminary of the Immaculate conception is a center of formation for ministry in the Roman Catholic Church. Although the faculty and facilities are at the service of various programs, under its direct responsibility are the following: (1) Master of Divinity program, which, in conformity with the directives of the appropriate ecclesiastical and academic bodies combines all the aspects of formation of men for ordination to priest-

ly ministry; (2) Master of Arts in Theology program, which offers a wide range of courses to men and women engagaed in, or preparing for, ministry, or interested in the pursuit of theology at the graduate level.

Community Environment. The Seminary of the Immaculate Conception is situated in Huntington Township, Suffolk County, Long Island, about 40 miles from New York City. It stands on over 200 acres of hilly land overlooking Cold Spring Harbor, Huntington Harbor, and Oyster Bay. The building is constructed in Spanish Romanesque style with a Byzantine tower.

Religious Denomination. Roman Catholic.

Accreditation. Middle States Association of Colleges and Schools; Association of Theological Schools in the United States and Canada.

Term System. Semester; summer term.

Enrollment in Degree Programs in Religion 1984–85. Total 180; men 106, women 74.

Degrees in Religion Awarded 1984–85. Master of Divinity 6; men 6. Master of Arts in Theology 25; men 6, women 19.

Faculty for Degree Programs in Religion. Total 31; full-time 16, part-time 15.

Admission Requirements. Bachelor of Arts degree or equivalent from an accredited institution.

Tuition and Fees. Tuition Master of Divinity $2,500 plus $20 registration fee; Master of Arts $100 per credit, $15 application fee, $5 registration fee.

Financial Aid. Applicants who wish to receive aid must file a request with the Associate Dean at least one month in advance of registration.

Housing. All Master of Divinity students live on campus during the academic year. Housing is available for Master of Arts students only during the summer.

Library Facilities. The library contains 52,634 volumes. It offers the student a wide range of reading in the various branches of the theological sciences.

Religious Services/Activities. The Seminary community places great emphasis on the Eucharistic Celebration as the focal point of each day. Other communal prayer, personal meditation, prayer groups, corridor prayer, scheduled days of recollection, and two annual community retreats are held.

Degree Programs

The Seminary has as one of its primary responsibilities the preparation of men for ordination to the priesthood. The Master of Divinity program is a first professional degree program consisting of 99 credits in courses required for all students and an additional 18 credits in elective courses or seminars. In addition, another two semesters of non-resident pastoral field education, normally done after the first two years of residency, are an integral part of the program. Courses are required in the areas of Sacred Scripture, Systematic Theology, Moral Theology, Historical Theology, Ministry of Word and Sacrament, and Ministry to Church and Society.

The Master of Arts in Theology is a graduate program designed as an academic preparation for those moving towards various professional, religious or ministerial careers or as part of an enrichment program for those already established in such careers. The degree requires one year of full-time study or its equivalent, i.e., 36 credit hours. Of these hours, 24 credit hours must be in theology (scripture, doctrine, moral) and 12 credit hours in an area of specialization (theology, liturgy, catachetics, youth ministry, or pastoral ministry). A final synthesis seminar is also required. A period of 5 years is allowed to complete the requirements for the degree.

Jewish Theological Seminary of America
3080 Broadway
New York, NY 10027   (212) 678-8000

Administration. Gerson D. Cohen, Chancellor and President of Faculties; Gordon Tucker, Dean, Rabbinical School; Paula Hyman, Dean, Seminary College of Jewish Studies; Morton Leifman, Dean, Cantors Institute - Seminary College of Jewish Music; Mayer E. Rabinowitz, Dean, Graduate School: Institute for Advanced Studies in the Humanities.

General Description. Founded in 1886, the Jewish Theological Seminary of America is the academic and spiritual center of the Conservative movement in Judaism. It includes five schools at its New York campus (the Seminary College of Jewish Studies; the Graduate School: Institute for Advanced Studies in the Humanities; the Rabbinical School; the Cantors Institute; and the Seminary College of Jewish Music), and a sixth in Israel (the American Student Center, housing both the year in Israel programs for Seminary students and Midreshet Yerushalayim, a yearlong institute for intensive study of Jewish classical texts). The Seminary has a student body exceeding 900 and a faculty of some 150 full- and part-time scholars. It offers degrees of Bachelor and Master of Arts; Doctor of Philosophy; Doctor of Hebrew Literature; and Bachelor, Master, and Doctor of Sacred Music. Related to the Seminary is the University of Judaism in Los Angeles, which also includes undergraduate and graduate programs. Extensive adult education programs emanate from both American campuses.

In the words of the original Charter, the Seminary was created for "the preservation in America of the knowledge and practice of historical Judaism." When Dr. Sabato Morais, rabbi of Mikveh Israel in Philadelphia, called for an institution for training American rabbis, the Jewish community in the United States was nearly 250 years old, but it depended for intellectual nourishment entirely on the European centers of Jewish learning. Dr. Morais and the influential rabbis, scholars, and laymen incorporated the Jewish Theological Seminary Association in 1886, and in January 1887 the first ten students began preparatory classes in the vestry rooms of Shearith Israel at 5 West 19th Street in New York City. In 1901 a group of prominent Jewish philanthropists, led by Jacob H. Schiff, Leonard Lewisohn, and Daniel Guggenheim, established a new corporation with a substantial endowment, The Jewish Theological Seminary of America, into which the older Association merged.

Community Environment. The Seminary moved to its present campus, extending along Broadway from 122nd to 123rd Streets in 1929. Its location makes the Seminary a member of that distinguished group of academic and ecclesiastical institutions on Morningside Heights which includes Barnard College, the Cathedral of St. John the Divine, Columbia University, Corpus Christi Church, Manhattan School of Music, the National Council of Churches, Riverside Church, Teachers College, and Union Theological Seminary.

Religious Denomination. Jewish.

Religious Emphasis. Conservative.

Accreditation. Middle States Association of Colleges and Schools.

Term System. Semester; summer term.

Enrollment in Degree Programs in Religion 1984–85. Total 900. Rabbinical School: total 142; men 111, women 31.

Degrees in Religion Awarded 1984–85. Bachelor and Master of Arts. Doctor of Philosophy. Doctor of Hebrew Literature. Bachelor, Master, and Doctor of Sacred Music.

Faculty for Degree Programs in Religion. Total 150. Rabbinical School: total 83; full-time 49, part-time 34.

Admission Requirements. College of Jewish Studies: open to men and women sixteen years of age or over who have completed high school and demonstrated outstanding academic ability; proficiency in the Hebrew language and familiarity with the Pentateuch and Former Prophets are desireable. *Cantors Institute:* men who are college graduates, members of the Jewish faith and loyal adherents of its observances, including the Sabbath and Holy Days, daily prayers, and dietary laws, and who have an adequate general Jewish background including knowledge of Hebrew, Bible, Jewish history, the Prayer Book, and customs of the synagogue. *Seminary College of Jewish Music:* men and women who are college graduates and who possess a general Jewish background, including knowledge of Hebrew, Bible, Jewish history, the Prayer Book, and customs of the synagogue. *Graduate School: Institute for Advanced Studies in the Humanities:* baccalaureate degree from an accredited college or university; GRE scores; three letters of recommendation, two of which must be from academics. *Rabbinical School:* Bachelor's degree; member of Jewish faith; GRE scores; interview; essays.

Tuition and Fees. Seminary College of Jewish Studies: Tuition $3,630 per academic year for students taking 9 or more credits; part-time students (8 credits or less) $200 per credit. *Cantors Institute:* Tuition $4,000 per academic year; students taking 11 credits or less $220 per credit.

Rabinnical School: Tuition $4,000 per academic year; students taking 11 credits or less $220 per credit. *Graduate School: Institute for Advanced Studies in Humanities:* Tuition $160 per credit; Ph.D. program where students are completing their two-year residence requirement $4,800 for the academic year (includes summer sessions). All students in residence have various miscellaneous fees.

Financial Aid. Financial aid is available in the form of tuition grants and loans based on needs.

Housing. Dormitory living is available; depending upon accommodations, cost can vary from $1,300 to $2,150 per academic year; apartments for married couples are available in limited number.

Library Facilities. The Ivan F. and Seema Boesky Family Library contains one of the largest and most exhaustive collections of Hebraica and Judaica in the world. It has been assembled over generations, and preserved through many vicissitudes of Jewish Life, including the great fire which attacked the library in 1966. The Library is rich in primary sources for research in Bible and its Jewish commentaries, rabbinics, Jewish philosophy, liturgy, history, and medieval and modern Hebrew literature. The manuscript division has several hundred codices and scrolls of the Bible and an extremely valuable collection of medieval Hebrew commentaries to Scripture. The library includes one of the major collections of fragments from the Cairo Geniza, a mine of primary research material. In addition, there are monographs and studies in related fields such as ancient Near Eastern history and Semitic philology. Total holdings of the Library number over 270,000 volumes.

The Cantors Institute has a collection of 1,400 albums of classical music, and a unique library of Jewish recorded music. Among the 1,000 records in this collection are many rare items. For purposes of instruction and research, the Cantors Institute reprints standard hazzanic and Jewish music materials not otherwise obtainable. An outstanding collection of tapes of authentic folk materials recently gathered in the Middle East is being regularly increased.

Religious Services/Activities. A unique atmosphere has developed at the Seminary through the interplay of formal studies and the extracurricular program. In a pluralistic Jewish environment, within the spectrum of the Conservative Movement, Seminary students have the opportunity to experience being a part of a smaller community within the context of New York City and Morningside Heights. The Student Life Office serves as a clearinghouse for all student activities whether originating from the students or the professional staff.

Degree Programs

Seminary College of Jewish Studies. The College is an undergraduate liberal arts college which specializes in Judaica and grants the Bachelor of Arts. It offers a full spectrum of courses in Bible, Hebrew language, Jewish education, Jewish history, Jewish literature, Jewish philosophy, Talmud, and Rabbinics. Texts are studied in the original language and classes are conducted in modern Hebrew.

Cantors Institute. The Institute trains *hazzanim* for congregational service. To men who complete the program, the Institute awards the diploma of *Hazzan,* the degree of Bachelor of Sacred Music, or both. All students are candidates for the BSM degree and are required to take courses in *hazzanut,* Jewish music, general music, and Jewish studies including Hebrew grammar and language, laws and customs, Bible, liturgy, and Jewish thought. Piano is a required part of the curriculum; students may be excused from piano on the basis of a proficiency examination by the instructor. Students continue studies in voice on a private basis.

Seminary College of Jewish Music. A coeducational school, the College trains teachers of Jewish music, choral directors, composers, and research scholars. It offers programs leading to the Bachelor, Master, and Doctor of Sacred Music.

The Bachelor of Sacred Music program is open to qualified college graduates and requires five years of full-time study. Students are expected to complete the prescribed curriculum of the Cantors Institute with the exception of vocal studies.

The Master of Sacred Music requires the completion of a minimum of thirty credits of graduate work in the Seminary College of Jewish Music and the submission of a satisfactory essay in either musicology or the history of Jewish music.

The Doctor of Sacred Music requires the completion of sixty credits of graduate work and a dissertation in either musicology or the history of Jewish music. Candidates who have unusual ability in composition may, with the permission of the faculty, submit a major work of Jewish content in place of the dissertation.

Rabbinical School. The School offers a program of graduate and professional studies leading to Master of Arts in rabbinics and then to ordination. The curriculum structures rabbinic education at the Seminary in four progressive levels: Level I Technical skills; Level II Introductory surveys; Level III Methodologies; Level IV Electives, professional skills, and thematic interdisciplinary ("synthesis") courses.

Graduate School: Institute for Advanced Studies in the Humanities. The Master of Arts program serves students who wish to prepare a career of service in the Jewish community, as well as those who wish to train for further research and scholarship in Judaica. It offers programs designed to provide advanced academic training in Ancient Judaism, Bible, Jewish history, Jewish literature, Jewish philosophy, Medieval Jewish studies, Talmud and Rabbinics, Interdisciplinary Studies, and professional training in the field of Jewish education.

The Doctor of Hebrew Literature program is designed for students who wish to pursue advanced academic work in a field of Jewish studies, but do not wish to pursue an academic career. The degree is intended to certify that its recipient is qualified to teach his/her field on an under-graduate level. The language requirements are English, Hebrew, and Aramaic.

The Doctor of Philosophy program provides advanced academic training in a broad area of Judaic scholarship with an intensive specialization in one area in preparation for an academic career. The degree certifies that the recipient is qualified to teach a wide range of Judaica on the undergraduate level and to train graduate students in their fields of specialization.

Special Programs

The Seminary's branch in Jerusalem, dedicated in 1962, is located in a cultural center near the Hebrew University, the Israel Museum, and the Knesset. The Center offers a wide range of courses which are integrated into the course of study in the Rabbinical Schools. It also provides special workshops and seminars designed to familiarize students with the religious, cultural, social, and political aspects of Jewish life in Israel. Some of these courses are open to other Seminary students studying in Jerusalem as well as to non-matriculating students from America and Israel, some of whom are in residence at the campus.

The University of Judaism, affiliated with the Jewish Theological Seminary, was founded in Los Angeles in 1947 as a teachers college and a school for adults who wished to continue their Jewish education. It has evolved into a leading center of higher Jewish education on the west coast. See: *Judaism, University of, Los Angeles, California.*

King's College
Department of Religion
Briarcliff Manor, NY 10510   (914) 941-7200

Administration. Dr. Robert A. Cook, President; Dr. Russell R. Fry, Chairman, Department of Religion.

General Description. The Department of Religion is within the Humanities Division of the College, and has two concentrations: Biblical Studies and Religious Education. The Department offers a major in Religion plus a minor in Biblical Studies or Religious Education. Those students who meet the requirements for graduation receive a Bachelor of Arts in Religion. The School is a member of the Institute for Holy Land Studies which allows the student to spend time abroad studying in Israel.

Parent Institution. The King's College is a 4-year, Christian liberal arts college, privately supported, independent, interdenominational, and coeducational. The arts, sciences and professional studies are taught from the perspective of classic Christian orthodoxy. The College's unique contribution to higher education is that its faculty ties together Biblical concepts of God, the world, the individual, and society, with the latest information in various fields of knowledge. The college community encourages students to broaden their minds through co-

curricular activities such as field experience, participation in the Christian service programs, and involvement in both intramural and varsity sports.

Community Environment. The King's College serves approximately 800 students on a beautiful 80-acre campus overlooking the Hudson River in Briarcliff Manor (suburban Westchester County) only 30 miles north of New York City.

Religious Denomination. Nondenominational.

Religious Emphasis. Evangelical.

Accreditation. Middle States Association of Colleges and Schools; Association of Christian Schools International.

Term System. Semester; summer term.

Enrollment in Degree Programs in Religion 1984–85. Total 35; men 23, women 12.

Degrees in Religion Awarded 1984–85. Bachelor of Arts in Biblical Studies 4; men 2, women 2. Bachelor of Arts in Religious Education 1; women 1.

Faculty for Degree Programs in Religion. Total 5; full-time 5.

Admission Requirements. High school diploma with a minimum of sixteen units, including three or more in English and six units from science, mathematics, or language; satisfactory scores on SAT or ACT.

Tuition and Fees. Tuition $5,525 full-time per academic year; $196 part-time per credit hour; room and board $2,300 per year.

Financial Aid. College, federal, and state financial aid are available in the form of scholarships, grants, loans, and employment.

Housing. On-campus housing is provided for single students. The Housing Office assists married students in securing off-campus housing.

Library Facilities. The library has current holdings of more than 90,000 volumes. Six hundred periodicals are received regularly, of which 350 are bound or retained on microfilm.

Religious Services/Activities. King's College gives a primary place in its co-curricular program to spiritual values and to the development of Christian responsibility and individual commitment. In addition to the required Bible courses, attendance at daily chapel services is expected of all students. Sunday morning worship and evening Bible study are conducted regularly. Students are encouraged to attend and participate in the Sunday activities of local churches. A college prayer meeting is held each Wednesday evening. A five-day Bible conference is held each fall and spring, with the guest speaker addressing the chapel and evening services. The Student Missions Fellowship sponsors an annual three-day missionary conference with mission leaders on campus to address forums, services, etc. All regular services and special religious meetings are interdenominational in character.

Degree Programs

The Religion major with a concentration in Biblical Studies leading to the Bachelor of Arts degree offers preparation for a lifetime of scholarly pursuits, personal growth, and cultural understanding. It is particularly helpful to those students who are planning to do graduate work either in a seminary or a graduate school of religion. Students are encouraged to explore the historical, doctrinal, and cultural implications of the Christian faith as revealed in the scriptures.

The major in Religion with a concentration in Religious Education engages students in the study of religious education and leadership and their roles in business, educational, social, and political institutions, and in the lives of persons, families, churches, communities, and the world. It is designed for students wishing to continue their education in seminary or graduate school with a view to assuming roles in local churches as Ministers or Directors of Christian Education, Educational Specialists, Youth Pastors, or in positions of leadership in parachurch organizations such as Young Life, Inter-Varsity, Campus Life, Campus Crusade, mission organizations, religious publishing houses, and in research or teaching.

Special Programs

The King's College Adult Learning Center offers workshops and courses in Biblical studies. The King's College is an affiliate college of The Institute of Holy Land Studies. Students are eligible for study at the Jerusalem campus and transfer credit is granted for courses completed in Hebrew, social studies, archaeology, and Bible.

Manhattan College
Department of Religious Studies
Manhattan College Parkway
Riverdale, NY 10471   (212) 920-0100

Administration. Brother J. Stephen Sullivan, F.S.C., President.

General Description. Manhattan College is a privately supported, independent college founded in 1853 by members of Brothers of the Christian Schools. The College is comprised of the Schools of Arts and Sciences, Business, Engineering, General Studies, Teacher Preparation, and the Graduate Division. The Department of Religious Studies offers a major in the field as well as the courses to satisfy the nine credits required of all students.

Community Environment. The campus of 47 acres is located on the heights above Van Courtlandt Park in the Riverdale section of New York City.

Religious Denomination. Roman Catholic.

Accreditation. Middle States Association of Colleges and Schools.

Term System. Semester.

Admission Requirements. Graduation from an accredited high school with a minimum of 16 units in academic subjects; SAT or ACT.

Tuition and Fees. Tuition and fees $5,400 per year; room and board $3,700.

Financial Aid. Assistance in many forms is available.

Housing. The College has living quarters for 1,200 students.

Library Facilities. The combined library facilities of the College include over 225,000 volumes, 230,000 microforms, and 6,000 audiovisual materials.

Religious Services/Activities. The Campus Ministry team coordinates the various ministries of the college community. Liturgical services are provided on a regularly scheduled basis. Programs including social action programs, off-campus retreats, discussion groups, lecture series, and ecumenical services are provided.

Degree Programs

The major in Religious Studies must complete the course in The Nature and Experience of Religion plus 21 credits in courses selected in consultation with the departmental chairman. The elective courses will ordinarily include at least one course from each of the areas of Scripture, Theology, Ethics, and Non-Christian Religions. Departmental course offerings are grouped under The Religious Traditions, Christian Theology, World Religious Traditions, Ethics, and Contemporary Issues. The major leads to the Bachelor of Arts degree.

Maryknoll School of Theology
Maryknoll, NY 10545   (914) 941-7590

Administration. Gerard McCrane, President.

General Description. The Maryknoll School of Theology is a graduate and professional school whose purpose is to serve the needs of the Catholic Foreign Mission Society of America (Maryknoll) and the Catholic Church in the United States in the areas of theological education and formation for ministry. The primary commitment of the School is to the education and ongoing formation of men and women for cross-cultural missionary ministry and to research related to Christian mission in all its dimensions. Through its various programs, students are helped to attain a critical understanding of the Christian faith in the light of its historical development and its contemporary challenges, to develop skills for evangelism, and to provide theological foundations for a spirituality which integrates personal faith and ministerial service.

The School, as part of its service to the Church, also welcomes students who will minister in the United States. In the light of Maryknoll's missionary charism, they receive a theological formation distinguished by cross-cultural sensitivity, a global vision, and an awareness of the Church's worldwide mission.

The School offers the degrees Master of Divinity, Master of Theology, and Master of Arts in Theological Studies. Also offered are the Certificate of Participation in Studies of Ritual, Symbolism, and World Religions and the Certificate of Participation in Studies of Justice and Peace.

Community Environment. The Maryknoll School of Theology is located about one hour's drive from New York City and near Ossining, New York on the banks of the Hudson River. All the cultural, recreational, educational, and community services of New York City are easily accessible.

Religious Denomination. Roman Catholic.

Accreditation. Middle States Association of Colleges and Schools; Association of Theological Schools in the United States and Canada.

Term System. Trimester.

Enrollment in Degree Programs in Religion 1984–85. Total 114; men 69, women 45.

Degrees in Religion Awarded 1984–85. Master of Divinity 46; men 46. Master of Theology 1; men 1. Master of Arts in Theological Studies 67; men 22, women 45.

Faculty for Degree Programs in Religion. Total 30; full-time 17, part-time 13.

Admission Requirements. Bachelor's degree from an accredited institution of higher education in the U.S. or its equivalent for overseas students; above average grades in undergraduate study; fulfillment of prerequisites for Master of Divinity program; for the Master of Theology, a student must have a Master of Divinity degree.

Tuition and Fees. Tuition $100 per credit; student fees $45; room and board $5,400.

Financial Aid. Limited financial assistance for tuition is available.

Housing. Limited accommodations are available. The Maryknoll Society dining room is open to all School of Theology students.

Library Facilities. The library contains over 92,000 volumes including the fields of theology, biblical studies, philosophy, church history, missions studies, church law, and English literature. In the past decade, concentrations have been extended in world religions, ecumenical studies, and the theology and liturgy of Protestant and Eastern churches. Substantial expansion has been accorded to area studies of Latin America, Asia and Africa, particularly in the fields of anthropology, sociology, politics, history, and education.

Religious Services/Activities. Daily Catholic liturgies.

Degree Programs

The Master of Divinity program provides the basic theological and professional preparation for those seeking to exercise ordained and other ministries in the Catholic Church. Its aim is to assist candidates to appropriate their Christian, theological, and ministerial identities in a way suited for missionary evangelization. The program has three stages: Stage 1 is foundational for developing the student's ministerial and missionary identity; Stage 2 gives the student an experience of inculturation in a missionary

context; and Stage 3 focuses on the appropriating and deepening of a cross-cultural and ministerial identity. The program consists of 111 credit hours of required and elective courses, including 18 credits as stipulated in the overseas/transcultural part of the program.

The Master of Theology program is offered to qualified students seeking to deepen their understanding of a particular area of theology and a developed competence in the skills of critical scholarship. Emphasis in the program is upon directed study and research. Students entering this program must hold a Master of Divinity degree or its equivalent from an accredited theological school. The program requires the completion of a minimum of 18 credit hours, ordinarily taken in the area of the student's specialization; a cumulative grade average of 3.25, and completion and defense of a thesis that demonstrates scholarly competence.

The Master of Arts in Theological Studies is an academic program. Three fields of concentration are offered: Christian Heritage; Theology of Justice and Peace; and Theology of Ritual, Symbolism, and World Religions. The program requires the completion of 48 credit hours, a written comprehensive examination, a cumulative grade average of 3.00, and a minimum of 36 credits hours in residence.

Special Programs

A Certificate of Participation is awarded for completion of special programs in Studies of Ritual, Symbolism, and World Religions and Studies of Justice and Peace. Each program requires the completion of 18 credits of coursework.

Nazareth College of Rochester
4245 East Avenue
Rochester, NY 14610   (716) 586-2525

Administration. Rose Marie Beston, President.

General Description. Nazareth College of Rochester was founded in 1924 by the Sisters of St. Joseph of Rochester as a college for the education of women. It is now a coeducational liberal arts college providing selected career programs at the undergraduate and master's levels. It is now governed by a lay Board of Trustees. The Department of Religious Studies offers a major program leading to the Bachelor of Arts degree. A Religious Studies Concentration (minor) is also offered for other majors.

Community Environment. The 75-acre campus is located in Pittsford, a suburb of Rochester.

Religious Denomination. Roman Catholic.

Accreditation. Middle States Association of Colleges and Schools.

Term System. Semester.

Admission Requirements. High school graduation; ACT or SAT.

Tuition and Fees. Tuition $2,650 per semester; association fee $30; room $807.50; board $675-$705.

Financial Aid. Qualifying students may receive a financial aid "package" composed of a combination of scholarship, grant, loan, and job assistance, which will vary according to demonstrated need and individual circumstances.

Housing. Two-thirds of the college's full-time enrollment live on campus in residence halls.

Library Facilities. The Lorette Wilmot Library has a collection of over 220,000 volumes.

Religious Services/Activities. Campus Ministry promotes a religious community through a program of liturgical and social activities. Catholic and Protestant chaplains work closely with students to design the regularly-scheduled religious services.

Degree Programs

The major leading to the Bachelor of Arts degree requires 30 credit hours, 24 of which must be upper-division courses. The option of an internship is available for majors. Majors are encouraged to minor in a related area, e.g., Bioethics, Social Work.

New York University
Washington Square
25 West 4th Street
New York, NY 10012   (212) 598-3591

Administration. John Brademas, President.

General Description. New York University is a privately supported, coeducational university founded in 1831. It now includes 21 colleges and schools at six major centers in Manhattan and enrolls over 27,000 full-time students. The Department of Cultural Foundations offers programs leading to the Master of Arts, Doctor of Education, and Doctor of Philosophy degrees, and to the Sixth Year Certificate. The Department of Hebrew Culture and Education offers a program in Hebrew and Judaic Studies under the sponsorship of the all-University Institute for Hebrew and Judaic Studies. This interdisciplinary center offers courses for undergraduates either individually or in a major or minor.

Community Environment. The chief center for undergraduate and graduate study is at the main campus on Washington Square in the Greenwich Village section of New York City.

Religious Denomination. None.

Accreditation. Middles States Association of Colleges and Schools.

Term System. Semester.

Admission Requirements. Graduation from high school or equivalent with completion of 16 academic units; SAT.

Tuition and Fees. Tuition $7,850 per year; room and board $4,100; student fees $300.

Financial Aid. The University residence halls accommodate 3,450 students.

Housing. Various types of assistance are available.

Library Facilities. The New York University Library System consists of eight distinct libraries. The combined holdings number over three million volumes.

Degree Programs

The Department of Cultural Foundations offers programs in Religious Education. Two emphases can be found in the courses offered: (1) Background courses on the philosophical and scientific bases for the relating of religion to life, including such courses as The World's Religions, Philosophical Foundations of Religion, Psychology of Religious Experience, and Moral Dilemmas in Classical and Modern Literature; (2) Courses relating the theories and methods of general education and the social sciences to the practice of educating in religion are intended primarily for professional workers in the field of religion. Various programs lead to the Master of Arts, Doctor of Education, and Doctor of Philosophy degrees. A cooperative program exists with the New York Theological Seminary leading to the degree of Master of Professional Studies conferred by the Seminary. In this program the student takes approximately 21 points in theological and Biblical studies at the seminary and 15 points in religious education at New York University.

The Department of Hebrew Culture and Education offers the undergraduate majors in Hebrew Language and Literature and Jewish History and Civilization.

Rabbi Isaac Elchanan Theological Seminary
2540 Amsterdam Avenue
New York, NY 10033   (212) 960-5344

General Description. The Rabbi Isaac Elchanan Theological Seminary is one of the leading Orthodox Jewish rabbinical schools in the United States. It offers a four-year graduate-level course leading to rabbinical ordination, post-graduate courses for rabbis, and an undergraduate program in Jewish music to train cantors. There is a Division of Communal Services and an academic center located in Jerusalem, Israel. The Seminary has an affiliate agreement with Yeshiva University for joint use of the library, classrooms, and other facilities.

Community Environment. New York City, the largest city in the nation, is also its business, entertainment, and industrial capital. This teeming city is considered by many as the greatest center of higher education in the country. It claims the largest library outside the Library of Congress. Nearby Yeshiva University, with which the Seminary has an affiliate agreement, is composed of 33 buildings located on 26 acres.

Religious Denomination. Jewish.

Religious Emphasis. Orthodox.

Accreditation. New York State Board of Regents.

Term System. Semester; no summer term.

Enrollment in Degree Programs in Religion 1984–85.

Total 156; men 156.

Degrees in Religion Awarded 1984–85. Ordination 20; men 20.

Faculty for Degree Programs in Religion. Total 25; full-time 13, part-time 12.

Admission Requirements. For graduate program leading to ordination: four years of intensive college-level study of Talmud and commentaries, and bachelor's degree with knowledge of Jewish Studies equivalent to major.

Tuition and Fees. Graduate tuition: $3,000 per year plus $125 registration fee.

Financial Aid. Financial aid during the recent past has been available to cover every graduate student's Seminary tuition.

Housing. Dormitories are available for unmarried students only; apartments are available for rental off-campus.

Library Facilities. The Seminary's library includes 6,-443 volumes. The Seminary has a cooperative arrangement with Yeshiva University under which their 850,000 volume library is open to Seminary students and faculty.

Religious Services/Activities. Services are held daily.

Degree Programs

A four-year graduate program leads to rabbinical ordination (Yoreh Yoreh) and advanced ordination (Yadin Yadin). Courses are required in Talmud and Codes, supplementary rabbinic studies (Jewish education, Homiletics, Chaplaincy), practical halakhah (Jewish law), and Jewish thought (Bible, philosophy).

Special Programs

An undergraduate program of the Philip and Sarah Belz School of Jewish Music is offered for the training of cantors. This course of study requires two to three years.

Postgraduate programs in Jewish law are offered for Rabbis.

Roberts Wesleyan College
Department of Religion and Philosophy
2301 Westside Drive
Rochester, NY 14624   (716) 594-9471

Administration. Dr. William C. Crothers, President; Dr. Oscar T. Lenning, Vice President for Academic Affairs, Academic Dean; Dr. Wesley E. Vanderhoof, Chairman, Division of Humanities.

General Description. The Department of Religion and Philosophy conceives its role in the fulfillment of the institutional objectives to be that of teaching Biblical literature, philosophy, and religion as an essential part of a student's arts education. In addition, the Department seeks to prepare students, in a preprofessional program, for advanced learning at a seminary or graduate school. The Department is made up of 5 complementing areas of discipline: Biblical Studies, Philosophy, Pastoral Studies, Religious Studies, and Missions. Generally, nine semester

hours in the areas of religion and philosophy are required of all students, and the Department furnishes these courses.

Parent Institution. Roberts Wesleyan College is an independent, coeducational, nonsectarian Christian liberal arts college founded by the Free Methodist Church of North America. The College offers a quality education to students of all denominations and a program designed to facilitate development in all dimensions of its students' lives. Since its Christian heritage is one of the most important components of Roberts Wesleyan's personalized education, its educational philosophy combines the historical Christian concern for the communication of human values with the development of the total person.

Community Environment. Roberts Wesleyan College is located in North Chili, New York, 8 miles southwest of Rochester and 12 miles from Lake Ontario. The College is near Niagara Falls, Watkins Glen, Letchworth Park, and the Finger Lakes. Rochester offers numerous cultural resources, all within convenient driving distance of the campus.

Religious Denomination. Nondenominational; maintains a relationship with the Free Methodist Church.

Religious Emphasis. Evangelical.

Accreditation. Middle States Association of Colleges and Schools.

Term System. Semester; summer term.

Enrollment in Degree Programs in Religion 1984–85. Total 40; men 40.

Degrees in Religion Awarded 1984–85. Bachelor of Arts 10; men 10.

Faculty for Degree Programs in Religion. Total 4; full-time 3, part-time 1.

Admission Requirements. Rank in the upper three-fifths from an approved high school; minimum of 12 academic units with no fewer than 4 units of English; 2 units of algebra/geometry; 1 unit of biology, chemistry, or physics; satisfactory scores on SAT or ACT; favorable character recommendations; good physical and mental health.

Tuition and Fees. Tuition and fees $5,934; room $1,478; board $1,030.

Financial Aid. Over 88 percent of students receive aid. Aid is available for dependents of ministers/missionaries, persons planning to enter Free Methodist ministry, and members of Free Methodist Church.

Housing. Dormitories are available for single students; on-campus apartments for married students. Housing is also available in the community.

Library Facilities. The library contains 86,500 volumes.

Religious Services/Activities. Chapel is held three times per week and attendance is required.

Degree Programs

The major in Religion-Philosophy leading to the Bachelor of Arts degree consists of 30 hours. The program is an interdisciplinary major designed to expose the student to the major areas of study offered by the department.

Rochester, University of
Department of Religious and Classical Studies
Wilson Boulevard
Rochester, NY 14627   (716) 275-2121

Administration. Dr. G. Dennis O'Brien, President; Dr. William Scott Green, Chairman, Department of Religious and Classical Studies.

General Description. In the Department of Religious and Classical Studies students explore the great, classical civilizations of West and East and the major religions that emerged from them. The Department offers programs of study in the history and philosophy of the world's major religions, in Greek, Latin, and Hebrew languages and literatures, and in ancient Mediterranean and Oriental civilizations. Through the study of important classical, Biblical, and religious writings, either in the original language or in translation, students critically examine the beliefs, ideas, values, rituals, and traditions that have shaped Western and Oriental cultures.

Parent Institution. Undergraduates from throughout the country take advantage of the University of Rochester's special nature: a richness and diversity of academic programs, opportunities to work with top faculty who are at the forefront of research, and the personal scale of its campuses. There are 4,550 undergraduates and 2,200 full-time graduate students at the University.

Community Environment. See: St. John Fisher College for information about the city of Rochester.

Religious Denomination. Nondenominational.

Accreditation. Middle States Association of Colleges and Schools.

Term System. Semester; summer term.

Admission Requirements. The University of Rochester does not use a specific minimum for high school or college grades or examination scores; students are evaluated in terms of their individual accomplishments.

Tuition and Fees. Tuition $9,400 per academic year; room double or triple occupancy $2,121 per year; board $1,750 per year; health fee $433 per year; student activity fee $80 per year.

Financial Aid. The University has made a commitment to provide a sound program of financial aid for undergraduate students.

Housing. About 85 percent of undergraduate students live on campus in residence halls or houses on the fraternity quadrangle. Freshmen are required to live on campus unless living with parents.

Library Facilities. The University library system is extensive, housing more than two million volumes and 12,000 current periodicals.

Degree Programs

The concentration in Religious Studies leading to the Bachelor of Arts degree includes a minimum of 10 courses, seminars, reading courses, and the Senior Tutori-

al. Students may enroll in selected courses at Colgate Rochester Divinity School.

St. Bernard's Institute
Colgate Rochester Divinity School
1100 South Goodman Street
Rochester, NY 14620   (716) 271-1320

Administration. Sebastian A. Falcone, S.T.L., Dean.

General Description. St. Bernard's Institute is a graduate school of theology, affiliated with and located on the campus of Colgate Rochester Divinity School. It provides, in an ecumenical setting, theological education, professional training, and spiritual development to students preparing for pastoral ministry within the Roman Catholic tradition. From its foundation in 1893 St. Bernard's has been committed to the education of seminarians for ordained priestly ministry; it now also is committed to the preparation of candidates for the permanent diaconate, the preparation of men and women for professional pastoral ministry within the Church, the continuing professional development of those involved in professional ministry, and the offering of educational opportunities to qualified individuals who wish to deepen their knowledge of theology and ministry. Drawing upon a relationship established in 1968 with the Colgate Rochester Divinity School, St. Bernard's took its place on the campus of the combined schools in 1981. The degrees Master of Divinity and Master of Arts in Theology are awarded. *See also:* Colgate Rochester Divinity School.

Religious Denomination. Roman Catholic.

Accreditation. Association of Theological Schools in the United States and Canada.

Term System. Semester; summer term.

Enrollment in Degree Programs in Religion 1984–85. Total 45; men 25, women 20.

Degrees in Religion Awarded 1984–85. Master of Divinity 13; men 13. Master of Arts in Theology 4; men 1, women 3.

Faculty for Degree Programs in Religion. Total 14; full-time 11, part-time 3.

Admission Requirements. Bachelor's degree; 24 prerequisite hours in theology/philosophy/religious studies; some credit may be given for life equivalency.

Tuition and Fees. Full-time Master of Divinity $1,850 per semester; Master of Arts $1,500 per semester; part-time $530 for one course, $990 for two courses; audit fee $190; registration $20.

Financial Aid. Assistance is available to all qualified students (Guaranteed Student Loans and local grants).

Housing. Available at Colgate Rochester Divinity School on a first-come, first-served basis.

Library Facilities. The 45,000 volumes of St. Bernard's Institute have been combined with the resources of the Colgate Rochester Divinity School library. The Bishop Fulton J. Sheen Archives are maintained here.

Religious Services/Activities. Daily ecumenical services.

Degree Programs

The Master of Divinity degree requires the completion of 96 credit hours, including two field education experiences, and comprehensive examinations. The Master of Arts degree requires the completion of 30 credit hours plus a thesis or 36 credit hours; comprehensive examinations are also required.

St. Bonaventure University
Theology Department
St. Bonaventure, NY 14778   (716) 375-2226

Administration. Very Rev. Mathias Doyle, O.F.M., President; Dr. E. Kieran Scott, Head, Theology Department.

General Description. The Department of Theology believes that the function of theology is to investigate and interpret the religious dimension of human experience. In order to observe this function the Department structures the 9 hour University requirement in Theology to provide an introduction, a study of religious traditions, and the investigation of the interactions of religion and broader cultural questions. In addition, the major in Theology program is designed for (1) general theological background, (2) professional background for further graduate studies in view of an advanced degree leading to the doctorate, (3) preparation for the field of religious education. The Bachelor of Arts degree is awarded.

Parent Institution. St. Bonaventure University is an independent, coeducational institution offering undergraduate programs through its Schools of Arts and Sciences, Business Administration, Education, and Graduate Studies. The Franciscan Institute, a graduate institute of specialized research and publication, grants the Master of Arts in Franciscan Studies.

Community Environment. The St. Bonaventure campus in southwestern New York is spread over 500 acres in a valley surrounded by the Allegheny foothills, between Olean and Allegany. Nearby is Bradford, PA.

Religious Denomination. Roman Catholic.

Religious Emphasis. Franciscan tradition.

Accreditation. Middle States Association of Colleges and Schools.

Term System. Semester; summer term.

Admission Requirements. High school graduate; academic attainment; recommendations from teachers; satisfactory CEEB or ACT scores.

Tuition and Fees. Tuition and fees $2,495 per semester; room and board $1,375-$1,420; books and supplies (estimated) $200; health insurance (optional) $90.

Financial Aid. Tuition scholarships and grants-in-aid are awarded on the basis of academic achievement, potential, and need. College Work-Study program.

Housing. All unmarried freshmen, sophomores, and ju-

niors, except those whose homes are within commuting distance, or who are 21 or over, are required to live in one of the residence halls. There are no facilities on campus for married students.

Library Facilities. The Friedsam Library and Resource Center contains over 200,000 volumes, 30,000 bound periodicals, 1,500 current periodicals, extensive microfilm collections.

Degree Programs

The Bachelor of Arts in Theology requires 30 credit hours in Theology, including The Nature of Religious Experience, A History of Christian Theology, Studies in Comparative Religion, Contemporary Study of the Bible, and Introduction to Contemporary Theology.

Special Programs

The Franciscan Institute concentrates upon Franciscan-related theology, philosophy, history, and spirituality. It specializes in research and extensive publication, but also grants the Master of Arts in Franciscan Studies. Through its library and resource people it is a principle American center for Franciscan research.

St. Francis College
Religious Studies Department
180 Remsen Street
Brooklyn, NY 11201   (718) 522-2300

Administration. Dr. Donald Sullivan, O.S.F., President of the College; Dr. John K. Hawes, Vice President for Academic Affairs - Academic Dean; Gerald A. Largo, Chairperson, Religious Studies.

General Description. St. Francis College's Department of Religious Studies has a two-fold approach to the study of religion. First, as an academic discipline, i.e., the instructional methods and content are analytical and scientific. Second, as the living experience exploring its relationship with present-day society, science, and one's quest for meaning. The major in Religious Studies provides a foundation for graduate study in religion, theology, and religious education.

Parent Institution. Established in the city of Brooklyn in 1884 by the Congregation of the Religious Brothers of the Third Order Regular of St. Francis, the College is today an independent, urban, nonresidential, coeducational college. Drawing its student body mainly from the New York City metropolitan area, the College also enrolls a significant number of foreign students. Having as an objective at its founding to provide higher education for young men of modest means from Brooklyn, it continues to attract the majority of its students from comparable economic circumstances.

Community Environment. The College campus consists of five interconnected buildings which provide instructional areas, library, student services, and office space for the College. The campus is within 2 blocks of the Borough Hall station of all subways and is easily accessible from all parts of the metropolitan area. It is located on Remsen and Joralemon Streets in Brooklyn Heights, a national historic landmark district. Within minutes are all the cultural advantages of New York City.

Religious Denomination. Nondenominational, but Roman Catholic in its roots and tradition.

Accreditation. Middle States Association of Colleges and Schools.

Term System. Semester; summer term.

Enrollment in Degree Programs in Religion 1984–85. Total 6; men 3, women 3.

Degrees in Religion Awarded 1984–85. Bachelor of Arts in Religious Studies 2; men 1, women 1.

Faculty for Degree Programs in Religion. Total 5; full-time 2, part-time 3.

Admission Requirements. Applicants seeking an Associate or Bachelor's degree should have completed a minimum of 16 academic high school units, including four years of English, three years of History/Social Science, two years of Mathematics, and one year of Natural Science; SAT.

Tuition and Fees. $134 per credit hour; matriculation fee $25 (one time only); service fee for students taking 12 or more credits $50, less than 12 credits $20; student activities fee $20; laboratory fees and other special fees where applicable.

Financial Aid. The College has a comprehensive financial aid program including a financial aid "package" offering some combination of scholarships, grants, loans, and student employment.

Housing. No campus housing is available.

Library Facilities. The McGarry Library houses in excess of 140,000 volumes and more than 800 periodicals are currently received. The James A. Kelly Institute for Local Historical Studies houses one of New York's largest collections of primary source records on local history including original charters of the Dutch and English governors, Indian deeds, and town records.

Religious Services/Activities. The Director of Campus Ministry endeavors to strengthen students' spiritual growth and development. He provides spiritual guidance and counseling, holds pre-Cana conferences for prospective marital partners, arranges an annual student retreat, and celebrates a weekly Mass in the College Chapel.

Degree Programs

The Religious Studies Department offers a major in religious studies leading to the Bachelor of Arts degree. Within the framework of liberal arts, religious studies majors are given a foundation for graduate study in religion, theology, and religious education, as well as for careers in related fields such as law, social work, religious education and journalism; service to church communities, and the like. Students are encouraged to draw upon the broad spectrum of course offerings from other disciplines

to broaden their base of knowledge.

St. John Fisher College
Department of Religious Studies
3690 East Avenue
Rochester, NY 14618   (716) 385-8000

Administration. Rev. Patrick O. Braden, C.S.B., President; Dr. H. Wendell Howard, Provost; Dr. Donald E. Bain, Dean of Faculty; Dr. John Murray, C.S.B., Chairman, Department of Religious Studies.

General Description. The Department of Religious Studies offers a major in Religious Studies. It consists of 30 credit hours in a program designed with the chairman or another member of the Department. Offerings include courses (1) which center on the historical development of religious ideas, movements, and institutions, (2) which center on analysis of religious thought and action in the light of religious beliefs, and (3) which examine the primitive literature of religions, in particular those of the Judaic and Christian traditions.

Parent Institution. St. John Fisher is an independent liberal arts institution in the Roman Catholic tradition, offering baccalaureate and selected graduate programs in the humanities, sciences, and management.

Community Environment. The 125-acre campus of St. John Fisher is located six miles southeast of Rochester, New York, in the suburb of Pittsford. The New York State Thruway runs south of the city. With Lake Ontario on its northern border and the scenic Finger Lakes to the southeast, the Rochester community of about three-quarters of a million people is located in an attractive setting. It offers a wide range of cultural, recreational, and entertainment opportunities, from concerts by the Rochester Philharmonic Orchestra and performances by local theatre companies, to professional baseball, soccer, and ice hockey. Local industry is highly diversified and weighted toward science and technology. Rochester has one of the highest concentrations of skilled technical and professional personnel of any major metropolitan area in the country. Recreational facilities within the area include golf, tennis, swimming, hockey, water sports, and skiing.

Religious Denomination. Roman Catholic.

Accreditation. Middle States Association of Colleges and Schools.

Term System. Semester.

Enrollment in Degree Programs in Religion 1984–85. Total 3; men 2, women 1.

Degrees in Religion Awarded 1984–85. Bachelor of Arts 3; men 2, women 1.

Faculty for Degree Programs in Religion. Total 7; full-time 5, part-time 2.

Admission Requirements. 16 units of high school work; college preparatory courses in English, language, mathematics, science, and social science; B average; combined SAT score of 1000.

Tuition and Fees. Full time tuition $5,750; fees $75; room and board $3,060.

Financial Aid. The financial aid programs at St. John Fisher College have been developed to assist students with their finances. Eligibility is based primarily on need and/or scholarship.

Housing. On-campus dormitories with single or double accommodations are available.

Library Facilities. The Charles J. Lavery Library has present holdings in excess of 135,000 volumes with a periodicals subscription of 800 titles. The library includes a full range of learning services as well as group study facilities, an After-Hours Study Area, the Bill Givens Multi-Media Center, and the Rochester-Genesee County Room which houses rare books and special materials on local history.

Religious Services/Activities. Campus Ministry provides programs and activities which contribute to the intellectual, social, spiritual, and religious growth of the College community. The activities include daily liturgy, prayer groups, retreat weekends, pre-Cana conferences, Bible study, and lectures.

Degree Programs

The Department of Religious Studies provides the opportunity for studying the religious dimensions of human life. It seeks to give students and professors of the department the opportunity of discovering and examining, through academic inquiry, the religious dimension of the human response to life in thought and action. The Bachelor of Arts with a major in Religious Studies is awarded.

St. John's University
St. John's College of Liberal Arts and Sciences
Grand Central and Utopia Parkways
Jamaica, NY 11439   (718) 990-6161

Administration. The Very Rev. Joseph T. Cahill, Ph.D., President; Rev. Joseph S. Breen, Ph.D., Dean, St. John's College of Liberal Arts and Sciences.

General Description. The Department provides the courses for the core requirements of 9 credit hours in Religion; Roman Catholic students must take specified courses. It also provides the requirements for the major, for which the degree Bachelor of Arts in Theology is awarded.

Parent Institution. St. John's University is a Roman Catholic institution of higher learning founded and sponsored by the Congregation of the Mission (Vincentian Fathers). The fundamental purpose of the University is to offer men and women, in a Catholic atmosphere, the opportunity to achieve for themselves a higher education in the liberal arts and sciences and to prepare for certain professions. The University is composed of St. John's College of Liberal Arts and Sciences, Institute of Asian Studies, Notre Dame College, School of Education and Human Services, College of Business Administration, College of Pharmacy and Allied Health Professions, St. Vincent's College, School of Continuing Education, and Evening and Weekend College Programs.

Community Environment. The principle administrative offices of the University are at the Queens (Jamaica) campus, a 95.5-acre tract in the Hillcrest section of the Borough. A branch campus is located on a 16.5-acre tract on Grymes Hill in the Borough of Richmond, at 300 Howard Avenue, Staten Island, NY 10301, phone (718) 390-4545.

Religious Denomination. Roman Catholic.

Accreditation. Middle States Association of Colleges and Schools.

Term System. Semester.

Admission Requirements. The Committee on Admissions considers scholastic record, results in intelligence and achievement tests, character and personal qualities, class standing, work experiences, honors and awards. Personal interview may be required. SAT or ACT.

Tuition and Fees. Tuition per semester $2,400; University fee $140.

Financial Aid. Extensive financial aid available. St. John's awards over $34 million in federal, state, university, and external funds each year. Almost $7 million of this amount is provided from St. John's own funds in grants-in-aid, scholarships, and tuition remissions.

Housing. The University has no campus housing.

Library Facilities. The University libraries contain approximately 701,000 volumes, 243,000 microforms, and 15,000 recordings.

Degree Programs

The degree Bachelor of Arts in Theology requires 36 semester hours in the major with 21 in required courses and 15 in electives. Language requirements should be in Biblical Languages.

St. Joseph's Seminary
School of Theology
Dunwoodie
Yonkers, NY 10704   (914) 968-6200

Administration. Rev. Msgr. Edward Connors, Rector/President.

General Description. Saint Joseph's Seminary, Dunwoodie, is the fifth in a series of educational institutions which have provided a clergy for the Archdiocese of New York. It began in 1896 and was founded for the exclusive purpose of educating candidates for the priesthood of the Roman Catholic Church.

Community Environment. The Seminary extends for 43½ acres atop Valentine Hill in Yonkers, north of New York City.

Religious Denomination. Roman Catholic.

Accreditation. Middle States Association of Colleges and Schools; Association of Theological Schools in the United States and Canada.

Term System. Semester.

Faculty for Degree Programs in Religion. Total 27.

Admission Requirements. Bachelor of Arts degree with at least 18 credits in Philosophy.

Tuition and Fees. Students are sponsored by their Archdioceses.

Housing. Living accommodations are available for 210 men.

Library Facilities. The Archbishop Corrigan Library has a book collection of over 90,000 volumes. It has been enriched by many outstanding collections, notably the libraries of Archbishop Corrigan, Cardinal Spellman, and the Rev. Patrick J. Brady. As a result, all areas of knowledge are broadly represented in the collection while the main concentration of research materials is to be found in the Sacred Sciences. The Archives of the Archdiocese of New York are located in the library.

Religious Services/Activities. The Spiritual Formation Program includes daily celebration of the Mass; Morning and Evening Prayers; daily meditation, spiritual conference with the Spiritual Director each week; Eucharistic Holy Hour each week; Nocturnal Adoration held monthly; at least five full Days of Recollection throughout the year; twice yearly retreats; and the daily practice of spiritual reading.

Degree Programs

The Master of Divinity Degree candidate must successfully complete all of the courses of the first six semesters of the theological curriculum. A comprehensive examination is given in the fall of the Fourth Theology to those who have fulfilled the requirements.

The Master of Arts in Religious Studies program offered by the Archdiocesan Catechetical Institute prepares men and women for various positions in religious education needs of the parishes and institutions of the Archdiocese of New York. It requires the completion of 30 credits, after which candidates may apply for the written comprehensive. Courses are required in Christology, Introduction to Old Testament, Introduction to Liturgy and Sacraments, Introduction to Theology of Christian Life - Morality, and Psychology of Religious Development. A minimum of 12 credit hours is recommended in the candidate's field of concentration.

Special Programs

A Permanent Diaconate Program is offered. It prepares men to assist the Bishop and priests as permanent deacons in the ministry of the liturgy, of the Word, and of charity. The program involves a three-year course of study.

St. Vladimir's Orthodox Theological Seminary

575 Scarsdale Road
Crestwood, NY 10707   (914) 961-8313

Administration. The Very Rev. John Meyendorff, Dean.

General Description. The need for a center of theological and pastoral training was felt since the days when the first seeds of Orthodoxy were sown in the American soil by eight Russian monks who, in the fall of 1794, landed in Alaska. Throughout the 19th century, while the number of Orthodox steadily grew, the Church remained fundamentally an "immigrant" community served by bishops and priests sent from abroad, primarily from Russia.

The St. Vladimir's Orthodox Theological Seminary was founded in 1938 after many years of planning, recovery, and reorganization. It is named for St. Vladimir, the prince who in 988 introduced Orthodox Christianity to Kievan Russia. In 1962, the new home of the Seminary was occupied at its present location. The Seminary prepares candidates for the priesthood in the Orthodox church, for missionary work, teaching, or other forms of service in the church. Non-Orthodox students may be admitted to the Seminary and receive academic credit for their work.

Community Environment. The 7-acre campus is located in the town of Crestwood in Westchester County. It is adjacent to the town of Yonkers.

Religious Denomination. Orthodox (Eastern).

Accreditation. Association of Theological Schools in the United States and Canada.

Term System. Semester.

Enrollment in Degree Programs in Religion 1984–85. Total 95; full-time men 57, women 10.

Faculty for Degree Programs in Religion. Total 20.

Admission Requirements. Bachelor of Arts degree or equivalent from an accredited college or university; for the Master of Divinity program, graduation from an approved theological school with a Bachelor of Divinity or equivalent.

Tuition and Fees. Tuition $850 per semester; room $300-$350; board $600; registration fee $25.

Financial Aid. Scholarships are awarded on the basis of the financial resources of the Seminary, the academic status of the applicants, and the student's financial situation.

Housing. Dormitory housing is available for 65 men and 25 women.

Library Facilities. The Florovsky Library has holdings of over 43,000 volumes. The collection is especially strong in the areas of Orthodox history, theology, philosophy, and culture. Through the acquisition of Archimandrite Anthony Repella's library in 1956, Metropolitan Makary's in 1957, and Fr. Florovsky's in 1979, the collection is unique in the field of Russian theological literature. Acquisition of the Kolchin collection of Russian liturgical music in 1973 and copies of the Ladd Johnson collection of sound recordings in 1979 has bolstered the Seminary's holdings in these areas.

Religious Services/Activities. Participation in the daily, weekly, and yearly cycles of services is the first spiritual obligation of every seminarian. The annual retreat for the entire Seminary community is held on the first three days of Great Lent. Students are expected to participate in the activities of the Seminary Choir.

Degree Programs

The Master of Divinity program is intended primarily for the professional education and training of those preparing themselves for the priesthood of the Orthodox Church or for other forms of church service. The program includes pastoral and practical training as well as academic preparation. It consists of 96 credits. A thesis project and a comprehensive examination are required.

The Master of Theology program is designed for students who have received the degree of Master of Divinity, or have completed equivalent graduate studies in theology and who desire to pursue their theological education with specialization in a particular area. The four fields available are Systematic Theology, Church History and Patristics, Liturgical Theology, and Orthodox Canon Law. The program normally requires two-years and requires the completion of 24 points in advanced studies and 6 points for the preparation of a thesis. A general oral comprehensive examination is also required.

Special Programs

A one-year program in liturgical music is offered by the Seminary and leads to the Diploma of Studies in Orthodox Liturgical Music. The program is open to high school graduates interested in preparing themselves for service in Orthodox parishes as choir directors and church readers. There is also a one-year program leading to a Diploma of Studies in Orthodox Religious Education. It consists of 32 units of undergraduate study divided between "content courses" and religious education courses.

Syracuse University
Department of Religion
College of Arts and Sciences
Syracuse, NY 13210   (315) 423-3511

Administration. Dr. Melvin A. Eggers, Chancellor-President; Dr. James B. Wiggins, Chair, Department of Religion.

General Description. The Department of Religion offers coursework leading to the Bachelor of Arts degree. It explores the manifestations of religion in various cultural contexts and examines the belief systems and practices found in several major religious traditions, particularly in the history and sacred writings of Christianity, Judaism, Hinduism, and Buddhism. The program combines reli-

gious thought and related concerns in psychology, literature, the arts, philosophy, mythology, and the social and natural sciences. Introductory and advanced courses are offered in Biblical and scriptural studies, religious history and thought, ethics and society, religion and culture, and history of religions.

The Department also offers graduate work leading to the Master of Arts and the Doctor of Philosophy degrees. The graduate program emphasizes not only the interdependence of religion and culture but the value of insights gained in the comparative study of religious traditions.

Parent Institution. Syracuse University is a privately supported, coeducational university founded in 1870 by the Methodist Church, with financial help from the city of Syracuse. It has become a nonsectarian academic community of 11 colleges and schools. The University grants undergraduate and graduate degrees.

Community Environment. The main campus of 200 acres is located in a residential section at the southeastern edge of Syracuse in the central part of the state.

Religious Denomination. Nonsectarian.

Accreditation. Middle States Association of Colleges and Schools.

Term System. Semester.

Faculty for Degree Programs in Religion. Total 14.

Admission Requirements. High school graduation with completion of 16 academic units; SAT or ACT; Graduate Record Examination required for some graduate programs.

Tuition and Fees. Tuition $7,750 per year; room and board $3,920; student fees $210.

Financial Aid. Various aid programs are available.

Housing. University housing is available for approximately 9,500 students on the main and south campuses.

Library Facilities. Library collections of more than two million volumes are housed primarily in the Ernest S. Bird Library.

Religious Services/Activities. Hendricks Chapel, on the main campus, is the focus of programs of the Dean of the Chapel. The St. Thomas More Chapel serves Roman Catholic students.

Degree Programs

The major in Religion leading to the Bachelor of Arts degree requires the completion of at least 30 credits, at least 18 of which must be in advanced courses taken during the junior and senior years. Students must study at least two different traditions and develop competence in at least two different methods of interpreting religion. Up to 9 of the 30 credits may be earned in approved courses in departments other than Religion.

Students seeking the Master of Arts in Religion must complete 30 credits of graduate study and must pass a set of comprehensive examinations. There is no thesis or foreign language requirement.

The student seeking the Doctor of Philosophy degree in

Religion must complete 54 credits of graduate work beyond the Master of Arts, including at least 18 credits of dissertation preparation. Competence in two foreign languages must be demonstrated and a set of five comprehensive examinations must be passed.

Union Theological Seminary

3041 Broadway
At Reinhold Niebuhr Place
New York, NY 10027   (212) 662-7100

Administration. The Rev. Donald W. Shriver, Jr., President; The Rev. Milton McCormick Gatch, Jr., Academic Dean.

General Description. Union Theological Seminary is a graduate school of Christian theology, the mission of which is to educate men and women for the ministries of the Christian faith and the issues it faces today. The Seminary was founded by a group of "new school" Presbyterian laity and clergy. Denominational in its orientation, it nevertheless welcomed students from all denominations from the outset and stressed the advantage of "the greatest and most growing community in America" as a site for training parish ministers, teachers of religion, missionaries, and workers in ecclesiastical and other benevolent agencies. In all of its work, Union "strives to serve the church and the world by encouraging, as its founders stated, learning, piety, and enlightended experience."

Other institutions with which Union Theological Seminary cooperates in various ways including cross-registration of some courses include Auburn Theological Seminary, Columbia University, Teachers College, General Theological Seminary, Jewish Theological Seminary, City University of New York, Manhattan School of Music, and Fordham University.

Degrees awarded include Master of Divinity, Master of Arts in Education and Theological Studies, Master of Sacred Theology, Doctor of Philosophy.

Community Environment. See: Barnard College for information about New York City.

Religious Denomination. Nondenominational (Christian).

Accreditation. Middle States Association of Colleges and Schools; Association of Theological Schools in the United States and Canada.

Term System. Semester.

Enrollment in Degree Programs in Religion 1984–85. Total 390 (academic year 1983-84).

Faculty for Degree Programs in Religion. Total 47; full-time 27, part-time 20.

Admission Requirements. The Seminary seeks a diverse student body. Ordinarily an applicant's baccalaureate program should show strong preparation in such liberl arts studies as English, philosophy, Bible or religion, history, natural science, social sciences, and foreign languages. Graduate of accredited college or graduate school as ap-

plicable. Personal recommendations. GRE.

Tuition and Fees. Tuition: Master's, annual $5,800; Ph.D., annual $9,700. Matriculation and Facilities fee $400. Health Insurance fee $158. Dormitory rooms $1,-320-$2,800.

Financial Aid. Assistance is provided in the form of grants, loans, and/or part time employment.

Housing. The Seminary owns and operates three buildings and some apartments in nearby Morningside Gardens for the purpose of housing students. Every effort is made to meet students' housing needs.

Library Facilities. The Burke Library contains over 600,000 carefully selected items, 1,500 currently received periodicals, and a reference section rich in bibliographies, indexes, handbooks, directories, encyclopedias, and key works of religious scholarship.

Degree Programs

The Master of Divinity degree requires 76 curriculum points distributed as follows: Biblical 15, Historical 9, Theological 12, Practical 10, Professional Development 6, Electives 20, Thesis 4. This program takes three years.

The Master of Arts in Education and Theological Studies degree is ordinarily a two-year program that includes studies in the Christian religion, the history and philosophy of education, and in the issues and practices in the field of religion and education.

The degree Master of Sacred Theology is a post-Master of Divinity degree, and consists of two programs: a general program and a research program. The former is with class work and seminary study; the latter is for more concentrated research and a thesis.

The Doctor of Philosophy degree is a post-Master of Philosophy degree. The Master of Philosophy is pursued upon acceptance into the Ph.D. program and includes the additional requirements of (1) matriculation examinations, (2) matriculation conference, (3) language requirements, (4) residency requirements, (5) field examinations, (6) award of the M.Ph. degree. Candidacy for the Ph.D. includes (1) dissertation proposal, (2) dissertation defense, (3) completion of requirements not later than six years after admission.

Special Programs

In cooperation with Columbia University the following degrees are awarded: Master of Arts, Doctor of Philosophy, Doctor of Education.

Wadhams Hall Seminary-College

Riverside Drive
R.R. 4, Box 80
Ogdensburg, NY 13669   (315) 393-4231

Administration. Rev. Msgr. Peter R. Riani, President; Rev. Leeward J. Poissant, Vice President and Dean of Students; Dr. Edward G. Clarke, Academic Dean.

General Description. Wadhams Hall Seminary-College is a 4-year liberal arts college with a major in philosophy offering a bachelor of arts degree. It is affiliated with the Roman Catholic Church and enrolls students considering the priesthood as their possible vocation. Wadhams Hall is a full-program (free-standing) seminary supported regionally by 12 dioceses in the United States and Canada.

Community Environment. Wadhams Hall Seminary-College is located on a 208-acre campus in Ogdensburg, New York, which is on the St. Lawrence River, on New York's (and the United States') northern border. It is about two hours from Syracuse and an hour and a half from Ottawa, Canada. All winter sports are available.

Religious Denomination. Roman Catholic.

Accreditation. Middle States Association of Colleges and Schools.

Term System. Semester.

Enrollment in Degree Programs in Religion 1984–85. Total 52; men 52.

Admission Requirements. High school graduation with average of C or better; SAT 400 verbal, 400 mathematical or ACT 19 minimum; desire to consider priesthood; on-campus interview and personal recommendations required.

Tuition and Fees. $2,795 per year, payable per semester; room and board $2,800 per year.

Financial Aid. Need-based scholarships, federal/state loans, and grants are available.

Housing. All students live on campus in furnished rooms.

Library Facilities. The library houses 97,582 volumes and has over 1,600 microforms. The entire 382-volume set of Greek and Latin Church Fathers edited by Jacque Migne is available on microfiche cards. The library has a rare book collection that includes special editions of the works of Augustine and Aquinas.

Religious Services/Activities. There is a daily schedule of required morning/evening prayer and Mass; monthly retreats and days of recollection; periodic special services.

Degree Programs

All students graduate with a Bachelor of Arts degree with a major in philosophy. The academic program is capped by philosophy, which serves to integrate the entire curriculum while developing the critical intellectual abilities necessary in all academic fields. Students are required to pursue courses in various "Teaching Areas." The primary purpose of the Religious Studies Teaching Area is to develop in each student a mature understanding and appreciation of the Christian faith-experience.

Special Programs

A pre-theologate program is offered for graduate students needing philosophy and religious studies background before entering a graduate school of theology.

Yeshiva University
Bernard Revel Graduate School
500 West 185th Street
New York, NY 10033   (212) 960-5253

Administration. Dr. Norman Lamm, President.

General Description. While nondenominational, the Bernard Revel Graduate School offers courses in Semitics and Jewish Studies that will be of interest to all students of religion. These courses, which lead to the degrees Master of Science, Master of Arts, and Doctor of Philosophy, are in the fields of Bible, Jewish History (Classical, Medieval, and Modern), Jewish Philosophy, and Talmudic Studies; also Semitic Languages, Literatures, and Cultures.

Parent Institution. Yeshiva University is an independent institution under Jewish auspices chartered by the State of New York. It offers programs leading to bachelor's degrees in the arts and sciences, and master's and doctorate degrees in law, medicine, Jewish studies, biological sciences, social work, and psychology.

Community Environment. The University is comprised of 33 buildings located on 26 acres. The Main, Midtown, and Bronx Centers have dormitory accommodations. New York City, the largest city in the nation, is also its business, entertainment, and industrial capital. This teeming city is considered the greatest center of higher education in the country and claims the largest library outside the Library of Congress. Its intellectual and cultural opportunities are limitless and virtually impossible to duplicate anywhere.

Religious Denomination. Nondenominational.

Accreditation. Middle States Association of Colleges and Schools.

Term System. Semester; summer term.

Enrollment in Degree Programs in Religion 1984–85. Total 82; men 59, women 23. (These figures represent degree programs in Semitics for fall 1985.)

Degrees in Religion Awarded 1984–85. Master of Science 13; men 7, women 6. Master of Arts 3; men 1, women 2. Doctor of Philosophy (Ph.D.) 1; men 1. (These figures represent degrees awarded in Semitics.)

Faculty for Degree Programs in Religion. Total 13; full-time 9, part-time 4. (These figures represent faculty for degree programs in Semitics.)

Admission Requirements. Bachelor's degree with major in Jewish Studies or equivalent knowledge of Hebrew language and literature.

Tuition and Fees. Tuition $175 per credit; $40 registration fee per semester.

Financial Aid. A limited number of fellowships and scholarships are available.

Housing. Off-campus housing only.

Library Facilities. The University's libraries house over 850,000 volumes, periodical, and other materials in all branches of the arts and sciences and Judaica. About 225,-

000 volumes are in the fields of Hebrew Language and Literature, Jewish Culture and Civilization, and Semitics.

Degree Programs

Students may work toward the degrees Master of Science which requires 30 credits properly distributed plus a comprehensive examination; the Master of Arts which requires 30 credits properly distributed and a research project; and the Doctor of Philosophy which requires 45 credits beyond the Master of Arts, knowledge of 3 foreign languages (Hebrew and 2 others), 3 written and 1 oral comprehensive examinations, and a dissertation. The areas of concentration available are Bible (Biblical and Cognate Studies); Semitic Languages, Literature, and Culture; Talmudic Studies (Talmud and Midrash); Jewish History (Classical, Medieval, and Modern); Jewish Philosophy (Medieval and Modern); and Hebrew Literature. Programs are planned jointly by the student and an advisor.

Atlantic Christian College
Department of Religion and Philosophy
Wilson, NC 27893   (919) 237-3161

Administration. Dr. Allan R. Sharp, Chairman, Department of Religion and Philosophy.

General Description. The Department of Religion and Philosophy offers a major in Religion and Philosophy leading to the Bachelor of Arts degree. The main purpose of the Department is to prepare students for seminary.

Parent Institution. Atlantic Christian College is a liberal arts college sponsored by the Christian Church (Disciples of Christ). It provides an environment in which the heritage of man's past is transmitted and in which students and faculty explore and examine critically man's intellectual, religious, and esthetic experience in order to realize their obligation to the past, present, and future. The College was incorporated in 1902.

Community Environment. The campus is located in the northern section of Wilson, a city situated 47 miles east of North Carolina's capital city of Raleigh. The city is accessible by way of highways U.S. 301, U.S. 264, N.C. 42, and N.C. 58. In addition, the city is served by AMTRAK and by two bus companies. Commercial air service is available at the Rocky Mount-Wilson air terminal and the Raleigh-Durham air terminal.

Religious Denomination. Christian Church (Disciples of Christ).

Religious Emphasis. Liberal.

Accreditation. Southern Association of Colleges and Schools.

Term System. Semester; 3 summer sessions.

Enrollment in Degree Programs in Religion 1984–85. Total 34; men 23, women 11.

Degrees in Religion Awarded 1984–85. Bachelor of Arts 3; men 2, women 1.

Faculty for Degree Programs in Religion. Total 6; full-time 4, part-time 2.

Admission Requirements. Graduate of an accredited high school or equivalent; SAT or ACT.

Tuition and Fees. Costs per year: tuition $3,750; activity fee $120; medical fee $60; room $800 to $900; board $1,-000.

Financial Aid. Eighty percent of study body received aid in 1984-85 totaling nearly $4 million.

Housing. Dormitories and fraternity houses are available on campus. Apartments are also available in the city of Wilson.

Library Facilities. The Willis N. Hackney Library includes 100,000 volumes, a substantial microforms collection, audio recordings, maps, filmstrips, and pamphlets. It subscribes to 600 periodicals and 17 newspapers. The C.L. Hardy Center contains the Carolina Discipliana Collection, a rich and unique research source pertaining to the Disciples of Christ and related religious movements.

Religious Services/Activities. The religious program is designed to undergird and permeate the total life experience of each student. The program finds expression through the Campus Christian Association. Directed by an advisor and a student-elected cabinet, the association provides a series of group discussions, plays, lectures, and programs of religious significance. Nondenominational vesper services are held each Wednesday. Several campus religious organizations offer opportunities for the development of leadership.

Degree Programs

The Bachelor of Arts with a major in Religion and Philosophy requires a total of 36 semester hours of both required and elective courses in the major field. Courses are in the General, Biblical, Historical, Practical, and Philosophy areas.

Belmont Abbey College
Belmont, NC 28012   (704) 825-3051

Administration. John R. Dempsey, President.

General Description. Belmont Abbey College was founded in 1876 and is operated by the Order of St. Benedict. It is one of the oldest Catholic institutions in the South. The college offers a four-year liberal arts and sciences curriculum and grants the Bachelor's degree. The College is a member of a Consortium including 10 colleges in the Charlotte area.

Community Environment. The campus of 60 acres is located in Belmont, 10 miles west of Charlotte, North Carolina.

Religious Denomination. Roman Catholic.

Accreditation. Southern Association of Colleges and Schools.

Term System. Semester.

Admission Requirements. Graduation from an accredited high school or equivalent; completion of 16 academic units; SAT or ACT.

Tuition and Fees. Tuition $1,948 per semester; room and board $2,488 per year; fees $45.

Financial Aid. Scholarships, grants, and state and federal loan programs are available.

Housing. Students live in residence halls on campus.

Library Facilities. The Abbot-Vincent Taylor Library contains more than 90,000 books, periodicals, and microforms.

Religious Services/Activities. The Campus Ministry program concerns itself with the spiritual life of the college community. Programs include regularly scheduled and ad-hoc Liturgies, weekend excursions, retreats, Knights of Columbus, reconciliation celebrations, and volunteer services.

Degree Programs

The Department of Theology offers Bachelor degree majors in Theology, Religious Education, and Religious Education with a concentration in Youth Ministry. The major in Theology is a traditional liberal arts major with a strong minor in Philosophy. The Religious Education/Youth Ministry concentration is designed to prepare directors of religious education, teachers of religion, and youth ministers.

Campbell University
Buie's Creek, NC 27506   (919) 893-4111

Administration. Norman A. Wiggins, President.

General Description. The Religion and Philosophy Department in the Division of Humanities offers required courses in the basic curriculum designed to acquaint students with their Judeo-Christian and Western philosophical heritage. It also offers advanced elected courses and concentrations plus the Bachelor of Arts degree with majors in Religion and in Religion and Philosophy as pre-vocational preparation for entering a religious or church-related vocation.

Parent Institution. Campbell University is a Baptist university affiliated with the Baptist State Convention of North Carolina. It was founded in 1885 and offers programs of study leading to the Bachelor's and Master's degrees.

Community Environment. The University occupies a 850-acre campus in the village of Buie's Creek, equidistant

from Fayetteville and Raleigh, North Carolina.

Religious Denomination. Baptist State Convention of North Carolina.

Accreditation. Southern Association of Colleges and Schools.

Term System. Semester.

Faculty for Degree Programs in Religion. Total 8.

Admission Requirements. Graduation from an accredited high school or equivalent; ACT or SAT.

Tuition and Fees. Tuition and matriculation fees $4,370 per year; room $620; board $1,065.

Financial Aid. A student loan program, state and federal grants and loans, and scholarships are available.

Housing. Men's and women's dormitories are provided on campus.

Library Facilities. The Carrie Rich Memorial Library contains over 166,000 volumes.

Degree Programs

The major in Religion may follow a general course of study consisting of 37 hours of Religion beyond the General College curriculum requirements. The student must complete 3 hours from each of the areas of Biblical Studies, Historical Studies, Theological Studies, and Religion and Society Studies. Ministry specializations are offered to the Religion major in Pastoral Ministry, Youth/Education Ministry, and Social Services/Missions Ministry. The Bachelor of Arts degree requires the completion of a total of 128 semester hours.

Catawba College
West Innes Street
Salisbury, NC 28144   (704) 637-4402

Administration. Stephen H. Wurster, President.

General Description. Catawba's religious affiliation is with the United Church of Christ, a Protestant body created in 1857 with the merger of the Evangelical and Reformed Church and the Congregational and Christian Churches. The College was founded in 1851 by the German Reformed Church, which in 1934 merged with the Evangelical Synod of North America. While the College stands in close relationship to the church, there are no sectarian restrictions. The College is a four-year liberal arts institution offering programs leading to the Bachelor's degree. The Religion and Philosophy Department spans two disciplines but offers a single major.

Community Environment. The campus of 210 acres is located in Salisbury, a city in the Piedmont section of North Carolina.

Religious Denomination. United Church of Christ.

Accreditation. Southern Association of Colleges and Schools.

Term System. Semester.

Admission Requirements. Graduation from an accredited high school with completion of 16 academic units;

ACT or SAT.

Tuition and Fees. Tuition and general fees $4,355; room and board $2,090.

Financial Aid. Through the combined resources of the student, parents, and federal, state, and institutional programs, the College makes every effort that students who demonstrate financial need and have the potential for success at Catawba obtain assistance in meeting expenses.

Housing. Dormitory accommodations are available on campus.

Library Facilities. The Corriher-Linn-Black Library houses over 150,000 volumes and 35,000 volume equivalents in microform.

Religious Services/Activities. Weekly worship is held in the Chapel and is open to all students regardless of denominational background. Catholic Mass is celebrated each week in the Chapel. The Campus Minister oversees campus ministry programs. Sharing groups, Bible study, and service projects, in addition to worship, are a few of the activities offered.

Degree Programs

Students may major in Religion and Philosophy requiring a total of 42 semester hours. Students may distribute their interest equally or weight it in the direction of either discipline.

Cranmer Seminary
323 Walnut Street
P.O. Box 128
Statesville, NC 28677   (704) 873-8365

Administration. Margaret D. Lane, Professor of Christian Education.

General Description. Cranmer Seminary was begun by the Anglican Orthodox Church for the purpose of training clergy for this denomination. The curriculum of the Seminary is concerned primarily and basically with the conversion of each student individually, and of all the students collectively, as much as possible, to the Living Person of Jesus Christ.

The Anglican Orthodox Church was founded in 1963 in Statesville, North Carolina by Bishop James Parker Dees who prior to that time had served as a priest in the Protestant Episcopal Church. The Anglican Orthodox Church is a conservative, evangelical church with a strong mission program and it has branches throughout the world. It was organized "to preserve the faith once delivered to the Saints" and to preserve our ancient ways of worship and their heritage. The Church continues in the tradition of the "low" Episcopal Church of the Reformers using only the 1928 *Book of Common Prayer* in its worship and adhering to the *Thirty-Nine Articles of Religion* compiled in the 1500s under the direction of Archbishop Thomas Cranmer and his associates.

Community Environment. The Seminary is located in Statesville in the piedmont section of North Carolina. It is an hour from Charlotte, an hour from Winston-Salem, and two hours from Asheville.

Religious Denomination. Anglican Orthodox.

Religious Emphasis. Fundamental in the Reformed tradition.

Accreditation. Cranmer Seminary does not seek accreditation. It is concerned with preparing men for living the Christian life and for Holy Orders in the Orthodox Anglican tradition.

Term System. Quarter; summer sesssion.

Enrollment in Degree Programs in Religion 1984–85. Total 2; men 2.

Degrees in Religion Awarded 1984–85. Master of Divinity 1.

Faculty for Degree Programs in Religion. Total 4; full-time 2, part-time 2.

Admission Requirements. High school graduation or equivalent; Christian commitment and a desire to serve Christ in the ordained ministry of the Anglican Orthodox Church.

Tuition and Fees. Tuition $500 per quarter (includes dormitory for single students, no meals); married students living in apartments $150 per quarter plus utilities; student activity fee $20; tuition includes cost of required books.

Financial Aid. Available based on need.

Housing. Students are assigned to private rooms (as available) in Tindale Hall dormitory; apartments for married students.

Library Facilities. The Lister Library contains approximately 7,000 volumes.

Religious Services/Activities. Chapel services are held daily; Morning Prayer 4 days a week; Holy Communion one day per week. Church and Sunday School each Sunday. Retreats are held usually once or twice per year. The Bishop meets with students once a week to discuss personal religion and commitment to Christ and to the holy life.

Degree Programs

The Bachelor of Theology is a three-year course of study which prepares students for Holy Orders in the Anglican Orthodox Church. This presupposes an Associate of Arts degree; for those who do not have the liberal arts work, the Associate of Arts degree may be acquired in a two-year program at Mitchell College, adjacent to the Seminary. The studies in Cranmer Seminary are Bible centered. The first year's concern is with the study and apprehension of the Word of God and of Christ. The second year's basic concern is with the understanding and application of the Word of God. The third year's basic concern is to sum up the first two years' studies in the study of dogmatic theology, which is a summation of the basic essentials of Biblical doctrine and its relation to the clergyman's complete ministry and witness.

The Master of Divinity program is for students who have already earned a Bachelor of Arts or Science degree.

The curriculum is the same as described above.

Special Programs

A limited correspondence program is offered only to branches of the Anglican Orthodox Church in foreign countries.

Duke University
Trinity College of Arts and Sciences
Department of Religion
Durham, NC 27706   (919) 684-3214

Administration. Dr. H. Keith H. Brodie, President; Dr. Ernestine Friedl, Dean, Trinity College; Dr. Bland, Chairman, Department of Religion.

General Description. The Department of Religion believes that the study of religion arises from and leads to the awareness that an understanding of religion is crucial to an understanding of persons and of human societies. The curriculum develops this understanding in two distinct but inseperable ways: first, through the examination of the particulars of specific religious traditions; and, second, through theoretical studies of an analytic, comparative, and constructive nature.

Parent Institution. Duke University, a privately supported, church-related (Methodist) institution, has over 9,000 students enrolled in degree programs. From its earliest days as an academy to its days as a large university, some of the basic principles have remained constant, namely a fundamental faith in the union of knowledge and religion, the advancement of learning, the defense of scholarship, the love of freedom and truth, a spirit of tolerance, and a rendering of the greatest service to the individual, the state, the nation, and the church.

Community Environment. Duke University is composed of 177 buildings on 878 acres in Durham, North Carolina. Durham, a large metropolitan area, is also a cigarette manufacturing industrial center where about 50 million pounds of tobacco are auctioned annually. Nationally known hospitals and clinics make this city a medical center. Other community facilities include numerous churches, museums, shopping areas, and major civic and service organizations.

Religious Denomination. The United Methodist Church.

Accreditation. Southern Association of Colleges and Schools.

Term System. Semester; summer term.

Faculty for Degree Programs in Religion. Total 18; full-time 17, part-time 1.

Admission Requirements. Duke University seeks, in each prospective student, not only evidence of intellectual promise and maturity of judgment, but also a degree of positive energy. Specific requirements: at least 12 units of acceptable college preparatory work; SAT; 3 Achievement Tests (1 must be English Compostition); ACT may be acceptable.

Tuition and Fees. Per academic year: tuition $8,270; single room $1,753-$2,300; double room $1,318-$1,734; board 100 percent $1,990, 75 percent $1,560; books and suplies $410; student health fee $190.

Financial Aid. Duke University has a comprehensive aid program that includes both merit and need-based scholarships, college work-study, NDSL, GSL.

Housing. Housing provided on campus for 85 percent of undergraduate students. Freshmen are required to live on campus.

Library Facilities. The libraries of Duke University consist of the William R. Perkins Library and its seven branches. The combined resources are 3,300,000 volumes, 10,000 periodicals, 11,000 serials, 166 newspapers, 7,450,-000 manuscripts, 82,000 maps, 39,000 music scores, 651,-000 sheets of microtext.

Religious Services/Activities. See: Duke University - Divinity School.

Degree Programs

The requirements for the major in Religion, leading to the Bachelor of Arts or Bachelor of Science degree, are eight courses from the Department. These must include at least two introductory courses. Also required is a distribution of courses to include at least one each from the categories African and Asian traditions; Jewish and Christian traditions; and analytic, comparative, and constructive studies. One of the eight must be a seminar. Four of the eight should constitute a thematic or methodological concentration on a particular aspect of religion.

Duke University - Divinity School
Duke Station
Durham, NC 27706   (919) 684-3214

Administration. Dr. H. Keith H. Brodie, President; Dr. Dennis M. Campbell, Dean of the Divinity School.

General Description. The Duke University Divinity School represents theological inquiry and learning within the greater University. By history and indenture, it stands within the Christian tradition, mindful of its distinctive lineage in and its continuing obligation to the United Methodist Church. The Divinity School, although United Methodist in tradition and dependency, receives students from many Christian denominations and offers its educational resources to representatives of the several communions who seek an education for church-related ministry. From its inception, it has been ecumenical in aspiration, teaching, and practice, as well as in its faculty. Educational policy has consistently aspired to foster a Christian understanding "truly catholic, truly evangelical, and truly reformed." The Divinity School awards the degrees Master of Divinity, Master of Religious Education, Master of Theology, Master of Arts, and Doctor of Philosophy (Ph.D.).

Parent Institution. See: Duke University.

Community Environment. Duke University is composed of 177 buildings on 878 acres in Durham, North Carolina. Durham, a large metropolitan area, is also a cigarette manufacturing industrial center where about 50 million pounds of tobacco are auctioned annually. Nationally known hospitals and clinics make this city a medical center. Other community facilities include numerous churches, museums, shopping areas, and major civic and service organizations.

Religious Denomination. The United Methodist Church.

Religious Emphasis. Ecumenical; Reformed.

Accreditation. Southern Association of Colleges and Schools; Association of Theological Schools in the United States and Canada.

Term System. Semester.

Enrollment in Degree Programs in Religion 1984–85. Total Divinity School 380; men 254, women 126. Total Graduate Division of Religion 53; Master of Arts 3, Ph.D. 50.

Faculty for Degree Programs in Religion. Divinity School Total 29; Graduate Program in Religion (University) Total 16; Adjunct Faculty 5.

Admission Requirements. Bachelor of Arts degree or its equivalent from a regionally-accredited college. The candidate should have a strong background in liberal arts, especially the humanities. A well-rounded background in English language and literature, history, philosophy, psychology, religion, social science, and foreign languages is especially desirable. The applicant must have an overall average of at least B- (2.65 on a 4.0 scale) and must be committed to some form of ordained or lay ministry.

Tuition and Fees. Tuition $575 per course; student health fee $95 per semster; meals $900 per semester.

Financial Aid. Financial aid is recommended on the basis of finacial need. In order to receive assistance in any form from the Divinity School, a student must be enrolled for at least three courses per semester and maintain an overall academic average of 2.0 or higher. A limited number of Divinity School scholarships are available.

Housing. Duke University operates Town House Apartments primarily for graduate and professional school students. It also operates a 500-unit housing facility on the central campus for single and married students. The Department of Housing Management maintains lists of rental apartments, rooms, and houses off campus.

Library Facilities. The Divinity School Library contains a collection of more than 210,000 volumes in the field of religion and related disciplines, and more than 600 religious periodicals subscriptions. Although an integral part of the University's eleven-unit library system, which possesses more than 3,000,000 volumes, the Divinity School Library has its own facilities in the Divinity School Building.

Religious Services/Activities. The Corporate Worship life of the Divinity School is centered in York Chapel where three services are held weekly—a service of prayer on Tuesday, a service of preaching on Wednesday, and a service of word and table on Thursday. Services are voluntary. Sunday morning worship services are held in Duke Chapel where special music programs are also presented throughout the academic year. The Chapel also sponsors committees on Faith and the Arts, Supportive Ministries, Worship, Prophetic Concerns, and Leadership and Development.

Degree Programs

The academic work of the Divinity School embraces three programs: (1) the Master of Divinity degree ordinarily of three academic years; (2) a one-year program beyond the basic degree, the Master of Theology; (3) a program of two academic years leading to the degree Master of Religious Education. All are graduate-professional degrees.

Students preparing for ordination to the Christian ministry may take advantage of (1) and (2) above, which form a natural sequence.

The Master of Religious Education is designed to prepare those not ordinarily seeking ordination, for a ministry of Christian education in local churches or other organizations.

The Doctor of Philosoophy (Ph.D.) degree is offered jointly by the Divinity School and the Graduate School. The latter in turn works jointly with the Duke University Department of Religion.

Special Programs

The Center for Continuing Education offers extensive opportunities for education for ministry. The Divinity School provides a program of year-round seminars, conferences and special consultation.

Elon College
Department of Religion
Elon College, NC 27244   (919) 584-9711

Administration. Dr. James Fred Young, President; Dr. James A. Pace, Chairman, Department of Religion.

General Description. The educational program at Elon and in the Department of Religion provides opportunities for students who wish to prepare for the various aspects of Christian ministry, including preministerial or other full-time Christian vocation. The Bachelor of Arts in Religion degree is granted.

Parent Institution. Elon College is a coeducational, residential, church-related (United Church of Christ) institution near Burlington, North Carolina. The College derives its name from the Hebrew name for "Oak," being founded in an oak forest. One aim of the College is to give all students the opportunity to acquire a philosophy of life which is founded upon and motivated by the beliefs and spiritual values of the historic Christian Church.

Community Environment. Fifteen miles west of Elon College is Greensboro, North Carolina. To the east are Duke University in Durham, the University of North Carolina at Chapel Hill, and North Carolina State University at Raleigh.

Religious Denomination. United Church of Christ.

Accreditation. Southern Association of Colleges and Schools.

Term System. Semester; summer term.

Faculty for Degree Programs in Religion. Total 5; full-time 4, part-time 1.

Admission Requirements. Rolling admissions plan; admission based upon high school record and class rank, SAT or ACT scores, and recommendations; interview preferred; applicant must demonstrate intellectual promise, and emotional and social stability.

Tuition and Fees. Tuition $1,750 per semester; room $460; board $675-$775 (fall), $525-$575 (spring); miscellaneous fees. Part-time tuition $70 per credit hour.

Financial Aid. Elon College operates on the policy that no student should be denied a college education because of limited funds. As far as possible, eligible students are aided in meeting costs through careful planning and through various forms of financial assistance.

Housing. On-campus housing available; assistance is offered for those needing off-campus housing.

Library Facilities. The McEwen Library contains more than 150,000 volumes.

Religious Services/Activities. Responsibility for college religious life rests with the Chaplain, who coordinates all on-campus religious programs. Voluntary religious services are held during the academic year. Groups meet regularly for Bible study, group discussions, and service projects.

Degree Programs

A major in Religion leading to the Bachelor of Arts degree requires 15 semester hours in specific Religion courses plus an additional 21 hours of Religion courses, preferrably including two to four courses in Greek.

Greensboro College
Department of Religion and Philosophy
815 West Market Street
Greensboro, NC 27401   (919) 272-7102

Administration. Dr. James S. Barrett, President; Dr. W. Barnes Tatum, Dean of the College.

General Description. The Department of Religion and Philosophy offers the major in Religion and Philosophy.

Parent Institution. Greensboro College is a four-year coeducational liberal arts college affiliated with The United Methodist Church. The Bachelor of Arts and the Bachelor of Science degrees are awarded.

Community Environment. The College occupies a 30-acre campus near the center of the city of Greensboro,

North Carolina. Textiles are the predominant industry for Greensboro, along with the manufacture of cigrettes.

Religious Denomination. The United Methodist Church.

Accreditation. Southern Association of Colleges and Schools.

Term System. Semester.

Admission Requirements. Graduate of an officially accredited secondary school; 16 acceptable HS units including 4 English, 2 college preparatory math, 10 additional college preparatory courses (such as history/social studies, foreign language, natural science); acceptable scores on SAT or ACT.

Tuition and Fees. Annual tuition and fees $4,130, room and board $2,170.

Financial Aid. Greensboro College is anxious to help every qualified student reach his/her educational goals and has designed an extensive program of financial aid to support this program.

Housing. Full-time students must live on campus except for commuting students residing in their parents' homes or married or veteran students.

Library Facilities. The library contains 80,000 volumes.

Degree Programs

The Bachelor of Arts in Religion and Philosophy requires 30 hours in the major. These must include the course Our Biblical Heritage (2 semesters), plus one course each in the following areas: Biblical Tradition, Theology, Contemporary Worship/Culture, Philosophy, Church History, Christian Education. Greek is a highly-recommended elective for those planning to continue at a seminary.

High Point College
933 Montlieu Avenue
High Point, NC 27262   (919) 885-5101

Administration. Jacob C. Martinson, Jr., President.

General Description. High Point College was founded in 1924 and is related to the United Methodist Church. The College is a four-year, coeducational liberal arts college offering the Bachelor of Arts and Bachelor of Science degrees. The Department of Religion and Philosophy offers courses to all students in fulfillment of a three-hour requirement and the major in Religion.

Community Environment. The campus is located on 75 acres in High Point, part of the Golden Triad (with Greensboro and Winston-Salem) at the industrial center of the state.

Religious Denomination. The United Methodist Church.

Accreditation. Southern Association of Colleges and Schools.

Term System. Semester.

Admission Requirements. Graduation from an accredited high school with rank in the upper fifty percent of graduating class; ACT or SAT.

Tuition and Fees. Tuition $3,800; general fee $100; campus center fee $100; student activity fee $50; room $500-$850; board $1,300.

Financial Aid. The College maintains various scholarship funds, grants, and loan and work programs which are intended to supplement the financial resources of the student and his family. Students presenting evidence of financial need, a record of scholastic ability, and leadership potential will be considered for financial aid.

Housing. Dormitory facilities are provided on campus.

Library Facilities. The Herman H. and Louise M. Smith Library houses over 100,000 volumes.

Religious Services/Activities. The College Chaplain is in charge of organized religious activities and groups, including denominational clubs. The Charles E. Hayworth Memorial Chapel is open daily and is used for worship on Sunday and at other times.

Degree Programs

The Bachelor degree major in Religion must complete 30 hours in the Department including specified courses, plus complete three departmental supporting courses. Courses required include Old and New Testament Studies, Christian Ethics, Religion and Myth, World Religions, History of Christianity, Christian Beliefs, and Seminar.

John Wesley College
Division of Biblical Studies
2314 North Centennial Street
High Point, NC 27260   (919) 889-2262

Administration. Dr. Clifford W. Thomas, President; John L. Lindsey, Chairman, Division of Biblical Studies.

General Description. John Wesley College is a four-year, interdenominational, coeducational, evangelical Bible college. Its goal is to enable students to become grounded in the Christian faith and to train them for Christian ministries. The College is committed to providing a strong Christian education in Biblical, professional, and general studies. Its theological position is Wesleyan Arminian.

Community Environment. A new building to house the College was designed as an all-purpose structure on land donated to the College, and has been occupied since 1982. The city, High Point, North Carolina, was named for the fact that it was the highest location, on the original survey, for the old North Carolina Railroad, between Goldsboro and Charlotte.

Religious Denomination. Nondenominational (Christian).

Religious Emphasis. Wesleyan-Arminian.

Accreditation. American Association of Bible Colleges.

Term System. Semester.

Admission Requirements. Each applicant's record

should reflect sound Christian experience and character, promise of growth, seriousness of purpose, and sense of responsibility—spiritually, academically, socially, and personally. High school graduation, 3 letters of recommendation, medical statement.

Tuition and Fees. Tuition $70 per semester hour for 12 hours or less; 13-17 hours $960 per semester flat rate; above 17 hours $50 per semester hour; miscellaneous fees.

Financial Aid. Federal and state aid programs; loan funds from the College; institutional scholarships and grants.

Religious Services/Activities. While the College is interdenominational, it strongly encourages the pursuit of Christian experience and growth in spritual maturity of every student. By having prayer at the opening of every class, required daily chapel services, and private devotions for each student, the College attempts to cultivate a continuous spiritual atmosphere on campus.

Degree Programs

The four-year Bachelor of Arts, the five-year Bachelor of Theology, and the one-year Christian Workers programs are primarily terminal.

Special Programs

The Associate of Arts, a two-year program, is preparatory.

Johnson C. Smith University
100 Beatties Ford Road
Charlotte, NC 28216   (704) 378-1010

Administration. Dr. Robert Albright, President.

General Description. Johnson C. Smith University was established in 1867. It is an independent private college of liberal arts offering varied fields of study. The University is affiliated with the Presbyterian Church (U.S.A.). Courses in Philosophy and Religion are offered which meet general education requirements as well as elective study in the liberal arts.

Community Environment. The campus of 85 acres is located in the western part of the city of Charlotte, a city with a population of more than 340,000.

Religious Denomination. Presbyterian Church (U.S.A.).

Accreditation. Southern Association of Colleges and Schools.

Term System. Semester.

Admission Requirements. Graduation from an accredited high school with 16 academic units; SAT.

Tuition and Fees. Tuition $1,290 per semester; student union fee $50; room $400; meals $420.

Financial Aid. A student must file an application for student financial aid each academic year.

Library Facilities. The James B. Duke Memorial Library has holdings of over 100,000 volumes.

Religious Services/Activities. The function of Religious

Life Programs exists to facilitate an environment in which persons in the campus community may realize as fully as possible their potential for spiritual growth.

Degree Programs

Courses are offered providing the opportunity for learning experiences in the content areas of the Judeo-Christian tradition, including Biblical literature, church history, Afro-American perspectives, the African influence, other major religious traditions in the contemporary world, and procedures in Christian education and worship. A major in the field of Philosophy and Religion has been discontinued.

Lenoir-Rhyne College
Department of Religion and Philosophy
Hickory, NC 28603   (704) 328-1741

Administration. John E. Trainer, President.

General Description. Lenoir-Rhyne College is an institution of the North Carolina Synod of the Lutheran Church in America providing programs of undergraduate and graduate study that offer the liberal arts as a basis for varied careers. It was founded in 1891 and carried the name Highland College. This name was changed to Lenoir College a short time later. In 1923, the present name was adopted. The Department of Religion and Philosophy offers majors in Religious Studies: Theology, in Religious Studies: Christian Education, in Philosophy, and in Theology and Philosophy. The Bachelor of Arts degree is awarded.

Community Environment. The campus of 60 acres is located in the town of Hickory in the western Piedmont section of North Carolina. The town is known as one of the state's major furniture manufacturing cities.

Religious Denomination. The Lutheran Church in America.

Accreditation. Southern Association of Colleges and Schools.

Term System. Semester.

Faculty for Degree Programs in Religion. Total 7; full-time 5, part-time 2.

Admission Requirements. Graduation from an accredited high school with rank in the upper half of graduating class; ACT or SAT.

Tuition and Fees. Tuition $2,095 per semester; room $352.50-$377.50; board plan available; general fee $119.50.

Financial Aid. Awards are need-based and granted on a yearly basis.

Housing. Students reside on campus in dormitories.

Library Facilities. The Carl Augustus Rudisill Library contains more than 119,000 accessioned volumes.

Religious Services/Activities. The Chapel Council serves as an advisory board to the Chaplain and implements religious activities on campus. Chapel is held one day each

week and Campus Communion is held Thursday evenings.

Degree Programs

Courses in Religious Studies are designed to help individuals clarify their religious convictions and life goals, as well as to provide preparation for persons who anticipate further study and possible entry into church-related professions. The major in Religious Studies: Theology requires the completion of 15 hours of foundational courses and 12 hours of electives from the course offerings in religion. The major in Religious Studies: Christian Education must complete 33 hours in religion plus two courses in sociology, one course in psychology, and an elective from the course offerings in religion. A student who completes this major is eligible upon graduation for certification by the Lutheran Church in America as a professional parish educator.

Mars Hill College
Department of Religion and Philosophy
Mars Hill, NC 28754   (704) 689-1189

Administration. Dr. Fred Blake Bentley, President; Dr. C. Earl Leininger, Chairman, Division of Humanities.

General Description. The Department of Religion and Philosophy, one of four departments in the Division of Humanities, contributes to the general college curriculum. Its courses are open to all students. The Department offers a major in religion as well as concentrations in religious education, in church music, church drama (in cooperation with the Division of Fine Arts), and in church recreation (in cooperation with the Division of Physical Education). All members of the Department hold the Ph.D. degree.

The Center for Christian Education Ministries, born out of a concern for churches in western North Carolina, was established by the College in 1975 to provide direct service to two special groups: students in on-campus and off-campus ministries, and pastors and other church leaders in the region. Located on campus, the Center aids these groups in 3 ways: through resources related to all areas of church life, through leadership training, and through shared ideas.

Parent Institution. Mars Hill College is a Christian liberal arts institution of higher education, founded and sustained by North Carolina Baptists since 1856. It accepts students regardless of race, creed, or national origin. The student body of 1,100 represents 28 states and 8 foreign countries. The College offers 35 academic majors, including some professional and preprofessional programs.

Community Environment. The 180-acre campus of Mars Hill College is located in Mars Hill, North Carolina, at an elevation of 2,300 feet, in the Blue Ridge Mountains of western North Carolina. The campus is about 19 miles north of Ashville and 10 miles from Marshall.

Religious Denomination. Baptist.

Religious Emphasis. Moderate.

Accreditation. Southern Association of Colleges and Schools.

Term System. Semester; summer term.

Enrollment in Degree Programs in Religion 1984–85. Total 41; men 28, women 13.

Degrees in Religion Awarded 1984–85. Bachelor of Arts 17; men 13, women 4.

Faculty for Degree Programs in Religion. Total 9; full-time 6, part-time 3.

Admission Requirements. High school transcript and recommendation; SAT or ACT scores. For regular admission, high school must be accredited and transcript must report at least 18 units with C average or better on college preparatory units. Limited early admission is available to high school students of exceptional academic ability who may begin their college work in summers or regular term while continuing high school studies. Limited special admission available to students whose high school grades or SAT/ACT scores are below minimum requirements (requires Supervised Developmental Studies program).

Tuition and Fees. Tuition $3,885; fees $215; on-campus housing averages $650 per year; board (dining hall) $1,100 per year.

Financial Aid. The College participates in both state and federal educational grant and loan programs. Financial Aid Form required. In addition, the College administers many institutional loan funds and scholarships, including some full-tuition scholarships. In the spring of 1985, the College granted over $300,000 in renewable awards to academically qualified students. Student employment is also available.

Housing. The College can guarantee on-campus housing in two-person rooms to all students accepted. Traditional separate dorms are available to men and women. An attractive complex of apartments and townhouses are assigned to honor students and upperclassmen. Limited off-campus housing is available to upperclassmen and married students. Limited campus housing available to married students.

Library Facilities. The Memorial Library contains a book collection of 85,000 volumes, subscriptions to 450 periodicals and serial titles, and a substantial microforms collection. The Appalachian Room, housing books and other resources related to the southern mountain region, represents the library's major special collection. Other special collections include the Southern Appalachian Photographic Archives, Bascom Lamar Lunsford Folk Music Collection, Ruskin Collection of Cherokee Indian artifacts.

Religious Services/Activities. The Christian Student Movement coordinates religious activities on campus, including pre-school retreat, weekly Thursday evening worship, weekend revival teams, special concerts and seminars, and regularly scheduled social ministries in regional institutions. Students are encouraged to participate in the life of local churches.

Degree Programs

The Bachelor of Arts degree with a major in Religion requires competence in biblical, historical, theological, and philosophical studies. Courses are designed to develop students toward competence in these four areas. Competence in Greek is recommended for all ministerial students and for those with a major in Religion. Students who are planning to move directly into an educational or youth ministry in a church are offered a major in Religion with a concentration in Religious Education. This major requires competence in biblical, historical, and theological studies as well as courses in Psychology, Religion, and a full semester internship. Those students who are interested in church music, church drama, or church recreation can major in Religion and take supportive studies in the area of their choice. The Department of Religion and Philosophy will assist in working out a special program with Music, Theatre Arts, or Physical Education. Majors are also offered in Church Music by the Division of Fine Arts and Church Recreation by the Physical Education Division.

Special Programs

The major in Religion as described above is also offered as part of the College's Continuing Education Program. Courses are offered in the evenings both on-campus and in seven Centers in the region. Requirements are identical to the on-campus program. Tuition is at a reduced rate. Students who enroll in 12 hours are considered full-time students and are eligible for financial aid. Continuing Education Program students may receive credit for prior learning by following specific procedures.

Meredith College
Department of Religion and Philosophy
3800 Hillsborough Street
Raleigh, NC 27607 (919) 829-8308

Administration. Dr. John Edgar Weems, President; Dr. Craven Allen Burris, Vice President and Dean of the College; Dr. Roger H. Crook, Head, Department of Religion and Philosophy.

General Description. Meredith College's Department of Religion and Philosophy strives to aid students in understanding and developing analytical skills and methods for examining various religious phenomena and philosophical perspectives. Exposure to the literature, thought, and divergent interpretations of religions and philosophies helps students to formulate and better understand their own perspectives. The strong emphasis on Biblical studies and Western religious thought reveals that a major concern of the Department is to bring students to a deeper appreciation of the Judaeo-Christian heritage. The Department grants the degree Bachelor of Arts in Religion.

Parent Institution. Meredith College is a church-related

(Baptist) liberal arts college for women. It enrolls approximately 1,700 students, most of whom live on campus. Although a majority of students come from North Carolina, a significant number come from other states and other countries. A growing number of older students are enrolling at Meredith, some of whom are entering college for the first time, and some of whom are resuming an interrupted educational program. Eighteen departments in the College offer baccalaureate majors; three departments (Music, Business, Education) offer graduate work.

Community Environment. Meredith's 225-acre campus is located in the western part of Raleigh, the capital city of North Carolina. In 1788, a state convention made plans for the building of North Carolina's capital. From this, Raleigh, named after Sir Walter Raleigh, was founded in 1792. A great number of parks, swimming pools, and 4 large auditoriums and amphitheaters are the facilities for recreation.

Religious Denomination. Baptist.

Religious Emphasis. The College strives for a balanced perspective appropriate to a liberal arts institution.

Accreditation. Southern Association of Colleges and Schools.

Term System. Semester.

Enrollment in Degree Programs in Religion 1984–85. Total 21; women 21.

Degrees in Religion Awarded 1984–85. Bachelor of Arts in Religion 9; women 9.

Faculty for Degree Programs in Religion. Total 5; full-time 4, part-time 1.

Admission Requirements. At least 16 units of secondary school credit earned in grades 9 through 12 (including 4 units in English and at least 9 additional credits chosen from English, foreign language, history, social studies, mathematics, and natural sciences); upper half of graduating class in high school; satisfactory scores on the SAT.

Tuition and Fees. Tuition $1,965 per semester; room and board $860 per semester.

Financial Aid. An assistance program is available to help meet the financial needs of students.

Housing. Dormitories are available for all resident students.

Library Facilities. The library houses over 150,000 volumes.

Religious Services/Activities. Student religious activities are under the sponsorship of the Meredith Christian Association and include vespers, prayer groups, and other worship services, as well as coordinating the annual Religious Emphasis Week. Campus facilities are often used for denominational meetings, particulary during the summer.

Degree Programs

The Bachelor of Arts with a major in Religion is offered and requires twenty-four hours in Religion, including one course from each of three categories: Religion and Society; Biblical Studies; and Religious History and Thought. The requirements for a major are sufficiently flexible to provide

for the student's personal development and choice of career preparation.

Methodist College
Department of Philosophy and Religion
5400 Ramsey Street
Fayetteville, NC 28301   (919) 488-7110

Administration. Dr. M. Elton Hendricks, President; Dr. Fred E. Clark, Dean, Academic Affairs; Dr. Garland Knott, Chair, Department of Philosophy and Religion.

General Description. The Department of Philosophy and Religion of Methodist College aspires to do two things: (1) acquaint the general student with the scholarly study of religion, (2) give Religion majors a strong academic base for graduate or professional study. Two majors, Religion and Religious Education, are offered. Religion courses include Bible, religious thought, and American and World Religions. Religious Education courses are strongly grounded in psychology, theology, philosophy, and methodology. The degree Bachelor of Arts is awarded.

Parent Institution. Methodist College is a four-year Christian liberal arts institution serving a diverse student population in an urban setting. It is the only such institution in the immediate area. Approximately 60 percent of the students are commuters, including a number of military and military dependents, mature persons returning to school, and area residents of usual college age.

Community Environment. The 600-acre campus of Methodist College is located 5½ miles north of Fayetteville, North Carolina in the Cape Fear Valley. North Carolina's farthest inland port, Fayetteville is at the head of navigation on the Cape Fear River. Principal industries here include chemicals, furniture, fabric, and lumber. Agriculture is of importance to the community.

Religious Denomination. The United Methodist Church.

Religious Emphasis. The spectrum from Neo-orthodox to Liberal.

Accreditation. Southern Association of Colleges and Schools.

Term System. Semester; summer term.

Enrollment in Degree Programs in Religion 1984–85. Total 15; men 9, women 6. (Figures are for the school year 1985-86.)

Degrees in Religion Awarded 1984–85. Bachelor of Arts in Religion 3; men 3. Bachelor of Arts in Religious Education 2; men 1, women 1.

Faculty for Degree Programs in Religion. Total 5; full-time 3, part-time 2.

Admission Requirements. High school graduation or equivalent; SAT or ACT; high school units should include 4 English, 2 mathematics, 1 history, 1 science, 6 electives, 2 foreign language (may be waived); no minimum on SAT or ACT but total record evaluated.

Tuition and Fees. $4,700 per year with small additional fees; room $850 per year; board $1,550 per year.

Financial Aid. The great majority of students receive substantial aid in the form of grants, scholarships, loans, and work programs. Students in or planning a church vocation (any denomination) receive a grant of one-half tuition.

Housing. Residence halls are available; on-campus apartments available for married students. There is abundant off-campus housing in the community (special permission required).

Library Facilities. The library houses over 73,000 volumes. Special collections include Children's Literature, Lafayette Collection, North Carolina Collection, Lee Collection of Rare Bibles, and Manuscript Collection.

Religious Services/Activities. Ecumenical Sunday services, Wednesday devotions, Student Christian Group, two annual retreats, and many other activities. The College Chaplain is Free Methodist.

Degree Programs

The Religion major leading to the Bachelor of Arts degree requires a total of 30 semester hours of work in the Department including prescribed courses. This program is especially helpful to students preparing for seminary or graduate school. The major in Religious Education is designed to prepare students for graduate programs for work as Education Assistants. Students must complete 32 semester hours of courses. The Methodist College program in Religious Education has been approved by the Division of Diaconal Ministry of the Board of Higher Education. Persons who graduate with a Bachelor's degree and a major in Religious Education will have fulfilled two of the four certification studies for Associate in Christian Education in the United Methodist Church.

A course of study providing preparation for the seminary, for graduate study of sociology, or for employment as a staff person in a church or human service agency is offered. The major requires 49-51 semester hours of which 18 semester hours meet Core Curriculum requirements.

Special Programs

Religion courses are offered in Continuing Education for academic credit. A number of church-related courses offered on campus and their successful completion result in the awarding of Continuing Education Units (CEUs).

North Carolina, University of - Charlotte
Department of Religious Studies
UNCC Station
Charlotte, NC 28223   (704) 597-4598

Administration. Dr. E.K. Fretwell, Jr., Chancellor; Dr. Robert Alan Gwaltney, Dean. Edward B. St. Clair, Chairman, Department of Religious Studies.

General Description. The Department of Religious Studies is an undergraduate department with a major in religious studies leading to the Bachelor of Arts degree. The Department also offers a minor in religious studies.

Parent Institution. The University of North Carolina at Charlotte is a comprehensive state university with an enrollment of over 10,000. It is composed of six colleges: Arts and Sciences, Architecture, Business Administration, Education, Engineering, and Nursing.

Community Environment. Despite its metropolitan setting, the campus covers approximately 1,000 acres of rolling hills with forests, streams, and ponds. Contemporary buildings of unique design and landscaping are clustered at the central campus which is easily accessible from major interstate and other highways. The setting is enhance by a planned community, University Place, University Research Park, and University Memorial Hospital, adjacent to the campus.

Religious Denomination. None.

Accreditation. Southern Association of Colleges and Schools.

Term System. Semester.

Enrollment in Degree Programs in Religion 1984–85. Total 26; men 14, women 12.

Degrees in Religion Awarded 1984–85. Bachelor of Arts 7; men 4, women 3.

Faculty for Degree Programs in Religion. Total 12; full-time 7, part-time 5.

Admission Requirements. Applicants for admission must present 16 acceptable units, 13 of which are to be academic (college preparatory) courses and are expected to include 4 units of English, 3 units of algebra and geometry, 2 units of social science, 1 unit of natural science, and 2 units of a foreign language; SAT or ACT.

Tuition and Fees. Tuition for in-state students $700 per year, out-of-state students $3,258 per year; room $647 to $785 depending upon accommodations; board $398 to $522 depending upon meal plan; other fees where applicable.

Financial Aid. Scholarships and work study programs are available.

Housing. There is on-campus housing for both single and married students.

Library Facilities. The J. Murrey Atkins Library houses an open-shelf collection which includes over 360,000 bound volumes, 675,000 units in microform, and approximately 131,000 manuscripts in closed stacks. The Rare Book Collection, numbering some 3,688 volumes, contains literary first editions, historical children's books, early printed works, fine press books, and a large number of 17th and 18th century English plays.

Religious Services/Activities. There is a United Religious Ministry under the Office of Student Affairs.

Degree Programs

The Bachelor of Arts in Religious Studies requires that 30 of 120 semester hours be in religious studies. The student must take Introduction to Religious Studies, Eastern

Religions, Western Religions, Senior Seminary, and six upper level electives. An interdisciplinary program in Religious Studies is an option intended to provide a course of studies that will make maximum use of the interdisciplinary aspects inherent in religious studies.

North Carolina Wesleyan College
College Station
Rocky Mount, NC 27801   (919) 971-7171

Administration. Dr. Bruce Petteway, President.

General Description. In 1956, the North Carolina Annual Conference of The United Methodist Church met in Goldsboro and approved a petition from the people of Rocky Mount to locate a college in their community. In 1964, the seniors of the first class received their degrees. The College grants the bachelor's degree. The Department of Religion offers a major leading to the Bachelor of Arts degree.

Community Environment. The campus occupies 200 acres in the city of Rocky Mount near the Atlantic coast.

Religious Denomination. The United Methodist Church.

Accreditation. Southern Association of Colleges and Schools.

Term System. Semester.

Admission Requirements. Graduation from an accredited high school or equivalent; upper half of graduating class; SAT.

Tuition and Fees. Tuition $2,000 per semester; activities fee $30; room $365; board $725.

Financial Aid. Students who excel in scholarship as well as those who cannot provide the entire cost of their education are encouraged to apply for financial aid.

Housing. Dormitory accommodations are available on campus.

Library Facilities. The College Library contains over 68,000 volumes. The Wesleyan Archives are maintained as a special collection.

Religious Services/Activities. The Interfaith Commission of the Student Government Association plans religious activities such as worship services, discussion groups, and retreats.

Degree Programs

The Bachelor degree major in Philosophy-Religion requires the completion of a minimum of 30 semester hours. The major in Religion requires a minimum of 24 semester hours in Religion courses including at least 3 semester hours each in Biblical, Historical, Systematic, and Sociocultural studies. Appropriate group and individualized studies may be substituted for courses in each area.

Pfeiffer College
Misenheimer, NC 28109   (704) 463-7343

Administration. Cameron P. West, President.

General Description. Pfeiffer College was founded in 1885 and is sponsored by the Western North Carolina Conference of the United Methodist Church. It is a liberal arts college offering programs leading to the Bachelor's degree. The Department of Religion offers a major through a variety of courses in Bible and Christian thought, taught from several perspectives.

Community Environment. The 365-acre campus is located in the rolling Piedmont area of North Carolina in the community of Misenheimer.

Religious Denomination. United Methodist Church.

Accreditation. Southern Association of Colleges and Schools.

Term System. Semester.

Admission Requirements. High school graduation or equivalent with rank in the upper 50 percent of graduating class; completion of 16 academic units.

Tuition and Fees. Tuition $3,865 per year; room and board $2,160; student fees $515.

Financial Aid. More than 90 percent of the students receive some form of aid. The average aid package exceeds $2,500 per student per year.

Housing. Students reside in dormitories on campus.

Library Facilities. The Gustavus A. Pfeiffer Library houses over 101,000 volumes.

Religious Services/Activities. All religious activities at the College are voluntary and many are ecumenical in nature. The Religious Life Council coordinates the religious life program on campus. The Brame Christian Life Convocations bring outstanding ministers or religious leaders to the campus each fall. Weekly chapel service, Sunday worship, and programs sponsored by denominational groups are regularly scheduled activities.

Degree Programs

Required courses for the Bachelor degree major in Religion include Old Testament, New Testament, Christian Beliefs, World Religions, Old Testament Life and Thought, New Testament Life and Thought, and Doing Philosophy - An Introduction. All courses carry credit equivalent to 3 semester hours.

Piedmont Bible College
716 Franklin Street
Winston-Salem, NC 27101   (919) 725-8344

Administration. Donald K. Drake, President; Ronald L. Reinert, Academic Vice President.

General Description. Piedmont Bible College is an undergraduate institution preparing students for pastoral and missionary work. Christian school teachers can receive North Carolina certification. A Missionary Aviation major is available. All students major in Bible and participate in Christian service. The College's general objectives are: (1) to cultivate Christian life and experience, (2) to inculcate a comprehensive knowledge of the Bible and an understanding of Christian doctrine, (3) to broaden and deepen the general education of its students for effective living as Christian citizens and Christian workers, (4) to instill vital missionary vision and dedication to worldwide service, (5) to teach students the specialized skills, knowledge, and attitudes necessary for competent Christian service, (6) to foster Christian refinement, appreciations, social attitudes, and skills, (7) to educate students in relation to health and Christian regard for the body.

Community Environment. Piedmont Bible College is in the rolling hills of North Carolina known as the Piedmont. Its home, Winston-Salem, is a multi-industrial, progressive city of about 150,000 population, enriched by its wealth of religious and general cultural traditions. Of special interest to both student and visitor is the restored 18th century Moravian community, Old Salem, located within walking distance of the campus.

Religious Denomination. Independent Baptist.

Religious Emphasis. Fundamentalist.

Accreditation. American Association of Bible Colleges; candidate for Southern Association of Colleges and Schools.

Term System. Semester; summer term.

Enrollment in Degree Programs in Religion 1984–85. Total 347; men 218, women 129.

Degrees in Religion Awarded 1984–85. Bachelor of Theology 14; men 14. Bachelor of Religious Education 20; men 15, women 5. Bachelor of Science 9; women 9.

Faculty for Degree Programs in Religion. Total 23; full-time 20, part-time 3.

Admission Requirements. High school diploma; Christian character references.

Tuition and Fees. $2,460 per year; room and board $1,950 per year.

Financial Aid. Pell Grant, Missionary Children Scholarship-Tuition Grant, and work-study are available.

Housing. Dormitories for single men or women; 30 apartments are available for married students (2 rooms, $150 monthly; 3 rooms, $190 monthly; includes utilities).

Library Facilities. The George M. Manuel Memorial Library houses over 46,000 volumes.

Religious Services/Activities. Daily chapel attendance is required. Attendance is compulsory at Mid-Winter Bible Conference, at the Thursday evening sessions of the annual missionary conference, and at all meetings scheduled in lieu of chapel. A Spiritual Life Week is held during the fall semester and an annual missionary conference in the spring.

Degree Programs

The Bachelor of Religious Education degree requires the completion of 129 semester hours of specified courses. The major is in Bible and minors are available in Administration, Youth Leadership, and Missions. The Bachelor of Science degree in Christian School Music Education requires a total of 171 credits and five years for completion. The Bachelor of Theology degree curriculum is primarily designed as a terminal degree program to prepare students for the pastoral office. This program requires a total of 166 semester hours. Within the program one may also minor in youth ministry (168 semester hours) or missions (167 semester hours), or major in missionary aviation (209 semester hours). Courses of instruction are organized into the divisions of Biblical Education, General Education, and Christian Ministries.

Special Programs

Adult level Bible and Bible-related classes are available at night on the main campus or in fifteen locations in nearby communities.

A three-year Christian Worker's Diploma course is offered which gives the student a basic knowledge of the Bible and educational activities of the local church. The diploma course requires satisfactory completion of 97 semester hours.

St. Andrews Presbyterian College
Laurinburg, NC 28352   (919) 276-3652

Administration. Dr. Alvin P. Perkinson, Jr., President.

General Description. St. Andrews Presbyterian College is a four-year coeducational residential college. It was established in 1958 by the Presbyterian Synod of North Carolina. The Department of Religion offers the major in the field leading to the Bachelor of Arts degree.

Community Environment. The campus of 700 acres is located in the city of Laurinburg at the southern edge of the peach belt and the Sandhills resort region of the state. Laurinburg is 100 miles from Charlotte.

Religious Denomination. Presbyterian Church (U.S.A.).

Accreditation. Southern Association of Colleges and Schools.

Term System. Semester (4-1-4 plan).

Admission Requirements. Graduation from an accredited high school; ACT or SAT.

Tuition and Fees. Tuition $5,800 per year; room $1,075-$1,612; board $1,775.

Financial Aid. The St. Andrews financial assistance program for students includes grants, workshops, scholarships, and loans.

Housing. All students are required to live on campus when rooms are available unless they are living with parents, guardians, or spouses.

Library Facilities. The DeTamble Library houses more than 100,000 volume and 18,000 microforms.

Religious Services/Activities. Religious activities are ecumenical in emphasis. The College Christian Union sponsors Sunday evening Vespers, Bible studies, Christian music concerts, special Christmas and Easter observances, and off-campus retreats.

Degree Programs

The Bachelor degree major in Religion requires the completion of 10 courses of which 6 are prescribed and 4 are elective. In addition to the regular major, the Department's program offers students options for designing and contracting a major which has an emphasis in some area(s) of study that the students wish to relate to religion. Internships in the field of religion combine supervised off-campus work in churches, hospitals, and social service agencies.

Southeastern Baptist Theological Seminary

P.O. Box 712

Wake Forest, NC 27587   (919) 556-3101

Administration. W. Randall Lolley, President; Morris Ashcraft, Dean of Faculty.

General Description. Southeastern Baptist Theological Seminary prepares men and women for Christian leadership in various ministries. These include preaching and pastoral care, missionary work at home and abroad, religious education, church music, the teaching of religion and other subjects in secondary schools and colleges, religious leadership on college campuses, the chaplaincy, social service, and other forms of ministry which require specialized preparation.

The Seminary opened for classes in 1951. When Wake Forest College moved to its new campus in Winston-Salem in 1956, the Seminary expanded to include the entire campus. Average enrollment during the history of the Seminary has been 725 students.

Community Environment. The campus dates from 1832 when the 615-acre plantation of Dr. Calvin Jones was purchased by the Baptists of North Carolina. The stone wall begun about 1885 still encloses the 25 acres of the campus proper. Wake Forest is located 15 miles north of Raleigh and 22 miles east of Durham.

Religious Denomination. Southern Baptist.

Religious Emphasis. Mainline Protestant.

Accreditation. Southern Association of Colleges and Schools; Association of Theological Schools in the United States and Canada.

Term System. Semester; summer term.

Enrollment in Degree Programs in Religion 1984–85. Total 1,134; men 933, women 201.

Degrees in Religion Awarded 1984–85. Master of Divinity 220; men 187, women 33. Master of Theology 6; men 5, women 1. Master of Religious Education 8; men 4, women 4. Doctor of Ministry 19; men 18, women 1. Associate of Divinity 29; men 27, women 2.

Faculty for Degree Programs in Religion. Total 68; full-time 38, part-time 30.

Admission Requirements. Students must have a baccalaureate degree from an accredited college or university with at least 75 hours in the liberal arts; must have the endorsement of their church or religious community, and must have three letters of reference which vouch for their commitment to Christian ministry and worthiness of character.

Tuition and Fees. The support of the Seminary by the Southern Baptist Convention through its Cooperative Program enables the Seminary to offer its programs of study without charging tuition. There is a matriculation fee per per semester of $300 for members of Southern Baptist churches and $600 for non-members. Dormitory housing $60 to $65 per month; apartment rentals $170 to $240 per month (does not include utilities).

Financial Aid. Financial aid and scholarships are available to a large number of students who need assistance.

Housing. The Seminary provides dormitory space for single students and apartments and townhouses for married students.

Library Facilities. The Library has a collection of more than 225,000 items including books, periodical volumes, music scores, music recordings, audiovisual materials, and Baptist documents. The microforms, containing approximately 90,000 volumes of books, periodicals, and dissertations make the Library's collection strong in Early American and Early British materials, including important Baptist history resources.

Religious Services/Activities. Worship is the center of the Seminary's life. Under the leadership of students, professors, and prominent visitors, devotional services are held at 10:00 a.m. each Tuesday, Wednesday, and Thursday. On special days, missionary speakers, scholars and other Christian leaders broaden the vision and deepen the commitment of students and others with lectures and addresses. The Conservative Evangelical Fellowship provides opportunities for support, fellowship, and the discussion of topics of interest to conservative, evangelical Christians. The Fellowship of Christians United in Service is a volunteer ministry designed to provide opportunities for ministry in churches in accord with their needs and the gifts of the team members. It sponsors a mission project for selected students and is open to all students. The Seminary chapter of The Hymn Society of America sponsors hymn festivals and workshops in the promotion and composition of new hymns and tunes. A variety of lecture series, conferences, and special days are scheduled throughout the academic year.

Degree Programs

The Master of Divinity degree is designed to be completed within three academic years of full-time attendance. It consists of entry level experiences, foundational studies, vocational and elective studies, and an integrative course or activity. The program is designed to assure an adequate understanding of scripture, theology, and the Christian tradition for the practice of Christian ministry with considerable latitude for the pursuit of competencies required in a variety of ministries. A candidate may concentrate in the fields of Christian Education or Church Music.

The Master of Arts in Christian Education program equips persons for service in Christian education and related ministries, usually in a local church. It is designed to be completed within two academic years and consists of 64 semester hours of courses.

The Master of Theology degree provides the student with an opportunity for guided research in a special area of theological study. Students in the program major in one of the four curriculum areas of Biblical, Historical, Theological, or Ministerial.

The Doctor of Ministry degree equips the student for the practice of ministry at a high level of professional competency. The program is complementary to work done for the Master of Divinity degree. The program provides opportunity for advanced study in interdisciplinary courses, seminars, and clinical settings. It combines academic study and experiential learning in an attempt to integrate theology and practice.

Special Programs

The Associate of Divinity is offered to men and women who feel the call to Christian service after a career in some other field. A balanced program of study in the biblical, historical, theological, and ministry areas is offered to them at the beginning college level. The program is designed to be completed in two years of full-time attendance.

Wake Forest University
Department of Religion
Box 7305, Reynolda Station
Winston-Salem, NC 27109   (919) 761-5201

Administration. Dr. Thomas K. Hearn, Jr., President; Dr. Thomas E. Mullen, Dean of the College; Dr. Gerald W. Esch, Dean of the Graduate School; Dr. Carlton T. Mitchell, Chairman, Department of Religion; Dr. Fred L. Horton, Jr., Director of Graduate Studies in Religion.

General Description. The Department of Religion offers courses designed to give every student an opportunity to acquire at least an introduction to the life, literature, and most important movements in the field of religion. It also seeks to give students preparing for specialized service as religion education directors, ministers, and missionaries the foundational courses needed for further study. The Bachelor of Arts with a major in Religion fulfills these objectives. The Department of Religion also offers work leading to the Master of Arts in Religion.

Parent Institution. A strong teaching and research emphasis is shared by Wake Forest College (which enrolls about 3,200 undergraduates) and the Graduate School (offering Master of Arts, Master of Arts in Education, Master of Science, and Doctor of Philosophy degrees). The three professional Schools of Law, Medicine, and Management complete the University community.

Community Environment. The Reynolda Campus of Wake Forest University is situated on approximately 320 acres; its physical plant consists of over 30 buildings, most of which are modified Georgian architecture and constructed of Old Virginia brick trimmed in granite and limestone. The Reynolda Gardens annex, consisting of about 150 acres and including Reynolda Woods, Reynolda Village, and Reynolda Gardens, is adjacent to the campus. The University is located in Winston-Salem, North Carolina, a historic city with a cultural and intellectual life disproportionate to its relatively small size of 145,000. The city grew out of the Moravian settlement that began in 1753 with the founding of Bethabara. Salem, which was founded by Moravians in 1766 and consolidated with Winston in 1913, has been reconstructed and is a popular place for sightseeing.

Religious Denomination. Baptist.

Religious Emphasis. Liberal.

Accreditation. Southern Association of Colleges and Schools.

Term System. Semester; summer term.

Degrees in Religion Awarded 1984–85. Bachelor of Arts in Religion 12. Master of Arts in Religion 3.

Faculty for Degree Programs in Religion. Total 13; full-time 10, part-time 3.

Admission Requirements. Admission as a freshman normally requires graduation from an accredited secondary school with a minimum of 16 units of high school credit. The SAT is required also and two letters of recommendation are requested to accompany the Wake Forest application form.

Tuition and Fees. Tuition $6,000 per year; room $1,060; board $1,030 to $1,450.

Financial Aid. Any student admitted to the University who demonstrates financial need will receive assistance commensurate with that need. Approximately five merit scholarships are available with varying stipends and numbers of awards.

Housing. Dormitories for single students and married student housing are available.

Library Facilities. The library collections total 927,286 volumes. Special collections cover the works of selected late nineteenth and early twentieth century English and American writers, and include pertinent critical material. Among the special collections are a Mark Twain collection, a Gertrude Stein collection, and the Ethel Taylor Crittenden collection in Baptist history. Also maintained is the Charles H. Babcock Collection of Rare and Fine Books.

Religious Services/Activities. Regular weekly services; Thursday chapel and Sunday services; retreats; seasonal celebrations; Bible study and discussion groups and both independent and church-related social service in Winston-Salem. Baptist, Roman Catholic, Episcopal, and Methodist chaplains represent their faiths.

Degree Programs

The Bachelor of Arts degree with a major in Religion requires thirty-two credits in the major, at least half of which must be upper division courses.

The Master of Arts degree in Religion offers the opportunity to pursue graduate study in religion in the broad and enriching context of the humanities, social sciences, and the natural sciences. Thirty semester hours are required for the degree of which twenty-four hours are in coursework and six hours in thesis credit.

The Master of Arts degree in Pastoral Care is offered in cooperation with the School of Pastoral Care at the North Carolina Baptist Hospital in Winston-Salem. A professional theological degree is a prerequisite.

Wingate College
Division of Humanities
Department of Religious Studies
Wingate, NC 28174   (704) 233-4061

Administration. Dr. Paul Richard Corts, President; Dr. Paul W. Beasley, Vice President for Academic Affairs and Dean; Dr. G. Byrnes Coleman, Chairman, Division of Humanities.

General Description. The Department of Religious Studies program involves concentrated academic study in religion, emphasizing the Judaeo-Christian heritage and expression. Its stance is Christian, involving an openness to truth and meaning from any and all mediating sources or disciplines. The degree Bachelor of Arts in Religious Studies is awarded.

Parent Institution. Wingate College exists to afford students educational opportunity in a setting characterized by Christian sensitivity and moral responsibility. The College seeks to relate the theories, data, and competencies of the curriculum to the cultural and interpersonal experiences of college life; and to lead the student to confront great moral issues. The college community promotes personal resolution to life's great issues, drawing on the wisdom of humane learning, the rigor of logical reasoning, the discipline of scientific observation, and the truth of Christian faith.

Community Environment. Wingate College is located in the village of Wingate, North Carolina, 4 miles east of Monroe and 28 miles southeast of Charlotte. Monroe, the county seat of Union County, has a population of approximately 13,000. Wingate is in the heart of the Piedmont Carolinas with the scenic Appalachian Mountains to the northwest and the Atlantic Coast with its beaches to the east.

Religious Denomination. Baptist.

Religious Emphasis. Conservative.

Accreditation. Southern Association of Colleges and Schools.

Term System. Semester; summer term.

Enrollment in Degree Programs in Religion 1984–85. Total 55; men 40, women 15 (the figures are approximate).

Degrees in Religion Awarded 1984–85. Bachelor of Arts 15; men 10, women 5 (the figures are approximate).

Faculty for Degree Programs in Religion. Total 5; fulltime 5. In addition, there are visiting lecturers from time to time.

Admission Requirements. High school graduation with minimum C average.

Tuition and Fees. Tuition $1,550; fees for boarding students $1,110.

Financial Aid. Various scholarships and aid are available.

Housing. Boarding students reside in dormitories; apartments are available in the community of Wingate for married students.

Library Facilities. The library houses over 100,000 volumes.

Religious Services/Activities. Chapel and vesper services are held once each week. Spiritual Awakening Week is held each January and there are frequent speakers throughout the school year.

Degree Programs

The Bachelor of Arts in Religious Studies requires the completion of 58 general education requirements plus 9 hours in Biblical Studies, 9 hours in Historical Studies, 9 hours in Theological and Philosophical Studies, 3 hours in a Religion elective, 18 hours of restricted electives (minor), and 19 general electives. A total of 125 hours is required.

Special Programs

A Bachelor of General Studies degree program is offered to nontraditional students and for individuals whose college careers may have been interrupted.

Jamestown College
Department of Religion
Jamestown, ND 58401   (701) 253-2545

Administration. Dr. James S. Walker, President; Dr. Richard H. Smith, Dean and Chief Academic Officer.

General Description. The Departments of Religion and Philosophy seek to serve students who desire to think seriously about human existence. The study of religion deepens and personalizes this thinking by exposing students to the content of revelation. The Bachelor of Arts in Religion/Philosophy is awarded.

Parent Institution. The objectives of Jamestown College are affirmed in its goal of academic excellence in a Christian environment. The College is determined to equip its students to face new problems and challenges in a changing world while never swerving from the insistence that the educational process be anchored to and constantly renewed by its Christian religious faith. The College is affiliated with the Presbyterian Church (U.S.A.) although most students are non-Presbyterian.

Community Environment. The Jamestown College campus of 107 acres of wooded land spreads across the plateau overlooking the city of Jamestown, North Dakota (population 16,000), located near the geographic center of North America. The city of Jamestown provides a variety of recreational facilities.

Religious Denomination. Presbyterian Church (U.S.A.).

Religious Emphasis. Reformed.

Accreditation. North Central Association of Colleges and Schools.

Term System. Semester, plus January interim term.

Enrollment in Degree Programs in Religion 1984–85. Total 10; men 5, women 5.

Faculty for Degree Programs in Religion. Total 1; full-time 1.

Admission Requirements. High school graduation in upper 50 percent of class; ACT score of 16 or above.

Tuition and Fees. Comprehensive fee $8,000.

Financial Aid. Assistance is based upon the student's completion of a financial inventory.

Housing. Dormitories are available for single students; on-campus housing for married students.

Library Facilities. The library has holdings of over 60,000 volumes.

Religious Services/Activities. Voluntary weekly chapel services.

Degree Programs

A major in Religion-Philosophy leading to the Bachelor of Arts degree consists of 10 courses in the Department, 3 of which must be taken in both fields, the remaining being elective. Required courses include Old Testament, New Testament, Ethics, Christian Beliefs, and the Philosophy of Religion.

Northwest Bible College
1900 8th Avenue, S.E.
Minot, ND 58701   (701) 857-3781

Administration. Donald M. Walker, President; Larry E. Perritte, Academic Dean/Registrar.

General Description. Northwest Bible College is an educational arm of the Church of God with international headquarters in Cleveland, Tennessee. The College is committed to an evangelical, biblical Christian concept of life. The College recognizes the need to relate to the entire person. To this end the spiritual life, social life, scholastic potential, and physical capabilities of each student are considered so that a well-balanced person may go forth as a living witness for Christ.

The College was founded in an environment of ministry and church growth. During the depression years of the 1930s the rapid growth of the Church of God in the Dakotas and surrounding areas created an acute need for trained ministers. An extended Bible study in the Lemmon, South Dakota, Church of God during January 1934 became the foundation. In the Fall of 1935, the College moved to Minot and became known as the Northwest Bible and Music Academy. After a move back to its point of origin in Lemmon, the College was permanently relocated to Minot, North Dakota in 1949. In 1956 the name Northwest Bible College was adopted.

Community Environment. The College enjoys a beautiful twenty-seven acre campus situated in southeast Minot. The campus becomes a "wonderland" in winter and has a park-like atmosphere in the summer. City bus and taxi services provide public transportation to the campus area. Minot is located within the eastern boundaries of the oil-rich Williston Basin in northwestern North Dakota, approximately 50 miles south of the Canadian border.

Religious Denomination. Church of God (Cleveland, Tennesee).

Religious Emphasis. Pentecostal.

Accreditation. American Association of Bible Colleges.

Term System. Semester; summer term.

Enrollment in Degree Programs in Religion 1984–85. Total 167.

Degrees in Religion Awarded 1984–85. Bachelor of Science in Bible 3; men 3. Bachelor of Arts in Bible 6; men 6. Bachelor of Science in Music 3; men 2, women 1. Bachelor of Science in Christian Education 2; men 1, women 1.

Faculty for Degree Programs in Religion. Total 15.

Admission Requirements. Applicants for admission to the College are considered on an individual basis. Admission is normally granted to graduates of an accredited high school or persons holding GED certificates and whose personal record reflects the moral, social, and ethical objectives of the College.

Tuition and Fees. Tuition per semester hour $85; room $415 per semester; board $450 per semester; other miscellaneous fees.

Financial Aid. Scholarships, federal assistance, and loans are available. Eligible students are selected for financial aid by the amount of financial need as determined by a "needs analysis," submission of proper forms, and the availability of Title IV, Federal Funds.

Housing. Residence halls are available for single students. A number of single dwelling and duplex units are provided on the campus for married students. Also, a trailer court is maintained for married housing.

Library Facilities. The Laud O. Vaught Learning Center is a 25,000 square foot brick structure housing classrooms, a 400-seat auditorium, and library. The library has stack space for 60,000 volumes and seating for 150 people.

Religious Services/Activities. Chapel services are conducted twice weekly and attendance is required of all students. Several times during the school year the Holy Sacrament is observed. Convocations and retreats are both scheduled during the Fall and Spring semesters. A Ministerial Club promotes fellowship among the ministerial students, encourages and assists members in obtaining ministerial rank and recognition, and provides instruction in practical areas of the ministry.

The Pioneers for Christ club is an evangelism organization giving special emphasis to personal witnessing, tract distribution, and jail and rest home services. Training sessions are held throughout the year to provide instruction in the skills of Christian service. Summer witness programs, holiday invasion teams, and weekend services to area churches complement the activities of this group. The organization is chartered with Pioneers for Christ International.

Degree Programs

The Bachelor of Arts or the Bachelor of Science with a major in Bible is offered by the Bible Division. The Bible curriculum consists of a three-fold foundation of grammatical, historical, and theological exegesis. The requirements for the degrees differ in the professional core of courses required.

The Bachelor of Science in Christian Education program is designed to prepare persons for ministry in church education. The program consists of an evaluation of the church's educational ministry in light of Biblical imperatives.

The Bachelor of Science with a Music and Christian Education major is designed to prepare persons for full-time church ministries. Upon completion of the program, the graduate should be qualified to lead the local church in both areas of education and music. The individual may serve in positions such as minister of Christian Education, Minister of Music, Youth Minister, Assistant Pastor, or as a leader of children, youth, or adults.

The Bachelor of Science with a major in Music offers course work which meets the needs of the general college student as well as the music major. Each course is designed to increase the student's musical sensitivity, understanding, and appreciation.

A Bachelor of Science in Elementary Education program is offered to supply qualified faculty for church-provided forms of education. The program will equip the graduate to serve in a teaching position in a Christian day school.

Special Programs

An Associate of Arts curriculum provides a unified two-year program which introduces the student to the fundamental areas of learning. The program provides basic Bible courses along with general education courses, so that the graduate will have sufficient background to be conversant in the Christian faith. An Associate of Arts in Secretarial Science is also offered. This program is designed to provide students with the opportunity to gain a marketable skill and a foundation in the Bible while living in a Christian environment.

The Christian Ministries certificate program is a one-year college level program of study designed primarily for individuals who may be unable to complete the more traditional two- and four-year programs. The 32 semester hours required include courses in Bible, Christian education, music, and general education.

OHIO

Allegheny Wesleyan College
2161 Woodsdale Road
Salem, OH 44460   (216) 337-6403

Administration. Robert E. Luther, President; Paul L. Kaufman, Academic Dean.

General Description. Allegheny Wesleyan College is a four-year undergraduate Bible college which grants the Bachelor of Arts degree with a major in Religion or a Bachelor of Theology degree with a major in Theology. The primary objective of the college is to prepare ministers, missionaries, and Christian day school teachers for the Allegheny Wesleyan Methodist Connection (Original Allegheny Conference) which is Arminian in doctrine, Wesleyan in emphasis, and evangelistic in outreach. The College traces its denominational heritage to the Methodist Episcopal church of 1843. The College was founded in 1956 under the name of Salem Bible College and Academy. In 1973, the Salem Bible College and Academy became a part of the Allegheny Wesleyan Methodist Connection as its denominational school and was renamed Allegheny Wesleyan College.

Community Environment. Salem, Ohio is located approximately 20 miles southwest of Youngstown in the rolling hills of northeastern Ohio. The 13-acre campus is two miles south of Salem.

Religious Denomination. Allegheny Wesleyan Methodist Connection.

Religious Emphasis. Fundamentalist.

Accreditation. American Association of Bible Colleges (Candidate).

Term System. Semester; summer term.

Enrollment in Degree Programs in Religion 1984–85. Total 51; men 32, women 19.

Degrees in Religion Awarded 1984–85. Bachelor of Arts 7; men 2, women 5.

Faculty for Degree Programs in Religion. Total 18; full-time 7, part-time 11.

Admission Requirements. Candidates for admission must give evidence of Christian character; ACT; final transcript of high school work; health certificate; recommendation from applicant's pastor and two from Christian friends; personal interview.

Tuition and Fees. $60 per semester hour; room and board $850 per semester; registration fee $50.

Financial Aid. Scholarships, grants, loans, and work opportunities are available.

Housing. Single students under 25 years of age are required to live in housing provided by the college except those residing with their parents.

Library Facilities. The library is housed in Blair Hall and contains over 11,000 volumes. A rare book collection of early Methodist writings and the archives of the Allegheny Wesleyan Methodist Connection are also housed here.

Religious Services/Activities. Highlights during the year are the Missionary Convention, the College Revival, and the Van Wormer Lectures. There are regular chapel services, an annual Ministerial Institute, and the College affiliates with the annual Youth Convention and Camp Meeting of the denomination.

Each student is required to select a church in the surrounding community within three weeks of enrollment, and regulary attend for the remainder of the year. Every student is expected to participate in some form of regular Christian service. Specific areas of opportunities for service include: preaching, evangelistic team outreach, Bible class teaching, Bible club supervision, and rest home visitation and ministry.

Degree Programs

The Bachelor of Arts degree program requires the completion of a major in Religion and the basic core course requirements. Majors are offered in the areas of Pastoral Ministries, Education, and Missions. Minors can be in the areas of Music, Music Education, and Biblical Languages.

The Bachelor of Theology degree allows the student to continue his/her studies beyond the Bachelor of Arts and permits the student an opportunity to intensify studies in Bible and Theology. In addition to all of the requirements for the Bachelor of Arts, the student must complete thirty-two semester hours of work with a grade point average of not less than 2.0 for the entire program.

Special Programs

Every attempt is being made by the Allegheny Wesleyan College Administration and the Board of Managers to correlate the Bachelor of Theology program with the Connectional Ministerial Course of Study. Every student completing this program should have completed the Connectional; however, the Itineracy and Orders Committee of the Allegheny Wesleyan Methodist Connection reserves the right to review the credits and will determine whether additional books should be required to complete the student's requirements for ordination. Although he will have met the basic academic requirements, not every student enrolled in the program is a candidate for the ministry and ordination.

Ashland Theological Seminary

Ashland, OH 44805 (419) 289-5038

Administration. Joseph Shultz, President.

General Description. Ashland Theological Seminary is a graduate school of Ashland College which was founded by The Brethren Church. The main emphases of the Seminary are complete and uncompromising loyalty to the Biblical and historical Christian Faith, the inculcation of competent Christian Scholarship, the nurture of a deeper spirituality in the Christian Life—all directed toward the goal of a practical Christian Ministry. The Seminary offers programs leading to the Master of Divinity and the Master of Arts degrees. The Seminary, the Methodist Theological School in Ohio, and the Trinity Lutheran Seminary in Columbus form a consortium for the offering of the Doctor of Ministry program.

Parent Institution. Ashland College was founded in 1878. It is a four-year liberal arts institution and grants the Associate, Bachelor, and Master's degrees. The Department of Religion in the School of Arts and Humanities offers a major requiring 24 hours of basic and advanced courses.

Community Environment. The Seminary campus is located in a former mansion on spacious grounds on Center Street in the city of Ashland. Ashland College is located in a residential section of the city.

Religious Denomination. Brethren Church (Ashland).

Religious Emphasis. Conservative.

Accreditation. North Central Association of Colleges and Schools; Association of Theological Schools in the United States and Canada.

Term System. Semester.

Admission Requirements. Bachelor's degree from an accredited college or university with a grade point average of 2.5 and a substantial foundation in the liberal arts.

Tuition and Fees. Tuition $800 per quarter, part-time $67 per credit hour.

Financial Aid. Alumni, Church, and endowed scholarships are available as well as Ministerial Student Aid by denomination, loans, and grants-in-aid.

Housing. Seminary apartments are available for Seminary students at moderate cost.

Library Facilities. The Seminary's theological library contains over 65,000 volumes. It maintains a special department for the preservation of Brethren books, manuscripts, pamphlets, tracts, sermons, legal documents, microfilm, periodicals, and memorabilia of the Church.

Religious Services/Activities. Worship services are held throughout the week.

Degree Programs

The Master of Divinity degree is the historic degree for pastoral training leading to ordination and is conferred upon the completion of the regular three-year program. The same degree with a special major in Pastoral Psychology and Counseling is conferred upon the completion of the regular three-year theological program and clinical studies and training at one of the four counseling programs offered at various centers.

The Master of Arts degree is conferred upon completion of a two-year program. The same degree with a special major in Pastoral Psychology and Counseling is conferred upon the completion of the two-year core plus clinical studies at one of the four participating centers.

The Doctor of Ministry degree is offered in participation with the consortium member schools. Requirements include completion of four core courses, two electives, participation in a peer group process, and completion of a project in ministry which culminates in a dissertation. Courses at the Seminary are grouped under Biblical Studies; Christian History, Theology, and Thought; Christian Ministries; Pastoral Psychology and Counseling.

Special Programs

As a member of the Institute of Holy Land Studies, students of the Seminary have the opportunity of supplementing their studies with a a program of studies in Israel.

Athenaeum of Ohio
Mt. St. Mary's Seminary of the West

Lay Pastoral Ministry Program

6616 Beechmont Avenue

Cincinnati, OH 45230 (513) 231-2223

Administration. Rev. James J. Walsh, President; Rev. Richard J. Sweeney, Dean.

General Description. Mt. St. Mary's Seminary of the West is that part of The Athenaeum of Ohio which provides for the education and formation of candidates for the ordained ministry as priests of the Roman Catholic Church. It is a full-time program which is available only to students sponsored by Roman Catholic dioceses or religious communities. The Master of Divinity degree is the basic program offered for those studying for the ordained priesthood. The Master of Arts in Theology and Master of Arts in Biblical Studies are academic in nature, providing the student with the experience of theological or biblical research and an initial graduate mastery of theology or biblical studies.

The Lay Pastoral Ministry Program is a response within The Athenaeum to the growing need for broadly based ministerial activity. Both men and women participate in the program, preparing for diverse forms of ministry emerging as the needs of the community change. Through the Lay Program participants may choose to work either on a Master of Arts in Religion or on a Certificate in Lay Ministry. Both of these lay program options engage participants in confronting the Biblical, magisterial, ecclesiological, and theological foundations of lay ministry, and provide participants with experience in responding appropriately to pastoral needs. Participation in either option is not limited to members of the Roman Catholic Church.

Parent Institution. The Athenaeum of Ohio, the religious center of the Archdiocese of Cincinnati, opened in 1829. It is an accredited center for education and formation, providing programs of preparation for and development in ministry within the Roman Catholic tradition. The various programs of The Athenaeum of Ohio embody the belief that preparation for ministry within the Roman Catholic Church must be faithful to the teaching of the Church. This mission is achieved through the three divisions of The Athenaeum: Mt. St. Mary's Seminary of the West, The Lay Pastoral Ministry Program, and the Division for Ministerial Development and Support. The latter provides support and programming not available through other resources to ordained and lay ministry. This includes Athenaeum alumni as well as the local churches its various programs serve. Such efforts include degree programs, lecture series, programs for lay ministers, programs for priests, sabbatical program, workshops, and adult education.

Community Environment. The Seminary is located in Cincinnati's suburban Mt. Washington. It occupies a campus of 45 acres. *See:* God's Bible School and College for information about Cincinnati.

Religious Denomination. Roman Catholic.

Accreditation. North Central Association of Colleges and Schools; Association of Theological Schools in the United States and Canada.

Term System. Quarter; summer term.

Enrollment in Degree Programs in Religion 1984–85. Total 99; men 64, women 35.

Degrees in Religion Awarded 1984–85. Master of Divinity 14; men 14. Master of Arts in Theology 3; men 3. Master of Arts in Biblical Studies 3; men 3. Master of Arts in Religion 13; men 2, women 11. Bachelor of Arts in Theology 1; men 1.

Faculty for Degree Programs in Religion. Total 41; full-time 18, part-time 23.

Admission Requirements. Sponsorship of a local church and its bishop or a religious superior; Bachelor's degree from an accredited institution.

Tuition and Fees. Comprehensive fee $6,200; orientation fee $135.

Financial Aid. Scholarships, loans, and work-study are available.

Housing. Housing is available only to full-time seminary students.

Library Facilities. The Eugene H. Maly Memorial Library emphasizes the fields of sacred scripture, liturgy, church history, bioethics, and current spiritual life. It houses over 70,000 volumes including a collection of 7,500 rare religious books.

Religious Services/Activities. Daily Eucharist; Liturgy of the Hours; Communal Penance services; retreats and days of renewal.

Degree Programs

The Master of Divinity program is the basic degree program offered for those studying for the ordained priesthood. The degree is professional in orientation. Is purpose is to provide an opportunity for the seminarian as a whole and believing person to acquire through study, research and supervised experience the knowledge, skills, and experience necessary for effective ministry; and to assist the student in the integration of the above in such a way that he can minister in the contemporary Roman Catholic Church as a qualified and learned priest. The degree requires that a student take 120 hours of specified and elective courses over a four-year, seminary-based program of ministerial education. The hours are distributed by departments as follows: Biblical Studies, Christian Living, Dogmatic-Liturgical Theology, Historical Theology/Church History, Interdisciplinary, Professional Courses, and Pastoral Courses.

The Master of Arts programs are academic in nature. Their objective is to provide the student with the experience of theological or Biblical research and an initial graduate mastery of theology and Biblical studies. Their purpose is to provide the church with scholars and teachers. These courses of study can be taken at the same time as pursuing the Master of Divinity degree. The Master of Arts in Theology and the Master of Arts in Biblical Studies are awarded upon completion of the programs.

The Bachelor of Arts in Theology is available to students who enter at age 23 or older with some previous college experience but who have not earned a degree. The total academic program consists of 139 semester credits.

Special Programs

There is a special program for casual students who may enroll in selected Seminary or Lay Pastoral Ministry Program courses or who may enroll in courses leading to a degree.

Baldwin-Wallace College
Department of Religion
Berea, OH 44017   (216) 826-2173

Administration. Dr. Neal Malicky, President; Dr. Mark H. Collier, Vice President for Academic Affairs and Dean of the College; Dr. Robert M. Fowler, Chairperson, Department of Religion.

General Description. Although the Department of Religion grants the degree Bachelor of Arts in Religion, the curriculum of the Department is designed for the total campus community. Studies offered are an integral part of the Humanities Division of the College, and reflect the College's commitment to a liberal arts education through humanistic studies. The courses offered by the Department are designed to acquaint students with the nature and function of religious thought and life. Several religious traditions in world culture are studied. Students aspiring to enter Christian vocations will finds specific courses of particular interest. Some courses may be clustered into study areas or concentrations (i.e., Biblical Studies, World Religions, Christian Theology).

Parent Institution. Baldwin University and German Wallace College were united as Baldwin-Wallace College in 1913. The privately-supported, coeducational, liberal arts institution is affiliated with the United Methodist Church.

Community Environment. The city of Berea, Ohio is located 15 miles southwest of Cleveland where sandstone was quarried for making grindstones. Community facilities include churches of all denominations, hospital, library, and a number of various civic and service organizations. A replica of Independence Hall with the Liberty Bell is on the campus.

Religious Denomination. United Methodist Church.

Religious Emphasis. No religious emphasis.

Accreditation. North Central Association of Colleges and Schools.

Term System. Quarter; summer term.

Enrollment in Degree Programs in Religion 1984–85. Total 7; men 4, women 3.

Degrees in Religion Awarded 1984–85. Bachelor of Arts in Religion 1; men 1.

Faculty for Degree Programs in Religion. Total 4; full-time 2, part-time 2.

Admission Requirements. An applicant must be a graduate of an accredited high school. Most of the students who are accepted rank in the upper half of their high school class; scores on the ACT or SAT; teacher's recommendation.

Tuition and Fees. Tuition $5,859 per year for 12 to 18 hours per quarter, less than 12 quarter hours $127 per credit hour; general fee $83 per quarter; room $425 to $637.50 per quarter; board plan $510 per quarter.

Financial Aid. Various types of financial aid are available.

Housing. Dormitory housing is available on campus.

Library Facilities. Ritter Library houses nearly 200,000 volumes and a wide selection of periodicals.

Religious Services/Activities. The College Chaplain conducts regular services in the College Chapel and also plans retreats. There is a Newman Center on campus with a full staff.

Degree Programs

The major in Religion leading to the Bachelor of Arts degree requires 45-50 hours. The required courses for the major are: Christian Faith and Thought, Hebrew Bible/Old Testament, New Testament, Eastern Religions, Western Religions, and Christian Ethics.

Borromeo College of Ohio
28700 Euclid Avenue
Cleveland, OH 44092   (216) 585-5900

Administration. Rev. James L. Caddy, President; Rev. Edward E. Mehok, Vice President; Rev. John E. Manning, Academic Dean.

General Description. Borromeo College is a baccalaureate-level seminary in which students are prepared in the liberal arts as they discern a calling to the Roman Catholic priesthood. Borromeo attempts to do this in a community environment through the integration of spiritual, apostolic, academic, and social experiences. The aim of the College is to help its students to mature as liberally-educated persons committed to Christian ideals and to the service of their neighbors, and to assist students in relating themselves personally and functionally to the Church and to the world. A core curriculum in Philosophy is required of all students. The degrees Bachelor of Arts and Bachelor of Philosophy are awarded.

Community Environment. Borromeo College is located in Wickliffe, Ohio, 14 miles from the center of Cleveland at the western extremity of Lake County. Access to several major interstate highways makes the college centrally located. The campus is no more than 20 minutes' travel time to cultural, civic, entertainment, and shopping centers of the Greater Cleveland area; local conveniences of the same sort are on the fringes of the campus.

Religious Denomination. Roman Catholic.

Accreditation. North Central Association of Colleges and Schools.

Term System. Semester; no summer term.

Enrollment in Degree Programs in Religion 1984–85. Total 91; men 91.

Degrees in Religion Awarded 1984–85. Bachelor of Arts 35; men 35.

Faculty for Degree Programs in Religion. Total 22; full-time 16, part-time 6.

Admission Requirements. High school diploma; ACT or SAT; letters of reference; acceptance by the Diocese of Cleveland, Capuchin community, or the Archdiocese of Washington.

Tuition and Fees. Tuition $3,500 per year; room and board $1,700.

Financial Aid. All financial aid is based upon the filing of the Confidential Financial Supplement and the application for Federal Student Aid. An Ohio resident should also file the Ohio Instructional Grant Form. Aid is available in the form of federal financial aid programs, state grants, and independent scholarships, grants, and loans.

Housing. All students are required to live on campus.

Library Facilities. The Vincent G. Marotta College Library houses over 60,000 volumes.

Religious Services/Activities. Students are required to attend morning and evening prayer and Mass each day. There are times set aside during the year for school retreats and days of formation.

Degree Programs

The Bachelor of Arts degree program requires the concentration in one major field and in at least one minor field. A minimum of 128 credit hours must be successfully completed and a quality point average of 2.00 must be maintained within the major field. Majors are offered in Philosophy, English, History, Classical Languages, and Social and Behavioral Sciences with a concentration of at least 30 credit hours. Eighteen credit hours in any field constitutes a minor. The requirements for the Bachelor of Philosophy Degree are the same, except that substitutions for the Science and Mathematics requirements are made with the approval of the Academic Dean. A basic core curriculum is required of all students. The Department of Religious Studies offers courses in Biblical Theology and Systematic Theology and recommends an absolute minimum of 15 credit hours in Religious Studies as a preparation for graduate studies in theology.

Capital University
Department of Religion and Philosophy
2199 East Main Street
Columbus, OH 43209   (614) 236-6307

Administration. Dr. Larry A. Gardner, Chair, Department of Religion and Philosophy.

General Description. The Department of Religion within the College of Arts and Sciences offers a program designed to help students examine the Christian way of life as based on an historical, literary, and theological understanding of the Scripture, as well as an understanding of other religious views. A primary purpose is to assist students to develop their own understanding of the basic questions of life.

Parent Institution. Capital University was founded in 1830 to offer a strong undergraduate program in pre-theology in order to provide an educated ministry for the Church. It is the oldest institution of the American Lutheran Church. The University consists of the College of Arts and Sciences, the School of Nursing, the Conservatory of Music, the Law School, and the Graduate School of Administration. As a Christian university, Capital seeks to harmonize the spiritual with the temporal development of the individual, as rooted in the heritage of the Reformation. It is committed to creating an environment in which liberal and professional disciplines flourish.

Community Environment. Capital's quiet location in suburban Bexley, four miles from downtown Columbus, gives the University's students the advantages of a residential campus with all the educational and cultural activities of Ohio's largest city nearby. Columbus is the headquarters of numerous corporations, government agencies, and private institutions. The city is situated in the center of Ohio.

Religious Denomination. American Lutheran Church.

Religious Emphasis. Reformation.

Accreditation. North Central Association of Colleges and Schools.

Term System. Semester; two summer sessions.

Enrollment in Degree Programs in Religion 1984–85. Total 27; 14 men, 13 women.

Degrees in Religion Awarded 1984–85. Bachelor of Arts 10; men 6, women 4.

Faculty for Degree Programs in Religion. Total 6; 5 full-time, 1 part-time.

Admission Requirements. Graduation from accredited high school with 12 units: 4 English, 2 Mathematics, 2 Natural Science, 2 Social Science, 2 or more of above or two units of foreign language; submission of results of ACT or SAT; submission of letters of recommendation, one from high school and one from church or community.

Tuition and Fees. Tuition $6,335 per school year (two semesters); room $1,150; board $1,470; orientation fee $35; pre-registration fee $50.

Financial Aid. Extensive financial aid is available in the form of scholarships, awards, grants, loans, and work-study opportunities.

Housing. Students are expected to live in dormitories unless living with relatives or unless residence is related to work. Married students may live in apartments available in the community.

Library Facilities. The library system contains over 250,000 volumes, 14,000 pamphlets, 1,500 periodicals, 8,000 microforms, and 10,000 recordings. Students majoring in Religion have access to the library of the Trinity Lutheran Seminary across the street.

Religious Services/Activities. The campus pastor leads and encourages a ministry of Word and Sacrament through worship, group encounter, counseling, and service. The Lutheran tradition and religious diversity on the campus have encouraged the development of varied approaches to Lutheran ecumenical witness.

The student-operated University Congregation gathers in worship on Sunday morning. Roman Catholic Mass is offered Saturdays or Sundays. In Wednesday morning Chapel, faculty, staff, and students come together to participate in worship. Student-conducted Vesper services are held Sundays. Bible study and other opportunities for faith development are offered periodically. Holy Communion is offered Tuesday evenings.

Capital Volunteers, operating out of the University pastor's office, provides a variety of ways by which students may serve others in a meaningful way. A large number of volunteers serve faithfully at several Columbus area institutions.

Special religious interest groups include the Baptist Student Union, Catholics on Campus, and the Fellowship of Christian Students.

Degree Programs

Three majors in the Bachelor of Arts program are provided: the Christian Staff Work major, which prepares the student for church vocations; the Religion major, which prepares the student for seminary or graduate school; and the World Religions and Philosophies major, which prepares the student for transcultural studies. A student wishing to teach in a Lutheran elementary school may concentrate in Religion.

Case Western Reserve University
Department of Religion
Mather House
Cleveland, OH 44106   (216) 368-2210

Administration. Eldon Jay Epp, Harkness Professor of Biblical Literature and Chairman, Department of Religion.

General Description. The Department of Religion is a liberal arts department in the Humanities and Arts Division of Western Reserve College, which is the liberal arts college of the University. The Department offers a major, a minor, and general education courses in the critical and historical study of religion.

Parent Institution. Case Western Reserve University is a private, moderately-sized, comprehensive university formed through the federation (in 1967) of Western Reserve University and the Case Institute of Technology. It was founded as Western Reserve College in 1826 by Yale alumni to offer a classical education and training for the ministry in the Western Reserve of Connecticut (now northeastern Ohio). The University offers undergraduate, graduate, and professional education in more than 60 fields.

Community Environment. The campus is located in University Circle, a 500-acre park-like concentration of educational, scientific, medical, artistic, musical, and cultural institutions located at the eastern end of the city of Cleveland. The city began nearly two centuries ago on the banks of the Cuyahoga River and has grown into a metropolis of almost 200 million people. The city is situated the southern shore of on Lake Erie.

Religious Denomination. Nondenominational (originally, the liberal arts college was Congregational/Presbyteri-

an).

Religious Emphasis. Pluralistic. There are endowed chairs in Protestant thought, Jewish studies, and Catholic studies. Courses in Asian religions are also taught.

Accreditation. North Central Association of Colleges and Schools.

Term System. Semester; summer term.

Enrollment in Degree Programs in Religion 1984–85. Total 270.

Degrees in Religion Awarded 1984–85. Bachelor of Arts 3; women 3.

Faculty for Degree Programs in Religion. Total 4; full-time 3, part-time 1.

Admission Requirements. High school preparation: 16 units of full credit high school work in solid academic subjects, including four years of English, at least three of mathematics, and one year of laboratory science. Current freshmen average SAT verbal of 543 and math 630, with 61 percent from top tenth and 81 percent from top twentieth of their high school classes.

Tuition and Fees. Costs per year: tuition $8,300; housing and meals $3,600; health fee $280; student activities fee $70.

Financial Aid. Excellent financial aid available; merit scholarships available. Average financial aid package equals tuition; about 65 percent of undergraduates receive financial aid.

Housing. Dormitories are available to all.

Library Facilities. The libraries of the University contain more than 1 million volumes, almost entirely on open shelves.

Religious Services/Activities. Campus ministries for Protestants, Roman Catholics, and Jewish students and faculty are on campus but separate from the Department of Religion.

Degree Programs

The Bachelor of Arts in Religion requires a major program of 30 hours (normally ten 3-hour courses) including Introduction to Asian Religions; Critical Moments in Christian History; Hebrew Scriptures: Literature and History of Ancient Israel; The New Testament and Christian Origins; and Introduction to Judaism; plus five additional courses.

Special Programs

Double majors with religion are conveniently arranged and popular, often with the sciences or social sciences.

Cedarville College
Department of Biblical Education
North Main Street
Box 601
Cedarville, OH 45314   (513) 766-5155

Administration. Dr. Robert G. Gromacki, Chairman; Department of Biblical Education.

General Description. The Department of Biblical Education is comprised of Biblical Studies, Philosophy and Religion, Theology, Practical Theology, Biblical Languages, and Church Education. The Department seeks to provide a Biblical foundation for a liberal arts education, presenting the great truths of the Scripture by studying correct principles of interpretation and proper application in order that the student may be an effective witness for Christ regardless of the vocation which he may be led to pursue. It also seeks to lay a good foundation for those persons called of God into full-time vocational Christian ministries.

Parent Institution. Cedarville College is a Baptist college of arts and sciences of approximately 1,800 students. A balanced liberal arts program is coupled with a fundamentalist and conservative theological position in regard to doctrine and patterns of conduct. The College was originally established by the Reformed Presbyterian Church. In 1953, the operation was transferred to the Trustees of Baptist Bible Institute of Cleveland. The name, Cedarville College, was retained.

Community Environment. The College is located in the rural community of Cedarville. It is within driving distance of Columbus, Dayton, Springfield, Cincinnati, and Xenia.

Religious Denomination. Baptist (General Association of Regular Baptist Churches).

Religious Emphasis. Fundamentalist.

Accreditation. North Central Association of Colleges and Schools.

Term System. Quarter; 2 five-week summer terms.

Enrollment in Degree Programs in Religion 1984–85. Total 107; men 97, women 10.

Degrees in Religion Awarded 1984–85. Bachelor of Arts 47; men 42, women 5.

Faculty for Degree Programs in Religion. Total 10; full-time 8, part-time 2.

Admission Requirements. Evidence of a personal relationship with Jesus Christ and a consistent, Christian lifestyle; academic record, recommendations, and rank in class; ACT preferred (SAT accepted).

Tuition and Fees. Tuition $3,552 for 48 quarter hours; fees $417 per year.

Financial Aid. The College has a broad program of financial aid to assist students who are accepted for admission and who demonstrate a need for such help. All grants and awards are made through the Financial Aid Office.

Housing. Accommodations include dormitories for single students and apartments for married students.

Library Facilities. The library houses over 100,000 volumes and provides over 900 current periodical subscriptions.

Religious Services/Activities. Students are urged to set aside a definite period each day for private devotions. Regular attendance at student prayer meetings aids the student in maintaining a healthy spiritual life. All students are required to attend church services regularly. In addition to private devotions and weekly residence hall prayer meetings, student prayer groups meet at various times each week to pray for missions. Several prayer days are designated each year as days of prayer.

The students and faculty meet together each day for worship and fellowship in a chapel service. Every student is required to attend. The Fall Bible Conference, the Staley Distinguished Christian Scholar Lecture Program, the Missionary Conference, and the Spring Enrichment Week are week-long features of the chapel program.

Degree Programs

The Bachelor of Arts with a preseminary Bible major is designed for students anticipating graduate work. It provides a sufficient foundation in Biblical subjects and the Greek language and enables the student to select elective courses from other departments which will enrich personal and professional development.

The Bachelor of Arts with a comprehensive Bible major is to provide an education for the person who upon graduation becomes a director of church education, a youth pastor or worker, a missionary candidate, an evangelist, or a pastor. Within this program, certain vocational emphases can be gained through course selection and supervised field experiences.

Special Programs

The College offers a concentrated program for the student who desires a formal education in Bible before he pursues his vocation or before he engages in a field of technical study not available in a Christian school. It is designed so that the student may function knowledgeably as a layman in his local church.

Cincinnati Bible College
Cincinnati Bible Seminary: Undergraduate
  Division
2700 Glenway Avenue
Cincinnati, OH 45204   (513) 244-8100

Administration. Harvey C. Bream, Jr., President; Earl W. Sims, Vice President and Academic Dean.

General Description. The Mission of Cincinnati Bible College is the promotion of Christian education and the training of men and women for Christian service. Preparation is provided for service as minister, missionary, educator, journalist, music director, secretary, and Biblical archaeologist. The education program consists of (1) a general education in the arts, letters, and sciences upon which other studies may be built, (2) a specialized education in Biblical history and doctrine with a view toward how these apply to life and a chosen profession, (3) a professional education providing a level of competence required for effective service. The College shares its campus with Cincinnati Christian Seminary, the graduate division, which offers Master of Arts, Master of Religious Education, Master of Ministry, and Master of Divinity degrees.

Cincinnati Bible College offers the degrees Bachelor of Arts, Bachelor of Science, and Associate of Science, with majors in Bible. A Bachelor of Music degree is also offered in Church Music or Bible. Second majors are available in Preaching, Ministry, Missions, Christian Education, Journalism, Deaf Education, Secretarial Science, Ancient Near East Studies, and Church Music.

Parent Institution. The Cincinnati Bible Seminary is the corporate name for Cincinnati Bible College and Cincinnati Christian Seminary. *See also:* Cincinnati Christian Seminary.

Community Environment. The College is located on 40 acres of hilltop land in the western side of Cincinnati overlooking the basin area of the city and northern Kentucky. Like Rome, Cincinnati is built on seven hills surrounding the downtown section. While the proximity to the downtown area is very convenient for employment and shopping, the relative isolation removes the campus from most of the disturbances and distractions of a major city.

Religious Denomination. Christian Churches and Churches of Christ.

Accreditation. American Association of Bible Colleges.

Term System. Semester; summer term.

Enrollment in Degree Programs in Religion 1984–85. Total 601; men 378, women 223.

Degrees in Religion Awarded 1984–85. Bachelor of Arts 30; men 29, women 1. Bachelor of Science 28; men 17, women 11. Bachelor of Music 4; men 1, women 3. Associate of Science 22; men 4, women 18.

Faculty for Degree Programs in Religion. Total 54; full-time 26, part-time 28.

Admission Requirements. High school graduation; good character; conditional admission is given to students of good character who rank in the lowest one fourth of their graduating class.

Tuition and Fees. $1,263 per semester; room $400 to $755 per semester; board $610 per semester.

Financial Aid. Pell Grant, Supplemental Educational Opportunity Grant, Guaranteed Student Loan Program, College Work-study program, school work program, school scholarships and grants.

Housing. Residence halls are available for both men and women; off-campus married student apartments also available.

Library Facilities. The library contains over 61,000 volumes.

Religious Services/Activities. Chapel services are held twice weekly; less formal inspirational service is held one evening per week.

Degree Programs

The Bachelor of Arts, Bachelor of Science, and Bachelor of Music degrees are offered by the College. Each degree requires a major of Bible and theology courses. Programs in Christian Ministries, Missions, Christian Education, Deaf Education, Journalism, Ancient Near Eastern Studies, Church Music, and English Bible are offered. Generally, 128 credits are required for the Bachelor's degree.

Special Programs

Programs leading to the Associate of Science degree are also offered by the College. A limited number of correspondence courses are available for persons unable to enroll in classroom work.

Cincinnati Christian Seminary
Graduate Division of Cincinnati Bible Seminary
2700 Glenway Avenue
Cincinnati, OH 45204   (513) 244-8120

Administration. Harvey C. Bream, Jr., President; Earl W. Sims, Vice President; Joe S. Ellis, Dean of the Graduate School.

General Description. The objectives of Cincinnati Christian Seminary are in keeping with the principles underlying all graduate study: (1) to provide depth of understanding in one's chosen field; (2) to introduce methods and tools necessary to continued research; (3) to encourage and develop initiative in one's studies and conclusions; (4) to provide application in advanced learning. In addition to these conventional reasons for graduate study, the are other reasons within the character and purpose of the Seminary: (1) to instill knowledge of God's word and desire for its firm defense; (2) to maintain an emphasis upon the salvation of souls; (3) to make available advanced education in various fields of service; (4) to stress the importance of the restoration of the New Testament pattern of the church. All courses of study are designed to meet the deepening need of the Bible college graduate without demanding repetition of his/her earlier studies as an undergraduate. The Seminary awards the degrees Master of Divinity, Master of Religious Education, Master of Ministry, Master of Arts, Master of Religious Education - International.

Parent Institution. The Cincinnati Bible Seminary is the corporate name for Cincinnati Bible College and Cincinnati Christian Seminary. *See also:* Cincinnati Bible College.

Community Environment. The Seminary is located on 40 acres of hilltop land in the western side of Cincinnati overlooking the basin area of the city and northern Kentucky. Like Rome, Cincinnati is built on seven hills surrounding the downtown section. While the proximity to the downtown area is very convenient for employment and shopping, the relative isolation removes the campus from most of the disturbances and distractions of a major city.

Religious Denomination. Christian Churches and Churches of Christ.

Accreditation. Associate member of the Association of Theological Schools in the United States and Canada.

Term System. Semester; summer term.

Enrollment in Degree Programs in Religion 1984–85. Total 324 (enrollment figure for school year 1982-83).

Faculty for Degree Programs in Religion. Total 40; full-time 7, part-time 33 (includes 13 from the Bible College who offer courses in the curriculum). Figures are for the school year 1982-83.

Admission Requirements. Baccalaureate degree from an approved college or university.

Tuition and Fees. Tuition $1,728; room and board $2,-200; student fees $506.

Financial Aid. Scholarships and loans are available.

Housing. Men's and women's dormitories are available on campus. Apartment accommodations are made available by the Seminary for a limited number of married students.

Library Facilities. The Seminary library consists of over 51,000 volumes. The Public Library and the libraries of the University of Cincinnati and of Hebrew Union College, containing nearly 5 million books, are located within 4 miles of the Seminary.

Religious Services/Activities. Graduate students participate in the chapel services held on Wednesdays and Fridays. A Conference on Evangelism is held annually and a fall retreat is planned.

Degree Programs

The Master of Divinity degree requires the successful completion of three years of academic work, including 90 semester hours, maintaining the required grade point average, and passing a comprehensive and oral examination. The 90 hours are divided among: core requirements in each of the four major fields of the Seminary curriculum (Biblical, Theological, Historical, and Practical Studies), studies in an area of concentration from one of those fields, language, and electives. Eight majors are offered: Bible, Old Testament, New Testament, Church History, Theology, Apologetics, Practical Theology, and Christian Education.

The Master of Ministry degree requires the successful completion of 60 semester hours. Approximately one-half of the enrolled hours are core requirements which include courses from the Biblical, Theological, Historical, and Practical fields. The other courses are taken in one of the chosen areas of concentration: preaching, counseling, church music, missions, journalism, and youth or campus ministry.

The Master of Arts degree requires the completion of 30 semester hours of study of which 15 must be devoted to one of the eight major areas of concentration. A thesis dealing with some problem in the area of concentration is required.

A Master of Religious Education degree requires the completion of 2 academic years of work including 60 semester hours. A candidate for the degree has the alternative of pursuing a program with a single major in Christian Education or a double major in Christian Education and some other area of practical studies such as deaf education. A special program leading to the Master of Religious Education is also offered to meet the special educational needs of international students whose native language is not English.

Circleville Bible College
P.O. Box 458
Circleville, OH 43113   (614) 474-8896

Administration. Douglas Carter, President; Lorraine Huffman, Registrar.

General Description. Circleville Bible College graduates serve in a variety of Christian careers. Each graduate has learned to apply the Word in his/her own life and to share it with others in real life situations. Graduates are involved in a variety of vocations ranging from church secretary to Christian school teacher to jungle missionary. In addition to Biblical studies which provide the foundation for all other learning, a general education program gives a dimension of learning which helps each person relate to other people. Professional studies furnish specific skills required to live and minister effectively. The College awards the Bachelor of Arts in Religion and Bachelor of Theology degrees.

The College is thoroughly evangelical in the Wesleyan-Arminian tradition.

Community Environment. Located in the heartland of central Ohio, 30 miles south of Columbus, the College has a 40-acre campus just east of the city limits of Circleville. The city has a sizeable population and offers shopping, recreational, and work opportunities.

Religious Denomination. Churches of Christ in Christian Union.

Religious Emphasis. Evangelical.

Accreditation. American Association of Bible Colleges.

Term System. Semester; summer term.

Enrollment in Degree Programs in Religion 1984–85. Total 148; men 95, women 53.

Degrees in Religion Awarded 1984–85. Bachelor of Theology 3; men 3. Bachelor of Arts 28; men 19, women 9. Bible Diploma 4; men 3, women 1.

Faculty for Degree Programs in Religion. Total 18; full-

time 13, part-time 5.

Admission Requirements. Three character references; health examination form; brief written account of Christian experience; high school transcript; photograph; ACT or SAT scores.

Tuition and Fees. Tuition $2,345 per semester for dormitory students (includes room, board, and all fees); $1,417 per semester. for commuting students.

Financial Aid. Financial aid is available in the form of discounts and grants, scholarships, federal student aid programs, loans, and student employment.

Housing. Dormitories are provided for all single students who are not commuting from home; limited housing from married students through the rental of apartments and mobile homes.

Library Facilities. The library houses 35,984 volumes.

Religious Services/Activities. Chapel services each day; various Christian service groups; on-campus organizations sponsor various activities.

Degree Programs

The Bachelor of Arts in Religion program has the following specializations: Christian Ministries, Christian Education/Church, Christian Education/Christian Day School, Christian Education/Missions Composite, Christian Education/Music Composite, Missions, Missions/ Christian Education Composite, Missions/Music Composite, Professional Church Music, Music/Christian Education Composite, and Music/Missions Composite.

The Bachelor of Theology is a five-year program.

Special Programs

A two-year program leads to a diploma in Bible.

Cleveland State University
Department of Religious Studies
East 22nd Street and Euclid Avenue
Cleveland, OH 44115   (216) 687-2170

Administration. Dr. Walter B. Waetjen, President; Dr. John a Flower, Provost and Vice President for Academic Affairs; Dr. Robert F. House, Associate Dean, College of Arts and Sciences; Dr. Lee W. Gibbs, Chair, Department of Religious Studies.

General Description. The Department of Religious Studies offers courses which enable students to understand the meaning and significance of religion as an important aspect of every civilization. The program supplies students with data, methods, and tools to facilitate an understanding of religion and to provide a preparation for a wide range of professional and graduate training. The Department grants the degree Bachelor of Arts in Religious Studies.

Parent Institution. Cleveland State University is an urban university with approximately 20,000 students. Established as a state-assisted university in 1964, Cleveland

State offers bachelor degrees in 60 major fields, 26 master's degrees, 5 Ph.D. and post-Master's programs, and 2 law degrees.

Community Environment. Cleveland State University's campus is undergoing a vigorous expansion program including acquiring land and erecting buildings in the city of Cleveland, Ohio. Students have easy access to many facilities provided by the city of Cleveland and the outlying areas.

Religious Denomination. None.

Accreditation. North Central Association of Colleges and Schools.

Term System. Quarter; summer term.

Enrollment in Degree Programs in Religion 1984–85. Total 15; men 11, women 4.

Degrees in Religion Awarded 1984–85. Bachelor of Arts in Religious Studies 2; men 1 (major), women 1 (minor).

Faculty for Degree Programs in Religion. Total 7; full-time 6, part-time 1.

Admission Requirements. All Ohio residents who have graduated from high schools chartered by the State Board of Education are eligible to enroll. Non-residents of Ohio must meet the admission requirements of CSU degree-granting colleges.

Tuition and Fees. Instructional and general fee $1,713; housing $810 per year.

Financial Aid. Through various financial aid programs, CSU seeks to help meet the educational expenses of students who have need, as measured by analysis of the Financial Aid Form.

Housing. CSU is primarily a commuter institution but a limited number of dormitory rooms are available.

Library Facilities. The library houses 662,403 bound volumes. Special collections include the Cleveland Press Collection, the Cleveland Union Terminal Archives, Contemporary Poetry Collection, and the Afro-American Cultural Collection.

Religious Services/Activities. Student religious life is supported by the United Christian Ministry, Newman, and Hillell organizations.

Degree Programs

The Department of Religious Studies requires 48 credit hours for a major leading to the Bachelor of Arts degree. Of the 48 required hours, at least 32 credits must be in upper division courses. The specific courses required for the major are determined on an individual basis in consultation with a departmental adviser.

Dayton, University of
Department of Religious Studies
300 College Park
Dayton, OH 45469   (513) 229-4321

Administration. Rev. James L. Heft, S.M., Ph.D., Chairman of the Department and Director of the Graduate Program.

General Description. The Department of Religious Studies sees itself as a community of scholars serving the University community and the local community by teaching, research, and action. The main concern of the department is an understanding and elucidation of the Judeo-Christian religious experience, as it is exemplified in the Roman Catholic tradition. This implies not only a deep investigation of the Roman Catholic position but also a dialogue with other Christian traditions and an exploration of the religious heritage of the human race.

The Graduate Department of Religious Studies is an ecumenical community of students and professors engaged in the study, research, and interpretation of religious issues. It considers these issues from the context of the more classical disciplines of the Judeo-Christian heritage, with particular emphasis on the Roman Catholic tradition, as well as the burgeoning areas of multicultural and cross-disciplinary concerns. It offers a Master of Arts individualized to meet each student's need, whether it be for an advanced degree or professional preparation. The student may therefore choose to follow one of two programs which lead to the Master of Arts degree.

Parent Institution. The University of Dayton is a private, coeducational school founded in 1850 by the Society of Mary (the Marianists), a Roman Catholic teaching order. It is among the nation's largest Catholic institutions of higher learning. Aware of the cultural richness of diversity, the University numbers among its students and faculty representatives of many faiths.

Community Environment. The main campus is seventy-six landscaped acres on a hill overlooking the city of Dayton, Ohio. The buildings are a pleasantly eclectic architectural mixture of old and new, all well equipped. The city of Dayton is one of Ohio's most progressive cities and is located where four shallow streams, draining the upper section of the rich Miami Valley, come together. Many nationally known firms have their world headquarters in Dayton.

Religious Denomination. Roman Catholic.

Accreditation. North Central Association of Colleges and Schools. Member of: Association of Catholic Colleges and Universities; Catholic College Coordinating Council; National Catholic Education Association.

Term System. Semester; summer term.

Degrees in Religion Awarded 1984–85. Bachelor of Arts 5; men 4, women 1. Master of Arts in Theological Studies 16; men 5, women 11. Master of Arts in Pastoral Ministries 7; men 2, women 5.

Faculty for Degree Programs in Religion. Total 23; full-time 15; part-time 8.

Admission Requirements. Undergraduate applicants must have graduated from an accredited high school or have a GED certificate; SAT or ACT. An applicant is admitted to graduate study if the admitting committee of the Department is satisfied that the applicant is fully qualified to undertake graduate study (twenty-four semester

hours in Philosophy and Theology with a 3.0 grade point average or their equivalent is recommended).

Tuition and Fees. Undergraduate tuition full-time $2,-490 per term, part-time $136 per semester hour; Graduate tuition $111 per semester hour; other fees may apply; residence halls $855 single, $660 double per term; food service varies from $199 to $593 per term depending upon option selected.

Financial Aid. The University desires to assist all qualified students who seek financial assistance in order to continue their education. In an effort to meet this goal, the University has established a complete financial aid program which includes scholarships, loans, grants, tuition reductions, and part-time employment.

Marianist Scholarships are offered to top-ranking students attending Marianist high schools in designated areas.

Housing. On-campus housing in University residence halls is required of all freshmen unless they are married, are 21 years of age or over, or are local residents living with their families.

Library Facilities. The Roesch Library houses the book, journal, government documents, and microform collections for both graduate and undergraduate students. Its book holdings number almost 850,000 volumes and its journal titles almost 3,000.

The Marian Library, on the seventh floor of the Roesch Library Building, houses the world's largest collection of works on the Virgin Mary. Its resources in over fifty languages include 66,000 books and pamphlets (some 6,000 printed before 1800), 125 periodicals, a clipping file of over 49,000 items, and a growing number of microforms. These works are supplemented by smaller collections: slides, medals, postcards, Marian postage stamps, and illustrations of various kinds. In addition to these materials dealing with Mariology, the library has significant holdings in national and regional bibliographies, reference works on the Bible, ecclesiastical and dogmatic history, church art (especially of the Eastern Churches and Medieval Europe), and the history of the book.

The Marian Library publishes a scholarly annual entitled *Marian Library Studies.* This multilingual journal is intended to promote the renewal and development of scientific studies in Mariology by integrating them with other spheres of research such as the critical edition of texts, historical bibliography, comparative studies in theology, psychology, and religious anthropology.

Religious Services/Activities. Campus Ministry seeks to lead the University in fostering a faith community among its members. It provides a number of services to all who are part of the University community. It cooperates with all segments of the university in fostering human development and the articulation and implementation of moral and religious values. It provides opportunities for prayer, for the celebration of the sacraments, for retreat experiences, and for pastoral counseling. It sponsors events, classes, and seminars that concern the deepening of faith, the awareness of human needs, and the practice of religious and moral values. It coordinates the efforts of more than fifteen student organizations that offer opportunities for community service. Though specifically Roman Catholic, it cooperates with and helps foster other religious groups on campus.

Degree Programs

The Bachelor of Arts with a major in Religious Studies requires 36 semester hours in the major field (Biblical Studies, Historical Theology; Systematic Theology; Christian Ethics-Religion and Culture) with a total of 120 semester hours.

The Master of Arts in Theological Studies program offers a comprehensive approach to the study of theology and religion. Each student is expected to develop an understanding of biblical sources, historical developments, moral and contemporary theologies, especially in the Roman Catholic tradition. Ecumenical perspectives, among Christians and world religions, provide an important matrix for study.

The Master of Arts in Pastoral Ministries program offers the student an opportunity to prepare for a variety of service careers emerging in the contemporary Church. Courses and Workshops, particularly in religious education and telecommunications, family and parish ministries, and the social teachings of the Church, ensure the vitality of the program. This program, grounded in the study of theology, shaped distinctively by general principles of pastoral ministry, is open to a variety of applications. It prepares students for pastoral positions in catechetics and religious education, family parish, and campus ministry. Taking into account the individual interests and needs of the students, the program responds to contemporary pastoral needs through an integration of theory and practice.

Special Programs

Professors can make arrangements for special class sessions at the Marian Library on such topics as the history of printing, Christian art, and the development of the Marian cult. A recently inaugurated International Marian Research Institute offers programs of study at the graduate level in Christology, Mariology, and Ecclesiology. It also prepares candidates for the Pontifical doctoral degree in theology.

The Center for Christian Renewal brings the resources of the University and the Catholic and Christian community into cooperation and dialogue with groups in the local community, the archdiocese, the nation, and the world. The Center is a collaborative effort of the Marianist community, the faculty, staff, and students of the University, and the Church community of the Archdiocese of Cincinnati. Activities of the Center and its constitutive organizations are made possible by the resources, contributed services, and financial support of the Marianist community. The following four organizations carry out

the mission of the Center: Center for Religious Telecommunications, Center for Creative Ministry (MORES), Office of Educational Services, and Strategies for Responsible Development.

Defiance College
Department of Philosophy, Religion and
Christian Education

701 North Clinton Street
Defiance, OH 43512   (419) 784-4010

Administration. Dr. Marvin J. Ludwig, President; Dr. Kenneth E. Christiansen, Head, Department of Philosophy, Religion and Christian Education.

General Description. The Department's program in Religion and Christian Education is concerned both with the academic study of Religion and with helping students to develop a well-reasoned theological understanding. In keeping with the general aims of Defiance College, the Judeo-Christian heritage is emphasised. However, some courses focus on the history, literature, and present influence of world religions and the general issue of understanding religious phenomena wherever they may be found.

Parent Institution. Defiance College is a four-year, coeducational, liberal arts college founded in 1850 and affiliated with The United Church of Christ.

Community Environment. Defiance's 150-acre campus is in Defiance, Ohio, a city of 17,000 in the northwest part of the state. It is an hour's drive from the airports in Toledo and Fort Wayne, Indiana, and 30 miles from the Ohio Turnpike.

Religious Denomination. United Church of Christ.

Accreditation. North Central Association of Colleges and Schools.

Term System. Semester (4-1-4 plan); 2 summer terms.

Admission Requirements. High school graduate in top 60 percent of graduating class; 2.0 ("C") grade point average based on a 4.0 scale; scores of 15 or better on ACT or 650 or better on SAT.

Tuition and Fees. Tuition per year $4,980 (includes student union fee of $60 and activity and health fee of $120); room double $1,040, single $1,850, small single $1,125; board $1,355.

Financial Aid. Over 80 percent of Defiance's students receive some type of financial aid. Help is available through college scholarships and grants.

Housing. Excluding married students, service veterans, and commuting students living with parents, all freshmen, sophomores, and juniors must reside in college housing.

Library Facilities. The Anthony Wayne Library and Instructional Center houses 90,000 volumes, a microfilm library, and A/V service.

Religious Services/Activities. The Office of Spiritual Life organizes weekly chapel services, sponsors discussion groups on moral issues, organizes retreats, and works closely with religiously-oriented student groups.

Degree Programs

The four majors leading to the Bachelor of Arts degree are: (1) Studies in Religion, (2) Philosophy and Religion, (3) Religion and Christian Education, (4) Religion and Society.

Special Programs

The Associate   degree in Christian Education is awarded.

Findlay College
Religion and Philosophy Departments
1000 North Main Street
Findlay, OH 45840   (419) 422-8313

Administration. Dr. Kenneth E. Zirkle, President; Dr. James A. Drake, Vice President for Academic Affairs.

General Description. A student majoring in Religion or Philosophy may choose one of the general degree programs listed below, or he/she may develop an individualized program of study in consultation with an advisor. Every effort is made to meet the student's individual needs and interests and to enrich the opportunities for the person's chosen career. Degree programs available: Bachelor of Arts with Religion Major; with Comprehensive Major in Religion, Christian Education, and Philosophy; with Philosophy Major. Associate of Arts in Religion (2-year program) with Religion Minor; with Philosophy Minor.

Parent Institution. Findlay College is a liberal arts institution founded in 1882. Although it is church related (Churches of God, General Conference), religious activity on campus is a matter of personal choice. The College is committed to Christian attitudes toward truth, beauty, and life.

Community Environment. Findlay College is located in Findlay, Ohio, a city of 40,000 residents, 45 miles south of Toledo on Interstate 75. The College itself is 10 blocks from the center of town. Living in Findlay provides the student with the best of two worlds: it offers many of the cultural, recreational, and commercial opportunities expected from a large city, plus the friendliness and accessibility of a small town.

Religious Denomination. Churches of God, General Conference.

Religious Emphasis. Personal choice.

Accreditation. North Central Association of Colleges and Schools.

Term System. Semester; summer term. There is also a Weekend College program.

Enrollment in Degree Programs in Religion 1984–85. Total 14.

Degrees in Religion Awarded 1984–85. Varies from year to year.

Faculty for Degree Programs in Religion. Total 10; full-time 6, part-time 4.

Admission Requirements. Completion of a college preparatory course of study in an accredited high school; ACT preferred (SAT accepted).

Tuition and Fees. Tuition $2,715 per semester; room and board $1,250 per semester.

Financial Aid. 75 percent of the student body receives financial aid. Need and no-need based scholarships are available to qualified applicants. Scholarship and financial assistance policy is based on the concept of awarding aid to the strongest academic high school seniors. Financial aid packages can range from $100 to as much as full tuition, room and board. In 1984-85, Findlay College provided over one million dollars in financial aid.

Housing. Students may live on campus in dormitory facilities or off-campus if married.

Library Facilities. The Shafer Library resources include 104,000 books, 600 periodicals and journal subscriptions, government publications, newspapers, microforms, and media.

Religious Services/Activities. Weekly chapel, Religious Emphasis Week; Christian Athletic Groups; Debutation drama and singing groups visit churches in various states.

Degree Programs

The Bachelor of Arts degree with a major in Religion requires the completion of general education requirements plus 33 semester hours in Religion. Students are encouraged to develop individualized programs of study in consultation with faculty advisors. The Comprehensive Major in Religion, Christian Education, and Philosophy includes 41 semester hours.

Special Programs

The Associate of Arts degree program in Religion is a flexible and interdenominational program for lay leaders and those interested in assuming lay leadership in the future. The program requires 60 semester hours of work, including an individualized major of at least 24 semester hours.

The College offers a travel seminar to the Middle East and Israel on an annual basis.

The Weekend College program at Findlay College offers an opportunity for students 23 years of age or older to enroll in college courses.

God's Bible School and College
God's Bible School, College, and Missionary
  Training Home
1810 Young Street
Cincinnati, OH 45210   (513) 721-7944

Administration. Bence C. Miller, President; Joe C. Brown, Academic Dean.

General Description. God's Bible School is located on Ringgold, Channing, and Josephine Streets on Mount Auburn, in Cincinnati, Ohio. It was founded in 1900 by the Rev. Martin Wells Knapp for the purpose of training Christian workers for service at home and abroad. The founder's vision was that of a school where emphasis should be on Bible and Missions. Interdenominational in religious affiliation and Wesleyan-Arminian in doctrinal teachings, the School has a long record of successful operation in producing leaders in both the religious and secular worlds of the United States and several other countries.

To meet the varying needs of those who desire a Christian education, the School offers a Bible College and a High School. It also has a home study course for those who desire to study at home. Several specific programs of study are offered. Each of these programs is planned for some type of preparation for Christian work, and contains varied combinations of subjects from four specific fields: Bible, General Education, Music, and Practical Studies related to one's profession. Degrees are offered in the areas of Ministerial Training, Missions, Christian Education, Christian Teacher Education, and Music.

Community Environment. Called by Longfellow "the Queen City of the West," Cincinnati was founded in 1788 and was named Losantiville. The following year the name was changed to Cincinnati after the Society of Cincinnati. The city is the third largest in Ohio, and is situated on a series of plateaus above the Ohio River, surrounded by hills. The altitude varies from 435 to 938 feet. The area is highly industrialized and has a very large variety of cultural activities and opportunities. The city is famous as a center of music and art.

Religious Denomination. Nondenominational - Wesleyan-Arminian.

Religious Emphasis. Evangelical - Fundamentalist.

Accreditation. Candidate for accreditation with the American Association of Bible Colleges.

Term System. Semester.

Enrollment in Degree Programs in Religion 1984–85. Total 301; men 148, women 153.

Degrees in Religion Awarded 1984–85. Bachelor of Arts 20; men 6, women 14. Bachelor of Religious Education 13; men 7, women 6.

Faculty for Degree Programs in Religion. Total 18; full-time 12, part-time 6.

Admission Requirements. Graduation from an accredited high school or equivalent; ACT or SAT.

Tuition and Fees. Tuition $600 per semester; $50 per semester hour if less than 12 or over 18 hours; room and board $1,025 per semester.

Financial Aid. Work-Study Program; Pell Grants, Guaranteed Student Loans; scholarships.

Housing. Dormitories for single students; a minimal number of apartments available for married students.

Library Facilities. The library houses 25,465 volumes.

Religious Services/Activities. Chapel is held in the forenoon each Monday, Wednesday, and Friday. The main emphasis of these chapel services is spiritual growth, but opportunity is also taken for the presentation of information that otherwise concerns the entire campus community. Attendance at chapel is required. Other religious services include a mid-week all-School prayer meeting, special meetings for prayer, fall and winter revivals, Camp Meeting, Missionary Convention, and special lecture series from time to time.

Degree Programs

The four-year programs leading to the degree of Bachelor of Religious Education are arranged especially for those planning to enter the ministry or other fields of Christian work. These programs can be arranged as a five-year course for those students who must work full-time jobs. Provision is made for two majors: one of 40 hours in Bible and one of at least 24 hours in one of the practical areas of Professional Studies. Emphasis may be placed on Ministerial Training, Christian Education, Christian Teacher Education, or Missions. Students preparing for the pastoral or evangelistic ministry should plan to major in Ministerial Training. The student must complete 128 semester hours with a grade point average of 2.0.

The five-year program leading to the degree of Bachelor of Theology is planned especially for those who intend to enter the ministry, whether as pastors, evangelists, or missionaries. Two majors, one of 45 hours in Bible and one of 30 hours in a professional field; one minor of 18 hours in General Education; and a minor of 15 hours in Doctrine are required. The student must complete 160 semester hours of work with a grade point average of not less than 2.0 for the entire course.

The four-year programs leading to the Bachelor of Arts degree are pre-graduate programs. The programs provide a Bible-centered program of education, a broad base of general education, and a group of basic professional subjects. The general requirements for the degree include the completion of 128 hours of credit with a grade point average of not less than 2.0. Christian Service credits (3-4) are also required for the Bachelor's programs.

The four-year Bachelor of Arts degree with a major in Music requires 60 hours of music, 30 in Bible and theology, and 40 hours of general education. It is a professional church music program.

The five-year Bachelor of Arts in Christian Education requires 77 hours in music, 30 hours in Bible and theology, and 40 hours in general education. The program is designed to train Christian music educators.

The Bachelor of Sacred Music degree in church music and performance requires 64 hours in music, 30 hours in Bible and theology, and 36 hours of general education. It is a performance degree in church music and also requires three Christian Service credits.

The five-year Bachelor of Sacred Music degree in Christian Education and Performance requires 81 hours in music, 30 hours in Bible and Theology, and 40 hours of general education. The program is designed to train Christian music educators. It requires three Christian Service credits.

Special Programs

The three-year programs leading to a Christian Workers Diploma give emphasis to Bible, doctrine, and related subjects, with a minimum of general education subjects. It is planned for any one who for some reason cannot spend the longer time required for the degree programs. A total of 90 semester hours is required with a grade point average of not less than 2.0. The student must also earn two Christian Service credits.

Correspondence courses are also offered.

Hebrew Union College - Jewish Institute of Religion, Cincinnati

3101 Clifton Avenue
Cincinnati, OH 45220   (513) 221-1875

Administration. Dr. Alfred Gottschalk, Rabbi, President; Dr. Samuel Greengus, Dean; Dr. Edward A. Goldman, Rabbi, Assistant Dean, Rabbinic School.

General Description. The Rabbinic School: The Rabbinic School offers a 5-year program of full-time graduate study leading to the Master of Arts degree and ordination. Students admitted to the rabbinic program are required to spend their first academic year in Israel. Upon completion of the first year of study in Jerusalem, students return to one of the 3 American campuses (Cincinnati, New York, Los Angeles) to which they were assigned upon admission. The Los Angeles school offers only the 2nd and 3rd years of the rabbinic program; students transfer to either Cincinnati or New York for their final 2 years of study. The second through fifth year program is divided between required and elective courses in various areas of specialization. The student's selection of electives and rabbinic thesis topic determines the area of specialization.

The School of Graduate Studies: The School of Graduate Studies offers a program leading to the Doctor of Philosophy degree on the Cincinnati campus. Graduate level work is regularly offered in the following areas: Bible and Ancient Near East; Bible: Texts and Versions; Hellenistics; Philosophy and Jewish Religious Thought; Rabbinics; Modern Jewish Thought. To be eligible, an applicant must have at least a Bachelor's degree and a working knowledge of Hebrew. Hebrew Union College and the Department of Classics at the University of Cincinnati offer a student interested in Jewish and Christian studies of the Greco-Roman world an opportunity to pursue advanced studies in both institutions and take advantage of their combined resources. The student whose emphasis is in intertestamental Jewish culture or early Christianity can matriculate in the program of the Hebrew Union College. The student whose interests lie primarily in the Greco-Roman world, but include Judaica or early

Christianity, can enroll in the Department of Classics in the University of Cincinnati. Students in either institution, therefore, are encouraged to include in their individual programs relevant courses offered at the other institution.

Parent Institution. Hebrew Union College - Jewish Institute of Religion is the institution of higher learning in American Reform Judaism. It is dedicated to the study of Judaism and related areas in the spirit of free inquiry. Nothing in the Jewish or general past or present is alien to its interest. Sensitive to the challenge imposed by a world of change, it believes that Jewish ideas and values, along with the contributions of other religions and civilizations are meaningful to the building of the future. The Cincinnati school and its sister institutions in New York City, Los Angeles, and Jerusalem comprise the 4-campus complex of Hebrew Union College - Jewish Institute of Religion. It is under the patronage of Reform Judaism's Union of American Hebrew Congregations.

Hebrew Union College was founded in 1875 in Cincinnati, the first institution of Jewish higher learning in America. Its founder was Rabbi Isaac Mayer Wise, the architect of American Reform Judaism, who had established the Union of American Hebrew Congregations two years earlier. In 1922, Rabbi Stephen S. Wise established the Jewish Institute of Religion in New York. The similar operation of the two schools led to their merger in 1950. A third center was opened in Los Angeles in 1954, and a fourth branch was established in Jerusalem, Israel, in 1963. (See also under entries in New York and California.)

Hebrew Union College is affiliated with the University of Cincinnati, the Greater Cincinnati Consortium of Colleges and Universities, the University of Southern California, Washington University in St. Louis, New York University, the University of Pittsburgh, and the Hebrew University in Jerusalem. These associations provide variously for cross-registration privileges, the use of libraries and other facilities, joint course offerings, and cooperative degrees.

Community Environment. The Cincinnati campus, situated adjacent to the University of Cincinnati, comprises 18 acres of land and 8 buildings. The Klau Library is one of the most extensive Jewish libraries in the world.

Religious Denomination. Jewish.

Religious Emphasis. Reform.

Accreditation. North Central Association of Colleges and Schools; Middle States Association of Colleges and Secondary Schools; Western Association of Schools and Colleges.

Term System. Semester; no summer term.

Enrollment in Degree Programs in Religion 1984–85. Total 140; men 107, women 33.

Degrees in Religion Awarded 1984–85. Rabbinic Ordination 18; men 11, women 7. Master of Arts in Hebrew Letters 15; men 10. women 5. Master of Arts 2; men 1, women 1. Doctor of Philosophy 5; men 5. Doctor of Hebrew Letters 2; men 2.

Faculty for Degree Programs in Religion. Total 37; full-

time 30, part-time 7.

Admission Requirements. Rabbinic School: Admissions procedures for the Rabbinic School are uniform for all three American campuses. A bachelor's degree from an accredited college or university or its equivalent is a prerequisite for admission. In addition, the Graduate Record Examination (GRE), interview with the Admissions Committee, and psychological testing are required. The Graduate School: Bachelor's degree from an accredited institution of higher education; GRE scores; letters of recommendation; essay for faculty consideration about academic background and aims.

Tuition and Fees. Tuition $5,100; application fee $35; room and board $2,550; ordination fee $75; dissertation fee $250; graduation fee $75.

Financial Aid. Whenever possible, financial aid is awarded as a combination of scholarship assistance and an interest-free loan. In cases of demonstrated need, financial aid is available for tuition, fees, and living expenses.

Housing. The Cincinnati campus is the only campus which maintains a dormitory. The Sisterhood Dormitory contains faculty and student dining rooms and various social rooms, as well as student housing.

Library Facilities. The Klau Library contains 330,000 volumes, among them 150 incunabula, 2,000 manuscript codices, and many thousands of pages of archival documents. Special collections include Jewish Americana, music, a Spinoza collection, and extensive microforms. The American Jewish Periodical Center, part of the Klau Library, preserves American Jewish periodicals and newspapers on microfilm. The American Jewish Archives has 8 million pages of documents, 2 million of which are from the archives of the World Jewish Congress.

Religious Services/Activities. Regular religious services, conducted by students or faculty, are held in the school chapel. The Cincinnati campus houses the S.H. and Helen R. Scheuer Chapel. Worship services following American Reform Jewish Liturgy are held once daily and on the Jewish Sabbath when classes are in session. Class retreats and an annual "Avivon" (Springtime Topical Workshops) are also held.

Degree Programs

The Rabbinic School offers a five-year program leading to the Master of Arts degree and ordination. Students admitted to the rabbinic program are required to spend their first academic year in Israel. Upon completion of the first year of study in Jerusalem, students return to Cincinnati to commence the four-year program which is divided between a required core program and elective courses in various areas of specialization. The student's selection of electives and rabbinic thesis topic determines the area of specialization. During the first two years of residence in Cincinnati, a student takes a total of twenty courses. Upon earning credit for the twenty courses, the student is awarded the Master of Arts in Hebrew Letters. In addition to the core program, each student takes twelve elec-

tive courses, of which at least four emphasize the use of Hebrew and Aramaic texts. All students are required to take three Professional Development Practica in the areas of education, human relations, community organization, and homiletics. For at least one year, each student serves as the student-rabbi of a biweekly congregation or in some equivalent role. A candidate for ordination must present an acceptable thesis on a subject which had previously been approved by the faculty. During the senior year, a student is required to deliver a sermon in the Scheuer Chapel.

The Graduate School offers a program leading to the Master of Arts degree that is designed to provide graduate level competency in one of the following areas of scholarship: Bible and Ancient Near Eastern Studies, History, Rabbinics, Hellenistics, Philosophy and Theology, and Contemporary Jewish Studies.

A program leading to the Doctor of Philosophy degree is offered in the areas of Bible and Ancient Near East, Bible: Texts and Versions, Hellenistics, Philosophy and Jewish Religious Thought, Rabbinics, and Modern Jewish Thought. Students must have a working knowledge of the Hebrew language.

The Doctor of Hebrew Letters degree is available only to rabbinic graduates of Hebrew Union College on the basis of the Master of Arts degree that they have earned and the two years of post-M.A. residency required for ordination.

Hebrew Union College - Jewish Institute of Religion, Jerusalem
American Headquarters
3101 Clifton Avenue
Cincinnati, OH 45220   (513) 221-1875

Administration. Dr. Alfred Gottschalk, Rabbi, President; Dr. Michael Klein, Dean; Dr. Avraham Biran, Director, Nelson Glueck School of Biblical Archaeology.

General Description. The address of the Israel branch of the Hebrew Union College - Jewish Institute of Religion is: 13 King David Street, Jerusalem, Israel 94101. The Jerusalem branch of the Rabbinic School provides the mandatory Year-in-Israel program for all entering rabbinic students. It concentrates on developing proficiency in modern Hebrew. It employs the Ulpan method which is designed to maximize Hebrew learning in a short period of time. Students also take courses in modern Jewish thought and in biblical archaeology. All Hebrew Union College students are also automatically enrolled at the Hebrew University and may take a limited number of courses for credit. The Year-in-Israel Program is also designed to deepen the students' understanding of the land, the people, and the institutions of Israel.

The Jerusalem campus also provides the first year of schooling for students of the Rhea Hirsch School of Education, Los Angeles. Here the emphasis is on Hebrew language acquisition, but the students also take electives in Judaic studies and education.

The School of Jewish Studies serves rabbinic and other students of the American campuses of the College and is the center for the National Federation of Temple Youth undergraduate programs ("College Academic Year" and "Reform Leadership Training Program"). Advanced students enroll in courses in Bible, Midrash, archaeology, and ancient Near East history. Arrangements have been made with Hebrew University to enable such students to attend courses offered there.

Undergraduate students of American universities may spend an academic year in Israel in a work-study program sponsored by the Youth Division of the Union of American Hebrew Congregations and the Jerusalem School of Hebrew Union College. Participants in the College Academic Year Program (Reform Leadership Training) live in Jerusalem and spend 6 weeks at Kibbutz Yahel. Their curriculum consists of courses in modern and biblical Hebrew, archaeology, and the history, sociology, and politics of modern Israel. Students may receive credit for this program at their home universities.

Parent Institution. Hebrew Union College - Jewish Institute of Religion is the Institution of higher learning in American Reform Judaism. It is dedicated to the study of Judaism and related areas in the spirit of free inquiry. Nothing in the Jewish or general past or present is alien to its interest. Sensitive to the challenge imposed by a world of change, it believes that Jewish ideas and values, along with the contributions of other religions and civilizations are meaningful to the building of the future. The Jerusalem school and its sister institutions in Cincinnati, New York City, and Los Angeles comprise the 4-campus complex of Hebrew Union College - Jewish Institute of Religion. It is under the patronage of Reform Judaism's Union of American Hebrew Congregations.

Hebrew Union College was founded in 1875 in Cincinnati, the first institution of Jewish higher learning in America. Its founder was Rabbi Isaac Mayer Wise, the architect of American Reform Judaism, who had established the Union of American Hebrew Congregations two years earlier. In 1922, Rabbi Stephen S. Wise established the Jewish Institute of Religion in New York. The similar operation of the two schools led to their merger in 1950. A third center was opened in Los Angeles in 1954, and a fourth branch was established in Jerusalem, Israel, in 1963. (See also under entries in New York and California.)

Hebrew Union College is affiliated with the University of Cincinnati, the Greater Cincinnati Consortium of Colleges and Universities, the University of Southern California, Washington University in St. Louis, New York University, the University of Pittsburgh, and the Hebrew University in Jerusalem. These associations provide variously for cross-registration privileges, the use of libraries and other facilities, joint course offerings, and cooperative degrees.

Community Environment. The Jerusalem campus is situated on five acres of land in the center of Jerusalem, on King David Street, overlooking the ancient, walled city. The main building houses the synagogue, the library, a pottery restoration room, classrooms, and administrative offices. The gatehouse at the entrance of the main building houses the records of the Gezer excavation conducted by the Nelson Glueck School of Biblical Archaeology. Adjacent to the main building, surrounded by gardens, stands the Rosaline and Meyer Feinstein Building. It contains the offices and workshops of the School of Biblical Archaeology and the headquarters of the World Union for Progressive Judaism. An impressive outdoor amphitheater adjoins the building. The Jerusalem School is currently engaged in a major building project.

Religious Denomination. Jewish.

Religious Emphasis. Reform.

Accreditation. Middle States Association of Colleges and Secondary Schools; North Central Association of Colleges and Schools; Western Association of Schools and Colleges.

Term System. Semester; summer term.

Enrollment in Degree Programs in Religion 1984–85. Total 19.

John Carroll University
Department of Religious Studies
20700 North Park Boulevard
University Heights, OH 44118 (216) 491-4911

Administration. Rev. Thomas P. O'Malley, S.J., President.

General Description. The Department of Religious Studies believes that the study of the religious experience of mankind is an academic discipline which it considers to be an integral part of a liberal education. The University, through its Department of Religious Studies, provides the opportunity for its students to choose elective courses designed to give them an understanding of their faith commensurate with their other learning.

Parent Institution. John Carroll University, founded in 1886, is a privately controlled, coeducational, Roman Catholic and Jesuit institution. It provides liberal arts programs in the arts, sciences, and business at the undergraduate level, and in selected areas at the Master's level. As a Jesuit university, John Carroll draws upon the intellectual resources and educational experience of the Society of Jesus.

Community Environment. The campus is located on 60 acres with 17 buildings in University Heights, a suburb 10 miles east of downtown Cleveland.

Religious Denomination. Roman Catholic.

Accreditation. North Central Association of Colleges and Schools.

Term System. Semester; summer term.

Admission Requirements. High school graduate; ACT

or SAT.

Tuition and Fees. Tuition $4,768 per year; room and board $2,720; student fees $300.

Financial Aid. The primary purpose of the Financial Aid Program is to assist, with some form of aid, as many as possible of the applicants accepted for admission who demonstrate financial need.

Housing. All students not commuting from home are required to live in a residence hall to the extent of available accommodations. All students living on campus must take their meals at the university cafeteria.

Library Facilities. The library houses 365,000 volumes as well as 500 periodicals, 5,000 microforms, and 2,700 recordings.

Degree Programs

The Bachelor of Arts in Religious Studies requires 33 hours in the major which includes an introductory course in at least one course in Scripture, historical theology, systematic theology, and religious ethics, and 7 other specified courses.

The Master of Arts is granted through the Department of Religious Studies and the Graduate School. It offers four tracks: (1) Scripture Specialization, (2) Theology Specialization, (3) Religious Education Concentration, (4) General Religious Studies.

Special Programs

The Department of Religious Studies of the Graduate School offers a Post-Master's program leading to the Certificate of Advanced Studies.

Malone College
Department of Religion and Philosophy
515 25th Street, N.W.
Canton, OH 44709   (216) 489-0800

Administration. Herbert R. Dymale, Chairperson, Department of Religion and Philosophy.

General Description. The Department of Religion and Philosophy considers Biblical knowledge essential in preparing the student for Christian leadership in his community and church. The student is involved in Biblical and philosophical studies early in his college experience and is later helped to synthesize his studies in a capstone course. A major is provided in Christian Ministries with an option in Christian Education, Religion, or Biblical Literature. Preparation is provided for the pre-seminary student, the individual who anticipates graduate school, or the one who plans to enter a church vocation.

Parent Institution. Malone College is affiliated with the Evangelical Friends Church - Eastern Region. It is a private four-year liberal arts college founded in 1892. Malone's program, policies, and people are founded upon a deep commitment to the evangelical Christian faith. Malone College recognizes that Biblical principles are the

standard for individual behavior and community life.

Community Environment. The 78-acre campus is situated in Canton, a city with a population of 125,000. Canton is the home of the Professional Football Hall of Fame and the birthplace of former President William McKinley.

Religious Denomination. Evangelical Friends.

Religious Emphasis. Evangelical Orthodox.

Accreditation. North Central Association of Colleges and Schools. Member of: Christian College Coalition; Christian College Consortium; Friends Association for Higher Education; Friends Council on Education.

Term System. Semester; two summer sessions.

Enrollment in Degree Programs in Religion 1984–85. Total 15; men 11, women 4.

Degrees in Religion Awarded 1984–85. Bachelor of Arts in Christian Ministries 15; men 11, women 4.

Faculty for Degree Programs in Religion. Total 9; full-time 4, part-time 5.

Admission Requirements. High school graduation; admission is based on applicant's high school program and grades, post-high school academic work, standardized test scores, motivation, maturity, and other personal qualifications.

Tuition and Fees. $160 per semester hour; room and board $2,510 per academic year (includes telephone); student activity fee $50 per semester.

Financial Aid. Grants, loans, college work-study, and off-campus job opportunities are available.

Housing. Unmarried students not commuting from the home of parents are expected to live in the College residence halls.

Library Facilities. The library of Malone College houses 111,000 volumes including a special Quaker Collection.

Religious Services/Activities. Regular chapel attendance is required of all full-time students.

Degree Programs

The Bachelor of Arts degree program with a major in Christian Ministries permits an option in Biblical Literature, Religion, or Christian Education. A student who carries a full major in some other division of the College may take a second major in Christian Ministries. Pre-seminary students are advised to take eleven hours of Greek and six hours of Psychology and Social Science.

Special Programs

The Christian College Consortium Visitor Program is designed to give students an opportunity to take advantage of course offerings and varied experiences on other Christian college campuses for an academic semester while maintaining regular standing at Malone College.

The American Studies Program offers students the opportunity to study in Washington, D.C. with peers from member institutions of The Christian College Coalition. Students serve as interns in government offices and/or participate in seminar programs that are designed to integrate faith, living, and learning.

Marietta College
Department of Religion
Marietta, OH 45750   (614) 374-4600

Administration. Dr. Sherrill Cleland, President; Dr. Dwight L. Ling, Provost and Dean of the College.

General Description. Marietta College, founded and nurtured in the Congregational tradition of the Christian faith is dedicated to the belief that religion is an indispensible part of true education. The College seeks to foster the spiritual as well as the intellectual growth of the student. The Department of Religion offers the Bachelor of Arts degree with a major in Religion.

Parent Institution. Marietta College is an independent and predominantly residential undergraduate institution. Committed to liberal arts education with a meaningful career orientation, the College attempts to add to the knowledge of its students and to provide them with the tools necessary to develop an effective life. It is privately supported and coeducational.

Community Environment. The College is located in Marietta, Ohio, a city of 17,000. Marietta, the county seat of Washington County, is 114 miles southeast of Columbus on the Ohio River.

Religious Denomination. Nondenominational. (Founded by the Congregational Church.)

Accreditation. North Central Association of Colleges and Schools.

Term System. Semester.

Enrollment in Degree Programs in Religion 1984–85. Total 4; men 3, women 1.

Degrees in Religion Awarded 1984–85. Bachelor of Arts 1; men 1.

Faculty for Degree Programs in Religion. Total 2; full-time 1, part-time 1.

Admission Requirements. High school graduation; ACT or SAT.

Tuition and Fees. Tuition $3,550 per semester; room $600 per semester; board $510-$550.

Financial Aid. Presidential Scholarships; other scholarships; Grimm Memorial Award in Religion.

Housing. Dormitories, fraternity and sorority housing. Off-campus housing for married students.

Library Facilities. The Dawes Memorial Library houses 260,755 volumes.

Religious Services/Activities. Extracurricular student religious organizations offer activities.

Degree Programs

The Bachelor of Arts degree with a major in Religion requires the completion of 124 semester hours. The major requires 30 hours in Religion, although with the approval of the department chairman, the student may substitute relevant and appropriate courses in other departments for 6 of the hours required in Religion. If a student elects a foreign language, it is recommended that German be chosen.

Methodist Theological School in Ohio
3081 Columbus Pike
Delaware, OH 43015   (614) 363-1146

Administration. Buford A. Dickinson, President.

General Description. The Methodist Theological School in Ohio, authorized by the 1956 General Conference of the Methodist Church, was founded primarily to provide professional education for ministry in and through the local church. The School pursues its principal aim of education for the professional ministry through courses in the basic disciplines of biblical studies, church history, theology, and ethics, as well as courses that integrate theory and practice in homiletics, worship and music, church administration, Christian education, and pastoral care. The School cooperates with United Methodist annual Conferences and several other judicatories in preparing and certifying candidates for ordained and lay ministries. Students are exposed to a rich diversity of theological perspectives and instructional styles, and are encouraged to develop their own concepts of faith and ministry. Since its doors were opened to the first class in 1960, more than twelve hundred graduates have scattered from the seminary to forty-five states and several nations to serve in churches and other professional positions related to ministry.

Community Environment. The seminary community lives and works fifteen miles north of Columbus, on a campus of wooded grounds and dignified buildings of Georgian architecture, designed to encourage study and spiritual growth. The campus consists of 70 acres, two miles south of Delaware, Ohio.

Religious Denomination. United Methodist.

Accreditation. North Central Association of Colleges and Schools; Association of Theological Schools in the United States and Canada. Approved by: University Senate of the United Methodist Church.

Term System. Quarter; summer term.

Enrollment in Degree Programs in Religion 1984–85. Total 252; men 149, women 103.

Degrees in Religion Awarded 1984–85. Master of Divinity and Master of Arts 240. Doctor of Ministry 17.

Faculty for Degree Programs in Religion. Total 18; full-time 18.

Admission Requirements. Baccalaureate degree from an accredited college or university is required for admission; special consideration may be given applicants who do not meet the normal academic requirements.

Tuition and Fees. Tuition for a full program of studies (3 units) $1,060 per quarter.

Financial Aid. The School provides assistance through grants, loans, and employment. Students are also urged to investigate sources of aid such as grants from their judicatories, home parishes, Eastern Star (Estarl Scholarships), and veterans' educational assistance.

Housing. There are accommodations for single students in a residence hall; one bedroom and efficiency apartments; town home of 1 and 2 bedrooms.

Library Facilities. The John W. Dickhaut Library offers a collection of more than 85,000 volumes, 340 theological and related journals, and audiovisual materials.

Religious Services/Activities. The Schola Cantorum, the seminary's main choral group, takes its name (School of Singing) from the church's first choral organization of sixth century Rome. The Campus Council involves representatives of the student body, spouses, faculty, staff, and administration. Any campus group is eligible to be represented on the Council. The work of the Council is intended to enhance communication and understanding within the community. The meetings facilitate discussion of pertinent issues and the dispensing of information to the community.

Degree Programs

The Master of Divinity curriculum educates candidates for ordained ministry in churches and requires students to complete 28 units of credit. The course of study maintains the classical framework of theological education and is oganized into four fields: Biblical Studies, Historical Studies, Theological Studies, and Practice Studies. Students working toward this degree may specialize in Christian Education by meeting the requirements for the Master of Divinity generally, including among their electives the required courses in Christian Education.

The Master of Arts in Christian Education is designed to prepare men and women for leadership in the church's educational ministry. Candidates must complete 20 units of work for the degree. Persons seeking this degree could be preparing for some of the following forms of ministry: a certified director or minister of Christian education, a diaconal minister, a curriculum designer, writer, or editor, a teacher of religion in public schools, a college seminary teacher (after completion of doctoral studies), a skilled lay educator, and a resource person on a district or conference staff. This degree is also granted in conjunction with the Master of Divinity degree to students who specialize in an interdisciplinary program, which requires them to complete the equivalent of four academic years (36 units of credit).

The Master of Arts in Liturgical Arts equips pastors and lay persons for knowledgeable and effective leadership in Christian worship.

The Master of Theological Studies is designed specifically for lay persons who desire to study theology at a postgraduate level. The program does not intend a professional outcome, but contains specific practical possibilities for lay persons who want to increase their participation in the life of the Church, who are devoted to lay teaching and service as volunteers, and who wish to integrate their scientific, technical, or professional understandings with an increased understanding of theology.

The Doctor of Ministry degree is offered cooperatively by Ashland Theological Seminary, Trinity Lutheran Seminary, and Methodist Theological School. The program offers formal coursework, supervised field educa-

tion, peer interaction, and periodic evaluation of progress. The program provides pastors the opportunity to continue theological studies in concert with their professional ministry.

Special Programs

The Center for Town and Rural Ministries is a joint venture with the United Theological Seminary in Dayton and the East and West Conferences of the United Methodist Church. The Center brings into focus existing and emerging needs and issues which confront town and rural churches and communities within the seminary communtiy through teaching, training, consultative, and research services.

The School requires students to enroll in courses offered by the Columbus Cluster of Theological Schools which comprises Methodist Theological School, Pontifical College Josephinum, and Trinity Lutheran Seminary. Cluster courses are frequently taught by an ecumenical team of faculty members, and students encounter a variety of Christian backgrounds through the interseminary program.

The Methodist Theological School is a founding member of the Commission on Interprofessional Education and Practice located at The Ohio State University. The Commission conducts research, develops and implements graduate curricula, continuing education events, and educates the nation in the issues and concerns of an interprofessional approach to human need.

The Clinical Practicum in Professional Ministry Project involves three to five Middler or Senior students from the School in the practice of professional ministry for the ten weeks of each Fall Quarter in the United Methodist Church of Berea (near the campus of Baldwin-Wallace College).

Students participate in the Clinical Pastoral Education program as well as the National Capital Semester for Seminarians (offered through Wesley Seminary in Washington, D.C.).

Mount Vernon Bible College
7516 Johnstown Road
Mount Vernon, OH 43050   (614) 397-9606

Administration. Harold A. Muetzel, President; Jerry M. King, Administrative Dean.

General Description. Since 1923, LIFE Bible College in Los Angeles, California has been serving the fellowship of Foursquare churches in preparing people for ministry. As graduates established works throughout the United States, it became apparent that another Bible college was needed in the eastern half of the nation to accomplish a similar work. In 1957, the answer to that need was resolved as Mount Vernon Bible College began its ministry.

Community Environment. Mount Vernon Bible College is located 5 miles southwest of the city of Mount Vernon,

Ohio. Within 650 miles live 75 percent of the combined populations of the United States and Canada. The 285-acre campus began with classes in a renovated county home. The facilities have expanded to include the main 4-story building, a student center and gymnasium, the chapel, various faculty housing, and 4 classroom buildings.

Religious Denomination. International Church of the Foursquare Gospel.

Religious Emphasis. Fundamentalist.

Term System. Quarter; no summer term.

Enrollment in Degree Programs in Religion 1984–85. Total 81; men 48, women 33.

Degrees in Religion Awarded 1984–85. Bachelor of Arts in Bible 8; men 8. Standard Ministerial 5; men 3, women 2.

Faculty for Degree Programs in Religion. Total 12.

Admission Requirements. High school diploma; applicants must give evidence of an established commitment to the ways of the Lord and of an approved Christian character; physical and emotional maturity.

Tuition and Fees. Matriculation fees $135; library fee $1 per credit hour; tuition $1,500 per year; room and board $595 per quarter.

Financial Aid. The College awards scholarships to worthy full-time students on the basis of their Christian character, academic ability, special talents, financial needs, and the availability of funds.

Housing. Both men's and women's dormitories are available in the main building and are overseen by a pastor of resident students.

Library Facilities. The library houses 12,172 volumes.

Religious Services/Activities. Three weekly chapel services; two Sunday services. It is required that during the first two years a student take an active part in the local fellowship of the campus church and to avail him/herself of a variety of ministry experiences. During the student's upper division studies, he/she is asked to serve on numerous student ministry assignments in various congregations in the Mount Vernon area.

Degree Programs

The Bachelor of Arts degree program is a four-year course in Bible and related education for which 180 quarter hours are required. The Bible is the major in this degree with a minimum of 52 hours of Bible required. Other requirements include 20 hours of Theology, 44 hours of general education, 26 hours of ministry courses, 10 hours of miscellaneous, and 28 hours of electives.

Special Programs

The Standard Ministerial Diploma program is a three-year course in Bible and related education. It is a basic program to prepare the student for general Christian service. Emphasis is placed on instruction in Bible and the important phases of Christian doctrines. Added to this is instruction in subjects of a practical nature which are related to the various fields of Christian work. A total of 136 quarter hours is required.

Mount Vernon is a member of the Evangelical Teacher Training Association. Students who complete the required work for a Teachers Certificate are entitled to teach the Preliminary Training Course of the association.

Mount Vernon Nazarene College
Division of Religion and Philosophy
800 Martinsburg Road
Mount Vernon, OH 43050   (614) 397-1244

Administration. Dr. William J. Prince, President; Dr. David L. Cuble, Chairperson, Division of Religion and Philosophy.

General Description. The Division of Religion and Philosophy has as its objectives, in part, (1) to acquaint the student with the Bible as great literature and as the inspired Word of God; (2) to aid the student to grow in the knowledge of Jesus Christ; (3) to introduce the student to the great thinkers, both philosophers and theologians, of the past and present; (4) to develop an understanding of and appreciation for the doctrine, tradition, and mission of the Church of the Nazarene; (5) to emphasize the relevance for the contemporary individual of the Biblical, theological, and philosophical principles preserved by the Christian Church, with special emphasis on those of the Wesleyan Arminian tradition; (6) to prepare the student for a life of Christian service; (7) to prepare people to administer effectively the policies and practices of the evangelical church, especially as these relate to the ministry within the Church of the Nazarene; (8) to assist the student in preparation for graduate studies in such fields as law, religion, history, literature, philosophy, and education.

Parent Institution. A coeducational college of the arts and sciences, Mount Vernon Nazarene is the official college of the East Central Educational Zone of the Church of the Nazarene. Primary responsibility for sponsorship and support of the College is charged to the Nazarene congrgations in Ohio, West Virginia, and the eastern half of Kentucky.

Community Environment. Mount Vernon Nazarene College is located about one mile south of the public square of Mount Vernon, Ohio. The county seat of Knox County, Mount Vernon has a population of 15,000. The campus of 210 acres is bordered by the Kokosing River.

Religious Denomination. Church of the Nazarene.

Religious Emphasis. Wesleyan Arminian.

Accreditation. North Central Association of Colleges and Schools.

Term System. Semester (4-1-4 plan); summer term.

Admission Requirements. Graduation from accredited high school with at least 15 units of academic work including 4 English, 2 math, 2 social studies, 1 science; 2 foreign language, 1 additional science strongly recommended;

ACT; personal recommendations; personal statement of interests.

Tuition and Fees. Tuition $1,815 per term; general fee $107; health services fee $68; room and board $1,193 (fall term including January term), $957 (spring term).

Financial Aid. The two-fold purpose of Nazarene's financial aid is financial need and academic acheivement. Assistance is basically of four types: loans, employment, grants, and scholarships.

Housing. Single students not living in their own homes are required to room in the college dormitories and take their meals in the college dining room.

Library Facilities. The library contains 75,000 volumes, 535 periodicals, 1,763 microforms, and A/V materials.

Religious Services/Activities. College chapel services are held three times a week when the entire college community meets together for worship. Throughout the year there are times of special emphasis upon evangelism, missions, and personal Christian living.

Degree Programs

The major in Religion, leading to the Bachelor of Arts degree has two tracks: (1) Ordination Track, which fulfills the educational requirements for ordination in the Church of the Nazarene; (2) Pre-Seminary Track, which includes the minimum requirements for entrance into a seminary Master of Divinity program.

The major in Christian Education, leading to the Bachelor of Arts degree, has two tracks: (1) Professional Track, which fulfills the education requirements for certification as a Minister of Christian Education in the Church of the Nazarene; (2) Pre-Seminary Track.

The Philosophy-Humanities major, for the Bachelor of Arts degree, emphasizes classical, Christian, modern, and contemporary philosophy.

Muskingum College
Department of Religion and Philosophy
New Concord, OH 43762   (614) 826-8211

Administration. Dr. Arthur J. De Jong, President; Dr. William L. McClelland, Chairman, Department of Religion and Philosophy.

General Description. The Department of Religion and Philosophy holds to the belief that the study of Religion and Philosophy since the Middle Ages reflects seriously upon those ultimate concerns that belong to each human person. The Department offers majors in Religion, Philosophy, or a combination of the two. The Religion major is firmly grounded in Biblical Studies, church history, and theology. The religion major is encouraged to consider aspects of personal religion, comparative religions, and interdisciplinary studies. The Department also furnishes the Liberal Arts Essentials course in Religion. Periodically, students have opportunities for field studies in Rome, Greece, Israel, India, and Nepal, and also internships in Princeton, Pittsburgh, and Chicago. The degree Bachelor of Arts is awarded.

Parent Institution. Muskingum College's mission is to be a liberal arts college dedicated to intellectual integrity, human dignity, and Christian commitment. Muskingum's direct religious affiliation is with the three-state Synod of the Covenant of the Presbyterian Church (U.S.A.). The degrees Bachelor of Arts and Bachelor of Science are awarded.

Community Environment. The Muskingum campus is located on 215 acres with 16 major buildings. The city of New Concord, Ohio is 70 miles east of Columbus, 115 miles west of Pittsburgh, and 125 miles south of Cleveland.

Religious Denomination. Presbyterian Church (U.S.A.).

Accreditation. North Central Association of Colleges and Schools.

Term System. Semester.

Faculty for Degree Programs in Religion. Total 4.

Admission Requirements. Fifteen units of high school including 4 units in English, 2 units foreign language, 3 units college prep math, 2 units science, 2 units social science, 2 others.

Tuition and Fees. Academic year: Tuition $6,450; board $1,550; room $870; fees $175.

Financial Aid. In order to assist the greatest number of needy students, financial aid resources are allocated equitably in packages consisting of gift aid (grants, scholarships) and self-help (loans, work). Muskingum's financial aid committment to a student is for four years, dependent upon the student's continued demonstrated need and satisfactory academic progress.

Housing. All unmarried, non-commuting students must live and take their meals in college housing unless otherwise authorized. The majority of the students live in the six residence halls.

Library Facilities. The library contains 176,000 volumes, 45,000 federal documents, 7,000 Ohio documents, 700 periodical subscriptions, 25,000 bound periodicals, 52,000 microforms, and a substantial non-print media center collection.

Religious Services/Activities. A multi-dimensional, unified campus ministry provides ample opportunity for religious worship. Thursday morning Common Hour is reserved for community worship in Brown Chapel, and occasional vesper services are scheduled on Wednesday evenings in the Chapel.

Degree Programs

The major in Religion, leading to the Bachelor of Arts degree, requires 26 credit hours in addition to the Liberal Arts Essentials course in Religion. It must include 2 courses in Biblical studies including both Old and New Testament literature, as well as History of Christianity, Global Issues and Values, and Senior Studies. One course in philosophy may be included as part of the major in Religion.

Ohio Wesleyan University
Department of Religion
South Sandusky Street
Delaware, OH 43015 (614) 369-4431

Administration. R. Blake Michael, Chairman, Department of Religion.

General Description. The goal of the Department of Religion is to make students aware of the role that religion has played and continues to play in the values of individuals and in the formation of social institutions. The study of religion is not confined to those planning to enter the professional ministry, nor to those who themselves have ardent personal religious convictions. Rather, students planning careers in diverse fields benefit from the careful study of religious phenomena and history.

Parent Institution. Ohio Wesleyan was founded by the Methodist Church in 1842. It is an independent, liberal arts institution with an enrollment of approximately 1,300 students, almost equally men and women, and a full-time faculty of 120. Some 40 percent of its students are from Ohio, the others coming from 37 states and 30 countries. Academic programs lead to a Bachelor of Arts degree, or to one of three professional degrees: Bachelor of Fine Arts, Bachelor of Music, and Bachelor of Science in Nursing. A wide variety of major and minor programs is available, including preprofessional study and interdepartmental work. In consultation with advisors, students also may design their own majors. Ohio Wesleyan is a member of the Great Lakes Colleges Association, a consortium of 12 leading independent institutions in Indiana, Michigan, and Ohio. Consortium members cooperatively administer educational programs, among them numerous off-campus opportunities.

Community Environment. The 200-acre campus of Ohio Wesleyan is located 20 miles north of Columbus. The city of Delaware is located midway between Cleveland and Cincinnati. It is the birthplace of President Rutherford B. Hayes for whom Hayes Hall is named.

Religious Denomination. United Methodist.

Accreditation. North Central Association of Colleges and Schools. Member of: Association of American Colleges; University Senate of the Methodist Church.

Term System. Semester; summer term.

Enrollment in Degree Programs in Religion 1984–85. Total 17; men 5, women 12.

Degrees in Religion Awarded 1984–85. Bachelor of Arts with Major 3; men 1, women 2. Bachelor of Arts with Minor 3; men 1, women 2.

Faculty for Degree Programs in Religion. Total 6; full-time 3, part-time 3.

Admission Requirements. Students interested in admission to Ohio Wesleyan should contact the Office of Admissions for information.

Tuition and Fees. Tuition $7,800 per academic year; other fees where applicable; room and board approximately $3,100 per academic year.

Financial Aid. Financial aid is available. Grants may be obtained through federal, state, and institutional programs. Among the Ohio Wesleyan grants are Special Recognition Awards that provide recipients with approximately 80 percent of their need-based aid as gift assistance. The University further recognizes outstanding academic potential and personal qualities by sponsoring several programs in which awards are made regardless of financial need.

Housing. Dormitory housing is provided for all students in one of five residence halls or seven small living units.

Library Facilities. The Leon A. Beeghly Library houses 400,000 volumes on open shelving and is a major depository for federal government documents. The Library also includes special collections of rare books and manuscripts as well as microcards, microfilm, microprint, and other instructional media. The Library contains the archives of the West Ohio Area of the United Methodist Church.

Religious Services/Activities. The University has a full-time Chaplain independent of the Department of Religion who is responsible for coordinating religious life activities on campus.

Degree Programs

The Bachelor of Arts degree with a major in Religion is offered. The program requires eight unit courses within the areas of Biblical Studies, Religion and Society, History of World Religions. The Bachelor of Arts degree with a minor in Religion requires five unit courses in the Department.

The Bachelor of Arts with Pre-Theology major is an interdisciplinary curriculum preparatory to graduate theological studies. In total, thirteen courses are required and must be distributed among courses in Religion, Philosophy, Cultural Studies, and Social Studies.

Otterbein College
Department of Religion and Philosophy
West College Avenue
Westerville, OH 43081 (614) 890-3000

Administration. Dr. Thomas Jefferson Kerr, IV, President; Dr. James Recob, Chairperson, Department of Religion and Philosophy.

General Description. Otterbein College seeks to sponsor a program of liberal arts education in the Christian tradition. It is a private, independent, coeducational, four-year liberal arts college affiliated with The United Methodist Church. The Bachelor of Arts degree in Religion is offered.

Community Environment. Otterbein College is located in Westerville, Ohio, a suburb of Columbus, the state capital. Westerville still retains its early advantages of a small town, while offering the amenities that go with a modern community.

Religious Denomination. The United Methodist Church.

Accreditation. North Central Association of Colleges and Secondary Schools.

Term System. Quarter; summer term.

Admission Requirements. Acceptable scores on the SAT or ACT, in upper half of high school class, solid high school academic record that meets state of Ohio certification requirements or its eqivalent.

Tuition and Fees. Tuition and fees $2,003 per term; room $349-$411; board $459. Special fees and deposits where applicable.

Financial Aid. In addition to financial aid based on demonstrated need, the College offers a number of scholarships based solely on academic merit, special ability, or potential. Part-time work-study is available.

Housing. Freshmen are housed in double-occupancy rooms; upperclassmen live in a "social pattern" arrangement of two or more rooms occupied by three or more students.

Degree Programs

The major in Religion consist of 45 quarter hours of course work in Religion, including certain required courses such as Philosophy and Greek leading to the Bachelor of Arts degree.

Payne Theological Seminary
1230 Wilberforce-Clifton Road
Wilberforce, OH 45384   (513) 376-2946

General Description. This graduate school of theology was established in 1856 and is supported by the African Methodist Episcopal Church. The interracial, interdenominational seminary trains men and women for the Christian ministry. Special programs are continally being developed to meet the needs of minority groups. Cooperation among Central State University, Wilberforce University, and Payne Theological Seminary greatly increases the facilities of the Seminary.

Community Environment. The Seminary is situated on 11 acres of wooded land in four buildings.

Religious Denomination. African Methodist Episcopal Church.

Term System. Quarter.

Admission Requirements. Bachelor degree from regionally-accredited college.

Tuition and Fees. Per year: Tuition $825; room and board $1,025; apartments for married students $1,350; student fees $25.

Financial Aid. Numerous assistance plans based upon need.

Housing. On-campus housing for single students; apartments for marrieds.

Library Facilities. The library contains 15,000 volumes.

Degree Programs

The Master degree is awarded.

Pontifical College Josephinum
Josephinum School of Theology
7625 North High Street
Columbus, OH 43085   (614) 885-5585

Administration. Most Reverend Pio Laghi, Chancellor; Reverend Monsignor Frank M. Mouch, Rector/President; Reverend Colin F. Bircumshaw, Vice Rector, School of Theology.

General Description. The School of Theology at the Pontifical College Josephinum is a Catholic seminary. Its primary purpose is to assist in preparing men for the services of Christ and His Church in the Roman Catholic priesthood. The Josephinum is the only Pontifical seminary outside Italy, which gives definition to the broad scope of its interests. It was not established to serve a single diocese. The Apostolic Pro-Nuncio is its Chancellor, and the seminary has certain direct ties to the center of the universal Church in Rome. It serves to educate young men for a great variety of dioceses, and is open also to the candidates for priesthood in religious orders and secular institutes. Since 1899 when six of the original twenty-three students were ordained, nearly 1,000 priests have received their training at the Pontifical College Josephinum.

The School of Theology offers two degree programs: one leading to a Master of Divinity and the other to a Master of Arts. Students may earn both degrees by completing the four-year program. Guided by the Catholic ecumenical principles outlined by the Second Vatican Council, the Josephinum has offered a complete program of Catholic seminary studies, and has enriched this program by its association with other seminaries in the Columbus area. The cooperation of Trinity Lutheran Seminary in Columbus and Methodist Theological School in Ohio, in nearby Delaware, Ohio, expands the academic program, the library resources, and the ecumenical perspective of the students.

Community Environment. The 120-acre campus is located two miles north of Worthington, Ohio.

Religious Denomination. Roman Catholic.

Accreditation. North Central Association of Colleges and Schools; Association of Theological Schools in the United States and Canada.

Term System. Quarter; no summer term.

Enrollment in Degree Programs in Religion 1984–85. Total 107; men 90, women 17.

Degrees in Religion Awarded 1984–85. Master of Divinity 22; men 21, women 1. Master of Arts in Theology 7; men 7.

Faculty for Degree Programs in Religion. Total 24; full-time 17, part-time 7.

Admission Requirements. Bachelor of Arts degree or its equivalent, with a 2.5 grade point average or higher.

Tuition and Fees. Resident tuition $2,510 per year, non-resident $837 per quarter; room $1,027.50 per year; board $1,027.50 per year; other fees $100.

Financial Aid. An annual $1,200 Josephinum Scholarship is awarded to all priesthood candidates. Information on financial aid is sent to all students after application for admission is received.

Housing. Priesthood candidates live on campus in dormitories.

Library Facilities. The A.T. Wehrle Memorial Library is located in the Pope John Paul II Education Center. The library collection numbers more than 96,000 volumes and receives 400 periodical titles. Archival material, rare books, and incunabula are housed in the Special Collections area.

Religious Services/Activities. The Spiritual Formation Program is an essential part of the School of Theology. At the heart of the program is spiritual direction. A one-on-one encounter between the seminarian and his director is encouraged no less than once a month. The program provides weekly conferences on the spiritual life, annual treats, periodic days of recollection, a daily horarium which includes time for interior prayer, and in cooperation with the Director of Liturgy, the daily celebration of the Eucharist, Liturgy of the Hours, and weekly opportunities for the Sacrament of Reconciliation.

The Josephinum has designed a ten-week program of intense spiritual formation with is called "The Discipleship Journey." It consists of a thirty-day retreat made according to the Spiritual Exercises of St. Ignatius Loyola, followed by five weeks of spiritual formation adapted to the needs of future diocesan priests. Participation in the program is strongly encouraged, but remains optional.

A lecture program brings to the campus speakers whose specialties range over wide fields, including theology, sacred scripture, and its allied fields, missionary endeavor, ecumenics, philosophy, sociology, science, literature, and the fine arts.

Degree Programs

A Bachelor of Arts degree with a major in Religious Studies is offered as part of the four-year undergraduate program. In 1984-85, five graduates of the College majored in Religious Studies.

The Master of Divinity degree is conferred by the School of Theology as the graduate degree of the first level which prepares the student for pastoral ministry in the Church. It is adapted to the needs of any person in the program who is not a candidate for ordination and readies one to pursue the terminal degree of Doctor of Ministry.

The Master of Arts in Theology degree signifies that a student has attained a notable degree of competence in the study of theology on the first level of graduate school. Although the program provides the opportunity for the student to specialize in one of three areas (Biblical Studies,

Systematic Dogma, or Systematic Moral), it is designed to cover the basic truths of theology as a whole and to prepare the student for higher studies in sacred science.

Special Programs

The Introductory Year in Theology program offers the necessary philosophical and theological courses to college graduates who have no previous seminary experience. The program includes Old Testament Studies, Philosophical Studies, Introduction to Pastoral Ministry, Mystery of Salvation, Latin (optional), Christian Doctrine, and electives. Introductory Year men live in the theologate and take part in the life of that community, especially in the spiritual exercises of Mass and the Liturgy of the Hours. The spiritual program also includes weekly conferences by the Spiritual Director of the theologate, monthly consultation with a personal spiritual director approved by the Rector, and during the Fall quarter, a special weekly conference for the Introductory Year students.

St. Mary Seminary
1227 Ansel Road
Cleveland, OH 44108   (216) 721-2100

Administration. The Rev. Msgr. Robert E. Bacher, Ph.D., President-Rector; The Rev. Allan R. Laubenthal, S.T.D., Vice Rector and Dean.

General Description. As the School of Theology of the Diocese of Cleveland, St. Mary Seminary has as its primary objective to seek to fulfill in a contemporary manner the purpose of enabling men who aspire to serve as diocesan priests to prepare themselves for that ministry and to provide them with opportunities to demonstrate in a positive manner the reality of their priestly vocation.

Community Environment. The Seminary is located on an 11-acre site on the east side of Cleveland adjacent to the University Circle Area. It is within easy access of many cultural and educational facilities such as the libraries and facilities of Case Western Reserve University, The Cleveland Institute of Music, the Cleveland Museum of Art, and the Western Reserve Historical Museum. The Seminary building on campus serves the needs of the students under one roof. It has private rooms for 150 students with suites for professors, classrooms, library, gymnasium, and chapel.

Religious Denomination. Roman Catholic.

Accreditation. North Central Association of Colleges and Schools; Association of Theological Schools in the United States and Canada.

Term System. Quarter.

Enrollment in Degree Programs in Religion 1984–85. Total 10; men 10 (June 1983).

Faculty for Degree Programs in Religion. Total 23; full-time 14, part-time 9.

Admission Requirements. Bachelor of Arts degree or equivalent; A.T.S. statement on Preseminary Studies; at least 12 semester hours of Old and New Testaments, World Religions, Catholic Theology, Principles of Liturgical and Ascetical Theology; 18 semester hours of philosophy; a parish live-in experience.

Tuition and Fees. Tuition $90 per credit hour; residential students from other dioceses and religious communities: tuition $3,510; room and board $1,900.

Housing. Housing is available for 150 students in the Seminary Building.

Library Facilities. The Seminary library contains 45,000 volumes and receives over 335 current periodicals; it also contains a substantial collection of incunabula and other precious volumes. Seminarians also make frequent use of the near-by university libraries and the Cleveland Public Library.

Degree Programs

The Master of Divinity degree follows a five-year sequence of theological study and formation for the priesthood. Included in the five years is a six month pastoral internship. The basic sequence is 155 quarter hours organized into Biblical Studies, Historical Studies, Systematic Theology, and Professional Practice. A cumulative academic average of at least a "C" (2.00) in all course work. An oral comprehensive examination. A pastoral project in some phase of the ministry.

The Master of Arts degree has been designed for the purpose of the development of a mature understanding of Catholic Thought and Practice in its sources, development, and contemporary expression. This study of Biblical, Historical, and Systematic Theology enables the participant (either men or women) to come to a personal integration of the authentic experience of faith and provides a solid theological base for an active role in Church life. The basic requirement is 72 quarter hours; 32 quarter hours of core courses (Biblical studies, 16 hours; historical studies, 9 hours; systematics, 13 hours); 34 hours of electives; language requirements; a grade of "B" or better in all area electives and a cumulative average of 3.0 on a scale of 4.0.

Special Programs

In cooperation with the United Theological Seminary of Dayton, Ohio, St. Mary Seminary provides faculty to assist with United's Doctor of Ministry Program.

Trinity Lutheran Seminary
2199 East Main Street
Columbus, OH 43209   (614) 235-4136

Administration. Dr. Fred W. Meuser, President; Dr. James M. Childs, Jr., Dean of Academic Affairs.

General Description. Trinity Lutheran Seminary is an historic first for Lutherans in the United States, in that it is the first seminary owned and operated jointly by the Lutheran Church in America and the American Lutheran Church. Its purpose is to train committed and competent men and women for the ministry of Jesus Christ in the Lutheran church and other Christian communions. This ministry includes ordained ministry, non-ordained professional ministry, the equipping of lay persons for Christian service, as well as continued education for professional ministry. The Seminary also functions as a resource for congregations in their understanding of Christian faith and their faithful fulfillment of their mission under Christ. Degrees offered are: Master of Divinity, Master of Arts in Theology, Master of Theological Studies, Master of Sacred Theology, and Doctor of Ministry.

Community Environment. Trinity Luthern Seminary is located in Bexley, Ohio, a suburb on the east side of Columbus. The campus is about 4 miles from the center of Columbus. Across College Avenue from the Seminary is the main campus of Capital University. Other educational institutions located in close proximity are Ohio State University, Ohio Dominican College, Franklin University, Methodist Theological School in Ohio, and Pontifical Seminary Josephinum.

Religious Denomination. Lutheran Church in America; American Lutheran Church.

Religious Emphasis. Combines traditional Lutheranism and contemporary theology and method.

Accreditation. North Central Association of Colleges and Schools; Association of Theological Schools in the United States and Canada.

Term System. Quarter; summer term.

Enrollment in Degree Programs in Religion 1984–85. Total 297; men 201, women 96.

Degrees in Religion Awarded 1984–85. Master of Theological Studies 10; men 5, women 5. Master of Arts in Theology 1; men 1. Master of Divinity 52; men 38, women 14. Master of Sacred Theology 1; men 1. Doctor of Ministry 1; men 1.

Faculty for Degree Programs in Religion. Total 26; full-time 24, part-time 2.

Admission Requirements. Bachelor of Arts or equivalent from an accredited college or university; GRE required.

Tuition and Fees. Tuition $1,800 per year; housing $585; life insurance $7.50; health insurance $225; community life fee $33; Capital University service fee $95; parking (per car) $60; books (estimate) $500; telephone service charge $58.

Financial Aid. All financial aid, except the Presidential Scholarship, is based on need verified by the Graduate and Professional Student Financial Aid Service form which is available from the financial aid office.

Housing. Residence for unmarried students is provided in dormitory housing. Apartments for married students are allocated on a space available basis.

Library Facilities. The Seminary library houses a collection of over 85,000 books and bound periodicals, and 3,000 units of audiovisual materials. It receives over 600 current periodicals. There are several nearby libraries which extend privileges to seminarians. The Methodist Theological School in Ohio has a collection of more than 85,000 theological books and other materials. At the Pontifical College Josephinum there is a library of over 100,000 volumes. The Capital University library has more than 250,000 units, including pamphlets, recordings, films, and tapes.

Religious Services/Activities. Daily chapel; weekly Eucharist; occasional evening services. Requests are frequently received for seminarians to conduct worship services in congregations in the Ohio region. Students who have completed the basic courses in preaching and worship are eligible to accept such assignments.

Degree Programs

The Master of Divinity program accounts for the largest percentage of student enrollment. The faculty of the Seminary certifies those graduates who qualify for call and ordination to the ministry of The American Lutheran Church, and also prepares students for the professional ministry of the Lutheran Church in America.

A Master of Arts in Theology degree is awarded to those students who satisfactorily complete the academic part of the Master of Divinity program, but not the year of internship required for the latter degree. This degree does not lead to certification for ordination.

A Master of Theological Studies degree, with concentrations in theological studies, counseling, or lay ministries, may be earned in two years of study.

The Master of Sacred Theology degree is offered to those candidates who hold the Master of Divinity degree and who engage in a rigorous program of post-graduate study.

The Doctor of Ministry degree is offered in conjunction with Ashland Theological School and the Methodist Theological School in Ohio. It is an advanced degree for persons engaged in the practice of ministry.

Special Programs

Continuing education workshops and summer courses are offered.

United Theological Seminary
1810 Harvard Boulevard
Dayton, OH 45406   (513) 278-5817

Administration. Dr. John R. Knecht, President; Dr. Newell J. Wert, Vice President for Academic Affairs and Dean.

General Description. United Theological Seminary is a graduate professional school of the United Methodist Church. Its purpose is to educate persons for Christian ministry. The distinguishing characteristic of the Seminary is the educational process that joins academic study and professional practice. A full range of theological subjects is taught. The student-faculty ratio is 10:1. Set in a

major urban center, the Seminary expects its student to have field experience in both the church and the community. Specializations are possible in a number of areas of study and practice. Degrees granted are Master of Divinity, Master of Arts in Theological Studies, Master of Arts in Religious Education, and Doctor of Ministry.

Community Environment. United Theological Seminary is located in the northwest area of Dayton, Ohio. The 35-acre campus is a wooded and landscaped area in the heart of a residential section. Dayton, one of Ohio's most progressive cities, is located where 4 shallow streams, draining the upper section of the rich Miami Valley, come together.

Religious Denomination. United Methodist.

Accreditation. North Central Association of Colleges and Schools; Association of Theological Schools in the United States and Canada.

Term System. Quarter; summer term.

Enrollment in Degree Programs in Religion 1984–85. Total 302; men 217, women 85.

Degrees in Religion Awarded 1984–85. Master of Divinity 53; men 37, women 16. Master of Arts in Theological Studies 2; women 2. Master of Arts in Religious Education 3; men 1, women 2. Doctor of Ministry 6; men 5, women 1.

Faculty for Degree Programs in Religion. Total 26; full-time 21, part-time 5.

Admission Requirements. Baccalaureate degree for Master's programs; Master of Divinity or equivalent for doctoral program.

Tuition and Fees. Tuition $3,528 per year; fees $33; housing $157 to $200 per month.

Financial Aid. Types of aid available include tuition grants, college work-study program, and field education remuneration.

Housing. Apartments are available on the campus with separate bath and kitchen for single or married students.

Library Facilities. The library contains over 103,000 volumes and houses a special collection of Evangelical United Brethren materials.

Religious Services/Activities. Chapel services are held twice weekly. There is also a weekly Eucharist service plus an annual retreat.

Degree Programs

The Master of Divinity is a three-year program preparing persons for ordination.

The Master of Arts in Theological Studies is a two-year program for persons seeking academic competence in the field of theological study. A specialization and final major paper are required.

The Master of Arts in Religious Education is a two-year professional degree for persons seeking positions in religious education.

The Doctor of Ministry program provides advanced education leading to increased professional competence in ministry. The program is highly individualized and directed to the fulfillment of educational needs determined by the participants as they minister within their own contexts.

Special Programs

Special programs including continuing education, evening courses, internships, supervisory training, and lay education events.

Wilberforce University
Philosophy and Religion Department
Wilberforce, OH 45384   (513) 376-2911

Administration. Dr. Charles E. Taylor, President; Jane Ball, Chairperson, Humanities Division.

General Description. The Philosophy and Religion Department of the Humanities Division offers a concentration in Religion and Biblical Studies for the Liberal Studies Major.

Parent Institution. Wilberforce University was founded in the state of Ohio in 1856 as the first Black college in America. It was named for the noted abolitionist William Wilberforce. Since 1863 the University has been under the auspices of the African Methodist Episcopal Church.

Community Environment. Wilberforce is located in rural southern Ohio, yet close to the urban centers of Dayton, Springfield, Columbus, and Cincinnati, all of which offer supplemental facilities, cultural advantages, and employment opportunities.

Religious Denomination. African Methodist Episcopal Church.

Accreditation. North Central Assciation of Colleges and Schools.

Term System. Trimester.

Admission Requirements. High school graduate in the upper two-thirds of graduating class; minimum of 12-15 acceptable high school credits; ACT (SAT may not be substituted for ACT).

Tuition and Fees. (Costs listed are for 1983-84.) Per trimester: tuition and fees $1,720; board $483; room $445.

Financial Aid. Assistance is available based upon need.

Housing. On-campus housing available for most students.

Library Facilities. The Learning Resources Center contains a library of 55,000 volumes, 240 reading stations, workshops, and classrooms.

Degree Programs

The Concentration in Religion and Biblical Studies of the Liberal Studies major requires 14 credit hours in the subject. The Bachelor of Arts degree is awarded.

Winebrenner Theological Seminary
701 East Melrose Avenue
P.O. Box 478
Findlay, OH 45839   (419) 422-4824

Administration. George E. Weaver, President; J. Harvey Gossard, Dean of Academic and Student Affairs.

General Description. Winebrenner Theological Seminary, established as a graduate school of theology of Findlay College in 1942, received its charter from the state of Ohio in 1961 as an independent degree-granting institution. Winebrenner remains associated with the Churches of God, General Conference, but also welcomes students from other denominations. Its primary mission is to provide theological education for ministerial candidates in the Church, either as pastors or in pastoral-related activities. The Master of Divinity degree is awarded.

Community Environment. See: Findlay College for information about the city of Findlay, Ohio.

Religious Denomination. Churches of God, General Conference.

Religious Emphasis. Conservative and Evangelical.

Accreditation. Candidate for accreditation the the North Central Association of Colleges and Schools; Associate member of the Association of Theological Schools in the United States and Canada.

Term System. Semester; no summer term.

Enrollment in Degree Programs in Religion 1984–85. Total 44; men 39, women 5.

Degrees in Religion Awarded 1984–85. Master of Divinity 9; men 9.

Faculty for Degree Programs in Religion. Total 8; full-time 6, part-time 2.

Admission Requirements. A Bachelor of Arts or Bachelor of Science degree, or its equivalent in semester credit hours is required for admission. An exception to this policy may be given to students, age 35 or older, who give evidence of vocational and personal experience strongly suggesting that they will satisfactorily complete at least 5 college-level course, including English composition, speech, history, introduction to philosophy, and introduction to either psychology or sociology. Such applicants are admitted as special students.

Tuition and Fees. $110 per course (less than 10 hours), or $1,000 per semester (10-15 hours). Audit fees are $50 per course hour unless also enrolled for credit; $25 per course hour (less than 10 hours); and $15 per course hour (10 or more hours).

Financial Aid. Grants and work-study grants are available to those applicants who can demonstrate financial need. Also available are the Kreager Interest-free loan fund and benefits for qualified veterans, and guaranteed student loans.

Housing. There are 8 apartments on campus. They are all 2-bedroom apartments that include appliances for $225 per month. They provide water/sewage, and trash removal, but other utilities must be covered by the renter. In addition, there are several apartment complexes located nearby with comparable facilities and price.

Library Facilities. The library houses approximately 30,000 volumes.

Religious Services/Activities. Chapel services are held on Tuesday and Friday mornings in Ritz Chapel. A variety of worship experiences are scheduled for the inspiration and edification of the Seminary community. Once a month during the academic year, Winebrenner sponsors the Minsters in Society Program to acquaint prospective ministers with important aspects of the society and culture which the church serves. The Ritz Lectures and an annual Ministers Conference are also held.

Degree Programs

The program of the Seminary is a course of studies leading to the Master of Divinity degree. This is the standard professional degree for the Christian ministry, representing three years of graduate level work beyond a four-year college program, and normally fulfills the academic requirements for ordination by most judicatories.

Special Programs

The Institute for Biblical Studies provides theological education for (1) ministerial candidates who are age 32 or older, have not had college preparation, and/or are unable to undertake a traditional program of college and seminary professional education; (2) lay persons who wish to be better equipped for Christian service. The Institute's objective for theological education is to enable persons to develop as spiritually mature and competent leaders in the church. The programs of study lead to the the Diploma in Pastoral Studies and the Certificate in Biblical Studies.

Winebrenner Theological Seminary - Institute for Biblical Studies
701 East Melrose Avenue
Findlay, OH 45839   (419) 422-4824

Administration. George E. Weaver, President of Winebrenner Theological Seminary and Director of the Institute for Biblical Studies.

General Description. The Institute for Biblical Studies has been established by Winebrenner Theological Seminary to provide theological education for (1) ministerial candidates who are age 32 or older, have not had college preparation, and/or are unable to undertake a traditional program of college and seminary professional education, and (2) lay persons who wish to be better equipped for Christian service. The Institute's objective for theological education is to enable persons to develop as spiritually mature and competent leaders in the church. The Institute offers the Certificate in Biblical Studies and the Diploma in Pastoral Studies.

Parent Institution. Winebrenner Theological Seminary,

established as a graduate school of theology of Findlay College in 1942, received its charter from the state of Ohio in 1961 as an independent degree-granting institution. Winebrenner remains associated with the Churches of God, General Conference, but also welcomes students from other denominations. Its primary mission is to provide theological education for ministerial candidates in the Church, either as pastors or in pastoral-related activities. The Master of Divinity degree is awarded by the Seminary.

Community Environment. See: Findlay College for information about the city of Findlay, Ohio.

Religious Denomination. Churches of God, General Conference.

Religious Emphasis. Conservative and Evangelical.

Accreditation. Candidate for accreditation with the Commission on Institutions of Higher Education of the North Central Association of Colleges and Schools; Associate Member of the Association of Theological Schools in the United States and Canada.

Term System. Semester; most classes are given in the evenings.

Faculty for Degree Programs in Religion. Total 8; full-time 6, part-time 2 (faculty of the Seminary).

Admission Requirements. Admission to the Institute is by approval of the faculty upon receipt of the application form and the recommendations forms. For Diploma students, a letter of recommendation or endorsement from the appropriate conference, commission, committee, or association, which oversees ministerial training, licensing, and ordination; for those students who do not have a denominational affiliation, the letter of endorsement should be from the chairperson of the ruling body of the local church to which he or she belongs).

Tuition and Fees. Certificate Program tuition per course $125; Diploma Program tuition per course hour (less than 10 hours) $110; Diploma Program tuition per semester (10-15 hours) $1,000; Diploma Program tuition per course (hours above 15), except choir, $110. Audit fees: per course (except students enrolled for academic credit) $50; per course for students and spouses enrolled for less than 10 hours ($25); per course for students and spouses enrolled for 10 or more hours $15.

Financial Aid. A number of possibilities for financial assistance are available to students enrolled in the Diploma in Pastoral Studies Program.

Housing. See: Winebrenner Theological Seminary.

Library Facilities. See: Winebrenner Theological Seminary.

Religious Services/Activities. See: Winebrenner Theological Seminary.

Special Programs

The Certificate in Biblical Studies is a program in adult education intended specifically for laypersons wishing to enrich their personal knowledge of the Bible and related skills for service in the church. Participants may choose to audit courses without completing the written assignments or may take the courses for credit. Those taking the courses for credit will receive a Certificate in Biblical Studies when they have completed the requirements for graduation. Classes are offered in English Bible, theology, Church history, Christian ministries, and spiritual formation.

The Diploma in Pastoral Studies is a program intended for persons who are 32 years of age or older, have not had college preparation, and/or are unable to undertake a full program of college and seminary education. This program is primarily intended as an alternative course of studies meeting the requirements of ordination for members of the Churches of God General Conference. Persons who are not members of the Churches of God are advised to confer with their appropriate judicatory regarding the requirements for ordination in their denomination or church. Courses in English Bible, History, Theology, Field Education, and others will be offered in classes which are not part of the program of instruction at the Winebrenner Theological Seminary.

Wittenberg University
Department of Religion
P.O. Box 720
Springfield, OH 45501   (513) 327-6314

Administration. Dr. William A. Kinnison, President; Dr. Eugene R. Swanger, Chairman, Department of Religion.

General Description. Wittenberg University's purpose is to provide a learning environment of superior quality committed to liberal arts education. Wittenberg, related to the Lutheran Church in America, seeks to manifest its Christian commitment and Lutheran heritage. It is partially supported by the Ohio and Indiana-Kentucky Synods of that church.

Community Environment. Wittenberg University is located in Springfield, Ohio, which is 45 miles west of Columbus and 25 miles northeast of Dayton, on a campus of 31 buildings on 71 acres.

Religious Denomination. Lutheran Church in America.

Accreditation. North Central Association of Colleges and Schools.

Term System. Trimester, consisting of 3 eleven-week terms; one 6-week summer term.

Faculty for Degree Programs in Religion. Total 5.

Admission Requirements. High school graduate, with college preparatory curriculum consisting of 4 units of English, 3 units each of math, social studies, science, and foreign language; ACT or SAT.

Tuition and Fees. Costs per term: Tuition $2,475; room $420; board $430; Health Center fee $40; other fees $97.

Financial Aid. Numerous scholarships available as well as loan plans. Employment opportunities on and off campus.

Library Facilities. The Thomas Library has a collection of over 310,000 volumes, 1,400 periodicals, 52,000 microforms, and 37,000 A/V materials.

Degree Programs

A major in Religion consists of a minimum of ten courses in the Department, leading to the degree Bachelor of Arts.

Wooster, College of
Department of Religious Studies
Wooster, OH 44691   (216) 263-2000

Administration. Dr. Henry J. Copeland, President; Dr. Donald W. Harward, Vice President for Academic Affairs; Dr. Glenn R. Bucher, Dean of the Faculty; Dr. Robert Houston Smith, Chairman, Department of Religious Studies.

General Description. Courses in the Department of Religious Studies examine the phenomenon of religion in the religions of the world, with special attention to the Jewish and Christian traditions. The Department offers courses in four main areas: (1) Phenomenology of Religion, (2) Biblical Studies, (3) Christian Thought, and (4) Religion in Social and Cultural Perspective. In addition to the major in Religion for the Bachelor of Arts degree, the College provides for a course of study which serves the educational needs of those students interested in seminary or graduate study in religion as preparation for religious vocations or other person-oriented professions.

Parent Institution. The College of Wooster was founded in 1866 by Presbyterians who wanted to do "their proper part in the great work of educating those who are to mold society and give shape to all its institutions."

Community Environment. The city of Wooster, Ohio is in the north-central part of the state. Cleveland is about 60 miles northeast, Columbus 90 miles southwest, and Pittsburgh 120 miles east. A city of 20,000, Wooster is the county seat of Wayne County, with representative industrial activity, and is the business center for a rich agricultural district. The College grounds comprising some 300 acres are in a residential section about a mile north and east of the public square.

Religious Denomination. Presbyterian Church (U.S.A.).

Religious Emphasis. Liberal Protestant.

Accreditation. North Central Association of Colleges and Schools.

Term System. Semester; summer term.

Enrollment in Degree Programs in Religion 1984–85. Total 28; men 9, women 19.

Degrees in Religion Awarded 1984–85. Bachelor of Arts 17; men 6, women 11.

Faculty for Degree Programs in Religion. Total 6; full-time 6.

Admission Requirements. High school graduation. In determining admission, consideration is given to the many different expressions of a student's qualities and abilities:

scholastic achievements, performance on standardized tests, extracurricular activities, and promise to profit from and contribute to the intellectual life of the community.

Tuition and Fees. Comprehensive unit fee $11,245; without room $10,235; without meals $9,670; without meals and room $8,545.

Financial Aid. The College has a broad program of financial aid to assist students of high caliber who demonstrate a need for such help. All grants and awards are made through the Financial Aid Office.

Housing. All new students and most upperclass students are expected to live in College-operated residence halls, as determined by the Dean of Students. A variety of housing options for individuals and groups is available.

Library Facilities. The Andrews Library has recorded holdings of over 740,000 items: 318,000 volumes of books; 168,000 microforms, recordings, and other audiovisual materials; 1,250 journals and newspapers; and over 240,-000 United States government documents.

Religious Services/Activities. Westminster Presbyterian Church is the "congregation-in-residence" at The College of Wooster. It is a congregation of students, faculty, and townspeople who share a common life of worship and fellowship. Students participate as full members, affiliate members, and non-members. Students serve on the boards and committees of the church, teach church school, and work in the mission programs. Regular Sunday worship services are held in McGaw Chapel. The Newman Catholic Community and the Jewish Student Association also sponsor a number of activities on the campus.

Degree Programs

The Bachelor of Arts with a major in Religion is offered through the Department of Religious Studies. While the Department provides opportunities for the in-depth study of Judaism and Christianity, it does not seek to indoctrinate students with a particular creed or religious position. It is the Department's strong desire to provide a climate in which students will raise and reflect upon serious religious questions, and find for themselves satisfactory answers. The major consists of eight courses plus the Independent Study thesis.

Special Programs

Study-travel seminars for selected participants are conducted abroad (Israel, Europe, India, Mexico) or in the U.S. at American Indian reservations.

A Layman's Academy of Religion and the Clergy Academy of Religion, both 8-week continuing education programs, are held annually. An Ethics and Society Internship, providing off-campus experience in business and industry is also offered.

OKLAHOMA

Bartlesville Wesleyan College
Division of Religion and Philosophy
2201 Silver Lake Road
Bartlesville, OK 74006   (918) 333-6151

Administration. Dr. Paul R. Mills, President; Dr. Larry Hughes, Vice President for Academic Affairs; Yvonne Abatson, Chairman, Continuing Studies Division; Dr. Robert Black, Chairman, Division of Religion and Philosophy.

General Description. The Division of Religion and Philosophy has two main purposes: to teach religion courses generally for all students of the College and particularly those majoring in religion, and to train persons for specific ministries in the church. The Division offers a four-year Bachelor of Arts degree, a four-year Bachelor of Science degree, and a non-degree four-year program leading to a diploma.

Parent Institution. Bartlesville Wesleyan College is a private Christian liberal arts school sponsored by The Wesleyan Church. Born out of several mergers and relocations dating back to 1909, the College was established as a 4-year college in 1972. More than 20 majors are available in 6 divisions — Business, Education, Humanities, Religion/Philosophy, Science/Mathematics, and Behavioral/Social Sciences. There is a full-time faculty of 28; adjunct and part-time faculty increase that number to approximately 70. Current enrollment is 533. The College grants the Bachelor of Arts, the Bachelor of Science, and the Associate of Arts degrees.

Community Environment. The 27-acre campus is located on a knoll overlooking the city of Bartlesville, Oklahoma, 50 miles north of Tulsa. There are 22 college buildings. A major oil- and gas-producing company is located in Bartlesville. The first oil well of commercial importance drilled in Oklahoma is in Johnstone Park which adjoins the city limits. The area has a temperate climate and an average temperature of 59.9 degrees. Bartlesville has a population of 40,000, with a public library, a museum, and an art center.

Religious Denomination. The Wesleyan Church.

Religious Emphasis. Evangelical.

Accreditation. North Central Association of College and Schools.

Term System. Semester; summer term; May term.

Enrollment in Degree Programs in Religion 1984–85. Total 95; men 88, women 7.

Degrees in Religion Awarded 1984–85. Bachelor of Arts in Christian Ministries 13; men 13. Bachelor of Science in Christian Ministries 9; men 9. Bachelor of Science in Christian Education 2; men 1, women 1.

Faculty for Degree Programs in Religion. Total 6; full-time 4, part-time 2.

Admission Requirements. High school courses: English 4 units; Laboratory Science 1 unit; Math, Algebra I plus one of the following - Algebra II, geometry, trigonometry, calculus; History/Social Science 2 units; academic electives 6 units. In addition, the student must satisfy at least two of the following: an ACT composite score of 15, ranking in the upper two-thirds of class, and a high school grade point average of 2.0. Probational admission is available for students with deficiencies in these requirements.

Tuition and Fees. Tuition $3,450 per year for a full load (12-16 hours; per credit hour rate $115; all regular fees $450; room and board $2,150 per year.

Financial Aid. In addition to federal and state grants and loans, the College offers a variety of academic scholarships.

Housing. Housing on-campus is provided for unmarried students. The College will assist married students in finding off-campus housing.

Library Facilities. There are over 110,000 catalogued volumes in the library. The Cox Collection of Wesleyana is currently being established in honor of retired professor and president Dr. Leo G. Cox.

Religious Services/Activities. As an institution of The Wesleyan Church, Bartlesville Wesleyan College considers spiritual development a top priority in a community of teacher-learners. Attendance is required at three chapels per week, and a Spiritual Emphasis Week is scheduled for each semester. Regular church attendance is expected as well.

Degree Programs

The Bachelor of Arts in Christian Ministries degree requires a total of 126 hours including 61 hours of general education (including 12 hours of Greek), 54 hours in pastoral ministry, Bible, church history, Christian education, and theology, and 11 elective hours. The Bachelor of Science in Christian Ministries is identical to the Bachelor of Arts except that science/math/social science/behavioral science hours are substituted for the foreign language requirement. The Bachelor of Science/Bachelor of Arts in Missions degree program represents the full Christian Ministries program plus 15 hours of additional missions courses for a total of 130 hours. Minors are available in Bible, Youth Ministry, and Missions.

Special Programs

A four-year Ministerial program is offered which is basically the same as the Bachelor of Arts degree with the religion major except for the language and science requirements. Designed for those students who want ministerial training but who are not interested in the degree, the total program must include specified courses and electives for a total of 120 hours.

Under the Division of Continuing Education, credit is available for prior experiential learning under a supervised portfolio program. In certain cases and with certain restrictions, correspondence work may also be accepted to a limited degree.

Bethany Nazarene College
Division of Philosophy and Religion
6729 Northwest 39th Expressway
Bethany, OK 73008   (405) 789-6400

Administration. W. Stephen Gunter, Chairman, Division of Philosophy and Religion.

General Description. The Department of Religion of the Division of Philosophy and Religion serves in two main functions. First, it provides basic courses surveying the heritage, resources, and practices of the Christian faith for the General Education program of the college. Second, the Department provides pre-professional and professional training for students wishing to enter traditional forms of Christian ministry. Provision is made for members of the Church of the Nazarene to be able to meet present ordination requirements.

Parent Institution. Bethany Nazarene College is a liberal arts institution founded in 1899 under the auspices of the Church of the Nazarene - a Wesleyan denomination in the tradition of classical Methodist theology. The present college is the result of mergers of various educational institutions during the period of 1920 through 1929. From 1920 to 1955 the College was known as Bethany-Peniel College and the present name was adopted in 1955. The College is under the ownership, control, supervision, and patronage of the South Central Educational Region of the Church of the Nazarene. In doctrinal emphasis the College subscribes to the statement of the belief and practice of Christianity in our day, which can only be achieved by personal salvation through faith in the Lord Jesus Christ. While Bethany Nazarene College is an institution of the Church of the Nazarene, it is not sectarian to the exclusion of people from other denominations.

Community Environment. The College occupies a campus of forty acres located in the center of Bethany, Oklahoma. The city is located in central Oklahoma and has a population of over 20,000.

Religious Denomination. Church of the Nazarene.

Religious Emphasis. Evangelical-Wesleyan.

Accreditation. North Central Association of Colleges and Schools.

Term System. Semester; January miniterm; May miniterm; summer session.

Degrees in Religion Awarded 1984–85. Bachelor of Arts 18; men 12, women 6. Bachelor of Science 7; men 5, women 2. Master of Arts 6; men 5, women 1.

Faculty for Degree Programs in Religion. Total 9; full-time 5, part-time 4.

Admission Requirements. High school diploma or equivalency examination.

Tuition and Fees. Tuition $104 per semester hour; general fee $90 per semester; single room (on board plan) $635 per semester; single room (not on board plan) $730.25 per semester; double room (on board plan) $555 per semester; double room (not on board plan) $638.25 per semester; board $554 to $604 per semester depending upon meal plan selected (10, 15, or 21 meals per week); other fees where appropriate.

Financial Aid. Full range of federal and state programs as well as institutional scholarships for academic excellence. President's and Dean's scholarships, $1,000 and $500 respectively. Over 60 percent of the students receive financial aid and/or scholarships.

Housing. Two apartment complexes and various local dwellings are available for married students. Two dormitories are reserved for male students and two dormitories are restricted to female students.

Library Facilities. The Learning Resources Center houses over 104,000 volumes, 12,415 bound periodicals, 125,821 microfiche units, 34,147 government documents, and 2,996 non-print items. Special collections include the R.T. Williams Holiness Collection of Wesleyana; the American Holiness Movement contains 1,725 volumes. The Hymnology Collection contains 1,177 volumes. The Ross W. Hayslip Bible Collection is also maintained.

Religious Services/Activities. Chapel is viewed as an integral part of the Bethany Nazarene College experience. Attendance at services twice per week is required. Class Convocations under the supervision of the College Chaplain in conjunction with Class Chaplains are held simultaneously once each month during the semester. Week-long "Revival" services are held each semester and class retreats occur each Spring. All religious organizations are under the coordination of the Vice-President of Religious Life of the Student Council in consultation with the Chairman of the Department of Religion. Each organization carries on a distinct program and fills a specific need in the religious life of the campus. The five organizations are Mission Crusaders, Prayer and Fasting, Gospel Team, Timothean Society, and Reachout.

The Rothwell Theological Lectures, established in 1981, are funded by Paul David Rothwell, M.D., as a tribute to his father, Dr. Mel Thomas Rothwell. Dr. Rothwell served Bethany Nazarene College from 1959-73 as Professor of Philosophy and ultimately as Chairman of the Division of Philosophy and Religion. In keeping with the teaching ministry of Dr. Rothwell, the lectures seek to present the best academic scholarship in integration with the highest expectations of Christian living, exposing the campus to able, sound Christian scholars who deal with relevant facets of theology and religion.

The Staley Lectures, founded by the Staley Foundation, are scheduled in the Fall and bring notable religious leaders to the campus to speak on vital themes.

Degree Programs

The Bachelor of Arts with a major in Religion offers various patterns of concentration including Religion, Philosophy, Christian Education, Missions, and Bible. The Religion concentration may be used to fulfill the course of study requirements for ordination in the Church of the Nazarene.

The Bachelor of Science in Religion does not meet all the course of study requirements for ordination in the Church of the Nazarene. The major requires a minimum of 41 hours in the Division of Philosophy and Religion.

The Bachelor of Science in Christian Education requires the completion of a Christian Education core of courses in addition to the general education program and the required courses in Religion.

The Master of Arts in Religion seeks to meet the needs of ministerial students, active ministers, and laymen interested in religious studies. The College gives full support to the Nazarene Theological Seminary of Kansas City, Missouri, and encourages its graduates to take advantage of the broad, three-year professional program offered by that institution. The Master of Arts program provides for concentrated advanced study in the areas of Old Testament, New Testament, and Theology, with some work in related studies in Religion, and with limited supporting work in advanced courses in the cognate fields of Biblical languages, Christian education, education, history, literature, missions, philosophy, practical theology, psychology, sociology, or speech communication.

The Master of Ministry is designed specifically to meet the continuing education needs of men and women who have been in full-time ministry for a minimum of three years. The program requires a Bachelor degree and will take a minimum of two years to complete, since partici-

pants are expected to remain in full-time ministry while completing the program.

Hillsdale Free Will Baptist College
3701 South I 35
P.O. Box 7208
Moore, OK 73153   (405) 794-6661

Administration. Edwin L. Wade, President; Thomas L. Marberry, Vice President of Academic Affairs.

General Description. The Religion programs of the College offer a two-year program leading to the Associate of Arts in Biblical Studies and a four-year program leading to the Bachelor of Arts in Theology.

Parent Institution. The College has as its goal to serve the Free Will Baptist denomination by providing needed educational opportunities to both clergy and laity. The College has the responsibility of perpetuating not only the general tenets of the Christian religion but also those distinctives unique to Free Will Baptists.

Community Environment. Hillsdale College is located on a 41-acre campus adjacent to Interstate 35, in the city of Moore, Oklahoma, a suburb of Oklahoma City. Listed recently in the National Homebuilder's Magazine as the fastest growing city in the United States, Moore is a young town. Will Rogers International Airport is 10 minutes away. The city has many churches, a library, and health facilities. Nearby Lake Draper offers water skiing and fishing.

Religious Denomination. Free Will Baptist.

Religious Emphasis. Fundamentalist.

Accreditation. Oklahoma State Regents for Higher Education.

Term System. Semester; summer term.

Enrollment in Degree Programs in Religion 1984–85. Total 66; men 49, women 17.

Degrees in Religion Awarded 1984–85. Bachelor of Arts in Theology 22; men 15, women 7. Associate of Arts in Christian Education 3; men 1, women 2.

Faculty for Degree Programs in Religion. Total 8; full-time 6, part-time 2.

Admission Requirements. High school graduate; student must take ACT but no minimum score is required for admission.

Tuition and Fees. Tuition $1,500 per year; room and board $1,950 per year; fees $200 per year.

Financial Aid. Pell Grant, NDSL, Guaranteed Student Loan, Oklahoma Tuition Aid Grant, and institutional scholarships are available.

Housing. Dormitory housing is provided for single students and one-bedroom apartments are available for married students.

Library Facilities. The library houses 12,568 volumes and holds 8,624 microfiche.

Religious Services/Activities. Bible and missionary conferences, days of prayer, dormitory devotions, and mandatory chapel services are held. Active involvement in the local church is a requirement for every student. Visitation, teaching opportunities, evangelistic outreach, and other ministries are pursued by students.

Degree Programs

The Bachelor of Arts in Theology degree consists of a Biblical Studies major and a minor selected by the student from among Pastoral Ministries, Christian Education, Missions, and Church Music. A total of 124 semester hours is required for the degree.

Special Programs

The Associate in Arts degree requires a minimum of 64 semester hours. A student may complete a program in Biblical Studies, Christian Education, Missions, Church Music, Music, Business, Elementary or Secondary Education, Social Studies, English, or Physical Education.

Ordained and licensed ministers who are over the age of thirty may enroll in a one-year program of studies leading to a Certificate in Bible.

The Evangelical Teacher Training Association Certificate is awarded in cooperation with the Association to graduates who meet specific requirements. The purpose of the program is to prepare the recipient to teach workers in the local church. The program requires that the student must have completed college courses in the areas of Bible, Christian Education, and Missions.

A limited program of correspondence courses is offered.

Mid-America Bible College
3500 SW 119th Street
Oklahoma City, OK 73170   (405) 691-3881

Administration. John W. Conley, President.

General Description. Mid-America Bible College is a coeducational institution of higher education in the Church of God. It began in 1953 as the South Texas Bible Institute in Houston. In 1955 the curriculum was expanded to that of a four-year college and the name was changed to Gulf Coast Bible College. In 1983, 35 acres of land were purchased in Oklahoma City and the move to the new campus was accomplished in 1985.

Parent Institution. The College is a special purpose institution whose aim has been since its inception to prepare persons for entry into church-related vocations. The College offers two degree programs: The Bachelor of Arts, with language, and the Bachelor of Science, without language. Programs in Christian vocations include pastoral ministry, professional ministries, missions ministry, music ministry, youth ministry, evangelistic ministry, nursing ministry, social ministries, teaching ministry in Christian higher education, day care administration, and recreational ministries.

Community Environment. The campus is located in Oklahoma City, the capital of the state. The city is a leading wholesale and distributiing point and ranks as one of eight primary livestock markets in the country. Two of the world's largest high gravity oil fields are within the city and surrounding area.

Religious Denomination. Church of God.

Accreditation. Southern Association of Colleges and Schools; American Association of Bible Colleges.

Term System. Semester.

Enrollment in Degree Programs in Religion 1984–85. Total 265 full-time; men 163, women 102.

Faculty for Degree Programs in Religion. Total 21; full-time 16, part-time 5.

Admission Requirements. High school graduation; ACT; references.

Tuition and Fees. Tuition $1,600 per semester; room $364; board $574-$674.

Financial Aid. Aid awards are made only after a student has been admitted to the College. Scholarships, loans, federal grants, and employment are available.

Housing. Dormitory accommodations are available on campus.

Library Facilities. The Charles Ewing Brown Library has holdings of over 38,000 volumes. The Charles Ewing Brown special collection emphasizes items of historical significance to the Church of God Movement.

Religious Services/Activities. The College has its own campus pastor who attends to the spiritual needs of the student body. He provides for counseling services and arranges for speakers and programs for the three chapel services each week. Many campus organizations are available for student participation.

Degree Programs

The purpose of the major in Christian education is to prepare the student who plans to minister in one of the broad variety of ministries available in the field of Christian Education. This program requires a minimum of 30 hours of courses germane to the field. The Bachelor's degree which includes this program will require a minimum of 126 semester hours. The major is comprised of two parts: the core requirements and the core specialty concentrations. The student may combine the core requirements with the selected career specialty concentration to complete the thirty hours for the major.

Oklahoma Baptist University
School of Christian Service
500 West University
Shawnee, OK 74801   (405) 275-2850

Administration. Dr. Bob R. Agee, President; Dr. Dick Rader, Dean, School of Christian Service.

General Description. The School of Christian Service was inaugurated at Oklahoma Baptist University in 1981 to promote the Christian growth and development of all University students and to prepare and encourage, both spiritually and academically, those students who are responding to a divine call to vocational or bi-vocational Christian ministry. To achieve this purpose the School of Christian Service cooperates with the various academic departments of the University by offering introductory courses in Biblical studies and philosophy in the Unified Studies program as well as a wide range of major emphases in Religion and Philosophy leading to the Bachelor of Arts degree. The School of Christian Service also offers minors in both philosophy and religion, and the Associate of Arts in Christian Studies degree.

Parent Institution. Oklahoma Baptist University is a senior coeducational institution with an enrollment of approximately 1,500 students. A Christian institution, its primary purpose is to conduct educational programs in the traditional arts and sciences designed to prepare students for effective service and leadership in the various vocations. The University offers 8 degrees: Bachelor of Arts, Bachelor of Science, Bachelor of Science in Education, Bachelor of Business Administration, Bachelor of Humanities, Bachelor of Music Education, and Bachelor of Fine Arts. The curriculum features strong general studies requirements and more than 75 areas of concentration and majors in departments of instruction.

Community Environment. Oklahoma Baptist University is located in Shawnee, Oklahoma, a city of 35,000 residents, 35 miles east of Oklahoma City and 90 miles southwest of Tulsa, near the geographical center of the state. The 125-acre campus is on the northwest edge of Shawnee, just 2 miles south of Interstate Highway 40.

Religious Denomination. Baptist (Southern Baptist Convention).

Religious Emphasis. Conservative.

Accreditation. North Central Association of Colleges and Schools.

Term System. Semester; summer term.

Enrollment in Degree Programs in Religion 1984–85. Total 221; men 182, women 39.

Degrees in Religion Awarded 1984–85. Bachelor of Arts in: Religion 23; men 19, women 4. Pastoral Ministry 9; men 9. Youth Ministry 2; men 2. Educational Ministry 1; women 1. Church Recreation 1; men 1. Christian Ministry 1; men 1.

Faculty for Degree Programs in Religion. Total 12; full-time 8, part-time 4.

Admission Requirements. ACT of at least 16 (SAT of 720); high school grade point average of at least 2.00 or class rank in the upper half; transfers from an accredited college or junior college with a minimum of a C average.

Tuition and Fees. $1,500 per semester (12-16 credit hours); housing costs range from $420 to $475 per semester for single students to $190 per month for married student apartments.

Financial Aid. Aid is available in the form of scholarships (academic, athletic, leadership, music, etc.), long-term loans, grants, part-time employment, and various educational assistance programs. Special scholarships are available for all Southern Baptist students entering vocational Christian ministry.

Housing. Off-campus housing is available for single and married students, as well as some private accommodations off-campus.

Library Facilities. The library houses 155,000 bound and catalogued volumes, 75,000 microfilms. A rare book collection contains 3,000 volumes. Special collections include the W.B. Bizzell Collection of Literature and History, E. C. Routh Library of Missions, the J.W. Storer Collection, and the H.H. Hobbs Collection.

Religious Services/Activities. Annual religious events include Campus Revival, Mission Day, Christian Focus Week, and Spiritual Retreat. Chapel, noonday devotionals, Prayer Breakfast, and Bible study are held weekly.

Degree Programs

The Bachelor of Arts degree with a major in Religion requires the completion of 128 hours. Emphases available are general, Bible, history, theology, ethics, youth ministry, pastoral ministry, educational ministry, home missions, foreign missions, children ministry, and church administration.

Special Programs

An Associate of Arts in Christian Studies degree program provides basic preparation in the area of Christian Studies. Students completing this degree receive an introduction to liberal arts studies and have a major emphasis in distinctly Christian studies. This degree requires the completion of 64 hours and work taken in the program will count toward a baccalaureate degree. Ordinarily persons must be at least 30 years of age to enroll in this degree program.

In an effort to make personnel and services of the institution available to meet appropriate educational needs of the Baptist constituency, the School of Christian Service cooperates with the Office of Ministerial Services of the Baptist General Convention of Oklahoma in providing college-level training for ministers and other church leaders through Ministry Training Institutes and the Northeastern Oklahoma Center in Tulsa. Courses leading to a Certificate or Diploma in Christian Studies are offered in off-campus centers around the state of Oklahoma in addition to the regular on-campus curriculum. The content of the off-campus courses is prepared by the School of Christian Service faculty and taught by qualified adjunct faculty members under the direction of the Dean of the School of Christian Service. Courses taken in the Diploma level can apply to either the Associate or Bachelor of Arts degrees.

Oklahoma Christian College
Division of Bible
Rt. 1, Box 141
Oklahoma City, OK 73111   (405) 478-1661

Administration. Dr. J. Terry Johnson, President; Dr. Raymond Kelcy, Chairman, Division of Bible.

General Description. Through the courses of the Division of Bible and through various other activities, the college seeks to develop in the individual a desire for truth and to guide in the path which leads to a discovery of the truth. Bible courses present the Bible as the inspired word of God. Related courses are offered which deal with introductory background materials in order that the message of the Bible be better understood. The Division of Bible includes the Departments of Bible, Biblical Languages, Missions, Religious Education, and Youth Ministry. The Division awards the degrees Bachelor of Arts in Bible, Bachelor of Science in Bible, Bachelor of Arts in Missions, Bachelor of Arts in Preaching, Bachelor of Science in Religious Education, and Bachelor of Science in Youth Ministry.

Parent Institution. Oklahoma Christian College is a four-year, private, coeducational liberal arts college whose faculty and a majority of the students are members of the Church of Christ.

Community Environment. The College occupies a 200-acre campus in Oklahoma City, Oklahoma, with a metropolitan area population of 800,000.

Religious Denomination. Church of Christ.

Accreditation. North Central Association of Colleges and Schools.

Term System. Trimester.

Faculty for Degree Programs in Religion. Total 8.

Admission Requirements. High school graduate with a minimum of 15 high school units.

Tuition and Fees. Tuition 12-16 semester hours (one trimester) $1,375; room $455-$595; board $440-$495; mandatory fees $50.

Financial Aid. Financial assistance is available; more than 80 percent of OCC students receive financial aid; more than 50 percent were eligible for federal aid.

Housing. Residence halls can house approximately 900 students. Apartments adjacent to the campus are available for married students.

Religious Services/Activities. Required chapel attendence daily; voluntary devotionals conducted by students in the residence halls and on campus.

Degree Programs

The degree requirements are: B.A. in Bible, 58 hours; B.S. in Bible, 50 hours; B.A. in Missions, 58 hours; B.A. in Preaching, 68 hours; B.S. in Religious Education, 66 hours; B.S. in Youth Ministry, 66 hours. Minors are also available in Bible, Biblical Languages, Church History, Missions, Non-textual Bible, Religious Education, and

Youth Ministry.

Oklahoma City University
School of Religion and Church Vocations
2501 North Blackwelder
Oklahoma City, OK 73106   (405) 521-5284

Administration. Dr. Richard C. Bush, Dean, School of Religion and Church Vocations.

General Description. The School of Religion and Church Vocations has been developed to serve the needs of Oklahoma City University students and congregations. Students wishing to attend seminary, prepare for the diaconal ministry, serve the Church in youth ministry, Christian education, music ministry, and deepen their knowledge of their religious heritage, attend the School. The School grants the Bachelor of Arts in Religion and the Master of Arts in Religion. Most graduate-level courses are taught in the late afternoon and early evening.

Parent Institution. Oklahoma City University was Methodist-established in 1904 to serve as a distinguished academic community for learning and personal growth for the sons and daughters of the Church and citizens of the region. Over the past 82 years the Church and the University have developed a special partnership of service. The University currently has 3,000 students in both undergraduate and graduate programs, with 79 percent from the state of Oklahoma. Students may study in Petree College of Arts and Sciences, the School of Religion and Church Vocations, the School of Management and Business Sciences, the School of Music and Performing Arts, the School of Law, and the OCU/St. Anthony School of Nursing. The University has a church-related, small-campus atmosphere and offers numerous academic, religious, cultural, and athletic opportunities for students. It is committed to quality, personalized, value-centered higher education.

Community Environment. The University occupies a campus of 64 acres in the northwest section of Oklahoma City, which is the capital of the state. A leading wholesale and distributing point for the state, the city ranks as one of the 8 primary livestock markets in the country. Two of the world's largest high gravity oil fields are within the city and surrounding area.

Religious Denomination. United Methodist.

Accreditation. North Central Association of Colleges and Schools.

Term System. Semester.

Degrees in Religion Awarded 1984–85. Bachelor of Arts in Religion 2; men 1, women 1. Master of Arts in Religion 3; men 1, women 2.

Faculty for Degree Programs in Religion. Total 12; full-time 8, part-time 4.

Admission Requirements. Factors which are considered include high school record, achievement on scholastic aptitude tests, desirable traits of character and personality, and the interests and goals of the applicant in relation to the programs of study offered by the University.

Tuition and Fees. Tuition $118 per credit hour; graduate tuition $139 per credit hour; application fee $20.

Financial Aid. The University is committed to making the utmost effort to assist students who are seeking an education at OCU. Every student, regardless of his/her family's income, probably is eligible for some form of financial aid, and no qualified student should fail to apply because of financial circumstances.

Housing. All unmarried undergraduate students must live in University residence halls unless they are living with their parents or legal guardian. Veterans, divorced persons, and persons at least 24 years of age may be excused from the housing regulations upon authorization of the Dean of Students.

Library Facilities. The Dulaney-Browne Library houses over 240,000 volumes, 1,138 periodicals, 9,208 microforms, and 528 audiovisual materials.

Religious Services/Activities. Students are urged to join and work with the United Methodist Student Fellowship, Kappa Phi for women, and other religious groups designed to support faith in the university setting. The Dean of the Chapel counsels with students and gives leadership to campus religious life activities.

Degree Programs

The Bachelor of Arts with a major in Religion requires a minimum of 124 semester hours. Up to 24 hours in the Foundation Curriculum and/or elective courses may be taken under the Credit/No Credit option. A student majoring in Religion must complete at least 36 hours in the major field, and no more than 40. This total includes the 6 hours in Religion and related areas in section five of the Foundation Curriculum. Courses in the major are structured in five basic areas: Bible; History; Theology; Religion, Ethics, and Culture; and Applied Studies.

The Master of Arts degree is offered with two options: Option A: For the Church Professional and Option B: For Individual enrichment. Each option requires the completion of 36 hours. the common pattern for Option A includes 18 hours of Foundation courses; 12 hours of Certification courses (Christian Education, Church Music, Business Management); 3 hours in Methodology and Readings; and 3 hours in Thesis/Project. The usual pattern for Option B includes 18 hours of Basic courses; 12 hours of Elective and Interdisciplinary courses 3 hours; and 3 hours in Thesis/Project. Option A includes the common core of Foundational courses required for consecration as Diaconal Minister in the United Methodist Church.

Special Programs

Various programs offered by the University include the European Study-Tour; student exchange with University of Goettingen, West Germany; English Language Services Center, Mid-Year Institute; The Washington Semester

Program; Drew University Semester on the United Nations; Harlaxton College Semester (England); Hawaii Loa College Semester; George Shirk Oklahoma History Center.

Oral Roberts University
School of Christian Theology and Ministry
7777 South Lewis Avenue
Tulsa, OK 74171   (918) 495-6057

Administration. Oral Roberts, President; Dr. William W. Jernigan, Vice-President for Academic Affairs; Dr. Robert G. Voight, Dean of Instruction; Dr. Robert J. Stamps, Dean, School of Christian Theology and Ministry.

General Description. The purpose of the School of Theology at Oral Roberts University is to provide graduate professional theological education for the equipping of men and women for effective leadership in Christian ministries throughout the world. Combining classical theological education with charismatic concern, the School endeavors to prepare students from a broad cultural and religious spectrum for competent service in the Church, the classroom, and the world. The School of Theology is a multidenominational seminary seeking to prepare students for ministry within their own particular tradition, church, and culture. Although intentionally evangelical, the School believes it is important to embrace a diversity of theological understanding. Three degrees are offered: Master of Arts, Master of Divinity, and Doctor of Ministry.

Parent Institution. Oral Roberts University began in 1965 as an outgrowth of evangelist Oral Roberts' ministry. Subsequently, the University has become one of America's premier Christian universities, with almost 5,000 students. Noted for its 21st century facilities and innovative educational programs, the University is one of the leading tourist attractions in Oklahoma. The educational philosophy of Oral Roberts University is summarized with the words "wholeness" and "excellence." Students are encouraged to develop spiritually, mentally, and physically, and are challenged to maintain high standards of excellence. The University's key distinctive is the emphasis upon the work and ministry of the Holy Spirit.

Community Environment. Oral Roberts University is located on 500 acres of scenic, rolling countryside in suburban Tulsa, Oklahoma, one mile from the Arkansas River. Twenty major buildings grace the $250-million campus. Tulsa, which has been called "one of America's most beautiful cities," offers many cultural opportunities for the students of its two universities and one junior college. A growing city with 400,000 residents, Tulsa has an extensive system of libraries, art centers, theater groups, and its own philharmonic orchestra. The city has a dynamic downtown building project and an ongoing parks and recreation program.

Religious Denomination. Nondenominational.

Religious Emphasis. Evangelical, Charismatic.

Accreditation. North Central Association of Colleges and Schools; Association of Theological Schools in the United States and Canada.

Term System. Semester; May and June Sessions.

Enrollment in Degree Programs in Religion 1984–85. Total 282; men 237, women 45.

Degrees in Religion Awarded 1984–85. Master of Arts in Biblical Literature 8; men 7, women 1. Master of Arts in Theological and Historical Studies 1; men 1. Master of Divinity 42; men 37, women 5. Doctor of Ministry 12; men 12.

Faculty for Degree Programs in Religion. Total 21; full-time 18, part-time 3.

Admission Requirements. Master's level: Bachelor of Arts or Bachelor of Science from an accredited program; Master of Arts - minimum grade point average 3.0, GRE; Master of Divinity - minimum grade point average 2.5. Doctoral level: Master of Divinity or equivalent from a seminary accredited by the Association of Theological Schools, grade point average 3.0, at least 2 years ministry experience subsequent to completion of Master of Divinity, must plan on continuing in full-time ministry throughout the course of the program.

Tuition and Fees. Tuition: Master of Arts $130 per credit hour; Master of Divinity $110 per credit hour; Doctor of Ministry $1,700 per year, $600 continuation fee for third year; fees $80 per year.

Financial Aid. Academic scholarships, grants, work-study, assistantships, fellowships, and student loans are available.

Housing. Graduate student apartments are available with one or two bedrooms. Rates for single with roommate (two bedrooms) $185; single, or married, one bedroom $235; married, two bedroom $299 (utilities not included).

Library Facilities. The University library houses 600,-000 volumes; the Seminary library contains 110,000 volumes. The Holy Spirit Research Center at the University is one of the most comprehensive collections of Pentecostal/Charismatic resources in existence.

Religious Services/Activities. Required University Chapel service once weekly; required Seminary Chapel service once weekly. Students are encouraged to participate in local churches, retreats, conferences, and television tapings for Oral Roberts' and Richard Roberts' programs.

Degree Programs

The Master of Arts degree focuses upon a concentration in either Biblical Studies or Theological and Historical Studies with a cognate in the second of these areas. The degree is especially suited for students who will use this degree as the foundation for a Ph.D. in one of the related disciplines and/or plan to teach in churches and educational institutions.

The Master of Divinity degree is the basic professional ministry degree. It prepares persons for effective ministry as pastors, evangelists, ministers of Christian education, missionaries, counselors, or other ministries. The program is designed to enable the student to take the initiative in learning.

The Doctor of Ministry program of studies is designed for qualified men and women who are engaged in pastoral and related ministries. The purpose of the program is to help the candidates grow in their understanding and interpretation of the Church's ministry in relation to biblical, historical, theological, ethical, and practical areas. The candidates are also challenged to develop their ministerial skills and to refine and articulate a theology of ministry while in a setting of ministry. A special feature of this program is to enable the candidates to understand the positive and problematic developments in the charismatic dimensions of the ministry.

Beginning in the fall of 1986, the University will offer Master of Arts programs in Pentecostal and Charismatic Studies, Religious Education, Christian Counseling, and Sacred Music.

Special Programs

Annual Conference on Divine Healing and Charismatic Renewal; Clinical Pastoral Education at the City of Faith.

Phillips University
The Graduate Seminary

P.O. Box 2000 University Station

Enid, OK 73702   (405) 237-4433

Administration. Dr. Joe R. Jones, President; Dr. C. William Bryan, Interim Dean of the Graduate Seminary.

General Description. The Graduate Seminary is one of the theological schools founded and maintained by the Christian Church (Disciples of Christ). As such, it is committed to the ideals and principles of this communion. While its primary function is to serve its own theological family, it is ecumenical in spirit and in its approach to theological education. Two academic degree programs are offered, the Master of Divinity, and Doctor of Ministry.

Parent Institution. Phillips University is a private, co-educational institution founded in 1906 by the Christian Church (Disciples of Christ) in Enid, Oklahoma. It is comprised of the University College (includes undergraduate and graduate programs) and the Graduate Seminary. The primary mission of the University focuses on the liberal arts curriculum integrated with many career-oriented programs in a value-structured Christian context that seeks to nurture scholarship, social responsibility, religious awareness, cultural appreciation, and individual opportunity. The preparation of students for some form of Christian ministry is an important dimension of the curriculum of the University.

Community Environment. The University is comprised of 25 buildings located on 35 acres on the east side of the city of Enid, Oklahoma's fifth largest city. The principle crop of the area is wheat, which is handled in Enid's large flour mills and huge grain elevators.

Religious Denomination. Christian Church (Disciples of Christ).

Accreditation. North Central Association of Colleges and Schools; Association of Theological Schools in the United States and Canada.

Term System. Semester; summer term.

Admission Requirements. Baccalaureate degree from an accredited college or university; must present evidence of fitness to carry on graduate work.

Tuition and Fees. Tuition $125 per credit hour; student activity fee $83; room, single occupancy $600 per semester, double occupancy $475; 15-meals/week plan $525, 10 meals/week plan $500.

Financial Aid. Numerous financial aid plans are available.

Housing. Residence halls and apartments are available.

Library Facilities. The University libraries are composed of three active divisions: Zollars Memorial Library, the John Rogers Graduate Seminary Library, and the Audio-Visual Center. The libraries contain well over 300,000 volumes and more than 30,000 microforms, plus thousands of slides, sound recordings, cassettes, video tapes, filmstrips, pictures, and kits.

Religious Services/Activities. Fellowship of Christian Athletes, Intervarsity Christian Fellowship, and Baptist Student Union.

Degree Programs

The Master of Divinity is the basic degree program in the Seminary and is designed to provide the essentials for an educated ministry.

The Doctor of Ministry program is designed to extend and refine the student's understanding and ministerial practice.

Special Programs

Through the Field Education Director's office, the Graduate Seminary provides a placement service for locating current students into nearby churches in various capacities, such as weekend ministers, assistant ministers, youth directors, education directors, or music directors. A main purpose of this service is to promote the greatest educational benefit to students from their service with churches.

Tulsa, University of
Faculty of Religion
600 South College Avenue
Tulsa, OK 74104   (918) 592-6000

Administration. Dr. J. Paschal Twyman, President; Dr. Thomas F. Staley, Provost and Vice President for Academic Affairs; Dr. Robert W. Henderson, Chairperson,

Faculty of Religion and Humanities.

General Description. Courses offered by the program in Religion are designed to permit students to deepen their knowledge and understanding of all mankind's personal and cultural experience of religion as well as their own. Students may profit from these courses regardless of their major field of study or career intentions. The beliefs and practices of all past and present principal cultures are presented in 4 curriculum areas: (1) religion and ideas; (2) religion and history; (3) religion, the individual, and society; (4) literature, art, and religion. The Bachelor of Arts degree is offered for students majoring in Religion.

Parent Institution. The University of Tulsa, a Presbyterian-related institution, is a major private university in the Southwest, with an undergraduate enrollment of more than 5,000 and a graduate enrollment of about 1,500. It is known for its strong humanities-based undergraduate curriculum as well as for its energy technology programs.

Community Environment. The University's Henry Kendall Campus lies a little more than 2 miles from the heart of downtown Tulsa, a city whose metropolitan area exceeds 500,000 population.

Religious Denomination. Presbyterian related.

Religious Emphasis. Liberal.

Accreditation. North Central Association of Colleges and Schools.

Term System. Semester; summer term.

Enrollment in Degree Programs in Religion 1984–85. Total 15; men 10, women 5.

Degrees in Religion Awarded 1984–85. Bachelor of Arts 3; women 3.

Faculty for Degree Programs in Religion. Total 8; full-time 3, part-time 5.

Admission Requirements. The University seeks students for whom reasonable academic success can be predicted. Admissibility is determined in part by analysis of academic records and, in the case of freshmen, SAT and/or ACT scores.

Tuition and Fees. Undergraduate tuition per semester hour for part-time students $165 per credit, full-time students $2,350 per semester; application fee $15; student association fee $20 per semester; athletic fee $15 per semester; graduation fee $20; there are special fees for international students and for certain classes.

Financial Aid. Financial assistance is available in the form of scholarships, grants, loans, and part-time employment.

Housing. Residence halls are available for single students; there are nearby apartment units for married students.

Library Facilities. The McFarlin Library houses over 1,200,000 volumes. There are several rare book collections housed here. The Rare Books Room contains the library's single most valuable item, a copy of the Eliot Bible, published in an obscure Indian language between 1680 and 1685.

Religious Services/Activities. Sharp Memorial Chapel is the center of religious activities on campus. There are special Lenten and Advent services held each year at Easter and Christmas and a Catholic Mass each Sunday. The Meditation Room is open daily. Several church organizations have their own centers and staffs near campus to provide activities for college students. The Council on Religious life coordinates activities.

Degree Programs

The major in Religion leading to the Bachelor of Arts degree requires 27 semester hours in Religion with at least 18 hours at the upper division level. A minor in Religion is an option for students majoring in any number of disciplines and consists of at least 12 semester hours of coursework, half of which must be at the upper division level.

OREGON

Columbia Christian College
Division of Bible and Religion
200 N.E. 91st Avenue
Portland, OR 97220   (503) 255-7060

Administration. Michael C. Armour, President; Dr. M. Patrick Graham, Chairman, Division of Bible and Religion.

General Description. The Division of Bible and Religion serves two vital functions in the life of Columbia Christian College. First, Bible is taught to every student who attends the College. Biblical study for the general student is designed to help him grow toward Christian maturity. Second, the Division exists to prepare students for effective Christian ministry, however that ministry might be expressed.

Parent Institution. Historically, Columbia Christian College has pursued three primary instructional objectives: first, to provide values-centered liberal arts education in a limited range of specializations in Biblical studies, business, education, humanities, music, natural science, and the social sciences; second, to prepare young people for church-related careers at home or abroad; third, to develop in students a sense of civic and social responsibility.

Community Environment. Columbia Christian College is located in the northeast section of Portland, Oregon. Metropolitan Portland is laced by rivers and surrounded by snow-capped mountain peaks. It is within 75 miles of the Pacific coastline.

Religious Denomination. Church of Christ.

Accreditation. Northwest Association of Schools and Colleges.

Term System. Quarter.

Admission Requirements. High school graduation to include 4 years of English, 2 of social studies, 2 of science, 2 of mathematics, 1 of health and physical education. A minumim G.P.A. of 2.0 is required.

Tuition and Fees. Tuition $76 per credit hour; medical fee $10/quarter; student activities fee $75. Estimated costs for academic year: Tuition and fees $3,883; room and board $2,175; books and personal expenses $1,271.

Financial Aid. Several student aid plans; most require full-time enrollment and 1.85-2.00 G.P.A. On-campus and off-campus work programs.

Housing. All unmarried students are expected to live on campus. Residence halls for both men and women are located here.

Library Facilities. The College library contains more than 61,000 volumes, 250 current periodicals, A-V materials, phonograph records.

Religious Services/Activities. Chapel attendance required; local church attendance recommended.

Degree Programs

The major in Bible and Religion prepares individuals for competent, effective ministry in the service of the church. It might find expression in preaching, missions, educational ministry in a college or university, or teaching in a Christian elementary or high school. Emphases within the major include Christian education, congregational ministry, missions, and textual studies. Majors require 37 credit hours in Bible, 19 in Religion, 2 in Practicum, 9 in other areas (Education, Business, Music), 12 in electives in Bible/Religion, 12 in humanities. The degree Bachelor of Arts in Bible/Religion is awarded.

Concordia College
2811 N.E. Holman Street
Portland, OR 97211   (503) 288-9371

Administration. Dr. Charles E. Schlimpert, President.

General Description. Concordia College was founded as a four-year academy in 1905 and became coeducational in 1964. It is owned and operated by the Lutheran Church-Missouri Synod. The College grants baccalaureate degrees.

Community Environment. The 11-acre campus is located on the valley slope of the Columbia River in northeast Portland, two miles east of Interstate 5. Downtown Portland is only minutes away from the campus.

Religious Denomination. The Lutheran Church-Missouri Synod.

Accreditation. Northwest Association of Schools and Colleges.

Term System. Quarter (3-3-3 plan).

Admission Requirements. Graduation from an accredited high school; SAT or ACT.

Tuition and Fees. Tuition $4,800 per year; capital use fee $60; student activity fee $270; room $1,200; food service $1,480-$1,920.

Financial Aid. Need-based financial aid funds are available in the form of scholarships and grants, loans, and work study. Concordia prepares a financial aid "package" to offer each eligible student.

Housing. There are several residence halls available on campus.

Library Facilities. The Hagen Center Library houses over 40,000 volumes.

Religious Services/Activities. Worship is placed at the center of life and activity at Concordia. Chapel attendance is encouraged on a daily basis in both mornings and evenings. Evening devotions are student-led, and residence hall chapels are available at all times for student use. Concordia encourages students to attend public congregational worship at the various churches throughout the city of Portland. St. Michael's Lutheran Church is within two blocks of the campus.

Degree Programs

The Director of Christian Education program is a baccalaureate level program with areas of concentration offered in Early Childhood Education, Elementary Education, Music, Outdoor Ministry, Secondary Education, Theatre Arts, Theology, and Visual Arts. A Religion composite major is also offered in the Liberal Arts program as well as a Pre-Theological program.

Eugene Bible College
2155 Bailey Hill Road
Eugene, OR 97405   (503) 485-1780

Administration. Donald R. Bryan, President; Larry R. Burke, Director of Christian Ministries.

General Description. Eugene Bible College was originally founded in 1925 to provide terminal Biblical and professional training both for persons wishing to enter the Christian ministry vocationally and for laymen seeking to engage more effectively in a variety of Christian service opportunities. The College is the official conference college of the Pacific Division of the Open Bible Standard Churches, Inc. and is incorporated under the by-laws of that organization by the State of Iowa as a non-profit organization. The College operates under the supervision of the Committee on Higher Education of the Open Bible Standard Churches, Inc., and is represented on that committee by its president.

Community Environment. The College is located on a

picturesque 20-acre campus in the west hills of Eugene overlooking the southern Willamette Valley. The city, Oregon's second largest with a population of just over 100,000, covers a land area of 28 square miles including many attractive urban residential areas, parks, and recreational facilities.

Religious Denomination. Open Bible Standard Churches, Inc.

Religious Emphasis. Evangelical.

Accreditation. American Association of Bible Colleges.

Term System. Quarter; summer term.

Enrollment in Degree Programs in Religion 1984–85. Total 178; men 105, women 73.

Degrees in Religion Awarded 1984–85. Bachelor of Arts 15; men 13, women 2. Bachelor of Science 12; men 9, women 3. Bachelor of Sacred Music 1; women 1. Bachelor of Religious Education 2; women 2.

Faculty for Degree Programs in Religion. Total 12; full-time 9, part-time 3.

Admission Requirements. Evidence of having received Jesus Christ as Savior and Lord both by profession of faith and by approved Christian character; graduate of an accredited high school or equivalent; SAT; health record.

Tuition and Fees. Costs per year: tuition $2,325; room and board $2,070; general fees $180; special fees $56.

Financial Aid. Federal financial aid programs (Pell Grants, SEOG, Work-Study, GSL); honor scholarships; married student discounts; children of active ordained minister discount; several general scholarships.

Housing. On-campus housing available for single students.

Library Facilities. The library contains 22,098 volumes.

Religious Services/Activities. Chapel is conducted twice each week . Once during each term a week is selected for spiritual commitment and a guest speaker is invited to share in a special worship-preaching service. Students are required to attend church on a regular basis throughout the year.

Degree Programs

The Bachelor of Arts or Bachelor of Science are awarded for completion of a professional program, each having Bible as its major plus a professional requirement with three alternative emphases which determine the type of degree earned (B.A. or B.S.). The programs are offered in Pastoral Studies, Missionary Studies, Christian Education, and Music Education.

Special Programs

A special one-year program of study has been developed for students who will be able to attend Bible college for only one year and who are seeking a short-term concentrated course in Bible and Theology to provide them with greater spiritual growth, stability, and insight. A Bible Certificate is awarded upon successful completion of the 48-hour program if a 2.00 grade point average is maintained.

Lewis and Clark College
Religious Studies Department
0615 S.W. Palatine Hill Road
Portland, OR 97219   (503) 244-6161

Administration. Dr. James A. Gardner, President; Dr. Richard Rohrbaugh, Chair, Religious Studies Department.

General Description. The Religious Studies Department of Lewis and Clark College offers both an undergraduate major and minor in Religion. The Departmental curriculum concentrates in three areas: (1) the history, culture, literature, and religion of the ancient Near East (including Biblical studies); (2) the history and theology of religion in the West (including Christianity, Judaism, and Islam); (3) world religions (especially those of India and East Asia). A variety of introductory courses are offered along with upper division seminars in each of the areas of concentration. Additional electives are offered on a periodic basis in a variety of areas including Jewish studies, social ethics, contextual theologies, and feminism. Hellenistic Greek is taught in alternate years.

Parent Institution. Lewis and Clark College is a selective institution including a Liberal Arts College, a Graduate School of Professional Studies, and the Northwestern School of Law. The undergraduate college offers majors in 38 areas of study, with additional cross-disciplinary majors available in gender studies and a variety of international area studies. With large numbers of students from other countries and an extensive overseas study program in which much of the student body participates, the international emphasis of the undergraduate college is central.

Community Environment. The campus of Lewis and Clark College occupies a country estate of 130 acres, which contains 40 college buildings, in the city of Portland, Oregon. Portland lies along both sides of the Willamette River at its juncture with the Columbia where there is a splendid port deep enough for the largest ships to dock.

Religious Denomination. Informally affiliated with the Presbyterian Church (U.S.A.).

Religious Emphasis. Liberal, Ecumenical.

Accreditation. Northwest Association of Schools and Colleges.

Term System. Quarter; summer term.

Enrollment in Degree Programs in Religion 1984–85. Total 27; men 11, women 16.

Degrees in Religion Awarded 1984–85. Bachelor of Arts 9; men 4, women 5.

Faculty for Degree Programs in Religion. Total 5; full-time 3, part-time 2.

Admission Requirements. Admissions procedures require application forms, high school transcripts, counselor's reference, teacher's reference, SAT or ACT scores, and a personal statement from the applicant.

Tuition and Fees. Total $11,409 for fall, winter, and spring terms.

Financial Aid. Financial aid is given primarily on the basis of need through a variety of sources: scholarships, grants, loans, and employment. Non-need scholarships are also available to outstanding students selected as Presidential scholars and those demonstrating exceptional talent in music or forensics.

Housing. Both dormitory and off-campus housing is available to single students. Off-campus housing is available for married students.

Library Facilities. The library contains over 200,000 volumes. Special collections include the Chuinard Collection of Lewis and Clark Expedition Materials, the NAPCU Microform Center, and a Federal Document Depository.

Religious Services/Activities. Ecumenical religious services are held weekly. Sectarian or denominational groups usually meet weekly as well. Study groups, intern projects, and service opportunities in the city of Portland are also available.

Degree Programs

The Bachelor of Arts degree in Religion requires 11 course credits in the major, 9 course credits in the college-wide core curriculum, two years of college-level work in a foreign language, and basic competence in college-level mathematics. A minimum of 37 course credits is required for graduation.

Special Programs

Student-designed majors, area studies, gender studies, and a variety of international programs can be coordinated through the Religious Studies Department. Overseas study in Germany, France, and Costa Rica is available on a full year basis. Study in other countries (six per year) is available for one or two quarters. Additional off-campus study opportunities exist in New York City and Washington, D.C.

Mount Angel Seminary
St. Benedict, OR 97373   (503) 845-3030

Administration. Fr. J. Terrence Fitzgerald, President-Rector; Fr. Henry LaCerte, O.S.B., Academic Dean; Fr. Gregory Duerr, O.S.B., Dean of the Graduate School.

General Description. The undergraduate curriculum at Mount Angel Seminary is shaped by convictions that result in (1) a program that seeks to give academic information optimal for the development of free Christian men, and (2) a program that seeks to provide a foundation for the study of theology. It emphasizes the great strengths of the Catholic tradition: its heritage of intellectual integrity, its discipline, its cohesiveness. The Bachelor of Arts degree is awarded to majors in philosophy or in liberal arts.

Graduate studies at Mount Angel have been designed both to prepare candidates for priestly ministry and to serve the needs of continuing education for many kinds of adult people interested in pursuing theological studies. The Master of Arts program offers the opportunity for advanced theological training by means of independent study. The Master of Divinity program focuses more specifically on coordinating theology with pastoral skills. The Master of Theological Studies offers the students an academic background in the ecclesiastical disciplines in order to prepare them to use the religious sources of the Church in their work.

Community Environment. Located in northeast Oregon between the Blue and Wallowa Mountains, St. Benedict is near the city of La Grande. The county seat of Union County, La Grande's principal industries are agriculture and lumbering. Hunting, fishing, and winter sports may all be enjoyed in the area.

Religious Denomination. Roman Catholic.

Accreditation. Northwest Association of Schools and Colleges; Association of Theological Schools of the United States and Canada.

Term System. Semester; no summer term.

Enrollment in Degree Programs in Religion 1984–85. Total 64; men 60, women 4.

Degrees in Religion Awarded 1984–85. Master of Arts 4; men 3, women 1. Master of Theological Studies 1; men 1. Master of Divinity 11; men 11.

Faculty for Degree Programs in Religion. Total 17; full-time 7, part-time 10.

Admission Requirements. Graduation from an accredited high school with a cumulative grade point average of 2.25 or higher and a combined score of 890 or higher on the SAT.

Tuition and Fees. Tuition resident students $2,500 per year; room $700; board $1,700; personal expenses approximately $600 per year; student services fee $125.

Financial Aid. To insure that all qualified candidates regardless of financial circumstances may consider enrolling at Mount Angel, the Seminary makes available the services of a Financial Aid Office. Oregon State Scholarship and Need Grants, Basic Education Opportunity Grants, insured student loans, employment, and Bishop's Scholarships are among the types of aid available.

Housing. Dormitory accommodations are available for students pursuing ordination to Catholic priesthood. Other students are required to arrange for their own housing.

Library Facilities. The library houses over 139,000 volumes.

Religious Services/Activities. Mass or prayer is held daily.

Degree Programs

The Bachelor of Arts degree is awarded to majors in philosophy or in liberal arts. Liberal arts majors concentrate either in a particular discipline or in the area of interdisciplinary studies. Those concentrating in a discipline choose behavioral sciences, history, literature, or philosophy. Those concentrating in an interdisciplinary

area focus on Classical Studies, Medieval and Renaissance Studies, American Studies, or Religious Studies. The degree requires a minimum of 124 semester hours.

Graduate courses are arranged so that the student moves gradually from introductory courses to concentrations on particular themes. After a foundation in basic concepts, doctrinal courses consider the Church as the milieu for faith and for the development of doctrine on Christ and the Trinity. Toward the end of the program the pastoral implications of theology are made more explicit, after the foundation in theory is firm, after the history of the tradition is traced, after one has learned to read the scriptures critically and as a testament of faith. The pastoral dimensions of theology are actively considered throughout the course of graduate studies. In the Field Education Program, academic learning is harmonized with the learning of pastoral skills.

The Master of Arts program offers the opportunity for advanced theological training by means of indepth study.

The Master of Divinity program focuses more specifically on coordinating theology with pastoral skills.

The Master of Theological Studies offers the students an academic background in the ecclesiastical disciplines in order to prepare them to use the religious resources of the Church in their work.

Multnomah School of the Bible
8435 N.E. Glisan Street
Portland, OR 97220   (503) 255-0332

Administration. Dr. Joseph C. Aldrich, President; Dr. Joseph Y. Wong, Vice President and Academic Dean.

General Description. The Bible is the central focus and the curriculum major of Multnomah School of the Bible. The Bible also serves as the guiding standard in Multnomah's specialized program of instruction. Other curricular areas, whether general education or professional studies, develop from a Biblical world view. Further, programs of the Graduate Division either provide a full Bible major in one year or rest upon a full Bible major of undergraduate study. The School grants the degrees Associate of Arts, Bachelor of Arts, Bachelor of Science, Bachelor of Religious Education, Bachelor of Sacred Music, Master of Arts, Master of Sacred Ministry, and the Graduate Certificate in Bible.

Community Environment. Multonmah School of the Bible is located in the city of Portland, Oregon — "The City of Roses" — which offers the ideal combination of an urban sports and cultural center with an area of startling natural beauty. Portland spans the juncture of the mighty Willamette and Columbia rivers. Adjacent to a 9-acre city park, Multonmah's 17-acre campus is located in a residential area of east Portland, near the main arteries of 82nd Avenue (Oregon Highway 213), the Banfield Expressway (Interstate 84), and I-205. Buses are available to and from the heart of the city's business district.

Religious Denomination. Nondenominational (Christian).

Accreditation. American Association of Bible Colleges.

Term System. Semester; summer term.

Enrollment in Degree Programs in Religion 1984–85. Total 673; men 398, women 275.

Degrees in Religion Awarded 1984–85. Associate of Arts 56; men 26, women 30. Bachelor's 77; men 48, women 29; Master's 23; men 21, women 2. Graduate Certificate 74; men 40, women 34.

Faculty for Degree Programs in Religion. Total 52; full-time 32, part-time 20.

Admission Requirements. Associate: High school graduation with a minimum 2.0 grade point average; satisfactory SAT scores. Bachelor: 32 semester hours of academic work in an accredited liberal arts college.

Tuition and Fees. Tuition $1,840 per semester; room $445; board $585; Master's program $120 per credit hour.

Financial Aid. Federal aid programs, institutionally administered federal programs, and Multnomah financial aid programs are among the resources available.

Housing. Unless living with their parents, single students are required to live in school housing. A limited number of houses for married students are available.

Library Facilities. The John and Mary Mitchell Library contains over 37,000 volumes.

Religious Services/Activities. Chapel is held daily except on Tuesday. Attendance is required of all students at Chapel, Student Ministries Workshop, Student Missionary Union, Days of Prayer and Praise, Christian Life Conference, and the Annual Missionary Conference.

Degree Programs

The College offers the Bachelor of Theology, the Bachelor of Arts in Biblical Literature, the Bachelor of Science in Biblical Education, the Bachelor of Religious Education, and the Bachelor of Sacred Music. The three-year Bible major of the bachelor's programs builds upon a one-year requirement in general education completed at an accredited college of the student's choice. Along with the total core curriculum of 73 semester hours (including 52 hours in Bible and doctrine), a varied program of minor emphases is provided to enable the students to specialize in a particular area of interest. These minor emphases include: Christian Education, Music, Missions, Journalism, Pastoral, Youth Ministry, Women's Ministry, and Biblical Languages.

The Master of Arts in Biblical Studies program is designed to offer a specialization in Bible, Biblical Interpretation, and Theology. It requires a minimum of 32 credit hours.

The Master of Sacred Ministry program is a one-year graduate program designed to develop an expository preacher whose ministry is able to effect numerical and spiritual growth of a local church. The program requires the completion of 32 hours of coursework.

Special Programs

The Graduate Certificate in Bible is a one-year program designed to offer graduates of universities, colleges, or nursing and other professional schools a major in Bible in one year. A bachelor's degree or comparable professional training is a prerequisite.

The Associate of Arts in Biblical Studies is a three-year course giving special emphasis to the study of the Bible. Available to high school graduates, the program offers a higher concentration of Bible study during the three-year curriculum. The program requires the completion of 96 semester hour credits.

The Adult Education Division offers Bible classes each Monday and Thursday night on a fourteen-week semester basis.

Northwest Christian College
828 East 11th Avenue
Eugene, OR 97401   (503) 343-1641

Administration. Dr. William E. Hays, President.

General Description. The mission of Northwest Christian College is to provide a Biblically-based education to equip men and women to serve the church and the world through a variety of vocations and professions. The educational philosophy of the College incorporates Biblical studies and general studies utilizing several majors to prepare students for professional or lay ministries in a particularly strong way. Coordinate programs with the University of Oregon and Lane Community College expand the offerings. Northwest Christian College is institutionally affiliated with the Christian Church (Disciples of Christ) and the Christian Churches and Churches of Christ.

Community Environment. Northwest Christian College campus is adjacent to the western boundary of the University of Oregon, in the city of Eugene. Eugene is the center of a vast recreational area and an important lumbering center.

Religious Denomination. Christian Church (Disciples of Christ); Christian Churches and Churches of Christ.

Accreditation. Northwest Association of Schools and Colleges.

Term System. Quarter.

Admission Requirements. Must provide satisfactory credentials relative to character and Christian purpose; high school graduation; CEEB tests, including SAT.

Tuition and Fees. Tuition 1-15 hours $86 per term hour; 15-18 hours $1,290 per term. Room and board single $2,597 per year, double $2,386 per year.

Financial Aid. Aid in the form of scholarships, grants, loans, and employment is available to eligible students who need assistance to attend school.

Housing. All single students under 21 not living with parents are required to live in a residence hall through the

Junior year. A limited number of apartments are available for married students off campus.

Library Facilities. The Learning Resource Center has a collection of 58,000 volumes, extensive A/V resources, microfilm, and rare periodicals, books, and Bibles.

Religious Services/Activities. The entire campus community cooperates in promoting an atmosphere conducive to spiritual growth and maturity. Individuals and groups within the residence halls have regular times for devotion, prayer, and study. Most classes are opened by scripture reading, meditation, or prayer. Students are expected to be actively involved in the local church of their choice. Chapel services play an important role on the campus, and all students are required to attend.

Degree Programs

Degree programs are offered at three levels: (1) Two-year programs (see Special Programs, below); (2) Four-year programs leading to the degrees Bachelor of Arts, Bachelor of Science, Bachelor of Theology, Bachelor of Sacred Music; (3) Graduate programs leading to the degrees Master of Arts in Christian Ministry, Master of Arts in Christian Service.

The Bachelor programs require 186 credit hours. Major subject fields for the Bachelor program are (1) Pastoral Ministry, (2) Educational Ministries, (3) Cross-Cultural Ministry, (4) Music Ministry, (5) Communication Ministry, (6) Biblical Languages and Interpretation, and (7) Interdisciplinary Studies: Church, Society, and Family.

Special Programs

Programs at the Associate level lead to the degrees Associate in Arts in Bible and General Studies and Associate in Arts in Bible and Early Childhood Education. The Associate in Arts programs require 96 credit hours.

Oregon State University
Department of Religious Studies
Social Science Building - No. 200
Corvallis, OR 97331   (503) 754-2921

Administration. Dr. John V. Byrne, President; Dr. Theran D. Parsons, Vice President for Administration; Dr. David B. Nicodemus, Dean of Faculty; Dr. Nicholas J. Yonker, Chair, Department of Religious Studies.

General Description. The Department of Religious Studies offers a major program leading to the Bachelor of Arts or Bachelor of Science degree, and a minor program which a student may pursue concurrently with a major in another academic discipline. The Department regards the study of religion as an essential part of liberal, humane learning and seeks to assist students in understanding the role religion plays in human existence. Special attention is given to contemporary religious movements and to non-Western religious thought. The Department participates in the Master of Arts in Interdisciplinary Studies degree program of the Graduate School.

Parent Institution. Oregon State University (OSU), located in Corvallis, Oregon, is a comprehensive research university and the state's land- and sea-grant university. The University's liberal arts and science programs provide high quality educational and research programs and also serve as the core disciplines for the University's professional schools. OSU offers programs in atmospheric and geosciences, biological and physical sciences, computer and mathematical sciences, oceanography, agriculture, business administration, education, engineering, health and physical education, forestry, home economics, pharmacy, and veterinary medicine. OSU provides services in research and extension in areas related to agriculture, forestry, fisheries, home economics, natural resource preservation and development, and energy conversation.

Community Environment. The 400-acre main campus of OSU is located in the heart of the Willamette Valley between the Cascade Mountains on the east and the Coast Range on the west, 80 miles south of Portland, in the city of Corvallis. The Willamette Valley is noted for truck crops and dairy goods. Plane, bus, and rail transportation are available. Community facilities include churches of major denominations, a hospital, library, shopping areas, and the major civic, fraternal, and veterans organizations. The Willamette River is available for fishing and boating, and the Pacific Coast is a 45-mile drive from the campus.

Religious Denomination. None.

Accreditation. Northwest Association of Schools and Colleges.

Term System. Quarter; summer term.

Enrollment in Degree Programs in Religion 1984–85. Total 14; men 8, women 6.

Degrees in Religion Awarded 1984–85. Bachelor of Science 5; men 2, women 3.

Faculty for Degree Programs in Religion. Total 5; full-time 5.

Admission Requirements. High school graduation; overall grade point average of 2.75; minimum score of 30 on Test of Standard Written English (SAT) or a score of 12 on the English portion of the ACT; 4 units English, 3 units Mathematics, 3 units Social Studies, 2 units Science, 2 units other college preparatory courses, recommended 1 year of Laboratory Science; SAT or ACT.

Tuition and Fees. Tuition (12-21 credit hours) resident $470 per term, nonresident $1,345; graduate resident (9-16 credit hours) $691 per term, graduate nonresident $1,-107; residence hall rates include meal plan (any 15 meals) and range from $1,940 to $2,670 per term.

Financial Aid. Scholarships, grants, loans, and part-time employment are available singly or in various combinations to meet the difference between what the student and the student's family could reasonable be expected to provide and the expected cost of attending OSU.

Housing. Through its 12 residence halls and the College Inn, the University offers a variety of living environments including halls for women only, two halls for men only, and several coeducational living areas.

Library Facilities. The William Jasper Kerr Library houses over 1 million volumes, 340,000 government documents, and over 1,110,000 microform pieces. Approximately 20,000 volumes are in the fields of philosophy and religion. Most materials are on open shelves directly available to faculty and students.

Religious Services/Activities. Campus Centers for Ministry to Students include: Baptist Student Union, B'nai B'rith Hillel Foundation, Canterbury House (Episcopal), LDS Institute of Religion, Luther House, Newman Center (Catholic), Salman Afarici Islamic Center, University Christian Center (Church of Christ), and Westminster House (United Campus Ministry).

Degree Programs

Religious Studies at OSU is a comprehensive, reflective, and nonsectarian exploration of religion as a significant human and cultural phenomenon. Course work examines the full range of religious expression in an atmosphere of free and open inquiry: historical, contemporary, and alternative religious traditions; belief systems; lifestyles; and experiences. Teaching and research draw on both the liberal arts and the relevant social and behavioral sciences. A major is a 43-credit program leading to the Bachelor of Arts or Bachelor of Science degree.

The Master of Arts in Interdisciplinary Studies is a program that permits selection of graduate-level courses in religious studies to complement work in other fields.

Oregon, University of
Religious Studies Department
Eugene, OR 97403   (503) 686-4971

Administration. Dr. Paul Olum, President; Dr. Richard Hill, Vice President for Academic Affairs and Provost; Dr. John E. Lallas, Executive Dean; Dr. Jack T. Sanders, Department Head, Religious Studies Department.

General Description. The Department of Religious Studies offers courses concerning the religious beliefs and practices of the world's major religions. The Department does not represent the viewpoint of any religious group, nor does it acknowledge any religion to be superior to others. The Department offers both a general and a specialized major leading to the Bachelor of Science degree.

Parent Institution. The University of Oregon is a state university enrolling a total of about 16,500 students. A major research facility, the University is also the primary liberal arts institution in the Oregon state system of higher education.

Community Environment. The main campus of the University of Oregon is located on 185 acres in Eugene, 109 miles south of Portland, at the head of the Willamette Valley. Eugene, the center of a vast recreational area, is an important lumbering center. Eugene's facilities include more than 80 churches, a large public library, and 3 hospitals.

Religious Denomination. None.

Accreditation. Northwest Association of Schools and Colleges.

Term System. Quarter; summer term.

Enrollment in Degree Programs in Religion 1984–85. Total 16; men 10, women 6.

Degrees in Religion Awarded 1984–85. Bachelor of Science 3; men 2, women 1.

Faculty for Degree Programs in Religion. Total 3; full-time 3.

Admission Requirements. High school graduation; certain courses in English, mathematics, science, social studies, and language (or substitute) required in high school; minimum score of 30 on TWSE or 12 on English portion of ACT; grade point average minimum 2.75.

Tuition and Fees. Resident tuition $480.50 per term, nonresident $1,355.50; residence halls $1,957-$2,277 per year.

Financial Aid. All forms of aid are available through the Financial Aid office.

Housing. Residence halls are available on campus; family housing and off-campus housing available through the Student Housing Office.

Library Facilities. The University of Oregon Library collections consist of about 1,670,000 volumes.

Degree Programs

The Bachelor of Arts and the Bachelor of Science degrees are offered with both a general and a specialized major. Students may choose either option, but those planning to teach in public schools and to qualify for a secondary social studies endorsement are advised to select the general option. Students planning on graduate school, research, and college and university teaching are advised to follow the specialized option. This option includes focusing in one of the following areas: Ancient Near Eastern and Mediterranean Religions, History of Christianity, Asian Religions, and Philosophy of Religion and Theology. The Bachelor's degree requires 186 credits with passing grades.

Warner Pacific College
Department of Religion and Christian
Ministries
2219 S.E. 68th Street
Portland, OR 97215   (503) 775-4366

Administration. Dr. Marshall K. Christensen, President; Dr. Joyce Quiring Erickson, Dean of Faculty; Dr. John Stanley, Chair, Department of Religion and Christian Ministries.

General Description. The Department of Religion and Christian Ministries provides new perspectives for training men and women for Christian service in church-related vocations. It has three specific roles: (1) providing academic studies in religion and Christian ministries at the undergraduate and graduate levels; (2) fostering research and development efforts aimed at increasing the effectiveness of church leaders in evangelism, Christian education, missions,and other areas of ministry; (3) encouraging students to join faith and practice by facilitating Christian service opportunities in Portland and Northwest churches and outreach programs. Degrees offered include: Associate of Arts in Christian Education, Associate of Arts in Youth Ministries; Bachelor of Arts in Religion with concentrations in Christian Education, Christian Ministries, Pastoral Ministries, Religions of the World, Religion, and Theology; Bachelor of Arts in Church Music/Youth Ministry; Master of Religion.

Parent Institution. Warner Pacific College is a Christian liberal arts institution sponsored by the Church of God (Anderson, Indiana) as a place of education and service for people, regardless of their denomination, who desire a quality liberal arts education in a vital Christian community. Although interdenominational in student body, faculty, and spirit, the standards of the College are founded in evangelical Christianity.

Community Environment. The physical setting of the campus on the slopes of Mt. Tabor and its location in Portland, Oregon provide a fascinating context in which to live and learn. From the campus one can enter Mt. Tabor Park, a city recreational park of 167 acres with walking trails and a view of Mt. Hood. The urban setting also provides convenient access to the cultural events that enrich campus activities.

Religious Denomination. Church of God (Anderson, Indiana).

Religious Emphasis. Holiness, Evangelical.

Accreditation. Northwest Association of Schools and Colleges.

Term System. Quarter; summer term.

Enrollment in Degree Programs in Religion 1984–85. Total 12; men 10, women 2.

Degrees in Religion Awarded 1984–85. Bachelor of Arts in Religion 17; men 16, women 1. Master of Religion 2; men 2.

Faculty for Degree Programs in Religion. Total 8; full-time 4, part-time 4.

Admission Requirements. Graduation from an accredited high school or equivalent; SAT; character references.

Tuition and Fees. Tuition $120 per credit hour or $1,800 block tuition for 12-18 credit hours per quarter; room and board $2,500 per academic year.

Financial Aid. Financial resources for aid come from various sources and in various forms from federal, state, institutional, and private programs.

Housing. Dormitories, married student apartments, and off-campus houses and apartments are available.

Library Facilities. The Otto F. Linn Library houses over 60,000 volumes.

Religious Services/Activities. Chapel is held twice a week and attendance is required. Fall Spiritual Life Week, Winter Spiritual Life Retreat, and Spring Mission Days are major student-planned and student-led religious emphases during the year.

Degree Programs

The major in Religion leading to the Bachelor of Arts degree requires the completion of 48 hours in specified courses in the Department. Ministry career clusters are offered in Pastoral Ministry, Youth Ministry, Christian Education, and Missions.

The Master of Religion degree requires the completion of graduate courses in Bible (12 credits), Theology (8 credits), Applied Theology (8 credits), The Minister's Spiritual Life (2 credits), electives (12 credits), and internship, thesis, or project (6 credits).

Special Programs

Associate of Arts programs are also offered by the Department.

An Interfaith Conference on Biblical Studies is held annually in April and is sponsored by the College, Ecumenical Ministries of Oregon, and other local groups. A Ministers Seminar is held in the fall.

Western Baptist College
Biblical Studies Division; Christian Ministries Division
5000 Deer Park Drive S.E.
Salem, OR 97301   (503) 581-8600

Administration. Dr. John G. Balyo, President; Dr. Richard Caulkins, Academic Dean.

General Description. The Biblical Studies Division provides training on two levels. First, all students must take the basic Biblical Studies Core which covers the Word of God from a broad perspective. Second, more detailed programs in Bible, theology, and Biblical Studies are provided for the in-depth study of specific areas. The Christian Ministries Division provides courses designed for those preparing for the various areas of Christian work.

Parent Institution. Western Baptist College has a threefold purpose: educational, professional, and personal. The educational purpose emphasizes the advancement of knowledge within a Christian context. The professional purpose provides a foundation for the student to enter any life work as a Christian and exercise Christian principles within that vocation. The personal purpose emphasizes education for life, producing the "whole man," which encompasses spiritual maturity, intellectual competence, cultural and social awareness, aesthetic growth, and physical development. Western Baptist College's academic programs are divided into three divisions: Biblical Studies, Christian Ministries, and Letters and Science. The latter is designed to fulfill the basic general education requirements for an undegraduate degree.

Community Environment. Salem, the capital of Oregon, has a population of 90,000. All forms of commercial transportation are available. Recreational activities include tennis, fishing, swimming, boating, riding, and bowling. Ski areas are nearby. Points of interest are the Bush Pasture, which is a city park planted with rare trees and shrubs, and Bush Barn Art Center and Museum.

Religious Denomination. Baptist.

Accreditation. Northwest Association of Schools and Colleges.

Term System. Quarter; no summer term.

Enrollment in Degree Programs in Religion 1984–85. Total 282; men 145, women 137.

Degrees in Religion Awarded 1984–85. Bachelor of Arts in Theology 2; men 2. Bachelor of Science 20; men 18, women 2.

Faculty for Degree Programs in Religion. Total 6; full-time 4, part-time 2.

Admission Requirements. Graduation from secondary school or equivalent; SAT, ACT or Washington Pre-College Aptitude Test; adequate academic achievement.

Tuition and Fees. Tuition $1,391 per quarter; less than 13 units $107 per unit; over 17 units $70 per unit; residential fee (housing and 19 meals per week) $820 per quarter; general fee $25; library fee $23 (part-time student $10); health service fee $10; student activities fee $42.

Financial Aid. A student who applies for aid and has been accepted for admission is considered for all types of aid for which he is eligible. Types of financial aid include federal and state programs, scholarships, loans, and employment.

Housing. Students not living with their families are normally expected to live in residence halls. A current listing of housing for off-campus married students is provided by the Office of Student Services.

Library Facilities. The Library-Media Center has holdings of over 56,000 items of which 42,000 are book stock. Forty-two percent of the collection is in the field of religion.

Religious Services/Activities. Daily chapel services provide students with a variety of opportunities for worship, for sharing, and for learning. Three Bible conferences are held throughout the academic year. Every student enrolled in a four- or five-year program takes a minimum of eight hours of "field education," which involves service in a local church and in the community. All students are expected to attend and participate in the activities of a local church.

Degree Programs

The Bachelor of Arts or Bachelor of Science program is a standard four-year course of study. It allows the student to prepare for a vocation or to enrich his/her personal life to be more effective in daily life or service. A minimum of 192 academic units is required for either degree. Students must complete 60 units in Biblical Stud-

ies/Ministries and Theology plus 64 units in general education requirements and 68 units in major/minor electives.

The Bachelor of Education degree is award for to the elementary and secondary education major and prepares the student for a teaching ministry, with special emphasis upon teaching in the Christian School.

The Bachelor of Theology is a five-year program for students desiring to become pastors or missionaries. Majors are available in theology, Biblical studies, pastoral education, and missions. The degree normally requires 48 quarter units beyond the B.S. or B.A. degree.

The Bachelor of Religious Education program is for students desiring to become Ministers of Christian Education. The degree normally requires 36 quarter units beyond the B.S. or B.A. degree.

Special Programs

The Associate of Arts degree is designed for (1) those students desiring more limited training as a Christian layperson for more effective life and service; (2) students desiring a strong Biblical and academic foundation before continuing career education; (3) students who feel that they will not, for financial reasons, be able to continue beyond two years and would like a terminal degree; and (4) older students desiring to enter Christian service, but who do not feel able to take the four-year program.

Western Conservative Baptist Seminary
5511 S. E. Hawthorne Boulevard
Portland, OR 97215   (503) 233-8561

Administration. Dr. Earl D. Radmacher, President; Dr. W. Robert Cook, Vice President and Dean of Faculty.

General Description. At Western Conservative Baptist Seminary a strong emphasis is placed on depth in basic preparation on which practical application is built. The Seminary provides a program strongly oriented toward biblical understanding, ability to use Greek and Hebrew in exegesis, and a theological undergirding on which to build a lifetime of ministry. Application of these basics is made in various areas of ministry such as pastoral, missions, church education, and church music. In addition, graduate training is provided for specializing in basic languages, theology, and clinical/counseling psychology from a Christian perspective.

The programs offered at Western come under the headings of Professional, Graduate, and Doctoral. Under Professional are the degrees Master of Divinity, Master of Church Music, Master of Arts in Church Education, and Master of Christian Leadership. Within the Graduate heading are the degrees Master of Arts - Old Testament, Master of Arts - New Testament, Master of Arts - Theology, Master of Arts - Psychology, and Master of Theology. Under the Doctoral program are the degrees Doctor of Ministry and Doctor of Philosophy (Ph.D.).

Community Environment. Located in a residential area on the western slope of Mt. Tabor and overlooking the beautiful city of Portland, the campus is an enjoyable place for study, discussion, discipleship, and learning.

Religious Denomination. Conservative Baptist.

Religious Emphasis. Evangelical.

Accreditation. Northwest Association of Schools and Colleges.

Term System. Quarter; intersession; eight-week summer term.

Enrollment in Degree Programs in Religion 1984–85. Total 462; men 427, women 35.

Degrees in Religion Awarded 1984–85. Master of Divinity 46; men 45, women 1. Master of Church Music 7; men 6, women 1. Master of Church Education 11; men 8, women 3. Master of Arts 30; men 27, women 3. Master of Arts in Counseling 15; men 13, women 2. Master of Theology 10; men 10. Doctor of Ministry 12; men 12. Doctor of Philosophy 5; men 5.

Faculty for Degree Programs in Religion. Total 42; full-time 32, part-time 10.

Admission Requirements. Baccalaureate degree; Christian experience statement; personal and church references.

Tuition and Fees. Tuition $115 per semester hour; application fee $25; registration fee $30.

Financial Aid. Minimal assistance is available.

Housing. No on-campus housing available; Dean of Students Office assists applicants in locating housing.

Library Facilities. The Cline-Tunnell Library holdings include 45,000 books and bound periodicals, as well as 625 periodicals covering biblical, theological, missionary, educational, and general fields of interest.

Religious Services/Activities. Chapel services are designed to give opportunities for worship, edification, and instruction concerning various Christian ministries. Students are requested to attend 80 percent of all regularly scheduled chapel services (three days weekly).

Degree Programs

The Master of Divinity degree is given in four areas of concentration: pastoral, Christian Education, Missions, and General Ministry. The program is designed to provide students with the training which will enable them to function as ministers of the gospel in a local church, as missionaries with Biblical and theological awareness, or in vocations related to the field of Christian education. The basic program is built around a common core of foundational (Biblical Literature), formulational (Theology and History), and functional (Ministry) studies. A total of 144 quarter hours is required.

The Master of Church Music is designed to prepare the student for a professional ministry in the music program of the local church. The 92 quarter hours required are divided between the core courses and courses in the area of concentration. An option with Church Education as a minor is also offered.

The Master of Arts in Church Education consists of coursework in church education, Bible, theology, and related studies. It requires 91-93 quarter hours divided between required core courses and elective courses that are selected from within prescribed divisional requirements.

The Master of Christian Leadership program trains those people who carry key leadership positions in professional, business, and executive roles. It requires the completion of 36 quarter hours in a curriculum of specified courses. The prescribed courses include Hermeneutics, Theology, Biblical Studies, Christian Ethics, Personal Ministry, and Communications Skills. An integrative paper is required.

The Master of Arts program is designed to give specialized training in theology and Biblical languages. It requires the completion of 84 quarter hours over a two-year period, including core courses and a major in Old Testament, New Testament, or Theology. A special program of study in Bible, theology, and psychology also leads to the Master of Arts in Counseling.

The Master of Theology degree program fosters advanced theological study by means of greater bibliographic facility, scholarly research, and logical and critical writing, with a view toward a successful profession in any one of a number of church and related ministries. Courses of study may be pursued in the divisions of Biblical Studies, Theological Studies, or Ministerial Studies. The program requires the completion of 36 quarter hours and an acceptable thesis of not less than 15,000 words or an acceptable field project/product.

The Doctor of Ministry program is an educational opportunity for experienced professional Christian workers to enlarge their ministerial vision and ability. The degree is awarded upon satisfactory passing of the written candidacy examination, satisfactory passing of the oral comprehensive examination, meeting general graduation requirements, and the recommendation of the faculty. The course of study includes 4 core courses, 3 independent studies, a field project/product, and the comprehensive exams. A Doctor of Philosophy program is also offered.

Special Programs

The Seminary offers an opportunity of spending selected summer quarters on location in Israel.

Western Evangelical Seminary
4200 S.E. Jennings Avenue
Portland, OR 97267   (503) 654-5466

Administration. Dr. Leo M. Thornton, President; Dr. William H. Vermillion, Dean.

General Description. Western Evangelical Seminary is a professional school for the training of men and women in Christian ministries. It is interdenominational with a Wesleyan-Arminian heritage. The Seminary has relationships with the following churches: Brethren in Christ, Evangelical, Evangelical Methodist, Free Methodist, and Wesleyan. Relationships also exist with two missionary groups: O.M.S. International and World Gospel Mission.

The actual teaching ministry of the Seminary began in 1947. The primary purpose of Western Evangelical Seminary is to prepare preachers and teachers of the Word who can effectively serve the churches of the supporting constituency as pastors, teachers, missionaries, and in other areas of Christian service.

Community Environment. The campus is located at Jennings Lodge, six miles south of the city limits of Portland, near the Willamette River. City bus routes 33 and 34 both stop at Jennings Avenue within walking distance of the four and one-half acre campus.

Religious Denomination. Interdenominational.

Religious Emphasis. Evangelical, Wesleyan, and Arminian.

Accreditation. Northwest Association of Schools and Colleges; Association of Theological Schools in the United States and Canada.

Term System. Quarter; summer term.

Enrollment in Degree Programs in Religion 1984–85. Total 143; men 121, women 22.

Degrees in Religion Awarded 1984–85. Doctor of Ministry 2; men 2. Master of Arts in Theological Studies 6; men 5, women 1. Master of Arts in Christian Education 3; men 3. Master of Arts in Christian Counseling 6; men 5, women 1. Master of Arts in Missions 2; men 2. Master of Divinity 18; men 17, women 1.

Faculty for Degree Programs in Religion. Total 16; full-time 7, part-time 9.

Admission Requirements. Good Christian character; Bachelor of Arts or its equivalent academic degree; grade point average of 2.5; students with a cumulative grade point average of 2.0-2.5 may be admitted on probation.

Tuition and Fees. A full academic load of 16 hours including fees and books is $1,540 per term; $85 per quarter hour.

Financial Aid. The Seminary is an approved institution for the training of Veterans. Denominational scholarships are available. In addition, special Seminary tuition scholarships are available.

Housing. The Seminary has an apartment complex with 12 two-bedroom apartments and 4 three-bedroom townhouse units. A number of houses and duplex units are available at reasonable rates. Eligibility is based upon being regularly enrolled in a degree program. Other economical housing is available on the Conference grounds adjacent to the campus.

Library Facilities. The George Hallauer Memorial Library houses more than 48,000 volumes.

Religious Services/Activities. Daily chapel services provide opportunity to communicate information of common interest and to share the concerns of guest speakers, but also are designed primarily to provide corporate worship and spiritual fellowship for the entire Seminary family. Other devotional meetings for prayer and praise, spon-

sored by student organizations, provide additional opportunities for spiritual fellowship. Annual retreats also afford excellent occasions for Christian fellowship. Spiritual emphasis weeks have been designed as the Spiritual Life Lectures in the fall, Christian Holiness Week in the winter, and Christian Missions Week in the spring.

Degree Programs

The Master of Divinity program aims to develop the student's values, understanding, and skills in the many aspects of the life of the Christian Church. A major is not required in the program but a student may elect a major in one of the following fields: Biblical Studies (Old Testament or New Testament), Christian History, Christian Thought, Pastoral Studies, Counseling, Christian Education, or Missions.

The Master of Arts program aims through graduate education to assist the student to develop competencies necessary for effective ministry, acquire basic tools of scholarly research and learning, and serve with a clear sense of identity and purpose as a Christian minister in contemporary culture. The Seminary offers four major areas of study leading to the degree: Christian Education, Christian Missions, Christian Counseling, and Theological Studies (including Biblical Studies, Christian History, and Thought).

Special Programs

A complete program for training hearing impaired students and students desiring to minister in this area is available. Interpreters are provided.

A Pastoral Renewal program designed to encourage continuing education is also offered by the Seminary. Any course may be taken for credit for $100 in a non-degree program.

A Spouse Certificate Program is a special offering for spouses of students enrolled in 12 or more hours. The program allows the spouse to take a course for $10 a quarter hour.

A Mature Adult Education program gives special consideration to students over 35 years of age. Also, students over 55 years of age may take courses at one-half the normal tuition charge.

PENNSYLVANIA

Academy of the New Church
Bryn Athyn, PA 19009   (215) 947-4200

Administration. Rev. Peter M. Buss, President; Robert S. Junge, Dean of the Theological School; Robert W. Gladish, Dean of the College; N. Bruce Rogers, Head, Division of Religion and Sacred Languages.

General Description. The Theological School offers a three-year post-baccalaureate course for male students that is designed to give students for the priesthood instruction on a graduate level in the Theology of the New Church, Homiletics, Pastoral Theology, and Church History, as preparation for the priestly office. The Bachelor of Theology degree is awarded. The College of the Academy offers a Religion major leading to the Bachelor of Arts degree.

Parent Institution. The Academy of the New Church comprises four schools, a library, and a publication office. The schools are: (1) The Theological School, established to educate young men for the ministry of the General Church of the New Jerusalem; (2) The College, which provides education in the doctrines and philosophy of the New Church and in the arts and sciences; it is composed of the Junior College and the Senior College; (3) The Girls School, which offers a 4-year secondary school; (4) The Boys School, which offers a 4-year secondary school.

Community Environment. The 130-acre campus has 13 buildings in Bryn Athyn, Pennsylvania, 15 miles northeast of Philadelphia. Bryn Athyn is a distinctive New Church community, but with all the cultural, recreational, and civic advantages of the bigger city easily available.

Religious Denomination. Swedenborgian (The New Jerusalem).

Accreditation. Middle States Association of Colleges and Schools.

Term System. Semester.

Admission Requirements. For the Theological School: a baccalaureate degree awarded by an accredited college, or the equivalent; will have covered in the undergraduate studies a pre-theological program which includes courses in New Church Religion, Hebrew, New Testament Greek, the Latin of Swedenborg, Education, and Philosophy. For

the Bachelor's major in Religion, sufficient prepation at the junior college level with an overall average of 1.9, with 2.5 in religion courses.

Tuition and Fees. Theological School: tuition $1,815 per year; board and room $1,974. The College: tuition $1,815 per year; comprehensive fees $264; board and room $1,974.

Financial Aid. Financial assistance is available in rebates, student work, scholarship grants, and student loans.

Housing. Students who are under 20 and are too far away from their homes to commute are required to live in the dormitories provided on campus. Theological students may live in the men's dormitory; approximately four hours of student work per week are required of first-year theological students who reside in the dorm.

Library Facilities. The Academy of the New Church Libraries are organized to meet the educational needs of the institution, to provide a center of research for scholars of the New Church, and to serve the general public of the Bryn Athyn Borough. The libraries house over 104,300 volumes.

Degree Programs

The Bachelor of Arts in Religion requires 42 credits in religion and major related subjects (15 credits in subjects such as philosophy, educational philosophy, history of Israel, sacred language).

The Bachelor of Theology degree requires completion of the Bachelor of Arts degree plus three years of study in the following categories: Theology, Applied Theology, Homiletics, Church History, and Senior Dissertation.

Albright College
Department of Religion
P.O. Box 516
Reading, PA 19603   (215) 921-2381

Administration. William R. Marlow, Chairperson, Department of Religion.

General Description. The Department of Religion is organized to meet four major objectives: (1) to deepen and enrich the faith of all students through careful examination of the religion for the individual and for contemporary society; (2) to give all students a sympathetic understanding of a wide range of religious ideas, communities of revelation, traditions, and culture; (3) to provide each student with an understanding of the Judaeo-Christian tradition of Western culture; (4) to lay foundations for those planning to enter Christian vocations, especially pre-theological students and potential active lay leaders in the Christian church. This foundation presumes and values an atmosphere of dialogue with all other disciplines, life-styles, and world-views.

The area of concentration is designed for those who plan a career in Christian education or a non-ministerial church vocation as well as those pre-theological students who plan to enter seminary. This program should enable the latter to progress more rapidly in graduate study during the seminary years.

Parent Institution. Albright College traces its origin from 1856 when Union Seminary was founded by the Central Pennsylvania Conference of the Evangelical Association of New Berlin, Pennsylvania. In 1929, it consolidated with Schuylkill College under the name of Albright College. The present church relationship of Albright College is the result of the 1946 and 1968 mergers of the Evangelical Church, the Church of the United Brethren in Christ, and the Methodist Church, which formed the United Methodist Church.

Community Environment. Thomas and Richard Penn, sons of William Penn, founded the city of Reading in 1748 and named it for their ancestral home in England. Located in the eastern foothills of the Appalachian Mountains, the city has a population of 80,000. The campus is located at the edge of a residential section of the city. Although located in the city proper, fields and woodlands are within walking distance of the campus. Consisting of more than 80 acres of land, the campus has outstanding facilities for academic learning, comfortable housing, recreation, and athletic activities.

Religious Denomination. United Methodist Church.

Accreditation. Middle States Association of Colleges and Schools.

Term System. Semester; summer sessions.

Enrollment in Degree Programs in Religion 1984–85. Total 14; men 8, women 6.

Degrees in Religion Awarded 1984–85. Bachelor of Arts 4; men 2, women 2.

Faculty for Degree Programs in Religion. Total 7; full-time 2, part-time 5.

Admission Requirements. All applicants must submit fifteen units of secondary school credit, beginning with ninth grade; SAT or ACT.

Tuition and Fees. Per academic year: tuition (comprehensive fee) $7,575; board $1,250; room $1,475; activities fee $100.

Financial Aid. Special grants are given to pre-theological students; loans, grants, and work-study programs

available.

Housing. Dormitories, senior apartments, senior houses, fraternity and sorority houses constitute the housing accommodations on the campus.

Library Facilities. The F. Wilbur Gingrich Library houses a collection of more than 180,000 books, periodicals, records, microfilms, and audiovisual materials.

Religious Services/Activities. Organizations for Roman Catholic, Jewish, and Protestant students provide many study, worship, service, and fellowship opportunities. Regular services are conducted by the college chaplain.

Degree Programs

The Bachelor of Arts with an area of concentration in Religion requires 24 credits in religion beyond the courses taken to satisfy the General Studies requirements. Courses in New Testament Greek may be included in the 24 credits provided they have not been used to meet General Studies language requirements. Eighteen additional credits in related courses are required.

Allegheny College
Department of Religious Studies
Meadville, PA 16335   (814) 724-3100

Administration. Dr. David Baily Harned, President.

General Description. The Department of Religious Studies presents courses whose functions are the study of the sources, history, nature, and relevance of religion. Majors may choose from the following groupings of courses: Biblical Studies, History of Religions, Theology and Philosophy of Religion, and Theology of Culture and Ethics. The Department also features seminars and independent study courses. The Bachelor of Arts in Religious Studies degree is offered.

Parent Institution. Allegheny College is a liberal arts, residential, coeducational college offering the degrees Bachelor of Arts, Bachelor of Science, and Master of Arts in Education. The College is affiliated with The United Methodist Church.

Community Environment. Allegheny College is located on a 165-acre campus in Meadville, in northwestern Pennsylvania. The College also owns a 324-acre recreational area about seven miles from Meadville where there are facilities for camping, hiking, and skating. Meadville is the county seat of Crawford County, a rich agricultural and active vacation area.

Religious Denomination. The United Methodist Church.

Accreditation. Middle States Association of Colleges and Schools.

Term System. Three terms of 10 weeks each; summer school of two 5-week sessions.

Admission Requirements. Strong college-preparatory program in high school with at least 4 major academic subjects in each of the final 3 years of high school. These should include 4 years of English, 3 social studies, 3 math, 3 science, 2 language; SAT or ACT; Achievement Test of CEEB recommended.

Tuition and Fees. Tuition $2,350 per term; room $390; board $405.

Financial Aid. Financial aid is available to students who qualify on the basis of both need and merit. Included are state grants, federal aid, Pell Grant, scholarships, and several more.

Housing. Approximately 75 percent of students are housed in campus residences. All freshmen who do not commute are required to live in a campus residence.

Library Facilities. The library contains over 190,000 volumes, 156,000 pamphlets, 1,265 periodicals, 31,000 microforms, recordings.

Religious Services/Activities. In addition to ecumenical services Sundays and several times during the week, Jewish, Episcopal, and Roman Catholic services are offered. A number of groups hold Bible study sessions, discussions, and conferences on campus.

Degree Programs

The Bachelor of Arts in Religious Studies requires the satisfactory completion of a minimum of ten term-courses in Religious Studies. These must include: Seminar in Religious Studies, Junior Group Tutorial, Senior Tutorial and Project, and three other advanced courses.

Allentown College of St. Francis de Sales
Department of Theology
Center Valley, PA 18034   (215) 282-1100

Administration. V. Rev. Daniel G. Gambet, O.S.F.S., President.

General Description. The Department of Theology offers an area of academic concentration and general elective courses. The concentration in Theology facilitates the formation of a comprehensive, systematic understanding of and appreciation of the Christian faith vision into the many dimensions of human experience so that students will be prepared for further theological study and/or immediate activity in teaching pastoral ministry. It also facilitates within all students the formation of a basic understanding of the central tenets of Catholic theology. Courses are offered on the introductory, intermediate, and advanced levels. The concentration in Theology leads to the Bachelor of Arts degree.

Parent Institution. Allentown College of St. Francis de Sales is a privately-supported, coeducational Roman Catholic liberal arts college. It began in 1965 and is conducted by the Oblate Fathers of St. Francis de Sales. The College grants the Bachelor's degree.

Community Environment. The campus of 300 acres is located in Center Valley, a rural area 15 minutes south of Allentown and Bethlehem and one hour from Philadelphia.

Religious Denomination. Roman Catholic.

Accreditation. Middle States Association of Colleges and Schools.

Term System. Semester.

Enrollment in Degree Programs in Religion 1984–85. Total 22; men 18, women 4.

Degrees in Religion Awarded 1984–85. Bachelor of Arts 11; men 9, women 4.

Faculty for Degree Programs in Religion. Total 6; full-time 3, part-time 3.

Admission Requirements. High school graduation from an accredited high school; 16 academic units; SAT or ACT.

Tuition and Fees. Tuition $4,950 per year; room and board $2,940; student fee $40.

Financial Aid. Over 80 percent of the students receive some form of financial aid. Along with government-funded aid, the College has resources to assist students with their college expenses through a combination of grants, loans, and campus employment programs. Full and partial tuition scholarships are also available for those who qualify.

Housing. Residence halls provide dormitory facilities for men and women.

Library Facilities. The library houses over 110,000 volumes of which 6,000 are in theology and religion. There is a special collection for Salesian Studies.

Religious Services/Activities. The Campus Minister/Chaplain serves the religious needs of the Allentown College community. He develops and implements programs of personal growth, community building, spiritual growth, and service. He and other priests on campus provide daily mass, the sacraments, and religious counseling, assisted by the Campus Ministry Organization.

Degree Programs

The program of concentration in Theology consists of a core of eight required courses: all five introductory courses, two intermediate courses, and a senior seminar. In addition, the Theology concentrator must choose four electives from among the intermediate and advanced courses. These electives present the possibility for two distinct specializations: (1) to pursue further theological studies and (2) to teach and/or engage in pastoral work. Internships are available to suit individual student needs.

Alvernia College
Theology/Philosophy Department
Reading, PA 19607   (215) 777-5411

Administration. Sr. Mary Dolorey, C.S.B., President.

General Description. The Theology/Philosophy Department at Alvernia College is primarily a service department. It serves the entire student body and fulfills its responsibility by and large through the liberal arts core. Approximately 300 students enroll in its programs per semester. The Department grants the degree Bachelor of Arts in Theology/Philosophy. The mission of the Theology/Philosophy Department, in keeping with the mission of the College, is commitment to the development of mature faith and sound philosophy of life by integrating systematic knowledge and Christian values through active learning and personal quest for objective truth. The Department aims to guide the student's pursuit of personal excellence and integrity through a study of philosophical ideals and the sound teachings of the Roman Catholic Church. In the context of this orientation, the Department attempts to prepare students for life, and its majors for graduate studies or for their ministries.

Parent Institution. Alvernia College, under the sponsorship of the Bernardine Sisters of St. Francis, continues to provide its students with a quality Catholic liberal arts education. It also prepares them for careers and professions to enhance their fullness of life. The College remains dedicated to Christian values. It sees its mission as integrating Christian faith, learning, and commitment. It concentrates on the total education and development of its students by stressing academic knowledge, professional competency, and value-oriented moral integrity according to the principles of the Roman Catholic Church.

Community Environment. The College is situated on an 85-acre campus overlooking Angelica Lake, in Reading, Pennsylvania. Reading, with a population of 80,000, was founded by Thomas and Richard Penn, sons of William Penn, in 1748. It was named for their ancestral home in England. Modern-day Reading has many churches representing most major denominations, and three hospitals. There are outreach programs available to the community by on-campus service groups.

Religious Denomination. Roman Catholic.

Accreditation. Middle States Association of Colleges and Schools.

Term System. Semester; summer term.

Enrollment in Degree Programs in Religion 1984–85. Total 6; men 5, women 1.

Faculty for Degree Programs in Religion. Total 6; full-time 3, part-time 3.

Admission Requirements. Academic high school diploma with 16 units comprising the following subjects: English (4 units), mathematics (2 units), science (2 units), social studies (2 units), modern languages (2 units), electives (4 units). Applicants to the freshman class are advised to take either the ACT or SAT.

Tuition and Fees. Tuition $3,690; room and board $2,770.

Financial Aid. The financial aid program offers assistance to qualified students in need through grants, loans, and employment.

Housing. Dormitory facilities are available.

Library Facilities. The library houses over 70,000 volumes. It maintains a special collection of 2,000 volumes in Polish Culture.

Religious Services/Activities. Persons in the college community of all faiths are welcome to use any of the services which the campus ministry provides. The college chaplain is available for spiritual guidance and counseling. Days of recollection, weekend retreats, and search weekends are scheduled every semester.

Degree Programs

A major in Theology/Philosophy leading to the Bachelor of Arts degree requires 24 credits in Theology and 18 credits in Philosophy. Majors have the opportunity to select advanced courses that best serve their needs.

Special Programs

A Continuing Education program offers adults the opportunity to complete a Bachelor's degree in less than four years. The program is composed of 6 eight-week modules with classes meeting two evenings per week.

Baptist Bible College of Pennsylvania
538 Venard Road
Clarks Summit, PA 18411   (717) 587-1172

Administration. Dr. Mark E. Jackson, President; Dr. John R. Master, Vice President - Academic Affairs.

General Description. Baptist Bible College was founded as Baptist Bible Seminary in 1932 by a group of pastors. Its original purpose of "training young people for the Gospel ministry and other lines of Christian service" has not changed. It grants the bachelor degree, three year diploma, and associate degree. In 1972 classes began in the graduate division known as the School of Theology, now known as the Theological Seminary. It grants the Master of Divinity and Master of Theology degrees. An alternative course of study is available for students not having a Bible college background.

Community Environment. The 145-acre campus of Baptist Bible College, containing 16 major buildings, is located in Clark's Summit, Pennsylvania, a residential suburb of about 8,000 people. This suburb is part of the greater Scranton-Wilkes Barre area with a population exceeding 500,000. Scranton is at a crossroads of the interstate highway system of the northeastern United States. The College is easily reached by all modes of transportation.

Religious Denomination. Independent Baptist.

Religious Emphasis. Fundamentalist.

Accreditation. Middle States Association of Colleges and Schools; American Association of Bible Colleges.

Term System. Semester; summer term.

Enrollment in Degree Programs in Religion 1984–85. Total 638; men 314, women 324.

Degrees in Religion Awarded 1984–85. Associate in Arts 23; men 4, women 19. Bachelor of Science in Bible 124; men 57, women 67. Non-degree program 73.

Faculty for Degree Programs in Religion. Total 10; full-time 7, part-time 3.

Admission Requirements. High school diploma or

equivalency diploma; SAT or ACT scores.

Tuition and Fees. Tuition $115 per credit hour; fees $550 per year; dormitory housing $888 per year.

Financial Aid. Grants, institutional aid, and scholarships in combination.

Housing. Dormitory accommodations for single students; no on-campus housing for married students.

Library Facilities. The Richard J. Murphy Memorial Library houses 78,179 volumes.

Religious Services/Activities. Students are required to regularly attend one of the approved fundamental churches in the area. Each school day the entire College meets for prayer, worship, spiritual instruction, and challenge. Daily chapel services feature faculty members, pastors, missionaries, student programs, and other special speakers. The Pastoral Interest Fellowship promotes interest in the pastoral ministry and provides an introduction to pastoral problems. The Student Missions Fellowship cultivates a burden for missions, creates an active interest in world missions fields, and provides students an opportunity to get involved in various missionary activities. Christian School Teachers Fellowship provides practical and helpful information concerning Christian school education.

Degree Programs

The Master of Divinity degree program offers courses in the following departments of study: Theology, Old Testament, New Testament, History, and Pastoral Theology. The program is of three years length.

The Master of Theology degree is designed for students holding a Master of Divinity degree or its equivalent.

The Bachelor of Science in Bible is a professional program of four years in length. The programs include Pastoral, Missions, Local Church Education, Christian School Education, Music Ministry, and Pre-Seminary. The Bachelor of Sacred Music is awarded to students completing the church music program with 65 credit hours in music following the professional four year program.

Special Programs

The Associate in Arts requires two years of study. Forty semester hours of courses in the arts and sciences are distributed over at least eight different academic fields. Also include are introductory courses in Biblical background studies.

A Diploma program represents three years of study in courses which could later be credited toward a degree. The Certificate program requires only one year of training.

Bucknell University
Department of Religion
Coleman Hall
Lewisburg, PA 17837   (717) 524-1205

Administration. Joseph A. La Barge, Ph.D., Chairman, Department of Religion.

General Description. The Department of Religion at Bucknell University offers courses in religion designed to contribute to a liberal education. The major in religion is selected by students who see the study of religion as a doorway to understanding human nature and history, and hence an appropriate focus for a liberal education. Other students choose the major as a more direct preparation for a career, general in such fields as social work, education, youth work, law, or some form of denominational religious work. The Bachelor of Arts degree is awarded.

Parent Institution. Bucknell University was born from the concerns of the church. With the opening of the Northwest Territory to settlement in the 1830s, the Baptists of Pennsylvania were intent on providing missionaries for an expanding frontier. After much discussion, Lewisburg was chosen as the site of the university, and in 1846 the University at Lewisburg opened in the basement of the local Baptist Church. In 1886, the name was changed in honor of William Bucknell of Philadelphia, a generous patron and chairman of the board of trustees. From a denominational beginning, Bucknell has emerged as a broad, diverse, nondenominational institution seeking talented students of all religious persuasions, ethnic backgrounds, and social circumstances.

Community Environment. Lewisburg, Pennsylvania is no longer the isolated retreat of the founders of Bucknell University. It is located on the bank of the Susquehanna River approximately 100 miles northwest of Philadelphia. Modern transportation has placed the University within three and a half hours of most of the major cities of the Mid-Atlantic region. The hill towns of the immediate area around Lewisburg are graced with the onion-domed churches of the Russians and beautifully crafted small synagogues which served a significant Jewish population in central Pennsylvania. A major portion of the 300-acre campus and most of the academic buildings are situated on College Hill. The Tidewater colonial style of architecture has been followed throughout most of the campus.

Religious Denomination. Nondenominational.

Religious Emphasis. Ecumenical.

Accreditation. Middle States Association of Colleges and Schools.

Term System. Semester (4-1-4) with interterm; summer term.

Enrollment in Degree Programs in Religion 1984–85. Total 9; men 6, women 3.

Degrees in Religion Awarded 1984–85. Bachelor of Arts 7; men 5, women 2.

Faculty for Degree Programs in Religion. Total 9; full-

time 4, part-time 5.

Admission Requirements. Applicants must be graduates of an approved four-year secondary or senior high school; completion of a minimum of two years of foreign language; SAT must be taken prior to January of senior year in high school; English Achievement test, foreign language achievement test (Arts and Science applicants).

Tuition and Fees. Tuition full-time $9,765 per year; room $1,135 per year; board $1,315 per year (typical); activities fee $100 per year.

Financial Aid. Approximately 55 percent of the student body received some form of financial assistance in 1984-85, ranging from grants and loans to work-study assistance.

Housing. Dormitory housing is required for all freshmen students. Upperclass students have the choice of dormitory, fraternity, or off-campus (privately owned) housing.

Library Facilities. The Ellen Clarke Bertrand Library collection contains over 430,000 volumes, 4,600 periodical titles, 230,000 government documents, and 167,000 items in microform.

Religious Services/Activities. A Protestant chaplain is in residence with a wide range of liturgical functions and counseling services. Chapel services are held in The Charles M. and Olive S. Rooke Chapel. A Catholic chaplain and a Jewish rabbi minister to the needs of the respective student groups.

Degree Programs

The Bachelor of Arts degree program with a major in Religion consists, in addition to the general requirements for the degree, of eight courses. The student, in consultation with a departmental adviser, will design a program of courses in accord with his/her educational aims. The program will include at least one, but not more than two, introductory courses; at least one course from each of the four curricular areas (The Bible, Western Religious Traditions, Asian Religious Traditions, Religion and Culture); at least one seminar course.

Cabrini College
Department of Religion
King of Prussia Road
Radnor, PA 19087   (215) 687-2100

Administration. Dr. Richard D. DeCosmo, President; Dr. Thomas P. McNicholas, Dean, Liberal Arts/Sciences and General Studies Division; Dr. Margaret Mary Reher, Chair, Department of Religion.

General Description. The objectives of the Department of Religion are to deepen the student's understanding of the religious dimension of humanity in its past and present historical manifestations, and to investigate the implications of the Christian message for today's society. Special emphasis is on the Christian tradition as interpreted by the Roman Catholic Church and its relationship with other Christian and non-Christian religions. The Department offers the degree Bachelor of Arts in Religion.

Parent Institution. Cabrini College, a coeducational, Catholic college of liberal arts and sciences, is committed to excellence in teaching and the development of the student as a liberally educated person who can meet the demands of professional growth and who has a concern for values. The College was established in 1957 by the Missionary Sisters of the Sacred Heart, who named it for their order's foundress, Frances Xavier Cabrini, the first American citizen saint. Undergraduate enrollment in all divisions of the College currently numbers approximately 900. Cabrini College grants the degrees Bachelor of Arts, Bachelor of Science, Bachelor of Science in Education, and Master of Education.

Community Environment. Cabrini College is located on 116 acres of the former Dorrance Estate in Radnor, Pennsylvania. Radnor is a part of the "Main Line" area of suburban residential Philadelphia. The other towns making up this area are Rosemont, Villanova, St. Davids, Wayne, Haverford, and Merion Station. The total locale encompasses over 200 civic, social, and church groups.

Religious Denomination. Roman Catholic.

Accreditation. Middle States Association of Colleges and Schools.

Term System. Semester; 2 summer sessions.

Enrollment in Degree Programs in Religion 1984–85. Total 5; men 1, women 4.

Degrees in Religion Awarded 1984–85. Bachelor of Arts 1; men 1.

Faculty for Degree Programs in Religion. Total 4; full-time 2, part-time 2.

Admission Requirements. Graduation from an accredited secondary school (or its equivalent) with between 17 and 21 units of credits in specific areas; satisfactory average and rank in secondary school class; recomendations of the guidance counselor, principal, or teachers; SAT or ACT scores.

Tuition and Fees. Tuition (maximum of 18 credit hours) $2,345 per semester; general fee $150; room and board $1,800.

Financial Aid. Cabrini Grants, National Direct Student Loan, Supplemental Educational Opportunity Grant, Pell Grant, and College Work-Study are among the many forms of financial aid available. Scholarships are available on a competitive basis.

Housing. Resident houses and dormitories are available on campus.

Library Facilities. The Holy Spirit Library contains 76,-718 volumes.

Religious Services/Activities. Campus Ministry is an organization of students, faculty, and staff that works to develop the Christian life and lifestyle for the college as a whole and for each member of the college community. There are many campus ministries—prayer, liturgy, discussion groups, service to those in need, concern for one another, and many other ways of making the gospel live.

Degree Programs

The major in Religion leading to the Bachelor of Arts degree requires the completion of 52-55 credits in general education requirements, 48-51 credits in electives, 2 credits in physical education, plus required courses. These courses include Introduction to the Old Testament; Ethical Issues; Jesus: His Meaning and Message (alternate, Introduction to the New Testament); The Catholic Church in America (alternate, The Church in in a Changing World); Towards a Theology of Peace (alternate, Faith and Justice); World Religions; and Religion electives. A total of 130 credits is required for the degree.

Duquesne University
Department of Theology
600 Forbes Avenue
Pittsburgh, PA 15282   (412) 434-6530

Administration. Dr. James P. Hanigan, Director of Graduate Studies; Dr. John F. O'Grady, Chair, Department of Theology.

General Description. The Department of Theology affirms that the academic study of religious experience is essential to a complete education. The Department fulfills its role in theological studies by the pursuit of the following aims: (1) it emphasizes Catholic theology, in dialogue with other Christian traditions, non-Christian traditions, and Judaism, as the key element in Duquesne's commitment to Catholic education on the university level; (2) it acknowledges the fact of the universal search for religious meaning and experience, and seeks not only to offer the possibility of a study of the varying approaches to religious witnesses in history, but also to place Catholic theology in communion with that quest; and (3) it aspires to a fruitful encounter with other university disciplines, since the department is convinced that theology's concerns are related to all vital human issues. Both undergraduate and graduate programs are offered.

Parent Institution. Duquesne University opened its doors as Pittsburgh Catholic College of the Holy Ghost in 1878. Founded by the Fathers and Brothers of the Congregation of the Holy Ghost, the university has provided the opportunity for a superior private education for students from many backgrounds. In 1911, a university charter was obtained and the name Duquesne University was adopted. The University now offers degree programs in 89 areas - 34 at the baccalaureate level, 47 at the master's, and 9 at the doctorate.

The original number of 40 students has expanded to more than 6,500. In the past twenty-five years, the University has undergone a dramatic transformation into a modern, highly functional educational facility that is located on its own self-enclosed 39-acre hilltop overlooking downtown Pittsburgh.

Community Environment. Pittsburgh, Pennsylvania is the third largest corporate center and one of the ten largest metropolitan areas in the United States. The city is renowned for its ethnic diversity, its lead in urban renewal, and its liveability. Within walking distance of the Duquesne campus are Heinz Hall for the Performing Arts, the Civic Arena, Three Rivers Stadium, Market Square, and the new Convention Center. The libraries, museums, art galleries, and music hall of Carnegie Institute in the Oakland area are easily accessible by public transportation or by private automobile. In recent years, the city has also developed a vibrant public theater and a number of experimental theater groups whose productions throughout the year have added to the cultural life of Pittsburgh.

Religious Denomination. Roman Catholic.

Religious Emphasis. Mainstream Catholic theology in an ecumenical context.

Accreditation. Middle States Association of Colleges and Schools. Member of: Catholic Educational Association of Pennsylvania; National Catholic Educational Association.

Term System. Semester; summer session.

Enrollment in Degree Programs in Religion 1984–85. Total 157; men 60, women 97.

Faculty for Degree Programs in Religion. Total 15; full-time 10, part-time 5.

Admission Requirements. Undergraduate applicants must fulfill all requirements for admission to Duquesne University as specified in their catalog. Graduate students must possess a B.A. with a major in theology or its equivalent to enter the M.A. program; possess a M.A. degree in theology or religious studies or their equivalent to enter the Ph.D. program; submit transcripts of all undergraduate and graduate work; submit three letters of recommendation from former Professors.

Tuition and Fees. Graduate level tuition $194 per semester hour credit; university fee $11 per credit; room and board per semester $1,701 single, $1,421 double. All clergy receive 50 percent tuition discount for all programs through the master's level.

Financial Aid. Graduate assistantships, scholarships, federally funded institutional aid (need based) and guaranteed student loans represent the variety of financial aid available to students.

Housing. Room and board in University dormitories are available upon application. The University does not provide dormitory accommodations for married students. The Housing office maintains a list of available off-campus rentals.

Library Facilities. The Library Resource Center houses over 445,000 volumes, more than 3,600 periodicals and journals, and a large collection of microprint and audiovisual materials. The Rabbi Herman Hailperin Collection contains nearly 3,600 volumes reflecting the history of Christian and Jewish scholarship during the Middle Ages. The Catherine H. Balkey Technology Collection is an extensive and ongoing collection of major books and journals in theology, with an emphasis on Catholic tradition. It is the largest of its kind in the region and is available to students and scholars. All graduate students have access to the library of the Pittsburgh Theological Seminary.

Religious Services/Activities. There are no requirements for mandatory participation in religious services. Numerous organizations of religious context are available for participation by students as well as Daily Mass.

Degree Programs

For the Bachelor of Arts in Theology, The Department of Theology has organized its undergraduate courses into three divisions: Biblical Studies, Christian Studies, and Selected Religious Studies. The major program consists of 27 semester credits with 6 basic required courses and the remaining credits chosen in consultation with the student's advisor.

The Master of Arts in Pastoral Ministry was initiated to provide persons who want to be involved in the ministry of their Church with a solid knowledge of theology as well as with a contemporary and professional understanding of the ministry in which they intend to work. The program consists of 36 academic credits and offers two specializations: Family Life Ministry and Health Care Ministry.

The Master of Arts in Theology will acquaint students with the broad areas of theology enabling them to both experience and research the Christian tradition and to provide a professional competence that will be of service to others. It also offers a basis for continual theological studies on a doctoral level. All students are required to take graduate courses totaling 30 credit hours.

The Ph.D. in Roman Catholic Theology specializes in systematic theology, encompassing the fields of doctrinal and moral theology. Since Vatican Council II, the Catholic Church has urged the development of a contemporary systematic theology which incorporates the best of the theological disciplines with the best of the human and physical sciences. The Department of Theology is committed to the development of a Ph.D. program in theology which listens to the other voices of human learning, including history, the history of religion, philosophy, anthropology, spirituality, sociology and the physical sciences. The Ph.D. program offers a perspective and identity which has, as its origin and focus, the Roman Catholic faith-tradition. A minimum of thirty-six credit hours (excluding the Dissertation) beyond the Master's Degree is required of all students.

Special Programs

Non-degree participation in the Pastoral Ministry program is available through a Certification Program and individual courses for credit or audit are open to all qualified persons.

A Master of Science in Religious Education, offered by the Graduate School of Education, is available at Duquesne University. Some of the required courses are taught by faculty members of the Department of Theology.

A Master of Arts in Theology satellite program is offered in Youngstown, Ohio.

Eastern Baptist Theological Seminary
City Line and Lancaster Avenue
Philadelphia, PA 19151   (215) 896-5000

Administration. Robert A. Seiple, President.

General Description. The Seminary is a privately supported, coeducational graduate theological school founded in 1925 and affiliated with the American Baptist Churches in the U.S.A. Admission to the Seminary is open to all qualified persons of all evangelical denominations. It is affiliated with Eastern College (formerly Eastern Baptist College) in St. Davids, Pennsylvania.

Community Environment. The campus of seven acres is located in Philadelphia, a major eastern city in southwestern Pennsylvania.

Religious Denomination. American Baptist Churches in the U.S.A.

Accreditation. Middle States Association of Colleges and Schools; Association of Theological Schools in the United States and Canada.

Term System. Semester (4-1-4 plan).

Enrollment in Degree Programs in Religion 1984–85. Total 391.

Faculty for Degree Programs in Religion. Total 33; full-time 15, part-time 18.

Admission Requirements. Baccalaureate degree from an accredited college or university; aptitude and personality tests.

Tuition and Fees. Tuition $3,040 per year; room and board $1,700; student fees $25.

Financial Aid. Assistance is available.

Housing. Living accommodations are available for 44 men, 16 women, and 32 families.

Library Facilities. The Seminary library contains over 84,000 volumes.

Degree Programs

The Seminary offers programs leading to the Master of Divinity and Doctor of Ministry degrees.

Eastern College
Religion/Philosophy Department
St. Davids, PA 19087   (215) 341-5810

Administration. Robert A. Seiple, President; Dr. Jean B. Kim, Vice President and Academic Dean.

General Description. The Religion-Philosophy Department has a special obligation to aid the College in its plans for Christian integration of academic subject areas and provide knowledge and training for students who plan to participate in the outreach of the Church throughout the world. To this end, two majors (Biblical Studies and Religion-Philosophy) are offered and the courses provided give those who major in other fields a means of enlarging and clarifying their religious understanding.

Parent Institution. As a Christian college of the arts and sciences, Eastern College is an academic community which strives to be characterized by Christian principles in all facets of its common life. The College exists to provide educational opportunities rooted in a unifying Christian world view that can serve as a foundation for a life of service. In order to do this, the College attempts to maintain the kind of atmosphere that is conducive to the development and maturing of Christian faith and character.

Community Environment. Eastern College's 92 acres of rolling wooded land and small lakes are minutes from historic Valley Forge and Independence Hall. Situated at the crossroads of the symbols of our nation's heritage and the intellectually vibrant urban center of Philadelphia, the campus and the area of Valley Forge-Philadelphia provide an ideal laboratory for a quality academic program.

Religious Denomination. American Baptist Churches in the U.S.A.

Religious Emphasis. Evangelical.

Accreditation. Middle States Association of Colleges and Schools.

Term System. Semester; summer term.

Enrollment in Degree Programs in Religion 1984–85. Total 12. (About 400 students are enrolled in religion courses.)

Degrees in Religion Awarded 1984–85. Bachelor of Arts in Religion/Philosophy 3; men 3. Bachelor of Arts in Biblical Studies 1; men 1.

Faculty for Degree Programs in Religion. Total 6; full-time 4, part-time 2.

Admission Requirements. High school graduation; SAT or ACT; the College selects those candidates whom it believes to be suited for its work and most likely to profit from it.

Tuition and Fees. Tuition $5,990; room and board $2,120; comprehensive fee $380.

Financial Aid. The College cooperates with the College Scholarship Service of the College Entrance Examination Board and the Pennsylvania Higher Education Assistance Agency and subscribes to the principle that the amount of financial aid granted a student should be based upon financial need. Types of aid include grants, loans, and campus work-study.

Housing. Residence halls are available for single students. No on-campus housing for married students.

Library Facilities. The Frank Warner Memorial Library maintains a collection of 90,000 books, bound periodicals, microforms, audio recordings, and over 500 current periodical subscriptions.

Religious Services/Activities. Christian activities at Eastern cover a wide range of projects, from musical and

prayer groups to political action to Bible studies. Residence hall Bible studies and prayer groups are active across the campus. Missions Fellowship promotes interest in Christian missions around the world. The Evangelicals for Social Action promote interest in critical social issues. The Fellowship of Christian Athletes, the Daily Meditations Tape Program, and the Intervarsity Christian Fellowship are other activities for student involvement. A weekly voluntary worship service is also held.

Degree Programs

The Bachelor of Arts with a Biblical Studies major is recommended for those who plan to become leaders in the life of the church without necessarily going on into seminary training. Opportunities exist for participation and leadership in Christian youth organizations, denominational organizations, home and foreign missionary organizations, and positions of lay leadership in the work of the local church. The Bachelor of Arts with a Religion-Philosophy major combines theology and philosophy providing a broad cultural basis for reflective awareness and intellectual discipline that can enrich the life of any person going into any vocation. It is valuable in preparation for the extensive use of philosophical themes and studies found in the seminary curricula. It leads to graduate studies in Religion.

Special Programs

Qualified junior or senior students may take course work at Eastern Baptist Theological Seminary.

Elizabethtown College
Department of Religion and Philosophy
College Avenue   •
Elizabethtown, PA 17022   (717) 367-1151

Administration. Dr. Gerhard E. Spiegler, President; Dr. Frederick F. Ritsch, Dean of the Faculty; Dr. Stanley T. Sutphin, Chair, Department of Religion and Philosophy.

General Description. The Department of Religion and Philosophy seeks to broaden the student's liberal arts curriculum by pursuing creative ventures which often cross over traditional disciplinary lines. While committed to the Judaeo-Christian tradition, the Department does not profess a single denominational consensus; it operates in the midst of a complex and pluralistic religious field. The Department encourages in the student a reflective stance which focuses on the basic philosophies, value systems, and faith expressions of mankind as a means of preparing the student for seminary, graduate school, social work, counseling, and journalism, among other fields. The College awards the degree Bachelor of Arts in Religion and Philosophy.

Parent Institution. Elizabethtown College is a four-year, coeducational college associated with the Church of the Brethren, offering a liberal arts education as well as preparation for specific careers. There are about 1,450 students. The purpose of Elizabethtown College has historically been expressed in the phrase "education for service." The College provides an education which should enable the student to develop as an intelligent and moral citizen who can be a productive member of society. The College awards the degrees Bachelor of Arts and Bachelor of Science.

Community Environment. The College is located in Elizabethtown, Pennsylvania, in the south central part of the state, midway between Harrisburg and Lancaster. The campus comprises 110 acres and 16 major buildings.

Religious Denomination. Church of the Brethren.

Religious Emphasis. Liberal.

Accreditation. Middle States Association of Colleges and Schools.

Term System. Semester.

Enrollment in Degree Programs in Religion 1984–85. Total 7; men 3, women 4.

Degrees in Religion Awarded 1984–85. Bachelor of Arts 4; men 3, women 1. Bachelor of Science 1; women 1.

Faculty for Degree Programs in Religion. Total 5; full-time 4, part-time 1.

Admission Requirements. Graduation from a senior high school accredited by the regional accrediting agency or by the Department of Education agency of the state in which the student resides; recommendation from high school principal or guidance counselor in regard to academic ability and character.

Tuition and Fees. Tuition, room, and board $4,807 per semester for resident students; $3,382.50 for commuting students.

Financial Aid. Over 80 percent of the students receive some form of assistance, usually in a package that combines grants, scholarships, loans, and on-campus jobs.

Housing. Campus residence halls; cooperative houses for selected groups of senior students. No on-campus provisions for married students.

Library Facilities. The library has holdings of 172,985 items which include 144,200 bound volumes in open stacks, 850 periodicals, a collection of musical recordings, art slides, and microforms. A Brethren Reading Room (Archive) is housed in the library.

Religious Services/Activities. Programs sponsored by the Chaplain's Office are ecumenical in nature. Major campus-wide religious programming is the responsibility of the Religious Life Committee, a representative body convened by the Chaplain.

Degree Programs

A major in Religion and Philosophy leading to the Bachelor of Arts degree must complete 33 hours of coursework in the Department beyond the 6 hours required in the General Education core. A major is required to complete a six-hour senior research project by independent study to be supervised and read by at least two members of the department.

Evangelical School of Theology
121 South College
Myerstown, PA 17067   (717) 866-5775

Administration. Dr. Ray A. Seilhamer, President; Dr. J. Duane Beals, Vice President for Academic Affairs.

General Description. The major objective of Evangelical School of Theology is to educate those who are called of God to the Christian ministry in its many and varied dimensions. It is a graduate school offering courses of study which lead to the Master of Arts in Religion and the Master of Divinity degrees. The School grants the Teacher's Diploma of the Evangelical Teacher Training Association, indicating one's preparation for local church lay ministry.

Community Environment. The School of Theology campus is located in Myerstown, Pennsylvania, on a gently rolling limestone ridge shaded by magnificent trees, providing an ideal setting for study and reflection. Myerstown is a Lebanon County community situated about 7 miles east of the city of Lebanon, with Harrisburg, Lancaster, and Reading within convenient driving distance. College, state, and theological libraries located in these centers together with the almost limitless intellectual and cultural facilities of Philadelphia, New York City, and Washington (all within a few hours' driving distance) amply supplement the resource needs of the serious student.

Religious Denomination. Evangelical Congregational Church.

Religious Emphasis. Conservative, Evangelical.

Accreditation. Middle States Association of Colleges and Schools.

Term System. Semester; no summer term.

Enrollment in Degree Programs in Religion 1984–85. Total 65; men 60, women 5.

Degrees in Religion Awarded 1984–85. Master of Divinity 4; men 4. Master of Arts in Religion 4; men 3, women 1.

Faculty for Degree Programs in Religion. Total 15; full-time 9, part-time 6.

Admission Requirements. Bachelor's degree or equivalent.

Tuition and Fees. Tuition $3,200 per year; dormitory room $150 per semester.

Financial Aid. Scholarships and loan endowment funds are the sources of aid available.

Housing. Dormitory housing available.

Library Facilities. The library contains over 47,000 volumes. It is affiliated with the Theological Libraries of Southeastern Pennsylvania.

Religious Services/Activities. Chapel is held each morning Tuesday through Friday during the fall and spring semesters. The Seminary Chaplain is responsible for the chapel schedule.

Degree Programs

The Master of Divinity curriculum is offered in a three- or a four-year program. Each program requires the completion of 96 credit hours in specified courses and electives. The four-year program is designed for those students planning to serve a church, or to work more than 20 hours in secular employment while a student at the Seminary.

The Master of Arts in Religion is designed for lay men and women whose major field or vocation is elsewhere, or who desire competency in the several fields of theological study. Each student must complete the 34 semester hour requirement in the core curriculum (Bible, Theology, Church History) and complete one of two options: General Studies which requires 18 semester hours (with a minimum of 4 semester hours in each of 3 selected fields) or Academic Studies which requires the completion of 18 semester hours in one of the fields (Biblical Studies, Theological Studies, Historical Studies).

Grove City College
Department of Philosophy and Religion
Grove City, PA 16127   (412) 458-6600

Administration. Dr. Dale R. Bowne, Chairman of the Department of Philosophy and Religion.

General Description. The Department of Philosophy and Religion offers a major in Religion for the benefit of those who plan to pursue graduate work (e.g. seminary) or seek careers in para-church ministries or Christian education. The religious program of Grove City College, evangelical in its orientation, offers ample opportunity for young people to fellowship with trained Christian leaders who are dedicated to helping youths to discover themselves through encounter with Jesus Christ and to understand their roles in life by the application of Christian principles to everyday life. Weekday convocation programs and Sunday vespers are designed to stimulate the campus community to think creatively and critically about ultimate issues in the light of the Word of God.

Parent Institution. Grove City College is an independent Christian college of liberal arts and sciences. It is affiliated with the Presbyterian Church, U.S.A. and observes the Presbyterian Standards for Colleges. The College was founded in 1876 and for many years was located near the center of Grove City on what is now known as the Lower Campus. In 1929, a farm across Wolf Creek from the old downtown campus was purchased, and the effort was begun to move the school from its limited area within the heart of Grove City, up onto the hill across Wolf Greek. Today, Grove City College has one of the finest and most modern campuses in the United States.

Community Environment. Grove City, Pennsylvania, a town of eight thousand population, is situated about sixty miles north of Pittsburgh. The town has diversified industries, is a strong church community, and has great pride in its college.

The campus comprises over 150 beautifully landscaped acres, divided into two sections by Wolf Creek. The two areas are connected by a stone arch footbridge and by city streets.

Religious Denomination. Presbyterian Church (U.S.A.).

Religious Emphasis. Evangelical.

Accreditation. Middle States Association of Colleges and Schools. Member of: Presbyterian College Union.

Term System. Semester; summer term.

Enrollment in Degree Programs in Religion 1984–85. Total 33; men 21, women 12.

Degrees in Religion Awarded 1984–85. Bachelor of Arts 8; men 5, women 3.

Faculty for Degree Programs in Religion. Total 9; full-time 5, part-time 4.

Admission Requirements. Graduation from and recommendation by an approved secondary school; acceptable test scores from either SAT or ACT; references evidencing excellent character, wholesome social conduct, and spiritual interest; a personal interview where such is possible; nonrefundable application fee $15.

Tuition and Fees. Tuition for Bachelor of Arts students $1,615 per semester; room and board $910 per semester; board alone $595 per semester; various other fees where applicable.

Financial Aid. Scholarship, loan funds, and work opportunities are awarded by the College on a year-to-year basis. The Grove City College Financial Assistance Program is based on the need and achievement of qualified full-time students and is reviewed each semester.

Housing. Grove City College is a residential college. The residence halls for men and for women were built not only to insure convenient and adequate quarters for students, but also to foster the social unity of the College, and to enhance the total learning environment and experience. All students except commuter students and those residing with their families are required to room and board in College residence halls.

Library Facilities. The Henry Buhl Library houses 148,000 books and bound periodicals, and a sizable collection of newspapers, periodicals, and documents in microform. The reading rooms have a seating capacity of four hundred and the Rare Book Room and Exhibit Lounge contain valuable books, documents, paintings, and objects of art.

Religious Services/Activities. Grove City College believes that regular attendance at the Chapel convocations is an essential part of the student's educational experience, and of college life. Attendance is required. The Chapel convocation program is diversified, and offers several types of services and activities. A student has freedom to choose those which best suit his interests and needs, but is required to attend a specified number of times (presently 16) each semester. A student may fulfill this requirement by attending either Chapel services or convocations, or both. Students coming to Grove City College should anticipate the Chapel convocation experience as an important part of college life.

There are seventeen religious groups and activities, united under the Grove City College Salt Company, which afford opportunities for Christian study, fellowship, and service.

Degree Programs

The Bachelor of Arts degree requires the completion of 128 semester hours. Pre-theological students are advised to follow the course of studies recommended by the American Association of Theological Schools. Students interested in the fields of Christian Education and/or Church Music should plan their programs with the help of the chairman of the Department of Philosophy and Religion and/or with the help of the Chairman of the Department of Music and Fine Arts.

Haverford College
Department of Religion
Haverford, PA 19041   (215) 896-1031

Administration. Dr. Robert B. Stevens, President; Dr. Freddye L. Hill, Dean of the College; Dr. Richard Luman, Acting Chairperson, Department of Religion.

General Description. The Religion Department at Haverford College offers work in Scripture (especially New Testament and the Koran), in the history of thought and institutions of both Eastern and Western religions, and in cross-cultural study of religious ideas and institutions. The program is organized around the three pillars of theology, history, and sacred text, with a strong emphasis on teaching students how to ask and answer questions, how to think critically, and how to plan and carry out a research project. The Department works with a cross-cultural program established independently of the Department which invites speakers and programs in various religious traditions, supports temporary appointments of distinguished scholars to the faculty, and sponsors a large colloquium which includes representatives of many traditions.

Further cooperation with faculty at Bryn Mawr, Swarthmore, and the University of Pennsylvania allows students to take courses at any one of the four institutions. Bryn Mawr, for example, maintains a program in Judaica, and in Hebrew and Arabic languages and literature.

Parent Institution. Haverford is a small, selective four-year liberal arts college of Quaker background, located 8 miles west of Philadelphia. The College places strong emphasis on the quality of students, the quality of teaching, and the active continuation of the life of the mind, as evidenced by active research programs by faculty, and a very extensive distinguished visiting program designed to keep people abreast of new developments in the fields the College teaches. The Quaker identification of the College

is evidenced by the close historic relation with the American Friends Service Committee, the conducting of public business in the Quaker fashion, and the encouragement of certain Quaker values among its students. The College has one of the highest rates in the United States of graduates going on to further work.

Community Environment. The 216-acre campus is located in the Main Line suburbs 10 miles west of Philadelphia, with 26 major college buildings. With a population of over 2,000,000, Philadelphia, the birthplace of the Nation, has retained much of the charm of its colonial origins even while developing into one of the greatest industrial cities of the world. The city has 19 museums and many churches of all denominations. All the cultural and community service facilities of a large metropolis are to be found here.

Religious Denomination. Religious Society of Friends.

Religious Emphasis. The College explains, concerning its religious emphasis, that "Quakers are probably *sui generis* in these matters; for example, the College never had a chapel: students were to belong to the worshipping community of a Meeting; Quakers do not have the same theological emphasis as many other groups."

Accreditation. Middle States Association of Colleges and Schools.

Term System. Semester; no summer term.

Enrollment in Degree Programs in Religion 1984–85. Total 28; men 14, women 14. (Figures are for the school year 1985-86.)

Degrees in Religion Awarded 1984–85. Bachelor of Arts 11; men 3, women 8. Religion majors may be from either Haverford or Bryn Mawr Colleges, and may graduate from either.

Faculty for Degree Programs in Religion. Total 4; full-time 4. There are many others on a part-time basis since many faculty are interested participants in religion programs, as are those from the guest lecturer programs.

Admission Requirements. The policy of Haverford College is to admit to the freshman class those applicants who, in the opinion of the College, are best qualified to profit by the opportunities which Haverford offers and at the same time to contribute to undergraduate life. Due regard is given not only to scholarly attainment as shown by school record and examination, but also to character and personality, plus interest and ability in extracurricular activities.

Tuition and Fees. Tuition $9,990 per academic year; residence fee $3,700; Students' Association fee $150 per year.

Financial Aid. Financial aid is administered by a committee chaired by the Director of Financial Aid and is awarded on the basis of financial need. The financial aid program principally rests upon a large number of endowed scholarships.

Housing. Most student live in dormitories or apartments on campus.

Library Facilities. The Library holds 445,000 volumes

and receives 1,703 periodicals and serials. The Quaker Collection consists of 220,000 manuscripts, documents, maps, and pictures and includes the journals of about 700 important Friends, the papers of leading Quaker families as well as papers of individual men and women, Meeting records, archives of Quaker organizations, and material on Friends' relationships with Indians. The Roberts Collection contains more than 20,000 manuscript items such as a complete set of the signers of the Declaration of Independence and letters of famous authors, statesmen, educators, artists, scientists, and ecclesiastics and monarchs, and valuable papers on religious, political, and military history. The Philips Collection of rare books and manuscripts, mostly of the Renaissance period, includes among its outstanding items first editions of Dante, Copernicus, Spenser, Leo Africanus, Cervantes, the King James Bible, Milton, Newton, and the four folios of Shakespeare. The Rufus M. Jones Collection contains 1,400 books on mysticism. Other special collections are also housed in the Library.

Religious Services/Activities. Several religious organizations initiated by students reflect various traditions and faiths and practices. A Friends Meeting open to the College community is held on Thursday mornings. The Quaker Activities Committee meets every other Sunday for dinner and discussion and serves as a place where the Quaker concerns of the student body are considered. The Catholic Student Union and the Haverford-Bryn Mawr Christian Fellowship meet on alternate weeks. Both conservative and reform services are held weekly for Haverford and Bryn Mawr members of Hillel.

Degree Programs

The Bachelor of Arts with a major in Religion is offered. The exact structure of the student's program must be determined in consultation with the major advisor. The Department of Religion is concerned with the historical study of religious traditions in the archaic, ancient, classical, and Judeo-Christian-Islamic West and with the philosophical study of religious thought, particularly in its modern forms of expression.

Special Programs

The Margaret Gest Center for the Cross-Cultural Study of Religion is a program that includes several interrelated dimensions: seminars for registered students, an Annual Lecture series on the Unity of Religions, an annual Spring Dialogue, and a Community Seminary on varying themes in comparative religion.

La Salle University
Graduate Religion Department
20th Street and Olney Avenue
Philadelphia, PA 19141   (215) 951-1350

Administration. Dr. F. Patrick Ellis, F.S.C., President; Dr. James J. Muldoon, F.S.C., Dean of Arts and Sciences.

General Description. The Department of Graduate Religion offers graduate education toward the revitalization of the Christian life as ministry. Its programs in theological and ministerial studies aim to be of service to all Christians, lay, vowed, or ordained. Open to the challenge of these times, the programs offer knowledge and skills for deepening personal faith in ministry, renewing Christian community, and acting for the renewal of society in peace and justice.

Parent Institution. La Salle University is administered by the Christian Brothers. It is committed to a liberal education within the Catholic and Christian Brothers' traditions.

Community Environment. La Salle University is located in 42 buildings on a 70-acre campus in Philadelphia, Pennsylvania. The cultural and entertainment facilities of Philadelphia's metropolitan area are abundant and accessible. Plays, concerts, opera, art and science museums, zoos, libraries, historical landmarks, major league sports, and a wide variety of recreational areas are all readily available to enrich a student's leisure time.

Religious Denomination. Roman Catholic.

Religious Emphasis. Contemporary.

Accreditation. Middle States Association of Colleges and Schools.

Term System. Trimester; summer term.

Enrollment in Degree Programs in Religion 1984–85. Total 400; men 125, women 275.

Degrees in Religion Awarded 1984–85. Master of Arts in Religion 33; men 10, women 23. Master of Arts in Pastoral Counseling 21; men 10, women 11.

Faculty for Degree Programs in Religion. Total 37; part-time 37.

Admission Requirements. Master of Arts in Theology or in Ministry: Bachelor of Arts degree with 3.0 cumulative average and 26 credits in theology or humanistic sciences. Master of Arts in Pastoral Counseling: Bachelor of Arts with 3.0 cumulative average; Miller Analogies Test or Graduate Record Examination; 12 credits in psychology and 12 credits in theology.

Tuition and Fees. Tuition for M.A. in Theology or in Ministry $133 per credit; M.A. in Pastoral Counseling $178 per credit.

Financial Aid. All Theology or Ministry students receive a 25 percent subsidy from the University.

Housing. Dormitory accommodations are available on campus.

Library Facilities. The David L. Lawrence Library houses over 300,000 volumes.

Religious Services/Activities. All services of the Roman Catholic Church are held daily.

Degree Programs

Programs are offered leading to the Master of Arts in Theology, Master of Arts in Ministry and the Master of Arts in Pastoral Counseling.

Lafayette College
Religion Department
Easton, PA 18042   (215) 250-5184

Administration. Dr. David W. Ellis, President; Dr. Stephen E. Lammers, Head, Department of Religion.

General Description. The Department of Religion offers courses for students who wish to learn something about general religious phenomena. In addition, it offers a Religion major which can prepare students for graduate work in religious studies and is often used by students as preparation for seminary work. Most majors in Religion design their own programs with the help of an advisor from the Department of Religion. The Bachelor of Arts in Religion is offered.

Parent Institution. Lafayette College is a small (2,050 students) undergraduate institution which has programs in humanities, social sciences, science and engineering. Originally an all-men institution, Lafayette admitted women in 1970.

Community Environment. Lafayette College is located in 55 buildings on a 110-acre campus overlooking the community of Easton, Pennsylvania. With a population of 26,000, Easton is situated at the confluence of the Lehigh and Delaware Rivers. The city has many churches, three hospitals, and two public libraries.

Religious Denomination. Presbyterian.

Accreditation. Middle States Association of Colleges and Schools.

Term System. Semester.

Enrollment in Degree Programs in Religion 1984–85. Total 2; women 2.

Degrees in Religion Awarded 1984–85. Bachelor of Arts in Religion 2; women 2.

Faculty for Degree Programs in Religion. Total 7; full-time 3, part-time 4.

Admission Requirements. High school transcripts; letters of recommendation; SAT scores.

Tuition and Fees. Tuition $9,200 per year; housing $1,500 per year.

Financial Aid. Assistance is available on a need basis to qualified students.

Housing. A variety of styles of dormitory living are available on campus.

Library Facilities. The library contains over 360,000 volumes.

Religious Services/Activities. There is a Newman Center, Hillel Society, and a College Church. In addition, various denominations maintain student groups and clubs on campus.

Degree Programs

A major in Religion leading to the Bachelor of Arts degree consists of ten courses, at least seven of which are at the intermediate and advanced levels. In developing programs of study, the Religion Department may accept for major credit appropriately related courses in other departments. The minor in Religion consists of six courses in religious studies chosen from a broad survey of the field or with a concentration in a particular area.

Lancaster Bible College
901 Eden Road
Lancaster, PA 17601   (717) 569-7071

Administration. Dr. Gilbert Peterson, President; Dr. Ray A. Naugle, Vice President and Academic Dean.

General Description. Lancaster Bible College exists for the purpose of educating Christian men and women to live according to the Biblical world view and to serve through Christian ministries. The College believes that a true education is one that includes the development of the person spiritually, academically, socially, and physically. The College is unaffiliated with any denomination or association but seeks to function in cooperation with all churches that are committed to the historic, fundamental Christian faith and that share its standards. The following programs of study are available: (1) Four-year degree program, Bachelor of Science in Bible. (2) Five-year program, Bachelor of Science in Bible with teaching certificate for teaching on the elementary school level. (3) Two-year program, Associate of Science in Bible. (4) One-year Concentrated Bible Course.

Community Environment. The 36-acre campus is located in Lancaster, in southeastern Pennsylvania. Ten miles from the Susquehanna River, Lancaster is the trading and financial center of one of the most fertile agricultural regions of the nation.

Religious Denomination. Nondenominational (Christian).

Accreditation. Middle States Association of Colleges and Schools; American Association of Bible Colleges.

Term System. Semester.

Admission Requirements. Candidates must give satisfactory evidence of Christian conversion; a 500-word autobiographical sketch; high school graduation with college preparatory courses and a "C" average; SAT or ACT; two personal references.

Tuition and Fees. Tuition per semester $1,900; room $450; board $625; comprehensive fee $113.

Financial Aid. Financial aid available through scholarships, discounts, federal assistance grants, loans, work-study, off-campus employment.

Housing. Single students not residing with parents or

relatives are expected to live in the residence halls on campus. Some off-campus housing is available for marrieds.

Library Facilities. The Stoll Memorial Library serves as a learning resource center for the entire campus. The library contains over 35,000 volumes and 325 periodicals. A teacher education resource center is also located in the library.

Degree Programs

The curriculum leading to the degree Bachelor of Science in Bible requires a minimum of 120 semester credit hours. Included are studies in the three basic areas of instruction representing the three academic divisions of the College: Bible Education, General Education, and Professional Education. Every student majors in Bible. Each student also takes a Professional specialization or a General Ministries specialization.

Special Programs

The curriculum leading to the Associate of Science in Bible requires a minimum of 60 semester hours of study, with the same three general areas as required in the Bachelor program.

The One-Year Concentrated Bible Course is for (1) college students or graduates who feel a real lack of Bible knowledge and (2) high school students or graduates who have maintained a "C" average in high school and want a one-year Bible course before entering a secular or liberal arts college.

Lancaster Theological Seminary

555 West James Street
Lancaster, PA 17603   (717) 393-0654

Administration. Dr. Peter Schmiechen, President; Dr. Elizabeth C. Nordbeck, Dean.

General Description. Lancaster Seminary is a graduate school specializing in the education of clergy and laity for leadership in local congregations. It offers educational programs leading to the degrees Master of Divinity, Master of Arts in Religion, and Doctor of Ministry, and provides continuing education opportunities for both parish ministers and lay persons. Founded in 1825 by the German Reformed Church in the United States, Lancaster Seminary is now closely related to the United Church of Christ.

Community Environment. The location of Lancaster Seminary offers a wide range of opportunities for cultural and religious enrichment, and for learning the work of parish ministry in a variety of settings: town and country, urban and suburban. The city of Lancaster is the hub of an agricultural and industrial region of over 360,000 population. Contributing to the community life are 4 colleges, several musical performance organizations, theaters and dramatic groups, and various folk, craft, and art mu-

seums. Lancaster County is the home of many religious traditions, including those of the "Pennsylvania Dutch" — Amish, Mennonite, Moravian, Brethren, Lutheran, and Reformed — as well as United Methodist, Presbyterian, Episcopalian, Greek Orthodox, Roman Catholic, Friends, and others. Lancaster is 3½ hours from New York City, 1½ from Philadelphia, and 2½ from Washington, D.C.

Religious Denomination. United Church of Christ.

Religious Emphasis. Liberal.

Accreditation. Middle States Association of Colleges and Schools; Association of Theological Schools in the United States and Canada.

Term System. One-three-one-three system; no summer term.

Enrollment in Degree Programs in Religion 1984–85. Total 215; men 168, women 47.

Degrees in Religion Awarded 1984–85. Master of Divinity 30; men 15, women 15. Master of Arts in Religion 6; women 6. Doctor of Ministry 6; men 5, women 1.

Faculty for Degree Programs in Religion. Total 30; full-time 12, part-time 18.

Admission Requirements. Bachelor's degree from an accredited college or university.

Tuition and Fees. Tuition $115 per credit; application fee $30; graduation fee $30; room and board (dormitory) $2,660; apartments $240-$260 per month; houses $230 per month. Total minimum charges for Doctor of Ministry program $3,530.

Financial Aid. Any full-time Master of Divinity or Master of Arts in Religion students are eligible for grants from the Seminary (if they are at least a half-time student). Aid is based on need. Any student who is at least a half-time student may apply for a Guaranteed Student Loan.

Housing. The Seminary has some one-bedroom and two-bedroom apartments for students, as well as dormitory facilities. Several houses are also available for married students with children.

Library Facilities. The Philip Schaff Library houses a book collection of over 128,000 volumes and more than 350 periodical subscriptions. Special strengths of the collection include Bible, Reformation church history, history of the Reformed Church in the United States, and Mercersburg Theology. The Raymond F. Albright Collection, containing about 7,000 volumes and including a number of rare books, is especially strong in English and American church history and liturgics.

Religious Services/Activities. Chapel is held daily. The services may be United Church of Christ, Methodist, Presbyterian, Episcopal, Baptist, Pentecostal, or Lutheran depending upon who is responsible for the Chapel service that day.

Degree Programs

Master's studies at the Seminary may lead to either the Master of Divinity or Master of Arts in Religion degree. While each degree draws essentially the same course offerings, admission to the programs and degree requirements are distinct. The degree program selected is dependent upon the student's goals for ministry. Curricular fields include Biblical Studies, Historical Studies, Theological Studies, Studies in Church Life and Work, and Integrated Ministry Studies.

The Doctor of Ministry degree is designed to enable qualified candidates to advance in competency to a high level of performance in the practice of ministry and to improve the profession through research and publications. As the second professional degree for the practice of ministry, the Doctor of Ministry builds upon the basic skills learned in a Master of Divinity program together with the subsequent years of experience in exercising those skills and reflecting upon them. There are three basic components to the program: the Seminar on Ministry, Independent Study, and the Doctoral Project.

Special Programs

Continuing education at the Seminary is designed to offer programs of direct relevance to the development of professional competence in ministry. Seminar and workshop offerings are developed and administered by the Center for Professional Development in Ministry.

The *Spectrum* program is designed to help lay persons develop an ability to articulate a personal faith and develop a life style expressive of that faith. Courses are taught by Seminary faculty, visiting professors, and other leaders in all forms of ministry.

Lincoln University
Department of Religion
Lincoln University, PA 19352   (215) 932-8300

Administration. Dr. Herman R. Branson, President; Rev. John A. West, III, Instructor in Religion.

General Description. The Department of Religion is situated in the Division of Humanities, and offers a major in Religion. It also prepares the student for further professional study of religion and theology, including seminaries.

Parent Institution. Lincoln University, founded in 1854, is the oldest college in the United States having as its original purpose the higher education of Afro-American youth. Since 1857, it has provided a superior liberal arts education to students "of every clime and complexion." Moreover, few universities of its size in this country enroll as large a percentage of students from other countries. The University is a general, multi-purpose, state-related, co-educational institution of higher education, providing undergraduate and graduate study serving the academic, cultural, and vocational needs of students who present a wide range of academic preparedness and definitions of purpose. Degree programs are offered in the arts and sciences, business, music, and other fields as the demand arises.

Community Environment. Lincoln University is surrounded by the rolling farmlands and wooded hilltops of southern Chester County, Pennsylvania. Its campus of 422 acres is conveniently located on U.S. Route 131, about one mile off U.S. Route 1, 45 miles southwest of Philadelphia, 15 miles west of Newark, Delaware, 25 miles west of Wilmington, Delaware, and 55 miles north of Baltimore, Maryland.

Religious Denomination. None.

Accreditation. Middle States Association of Colleges and Schools.

Term System. Trimester.

Enrollment in Degree Programs in Religion 1984–85. Total 3; men 2, women 1.

Degrees in Religion Awarded 1984–85. Bachelor of Science 1; men 1.

Faculty for Degree Programs in Religion. Total 2; full-time 1, part-time 1.

Admission Requirements. Completion of an accredited secondary school or GED; SAT; two recommendations.

Tuition and Fees. Tuition, fees, room and board for in-state students $2,115 per term; out-of-state students $2,615.

Financial Aid. An eligible student will be considered for a number of financial aid opportunities. Pell Grants, Supplementary Educational Opportunity Grants, National Direct Student Loans, Guaranteed Student Loans, Parent Loan for Undergraduate Students, as well as College Work-Study and Students' State Incentive Grants are a few of the possibilities.

Housing. Students who desire housing would stay in one of the 12 dormitories provided for the general student body. There is no housing available for married students.

Library Facilities. The Langtson Hughes Memorial Library, named after the late distinguished alumnus, houses a collection of over 150,000 volumes. There is a special collection on Afro-American and African literature representing all aspects of the Black Experience. The library also houses a part of the Susan Reynolds Underhill Collection, and selections from other collections of African art and artifacts.

Religious Services/Activities. The program of religious life is ecumenical. Campus organizations include the Chapel Usher Board, Fellowship of Catholic Students, Gospel Ensemble, Islamic Student Association, and Militants for Christ.

Degree Programs

The requirement for a major in Religion in the Bachelor of Arts program is the completion of eight courses in religion and two years of a modern foreign language. A major is required to complete a major research project or to pass a comprehensive examination in the major field. A Bachelor of Science degree may be granted in Religion when the student has not completed the two years' foreign language requirement. The student is encouraged, however, to follow the Bachelor of Arts program.

Lutheran Theological Seminary
Gettysburg, PA 17325   (717) 334-6286

Administration. Dr. Herman G. Stuempfle, Jr., President; Dr. Gerhard Krodel, Dean.

General Description. Lutheran Theological Seminary is an institution of the Lutheran Church in America, whose primary mission is the preparation for ordained and other professional ministries. It also sponsors graduate programs and continuing education programs for clergy and laity. Degrees conferred are: Master of Divinity, Master of Arts in Religion, Master of Sacred Theology, and Doctor of Ministry.

Community Environment. Founded in 1826, the Seminary is the oldest Lutheran school of theology in America. The school is located in a town of approximately 10,000 inhabitants, a town made famous by one of the most important battles of the Civil War and by one of the most significant speeches in the history of man. Situated in the rolling hills of central Pennsylvania's picturesque farm and orchard country, Gettysburg is encircled by the Battlefield National Park with its splendid drives and charming natural history. The Seminary is within easy access of a number of metropolitan academic, cultural, and recreational centers, with Harrisburg (capital of Pennsylvania) 35 miles away, Baltimore 60 miles distant, and Washington, D.C. 75 miles away.

Religious Denomination. Lutheran Church in America.

Accreditation. Middle States Association of Colleges and Schools; Association of Theological Schools in the United States and Canada.

Term System. Four-one-four.

Enrollment in Degree Programs in Religion 1984–85. Total 288.

Degrees in Religion Awarded 1984–85. Master of Divinity 180; men 120, women 60. Master of Arts in Religion 17; men 5, women 12. Master of Sacred Theology 2; men 2. Doctor of Ministry 5; men 5.

Faculty for Degree Programs in Religion. Total 20; full-time 18, part-time 2.

Admission Requirements. Bachelor's degree from an accredited college or university.

Tuition and Fees. General fee $1,900; annual room rent $410-$600; board $1,125 (estimate); apartment housing $110-$200 per month; cooperative health fund fee $12; student association dues $20.

Financial Aid. Both academic and need-based scholarships are available.

Housing. On-campus housing is available for all single students; apartment housing available for married students.

Library Facilities. The Abdel Ross Wentz Library contains 133,000 volumes and subscribes to 600 periodicals. The library is the beneficiary of the collection once belonging to the Lutheran Historical Society. This collection is rich in nineteenth century materials.

Religious Services/Activities. An active ministry to both the Seminary and local communities is carried out through a multichoir program. The program of worship in the Seminary is planned and administered by the associate chaplain in consultation with the chaplain and with the help of a student-faculty committee on worship. The Seminary community worships together at services held daily Monday through Friday. The Eucharist is celebrated each Wednesday during the academic year and on major Christian festivals.

Degree Programs

The Master of Divinity program is designed for students planning to enter the ordained ministry. Requirements for the degree are normally completed through four years of study and include both course work and field education. Courses in various disciplines are offered primarily within three divisions: Biblical Studies, Historical-Theological Studies, Studies in Ministry.

The Master of Arts in Religion program is a two-year curriculum which can be completed on one of two tracks: (a) a track intended for persons preparing for professional service in the church without ordination; or (b) a track intended for persons desiring study in the theological disciplines but not necessarily preparing for professional service in the church.

The Master of Sacred Theology degree provides holders of a first theological degree an opportunity to specialize in a given area of theological education. A total of eight courses with an average grade of B or higher and an acceptable thesis constitute the major degree requirements.

The Doctor of Ministry is an advanced professional degree designed for men and women in the ordained ministry of the church. The program is sponsored jointly by the Lutheran Theological Seminaries at Gettysburg and Philadelphia. The candidate for this degree is expected to demonstrate achievement at a level signficantly in advance of first degree programs with respect to three goals: (1) competence in the practice of ministry; (2) depth understanding of a particular issue or task of ministry; and (3) an independent study project in which the candidate will devote intensive study to some task or issue in his or her ministry.

Special Programs

Regular continuing education events are held for both clergy and laity.

Lutheran Theological Seminary at Philadelphia
7301 Germantown Avenue
Philadelphia, PA 19119   (215) 248-4616

Administration. The Rev. Raymond M. Bost, Chairman; The Rev. John A. Kaufmann, Registrar.

General Description. The Lutheran Theological Seminary at Philadelphia is a community of faculty and students whose task within the total mission of the Church is the broad and inclusive one of providing theological leadership and guidance in the Church under the Word of God. Basic to this task is the education of men and women for the parish ministry and also for those specialized ministries which have become vital to the Church's life.

The Seminary is also known as the Philadelphia or Mt. Airy Seminary. It is one of nine seminaries supported by the Lutheran Church in America. The Seminary was founded in 1864 by the Ministerium of Pennsylvania, and the first classes were held in facilities located in central Philadelphia. In 1889, the school was relocated to its present location.

Community Environment. The Seminary is located on a tree-shaded campus of 13-1/2 acres in the Mt. Airy section on the northwestern outskirts of Philadelphia. The cultural and entertainment facilities of Philadelphia's metropolitan area are abundant and accessible. Plays, concerts, opera, art and science museums, zoos, libraries, historical landmarks, major league sports, and a wide variety of recreational areas are all readily available to enrich a student's leisure time.

Religious Denomination. Lutheran Church in America.

Religious Emphasis. Confessional.

Accreditation. Middle States Association of Colleges and Schools; Association of Theological Schools in the United States and Canada.

Term System. Semester; January term; summer term.

Enrollment in Degree Programs in Religion 1984–85. Total 339; men 220, women 119.

Degrees in Religion Awarded 1984–85. Doctor of Ministry 1; men 1. Master of Divinity 34; men 20, women 14. Master of Arts in Religion 5; men 1, women 4. Master of Sacred Theology 9; men 9.

Faculty for Degree Programs in Religion. Total 41; full-time 19, part-time 22.

Admission Requirements. Baccalaureate degree with appropriate academic average and ecclesiastical endorsement; for Master of Sacred Theology and Doctor of Ministry programs the applicant must have a Master of Divinity degree or its equivalent with appropriate academic average.

Tuition and Fees. Tuition $190 - $210 per unit; room and board per academic year $2,410 to $2,440; campus apartments per month $195 to $286; other fees appropriate to the program.

Financial Aid. Financial aid is available in Master of Divinity and Master of Arts in Religion programs (normal maximum grant as determined by need is full tuition); several merit scholarships are awarded by the Faculty.

Housing. Dormitory rooms, apartments, and off-campus housing are available.

Library Facilities. The Krauth Memorial Library is located at the focal point of the campus. The Library houses over 145,000 volumes and is one of the finest scholarly collections in any Lutheran institution in America.

The archives of five supporting synods are included on the Library shelves. Special collections in Worship and Reformation History are also maintained.

Religious Services/Activities. The keystone of community life at the Seminary is common worship. In Chapel, services of the Church as well as experimental liturgies are used. Services are conducted by students with frequent participation by faculty and administration members as well as guest preachers. Attendance is encouraged for all members of the community. Holy Communion is administered regularly. The weekly campus paper, *The Seminarian* and the annual *Student Body Handbook* are published by an editorial committee under the auspices of the Student Body.

Degree Programs

The Master of Divinity is the basic degree program and is the degree normally required for ordination in the Lutheran Church in America. The normal period of Seminary enrollment to complete this program is four years.

The Master of Arts in Religion prepares the candidate for professional church leadership or further graduate study. Majors are available in the areas of Biblical, Historical-Systematic, and Practical.

The Master of Sacred Theology is a degree at the second professional level which emphasizes academic accomplishment. It is course/seminar/research-oriented and provides for both a broad exposure to all theological disciplines and a detailed examination of a particular discipline through its major and thesis requirements.

The Doctor of Ministry is an advanced professional degree designed for persons in the ordained ministry of the church. It presupposes both the completion of a first professional degree in theology and experience in a field of full-time ministry. It provides a discipline through which the active pastor can reflect critically on his/her ministry and further develop professional skills. The program is constituted through a learning contract negotiated between the candidate and the Seminary. This contract varies according to the context and the goals of each candidate.

Special Programs

The Urban Theological Institute is a program sponsored by Black pastors from the greater Philadelphia area and the Seminary. It is designed to provide training for college graduates who wish to earn a theological degree on a part-time basis. Both the Master of Arts in Religion with a major in Urban Ministry and the Master of Divinity degree are available through this program.

A one-year course, offering no formal degree, is designed as a basic orientation in Lutheran theology for qualified lay persons desiring to relate the Christian faith more closely to their chosen occupations.

Mary Immaculate Seminary

300 Cherryville Road
P.O. Box 27
Northampton, PA 18067   (215) 262-7866

Administration. Rev. Thomas F. Hoar, C.M., Ph.D., President.

General Description. The purpose of Mary Immaculate Seminary is to prepare men and women to enter into various ministries in dioceses and communities of the Roman Catholic Church. The Seminary's primary thrust is toward assisting men to become priests. It also offers opportunities for priests, religious, and lay people who are interested in on-going theological, spiritual, and pastoral development. The degrees Master of Divinity and Master of Theology are awarded.

Community Environment. The Seminary is situated on a 460-acre campus on a high hill overlooking the Lehigh River. Northampton lies a short distance northwest of Bethlehem and Allentown.

Religious Denomination. Roman Catholic.

Accreditation. Middle States Association of Colleges and Schools; Association of Theological Schools in the United States and Canada.

Term System. Semester.

Faculty for Degree Programs in Religion. Total 23; full-time 9, part-time 14.

Admission Requirements. For the Master of Divinity: bachelor's degree from an accredited institution; 12 credit hours in religious studies; GRE, basic reading skills in modern foreign language; knowledge of Latin or Biblical Greek recommended. For the Master of Theology: M.Div. degree or equivalent; point-hour ratio of 2.50 from accredited school of theology.

Tuition and Fees. Tuition $2,300; room and board $2,-300; miscellaneous fees $87.50.

Housing. Eighty student rooms are located in the main Seminary building.

Library Facilities. The library houses 67,000 volumes; also periodicals, microfilm, microfiche, and other media.

Degree Programs

The Master of Divinity degree is designed to provide the theological knowledge, attitudes, and skills for basic ministerial competence. It consists of three years (six semesters) of theological studies; 90 degree credits, 84 earned through core and elective courses, 6 though pastoral placements; a minimum point-hour ratio of 1.50 as a cumulative average for all credits earned; written comprehension examinations; oral review.

The Master of Theology degree aims at advanced theological competence. It is a post-Master of Divinity degree. It consists of one year (two semesters) of theological studies; 30 degree credits, 18 of which must be in advanced course work in theology and Bible, 2 in the intermester program, and 2 in practical pastoral course; a thesis of at least 60 pages; a reading knowledge of a modern foreign language: French, German, Spanish, or Italian; cumulative average of 3.0 for all Th.M. courses. A variation is possible with more degree credits and a shorter research paper.

Messiah College
Department of Religion and Philosophy

Grantham, PA 17027   (717) 766-2511

Administration. Dr. D. Ray Hostetter, President; Dr. H. David Brandt, Vice President for Academic Affairs and Dean of the College; Dr. Luke L. Keefer, Jr., Chairman, Department of Religion and Philosophy.

General Description. The Department of Religion and Philosophy is one of ten departments at Messiah College, all at the undergraduate level. It has a strong connection with the liberal arts tradition of the institution. Studies in Bible, theology, church history, philosophy, and practical Christian ministries are joined to a strong component of courses in integrated humanities and general education. The purpose is two-fold: to prepare students for graduate study in religion and to train students for ministry vocations requiring only a collegiate degree.

Parent Institution. Founded by the Brethren in Christ Church in 1909 as a Bible school and missionary training school, Messiah College has passed through the years to a junior college and finally to a four-year, accredited Christian liberal arts college. Since 1972 the College has been legally independent from the church, but is still has a covenantal relationship with the denomination. Present student enrollment is above 1,800, and the College maintains a satellite campus in conjunction with Temple University in Philadelphia. The College is also associated at the baccalaureate level with Daystar University College in Nairobi, Kenya. Thus, a much wider range of majors and enrichment programs is available than is usual for a school of this size.

Community Environment. Grantham, Pennsylvania, 10 miles southwest of the capital city, Harrisburg, provides Messiah College with a semi-rural setting and easy access to such urban centers as Harrisburg, Philadelphia, Baltimore, and Washington. Since 1910, the Grantham campus has gradually developed into a 300-acre site with modern, attractive facilities accommodating academic, social, religious, and athletic activities. Sixteen of the 20 buildings have been constructed since 1964.

Religious Denomination. Brethren in Christ.

Religious Emphasis. Evangelical (with specific flavoring from its Anabaptist, Pietist, and Wesleyan rootage).

Accreditation. Middle States Association of Colleges and Schools.

Term System. Semester; summer term.

Degrees in Religion Awarded 1984–85. Bachelor of Arts in Bible 6; men 6. Bachelor of Arts in Christian Education 13; men 9, women 4. Bachelor of Arts in Religion 3; men

2, women 1.

Faculty for Degree Programs in Religion. Total 14; full-time 8, part-time 6.

Admission Requirements. High school graduation from an approved senior high school or the equivalent in upper half of class; SAT scores totaling 850 or more, or minimum composite ACT score of 19.

Tuition and Fees. Tuition $2,600 per semester; student activity fee $30; room $600 to $665; board $675.

Financial Aid. State, federal, institutional, and community scholarships; grants, loans, and work-study programs available. Pennsylvania residents should use the Pennsylvania Higher Education Assistance Agency (PHEAA) grant application to determine eligibility for the Pennsylvania State Grant, the Pell Grant, and Messiah College need-based financial aid.

Housing. Most students room in one of the College's nine residences, with options available between traditional dormitories or townhouse apartments.

Library Facilities. The Murray Learning Resources Center houses more than 140,000 books, 100 periodical titles, 15,000 microforms, and 25,000 audiovisual items. Over 18,000 volumes are in the area of religion. The Center also contains the archives of the College and the Brethren in Christ Archival Collection.

Religious Services/Activities. A Brethren in Christ congregation meets on campus. Students attend many different community churches of various denominations. College Chapel meets twice weekly (required attendance). Many student participate in gospel team and mission group activities.

Degree Programs

The Bachelor of Arts with a major in Bible is for persons anticipating Christian ministry, persons desiring a strong biblical background as lay Christians, and persons desiring to supplement other majors with a biblical studies background. It stresses a thorough knowledge of the Scriptures and the biblical context. Courses in methods of Bible study, content of the Bible, and New Testament Greek assist students in furthering their understanding and appreciation of God's Word and its application to the issues that confront mankind.

The Christian Education major leading to the Bachelor of Arts degree combines knowledge of the Christian faith with principles and methods of education in a program to equip students for service in the educational ministry of the church. In addition to courses from the Religion Department, it involves courses in the behavioral sciences. The major is particulary helpful to persons anticipating service in Christian education, youth ministry, Christian camping, and parachurch organizations.

The Bachelor of Arts major in Religion gives the student a broad background to the study of religion generally and the Christian faith in particular. An understanding of the Christian faith is approached through studies in biblical language and literature, philosophy, church history,

and religious thought. The major is appropriate preparation for more advanced training in seminary or graduate school.

Special Programs

The College offers a two-year Certificate in Religious Studies involving 60 semester hours of credit. The needs and interests of each student are the primary consideration in course selection.

Several Bible and religion courses are available in correspondence format.

Moravian College
Moravian Theological Seminary
60 West Locust Street
Bethlehem, PA 18018   (215) 861-1516

Administration. Dr. Herman E. Collier, President; Dr. William W. Matz, Dean, Moravian Theological Seminary.

General Description. The stated goals of Moravian Theological Seminary are to provide the best possible preparation for the ordained parish ministry in the contemporary church; to give special attention to the needs of the Moravian Church; to be a theological resource for the Moravian Church. The degrees granted are Master of Divinity, Master of Arts in Pastoral Counseling, Master of Arts in Theological Studies, Master of Arts in Christian Education, Doctor of Ministry. The Certificate in Theological Studies is also offered.

Parent Institution. Moravian College is a privately-supported coeducational liberal arts college, and one of the oldest in the nation.

Community Environment. Bethlehem is at the center of a metropolitan area known as the Lehigh Valley. Within a 35-mile radius of the Seminary are 13 institutions of higher learning including Lehigh University. Many ethnic and diverse religious backgrounds of the area residents make this an ideal location for the study of religion; Protestantism, Roman Catholicism, Eastern Orthodoxy, and the Jewish religion are strongly represented.

Religious Denomination. Moravian.

Accreditation. Middle States Association of Colleges and Schools; Association of Theological Schools in the United States and Canada.

Term System. Semester (4-1-4- plan); summer terms.

Admission Requirements. Baccalaureate degree with the following subjects as a basic preparation: Bible and Religion (Old Testament, New Testament, Comparative Religion), English literature and composition, Speech, History (Ancient, Medieval, European, American), Philosophy, Natural Sciences, Social Sciences, Management, Fine Arts, Foreign Languages (one or more of Latin, Greek, Hebrew, German).

Tuition and Fees. Master of Divinity: per semester tuition $1,700; board $635; room $665. Master of Arts: per credit hour tuition $145. Doctor of Ministry: tuition is paid for 2 academic years; consult Seminary.

Financial Aid. Candidates for the ministry of the Moravian Church in America may receive financial aid toward tuition, board, room, and other expenses according to their need through scholarships. Student loans may be arranged.

Housing. Three residences for single students are available as well as limited housing for marrieds.

Library Facilities. The Reeves Library collection numbers 176,000 volumes, and cooperation with other Lehigh Valley colleges makes one million volumes readily accessible to Moravian students.

Degree Programs

The Master of Divinity degree is a three-year program requiring a minimum of 102 credit hours.

The Master of Arts in Pastoral Counseling degree is primarily for clergy or laypersons seeking to develop counseling competence. Normally requires two years and 62 credit hours.

The Master of Arts in Theological Studies degree normally requires a minimum of four semesters of full-time study totaling 53 credit hours. (The Master of Theological Studies is designed for those who are not intending to enter the ordained ministry.)

The Master of Arts in Christian Education is offered in a cooperative program with the Presbyterian School of Christian Education, Richmond, Virginia. A student may complete the first year of study (32 semester hours) at Moravian Theological Seminary and the second year (30 semester hours) at PSCE and be awarded the degree Master of Christian Education by the latter institution.

The Doctor of Ministry degree, carried out in joint sponsorship with the Theological School of Drew University, is a part-time, regionally-based, in-ministry program of continuing education. The first year's classes are on the Moravian campus and the summer session is on the Drew campus. Degrees are conferred by Drew. The program requires at least 2 academic years, and may extend to five years.

Special Programs

The Certificate in Theological Studies program is for a very limited number of students who are approved candidates for ministry in their respective denominations but who lack an accredited baccalaureate degree.

Muhlenberg College
Religion Department
2400 Chew Street
Allentown, PA 18104   (215) 433-3191

Administration. Dr. Johnathan C. Messerli, President; Dr. Darrell Jodock, Head of Religion Department.

General Description. The Religion Department offers three first-level courses which seek to introduce the West-

ern religious tradition, the Bible, and the procedures employed in the academic study of religion. It also offers a wide variety of second-level courses that permit more intensive work in the student's own or a different religious tradition. The Department offers a major in the study of Religion.

Parent Institution. Muhlenberg College is an independent, undergraduate, coeducational institution affiliated with the Lutheran Church in America. Founded in 1848 to provide a liberal arts education in the Christian humanistic tradition, the College is committed to high standards of academic integrity and excellence. The College grants the Bachelor's degree.

Community Environment. The 78-acre campus is located in Allentown, on the edge of the picturesque "Pennsylvania Dutch" country, approximately 55 miles north of Philadelphia and 90 miles west of New York City.

Religious Denomination. Lutheran Church in America.

Accreditation. Middle States Association of Colleges and Schools.

Term System. Semester.

Faculty for Degree Programs in Religion. Total 5.

Admission Requirements. High school graduation with rank in the upper 30 percent of graduating class; completion of 16 academic units; SAT or ACT; two achievement tests.

Tuition and Fees. Tuition $8,095 (two semesters); activity fee $90; room $1,200-$1,300; board $1,240-$1,315.

Financial Aid. All assistance is awarded on the basis of financial need together with demonstrated and potential academic and non-academic achievement.

Housing. Dormitory accommodations are available for 589 men and 602 women.

Library Facilities. The John A.W. Haas Library and Cedar Crest College's Cressman Library, operating as a joint system, contain 295,000 volumes.

Religious Services/Activities. The College community is religiously diverse. Services, programs, and organizations are open to all students. Services of worship include worship according to the Lutheran tradition on Sundays, Masses according to the Roman Catholic rite during the weekend or Sundays, and Jewish services on Friday evening. A midweek evening informal ecumenical Christian service is planned and led by students.

Degree Programs

The major in Religion leading to the Bachelor of Arts degree requires a minimum of 12 courses. Courses are grouped as follows: Introductory; Specific Religious Traditions; Perspectives on Religion; and Seminars.

Special Programs

In cooperation with the Luther Institute, the Religion Department sponsors a semester-long program in "Religion and Public Affairs" in Washington, D.C.

Neumann College

Aston, PA 19014   (215) 459-0905

Administration. Sr. M. Margarella O'Neill, O.S.F., President.

General Description. Neumann College is a privately supported, Catholic, liberal arts college. It began in 1965 and offers degree programs in Behavioral Science, Biology, English, Arts and Letters, Business Administration, Communication, Medical Technology, Nursing, Social Sciences, and Religious Studies.

Community Environment. Situated in suburban Aston, Neumann College is located on a campus of 14 acres, serving the lower Delaware Valley.

Religious Denomination. Roman Catholic.

Accreditation. Middle States Association of Colleges and Schools.

Term System. Semester.

Admission Requirements. Graduation from an approved high school or equivalent; rank in upper 60 percent of graduating class; SAT or ACT.

Tuition and Fees. Tuition $3,850 per year; student fees $150.

Financial Aid. The College offers several forms of financial aid to assist needy students. Assistance given by the College is intended to supplement the family's funds.

Housing. There are no dormitory facilities available.

Library Facilities. The library contains a balanced collection of over 72,000 volumes and receives 625 periodical subscriptions.

Religious Services/Activities. A Campus Ministry Committee composed of chaplain, faculty, and students seeks to meet the spiritual needs of the entire campus community. All activities are voluntary. Liturgical services are arranged daily.

Degree Programs

The Department of Religion in the Division of Humanities offers the major in Religious Studies leading to the Bachelor of Arts degree. The degree requires a total of 121 credits.

Pennsylvania, University of
Department of Religious Studies

36 College Hall
Philadelphia, PA 19104   (215) 898-7507

Administration. Professor Guy R. Welbon, Chair, Department of Religious Studies.

General Description. The Department of Religious Studies has a threefold aim: (1) to acquaint the student with the major theories and methods of the interpretation of religious phenomena and the problems that arise therein; (2) to enable the student to gain a relatively mature understanding of the major religious traditions; and (3) to promote serious and independent research in some aspects

of religious studies of interest to the student. There are several emphases possible within the religious studies concentration and opportunities for intensive concentration in certain religious traditions such as Judaism, Christianity, Islam, or Hinduism.

Parent Institution. The University is a privately supported, coeducational university that was founded in Philadelphia in 1740. It is independent and nonsectarian.

Community Environment. The University occupies a 260-acre campus in west Philadelphia.

Religious Denomination. None.

Accreditation. Middle States Association of Colleges and Schools.

Term System. Semester.

Faculty for Degree Programs in Religion. Total 10.

Admission Requirements. High school graduation with high rank in graduating class; SAT; three Achievement Tests required; GRE required for graduate programs.

Tuition and Fees. Tuition $9,600 per year; room and board $4,225 (average).

Financial Aid. Assistance is available and is based on need.

Housing. Living accommodations in dormitories are available to single students and families.

Library Facilities. The university libraries include more than 3 million books. The University Library Center houses the largest portion of the collection.

Degree Programs

The major program in Religious Studies leading to the Bachelor of Arts degree requires 12 credit units in the field and major-related subjects. Each student's program is prepared in consultation with the undergraduate chairman.

The graduate program leading to the Master of Arts and Doctor of Philosophy degrees draws widely on the interdisciplinary resources of the University. Available fields include primitive religions; ancient religions and archaeology of the Near East and/or Mediterranean world; contemporary religions, in particular religious traditions such as Judaism, Christianity, Islam, Hinduism, Buddhism, Taoism; Western academic approaches to religion; and Western contemporary religious thought.

Philadelphia College of Bible

Langhorne Manor
Langhorne, PA 19047   (215) 752-5915

Administration. W. Sherrill Babb, President; David C. Smith, Director of Admissions and Records.

General Description. Philadelphia College of Bible is the result of the merger in 1951 of the National Bible Institute (founded in 1913) and the Philadelphia School of the Bible (founded in 1914). The combined school was known as the Philadelphia Bible Institute until 1958 when the present name was adopted. The doctrinal position of the College is historically that of conservative, evangelical Christianity.

The College is distinctively a Bible College. Every student is a Bible major who receives a thorough grounding in Bible and doctrine. The professional specializations available to the student offer preparation for a career of Christian ministry. Every student is required to have a field experience in Christian ministry each semester. The practices and policies of the College are designed to prepare students to meet the standards that will be expected of them as full-time Christian workers dedicated to a ministry for Christ.

Community Environment. Philadelphia College of Bible is located in Langhorne Manor, a suburban community in Lower Bucks Country, Pennyslvania. Four miles from the northeast boundary of Philadelphia, the College is just a short drive from some of America's prime farm, forest, and resort areas. The 115-acre wooded campus has eight educational buildings clustered on a hill which overlooks a 2-acre pond.

Religious Denomination. Nondenominational.

Religious Emphasis. Fundamentalist.

Accreditation. Middle States Association of Colleges and Schools; American Association of Bible Colleges.

Term System. Semester.

Enrollment in Degree Programs in Religion 1984–85. Total 544; men 305, women 239.

Degrees in Religion Awarded 1984–85. Bachelor of Science in Bible 88. Bachelor of Social Work 4. Bachelor of Music 3.

Faculty for Degree Programs in Religion. Total 40; full-time 30, part-time 10.

Admission Requirements. Confidential references from a pastor and an employer or business acquaintance; concise statement of family background, conversion experience, and purpose for wanting to attend the College; high school diploma representing a minimum of 15 units; SAT or ACT scores.

Tuition and Fees. Costs for a dormitory student per academic year are approximately $6,563, for a commuting student $4,033; miscellaneous and music fees are extra.

Financial Aid. Applicants for financial aid are selected on the basis of need. There are grants, scholarshare/student aid, endowed scholarships, awards, loans, and student employment.

Housing. On-campus dormitories for single students; no married student housing available on campus.

Library Facilities. The library contains over 50,000 volumes and subscribes to more than 500 periodicals. The Jamieson Missionary Research Collection and the Douglas B. MacCorkle Microform Collection represent special research materials. The library's holdings also include a collection of 3,500 color slides of Bible lands, geography, and civilization.

Religious Services/Activities. Spiritual maturity is stressed at the College. Daily chapel services, class devotions, annual conferences, and regular church attendance provide opportunities for worship, instruction, and challenge. Class meetings, residence hall meetings, and Student Missionary Fellowship meetings offer the student the privilege and responsibility of regular intercessory prayer. Christian Service requirements involving the student in outreach stimulate personal spiritual development.

Degree Programs

The Bachelor degree programs are structured to provide every student with a thorough grounding in Bible and doctrine. In addition to the 45 credits of specified Bible and doctrine requirements there are 7 additional credits of Bible-related subjects required; thus, every student, regardless of professional specialization, is a Bible Major. The curriculum also provides the student with a complementary foundation in general education through a knowledge of the history, language, behavior, expressions, and thought of both past and present cultures. To complete the undergraduate curriculum, the student specializes in an elected professional area. The curriculum in the Professional Division provides a balance of theory and skill courses in the areas of Communications, Local Church Christian Education, Missions, Music, Pastoral Studies, Social Work, and Teacher Education.

Special Programs

The College has an affiliation with the Institute of Holy Land Studies in Jerusalem which makes it possible for qualified students to take part of their studies in the Holy Land.

Continuing Education and a Correspondence Program are also offered by the College whereby a two-year Certificate and a four-year Diploma are offered.

Pittsburgh Theological Seminary
616 North Highland Avenue
Pittsburgh, PA 15206   (412) 362-5610

Administration. Dr. Carnegie Samuel Calian, President; Dr. Ulrich W. Mauser, Dean of the Faculty.

General Description. Pittsburgh Theological Seminary is a graduate professional institution of the Presbyterian Church (U.S.A.). Located in the heartland of Presbyterianism and part of a thriving city, the Seminary seeks to prepare men and women for dynamic pastoral ministry and Christian lay leadership in all phases of the Church's outreach. Dedicated to excellence in theological education, the faculty strives to prepare graduates who will demonstrate both personal piety and the keenest possible intellectual understanding of the Gospel and its implications for individual and social living.

The Seminary was formed in 1959 by the consolidation of two previously separate institutions: Pittsburgh-Xenia Theological Seminary of the United Presbyterian Church of North America and Western Theological Seminary of the Prebyterian Church in the United States of America. The union of the two denominations led to the consolidation of the seminaries.

The Seminary grants the degrees Master of Divinity, Master of Arts, Master of Sacred Theology, and Doctor of Ministry. In cooperation with the University of Pittsburgh, the Seminary has several joint graduate degree programs in the study or religion.

Community Environment. The city of Pittsburgh, in southwestern Pennsylvania, is built on and surrounded by the broken hills and wooded slopes which run along her three rivers. Downtown Pittsburgh, located at the point where the Allegheny and Monongahela Rivers merge to form the Ohio, is one of the largest corporate headquarters cities in the United States. The Seminary campus is in the Highland Park/East Liberty section of Pittsburgh.

Religious Denomination. Presbyterian Church (U.S.A.).

Accreditation. Middle States Association of Colleges and Schools; Association of Theological Schools in the United States and Canada.

Term System. Quarter.

Enrollment in Degree Programs in Religion 1984–85. Total 436; men 322, women 114.

Degrees in Religion Awarded 1984–85. Master of Divinity 48; men 31, women 17. Master of Arts 7; men 2, women 5. Master of Sacred Theology 2; men 1, women 1. Doctor of Ministry 25; men 24, women 1.

Faculty for Degree Programs in Religion. Total 29; full-time 19, part-time 10.

Admission Requirements. Bachelor of Arts or Bachelor of Science degree; personal interview; letters of reference from local church.

Tuition and Fees. Tuition $3,474 per year; dormitory room $75 per month, apartments for singles $160-$200 per month, apartments for married students $215-$345 per month.

Financial Aid. Grants up to cost of tuition, work-study, and loans are available.

Housing. On campus housing is available.

Library Facilities. The Clifford E. Barbour Library houses a collection of over 200,000 volumes. The John M. Mason Memorial Collection contains a collection of classical theological works dating from the reformation period. The James Warrington Collection of Hymnology includes several thousand hymn and song books which came from the estate of James Warrington of Philadelphia. The archive room of Barbour Library contains materials relating to Associate, Associate Reformed, and United Presbyterian congregations, presbyteries, synods, and general assemblies.

Religious Services/Activities. There is worship on campus every weekday throughout the academic year.

Degree Programs

The Master of Divinity degree is designed to prepare men and women for the various ministries of the Presbyterian Church (U.S.A.) and other denominations. The curriculum integrates theological studies and the work of ministry so that theory and practice, academy and parish,

are complementary components in the education process. The degree requires 108 term hours.

The Master of Arts program is designed for men and women who wish to engage seriously in religious studies at the graduate level, but do not need the full range of courses required in the Master of Divinity Program. The goals of the course of study include: (1) providing the opportunity for an academic inquiry into some aspects of the Christian religion; (2) enabling students to concentrate their studies in one or at most two areas of research, under the guidance of a member of the faculty, in preparation for the writing of a thesis; and (3) affording specialized work in the field of Christian education. Seventy-two term hours are required for the degree. A special track is available for candidates who wish to prepare for nonordained educational ministries.

The Master of Sacred Theology degree is an advanced degree in International Christian Studies that is designed to assist both overseas and North American students to study Christianity as an international faith.

The Doctor of Ministry program is designed to develop greater competency in professional ministry through systematic and disciplined study that will lead to a higher competence in integrating all aspects of ministry. Four areas are available for emphasis: Parish Focus, Reformed Focus, Pastoral Care Focus, and the Chaplaincy Focus.

Special Programs

Eight Joint Degree programs with the University of Pittsburgh, Duquesne University, and Carnegie-Melllon University are offered. Continuing education programs are also available.

Pittsburgh, University of
Department of Religious Studies
2604 Cathedral of Learning
Fifth and Bigelow
Pittsburgh, PA 15260   (412) 624-5990

Administration. Dr. Wesley W. Posvar, Chancellor; Dr. John Bolvin, Dean, General Studies; Dr. Fred W. Clothey, Chairman, Department of Religious Studies.

General Description. The Department of Religious Studies, founded in 1972, studies religion from an interdisciplinary and intercultural perspective. All its graduates are expected to have a mature theoretical framework for the study of religion and must know more than one religious tradition well. The Department offers a baccalaureate major in Religion. Also, in offering the Ph.D. degree in Religion, the Department works cooperatively with Pittsburgh Theological Seminary, Duquesne University, and Carnegie-Mellon University. The Department headquarters a research center which coordinates and generates research in religion and culture.

Parent Institution. The University of Pittsburgh is a

nonsectarian state-related university founded in 1787. It includes 5 separate campuses, with some 35,000 students (about 21,000 of them are full-time) and 3,000 faculty (of which 2,400 are full-time). The main campus in Pittsburgh includes 16 separate schools and a library system housing 4 million volumes. The University is a major research center in a wide range of fields, from organ transplant and resuscitation technology to American Indian mythology and ritual studies.

Community Environment. The main campus of the University of Pittsburgh is located on a 125-acre site in Oakland, the cultural center of Pittsburgh. A 42-story building known as the Cathedral of Learning houses many of the classrooms and administrative facilities of the University's Oakland location. With a population of over 500,000, Pittsburgh is a large industrial complex and a major corporate headquarters center. Smoke control, the revamping of the "Golden Triangle," and a surge of building has spearheaded a kind of renaissance in Pittsburgh since the end of World War II.

Religious Denomination. None.

Accreditation. Middle States Association of Colleges and Schools.

Term System. Semester; summer term.

Enrollment in Degree Programs in Religion 1984–85. Total for the Ph.D. 26; men 18, women 8. Undergraduate class enrollments are 803 students.

Degrees in Religion Awarded 1984–85. Doctor of Philosophy (Ph.D.) 3; men 3.

Faculty for Degree Programs in Religion. Total 34; full-time 19, part-time 15.

Admission Requirements. For Ph.D.: Bachelor of Arts and Master's equivalency preferred; 590 GRE verbal; strong transcripts, recommendations, and research paper.

Tuition and Fees. Tuition undergraduate in-state $1,445 per term (12-18 credits), otherwise $97 per credit; out-of-state $2,890 per term (12-18 credits), otherwise $194 per credit; graduate in-state $1,775 per term (9-15 credits), otherwise $145 per credit; graduate out-of-state $3,510 per term (9-15 credits), otherwise $290 per credit.

Financial Aid. University-wide fellowships (e.g., Mellon; Provost's Humanities fellowships); teaching assistantships and fellowships; small department grants (e.g., for the study of religion in India); tuition remissions.

Housing. Dormitories and off-campus rooms and apartments are available.

Library Facilities. The library houses over 4 million volumes inlcuding microtexts. Students have access to the theological library of Pittsburgh Theological Seminary. Special collections include those in Latin American mythology, religion in China, Judaica, and the study of religion.

Religious Services/Activities. The Department is nonsectarian but hosts periodic scholarly colloquia for students, faculty, and other interested persons. Access to chaplains and religious institutions are at the students' discretion.

Degree Programs

The Religious Studies major leading to a Bachelor of Arts degree consists of four components: at least one course in the theory or method of religious study; at least four courses in one area of specialization (e.g., religion in America, religion in Asia, Christian studies, Jewish studies, classical religion); at least two courses in alternate traditions of a comparative nature (e.g., Islamics for the Jewish studies specialist); and a senior colloquium/independent study. The cognate courses can encompass study of (1) the literature, language, art, society, or history of a culture the student is seeking to understand, or (2) disciplines or processes that are related to religion, such as social change, mythology, symbolism, literature.

A Cooperative Ph.D. Program in the Study of Religion is offered jointly by the University and the Pittsburgh Theological Seminary in cooperation with Duquesne University and Carnegie-Mellon University. The program leads to the Ph.D. degree awarded by the University of Pittsburgh. The aim of the program is to develop interdisciplinary scholars broadly trained in scriptural, historical, ethical, theological, sociological, and phenomenological fields. Areas of specialization include Old Testament; New Testament; history of Christianity in various eras and contexts; history of Judaism; Jewish-Christian and Jewish-Muslim relations; systematic theology, particularly modern protestant; ethics with primary emphasis on analysis of contemporay social issues; sociology and anthropology of religion; and phenomenological and comparative approaches to religion. Graduate work in specific areas of theoretical and thematic study is encouraged: religion and politics; religious acculturation; religions in encounter; myth and ritual studies; and methodologies in the study of religion.

Reformed Presbyterian Theological Seminary
7418 Penn Avenue
Pittsburgh, PA 15208   (412) 731-8690

Administration. Dr. Bruce C. Stewart, President; Dr. Wayne R. Spear, Dean of the Faculty.

General Description. The Reformed Presbyterian Theological Seminary is a graduate professional institution of the Reformed Presbyterian Church of North America. The Church has commissioned the Seminary with the primary purpose of preparing men to serve as pastors of congregations in the Church. The Seminary is also entrusted with the responsibility to equip those who will serve as missionaries or in other areas of Christian service. While special reference is made to the ministries of the Reformed Presbyterian Church, the Seminary welcomes and receives students from many other denominations (currently 20). It grants the Master of Divinity degree.

Community Environment. The Seminary is located in Pittsburgh, Pennsylvania, in a completely renovated 3-

story brick building with an added 2-story wing to supplement the library. *See:* Pittsburgh Theological Seminary for information about Pittsburgh.

Religious Denomination. Reformed Presbyterian.

Religious Emphasis. Reformed.

Accreditation. Candidate for associate membership in the Association of Theological Schools in the United States and Canada; Commonwealth of Pennsylvania.

Term System. Quarter; summer term.

Enrollment in Degree Programs in Religion 1984–85. Total 31; men 31.

Degrees in Religion Awarded 1984–85. Master of Divinity 9; men 9.

Faculty for Degree Programs in Religion. Total 9; full-time 5, part-time 4.

Admission Requirements. Baccalaureate degree; personal interview. Applications and credentials are acted upon by the faculty.

Tuition and Fees. Tuition $500 per quarter; fees $135; dormitory fee $200 per quarter; accommodations for married students in the community $260 per month.

Financial Aid. Primarily for Reformed Presbyterian students; other limited scholarships based on need are available.

Housing. Dormitory for men; off-campus apartments for married students.

Library Facilities. The Library collection consists of over 28,000 volumes and 160 periodicals and journals. The collection includes materials in exegetical and expository Scripture study, systematic and historical theology, and in the practical fields of the Church's service.

Religious Services/Activities. Students are expected to attend chapel each day they have classes and are expected to become involved in the church life and ministry of the congregation of their choice. Prayer groups with advisor and advisees are held once each week.

Degree Programs

The Master of Divinity degree is designed to provide a complete and balanced preparation for the pastoral ministry or other forms of Christian service. Completion of the course ordinarily requires at least three academic years and one summer field work program. The course is organized within six areas of study: Old Testament Studies, New Testament Studies, Systematic Theology, the History of the Church, Speech and Homiletics, and Pastoral Theology.

Special Programs

A Diploma Program is offered for students who do not have a baccalaureate degree, but have demonstrated that they can do satisfactory work at a seminary level.

A Missionary Candidate Certificate is awarded upon the completion of one year of special training for missionary service.

A Training in Ministry Certificate is awarded upon completion of a two year program to enrich specific areas of ministry.

St. Charles Borromeo Seminary
Overbrook
Philadelphia, PA 19151   (215) 839-3760

Administration. Msgr. Francis X. DeLorenzo, President and Rector.

General Description. St. Charles Borromeo Seminary is a privately supported, Roman Catholic undergraduate and graduate seminary. It was founded in 1832 and was granted its charter by the Commonwealth of Pennsylvania in 1838. The Seminary is owned and operated by the Roman Catholic Archdiocese of Philadelphia to prepare men for the Roman Catholic priesthood. It accepts men from other Dioceses. The college department of the Seminary admits women on a part-time basis and is a four-year liberal arts college granting the Bachelor of Arts degree.

Community Environment. The Seminary occupies a campus of 137 acres in Overbrook, a suburban area of Philadelphia. The entire physical plant of the College is independent of the Theology Department.

Religious Denomination. Roman Catholic.

Accreditation. Middle States Association of Colleges and Schools; Association of Theological Schools in the United States and Canada.

Term System. Semester.

Enrollment in Degree Programs in Religion 1984–85. Total 168.

Faculty for Degree Programs in Religion. Total 50; full-time 31, part-time 19.

Admission Requirements. High school graduation with rank in upper half of graduating class; SAT and psychological aptitude tests required. Residents of the Archdiocese of Philadelphia should write to the Director of Admissions at the Seminary; residents of Allentown should write to the Director of Vocations, 1729 Turner Street, Allentown, Pennsylvania 18104.

Tuition and Fees. Tuition $2,600; room and board $2,-400; student fees $40.

Financial Aid. Assistance is available.

Housing. Dormitory accommodations are provided.

Library Facilities. The Seminary Library contains over 180,000 volumes and subscribes to 542 periodicals.

St. Francis College of Pennsylvania
Philosophical and Religious Studies
Department
Loretto, PA 15940   (814) 472-7000

Administration. Rev. Christian R. Oravec, T.O.R., President; Dr. Thomas Maher, Vice President for Academic Affairs.

General Description. The Philosophical and Religious Studies Department is one of the largest on campus, although there are few actual majors. All students attending the College must take at least 2 religious studies courses to complete a core curriculum requirement. Recently joined together, the Philosophy and Religious Studies Departments have added the Graduate Program in Pastoral Ministry. The Bachelor of Arts in Religious Studies is offered.

Parent Institution. Founded in 1847 by six Franciscan Brothers from Ireland, Saint Francis College is a 4-year, private, liberal arts, coeducational college governed by a board of lay persons and Franciscans of the Third Order Regular of Saint Francis of Assisi. There are 13 departments in the College with 33 different majors. Master's degrees are offered in Pastoral Ministry, Education, and Industrial Relations. The average class size in the College is 27, with a student-faculty ration of 15-1.

Community Environment. Loretto, Pennsylvania, with a population of 1,661, was founded in 1799 as a Catholic colony by Prince Gallitzin, a priest later disinherited by the Russian emperor because of his religion. It is located in the western part of the state between Altoona and Johnstown. The climate is temperate. The campus of 600 acres contains 20 buildings, athletic fields, a golf course, tennis courts, and a lake.

Religious Denomination. Roman Catholic.

Religious Emphasis. Emphasis is on the tradition of Francis of Assisi.

Accreditation. Middle States Association of Colleges and Schools.

Term System. Semester; 2 summer sessions.

Enrollment in Degree Programs in Religion 1984–85. Total 10; men 8, women 2. Recent enrollment has totally changed because of the recent consolidation of the two departments (Philosophy and Religious Studies); the Department has rebuilding in process.

Degrees in Religion Awarded 1984–85. Bachelor of Arts in Religious Studies 3; men 1, women 2.

Faculty for Degree Programs in Religion. Total 5; full-time 2, part-time 3.

Admission Requirements. SAT scores; high school transcript; campus interview and visit recommended.

Tuition and Fees. Tuition $4,992; room and board $2,-780; fees $369; application fee $20.

Financial Aid. Grants, loans, work-study, and student employment available. Deadline for financial aid is May 1; scholarship March 1.

Housing. Dormitory housing; fraternity and sorority houses. Off-campus housing depends upon the particular situation and varies.

Library Facilities. The library houses 175,000 volumes, periodicals, and microfilm collection. Two special collections are available to religious studies students: Franciscan Archives and Studies and the Seminary collection currently being incorporated into the regular collection.

Religious Services/Activities. About 90 percent of the student body is Roman Catholic. Campus Ministry, daily and weekend Liturgies, prayer meetings, Bible study, and

on-going formation; secular Franciscan group holds retreats each semester; candlelight liturgies during Lent and Advent.

Degree Programs

The Bachelor of Arts in Religious Studies requires the completion of specified courses in the major field. A practicum is offered that gives students an opportunity for service in neighboring agencies or in summer volunteer work.

Special Programs

A Continuing Education program offers many religious studies courses during the two semesters at night for the working student and/or the adults of the community. Two different religious studies courses are offered during the summer sessions.

A Franciscan Workshop Program is offered in the summer for interested individuals in Franciscan Studies and there is a Summer Conference on Pastoral Ministry.

St. Joseph's University
Department of Theology
5600 City Avenue
Philadelphia, PA 19131   (215) 879-7565

Administration. Dr. Donald I. MacLean, S.J., President; Dr. James J. Neville, S.J., Dean, College of Arts/Sciences; Dr. Martin R. Tripole, S.J., Chairperson, Department of Theology.

General Description. At St. Joseph's University the Theology Department takes seriously the place of religious experience and inquiry. Religion, dealing as it does with the human person's relation to the transcendent and the quest for ultimate meaning and fulfillment, is a significant part of human life and history. Thus, the academic study of religion is viewed as an important discipline within the liberal arts curriculum of the University. Three courses in theology and religious studies are required of all students as part of their general education requirement. A major and a minor in theology are offered as well as preparation of teachers for Catholic schools. The Bachelor of Arts is awarded.

Parent Institution. St. Joseph's University, a private liberal arts institution for men and women, founded by members of the Society of Jesus in 1851, has been conducted by the Jesuits for more than a century and a quarter as a Catholic educational institution in the Ignatian tradition.

Community Environment. Situated on the western boundary of Philadelphia, St. Joseph's 41-acre campus combines urban accessibility with the charm of the suburban Main Line. In this urban-suburban environment students share in the cultural, educational, and entertainment resources of a great metropolitan area.

Religious Denomination. Roman Catholic.

Accreditation. Middle States Association of Colleges

and Schools.

Term System. Semester.

Enrollment in Degree Programs in Religion 1984–85. Total 12; men 6, women 6.

Degrees in Religion Awarded 1984–85. Bachelor of Arts 4; men 2, women 2.

Faculty for Degree Programs in Religion. Total 23; full-time 7, part-time 16.

Admission Requirements. Academic record from all high schools and preparatory schools and from all colleges and universities attended; SAT; letter of recommendation from a faculty member or guidance counselor from the applicant's high school.

Tuition and Fees. Tuition $2,675 per semester; room and board $1,740 per semester.

Financial Aid. The University offers opportunities for scholarships, grants, loans, and employment, either singly or in combination.

Housing. Residence halls are available on campus. The University also owns three conventional apartment buildings one-half mile from campus. These are designed primarily as an upper-class experience.

Library Facilities. The Francis A. Drexel Library contains a collection of more than 200,000 volumes and substantial holdings in microform and audiovisual materials. It receives more than 1,500 periodicals and newspapers.

Religious Services/Activities. Through liturgical worship, weekend retreats, prayer groups, or community service projects, all the members of the college community are encouraged to express and strengthen their faith in the ways best suited to each. The Office of Campus Ministry organizes various programs.

Degree Programs

The major in Theology leading to the Bachelor of Arts degree must complete seven Theology courses in addition to the 3 required in the general education requirements. The curriculum of the department is organized into five principal areas: Biblical, Historical, Systematic, Ethical, and Cultural-Comparative. The major must complete courses in each of the five areas plus two additional courses consisting of seminars. The course offerings are on three distinct but interrelated levels. The first level introduces theological study by exploring various aspects of religious experience and reflection. Courses on the second level concentrate on the major topics of Christian theology and on interpreting the meaning of Christian faith for today. The third level courses engage the student in either a more specialized treatment of historical and theological questions within the Christian tradition, or in studies of a comparative and interdisciplinary nature, an in-depth study of other religious traditions.

St. Tikhon's Orthodox Theological Seminary
P.O. Box 11
South Canaan, PA 18459   (717) 937-4411

Administration. His Beatitude, The Most Blessed Metropolitan Theodosius, Primate of the Orthodox Church in America, President; His Grace, The Right Reverend Bishop Herman, Rector; The Very Reverend Vladimir S. Borichevsky, Dean of Faculty.

General Description. St. Tikhon's Seminary was founded in 1938 and is located at St. Tikhon's Orthodox Monastery, America's first Orthodox monastery, in the mountain village of South Canaan, Pennsylvania. It received a charter from the Commonwealth of Pennsylvania in 1967. In 1975 the Seminary entered into a formal affiliation with Marywood College in Scranton, Pennsylvania so that a St. Tikhon's student can earn a bachelor degree from Marywood and a Diploma in Orthodox Theology from St. Tikhon's, having completed 5 years of intensive work in pre-theological and theological fields of study. The goal of the Seminary is: to provide a structured program of theological study and training, approved by the Holy Synod of Bishops of the Orthodox Church in America; for the training of candidates for the priesthood; to carry on research in Orthodox theology and Church history; to promote by publication and lectures the knowledge of the Eastern Orthodox Faith; and to develop other areas of study including religious education and liturgical music.

Community Environment. South Canaan, Pennsylvania is located in the hilly lake country of the northeastern part of the state, near Scranton. Scranton is little more than 100 miles from New York City and is easily accessible by airlines and a network of superhighways connecting it with major cities within Pennsylvania and in adjoining states.

Religious Denomination. Orthodox Church in America.

Religious Emphasis. Eastern Orthodox Faith.

Accreditation. The Holy Synod of Bishops of the Orthodox Church. Marywood College, St. Tikhon's affiliate, is accredited by the Middle States Association of Colleges and Schools.

Term System. Semester.

Enrollment in Degree Programs in Religion 1984–85. Total 50; men 50.

Degrees in Religion Awarded 1984–85. Diploma in Orthodox Theology 4; men 4.

Faculty for Degree Programs in Religion. Total 9; full-time 5, part-time 4.

Admission Requirements. The applicant must give evidence that he is prepared to successfully undertake the programs of study offered by St. Tikhon's Seminary and Marywood College. This evidence, provided by the credentials and information required with the application, is submitted to the Board of Admissions for action. The following documents and information must be submitted with the application form: a certified copy of the Baptismal record; a photograph of the applicant; an official high school and/or college grade transcript; completed health form; letter from the applicant's Pastor; a brief biographical essay; and a $15 fee.

Tuition and Fees. Tuition $600 per semester; registration fee $10; dormitory fee $225 per semester; board fee $425 per semester; Extension Program $50 per credit; non-dormitory students $675 per semester.

Financial Aid. Orthodox Church in American Grant for students who qualify; the Federated Russian Orthodox Clubs of America Scholarship Program. Limited scholarships are available from the following Dioceses of the Orthodox Church in America: Diocese of Canada; Diocese of Eastern Pennsylvania; Diocese of the Midwest; Diocese of New England; Diocese of New York and New Jersey; Diocese of Western Pennsylvania.

Housing. Limited housing for married students on campus; nearby housing is available through the Seminary's Office of the Registrar.

Library Facilities. The Seminary library contains more than 15,000 volumes of Orthodox theology, philosophy, culture, and history. Assembled with particular attention to Seminary needs, the library is also rich in Russian literature. Also at the student's disposal is the Marywood College library with more than 125,000 volumes and 1,100 periodicals.

Religious Services/Activities. Daily liturgical services are observed at the Monastery Church. An active Campus Ministry program serves the personal and religious needs of all members of the Seminary.

Special Programs

A Diploma in Orthodox Theology is awarded upon the completion of the pre-theological and theological programs of specified courses at the Seminary. Students pursuing an undergraduate degree must select a major area of study at Marywood College and will be required to coordinate Marywood class schedules with the Seminary Registrar.

In addition to the resident program of studies, the Seminary conducts a Theological Extension Program from September through May. The Seminary also conducts an annual Adult Education Lecture Series on Tuesday evenings during October. A Liturgical Music Conference/Seminar is held during the month of August and a Youth Camp Program during the month of July.

St. Vincent Seminary
Latrobe, PA 15650   (412) 539-9761

Administration. Paul R. Maher, O.S.B., Chancellor; John E. Haag, O.S.B., Rector; Cecilia Murphy, R.S.M., Academic Dean.

General Description. Saint Vincent Seminary, grounded in the tradition of the Catholic Church and shaped by the Benedictine heritage of liturgical prayer, study, hospital-

ity, and community, is a center for the spiritual formation, human development, and academic and pastoral preparation of candidates for the priesthood. It is also a graduate school of Theology that offers the Master of Divinity degree and the Master of Arts degree. The goal of the Master of Arts program is to develop in the student an academic competency in theology with a concentration in either systematic theology or Biblical studies.

Community Environment. The Seminary's campus is shared by the Seminary with a monastery of Benedictine monks, a liberal arts college, and a parish. This affords opportunities for living and learning that are unique among seminaries on the East coast. The coeducational liberal arts college for about 1,000 students affords ready access to many cultural and educational events.

Religious Denomination. Roman Catholic.

Accreditation. Middle States Association of Colleges and Schools; Association of Theological Schools in the United States and Canada.

Term System. Semester; no summer term.

Enrollment in Degree Programs in Religion 1984–85. Total 63; men 57, women 6.

Degrees in Religion Awarded 1984–85. Master of Divinity 10; men 10. Master of Arts 4; men 4.

Faculty for Degree Programs in Religion. Total 14; full-time 4, part-time 10.

Admission Requirements. Master of Divinity: Bachelor's degree from an accredited college; 18 credits in philosophy; letters of recommendation may be requested. Master of Arts: Bachelor's degree from an accredited college and indication of aptitude for advanced study; 24 credits in philosophy and religion; letters of recommendation and GRE scores may be requested; language requirement in Hebrew, Greek, Latin.

Tuition and Fees. Tuition $150 per credit; comprehensive fee $10 per credit; room $630 per semester (ordination students); board $700 per semester (ordination students).

Financial Aid. Some student aid is available.

Housing. Housing is available for ordination students only.

Library Facilities. The library contains 218,000 volumes with special collections in Catholic Theology and History.

Religious Services/Activities. Daily liturgy; annual retreat; quarterly days of recollection.

Degree Programs

The Master of Divinity degree requires 75 credits in specific areas; an introductory New Testament Greek course; and a quality point average of 2.0. A minimum of 24 credits must be earned at Saint Vincent Seminary.

The Master of Arts degree requires the completion of 30 credits of specified courses; a seminar on scholarly method; 3 Master of Arts seminars; quality point average of 3.0 in Master of Arts courses in area of concentration; and written and oral comprehensives.

Susquehanna University
Department of Philosophy and Religion
Selinsgrove, PA 17870   (717) 374-0101

Administration. Dr. Johnathan C. Messerli, President; Dr. Joel L. Cunningham, Dean of the Faculty; Rev. John C. Cooper, Ph.D., Head, Department of Philosophy and Religion.

General Description. The Department of Philosophy and Religion is a co-department offering majors in both Religion and Philosophy, as well as minors in both subjects. A student in Religion may minor in the Biblical, Historical, or Contemporary areas. Major attention is given to the Judaeo-Christian tradition because of its pervasive influence in Western society. While the University has a stance within the context of the Christian tradition, students are encouraged to study other aspects of religious phenomena, especially as found in Asian religions. The Bachelor of Arts is awarded.

Parent Institution. Susquehanna University is a four-year private university sponsored by the Lutheran Church in America. It contains the School of Arts and Sciences, the School of Fine Arts and Communications, and the Sigmund Weis School of Business.

Community Environment. Susquehanna University is located on a 155-acre campus approximately 50 miles north of Harrisburg, Pennsylvania, in Selinsgrove (population 5,116). The Susquehanna River winds through this quiet town.

Religious Denomination. Lutheran Church in America.

Religious Emphasis. Mainstream Protestant.

Accreditation. Middle States Association of Colleges and Schools.

Term System. Semester; summer term.

Enrollment in Degree Programs in Religion 1984–85. Total 6; women 6.

Faculty for Degree Programs in Religion. Total 6; full-time 4, part-time 2.

Admission Requirements. Secondary school records and recommendations; SAT or ACT.

Tuition and Fees. Tuition $5,640 per year; room and board $2,445.

Financial Aid. Endowed and restricted scholarships, grants, loans, and employment are among the types of assistance available.

Housing. Dormitory accommodations are available on campus.

Library Facilities. The Roger M. Blough Learning Center contains the University Library whose collection numbers more than 125,000 volumes, 25,000 microforms, 7,000 recordings, and 2,500 pieces of printed music, plus extensive pamphlet and report holdings. The library subscribes to 1,150 periodicals.

Religious Services/Activities. Opportunities for participation in one's religious faith are available in the churches, temples, and other religious institutions in the area. Campus Ministry programs of several religious groups are also active. Services are held in the Chapel each Sunday and at other times throughout the week as announced.

Degree Programs

The major in Religion leading to the Bachelor of Arts degree requires a minimum of eight courses. At least two courses must be taken in each of the following areas, with at least half in each area from upper level courses: Biblical Studies, History of Religion, Contemporary Religious Issues.

Swarthmore College
Department of Religion
Swarthmore, PA 19081   (215) 447-7000

Administration. Dr. David W. Fraser, President; Dr. James W. England, Provost; Dr. Janet Smith Dickerson, Dean of the College; Dr. P. Linwood Urban, Chairperson, Department of Religion.

General Description. The Department of Religion applies several methodologies to the study of the religious traditions of the West and of Asia — historical investigation, textual criticism, philosophical analysis, and empirical description — in the interests of a holistic understanding of religion. Further, the Department strives for an empathetic and responsible treatment of the normative issues encountered in the subject matter and raised by its students. The Bachelor of Arts is awarded.

Parent Institution. Swarthmore College, founded in 1864 by members of the Religious Society of Friends as a coeducational institution, is a small college by deliberate policy. Although it has been nonsectarian in control since the beginning of the present century, and although Friends now compose a minority of the student body, the faculty, and the administration, the College seeks to illuminate the lives of its students with the spiritual principles of that Society.

Community Environment. Swarthmore's campus occupies 300 acres of rolling wooded land in and adjacent to the borough of Swarthmore in Delaware County, Pennsylvania. The borough is a suburb within half an hour's commuting distance of Philadelphia. The College's location also makes possible cooperation with nearby institutions, Bryn Mawr College, Haverford College, Temple University, and the University of Pennsylvania.

Religious Denomination. Religious Society of Friends.

Religious Emphasis. The majority of the members of the college community can be described as liberal.

Accreditation. Middle States Association of Colleges and Schools.

Term System. Semester; no summer term.

Enrollment in Degree Programs in Religion 1984–85. Total 7; men 2, women 5.

Degrees in Religion Awarded 1984–85. Bachelor of Arts 11; men 4, women 7.

Faculty for Degree Programs in Religion. Total 7; full-

time 4, part-time 3.

Admission Requirements. Applicants must have satisfactory standing in school, in aptitude and achievement tests, and strong intellectual interests. Other factors of interest to the College include strength of character, promise of growth, initiative, seriousness of purpose, distinction in personal and extracurricular interests, and a sense of social responsibility.

Tuition and Fees. Tuition $10,080 per year; room $1,-940; board $1,940; student activities fee $140.

Financial Aid. Most financial aid awarded by the College is based upon a demonstrated financial need and is usually a combination of grant, loan, and student employment.

Housing. Most students live in College dormitories which include coeducational housing as well as single-sex dormitories and sections.

Library Facilities. The Thomas B. and Jeannette E.L. McCabe Library has holdings of over 600,000 volumes. It maintains the Friends Historical Library of approximately 35,000 volumes. The Peace Collection, formed around the original nucleus (1930) of the personal papers of Jane Addams of Hull-House, Chicago, is also maintained.

Religious Services/Activities. Religious life at the College is a matter of individual choice, as is consistent with Quaker principles. The Swarthmore Friends Meeting House is located on the campus and students are cordially invited to attend its meeting for worship on Sunday. Extracurricular groups with faculty cooperation exist for the study of the Bible and the exploration of common concerns of religion. These groups include the Christian Fellowship and Charitas, both Christian groups; Young Friends, Ruach (Jewish Collective), Newman Club, and Ba'hai.

Degree Programs

The major in Religion leading to the Bachelor of Arts degree is planned through consultation with faculty members in the Department. Majors in both the Course and External Examination Programs select an area of concentration, either Religious Traditions of the West or Religious Traditions of Asia, but also do some work in the other area. For advanced work in some areas of religion, foreign language facility is desirable. An import part of the Course major is the production of a sustained piece of writing. Normally, students in the Course program will elect the Senior Comprehensive Paper. With the consent of the Department, students may substitute a two-credit Thesis.

Temple University
Department of Religion
Philadelphia, PA 19122   (215) 787-7707

Administration. Dr. Peter J. Liacouras, President; Dr. Barbara Lavin Brownstein, Provost; Dr. Norbert Samuel-

son, Director of Graduate Studies; Dr. Gerard Sloyan, Chairman, Department of Religion.

General Description. Graduate studies in the Department of Religion include work toward the Master of Arts and Doctor of Philosophy degrees. The Department lays major emphasis upon 2 dimensions of the study of religion. First, the faculty and course offerings are constituted so as to provide the students confrontation with and study of the major religions of the world. Instruction is offered in Buddhism, Hinduism, Christianity, Judaism, Islam, Confucianism, Taoism, and native African religions. Second, the relation of religion to the major forces in modern society is stressed. Study is available in the phenomenology and philosophy of religion, in the relation of religion to language, literature, and the arts, in ethics, and in psychology and religion.

Parent Institution. Enrolling nearly 30,000 students, Temple University is one of the nation's largest institutions of its kind. Its curricula span a broad spectrum. Students earn bachelor's degrees in more than 95 different fields, master's degrees in 72, and doctorates in 52. The faculty numbers more than 2,500. Eleven schools and colleges offer associate and baccalaureate degree programs; the Graduate School awards master's and doctoral degrees in cooperation with 13 schools and colleges in the University. Professional degrees are also available in dentistry, law, and medicine. As a Commonwealth University, Temple serves not only Philadelphia but also the eastern portion of Pennsylvania and in many cases the state as a whole.

Community Environment. The academic program of Temple University is conducted on 7 campuses, located in central and northern Philadelphia, its nearby suburbs, and in a foreign country. The Academic Center is located on Broad Street and Montgomery Avenue, situated at a point approximating the geographic center of the Delaware Valley Region. With a population of over 2,000,000, Philadelphia, birthplace of the nation, has retained much of the charm of its colonial origins even while developing into one of the great industrial cities of the world. The city has 19 museums and many churches of all denominations.

Religious Denomination. None.

Accreditation. Middle States Association of Colleges and Schools.

Term System. Semester.

Enrollment in Degree Programs in Religion 1984–85. Total 153; men 101, women 52.

Degrees in Religion Awarded 1984–85. Master of Arts 19; men 12, women 7. Doctor of Philosophy (Ph.D.) 4; men 4.

Faculty for Degree Programs in Religion. Total 20; full-time 17, part-time 3.

Admission Requirements. Applicants should be graduates of accredited institutions of higher learning who have completed an undergraduate concentration in religion or who hold graduate degrees in the study of religion. Domestic applicants must submit scores from the Graduate Record Examination.

Tuition and Fees. Tuition in-state $142 per semester hour, out-of-state $179 per semester hour.

Financial Aid. The Department has an active Scholarship and Award Program. Successful students may anticipate considerable support, including living expenses and tuition remission, during the time of their doctoral program. Awards are made and renewed annually. Besides Departmental funds, the University has a Financial Aid Program which it administrates solely on the basis of financial need.

Housing. One- and two-bedroom and den air-conditioned, unfurnished apartments are situated at the southern end of the Main Campus. These apartments are available for occupancy with graduate students receiving first preference.

Library Facilities. The Samuel Paley Library on the Main Campus plus the various other division libraries house over 1.8 million volumes.

Degree Programs

Unit I of the graduate program in Religion consists of 24 semester hours of residence courses (12 of which are in proseminars), the qualifying examination, and, for students intending to pursue the Ph.D. program, a demonstration of competence in a first foreign language. A review of a student's program is made at the conclusion of Unit I. Upon recommendation of the faculty, students may proceed to the degree programs.

The Master of Arts requires the successful completion of Unit I plus two additional courses for a total of 30 semester hours. Two courses may be transferred from graduate work taken elsewhere.

The Doctor of Philosophy degree requires the completion of Unit I with distinction, the remaining professional and research languages, and additional courses which contribute to gaining competence in several areas of specialization. At the completion of the course requirements, a Preliminary Examination is scheduled, during which students should demonstrate competence in their concentration and readiness to proceed to the dissertation. This examination is both written and oral. In Unit III the dissertation is written and, at its completion, defended before an examining committee. Upon acceptance of the dissertation and its successful defense, the candidates are recommended to the University for the Ph.D. degree.

Theological Seminary of the Reformed Episcopal Church
4225 Chestnut Street
Philadelphia, PA 19104   (215) 222-5158

Administration. Dr. Milton C. Fisher, Academic Dean.

General Description. The Theological Seminary of the Reformed Episcopal Church was established in 1886 with fewer than a dozen students. Both faculty and student body remained very small until World War II. Peak enrollment of over 100 was reached in the early 1970s. Men and women of many denominations and from independent churches attend the Seminary. Its alumni work in churches and schools throughout America and overseas upon graduation or after completion of further education. The 3-year core program leads to the Master of Divinity degree for college graduates, and the Diploma for those not yet holding an undergraduate degree.

Community Environment. The Seminary is housed in a building which forms part of a superb church architectural group at 43rd and Chestnut Streets in West Philadelphia, Pennsylvania. This is an urban location, at the western edge of Philadelphia's "University City," and affords easy commuting and varied part-time employment, both secular and church-related. The students have access to the libraries of the University of Pennsylvania, Drexel University, Temple University, and public libraries. The city provides outstanding examples and facilities in the cultural areas of history and the arts and sciences. Not far from the Seminary are institutions such as the Pennsylvania Academy of the Fine Arts, the Academy of Natural Sciences, the Franklin Institute, the University Museum, the American Philosophical Society, and the Academy of Music. Social service opportunities abound in the immediate neighborhood, among minority groups, international studies, and resident refugees.

Religious Denomination. Reformed Episcopal Church.

Religious Emphasis. Reformed.

Term System. A semester system has been followed with a required 2-week "Winterim" session at the start of the second semester in January. A quarterly system will be introduced in the 1986-1987 academic year.

Enrollment in Degree Programs in Religion 1984–85. Total 53; men 46, women 7.

Degrees in Religion Awarded 1984–85. Master of Divinity 13; men 13.

Faculty for Degree Programs in Religion. Total 8; full-time 5, part-time 3.

Admission Requirements. High school diploma or GED; open enrollment; formal interview; no entrance exam; early decision and rolling admissions; $25 application fee. College graduates may enter as candidates for Master of Divinity upon examination of transcripts.

Tuition and Fees. Tuition $1,800; library fee $40; housing $1,600.

Financial Aid. Several scholarship funds exist for partial tuition grants to needy and deserving students, determined by application to the officers of the faculty.

Housing. A dormitory for single male students is the only facility available.

Library Facilities. The library houses over 30,000 volumes. The Rare Book Room contains collections of 18th Century Church of England History, Early New England Church History; and Reformed Episcopal Church History.

Religious Services/Activities. Opportunities are offered

for participation in camp and retreat programs or local congregations of the Reformed Episcopal Church. The majority of students come from other denominations and generally seek out their own service opportunities.

Degree Programs

The first professional graduate degree, the Master of Divinity, is offered to those who hold a liberal arts or sciences degree upon completion of the full required program. Otherwise, a non-college graduate may apply for the Master of Divinity upon completion of a baccalaureate degree. A Master's thesis is required of those diploma recipients who graduated since the replacement of the Bachelor of Divinity degree by the Master's degree in January, 1983.

Thiel College
Religion Department
Greenville, PA 16125   (412) 588-7700

Administration. Dr. William A. Good, Chairperson.

General Description. The purpose of the Department of Religion is to provide the student with an academic understanding of the religious experience of humankind. This purpose is fulfilled through courses which are designed (1) to familiarize the student with the biblical record of the Judeo-Christian tradition, (2) to interpret the nature of religious experience, especially Christian, (3) to introduce the student to the chief persons, works, and movements in the history of Christianity, and (4) to show the interrelatedness of religion and culture.

Parent Institution. Thiel College is a four-year, coeducational, liberal arts college which was chartered as a private, independent, degree-granting corporation in 1870 by the Commonwealth of Pennsylvania. It is the college of the Western Pennsylvania-West Virginia Synod, Lutheran Church in America.

The college was founded as Thiel Hall in Monaca (Philipsburg) on the Ohio River in 1866 by Reverend Dr. William A. Passavant, using the $4,500 tithe of A. Louis Thiel, retired Lutheran oil man. Accepting gifts of land and construction money, the institution moved to Greenville in 1871.

Community Environment. The college campus of 135 acres is located on College Heights in Greenville, an attractive community of 10,000 in northwestern Pennsylvania. The college buildings and grounds represent an investment of approximately seventeen million dollars.

Religious Denomination. Lutheran Church in America.

Religious Emphasis. Moderate.

Accreditation. Middle States Association of Colleges and Schools.

Term System. Semester; summer session.

Enrollment in Degree Programs in Religion 1984–85. Total 14; men 5, women 9.

Degrees in Religion Awarded 1984–85. Bachelor of Arts

in Religion 2; men 1, women 1. Bachelor of Arts in Parish Education 1; women 1.

Faculty for Degree Programs in Religion. Total 4; full-time 2, part-time 1.

Admission Requirements. High school graduation; recommendations; seriousness of purpose; personal interview in most cases.

Tuition and Fees. Tuition per academic year $6,058; room and board $2,932 per academic year; additional fees where applicable.

Financial Aid. All programs of financial assistance at Thiel are designed to aid qualified students in obtaining a superior education. There are three categories of gift aid at Thiel College: academic scholarships, financial need grants, and no-need grants. Clergy Grants of up to 50 percent tuition are allocated each year to the children of active pastors of the Lutheran Church in America's Western Pennsylvania/West Virginia Synod. Grants of up to 25 percent are allocated each year to the children of active pastors of the American Lutheran Church and of the Association of Evangelical Lutheran Churches whose congregations fall within the boundaries of the Lutheran Church in America's Western Pennsylvania/West Virginia Synod.

Housing. Thiel College is a resident campus. All students must live on campus and will be assessed room and board. Those students residing within 35 miles of the campus who are independent, veterans, married, or living with relatives are given permission to commute. Student housing includes residence halls and fraternity houses.

Library Facilities. The Langenheim Memorial Library, completed in 1952, houses a collection of 125,000 books, 202,654 government documents, 941 periodical titles, as well as 7,000 microfilm reels and 15,000 microfiche items.

Religious Services/Activities. Participation in the religious life of the College is voluntary. The College has a full-time college pastor who provides pastoral care and counseling for members of the Thiel community. The College ministry schedules both regular services and worship opportunities for holidays. The Holy Communion is celebrated twice each week in Burgess Chapel which is located in the William Passavant Memorial Center on the campus. These services are conducted within the guidelines of the Lutheran tradition, with a more formal liturgical service held on Sunday mornings and an informal eucharist held on Wednesday evenings. Mass is celebrated by a local Roman Catholic priest in Burgess Chapel in the late afternoon on Saturdays.

A variety of faith-oriented programs is scheduled at Thiel during each year. This includes informal fellowship and educational gatherings, lectures, Bible study, retreats, conferences, service projects, and leadership training events. A major weekly forum entitled "50 Minutes," is held on Thursday mornings during the academic terms. Issues and events of the day are discussed by visiting experts, members of the Thiel community, and other program resources to facilitate growth in matters relating faith and life. An all-college Faith and Life Committee, appointed by the College president, and including student, faculty, staff, and administrative representation from a cross-section of the denominations at the College, works with the college pastor in developing and carrying out programming and ministry on the campus.

Degree Programs

The Bachelor of Arts degree program includes two majors: (1) Religion and (2) Parish Education. The first of these is a general liberal arts major suitable for any student interested in such a liberal arts background. Both majors also provide depth in the fields and opportunities to prepare for a professional career or graduate study.

Special Programs

Thiel's Center for Lifelong Learning provides for the educational needs of adults by providing professional consultant service; developing professional certificate and degree programs, and providing a wide range of personal enrichment programs. Among these offerings are the Advent-Christmas Sermon Seminars.

United Wesleyan College
1414 East Cedar Street
Allentown, PA 18103   (215) 439-8709

Administration. Earle L. Wilson, President.

General Description. The College provides professional training, especially for Christian ministries, with three baccalaureate degree programs: Bachelor of Theology, Bachelor of Science, and Bachelor of Arts. Students major in Bible and theology in all of these degree programs and select a program in one of the areas of Pastoral Ministry, Christian Education, Sacred Music, Missiology, or Pre-Seminary Studies.

Parent Institution. United Wesleyan College is a privately supported, coeducational college established in 1921 as Beulah Park Bible School. It was reorganized in 1934 and was named the Allentown Bible Institute. The name Eastern Pilgrim College was adopted in 1954, the name Penn Wesleyan in 1970, and as the result of a merger in 1972, the present name was adopted. The college is affiliated with the Wesleyan Church.

Community Environment. The campus of 17 buildings is located in Allentown, 60 miles north of Philadelphia and 90 miles west of New York City.

Religious Denomination. The Wesleyan Church.

Religious Emphasis. Wesleyan-Arminian.

Accreditation. American Association of Bible Colleges.

Term System. Semester (4-1-4 plan).

Admission Requirements. High school graduation or the equivalent; ACT or SAT required.

Tuition and Fees. Tuition $3,100 per year; room $800; board $1,200; fees $440.

Financial Aid. Scholarships, grants, loans, and part-time employment are available.

Housing. Dormitory accommodations are available on campus.

Library Facilities. The Etta G. Hoffman Memorial Library houses over 30,000 volumes.

Religious Services/Activities. The Campus Ministerial Association, Christian Education Ministries Association, and the Student Missions Fellowship are among the organizations available for student participation.

Degree Programs

The degree programs Bachelor of Theology, Bachelor of Science, and Bachelor of Arts require a total of 132 semester hours each.

Special Programs

Special programs in missiology have been structured for medical personnel, educators, and mission aviation, in addition to the evangelistic emphasis.

Ursinus College
Department of Religion
5th and Main Street
Collegeville, PA 19426   (215) 489-4111

Administration. Dr. Richard P. Richter, President; Dr. Donald L. Helfferich, Chancellor; Dr. William E. Akin, Dean of the College.

General Description. The offerings of the Department of Religion are open to all students, but will be of special interest to pre-theological students, prospective teachers in the fields of philosophy, religion, and ethics, and all of those interested in the general humanities. The Department offers an undergraduate major in Religion, combined with Philosophy, and the student may specialize in either or both.

Parent Institution. Ursinus College was founded in 1869 by the German Reformed Church, and maintains some ties still with its successor, the United Church of Christ. There are no limitations on its student body, which is quite diverse.

Community Environment. Ursinus College is located in Collegeville, a borough in Montgomery County, Pennsylvania, 25 miles northwest of Philadelphia, and a few miles from Norristown and Valley Forge.

Religious Denomination. United Church of Christ.

Religious Emphasis. Reformed.

Accreditation. Middle States Association of Colleges and Schools.

Term System. Semester; summer term.

Enrollment in Degree Programs in Religion 1984–85. Total 15; men 9, women 6.

Degrees in Religion Awarded 1984–85. Bachelor of Arts in Religion 7; men 4, women 3.

Faculty for Degree Programs in Religion. Total 3; full-time 2, part-time 1.

Admission Requirements. High school graduation; SAT.

Tuition and Fees. Tuition $6,300; room and board $3,-000.

Financial Aid. The Colleges administers a variety of scholarship, loan, and student employment funds.

Housing. Residence halls for men and women are available on campus.

Library Facilities. The Myrin Library library houses over 140,000 volumes.

Religious Services/Activities. Voluntary worship services and other religious programs are held on the campus under the supervision of the Campus Minister of the College. A number of student-led religious organizations, representing a wide range of beliefs, are active on the campus.

Degree Programs

A major in Philosophy and Religion leading to the Bachelor of Arts degree requires 36 hours of work within the Department. Each major is encouraged to earn a minor in another field of study, or to elect 18 hours of coursework in an area of concentration which will broaden skills and interests, e.g., Literature, the Classics, the Arts, and the Social Sciences.

Valley Forge Christian College
Charlestown Road
Phoenixville, PA 19460   (215) 935-0450

Administration. Wesley W. Smith, President.

General Description. The purpose of Valley Forge Christian College is to offer systematic training on the collegiate level to men and women for Christian service as either ministers or laypersons. Four-year degree programs, three-year and two-year diploma programs, and a one-year certificate program are offered.

Parent Institution. The College was established in 1939 as the Eastern Bible Institute for the training of pastors, evangelists, missionaries, Christian education workers and lay workers. It is now operated under the supervision of a Board of Regents representing the six districts of the Assemblies of God in the northeastern part of the U.S.

Community Environment. The 80-acre campus includes 70 buildings. It is located in Phoenixville, 250 miles northwest of Philadelphia.

Religious Denomination. Assemblies of God.

Accreditation. American Association of Bible Colleges.

Term System. Semester.

Admission Requirements. High school graduation from an accredited school or equivalent.

Tuition and Fees. Tuition $1,104 per semester; room $448; board $560; fees $77.50.

Financial Aid. Assistance is available in the form of grants, scholarships, loans, and employment.

Housing. Dormitory accommodations vary from a four-occupant to a single-occupant arrangement. A limited number of on-campus apartments are available for married students.

Library Facilities. The library contains over 33,000 volumes.

Religious Services/Activities. Daily chapel services are held. All students are expected to include a period in their daily schedule for personal devotions.

Degree Programs

The Bachelor of Science in Bible is offered with specializations in Pastoral Studies, Pre-Seminary, Missions, Jewish Studies (for those who wish to prepare for ministry among Jewish people), Church Music, and Combined Special Ministries.

The Bachelor of Religious Education program offers specialization in Minister of Education and Private School Teaching. The Bachelor's programs require a total of 126 credits.

Special Programs

Three-year Diploma programs are offered in Pastoral Studies, Missions, Christian Education, and Church Music. A two-year Diploma program in Jewish Studies is also offered. The one-year Certificate Program is offered primarily for those who desire personal enrichment in Bible and theology.

Westminster Theological Seminary
P.O. Box 27009
Philadelphia, PA 19118   (215) 887-5511

Administration. Dr. George C. Fuller, President; Dr. Samuel T. Logan, Jr., Academic Dean.

General Description. Westminster Theological Seminary is a graduate institution which has as its purpose the formation of men and women for the Gospel ministry as pastors, evangelists, and teachers. The Seminary has as its motive and aims the provision of theological training for other church members and officers and the communication of the fruits of biblical, theological, apologetic, historical, and practical studies. All members of the Faculty and Board of Trustees must indicate in writing their agreement with the Westminster Confession of Faith.

The Seminary was founded in 1929 as the result of the efforts of four former teachers at the Princeton Theological Seminary where the modernist and indifferentist forces of the Presbyterian Church in the U.S.A. accomplished a reorganization. These men were of the old biblical faith and created Westminster Theological Seminary in Philadelphia. Westminster has remained constant in her loyalty to the Bible and to the systematic exposition of biblical truth which is known as the Reformed faith.

Community Environment. The Seminary is located on a suburban campus of seventeen acres at the intersection of Church Road (Route 73) and Willow Grove Avenue in

Cheltenham Township, approximately three miles from the Fort Washington exit of the Pennsylvania turnpike. The campus is within a half hour of center city Philadelphia.

Religious Denomination. Reformed and Presbyterian.

Religious Emphasis. Conservative.

Accreditation. Middle States Association of Colleges and Schools; Association of Theological Schools in the United States and Canada (Candidate).

Term System. Semester; January and June terms.

Enrollment in Degree Programs in Religion 1984–85. Total 470; men 441, women 29.

Degrees in Religion Awarded 1984–85. Master of Arts in Religion 48; men 44, women 4. Master of Divinity 27; men 27. Master of Theology 9; men 8, women 1. Doctor of Ministry 9; men 9. Doctor of Philosophy 5; men 5.

Faculty for Degree Programs in Religion. Total 32; full-time 16, part-time 16.

Admission Requirements. A baccalaureate degree is required for admission to the M.A. in Missiology, M.A. in Religion, and Master of Divinity programs. A first theological degree is required for admission to the Master of Theology and Doctor of Philosophy programs. A Master of Divinity degree is required for admission to the Doctor of Ministry program.

Tuition and Fees. Tuition $3,500 per year for M.A. in Missiology, M.A. in Religion, and Master of Divinity programs; $3,450 per year for Master of Theology program; $4,600 for Ph.D. program; varying amounts for different Doctor of Ministry programs; dormitory rooms for single students $1,050 per year; meals are provided by the Westminster Dining Club under a variety of plans.

Financial Aid. Over $100,000 in financial aid was awarded for 1985-86.

Housing. Dormitory rooms are available for single students. Assistance in finding off-campus housing is provided for married students.

Library Facilities. The Seminary has holdings covering all branches of biblical and theological study, as well as related disciplines. Containing approximately 86,000 volumes and regularly receiving approximately 500 periodicals, the library has particular strengths in Reformed theology and in biblical interpretation and exegesis. The holdings of major collected works of great theological writers include the entire Migne edition of the fathers, the *Corpus Christianorum,* the Weimar edition of Luther, and the *Corpus Reformatorum* edition of Calvin, Zwingli, and Melanchthon. In addition, the library has extensive holdings on microfilm and microfiche of early documents and books of the Reformation period, as well as many scholarly periodicals. The library's rare book room houses a strong collection of early works on Reformed theology and biblical exegesis. There is an extensive collection of Latin, Greek, and English Bibles.

Religious Services/Activities. Daily chapel service; Day of Prayer each semester; Missions Emphasis Week; weekly faculty-student prayer meetings; occasional special conferences. Each student is urged to associate with the life and work of a particular congregation of his choice.

Degree Programs

The Master of Arts in Missiology is a terminal degree program. It is a professional degree program designed to prepare the student for ministry in the Philadelphia area, in other North American cities, and in cities around the world. Using the resources of Philadelphia's urban complex, a program of study has been developed which seeks to integrate traditional features of Westminster Seminary's academic curriculum with involvement in, and reflection on, urban community and church life.

The Master of Arts in Religion program is designed for men and women who desire a theological background and training for various callings other than the gospel ministry or for advanced study in religion or other disciplines.

The Master of Divinity program prepares for the gospel ministry and enables the student to meet ecclesiastical requirements for ordination. The program provides a complete and symmetrical training for the gospel ministry.

The Master of Theology program is designed to increase the student's knowledge of a major field of theological learning, particularly through training and practice in the use of the methods and tools of theological research, and thus to further preparation for a pastoral or teaching ministry or for more advanced graduate study. The following majors are offered: Old Testament, New Testament, Church History, Systematic Theology, and Apologetics.

The Doctor of Philosophy program is designed to develop in a limited number of advanced students of high intellectual ability the capacity for independent inquiry and criticism required for doing original research in a particular area of theological study, teaching in a seminary or a college, or providing specialized leadership in the church. The degree is offered in two areas: (1) Reformation and Post-Reformation Studies and (2) Hermeneutics and Biblical Interpretation.

The Doctor of Ministry is offered in three areas of emphases: pastoral ministry, pastoral counseling, and the urban missions. The goal of the program is not merely the attainment of personal skills but also the achievement of a substantial contribution toward the advancement of ministry.

Special Programs

An Urban Missions program is offered in coordination with the Center for Urban Theological Studies in Philadelphia. Designed for urban church leaders, courses are scheduled on weekday evenings and Saturday mornings. These courses are part of a curriculum which leads to a Master of Arts in Missiology degree.

The Seminary participates in The Institute on the Religious Roots of America which is operated in Great Britain during the summers of even numbered years and in New

England, Virginia, and Pennsylvania during the summers of odd numbered years.

The Seminary is associated with the Institute of Holy Land Studies.

PUERTO RICO

Antillian College

Mayaguez, PR 00708   (809) 834-9595

Administration. Angel M. Rodriquez, President.

General Description. Antillian College is a private, multipurpose, coeducational college offering liberal arts, professional, preprofessional, and vocational curriculum to those who prefer to study in a Christian environment. The College is owned and operated by the Seventh-day Adventist Church. It opened in 1961 as Puerto Rico Adventist College and adopted the present name in 1962. An extension campus is located in Rio Piedras. The Department of Theology offers the major leading to the Bachelor's degree and also oversees the Program of Ministerial Studies.

Community Environment. The campus is located high on a mountainous 284-acre site overlooking the city of Mayaguez and the Atlantic Ocean.

Religious Denomination. Seventh-day Adventist Church.

Accreditation. Middle States Association of Colleges and Schools.

Term System. Semester.

Admission Requirements. High school graduation.

Tuition and Fees. Tuition $928 per semester; room $190; board $530; health insurance $37.50; registration fee $45.

Financial Aid. The Office of Student Aid provides guidance and materials for those who need grants.

Housing. Dormitory facilities are available on campus.

Library Facilities. The Antillian College Library maintains a book collection of over 56,000 volumes and subscribes to 400 periodicals.

Degree Programs

The Bachelor degree major in Theology requries 67 credits. This major is suggested for the student who desires to benefit from the double Major Program in the areas of Administration and Secondary Education, or from the two Minors in Nursing or Computer Science. This program is tailored to the needs of the modern church. Courses required included 18 credits in Pastoral Theology, 17 credits in Old Testament, 15 credits in New Testament, 17 credits in Systematic Theology, and 18 credits in cognates.

The student whose goal is to become a Seventh-day Adventist minister must apply for entrance and seek formal acceptance to the Program of Ministerial studies of the Theology Department.

Special Programs

The Associate in Arts in Religion requires 30 credits in the major field and 31 in general requirements.

Catholic University of Puerto Rico
Theology and Philosophy Department

Seminary Regina Cleri

Ponce, PR 00731   (809) 844-4150

Administration. Dr. Francisco J. Carreras, President; Rev. Tosello Giangiacomo, C.S.Sp., Vice President for Academic Affairs; Msgr. Frederico Abad, Dean, College of Arts and Humanities; Dr. Carl B. Sauder, Director, Department of Theology and Philosophy.

General Description. The Department of Theology is the central nucleus which gives meaning to the University as a Catholic university. To attain this end, the Department has formulated the following objectives: (1) to be the reference point of theological thought for the other disciplines of the University; (2) to present to the University student a basic understanding of the religious dimension of man and the answers which Christianity and the Catholic Church offer him; (3) to prepare the laity to face the challenge of the modern apostate.

Parent Institution. Catholic University of Puerto Rico is a private university established in 1948; it has been affiliated from the beginning of its history with the Catholic University of America in the United States. In addition to the main campus, the University operates educational centers in Aguadilla, Arecibo, Bayamon, Caguas, Guyama, and Mayaguez. The University includes a seminary, Seminary Regina Cleri, for the education of Puerto Rican clergy, and operates a seminary center at

Aibonito.

Community Environment. The campus of the University occupies 92 acres in the city of Ponce from which transportation facilities are available to all parts of the island of Puerto Rico. Community facilities include a public library, museums, churches of the major denominations, hospitals, and excellent shopping facilities.

Religious Denomination. Roman Catholic.

Accreditation. Middle States Association of Colleges and Schools.

Term System. Semester; summer term.

Enrollment in Degree Programs in Religion 1984–85. Total 150; men 50, women 100 (these figures are estimated).

Faculty for Degree Programs in Religion. Total 21; full-time 15, part-time 6.

Admission Requirements. Accredited high school graduation, minimum C average and completion of 15 units including 4 English, 2 mathematics, 2-3 foreign language, 1 science, 1 social science; SAT with a minimum of 450 verbal and 450 math, and 3 Achievement Tests. GRE required for graduate school.

Tuition and Fees. Tuition $40 per credit undergraduate, $80 per credit for Master's students, non-resident students $4,000 per semester; University fees $47.80 undergraduate, graduate $28; first-year day students $77.30; housing $200 per semester.

Financial Aid. The University tries to offer needy students financial assistance by obtaining available funds from different sources such as the Federal Government, the Government of Puerto Rico, and private donors.

Housing. The University has limited campus residence facilities for out-of-town students.

Library Facilities. The Encarnacion Valdes Library which serves as a center to house teaching materials, is located in the heart of the campus.

Religious Services/Activities. There are several religious organizations on the campus including the Knights of Columbus, Catholic Action Youth, and the Liturgy Circle.

Degree Programs

The Bachelor of Arts in Theology is offered by the Department of Theology and Philosophy. The basic program includes courses in Introduction to the Critical Study of the Bible; God, Christ, Church; Grace, Sacraments, and Eschatology; and Moral Theology. A Master of Arts in Religious Education is also offered by the Department.

Special Programs

The Department offers two Catechetical programs, one for 40 credits, and one for 20 credits. The 40-credit programs lead to a diploma of theological capability.

Evangelical Seminary of Puerto Rico
776 Ponce de Leon Avenue
Hato Rey, PR 00918   (809) 751-6483

Administration. Dr. Luis Fidel Mercado, President.

General Description. The goal of the Evangelical Seminary of Puerto Rico is to act as a servant of the Church of Jesus Christ in training clergy and lay leaders for the growing Protestant Spanish-speaking communities of Puerto Rico, the Caribbean, Latin America, and the United States. As a center for theological education, it seeks to be faithful to the Biblical revelation and to be relevant to the contemporary world. As a graduate center for the study of religions the Seminary also offers lay persons from a variety of backgrounds theological education with an interdisciplinary perspective. This will enable them to be more effective in their personal witness and service to the Christian Church and the community at large. Founded in 1919 by the joint effort of six protestant denominations, now the Seminary is sponsored by The American Baptist Churches, The Christian Church (Disciples of Christ), The Presbyterian Church (USA), the United Church of Christ, and The United Methodist Church. It is supported by The Community Churches and the Lutheran Church in America.

Community Environment. The Evangelical Seminary of Puerto Rico is located in the San Juan metropolitan area adjacent to the Rio Piedras campus of the University of Puerto Rico. It consists of a 4-acre compound, beautifully landscaped, containing classrooms, administrative offices, a modern library, faculty housing, and dormitory space. The majority of students are commuters. The Seminary is the only fully-accredited Hispanic school of theology within the jurisdiction of the Association of Theological Schools in the United States and Canada.

Religious Denomination. Nondenominational (sponsored by 5 Protestant denominations).

Religious Emphasis. Ecumenical.

Accreditation. Association of Theological Schools in the United States and Canada.

Term System. Semester; 2 summer sessions.

Enrollment in Degree Programs in Religion 1984–85. Total 186; men 130, women 56.

Degrees in Religion Awarded 1984–85. Master of Arts in Religion 5; men 3, women 2. Master of Divinity 22; men 16, women 6.

Faculty for Degree Programs in Religion. Total 16; full-time 6, part-time 10.

Admission Requirements. Bachelor's degree or equivalent from a duly accredited institution; results of TOEFL.

Tuition and Fees. Tuition $60 per credit; room $60 per month (men's dormitory), $65 per month (women's apartments).

Financial Aid. A majority of students receive financial aid from the denominations that sponsor them. This is usually in the form of direct scholarships or employment in churches, or both.

Housing. Men's and women's dormitories are available; there are a few apartments for married students.

Library Facilities. The Juan de Valdes Library has a collection of over 34,000 volumes and receives 285 periodical journals. Special collections include the collections of Harry Emerson Fosdick, Robert MacCracken, Angel M. Mergal, and Domingo Marrero. The Historical Archives of Protestantism in Puerto Rico are also maintained.

Religious Services/Activities. The Seminary considers the devotional life of the students to be of prime importance. There are weekly chapel service and annual retreats. Most of the students have pastoral responsibilities in the churches of Puerto Rico.

Degree Programs

The Master of Divinity program is designed to prepare men and women for the ordained ministry of the Church. The program includes Biblical Studies, Studies in Theology and History, Interdisciplinary Studies, and Studies in Church Ministry. A total of 90 credits is required. Students must also participate each semester in a Church Ministry Colloquium and in the second semester of the third year must present an integration essay.

The Master of Arts in Religion program fosters an atmosphere of study and reflection about religion, using the appropriate graduate-level curricular resources, within the Judeo-Christian tradition, from an ecumenical perspective. Special attention is given to the Puerto Rican historical and cultural context, wherein religion plays a significant role. This program is academic in nature and does not aspire to prepare professional ministers for the church. Its distinctive focus is the study of religion in its multiple aspects and the relation between such a study and other fields of knowledge. A comprehensive understanding of religious experience is offered, which includes Biblical, theological, historical, philosophical, psychological, sociological, and anthropological studies. A total of 60 credits and a research paper are required.

Special Programs

The Seminary offers a series of continuing education workshops in the fields of Pastoral Counseling, Leadership and Group Dynamics, Christian Communications, and Evangelism.

RHODE ISLAND

Brown University
Department of Religion
Providence, RI 02912   (401) 863-1000

Administration. Howard R. Swearer, President.

General Description. The Department of Religion offers a concentration in Religious Studies. Each student, in consultation with appropriate faculty members, devises a concentration program which may include courses given outside the Department. The student presents for approval by the concentration advisor a written statement of the objectives of the program and a list of the component courses. The program is expected to encompass the study of at least two major religious traditions and to take account of more than one approach to the study of religions, e.g., philosophical, historical.

The Department of Judaic Studies offers a concentration dealing with several academic disciplines in the subject. The principle disciplines represented include History, Literature, Religious Studies, Sociology, and Political Science. All concentrators in this program must have one full year of Hebrew.

The University grants the Bachelor, Master, and Doctorate degrees.

Parent Institution. Brown University is a privately supported coeducational liberal arts college founded in 1764. The University's curriculum emphasizes interdisciplinary majors, independent studies, and small seminar courses.

Community Environment. The 52-acre campus consists of 100 buildings. It is located in Providence, the capital city of Rhode Island. The city is the second largest in New England and is the industrial and commercial center of the state.

Religious Denomination. Nondenominational.

Accreditation. New England Association of Schools and Colleges.

Term System. Semester.

Admission Requirements. High school graduation with 16 units (English 4, mathematics 3, foreign language, science 3, social science 1); ACT or ACT; three achievement tests required.

Tuition and Fees. Tuition $8,200 per year; room and board $3,135.

Financial Aid. Various types of financial assistance are available to qualified students.

Housing. All students not living with parents are required to live in a University dormitory.

Library Facilities. The University Library contains over 1,800,000 volumes.

Providence College
Department of Religious Studies
Eaton Street and River Avenue
Providence, RI 02918   (401) 865-2140

Administration. Dr. Thomas R. Peterson, O.P., President.

General Description. The Department of Religious Studies program pursues two objectives: (1) it provides all students fulfilling the two courses general requirement with a large selection of courses dealing with a variety of pertinent areas and aspects of religion: Biblical literature, Roman Catholic theology, Protestant Christianity, and Jewish religious thought; (2) it provides majors in Religious Studies with a program that is flexible and professional, designed to meet the particular and personal objectives of each student.

Parent Institution. Providence College is primarily a four-year college of liberal arts and sciences with an undergraduate enrollment of approximately 3,500 men and women. It is conducted under the auspices of the Order of Preachers of the Province of St. Joseph, commonly known as the Dominicans. It was founded in 1917.

Community Environment. The campus is situated on a 93-acre site and consists of 30 buildings. The city of Providence is the capital of Rhode Island and is the second largest city in the state.

Religious Denomination. Roman Catholic.

Accreditation. New England Association of Schools and Colleges.

Term System. Semester system.

Admission Requirements. High school graduation or equivalent; SAT or ACT; GRE required for graduate school.

Tuition and Fees. Tuition $6,358 per year; room and board $3,550.

Financial Aid. Federal, state, and institutional programs are administered by the Office of Financial Aid.

Housing. Residence accommodations are available on campus.

Library Facilities. The Phillips Memorial Library has holdings of over 236,000 volumes.

Religious Services/Activities. Opportunities are given to all students to engage in voluntary service programs on campus and within the city of Providence. The Chaplain is available to discuss with or advise students on religious matters. Masses are scheduled in the Chapel on weekdays and on Sundays.

Degree Programs

Programs offered lead to the degrees Bachelor of Arts and Master of Arts in Religious Studies, Biblical Studies, and Religious Education. The Religious Studies major in the Bachelor of Arts program requires a minimum of 36 hours in courses and/or seminar.

SOUTH CAROLINA

Baptist College at Charleston
Department of Religion and Philosophy
P.O. Box 10087
Charleston, SC 29411   (803) 797-4394

Administration. Dr. Jairy C. Hunter, Jr., President; Dr. A. Kennerly Bonnette, Jr., Vice President for Academic Affairs; Dr. Sherley Mervin Mayo, Chairman, Department of Religion and Philosophy.

General Description. The Department of Religion and Philosophy is one of 24 departments in a liberal arts college. It supports the broad liberal arts curriculum as well as providing courses for majors and minors in Religion. The course offerings center around biblical courses with additional offerings in church history and theology. The major in Religion is primarily pre-professional with only slight emphasis on ministry. The Bachelor of Arts degree is awarded.

Parent Institution. Baptist College at Charleston is a private liberal arts college whose mission is "academic excellence in a Christian environment" with a variety of liberal arts, pre-professional, professional, and graduate programs of study. The College is affiliated with and supported by the South Carolina Baptist Convention.

Community Environment. Built on 500 acres of land in Charleston County, South Carolina, the institution is composed of mostly new buildings, and is continuing to expand its facilities. Noted for its splendid harbor, Charleston is on a peninsula formed by two rivers. This is one of America's oldest cities and retains many of its eighteenth century historical features.

Religious Denomination. Southern Baptist Convention.
Religious Emphasis. Conservative/Moderate.
Accreditation. Southern Association of Colleges and Schools.
Term System. Semester; January Interterm; summer term.
Enrollment in Degree Programs in Religion 1984–85. Total 53.
Degrees in Religion Awarded 1984–85. Bachelor of Arts 19; men 10, women 9.

Faculty for Degree Programs in Religion. Total 4; full-time 2, part-time 2.
Admission Requirements. Graduation from an approved secondary school or equivalent; character references; SAT or ACT scores.
Tuition and Fees. Tuition $2,112 per semester; general fees $325 per semester; room and board $1,280.
Financial Aid. The student aid program includes funds for scholarships, grants, loans, and employment.
Housing. On-campus dormitories are provided for men and women; one quad is available for married students.
Library Facilities. The L. Mendel Rivers Library houses 135,425 volumes. The South Carolina Collection is maintained here.
Religious Services/Activities. Weekly meetings of the Baptist Student Union, Fellowship of Christian Athletes, and the Campus Crusade for Christ are held. The Staley Foundation Distinguished Christian Scholar Lectures are held one or two times per year. Attendance at convocation is required of all students.

Degree Programs

A major in Religion leading to the Bachelor of Arts degree consists of 36 semester hours of which 12 hours must be in courses numbered 300 and above. Basic Studies include Religion, Old Testament Survey, and New Testament Survey. Major Studies include Religion, Life and Teaching of Jesus, Life and Letters of Paul and 24 hours of approved Religion electives. The courses offered by the Department are liberal arts courses and not professional by nature.

Bob Jones University
School of Religion
Division of Graduate Studies and Seminary
Wade Hampton Boulevard
Greenville, SC 29614   (803) 242-5100

Administration. Dr. Bob Jones, Chancellor; Dr. Bob Jones III, President; Dr. Thurman W. Wisdom, Dean,

School of Religion.

General Description. The School of Religion is designed to provide high quality training in the knowledge of the Word of God, its practical application, and its effective proclamation to the world. Undergraduate courses are for students preparing for full-time Christian ministry as evangelists, pastors, Bible teachers, missionaries, and other Christian workers, and for students who do not feel called to full-time Christian service but who wish to acquire a thorough knowledge of the Bible. The graduate courses are intended primarily for those who wish advanced preparation for full-time work as evangelists, pastors, missionaries, or teachers of the Bible. The School is divided into three divisions: (1) Bible, (2) Practical Studies, (3) Graduate Studies and Seminary which contains the Departments of Old Testament, New Testament, Church Administration, Church History, and Theology.

At the undergraduate level the Bachelor of Arts degree with majors in Bible, Bible Education, Church Ministries, Pastoral Studies, and Christian Missions is available. The Bachelor of Science degree with a major in Missionary Aviation is also available. The Division of Graduate Studies and Seminary offers the Master of Arts degree with majors in Bible, Pastoral Studies, Church Administration, Theology, and Church History; the Master of Divinity degree; the Doctor of Philosophy (Ph.D.) degree with majors in Old Testament, New Testament, Church Administration, Theology, and Church History; and the Doctor of Ministry degree.

Parent Institution. Bob Jones University is a nondenominational, coeducational institution of learning for the general education of youth in the essentials of culture and in the arts and sciences, giving special emphasis to the Christian religion.

Community Environment. Bob Jones University is located on a 200-acre tract of rolling land just within the city limits of Greenville, South Carolina, an industrial city in an important textile manufacturing region.

Religious Denomination. Nondenominational.

Religious Emphasis. Fundamentalist.

Accreditation. Recognized by the Attorney General's Office and the state of South Carolina.

Term System. Semester.

Enrollment in Degree Programs in Religion 1984–85. Total 884; men 749, women 135.

Degrees in Religion Awarded 1984–85. Bachelor of Arts 243; men 146, women 97. Master of Divinity 18; men 18. Master of Arts 54; men 41, women 13. Doctor of Philosophy (Ph.D.) 6; men 6.

Faculty for Degree Programs in Religion. Total 34; full-time 23, part-time 11.

Admission Requirements. Undergraduate: High school graduation; SAT. Graduate: Baccalaureate degree in Religion with a minimum of 30 semester hours in Religion and a 1.6 grade point average on a 3.0 scale.

Tuition and Fees. Tuition, room, and board $2,539 per semester.

Financial Aid. Aid through government-sponsored programs is not available. The University has a variety of loan funds, scholarships, and work-study programs. Graduate assistantships are available to a limited number of qualified applicants.

Housing. Dormitory housing on campus. Off-campus is housing is available at reasonable rates in the community for married students.

Library Facilities. The Mack Library contains over 182,000 books and subscribes to 750 periodicals. It houses the Bowen Collection of Biblical Antiquities and the University Collection of Sacred Art.

Religious Services/Activities. Sunday morning worship services; Sunday evening vespers; daily chapel; and various student and extension opportunities.

Degree Programs

The Bachelor of Arts degree is offered with majors in Bible, Education, Church Ministries, Pastoral Studies, and Christian Missions. The Bible major requires 71-79 hours devoted to the study of the Bible and to the development of ministerial and Christian service skills. The Bible Education program is for the ministerial student who wants a B.A. degree with a Bible major, academic minor, and a teacher's certificate for Tennessee. The Church Ministries major is designed to prepare students to serve as youth pastors, youth leaders, camp directors, counselors, recreational leaders, and children's workers or adult workers. It requires 50-66 hours devoted directly to Christian service studies and skills. The major in Pastoral Studies is primarily intended to prepare students to serve in pastoral and associate pastoral ministries which support the preaching ministry of the senior pastor of a large church. It requires 79 hours devoted directly to the development of pastoral and Christian service skills. The Christian Missions major is designed to prepare students for foreign mission fields, though the program gives some attention to home missions. It requires 73-81 hours devoted to the development of knowledge and skills necessary for service in the field. (A Missionary Aviation program leading to the Bachelor of Science degree is offered). All bachelor degree programs require a total of 130 semester hours.

The Master of Divinity is the regular seminary degree for ministerial students, awarded upon the successful completion of the standard theological course beyond a college Bachelor's degree. The degree requires the completion of a three-year program consisting of 91 credit hours. The extension course, Practical Theology (2 hours) is taken for two summers.

The Master of Arts degrees in Bible, Church Administration, Practical Theology, Pastoral Studies, Church History, and Theology require the completion of 32 hours of courses. One summer of the extension course, Practical Theology, is also required.

The Doctor of Philosophy (Ph.D.) degree may be earned in the Department with a major in Old Testament or New Testament Interpretation, Church Administration, Church History, or Theology. Specific course requirements are be worked out under the direction of the Dean and the Chairman of the Division of Graduate Studies.

Special Programs

The Certificate of Biblical Studies program is designed for students with at least a Bachelor's degree from a recognized college who are interested in pursuing graduate studies in religion but who do not intend to enter a pulpit ministry. The program is not open to students preparing for the ministry; candidates must be approved by the Dean of the School of Religion.

Central Wesleyan College
Division of Religion
Wesleyan Drive
Central, SC 29630   (803) 639-4169

Administration. Dr. John M. Newby, President; Kenneth Foutz, Chair, Division of Religion.

General Description. The Division of Religion offers a major in Religion with concentrations in Bible, Theology, Christian Education, and New Testament Greek. The programs lead to the Bachelor of Arts degree.

Parent Institution. The purpose of Central Wesleyan College is to provide postsecondary education guided by a Christian understanding of the liberal arts. This purpose underlies an academic program that endeavors to combine the broad base of the liberal arts with the preparation for various professional careers and graduate studies, including the preparation of individuals for Christian ministry. The College is committed to the ideals (educational philosophy, doctrinal convictions, ethical commitments, and social sensitivity) of The Wesleyan Church, its sponsoring denomination. The College is a coeducational liberal arts college founded in 1906.

Community Environment. The campus is located in Central, a community in the Piedmont section of South Carolina between Atlanta, Georgia and Charlotte, North Carolina.

Religious Denomination. The Wesleyan Church.

Accreditation. Southern Association of Colleges and Schools.

Term System. Semester.

Admission Requirements. Graduation from high school or equivalent; SAT or ACT.

Tuition and Fees. Tuition $2,200 per semester; room $335; board $730; activity fee $30.

Financial Aid. All scholarships, grants-in-aid, loans, and campus employment are awarded by the director of financial aid working with the Committee on Scholarships Financial Aid.

Housing. Dormitory accommodations are available for 175 men and 200 women.

Library Facilities. The Library-Learning Center contains over 58,000 volumes including the Wesleyana Collection.

Religious Services/Activities. Students are expected to be present at daily chapel exercises and all students are encouraged to attend the annual missions convention and the special emphasis services conducted once each semester. Attendance at this convention and these services is required of resident students.

Degree Programs

The concentration in Bible requires 36 hours of specified courses and 18 more hours in Bible including Greek Bible. These must include at least nine hours in Old Testament and nine hours in New Testament. The concentration in Theology requires 33 hours, including 12 hours of doctrinal studies, 12 hours of pastoral studies, and 9 hours of historical studies. Additional electives are required for ordination in The Wesleyan Church. The concentration in Christian Education requires 33 hours and the concentration in New Testament Greek requires 42 hours in Bible and 18 hours of Greek Bible.

Claflin College
Department of Religion and Philosophy
College Avenue, N.E.
Orangeburg, SC 29115   (803) 534-2710

Administration. Dr. Douglas Johnson, Chairman, Department of Religion and Philosophy.

General Description. The Department of Religion and Philosophy aims to serve as an integrated force in the college curriculum and to educate an informed laity. It offers undergraduate preparation for preseminarians and others interested in professional service in the church. The Bachelor of Arts degree is offered.

Parent Institution. Claflin College was founded in 1869 and is privately controlled by the United Methodist Church. It offers the Bachelor of Arts and Bachelor of Science degrees in the various liberal arts and sciences disciplines.

Community Environment. The 25-acre campus is located near the business district of Orangeburg in an agricultural area of South Carolina.

Religious Denomination. United Methodist Church.

Accreditation. Southern Association of Colleges and Schools.

Term System. Semester.

Admission Requirements. High school graduation or equivalent; SAT or ACT.

Tuition and Fees. Tuition $1,174 per semester; room and board $183-$190 per month; general fees $233.

Financial Aid. Assistance is available in the form of scholarships, loans, grants, and employment.

Housing. Dormitories are available on campus.

Library Facilities. The Hubert Vernon Manning Library houses over 72,000 volumes.

Religious Services/Activities. The Director of Religious Life assists in organizing and coordinating the religious programs of the college. Emphasis is placed upon chapel and church attendance.

Degree Programs

The major in Religion and Philosophy requires the completion of 24 hours of prescribed courses. A total of 124-126 semester hours is required for the Bachelor of Arts degree.

Columbia Bible College
7435 Monticello Road
Columbia, SC 29203   (803) 754-4100

Administration. Robertson McQuilkin, President; Edward B. Germann, Director of Enrollment Development.

General Description. Columbia Bible College is a private, coeducational institution offering professional training for Christian Service. The curriculum and community life of the school are designed to provide a dynamic context in which the student is assisted and encouraged to know Christ, know the Bible by gaining mastery of its content and understanding of its meaning and application, and to know the people and culture to be reached by the gospel.

The College was founded in 1923 as Columbia Bible School, offering a two-year course in biblical studies. In 1927 the College occupied its former campus in downtown Columbia and moved to its present location in 1960. Many of the more than 9,000 alumni serve in Christian ministries today in more than 100 countries.

Community Environment. The College is located on a modern 350-acre campus on the edge of metropolitan Columbia. An outstanding characteristic of the campus is the environment of uncluttered forestry, a lake, and the Broad River.

Religious Denomination. Nondenominational.

Religious Emphasis. Evangelical.

Accreditation. Southern Association of Colleges and Schools; American Association of Bible Colleges.

Term System. Quarter; summer term.

Enrollment in Degree Programs in Religion 1984–85. Total 559; men 330, women 229.

Degrees in Religion Awarded 1984–85. Bachelor of Arts in Biblical Studies 107; men 64, women 43. Associate of Arts in Biblical Studies 13; men 3, women 10.

Faculty for Degree Programs in Religion. Total 21; full-time 19, part-time 2.

Admission Requirements. High school diploma or GED; SAT; definite Christian conversion.

Tuition and Fees. Tuition $3,300 per year; room and board $2,175 per year; registration, medical, and activity fees approximately $100.

Financial Aid. Financial aid is available in the form of

grants, work-study, federal programs, some state programs, and sponsorship by foundations.

Housing. On-campus dormitories for single students; Mobile Home Village on campus for married students.

Library Facilities. The library has holdings of 68,300 books.

Religious Services/Activities. The College practices a lifestyle that is aimed at helping the student to understand and apply the implications of scriptural standards. Personal godliness should be the aim of every student. A time is set aside daily for personal fellowship with God. Daily chapel services and monthly days of prayer provide opportunity for inspiration, fellowship, and spiritual growth. Students associate themselves with a local church of their choosing for fellowship and service. Sunday is a day of worship, rest, and ministry, free from recreation, work, and study.

The Student Foreign Missions Fellowship gives students the opportunity to investigate missions as a career or to receive information and inspiration concerning world missions. Geographical prayer groups meet regularly to learn about and pray for missions in specific areas of the world.

Degree Programs

The Bachelor of Arts and Bachelor of Science degrees are offered through nine programs. The curriculum of Columbia Bible College differs from the usual Christian liberal arts college curriculum in the proportion of time devoted to the study of the Bible and to the study of man. Here the chief study is the Bible, and the secondary study is that of man. It also differs in the approach to communication skills, in that these are essential for all training for a church-related vocation. In order to allow for variation according to different gifts and callings, Columbia Bible College provides nine sequences in the curricula: Missions Minor, Pastoral Ministries Minor, Christian Education Minor, Church Music Major and Minor, Church Music-Christian Education Minor, General Ministries Minor, Pre-Seminary Minor, Bible Teaching Minor, and Elementary Education Major and Minor. In each of the curricula is a common core of subjects that includes English, Bible, theology, communication skills, and certain other courses deemed essential to all Christian workers.

Special Programs

The Associate of Arts program is offered for those who desire to obtain a basic understanding of the Bible, the principles of Bible interpretation, and the essential tool and background courses.

Erskine College
Erskine Theological Seminary
P.O. Box 171
Due West, SC 29639   (803) 379-8885

Administration. Dr. William Bruce Ezell, Jr., President; Dr. Jimmy Knight, Vice President and Dean of the College; Dr. Randall T. Ruble, Vice President and Dean of the Theological Seminary.

General Description. Erskine Theological Seminary offers a three-year post-graduate curriculum leading to the Master of Divinity degree. Its purpose is to provide studies leading to ordination. While the Seminary is conducted under the auspices of the Associate Reformed Presbyterian Church and has a special obligation to equip men for the ministry in that church, it admits persons of Christian character from other Christian denominations. The Seminary also offers the Doctor of Ministry degree.

Parent Institution. Founded in 1839, Erskine College is the oldest private college in South Carolina. It is a church-related liberal arts institution, operated by the Associate Reformed Presbyterian Church. Through its undergraduate Department of Bible, Religion, and Philosophy, the College offers a major in Bible and Religion and one in Christian Education both leading to the Bachelor of Arts degree.

Community Environment. Erskine College is in Due West, a town of 1,350 residents located in historic Abbeyville County, South Carolina, an area rich in colonial, Revolutionary War, and Civil War history. The town and college, with a number of antebellum buildings, are listed in the National Register of Historical Places. Erskine is near a number of lakes and recreational areas. The 85-acre campus is divided into east and west sections connected by a mall.

Religious Denomination. Associate Reformed Presbyterian.

Religious Emphasis. Reformed.

Accreditation. Southern Association of Colleges and Schools; Association of Theological Schools in the United States and Canada.

Term System. Four-one-four; summer term.

Enrollment in Degree Programs in Religion 1984–85. Total 134; men 114, women 20.

Degrees in Religion Awarded 1984–85. Master of Divinity 21; men 18, women 3. Doctor of Ministry 3; men 3.

Faculty for Degree Programs in Religion. Total 16; full-time 9, part-time 7.

Admission Requirements. Master of Divinity: Baccalaureate degree from an accredited college. Doctor of Ministry: Bachelor's and Master's degrees with a B average.

Tuition and Fees. Tuition Master of Divinity $80 per semester hour, Doctor of Ministry $90 per semester hour; dormitory $1,150 per year for seminary students.

Financial Aid. Assistance is available and is based on demonstrated need.

Housing. Dormitory accommodations for single students; no campus housing for married students.

Library Facilities. The McCain Library houses a collection of over 110,000 volumes. The Erskine Theological Seminary collection contains more than 30,000 volumes in theology and related fields.

Religious Services/Activities. The Student Christian Association is open to all students. Each year, a Christian Emphasis Week is observed on the campus with a program of speakers, music, and films. Convocations are held each Monday and Wednesday. Campus Fellowship and other worship and Bible study groups meet periodically. A Foreign Missions Fellowship provides college and seminary students an opportunity to learn about service in this field. Several denominations sponsor groups at Erskine. The faculty and students are welcomed into the membership of local churches.

Degree Programs

The Master of Divinity degree requires completion of 90 semester hours in the areas of Bible, Theology, Church History, and Ministry. It is a three-year program.

The Doctor of Ministry degree requires the completion of 36 semester hours and a project dissertation.

Special Programs

The Seminary sponsors an extensive program of continuing education.

Furman University
Department of Religion
Poinsett Highway
Greenville, SC 29613   (803) 233-5386

Administration. Dr. Robert Wilson Crapps, Chairman, Department of Religion.

General Description. In keeping with the liberal arts tradition, the Department of Religion offers a major including studies in Bible, Christian history and thought, religion and literature, world religions, psychology of religion, and Christian education. The specific courses of the major are agreed upon in conference with the student's departmental advisor.

Parent Institution. Furman University was founded in 1826 and is affiliated with the South Carolina Baptist Convention. It is a liberal arts college committed to Christian ideals and offers programs in a variety of disciplines.

Community Environment. The 750-acre campus is located in Greenville, a city of diverse industries.

Religious Denomination. South Carolina Baptist Convention.

Accreditation. Southern Association of Colleges and Schools.

Term System. Semester (3-2-3 plan).

Admission Requirements. High school graduation with completion of 18 units including 4 English, 3 mathematics, 2 science, 2 foreign language, 3 social studies, SAT.

Tuition and Fees. Tuition $5,984 per year; room $1,328-$1,440; board $1,472-$1,608.

Financial Aid. Furman's program of financial assistance includes scholarships, employment on campus, grants, and loans.

Housing. The University maintains traditional residence halls for men and women.

Library Facilities. The James Buchanan Duke Library contains more than 290,000 volumes, including the South Carolina Collection and the Baptist Historical Collection.

Religious Services/Activities. The Religious Council provides coordination for the religious organizations of many denominational groups on the campus. A service of worship, led by the University Chaplains, is held each Sunday morning in the Watkins Student Center.

Degree Programs

The major in Religion leading to the Bachelor of Arts degree requires the completion of eight courses and must include Religions of the World. A program of study is also available which is designed for those who wish to work with elementary and youth programs of the church.

The educational program at Furman provides opportunities for students who wish to prepare for the various aspects of Christian ministry. In general, for church-related vocations, students should expect to major in Religion.

Limestone College
Department of Religion
College Drive
Gaffney, SC 29340   (803) 489-7151

General Description. Limestone College is a privately supported, coeducational, liberal arts college founded in 1845. It is an institution that historically is grounded in the Western ideals of higher education, the democratic principles of government, and the Judeo-Christian philosophy of moral responsibility. The college grants the Bachelor's degree and will coordinate programs for students who plan to enter religious vocations.

Community Environment. The campus consists of 23 buildings on 115 acres and is located in Gaffney, a city of diversified industries and a surrounding agricultural area.

Religious Denomination. Nondenominational.

Accreditation. Southern Association of Colleges and Schools.

Term System. Semester.

Admission Requirements. High school graduation; ACT or SAT; non-high school graduates considered.

Tuition and Fees. Tuition $2,480 per semester; room and board $1,070-$1,120.

Financial Aid. Grants, scholarships, loans, and work-study programs are available.

Housing. Men's and women's dormitories are available as well as some accommodations for families.

Library Facilities. The A.J. Eastwood library has a collection of over 73,000 volumes.

Degree Programs

The major in Religion leading to the Bachelor of Arts degree requires 30 hours of Religion. Students pursuing this major are encouraged to strengthen their program of study by taking courses in several supporting disciplines and at least one foreign language.

Lutheran Theological Southern Seminary
4201 North Main Street
Columbia, SC 29203   (803) 786-5150

Administration. Dr. Mack C. Branham, Jr., President; Dr. Paul T. Jersild, Dean, Academic Affairs; Dr. Martin F. Saarinen, Director of Doctor of Ministry Program and Continuing Education.

General Description. The purpose of Lutheran Theological Southern Seminary is education for the church's ministry, primarily in the Lutheran Church in America, including theological preparation for ordained and lay ministry and continuing theological education of laity and clergy. This theological education is evangelical in content, relevant to contemporary society, and ecumenical in scope, with the intent of developing persons to become spiritually mature, theologically competent, and ethically sensitive within an inclusive and caring community. Special emphasis is given to preparing men and women for the parish ministry. The Seminary's basic degree program, the Master of Divinity is devoted to this purpose. The Seminary also offers the Master of Arts in Religion degree for persons who are preparing to be lay professionals in the Church and for others in non-professional religious studies. The Doctor of Ministry degree, a professional doctorate, provides advanced studies for persons who have completed the first professional degree in ministry and are employed full time in a ministry setting.

Parent Institution. The Lutheran Church in America, with headquarters in New York City, owns and operates nine theological seminaries through its synods.

Community Environment. Lutheran Theological Southern Seminary is located in Columbia, the capital city of South Carolina. It occupies a beautiful campus at the northern edge of the city, in the residential community of Eau Claire. Columbia, a rapidly growing business center, is a natural stop-over point for north-south travel. Columbia is a city of strikingly beautiful homes, churches, schools, and colleges. Its garden trails lure hundreds of visitors in azalea time. There are 15 Lutheran churches in the Columbia area and at least fifty within a 50-mile radius of the city.

Religious Denomination. Lutheran Church in America.

Religious Emphasis. Strong confessional emphasis

shaped by the Reformation heritage.

Accreditation. Southern Association of Colleges and Schools; Association of Theological Schools in the United States and Canada.

Term System. Semester; 2-week summer term.

Enrollment in Degree Programs in Religion 1984–85. Total 158; men 125, women 33.

Degrees in Religion Awarded 1984–85. Master of Arts in Religion 9; men 6, women 3. Master of Divinity 24; men 20, women 4.

Faculty for Degree Programs in Religion. Total 20; full-time 14, part-time 6.

Admission Requirements. Bachelor's degree; statement from applicant's denominational officials approving the applicant as a student for the ministry; physician's certificate indicating the applicant's physical ability to pursue theological studies.

Tuition and Fees. Tuition for Lutheran students $1,840 per year, non-Lutheran $2,785 per year, part-time $94.50 per semester hour; internship $400; room and board $1,-608 to $1,878; married student apartments $170 to $205.

Financial Aid. The amount of assistance given to each student making application for aid will be determined by the student's need, the number of students applying, and the funds available.

Housing. Rooms for single students are provided in the dormitory; apartments and some houses available for married students.

Library Facilities. The library houses a collection of over 87,000 volumes and 450 periodicals. The library also houses a special collection in Southern Lutheran Church History.

Religious Services/Activities. Daily chapel services are held. The service of Holy Communion is offered each full week of the school year.

Degree Programs

The Master of Divinity degree is a first professional degree which is earned by completion of a four-year curriculum. Three years are spent in residence in courses, field education, and in other learning situations. One year is spent in a supervised internship setting, which is normally a congregation. The curriculum is designed to prepare persons for ordained ministry.

The Master of Arts in Religion degree can be earned after two years of study. Students design their own curricula with the aid of faculty advisors. Persons who desire to study theology without specific career goals or who seek certification as lay ministers within their denominations would normally enroll in this degree program.

The Doctor of Ministry Degree is a second professional degree that can be sought by all persons who have earned the Master of Divinity degree (or its equivalent) and who have two years of experience in ministry. The program includes both on-campus and off-campus units and can be completed in three years. The purpose of the degree is to provide recognition of superior competence in the practice

of ministry. The program enables the participant to develop and implement a self-guided "Learning Plan" based on an issue which is integral to one's ministry.

Special Programs

The Academy of Bible and Theological Studies for clergy and laity is a continuing education program of the Seminary. It offers short courses and workshops in the summer, fall, and spring.

Morris College
Department of Religion Education
North Main Street
Sumter, SC 29150   (803) 775-9371

Administration. Luns C. Richardson, President.

General Description. From its beginning in 1908, Morris College has been a center for training ministers and teachers for the pulpits and schools of the state and the nation. The College offers programs of study leading to the baccalaureate degree with major programs in various disciplines in the liberal arts. It is operated by the Baptist Education and Missionary Convention of South Carolina.

Community Environment. The campus has 12 buildings on 44 acres on the north side of the city of Sumter, 45 miles east of Columbia, the state capital.

Religious Denomination. Baptist Education and Missionary Convention of South Carolina.

Accreditation. Southern Association of Colleges and Schools.

Term System. Semester.

Enrollment in Degree Programs in Religion 1984–85. Total 5.

Admission Requirements. High school graduation with 18 units including 4 English, 2 mathematics, 1 science, and 3 social science; non-high school graduates considered.

Tuition and Fees. Tuition $1,331 per semester; room $393.50; board $498.50.

Financial Aid. Assistance is offered to the extent that funds are available for grants, loans, and a limited number of scholarships.

Housing. Students reside in campus dormitories or off campus with permission.

Library Facilities. The L.C. Richardson - W.A. Johnson Learning Resources Center contains the College's library collection of over 37,000 volumes and its media facilities.

Degree Programs

The Department of Religious Education offers a program of study with a major in Religious Education leading to the Bachelor of Arts degree. It requires 58 hours in general education, 30 hours in the major, 12 hours from prescribed courses, and 24 hours in electives.

Newberry College
College Street
Newberry, SC 29108 (803) 276-6974

Administration. Paul Tilquist, President.

General Description. Newberry College was founded in 1856 and is privately supported by the South Carolina, Southeastern, and Florida Synods of the Lutheran Church in America. Its purpose is to provide students with opportunities for liberal and culturally relevant education enriched by a clear consciousness of Christian values. This purpose underlies an academic program that endeavors to combine the broad base of the liberal arts with preparation for careers in a number of specialized fields. The Bachelor's degree is awarded.

Community Environment. The 60-acre campus is located in Newberry, a city with a population of approximately 10,000. It is 40 miles northwest of Columbia, the state capital.

Religious Denomination. Lutheran Church in America.

Accreditation. Southern Association of Colleges and Schools.

Term System. Semester.

Admission Requirements. High school graduation or equivalent; ACT or SAT.

Tuition and Fees. Tuition $4,700 per academic year; general fee $300; room $950-$1,050; board $1,350.

Financial Aid. Need is the primary factor in determining the amount of financial aid a student receives.

Housing. Dormitories and fraternity/sorority houses are available on campus.

Library Facilities. The Wessels Library houses over 80,000 volumes. It maintains a special collection of historical documents pertaining to Lutheranism.

Religious Services/Activities. The College Chaplain serves as the campus worship leader as well as providing both formal and informal ministry of counseling. Worship services are conducted each Sunday and Tuesday morning. Holy Communion is offered twice each month on Thursday mornings. Worship and study are also vital parts of the weekly denominational group meetings.

Degree Programs

A major in Religion and Philosophy requires, in addition to the Core curriculum, 27 hours of department courses including at least two Religion courses and at least three Philosophy courses. The major is designed so that the student may weight his studies on the side of religion or philosophy according to his interest.

Students who expect to become pastors or to serve churches in other full-time positions should plan to enroll in a seminary or divinity school after graduation from Newberry College. The pre-theological student is advised to take courses in English literature, Greek, history, philosophy, psychology, religion, sociology, and speech.

Presbyterian College
Department of Religion
Clinton, SC 29325 (803) 833-2820

Administration. Dr. Kenneth Bradley Orr, President; Kenneth N. Creel, Acting Dean.

General Description. The Department of Religion offers a program of study leading to the Bachelor of Arts degree with a major in Religion. A concentration in Christian Education is also available.

Parent Institution. Presbyterian College is a fully accredited, four-year institution of higher learning with a program of liberal arts and sciences designed to develop the full capacity of each student. The College is related to the Presbyterian Synod of the Southeast (Georgia and South Carolina) which supports the school and provides direction through the board of trustees.

The College had its beginning in 1880 when it was founded as Clinton College. In 1890, the name was changed to Presbyterian College of South Carolina. In 1904, the College came under the full control of the South Carolina Synod.

Community Environment. Presbyterian College is a located in Clinton, a progressive city of 10,000 located in the heart of the South Carolina Piedmont. The campus is situated on an oak-shaded 175-acre campus within the corporate limits of Clinton. The campus has 20 major buildings of Georgian colonial-style architecture built around two central plazas, east and west. Oaks predominate, but the great variety of trees and rare shrubs is arranged to assure grounds of beauty throughout the year.

Religious Denomination. Presbyterian.

Accreditation. Southern Association of Colleges and Schools. Member of: Association of Presbyterian Colleges.

Term System. Semester; two summer sessions.

Degrees in Religion Awarded 1984–85. Bachelor of Arts 8; men 3, women 5.

Faculty for Degree Programs in Religion. Total 6; full-time 4; part-time 2.

Admission Requirements. Completion of a four-year high school course of study (four units of English; two or more units of foreign language; three units of mathematics; two or more units of laboratory science; two or more units of history and the social sciences).

Tuition and Fees. Charges for the school year include tuition $4,555; general fee $365; room rent and service $1,050; meals $1,250.

Financial Aid. The College offers a variety of scholarships, grants-in-aid, work opportunities, and loan funds to help defray expenses.

Housing. All students are required to live in the College-provided facilities with these exceptions: (1) seniors, who are free, with the concurrence of their parents, to make their own arrangements; (2) students who have homes in Clinton or the near vicinity; (3) students who live with relatives; and (4) married students.

Library Facilities. The library houses a total of 135,000

volumes of which 13,031 are in the field of Religion.

Religious Services/Activities. Students are encouraged to worship and participate regularly in the life of a local church of their choice within the community. The churches of Clinton extend a warm welcome. On campus, in addition to the classroom Bible instruction, religious leaders address the student body on occasion. Special worship services call the entire college community to worship together. Student fellowship groups meet regularly for mutual encouragement and growth in Christian maturity. An ordained minister serves as chaplain and is available to all students who need his counsel.

Degree Programs

The Bachelor of Arts with a major in Religion requires the completion of the general education requirement, basic courses in Religion, 30 additional hours in Religion, and six hours in a related field to be approved by the advisor. The concentration in Christian Education requires basic courses, 15 hours of Christian education courses, 15 hours in religion, plus 6 hours in a related field. A pre-theological student should schedule at least six hours of Greek and will usually major in Religion or Religion and Philosophy. Where a pre-theological student selects a different major, a member of the Department of Religion and will be designated by the academic dean to serve, in addition to the major advisor, as a second advisor to keep his program pointed toward graduate study in theology.

All students of Presbyterian College are required to take six hours of religion as part of the general education program.

South Carolina, University of
Department of Religious Studies
Columbia, SC 29526   (803) 347-3161

Administration. Donald L. Jones, Chairman, Department of Religious Studies.

General Description. The major in religious studies is provided for students seeking a broad liberal arts education focused on the study of religion as an academic discipline and its relation to other fields of study. This is ordinarily accomplished through a program of interdisciplinary study developed in close consultation between the departmental faculty and the individual student. In each case the purpose is to provide an integrated program that will meet the needs and interests of the particular student by including in the major-cognate sequence appropriate courses. Such a program can provide a foundation for graduate study on the part of those interested in the teaching of religion or any of the various religious vocations.

Parent Institution. Chartered in 1801 as South Carolina College, the University of South Carolina is among the oldest state universities. It is a publicly supported coeducational institution serving the state through a statewide university system, with the Columbia campus as its center

and additional University and four-year campuses located throughout the state.

Community Environment. The main 242-acre campus is located in downtown Columbia, the state capital.

Religious Denomination. None.

Accreditation. Southern Association of Colleges and Schools.

Term System. Semester.

Admission Requirements. High school diploma or equivalent (GED); entrance examinations required.

Tuition and Fees. Tuition resident $720 per semester, nonresident $1,485; University fee $89.50; room and board $1,277.

Financial Aid. Scholarships, grants, loans, and part-time employment are available to undergraduate students.

Housing. A variety of residence hall accommodations is available.

Library Facilities. The University libraries in Columbia house over 7 million process items including 2 million volumes and approximately 2 million units in microform.

Religious Services/Activities. Students are invited to participate in a wide range of religious activities on campus. Several denominations provide religious centers with full-time chaplains.

Degree Programs

The basic degree requirements in Religious Studies are 53-54 hours in general education, 24-18 hours in upper division Religious Studies courses including an Advanced Project, 12-18 hours in cognates, and electives. The Bachelor of Arts degree requires a total of 120 hours.

Southern Methodist College
760 Broughton Street
P.O. Box 1027
Orangeburg, SC 29116   (803) 534-7826

Administration. Charles O. Bennett, President.

General Description. Southern Methodist College offers the Bachelor of Arts degree in religion through the following majors: Bible, Christian Ministries, Missions, and Christian Education. Each major is offered to the student who desires a concentration in his/her chosen field and who is strongly considering graduate studies. The Master of Biblical Studies is a fifth-year program providing further preparation for the Christian worker who wishes to perform professional ministry tasks more effectively.

Parent Institution. The basic mission of Southern Methodist College is to provide a quality Christian education which meets the vocational, emotional, physical, social, intellectual, and spiritual needs of the Christian public in the South. A special emphasis is given to training individuals in a Wesleyan-Arminian perspective for the ministries of the Christian Church.

Community Environment. The College occupies one of the most attractive sites in the city of Orangeburg and is located on a beautiful 20-acre tract of rolling land. Orangeburg is in an agricultural and dairying area. Its industries include textiles, wood products, meat packing, chemicals, and baking goods. This is a suburban community with a temperate climate. Orangeburg is about 40 miles south of Columbia, the state capital.

Religious Denomination. Southern Methodist Church.

Religious Emphasis. Wesleyan-Arminian (Fundamental).

Accreditation. Licensed by the state of South Carolina.

Term System. Semester; summer term.

Enrollment in Degree Programs in Religion 1984–85. Total 49; men 31, women 18.

Degrees in Religion Awarded 1984–85. Bachelor of Christian Ministries 1; men 1. Bachelor of Arts in Missions 1; women 1. Bachelor of Arts in Christian Education 2; women 2. Master of Biblical Studies 2; men 2.

Faculty for Degree Programs in Religion. Total 5; fulltime 4, part-time 1.

Admission Requirements. High school diploma; health certificate.

Tuition and Fees. Tuition $650 per semester; matriculation fee $60 per semester; library fee $25; part-time students $60 per semester hour; room and board $850 per semester.

Financial Aid. Every full-time student enrolled at the College is eligible to apply for financial aid which is granted on the basis of financial need, scholastic ability, and promise of future growth and service. Aid is available as scholarships, work scholarships, and loans.

Housing. Dormitory housing is available for single students; married student housing in a mobile home cluster is available with lot rent of $25 per month (unit rent varies).

Library Facilities. The Corbett Library houses a collection of 16,000 volumes.

Religious Services/Activities. Attendance is required at Chapel, held each day Monday through Friday. Although no Sunday services are conducted on campus, each dormitory student is required to attend Sunday School and Morning Worship locally. Student prayer meeting is held each week under the direction of Gamma Alpha Bible Society. Annual events include Bible Conference, Spring Retreat, Missions Emphasis Week, and Christian Education Week.

Degree Programs

The Bachelor of Arts in Bible, Christian Ministries, Christian Education, Missions, English, History, and Social Studies is offered at the College. Students earning the Bachelor of Arts degree will take a major of at least 30 semester hours in one of the divisions and a minor of at least 24 semester hours. A course in Bible must be elected each semester by all students.

The Master of Biblical Studies degree is intended to further prepare the Christian worker through intensive study in Bible and related areas so that he may perform professional ministry tasks more effectively. It will also help the minister complete the Conference Course of Study for Elder's orders in the Southern Methodist Church.

Special Programs

The Associate of Arts degree in Bible is also offered. The program is designed to present a concentrated study of the Bible for those who wish to expand their Biblical knowledge.

The One Year Certificate of Biblical Studies is designed to provide a basic, Biblical education for a high school graduate who desires a Biblical foundation for life before pursuing a career, or technical training, or a university education.

Wofford College
Department of Religion
North Church Street
Spartanburg, SC 29301   (803) 585-4821

Administration. Dr. Joab M. Lesesne, Jr., President; Dr. Dan B. Maultsby, Dean of the College and Vice President for Academic Affairs; Dr. John M. Bullard, Chairman, Department of Religion.

General Description. The Department of Religion is an undergraduate department offering introductory and advanced courses in a liberal arts curriculum to students wishing to view religion as an element in human culture preserving cherished values. The Department always has offered pre-seminary, pre-professional religious instruction to students intending to continue their work in accredited theological seminaries, many of whom have earned high distinction in the Christian ministry.

Parent Institution. Wofford College is a 4-year liberal arts college founded in 1854 by a Methodist minister who bequeathed $100,000 for the purpose of establishing and endowing it for the benefit of area youth. Since 1973, it has been coeducational and, since 1962, has maintained an enrollment of 1,000 students. It is the only college in South Carolina with a chapter of Phi Beta Kappa (the University of South Carolina and Furman University are the only other chapters), and Wofford's chapter dates back to 1940. Religion and Bible have been stressed in the College's curriculum since the very beginnings. The College is supported by the South Carolina Conference of the United Methodist Church.

Community Environment. One of the leading textile manufacturing cities in the South, Spartanburg is also one of the largest peach shipping centers of the world. The city was named after the Spartan Regiment which represented this community in the Revolutionary War. The community is located in the Piedmont section of South Carolina and has an average temperature of 60 degrees.

Religious Denomination. United Methodist.

Religious Emphasis. Liberal and Neo-Orthodox.

Accreditation. Southern Association of Colleges and Schools.

Term System. Semester, plus January Interim Term (4-1-4); two summer sessions.

Enrollment in Degree Programs in Religion 1984–85. Total 27; men 23, women 4.

Degrees in Religion Awarded 1984–85. Bachelor of Arts 8; men 5, women 3.

Faculty for Degree Programs in Religion. Total 6; full-time 4, part-time 2.

Admission Requirements. Admission is based on predicted success in college work determined by rank in high school class, scores on verbal and math portions of the Scholastic Aptitude Tests (SAT), and overall academic record. Promise of leadership and service are also considered.

Tuition and Fees. Comprehensive Fee per academic year of approximately $8,000 for boarding students and $5,175 for commuting students.

Financial Aid. Very generous financial aid packages make attendance at Wofford a realistic possibility for nearly all qualified students.

Housing. Dormitory space in air-conditioned buildings is available to all students.

Library Facilities. The Wofford library collections are housed in the Sandor Teszler Library. There are more than 220,000 volumes including 3,800 periodicals and microforms. Also housed in the library are 20,000 rare books including holdings in hymnology, Bible polyglots, printing, and several holdings from the 16th and 17th centuries. Also housed in the library are the records and historical material of the South Carolina Conference of the United Methodist Church.

Religious Services/Activities. Wofford College strives to create an atmosphere congenial to the development of Christian character. Students receive encouragement and guidance from the faculty, worship services, religious programs, and frequent public lectures, periods of religious emphasis, and the activities of student religious organizations.

Degree Programs

The Bachelor of Arts degree with a major in Religion requires the completion of 124 semester hours with 24 semester hours in Religion (introductory courses, The Bible, Theology and Ethics, Religious Traditions, and advanced studies).

SOUTH DAKOTA

Augustana College
Department of Religion
29th and Summit Avenue
Sioux Falls, SD 57102   (605) 336-5516

Administration. Dr. Frederick Rusch, Chairman, Department of Religion.

General Description. The curriculum of the Department of Religion is designed to introduce students to the study of religion and to prepare them to respond creatively to their religious and theological heritage. Courses are offered in the areas of Biblical Studies, Church History, Theology and Ethics, World Religions, and Parish Ministries in an effort to inform students in the fundamentals of Christian faith and life and to acquaint them with major religions of the world. Students may choose a religion major in preparation for graduate study, for church-oriented vocations, or as a liberal arts major. The Bachelor degree is awarded.

Parent Institution. Augustana College is a liberal arts college of the American Lutheran Church. It was founded 1835. The name Augustana is drawn from the origin of the Lutheran Church in the Augsburg Confession in 1530 during the time of the Reformation.

Community Environment. The campus of the College contains 18 buildings on 100 acres. It is located in the city of Sioux Falls in the southeastern corner of South Dakota.

Religious Denomination. The American Lutheran Church.

Accreditation. North Central Association of Colleges and Schools.

Term System. Semester (4-1-4 plan).

Admission Requirements. High school graduation or the equivalent; ACT.

Tuition and Fees. Tuition $5,795 per year; room $1,116; board $1,075.

Financial Aid. The College provides financial assistance to promising and qualified students through scholarships, grants, campus work opportunities, and placement services.

Housing. Dormitory living accommodations are available on campus.

Library Facilities. The Mikkelsen Library houses over 185,000 volumes.

Religious Services/Activities. The activities of the Student Congregation are planned for the entire campus and include worship, mid-week communion, concerts, lectures, discussions, Bible study groups, outreach, and fellowship.

Dakota Wesleyan University
Religion/Philosophy Department
1200 West University Avenue
Mitchell, SD 57301   (605) 996-6511

Administration. Dr. James B. Beddow, President.

General Description. The Department of Religion and Philosophy provides the opportunity for the student to examine a broad range of spiritual and intellectual views of the nature of existence and of the principles for living a meaningful life. The programs have special value for those planning church-related vocations. Pre-theological students may major in Religion/Philosophy. The Department awards the Bachelor of Arts in Religion/Philosophy.

Parent Institution. Dakota Wesleyan University is a 4-year liberal arts institution related to the United Methodist Church. It offers the Bachelor degree.

Community Environment. Dakota Wesleyan's 40-acre campus is located in Mitchell, South Dakota (population 14,500), in the James River Valley. Mitchell is a trading and agricultural center.

Religious Denomination. United Methodist.

Religious Emphasis. Pluralistic.

Accreditation. North Central Association of Colleges and Schools.

Term System. Semester; summer term.

Degrees in Religion Awarded 1984–85. Bachelor of Arts in Religion-Philosopgy 1; men 1.

Faculty for Degree Programs in Religion. Total 2; full-time 1, part-time 1.

Admission Requirements. High school graduation or

GED; ACT score of 18.

Tuition and Fees. Total tuition, fees, room and board $6,330 per year.

Financial Aid. Contributions of generous donors, United Methodist Conference support, alumni gifts, and earnings from endowment are sources of assistance available to students. There are numerous scholarships, grants, and activity awards. Federal aid, state grants, loans, and employment are available.

Housing. Freshmen and sophomores are required to live on campus.

Library Facilities. The Layne Library houses 65,000 volumes.

Religious Services/Activities. The Religious Life Council works with the campus minister in programming religious activities on campus which include weekly chapel services, fellowship groups, outreach, social events, and social concerns. Both Protestant and Catholic worship services are held each week on campus.

Degree Programs

The major in Religion/Philosophy leading to the Bachelor of Arts degree requires no specific course requirements as a projected plan is designed with the Department staff. A total of 7 units in the major is required. Pre-theological students may take a major or minor in Relgion/Philosophy or in some other related department.

North American Baptist Seminary
1321 West 22nd Street
Sioux Falls, SD 57105   (605) 336-6588

Administration. Charles M. Hiatt, President; James Gordon Harris, III, Vice President for Academic Affairs.

General Description. A fully-accredited graduate professional school, North American Baptist Seminary began as Rochester Theological Seminary, Rochester, New York, in 1858. The school was moved in 1949 to Sioux Falls, South Dakota, and took its present name. The Seminary is owned and supported by the North American Baptist Conference. The Seminary offers a flexible curriculum, a 3-3 program in cooperation with nearby Sioux Falls College and Augustana College, by which students may shorten their normal college/seminary studies by 1 year. Students receive both the Bachelor of Arts and Master of Divinity degrees in a 6-year period. The 4-1-4 curriculum offers study programs in Israel, Japan, Africa, and Mexico. Also available for students is an opportunity to spend one year in an inner-city program in Chicago.

The Seminary offers three basic degree programs: The Master of Divinity (3-year program); the Master of Arts (2-year program) with specialties in Christian Education and Counseling; Religious Studies (non-degree, for the secular community). Also, the Doctor of Ministry degree is an "in-ministry" program designed for people with superior ability in the practice of ministry.

Community Environment. Sioux Falls is located in the southeastern corner of the state of South Dakota. It is the major cultural, educational, and commercial hub of the Great Plains area, with an estimated metropolitan population of 100,000. The advantages of progressive educational resources are available in Sioux Falls, with Augustana and Sioux Falls Colleges both within walking distance of the Seminary. Libraries of these two colleges are available to students of North American. In addition, North Central University Center, a community college without walls, has been developed by the two Colleges and the Seminary. Two universities, the University of South Dakota and South Dakota State University, are within an hour's drive.

Four distinct seasons make possible a variety of sports and hobbies. Sioux Falls has approximately 52 parks, a number of modern swimming pools, golf courses, tennis courts, skating rinks, picnic areas, and other recreational facilities. Programs of the Sioux Falls Symphony Orchestra, the Community Playhouse, and the Community Concert Series bring to the city outstanding artists and performers.

Religious Denomination. North American Baptist Conference.

Accreditation. North Central Association of Colleges and Schools; Association of Theological Schools in the United States and Canada.

Term System. Semester; no summer term.

Enrollment in Degree Programs in Religion 1984–85. Total 146; men 117, women 29. There are 34 men in the Doctoral program; 72 full-time men and 20 full-time women in degree programs; 11 part-time men and 9 part-time women in degree programs.

Degrees in Religion Awarded 1984–85. Doctor of Ministry 4; men 4. Master of Divinity 20; men 17, women 3. Master of Arts 12; men 8, women 4.

Faculty for Degree Programs in Religion. Total 16; full-time 15, part-time 1.

Admission Requirements. Application to a Master's level program at the Seminary includes the following requirements: (1) a Bachelor's degree with official transcripts; (2) a written testimony of Christian experience; and (3) a church letter of endorsement and letters of recommendation. Application data will be reviewed by the Admissions Committee.

Tuition and Fees. Tuition for full-time students $3,100 per year; application fee $20; commencement fee $25; health insurance required for all full-time students who are not members of a plan.

Financial Aid. Those students who are members of North American Baptist Conference Churches and intend to serve in NAB ministry for at least 3 years are eligible to apply for a $500 grant for the school year ($250 per semester). The Wesseler Fellowship Program attracts students with outstanding ministry potential to prepare for ministry within the NAB Conference. It is awarded to an incoming full-time student on or before June 1 of each year. The Guaranteed Student Loan program is available (loans can be made of up to $5,000 with an interest rate of 9 percent). There are a limited number of on-campus employment opportunities and secular employment is available in the community.

Housing. Ample and attractive housing in apartment buildings is available as well as an on-campus dormitory for male students.

Library Facilities. The library contains 56,480 volumes. Under development is a special collection entitled the James G. Harris Memorial Collection in Homiletics.

Religious Services/Activities. Chapel services are held three times each week. Students in professional programs are given field education assignments. The Annual Day of Prayer, Annual Week of Spiritual Renewal, and Annual Mission Conference are scheduled events. Weekly spiritual development groups are also organized.

Degree Programs

The Master of Divinity program is designed primarily to prepare the student for the pastoral ministry. There is sufficient flexibility in the program to equip the student for a variety of other church-related ministries, such as the chaplaincy and missionary service. The program normally requires study of one of the Biblical languages and provides sufficient academic stimulus to prepare capable students for continuation in graduate studies. The student must satisfactorily complete 94 semester hours with maintenance of a 2.25 grade point average.

The Master of Arts in Christian Education program seeks to prepare students to be qualified directors or ministers of Christian Education. It requires the completion of 62 semester hours including 27 hours in Christian Education.

The Master of Arts in Counseling program seeks to prepare students to actualize their God-given potential and gifts as healers in the role of counselor. The course of study will equip the student with a Biblical foundation, a meaningful Christian and counseling philosophy, coupled with counseling skills. The degree requires completion of 62 semester hours of work of which 27 hours must be in counseling or in an approved related field.

The Master of Arts in Religious Studies is a two-year program designed primarily for those who desire to prepare more adequately to serve God in the secular community. It may also be pursued as a basis for work toward advanced academic degrees in religion, a professional ministerial degree for those who are vocationally uncertain, or as a continuing education degree for those already in a ministry vocation. The degree program requires satisfactory completion of 60 semester hours of work and maintenance of a 2.25 grade point average.

The Doctor of Ministry program is professionally oriented and is designed for the continuing development of persons who have exhibited high ministerial and academic ability. It is an in-ministry program, primarily of the generalist variety, which seeks to integrate within the candidate academic excellence and competence in skills for the

various aspects and types of contemporary Christian ministry. The requirements for completion of the program include 30 credit hours of study, completion of a final written statement; and the completion of a graduation examination.

Special Programs

Evening courses are offered for laity each semester. Several continuing education unit courses are also offered. Distance learning courses are offered in several cities in the U.S. and Canada. An Israel travel course occurs biennially and a Japan course annually.

Sioux Falls College
Department of Religion and Philosophy
1501 South Prairie
Sioux Falls, SD 57105   (605) 331-5000

Administration. Dr. Owen P. Halleen, President; Dr. Dennis Tanner, Vice President for Academic Affairs.

General Description. The Department of Religion and Philosophy has as its goals for the Religious Studies major: (1) to provide students with a broad understanding of religious studies in their biblical, historical, theological, and philosophical aspects; (2) to prepare certain students for advanced study in seminaries and university graduate programs; (3) to present students with the opportunity to develop a Christian worldview. As for vocational applications, the Religious Studies major can be a foundation for graduate and professional training leading to careers in pastoral ministry, Christian education, missionary service, campus ministry, institutional chaplaincy, and teaching.

Parent Institution. Sioux Falls College is a Christian liberal arts institution affiliated with the American Baptist Churches in the U.S.A. and dedicated to providing a selection of associate, baccalaureate, and master degree programs in the liberal arts and selected professional disciplines.

Community Environment. Located in Sioux Falls, the largest city in South Dakota, the College's campus is in the residential section. At a population of 85,000, Sioux City is large enough to provide the entertainment and job possibilities of a city and small enough to retain the warmth and friendliness of its rural setting.

Religious Denomination. American Baptist Churches in the U.S.A.

Religious Emphasis. Evangelical.

Accreditation. North Central Association of Colleges and Schools.

Term System. Four-one-four (with January term).

Enrollment in Degree Programs in Religion 1984–85. Total 38; men 22, women 16.

Degrees in Religion Awarded 1984–85. Bachelor of Arts in Religious Studies 7; men 4, women 3. Bachelor of Arts in Pre-Seminary Studies 3; men 2, women 1.

Faculty for Degree Programs in Religion. Total 3; full-

time 2, part-time 1.

Admission Requirements. Top half of high school graduating class; ACT of 19 or SAT of 800.

Tuition and Fees. Comprehensive education fee $4,600;
room and board $2,296.

Financial Aid. Scholarship and grant funds are awarded
to promising and qualified students according to policy
and procedure established by the Faculty's Student Affairs
Committee. The College also cooperates with federal,
state, church, and private agencies in providing various
forms of scholarship, grant, loan, and work assistance.

Housing. Dormitory accommodations are available on
campus.

Library Facilities. The Norman B. Mears Library contains approximately 75,000 volumes and other learning
resources. Students also have access to the libraries of the
North American Baptist Seminary and Augustana College.

Religious Services/Activities. The College employs a
Chaplain responsible for directing and coordinating religious activities.

Degree Programs

In addition to the regular degree requirements of the
College, the major in Religious Studies leading to the
Bachelor of Arts degree requires at least 33 semester hours
of study that includes specific courses in religion and
philosophy. Students must maintain a 2.5 grade point average or higher in the courses for the major. Courses are
offered in the areas of Biblical Studies, Historical Studies,
and General Courses (Introduction to Ministry, Senior
Seminary, Independent Study in Religion).

A joint Bachelor of Arts and Master of Divinity program is offered by the College and the North American
Baptist Seminary.

Special Programs

An Associate of Arts in Religious Theatre program
seeks to enable the student to lay the foundation for a
career in religious education, the ministry, or the lay ministry.

TENNESSEE

American Baptist College
American Baptist Theological Seminary
1800 White's Creek Road
Nashville, TN 37207   (615) 262-3433

Administration. Dr. Odell McGlothian, Sr., President.

General Description. The founding of the American Baptist Theological Seminary was the result of an interracial venture undertaken cooperatively by the National Baptist Convention and the Southern Baptist Convention in the early 1900s. It is operated jointly by both groups through a Board of Trustees representing both conventions. The College specializes in training pastors, denominational workers, Christian education directors, and other Christian workers for Christian ministry. It offers two degree programs: the Bachelor of Arts and the Bachelor of Theology.

Community Environment. The campus occupies a 53-acre campus near the Cumberland River in Nashville, the capital of the state of Tennessee. Nashville is a national center of religious publishing activities.

Religious Denomination. National Baptist Convention, U.S.A., Inc. and Southern Baptist Convention.

Accreditation. American Association of Bible Colleges.

Term System. Semester.

Admission Requirements. High school graduation; SAT; three references.

Tuition and Fees. Tuition, room, and board $2,500 per year.

Financial Aid. The College provides some financial assistance to worthy students through scholarships, campus employment, grants, and loans.

Housing. Single students are housed in Griggs Hall. Apartments for married students are located on the lower end of the campus.

Library Facilities. The T.L. Holcomb Library houses over 24,000 volumes, including a large Biblical and Theological section. The library has a collection of Bibles in more than thirty languages.

Religious Services/Activities. The Baptist Student Union is a voluntary organization which promotes prayer, Bible study, local church membership, missions, and Christian fellowship. It sponsor a regular mid-week prayer service. Worship services or assemblies are held twice each week.

Degree Programs

The Bachelor of Arts program includes a core curriculum of 68 semester hours, a Biblical-Theological Studies major of 30 semester hours, a divisional minor of 20 semester hours plus 10 semester hours of open electives. The curriculum is grouped into four divisions: Biblical-Theological Studies; Church Vocations; Humanities; and General Education.

The Bachelor of Theology program is designed for those who do not anticipate seminary study and who want the fullest possible preparation that the institution offers. The fifth year makes possible greater depth in one of two main areas of study: Biblical-Theological Studies or Pastoral Studies-Missions. A baccalaureate degree is a prerequisite to this program.

Bethel College
Department of Religion
Cherry Street
McKenzie, TN 38201   (901) 352-5651

Administration. John N. Langfitt, Academic Dean, Professor of Religion; L.C. Waddle, Professor of Religion; William McDowell Ramsay, Hannibal Seagle Professor of Religion and Philosophy.

General Description. The Department of Religion offers programs with a major in Religion, a major in Christian Education, and a pre-seminary curriculum which provides the intellectual foundations essential to an effective theological education.

Parent Institution. Bethel College is the only college sponsored by the Cumberland Presbyterian Church. It is supported by the Church and in turn provides leadership in the denomination through its graduates. The College was founded in 1842 in McLemoresville (12 miles from McKenzie) by the West Tennessee Synod of the Cumberland Presbyterian Church. Granted a charter by the State of Tennessee in 1847, Bethel moved to its present site in 1872.

Community Environment. Situated in McKenzie, a town of 5,400, Bethel is halfway between Memphis and Nashville, 110 miles from each. The city of Jackson is 40 miles south and Paris Landing State Park on Kentucky Lake is 30 miles to the east. The college buildings are set on a 100-acre campus.

Religious Denomination. Cumberland Presbyterian Church.

Religious Emphasis. Reformed.

Accreditation. Southern Association of Colleges and Schools.

Term System. Quarter; 5-week summer term.

Enrollment in Degree Programs in Religion 1984–85. Total 25; men 19, women 6.

Degrees in Religion Awarded 1984–85. Bachelor of Arts 6; men 3, women 3.

Faculty for Degree Programs in Religion. Total 4; full-time 2, part-time 2.

Admission Requirements. ACT composite of 16 minimum or SAT 800 minimum; or in top half of high school graduating class; or a counselor's recommendation; or personal interview and recommendation by Bethel's Academic Dean.

Tuition and Fees. Costs per quarter: $950 for full-time student (12-17 hours); $30 per quarter hour above 17 hours; meals $380; room $225; fees are applied in some discipline areas.

Financial Aid. Scholarships, grants, and loans are available.

Housing. Dormitory facilities for single students; limited apartments for married students and/or apartments in McKenzie.

Library Facilities. The library houses 80,000 volumes with large holdings in Religion and Philosophy.

Religious Services/Activities. Weekly chapel; student vespers; Religion Majors Organization; quarterly conferences in College/Denominational Events.

Degree Programs

The Bachelor of Arts with a major in Religion or a major in Christian Education have the following goals: knowledge of what the Bible is, including its contents and basic teachings; ability to employ sound principles of interpretation in the study of the Bible; knowledge of the history of Christianity; ability to describe and evaluate basic Christian doctrines as variously interpreted and in comparison with other religions; knowledge of the basic concepts, goals, and methods of Christian Education; and preparation for graduate study in religion and Christian Education.

Bryan College
Division of Biblical Studies and Philosophy
Dayton, TN 37321   (615) 775-2041

Administration. Dr. Brian Richardson, Chairman, Division of Biblical Studies and Philosophy.

General Description. The curriculum of the Division of Biblical Studies and Philosophy has the specific responsibility to communicate Biblical, theological, and philosophical thought on the campus. The Division provides exegetical, doctrinal, and historical instruction in the content of scripture and instruction in its practical application so that the student will be led to a personal commitment and acceptance of a Biblically theistic, Christian view of the world. The Division has four departments: Ancient Languages, Bible, Christian Education, and Philosophy.

Parent Institution. Bryan College was founded in 1930 and is nonsectarian in character. It is a four-year Christian liberal arts college named after William Jennings Bryan who defended the authority of the Bible in the famed Scopes trial.

Community Environment. The 100-acre campus consists of 17 buildings and overlooks the Richland embayment of TVA Lake Chickamauga in the town of Dayton, 38 miles north of Chattanooga.

Religious Denomination. Nondenominational (Christian).

Accreditation. Southern Association of Colleges and Schools.

Term System. Semester.

Admission Requirements. High school graduation; ACT or SAT.

Tuition and Fees. Tuition $1,950 per semester; room $620; board $820.

Financial Aid. Assistance is provided through scholarships and grants, loans, and student employment.

Housing. The College has four main residence halls plus auxiliary housing for single students beyond the normal age for dormitory housing.

Library Facilities. The Ironside Memorial Library houses over 69,000 volumes. Special collections include the Rader Bible and Rare Book Collection, the William Jennings Bryan Mementos, and the Birch Arnold Memorial Library of Freedom Collection.

Religious Services/Activities. Men and women of Bryan are encouraged to attend Sunday school, prayer meetings, youth groups, and Sunday evening services in the local churches. Chapel programs with a spiritual emphasis are held. A Spiritual Life Conference, Missionary Conference, and Christian Life Conference are held as scheduled events.

Degree Programs

The major in Bible includes 31 semester hours of Bible plus collateral requirements in Philosophy, History, and Greek. The requirements for a major in Christian Education are 36 semester hours in core courses plus electives.

465

The requirements for a Christian Education-Church Music major are 24 hours of Christian Education and 29-35 hours of Music. The major areas lead to the Bachelor of Arts degree.

Carson-Newman College
Division of Religious Studies
Jefferson City, TN 37760   (615) 475-9061

Administration. Dr. William L. Blevins, Chairman, Division of Religious Studies.

General Description. The academic program of the Religious Studies Department is designed to consider, within a Christian context, questions of ultimate concern to people. The course of study centers upon the origin and development of Christianity. The six divisions of the curriculum are intended to provide majors with a broad exposure to several areas of religious studies. These include Biblical Studies, Baptist Studies, Discipleship Studies, Historical Studies, Theological Studies, and Practical Studies. The programs offered lead to the Bachelor of Arts degree.

Parent Institution. Carson-Newman College was founded in 1851 and is affiliated with the Southern Baptist Convention. It is a four-year, liberal arts college with a Christian commitment.

Community Environment. The campus of 88 acres contains 34 buildings in the town of Jefferson City, 30 miles east of Knoxville.

Religious Denomination. Southern Baptist Convention.

Accreditation. Southern Association of Colleges and Schools.

Term System. Semester.

Admission Requirements. High school graduation with rank in the upper 50 percent of graduating class; ACT score of 17 required; non-high school graduates may be considered under certain conditions.

Tuition and Fees. Tuition $2,000 per semester; room $350-$385; board $510-$535; student activity fee $25.

Financial Aid. Federal and state programs are available to assist students.

Housing. College residence halls are available.

Library Facilities. The library houses a collection of approximately 150,000 volumes, 1,000 journal and periodical titles, and numerous microforms.

Religious Services/Activities. Students are encouraged to become active in a local church. The Baptist Student Union sponsors activities such as weekly meetings, retreats, campus outreach, community ministries, discipleship groups, fellowships, and involvement in state and national conferences. The Ministerial Association is open to all students who plan to purse a career in vocational ministry.

Degree Programs

The major in Religion consists of 33 semester hours in the field and 3 hours in Philosophy. The major in Church

Recreation is an interdisciplinary program designed to train prospective ministers of church recreation for immediate employment or to provide a basis for graduate study in the field. The program involves several departments in the college but is directed by the Religion Department. The majors plus general education requirements lead to the Bachelor of Arts degree.

Covenant College
Biblical Studies Department
Lookout Mountain, TN 37350 (404) 820-1560

Administration. Dr. Martin Essenburg, President; Dr. Nicholas P. Barker, Vice President for Academic and Student Affairs; Dr. Donovan L. Graham, Dean of Faculty.

General Description. The goals of the Biblical Studies Department are: to provide the tools by which the student will gain increasing knowledge of the message and content of the Bible; to acquaint students with problems connected with Biblical scholarship and the content of Christian faith against the belief system of the modern world; to equip students with a basis on which to develop a consistent apologetic; to encourage students with apparent gifts and talents for the ministry to pursue such a calling. The Bachelor of Arts and the Associate of Arts degrees are awarded.

Parent Institution. Covenant College, a part of the Presbyterian Church in America, is dedicated to training Christian men and women; professional excellence in a Christian context is its goal. Covenant bases its liberal arts program on the Bible, the written Word of God.

Community Environment. The Covenant College campus is located on the very top of Lookout Mountain, in the town of Lookout Mountain, a suburban community that enjoys the cultural, recreational, and social facilities of nearby Chattanooga. The campus is actually just across the state border, in Georgia. Community facilities include churches of major denominations.

Religious Denomination. The Presbyterian Church in America.

Religious Emphasis. Reformed.

Accreditation. Southern Association of Colleges and Schools.

Term System. Semester; summer term is a 3-week session in May.

Enrollment in Degree Programs in Religion 1984–85. Total 40; men 33, women 7.

Degrees in Religion Awarded 1984–85. Bachelor of Arts 14; men 12, women 2. Associate of Arts 4; men 1, women 3.

Faculty for Degree Programs in Religion. Total 5; full-time 5.

Admission Requirements. A candidate for admission should have completed 15 units from an approved secondary school. The candidate should present marks of A,B, or C in secondary subjects with a combined score of 800

or higher in the SAT or a composite score of 17 or more in the ACT.

Tuition and Fees. Tuition $4,800 per year; fees $100 per year; average room and board $2,635 per year.

Financial Aid. Federally funded programs and institutionally funded academic scholarships, and church grants are among the types of assistance available.

Housing. Single freshmen, sophomores, and juniors are required to live on campus unless they are 21 years of age or older. One duplex is available for rent by married students. The Student Development Office will assist married students in finding off-campus housing.

Library Facilities. The library contains over 105,000 volumes and houses the T. Stanley Soltau Missions Collection and the Kresge Collection for Christian Learning.

Religious Services/Activities. There is a required daily chapel service. Outreach Ministries helps students become aware of ministries in the Chattanooga area. Some of the ministries students work with Young Life, Prison Ministries, and Bethany Christian Services.

Degree Programs

The Biblical Studies Department offers a variety of courses in theology, missions, and Bible "book study" courses, and also offers two years of Greek. A Pre-Ministerial Studies program leading to the Bachelor of Arts degree requires a minimum of 126 hours and a grade point average of 2.0. Students may select any of several majors, including Biblical Studies and Missions.

Special Programs

The Associate of Arts degree may be obtained in Biblical Studies.

David Lipscomb College
Department of Bible
3901 Granny White Pike
Nashville, TN 37203   (615) 385-3855

Administration. Howard Horton, Chairman, Department of Bible.

General Description. David Lipscomb College is a Christian, coeducational, liberal arts college offering three degrees: Bachelor of Arts, Bachelor of Science, and the Master of Arts. The Department of Bible offers majors with emphases in Biblical Languages, Missions, Preaching, Religious Education, and Youth Ministry. The Master of Arts in Bible is offered in its graduate program. All students in the College must take daily Bible courses.

Parent Institution. The College is affiliated with the Church of Christ. It had its beginning as the Nashville Bible School in 1891 and bore that name until 1918.

Community Environment. The campus is located in a residential area near Harpeth Hills just south of Nashville, Tennessee.

Religious Denomination. Churches of Christ.

Accreditation. Southern Association of Colleges and Schools.

Term System. Quarter.

Admission Requirements. High school graduation; GED accepted for students over 18 years of age; ACT required.

Tuition and Fees. Tuition $64 per quarter hour; general fee $55; room and board $732.50 per semester.

Financial Aid. The financial aid program includes scholarships, grants, loans, and employment.

Housing. There are four residence halls for women and two for men.

Library Facilities. The library houses over 147,000 volumes.

Religious Services/Activities. Attendance at daily chapel services is required.

Degree Programs

All candidates for Bachelor degrees must complete a minimum of 198 quarter hours including the daily Bible requirement, general education courses, electives, and the major and minor areas of study.

Emmanuel School of Religion
Route 6, Box 500
Johnson City, TN 37601   (615) 926-1186

Administration. Calvin L. Phillips, President; Delno W. Brown, Dean-Registrar.

General Description. The Emmanuel School of Religion was founded in 1961. It is an independent legal entity and is fraternally related to the brotherhood of Christian Churches. The School opened for classes in 1965. The purpose of the School is indicated by its name. "Emmanuel" states the confidence in the revelation of God in Christ which must permeate all studies. It points to the expectant reception by faculty and students of the presence of the Holy Spirit in the pursuit of theological learning. The School offers two degree programs for those who have attained a baccalaureate degree.

Community Environment. The School is housed in a $3.5 million facility built by funds provided by the B.D. Phillips Charitable Trust of Butler, Pennsylvania. It is located across from Milligan College in a growing suburban area in the Appalachian Mountains between Johnson City and Elizabethtown, Tennessee.

Religious Denomination. Christian Churches and Churches of Christ.

Religious Emphasis. Conservative.

Accreditation. Association of Theological Schools in the United States and Canada.

Term System. Semester; January intersession; 4 summer sessions.

Enrollment in Degree Programs in Religion 1984–85. Total 152; men 137, women 15.

Degrees in Religion Awarded 1984–85. Master of

Divinity 18; men 17, women 1. Master of Arts in Religion 5; men 2, women 3.

Faculty for Degree Programs in Religion. Total 11; full-time 9, part-time 2.

Admission Requirements. Baccalaureate degree; GRE general test; English and Bible tests.

Tuition and Fees. Tuition $80 per semester hour for credit, $35 for audit; annual fees $120; room $150 and up per month.

Financial Aid. College work-study, scholarships, and loans available.

Housing. Both on-campus and off-campus apartments available.

Library Facilities. The Library collection contains more than 70,000 volumes. The Beauford H. Bryant New Testament Seminar Library contains 4,500 volumes primarily concerned with the New Testament and its background. Students of early Christianity make use of the private collection of the late Dr. Paul Schubert. The Restoration Movement Archives Collection was established as a research facility for the examination of past and present aspects of the Campbell-Stone tradition. This Discipliana collection consists of a wide range of books, periodicals, pamphlets, and memorabilia.

Religious Services/Activities. Emmanuel offers various programs which are structured, and other, more spontaneous, events which grow out of the atmosphere of freedom and responsibility within the School. Worship services are held in the chapel each class day. Several times each month the community is divided into small groups of approximately ten persons for sharing personal and relational concerns during the chapel period. Individual devotional life is encouraged, as is involvement in and service to local congregations.

Degree Programs

The Master of Divinity degree curriculum is considered the standard for ministerial education. The program can be completed in three years, but a student usually completes it in from four to five years because of employment or ministerial responsibilities. The degree requires the completion of 90 semester hours of graduate studies and a thesis.

The Master of Arts in Religion is an academic degree for persons interested in intensive graduate study in one area. It is designed to help them to acquire deeper biblical and theological understanding in preparation for further advanced study or for more effective service in the church and in the world through the practice of various professions. It is not a substitute for the Master of Divinity as preparation for full-time church ministry. The degree program may be taken with a preaching major in Christian Ministries only by students with an undergraduate major in Bible or Christian doctrine.

The Master of Divinity in Honors is offered for those who have demonstrated the capacity for disciplined independent study and who desire to pursue more concen-

trated study in a particular area, issue, or period.

Special Programs

Continuing education courses for students' wives and laypersons are offered during the evening hours. During January and the summer months, courses are offered for ministers.

Free Will Baptist Bible College
3606 West End Avenue
Nashville, TN 37205   (615) 383-1340

Administration. Robert E. Picirilli, Academic Dean.

General Description. Free Will Baptist Bible College requires a Bible-Theology major in all degree programs, emphasizing preparation for various church ministries.

Community Environment. Free Will Baptist Bible College includes 12 major buildings, 5 of which are of modern, new construction, in the city of Nashville, Tennessee. Nashville is the capital of Tennessee, and a manufacturing center whose products range from synthetic fabrics and materials to household appliances. Surrounding the city is an agricultural area raising corn, tobacco, wheat, dairy products, garden vegetables, and livestock.

Religious Denomination. Free Will Baptist (National Association of Free Will Baptists).

Religious Emphasis. Fundamentalist.

Accreditation. American Association of Bible Colleges.

Term System. Semester; summer term.

Enrollment in Degree Programs in Religion 1984–85. Total 417; men 210, women 207 (reflects enrollment in fall, 1984).

Degrees in Religion Awarded 1984–85. Associate of Science in Business 9; men 2, women 7. Associate of Christian Ministries 4; men 2, women 2. Bachelor of Science 34; men 13, women 21. Bachelor of Arts 29; men 21, women 8. Master of Arts in Pastoral Studies 1; men 1.

Faculty for Degree Programs in Religion. Total 34; full-time 27, part-time 7 (figures from fall 1985, and include all with "faculty" status, whether instructional or not).

Admission Requirements. High school graduation; Christian character; references.

Tuition and Fees. $2,050 per year; room and board $2,120.

Financial Aid. Loans, limited scholarships, and work available.

Housing. Dormitories are available for unmarried students; married students assisted in finding off-campus housing.

Library Facilities. The library contains a collection of 48,000 volumes and maintains the Free Will Baptist Historical Collection.

Religious Services/Activities. Weekly services on campus; weekly Christian service activities required.

Degree Programs

The Bachelor of Arts with a major in Bible is offered with second majors in English or Pastoral Training. Minors are offered in English, Music, Christian Education, Pastoral Training, Missions, Elementary Education, and Foundations in Education. The Bachelor of Science with a major in Bible is also offered with second majors in Elementary Education, Secondary Education, Pastoral Training, Church Music and Christian Education, Church Music, and Nursing (by transfer).

A Master of Arts in Pastoral Training is offered by the Graduate School.

Freed-Hardeman College
Department of Bible
Henderson, TN 38340   (901) 989-4611

Administration. Dowell Flatt, Chairman, Department of Bible.

General Description. The Department of Bible seeks to teach the Bible to all students, to provide a unifying core of truth and Christian ideals for the college, and to help educate capable preachers of the gospel. The Department offers the Bachelor of Arts and the Bachelor of Science degrees with a major in Bible. Courses are offered in the areas of Old Testament, New Testament, Practical, Doctrinal, History, and Biblical Languages.

Parent Institution. Freed-Hardeman College is an endowed, independent, nonprofit institution. It is not owned or operated by a church or combination of churches. It is governed by a self-perpetuating board of trustees who are members of the Churches of Christ and who hold the institution in trust for its founders, alumni, and supporters. Most of the students are members of the Churches of Christ. The College enrolls, however, students of any or no religious affiliation.

Community Environment. The campus of 95 acres is located in the West Tennessse county seat town of Henderson.

Religious Denomination. Churches of Christ.

Accreditation. Southern Association of Colleges and Schools.

Term System. Semester.

Admission Requirements. High school graduation or equivalent; ACT.

Tuition and Fees. Tuition $1,425 per semester; room $470; board $590.

Financial Aid. Scholarships are awarded primarily on the basis of demonstrated ability and are restricted to full-time students. Federal and state aid are available.

Housing. Dormitory facilities are provided on campus.

Library Facilities. The Loden-Daniel Library and the Lawhorn Library house more than 112,000 volumes.

Religious Services/Activities. Each student attends chapel each morning. Many religious activities and groups are available for voluntary participation.

Harding Graduate School of Religion
1000 Cherry Road
Memphis, TN 38117   (901) 761-1353

Administration. Dr. Clifton L. Ganus, Jr., President; Dr. Harold Hazelip, Dean; Dr. Bill Flatt, Registrar, Assistant to the Dean.

General Description. The Harding Graduate School of Religion is a branch school of Harding University in Searcy, Arkansas. Harding began as a senior college in 1924, when two junior colleges merged. The College moved to its present location in Searcy in 1934, and was renamed Harding University in 1979. Harding Graduate School of Religion is an outgrowth of graduate studies in religion which began on the Searcy campus in 1952. An extension program offering such courses in Memphis was begun in 1955. In 1958, the Memphis program was officially expanded into a branch of Harding University.

The School has two purposes: to provide professional training for students who expect to enter some area of Christian service upon completion of their programs and to provide introductory graduate studies for students, including those who plan to seek advanced degrees in other institutions. Emphasis is placed upon both teaching and research in the Biblical, Historical, Doctrinal, and Ministerial fields of theological study.

Community Environment. The School occupies a wooded thirty-five acre campus situated in a residential section of East Memphis at the corner of Park Avenue and Cherry Road. It is easily accessible to shopping centers and restaurants and is within thirty minutes of downtown Memphis. The city is the fourteenth largest in the United States. Metropolitan Memphis, with more than 875,000 citizens, is a modern, cultural, medical, and educational center with abundant opportunities for personal growth.

Religious Denomination. Churches of Christ.

Religious Emphasis. Conservative.

Accreditation. Southern Association of Colleges and Schools.

Term System. Semester; 4 summer sessions.

Enrollment in Degree Programs in Religion 1984–85. Total 205; men 198, women 7.

Degrees in Religion Awarded 1984–85. Doctor of Ministry 1; men 1. Master of Arts 1; men 1. Master of Arts in Religion 15; men 14, women 1. Master of Theology 24; men 23, women 1.

Faculty for Degree Programs in Religion. Total 15; full-time 12, part-time 3.

Admission Requirements. For the Master of Arts or Master of Arts in Religion: Bachelor of Arts or Bachelor of Science degree with at least 2.30 grade point average; 24 hours of undergraduate Bible; GRE if from unaccredited school; meet biblical languages requirement. For Master of Theology: Bachelor of Arts or Bachelor of Science degree with at least 2.00 grade point average; GRE if from unaccredited school; meet undergraduate Bible and biblical languages requirement. For Doctor of Ministry: Master of Theology degree or equivalent; GRE scores; ministry experience; 3.00 grade point average in Master of Theology or equivalent.

Tuition and Fees. Tuition $100.50 per semester hour; registration fee $69; dormitory room $434 per semester.

Financial Aid. Loans and some scholarships available.

Housing. Dormitory rooms available for single students; apartments for married students, both furnished ($235 to $265 per month) and unfurnished ($235 to $245) per month; off campus apartment complexes available.

Library Facilities. The L.M. Graves Memorial Library contains 78,000 volumes. Significant holdings of religious literature include facsimiles of the Sinaiticus, the Alexandrian, the Vatican; Chester Beatty, Bezae, Bodmer, Nag Hammadi manuscripts; the Aleppo Codex and the Leningrad Bible. The library holds the Migne Patrology series and the printed catalogs of the Ecole Biblique in Jerusalem, the Missionary Research Library, and the Library of the Oriental Institute of the University of Chicago. Special collections include Greek manuscripts on film, Restoration literature, missions, dissertations produced by members of the Churches of Christ, and the curriculum library of religious educational materials.

Religious Services/Activities. Daily chapel service is held in Pittman Chapel. The W.B. West, Jr. Lectures, held in the fall, bring outstanding Christian scholars to the campus for lectures on subjects of current interest in the church. The Graduate School conducts a preachers' forum each spring on some area of interest to ministers. Topics for this forum are chosen by the alumni through their officers.

Degree Programs

The Master of Arts degree requires one year of graduate study with a major in any one of the four divisions of the curriculum: the Biblical, the Doctrinal, the Historical, and the Ministerial. A thesis is required.

The Master of Arts in Religion is designed primarily for students whose life work may be best served by additional course hours instead of a thesis.

The Master of Theology degree is designed to prepare students for ministry. It also is the basic degree required by most schools of religion for admission to Ph.D. or Doctor of Theology programs. A student may concentrate in one of the subdivisions of the field: Counseling, Communications, or Church Planting and Growth.

The Doctor of Ministry degree is designed to prepare students for productive Christian ministry. A degree in the continuing education trend, the program emphasizes ministry and its practical application. The degree is not based so much upon a required number of courses in classical theological disciplines, but on whether one can sense how Biblical content is integrated into the practice of ministry. The program utilizes faculty and resources in advanced ministerial preparation, with a strong sense of responsibility to and for the Restoration tradition of which it is a part. One of three areas of concentration is pursued: Counseling, Communications, and Church Planting and Growth. Two patterns are available for completing degree requirements: a continuous 12-month study and an open-ended period not to exceed five years.

Special Programs

The Institute for Church Planting is the framework for offering services to churches, schools, and individuals interested in church planting and development. It operates as a function of the Ross Road Church of Christ and the Harding Graduate School of Religion. The Training division sponsors one-day seminars in church planting, continual classes at Ross Road Church, extension courses, and specialized growth workshops. The Graduate division is limited to select courses offered by Harding Graduate School for graduate and degree credit.

Johnson Bible College
Knoxville, TN 37998   (615) 573-4517

Administration. Dr. David L. Eubanks, President; Dr. William R. Blevins, Academic Dean.

General Description. Johnson Bible College was founded in 1893 by Ashley S. Johnson because of his strong conviction that the one great need of the cause of Christ was more laborers and as a fulfillment of his dream to furnish an education for worthy young men who could not afford it. The marble plaque beside the entrance to the Main Building still reads, "Open day and night to the poor young man who desires above every other desire, to preach the gospel of Christ." After more than ninety years of continuous operation, Johnson is still fulfilling these two purposes of its founder. The curriculum has been expanded to meet the Christian educational needs of women students who are interested in giving their lives to a specialized ministry in some field of Christian service.

The College is a special-purpose, undergraduate institution. That purpose is to educate students in specialized Christian ministries, with primary emphasis on the preaching ministry, through a program of Biblical, general, and special studies.

Community Environment. The College is located almost in the exact center of that portion of the United States lying east of the Mississippi River and south of the Great Lakes. The campus is seven and one-half miles from the city limits of Knoxville, the metropolitan hub of East Tennessee. The College campus contains 50 acres on a hill overlooking the French Broad River.

Religious Denomination. Christian Churches and Churches of Christ.

Religious Emphasis. Biblical (Conservative).

Accreditation. Southern Association of Colleges and Schools; American Association of Bible Colleges.

Term System. Semester; summer term.

Enrollment in Degree Programs in Religion 1984–85. Total 380; men 194, women 186.

Degrees in Religion Awarded 1984–85. Bachelor of Arts 18; men 17, women 1. Bachelor of Science 33; men 17, women 16. Associate of Science 2; men 1, women 1.

Faculty for Degree Programs in Religion. Total 23; full-time 15, part-time 8.

Admission Requirements. Commitment to specialized Christian service or possessing a serious purpose to profit from Bible college education.

Tuition and Fees. Costs per semester: tuition $875; fees $125; room and board $1,020.

Financial Aid. The College has a long tradition of providing financial aid to those students who are unable to pay for the total cost of their education. Financial aid is available in the form of grants, scholarships, special programs, and college work-study program.

Housing. Both dormitories for single students and apartments for married students are available on campus.

Library Facilities. The Glass Memorial Library houses a book collection of 75,000 volumes.

Religious Services/Activities. Students are required to participate in the Christian Service program. In order to remain in good standing, a student must satisfactorily complete each semester's Christian service requirements, submitting a report of activity at midterm and at the end of each semester.

On frequent occasions during the year, guest speakers are invited to address the student body. Through the Alumni Preaching Lectureship and the Homecoming and Preaching Rally, outstanding Christian leaders are engaged each year for a series of addresses.

Degree Programs

The Bachelor of Arts and the Bachelor of Science degree programs have a major study requirement of at least thirty semester hours of Biblical studies courses incorporated into every program. All of these single major programs also require a specialty (commonly called a minor) in one of nine areas of ministry. Double major Bachelor of Science programs are also offered in Bible and Elementary Education, Bible and Church Music, and Bible and Nursing. Whether the student is interested in preaching, missionary service, ministering to youth, church music, Christian education, youth ministry, media communications, deaf missions, microcomputer skills, elementary teaching from a Christian perspective, and/or nursing, there is a program of study which will help fulfill each vocational goal.

The Bachelor of Theology degree is open to those who desire another year of study beyond the normal four-year curriculum. Students have an opportunity to take additional courses in Biblical studies in one or more areas of specialty beyond what they have taken in their regular B.A. or B.S. programs.

Special Programs

An Associate of Science degree and a certificate program for students who desire shorter courses of study are also offered by the College.

King College
Bristol, TN 37620   (615) 968-1187

Administration. Dr. Donald Rutherford Mitchell, President.

General Description. The Department of Bible and Religion offers a major that prepares students to enter theological seminaries or graduate schools of religion in preparation for careers in pastoral ministry, teaching, or administration. The Department of Christian Education offers a minor in the field. The Bachelor of Arts degree requires the completion of a total of 130 semester hours.

Parent Institution. King College is a private, coeducational, four-year liberal arts college founded by Presbyterians and largely supported by them since 1867. It confers the degrees Bachelor of Arts, Bachelor of Science, Bachelor of Science in Education, and Bachelor of Science in Health Science.

Community Environment. The college has a campus of 135 acres. It is located in the town of Bristol in the foothills of the Appalachian Mountains. The main street of the town is bisected by the Virginia-Tennessee state line.

Religious Denomination. Presbyterian Church (U.S.A.).

Accreditation. Southern Association of Colleges and Schools.

Term System. Semester (4-1-4 plan).

Admission Requirements. High school graduation in the upper 50 percent of the graduating class; ACT; non-high school graduate are considered under certain circumstances.

Tuition and Fees. Comprehensive fees $3,265 per semester.

Financial Aid. The College has a comprehensive financial aid program.

Housing. All students enrolled full-time who do not reside locally with parents are required to live in a college residence hall.

Library Facilities. The library houses over 62,000 volumes.

Religious Services/Activities. Chapel is held regularly each Tuesday morning and a convocation is held each Thursday morning.

Degree Programs

A major in Bible and Religion leading to the Bachelor of Arts degree requires the completion of 24 semester hours in Bible and 6 semester hours of a foreign language.

Lambuth College
Department of Religion
Lambuth Boulevard
Jackson, TN 38301   (901) 427-1500

Administration. James Kenneth Wilkerson, Chairman, Department of Religion.

General Description. The Department of Religion offers a major leading to the Bachelor of Arts degree. Students may also take courses leading to the ministry or the religious education professions.

Parent Institution. Lambuth College is an institution of the United Methodist Church. It had its beginning in 1843 as the Memphis Conference Female Institute. The College became coeducational in 1923 and adopted its present name. Approximately 800 students are enrolled annually. All students are required to take two courses in religion.

Community Environment. The 50-acre campus is located in the city of Jackson, a trading and shipping center for agricultural products.

Religious Denomination. United Methodist Church.

Accreditation. Southern Association of Colleges and Schools.

Term System. Semester.

Admission Requirements. High school graduation; non-high school graduates considered.

Tuition and Fees. Tuition $1,800 per semester; matriculation and student activities fee $85; room $370; board $580.

Financial Aid. The College offers a number of ways for a student to finance a college education, including federal grants, loans, and scholarships.

Housing. Students reside in residence halls on campus.

Library Facilities. The Luther L. Gobbel Library houses a collection of over 135,000 volumes.

Religious Services/Activities. Under the direction of the Minister to the College, students attend worship services on and off campus and plan other activities which reflect their religious interests and concerns.

Degree Programs

The Bachelor of Arts major requires 30 hours in Religion including prescribed courses plus 3 hours each in Philosophy, Literature, Music-Art-Drama, and History.

Lee College
Department of Bible and Christian Ministries
North Ocoee
Cleveland, TN 37311   (615) 472-2111

Administration. Dr. John Sims, Chairman, Department of Bible and Christian Ministries.

General Description. The Department of Bible and Christian Ministries came into being in 1984 as a result of the combining of the former Department of Bible and

Theology and the Department of Christian Education. The new Department is large in scope and is designed to coordinate the preparation previously offered in both areas. The Department offers majors in Biblical Education, Christian Education, and Intercultural Studies. The Bachelor of Arts and the Bachelor of Science degrees are awarded. The Evangelical Teacher Training Diploma is also offered.

Parent Institution. Lee College began in 1918 as a Bible training school affiliated with the Church of God. In 1925, plans were initiated to expand the then junior college to a four-year college of liberal arts. The College enrolls approximately 1,200 students annually.

Community Environment. The 20-acre campus is located in Cleveland in the heart of the Tennessee Valley. TVA lakes nearby offer outdoor recreational opportunities.

Religious Denomination. Church of God.

Accreditation. Southern Association of Colleges and Schools.

Term System. Semester.

Admission Requirements. High school graduation.

Tuition and Fees. Tuition $1,320 per semester; room $377; board $540.

Financial Aid. The College offers a broad program of financial aid to students, including scholarships, loans, employment, and combinations of these programs.

Housing. Dormitory accommodations are available on campus.

Library Facilities. The library contains over 82,000 volumes.

Religious Services/Activities. All students are required to attend chapel services. Twice each year, a week is set aside for special convocation. Practical Christian service activities are provided through the office of the Director of Christian Services and the Campus Pastor.

Maryville College
Department of Religion and Philosophy
Maryville, TN 37801   (615) 982-6412

Administration. Professor Cartlidge, Chairman, Department of Religion and Philosophy.

General Description. The Department of Religion and Philosophy focuses on concerns and questions that have long been regarded as fundamental to human existence. At Maryville, the course offerings emphasize the history of thought and the sub-field of ethics. Students interested in the ministry, religious education, church music, or other church-related vocations pursue a variety of majors.

Parent Institution. Maryville College is a church-related institution of liberal arts and sciences. It is affiliated with the Presbyterian Church (U.S.A.). The College was founded in 1819 and is one of the eleven oldest church-related colleges in the United States.

Community Environment. The 375-acre campus is located in Maryville, founded in 1790. The town is near the entrance to the Great Smoky Mountains National Park.

Religious Denomination. Presbyterian Church (U.S.A.).

Accreditation. Southern Association of Colleges and Schools.

Term System. Semester (4-1-4).

Admission Requirements. High school graduation with rank in the top 50 percent of the graduating class; ACT or SAT required.

Tuition and Fees. Tuition $1,920 per semester; room $1,020; board $1,020; activity fee $85.

Financial Aid. The College makes every effort to aid qualified students who could not attend college without financial assistance.

Housing. Students are expected to live on campus during all four years at the College unless the student lives with family.

Library Facilities. The Lamar Memorial Library contains over 116,000 volumes.

Religious Services/Activities. The College maintains a covenant relationship with the Presbyterian Church (U.S.A.). The Center for Campus Ministry coordinates activities for the religious life at Maryville.

Degree Programs

The major in Religion leading to the Bachelor of Arts degree consists of 45 hours in religion and related areas.

Memphis Theological Seminary
168 East Parkway South
Memphis, TN 38104   (901) 458-8232

Administration. Dr. J. David Hester, President; Dr. Hubert W. Morrow, Academic Dean.

General Description. Memphis Theological Seminary is a graduate professional school of religion offering the degrees Master of Divinity, Master of Arts in Religion, and the Master of Arts. The purpose of the Seminary is to provide graduate, professional education as preparation for persons seeking ordination to the ministry and to lay persons who want to serve in positions in the church. It is owned and operated by the Cumberland Presbyterian Church. Its roots are in the Reformed tradition and it reflects the evangelical character of American Protestantism. It is ecumenical in spirit, welcoming students of all denominations, persons of both sexes, and those of various cultural and ethnic backgrounds.

Community Environment. The Seminary is located in Memphis, Tennessee, a city of 650,000 people. Situated on the Mississippi River, Memphis is the center of a region called the Mid-South. The Seminary is in the section of the city called Mid-Town.

Religious Denomination. Cumberland Presbyterian Church.

Religious Emphasis. Reformed tradition as this has been modified by the evangelical character of American Protestantism.

Accreditation. Association of Theological Schools in the United States and Canada.

Term System. Semester; summer term.

Enrollment in Degree Programs in Religion 1984–85. Total 193; men 149, women 44.

Degrees in Religion Awarded 1984–85. Master of Divinity 39; men 32, women 7. Master of Arts in Religion 3; men 3.

Faculty for Degree Programs in Religion. Total 22; full-time 8, part-time 14.

Admission Requirements. Bachelor's degree from an accredited college or university.

Tuition and Fees. Tuition $80 per semester hour; fees $75 annually; apartment housing $190 per month (without utilities).

Financial Aid. Service loans to Cumberland Presbyterian students; limited number of scholarships for Blacks; approved for Veterans' benefits and federally guaranteed student loans.

Housing. A limited number of apartments are available for married and single students on an annual lease basis.

Library Facilities. The library houses over 70,000 volumes and maintains a special collection in Black Studies.

Religious Services/Activities. Ecumenical worship services; morning prayers daily and chapel service on Thursdays.

Degree Programs

The Master of Divinity degree is designed for persons preparing for ordination to the office of the ministry. It requires the completion of 90 semester hours. The Master of Arts in Religion degree is designed for lay persons who want to do academic study of religion for personal enrichment and to aid them in serving in helping roles in the church. The degree requires 60 semester hours. The Master of Arts degree is designed for persons who want to teach religion in secondary schools and in higher education, or to prepare for doctoral study. Majors are offered in New Testament, Old Testament, Theology, and Church History.

Mid-America Baptist Theological Seminary
1255 Poplar Avenue
Memphis, TN 38104   (901) 726-9171

Administration. B. Gray Allison, President.

General Description. The Seminary began in the fall of 1971 as "The School of the Prophets." It is not owned or controlled by, nor has any formal affiliation with, the Southern Baptist Convention. It is, however, committed to the Southern Baptist doctrinal beliefs. The Seminary's primary purpose is to provide graduate theological training and other levels of training for effective service in church-related vocations. The emphasis of the entire school is geared directly to Southern Baptist churches and missions.

Community Environment. The campus is located directly north of Bellevue Baptist Church in the midtown area of Memphis. The city is an inland port, industrial center, and a distributing point.

Religious Denomination. Southern Baptist.

Accreditation. Southern Association of Colleges and Schools.

Term System. Semester.

Admission Requirements. Associate of Divinity program: High school graduation or equivalent; Master's programs: Bachelor of Arts degree or equivalent from an accredited college or university.

Tuition and Fees. Matriculation fee $180 per term (varies depending upon course load).

Financial Aid. The Student Financial Affairs Committee has the responsibility of selecting recipients for the various scholarships and student aid money available.

Housing. A limited number of apartments and dormitory facilities are owned by the Seminary.

Library Facilities. The Ora Byram Allison Memorial Library houses over 87,000 books, microforms, and audiovisual materials.

Religious Services/Activities. Chapel services are held daily. Student Mission Fellowship, the Student Theological Forum, and the Mid-America Women's Fellowship are among the organizations available for student participation.

Degree Programs

The Master of Divinity program is designed to equip the student for the gospel preaching ministry as a pastor, assistant pastor, church planter, evangelist, or missionary. It is a three-year program requiring 96 semester hours of academic credit.

The Master of Arts in Religion and Education program is designed to equip the student for service as an education director, age-group director, or administrator in the local church; as a missionary in the area of religious education; or as a teacher/administrator in a Christian school. It is a two-year program requiring 64 semester hours of academic credit.

The Doctor of Theology degree is designed to equip the student for creative scholarship, independent research, and effective teaching and preaching. It involves a minimum of two years of study beyond the Master of Divinity degree or its equivalent.

Special Programs

The Associate of Divinity program is designed to equip the student who has not completed college for the gospel preaching ministry as pastor, assistant pastor, church planter, or evangelist. It is a three-year program requiring 96 semester hours of academic credit. The Associate program's courses are generally parallel in content and format to the courses offered in the Master's degree programs.

Mid-South Bible College
2485 Union Avenue Extension
P.O. Box 12144
Memphis, TN 38182   (901) 458-7526

Administration. Dr. Robert J. Hilgenberg, President; Dr. Raymond L. Waddell, Academic Dean.

General Description. Mid-South Bible College is an evangelical Christian institution of higher education whose purpose is to help Christian men and women prepare themselves spiritually, academically, vocationally, and professionally to serve as Christian servant-leaders. Degrees offered are: Bachelor of Arts, Bachelor of Science, and Bachelor of Music Education.

Community Environment. Mid-South Bible College is located in an area that provides many unusual advantages for its students. Memphis, Tennessee possesses a public library system with 19 branches throughout the area, and a strong and balanced educational system at every level. Major facilities include 11 colleges and universities, 4 vocational and technical schools, 5 schools of nursing, 11 business schools, 7 schools of theology, 3 major elementary and secondary educational systems, and numerous private schools. The wide selection of cultural attractions includes the Metropolitan Opera, touring symphony orchestras, and concert artists. There are over 750 denominational and independent churches in Memphis alone, and an even larger number in the surrounding Tri-State area.

Religious Denomination. Nondenominational.

Religious Emphasis. Conservative Christian Evangelical.

Accreditation. American Association of Bible Colleges; candidate for Southern Association of Colleges and Schools.

Term System. Semester; summer term.

Enrollment in Degree Programs in Religion 1984–85. Total 209; men 123, women 86.

Degrees in Religion Awarded 1984–85. Bachelor of Arts 5; men 5. Bachelor of Science 12; men 5, women 7.

Faculty for Degree Programs in Religion. Total 6; fulltime 4, part-time 2.

Admission Requirements. High school graduation with a scholastic average of at least C; satisfactory scores on ACT or SAT.

Tuition and Fees. Tuition $1,344 per semester (1-11 credit hours $112 per credit hour); activity fee $25 per semester; room and board $1,050 per semester.

Financial Aid. Programs include scholarships, grants, loans, and work programs to qualified students.

Housing. Dormitory facilities for single students are available.

Library Facilities. The library contains approximately 30,000 volumes.

Religious Services/Activities. Each student who attends

classes during the day and takes 8 or more hours is required to attend chapel services daily. The College maintains a Christian Service Department which provides opportunities for practical experience in a wide variety of Christian ministries. Special Conferences, including the Christian Life conference in the fall, are scheduled throughout the course of the school year. One day is also set aside each semester for praying together as a College family.

Degree Programs

The content of the degree programs (Bachelor of Arts, Bachelor of Science, Bachelor of Music Education) may be divided into three areas: (1) Bible and Theology, (2) General Education, (3) Professional Courses. Students earning one of these degrees must satisfy the requirements for a major in Bible and Theology, and also the requirements for one of the programs of study. Those pursuing a B.A. degree must also satisfy a twelve-hour foreign language requirement. All degree candiates must complete a minimum number of hours in each of the areas as specified in the programs. A major consists of a minimum of 30 semester hours' credit; an emphasis consists of not less than 12 or more than 29 semester hours' credit. Majors are offered in Bible and Theology, Natural Science, Social Studies, Music, Psychology, and Elementary Education. Concentrations may be pursued in Church Ministries and Secondary Education.

Special Programs

Adult Education Bible classes are offered free to the public by the College.

Milligan College
Area of Biblical Learning
Milligan, TN 37682   (615) 929-0116

Administration. Dr. Henry E. Webb, Chairman, Area of Biblical Learning.

General Description. The first aim of Biblical study is to introduce each student to the content of the Christian revelation in such a way as to assist in effective living and service in any vocation. The vocational aim is also met by such study directed toward specialized ministries. Bible courses are required of all students in Milligan College and are also offered as areas of concentration for majors.

Parent Institution. Milligan College is a privately-controlled institution of the Christian Churches and Churches of Christ. It was founded in 1886 with the expressed motto "Christian Education - the Hope of the World."

Community Environment. Milligan is located in the suburban areas of Johnson City and Elizabethton. Five TVA lakes are nearby and offer many recreational opportunities.

Religious Denomination. Christian Churches and Churches of Christ.

Accreditation. Southern Association of Colleges and Schools.

Term System. Semester.

Admission Requirements. High school graduation or equivalent; ACT or SAT.

Tuition and Fees. Tuition $2,148 per semester; room $378-$525; board $726.

Financial Aid. A comprehensive financial aid program is available for qualified students in the form of grants, campus employment, loans, and scholarships.

Housing. Dormitory housing is available on campus.

Library Facilities. The P.H. Welshimer Library has holdings of more than 115,000 volumes. The library was first occupied in November 1961 and was the gift of the T.W. Philips, Jr. Charitable Trust and the Phillips family of Butler, Pennsylvania, after an initial gift by the Kresge Foundation of Detroit, Michigan.

Religious Services/Activities. Regular church attendance is encouraged of all Milligan students. Prayer services are held frequently in the dormitories and in Seeger Memorial Chapel. Participation in the Christian Service Club, Missions Club, and the Association of Christian Ministries is open to all students.

Degree Programs

The major in Bible leading to the Bachelor of Arts degree consists of 30 hours which must include 6 hours of New Testament, 6 hours of Old Testament History, 2 hours Christian Ministries, and Homiletics.

The program in Religious Education is designed to serve persons who wish to combine a strong Bible program with work in both Christian Education and professional education. The Religious Education major consists of courses in that field in addition to those courses required for the Bible major. This program is correlated closely with the program in teacher education.

Scarritt College
1008 19th Avenue, South
Nashville, TN 37203   (615) 327-2700

Administration. Donald J. Welch, President.

General Description. Scarritt College is an institution of the United Methodist Church whose primary mission is a Christian commitment to provide graduate education in Christian education and church music as preparation for professional leadership in pursuit of the mission of the Church. The College was founded in 1892 in Kansas City, Missouri and moved to its present site in Nashville in 1924. Scarritt began through the leadership of Belle Harris Bennett, a young Kentucky woman active in the turn-of-the-century Woman's Society of the Methodist Episcopal Church, South. Its name is that of Kansas preacher Nathan Scarritt, who gave $25,000 and the original tract of land on which the College was built.

Parent Institution. Scarritt offers the Master of Arts degree in Christian Education and the Master of Church Music degree. These degree programs, which take approximately two full years to complete, are designed to prepare for professional church careers. They also enable their graduates to understand these disciplines and to be at the forefront of shaping Christian education and church music as professions. A joint Master of Arts in Christian Education/Master of Divinity program is offered in cooperation with the Divinity School of Vanderbilt University.

Community Environment. The campus buildings are of Gothic architecture. Ramps and elevators provide access for students with handicapping conditions to the library, chapel, campus center, administrative offices, and the first floors of housing structures. Nashville is a progressive city of great educational, spiritual, and cultural resources. The community of Vanderbilt University, within one block of the Scarritt campus, welcomes Scarritt students to attend the many activities on that campus.

Religious Denomination. United Methodist Church.

Accreditation. Southern Association of Colleges and Schools; Association of Theological Schools in the United States and Canada.

Term System. Semester.

Admission Requirements. Bachelor of Arts degree; recommendation from local pastor.

Tuition and Fees. Tuition $150 per semester hour; dormitory $640-$850 per semester; apartment $225-$300 per month; board $300-$750 per semester depending upon meal plan selected.

Financial Aid. The basic sources of financial aid are campus employment, scholarships, grants, and loans.

Housing. Dormitory and apartment housing is available on campus.

Library Facilities. The Virginia Davis Laskey Library contains material outlining the evolution and practice of the church's educational ministry. It houses over 54,000 volumes. The Rare Book Collection contains English Bibles including a 1613/11 Bible known as the "Great She Bible," a 1599 "Geneva" or "Breeches" Bible, and several other rare English Bibles. Some material in Methodism is also included in this collection.

Religious Services/Activities. Forum Hour at Scarritt, a morning hour each week during which no classes are conducted, offers a variety of lectures and workshops in Christian Education and church music as well as related disciplines. There are campus chapters of the American Guild of Organists; the Christian Educators Fellowship; and the Fellowship of United Methodists in Worship, Music, and Other Arts. There is a weekly chapel service, observance of morning prayer, and Bible study.

Degree Programs

The Master of Arts degree in Christian Education is designed for persons preparing for leadership in the educational ministry of the church in local congregations,

denominational agencies, and ecumenical organizations. The program provides a balance and integration of theological, educational, and ministerial sources of the church's educational ministry. The program includes coursework in the heritage of the Christian tradition, the ministry of the church in the world, and the nature and function of educational ministry.

The Master of Church Music degree combines disciplined musical training with theological study to prepare students for leadership in music ministry. The degree, which offers either a choral or organ emphasis, provides a balance of coursework, field education, applied music study, and musical performance.

South, University of the
The School of Theology
Sewanee, TN 37375   (615) 598-5931

Administration. Dr. John Everitt Booty, Dean of The School of Theology; Elizabeth Sowar Camp, Registrar and Master of Divinity Admissions Officer.

General Description. The School of Theology is at present the only graduate division of the University of the South. Its main program, the Master of Divinity, is a professional one which trains persons for ordination to the priesthood in the Episcopal Church. The Doctor of Ministry and the Master of Sacred Theology programs both operate during the 5-week summer session. These students are post-Master of Divinity and generally are clergy who use this a means of continuing education.

Parent Institution. The University of the South opened in 1868. It is owned by 28 dioceses of the Episcopal Church and is a liberal arts coeducational institution with 1,000 undergraduate men and women students.

Community Environment. The campus of the University of the South (known locally as the "Domain") covers ten thousand acres of rolling woodland on the Cumberland Plateau. The municipality of Sewanee, consisting of about eight hundred residences scattered over the Domain and a small shopping area, has a permanent population of about 2,000. The urban centers of Chattanooga and Huntsville can be reached in about an hour.

Religious Denomination. The Episcopal Church.

Accreditation. Southern Association of Colleges and Schools; Association of Theological Schools in the United States and Canada.

Term System. Semester; summer term.

Enrollment in Degree Programs in Religion 1984–85. Total full-time 75, part-time 62; men full-time 63, part-time 60; women full-time 12, part-time 2.

Degrees in Religion Awarded 1984–85. Master of Divinity 16; men 14, women 2. Doctor of Ministry 2; men 2.

Faculty for Degree Programs in Religion. Total 20; full-time 11, part-time 9.

Admission Requirements. Applicants for admission to

the School of Theology require the following: Bachelor or equivalent degree; college transcripts; General Test of the GRE; a psychiatric or psychological report; 5 recommendations from: student's bishop, his/her rector, one other ordained minister, one lay person, and one teacher or associate; visit School for interviews. For the Doctor of Divinity: completion of Master of Divinity degree or equivalent with minimum grade average of B; official transcripts of all previous college, seminary, and graduate work; letters of reference from at least 2 theological school professors and one church official; an extended paper detailing applicant's academic and religious pilgrimage, commitment to the ministry, and goals.

Tuition and Fees. Master of Divinity tuition $5,150 per year plus approximately $215 in fees; single apartment rentals $1,500 per year; University housing for families $255 to $475 per month. Doctor of Ministry tuition $130 per semester hour.

Financial Aid. Financial aid offered by the University of the South is awarded on the basis of financial need.

Housing. Master of Divinity students may live in apartments which are furnished with dormitory-type bedroom furniture, plus kitchen appliances. Housing for students with families is available for approximately three-fourths of those needing housing; most housing is 2- or 3-bedroom duplexes. There are some private rentals.

Library Facilities. The Library houses a collection of more than 88,000 volume, diocesan and General Convention journals, and approximately 900 periodical subscriptions. This collection supplements and is supplemented by some 325,000 volumes in the general undergraduate library. A carrel for each theological student and faculty member is available.

Religious Services/Activities. During the nine month academic year, there is Eucharist twice a week plus on Holy Days; daily morning and evening prayer, Monday through Friday; three retreats a year (all Episcopal). During the 5-week summer program, Eucharist is celebrated once a day, according to rite of student celebrant; students are four-fifths Episcopal and one-fifth ecumenical.

Degree Programs

The Master of Divinity curriculum has as its purpose the preparation of the whole person, through the unity given in Christ, for parish ministry and mission within the context of Christian community. Academic studies are developed within the broader perspective of spiritual formation and training in ministerial skills. The curriculum includes four integrated components, all of which are required. The first constitutes those areas of learning that continue through all three years of the program. The second covers those disciplines that are of fundamental importance to the more academic aspects of theological education from the perspective of historical development. The third stresses personal growth and the development of skills in pastoral ministry. A program of electives is offered to provide more flexibility and the opportunity for

study in greater depth one discipline.

Regular students who do not have a bachelor's degree may become candidates for the Licentiate in Theology by taking this program.

The Master of Sacred Theology program requires 30 semester hours and is an academic research degree based primarily on courses taken in the summer at the School of Theology, although students may take courses at the Vanderbilt Divinity School and electives at the School of Theology. The student must have a major area of concentration and must write a thesis for six hours' credit.

The Doctor of Ministry program is an effort to make the degree available to students who wish to study during the summer months. It will also make available a number of continuing education opportunities for ministers who are unable to be released from their work during the academic year. The courses of study are designed to enable participants to attain excellence in the practice of ministry and to provided persons actively engaged in some form of professional ministry the opportunity to develop further the attitudes, skills, and knowledge which are essential to their ministry. The program stresses the relationship between the practice of ministry and biblical, historical, and theological knowledge.

Southern College of Seventh-day Adventists Division of Religion
Collegedale, TN 37315   (615) 238-2111

Administration. Dr. John Wagner, President; Dr. William Allen, Vice President for Academic Administration; Dr. Gordon Hyde, Chairman, Division of Religion.

General Description. The Division of Religion offers an undergraduate program preparing pre-seminary candidates for the ministry and also for secondary Bible teaching in the school system operated by Seventh-day Adventists. The Division contains a full-time faculty of six, each holding an earned doctorate either in Biblical Studies, Theology, or Practics. There are about 100 majors presently, and the College has an excellent record of placement of graduates. The Division is about to move into a Religious Center for the first time, with chapel, offices, classrooms, and a reference library. The Division is affiliated with the Theological Seminary of Andrews University, Berrien Springs, Michigan. The Division's Bachelor of Arts in Religion serves candidates for the ministry of the Seventh-day Adventist Church, providing the undergraduate academic preparation for the Andrews Seminary.

Parent Institution. Southern College of Seventh-day Adventists is a denominational liberal arts college offering the range of baccalaureate and associate degrees. The College has the advantages of a delightful location 18 miles from Chatanooga, Tennessee, and a complete modern campus, striking for its immediate setting. The faculty is qualified and experienced. There are approximately 1,250 full-time students.

Community Environment. Southern College's Collegdale campus is nestled in a valley 18 miles northeast of Chattanooga, Tennessee, located on over 1,000 acres of school property. The quietness and beauty of the peaceful surroundings are in keeping with the College's educational philosophy. Collegedale is within 10 miles of the TVA lake system recreation areas.

Religious Denomination. Seventh-day Adventist.

Religious Emphasis. Protestant Evangelical, Biblical.

Accreditation. Southern Association of Colleges and Schools.

Term System. Semester; summer term.

Enrollment in Degree Programs in Religion 1984–85. Total 100.

Degrees in Religion Awarded 1984–85. Bachelor of Arts in Religion 12; men 12. Bachelor of arts in Theology 11; men 11.

Faculty for Degree Programs in Religion. Total 6; full-time 6.

Admission Requirements. Four-year high school diploma or equivalent, adequate character references, and commitment to school philosophy and objectives.

Tuition and Fees. Tuition $5,248 per semester; room and board $2,450; books and supplies $300; dormitory housing $1,030 (two semesters); apartments $95 to $210 per month; trailer space $72.

Financial Aid. Work incentive scholarships, loans, grants, and scholarships are available.

Housing. Modern dormitories, married student apartments, and a trailer court are available on-campus.

Library Facilities. The library houses over 180,000 volumes and 1,000 periodicals.

Religious Services/Activities. Convocation exercises in the residence halls and for the entire student body serve educational and religious purposes. The religious emphasis week and the weekend church services assist in the spiritual growth of the students comprising the college community. Students are required to attend these services regularly.

Degree Programs

The Bachelor of Arts degree in Religion serves candidates for the ministry of the Seventh-day Adventist Church, providing the undergraduate academic preparation for the Theological Seminary of Andrews University in Berrien Springs, Michigan. The degree is also suitable for students who may be preparing to serve as secondary Bible teachers, Bible instructors, chaplain's assistants, and for those who may be preparing for various other professions. Each student's program is individualized. Students who wish to be admitted to the religion program in preparation for the ministry must file a formal application with the Division of Religion during the first semester of the sophomore year. Religion majors are required to attend professional chapels for the information and inspiration provided. The program offerings include a major (30

hours) with two tracks: Ministerial Track - Seminary with a Biblical languages minor and cognate courses; Ministerial Track - Non-Seminary with a Practical Theology minor and cognate courses. The Division of Religion strongly recommends that ministerial students choose the Seminary track.

Special Programs

Evangelism field schools are conducted during the summer session.

Temple Baptist Theological Seminary
Tennessee Temple University
1815 Union Avenue
Chattanooga, TN 37404   (615) 624-2947

Administration. Dr. Lee Roberson, Founder/Chancellor; Dr. James R. Faulkner, President; Dr. Roger Martin, Dean, Temple Baptist Theological Seminary.

General Description. The Temple Baptist Theological Seminary of Tennessee Temple University offers advanced training in theological and practical areas in order to equip ministers for their tasks. Programs are offered for both professional and lay leaders. Courses are open to both men and women. Degrees offered include: Bachelor of Divinity, Master of Divinity, Master of Theology, Master of Religious Education, Master of Biblical Studies (for lay men and women), Doctor of Theology, Doctor of Religious Education, Doctor of Ministry.

Parent Institution. The purpose of Tennessee Temple University is to train Christian leaders and workers (both secular and religious) academically and spiritually, for service at home and abroad. Mainly, Temple students are preparing to be preachers, missionaries, evangelists, Christian workers, church choir directors, song leaders, educational directors, Bible teachers, and school teachers. Temple considers itself to be a Bible college with a heavy liberal arts emphasis.

Community Environment. Located in southeastern Tennessee, on the Tennessee River, Chattanooga is an important industrial center with over 500 manufacturing plants.

Religious Denomination. Baptist.

Religious Emphasis. Fundamentalist, Evangelical.

Accreditation. American Association of Bible Colleges.

Term System. Semester, summer term.

Enrollment in Degree Programs in Religion 1984–85. Total 130; men 125, women 5.

Degrees in Religion Awarded 1984–85. Bachelor of Divinity 1; men 1. Master of Biblical Studies 2; men 2. Master of Religious Education 5; men 5. Master of Divinity 14; men 14. Master of Theology 3; men 3.

Faculty for Degree Programs in Religion. Total 12; full-time 10, part-time 2.

Admission Requirements. Bachelor of Arts or Bachelor of Science degree with at least 50 hours of liberal arts credit.

Tuition and Fees. Tuition $715 (6 to 18 hours), $109.50 per hour for more than 18 or less than 6 hours; matriculation fee $50; application fee $15; graduation fee $33.

Financial Aid. Limited scholarships are available.

Housing. The Office of Housing and Employment aids students in locating low-cost housing. Single students may reside in the University dormitory.

Library Facilities. The Cierpke Memorial Library houses 138,473 volumes.

Religious Services/Activities. Chapel is held three times weekly (twice with the University). The Douglas Cravens Seminary Lectures of two days' duration are offered each semester. A Day of Prayer is held once each semester.

Degree Programs

The degrees Bachelor of Divinity (3 years), Master of Divinity (3 years), Master of Theology (4 years), Master of Religious Education (2 years), and Master of Arts in Biblical Studies (2 years, for lay men and women) are offered by the Seminary. The degrees Doctor of Theology (4 years) and Doctor of Ministry (1 year beyond the Master of Divinity degree) are also offered. These programs have been subject to major revision as of December 1985. Contact the Seminary for the revised program descriptions and requirements.

Tennessee Temple University
Bible and Christian Ministries Division
1815 Union Avenue
Chattanooga, TN 37404   (615) 698-6021

Administration. Dr. Lee Roberson, Founder/Chancellor; Dr. James R. Faulkner, President; Dr. James A. Price, Dean, Bible and Christian Ministries Division.

General Description. The Division of Bible and Christian Ministries offers programs for both degree and non-degree majors and also a pre-seminary program. Majors are available in Bible, Christian Education, Missions, and Pastoral Studies. The Bible major is the pre-seminary course, preparing students for graduate work.

Parent Institution. The purpose of Tennessee Temple University is to train Christian leaders and workers (both secular and religious) academically and spiritually, for service at home and abroad. Mainly, Temple students are preparing to be preachers, missionaries, evangelists, Christian workers, church choir directors, song leaders, educational directors, Bible teachers, and school teachers. Temple considers itself to be a Bible college with a heavy liberal arts emphasis.

Community Environment. Located in southeastern Tennessee, on the Tennessee River, Chattanooga is an important industrial center with over 500 manufacturing plants.

Religious Denomination. Baptist.

Religious Emphasis. Fundamentalist, Evangelical.

Accreditation. American Association of Bible Colleges.

Term System. Semester; summer term.

Enrollment in Degree Programs in Religion 1984–85. Total 615; men 448, women 167.

Degrees in Religion Awarded 1984–85. Bachelor of Science in Christian Ministries 4; men 1, women 3. Bachelor of Arts in Bible 22; men 22. Bachelor of Religious Education in Pastoral Missions and Christian Education 59; men 46, women 13. Diploma (3-year) in Christian Ministries 4; men 1, women 3.

Faculty for Degree Programs in Religion. Total 21; full-time 18, part-time 3.

Admission Requirements. High school graduation and acceptable ACT for a 4-year degree program; high school diploma not required for the 3-year diploma program.

Tuition and Fees. Tuition $1,245 per semester; fees $50; room and board $1,200 per semester.

Financial Aid. Students may apply for government loans and Pell grants through the University. Student employment services are available through the University for students who qualify.

Housing. Dormitories are provided for single students. The Office of Housing and Employment aids married students in finding available low-cost housing in nearby areas.

Library Facilities. The Cierpke Memorial Library houses 138,473 volumes and receives 1,040 periodicals.

Religious Services/Activities. Sunday school, Sunday morning worship service, and mid-week prayer service are offered. University chapel services are held 3 days per week.

Degree Programs

The Bachelor degree programs require the completion of a minimum of 130 semester hours. The major in Bible leading to the Bachelor of Arts degree is designed to prepare students for graduate work in a seminary. The major in Christian Education, Missions, or Pastoral Studies leads to the Bachelor of Religious Education degree. A Bachelor of Science program is offered for the Christian worker who desires more of a liberal arts foundation than the Bachelor of Religious Education program would provide. All programs are offered by the Division of Bible and Christian Ministries.

A Bachelor of Arts in Pulpit Communications is a pre-seminary and interdisciplinary academic program with an emphasis on the study of speech communication and Bible. The Bachelor of Science in Missionary Health is a five-year program. It is designed to prepare students for a career in medical missions. The first and fifth years are totally at the University; the second, third, and fourth years are in both the University and the Baroness Erlanger Hospital School of Nursing.

Special Programs

A three-year Diploma in Christian Education is also offered by the Division of Bible and Christian Ministries for students of advanced age. Majors are available in Christian Education, Missions, and Pastoral Studies.

Tennessee Wesleyan College
Department of Religion
P.O. Box 40
Athens, TN 37303   (615) 745-5872

Administration. Dr. James E. Cheek, President.

General Description. The Department of Religion offers a major in Church Vocations and a Pre-Seminary major. These programs lead to the Bachelor of Science and Bachelor of Arts degrees, respectively.

Parent Institution. Tennessee Wesleyan College was founded in 1857 and is affiliated with the United Methodist Church. It offers a four-year liberal arts curriculum.

Community Environment. The campus of 24 acres is located in Athens, a city of 7,000 people, located between Chattanooga and Knoxville, Tennessee.

Religious Denomination. United Methodist Church.

Accreditation. Southern Association of Colleges and Schools.

Term System. Quarter.

Admission Requirements. High school graduation.

Tuition and Fees. Tuition $2,400 per year; room and board $1,710.

Financial Aid. Assistance in various forms is available.

Housing. All students not residing with parents are required to live in campus dormitories.

Library Facilities. The Merner-Pfeiffer Library houses over 76,000 volumes.

Religious Services/Activities. Weekly chapel services are held and convocation programs are provided. Full-time students are required to attend five convocations per quarter.

Degree Programs

In order to major in a Church Vocation, the student completes the core Religious Studies course and one or more of the following areas: Church School Education, Church Camps and Recreation, Church Business Management. The major leads to the Bachelor of Science degree. The requirements for the Pre-Seminary major include English, Social Science, Economics, Education, History, and Religion (including one course in Bible). This major leads to the Bachelor of Arts degree.

Trevecca Nazarene College
Department of Religion and Philosophy
333 Murfreesboro Road
Nashville, TN 37203   (615) 248-1200

Administration. Dr. Homer J. Adams, President; Dr. William J. Strickland, Dean of the College; Dr. H. Ray Dunning, Chairman, Department of Religion and Philosophy.

General Description. The Department of Religion and Philosophy provides a curriculum to prepare persons for various areas of Christian service as well as for graduate study in religion. In addition to implementing its own goals, the Department services the curricular commitment of the institution to general education studies in Bible, doctrine, and philosophy. The degree Bachelor of Arts in Religion is offered.

Parent Institution. The fundamental purposes for Trevecca Nazarene's being are a high quality education in the liberal arts, and selected professional, para-professional, and pre-professional programs. Its stated objectives are: (1) To reflect Christian principles; (2) To provide a quality academic program; (3) To continue to be a person-centered institution; (4) To be service oriented.

Community Environment. Trevecca Nazarene College is set amidst the city of Nashville, Tennessee, a bustling city with a diverse and well-balanced economy, containing industry, education, music, parks, innumerable churches, temples, and shrines. Known as "Music City, U.S.A.," Nashville is the home of the internationally known "Grand Ole Opry."

Religious Denomination. Church of the Nazarene.

Religious Emphasis. Wesleyan.

Accreditation. Southern Association of Colleges and Schools.

Term System. Presently under the Quarter system, Trevecca is in the process of changing to the Semester system; summer term.

Enrollment in Degree Programs in Religion 1984–85. Total 120.

Faculty for Degree Programs in Religion. Total 7; full-time 5, part-time 2.

Admission Requirements. Students with an ACT Standard Composite Score of 15 or above will be given Regular Admission; $15 nonrefundable admission fee; confidential health form; official certification of high school graduation.

Tuition and Fees. Tuition $1,205 per term; general fee $70 per term; room and board $1,965 per year.

Financial Aid. The Director of Student Financial Aid assists students in obtaining employment on or off campus and accepts and processes students' applications for assistantships, scholarships, loans, and other grants-in-aid.

Housing. Dormitories and married student housing are available.

Library Facilities. The Mackey Library has holdings of over 85,000 volumes, 18,000 microforms, and 3,000 audiovisual materials.

Religious Services/Activities. The Religious Life Committee, Christian Workers Association, Ministerial Association, and Missions-in-Action are among the organizations available for student participation. Chapel services are held four days a week and students are required to attend three of the four services.

Degree Programs

The Bachelor of Arts degree in Religion is offered in six areas of concentration: Pastoral Ministry, Pre-Seminary, Religious Studies, Christian Education, Youth Ministry, and Youth and Music. A total of 192 quarter hours is required for the degree including prescribed courses depending upon the major pursued.

Vanderbilt University
The Divinity School
Nashville, TN 37240   (615) 322-2776

Administration. Dr. H. Jackson Forstman, Dean of the Divinity School.

General Description. The Divinity School began in 1875 as the Biblical Department of Vanderbilt University. The School seeks to fulfill two basic objectives: education of men and women for the practice of Christian ministry; and education, through the Department of Religion of the Graduate School, of future scholars and teachers of religion. Degree programs enable students to plan a course of study in light of their talents, interests, and professional objectives. Although the Divinity School is independent of any church or denomination, it enjoys the recognition and favor of several and welcomes faculty and students of all.

Parent Institution. Vanderbilt University is an independent, privately-supported university. It was under the auspices of the Methodist Episcopal Church, South until 1914.

Community Environment. The University has 50 buildings on a 260-acre campus in the city of Nashville, the capital of Tennessee. Religious publishing is a major industry in the city.

Religious Denomination. Nondenominational.

Accreditation. Southern Association of Colleges and Schools; American Association of Theological Schools in the United States and Canada.

Term System. Semester.

Admission Requirements. Baccalaureate degree from an accredited institution. Doctor of Ministry program: Master of Divinity degree.

Tuition and Fees. Graduate School: Tuition $354 per credit hour; after 72 semester hours, $200 per semester if in residence, or $50 per semester if out of residence. Divinity School: Tuition $223 per credit hour. Student activities fee $52.

Financial Aid. Scholarships, grants-in-aid, and loans are available.

Housing. Housing is available in residence halls and apartments.

Library Facilities. The Jean and Alexander Heard University Library has holdings numbering over 1,600,000 volumes. The Divinity Library houses 135,000 volumes and receives more than 900 serials in a wide variety of languages. The collection is particularly strong in Biblical studies and maintains a distinguished special collection in Judaica. The Thomas W. Phillips Memorial Building houses the headquarters, library, and archives of the Disciples of Christ Historical Society.

Religious Services/Activities. Worship at Vanderbilt is a shared responsibility of faculty and students. A variety of worship services are available on a regular basis. Acts of worship are scheduled each Thursday for the entire Divinity School community. Other services of worship open to the community are provided by the Roman Catholic and Episcopal traditions.

Degree Programs

The Master of Divinity program aims to begin a process of education focusing on understanding the Christian faith and its implications for human life. It is designed to prepare men and women for the practice of ministry, although a definite commitment to the ministry is not prerequisite to admission. A minimum of 84 semester hours of coursework is required. Students may select a focus from the following: Pastoral Ministry, Specialty Ministry, Special Problem, Bi-Professional, Liberation Theology, or Pre-Teaching. Field education is required.

The Doctor of Ministry program is designed to provide advanced professional training for men and women who anticipate a life vocation in the service of the church. Students must complete a minimum of 30 semester hours with a grade point average of B or better and are required to complete a project of substantial scope as part of their plan of study. Students may complete all requirements in one academic year.

The Department of Religion in the Graduate School offers work leading to the Master of Arts and Doctor of Philosophy (Ph.D.) degrees. Programs of study are available in the following areas: Asian and African religions, Biblical studies (Old Testament, New Testament), European and American church history, history of Christian and Jewish thought, systematic and philosophical theology, religious and social ethics, and religion and personality. A minimum of 24 semester hours of graduate work is required for the Master of Arts. The Doctor of Philosophy formally requires 72 hours of graduate study.

TEXAS

Abilene Christian University
College of Biblical Studies
1600 Campus Court
ACU Station Box 7768
Abilene, TX 79699   (915) 674-2317

Administration. Dr. William J. Teague, President; Dr. John C. Stevens, Chancellor; Dr. C.G. Gray, Vice President for Academic Affairs and Dean of the University; Ian A. Fair, Chairman, Department of Bible (College of Liberal and Fine Arts); B.J. Humble, Chairman, Department of Bible (Graduate School).

General Description. Abilene Christian University is divided into 6 academic colleges, of which one is the College of Biblical Studies. Established on February 18, 1985, the College stands in a long line of Christian service. Continuing the University's 79-year commitment to the Bible as the inspired and infallible word of God, the College is committed to a concept of ministry and service that has deep roots in the restoration movement. Intensive study of the Bible lies at the core of every religious program offered by the College. The College of Biblical Studies includes the following three departments: Department of Bible, the Department of Marriage and Family, and the Department of Graduate Studies.

For those wishing to prepare for the ministry, the Department of Bible offers 11 degrees on the undergraduate level through the Bachelor of Arts degree and the Bachelor of Science degree programs. The Department of Graduate Studies offers 19 graduate degrees through the Master of Arts degree or Master of Science degree programs.

Parent Institution. Abilene Christian University was founded in 1906 by A.B. Barret, a Tennessee preacher, who envisioned a center of Christian education in the Southwest, and has been closely related to the Church of Christ throughout its history. Its purpose remains to educate its students for Christian service throughout the world. As such, the University emphasizes a curriculum of liberal studies, exalts the Bible as the Word of God, and strives for Christian values in contemporary life. The

Graduate School was established on 1953 and now enrolls about 600 students each semester.

Community Environment. The 102-acre campus has 26 buildings on a site overlooking the city from the northeast, plus a 27-acre residential park with 7 buildings. In the early history of Texas, the buffalo lured settlers to this west Texas city and the railroad encouraged them to stay. Today, this community of over 100,000 serves the agricultural, marketing, and oil interests in the area. It is the site of Dyess Air Force Base. The climate is high and dry. Recreational facilities include swimming, boating, fishing, water sports, golf courses, zoo, roller rink, tennis, and bowling alleys.

Religious Denomination. Church of Christ.

Religious Emphasis. Evangelical, Restorationist.

Accreditation. Southern Association of Colleges and Schools.

Term System. Semester; summer term.

Enrollment in Degree Programs in Religion 1984–85. Total 260; men 250, women 10.

Degrees in Religion Awarded 1984–85. Bachelor of Arts 10; men 8, women 2. Bachelor of Science 18; men 18. Bachelor of Biblical Studies 6; men 6. Master of Arts 18; men 18. Master of Science 15; men 12, women 3. Master of Divinity 7; men 7. Master of Religious Education 1; men 1. Master of Missiology 2; men 2. Master of Marriage and Family Therapy 12; men 10, women 2. (Statistics are for May and August, 1985.)

Faculty for Degree Programs in Religion. Total 36; full-time 25, part-time 11.

Admission Requirements. Undergraduate: High school diploma with rank in the 1st, 2nd, or 3rd quarter of class; minimum of 15 high school units including 3 in English, 2 in pure social science, 2 in mathematics, 1 in science, and 7 electives selected from the list approved by the State Department of Education. Graduate: Bachelor of Arts degree or the equivalent; knowledge of a foreign language.

Tuition and Fees. Tuition $95 per semester hour; general fee $20 per semester hour; board with various meal plans $535 to $610 plus tax per semester; room rates range from $410 to $610 depending upon accommodations; health services fee $10 per semester; other fees where applicable.

Financial Aid. Grants and scholarships available; scholarships for Bible majors; work opportunities and loans.

Housing. The University has on-campus dormitory accommodations for single students. There is no housing for married students, but numerous apartments are available near the campus.

Library Facilities. The Margaret and Herman Brown Library holds a collection of 750,000 titles. The library is a federal depository for selected government publications. Special collections include Robbins Railroad Collection, Omar Burleson Archives, a rare Bible collection, church and Abilene Christian University archival material, collections for Restoration Studies.

Religious Services/Activities. Activities include required daily assembly (chapel), spontaneous worship as in the Tuesday Night Devotionals, Mission Outreach, the annual "Lectures on Preaching" (October), and the Bible Lectureship (February) which attracts thousands of visitors from throughout the United States. In addition, a number of Abilene congregations provide special programs for students.

Degree Programs

The Bachelor of Arts or Bachelor of Science programs are offered with a major in Biblical, Greek, Ministry, Missions, Religious Education, Pulpit Ministry, and Youth Ministry. The various majors provide knowledge of the Bible and related studies so that the student will be well-grounded intellectually in the Christian faith and that his/her own faith will be a personal experience to be lived and shared. Courses are grouped into the areas of Greek, Hebrew, Latin, Biblical Division, Doctrines Division, Church History Division, Christian Ministry, and Missions.

The Master of Arts degree program offer major field concentrations in Old and New Testament, Ancient Church History, Restoration History, Doctrinal Studies, Biblical Greek, and Missions. Major field concentrations in the Master of Science program are offered in Ministry and Evangelism, Religious Education, and Missions. These programs are intended to provide a background for further graduate study, teaching careers in colleges and schools, and for specific ministries in the church.

The Master of Missiology degree serves the needs of specialists in Missions who need both a broad training in mission work and Biblical studies and yet cannot afford the time for more extensive training.

The Master of Religious Education degree is offered primarily to provide a higher degree of specialization and efficiency for education directors, directors of elementary, youth, and adult work, college professors of religious education, and writers of Bible class literature. The degree also provides excellent training for directors of Bible chairs in state colleges and universities, preachers, elders, and Bible school teachers. The course of study is structured to give a strong foundation in the Bible with such

other studies which deal with the practicalities of planning and administering a program of work in the area of the student's interest and preparation.

The Master of Divinity degree allows a breadth of preparation not possible in the other degree programs and is intended primarily to prepare men for more effective ministry of the work in preaching, in the educational work of the local church, and in missionary work at home and abroad. The degree also represents excellent preparation for teaching in Bible chair situations and for doctoral work in Biblical studies.

A Master of Arts degree in Religious Communication is an interdepartmental program. It provides for substantial courses in Biblical content from the Bible department and for methodology and communication theory from the Communication Department. The program requires 36 hours, 18 of which are in Bible courses and 18 in Communication courses.

Special Programs

By means of a correspondence study service, college courses from the regular curriculum are made available to students away from the campus.

Arlington Baptist College
Division of Biblical Education
3001 West Division
Arlington, TX 76012   (817) 461-8741

Administration. Wayne Martin, President.

General Description. The Division of Biblical Education seeks to impart a thorough Biblical knowledge, a language basis for a sound exegesis of the Bible, and an understanding of the basic doctrinal and theological concepts of the Christian faith. The Division is divided into the Departments of Bible, Biblical Language, and Theology. All students major in Bible. The degrees Bachelor of Arts and Bachelor of Science are awarded as well as the Bible Certificate and the Diploma of Bible.

Parent Institution. The primary purpose of Arlington Baptist College is to offer instruction in the English Bible and other subjects necessary for a proper approach to and presentation of the Word of God. Graduates are qualified for leadership in soul winning, church building, missionary endeavors, church music, Sunday school administration, and Christian education.

Community Environment. Arlington Baptist College occupies 55 acres of some of the choicest property between Fort Worth and Dallas. Native trees and shrubs combine with scenic walks to provide the student with an appropriate setting for meditation. The College is within minutes of downtown Fort Worth, Arlington, Grand Prairie, Hurst, Euless, Irving, and Dallas.

Religious Denomination. Baptist.

Religious Emphasis. Fundamentalist.

Accreditation. American Association of Bible Colleges.

Term System. Semester.

Enrollment in Degree Programs in Religion 1984–85. All students (approximately 244) major in Bible.

Degrees in Religion Awarded 1984–85. Bachelor of Arts 8; men 6, women 2. Bachelor of Science 32; men 22, women 10. Diploma 1; men 1.

Faculty for Degree Programs in Religion. Total 20; full-time 16, part-time 4.

Admission Requirements. Graduation from an accredited high school with minimum of three years of English, two years of social science, two years of mathematics, and one year of science; ACT or SAT; GED equivalency accepted; 18 years of age. Applicant must be a Born-Again Christian.

Tuition and Fees. Tuition $50 per semester hour; fees approximately $100; room and board approximately $1,-550 per year.

Financial Aid. Financial aid is offered to those students who can document their need for such assistance and who would not otherwise be able to attend Arlington Baptist College.

Housing. All single students are required to live in one of the dormitories and to take their meals in the cafeteria.

Library Facilities. The Earl K. Oldham Library houses a collection of over 25,000 volumes. The J. Frank Norris papers on microfilm are maintained and other historical materials on the College and its founders are located in the Heritage Collection.

Religious Services/Activities. Chapel services are conducted three times a week and are compulsory for all students. All students are urged to unite with a local church as soon as possible after arriving in the area. There are group prayer meetings and semester days of prayer.

Degree Programs

A minimum of 128 semester hours is required for graduation with a Bachelor of Arts or Bachelor of Science degree. The curriculum is structured in three divisions: Biblical Education (40 hours), Professional Education (6-10 hours), and General Education (52 hours); in addition are the Minor (18-20 hours), and electives (6-12 hours). The Biblical Education Division includes the Departments of Bible, Biblical Language, and Theology. The Division of Professional Education includes the Departments of Christian Education, Missions, Music, and Pastoral Studies. The Division of General Education is comprised of the Departments of Business, Communications, Language Arts, Science, and Social Sciences.

Special Programs

A Bible Certificate is awarded upon the completion of a prescribed program of 32 hours. A Diploma of Bible is awarded to students completing a prescribed program of 92 semester hours.

Austin College
Department of Religion and Philosophy
900 North Grand Avenue
Sherman, TX 75090   (214) 892-9101

Administration. Harry E. Smith, President.

General Description. Austin College throughout its history has played a vital role in the education of students preparing for a profession in the field of theology. Students who contemplate the graduate study of theology, professional training for a church vocation, or the study of religion should register with the College chaplain who serves as pre-theology adviser.

Parent Institution. Austin College is a privately supported, coeducational liberal arts college. It is affiliated with the Presbyterian Church. The 60-acre campus is located in northeast Sherman, 60 miles north of Dallas.

Community Environment. Austin has a population of over 370,000. It is located on the Colorado River in the heart of Texas and is capital of the state.

Religious Denomination. Presbyterian Church (U.S.A.).

Accreditation. Southern Association of Colleges and Schools.

Term System. Semester (4-1-4 plan).

Admission Requirements. High school graduation from an accredited school; upper half of graduating class.

Tuition and Fees. Tuition $5,500 per year; room $1,300; board $1,400; student activity fee $40.

Financial Aid. Scholarships, grants, and loans are available.

Housing. Residence halls are available on campus.

Library Facilities. The Arthur Hopkins Library houses over 185,000 volumes.

Religious Services/Activities. The Religious Program at the College is coordinated through the college chaplain and the Chapel office. Ecumenical in style, the program focuses on activities and programs of worship, community building, study, and service.

Degree Programs

The curriculum in Religion and Philosophy is structured to permit a concentration in either field or in a combined program of studies which enables a student to pursue a special interest in both disciplines. A concentration in Religion requires a minimum of eight approved courses. The Bachelor of Arts degree is awarded upon the completion of a total of 34 course credits.

Austin Presbyterian Theological Seminary
100 East 27th Street
Austin, TX 78705   (512) 472-6736

Administration. Dr. Jack L. Stotts, President; Dr. Robert M. Shelton, Academic Dean.

General Description. Austin Presbyterian Theological Seminary is a seminary in the Presbyterian-Reformed tradition whose mission is to educate and equip individuals for the ordained Christian ministry and other forms of Christian service and leadership. The Seminary grants the degrees Master of Divinity, Master of Theology, and Doctor of Ministry.

Community Environment. Austin Presbyterian Theological Seminary is located in one of the most rapidly growing areas in the country and the fastest growing metropolitan area in Texas. The Seminary is ideally situated in the city of Austin, on the north edge of the University of Texas and 2 blocks away from the Episcopal Seminary of the Southwest. It enjoys a rich community life in the midst of an intensive educational setting. The atmosphere and the curriculum provide opportunities for maximizing the experience of each student.

Religious Denomination. Presbyterian.

Religious Emphasis. Reformed.

Accreditation. Southern Association of Colleges and Schools; Association of Theological Schools in the United States and Canada.

Term System. Three-one-three; summer term for intensive Greek for first year students.

Enrollment in Degree Programs in Religion 1984–85. Total 168; men 132, women 36; does not include special students or audits.

Degrees in Religion Awarded 1984–85. Master of Divinity 21; men 15, women 6. Master of Theology 1; men 1. Doctor of Ministry 9; men 9.

Faculty for Degree Programs in Religion. Total 15; full-time 13, part-time 2.

Admission Requirements. Graduate of an accredited college or university with baccalaureate degree and cumulative grade point average of at least 2.5 on a 4.0 scale; full communion with some branch of Christian church; exhibit fitness and promise for ministry.

Tuition and Fees. Tuition $2,375 (September-May) for Master of Divinity program; $2,325 for Doctor of Ministry program; dormitory room $80-$100 per month; board $140 per month; apartments $175-$300 per month.

Financial Aid. Work scholarships, tuition grants, short- and long-term loans represent the resources available for financial aid.

Housing. Dormitories and apartments are available. Single students must live and eat in the dining hall.

Library Facilities. The Stitt Library holdings are in excess of 118,000 volumes of books and periodicals, 2,150 reels of microfilm, and hundreds of microfiche. The library is particulary strong in biblical studies, biblical archaeology, patristics, the continental Reformation, Calvin, and Presbyterianism.

Religious Services/Activities. Chapel service is held five days per week, three of which are prayer and praise and two of which are full worship services.

Degree Programs

The Seminary intends its Master of Divinity program to prepare men and women to enter the office of Minister of the Word in the Church for the sake of the Church's obedient service in the world. The program acknowledges the real differences which exist in student needs, interests, and goals, and therefore endeavors to mediate that knowledge and to allow for the development of those skills which together provide the essential foundation for a variety of ministries. Students participate in three modes of learning: classroom study, supervised practice of ministry, and reflection. A total of 200 credits of required and elective work must be accomplished.

The Master of Theology program is a post-Master of Divinity opportunity to pursue further study and research under close faculty supervision. Ordinarily it requires residence for a nine-month academic year. During this time the candidate focuses on one theological discipline, or on a field of inquiry which integrates two of the usual theological disciplines (biblical, historical, theological, church's ministry) or which integrates one of these with a field of human studies. The program is designed to enable a candidate to obtain greater competence in one or more disciplines beyond the Master of Divinity level. Each program will be designed in accord with the candidate's goals.

The Doctor of Ministry program is designed for persons who already hold the Bachelor of Divinity, Master of Divinity, or their equivalent, and who are actively engaged in the practice of ministry. The program provides ministers the opportunity to significantly increase their competence in areas of particular interest.

Special Programs

The Seminary offers continuing education programs; an extension program in Houston, a lecture series, and a Lay Academy.

Baylor University
Department of Religion
Box 150, Baylor University
Waco, TX 76798   (817) 755-3735

Administration. Dr. Herbert H. Reynolds, President; Dr. John S. Belew, Provost; Dr. Robert G. Collmer, Dean of Graduate Studies; Dr. Glenn O. Hillburn, Chairman, Department of Religion.

General Description. The Graduate Program in Religion is designed to offer a range of educational opportunities for the serious student of religion. Various programs at both the Master of Arts and Doctor of Philosophy levels are structured to meet diverse needs and objectives.

Parent Institution. Baylor University is a coeducational institution of higher learning where education may be gained under Christian influences and ideals. The University's paramount, all-inclusive aim is to prepare students for effective living in a democratic society. As an educational institution striving for academic excellence, the University's immediate purpose is to offer a program of liberal arts and professional education that will challenge and guide students in their quest for knowledge, that will motivate them toward self-realization, that will help them improve their abilities, and that will enable them to cultivate a greater appreciation of the highest values. In this pursuit of learning, scholarship is considered to be not an end in itself, but a vital means by which students may develop a high degree of usefulness.

The University seeks to provide a democratic and Christian atmosphere on the campus and in classrooms and laboratories, whereby students and faculty may work together with inquiring minds in the discovery and propagation of ideas. Students are taught to think for themselves, to develop intellectual curiosity, and to be self-reliant in their search for truth.

Community Environment. The 350-acre campus has 55 buildings, located in Waco, Texas, population over 100,-000. An industrial center located on the Brazos River, the city is surrounded by rich agricultural and dairying country. The climate is temperate with a mean annual temperature of 67.4 degrees, and average rainfall of 35 inches. There are almost 200 churches of various faiths, public hospitals and a veterans hospital, as well as excellent libraries. Local recreation includes boating, swimming, fishing, picnicking, bowling, tennis, parks, a zoo, and Lake Waco.

Religious Denomination. Southern Baptist.

Religious Emphasis. Ecumenical.

Accreditation. Southern Association of Colleges and Schools.

Term System. Semester; summer term.

Enrollment in Degree Programs in Religion 1984–85. Total 99; men 95, women 4.

Degrees in Religion Awarded 1984–85. Master of Arts 1; men 1. Doctor of Philosophy 13; men 13.

Faculty for Degree Programs in Religion. Total 10; full-time 10.

Admission Requirements. Master of Arts: Eighteen semester hours of undergraduate study in religion; Graduate Record Examination; superior grade point average. Doctor of Philosophy: Equivalent of Master's degree in Religion; at least two foreign languages; Graduate Record Examination; superior grade point average.

Tuition and Fees. Tuition $125 per semester hour; matriculation fee $25.

Financial Aid. Graduate assistantship valued up to $7,-250; University funded scholarships valued up to $9,000 per year; E.L. Dwyer endowed scholarships valued up to $1,500; partial tuition-remission scholarships.

Housing. Adequate off-campus housing is available at moderate rates.

Library Facilities. The general library has holdings of 1.3 million volumes plus 500,000 microforms. The holdings in religion number over 250,000 volumes.

Degree Programs

At the Master of Arts level, two programs meet the goals of students. The General Program is a broad course of study for those whose purpose is to acquire a comprehensive study of religion at the graduate level. This program is designed to satisfy the needs of either those who want a broad foundation from which to do further graduate study or those who desire a deeper understanding of the Christian religion for personal or vocational purposes. In this program the student will take at least six hours of study in each of three major divisions (Biblical, Historical, and Theological) of the Department. The Specialized Program is designed for the student with adequate undergraduate background in religion who wants to pursue intensive study and research within one of the three major divisions.

The Doctor of Philosophy with a major in religion provides an opportunity for qualified students to do graduate work in this discipline at the highest level and in the university setting. It provides preparation for research and teaching in the college and university setting where religion is taught as one of the liberal arts and in relation to other such disciplines, particularly the humanities, the social sciences, and the natural sciences.

Bishop College
3837 Simpson-Stuart Road
Dallas, TX 75241   (214) 372-8057

Administration. Dr. Wright L. Lassiter, Jr., President.

General Description. The curriculum area of Religion offers major programs in Religion and Philosophy with program emphasis in Christian Education, Philosophy, and Religion. The programs lead to the Bachelor of Arts degree.

Parent Institution. Bishop College was established in 1881 in Marshall, Texas by freedmen from Texas and Louisiana and missions from the Home Mission Society of the Northern Baptist Convention (now the American Baptist Churches). The institution has affiliations with most major Black Baptist conventions throughout the country.

Community Environment. The College is located in the South Oak Cliff section approximately eight miles south of downtown Dallas. The 200-acre campus has 27 buildings.

Religious Denomination. American Baptist Churches in the U.S.A.

Accreditation. Southern Association of Colleges and Schools.

Term System. Semester.

Admission Requirements. High school graduation from an accredited school; SAT; college entrance examinations.

Tuition and Fees. Tuition $1,320 per semester; general fees $180; room $468; board $642.

Financial Aid. The College participates in federally funded program as well as various grant and aid programs for Texas residents. Honor scholarships and work-study programs are also available.

Housing. The College has eight modern dormitories.

Library Facilities. The Zale Library houses approximately 174,000 volumes.

Religious Services/Activities. Student Convocation is the opportunity for the College community to come together in both worship services and in special programs.

Degree Programs

The Bachelor of Arts degree is offered with majors in Religion, Philosophy, and Christian Education.

Dallas Baptist University
College of Christian Faith and Living
7777 West Kiest Boulevard
Dallas, TX 75211   (214) 331-8311

Administration. Dr. William E. Bell, Jr., Dean, College of Christian Faith and Living.

General Description. The College of Christian Faith and Living fulfills a significant role in the curriculum of Dallas Baptist University through the course offerings in religion, Greek, philosophy, and religious education. It provides general studies courses in religion for all students, a program of courses for majors in religion and religious education, and electives for all students who desire them. The programs of study for religion and religious education are designed to prepare students for further study in a seminary or university, or for a lifetime of study and service without further formal training. The school provides on-the-job training for religion majors in cooperation with local churches, hospitals, missions, and other religious institutions.

Parent Institution. Dallas Baptist University was established as a two-year institution in 1898. Beginning with the fall semester of 1968, the school entered transition to senior college status. The first bachelor's degrees were awarded in 1970. The University is a Christian, coeducational college cooperating with the Baptist General Convention of Texas.

Community Environment. The 200-acre campus has 11 buildings. It is located in Dallas, a financial, manufacturing, and distributing center with a population of approximately 850,000 people. The campus is 13 miles from downtown Dallas and 19 miles from Fort Worth.

Religious Denomination. Baptist General Convention of Texas.

Accreditation. Southern Association of Colleges and Schools.

Term System. Semester.

Admission Requirements. High school graduation from an accredited school with rank in the upper 70 percent of class; GED accepted; ACT required.

Tuition and Fees. Tuition $120 per semester hour; room $430 per semester; board $732.25 per semester.

Financial Aid. Scholarships, awards, grants, loans, and employment are types of assistance available. Ministerial Career Scholarships and Christian Participation Scholarships are also available.

Housing. Dormitories for men and women are located on campus.

Library Facilities. The library houses over 129,000 volumes.

Religious Services/Activities. Service organizations on campus include Fellowship of Christian Athletes, Ministerial Alliance, and Baptist Student Union. The Baptist Student Union promotes the students' religious and spiritual development.

Degree Programs

The major in Religion leading to the Bachelor of Arts degree must complete 27 hours of specified religion courses and 9 hours of specified philosophy courses. The Bachelor of Arts degree requires a minimum of 126 hours.

The major in Religious Education leads to either the Bachelor of Arts or Bachelor of Science degree and requires a minimum of 30 hours of required and elective courses.

Dallas Christian College
2700 Christian Parkway
Dallas, TX 75234   (214) 241-3371

Administration. Gene Shepherd, President.

General Description. The primary purpose of Dallas Christian College is to prepare students for Christian ministries or church vocations through a program of Biblical, general, and practical studies. Its educational objective is to provide a curriculum designed to develop an individual capable of reaching the fullness for which he was created. The College grants the degrees Bachelor of Arts, Bachelor of Science in Religion, Bachelor of Science in Education, Bachelor of Science in Music, Associate of Arts, Associate of Ministry, and Associate of Applied Science.

Community Environment. Dallas Christian College is located on a 22-acre campus in Farmer's Branch, just 600 feet from Dallas' northwest boundary line. This is a rapidly developing section of the North Dallas metropolitan area. It is convenient to transportation, business areas, cultural centers, and recreational areas.

Religious Denomination. Nondenominational; supported by the Independent Christian Churches.

Accreditation. American Association of Bible Colleges.

Term System. Semester.

Enrollment in Degree Programs in Religion 1984–85. Total 113; men 63, women 50.

Degrees in Religion Awarded 1984–85. Bachelor of Arts 7; men 6, women 1. Bachelor of Science in Religion 2; men 2. Bachelor of Science in Education 2; women 2. Bachelor of Science in Music 1; men 1. Associate of Arts 2; women 2. Associate of Ministry 1; women 1. Associate of Applied Science 3; women 3.

Faculty for Degree Programs in Religion. Total 21; full-time 8, part-time 13.

Admission Requirements. Top¾ of high school graduating class; score above the 20th percentile on the ACT composite.

Tuition and Fees. Tuition $59 per semester hour; special fees up to $125; books and supplies $100-$150.

Financial Aid. Grants, loans, and college work-study are available to qualified students.

Housing. Men's and women's dormitories are available.

Library Facilities. The library contains over 30,000 volumes.

Religious Services/Activities. Chapel services are held 3 times a week.

Degree Programs

The Bachelor of Arts program prepares the student to minister in a local congregation and also contains the course prerequisites for entrance into a seminary or graduate school. The program requires 128 hours for graduation, including 41 hours in general education, 32 hours in Bible, 18 hours in the Biblical Language minor, and 18-19 hours in another minor of the student's choice.

The Bachelor of Science in Education program prepares the student to teach in a Christian or private day school. It requires 130 hours for graduation, including 50 hours in general education, 8 hours in language, 32 hours in Bible, 35 hours in specialized education courses, and 5 hours in ministerial education. The Bachelor of Science in Music program equips the student with a working knowledge of the English Bible and develops the student as a competent musician, capable of directing the music program of the local congregation. The 128-hour program requires 38 hours in general education, 40 hours in Bible, 27 hours in music theory and education, 8 hours in applied music, 6 hours in concert choir, 2 hours in performing groups, and 7-8 hours in ministerial education.

The Bachelor of Science in Religion program equips the student for a general or specialized ministry in the local congregation. The program requires 128 hours for graduation, including 41 hours in general education, 40 hours in Bible, and a choice of two minor areas of study of 18-19 hours each. The Bachelor of Science in Religion (Missions and Nursing) prepares the student to serve as a nurse in a foreign or home mission. The program of study includes courses at both Dallas Christian College and the Brookhaven College campus of the Dallas County Community College System. The program requires 131 hours for graduation including 43 hours in general education and science, 36 hours in nursing, 32 hours in Bible, and 22 hours in missions and ministry education.

Special Programs

The degrees Associate of Arts, Associate of Ministry, and Associate of Applied Science with emphasis in Secretarial Science are offered.

Dallas Theological Seminary
3909 Swiss Avenue
Dallas, TX 75204   (214) 824-3094

Administration. Dr. John F. Walvoord, President; Dr. Roy B. Zuck, Academic Dean; Dr. Thomas L. Constable, Director of D.Min. Studies; Dr. Harold W. Hoehner, Director of Th.D. Studies.

General Description. The purpose of Dallas Theological Seminary is to prepare students, through graduate-level biblical, theological, ministerial, and spiritual instruction, to expound the Scriptures while serving in various ministries throughout the world. It grants the degrees Master of Theology, Master of Sacred Theology, Master of Arts in Biblical Studies, Master of Arts in Christian Education, Doctor of Ministry, and Doctor of Theology. The Seminary furthers its purpose by offering on-campus and off-campus continuing education courses for alumni and other Christian workers. It also publishes *Bibliotheca Sacra*, designed to provide continuing biblical and theological instruction to biblical scholars, alumni, pastors, teachers, and serious lay Bible students. The Seminary also serves as a theological resource center for the Christian public.

Dallas Theological Seminary is denominationally unrelated. It seeks to serve those of like Biblical faith in evangelical Protestantism and welcomes to its student body qualified persons who are in sympathy with its doctrinal position.

Community Environment. Dallas Theological Seminary is located in Dallas, Texas, one of the fastest growing cities in the thriving Southwest. Dallas is a city of almost 1 million people with a metropolitan area population of more than 2.5 million. The city boasts beautiful residential areas, parks and playgrounds, fine schools and universities, and an outstanding zoo. The Seminary campus includes 19 buildings on 13 acres of land, within minutes of downtown Dallas and 25 miles from the Dallas-Fort Worth International Airport.

Religious Denomination. Nondenominational (Protestant).

Religious Emphasis. Evangelical, Dispensational.

Accreditation. Southern Association of Colleges and Schools.

Term System. Semester.

Enrollment in Degree Programs in Religion 1984-85. Total 1,186; men 1,058, women 128.

Degrees in Religion Awarded 1984-85. Master of Arts in Biblical Studies 87; men 65, women 22. Master of Arts in Christian Education 16; men 15, women 1. Master of Theology/Doctor of Theology 219; men 219. Doctor of

Ministry 6; men 6.

Faculty for Degree Programs in Religion. Total 68; full-time 60, part-time 8.

Admission Requirements. Bachelor of Arts degree or its equivalent with at least 60 hours in Arts and Sciences.

Tuition and Fees. Master's courses $115 per semester hour; Doctor of Theology courses $145 per semester hour; Doctor of Ministry courses $120 per semester hour; room and board $1,155 per semester.

Financial Aid. Over 20 scholarship funds are administered for student aid.

Housing. Dormitory space is available for single men; one-bedroom apartments are available for married students and single women.

Library Facilities. The Mosher Library contains a book collection of approximately 95,000 volumes.

Religious Services/Activities. Chapel is held four days a week. Faculty-led advisee groups provide opportunity for individual spiritual development.

Degree Programs

The program leading to the Master of Arts degree in Biblical Studies is designed to give men and women a Biblical and theological foundation for various kinds of Christian service other than pulpit ministry. The Seminary considers the degree a terminal degree which is not designed to prepared students for doctoral studies at the Seminary.

The Master of Arts degree in Christian Education is designed to provide a graduate-level biblical and theological education for men and women who anticipate a vocational ministry as Christian education specialists. This program helps prepare its graduates to assume positions such as ministers of Christian education, ministers of youth, children's workers, ministers of adults, directors of family life education, administrators in Christian higher education, camp leaders, Christian school administrators, or parachurch youth leaders.

The Master of Theology four-year degree program is the Seminary's major curriculum. It is designed to produce competent Bible expositors who are qualified to serve effectively as pastors, missionaries, and leaders in other areas of Christian ministry. The prescribed curriculum involves extensive preparation in Hebrew, Greek, Bible, systematic and historical theology, along with preparation in other disciplines including pastoral ministries, Christian education, missions, and field education. Majors for the program include Semitics and Old Testament Studies, New Testament Literature and Exegesis, Bible Exposition, Systematic Theology, Historical Theology, Pastoral Ministries, Christian Education, or World Missions.

The Master of Sacred Theology Program is open to those who have graduated from a standard three-year seminary course. The program is designed to provide an opportunity for additional and advanced studies in the theological disciplines in preparation for Christian service.

The Doctor of Ministry program is designed to equip those actively involved in a vocational ministry with a higher level of competence in the practice of a biblically and theologically oriented ministry. The program concentrates on developing expertise in the theory and practice of ministry.

The Doctor of Theology degree is designed for those who are capable of doing research at the highest level with a view to their becoming scholars and educational leaders in various fields of Christian ministry. The program includes three years of study, two of which (as a minimum) must be spent in residence.

Special Programs

A Lay Institute is held during which advanced students teach lay persons from the community on Monday evenings.

Several continuing education seminars are held around the country each year and are taught by faculty members.

Dallas, University of
Department of Theology/Holy Trinity Seminary
1845 East Northgate Drive
Irving, TX 75062   (214) 721-5219

Administration. Dr. Robert F. Sasseen, President; Dr. John E. Paynter, Provost and Dean of the College; Dr. Peter C. Phan, Chairman, Department of Theology, and Director of Graduate Programs.

General Description. The Theology Department contributes to the general educational effort of the University on the following levels: a basic program of core curriculum courses designed for all students, an undergraduate major program for those who plan to concentrate on theological studies, graduate programs (Master of Arts, Master of Divinity, Master of Religious Education) for those who intend to cultivate theology in teaching, priestly ministry, scholarship, and other forms of professional activities.

Through its graduate programs the Department of Theology fosters advanced theological studies, scholarship and research, and the development of pastoral and catechetical skills. The Department is privileged to participate in the theological formation of candidates for the priesthood, in particular the seminarians of Holy Trinity Seminary, and of several religious orders. It offers degree programs for men and women who plan careers in teaching and research.

Parent Institution. The University of Dallas is sponsored by the Roman Catholic Diocese of Dallas. It is dedicated to the renewal of the Western heritage of liberal education and to the recovery of the Christian intellectual tradition. The University is open to faculty and students of all denominations, and supports their academic and religious freedom. The educational mission of the University is carried out in the Constantin College of Liberal Arts and in the Braniff Graduate School.

Community Environment. The University of Dallas occupies a 1,000-acre tract of rolling hills located northwest of the city of Dallas, in Irving, Texas (population 120,-000). From this campus, one of the highest points in the area, the skyline of Dallas dominates the view. In the center of the burgeoning metroplex, the campus is ten miles from the huge Dallas-Fort Worth Regional Airport, fifteen minutes from downtown Dallas, and forty minutes from Fort Worth by interstate highways. L.B. Houston nature preserve, along the Elm Fork of the Trinity River, forms part of the eastern boundary of the campus.

Religious Denomination. Roman Catholic.

Accreditation. Southern Association of Colleges and Schools.

Term System. Semester; summer term.

Enrollment in Degree Programs in Religion 1984–85. Total 64; men 56, women 8.

Degrees in Religion Awarded 1984–85. Bachelor of Arts 1; men 1. Master of Divinity 9; men 9. Master of Religious Education 1; women 1. Master of Arts 5; men 3, women 2. Doctor of Philosophy 1; women 1.

Faculty for Degree Programs in Religion. Total 16; full-time 6, part-time 10.

Admission Requirements. High school transcript showing at least six semesters of work and rank in the top fifteen percent of the junior class; one academic letter of recommendation; SAT or ACT with rank in the upper fifteen percent of college-bound students. Graduate students must have a Bachelor's degree and submit Graduate Record Examination scores.

Tuition and Fees. Tuition $2,015 per semester; part-time $168 per credit hour; room and board $1,195 to $1,520 depending upon accommodations and meal plan; apartment housing $745 to $955 per semester; general fee $200 per semester.

Financial Aid. Scholarships and awards, grants, federal and state aid programs, and work-study programs are available.

Housing. On-campus dormitories and apartment accommodations (for upper division and graduate students) are offered. Dormitory contracts include food service.

Library Facilities. The William A. Blakley Library contains more than 150,000 volumes in book form, over 70,-000 volumes in microforms, and over 800 current titles of periodicals.

Religious Services/Activities. Mass is offered at noon and at five daily and several times during the weekend. In addition to the regular schedules of Masses, other religious events such as the Mass of the Holy Spirit, Advent Masses, and Easter Week services mark the liturgical and academic seasons. The University community is also welcome at liturgies at Holy Trinity Seminary, the Cistercian Abbey, Dominican Priory, and the School Sisters of Notre Dame.

Degree Programs

The Bachelor of Arts with a major in Theology is a coordinated sequence of advanced courses in Biblical Theology; History of Dogma; Dogmatic, Liturgical, and Moral Theology. Further advanced courses are offered as electives.

The course of studies leading to the Master of Arts in Theology is designed to impart to qualified students a deeper understanding of and graduate-level professional competence in theology and thus prepare them ordinarily for careers in research and teaching or for further graduate studies.

The Master of Religious Education is offered in cooperation with the Department of Education. The curriculum intends to prepare the students academically for the ministry, especially in the field of religious education, by providing them with an opportunity to gain an advanced knowledge of theology and of the theories and techniques of teaching.

The Master of Divinity degree is a professional degree designed for candidates for the priesthood. It is a four-year program.

East Texas Baptist University
Department of Religion
1209 North Grove Street
Marshall, TX 75670   (214) 935-7963

Administration. Dr. Jerry F. Dawson, President; Dr. C. Gwin Morris, Executive Vice President and Dean of the University; Dr. Donald R. Potts, Chairman, Department of Religion.

General Description. The program of the Department of Religion is designed to equip ministers and church leaders for Christian service within the local church and with the institutional church. Emphasis is placed upon both an academic and a practical study of religion within the context of a liberal arts degree. Through this approach students are not only equipped for immediate places of service in church vocations, but they are also prepared for advanced studies at seminaries or other graduate schools. A major may be obtained in Religion, Christian Ministry, Administrative Careers, or Ministry Careers. In addition to these four areas of religion majors, there are ten areas of specialization which include Church Administration, Counseling Ministries, Education Ministries, Children's Ministries, Youth Ministries, Church Recreation, Church Secretarial Services, Social Ministries, Christian Missions, and Institutional Services.

Parent Institution. East Texas University is a private, coeducational, liberal arts college owned by the Baptist General Convention of Texas and is operated by a Board of Trustees elected by the Convention. The purpose of the University is based upon two guiding principles: that the liberal arts form the surest foundation for education, and that the Christian faith provides the surest foundation for life.

Community Environment. Located on Van Zandt Hill in Marshall, Texas, the 180-acre campus of East Texas Baptist University occupies a site of scenic beauty. The buildings are grouped in a setting of native oaks and pines surrounded by sloping lawns. Marshall (population 23,-000) is 40 miles west of Shreveport, Louisiana. There are many churches of various faiths, hospitals, a radio station, and a public library.

Religious Denomination. Southern Baptist.

Religious Emphasis. Conservative.

Accreditation. Southern Association of Colleges and Schools.

Term System. Semester; summer term.

Enrollment in Degree Programs in Religion 1984–85. Total 122; men 105, women 17.

Degrees in Religion Awarded 1984–85. Bachelor of Arts in Religion 4; men 3, women 1. Bachelor of Arts in Christian Ministries 19; men 19. Bachelor of Arts in Administrative Careers 8; men 5, women 3. Bachelor of Arts in Ministerial Careers 5; men 2, women 3.

Faculty for Degree Programs in Religion. Total 6; full-time 4, part-time 2.

Admission Requirements. In determining the applicant's qualifications for admission, the Admissions Committee considers motivation, intellectual capacity, previous academic achievement, personality and character, vocational interests, and health. An applicant who ranks in academic achievement in the upper half of high school graduating class or has an ACT composite score of 15 or above, and has the units required may be accepted upon submission of his high school grades. Those in the lower half may be admitted on a trial enrollment of one semester.

Tuition and Fees. Tuition $1,500 (15 credit hours), $1,-245 (12 credit hours), $855 (9 credit hours).

Financial Aid. A program of scholarships, grants, loans, and campus employment is available to help students meet expenses while enrolled in University courses.

Housing. Housing for single men and women is provided in campus dormitories. Married students may find housing in unfurnished apartments belonging to the University.

Library Facilities. The Mamye Jarrett Learning Center, the university library, contains over 100,000 volumes of which 8,933 are in Religion.

Religious Services/Activities. The Baptist Student Union sponsors Time Out, a student-led worship service, each week. There are also other on-campus activities calculated to help the student develop and mature spiritually. Fall Retreat, Texas Baptist Student Union Convention, Leadership Training Conference, Missions Conference, and the International Student Conference are among the activities offered. Chapel services are held twice a week.

Degree Programs

The major in Religion leading to the Bachelor of Arts degree requires 33 hours and is a general, theoretical major designed for those who are interested in the fundamentals of the Christian faith. Courses in Biblical Studies, Theological Studies, Historical Studies, and electives are required. The major in Christian Ministry is a composite major of 54 hours which includes Biblical Studies, Theological Studies, and courses in an area of specialization or a minor in another Department. The major in Administrative Careers is also a composite major of 54 hours which requires courses in Biblical Studies, Church-Denominational Ministries, and courses in an area of specialization. The major in Ministry Careers requires a total of 48 hours which includes Biblical Studies, Religious Education, and an area of specialization. All Bachelor of Arts degrees require a total of 128 hours for graduation.

Special Programs

The University provides a program of continuing education in both Marshall and Longview, Texas. Upon demand the program has been extended and expanded in areas within a seventy-five mile radius of Marshall.

Episcopal Theological Seminary of the Southwest

606 Rathervue Place
P.O. Box 2247
Austin, TX 78768   (512) 472-4133

Administration. The Very Rev. Durstan R. McDonald, Dean; William Milton Bennett, Provost.

General Description. The Episcopal Theological Seminary of the Southwest exists to serve the mission of the Church by preparation of men and women for effective leadership as parish clergy in the context of today's world. Students immerse themselves in the study of the classical theological disciplines of scripture, church history, theology, and ethics. An emphasis on pastoral theology, homiletics, clinical pastoral education, and field work enables graduates to apply theological and ethical perspectives to the cultural context in which they are serving. There is a special emphasis on Hispanic studies and cross-cultural awareness. The Seminary's unique position in the Southwest provides for this emphasis. The Seminary grants the degrees Master of Divinity and Master of Arts in Religion, the Diploma in Sacred Theology, and the Certificates of Special Studies, Individual Theological Study, and Continued Professional Studies.

The Seminary has a close working relationship with nearby Austin Presbyterian Theological Seminary. Students cross register for courses; faculty members exchange classrooms; courses are jointly offered by members of both faculties; and the libraries of the two institutions cooperate in the acquisition of books.

Community Environment. Episcopal Theological Seminary of the Southwest is located on a 5-acre campus in Austin, Texas. Austin is a major center of government, education, and high tech industry. The state capitol and over a hundred state offices are located here, as well as the regional headquarters of many federal agencies. There are 7 colleges and universities within a 30-mile radius of the capitol, the largest being the Austin campus of the University of Texas with over 45,000 students. To the west of Austin lies the Hill Country with its 7-lake chain, one of the most attractive tourist areas in Texas.

Religious Denomination. Episcopal.

Accreditation. Southern Association of Colleges and Schools; Association of Theological Schools in the United States and Canada.

Term System. Two semesters, January term (4-1-4 plan); summer term.

Enrollment in Degree Programs in Religion 1984–85. Total 74; men 44, women 30.

Degrees in Religion Awarded 1984–85. Master of Arts 5; men 2, women 3. Master of Divinity 21; men 14, women 7. Certificate of Special Studies 1; women 1. Certificate of Individual Theological Study 3; men 3.

Admission Requirements. Baccalaureate degree.

Tuition and Fees. Tuition $1,650 per semester or $140 per credit hour, whichever is lower; January term $300; housing $160 per month.

Financial Aid. The Seminary is prepared to provide substantial financial aid to needy students to help fill the gap between total costs and resources available from the student, his or her diocese and parish, and other sources. To qualify for consideration for a scholarship grant, the applicant must complete a proper application form, including full disclosure of available financial resources and a proposed budget for the period for which the grant is sought.

Housing. Most students live off-campus. Some dormitory housing is available. The Seminary does not provide board.

Library Facilities. The Seminary Library numbers more than 85,000 volumes and subscribes to 300 periodicals. The library maintains the 17,300 volume collection of the former Episcopal Seminary of the Caribbean. The library also houses the Archives of the Episcopal Church.

Religious Services/Activities. Services are held daily in Christ Chapel. The daily worship schedule is augmented by regular quiet days and festival services. There is an active student association which augments the social and spiritual life of the community in a variety of ways, and there is also an organization for women of the Seminary which sponsors activities of special interest to its members.

Degree Programs

The Master of Divinity program is designed to provide the first level of professional competency for those planning to enter the parish ministry. The three-year program includes at least one summer of supervised training, and requires a total of 107 credits, of which 87 are required and 14 are electives.

The Master of Arts in Religion program is generally designed for those who desire a theological education, but who require neither the comprehensiveness in every area of the curriculum nor the emphasis on professional training characteristic of the Master of Divinity program. The degree requires a minimum of four semesters of full-time study during which a total of 48 credits must be earned. There are three tracks available: Track I is intended for those who wish to study religion; Track II is intended for those who wish to pursue a general theological education to inform the exercise of their ministries as baptized Christians; and Track III is intended for those who wish to begin or further a general theological education in connection with some form of ordained ministry.

Special Programs

The Diploma in Sacred Theology is awarded to those who complete the requirements for the Master of Divinity degree but who do not hold the prerequisite bachelor's degree or its equivalent.

The Certificate in Special Studies and the Certificate of Continued Professional Studies are awarded to a regularly admitted student who has earned at least eighteen credits at or through the Seminary within a two-year period. The Certificate of Individual Theological Study is awarded to those students who have satisfactorily completed a program of study designed especially to meet their individual needs and purposes.

Special Studies programs include: Preparatory Course for New Students; Independent Directed Study Projects; Specialized Curriculum for Lutherans; Courses for United Methodist Ordinands; Theological Studies for Hispanic Ministry; Center for Hispanic Ministries; Spanish Language Study; English Language Instruction for Foreign Students; and Special Assistance.

Hardin-Simmons University
Logsdon School of Theology
Drawer O, HSU Station
Abilene, TX 79698   (915) 677-7281

Administration. Dr. Jesse C. Fletcher, President; Dr. Ronald A. Smith, Vice President for Academic Affairs; Dr. H. K. Neely, Dean, Logsdon School of Theology; Dr. W. Ray Ellis, Dean, Graduate School.

General Description. The Logsdon School of Theology is one of the six schools/colleges of Hardin-Simmons University. Although its primary thrust is pre-seminary undergraduate education in religion, the School of Theology also offers the graduate program Master of Arts in Religion. Undergraduate courses are offered in Old Testament, New Testament, Greek, Hebrew, theology, church history, missions, world religions, comparative Christianity, church recreation, sociology of religion, psychology of religion, several phases of religious education, the work of the minister, evangelism, and sermon preparation — as well as other subjects when need demands. An additional program offered by the School is the Lay Academy, one more way in which Hardin-Simmons University is a partner with Texas Baptist churches in the work of education. The program is designed specifically for the lay person over 25 years of age who desires to learn more about the Christian faith, and covers such topics as theology, Christian history, Baptist life, and other areas of Christian concern.

The Graduate School offers the Master of Arts in Religion and the Master of Arts in Family Ministry.

Parent Institution. Hardin-Simmons University is a comprehensive four-year coeducational liberal arts university owned by the Baptist General Convention of Texas. Current student enrollment is around 1,800 students. Courses are offered through six schools/colleges: College of Arts and Sciences, School of Business and Finance, Irvin School of Education, School of Music, School of Nursing, and Logsdon School of Theology. In addition, the Graduate School grants the degrees Master of Arts, Master of Business Administration, Master of Education, and Master of Music; and the Division of Continuing Education offers non-credit courses designed to meet specific needs.

Community Environment. Hardin-Simmons' compact and beautiful campus, known as "The Forty Acres," contains 26 buildings, two athletic fields, rodeo grounds and stadium, dormitories, and married students' housing. See also: Abilene Christian College for information about the city of Abilene.

Religious Denomination. Southern Baptist.

Religious Emphasis. Mainline Baptist.

Accreditation. Southern Association of Colleges and Schools.

Term System. Semester; May Term and summer term.

Enrollment in Degree Programs in Religion 1984–85. Total 150; men 133, women 17.

Degrees in Religion Awarded 1984–85. Bachelor of Arts 17; men 17. Bachelor of Behavioral Science 13; men 12, women 1.

Faculty for Degree Programs in Religion. Total 10; full-time 7, part-time 3.

Admission Requirements. Applicants submit: completed application for admission with $25 fee; transcript of high school graduation or for transfer students, transcript of accredited junior or senior college work; scores on either ACT or SAT; immunization record.

Tuition and Fees. Tuition $107 per semester hour; activities fee $42; auto permit $20 to $25; room and meals (20 per week) $1,125 to $1,150 per semester.

Financial Aid. A comprehensive financial aid program is offered through the Office of Financial Aid, Hardin-Simmons University. Also, the In-Service Training Office of the Logsdon School of Theology has access to a limited amount of financial aid.

Housing. The following types of housing are available: dormitories for single students, a limited number of apartments and houses for married students, and off-campus privately owned apartments and houses.

Library Facilities. The Richardson Library contains 347,363 items and includes books, bound periodicals, and U.S. documents. Special collections include Southwest History of U.S., Printing of Carl Hertzog, and the Abilene, Texas Photo Collection.

Religious Services/Activities. Chapel is held twice weekly. In addition, there is a religious emphasis week in the fall and a lectureship in the spring.

Degree Programs

Undergraduate degrees include the Bachelor of Arts in Bible, the Bachelor of Arts in Religious Education, the Bachelor of Behavioral Science in Applied Theology, and the Bachelor of Behavioral Science in Church Recreation. Each program has specific course requirements. The courses in Bible and Biblical Languages are designed to give the student a knowledge of and appreciation for the Bible. The courses in Theology provide the student with an understanding of the basic doctrinal positions of the Christian faith, an understanding of alternative views, and an understanding of the Christian past. The courses in Religious Education/Applied Christianity are designed to serve the educational and vocational guidance needs of those planning church-related careers as ministers and other local staff members, missionaries, social workers, denominational personnel, counselors, community and family service workers, and other Christian ministers.

The Graduate School offers the Master of Arts in Religion and the Master of Arts in Family Ministry. The latter degree has three emphases: (1) Theology/Religion, (2) Marital and Family Therapy, and (3) Family Enrichment/Education. Graduates of this program will satisfy all of the course work requirements and half of the clinical experience and supervision requirements for clinical membership in the American Association for Marriage and Family Therapy (AAMFT) and certification in Texas as Marriage and Family Therapists.

Special Programs

The Lay Academy is designed specifically for the lay person over 25 years of age who desires to learn more about the Christian faith. Classes are offered in church facilities where there is demonstrated interest as well as on campus. The courses lead toward Lay Academy Awards.

In-Service Training is offered including special guidance in connection with field apprenticeships.

Houston Baptist University
College of Humanities

Department of Christianity and Philosophy
7502 Fondren Road
Houston, TX 77074   (713) 774-7661

Administration. Dr. W.H. Hinton, President; Dr. Don Looser, Vice President for Academic Affairs; Dr. Calvin Huckabay, Dean, College of Humanities; Dr. A.O. Collins, Chairman, Department of Christianity and Philosophy.

General Description. Houston Baptist University is committed to providing a liberal arts undergraduate education dedicated to the view that Christian ideals and principles provide the perspectives, goals, and values most essential in higher education. The implementation of this view is the responsibility of the entire University but it is the province of the Department of Christianity to offer the specific courses that enable the students to gain an intelligent and meaningful acquaintance with the Christian religion and the writings of the Old and New Testaments. Nine semester hours in Christianity are required for graduation; a major in Christianity requires 34 semester hours.

As preparation for the student who is committed to or considering church vocations, the University provides a program of field-based practical studies through the newly-created (1984) Center for Exploring Ministry Careers. This exposure to ministry settings is designed to complement classroom experiences to help the student learn more about him/herself, his/her denomination, and the field of ministry. Through field trips, seminars, personal counseling, apprenticeship experiences, and ministry projects, the student is able to integrate classroom and field experience with his/her developing self concept.

Parent Institution. Houston Baptist University is a private institution of higher learning related to the Baptist General Convention of Texas. The University offers to students of all persuasions a program directed toward intellectual development characterized by breadth and depth and toward moral and spiritual growth based on the Christian faith and message. Bachelor and Master degrees are offered through the Colleges of: Business and Economics, Education and Behavioral Sciences, Fine Arts, Humanities, Science and Health Professions, and Graduate Studies.

Community Environment. Houston, Texas supports a metropolitan area population of 2,300,000. Although the city lies 50 miles inland, it is a major seaport due to the conversion of Buffalo Bayou into the Houston Ship Channel. The city was named in honor of Sam Houston, hero of the Battle of San Jacinto. There are over 1,000 churches representing all the major denominations, excellent medical facilities, ample shopping centers, and good student housing in the area.

Religious Denomination. Southern Baptist.

Religious Emphasis. Conservative.

Accreditation. Southern Association of Colleges and Schools.

Term System. Quarter system, but the University uses semester hours in determining credits; summer term.

Enrollment in Degree Programs in Religion 1984–85. Total 125; men 100, women 25.

Degrees in Religion Awarded 1984–85. Bachelor of Arts 17; men 15, women 2. Bachelor of Science 3; men 2, women 1.

Faculty for Degree Programs in Religion. Total 8; full-time 6, part-time 2.

Admission Requirements. An applicant is considered for admission if he/she has graduated in the top quarter of his class from an accredited high school or has a total score of 900 on the SAT; a composite of 20 on the ACT will be accepted but is not preferred; $25 nonrefundable fee.

Tuition and Fees. Tuition $1,265 per quarter; room and board (15 meals per week) $721 per quarter; other fees where applicable.

Financial Aid. There is much financial aid for church vocations students through Support for Every Religious Vocation program.

Housing. During the summer of 1984, both the Men's and Women's Residence Colleges were renovated. Each college is divided into four-room suites with common living room and kitchen facilities. Each pair of rooms has its own bath facility, and each room has its own lavatory.

Library Facilities. Moody Library is composed of a book collection of approximately 135,000 volumes with 5,000 titles being added annually. Supplementary materials include 3,00 audiovisual materials, 2,900 reels of microfilm, and 165,000 sheets of microfiche. The library subscribes to 750 journals.

Religious Services/Activities. The Christian Life on Campus is the branch of the Student Association which is responsible for the coordination of religious activities. These activities include Bible study, evangelism, worship, prayer, mission involvement, Christian citizenship training, retreats, participation in Baptist Student Union programs, etc. The program is Christ-centered, church-related, and student-led. Special emphasis weeks are promoted twice during the school year whereby the challenge of Christian discipleship is presented to all students. Weekly convocations are also held.

Degree Programs

The Bachelor of Arts degree with a major in Christianity requires a minimum of 130 semester hours with thirty-four hours of Christianity, nine of which are required of all students. Courses are required in various categories: Practical and Functional Studies; Biblical Studies; Historical and Theological Studies; Philosophical Studies. Other courses in Philosophy, Senior Seminars, and elective Christianity course offerings are also taken. Because of a double major requirement at the University, there are Christianity majors who select the field but who are entering other professions or types of work.

Special Programs

The Center for Exploring Minstry Careers offers four-year comprehensive vocational guidance and placement through many field-based learning experiences.

A special missionary internship program provides cross-cultural ministries in the international setting of Houston.

Howard Payne University
School of Christianity
Brownwood, TX 76801   (915) 646-2502

Administration. Joseph T. McClain, Dean.

General Description. The School of Christianity is comprised of a Division of Biblical Studies with a Department of Bible and a Department of Biblical Languages; a Division of Practical Studies with a Department of Practical Theology, a Department of Preaching and Evangelism, and a Department of Religious Education; and a Division of Philosophical Studies with a Department of Philosophy.

Parent Institution. Howard Payne University is a church-related, liberal arts centered institution. While the University's primary obligation is to her parent body, The Baptist General Convention of Texas, it has no restrictions as to the beliefs or locations of persons whom it serves.

Community Environment. The University is located in Brownwood, Texas, 120 miles southwest of Fort Worth and 80 miles southeast of Abilene. The city has a population of 20,000. The 45-acre campus has nineteen buildings, most of which are red brick and of modern or colonial styles of architecture.

Religious Denomination. Southern Baptist.

Accreditation. Southern Association of Colleges and Schools.

Term System. Semester.

Admission Requirements. Accredited high school graduation with completion of 15 units including 3 English, 2 mathematics, 1 laboratory science, 2 social science; SAT or ACT required.

Tuition and Fees. Tuition $2,250; room and board $2,180; student fees $200.

Financial Aid. Special financial aid is available.

Housing. All single students except those close enough to live at home are required to live in the residence halls provided by the University. A limited number of houses and apartments are available for rent by married students.

Library Facilities. Walker Library has holdings of more than 103,000 volumes.

Religious Services/Activities. Chapel is required of all students and is held twice weekly. Activities include the Baptist Student Union, Campus Baptist Young Women, Fellowship of Christian Athletes, International Club, La

Hora Bautista, and the Ministerial Association.

Degree Programs

Ministerial students are encouraged to take the area of concentration in the School to meet the suggested requirements of the American Association of Theological Schools. The School strongly recommends that ministerial students take a core in Bible, Practical Theology, Biblical Languages, Philosophy or Religious Education as the best preparation for graduate study. Baptist students who are receiving the ministerial scholarship are required to earn the Bachelor of Arts degree from the School of Christianity or take eighteen hours in the departments of the School. A minimum of 128 semester hours is required for the Bachelor's degree with an area of concentration of at least 50 hours.

Special Programs

The Corpus Christi Learning Center is operated in Corpus Christi, Texas for the purpose of educating men and women for full-time Christian service.

Jarvis Christian College
Division of Humanities and Social Science
Area of Religion
U.S. Highway 80
Hawkins, TX 75765   (214) 769-2174

Administration. Claude Walker, Professor of Religion.

General Description. In support of the general mission of the College and that of the Division of Humanities and Social Science, the mission of the Area of Religion is to provide students the opportunity to develop an understanding of the Judeao-Christian Religious Tradition and its value system and to appropriate these values in a democratic society. In addition, this Area provides resources for the recruitment and training of students for the pastoral ministry and other church-related vocations. It further provides, through religious activities on campus, the opportunity for students, faculty, and staff to share in a living Christian community.

Parent Institution. Jarvis Christian College is an historically Black institution that has been affiliated with the Christian Church (Disciples of Christ) since its inception in 1912.

Community Environment. The 425-acre campus is located one mile east of Hawkins and four miles west of Big Sandy. There are 57 college buildings including the James Nelson Ervin Religion and Cultural Center.

Religious Denomination. Christian Church (Disciples of Christ).

Accreditation. Southern Association of Colleges and Schools.

Term System. Semester system.

Admission Requirements. High school graduation from

an accredited school with rank in upper half of graduating class; completion of 16 units including 3 English, 2 mathematics, 1 science, 3 social science; college entrance examinations and ACT required.

Tuition and Fees. Tuition $1,140 per year; room and board $972; student fees $110.

Financial Aid. Assistance is based on established financial need and satisfactory academic performance.

Housing. Housing is available in campus residence halls.

Library Facilities. Library holdings are housed in the Olin Library and Communication Center.

Religious Services/Activities. Activities are coordinated by the Area of Religion.

Degree Programs

A major in Religion leading to the Bachelor of Arts degree requires 33 semester hours in specified courses. The degree also requires twelve semester hours of foreign language. Course offerings include religion and philosophy.

Special Programs

An Associate of Arts program is designed to provide some basic college level coursework for persons interested in church-related vocations.

LeTourneau College
Division of Biblical Studies and Missions
Mobberly Avenue
P.O. Box 7001
Longview, TX 75607   (214) 753-0231

Administration. Dr. Richard H. LeTourneau, President; Richard C. Berry, Vice President, Dean of the College; Donald R. Connors, Chairman, Division of Liberal Arts.

General Description. LeTourneau's Biblical Studies program provides courses designed to give the student a clear understanding of the scriptures according to conservative, evangelical theology, and to develop facility in the use of the scriptures applicable to personal experience and practical Christian service. The Biblical Studies major provides pre-ministerial preparation for seminary, as well as training for church planting missionaries.

Parent Institution. The purpose of LeTourneau College is to provide programs in higher education stressing academic quality, practical application, and spiritual development. The Scriptures are seen as the integrating core for Christian education. Therefore, courses in Bible are required to help the student understand more fully the bearing of the Christian faith on life and thought. Bachelor of Arts, Bachelor of Science, and Associate of Science degrees are granted.

Community Environment. LeTourneau College occupies a 162-acre campus in Longview, Texas, which is located in the beautiful pine tree forests and hills of east Texas. The community has a population in excess of 60,-000 and is one of the fastest growing areas of Texas. Currently, Longview has approximately 260 manufacturing and processing plants and is second in the state in industrial expansion. Students find better than average employment opportunities in Longview because of the community's industrial growth. The community is favored with more than 100 churches representing many denominations. Longview is served by Interstate 20 between Shreveport, Louisiana and Dallas, Texas.

Religious Denomination. Nondenominational.

Religious Emphasis. Evangelical.

Accreditation. Southern Association of Colleges and Schools.

Term System. Semester; summer term.

Enrollment in Degree Programs in Religion 1984–85. Total 17.

Degrees in Religion Awarded 1984–85. Bachelor of Arts in Bible 3; men 1, women 2. Bachelor of Arts in Missions 3; men 3.

Faculty for Degree Programs in Religion. Total 7; full-time 4, part-time 3.

Admission Requirements. LeTourneau College bases its admissions evaluation on two major considerations: character and ability to do academic work. Graduation from an approved high school with a minimum 16 units credit in college preparatory work is required of freshman class applicants. The high school program should consist of 4 units of English, journalism, or speech; 2 social science; 1 natural science; 2 mathematics (exclusive of general math); 7 electives. ACT or SAT scores are required.

Tuition and Fees. Tuition $2,245 per semester; general fees $28; residency fees (includes room and board) $1,250 per semester.

Financial Aid. Assistance consists of employment, grants, loans, and scholarship programs.

Housing. Dormitory accommodations are available for single students, apartments for married students.

Library Facilities. The Margaret Estes Library collection contains approximately 91,000 bound volumes, 477 periodical subscriptions, 2,198 phonorecords and tapes, and 57,928 varied forms of micromaterials.

Religious Services/Activities. Devotions, chapel, Spiritual Emphasis Week, Missions Emphasis Week, Fall Retreat, church services, Christian Service opportunities, and Bible courses are among the many religious activities at the College.

Degree Programs

The Bachelor of Arts in Biblical Studies program requires the completion of a minimum 126 semester hours including specific Biblical Studies course requirements. Students training for church planting ministries will normally take the Biblical Studies major with the Cross-Cultural Studies minor. A Christian service assignment is required for the major in consultation with the division.

At least half of the total semesters as a Biblical Studies major are to be spent in a Christian service assignment.

A Bachelor of Science degree program is available as an option with Aviation Technology in combination with Biblical Studies. This option is designed primarily for the student preparing for missionary aviation who wants a clear understanding of the Scriptures for personal application and use on the mission field along with the requirements of the Associate degree in Aviation.

A Bachelor of Science degree in Biblical Studies with a Camp Administration Option is designed to prepare students for leadership roles in Christian campus, conferences, and retreat centers both in the United States and abroad.

Lubbock Christian College
Biblical Studies Division
5601 West 19th Street
Lubbock, TX 79407   (806) 792-3221

Administration. Dr. Stephen S. Lemley, President; Dr. Jerry D. Perrin, Executive Vice President; Dr. E. Don Williams, Dean of the College; Dr. Charles B. Stephenson, Chairman, Biblical Studies Division.

General Description. At Lubbock Christian College every academic department is placed in the context of the Christian commitment of the College. As a part of the college community, the Biblical Studies Division is the focal point for the academic study of the Bible and ministry as well as an initiator of activities conducive to the spiritual growth of the college community. The Division also contributes to the College requirement of 14 credit hours in Biblical Studies for every student. The Bachelor of Arts degree is offered with a major in Bible; areas of emphasis may be Bible, Missions, Biblical Languages, Religious Education, Youth Ministry.

Parent Institution. Lubbock Christian College is a four-year institution of higher learning which seeks to continue its founding commitment to the principles of Christ as taught in the Bible. The mission of the College, as broadly expressed in the words on its seal, is to stimulate "Learning, Character, Citizenship" in a Christian environment.

Community Environment. The College is located on a 120-acre campus in Lubbock, Texas (population 165,000), the industrial, agricultural, and educational center of the South Plains of Texas. The climate is mild and arid. There are over 200 churches.

Religious Denomination. Churches of Christ (related).
Religious Emphasis. Conservative.
Accreditation. Southern Association of Colleges and Schools.
Term System. Semester; summer term.
Enrollment in Degree Programs in Religion 1984–85. Total 62; men 59, women 3.
Degrees in Religion Awarded 1984–85. Bachelor of Arts 13; men 13.

Faculty for Degree Programs in Religion. Total 10; full-time 5, part-time 5.
Admission Requirements. High school graduation or college transfer in good standing.
Tuition and Fees. Tuition including fees $1,723 per semester.
Financial Aid. Grants, loans, and scholarships are available.
Housing. There are three dormitories on campus plus college-owned off-campus apartments.
Library Facilities. The Moody Library houses over 80,000 volumes.
Religious Services/Activities. The annual Bible Lectureship, annual Willson-Morris Lectures, the Summer Minister's Renewal Program, and the Summer Mission Campaign Program are among the various activities offered on the campus. All students are required to attend daily chapel.

Degree Programs

The Bachelor of Arts degree requires the completion of 132 semester hours. Emphasis may be followed with six courses in any of the following areas: Bible, Biblical Languages, Missions, Religious Education, or Youth Ministry. Each emphasis also prepares the graduate for advanced work in a graduate school. The curriculum that each Bible major studies is, however, designed to prepare for immediate service in the church upon graduation.

Mary Hardin-Baylor, University of
Department of Religion
Belton, TX 76513   (817) 939-5811

Administration. Dr. Bobby E. Parker, President; Dr. George Andreason, Executive Vice President; Rachael LaRoe, Dean, School of Arts and Sciences; Dr. J.A. Reynolds, Chairperson, Department of Religion.

General Description. The Department of Religion provides courses in various areas in religion for both lay people and those preparing for religious vocations. A major is offered for the latter group who are recommended to follow the Department's Religion and Life Curriculum which includes a major in religion and minors in sociology and psychology. Through a program of field-based education students are given practical experience in various areas of ministry.

Parent Institution. The University of Mary Hardin-Baylor is owned and operated by the Baptist General Convention of Texas which cooperates with the Southern Baptist Convention. Thus, the University is a private, denominational school. The fall 1985 enrollment was a little over 1,300. The University grants Master and Bachelor degrees.

Community Environment. The University's spacious 101-acre campus has all the natural beauty of central Texas as well as its mild climate. Dallas and Fort Worth are a two and a half hour drive from the campus. The Scott and White medical complex is 15 minutes from the campus. Belton has a population of about 8,700.

Religious Denomination. Southern Baptist.

Religious Emphasis. Conservative in theology.

Accreditation. Southern Association of Colleges and Schools.

Term System. Semester.

Enrollment in Degree Programs in Religion 1984–85. Total 47; men 45, women 2.

Degrees in Religion Awarded 1984–85. Bachelor of Arts 10; men 9, women 1. Bachelor of Science 1; men 1.

Faculty for Degree Programs in Religion. The total varies depending upon the number of part-time faculty; full-time 2.

Admission Requirements. Applicants must rank in upper half of high school graduating class or score 15 or above on the ACT or 700 or above on the SAT and have graduated from an accredited high school with 15 units or received the General Education Diploma (GED). Seven units from an accredited high school must be of the following: 3 units English, 2 units social science, and 2 units mathematics.

Tuition and Fees. Tuition $95 per semester hour (graduate $110); board $700 per semester for a 20-meal plan; room $295 to $525 depending upon accommodations.

Financial Aid. The University makes available a broad range of financial assistance to worthy and qualified students. Most financial aid is awarded in accordance with demonstrated need for assistance as determined by use of the American College Testing (ACT) Program's Family Financial Statement.

Housing. Dormitories are available on campus for single students; apartments are available in a subsidized complex adjacent to the campus.

Library Facilities. The Townsend Memorial Library contains approximately 108,000 volumes, including bound periodicals and microfilms, and receives 650 current periodicals and newspapers.

Religious Services/Activities. Chapel attendance is an integral part of the educational process and is required of all students. The Baptist Student Union is organized to assist every student in that religious activity which he/she needs for the highest Christian development and spiritual growth. The participation of any student of any denomination in one or more unit organizations on the campus or in a local church is encouraged. The Crusaders for Christ, an organization for church-related vocations students of all denominations, meets monthly.

Degree Programs

The Bachelor of Arts degree with a major in Religion is offered by the Department of Religion. The objective of the curriculum is two-fold: it offers courses which will enable the student to be an effective member of a local church; the courses offered provide training for the student who plans to enter a church-related vocation. A ma-

jor in Religion requires 30 semester hours; a minor 24 hours. The Religion and Life Curriculum seeks to provides a foundation for both those who continue their training in seminary and those who may not be able to attend seminary. Students who enter the curriculum major in religion and minor in sociology and psychology. The Bachelor of Science in Religion is designed for those who plan to pursue a career in religious education or youth work.

Special Programs

The Department of Religion also provides training for the church members of Belton, Texas and nearby towns. For those who cannot attend during the day, at least one night course is offered each semester.

A program of In-Service Guidance is provided by the University in cooperation with the Baptist General Convention of Texas and the Home Mission Board of the Southern Baptist Convention to train and develop church leadership.

McMurry College
Department of Religion
14th and Sayles
Abilene, TX 79605   (915) 692-4130

Administration. Professor Philip L. Shuler, Jr., Chairperson.

General Description. The curriculum in the Department of Religion is designed to give students the opportunity to: (1) understand the experience of faith as an integral element of human life, (2) understand the literature of faith in relation to cultural and historical influence, (3) discover the relevance of religion for contemporary thought and practice, (4) think through their own faith in the light of alternative views, and (5) prepare for the theological and other graduate disciplines.

Parent Institution. McMurry College was founded in 1920 at Clarendon, Texas. It is the legal and spiritual successor to four historic educational institutions of west Texas and New Mexico: Stamford College, Clarendon College, Seth Ward College, and Western College of Artesia. The College is supported by the United Methodist Church.

Community Environment. The College occupies a 51-acre campus in Abilene, a west Texas city with a population of 100,000. The community serves the agricultural, marketing, and oil interests of the area.

Religious Denomination. United Methodist Church.

Accreditation. Southern Association of Colleges and Schools.

Term System. Semester system.

Faculty for Degree Programs in Religion. Total 3.

Admission Requirements. High school graduation from an accredited school; completion of 16 units in high school including 4 English, 2 mathematics, 2 science, 3 social science, 2 foreign language; ACT.

Tuition and Fees. Tuition $3,000 per year; room and board $1,710; student fees $320.

Financial Aid. Ministerial, endowed, and United Methodist scholarships are available. Federal, state, private, and institutional sources are also available.

Housing. All unmarried freshmen students whose parents do not reside in Abilene or within commuting distance are required to live in a residence hall.

Library Facilities. The Jay-Rollins Library contains over 125,000 bound volumes. There are four special collections housed in the library: Scarborough Library of Genealogy, the McMurry College Archives, the Archives of the Northwest Texas Conference of the United Methodist Church, and the J.W. Hunt Library of Texana and the Southwest.

Religious Services/Activities. Students are encouraged to take an active part in the religious activities on campus and to attend regularly the services of a local church of their denomination. Each week a worship for the entire College is conducted in the campus center. Services of Holy Communion are conducted from time to time. The Christian Life Fellowship functions to coordinate a variety of committees and groups on campus.

Degree Programs

The major in Religion leading to the Bachelor of Arts degree requires the completion of a minimum of thirty hours, eighteen of which must be advanced. Majors are required to incorporate in their advanced coursework at least one course from each of the following areas: Biblical studies, religious education/psychology of religion, church history, and history of religions. The Church Ministries Program is designed for persons with vocational or avocational interests in Christian education, sacred music, or ordained ministry. The offerings are structured for three types of persons: those who want a religion major with concentration in Christian education; those who want to combine a Christian education concentration with sacred music, and those who want to combine a music major with Christian education. A Pre-Seminary Studies program is also offered.

Oblate School of Theology
285 Oblate Drive
San Antonio, TX 78216   (512) 341-1366

Administration. Rev. Patrick Guidon, O.M.I., President; Rev. Robert E. Lampert, Academic Dean; Lillian T. Younker, Director of Continuing Education.

General Description. Oblate School of Theology, a Catholic, graduate/professional school of theology, seeks to serve the community of God by providing for a variety of ministries. In particular, it focuses on preparation for ordained ministry by providing the necessary academic studies and pastoral practice. While the primary focus remains the preparation for the first graduate or professional degree in theology, the School, attentive to the signs of the times, places special emphasis on developing new programs in lay ministry, spiritual renewal, and continuing education of the clergy.

Community Environment. Oblate School of Theology is located in San Antonio, Texas on a 25-acre campus. The large administration building houses the administrative offices, classrooms, a lecture hall, and library. A chapel graces the campus and the beautiful grounds provide ample space for enjoying the outdoors and finding a quiet place for study and reflection. With a population of 850,-000, San Antonio is called the cradle of Texas because of its history of being the birthplace of the Rough Riders. It is presently a mixture of its early Spanish background and a modern metropolis. Skyscrapers exist alongside 18th century adobe restorations. Over 500 churches representing most denominations, many civic and fraternal organizations, hospitals, and museums serve the community.

Religious Denomination. Roman Catholic.

Accreditation. Southern Association of Colleges and Schools; Association of Theological Schools in the United States and Canada.

Term System. Semester; summer term.

Enrollment in Degree Programs in Religion 1984-85. Total 107; men 71, women 36.

Degrees in Religion Awarded 1984-85. Master of Divinity (First Professional) 6; men 5, women 1. Master of Theological Studies 9; men 1, women 8.

Faculty for Degree Programs in Religion. Total 19; full-time 13, part-time 6.

Admission Requirements. Bachelor's degree with a grade point average of 2.0 (C).

Tuition and Fees. Tuition $120 per credit hour; registration fee $10 per semester; activity fee (dependent upon number of hours taken) $12 to $45; matriculation fee $15.

Financial Aid. Federally Insured Student Loans; Hinson-Hazelwood College Student Loan.

Housing. There is no housing available through Oblate School.

Library Facilities. The library contains 21,959 volumes.

Religious Services/Activities. Tuesday liturgy (Mass) of the School Community (students, faculty, and staff) with luncheon following; Sunday Mass for extended Community.

Degree Programs

The Master of Divinity program leads to the first professional degree in ministry and is designed primarily for candidates for the priesthood and for professional ministerial service to the Church. The program requires 89 credit hours in courses from the areas of Historical and Cultural Studies, Scriptural Studies, Theological Studies, and Pastoral Studies.

The Master of Divinity for Clergy provides a professional post-baccalaureate degree in theology for ministers who take adequate updating in theology and advance their professional proficiency in ministry. A substantial portion of the degree represents official approbation of non-accredited seminary training in theology. Further proficiency is gained by participation in a program consisting of academic and pastorally oriented courses.

The Master of Theological Studies degree is a 42-semester-hour graduate degree in theology which is oriented to provide theological education both to those preparing for professional ministry in the Church and to those seeking personal enrichment. It seeks to discern the theological meaning and significance of human events, and to offer theological perspectives on life situations for women and men, laity, religious, and clergy.

Special Programs

The Certificate of Pastoral Studies is a program of studies for a small number of special students who do not quality to enter one of the regular degree programs. The program is intended to parallel the Master of Divinity plan in purpose and scope. It is intended primarily for students who lack a Bachelor of Arts degree, or its equivalent.

The Lay Ministry Institute prepares the laity, including Sisters and Brothers, for pastoral ministry. The two options for preparing for lay ministry are the Certificate program of the Lay Ministry Institute or the Master's degree program.

The Ministry to Ministers program provides a four-month period of living and sharing together as a faith-community.

Oblate's faculty offers short courses, seminars, workshops, and lectures during the fall and spring semesters and during the summer school.

Rice University
Department of Religious Studies
6100 South Main
P.O. Box 1892
Houston, TX 77251   (713) 527-4995

Administration. Dr. George E. Rupp, President; Dr. Allen J. Matusow, Dean, School of Humanities; Dr. Niels C. Nielsen, Chairman, Department of Religious Studies.

General Description. The Rice University Department of Religious Studies was established in 1968. Study in the Department includes the areas of Biblical Studies, History and Philosophy of Religion, Ethics, and Church History. Degrees offered are Bachelor of Arts, Master of Arts, and Doctor of Philosophy.

Parent Institution. Dedicated to "the advancement of letters, science, and art," Rice University is private, non-sectarian, and coeducational. It includes among its academic divisions both undergraduate and graduate studies in humanities, social sciences, natural sciences, engineering, architecture, administrative sciences, and music.

Community Environment. A look through the archway of Lovett Hall shows even the casual visitor why the 300-acre Rice University campus is widely acclaimed for its dignified yet casual beauty. Approximately 40 permanent buildings are conveniently grouped in quadrangles under graceful live oak trees. The city's large stadium, the Fondren Library, the Media Center, the gymnasium, and the computer center, as well as the University's dramatic and musical presentations make Rice "behind the hedges" a community unto itself. Yet, only three miles from downtown Houston, Rice students enjoy all the commercial and cultural advantages of a major metropolitan center.

Religious Denomination. None.

Religious Emphasis. Students majoring in the area of Religious Studies come from a full range of confessional backgrounds. The Department of Religious Studies and its staff are interfaith in character.

Accreditation. Southern Association of Colleges and Schools.

Term System. Semester; no summer term.

Enrollment in Degree Programs in Religion 1984–85. Undergraduate total 11; men 6, women 5. Graduate total 27; men 24, women 3.

Degrees in Religion Awarded 1984–85. Bachelor of Arts 2; women 2. Master of Arts 4; men 3, women 1. Doctor of Philosophy 2; men 1, women 1.

Faculty for Degree Programs in Religion. Total 10; full-time 5, part-time 5.

Admission Requirements. There are five basic measures used in evaluation of candidates for undergraduate admission: high school record, SAT scores, recommendations from teachers and counselors, personal interview, the application itself. The Rice University graduate program has selective admissions. Persons applying should submit Graduate Record Examination scores, both aptitude and achievement. Final selection of candidates is made by the Graduate Council of the University. The Department is prepared to consider persons with a variety of backgrounds and institutions. It offers an ecumenical program with positive emphases on the religious heritage in a non-church university.

Tuition and Fees. Tuition $4,100 per year; basic fees $213; room and board in residential colleges $3,650; other special charges where applicable.

Financial Aid. Through grants, low interest loans, campus work opportunities, or a combination of these programs, the University attempts to give students sufficient aid to meet educational expenses.

Housing. All students on campus share the same residential facilities. Every undergraduate student, whether living on campus or not, is a member of eight residential colleges. The buildings of each college include a dining hall and living rooms, which are available to both resident and nonresident members, and living quarters for approximately 215 students from all classes of the University and all academic disciplines.

Library Facilities. The Fondren Library comprises

more than 1,142,000 volumes plus 1,337,000 microforms and 11,000 serial titles.

Degree Programs

All undergraduates majoring in Religious Studies are expected to enroll in one of the introductory courses offered at the first- or second-year level. A total of 24 semester hours in advanced courses are required for completion of the major. At least six semester hours are to be elected in each of the following areas represented in the department: (1) Historic and Biblical studies; (2) Interpretation, theology, comparative religions; (3) Religion in the modern world.

The Master of Arts and the Doctor of Philosophy degrees are given in Religious Studies, with specialization in Biblical Studies, Church History, Philosophy of Religion (including Theology), and Ethics. There is no required course sequence and graduate students are expected to be self-directed.

Rio Grande Bible Institute and Language School
Rio Grande Bible Institute
4300 South Business Highway 281
Edinburg, TX 78539   (512) 383-3806

Administration. Gordon Johnson, President; Steve Pelphrey, Administrative Vice President; George Parker, Academic Dean.

General Description. The Rio Grande Bible Institute offers a four-year program of Biblical and theological studies, taught entirely in Spanish for Spanish-speaking students from Mexico, United States, and countries in Latin America.

Parent Institution. The parent institution is a combination of two schools: one, the 4-year Bible Institute for preparation of pastors and church leaders in Latin America and the United States; the other, a school offering an intensive Spanish language course of nine months, intended to equip missionaries to work in Spanish speaking countries.

Community Environment. Edinburg, Texas is situated in the populous tip of Texas along the Texas-Mexican border. It is located 540 miles south of Dallas, Texas, and only 16 miles from Reynosa, Mexico, a city of 200,000 people. Monterrey, the third largest city in Mexico, is located 145 miles southwest of Edinburg. On both sides of the immediate border live a half a million people to whom the Gospel is both strange and new. The Institute shares in the bilingual and bicultural advantages of this area that give to the prospective worker bound for Latin America an unparalleled opportunity to prepare him/herself for the mission field.

Religious Denomination. Nondenominational.
Religious Emphasis. Fundamentalist.

Term System. Semester.
Enrollment in Degree Programs in Religion 1984–85. Total 105; men 55, women 50.
Degrees in Religion Awarded 1984–85. Diploma 12; men 8, women 4.
Faculty for Degree Programs in Religion. Total 19; full-time 13, part-time 6.
Admission Requirements. The following factors will establish the possibility of acceptance as a full-time student: Affiliation in good standing with a responsible mission board; anyone over the age of 40 will be considered on the strength of need and merit; previous educational background; willingness to respect the doctrinal position and emphasis of the Rio Grande Bible Institute.
Tuition and Fees. $180 per year.
Financial Aid. Work scholarship available for room and board.
Housing. Dorms and apartments are available.
Library Facilities. The library houses 5,200 books. There is currently a library expansion program.
Religious Services/Activities. Occasional special seminars are held on themes relevant to the objectives of the Institute; one Bible conference in English and one in Spanish each year; two devotional series per year in Spanish.

Special Programs

The Institute offers a four-year Bible course taught wholly in Spanish by national brethren and missionaries. More than 140 hours of Bible and Bible-related subjects are offered with a strong emphasis on Practical Theology, Greek, Christian Education, and Music. A diploma is awarded upon successful completion of the program.

The Institute offers an intensive nine-month, two-semester Spanish Language School. It is open to accepted or prospective missionary candidates who plan on Christian work in Spanish America.

The Institute also offers a one-year concentrated Bible course to equip Latin Christians who are in special careers that may not allow them to take four years out of their secular preparation. The course is open only to those who, in the judgment of the registrar, have had advanced academic instruction.

Intensive week-long post-graduate seminars are held in different locations in Mexico each summer.

St. Mary's University
Department of Graduate Theology
One Camino Santa Maria
San Antonio, TX 78284   (512) 436-3310

Administration. Rev. John A. Leies, S.M., S.T.D., Acting President, and Vice President of Academics; Dr. Ronald D. Merrell, Dean of Graduate School; Rev. Charles H. Miller, S.M., S.T.D., Professor of Theology and Graduate Advisor.

General Description. The Department of Graduate

Theology offers a program during the school year and during the summer leading to the degree Master of Arts in Theology, with specializations in Biblical Theology, Systematic Theology, Christian Spirituality, and Religious Education. The Department participates in the University's mission in a specific way. The students who enter the program are encouraged in a faith context to develop a contemporary foundation in advanced critical theological study and reflection for their particular church ministries. The Graduate Theology programs provide an adequate foundation in Scripture, Systematics, Spirituality, and Catechesis, as well as more in-depth study in the participant's area of choice. The program also offers continuing studies for persons already having an advanced theological formation but seeking contemporary insights. These persons can elect to take courses for enrichment or to work toward a certificate of advanced studies.

Parent Institution. St. Mary's University of San Antonio, Texas, is an independent Catholic institution inspired by the Gospels and shaped by the rich tradition of the Society of Mary (Marianists). Founded and fostered as a community of faith for the advancement of the human family, the University gives Christian purpose and dynamism to a pursuit which people of varied traditions and experiences unite in commitment to an educated venture, in dedication to a life of scholarship, and in the extension of service to society. The University includes: School of Humanities and Social Sciences, School of Business and Administration, School of Law, Graduate School, Institute of International and Public Affairs, and School of Science, Engineering, and Technology.

Community Environment. St. Mary's 135-acre campus is located in the Woodlawn Hills section of San Antonio, Texas, with 30 permanent buildings. San Antonio, with its population of 850,000, is called the cradle of Texas liberty because of its history. It is also the birthplace of the rough riders and the deathbed of such heroes as Davy Crockett and Jim Bowie. San Antonio is a mixture of its early Spanish background and a modern metropolis.

Religious Denomination. Roman Catholic.

Accreditation. Southern Association of Colleges and Schools.

Term System. Semester; summer term.

Enrollment in Degree Programs in Religion 1984–85. Total 40; men 17, women 23.

Degrees in Religion Awarded 1984–85. Master of Arts in Theology 19; men 7, women 12.

Faculty for Degree Programs in Religion. Total 6; full-time 3, part-time 3.

Admission Requirements. Bachelor's degree or its equivalent from an accredited college or university; the Aptitude or Subject Test of the Graduate Record Examination (GRE).

Tuition and Fees. Tuition $168 per semester hour; room $570 to $700 per semester; board $450 to $800 per semester.

Financial Aid. Sources of aid include grants, assistant-ships, employment, loans, and payment plans. Grants of 25 per cent tuition are available to persons in or preparing for church ministry.

Housing. Single students are housed in residence halls. There are no on-campus facilities for married couples or families.

Library Facilities. The Academic Library houses more than 200,000 volumes, 25,000 microfilms, and a Learning Resources Center.

Religious Services/Activities. Daily Liturgy; retreats; prayer services.

Degree Programs

The Master of Arts is a first level graduate degree involving a minimal level of professional practice but a major concentration on critical theological study and reflection. It aims at developing the general theological understandings which lay and ordained Christians need as the reflective religious basis for their life and work. The degree program requires a basic core of 24 hours of graduate-level work distributed as follows: Biblical Theology (6 hours); Systematic Theology (6 hours); Christian Spirituality (6 hours); and Religious Education (6 hours). Specializations in biblical Theology, Systematic Theology, and Christian Spirituality offer two options: 36 hours of coursework without thesis, or 30 hours of coursework with thesis. The non-thesis option in these areas requires, in addition to the coursework, the research and writing of three scholarly essays. Specialization in Religious Education involves 34 hours of coursework and a project. Specialization means that one-third of the work is done in that field.

Special Programs

A Certificate of Graduate Theological Studies may be earned by a student holding a Bachelor of Arts or equivalent. The program requires 12 hours of coursework at St. Mary's University, approved by the Graduate Advisor, and the writing of a project or research paper under the direction of a professor.

A Certificate of Postgraduate Theological Studies may be earned by a student holding the Master of Arts in theology or equivalent. This program requires 12 hours of coursework at St. Mary's University, approved by the Graduate Advisor, and the writing of a project or research paper under the direction of a professor.

St. Thomas, University of
St. Mary's Seminary - School of Theology
9845 Memorial Drive
Houston, TX 77024   (713) 686-4345

Administration. Rev. William J. Young, C.S.B., President; Rev. Richard J. Schiefen, C.S.B., Senior Vice President and Vice President for Academic Affairs; Rev. J. Michael Miller, C.S.B., Dean, School of Theology.

General Description. The School of Theology of the University of St. Thomas seeks to advance the study of theology and related disciplines at the post-baccalaureate level in a three-fold manner. It provides: (1) the academic and professional preparation for those whose objective is the priesthood or other Christian ministries (M.Div.); (2) a program of studies in theology and related disciplines for those whose interest is primarily academic rather than professional (M.A.); (3) a distinctive program for those engaged in religious education (M.R.E.).

In keeping with its special tradition, its location on the Seminary campus, and its close relationship with the Diocese of Galveston-Houston, the School of Theology has constructed its programs with a specifically Roman Catholic orientation and emphasis. However, the School seeks to foster an ecumenical perspective and so welcomes qualified students of other denominations who wish to take advantage of its courses and degree programs. It undertakes courses and seminars/workshops to further the continuing theological education of both clergy and laity.

Parent Institution. The University of St. Thomas is a coeducational institution of higher learning founded in 1947 by priests of the Congregation of St. Basil (Basilian Fathers). As an academic institution, it exists to cultivate the life of the mind, i.e., to foster the intellectual virtues and to inculcate sound habits of learning; above all, it seeks to instill a thirst, love, and reverence for truth. As a religious institution, it strives to constitute a community of learners and teachers who are animated and brought together by a shared world-view which has been formed in the context of the Roman Catholic faith.

Community Environment. The administrative and instructional facilities of the School of Theology are located on the campus of St. Mary's Seminary in a suburban residential area within the city limits of Houston, Texas. The campus is approximately 8 miles from the University of St. Thomas central campus at 3812 Montrose Boulevard. Although most classes are conducted on St. Mary's campus, some night and all summer courses are taught on the central campus. The metropolitan area of Houston has a population of 2,300,000. Although Houston lies 50 miles inland, it is a major seaport due to the conversion of Buffalo Bayou into the Houston Ship Canal.

Religious Denomination. Roman Catholic.

Accreditation. Southern Association of Colleges and Schools; Associate Member of the Association of Theological Schools in the United States and Canada.

Term System. Semester.

Enrollment in Degree Programs in Religion 1984–85. Total 50; men 38, women 12.

Degrees in Religion Awarded 1984–85. Master of Divinity 1; men 1. Master of Arts 2; women 2.

Faculty for Degree Programs in Religion. Total 12; full-time 4, part-time 8.

Admission Requirements. An applicant for the Master of Divinity program must have (1) a B.A. or B.S. (or an equivalent first degree) from an accredited college or uni-

versity; (2) at least 12 hours of undergraduate courses in philosophy which in the judgment of the dean and/or the admissions committee are adequate preparation for admission to the School; (3) some general background in humanities and social sciences. It is recommended that students who intend to apply for admission have introductory undergraduate courses in theology, sacred scripture, a reading knowledge in Latin or Greek, and a modern language.

Tuition and Fees. Tuition $135 per semester hour for up to 12 hours; for 13-16 hours, $1,700 per semester; for 17 hours and up, each additional hour $75; adult students $100 per credit hour; registration fee $50 per semester.

Financial Aid. Students are encouraged to seek information from the Financial Aid Office on the central campus concerning Educational Opportunity Grants, government loans, and other forms of student aid.

Housing. Housing is available on campus for seminarians only.

Library Facilities. The Cardinal Beran Library is a specialized collection devoted primarily to materials in theology and closely related subjects. The holdings number approximately 39,000 volumes and 3,700 items of audiovisual materials. Periodical subscriptions total 305. Students of the School enjoy full access to the wider resources of Doherty Library, located on the central campus. This collection holds more than 125,000 titles and subscribes to 700 periodicals.

Degree Programs

The Master of Divinity degree is awarded upon a student's completion of a four-year professional program of full-time study or its equivalent. It is a basic degree in theology and related disciplines, intended for those whose objective is Christian ministry. The degree requires the completion of 110 semester hours and a 2.0 average in core courses. Specific requirements for Roman Catholic seminarians may be demanded by ecclesiastical authorities for candidates to the priesthood. The 110 hours expected of all candidates will be supplemented by additional noncredit courses determined by the Seminary and the School of Theology. The core curriculum includes courses in Sacred Scripture (20 credit hours), Systematic Theology (31 credit hours), Church History (12 credit hours), Moral Theology and Canon Law (15 credit hours), and Pastoral Theology and Field Education (27 credit hours).

The Master of Arts in Theological Studies program consists of 36 hours of courses selected in consultation with a faculty advisor and approved by the Dean. The program will include two basic courses in systematic theology; two basic courses in sacred scripture; two courses in the History of Christian thought. A non-thesis program requires an additional 18 hours selected from approved courses; the thesis program requires an additional 12 hours selected from approved courses and a thesis. A reading knowledge is required in a language other than English and the student must have an overall average of B (3.0).

The Master of Religious Education program is intended to prepare teachers and administrators in Catholic schools, directors of religious education, youth ministers, and liturgical and pastoral ministers with the necessary professional competence and expertise in Catholic doctrine and theology according to the teaching of the Church and modern catechetical and pastoral techniques. A specialization in liturgy is offered to prepare liturgical ministers for work in parishes and schools. The degree requires participants to take 30 hours of graduate credit. One of the following is also required: (1) a creative project designed by the student to meet the needs of his/her particular ministry focus; (2) additional master's coursework at the University of St. Thomas or at another university; or (3) comprehensive exams.

Southern Methodist University
Dedman College
P.O. Box 296
Dallas, TX 75275   (214) 692-2058

Administration. R. Hal Williams, Dean of Dedman College.

General Description. Dedman College offers the major in Religious Studies leading to the Bachelor of Arts degree.

Parent Institution. Southern Methodist University is a privately supported, coeducational university located in Dallas, Texas. The University is composed of Dedman College, Meadows School of the Arts, the School of Business Administraton, the School of Continuing Education, the School of Engineering/Applied Science, the School of Law, Perkins School of Theology (*See:* separate entry), and the Department of International Programs. The University is affiliated with the United Methodist Church.

Community Environment. Dallas has a population of approximately 850,000 and is a center for scientifically oriented industry in the electronics and aerospace fields and ranks high in cotton, oil, and consumer goods production. The city is a transportation hub for rail, bus, and airlines.

Religious Denomination. The United Methodist Church.

Accreditation. Southern Association of Colleges and Schools.

Term System. Semester; summer sessions.

Admission Requirements. Graduation from an accredited high school or equivalent; completion of 13 college preparatory units; SAT or ACT. Admission is based upon high school record, SAT scores, and recommendations.

Tuition and Fees. Tuition $3,265 per semester; general student fee $417; room $931; board $1,032.

Financial Aid. The University has a diverse program of merit scholarships, grants, loans, and part-time jobs.

Housing. The University has housing accommodations for 1,708 women, 1,311 men, and 200 families.

Library Facilities. The holdings of the library system number over 2 million volumes.

Religious Services/Activities. Under the direction of the Office of the Chaplain, the Campus Ministry Council coordinates plans and activities for denominational groups and others interested in religious life on the campus.

Degree Programs

The major in Religious Studies is offered in Dedman College and leads to the Bachelor of Arts degree. Courses offered include the study of various religious traditions and experience.

Southern Methodist University - Perkins
School of Theology
Dallas, TX 75275   (214) 692-2152

Administration. James E. Kirby, Dean; Guy Garrett, Director, Academic Procedures.

General Description. The Perkins School of Theology of Southern Methodist University grew out of a movement led by Bishop Seth Ward to establish a theological school west of the Mississippi River. Before 1908, there had been a professor of Bible and kindred subjects in many of the church colleges of the Methodist Episcopal Church, South, but no theological seminary. When Southern Methodist University was opened in 1915, the School of Theology began its work as an integral part of the institution. By an act of the United Conference of the Methodist Church in 1939, ownership of the University was vested in the South Central Jurisdictional Conference, and the School of Theology became the official seminary in the jurisdiction. The School is named for Mr. and Mrs. J.J. Perkins of Wichita Falls, Texas who provided major endowment funds for its support.

The primary purpose of the School is to prepare men and women for effective ministry in the church and to serve the church through disciplined reflection on its life and witness. The School is a constituent part of Southern Methodist University which is owned by the South Central Jurisdiction of The United Methodist Church.

Parent Institution. Southern Methodist University is a privately supported, coeducational university located in Dallas, Texas. The University is composed of the College of Liberal Arts, Meadows School of the Arts, the School of Business Administration, the School of Continuing Education, the School of Engineering/Applied Science, the School of Law, Perkins School of Theology, and the Department of International Programs.

Community Environment. Dallas has a population of approximately 850,000 and is a center for scientifically oriented industry in the electronics and aerospace fields and ranks high in cotton, oil, and consumer goods production. The city is a transportation hub for rail, bus, and airlines.

Religious Denomination. The United Methodist Church.

Accreditation. Southern Association of Colleges and Schools; Association of Theological Schools in the United States and Canada.

Term System. Semester; summer sessions.

Enrollment in Degree Programs in Religion 1984–85. Total 508; men 365, women 143.

Degrees in Religion Awarded 1984–85. Master of Divinity 67; men 47, women 20. Master of Sacred Music 15; men 8, women 7. Master of Theological Studies 10; men 5, women 5. Doctor of Ministry 10; men 9, women 1.

Faculty for Degree Programs in Religion. Total 43.

Admission Requirements. Bachelor of Arts degree with a 2.5 grade point average.

Tuition and Fees. Tuition $157 per semester hour; student fee $36 per semester hour; board (full meal ticket plan) on campus $1,032 per semester (other meal ticket plans available); housing $511 to $1,095 per semester depending upon accommodations.

Financial Aid. Up to 50 percent in aid depending upon need; additional aid for ethnic minority students.

Housing. Dormitories, efficiency apartments, and one bedroom apartments available.

Library Facilities. The holdings of the Bridwell Library number 231,000 volumes. The Bridwell-DeBellis Collection of Fifteenth Century Printing is housed here.

Religious Services/Activities. Theological reflection and training for ministry are the purpose of the school. However, these purposes imply a total concern for the development of persons in community. This concern is manifest not only in the classroom and the library, but also in a wide range of activities and associations that make up the life of the School. Worship is a central element in the life of the School. Each day students and faculty members are afforded a variety of worship opportunities. Monday through Friday the day begins at 7:30 a.m. with a brief Eucharist service and ends at 10:00 p.m. with a Compline service or a service of evening prayer. At 11:15 each day, except Wednesday, there is a community service of prayer, communion, and/or preaching. Regular convocations are held on Thursday afternoons. These include lectures by visiting scholars and church and community leaders, and discussion on a wide variety of issues. All Perkins students are encouraged to participate in the events of Ministers' Week and Laity Week which occur annually in February.

Degree Programs

The Master of Divinity degree is designed primarily for students who plan to enter the ministry of the local church, though it also provides preparation for other specialized ministries. Each candidate for the degree is required to serve a full-time Internship of no less than 18 weeks duration. Internships are served in congregations, college teaching, campus ministry, hospital chaplaincy, Federal Prison, Army and Air Force Chaplaincy, homes for the elderly, and other sites.

The Master of Theological Studies degree is designed primarily for those persons who wish to pursue a program of theological study but do not seek ordination or the sort of professional preparation offered by the other degree programs of the School. The requirements are designed to insure some breadth of exposure to the various disciplines of theological study, while at the same time allowing each student to fashion a plan of study which serves his or her individual interests and goals.

The Master of Sacred Music degree program of study is jointly sponsored by the School and the Division of Music and is for the preparation of professional music leadership in the church. The program provides a wide range of graduate-level training in performance, professional, and academic skills.

The Master of Religious Education degree prepares men and women for church leadership as directors of religious education. It provides the basic educational qualifications for consecration to diaconal ministry. The degree combines study in the Biblical, theological, historical, and ethical disciplines with training in religious education.

The Doctor of Ministry program enables specially qualified and promising persons to achieve advanced competence in ministry for leadership in the church, both in the theological fields and in the practice of ministry. The degree is oriented toward the professional ministry and presupposes experience in and expectations for ministry in the church.

Special Programs

The Course of Study School is offered for those pastors who are ineligible or otherwise find it impossible to undertake a program leading to the Master of Divinity degree. The full four-year curriculum of basic studies, as well as the fifth year of advanced studies, are provided in both English and Spanish. The Boards of Ministry of the various annual conferences pay the costs of room and board and textbooks for their students. Tuition and instructional costs are paid by the Division of Ordained Ministry and Perkins, while facilities and administrative costs are provided by Perkins.

Southwestern Adventist College
Department of Religion
Keene, TX 76059   (817) 645-3921

Administration. Dr. Marvin E. Anderson, President; Dr. Harold L. Wright, Vice President for Academic Affairs; Dr. Rob Sheppard, Chairman, Department of Religion.

General Description. The Department of Religion seeks to introduce the student to a personal, vital, and living experience with Jesus Christ, and to foster the growth of that experience. Besides providing courses designed to develop religious insights and skills in all students of the College, the Department offers several programs to meet specific needs. Included are: Major in Religion, Major in Religion with emphasis in Ministry of Music, Minor in Religion, Minor in Biblical Language, and a Pre-Ministerial curriculum to prepare the student for admission to the Seventh-day Adventist theological seminary and the gospel ministry. The Department also provides training for professional Bible instructors. The degree Bachelor of Arts is awarded.

Parent Institution. Founded in 1893, Southwestern Adventist College is a coeducational institution of higher learning established by the Seventh-day Adventist Church as an instrument essential to the fulfillment of the teaching ministry. Owned and operated by the Southwestern Union Conference of Seventh-day Adventists, the College has the philosophy that true education consists of harmonious development of the mental, physical, social, and spiritual nature of man. In response to that philosophy, the College educational program has these objectives: spiritual, intellectual, social, aesthetic, civic, health, and vocational.

Community Environment. The location of Southwestern Adventist College offers its students the best of country and city life. Situated in the suburban college community of Keane, Texas, the College is just 28 minutes from the Dallas-Fort Worth Metroplex. As one of the nation's most progressive centers, the Metroplex offers culture, finance, shopping, entertainment, and work opportunities. Dallas-Fort Worth International Airport is just 55 minutes from the campus.

Religious Denomination. Seventh-day Adventist.

Religious Emphasis. Fundamentalist.

Accreditation. Southern Association of Colleges and Schools.

Term System. Semester.

Enrollment in Degree Programs in Religion 1984–85. Total 75; men 71, women 4.

Degrees in Religion Awarded 1984–85. Bachelor of Arts in Religion 16; men 16.

Faculty for Degree Programs in Religion. Total 6; full-time 3, part-time 3.

Admission Requirements. High school graduation or equivalent.

Tuition and Fees. Comprehensive fee for dormitory students $3,893 per semester; village students $2,560 per semester.

Financial Aid. Besides numerous scholarships, there are various loans and federal and state grants (Texas Equalization Grants are not available to Religion majors).

Housing. Dormitory facilities for single students; married students may rent apartments from the College or in the village.

Library Facilities. The Findlay Memorial Library contains over 125,000 volumes and subscribes to 500 current periodicals.

Religious Services/Activities. Regular attendance at chapel exercises and worship services is expected of all students.

Degree Programs

The Religion major leading to the Bachelor of Arts degree requires the completion of 30 hours of prescribed courses. The student may elect the major with an emphasis in Ministry of Music. A pre-ministerial curriculum can be followed to prepare for admission to the Seventh-day Adventist theological seminary and the gospel ministry. Students preparing for the ministry must complete the requirements for the Bachelor of Arts degree, meet the language requirement with New Testament Greek, and in addition to the Religion major requirements, include courses in Christian Witnessing, Homiletics, Christian Ministry, and a Pastoral Practicum.

Special Programs

The College offers an Adult Degree Program for off-campus work. This program leads to a degree in most disciplines and involves a two-week seminary conducted on campus followed by correspondence courses.

Southwestern Assemblies of God College
1200 Sycamore
Waxahachie, TX 75165   (214) 937-4010

Administration. Dr. Delmer R. Guynes, President; Dr. J. Paul Savell, Academic Dean.

General Description. Southwestern Assemblies of God College is a 4-year Bible college offering degrees in Pastoral Ministry and Evangelism, Missions, Christian Education, Biblical Languages, Elementary Education, and Music. Southwestern serves the states of Mississippi, Louisiana, Arkansas, Oklahoma, Texas, and New Mexico as a regional college of the Assemblies of God. During its 59-year history the school has become a training center for world-wide evangelism. The alumni of Southwestern may be found in every part of the world spreading the gospel through various means.

Community Environment. Southwestern is located in the heart of the rich black lands of central Texas in Waxahachie, the county seat of Ellis County. This unique city of about 20,000 provides an excellent setting for a college, since it is outside big-city congestion yet affords the benefits of a large industrial center, being situated just beyond the Dallas-Fort Worth Metropolitan area. The College occupies a 70-acre plot on the north perimeter of Waxahachie. The spacious campus provides ample area for the plant, recreational facilities, and future growth.

Religious Denomination. Assemblies of God.

Religious Emphasis. Conservative.

Accreditation. Southern Association of Colleges and Schools (first two years); American Association of Bible Colleges (4 years).

Term System. Semester; summer term.

Faculty for Degree Programs in Religion. Total 31; full-time 22, part-time 9.

Admission Requirements. Applicants graduating from an accredited secondary school or the equivalent are eligible for admission; ACT required; campus visit recommended.

Tuition and Fees. Tuition $1,950 per year; room and board $2,450; required fees $155.

Financial Aid. The College participates in ACT Financial Aid Services. Scholarships, grants, loans, and student employment available.

Housing. Single students under 25 who are not living at home must live on campus in dormitory housing. Married-student housing available.

Library Facilities. The Nelson Memorial Library contains over 90,500 volumes and represents one of the largest collections in Pentecostal circles. In addition to books, the library has files of several newspapers and over 500 periodicals. The Southwestern Alumni Association sponsors the Pentecostal Alcove which holds an array of materials pertaining to the modern Pentecostal movement.

Religious Services/Activities. Spiritual life on the campus finds outlets in several campus organizations such as missionary prayer groups. It is related to the student's Christian service activities where participation in practical church service is expected. Annual world ministries convention is featured at which time Christian stewardship and consecration are stressed. The campus also sponsors fall and spring revivals. Speakers are brought to the campus who are outstanding preachers and Bible expositors.

Degree Programs

The Bachelor of Arts, Bachelor of Science, and Bachelor of Sacred Music degrees are offered with major programs in Biblical Languages, Christian Education, Elementary Education, Missions, Pastoral Ministry/Evangelism, and Sacred Music.

Special Programs

The Associate of Arts degree is awarded with Junior College courses offered in bible, business administration, communication arts, education, music, psychology, and social science.

A Diploma is granted after a student has completed 93 hours that place emphasis on the Bible and practical training. This course is intended primarily for the older student who does not care to fulfill the requirements of the regular four-year degree program.

Southwestern Baptist Theological Seminary
School of Theology
2001 West Seminary Drive
Fort Worth, TX 76122   (817) 923-1921

Administration. Dr. Russell H. Dilday, President; Dr. John P. Newport, Vice President for Academic Affairs and Provost; Dr. William B. Tolar, Dean, School of Theology; Dr. Jack D. Terry, Dean, School of Religious Education; Dr. James McKinney, Dean, School of Church Music.

General Description. The preparation of ministers is the major emphasis of Southwestern Baptist Theological Seminary which believes that the ever-widening circle of Christian ministry finds its focal point in a continuing emphasis on evangelism and missions. Consequently, the School of Theology provides a program of study which will prepare the student for the complex ministries in the closing years of the 20th century. The School of Theology offers the degrees Master of Divinity, Master of Arts in Missiology, Doctor of Ministry, and Doctor of Philosophy. The Associate of Divinity is for those who do not have a baccalaureate degree and are 30 years of age or over.

Parent Institution. Southwestern Baptist Theological Seminary is one of the country's (if not the world's) largest theological seminaries, with over 5,000 students enrolled annually. One estimate holds that Southwestern prepares 1 of every 12 students enrolled in accredited theological seminaries in the United States and Canada. More than 40 percent of all students in Southern Baptist seminaries are enrolled at Southwestern. Almost 50 percent of all missionaries trained in Southern Baptist seminaries are former Southwestern students. This love for missions and evangelism continues the dream of B.H. Carroll, the Seminary's founder. Carroll started Southwestern as an outgrowth of Baylor University's theological department in Waco, Texas. The Seminary was chartered in 1908 and functioned on the Baylor campus until 1910. Since that first year, Southwestern has enrolled more than 50,000 students. The Seminary is composed of the Schools of Theology, Religious Education, and Church Music. Other degrees offered by the Seminary are Doctor of Education, Doctor of Musical Arts in Church Music, Master of Arts (Church Social Services, Social Work, Communication, Marriage and Family Counseling, Religious Education), and Master of Music in Church Music.

Community Environment. The main facility of the Southwestern Baptist Theological Seminary is in Fort Worth, Texas, on a beautiful 200-acre campus located on one of the highest spots in Tarrant County, known as Seminary Hill. Three off-campus centers are located in Houston and San Antonio, Texas, and Shawnee, Oklahoma. Fort Worth, with a population of 400,000, is the leading industrial and petroleum capital of the state. Community service facilities include libraries, two art museums, many churches representing over 45 religious denominations, a civic opera, symphony orchestra, ballet theatre, hospitals, and clinics. The Fort Worth-Dallas area is home to over 2,000,000 people.

Religious Denomination. Southern Baptist.

Accreditation. Southern Association of Colleges and Schools; Association of Theological Schools in the United States and Canada; National Association of Schools of Music.

Term System. Semester; summer term.

Enrollment in Degree Programs in Religion 1984–85. Total 2,866; men 2,679, women 187.

Degrees in Religion Awarded 1984–85. Degrees awarded by the School of Theology: Master of Divinity 405; men 376, women 29. Doctor of Ministry 34; men 33, women 1. Doctor of Philosophy (Ph.D.) 22; men 21, women 1. Associate of Divinity 64; men 39, women 25.

Faculty for Degree Programs in Religion. Total 77; full-time 49, part-time 28.

Admission Requirements. Candidates for admission to Southwestern must present evidence of a divine call to the Christian ministry through references and church endorsement. Also required are a record of solid academic achievement, a mature Christian character, and promise of continued intellectual and spiritual growth. A baccalaureate degree from an accredited college or university is prerequisite to all graduate degrees from the Seminary. Persons who are thirty years of age or older and high school graduates may apply for an Associate degree program of study.

Tuition and Fees. Matriculation fee $300 per semester ($600 for non-Southern Baptist students); student service fee $40; residence hall $75 to $120 per month; Seminary housing for married students $195 to $340 per month; semester meal ticket $220 to $428 depending on meal plan.

Financial Aid. Financial assistance is granted on the basis of need on a year-to-year basis with reapplication and review each year.

Housing. Housing for students consists of dormitories, a student village, married housing apartments, a trailer park, and privately owned rental property around Fort Worth.

Library Facilities. The A. Webb Roberts Library contains more than 300,000 volumes and 100,000 annuals and associational minutes. The library has been judged to be one of the outstanding theological libraries in the United States based on the strength of its collections, diversity of materials, accessibility of resources, and service concepts of its staff. The library has served as the official repository for historical materials of the Baptist General Convention of Texas since 1933.

Religious Services/Activities. Chapel services are held four days a week; attendance is not required. Each semester there is a school revival on campus, led by leading personnel in the Convention. There are many opportunities for service in local churches, paid and volunteer.

Many opportunities for active involvement in missions and evangelism exist.

Degree Programs

The Master of Divinity degree is the basic degree in the School of Theology for those preparing for Christian ministry in its pastoral or preaching dimensions. It is predicated on a Bachelor of Arts degree or its equivalent. Beside the basic Master of Divinity degree, there are four areas of concentration a student may choose: Master of Divinity with Missions-Evangelism Concentration; Master of Divinity with Religious Education Concentration; Master of Divinity with Communication Arts Concentration; Master of Divinity with Church Music Concentration. The student, to be eligible for admission to the latter program, must have a bachelor's degree with a major in music from an accredited college or university.

The Master of Arts in Missiology is an in-service degree designed exclusively for missionary practitioners on furlough or leave-of-absence who desire mid-career training in order to develop more effective skills.

The Doctor of Ministry degree is advanced professional education for the practice of Christian ministry. The program seeks the correlation of classical theological studies with the development of professional skills in ministry.

The Doctor of Philosophy degree is an advanced academic degree offered by the School of Theology. It is designed to prepare persons to serve as teachers in specialized areas of religion, as pastors of churches, or in denominational leadership as administrators, editors, authors, etc. It emphasizes quality in research and the development of the capacity for critical evaluation.

Special Programs

An Associate of Divinity degree is awarded students upon successful completion of a two-year courses. Persons thirty years of age and over who have a high school diploma or its equivalent may enter this course of study without college preparation.

Southwestern University
Religion and Philosophy Department
Georgetown, TX 78626   (512) 863-1200

Administration. Farley W. Snell, Chairman, Religion and Philosophy Department.

General Description. The program in Religious Studies offers students the opportunity to deepen understanding of their own religious heritage, to encounter sympathetically the religious traditions of others (e.g., Asian peoples), and to develop constructive approaches to religious issues. The Department also offers a program in Christian Education designed to train a person for staff leadership in either the educational or music program of the local church.

Parent Institution. Southwestern University traces its roots to 1840 when the forerunner of the University, Rutersville College, was chartered by the Republic of Texas. Three other colleges founded by pioneer Methodists united into one central college in Georgetown in 1873. When the five Methodist Conferences of Texas located the central institution in Georgetown, it was known as Texas University. In 1875 the present name was adopted.

Community Environment. Georgetown is a city of 13,-500 residents located 28 miles north of Austin, the state capital. The campus is situated in a residential area on the eastern edge of the city on 500 acres.

Religious Denomination. United Methodist.

Accreditation. Southern Association of Colleges and Schools.

Term System. Semester.

Faculty for Degree Programs in Religion. Total 6.

Admission Requirements. Accredited high school graduation or equivalent; rank in upper half of graduating class; completion of 16 units including 4 English, 3 mathematics, 2 science, 2 foreign language, 2 social science; SAT or ACT required.

Tuition and Fees. Tuition $2,450 per semester; room $605-$790 depending on accommodations; board $625-$785 depending on meal plan selected.

Financial Aid. Scholarships and other types of aid are available.

Housing. Students are housed in residence halls on campus.

Library Facilities. The Cody Memorial Library contains over 143,000 volumes and subscribes to 500 periodicals and newspapers.

Religious Services/Activities. Weekly chapel services are provided. Students are encouraged to become involved in organizations related to denominational interests.

Degree Programs

A major in Religion leading to the Bachelor of Arts degree consists of 33 hours, including no more than three introductory level courses. The distribution of courses includes two in religious thought, two in Biblical studies, three in comparative religion, one in Christian history, and three electives. The degree requires a minimum of 124 semester hours. The Department will work with any student in planning a course of study for a church-related career. This includes a program designed to meet seminary requirements as well as a program in Christian Education that offers a major in church music or Christian education.

Texas Christian University
Brite Divinity School
Forth Worth, TX 76129   (817) 921-7577

Administration. M. Jack Suggs, Dean.

General Description. Brite Divinity School is the graduate professional theological school of Texas Christian University. Its primary focus is preparing men and women for

ministry in the Church of Jesus Christ. A seminary of the Christian Church (Disciples of Christ), it is ecumenical in outlook; almost half of both faculty and students come from denominations other than the Disciples. Nearly one-fourth of the student body is affiliated with the United Methodist Church. The courses taught at Brite in Methodist history, doctrine, and polity - which are required for ordination in the United Methodist Church - have been officially approved by appropriate denominational offices.

Parent Institution. Texas Christian University is an independent, coeducational university enrolling about 7,000 students in six colleges. It was founded in 1873 as AddRan College.

Community Environment. The University is situated on a 243-acre campus in the southwestern residential district of Fort Worth. It is easily accessible to a variety of recreational, educational, and professional opportunities in the Forth Worth/Dallas metroplex. Major museums, parks, theatres, and churches are within a few miles of the campus.

Religious Denomination. Christian Church (Disciples of Christ).

Religious Emphasis. Mainline Protestant.

Accreditation. Southern Association of Colleges and Schools; Association of Theological Schools in the United States and Canada.

Term System. Semester; summer term.

Enrollment in Degree Programs in Religion 1984–85. Total 232; men 162, women 70.

Degrees in Religion Awarded 1984–85. Master of Divinity 85; men 64, women 21. Master of Religious Education 2; women 2. Master of Theology 1; men 1. Doctor of Ministry 14; men 13, women 1.

Faculty for Degree Programs in Religion. Total 25; full-time 18, part-time 7.

Admission Requirements. Baccalaureate degree; promise for ministry; good moral character.

Tuition and Fees. Tuition $162 per semester hour; House of Student Representatives fee $15 per semester; general university fee $260 per semester ($12 per semester hour for part-time students taking less than 9 semester hours).

Financial Aid. Standard tuition grants are made in the amount of 80 percent of tuition. Fifteen full tuition scholarships awarded for scholastic merit annually. Small grants on basis of need. Full-tuition ethnic minority awards.

Housing. Apartments for single and married students are available in graduate housing complexes.

Library Facilities. The Mary Couts Burnett Library houses more than 1.2 million volumes of which 200,000 volumes are in religion and theology. The Library maintains a significant collection of materials related to the history and thought of the Christian Church (Disciples of Christ). Most of the important American and European theological journals are available for student use.

Religious Services/Activities. Seminary chapel is held on

Tuesday morning; worship leaders are faculty members, students, and distinguished guests. There are also weekly university-wide services.

Degree Programs

The Master of Divinity program of study is designed to prepare students for one of the various forms of ministry in the church. In recognition of the great diversity of students' undergraduate preparation and vocational goals, the curriculum is flexible and allows much freedom in the selection of courses. A major concentration of elective courses in management, music, pastoral care, and pastoral psychology, or religious education is available within the structure of the program.

The Master of Religious Education program prepares students for the ministry of Christian Education. The curriculum includes courses in Orientation to Ministry, Foundation Disciplines, Religious Education, Parish Ministries, and electives.

The Master of Theology degree is available for advanced students who wish to pursue specialized professional study in the area of Pastoral Care and Pastoral Psychology. The program requires a minimum of thirty semester hours of graduate work beyond the Master of Divinity degree.

The Doctor of Ministry program provides work at the doctoral level for men and women of high potential who wish to develop more effective expressions of the church's ministry in the world. The program is designed to prepare persons for creative forms of Christian ministry other than teaching and research in colleges, universities, or seminaries. The objectives of the program are to facilitate thoughtful examination of the meaning of ministry in the minister's specific setting, to provide the opportunity for the minister to integrate formal theological education and understanding with practical experience and professional skills in the process of maturing ministry, and to involve the minister in acquiring a discipline and pattern for continuing growth in ministry. While most of the program is carried on "in ministry," normally fifteen weeks of work at Brite are required.

Texas Lutheran College
Department of Theology and Philosophy
1000 West Court Street
Seguin, TX 78155   (512) 379-4161

Administration. Dr. Charles Oestreich, President; Dr. James A. Halseth, Vice President for Academic Affairs and Academic Dean; Dr. Norman A. Beck, Chairperson, Department of Theology and Philosophy.

General Description. In the study of theology, the Department of Theology and Philosophy of Texas Lutheran College seeks to utilize the disciplines of theology to strengthen and illumine programs in general education for all students of the College, to provide major concentra-

tions of study in religion, to provide for lay and ordained ministers in the church, to provide support and stimulation for the Christian and academic communities at the College, and to serve the general community and its churches in modes relevant to their resources and needs. The Bachelor of Arts is awarded in: Theology, Pre-Ministry, and Church Staff Associate. The latter is a special four-year, flexible program for men and women interested in professional, non-ordained service in the church.

Texas Lutheran College also supports the Lutheran Institute for Religious Studies, an inter-Lutheran continuing education center based at the College. The Institute exists to foster growth and renewal for clergy and laity in Biblical studies, doctrinal and historical theology, personal and spiritual growth, skills for ministry, issues in church and society, and career development.

Parent Institution. Texas Lutheran College is a small, church-related liberal arts college in south-central Texas near San Antonio. It offers majors and programs in the Arts and Sciences, Teacher Education, and professional and pre-professional areas.

Community Environment. The Texas Lutheran College campus is situated on the western edge of Seguin, Texas. Located in the city, on the Guadalupe River, is Starcke Park, one of the best-known and most scenic parks in the state. Within a few hours' drive are the attractive Texas "Hill Country," the Gulf Coast and Padre Island seashore area, the state capital in Austin, the metropolis of Houston, and the important international border with Mexico. The spacious 120-acre campus features modern physical facilities that contribute to the invigorating atmosphere of a community of learning.

Religious Denomination. American Lutheran Church.

Accreditation. Southern Association of Colleges and Schools.

Term System. Semester; summer term.

Enrollment in Degree Programs in Religion 1984–85. Total 20; men 14, women 6.

Degrees in Religion Awarded 1984–85. Bachelor of Arts 7; men 5, women 2.

Faculty for Degree Programs in Religion. Total 5; full-time 2, part-time 3.

Admission Requirements. Students graduating from an accredited high school will be considered for admission to Texas Lutheran. The applicant should have completed a minimum of 16 acceptable units of high school work, including 13 from academic areas. All applicants must present SAT or ACT score reports.

Tuition and Fees. Tuition $3,600 per year; room $950; board $1,050 to $1,209 depending upon meal plan; other fees where applicable.

Financial Aid. A student who wishes to be considered for need-based financial assistance must submit the completed Financial Aid Form to College Scholarship Service for analysis.

Housing. The majority of students live in residence halls.

Library Facilities. The Blumberg Memorial Library contains approximately 130,000 volumes. In addition, resources of over 2 million volumes are available through cooperative arrangements with a San Antonio-area library consortium.

Religious Services/Activities. Opportunities for corporate worship are provided in the College Chapel on Monday, Wednesday, and Friday mornings each week. The Campus Congregation conducts Sunday morning worship, periodic evening vespers, and festive seasonal worship experiences. Dayagim, an organization of students who are preparing for church-related ministries, plus a chapter of the Lutheran Student Movement that is made up of students who are affiliated with Lutheran students of other campuses, conduct regular meetings and discussion forums in order to promote a greater awareness of Christian responsibility among students. Campus Ministry also includes opportunities provided by area congregations and by on-campus student groups representing the Baptist, Episcopal, Methodist, and Roman Catholic traditions.

Degree Programs

The College offers a flexible four-year program for men and women interested in professional, non-ordained service in the church. The program leads to a Bachelor of Arts degree and may be taken with a view to a broad, general preparation for church staff work; or it may be taken with more particular career aspirations in mind, such as educational, group, social service, music, or administrative ministries.

A Pre-Ministry program leading to the Bachelor of Arts degree is also offered through the Department of Theology and Philosophy. Students who anticipate continuing their programs of study at a school of theology plan their current programs to meet the requirements of the particular school they expect to enter. The Bachelor of Arts degree with a major in Theology is also offered. The major requires 28 semester hours in required and supporting courses.

Special Programs

The Lutheran Institute for Religious Studies is an inter-Lutheran continuing education center based at Texas Lutheran College. It exists to foster growth and renewal for clergy and laity in Biblical studies, doctrinal and historical theology, personal and spiritual growth, skills for ministry, issues in church and society, and career development. Programs are offered in conjunction with regional and national church agencies, as well as seminaries.

Texas Wesleyan College
Department of Religion and Philosophy
Wesleyan at Rosedale
Fort Worth, TX 76105   (817) 732-5087

Administration. Dr. Jon H. Fleming, President; Dr. W.L. Hailey, Provost; Dr. Ronald D. Ballard, Dean, School of Science and Humanities.

General Description. The College grants the Bachelor of Arts degree in Humanities/Religion, The Bachelor of Science in Christian Education, and the Bachelor of Science in Religion. The Pre-Professional Program allows the pre-ministerial student to participate in an off-campus mentorship with a respected clergyman. During the program the student is afforded the opportunity to experience first-hand the demands and rewards of professional activity.

Parent Institution. Texas Wesleyan College was founded in 1891 by the Methodist Episcopal Church, South, and was named Polytechnic College. The College was sponsored by Bishop Joseph S. Key, and land was donated by A.S. Hall, W.D. Hall, and George Tandy, Fort Worth area businessmen. In 1914 the College became the women's college of the Methodist Church and was named Texas Woman's College. In 1934 it again was made coeducational and became Texas Wesleyan College. Throughout its history the College has maintained a close relationship with the United Methodist Church. The College contains the Schools of Business, Education, Fine Arts, and Science and Humanities.

Community Environment. Texas Wesleyan College is located on more than 74 acres four miles southeast of downtown Fort Worth, on one of the highest points in the city. The heritage of Wesleyan is reflected in some of the old buildings on campus with their Georgian-style columns, while progress is seen in the contemporary design of the newer buildings. Fort Worth, with a population of 393,476 lies in the rich backland prairie and is the leading industrial and petroleum capital of the state. The area contains many churches representing over 45 religious denominations, and many cultural activities.

Religious Denomination. United Methodist Church.

Accreditation. Southern Association of Colleges and Schools.

Term System. Semester; summer term.

Enrollment in Degree Programs in Religion 1984–85. Total 28; men 12, women 16.

Degrees in Religion Awarded 1984–85. Bachelor of Science in Christian Education 3; men 1, women 2. Bachelor of Science in Religion 1; men 1. Bachelor of Arts in Humanities/Religion 2; men 1, women 1.

Faculty for Degree Programs in Religion. Total 6; full-time 4, part-time 2.

Admission Requirements. The student who graduates in the upper half of the high school senior class of an accredited high school or its equivalent may be admitted to the freshman class. Also, proficient college examinations scores must be submitted by each freshman applicant.

Tuition and Fees. Tuition $1,825 per semester, part-time students (1-11 hours) $125 per semester hour; general fees $100 (1-5 semester hours $30, 6-11 hours $40); other applicable fees; room $475 to $675 per semester; board $240 to $825 depending upon meal plan.

Financial Aid. The program of student financial aid includes grants, loans, and campus employment. The College annually provides a number of scholarships to students who have exhibited outstanding academic performance. Religion majors with exceptional ability should contact the Department of Religion for information on religion scholarships.

Housing. Student residence halls are available.

Library Facilities. The Judge George W. Armstrong Library offers excellent facilities for study and research.

Religious Services/Activities. The Methodist Student Movement meets weekly.

Degree Programs

The Bachelor of Arts in Humanities-Religion is a pre-ministerial program which offers an interdepartmental major. This gives the student an introduction to many fields of study (history, English, languages, philosophy, psychology, sociology, and religion) without being required to accumulate a large number of credit hours in any one field. The program is recommended for pre-ministerial students. The Bachelor of Science in Religion requires the completion of core courses plus electives and courses in Religion. The Bachelor of Science in Christian Education also requires core courses plus electives and courses in Religion and Biblical Studies.

Special Programs

The Wesleyan Program for Church Administration offers specialized training for the church professional. The three major components of this specialty are: Church Careers Studies, Church Management Summer Studies, and Church Business Administration Continuing Education Studies.

Trinity University
Department of Religion
715 Stadium Drive
San Antonio, TX 78284   (512) 736-7207

Administration. Dr. William O. Walker, Jr., Chair, Department of Religion.

General Description. The Department of Religion offers a variety of courses and a major concentration in Religion leading to the Bachelor of Arts degree. Upper division courses are offered in the area of Western Religious Traditions; Eastern Religious Traditions; Theological, Philosophical, and Comparative Studies; Religion, the Individual, and Society; Religion and the Arts; and Special Courses.

Parent Institution. Trinity University is an independent coeducational institution of higher learning founded in 1869 by Texas Presbyterians. It is now non-sectarian in its policies. The institution served a full century as "the college of The Synod of Texas." In 1969 a covenant was adopted between the Synod and the University, and the previous legal ties were dissolved.

Community Environment. The 107-acre Skyline Campus sits atop Trinity Hill overlooking historic, multicultural San Antonio.

Religious Denomination. Nondenominational.

Accreditation. Southern Association of Colleges and Schools.

Term System. Semester.

Faculty for Degree Programs in Religion. Total 7.

Admission Requirements. High school graduation or equivalent; SAT or ACT; GRE required for graduate programs.

Tuition and Fees. Tuition $5,400 per year; activity fee $90; room $1,475 and board $1,400 per year.

Financial Aid. State and federal grants, college work-study grants, scholarships, and loans represent the types of aid available.

Housing. Dormitory accommodations are available on campus.

Library Facilities. The Library houses over 450,000 books and bound periodicals.

Degree Programs

The requirements for the degree of Bachelor of Arts with a major in Religion are completion of the general curriculum, completion of 30 semester hours in Religion (at least 15 semester hours must be in upper-division courses), and electives, to total 124 semester hours.

Wayland Baptist University
Division of Christian Studies
1900 West 7th
Plainview, TX 79072   (806) 296-5521

Administration. Dr. David L. Jester, President; Dr. M. Daniel McLallen, Academic Vice President and Dean of the University; Dr. Fred D. Howard, Chairperson, Division of Christian Studies.

General Description. The Division of Christian Studies offers courses in the academic areas of Religious Education, Theology, Bible, Christian Leadership. The degree Bachelor of Arts is awarded.

Parent Institution. Wayland Baptist University was founded to meet a need for Christian higher education on the South Plains of West Texas. It remains today a coeducational, multi-purpose institution, and is the only Baptist senior college in the area.

Community Environment. Wayland Baptist University's 80-acre campus is located in the heart of Plainview,

Texas, a small city of 25,000 in the center of a highly developed agricultural area on the South Plains. A prosperous city with a variety of cultural and recreational opportunities, Plainview offers excellent medical facilities and churches of all denominations.

Religious Denomination. Southern Baptist.

Accreditation. Southern Association of Colleges and Schools.

Term System. Semester; 5 summer terms.

Enrollment in Degree Programs in Religion 1984–85. Total 62; men 42, women 20.

Degrees in Religion Awarded 1984–85. Bachelor of Arts in Religion 4; men 4. Bachelor of Arts in Christian Ministries 3; men 3. Bachelor of Arts in Bible 2; men 2. Bachelor of Arts in Religious Education 3; women 3. Bachelor of Arts in Theology 6; men 6.

Faculty for Degree Programs in Religion. Total 10; full-time 6, part-time 4.

Admission Requirements. Graduation from an accredited high school or GED.

Tuition and Fees. Tuition $70 per credit hour; activity fee $60; room and board rates vary depending upon accommodations and meal plan selected (approximately $974-$1,231).

Financial Aid. Seventy-five percent of the student body receives some financial aid from private, institutional, federal, and state sources. Academic and endowed scholarships are available.

Housing. Single undergraduate students are required to live in campus dormitories. Married student housing is available.

Library Facilities. The Van Howeling Memorial Library houses a collection of over 97,000 volumes. Special collections maintained include Local and Denominational History and the University Archives.

Religious Services/Activities. Student Ministries is the responsibility of the Baptist Student Union Executive Council, working with the Director of Student Ministries. The Council supervises and coordinates the religious emphases at the University.

Degree Programs

The major in Bible leading to the Bachelor of Arts degree requires 30 hours in specified courses plus advanced Old Testament and New Testament, philosophy, and advanced Bible electives. Course offerings are designed to meet student needs as follows: (1) a carefully designed curriculum of pre-seminary training for ministerial students, (2) an extensive preparation in Biblical knowledge for ministerial students whose Wayland degree will be their terminal formal training, and (3) survey courses in both Old and New Testament for all students.

The Department of Religious Education offers a major that includes academic studies in the administration of the church's leadership and educational programs, church and denominational activities, and ministry skills for persons entering specialized church-related vocations other than pastor.

The Department of Theology offers a major that includes academic studies in church history, theological method and diversity, and the theological basis for a church-related ministry. The major requires the completion of 30 hours. All baccalaureate degrees require the completion of a total of 124 semester hours.

Woodcrest College
(Formerly Dallas Bible College)
Route 1, Box 106
Lindale, TX 75771   (214) 882-7566

Administration. Dr. U.A. Doiron, President; Thomas Houston, Executive Vice President.

General Description. Woodcrest College is the new identity of Dallas Bible College, a name respected in the field of Christian postsecondary education. Founded in 1941, it has expanded its programs and pursued the goal of integrating Biblical truth in every area of the curriculum. It also has established extension classes in Houston in cooperation with the Houston Bible Institute, and in San Antonio in cooperation with the Texas Bible Institute.

In 1984, the board of directors of the College decided to move the main campus to a beautiful, 68-acre site in east Texas. They also changed the name of the institution to Woodcrest College and voted to continue expansion of the curriculum to meet current needs of the Woodcrest constituency. The first classes at the new campus began in August 1985. A Dallas campus will remain, at 8733 La Prada, Dallas, TX 75228, telephone (214) 328-7171. The Dallas campus will also be served by members of the Woodcrest faculty.

The educational philosophy of Woodcrest College is Biblical, evangelical, developmental, and ministry-oriented. It undergirds every aspect of the life of the college, both in academic and non-academic matters. The academic programs include one-year programs (Bible Certificate, Bible Diploma), two-year programs (Associate of Arts degree), four-year programs (Bachelor of Science, Bachelor of Arts), and a five-year program (Bachelor of Theology).

Community Environment. The new main campus of Woodcrest College is located in Lindale, Texas, on State Highway 110 in the picturesque, rolling woodlands of east Texas. It is 1 mile north of Interstate 20 and 17 miles northwest of downtown Tyler, one of the most rapidly growing cities in the eastern part of Texas, and 80 miles from Dallas.

Religious Denomination. Nondenominational.

Religious Emphasis. Fundamentalist.

Accreditation. American Association of Bible Colleges.

Term System. Semester.

Degrees in Religion Awarded 1984–85. Certificate (1-year) 9; men 5, women 4. Associate of Arts 13; men 9, women 4. Bachelor of Arts and Bachelor of Science 31;

men 21, women 10. Bachelor of Theology (5-year) 3; men 3.

Faculty for Degree Programs in Religion. Total 20; full-time 11, part-time 9.

Admission Requirements. High school education or its equivalent; ACT test; minimum age requirement 18 (unless special circumstances); testimony of having been saved at least a year and of having dedicated their lives to the Lord's will; completed medical form; resident students must get medical release signed by parent or guardian; resident students must have hospitalization; students admitted of any sex, race, color and national or ethnic background.

Tuition and Fees. Tuition $90 per semester hour for students taking 8 hours or more, $95 per semester hour for 1-7 hours; student fees $60; library fee $2; room and board $1,100 per semester.

Financial Aid. Veterans Assistance, Pell Grants, Supplementary Educational Opportunity Grants, College Work-Study, National Direct Student Loans, Guaranteed Student Loan Program, scholarships, and regular on-campus employment are available.

Housing. Single students under 25 years of age are required to live in the residence halls located on campus unless they live with their parents or are granted special permission to live elsewhere. Students taking less than eight hours can live in the residence halls only by action of the Student Housing Committee. Although housing facilities for married students are not provided by the College, suitable housing accommodations in the surrounding area are sought by the College on behalf of the students.

Library Facilities. The W. Howard Gould Library houses over 35,000 volumes, 4,000 audio media and visual aids, plus over 200 periodicals. An education lab includes tape recordings, filmstrips, records, flannel graph, and textbook materials.

Religious Services/Activities. Chapel is held each day for 35 minutes featuring area pastors, missionaries, and faculty and staff. Student Missions Fellowship sponsors prayer bands, SMR chapels, and summer missionary internships. Wives Fellowship fosters close fellowship among college families. The student Congress provides channels of communication. The JOY Musical Team represents Woodcrest to outside organizations.

Degree Programs

Every program at Woodcrest College involves a major in Bible and theology; individual programs are designated by student's vocational or professional objectives. The Bachelor of Science programs are: Business, Counseling, General Missons, General Studies, Music, Occupation Education, Christian Ministries Program for Nurses, Pastoral Studies, Teacher Education, and Youth Ministry. All programs require 130 semester hours of study. The Bachelor of Arts programs include: Linguistic, Greek, and Pre-Seminary.

The Bachelor of Theology program seeks to meet the needs of students who have two years of liberal arts education and who desire a broad Biblical education. This five-year program of study enables students to prepare for a pastoral ministry and for graduate study at the same time.

Special Programs

The Associate of Arts degree is a two-year program designed to provide Biblical and professional training for students who desire additional education in subjects not offered at Woodcrest College. There are three different plans for this program: an elementary or secondary education concentration at one of the universities in the north or east Texas area or participation in a cooperative program with Fort Hays State University in Hays, Kansas; a plan designed for students who wish to enter various business or vocational occupations; and a third plan designed for students with musical abilities who desire training to enable them to serve as a leader in the music program of a local church.

A Bible Certificate can be earned for a year of training in Biblical studies.

A Bible Diploma program is designed for the graduate of a liberal arts college who desires intensive Bible training.

UTAH

Brigham Young University
Department of Religious Education
Provo, UT 84602   (801) 378-2507

Administration. Robert J. Matthews, Dean, Department of Religious Education.

General Description. All undergraduate students at the University must fulfill a 14-hour requirement in religion. Graduate study on the Master's and Doctoral levels is also offered. The Dean of Religious Education is also the Director of the Religious Studies Center which promotes research in Ancient Studies, Bible, Book of Mormon, Church History, Pearl of Great Price, and World Religions. The Center is a supporting and coordinating agency for religion-oriented research throughout the University. It is not involved in classroom instruction or degree programs.

Parent Institution. Brigham Young University began as an academy of The Church of Jesus Christ of Latter-day Saints in 1875 and became a university in 1903.

Community Environment. The campus is located in Provo, 45 miles from Salt Lake City.

Religious Denomination. The Church of Jesus Christ of Latter-day Saints.

Accreditation. Northwest Association of Schools and Colleges.

Term System. Semester system.

Admission Requirements. High school graduation; ACT. Graduate programs: Baccalaureate degree from an accredited university or college.

Tuition and Fees. Tuition $1,110 per semester for non-LDS members, $740 for members; room and board $1,200 per semester.

Financial Aid. Scholarships, awards, loans, and federal aid programs are available.

Housing. Campus housing includes room and board residence halls for men and women, and married student apartments.

Library Facilities. The library contains over 1,300,000 volumes, 67,000 pamphlets, 182,000 periodicals, 340,000 microforms, and 16,000 sound recordings.

Religious Services/Activities. High standards of honor, integrity, and morality as well as Christian ideals in every day living are required of every student.

Degree Programs

A minor for the Master of Arts and Doctor of Philosophy degrees is offered by the Department of Religious Education in a graduate program for Church History and Doctrine. Fields of study include Christian History, Doctrine and Covenants, and World Religions. A minimum of 9 hours of approved coursework is required for a minor in a Master's program. In a Doctoral program, the number of hours required is determined in consultation with the chairman of the department offering the major, but it must not be less than 12 hours.

Westminster College of Salt Lake City
Philosophy/Religion Program
1840 South 1300 East
Salt Lake City, UT 84105   (801) 484-7651

Administration. Dr. Charles H. Dick, President; Dr. Allan A. Kuusisto, Academic Vice President and Dean of the Faculty; Dr. Stephen R. Baar, Dean, School of Arts and Sciences; Dr. Michael Popich, Program Director, Philosophy and Religion Program.

General Description. Westminster College has a combined Philosophy and Religion program in which students may major, with an emphasis on Religion. All students of the College are required to take one course in Religion or Philosophy as a part of the graduation requirements.

Parent Institution. Westminster College is a private, independent, 4-year liberal arts college with graduate programs in education and management. The College is nonsectarian but maintains historical ties with the Presbyterian Church, U.S.A., the United Methodist Church, and the United Church of Christ.

Community Environment. Westminster's 27-acre campus is located in a pleasant residential area in Utah's state capital — Salt Lake City — within the shadows of the rugged Rocky Mountains. Student residing in the on-campus residence halls are just 10 minutes from downtown, 15 minutes from nearby canyons, and only 30 minutes from spectacular ski slopes. Music, ballet, professional sports, and other cultural events are available.

Religious Denomination. Nondenominational. The College welcomes students of all religious persuasions while maintaining historical ties with the Presbyterian Church, U.S.A., the United Methodist Church, and the United Church of Christ.

Accreditation. Northwest Association of Schools and Colleges.

Term System. Semester; May Term; summer term.

Enrollment in Degree Programs in Religion 1984–85. Total 2; men 1, women 1.

Degrees in Religion Awarded 1984–85. Bachelor of Arts 1; women 1.

Faculty for Degree Programs in Religion. Total 2; part-time 2.

Admission Requirements. High school grade point average of 1.0 (C) or higher; all students are required to take either the ACT or SAT and have the results sent to the Office of Admissions. Applicants with high school grade point averages below 2.0 (C) may be admitted on probation if they can demonstrate ability to successfully undertake college work.

Tuition and Fees. Tuition $4,160 per year; room and board $3,600.

Financial Aid. A significant program of merit-based and need-based aid is available to support new and continuing students.

Housing. On campus dormitory housing; no on campus housing for married students.

Library Facilities. The library houses over 63,000 volumes and maintains online access to computer records of over 4,500 other libraries throughout the country. Volumes in public college and university libraries in Utah are available on interlibrary loan.

Religious Services/Activities. Nondenominational activities held weekly and monthly during special seasons.

Degree Programs

A Bachelor of Arts degree with a Philosophy and Religion major is offered, with an emphasis in Religion. A minimum of 24 semester hours in Philosophy and Religion coursework must be completed. Students who intend to go on to graduate school are strongly advised to obtain proficiency in a foreign language.

Special Programs

Prior Learning Assessment is available to adult students whereby they may gain academic credit through a portfolio documenting college-level skills gained through career and life experience.

VERMONT

St. Michael's College
Department of Religious Studies
Winooski, VT 05404   (802) 655-2000

Administration. Dr. Joseph Kroger, Chairman, Department of Religious Studies.

General Description. Religious Studies are offered by the Department in keeping with the general objectives of the College to study systematically the meaning and relevance of Christian beliefs. Each student is required to take at least 6 credits in Religious Studies. In addition, the Department offers an undergraduate Religious Studies Concentration, granting the Bachelor of Arts degree. At the graduate level, the Master of Arts degree is offered with concentrations in Religious Education, Pastoral Ministry and Spirituality, Scripture, and Theology. The Certificate of Advanced Specialization is a post-degree certificate.

Parent Institution. St. Michael's is a private liberal arts and sciences college founded in 1904 and sponsored by the Society of Saint Edmund, a community of Catholic priests and brothers. Its mission is to provide a liberal education in the light of the Catholic faith and its developing tradition. However, it respects those of other beliefs and convictions, welcoming their contributions in the common pursuit of truth, goodness, and justice.

Community Environment. Viewed from St. Michael's campus, Mount Mansfield, Vermont's tallest peak, rises out of the morning mist to the east, and to the west is the spectacular view of Lake Champlain and the Adirondacks. The campus's own hilltop overlooks the winding Winooski River and covers a landscaped 430 acres, divided into main and north campuses. Nearby is Burlington, Vermont's largest city, as are the University of Vermont, Champlain College, and Trinity College, all within a 5-mile radius.

Religious Denomination. Roman Catholic.

Accreditation. New England Association of Schools and Colleges.

Term System. Semester.

Enrollment in Degree Programs in Religion 1984–85. Total 13; men 9, women 4.

Degrees in Religion Awarded 1984–85. Bachelor of Arts

in Religious Studies 5; men 5.

Faculty for Degree Programs in Religion. Total 8; full-time 6, part-time 2.

Admission Requirements. High school graduation; SAT or ACT; recommendations of counselors and teachers.

Tuition and Fees. Tuition $6,804 per year; room $1,423; board $1,339; student activities fee $70.

Financial Aid. Financial aid, consisting of scholarships, grants, loans, and work opportunities, is awarded on the basis of financial need.

Housing. Residence halls and student apartments are available on campus.

Library Facilities. The Jeremiah Durick Library contains over 140,000 volumes of bound books and periodicals, as well as an additional 48,000 volumes in microfilm.

Religious Services/Activities. The Office of Campus Ministry conducts a variety of spiritual, pastoral, and liturgical programs and activities such as catechetical and basic doctrinal instruction, Bible study, shared prayer, Christian fellowship, weekend retreats, and social justice education. The Chapel of Saint Michael the Archangel is the spiritual center of the campus.

Degree Programs

The Bachelor of Arts degree with a concentration in Religious Studies provides students with the opportunity for more extensive and intensive exploration of the Christian experience and the traditions of other religions. In the context of the College's overall curriculum, the Religious Studies concentrator is able to deepen and expand his understanding of the religious dimension of life, both culturally and personally. Concentrators must take ten courses and the senior seminar in Religious Studies.

Trinity College
Department of Religious Studies
208 Colchester Avenue
Burlington, VT 05401   (802) 658-0337

General Description. The Department of Religious Studies offers a concentration leading to the Bachelor of

517

Arts degree. Religious Studies explores the areas of Biblical Studies, Systematic Theology, and Theological Ethics. The Department emphasizes Biblical Studies (including opportunities to explore the Holy Land through on-site tours) and Theological Ethics.

Parent Institution. Trinity College is a small liberal arts college distinguished by over fifty years of academic achievements and is rooted in the Catholic religious tradition. It was founded in 1925 by the Sisters of Mercy of the Diocese of Burlington.

Community Environment. The 17-acre campus is 10 minutes from the center of Burlington, the largest city in Vermont, located on Lake Champlain.

Religious Denomination. Roman Catholic.

Accreditation. New England Association of Schools and Colleges.

Term System. Semester.

Admission Requirements. High school graduation with rank in the upper half of class; non-high school graduates considered.

Tuition and Fees. Tuition $5,040 per year; room and board $2,851; student fees $115.

Financial Aid. Aid is awarded on the basis of need.

Housing. Campus residency is required for all traditional, full-time degree students.

Library Facilities. The library houses over 36,000 volumes.

Religious Services/Activities. The goal of the Campus Ministry program is to utilize the skills, experience, and spiritual resources of the college community to build a community of faith and social awareness. Sunday Eucharist, residence hall Masses, prayer groups, retreats, ecumenical services, discussions, workshops, and outreach projects are among the activities available.

Degree Programs

The Department of Religious Studies grants the Bachelor of Arts degree in Religion.

Vermont, University of
College of Arts and Sciences
Department of Religion
481 Main Street
Burlington, VT 05405   (802) 656-3080

Administration. Dr. Lattie F. Coor, President; Dr. John G. Jewett, Dean, College of Arts and Sciences; Luther A. Martin, Chairman, Department of Religion.

General Description. The Department of Religion of the University of Vermont offers a major and a minor in Religion for the Bachelor of Arts degree. The courses are taught from a nonsectarian, academic prespective.

Parent Institution. Combining the heritage of a private university with that of a land-grant institution, the University of Vermont embraces a broad range of instruction-al and research programs in the liberal disciplines and in the professions.

Community Environment. Burlington is Vermont's largest city and, while the University is a significant resource, the city has manifold cultural, recreational, and social offerings. Burlington is a tourist and business center with a rich history and significant business development.

Religious Denomination. None.

Accreditation. New England Association of Schools and Colleges.

Term System. Semester.

Enrollment in Degree Programs in Religion 1984–85. Total 30.

Faculty for Degree Programs in Religion. Total 7; full-time 7.

Admission Requirements. Qualification for admission is determined on the basis of the secondary school record, rank in graduating class, recommendations, writing ability, strength of preparation in the area chosen as a major, SAT test results, and other supportive information.

Tuition and Fees. Tuition Vermont residents $1,275 per semester; non-resident $3,380; housing $1,898; board $1,-004; student health fee $114 per year; student activities fee $37.

Financial Aid. Aid is most often awarded in combinations of the various types of aid (scholarships, loans, and employment).

Housing. Any student may apply to live in University residence halls but priority is given to full-time undergraduate students. University-owned apartments designated for married students are located off-campus.

Library Facilities. The Bailey-Howe Library contains a collection of over 1 million volumes.

Degree Programs

The major in Religion leading to the Bachelor of Arts degree requires the completion of 36 hours in the Department (up to 9 hours in related courses may be substituted). Courses include the areas of Judeo-Christian traditions, Asian traditions, cultural, and comparative religion.

VIRGINIA

Bridgewater College
Department of Philosophy and Religion
East College Street
Bridgewater, VA 22812   (703) 828-2501

Administration. Dr. Wayne F. Geisert, President; Dr. Ben F. Wade, Provost and Professor of Religion; Dr. John W. Cooper, Dean for Academic Affairs.

General Description. The Department of Philosophy and Religion seeks to broaden the liberal arts education of all students in the College by a careful consideration of the methods and content of the study of religion and philosophy. A major in Philosophy and Religion is offered which may be focused on the study of either philosophy or religion, but requiring significant exposure to both disciplines. Many courses cross over traditional disciplinary lines.

Parent Institution. Founded in 1880, Bridgewater College was the first coeducational, senior-level college in the Commonwealth of Virginia. It seeks to be an academic community with a distinctively Christian atmosphere and with a wholesome balance of learning, service, and pleasure. Approximately 750 students are enrolled at the largely residential college. Twenty-eight majors are offered in programs leading to the Bachelor of Arts and Bachelor of Science degrees.

Community Environment. Bridgewater College is located in the Shenandoah Valley, a scenic and historic region in Virginia. The campus is comprised of 165 acres; the educational activities are focused on the primary campus of 40 acres. The town of Bridgewater is 7 miles south of Harrisonburg.

Religious Denomination. Affiliated with the Church of the Brethren.

Religious Emphasis. Liberal (mainline Protestant with Anabaptist influence).

Accreditation. Southern Association of Colleges and Schools.

Term System. Modified semester (3-3-1-3); summer term.

Enrollment in Degree Programs in Religion 1984–85. Total 11; men 7, women 4.

Degrees in Religion Awarded 1984–85. Bachelor of Arts 2; men 2.

Faculty for Degree Programs in Religion. Total 5.

Admission Requirements. High school graduation with 2.0 grade point average in college preparatory courses from an accredited high school; SAT score of 800 or equivalent; three letters of recommendation.

Tuition and Fees. Tuition $5,370 per year; room and board $2,880.

Financial Aid. All standard types of aid are available, including federal grants and loans, Virginia Tuition Assistance Grants, and non-need based academic scholarships.

Housing. Dormitories are available for single students; several apartments and houses may be rented by married students.

Library Facilities. The Alexander Mack Memorial Library houses over 125,000 volumes. Special collections include Church of the Brethren History and Conflict Resolution and Peace Studies.

Religious Services/Activities. The College Street Church of the Brethren is located on the campus. Among the organizations and activities offered to students are the Interdenominational Council of Religious Activities, Chapel Services, Baptist Student Union, Wesley Fellowship, Lutheran Student Association, Fellowship of Christian Athletes, and other denominational and interdenominational groups represented. Most have weekly meetings and semiannual retreats.

Degree Programs

A major in Philosophy and Religion leading to the Bachelor of Arts degree consists of not less than 30 units with a minimum of 12 units each from Philosophy and Religion, the remaining units composed of courses approved by the Department.

Special Programs

Telecourses and noncredit continuing education opportunities in Philosophy and Religion are frequently offered. Study abroad opportunities are available through Brethren Colleges Abroad at Marburg, West Germany; Strasbourg, France; Barcelona, Spain; Cheltenham, England;

and Dalian, China (PRC).

Eastern Mennonite College
Bible and Religion Department
Harrisonburg, VA 22801   (703) 433-2771

Administration. Dr. Richard C. Detwiler, President; Dr. Albert N. Keim, Dean of the College.

General Description. In order to meet the needs of the church, the interests of students in vocational ministries, and the concerns of both with issues in religion and philosophy, the Department offers a choice of three majors: (1) Biblical Studies and Theology offers a solid foundation in Biblical studies and is recommended as pre-seminary preparation; (2) Christian Ministries focuses on the church and missions and serves those with interests in pastoral or youth ministries; (3) Religion and Philosophy is for students with special interests in theology and philosophy. The Department awards the degrees Bachelor of Arts, Bachelor of Science, and Master of Education in Christian School Instruction.

Parent Institution. Eastern Mennonite College is responsible to the Mennonite Church to provide a liberal arts education from an Anabaptist/Mennonite perspective. However, while serving as an extension of the Mennonite Church and home in education, the College welcomes all persons who desire a Christian education within the framework of the College's philosophy. It educates persons for Christian mission and service.

Community Environment. The 89-acre campus of the College is located in Harrisonburg, Virginia, in the heart of the scenic and historic Shenandoah Valley. Harrisonburg (population 25,000) is fronted on the east by the Massanutten and Blue Ridge mountain ranges, and on the west by the Alleghenies. Only 125 miles from the nation's capital and 115 miles from Richmond, the College has an ideal location for historical and cultural field trips.

Religious Denomination. Mennonite.

Religious Emphasis. Evangelical Anabaptist.

Accreditation. Southern Association of Colleges and Schools.

Term System. Semester; summer term.

Enrollment in Degree Programs in Religion 1984–85. Total 44; men 43, women 1.

Degrees in Religion Awarded 1984–85. Bachelor of Science in Christian Ministries 5; men 5. Bachelor of Science in Biblical Studies and Theology 6; men 6. Bachelor of Arts in Biblical Studies and Theology 2; men 2.

Faculty for Degree Programs in Religion. Total 7; full-time 4, part-time 3.

Admission Requirements. High school graduation; SAT and ACT required; two personal references.

Tuition and Fees. Tuition $5,156 per year; activity fee $94; room and board $2,328 per year.

Financial Aid. Assistance may be a combination of personal and family resources, public and private grants and scholarships, the college work program, and a college grant or bank loan.

Housing. Dormitories and intentional communities are available for unmarried students. Apartments for married students are available in the surrounding community. The College operates a trailer park for students and staff.

Library Facilities. The library houses over 115,000 volumes of which 28,150 volumes are in Religion. The Anabaptist/Mennonite History special collection is maintained.

Religious Services/Activities. College Assembly meets 3 times weekly. Organizations offered for student participation include Young Peoples Christian Association, Peace Fellowship, Student Missionary Fellowship, and Amnesty International Campus Chapter.

Degree Programs

The Bachelor of Arts and the Bachelor of Science degrees require the completion of 128 semester hours. Majors are offered in Biblical Studies and Theology, Christian Ministries, and Religion and Philosophy. Each major requires the completion of 36 semester hours of core, optional, and designated courses.

Special Programs

The Associate in Arts in Bible is a two-year program which allows the student to combine 23 hours of core requirements with a 30-hour concentration in Biblical and Church Studies and 11 hours of electives.

A One-Year Bible Program is offered for students wanting concentrated Bible study for one year.

Emory and Henry College
Department of Religion
Emory, VA 24327   (703) 944-3121

Administration. Maurice S. Luker, Jr., Chairperson, Department of Religion.

General Description. The Department of Religion offers a concentration in the area of Religion leading to the Bachelor of Arts degree. The objective of the program is to investigate religious thought and action within a balanced context of approaches, utilizing psychological, sociological, literary, and historical insights to support a thorough study of religious traditions.

Parent Institution. Emory and Henry College is a four-year liberal arts college affiliated with the Holston Conference of the United Methodist Church. The College was founded in 1836.

Community Environment. The campus of 150 acres has 22 buildings. Emory is a village in the Virginia Highlands, approximately 20 miles north of Bristol.

Religious Denomination. United Methodist Church.

Accreditation. Southern Association of Colleges and Schools.

Term System. Fall, Winter, Spring terms; two summer

520

sessions.

Faculty for Degree Programs in Religion. Total 3.

Admission Requirements. High school graduation or equivalent; recommended rank in top 50 percent of high school class; ACT or SAT.

Tuition and Fees. Tuition and fees $4,500; room and board $2,400.

Financial Aid. Assistance in the form of grants and scholarships, loans, and employment is available.

Housing. Residence halls provide housing on campus.

Library Facilities. The Kelly Library houses over 140,-000 volumes and subscribes to 715 current periodicals.

Religious Services/Activities. The campus religious life program is ecumenical and open to all. Special convocations and worship services are provided in Memorial Chapel on campus. Many students meet regularly in a fellowship group for Bible study and discussion.

Degree Programs

The concentration in Religion requires the completion of four core courses plus four additional courses selected in consultation with the faculty advisor. Courses are offered in three areas: General Interest Courses, Advanced Religion Courses, and Christian Education. Each student must complete two projects: one in community service and one of a creative character.

Ferrum College
Department of Religion and Philosophy
Ferrum, VA 24088   (703) 365-2121

Administration. Joseph T. Hart, President.

General Description. The Department of Religion and Philosophy offers three majors that provide an opportunity for students to concentrate in religioius studies, philosophy, or in a combined major with a balance of the two disciplines. Majors are equipped for seminary or career opportunities, or they may pursue studies for advanced degrees.

Parent Institution. Ferrum College is a church-related college operating under the auspices of the Virginia Methodist Church. The nondenominational college was founded in 1913.

Community Environment. The campus occupies an area of 754 acres and has over 70 buildings. It is located in the rural village of Ferrum in the foothills of the Blue Ridge Mountains, 35 miles southwest of Roanoke.

Religious Denomination. United Methodist Church.

Accreditation. Southern Association of Colleges and Schools.

Term System. Semester.

Admission Requirements. High school graduation; SAT or ACT; non-high school graduates considered.

Tuition and Fees. Tuition and fees $4,230; room and board $1,940.

Financial Aid. A comprehensive assistance program in-

cluding campus jobs, scholarships, grants, and loans is available.

Housing. Student resident halls are available on campus.

Library Facilities. The Stanley Library houses over 73,-000 volumes. Special collections and archives of several organizations, including the Blue Ridge Institute, are maintained.

Religious Services/Activities. Individuals are encouraged to attend chapel services or the church of their choice and to participate in voluntary service activities and campus religious groups.

Degree Programs

The majors in Religion, Philosophy, or a combination thereof leading to the Bachelor of Arts or Bachelor of Science degree require the completion of 36 semester hours in prescribed courses.

Hampden-Sydney College
Department of Religion
Hampden-Sydney, VA 23943   (804) 223-4388

Administration. Josiah Bunting, III, President.

General Description. The Department of Religion offers a major in the field and provides a program for those who contemplate the Christian ministry by preparing for study at a theological seminary.

Parent Institution. Hampden-Sydney College is affiliated with the Presbyterian Church in the United States. It is a four-year liberal arts college for men and has been in continuous operation since 1776.

Community Environment. The college campus is situated on 566 acres in the rural area of Hampden-Sydney, 70 miles southwest of Richmond. Farmville, a town of 6,000, is located seven miles north.

Religious Denomination. Presbyterian Church (U.S.A.).

Accreditation. Southern Association of Colleges and Schools.

Term System. Semester system.

Admission Requirements. High school graduation or equivalent.

Tuition and Fees. Comprehensive fee $7,050 per year; room $700-$1,00; board $1,500.

Financial Aid. Various types of financial aid are available, both need-based and for academic achievement.

Housing. Dormitories and fraternity houses are available.

Library Facilities. The Eggleston Library has a book collection of 140,000 volumes. More than 800 periodicals and scholarly journals are received regularly.

Degree Programs

The requirements for a baccalaureate major in Religion are 30 hours in Religion courses in Biblical studies, one course in Christian religious tradition, one course in non-

Christian religious tradition, and one course in Christian theology or ethics. Six hours in Philosophy courses are recommended for Religion majors.

Liberty University
(Formerly Liberty Baptist College)
School of Religion and Liberty Baptist
 Theological Seminary
Box 20000
Lynchburg, VA 24506   (804) 237-5961

Administration. Dr. Jerry Falwell, Chancellor; Dr. A. Pierre Guillerman, President; Dr. Richard G. Fitzgerald, Academic Dean.

General Description. The School of Religion of Liberty University functions at the heartbeat of the institution's purpose. Since the University began in 1971, the School of Religion has led in its commitment to Biblical truth. It offers a variety of programs from the diploma to master's level. It includes the Institute of Biblical Studies, the Division of Religion, the Graduate School of Religion, and Liberty Baptist Theological Seminary. Biblical and theological studies are a vital part of the curricula at all levels.

Parent Institution. Liberty University was formed under the auspices of the Thomas Road Baptist Church and operates as one of the ministries of this local church. The belief of the University is that the primary focus of God's work in the world is the local church. The fundamental purpose of the local church is evangelism. Therefore, Liberty has as its pervasive aim the equipping of young people for evangelistic ministry in the local church. Liberty is probable distinctive among Christian colleges because it emphasizes evangelism, holds a fundamentalist position, and provides academic excellence with a liberal arts curriculum.

Community Environment. Liberty University is located in the heart of Virginia in Lynchburg (population 70,000) on the south bank of the historic James River with the scenic Blue Ridge Mountains as a backdrop. The city is almost 200 years old and noted for its culture, beauty, and educational advantages.

Religious Denomination. Baptist.

Religious Emphasis. Fundamentalist.

Accreditation. Southern Association of Colleges and Schools.

Term System. Semester; summer term.

Enrollment in Degree Programs in Religion 1984–85. Total 780; men 460, women 320.

Degrees in Religion Awarded 1984–85. Associate of Arts 14; men 10, women 4. Bachelor of Science 86; men 85, women 1. Bachelor of Arts 6; men 6. Master of Arts 26; men 20, women 6. Master of Religious Education 15; men 15. Master of Divinity 13; men 13.

Faculty for Degree Programs in Religion. Total 45; full-time 35, part-time 10.

Admission Requirements. Open admission. The Master of Arts program requires a 3.0 grade point average in undergraduate work; undergraduate work in the area of the Master's concentration; foreign language ability or coursework as determined by the department of study; and a combined score of 900 on the quantitative and verbal areas of the Graduate Record Examination.

Tuition and Fees. Tuition $1,250 per semester.

Financial Aid. Aid consists of scholarships, grants, loans, and a work-study program. Seminary programs have a scholarship available which reduces the tuition to $300 per semester.

Housing. Dormitories are available; assistance in locating off-campus housing is offered.

Library Facilities. The library contains over 250,000 volumes and maintains the Church League of America Collection.

Religious Services/Activities. The University is closely associated with Thomas Road Baptist Church which provides many opportunities for worship, service, and activities.

Degree Programs

The Bachelor of Science degree is offered with majors in Pastoral Ministries, Cross-Cultural Ministries, and Church Ministries (with concentrations in Counseling, Christian Education, and Youth Ministries).

The Bachelor of Arts degree includes majors in Cross-Cultural Ministries and Christian Thought.

The Master of Arts degree is offered with with concentrations in Biblical Studies, Church Growth and Cross-Cultural Studies, Counseling, and Christian Thought.

The Master of Religious Education includes concentrations in Christian Education and Counseling.

Special Programs

The School of Lifelong Learning of the University has the following programs in religion available on cassettes (the majority of coursework is non-resident): Bachelor of Science in Church Ministries, Master of Arts in Counseling, and Master of Religious Education.

Lynchburg College
Department of Religious Studies
Lynchburg, VA 24501   (804) 522-8331

Administration. Dr. Joseph L. Nelson, Jr., Chair, Department of Religious Studies.

General Description. The Department of Religious Studies offers: (1) introductory courses, (2) advanced general courses which are shared with other departments of the faculty, (3) seminars on an intermediate level, and (4) special courses involving either individual research or apprenticeships. Through an Advisory Committee on Pre-Ministerial Education, the College exercises a cooperative role with related church officials in supervising the pre-seminary education of students preparing for some ministerial vocation.

Parent Institution. Lynchburg College was founded in 1903 as Virginia Christian College, a liberal arts college related to the Christian Church (Disciples of Christ) but unusual in Virginia at that time because it was coeducational from the outset. The name was changed in 1919 to Lynchburg College. Church leaders serve on the Board of Trustees. While no sectarian authority exercises control over the educational enterprise, ties to a religious heritage have provided a continuing force in the humanitarian, moral, and spiritual character of the College.

Community Environment. The campus grounds extend over 214 acres. The Blue Ridge Mountains form the western skyline. Predominantly of colonial design, the buildings are grouped on the main campus oval. Lynchburg, Virginia was founded in 1786 and is a modern community with a population in its metropolitan area of 144,500. The city is approximately 4 hours from Washington, D.C.

Religious Denomination. Christian Church (Disciples of Christ).

Accreditation. Southern Association of Colleges and Schools.

Term System. Semester; winter term; 4 summer terms.

Degrees in Religion Awarded 1984–85. Bachelor of Arts 4; men 4.

Faculty for Degree Programs in Religion. Total 5; full-time 4, part-time 1.

Admission Requirements. Graduation from an approved secondary school with a minimum of 15 academic units or the equivalent as shown by examination.

Tuition and Fees. Tuition $6,250 per year; room and dining hall $3,200 per year.

Financial Aid. There are many forms and levels of financial aid, depending upon many different variables.

Housing. Campus dormitories available. Many students choose to live off-campus, but that is an individual choice and individual responsibility. There are very limited facilities for married students.

Library Facilities. The Knight-Capron Library has holdings of 200,800 volumes, 614 current periodical titles, and approximately 20,000 pieces of multimedia material. The Saxton Rare Book Room houses a valuable collection of fifteenth and sixteenth century illuminated manuscripts, eighteenth and nineteenth century volumes of religious history, and the Disciples of Christ Historical Collection for Virginia.

Religious Services/Activities. The Chapel program at the College includes a wide range of opportunities for growth and challenge. Various small groups meet throughout the year. Fellowship is the focus of some, while a highly disciplined structure for exploring the interrelationship of prayer and service provides the core of involvement with others. Opportunities for volunteer work in the community are available to all students throughout the year.

A weekly ecumenical worship service is held on Sunday mornings. A weekly Mass for Roman Catholic students is conducted on Sunday evenings.

The Chaplain of the College is responsible for giving shape to the Chapel program. Special lectures, forums, movies, weekend retreats, and other activities are planned by the Chaplain to increase a feeling of community on campus and to explore what it means to live as a Christian in the modern world.

Degree Programs

The Bachelor of Arts with a major in Religious Studies and the Bachelor of Arts with joint major in Religious Studies plus certain other fields (Sociology, Psychology, Philosophy, Theatre Arts, Speech Communication, Music, Business Administration, etc.) are offered through the Department of Religious Studies. For pre-ministerial education, students are advised by faculty of the Department of Religious Studies and the College Chaplain. The Advisory Committee appoints qualified students in supervised field education as "Apprentices-in-Ministry." This may entail service with church congregations, church-related agencies, or other social service agencies.

Presbyterian School of Christian Education
1205 Palmyra Avenue
Richmond, VA 23227   (804) 359-5031

Administration. Dr. Heath K. Rada, President; Dr. Paul W. Walaskay, Dean of the Faculty.

General Description. The Presbyterian School of Christian Education is a graduate center for educational ministry: "graduate" because it offers the Master of Arts and the Doctor of Education degrees, both with emphasis on Christian education; "center" because the campus is the home of programs other than degree studies which reach out to community, national church, and even the world; "educational ministry" because the academic programs are focused on preparing lay persons to function as leaders in teaching ministries. Being one of three schools in the Richmond Theological Center gives PSCE additional ecumenical contacts and provides a broader experience for students. The other schools are Union Theological Seminary in Virginia and the School of Theology of Virginia Union University.

Community Environment. The campus of PSCE is in Richmond, Virginia, the historical capital of the Confederacy. Virginia was also one of the original 13 colonies, so one will find in Richmond many places of historical interest. The city is conveniently located, 325 miles from New York, 100 miles from Washington, 50 miles from Williamsburg, 100 miles from Virginia Beach, and 95 miles from the Skyline Drive or the Shenandoah National Park.

Religious Denomination. Presbyterian.

Accreditation. Southern Association of Colleges and Schools; Association of Theological Schools in the United States and Canada.

Term System. Five terms: September, Fall, January,

Spring, and May; no summer term.

Enrollment in Degree Programs in Religion 1984–85. Total 138; men 32, women 106.

Degrees in Religion Awarded 1984–85. Master of Arts 50; men 11, women 39.

Faculty for Degree Programs in Religion. Total 21; full-time 13, part-time 8.

Admission Requirements. Master of Arts program: Bachelor's degree or its equivalent from an accredited college or university. Doctor of Education program: Bachelor of Arts degree or equivalent, Master's degree (M.A., M.Ed., M.Div., M.R.E. or equivalent) plus a minimum of two years of effective professional performance either in religious education or in a closely related area.

Tuition and Fees. Master of Arts tuition $3,000, Doctor of Education $3,500; dining hall fees $1,302 to $1,673.50 (depending upon meal plan); housing $680; married student's apartment $2,160.

Financial Aid. A financial aid package which may include a combination of grant, work, and loan may be appropriated to students who have explored other areas of funding and still need financial assistance. The School is also an eligible institution for low-interest Guaranteed Student Loans, available through lending institutions in the student's home state.

Housing. Dormitory accommodations are available for single students and there are on-campus apartments for married students.

Library Facilities. The library of the Union Theological Seminary, immediately adjacent to the School's campus, is utilized by PSCE students. Its holdings exceed 200,000 volumes.

Religious Services/Activities. The campus community gathers for worship four days each week in Sydnor Chapel.

Degree Programs

The Master of Arts degree includes the completion of 90 quarter hours of required courses and a program of a minimum of 10 weeks in supervised field education (not required of Master of Divinity graduates). A Christian Education and Social Work Program and a Church Music and Christian Education Program are dual degree programs offered in cooperation with Virginia Commonwealth Unviersity.

The Doctor of Education is a graduate professional degree. The program stresses preparation for advanced professional responsibilities by engaging in full-time study and independent research in religious education and its foundational disciplines, as well as in an area of specialization. A minimum of two full-time academic years in residence is required.

Protestant Episcopal Theological Seminary in Virginia
3737 Seminary Road
Alexandria, VA 22304   (703) 370-6600

Administration. Very Reverend Richard Reid, President and Dean; Dr. Allan M. Parrent, Associate Dean for Academic Affairs; Reverend Richard A. Busch, Director, Center for Continuing Education.

General Description. The Protestant Episcopal Theological Seminary in Virginia (commonly called "Virginia Theological Seminary") is a seminary of the Episcopal Church, located in northern Virginia near Washington, D.C. It was founded in 1823, provides graduate theological education, and serves as a theological resource for the church. It understands its primary mission to be the preparation of men and women for the ordained ministry, particularly for service in the parish ministry. It also provides continuing education for clergy of all denominations and theological education for laity. The Seminary is a member of the Washington Theological Consortium.

Community Environment. The campus expresses something of the traditional spirit of the seminary in the arrangement of its buildings: the chapel and 14 other buildings, including the library, form a widely-spaced quadrangle in the center of the campus. Circling these buildings in a wide arc are a dozen or more faculty homes, easily accessible to all students. The City of Alexandria, Virginia, in the Washington, D.C. metropolitan area, is a city in its own right, and was founded in 1749. The city was named for John Alexander; during the Revolutionary period it was one of the principal colonial ports as well as a trade, social, and political center. The Old Town area provides a very pleasant stroll into another century where the shady streets, some of which are cobblestoned, are closely flanked by 18th century houses. Fine shops are in the area.

Religious Denomination. Episcopal.

Accreditation. Association of Theological Schools in the United States and Canada.

Term System. Semester; no summer term.

Enrollment in Degree Programs in Religion 1984–85. Total 212; men 150, women 62.

Degrees in Religion Awarded 1984–85. Master of Theological Studies 13; men 11, women 2. Master of Divinity 54; men 39, women 15. Doctor of Ministry 5; men 5.

Faculty for Degree Programs in Religion. Total 32; full-time 17, part-time 15.

Admission Requirements. For admission to the M.Div. and M.T.S. degree programs, one must be a graduate of an accredited college or university. In addition one must have satisfactory scores on the Graduate Record Examination and show evidence of a satisfactory physical and psychological examination. Those who are seeking Holy Orders must also present credentials concerning their character and fitness for ordained ministry. To be admitted to the D.Min. program, one must have an M.Div. degree or equivalent and at least five years' experience in ordained ministry.

Tuition and Fees. Tuition $3,600 (Ecclesiastical endorsement is also required); room $860; board $1,700.

Financial Aid. Financial aid is available and is given strictly on the basis of need. Housing subsidies are available for married students living off campus.

Housing. Dormitory housing is available on campus. Subsidized housing for married students is provided by the Seminary at rates ranging from $110 to $185 per month.

Library Facilities. The Bishop Payne Library contains 109,375 volumes. The library also receives 560 periodicals. Through its participation in the Washington Theological Consortium, the extensive collections of the member libraries, numbering more than 900,000 volumes, are available for direct borrowing by students and faculty.

Religious Services/Activities. Worship is in accordance with the *Book of Common Prayer* of the Episcopal Church. Morning chapel is held daily and the participation of the whole academic community is a normal expectation. A daily service of Evening Prayer is also available. In addition, special worship services are offered on occasion in which the participation of the broader seminary community is encouraged.

Degree Programs

The Master of Divinity program is designed primarily to prepare men and women for the ordained ministry of the Episcopal Church. It is a 3-year course of study requiring completion of 93-1/2 hours of course work, plus 6 credit hours (11-12 weeks in the field) of Clinical Pastoral Education, usually taken during the first summer.

The Master of Theological Studies program is a 2-year course of study requiring 60 hours of course work. Candidates for the degree are required to select a field of concentration in either Bible, Theology, Church History, or Pastoral Theology.

The Doctor of Ministry program requires completion of a basic 6-week term in the Continuing Education program, 2 summer residential workshops of 4 weeks each, 4 action-reflection examinations and a thesis project. The focus of the program is the practice of the ordained ministry. The immediate purpose is to instill greater theological, spiritual, and behavioral understanding of particular situations in the candidates' ministry, supported by biblical and historical perspectives.

Special Programs

The Seminary conducts a Lay School of Theology on two evenings per week, offering basic non-degree-credit courses in the various theological disciplines. The Center for Continuing Education offers several 6-week terms per year, primarily for clergy, plus a variety of other short term courses. The Center for the Ministry of Teaching provides resources, consultations, and various training programs to meet the needs of the seminary, parish lead-

ers, and others involved in Christian education at the parish level.

Randolph-Macon College
Religious Studies Department
Ashland, VA 23005   (804) 798-8372

Administration. Dr. Ladell Payne, President; Dr. Jerome H. Garris, Dean of the College; Dr. Betty Jean Seymour, Chairperson, Religious Studies Department.

General Description. Courses offered by the Department of Religious Studies focus on three major areas: biblical studies, the world's religious traditions, and religion and culture. Religion is explored in its various manifestations, with particular emphasis given to the interaction of religion with human cultures, the place of religion in world history and literature, and the relation of religion to contemporary human problems.

Parent Institution. Randolph-Macon is an undergraduate, coeducational college of the liberal arts. The purpose of a Randolph-Macon education is to develop the mind and character of the student and to convey a sense of life defined by historical continuity and ethical responsibility. Founded by Methodists in 1830, Randolph-Macon is an independent college that maintains a relationship with the United Methodist Church. Through this living tie the College draws strength from a religious tradition that nurtures creative social change and personal accountability.

Community Environment. The Randolph-Macon campus is located in Ashland, Virginia, a community of 6,000 just 15 miles north of Richmond and 90 miles south of Washington, D.C. The College is within a day's drive of one-third of the population of the United States. The 100-acre campus, amid a fine grove of oaks and maples, has a total of 40 buildings and major facilities. Richmond, the capital of Virginia, is located on the James River. The city is an important industrial and commercial center. As one of the greatest tobacco markets in the world, it has various tobacco factories near by. Richmond has many historical shrines and a great many points of interest.

Religious Denomination. United Methodist.

Religious Emphasis. Liberal.

Accreditation. Southern Association of Colleges and Schools.

Term System. Semester.

Enrollment in Degree Programs in Religion 1984–85. Total 12; men 6, women 6.

Faculty for Degree Programs in Religion. Total 4; full-time 2, part-time 2.

Admission Requirements. The Committee on Admissions stresses the following factors when considering an application: secondary school record; standardized tests (SAT or ACT); recommendation of counselor, principal, or headmaster; personal characteristics.

Tuition and Fees. The College has a system of comprehensive fees which applies to all categories of students:

resident students $9,540; students residing in fraternity houses $8,240; those students who live in the new dormitories $9,790; day students (those students who do not live or board on-campus) $6,540. All fees per year. Other special fees where applicable.

Financial Aid. The College administers a diversified program of scholarships, grants, loans, student employment, and other forms of aid for students who need assistance in meeting their educational expenses. The College awards honor scholarships on the basis of merit and academic and leadership potential. Most financial aid, however, is awarded on the basis of demonstrated need.

Housing. All students are expected to live on campus in college housing except married students and those who commute from their parents' homes.

Library Facilities. The Walter Hines Page Library contains 122,000 volumes. Special collections include the Richard Beale Davis Collection in early American literature and history, the Dodd Collection in American history, and the Virginia Methodist Historical Collection. A fourth collection is devoted to the European eighteenth century including, in particular, the works of Giacomo Casanova and Ange and Sara Goudar, the most extensive of any in the world. Another collection is devoted to Henry Miller.

Religious Services/Activities. The following activities are important aspects of Randolph-Macon's effort to promote spiritual life and social awareness: regular worship services, ministry to students of various faiths, spiritual retreats and discussion groups, and volunteer service in many local projects. Students are also encouraged to become involved in efforts to deal with problems of hunger, war, and racism.

Degree Programs

The Bachelor of Arts with a major in Religious Studies requires the completion of the 112 semester hours with a minimum of 34 courses of three semester hours or more credit. The major program consists of 30 semester hours of work in Religious Studies and in related subjects. At least 21 hours must be taken in the Department, and at least six hours must be taken in each of three areas of emphasis.

Sweet Briar College
Department of Religion
Sweet Briar, VA 24595   (804) 381-6289

Administration. Dr. Nenah Elinor Fry, President; Dr. A. Robin Bowers, Dean of the College; Dr. Gregory T. Armstrong, Chairman, Department of Religion.

General Description. Sweet Briar College is a private, independent, four-year liberal arts college for women. Founded in 1901, the College offers 31 departmental majors plus various interdepartmental majors and programs. The enrollment is 675 students in residence and about 45

in off-campus study programs including England, Scotland, France, and Spain.

Community Environment. Located on an extraodinarily beautiful campus, Sweet Briar College is situated on 3,300 acres of rolling meadows and woodlands in central Virginia. The College is 12 miles north of Lynchburg, Virginia, and within easy reach of Charlottesville, Richmond, and Washington, D.C. The location, with its mountain vistas and its sense of space and spaciousness, contribute to an atmosphere of freedom, both intellectual and physical.

Religious Denomination. None.

Accreditation. Southern Association of Colleges and Schools.

Term System. Four-one-four; no summer term.

Enrollment in Degree Programs in Religion 1984–85. Total 4; women 4.

Degrees in Religion Awarded 1984–85. Bachelor of Arts 1; women 1.

Faculty for Degree Programs in Religion. Total 2; full-time 2.

Admission Requirements. High school diploma: at least 16 academic units in English, foreign languages, mathematics, science, social studies; SAT or ACT test scores; secondary school recommendations; advanced standing students also admitted from other colleges.

Tuition and Fees. Comprehensive fee for tuition, room, and board $11,300 per year; tuition alone $8,400; separate student activities fee $80.

Financial Aid. Need-based and merit awards are available as well as loans and campus jobs. The current average award is $6,000.

Housing. Dormitories available; no college-owned off-campus or married student housing.

Library Facilities. The Mary Helen Cochran Library collection includes more than 186,000 volumes with additional holdings in microprint and microfilm and a current periodical list of over 800 titles. Special collections are shelved in the Fergus Reid Rare Book Room, the Fanny B. Fletcher Archives Room, and the Kellogg Education Laboratory Library.

Religious Services/Activities. The ecumenical College chapel holds services six days per week during the academic year. Various other activities and community service projects are offered.

Degree Programs

A Bachelor of Arts candidate who elects Religion as her major subject must complete at least ten units in the department including Old Testament, New Testament, Introduction to Religion, Religions of Asia, and Senior Seminary.

Special Programs

The College offers various programs for off-campus study in the United States and overseas, including internships; certificate programs in management, public administration, and European Civilization; Turning Point Program for women 26 years of age or older who have had their formal education interrupted.

Union Theological Seminary in Virginia
3401 Brook Road
Richmond, VA 23227   (804) 355-0671

Administration. Dr. T. Hartley Hall, IV, President; Dr. William V. Arnold, Dean of the Faculty.

General Description. The history of Union Theological Seminary goes back to 1806 when the Presbytery of Hanover "taking into consideration the deplorable state of our country as to religious instruction, the very small numbers of ministers possessing the qualifications required by Scripture, and the prevalence of ignorance and error" established a religious library and a fund for educating youth for the ministry of the Gospel. Regarding its present mission as education for ministry, the Seminary offers a basic program, graduate studies, and a Doctor of Ministry degree. In addition, continuing education is provided to encourage and enable seminary graduates and others to study systematically as they engage in various forms of ministry.

Community Environment. Union Theological Seminary occupies a spacious site in Ginter Park, a residential suburb a few miles north of the city of Richmond, Virginia. On the 12-acre main quadrangle are situated academic buildings, the student center, dormitories, a continuing education center, faculty homes, the library, and a multipurpose building. On the Westwood tract, a 38-acre plot diagonally across Brook Road from the main campus, are located athletic fields for year-round sports and additional faculty homes. The Seminary has been located in Richmond since 1898. As the capital of Virginia, it is a city rich in historical tradition and is a growing, well-balanced metropolis which serves as a distribution center for a large area.

Religious Denomination. Presbyterian Church (U.S.A.).

Accreditation. Southern Association of Colleges and Schools; Association of Theological Schools in the United States and Canada.

Term System. Mini-terms: September Term, Fall Term, January Term, Spring Term, May Term, Summer Term.

Enrollment in Degree Programs in Religion 1984–85. Total 273; men 204, women 69.

Degrees in Religion Awarded 1984–85. Master of Divinity 13; men 10, women 3. Master of Theology 5; men 5. Doctor of Ministry 39; men 33, women 6. Doctor of Philosophy 6; men 6.

Faculty for Degree Programs in Religion. Total 23; full-time 19, part-time 4.

Admission Requirements. Bachelor's degree from a college or university accredited by one of the nationally recognized regional accrediting agencies; completed application packet with an on-campus interview by a member of the Admissions Committee; Graduate Record Examinations Aptitude Test is a requirement for applicants whose undergraduate grade point average is less than 3.0 on a 4.0 scale (the GRE is recommended for all other applicants).

Tuition and Fees. $455 per course or maximum tuition charge of $3,640 (excluding Greek School which carries an additional $455 charge). Master of Theology and Doctor of Philosophy tuition is $4,500 per academic year; other fees $5; dormitory rates range from $82 to $129 per month depending on accommodations; apartment rates range from $213 to $416 per month depending on size, furnishings, and location.

Financial Aid. Grants are based on unmet need, i.e., total expenses less total resources as computed on the financial aid application and approved by the Financial Aid Office.

Housing. Campus housing is available for all students; dormitories for single students, apartments for married students.

Library Facilities. The Seminary Library book collection numbers more than 238,000 volumes and grows at the rate of some 5,500 volumes per year. More than 1,200 periodicals and scholarly journals are regularly received. The Library is a major research library, with particular strengths in Presbyterian history and theology and Biblical studies. Within the Library there is a Reigner Recording Library, a free circulating library of recordings which includes more than 24,000 reels and cassettes of magnetic tape of sermons, worship services, theological lectures, and religious radio programs by leading church persons throughout the world. The Reigner Library serves as the official repository and circulating agent of the radio programs of the Broadcasting and Film Commission of the National Council of Churches.

Religious Services/Activities. All students, staff, and faculty have the opportunity to worship together on four weekday mornings. These services are led by students and faculty as well as occasional outside guests. Special worship services are planned to highlight the Christian year and the academic year. On three Sundays of September, the community gathers for worship followed by faculty open houses. Thanksgiving, Advent, and Holy Week are also marked by special services.

Degree Programs

The basic degree program of the Seminary is the Master of Divinity degree. This program contains a variety of learning experiences to enable graduates to undertake the work of ministry. The requirements for the degree include: three years or levels; two Biblical languages; 28 credits, of which 14 are required in: Hebrew, Old Testament, New Testament, Theology, Ethics, Church History, Pastoral, and Evaluative Review.

A program of studies leading to the degree of Master of Theology is offered by the Departments of Bible, Theology, and Church History, and by the faculty in the field of

Pastoral Counseling. The programs of the first three departments are planned so that they can be completed in once academic year. The program consists of graduate seminars and supervised research.

The program of studies leading to the degree of Doctor of Philosophy is designed to give the candidate a mastery of specialization and to equip him/her for resourceful and creative scholarship. Studies leading to this degree may be pursued in the Biblical, Historical, and Theology Departments.

The Doctor of Ministry degree is a program for ordained ministers who have completed a basic theological degree and are presently involved in the practice of ministry. It provides a structured, supervised, and evaluated program of study which builds upon prior theological education and sustained experience in the practice of ministry. A candidate for the degree must spend at least two academic years in the program before the degree is awarded; the maximum amount of time permitted for completing the degree is four years.

Special Programs

Under the sponsorship of The National Association of Church Business Administrators, the Office of Continuing Education and Doctor of Ministry Studies offers a certification program for church professionals. This certification is accomplished through two ten-day seminars and a project over a period of two summers.

The Seminary also offers a wide range of Continuing Education programs for both lay and ordained ministry.

Virginia Union University
School of Theology
1601 West Leigh Street
Richmond, VA 23220   (804) 257-5715

Administration. Dr. S. Dallas Simmons, President; Dr. Henry H. Mitchell, Dean, School of Theology.

General Description. The School of Theology of Virginia Union University is a graduate professional school for ministry, with single focus on the Master of Divinity degree and historic competence in preparation for ministry in the Black culture community. The School is open to all and its student body is cross-representative of not only ethnic groups but denominational affiliations. Its graduates serve in key places in the national bodies of Baptists and in the great churches of the nation, but they are also outstanding in chaplaincies and a vast variety of other ministries. Two of the three largest Black Baptist denominational bodies in America today have both Presidents and General Secretaries who are graduates of Virginia Union University.

Parent Institution. The Virginia Union University is the result of the merger of a number of institutions founded for Blacks after the Civil War. They were in Richmond and, in one case, Washington, D.C., and later, Harper's

Ferry where Storer College was founded. Their commitment was to the training of newly-freed Blacks for the leadership of their communities and churches. The University was and still is a church-related (Baptist) liberal arts college with a graduate school/seminary.

Community Environment. The 55-acre campus of the University has a combination of older buildings of Virginia granite and more recent ones of brick and Belgian tile. It is in Richmond, the capital of Virginia, on the James River, and 100 miles south of Washington, D.C. Richmond is an important industrial and commercial city.

Religious Denomination. Baptist; receives support from 6 Baptist bodies nationally.

Religious Emphasis. With firm commitment to Black culture, the University is heavily Bible centered and at the same time creatively activist on social issues.

Accreditation. Southern Association of Colleges and Schools; Association of Theological Schools in the United States and Canada.

Term System. Five-term system: September, Fall, January, Spring, May; summer term.

Enrollment in Degree Programs in Religion 1984–85. Total 142; men 118, women 24.

Degrees in Religion Awarded 1984–85. Master of Divinity 32; men 26, women 6.

Faculty for Degree Programs in Religion. Total 13; full-time 7, part-time 6.

Admission Requirements. Bachelor's degree from an accredited college or university; references from a variety of sources.

Tuition and Fees. Tuition $1,575.

Financial Aid. Limited scholarship, aid, work study, and a variety of loans.

Housing. Some dormitory space is available, plus limited access to space in other schools of the Richmond Theological Center. Many students reside off-campus in apartments ($300 per month and up).

Library Facilities. The library of the Union Theological Seminary in Virginia is utilized on a contact basis.

Religious Services/Activities. Services are not denominationally specific, but tend to fuse Afro-American and Western cultures. Chapel is held twice weekly and there is an annual spiritual retreat at the beginning of each year.

Degree Programs

The Master of Divinity is the single program of the University.

Special Programs

The University sponsors the annual Ellison Convocation which offers lectures and enrichment to alumni and others. The Evans-Smith Institute of Leadership Education is also sponsored jointly with the state Baptist convention. Certificates in all phases of church ministry are awarded.

WASHINGTON

Central Washington University
Religious Studies Program
Ellensburg, WA 98926 (509) 963-1818

Administration. Dr. Donald L. Garrity, President; Dr. Burton J. Williams, Dean of the College of Letters, Arts, and Sciences; Dr. Jay E. Bachrach, Director, Religious Studies Program.

General Description. The Religious Studies Program of Central Washington University offers a special major in the Philosophy Program so that the student may graduate with a Bachelor of Arts in Philosophy with a concentration in Religious Studies. The Program inquires into the nature of religion, its pervasive role in human life, and its contribution to understanding human existence and destiny.

Parent Institution. Central Washington University is one of six state-supported institutions offering baccalaureate and graduate degrees.

Community Environment. The 350-acre campus is 106 miles east of Seattle in a quiet setting at the foot of the Cascade Mountains. Ellensburg is a small city in a semi-urban section of central Washington State. The community has several churches.

Religious Denomination. None.

Accreditation. Northwest Association of Schools and Colleges.

Term System. Quarter.

Enrollment in Degree Programs in Religion 1984–85. Total 8; men 5, women 3.

Faculty for Degree Programs in Religion. Total 1; full-time 1.

Admission Requirements. High school graduation; Washington Pre-College Test; SAT or ACT.

Tuition and Fees. Tuition for state of Washington residents $25.50 per quarter; general and activity fees $288.50.

Financial Aid. The University will make every effort to provide financial assistance to eligible applicants commensurate with indicated need. Sources may take the form of a loan, work, scholarship, and/or grant, singly or in combination thereof.

Housing. Campus housing is available.

Library Facilities. The library houses over 400,000 books.

Religious Services/Activities. Religious activities and clubs are open to all students through interdenominational groups not directly a part of the University.

Degree Programs

The Religious Studies program leading to the Bachelor of Arts degree is an interdisciplinary program. It offers knowledge of the literature, history, and practice of religious traditions, the variety of religious world views, and the modes of religious thought and language. The major requires the completion of 31-35 credits. A minimum of 180 quarter credits is required for graduation.

Gonzaga University
Department of Religious Studies
East 503 Sharp
Spokane, WA 99258 (509) 328-4220

Administration. Dr. Bernard J. Coughlin, S.J., President; Dr. Peter B. Ely, S.J., Academic Vice President; Dr. John E. Byrne, Dean of the Graduate School; Dr. Charles D. Skok, Chairman, Department of Religious Studies.

General Description. The Department of Religious Studies has as its aim to help students develop an informed, reflective, critical, and articulate consciousness of their own developing faith in relation to the development of the modern world. This aim is pursued through the study of scripture and Christian tradition, and their application to major areas of contemporary life. The Department offers courses in the areas of scripture, historical and systematic theology, Christian moral theology, and spirituality. It helps to satisfy the University's core requirement for all undergraduate students of three religious studies courses (9 credits). The degree Bachelor of Arts in Religious Studies is offered; a minor in Religious Studies is available. The Department also offers a 15-credit Certificate of Ministry Program.

The Department of Religious Studies offers 3 programs

at the Master's level to meet the needs of persons seeking greater understanding and practical knowledge of Biblical and Christian studies, prayer, and spiritual direction. These programs are designed as terminal degrees and are characterized by the flexibility needed to meet the personal and professional needs and interests of each student. The degrees granted are Master of Arts in Religious Studies, Master of Arts in Spirituality, and Master of Divinity.

St. Michael's Institute, which is both a Pontifical Faculty of Philosophy owned and operated by the Society of Jesus and a School of Philosophy and Letters of Gonzaga University, provides the religious and academic formation of Jesuit scholastics who are candidates for the priesthood. The School has two divisions: a novitiate or preparatory division and a collegiate division. The primary purpose of the Institute is to give Jesuit students the basic liberal and philosophical education which will prepare them for their future apostolic and educational work.

Parent Institution. Gonzaga University is an independent Roman Catholic and Jesuit university governed by a Board of Trustees composed of Jesuits and laity. The University receives no regular support from the Roman Catholic Church, but depends on tuition revenues, outright gifts, the income from a modest endowment fund, and the contributed services of some 50 Jesuits among the faculty and administration for its operational needs. The University is composed of the College of Arts and Sciences and the Schools of Business Administration, Education, Engineering, Continuing Education, and Law, as well as a Graduate School and St. Michael's Institute.

Community Environment. The Gonzaga campus of 60 landscaped acres is situated along the Spokane River in Spokane, Washington. Students are within walking distance of the city center with easy access to department stores, shops, and restaurants. The campus lies some 14 blocks from the Spokane Opera House, the Memorial Coliseum, and Riverfront Park, the site of Expo '74. Spokane forms the hub of the Pacific Northwest's "Inland Empire." A four-state region relies on this area's business, service, and transportation facilities. With a population of 325,000 in the metropolitan area, the city of Spokane offers ample opportunities for work and relaxation for the students.

Religious Denomination. Roman Catholic.

Religious Emphasis. Traditional/Progressive.

Accreditation. Northwest Association of Schools and Colleges.

Term System. Semester; summer term.

Degrees in Religion Awarded 1984–85. Bachelor of Arts in Religious Studies 10; men 3, women 7. Master of Arts in Religious Studies 16; men 4, women 12. Master of Arts in Spirituality 5; men 2, women 3. Master of Divinity 1; men 1.

Faculty for Degree Programs in Religion. Total 23; full-time 19, part-time 4.

Admission Requirements. Decisions on admission to any undergraduate school or college of the University are made after a careful review of an applicant's academic achievement, scholastic aptitude, and personal characteristics which may predict success in the University. High school or college grades, course content, class rank, test scores, and recommendations from teachers, counselors, and principals play an important part in the whole admission procedure. All applicants are reviewed according to these criteria without regard to age, color, creed, marital status, national or ethnic origin, physical handicap, race, religion, or sex.

Tuition and Fees. Undergraduate tuition $3,080 per semester, part-time $190 per credit hour; graduate and post-graduate full- and part-time $180 per credit hour; room and board $1,370 to $1,780 depending on accommodations and meal plan.

Financial Aid. The University strives to provide as much financial aid as possible on an equitable basis.

Housing. The University operates eleven residence halls of various sizes. All full-time, single undergraduate students must reside and dine on campus unless living with immediate family, until age 21 (or will be during the academic year).

Library Facilities. The Crosby Library, the gift of Mr. Harry L. (Bing) Crosby, houses a collection of over 350,000 books, periodicals, and microform materials. It also contains a special collection of about 5,000 rare books.

Religious Services/Activities. Roman Catholic Eucharistic Liturgies are celebrated daily in the University Chapel and at various times in Jesuit House Chapel and in the residence halls. Attendance is optional. A variety of retreats including "Searches" and scriptural retreats are offered during the year.

Degree Programs

The Bachelor of Arts degree with a major in Religious Studies requires 128 credit hours of which 33 credit are in the major (12 credits from the required major core and 21 credits from the upper division courses).

The Master of Arts in Religious Studies degree provides graduate theological background for teaching, consulting, research, and development of theological resources for ministry in parishes, schools, adult education programs, and other services to the Church. A core of 4 theology courses is required: Biblical—Method in Scripture and Theology; Systematic—Modern Christian Thought; Applied—Theological Ethics; and Synthetic (integrating the program)— Religious Experience, Culture, and Theology. Eighteen additional hours are required, determined by the area of concentration: Biblical, systematic, or applied theology.

The Master of Arts in Spirituality degree is especially designed to prepare people for the many developing areas of spiritual ministry. In-depth study of spirituality within the Church for all walks of life (essential courses) is combined with study of various specialized areas for specific ministries (elective courses). A total of 30 hours of religious studies is required.

The Master of Divinity is a graduate professional program designed for students preparing for various areas of ministry in the Church today. It is a program which integrates theological instruction and effective pastoral practice. Courses are offered in scripture; doctrine; moral, pastoral, and spiritual theology; canon law; history; and philosophy (for those who need it for ordination). There is also a strong practical component in field work experience. The program will normally require three to four years and requires 18 credits of Philosophy (if necessary for ordination) and 115 credits in Theology with a specified distribution.

Special Programs

The University offers a special program of theological updating and renewal through the CREDO Program. It is open to laity, religious, and priests. FOCUS is a certificate program that prepares men and women for spiritual leadership in the Contemporary Church. Classes, seminars, and workshops blend Theology, Scripture, Human Development, Psychology of Leadership, Spiritual Direction, and Social Justice. The CHRISTUS Program at the University is designed for those interested in Biblical and Christian studies, spiritual growth, personal enrichment, and Christian service. A Diploma is awarded upon completing the ten-course program.

The Mater Dei Institute provides a program of priestly formation for men over 30 who have completed a Bachelor's degree.

Northwest College
Undergraduate School of Theology
11102 North East 53rd Street
Kirkland, WA 98033   (206) 822-8266

Administration. Dr. D. V. Hurst, President; Dr. Frank B. Rice, Academic Dean.

General Description. The Undergraduate School of Theology for the Assemblies of God is sponsored by the Assemblies of God denomination. The purpose of the School is to prepare professionals and church workers for the work of the sponsoring church and for other denominations of similar character.

Parent Institution. Northwest College is a coeducational Christian institution of higher learning operated under the control of the Alaska, the Montana, the Northwest, the Southern Idaho, and the Wyoming District Councils of the Assembly of God. The College offers educational opportunities for students who desire a general education, training for full-time Christian service, or basic preparation for other fields.

Community Environment. The campus of Northwest College has continually expanded, and is now on a 55-acre location in Kirkland, in the greater metropolitan area of Seattle. It is 10 miles from downtown Seattle.

Religious Denomination. Assemblies of God.

Religious Emphasis. Fundamentalist - Pentecostal.

Accreditation. Northwest Association of School and Colleges; American Association of Bible Colleges.

Term System. Quarter; Summer term.

Enrollment in Degree Programs in Religion 1984–85. Total 671; men 367, women 304.

Degrees in Religion Awarded 1984–85. Bachelor of Theology 3; men 2, women 1. Bachelor of Arts 88; men 67, women 21. Associate of Arts 49; men 17, women 32.

Faculty for Degree Programs in Religion. Total 42; full-time 23, part-time 19.

Admission Requirements. High school graduation; character references; religious commitment.

Tuition and Fees. $4,003 per year; room and board $1,941.

Financial Aid. Scholarships, federal grants and loans, and grants in aid are types of assistance available.

Housing. Housing is available for both single and married students.

Library Facilities. The library's holdings exceed 60,000 volumes.

Religious Services/Activities. Chapel is held daily and attendance is required. There is a Spiritual Emphasis Week and student retreats are held.

Degree Programs

The Bachelor of Arts degree is offered with majors in Biblical Literature, Christian Education, Missions, Pastoral Ministries, Religion and Philosophy, Sacred Music, and Youth Ministries. The degree requires the completion of 183 quarter credits with 36 included in the major. The Bachelor of Theology degree is a five-year program built on a major in Biblical Literature with special concentrations in Theology, Biblical Languages, interpretive skills, and in the History of the Christian Church. The degree requires 228 quarter credits.

Special Programs

The Diploma Program in Bible is a three-year non-degree program with concentration in Biblical subjects.

Pacific Lutheran University
Department of Religion
Park Avenue and 121st Street
Tacoma, WA 98447   (206) 531-6900

Administration. Dr. William O. Rieke, President; Dr. Paul O. Ingram, Chair, Department of Religion.

General Description. The Department of Religion offers the serious academic study of the Bible, of the Christian tradition, of attempts to understand God's continuing activity, and of God's promises for the future. A broad range of courses and opportunities are available. The Department also participates in a program of continuing theological education for clergy and laity in the Pacific Northwest through the Lutheran Institute for Theological Education

(LITE). The major in Religion leads to the Bachelor of Arts degree.

Parent Institution. Pacific Lutheran University was founded in 1890 by men and women of the Lutheran Church in the Northwest. It is a private, four-year, coeducational university and grants the baccalaureate and Master's degrees.

Community Environment. The 126-acre campus is located in Parkland, a suburb of Tacoma and seven miles south of the city.

Religious Denomination. The American Lutheran Church.

Accreditation. Northwest Association of Schools and Colleges.

Term System. Semester (4-1-4 plan).

Faculty for Degree Programs in Religion. Total 10.

Admission Requirements. Graduation from an accredited high school; rank in upper half of graduating class; 16 academic units; SAT or ACT.

Tuition and Fees. Tuition $2,775 per semester; room and board $1,410.

Financial Aid. The quantity and composition of awards are based upon demonstrated financial need, academic achievement, test scores, and other personal talents and interests.

Housing. Housing accommodations are available on campus for 750 men, 950 women, and 30 families.

Library Facilities. The Robert A.L. Mortvedt Library houses over 265,000 volumes. The library has a special collection devoted to the Scandinavian Immigrant Experience and contains the University and regional Lutheran Church archives.

Religious Services/Activities. Chapel worship is held Monday, Wednesday, and Friday mornings during each semester. The University Congregation meets in regular worship and celebrates the Lord's Supper each Sunday. Pastoral services of the University pastors are available to all students. Several denominations and religious groups have organizations on campus and there are numerous student-initiated Bible study and fellowship groups. The Campus Ministry Council coordinates these activities.

Degree Programs

The major in Religion leading to the Bachelor of Arts degree requires 28 semester hours, with 12 hours concentrated in one of five areas (Biblical Studies; History of Christianity; History of Religions; Theology and Ethics; and Religion, Culture, Society, and the Individual), and 16 hours distributed so that at least 4 hours are taken in each of two other areas.

Puget Sound Christian College
410 Fourth Avenue North
Edmonds, WA 98020   (206) 775-8686

Administration. Dr. Glen R. Basey, President; Delores Scarbrough, Registrar.

General Description. Puget Sound Christian College is a four-year Bible college founded in 1950 as the Puget Sound College of the Bible. The current name was adopted in 1984. The philosophy of education of the College presupposes both the centrality and authority of the Scriptures in the church; a commitment to the proposition that ability to function effectively in Christian leadership involves the full development of an explicit Christian view of the world; and a conviction that student development must occur in the areas of spiritual growth and personal responsibility and that the student must be equipped with the fundamental knowledge, discipline, and skills appropriate to his/her chosen ministry.

Community Environment. The College campus features three separate buildings, originally designed as a public high school. Edmonds, Washington is a suburban community of 28,000 located fifteen miles north of Seattle.

Religious Denomination. Independent Christian Church and Church of Christ.

Religious Emphasis. Conservative.

Accreditation. American Association of Bible Colleges.

Term System. Quarter.

Enrollment in Degree Programs in Religion 1984–85. Total 137; men 78, women 59.

Degrees in Religion Awarded 1984–85. Bachelor of Arts 15; men 5, women 10. Bible Certificate 11; men 6, women 5.

Faculty for Degree Programs in Religion. Total 14; full-time 8, part-time 6.

Admission Requirements. High school transcript or GED; college transcripts for transfer students; three references.

Tuition and Fees. Tuition $840 per term; room and board $752 per term.

Financial Aid. Pell Grants, guaranteed student loans, SEOG, and a limited number of scholarships constitute the variety of financial aid available.

Housing. On campus housing for single men and women; limited number of apartments for married students.

Library Facilities. The Charles H. Phillips Memorial Library contains 27,000 select volumes and receives more than 200 religious journals and secular periodicals.

Religious Services/Activities. Chapel attendance is mandatory. It is the desire of the faculty and administration that each student should find a regular place of worship and service in the local community or immediate area. One of the major special events of the College is Gospel Festival, the largest meeting of the year. It features some of the outstanding speakers and church leaders of the Pacific Northwest and of the nation. The Ambassadors is a group composed of students and faculty who are vitally interested in church growth and mission outreach. They help to sponsor an annual World Outreach Week and solicit student commitments to assist student interns and recruits in visiting a foreign mission field.

Degree Programs

The Bachelor of Arts program involves every degree-seeking student. The student must complete the core requirements which furnish the student with a Bible major. The student also becomes involved in one of the following second major options: Preaching, World Mission, Biblical Research, Christian Education, Christian Education/Youth Ministry, Christian Education/Preschool Ministry, Christian Education/Music, Christian Education/Social Science, Youth Ministry/Music, Youth Ministry/Social Science.

Special Programs

The Bible Certificate program is designed for the student who has completed a degree in another field or the student desiring Bible training prior to enrolling in a secular institution. The year of intensive study is best utilized by those whose occupational commitment is toward a position other than church leadership ministry.

A Missionary Aviation option is offered which includes the completion of the Bachelor of Arts in World Mission at Puget Sound Christian College and the Associate of Arts in Aircraft Technology from Everett Community College. Puget Sound Christian College teaches ground school; flight lessons are given at Paine Field in Everett, Washington.

Puget Sound, University of
Department of Religion
1500 North Warner
Tacoma, WA 98416   (206) 756-3288

Administration. Dr. Philip M. Phibbs, President; Dr. Thomas A. Davis, Dean of the University; Dr. John W. Phillips, Chair, Department of Religion.

General Description. The Department of Religion of the University of Puget Sound is devoted to the full and fair study of the religions of humankind, holding that these lie at the foundations of culture and history. As well as the major and minor in Religion, the Department offers service to the entire University, providing courses in the core curriculum and instruction useful to allied departments and schools. The Bachelor of Arts is offered.

Parent Institution. The University of Puget Sound is a private, coeducational university related to the United Methodist Church. It welcomes students, faculty, and staff of all religious faiths. It enrolls 2,800 undergraduate students.

Community Environment. The University occupies 37 Tudor structures conveniently spaced over the campus of 72 acres, a short distance from the shores of Puget Sound

and the Pacific Ocean, as well as the slopes of the Cascade and Olympic Mountains.

Religious Denomination. Partial support to the University is by The United Methodist Church, but the University itself does not reflect any denominational preference.

Religious Emphasis. Liberal.

Accreditation. Northwest Association of Schools and Colleges.

Term System. Semester; summer term.

Enrollment in Degree Programs in Religion 1984–85. Total 12; men 3, women 9.

Degrees in Religion Awarded 1984–85. Bachelor of Arts 6; men 1, women 5.

Faculty for Degree Programs in Religion. Total 6; full-time 4, part-time 2.

Admission Requirements. Graduation from an accredited high school.

Tuition and Fees. Full tuition $6,860; application fee $20; student government fee $100.

Financial Aid. There are special Religious Leadership Awards available. All of the other usual sources of assistance such as federal and state grants and loans, college work-study, and scholarships are also available.

Housing. Dormitories and off-campus university-owned housing are available, plus fraternity and sorority housing.

Library Facilities. The Collins Memorial Library contains over 310,000 volumes. It houses an extensive Music Library of scores and recorded music.

Religious Services/Activities. The University has a Religious Life Office and a full-time United Methodist Chaplain. These offices sponsor many religious activities for students of all faiths.

Degree Programs

The major in Religion leading to the Bachelor of Arts degree is offered by the Department of Religion. The faculty provides an introduction to the discipline followed by careful probing of two or more important religious traditions and exposure to major methods used in the study of religion. The major requires the completion of an introductory course, five intermediate courses to include at least one course in Asian religion, two advanced courses, and a seminar. The degree requires the completion of 32 units of which a minimum of 8 units are in the major.

St. Michael's Institute
Gonzaga University
East 502 Boone Avenue
Spokane, WA 99258   (509) 328-4220

Administration. John E. Costello, S.J., Dean.

General Description. St. Michael's Institute, which is both a Pontifical Faculty of Philosophy owned and operated by the Society of Jesus and a School of Philosophy and Letters of Gonzaga University, provides the religious and academic formation of Jesuit scholastics who are candidates for the priesthood. The School has two divisions, a novitiate or preparatory division and a collegiate division. The faculty at the Institute are also engaged in teaching in the College of Arts and Sciences or in the Graduate School of Gonzaga University.

Parent Institution. See: Gonzaga University.

Religious Denomination. Roman Catholic.

Religious Emphasis. Jesuit.

Degree Programs

The primary purpose of the Institute is to give Jesuit students the basic liberal and philosophical education which will prepare them for their future apostolic and educational work. After the Novitiate, the Jesuit students move into a full-time study program at the Institute and Gonzaga University. While continuing their religious training, they devote most of their time to a four-year program leading to the Bachelor of Arts or Bachelor of Science degree. Besides meeting the degree requirements of the College of Arts and Sciences at Gonzaga, the students must pass a one-hour comprehensive oral examination in philosophy before a board of three examiners. Those meeting the requirements set down in the official ecclesiastical documents may, after one or two years devoted mostly to philosophy, receive the canonical degree of Licentiate in Philosophy and a Master of Arts in Philosophy.

Seattle Pacific University
School of Religion

3307 West 3rd Avenue

Seattle, WA 98119   (206) 281-2158

Administration. Dr. David C. Le Shana, President; Dr. Curtis A, Martin, Executive Vice President; Dr. David O. Dickerson, Vice President for Academic Affairs and Dean of the Faculty; Dr. R. Larry Shelton, Dean, School of Religion.

General Description. The School of Religion upholds the University's commitment to a fully-integrated world view which looks at life as intimately related to all of God's creation. The School believes that Biblical truth is the integrating core of life and learning, and is best expressed in the philosophy of "unity in diversity." To that end, courses offered within the School contribute toward this educational philosophy. Conversely, subjects taught throughout the University provide breadth and perspective for fields of concentration available in religion. Thus, the School of Religion draws strength from its presence within the academic setting of the entire University.

In addition to providing Foundational Studies in General Education, the School offers undergraduate majors in Biblical Studies, Christian Education, Christian Mission, Religion, Religion/Greek, and Religion/Philosophy. Minors are also offered in the areas of Biblical Studies, Chris-

tian Education, and Christian Mission.

At the graduate level, the School coordinates Master of Arts and Master of Christian Ministries programs through the Graduate School.

Parent Institution. The year was 1891 when a handful of Free Methodist pioneers established a school in Seattle called Seattle Seminary, located on the north slope of what is now Queen Anne Hill. As the student body grew, so did the Seminary, becoming Seattle Pacific College in 1915 and Seattle Pacific University in 1977. Today the Free Methodist Church remains the sponsoring denomination for the University and its 3,000 students. In nine separate schools and 58 majors, Seattle Pacific places strong emphasis on an interdisciplinary approach.

Community Environment. Seattle Pacific University students enjoy aesthetically pleasing physical learning spaces. Spread over the 35-acre campus, the buildings, recognized by their traditional brick or modern faces, are better known for the many ways in which they meet the students' educational needs. Although located in a primarily residential district, The University is just minutes away from the heart of downtown Seattle shopping, entertainment, and restaurants. Students find the peace to study but still enjoy the opportunities of a large city. Also, only one and one-half hours away on Puget Sound's Whidbey Island is the University's 135-acre Camp Casey. This rural, beachfront property is used for environmental studies, recreation, and academic workshops. Blakely Island in the San Juans, just south of Vancouver Island, provides 965 acres of wilderness campus for marine field study and research.

Religious Denomination. Free Methodist.

Religious Emphasis. Evangelical.

Accreditation. Northwest Association of Schools and Colleges.

Term System. Quarter.

Degrees in Religion Awarded 1984–85. Bachelor of Arts in Christian Education 9; men 3, women 6. Bachelor of Arts in Christian Missions 3; men 2, women 1. Bachelor of Arts in Religion/Greek 3; men 3. Bachelor of Arts in Religion 2; men 2. Bachelor of Arts in Biblical Studies 1; men 1. Master of Arts/Master of Christian Ministries in Christian Education 3; men 2, women 1.

Faculty for Degree Programs in Religion. Total 14; full-time 10, part-time 4.

Admission Requirements. Students are admitted to Seattle Pacific University who exhibit the academic characteristics which predict their success in the University programs to which they seek enrollment and the personal qualities that indicate a contribution to the fulfillment of the objectives of the University. High school transcript; entrance examination (Washington Pre-College Test, SAT, ACT); recommendation from a minister (if not available, substitute a youth leader, teacher, or employer).

Tuition and Fees. Tuition for 5 or fewer credits per credit hour $77; 6-11 total credits $167 per credit hour; 12-17 total credits $1,999 per quarter; additional credits over 17 $167 per credit hour; evening-only tuition 9 or fewer credits $77 per credit hour. Graduate tuition for 5 or fewer credits $93 per credit hour; 6-11 total credits $194 per credit hour; 12-17 total credits $2,404 per quarter; evening-only tuition 9 or fewer credits $93 per credit hour; other fees where applicable; room and board $515 per quarter.

Financial Aid. Financial aid "packages" contain combinations of scholarships, grants, employment, and loans.

Housing. On-campus residence halls house both men and women and foster a balanced, "family" type atmosphere. Five residence halls on campus and five apartment complexes adjacent to the campus accommodate approximately 1,400 full-time students. Housing is also available for graduate, part-time, and married students as space permits.

Library Facilities. At the heart of the campus is the Learning Resource Center, which includes Weter Memorial Library and the Archer Instructional Media Center. Approximately 130,000 volumes are arranged on open shelves for each access and the collection grows by some 5,000 new titles each year. The University has an expanding microfiche collection currently numbering over 250,000 items.

Religious Services/Activities. Chapel is held three times weekly and Sunday services are held morning and evening. Mid-week programs are held on Wednesdays.

Degree Programs

The Bachelor of Arts programs offer majors in Religion, Biblical Studies, Christian Mission, Christian Education, Religion-Greek, and Religion-Philosophy. In order to be admitted to "Declared Major" status in the School of Religion, a student must have a cumulative grade point average of 2.00 or higher in all previous college credits, and have attained at least a C grade (2.3 grade point) in the introductory disciplinary course. Courses are offered in the areas of General Religion, Biblical Literature, Cognate Biblical Studies, Church History, Theology and Philosophy of Religion, Christian Education, the Christian Mission, and Interdisciplinary Courses.

The Master of Arts and Master of Christian Ministries programs are organized around a core of religion studies, and draw from strengths within the various disciplines at Seattle Pacific. The programs use experts in many areas of Christian ministries as internship supervisors.

Seattle University
Department of Theology and Religious Studies

Broadway and East Madison
Seattle, WA 98122   (206) 626-5896

Administration. Dr. William J. Sullivan, President; Dr. Thomas A. Longin, Vice President for Academic Affairs;

Dr. G. David Pollick, Dean, College of Arts and Sciences; Dr. Richard H. Ahler, SJ, Chairperson, Department of Theology and Religious Studies.

General Description. The Department of Theology and Religious Studies contributes to the fostering of students' human and personal growth by helping them develop skills, attitudes, and knowledge that will enable them to deal perceptibly, intelligently, and critically with the religious dimension of human life, especially with the beliefs, practices, and values of the Catholic Christian tradition. To this end the Department supplies two levels of courses for the core curriculum. Level I courses aim at recognition and appreciation of the existence and function of God's presence in human experience and history. Level II courses aim at enabling students to learn how to make a religious tradition their own, carefully and critically. The Department also offers a program of courses, some from core offerings, some special for majors, leading to a Bachelor of Arts degree in Theology and Religious Studies. Graduate studies are also offered. *See:* Institute for Theological Studies at Seattle University.

Parent Institution. Seattle University is an independent, coeducational institution of higher learning operated by its own board of trustees and administration, under the auspices of the Society of Jesus. It has for its object and purpose the conservation, interpretation, and transmission of knowledge, ideas, and values, the extension of the frontiers of knowledge, and the preparation of students for some of the professions. As a university conducted under the auspices of the Jesuits, it affirms its belief in and support of Christian ideals and values. It affirms its belief in the unity and totality of all human knowledge. It seeks to develop a truly liberated and enlightened intelligence in its faculty and student body.

Community Environment. Seattle University is located on a 52-acre campus on Seattle, Washington's historic First Hill. Within a short walking distance are the city's major education, business, and shopping centers, and the Elliott Bay waterfront. Seattle is a seaport city surrounded by unsurpassed natural beauty, and is the largest city in the Pacific Northwest. It has all the scenic and cultural variety of a metropolitan city with the unique advantage of mountains and water at its back door.

Religious Denomination. Roman Catholic.

Accreditation. Northwest Association of Schools and Colleges.

Term System. Quarter; summer term.

Enrollment in Degree Programs in Religion 1984–85. Total 20; men 5, women 15.

Degrees in Religion Awarded 1984–85. Bachelor of Arts & Bachelor of Science 11; men 5, women 6. Bachelor of Arts in Education 2; women 2.

Faculty for Degree Programs in Religion. Total 14; full-time 12, part-time 2.

Admission Requirements. Graduation from an accredited high school; grade point average in the 16 college preparatory units of 2.50 or above on 4.00 scale; SAT,

ACT, or Washington Pre-College Test.

Tuition and Fees. Tuition $136 per credit hour; matriculation fee $45; graduation fee $45; international student fee $12 per quarter; room $678 to $940 per quarter; board $600 to $1,200 for nine months.

Financial Aid. The University expects its students and their families to make a reasonable contribution toward the expense of a college education. The expected contribution is determined by the need analysis of the College Scholarship Service. The University then tries to supplement that contribution with an award of aid which may consist of a combination of grants, loans, and/or part-time employment.

Housing. Full-time freshman students are required to live in University housing unless they are married, living with parents, or have been granted a waiver.

Library Facilities. The A.A. Lemieux Library contains over 202,000 volumes. A collection of 17,150 volumes and 148 journals is available in theology and religious studies. This collection is strong in Scripture and Systematics.

Religious Services/Activities. Religious services are available daily in several places for Roman Catholics, and weekly for Protestants. The Campus Ministry team promotes collaboration among Jesuits, lay faculty, staff, and students through liturgical celebrations, retreats, volunteer programs, and education for peace and justice.

Degree Programs

The Bachelor of Arts and Science degree with a major in Theology and Religious Studies consists of the University's required core curriculum plus twelve courses (60 credit hours) distributed through Scripture and foundations, systematics, Christian ethics, the history of Christian thought, religious studies, and a senior seminary. A minor, similarly structured but requiring only six courses, is also available.

Special Programs

Occasional continuing education courses are sponsored by the University Continuing Education Department. There are also several on-going educational opportunities sponsored by the Roman Catholic Archdiocese of Seattle and accredited by the University.

Seattle University - Institute for Theological Studies
Seattle, WA 98122   (206) 626-5318

Administration. Dr. William J. Sullivan, S.J., President; Dr. Thomas C. Longin, Vice President for Academic Affairs; Dr. Marylou Wyse, Dean, Graduate School; Dr. Richard H. Ahler, S.J., Chairperson, Department of Theology and Religious Studies.

General Description. The Institute for Theological Studies is a joint venture of the Archdiocese of Seattle and Seattle University. It provides disciplined, developmental,

and holistic training for men and women who work or wish to work in the exciting and changing community of the church. Institute programs are rooted in the conviction that ministers and educators must combine personal and professional growth with a gospel vision of ministry in the world. The programs combine the development of theological and pastoral skills with provision for personal/spiritual formation of students. Each student in the Master of Pastoral Ministry, Master of Theological Studies, and Master of Divinity programs chooses a supervised internship in a specific area of ministry (e.g., parish, hospital, etc.). The internship is an opportunity to deepen an understanding of ministry and develop expertise. Weekly individual and group supervision sessions support and intensify this internship experience.

Parent Institution. Seattle University was founded in 1891 by the Jesuit fathers. As one of 28 Jesuit colleges in the United States, Seattle University joins other Jesuit schools in educating for leadership and service. Like students in Jesuit colleges worldwide, men and women of every culture find Seattle University a challenging and supportive environment. While Seattle University is the largest independent institution in the Pacific Northwest, students also enjoy the best of a small college atmosphere — academic rigor and personal attention. The faculty is strongly committed to teaching as its highest priority and utilizes dialogue as its primary education tool.

Community Environment. Seattle University is located on a 52-acre campus on Seattle, Washington's historic First Hill. Within a short walking distance are the city's major education, business, and shopping centers, and the Elliott Bay waterfront. Seattle is a seaport city surrounded by unsurpassed natural beauty, and is the largest city in the Pacific Northwest. It has all the scenic and cultural variety of a metropolitan city with the unique advantage of mountains and water at its back door.

Religious Denomination. Roman Catholic.

Accreditation. Northwest Association of Schools and Colleges; the Institute of Theological Studies will apply for accreditation from the Association of Theological Schools in the United States and Canada.

Term System. Quarter; summer term.

Enrollment in Degree Programs in Religion 1984–85. Total 180; men 47, women 133.

Degrees in Religion Awarded 1984–85. Master of Ministry 11; men 2, women 9. Master of Pastoral Ministry 7; men 1, women 6. Master of Religious Education 20; men 6, women 14.

Faculty for Degree Programs in Religion. Total 55; full-time 8, part-time 47.

Admission Requirements. Bachelor's degree with a 3.00 grade point average; liberal arts background equivalent to the undergraduate core at Seattle University; two undergraduate courses in theology; two letters of recommendation; autobiographical statement; two years of experience in some form of education, ministry, or church-related service as a professional or a volunteer; compatibility assessment (not necessary for SUMORE) personal telephone interview (not necessary for SUMORE).

Tuition and Fees. Tuition $135 per quarter hour.

Financial Aid. Students should contact the Institute for Theological Studies office for information about financial aid.

Housing. Students from out of the region may reside in student dormitories. There are no special provisions for married couples, nor is there off-campus housing.

Library Facilities. The A.A. Lemieux Library contains over 202,000 volumes. A collection of 17,150 volumes and 148 journals is available in theology and religious studies. This collection is strong in Scripture and Systematics.

Religious Services/Activities. Religious services are available daily in several places for Roman Catholics, and weekly for Protestants. The Campus Ministry team promotes collaboration among Jesuits, lay faculty, staff, and students through liturgical celebrations, retreats, volunteer programs, and education for peace and justice.

Degree Programs

The Master of Ministry and the Master of Religious Education are graduate programs offered in the SUMORE Program which is designed to assist lay people, religious, and priests achieve a high level of competence in the evolving ministries of the Christian churches. These degree programs are structured around a common core of courses including scripture, foundational theology, the social sciences, counseling, applied theology, and professional training. Electives are offered in a number of specialized areas of ministry such as youth, young adult, adult, family, and social justice ministry; and in liturgy, spirituality, and pastoral counseling. Students may complete the requirements for the degree in three eight-week summers or over four or more summers in a variety of options.

The Master of Pastoral Ministry is a CORPUS program of pastoral ministry formation and training combining theology, ministerial skills development, and a supervised internship. It is designed for men and women entering ministry for the first time, or making a transition in ministries, for those seeking a development of present knowledge and skills or wanting a deeper integration of spirituality and ministry. Required coursework (excluding the graduate project) may be completed in one year but must be completed within three years. Courses taken from the SUMORE Program may also be applied.

A Master of Theological Studies - Level II program is scheduled to begin in fall 1986 and a Master of Divinity - Level III program is scheduled to begin in fall 1987.

WEST VIRGINIA

Alderson-Broaddus College
Philippi, WV 26416   (304) 457-1700

Administration. Dr. Bill G. Fowler, Associate Professor of Religion and Philosophy.

General Description. Because Alderson-Broaddus is a church-related college, it is especially concerned with the undergraduate preparation of students planning to become ministers or other professional Christian workers. At the College, while there is no specific curriculum that all students preparing for church vocations are required to take, a major in Christian Studies is encouraged. Guidance is also given in the details of program planning so that such students will be adequately prepared for seminary or other graduate studies in theology or Christian Education.

Parent Institution. Alderson-Broaddus College is a private undergraduate institution chartered under the laws of the State of West Virginia and affiliated with the West Virginia Baptist Convention and with the American Baptist Churches, U.S.A. While the College is Baptist in heritage and relationship, it is not sectarian in outlook. The College is committed to Christian principles and strives to educate young men and women for responsible and creative participation in the society of a rapidly changing world.

Two institutions were united in 1932 to form Alderson-Broaddus. The older of the two, Broaddus College, was founded in Winchester, Virginia in 1871 as Broaddus Academy and was moved across the Allegheny Mountains to Clarksburg, West Virginia in 1876. Broaddus Academy was neither church founded nor church owned, but it became related to the West Virginia Baptist Convention after moving to West Virginia. Later it became associated with the American Baptist Convention. The other institution, Alderson Junior College, was founded at Alderson, West Virginia in 1901. The two institutions were merged in 1932.

Community Environment. The College campus occupies a rolling hilltop area above the valley of the winding Tygart Valley River. It overlooks Philippi, a county seat, where courthouse and church spires and a historic cov-

ered wooden bridge give old world atmosphere to the view. The first land battle of the Civil War took place on the slope to the front of the hilltop campus.

Religious Denomination. American Baptist Churches, U.S.A.

Accreditation. North Central Association of Colleges and Schools.

Term System. Semester; limited summer course offerings.

Enrollment in Degree Programs in Religion 1984–85. Total (Christian Studies majors) 20; men 17, women 3.

Degrees in Religion Awarded 1984–85. Bachelor of Arts 5; men 5.

Faculty for Degree Programs in Religion. Total 5; full-time 2, part-time 3.

Admission Requirements. Secondary school transcript; satisfactory test data (SAT or ACT).

Tuition and Fees. Costs per year: tuition $4,916; general fee $138; room and board $1,804; various miscellaneous fees.

Financial Aid. Financial aid in the form of scholarships, grants, and loans is available.

Housing. Dormitory facilities for unmarried students; married students live off-campus.

Library Facilities. The Pickett Library Media Center houses 92,000 volumes of print and nonprint materials.

Religious Services/Activities. A weekly chapel service and informal devotional groups enrich the religious atmosphere of the campus. Outstanding religious leaders are brought to campus for forum addresses and small group discussions. Kappa Delta Chi is an organization for preministerial students and others planning to enter church-related vocations. Students are encouraged to participate in the life of Philippi churches. Several of the churches have student classes and student youth groups, and pastors welcome the opportunity to counsel with students on religious matters.

Degree Programs

The Bachelor of Arts degree with a major in Christian Studies is designed for the preparation of students planning to become ministers or other professional Christian workers. The principle objectives of the courses offered are to acquaint the student with the whole range of the Judaeo-Christian tradition, to encourage the student to examine his faith carefully in light of modern needs, and to introduce the student to non-Christian religions.

Special Programs

External education courses in Religion and other areas of interest are offered during the evening hours off-campus.

Appalachian Bible College
Bradley, WV 25818   (304) 877-6428

Administration. Dr. Daniel L. Anderson, President; Dr. Paul C. Reiter, Dean of Education.

General Description. Appalachian Bible College specializes in teaching the Scriptures. It provides strong fundamentalist training in Bible and Theology, with 8 specialized academic programs geared toward Christian service professions. The College further provides its students with a broad grasp of Biblical literature, both Old and New Testaments, along with a definite framework from which to study and interpret Scripture. Distinctives of the Bible College include a major in Bible and Theology and a required Christian service assignment.

Community Environment. The campus of Appalachian Bible College is nestled in the hills of West Virginia, the Mountain State, in the small community of Bradley, just 3 miles from Beckley, and an hour's drive from Charleston, the state capital. The College is surrounded on all sides by rugged, wooded hills. The 110-acre campus is easily accessible via the West Virginia Turnpike and U.S. Route 16.

Religious Denomination. Nondenominational.

Religious Emphasis. Fundamentalist (moderate).

Accreditation. American Association of Bible Colleges.

Term System. Semester; no summer term.

Enrollment in Degree Programs in Religion 1984–85. Total 180; men 80, women 100.

Degrees in Religion Awarded 1984–85. Bachelor of Theology 2; men 1, women 1. Bachelor of Arts 15; men 10, women 5.

Faculty for Degree Programs in Religion. Total 20; full-time 16, part-time 4.

Admission Requirements. Evidence of receiving Christ as Savior; recommendations from friends, pastors, teachers, etc.; grade point average of 2.0; scores on ACT or SAT.

Tuition and Fees. $4,892 yearly.

Financial Aid. Grants, loans, student employment, scholarships, and awards are available.

Housing. Men's and women's dormitories; trailer courts on campus for married students; low rent apartments are available near campus.

Library Facilities. The library contains more than 30,-000 volumes and covers the entire field of Biblical, professional, and general education studies. Over 200 periodicals and missionary journals provide current literature. A Judaica Collection is also maintained.

Religious Services/Activities. Attendance at a scriptural and spiritual church both Sunday morning and evening is expected of each student. Attendance at a mid-week prayer meeting is also expected. Membership in a local church or affiliation with an organized assembly which does not offer membership is required of each student before graduation. Christian service assignments require weekly service in local churches or the community.

Degree Programs

The Bachelor of Arts program requires all students to major in English Bible and Bible Theology. The student will choose his/her program of concentration at the close of the second year of study. The areas of concentration offered are Family Counseling, Music, Youth and Music, Business Administration, Youth Ministries, Pastoral, Missions, and Elementary Education.

The Bachelor of Theology degree consists of the Bachelor of Arts in Bible and Theology plus two professional programs with a minimum of 160 semester hours taken at the College or some studies taken elsewhere and transferred in to achieve the same combination of elements.

Special Programs

The Diploma Program in General Bible has its first year courses identical with the degree students, except for the physical education requirements, and moves to a combination of required and elective courses thereafter.

The Bible Certificate Program provides a sense of accomplishment for the student who plans to attend the College for only one year.

Bethany College
Department of Religious Studies
Bethany, WV 26032   (304) 829-7611

Administration. Dr. Richard B. Kenney, Head of Department of Religious Studies.

General Description. Biblical studies form the central core of Departmental offerings. In addition, each student examines the relationship between religion and culture, both ancient and modern. The Department assists the student in learning how to acquire, evaluate, and use religious knowledge. Each course is designed to enhance the student's efforts to interrelate his/her varied academic, social, and personal experiences.

Parent Institution. Bethany College was founded in 1840 by Alexander Campbell, educator, celebrated debater, and Christian reformer who provided land and funds for the first building and served as first president. Since its inception, the College has remained affiliated with the Christian Church (Disciples of Christ). This religious body, of which Campbell was one of the principal founders, continues to support and encourage the College, although it exercises no sectarian control. Students of virtually every religious communion have been welcomed.

Community Environment. Bethany is located in the northern panhandle of West Virginia in the foothills of the Allegheny Mountains. Pittsburgh is 48 miles to the northeast, Wheeling, West Virginia and Washington, Pennsylvania are each a half-hour drive from the 1,600-acre campus.

Religious Denomination. Christian Church (Disciples of Christ).

Accreditation. North Central Association of Colleges and Schools.

Term System. Semester.

Admission Requirements. High school graduation with rank in upper half of graduating class; completion of 15 units including 4 English; SAT or ACT.

Tuition and Fees. Tuition and fees $6,380 per year; room and board $2,330; student board of governors $130, student union $60.

Financial Aid. All need-based aid is awarded through the Financial Aid Office. Outstanding students, regardless of demonstrated need, frequently receive scholarships and grants.

Housing. Housing in campus dormitories is available.

Library Facilities. The T.W. Phillips Memorial Library contains nearly 155,000 volumes. The Campbell Room contains books, periodicals, letters, paintings, photographs, and museum pieces related to Bethany's Founder and first President, Alexander Campbell.

Religious Services/Activities. Many religious backgrounds are represented in the study body and faculty. While participation in religious activities is voluntary, there are many opportunities for religious participation on campus.

Degree Programs

The field of concentration in Religious Studies leading to the Bachelor of Arts degree requires a minimum of 24 hours (excluding the general requirement of a course in religious studies), a Senior Project, and the successful completion of the Senior Comprehensive Examination. The Comprehensive Examination in Religious Studies emphasizes Biblical Studies, early Christianity, and contemporary religious thought and culture.

Davis and Elkins College
Department of Religion and Philosophy
Elkins, WV 26241   (304) 636-1900

Administration. William E. Phipps, Chairperson.

General Description. Courses in Religion are designed to introduce the student to basic religious concepts, problems, and terminology; to help students gain an accurate knowledge of and appreciation for the Bible; to introduce

the student to major developments in the Western religious tradition, both historical and contemporary; to afford opportunity to examine non-Western religious traditions; and to explore the relationship to other aspects of human behavior. The Bachelor of Arts degree and the Bachelor of Science degrees are awarded.

Parent Institution. Davis and Elkins College is sponsored by the recently reunited Presbyterian Church in the U.S.A. The first classes were held in 1904.

Community Environment. The community of Elkins has a rural setting and a population of 10,000. It is located in the foothills of the Alleghenies and is the headquarters for the nearby Monongahela National Forest. The campus is situated on 170 acres.

Religious Denomination. Presbyterian Church (U.S.A.).

Accreditation. North Central Association of Colleges and Schools.

Term System. Semester (4-1-4 plan).

Admission Requirements. High school graduation; ACT or SAT required.

Tuition and Fees. Tuition $5,096 per year; room $1,268; board $1,329.

Financial Aid. Federal and state loans and grants, scholarships, and college work-study are among the types of assistance available.

Housing. Men's and women's dormitories are available on campus.

Library Facilities. The College Learning Materials Center houses over 100,000 volumes.

Religious Services/Activities. The College provides many opportunities for voluntary participation in a wide range of religious activities, including chapel services, Bible study, student led discussions, special speakers, and service projects.

Degree Programs

The major in Religion and Philosophy consists of 36 semester hours of Religion and Philosophy courses. The major in Social Service leading to the Bachelor of Arts degree consists of 44-46 semester hours of courses in the Department and other curricular areas. The Bachelor of Science with a major in Social Service consists of 48-49 semester hours in the Department and other curricular areas. Generally, 124 semester hours are required for the Bachelor's degree.

Ohio Valley College
College Parkway
Parkersburg, WV 26101   (304) 485-7384

Administration. Keith Stotts, President.

General Description. Ohio Valley College is a Christian, coeducational, liberal arts college offering associate degrees in both transfer and terminal programs and baccalaureate degree programs in Bible to prepare students for active ministry and/or admission to graduate study in

Bible or Religious Studies.

Parent Institution. The College was established in 1958 and is operated by members of the Churches of Christ.

Community Environment. The campus of 127 acres is located in Parkersburg, a city of 50,000 people in the mid-Ohio Valley.

Religious Denomination. Churches of Christ.

Accreditation. North Central Association of Colleges and Schools.

Term System. Semester.

Admission Requirements. High school graduation from an accredited school; ACT with score of 14 or above; non-high school graduates considered.

Tuition and Fees. Tuition $2,820 per year; room $415-$465 per semester; board $800 per semester; activity fee $80; library fee $40.

Financial Aid. The College offers several types of scholarships. State and federal aid are also available.

Housing. Dormitory facilities for men and women are available on the campus.

Library Facilities. The library has holdings of over 21,000 volumes and subscribes to 196 current periodicals. More than 6,000 microforms complement the book collection.

Religious Services/Activities. All full-time students, faculty, and staff assemble every regular school day for a short period of devotion. Attendance at this chapel period is required. Various clubs and interest groups are available for student participation.

Degree Programs

The Department of Bible and Religion offers a Bible program to prepare men and women to serve effectively in areas of preaching, teaching, personal evangelism, counseling, and education or to pursue graduate studies. The general requirements for the Bachelor of Arts degree in Bible include general education core courses required for the Associate of Arts degree plus 71 hours in Bible and Religion areas. The Bachelor of Science in Bible requires the same general education core courses plus 81 hours in Bible and Religion. A total of 128 semester hours are required for the Bachelor's degree.

Special Programs

An Associate of Arts program is offered by the College and constitutes the first two years of work toward the baccalaureate degrees described above.

West Virginia Wesleyan College
Department of Religion
Buckhannon, WV 26201   (304) 473-8000

Administration. Hugh A. Latimer, President.

General Description. The Department of Religion offers courses that contribute to education in the humanities through their consideration of man in terms of his reli-

gious traditions, commitments, and questions. In keeping with the tradition of the College, Christianity receives particular attention as a basis for understanding the heritage of the Western world. The major or minor is appropriate for persons preparing for theological study and church-related vocations.

Parent Institution. The College is a privately supported, coeducational, liberal arts college. It was founded in 1890 as the West Virginia Conference Seminary. It is affiliated with the United Methodist Church.

Community Environment. The 60-acre campus is located in Buckhannon, near the geographical center of West Virginia.

Religious Denomination. United Methodist Church.

Accreditation. North Central Association of Colleges and Schools.

Term System. Semester (4-1-4 plan).

Faculty for Degree Programs in Religion. Total 4.

Admission Requirements. High school graduation from an accredited school; SAT or ACT required; non-high school graduates considered.

Tuition and Fees. Tuition $4,900 per year; room and board $2,887; student fees $550.

Financial Aid. Financial aid is available on the basis of scholastic achievement, special talents and abilities, and financial need.

Housing. Dormitories are available on campus.

Library Facilities. The library houses over 135,000 volumes and subscribes to 685 periodicals. The book collection is supplemented by over 11,000 microforms and audiovisual materials.

Religious Services/Activities. The Christian Life Council, advised by the Dean of the Chapel, coordinates the activities of campus Christian groups and plans special events and programs.

Degree Programs

The major in Religion leading to the Bachelor of Arts degree requires 24 semester hours beyond the introductory course (6 hours). Seniors must complete a comprehensive examination.

Wheeling College
Department of Theology/Religious Studies
310 Washington Avenue
Wheeling, WV 26003   (304) 243-2369

Administration. Fr. Thomas S. Acker, President; Dr. Eugene F. Laufer, Director, Master of Arts in Religious Education Program.

General Description. The Department of Theology/Religious Studies is primarily a support area on the undergraduate level. On the graduate level, the Department offers a Master's degree in Religious Education, a nontraditional program. The degrees Bachelor of Arts in Religion and Master of Arts in Religious Education are offered.

Parent Institution. Wheeling College is a small, Catholic, liberal arts institution. It is owned and operated by the Jesuit Fathers as one of a network of 28 Jesuit colleges and universities in the United States.

Community Environment. Wheeling College is located on 65 acres in Wheeling, West Virginia. It is a one hour drive from Pittsburgh, and a two hour drive from Columbus.

Religious Denomination. Roman Catholic.

Religious Emphasis. Liberal and Ecumenical.

Accreditation. North Central Association of Colleges and Schools.

Term System. Semester; 2 sessions of summer school.

Enrollment in Degree Programs in Religion 1984–85. Total 16; men 2, women 14. There are currently 11 in the Master's program and 5 in the undergraduate program.

Degrees in Religion Awarded 1984–85. Master of Arts in Religious Education 11; men 1, women 10. Bachelor of Arts 5; men 1, women 4.

Faculty for Degree Programs in Religion. Total 6; full-time 3, part-time 3.

Admission Requirements. Undergraduate: High school diploma or equivalent; 15 units of high school academic courses; upper half of high school class; SAT of at least 850 or composite score of 18 on ACT. Graduate: Baccalaureate degree; GRE exam.

Tuition and Fees. Tuition undergraduate $5,620 per year, graduate $150 per credit hour; room $1,425-$1,925; board $1,500.

Financial Aid. Financial aid is awarded on the basis of scholastic achievement or financial need or a combination of both. Several types of aid are available to graduate students in the form of loans, scholarships, and direct grants from federal and state sources.

Housing. Housing is available on campus for all undergraduates. Housing is also available for all graduate students at the off-campus center in Parkersburg where most of the graduate courses are taught.

Library Facilities. The library houses over 116,000 volumes and 35,000 microforms.

Religious Services/Activities. All religious activities are separate from the academic programs. There is a Campus Ministry Office that provides for regular Catholic services, retreats, and other activities.

Degree Programs

The Theology/Religious Studies major leading to the Bachelor of Arts degree requires 36 credits. The student selects any one of the three introductory courses and any one of the upper-level offerings to fulfill the core curriculum requirement. In addition, majors complete 24 credits in electives and 4 credits in a senior seminar. French or German is recommended for majors.

The Master of Arts in Religious Education is designed to prepare students for a variety of church-related educational ministries. A unique feature of the program is the nontraditional format which is tailored to meet the needs of persons holding full-time jobs. Its structure includes ten intense weekend sessions scheduled every fourth week during the academic year in Parkersburg and two one-week sessions during the summer months at Wheeling College. A person enrolled on a full-time basis may earn the 34-credit degree in two years and three summers of work.

WISCONSIN

Alverno College
Department of Religious Studies
3401 South 39th Street
Milwaukee, WI 53215   (414) 647-3999

Administration. Joel Read, President; Dr. Austin Doherty, Vice President and Dean, Academic Affairs; Dr. Margaret Earley, Coordinator, Department of Religious Studies.

General Description. Alverno College offers an undergraduate degree, Bachelor of Arts, in Religious Studies. In addition to the major, a minor is also offered. The Religious Studies major deals with the analysis of contemporary faith questions and scriptural interpretations, and engages in the process of examining one's own value and belief systems. The student focuses on expressions of religious consciousness across religious traditions and on the implications of religious beliefs, practices, and institutions for contemporary life. The program includes courses, off-campus experiences, and independent research. The Department of Religious Studies is a part of the Division of Arts and Humanities.

Parent Institution. In 1887, the School Sisters of St. Francis opened a teacher training institution that grew to become Alverno College, a liberal arts college for women with an enrollment of 1,650 students. Alverno's 35 areas of study are offered through the College's 6 academic divisions: Fine Arts; Arts and Humanities; Behavioral Sciences; Nursing; Natural Sciences and Technology; Education, Information Sciences, and Computer Studies. Woven through this "content" curriculum is a second curriculum designed to help students master such intellectual abilities as critical thinking, social interaction, valuing, aesthetic response, and communication. This "ability-based" education, unique to Alverno, has earned praise from educators throughout the United States and abroad.

Community Environment. Alverno's 52-acre, 9-building campus is located on the south side of Milwaukee, Wisconsin. Situated on the west shore of Lake Michigan, Milwaukee (population 718,000) is the largest city in Wisconsin, with all major forms of commercial transportation available. Milwaukee is the nation's brewing center and also a major grain market and manufacturing center.

Religious Denomination. Roman Catholic.

Religious Emphasis. Most positions are presented and respected.

Accreditation. North Central Association of Colleges and Schools.

Term System. Semester; summer term.

Enrollment in Degree Programs in Religion 1984–85. Total 10; women 10.

Faculty for Degree Programs in Religion. Total 3; full-time 2, part-time 1.

Admission Requirements. Graduation from an accredited high school or successful completion of a GED certificate program; completion of 10-12 academic units in high school; ranking in upper half of high school class; satisfactory scores on ACT test or Alverno College's pre-admission assessment.

Tuition and Fees. Tuition $2,334 per semester; room and board $1,000 per semester.

Financial Aid. Over 80 percent of Alverno's students receive some sort of financial aid. In addition to helping each student obtain all the federal, state, and other tuition assistance for which she qualifies, Alverno administers over 30 scholarship programs of its own for students.

Housing. Alverno's "Campus Center" offers single and double accommodations for students. The Student Services office helps students seeking off-campus housing choose from a plentiful supply of rental units close to the campus.

Library Facilities. The Alverno Library Media Center includes over 250,000 books, periodicals, and microfiche records. Its special collections include the Resource Center on Women and several special collections for college educators.

Religious Services/Activities. Roman Catholic Mass is celebrated on Saturday evenings and on special occasions such as Graduation and major holy days. Ecumenical services are held on occasion (Thanksgiving; some convocations). Lenten and Advent prayer services are held in the Chapel. Retreats, a Spirituality Interest Group, and a

Bible Study Group are also held.

Degree Programs

The Bachelor of Arts degree with a major in Religious Studies is offered by the Integrated Arts and Humanities program which is designed to help each student develop general professional abilities at the same time as she explores an area of specialized inquiry. The Religious Studies courses include Contemporary Issues in Religion: Control of Life and Death; Religious Experience; Myth and Symbol; The Biblical World View; Religion in America and the World; Interpreting the Christian Heritage; Religious Studies Design; Independent Study; and Off-Campus Experiential Learning Seminar.

Special Programs

The Institute for Parish Service offers programs to help people become more effective leaders in the Church community. Courses offered include The Role of Lay Women and Men in the Church, Christian Leadership, The Role of Faith in Personal Growth, and Ministering in Education and Worship. Certificates of Completion are awarded.

Cardinal Stritch College
Religious Studies Department
6801 North Yates Road
Milwaukee, WI 53217   (414) 352-5400

Administration. Sr. M. Camille Kliebhan, O.S.F., Ph.D., President; Dr. Robert F. Flahive, Vice President; Sr. Andree Gaspard, O.S.F., Academic Dean; Sr. Coletta Dunn, Professor, Religious Studies.

General Description. At Cardinal Stritch College the Religious Studies Department aims to provide the student with the resources needed to examine the symbols of religion and to evaluate their contribution to history, culture, and personal development. The Department seeks to provide knowledge, understanding, and appreciation of religious beliefs. Men and women of all ages, races, and creeds who are interested in personal enrichment, spiritual growth, professional development, and social service, enroll as majors. Graduates generally follow the professions of teaching, youth ministry, counseling, and church-related ministries.

Parent Institution. Cardinal Stritch College is a Catholic, coeducational, liberal arts college located in metropolitan Milwaukee. Chartered as a 4-year institution in 1937 and sponsored by the Sisters of St. Francis of Assisi, it is operated by both religious and lay personnel. The College provides its students with a liberal arts foundation, practical career preparation, and opportunities for service to others so that these individuals may develop as persons, family members, workers, and citizens. Rooted in the Judeo-Christian tradition, the Schools's value-oriented curriculum is organized to help students learn "to value

the better things" of life.

Community Environment. Cardinal Stritch College occupies a lovely, open site of over 40 acres, located in Milwaukee's northeast suburbs of Fox Point and Glendale, not far from Lake Michigan. Easy access from all parts of Milwaukee, southeastern Wisconsin, and northern Illinois is afforded by Highway I-43 that runs parallel to the western edge of the campus. See also: Alverno College for information about Milwaukee.

Religious Denomination. Roman Catholic.

Accreditation. North Central Association of Colleges and Schools.

Term System. Semester; summer term.

Enrollment in Degree Programs in Religion 1984–85. Total 30; men 14, women 16.

Degrees in Religion Awarded 1984–85. Bachelor of Arts in Religious Studies 4; men 2, women 2.

Faculty for Degree Programs in Religion. Total 7; full-time 2, part-time 5.

Admission Requirements. Open to men and women who have a high school education or its equivalent. Applicants are accepted for admission on the basis of past achievements and demonstrated ability to succeed in college work. For guidance purposes, it is recommended that students arrange to take ACT or SAT and have the scores sent to Stritch.

Tuition and Fees. Full-time tuition $2,320 per semester; part-time (1 through 11 credits) $145 per credit; room and board $1,150 to $1,200 per semester depending upon meal plan and accommodations; room only $498 to $528 per semester depending upon accommodations.

Financial Aid. Students and parents are encouraged to take advantage of financial aid plan programs sponsored by the federal government, the State of Wisconsin, and of Cardinal Stritch College. Grants, loans, scholarships, and service work contracts are available to qualified full- and part-time students through Stritch's Financial Aid Office.

Housing. Stritch offers comfortable living accommodations on campus for 200 resident students with both single and double rooms available. Five-day and seven-day meal plans in accordance with student's preference are available.

Library Facilities. The library houses over 100,000 volumes. There are special collections on Roman Catholicism, Scholastic Philosophy, and Youth Ministry.

Religious Services/Activities. Campus ministry personnel serve all students regardless of religious affiliation. Campus ministers and students work together to plan a variety of religious activities. For Catholics, daily liturgies, periodic penance celebrations, and spiritual retreats are scheduled throughout the school year.

Degree Programs

The Bachelor of Arts in Religious Studies requires a 24-credit major with Biblical, Theological, Religious Historical, and Applied Theology courses according to the students' needs in future ministry. Tracks available to majors include preparation for graduate theological studies, preparation as secondary teachers of religion, preparation as youth ministers, directors of religious education, and related careers.

A Master of Arts program in Special Education has a specialization in Special Religious Education.

Special Programs

Continuing Studies offerings in Biblical Studies is available annually in 6-week and 12-week blocks.

Carroll College
Department of Religion
100 North East Avenue
Waukesha, WI 53186   (414) 547-1211

Administration. Dr. Lawrence A. Sinclair, Professor and Chairperson, Department of Religion.

General Description. The objectives of the Department are (1) to provide the student with an opportunity for an encounter with the world today from a point of view which takes into account religious values and insights; (2) to provide the student with an opportunity for understanding, evaluating, and responding to the Judeo-Christian tradition; (3) to provide the student with an opportunity to understand and evaluate his or her own religious convictions, and (4) to provide the student with an opportunity to enter into dialogue with those who express various Christian and non-Christian points of view.

Parent Institution. Carroll College is a small, independent, coeducational four-year liberal arts college. Following the intent of its founders, the college emphasizes the combination of scholarly ideals and Christian culture. The first and oldest college in Wisconsin, Carroll is referred to as the "Pioneer College." Pioneers founded Prairieville Academy in 1841; an amending act of incorporation created Carroll College in 1846. The college is named for Charles Carroll, a signer of the Declaration of Independence and early American statesman from Carrollton, Maryland. The College, which is related to the Presbyterian Church (U.S.A.), is Christian but nonsectarian and ecumenical.

Community Environment. The name Waukesha comes from an Indian word meaning "by the Little Fox." The city has a population of 52,000 and is situated 40 minutes from metropolitan Milwaukee. The 30-acre campus is located in a residential section of the city.

Religious Denomination. Presbyterian Church (U.S.A.).
Religious Emphasis. Ecumenical.
Accreditation. North Central Association of Colleges and Schools.
Term System. Semester (4-1-4); two summer sessions.
Enrollment in Degree Programs in Religion 1984–85. Total 10; men 5, women 5.
Degrees in Religion Awarded 1984–85. Bachelor of Arts 7; men 5, women 2.

Faculty for Degree Programs in Religion. Total 3; full-time 3.

Admission Requirements. Admission is offered to those for whom academic and personal success seem likely. Each candidate is evaluated individually. Evidence of good character, interest in, and ability to do college-level work are essential.

Tuition and Fees. Basic expenses (not including cost of textbooks and student deposits) per year: tuition and incidental fee $7,030; activity fee $70; board (minimum plan) $1,160; room (double) $1,120.

Financial Aid. Financial aid at Carroll College is available to full-time students who are degree candidates, following guidelines established by the College, the U.S. Department of Education, and the Wisconsin Higher Educational Aids Board. All types of aid are awarded on the basis of the applicant's need as determined by the College Scholarship Service and by academic requirements for the type of aid requested.

Housing. Campus housing is available for about 900 students. All full-time freshmen, sophomores, and juniors not living at home must reside in a college residence.

Library Facilities. The library houses 160,000 volumes and subscribes to 600 periodicals. There is a special collection on 18th and 19th century English and American theologians.

Religious Services/Activities. Religious programs at Carroll are coordinated through the Office of the Dean of the Chapel and the student Interfaith Programs Committee. There are numerous opportunities for both students and faculty to explore and develop religious faith and action in accord with the liberal arts tradition of the college. Weekly worship services are open to the entire campus community. These worship services are ecumenical in nature and often make use of clergy and laity from area churches. An annual Confrontation Lecture Series (six lectures) gives attention to "moral and social issues in a religious context." Students are expected to attend at least three of the Confrontations each year. Various fellowship opportunities are also available on the campus. The Dean of the Chapel assists students with opportunities for service through volunteer agencies, special retreats, and provides crisis intervention service for the campus.

Degree Programs

The Bachelor of Arts with a major in religion prepares young men and women for: graduate education in a theological seminary leading to ordination and work as a pastor; graduate education in the field of religion leading toward teaching; and positions of reponsibility in church and community. The student who plans to enter the ministry will find the Religion major flexible to suit one's needs. The major is designed to provide breadth in the liberal arts, as well as depth in the study of the Bible and Christian faith.

Special Programs

The New Cultural Experiences Program sponsors overseas trips to Bible lands and ecumenical study tours to Western Europe (alternate during the January term).

Carthage College
Department of Religion
Kenosha, WI 53141   (414) 551-8500

Administration. Dr. Erno J. Dahl, President; Dr. Daniel N. Keck, Dean of the College; Dr. Allan Hauck, Chairperson, Department of Religion.

General Description. The purpose of the Department of Religion is to provide an understanding and appreciation of the Christian religion, its origin, history, doctrines, and ethics, and of non-Christian religions, and their place in the culture of America and other lands. All students are required to take courses in the Department of Religion. The Department offers lay professional, pre-seminary, and church management majors and minors. The degree Bachelor of Arts is awarded.

Parent Institution. Carthage College is a four-year, co-educational liberal arts college affiliated with the Lutheran Church in America (Michigan and Wisconsin-Upper Michigan Synods). The College also maintains a cooperative relationship with The American Luthern Church (Southern and Northern Districts in Wisconsin).

Community Environment. Though located in Illinois for more than a century, Carthage is now in Kenosha, Wisconsin, an urban-industrial city of 78,000 strategically situated midway between Chicago and Milwaukee.

Religious Denomination. Lutheran Church in America.

Religious Emphasis. Ecumenical.

Accreditation. North Central Association of Colleges and Schools.

Term System. Semester; summer term.

Enrollment in Degree Programs in Religion 1984–85. Total 12; men 7, women 5.

Degrees in Religion Awarded 1984–85. Bachelor of Arts 5; men 3, women 2.

Faculty for Degree Programs in Religion. Total 5; full-time 4, part-time 1.

Admission Requirements. High school graduation in upper third of class or special admission because of high ACT and SAT scores.

Tuition and Fees. $3,000 per semester; room $700; board $700.

Financial Aid. Assistance is available on basis of need and/or academic standing.

Housing. Dormitories are available on campus; local housing is available for married students.

Library Facilities. The library houses 217,793 volumes and its holdings are especially strong in the area of religion.

Religious Services/Activities. Ecumenical weekly chapel services; Sunday morning Lutheran services; Sunday evening Roman Catholic Mass; many organizational activities.

Degree Programs

Thirty-six credits constitute a major in Religion leading to the Bachelor of Arts degree. All students majoring in Religion must obtain, either by proficiency testing or by course completion, eight credits of college credit in a foreign language. Pre-seminary students are advised to take at least five courses in Religion as a background for graduate study. The Lay Church Worker major is for those who desire to prepare for lay professions in the church or for further study. The major applies to the certification requirements for Church Staff Associates of the American Lutheran Church and for Lay Professionals in the Lutheran Church in America. It is also applicable to vocations in other church denominations.

Concordia College
Division of Theology and Social Science
12800 North Lake Shore Drive
Mequon, WI 53091   (414) 243-5700

Administration. Norman P. Wangerin, Chairman, Division of Theology and Social Science.

General Description. The Division of Theology and Social Science offers required courses for the core curriculum, the major area of concentration, a Pastoral Ministry Program, and a Lay Ministry Program.

Parent Institution. Concordia College was founded in 1881 as one of 15 institutions in a system of schools owned and maintained by the Lutheran Church-Missouri Synod.

Community Environment. The campus is located on the north side of Mequon along Lake Michigan and is easily reached from downtown Milwaukee.

Religious Denomination. Lutheran Church-Missouri Synod.

Accreditation. North Central Association of Colleges and Schools.

Term System. Semester system (4-1-4 plan).

Faculty for Degree Programs in Religion. Total 8.

Admission Requirements. High school graduation from an accredited high school or equivalent; SAT or ACT.

Tuition and Fees. Educational fees $2,200 per semester; room and board $1,295.

Financial Aid. The amount of financial aid awarded is based mainly on the applicant's financial need.

Housing. Residence halls are available on campus.

Library Facilities. The library contains over 33,000 volumes and subscribes to 180 periodicals.

Religious Services/Activities. Chapel services are held Monday through Friday; worship service is held on Sunday morning. Devotions are held in the residence halls, and personal Bible study is encouraged.

Degree Programs

The Pastoral Ministry program is a liberal arts academic preparation to the study of Theology. The program requires a core curriculum and a concentration in either Theological Language or choice of major and concentration in any other professional collateral. The program leads to the Bachelor of Arts degree.

The Lay Ministry Program is designed to equip men and women to work under a pastor's guidance and direction in evangelism, visitation, education, group work, youth, elderly, administration, and as a Christian education director. The Bachelor of Arts degree is awarded.

The major in Theology requiring a minimum of 30 credits hours leads to the Bachelor of Arts degree (126 credit hours total required).

Holy Redeemer College
1701 Sharp Road
Waterford, WI 53185   (414) 534-3191

Administration. Dr. J. Robert Fenili, President and Rector.

General Description. Holy Redeemer College can trace its origins back to 1851 when the Redemptorist Congregation of Priests and Brothers established their first American seminary at Cumberland, Maryland. It opened its present site in 1968 when it combined the junior college program of St. Joseph's Preparatory Seminary of Edgerton, Wisconsin and the senior college program of Immaculate Conception Seminary of Oconomowoc. When the new college opened, it offered a four-year Bachelor of Arts program to candidates of the Redemptorist Congregation who were seeking to become Roman Catholic priests. The College also offered a non-degree academic program for individuals who wished to serve the Church as religious brothers. In 1980, Sacred Heart School of Theology entered into an agreement with the College that enables candidates for Sacred Heart Seminary to complete their undergraduate prerequisites at Holy Redeemer before beginning the program of studies at the Sacred Heart School of Theology. The College accepts non-seminarian commuter students from the surrounding area.

Community Environment. Waterford is a rural community 30 miles southwest of Milwaukee and 20 miles west of Racine.

Religious Denomination. Roman Catholic.

Religious Emphasis. Redemptorist.

Accreditation. North Central Association of Colleges and Schools.

Term System. Trimester.

Admission Requirements. High school graduation or equivalent; ACT required.

Tuition and Fees. Tuition $2,235 per year; room and board $1,935; student fees $165.

Financial Aid. Scholarships, loans, work-study grants, grants-in-aid, state aid are among the types of assistance available.

Housing. Resident students are housed in a dormitory facility on campus.

Library Facilities. The library has holdings of 34,600 volumes.

Religious Services/Activities. The Religious Life program seeks to give inspiration through instruction, experience, and reflection upon the beliefs and values of the Christian, Catholic, the Religious, and the Redemptorist communities. The life of the College seminarian is centered around prayer, charity, and community service to others. A Field Education program provides guided access to practical experience directed toward a career in pastoral ministry.

Degree Programs

The seminarian pursues philosophy as the equivalent of a major area of concentration by taking, in addition to the core liberal arts requirements in philosophy, additional courses in the field to constitute a total of 27 credits. A total of 128 semester hours is required for the Bachelor of Arts degree.

Immanuel Lutheran College
Immanuel Lutheran College and Immanuel
Lutheran Seminary
501 Grover Road
Eau Claire, WI 54701   (715) 834-3301

Administration. Gordon Radtke, President; Clifford Kuehne, Dean of the College; L.W. Schierenbeck, Dean of the Theological Seminary.

General Description. Immanuel Lutheran College is a one-campus unit offering a four-year high school department, a two-year general college course (Associate of Arts), a four-year college program (Bachelor of Science) to train Lutheran elementary school teachers for the Church of the Lutheran Confession (CLC), a four-year college program (Bachelor of Arts) offering pre-theological training for admission to the Seminary, and a three-year Seminary program (CRM — Candidate for the Holy Ministry) for the training of ministers for the Church of the Lutheran Confession.

Community Environment. The campus of Emmanuel Lutheran College is located on Grover Road, adjacent to Corydon Park, about two and one-half miles south of the business district of the city of Eau Claire, Wisconsin. The campus comprises 75 acres, of which the building area is beautifully landscaped. Eau Claire is a cultural, commercial, educational, and medical center in west central Wisconsin. The city, which is located at the confluence of the Eau Claire and Chippewa Rivers, is served by air and bus lines. The city and the surrounding area abound in colorful, natural beauty, and offer numerous year-round recreational activities.

Religious Denomination. Church of the Lutheran Confession.

Religious Emphasis. Conservative Lutheran.

Term System. Semester; no summer term.

Enrollment in Degree Programs in Religion 1984–85. Total 22; men 14, women 8.

Degrees in Religion Awarded 1984–85. Associate of Arts 6; men 1, women 5. Bachelor of Science 1; women 1. Bachelor of Arts 4; men 4. CRM (Candidate for the Holy Ministry) 4; men 4.

Faculty for Degree Programs in Religion. Total 11; full-time 11.

Admission Requirements. High School: by application and acceptance. College: high school graduation; ACT; complete physical history. Seminary: Bachelor of Arts degree.

Tuition and Fees. High School: $300 per semester; Associate of Arts $370 per semester; Bachelor of Arts/Bachelor of Science $327.50 per semester; Candidate for Holy Ministry $235 per semester; room and board $650 per semester; activity fee $20 per semester.

Financial Aid. Students who inquire about financial aid will be advised of the help that is presently available. There is an automatic grant of over $1,000 per year to all students through the Church Body Subsidy. This grant reduces the tuitions to the catalog listed amounts. Additional student aid (scholarships, grants, loans) available in limited amounts by individual application.

Housing. Students will be provided with sleeping and study rooms equipped with all the necessary furniture. Married students arrange for their own off-campus housing.

Library Facilities. The library contains over 12,000 volumes. Special collections include archaic and out-of-print periodicals, papers, works, books (much of the material in the German language) in the Theological Division of the library.

Religious Services/Activities. There are daily AM and PM chapel services. Sunday and special festival services are held at the local Church of the Lutheran Confession (CLC). The choir tours to congregations of the CLC.

Degree Programs

The Bachelor of Arts program prepares students for entrance into Immanuel Lutheran Seminary. The courses provide them with a broad liberal arts training and a working knowledge of Greek and Hebrew. The Bachelor of Science program provides a complete training for those young men and women preparing for teaching in Lutheran elementary schools. The students take courses in general subject areas and in professional education.

Special Programs

The Associate of Arts program serves not only those individuals who end their college education with a two-

year degree but also those who transfer to other institutions of higher learning.

The Seminary Program has as its sole aim and purpose the training of young men for the ministry of the Gospel. A Candidate for the Holy Ministry degree is awarded upon completion of the program.

Each year a number of high school graduates and adults may take religion or other courses at the College without committing themselves to a degree program.

Lakeland College
Humanities Division - Philosophy and
Religion Department
Sheboygan, WI 53081   (414) 565-1201

Administration. Dr. Reinhard Ulrich, Chairman, Humanities Division.

General Description. The role of the Humanities Division in the curriculum is to transmit Western culture, in both its historical and contemporary forms. The Division offers departmental programs in language, written communication, literature, philosophy, and religion. The Department of Philosophy and Religion seeks to assist students in developing a critical awareness of themselves and their world. Majors in Church Administration, Philosophy, and Religion are offered.

Parent Institution. Lakeland College is a privately supported liberal arts college. It was founded in 1862 and is affiliated with the United Church of Christ.

Community Environment. The campus of 145 acres is located in Sheboygan, 12 miles northeast of Milwaukee. The town of 50,000 population offers students off-campus opportunities for work and recreation.

Religious Denomination. United Church of Christ.

Accreditation. North Central Association of Colleges and Schools.

Term System. Semester.

Admission Requirements. High school graduation from an accredited school or equivalent; rank in upper 50 percent of graduating class; SAT or ACT required.

Tuition and Fees. Tuition $5,500 per year; room and board $2,600.

Financial Aid. Assistance is available.

Housing. Most students live on campus in residence halls.

Library Facilities. The library houses over 55,000 books.

Degree Programs

The major in Religion leading to the Bachelor of Arts degree requires the completion of five courses: Old Testament Theology or New Testament Theology, Contemporary Theology, and three additional courses in Religion. The major in Church Administration requires the completion of 12 courses in various curricular areas. The Bachelor of Arts degree requires 128 semester hours.

Marian College
Theology/Philosophy Department
45 South National Avenue
Fond du Lac, WI 54935   (414) 923-7600

Administration. Dr. Leo Krzywkowski, President; Dr. Daniel DiDomizio, S.T.D., Chairperson, Department of Humanistic Studies.

General Description. The Scripture and Theology courses of the Department of Theology provide settings in which students may examine the rational and historic bases of their life of faith. The variety of courses insures a broad exposure to the religious thought of many faith expressions. The Religious Studies major includes certification by the state for teaching religion in grades 7 through 12. The Religious Studies or Theology majors prepare persons for pastoral positions. Certain individual courses may lead to Archdiosesan certification in religious education.

Parent Institution. Marian College is a Catholic liberal arts institution founded by the Sisters of the Congregation of Saint Agnes. It is committed to the education of the whole person.

Community Environment. Situated 54 miles northwest of Milwaukee, Marian College of Fond du Lac, Wisconsin (population 36,000) is located on the edge of the scenic Kettle Moraine region, the dominant glacial formation of Wisconsin. It is less than a mile from Lake Winnebago.

Religious Denomination. Roman Catholic.

Religious Emphasis. Liberal.

Accreditation. North Central Association of Colleges and Schools.

Term System. Semester.

Enrollment in Degree Programs in Religion 1984–85. Total 8; men 2, women 6.

Degrees in Religion Awarded 1984–85. Bachelor of Arts in Religious Studies 4; men 2, women 2.

Faculty for Degree Programs in Religion. Total 3; full-time 3.

Admission Requirements. High school graduation in top 50 percent of class; 2.5 grade point average.

Tuition and Fees. $4,500 per year.

Financial Aid. 80 percent of the student body receives some form of aid.

Housing. Dormitories or apartments are available.

Library Facilities. The library houses over 66,000 volumes and maintains the Holocaust Collection.

Religious Services/Activities. Catholic Eucharistic Liturgies are celebrated daily; retreat/reflection opportunities are scheduled on a regular basis.

Degree Programs

The Bachelor of Arts in Theology degree requires the completion of 128 credits including 39-40 in general studies, 52-53 in electives, and 36 in Theology. Two courses in Philosophy are required. A major in Religious Studies requires 38 credits including two courses in Philosophy.

Marquette University
Theology Department
1201 West Wisconsin Avenue
Milwaukee, WI 53233   (414) 224-7170

Administration. Rev. William J. Kelly, S.J., Acting Chairman, Theology Department; Dr. Richard A. Edwards, Assistant Chairman.

General Description. The Graduate Program in Theology and Religious Studies is Roman Catholic in orientation, but the faculty, student body, and areas of study represent a significant commitment to the whole Christian theological tradition. (At present, one-third of the graduate students in residence are from Evangelical, Lutheran, Anglican, and other non-Roman Catholic Christian traditions.) Emphasis is on learning to theologize, not merely on the mastering of theological content. At the Master and Doctorate level, the student may concentrate in either the biblical, historical, or systematic/ethics areas. At the Doctorate level, it is also possible to do interdisciplinary studies in the Theology and Society Program. Also of note is a special departmental focus on Luther Studies in a Roman Catholic context; this builds on special strengths both in Reformation studies and in patristic and medieval theology.

Parent Institution. Marquette University is a Jesuit, urban institution committed to undergraduate, professional, and graduate education. The founders of Marquette were witness to their belief that, within the arena of higher education, there was room and there was reason for alternative approaches to the higher education mission. Specifically, they judged the propriety of and need for an institution which, in the Jesuit tradition, would provide a Catholic setting for liberal education.

The University was opened in 1881 and conducted under the auspices of the Society of Jesus. It is named for Pere Jacques Marquette, a renowned Jesuit who explored the upper Middle West and the Mississippi River in the 17th century. The University today consists of 13 colleges, schools, and programs.

Community Environment. The 68-acre campus of Marquette University contains 42 major buildings. The city of Milwaukee, the largest city in Wisconsin, is located on the west shore of Lake Michigan and has a population of approximately 718,000.

Religious Denomination. Roman Catholic.

Religious Emphasis. Liberal.

Accreditation. North Central Association of Colleges and Schools.

Term System. Semester; summer term.

Enrollment in Degree Programs in Religion 1984–85. Total 123; men 82; women 41.

Degrees in Religion Awarded 1984–85. Master of Arts 3; men 3. Doctor of Philosophy 8; men 6, women 2.

Faculty for Degree Programs in Religion. Total 36; full-time 27, part-time 9.

Admission Requirements. Preparation for graduate study should preferably be an undergraduate major in theology or religious studies or another appropriate field (e.g., philosophy, classics). Ample opportunities for supplementing incomplete undergraduate preparation in religious studies are available. Ideally, all students should have some familiarity with Scripture and basic Christian teachings. Documents required include GRE scores (aptitude); transcripts; two letters of recommendation (three if financial aid is requested); a statement of foreign language proficiency; for those without graduate degrees, a list of undergraduate theology courses taken; a brief statement of purpose of beginning graduate study in theology.

Tuition and Fees. Tuition $178 per credit hour; various other fees where applicable; room unfurnished $256 per month; board $255 to $790 per semester depending upon meal plan selected (5 to 19 meals per week).

Financial Aid. Several fellowships are available; these are restricted to doctoral candidates. Competition for teaching and research assistantships is open to all graduate students; assistantship awards involve free tuition and an annual stipend (presently about $6,000). Competition for tuition scholarships is open to all graduate students. Applicants for financial aid must submit a special financial aid application in addition to the regular application for admission. Financial aid deadline is February 15.

Housing. Although there is a limited number of one-bedroom and efficiency apartments available on campus, most married graduate and professional students live off-campus in private housing. Facilities on campus generally are not conducive to accommodating children beyond infancy, and families with more than one child may not reside on campus.

Library Facilities. The Marquette University Library system has over 700,000 volumes of books and bound journals and more than 10,000 periodicals, newspapers, and other serials. Theological resources include a basic reference section in theology and religious sources and extensive holdings in the biblical area, patristics, conciliar documents and collections, with special emphasis on the medieval, Reformation, and counter-Reformation sources. In collaboration with the Philosophy Department, a collection of primary sources, commentaries, translations, and critical monographs of the best medieval, modern, and contemporary authors has been developed. The Milwaukee Public Library is located just on the edge of the campus. The libraries of the University of Wisconsin-Milwaukee, St. Francis Seminary, and Nashota House have collections accessible to graduate students.

Religious Services/Activities. The University has established a Campus Ministry program with the specific purpose and responsibility of creating an environment favorable to spiritual growth, of developing a vital faith community, and of encouraging the integration of faith and reason. There are on campus many religiously-oriented organizations, sub-communities, and projects. Specific programs include many and varied liturgies in the Gesu Church, at the St. Joan of Arc Chapel, and in the residence halls; the Marquette University Community Action Program, a student volunteer organization serving the elderly, the sick, and the poor of the Milwaukee area; a program of weekend retreats; the presence of pastoral ministers in each of the residence halls; spiritual, vocational, and personal direction available for everyone interested; faculty dialogue sessions and spiritual enrichment groups such as the Pere Marquette Society; and religious educational opportunities such as Bible study groups, lectures, Lenten series, and different workshops.

Degree Programs

The Master of Arts in Theology candidate may concentrate in Scriptural, Historical, or Systematic Theology. An undergraduate major in theology is required. For those planning to work in Systematic Theology, a minor in philosophy is recommended.

The Doctor of Philosophy candidate may concentrate in Scripture (with emphasis on Old Testament or New Testament), in Historical Theology, or in Systematic Theology (including Christian Ethics). An additional option within the Theology Department exists for doctoral candidates in the area of Theology and Society. Doctoral students electing this option take at least 21 hours of theology courses (primarily in Systematic Theology) selected around this theme, a total of at least 18 hours in Scriptural and Historical Theology, and 15 hours in one or more related human sciences. A total of 60 hours is required, although students may also have to take additional courses to certify their qualifications in both Theology and the allied discipline. Qualifying examinations and dissertation topics for doctoral students in the area of Theology and Society are expected to reflect the cross-disciplinary nature of their course work.

Nashotah House Theological Seminary
2777 Mission Road
Nashotah, WI 53058   (414) 646-3371

Administration. Rt. Rev. Stanley Atkins, Dean and President of Nashotah House.

General Description. Nashotah House is an Episcopal seminary founded in 1842. The course of study is based upon the English system of three years of divinity. The curriculum covers all areas required by the Canon Law and includes classical Greek and Hebrew. The primary mission of the seminary is to introduce future parish priests to the fullness and richness of the Church's tradition by offering a solid grounding in the Biblical, theological, historical, and pastoral dimensions of the Church's heritage. The degrees Master of Divinity, Master of Theological Studies, and Master of Sacred Theology are offered.

Community Environment. Nestled on the shores of Upper Nashotah Lake, 35 miles west of Milwaukee, Nashotah House offers the best of both worlds: a serene campus on 460 wooded acres and a location just a short drive from a large city that offers many nationally recognized performing arts.

Religious Denomination. Episcopal.

Accreditation. Association of Theological Schools in the United States and Canada.

Term System. Trimester; no summer term.

Enrollment in Degree Programs in Religion 1984–85. Total 73; men 65, women 8.

Degrees in Religion Awarded 1984–85. Master of Divinity 22; men 19, women 3.

Faculty for Degree Programs in Religion. Total 16; full-time 8, part-time 8.

Admission Requirements. Persons admitted to the regular Master of Divinity or Master of Theological Studies degree programs must have a baccalaureate degree from an accredited college or university.

Tuition and Fees. Tuition $4,400; room $910; board $2,450.

Financial Aid. Various types of financial assistance are available.

Housing. Dormitories and married student housing are available on campus.

Library Facilities. The library houses over 80,000 volumes. The Underwood Collection of Prayer Books includes an illuminated manuscript.

Religious Services/Activities. The Seminary community gathers daily for Morning Prayer, the Eucharist, and Evensong which form the core of the corporate worship integral to the common life. Quiet Days are scheduled each term, with meditations given by members of the faculty or visiting clergy. One week-long retreat is scheduled each year in October.

Degree Programs

The Master of Divinity degree is a first professional degree program normally of three years duration. The curriculum covers all areas required by Canon Law.

The Master of Theological Studies degree is intended primarily for persons wishing to obtain a basic first professional degree in theological education, but do not plan to seek ordination. The program requires two years of study.

The Master of Sacred Theology program has two purposes: (1) to offer parish clergy an opportunity to extend and deepen their theological understanding and (2) to offer persons contemplating an academic career an opportunity to test that vocation.

Northwestern College
1300 Western Avenue
Watertown, WI 53094   (414) 261-4352

Administration. Carleton Toppe, President.

General Description. It is the purpose of Northwestern College to serve the needs of the Wisconsin Evangelical Lutheran Synod by assisting in the preparation of a preaching ministry qualified to proclaim the Word of God faithfully, effectively, and universally, in accord with the Lutheran Confessions. A fundamental objective is to prepare students qualified to enter Wisconsin Lutheran Seminary. Special emphasis is placed on the study of religion and history, and on ancient and modern languages.

Parent Institution. The College was founded in 1864 and is owned and maintained by the Wisconsin Evangelical Lutheran Synod. It offers a four-year college program.

Community Environment. Watertown has a population of 18,000 and is located in an agricultural and dairying area of Wisconsin. The city is situated in the southeastern resort area of the state.

Religious Denomination. Wisconsin Evangelical Lutheran.

Accreditation. North Central Association of Colleges and Schools.

Term System. Semester.

Admission Requirements. High school graduation or the equivalent of the courses outlined for Northwestern Preparatory School; prerequisites in Latin (four years) and German (two years) must be met.

Tuition and Fees. Tuition $1,610 per year (a portion is refundable); room $285 per semester; board $525 per semester; activities and services fee $42.50 per year.

Financial Aid. The College provides financial assistance to qualified and deserving students who demonstrate need.

Housing. There are three men's dormitories on campus.

Library Facilities. The library contains over 44,000 volumes.

Religious Services/Activities. Regular attendance at a church of the Wisconsin Evangelical Lutheran Synod is required.

Degree Programs

The College curriculum requires a minimum of 149 credit hours for graduation with the Bachelor of Arts degree. Required courses in Religion constitute 20 hours over 8 semesters.

Ripon College
Department of Religion
Ripon, WI 54971   (414) 748-8102

Administration. Professor H. Jerome Thompson, Chair, Department of Religion.

General Description. The Department of Religion offers a major in the field. Preprofessional studies in preparation for special study at a theological seminary are also offered in a balanced liberal arts education.

Parent Institution. Ripon College is a privately supported nondenominational liberal arts college founded in 1851. It is affiliated with the United Church of Christ. The College enrolls about 900 students each year.

Community Environment. Ripon, Wisconsn is the home of 7,000 citizens, several industries, and a modest business community. The Little White Schoolhouse, now a national landmark, is the birthplace of the Republican party founded there in 1854.

Religious Denomination. United Church of Christ.

Accreditation. North Central Association of Colleges and Schools.

Term System. Semester.

Admission Requirements. High school graduation or equivalent; SAT or ACT accepted but not required.

Tuition and Fees. Tuition $7,294 per year; room $780; board $1,320; student fees $100.

Financial Aid. The College has a comprehensive financial aid program.

Housing. Dormitory facilities are available.

Library Facilities. The Lane Library/Wehr Learning Resources Center houses over 150,000 volumes.

Religious Services/Activities. The services and counseling of a chaplain are available to all. The Chapel in Harwood Memorial Union may be used by any groups or individual. Numerous local churches welcome students.

Degree Programs

The major in Religion leading to the Bachelor of Arts degree requires 31 credits including 16 in religion and 12 in Philosophy. It is possible to integrate the major in Religion with off-campus programs at Newberry Library, Madrid, Bonn, or London-Florence.

Sacred Heart School of Theology
7335 South Lovers Lane Road
Hales Corners, WI 53130   (414) 425-8300

Administration. Rev. Thomas J. Garvey, SJC, President/Rector; Rev. Otto Bucher, OFMCap, Vice Rector/ Academic Dean.

General Description. Sacred Heart School of Theology is the largest seminary in the United States specializing in the priestly formation of adult candidates for priesthood in the Roman Catholic Church. It is, therefore, a professional school for the pastoral education of men of mature years and experience preparing for the priesthood. Located on the outskirts of the Milwaukee metropolitan area, the School is owned and maintained by the Sacred Heart Fathers and Brothers. At Sacred Heart, the educational experience has three principal components: academic preparation through theological studies, pastoral preparation through supervised experience, and spiritual and personal formation through community life, worship, and

personal and group spiritual guidance. The Seminary awards the Master of Divinity degree to students holding a BA or BS degree. A Certificate of graduation is awarded to those without the undergraduate degree.

Community Environment. See: Alverno College for information about Milwaukee.

Religious Denomination. Roman Catholic.

Accreditation. Association of Theological Schools in the United States and Canada.

Term System. Semester; summer term.

Enrollment in Degree Programs in Religion 1984-85. Total 100; men 100.

Degrees in Religion Awarded 1984-85. Master of Divinity 16; men 16. Certificate of Graduation 13; men 13.

Faculty for Degree Programs in Religion. Total 19; full-time 15, part-time 4.

Admission Requirements. Sponsorship by either a bishop of a diocese or the major superior of a religious community; Bachelor's degree from an accredited college or university (those older than age 30 with 60 credits from accredited college or university may apply); sponsored students with insufficiencies in academic prerequisites may live at the Sacred Heart School of Theology and enroll in special programs at Cardinal Stritch College; additional requirements available from Director of Admissions.

Tuition and Fees. Tuition per year $3,350; room and board $3,550 per year; nonrefundable application fee $25.

Financial Aid. Veterans Administration benefits available.

Housing. There is dormitory housing for candidates for priesthood.

Library Facilities. The library contains 66,145 volumes with a special collection of 500 volumes on Theology of Sacred Heart.

Religious Services/Activities. Roman Catholic Mass and Adoration celebrated daily; morning and evening prayer on school days; annual retreat; days of recollection (3 per semester); spiritual direction; sacrament of reconciliation by arrangement.

Degree Programs

The Master of Divinity program follows the guidelines of the American Bishops' *Program of Priestly Formation.* The curriculum is designed to provide a knowledge of the broad spectrum of the teaching of the Roman Catholic Church. The academic preparation for the priesthood includes 32 core courses in scripture, systematic theology, pastoral and historical studies, plus 10 hours of electives. Prior knowledge in any of these areas may be accepted through assessment of competence by the Academic Dean and his staff. For some students, a semester of survey courses in philosophy, introduction to theology, preaching and communication skills, plus liturgical music and introduction to worship may be required. Completion of the full academic program normally calls for four years' study before ordination to the diaconate. Each man has a seven-month full-time internship in a parish of his diocese or religious community.

Special Programs

Sacred Heart School of Theology also admits students who have not yet received an undergraduate degree. Men who are 30 years of age or older who have 60 hours of undergraduate credit from an accredited institution may be accepted into the program. Upon completion of all the other requirements of the Master of Divinity degree, these students receive a Certificate of Graduation from the School of Theology.

St. Francis Seminary
School of Pastoral Ministry
3257 South Lake Drive
Milwaukee, WI 53207   (414) 744-1730

Administration. Rev. Daniel J. Pakenham, Rector; Rev. James J. Jarumbo, Dean of Studies.

General Description. St. Francis Seminary is a graduate professional school for the training of priests and lay and religious persons for ministry. Its primary purpose is to provide a priestly formation program for the priesthood in the Archdiocese of Milwaukee and for any other dioceses or religious communities who choose to send candidates. The degrees Master of Divinity and Master of Theological Studies are offered.

Community Environment. St. Francis Seminary is located just south of the city of Milwaukee in the city of St. Francis, on a 100-acre tract of wooded land overlooking Lake Michigan.

Religious Denomination. Roman Catholic.

Accreditation. North Central Association of Colleges and Schools; Association of Theological Schools in the United States and Canada.

Term System. Semester; summer term.

Enrollment in Degree Programs in Religion 1984–85. Total 95; men 60, women 35.

Degrees in Religion Awarded 1984–85. Master of Divinity 12; men 11, women 1. Master of Theological Studies 9; women 9.

Faculty for Degree Programs in Religion. Total 15; full-time 11, part-time 4.

Admission Requirements. Baccalaureate degree; letters of recommendation; interview and psychological testing.

Tuition and Fees. Tuition $110 per credit; additional fees.

Financial Aid. Limited financial assistance is available.

Housing. Campus housing is available only for candidates for the priesthood.

Library Facilities. The Salzmann Library houses over 75,000 volumes with special collections in Theology and Rare Books.

Religious Services/Activities. Daily liturgies are held. The Spiritual Formation Committee assumes the major

responsibility for coordinating the formational activities.

Degree Programs

The Master of Divinity degree is the professional degree required prior to the final recommendation for priestly ordination. The candidate must present 106 credit hours with 90 in the various academic departments (Systematic Theology, Biblical Studies, Historical Studies, Liturgical Studies, Religious Education, Kerygmatic Theology, Theology and Behavioral Science), 2 in Integrating Seminars, 10 in Field Education, and 4 in the Comprehensive Requirement.

The Master of Theological Studies degree is the professional degree awarded to those interested in ministerial service, but not pursuing ordained ministry. The candidate must present 42 credit hours of which 18 credits must be in core curricular requirements and electives in the area of Theological Foundations for Ministry, 18 credits in core curricular requirements and electives in the area of Pastoral Applications to Ministry, and 6 additional elective credit hours.

Silver Lake College of the Holy Family
Religious Studies Department
2406 South Alverno Road
Manitowoc, WI 54220   (414) 684-6691

Administration. Sr. Anne Kennedy, President; Sr. Carol Diederich, Academic Dean; Sr. Ruth Ann Myers, Professor, Religious Studies.

General Description. The Religious Studies Department aims to promote an appreciation of the Judaeo-Christian heritage common to all Christians; to explain Catholic doctrine and give information about other religions so as to foster an ecumenical appreciation of the truths and values which all share; to instill an awareness of the impact of the Good News of salvation on one's personal life and on Christian living in society through theological reflection on Scripture, Church tradition and contemporary culture, and through the acquisition of skills to confront life issues; and to provide adequate preparation for Christian ministry, especially in the areas of catechesis and education.

Parent Institution. Silver Lake College is a four-year liberal arts coeducational college sponsored by the Franciscan Sisters of Christian Charity. It exists to share a liberal arts experience with its students, to provide a career direction fully integrated with the liberal arts, and to assist in the development of its students to become persons who are mature, free, responsible, and prepared both to assume leadership and to give service to others. Silver Lake is presently a commuter college and is the only bachelor degree-granting institution in Manitowoc County. As such, the College considers it a primary thrust of its mission to meet the higher education needs of the county and northeastern Wisconsin constituencies, both

Catholic and others, from whom it receives its greatest support.

Community Environment. The communities of Manitowoc and Two Rivers were founded in 1838 and are located on the shore of Lake Michigan with convenient access to major Wisconsin cities. This thriving industrial community has 37 churches, 3 modern hospitals, museums, and numerous parks and recreation areas.

Religious Denomination. Roman Catholic.

Accreditation. North Central Association of Colleges and Schools.

Term System. Semester; summer term.

Enrollment in Degree Programs in Religion 1984–85. Total 19; men 3, women 16.

Degrees in Religion Awarded 1984–85. Bachelor of Arts 2; women 2.

Faculty for Degree Programs in Religion. Total 5; full-time 1, part-time 4.

Admission Requirements. Applicants are considered individually by an evaluation of their scholastic achievements and potential for success in college. Students are admitted on the basis of high school record and ACT or SAT scores; candidates are expected to rank in the upper two-thirds of their class and have completed a minimum of 16 units of work from an accredited high school including 3 units of English, 2 units of Mathematics, 2 units of History and Social Studies, and 1 unit of Laboratory Science.

Tuition and Fees. Tuition full-time (12 or more credits per semester) $2,200 per semester; part-time tuition varies depending upon number of credits (fewer than 12) and ranges from $85 to $145 per credit. Graduate tuition is also based on number of credits and ranges from $120 to $150 per credit; other fees where applicable.

Financial Aid. In 1984-85, 100 percent of Silver Lake College's full-time students and 67 percent of the half-time students received some form of financial assistance. The average award for full-time students, consisting of grants, scholarships, loans, or campus jobs, was $4,231. The average of grant aid alone was $2,704.

Housing. College-sponsored off-campus housing is available.

Library Facilities. The library contains 57,220 volumes, 22,518 audiovisual materials, and 2,099 reference works. A special collection of juvenile literature numbers 2,919 volumes and a collection of music scores includes 1,073 items.

Religious Services/Activities. Eucharist is celebrated twice weekly. There is an overnight retreat once each semester, plus other religious services and activities as determined by Campus Ministry.

Degree Programs

The Bachelor of Arts with a major in Religious Studies consists of a liberal arts core plus 36 credit hours including Key Concepts in Catholicism I and II; The Mystery of the Church; Catholic Moral Principles; The Sacraments; Old Testament; New Testament; and 15 semester hours of electives in Religious Studies courses.

CANADA

ALBERTA

Alberta, University of
Department of Religious Studies
4-65 Humanities Centre
Edmonton, AB T6G 2E5   (403) 432-2174

General Description. The Department of Religious Studies covers five major religious fields: Judaism, Islam, Hinduism, Japanese and Chinese Religions, and Christianity. In addition, it offers over twenty courses in thematic subjects.

Parent Institution. The University of Alberta is over 80 years old with a full-time enrollment of around 25,000 students. It has Faculties of Agriculture and Forestry, Arts, Business, Dentistry, Education, Engineering, Home Economics, Law, Library Science, Medicine, Nursing, Pharmacy and Pharmaceutical Sciences, Physical Education and Recreation, Rehabilitation Medicine, Science. Graduate studies and research are available in all of these fields.

Community Environment. Edmonton is the provincial capital of Alberta and its largest city. It takes its name from Fort Edmonton, an early trading post of the Hudson Bay Company.

Religious Denomination. Nondenominational.

Accreditation. Provincial accreditation; Association of Commonweatlth Universities; Association of Universities and Colleges of Canada.

Term System. Semester system.

Enrollment in Degree Programs in Religion 1984–85. Total 15; men 8, women 7.

Faculty for Degree Programs in Religion. Total 9; full-time 5, part-time 4.

Admission Requirements. High school education and a provincial examination.

Tuition and Fees. Tuition $937.50 for full-time students; room and board $2,000; student fees $75.

Financial Aid. Some scholarships are available.

Housing. There is student housing for approximately 3,200 students.

Library Facilities. The University Libraries have holdings of over 2 million volumes.

Religious Services/Activities. Activities are at the discretion of campus chaplains and affiliated colleges.

Degree Programs

A major and an honors program in Religious Studies are offered by the Department.

Special Programs

Courses are given off-campus in various towns and cities in the Province of Alberta.

Calgary, University of
Department of Religious Studies
2500 University Drive, N.W.
Calgary, AB T2N 1N4   (403) 220-5886

General Description. The Department of Religious Studies is non-sectarian and intends to serve students who have religious affilations as well as those who do not. The purpose of the Department is educational and academic—one of fostering an informed understanding of the varied and important phenomena of religious belief and practice. Two aspects are stressed. First, there is the acquisition of basic knowledge of the world's major religious traditions (Judaism, Christianity, Islam, Hinduism, and Buddhism). Secondly, opportunity is provided for the discussion of the claims religion makes in relation to life.

The Department has from its inception served as a Biblical and theological resource to the Calgary and area religious communities. The religious communities, through Calgary Inter-Faith Community Action organization, have provided ongoing support for the development of the Department. The Department offers instruction in the field of Religious Studies only. Students may focus their studies on either Eastern Religions, Western Religions, or the Nature of Religion.

Parent Institution. The University of Calgary had its origin in 1945 when the former Normal School became a branch of the Faculty of Education of the University of Alberta in Edmonton. Subsequently, it gained full autonomy.

Community Environment. The 314-acre campus is located in the northwest section of Calgary. The city is the head office stronghold of Canada's oil, gas, and sulphur industries. It is home to more than a half million people and is the fifth largest city in Canada.

Religious Denomination. Nondenominational.

Accreditation. Provincially accredited; Association of Universities and Colleges of Canada.

Term System. Semester system.

Faculty for Degree Programs in Religion. Total 10.

Admission Requirements. High school graduation with 20 academic units required; SAT.

Tuition and Fees. Tuition $808; nonresident tuition $1,-212; room and board $2,800; student fees $92.

Financial Aid. Financial assistance may be available to qualified students.

Housing. Housing is available for 1,000 students.

Library Facilities. The University Libraries house over 1.2 million volumes.

Degree Programs

A major in Religious Studies leading to the Bachelor of Arts degree requires completion of seven to ten full-course equivalents in Religious Studies. If the majority of courses are in the Nature of Religion, the student's program must include at least two full-course equivalents in Eastern Religions and one full-course equivalent in Western Religions, or the reverse.

The Master of Arts degree is offered with focus on either Eastern Religions or Western Religions or the Nature of Religion. The program enables students to obtain the degree by two routes: thesis-based or non-thesis.

Camrose Lutheran College
Department of Religious Studies
4901 46th Avenue
Camrose, AB T4V 2R3   (403) 679-1100

Administration. Dr. Chester L. Olson, Academic Dean.

General Description. The Department of Religious Studies offers undergraduate courses in a liberal arts curriculum. Most of the courses pertain to the Christian tradition.

Parent Institution. Camrose Lutheran College is a residential liberal arts college of the Evangelical Lutheran Church in Canada. It was the first private college in Alberta to receive degree-granting authority under the provisions of legislation enacted in 1984 by the Alberta government. It provides a significant alternative in university education to the four provincial universities, while maintaining an affiliation agreement with the University of Alberta to accommodate transfer students. The College was founded in 1910 by the Alberta Norwegian Lutheran Association.

Community Environment. The College is located on a 40-acre campus in Camrose, a city of 13,000. It is an

hour's drive southeast of Edmonton.

Religious Denomination. Lutheran.

Accreditation. Provincially accredited.

Term System. Two 13-week terms plus examination periods.

Enrollment in Degree Programs in Religion 1984–85. Total 3; men 2, women 1.

Degrees in Religion Awarded 1984–85. Bachelor of Arts 1; men 1.

Faculty for Degree Programs in Religion. Total 5; full-time 3, part-time 2.

Admission Requirements. Grade 12 matriculation average of at least 60 percent in five appropriate subjects, or adult status.

Tuition and Fees. Tuition for Canadian students $1,898; visa students $2,198; room and board $2,808; student activity fees $86.

Financial Aid. An extensive program of financial aid is available. Approximately 75 percent of the student body receive some form of financial aid.

Housing. All students are required to live in College residences for the first two years of their programs. Exceptions are made for students over 21 years of age at the start of the term, married students, and students living with their families in the Camrose area.

Library Facilities. The library maintains a collection of over 50,000 volumes. Students have access to the University of Alberta Library.

Religious Services/Activities. The College community is invited to worship on a regular basis through the chapel program (three mornings and one evening each week) and in connection with important events in College life and the church year. Students also have the opportunity to be involved in a variety of Christian Life programs, including Bible studies, retreats, and service projects in area churches and institutions.

Degree Programs

A major in Religion leading to the Bachelor of Arts degree is offered by the Department.

Canadian Union College
Department of Religious Studies
Box 430
College Heights, AB T0C 0Z0 (403) 782-3381

Administration. Malcolm Graham, President; Reo E. Ganson, Academic Dean; Warren C. Trenchard, Chairman, Division of Humanities.

General Description. The Department of Religious Studies is one of several academic components of the Division of Humanities. The Department provides students with the opportunity for both the objective examination of the phenomenon of religion and its various specific forms as well as the subjective development of a religious experience, from the perspective of Seventh-day Adventist

Christianity. Students are under no obligation to move from the objective level to the subjective. The Department offers three degree programs: Bachelor of Arts in Religious Studies, Regular Track; Bachelor of Arts in Religious Studies, Pre-Ministerial Track; Bachelor of Education, Specialization in Religious Studies.

Parent Institution. Canadian Union College is an institution of higher education which is owned and operated by the Seventh-day Adventist Church in Canada. The College was started in 1907 in Leduc, Alberta, and moved to its present location near Lacombe, in 1909. It offers Baccalaureate degrees in the Arts, Sciences, and Education, as well as Associate Degrees in several disciplines. The College maintains affiliation agreements with the University of Alberta in Edmonton, and with Union College of Lincoln, Nebraska.

Community Environment. The present location of Canadian Union College is on a hilltop overlooking miles of the surrounding countryside and consisting of a campus and farm of almost 3,000 acres, two miles north of Lacombe, Alberta.

Religious Denomination. Seventh-day Adventist.

Religious Emphasis. Conservative.

Accreditation. Currently being reviewed for accreditation by the Alberta Private Colleges Accreditation Board.

Term System. Semester; summer term.

Enrollment in Degree Programs in Religion 1984–85. Total 52; men 51, women 1.

Degrees in Religion Awarded 1984–85. Bachelor of Arts 10; men 9, women 1.

Faculty for Degree Programs in Religion. Total 5; full-time 3, part-time 2.

Admission Requirements. Possession of an Alberta Advanced High School Diploma or equivalent.

Tuition and Fees. Tuition $2,375 per semester; room and board $1,235 per semester.

Financial Aid. The Department annually awards several scholarships of $500 each. In addition to this, the college provides most students with work opportunities in industrial and other types of jobs.

Housing. The College provides single student housing in dormitories and married student housing in apartments and separate homes.

Library Facilities. The library maintains special collections of 4,900 volumes in Religious Studies, approximately 1,000 volumes in Seventh-day Adventist heritage, and subscribes to 93 journals in Religious Studies.

Religious Services/Activities. Religious services conducted on the campus are administered by the Seventh-day Adventist Church. The Department also sponsors an annual retreat in a Rocky Mountain foothills setting.

Degree Programs

The regular track of the Bachelor of Arts degree in Religious Studies is designed to provide students with a broad introduction to the various subdisciplines in the field of religious studies, with particular emphasis on the

Christian religion. It may also be used as a first or second major by students pursuing a pre-professional curriculum. Students who complete this track will be prepared to engage in graduate studies in the field of Religion or to enroll in professional education, including seminary training.

The pre-ministry track of the Bachelor of Arts degree in Religious Studies is an extension of the regular track. It is designed to serve as the first step in training for the pastoral ministry as outlined by the North American Division of the Seventh-day Adventist Church. Students who complete this track will be specifically prepared to continue their professional training for the pastoral ministry at the seminary level. They will meet the entrance requirements of the Seventh-day Adventist Theological Seminary at Andrews University.

The Bachelor of Education degree with specialization in Religious Studies is a program intended to prepare the student to teach religion in secondary education.

Concordia Lutheran Seminary
7040 Ada Boulevard
Edmonton, AB T5B 4E3   (403) 474-1468

Administration. Dr. W. Theo Janzow, President.

General Description. The chief purpose of Concordia Lutheran Seminary is to prepare students for the pastoral ministry of the Lutheran Church-Missouri Synod and, in particular, for the Lutheran Church-Canada. Students who successfully complete the pastoral training program receive both a degree and certification for eligibility to receive a call into the pastoral ministry of the Synod and the Lutheran Church-Canada. The Seminary also offers a program for people who desire to grow in theological knowledge and understanding but who do not desire or are ineligible to enter the pastoral ministry of the Synod. The Seminary also seeks to provide helpful opportunities for continued learning to clergy and laity, through summer courses, institutes, and workshops.

The Seminary began its first academic year with a divine worship service held at Grace Lutheran Church, Edmonton, on Sunday, September 9, 1984. The first classes met on the following day. The Seminary currently operates out of two buildings. It has initiated a study to identify a future site and to make plans for a more permanent facility that would satisfy the Seminary's needs for many years to come.

Community Environment. Edmonton is the provincial capital of Alberta and its largest city. It takes its name from Fort Edmonton, an early trading post of the Hudson Bay Company. The city is the center of an important farming, oil and gas, and coal mining area, as well as manufacturing.

Religious Denomination. Lutheran Church-Missouri Synod.

Religious Emphasis. Confessional.

Accreditation. Association of Theological Schools in the

United States and Canada (Candidate).

Term System. Semester; winter and spring short terms; three summer terms.

Enrollment in Degree Programs in Religion 1984–85. Total 13; men 13.

Degrees in Religion Awarded 1984–85. Theology Diploma 1; men 1.

Faculty for Degree Programs in Religion. Total 5; full-time 3, part-time 2.

Admission Requirements. Bachelor of Arts degree plus one year each of Greek and Hebrew.

Tuition and Fees. Tuition $75 per semester credit hour; library fee $15 per semester; student activity fee $30 per semester; one time orientation fee $25 for full-time student.

Financial Aid. Grants-in-Aid are available. Ordinarily aid is offered only to students who are enrolled on a full-time basis. Students who are preparing for the pastoral ministry of the Lutheran Church-Missouri Synod receive a church worker scholarship of $10 per semester credit hour.

Housing. Students must arrange for their own housing accommodation.

Library Facilities. The library houses 4,000 volumes.

Religious Services/Activities. The College has a program of campus worship and personal counseling. It encourages informal Bible study and intercessory prayers. The Lutheran Life Lectures are held in October; the Timothy Lectures in March. There are daily chapel devotions.

Degree Programs

The Bachelor of Theology is a four-year degree designed for people who seek to serve in the pastoral ministry of the Lutheran Church-Missouri Synod but who are 35 years of age or older. The curriculum is the same as for the Master of Divinity program.

The Master of Divinity degree is a four-year program designed for people who seek to serve in the pastoral ministry of the Lutheran Church-Missouri Synod. Candidates must show evidence of their commitment to Christian ministry, be of good character, and enjoy satisfactory health. All students must complete a specified number of hours in each of the major theological disciplines: Exegetical, Systematic, Historical, Practical. All students must select a concentration in one major academic area from among the following: Old Testament Exegesis, New Testament Exegesis, Systematics, Historical Theology, Practical Theology. A total of 112 semester hours credit is required for the degree.

The Master of Theological Studies is a two-year program restricted to people not seeking certification for the Lutheran Church-Missouri Synod pastoral ministry. Students must complete 60 semester hours of work over a six-year period in specified courses.

Special Programs

Applying students who meet the criteria for admission to either the Master of Divinity or the Bachelor of Theology degree programs and who indicate a desire to be certified for the pastoral ministry of the Lutheran Church-Missouri Synod upon graduation, may be admitted as candidates for certification according to specific guidelines.

St. Stephen's College
University of Alberta Campus
Edmonton, AB T6G 2J6   (403) 439-7311

General Description. St. Stephen's College is an institution for graduate studies in the field of professional ministry and a center for continuing education for professional clergy. It also provides courses in theology and religious studies for undergraduate university students and maintains a number of national institute programs for clerical and lay leadership in the church. St. Stephen's College pre-dates the formation of Alberta as a province. Originally established when the area was among the Territories, it provided post-high school education in a variety of subjects until a university was founded. Then it subsequently became a theological school for the basic training of ministers, and since 1968 has pursued its present mandate. The College offers the degrees Master in Theology, Master of Theological Studies, and Doctor of Ministry. Also offered is the Certificate in Theological Studies.

Community Environment. Edmonton is the provincial capital of Alberta and its largest city. It takes its name from Fort Edmonton, an early trading post of the Hudson Bay Company.

Religious Denomination. United Church of Canada.

Religious Emphasis. Ecumenical in polity and practice; liberal (post-modern).

Term System. Semester.

Degrees in Religion Awarded 1984–85. Certificate in Theological Studies 2; women 2. Doctor of Ministry 1; men 1.

Faculty for Degree Programs in Religion. Total 15; full-time 3, part-time 12.

Admission Requirements. For advanced professional degrees at the Master's and Doctoral levels, a professional Master's degree is required. For undergraduate university courses, University admission is required. For special programs (continuing education and lay program), high school matriculation or its equivalent.

Tuition and Fees. Tuition $150 per course; Master's program $650 (plus course fees); Doctor of Ministry $3,800.

Financial Aid. Bursarization of course fee; no direct financial aid to students.

Housing. Guest House accommodation provided for participants in short-term courses ($15 per night, includes housekeeping facilities). No semester-long accommodation available.

Library Facilities. The library contains 12,626 volumes. The Dalgleish Collection includes old and rare religious books and Bibles.

Religious Services/Activities. An extensive and varied range of activities with a variety of denominations are offered, including retreats, collegia, and one-day events.

Degree Programs

The Master of Theology degree is designed for Albertans at any level of professional ministry who desire to follow disciplined and measurable academic and professional studies on a part-time basis while continuing in their regular vocational duties. The candidate undertakes a program of courses, directed reading, directed projects, or supervised experience equivalent to a full academic year of higher education. Normally this consists of 8 semester-length courses (approximately 40 hours each). Candidates select courses covering a broad spectrum of the classical theological disciplines with five courses in the area of specialization elected for the dissertation.

The Doctor of Ministry degree is pursued in phases: the Exploratory Phase and the Candidacy Phase. The Candidacy Phase offers two streams: (1) the Pastoral Ministry Stream which consists of an Interdisciplinary Study of Ministry, coursework, practicum, collegium, and a professional paper; (2) the Institutional Ministry Stream which consists of Interdisciplinary Study of the Ministry and Supervised Pastoral Education.

Special Programs

The Certificate in Theological Studies is for persons who do not seek ordination and is at the level of the Master of Divinity. The equivalent of two acadmeic years of study or 60 credits is required.

Other special programs include the Institute on Christian Education in the Canadian Context in conjunction with the Centre for Christian Studies in Toronto; the Canadian program for Supervision in Ministry at alternating locations across Canada; and an annual multi-staff workshop entitled The Institute on the Management of Ministry.

BRITISH COLUMBIA

Carey Hall Baptist College

5920 Iona Drive

Vancouver, BC V6T 1J6   (604) 224-4308

Administration. Philip Collins, Principal.

General Description. Carey Hall Baptist College is a small graduate college on the campus of the University of British Columbia. It was established in March 1959 by "an Act to incorporate Carey Hall" by the Provincial Legislature. The College began operations in 1960 and in 1980 a graduate program of studies was initiated as well as a program of continuing education. The College is evangelical and fully committed to the historic Christian faith. Its purpose is to serve the churches of the Baptist Union of Western Canada and to contribute to the renewal of the institutional church in Canada. The College is affiliated with the University of British Columbia through its Regent College.

Parent Institution. The College is in the truest sense a denominational school. Although normally administered by its Board of Administration and Senate, the Baptist Union of Western Canada has the final word on its ministry. The Baptist Union is one of the four conventions which make up the Canadian Baptist Federation. This parent body of 21,000 members and 164 churches reflects an evangelical faith with a strong commitment to mission and outreach, with ministry carried on in a spirit of liberty and mutual trust.

Community Environment. Vancouver is the the major city of western Canada. It has a superb natural harbor. Many cultural and historical attractions are available.

Religious Denomination. Baptist Union of Western Canada.

Religious Emphasis. Evangelical; Conservative; Centrist.

Accreditation. Association of Theological Schools in the United States and Canada.

Term System. Semester system.

Enrollment in Degree Programs in Religion 1984–85. Total 27; men 24, women 3.

Degrees in Religion Awarded 1984–85. Master of Divinity 6; men 5, women 1.

Faculty for Degree Programs in Religion. Total 3; 5 sessional lecturers.

Admission Requirements. Students are admitted through Regent College of the University of British Columbia.

Tuition and Fees. Tuition and fees $3,100.

Financial Aid. Financial aid is available through bursaries and special funds.

Housing. A residence is maintained for 38 men under the general supervision of the Residential Dean.

Library Facilities. Carey Hall is developing, along with Regent College, a separate entity to be known as the Regent College/Carey Hall Library Society. Currently, there are 25,000 circulating volumes. A special Baptist/Anabaptist Reference Library is also under development. Students have access to the University of British Columbia libraries.

Religious Services/Activities. The College participates in the chaplaincies on the campus of the University of British Columbia. Union churches maintain a special witness on campus.

Degree Programs

The Master of Divinity degree is a three-year program, particularly suited for those who intend to enter full-time Christian service, at home or overseas, whether ordained or not. This program is completed in cooperation with Regent College.

Special Programs

A Certificate in Ministry is a two-year program, open to those persons for whom normal requirements for ordination are not expected, who are past the age of 34, or for those pastors and lay people who seek growth and renewal in ministry. For each student, a program is designed to provide a balance of academic Biblical studies and competence in the practice of ministry.

Vancouver School of Theology
6000 Iona Drive
Vancouver, BC V6T 1L4   (604) 228-9031

Administration. The Rev. A. Van Seters, Principal; The Rev. T.R. Anderson, Vice Principal; The Rev. W.J. Phillips, Director of Advanced Study in Ministry.

General Description. Vancouver School of Theology is a graduate center for theological education, serving various Christian denominations. The main three participating (sponsoring) denominations are the Anglican Church of Canada, the United Church of Canada, and the Presbyterian Church in Canada. The School grants the degrees Master of Divinity, Master of Theological Studies, and Master of Theology.

Community Environment. Vancouver School of Theology is located on the campus of The University of British Columbia in Vancouver. The city is well favored in its setting of ocean and mountains. It is a cosmopolitan city with many ethnic groups comprising its population.

Religious Denomination. Ecumenical Christian Churches; sponsored by the Anglican Church of Canada, the United Church of Canada, and the Presbyterian Church in Canada.

Religious Emphasis. Liberal.

Accreditation. Association of Theological Schools in the United States and Canada.

Term System. Semester; summer term.

Enrollment in Degree Programs in Religion 1984–85. Total 113; men 43, women 70.

Degrees in Religion Awarded 1984–85. Master of Divinity 19; men 8, women 11. Master of Theological Studies 4; men 3, women 1.

Faculty for Degree Programs in Religion. Total 18; full-time 15, part-time 3.

Admission Requirements. Bachelor's degree.

Tuition and Fees. Tuition $1,500.

Financial Aid. Bursaries and student aid are available as determined by the Student Aid Officer.

Housing. Dormitory rooms are available for single students as well as some suites for married students. Off-campus housing is readily available.

Library Facilities. The library contains over 71,000 volumes and subscribes to 325 current periodicals. A special slide collection of Religious Art is maintained.

Religious Services/Activities. Morning and Evening Prayer (Anglican); once weekly United Church service; once weekly community worship; fall and spring retreats.

Degree Programs

Studies in theological education are pursued at four levels. Level I refers to the student's lengthy period of growth in understanding in family, church, and general experience together with academic education to a first university degree. Level II presupposes the preparation provided by Level I and involves intensive study in the basic theological disciplines. Level III provides specialized training for ministry which will sharpen theological awareness and increase competence in various forms of professional ministry. It involves responsible field work in parish and community and in hospital settings, together with continuing study in the various theological disciplines. The Level III program requires one year. Graduating students receive the degree of Master of Divinity in recognition of the completion of Levels II and III. Selected older students who do not hold a prior degree receive the degree of Bachelor of Theology in recognition of the completion of Levels II and III together with a program of university level courses. Level IV programs include continuing education and degree study leading to the Master of Theology degree.

MANITOBA

Brandon University
Department of Religion
270 - 18th Street
Brandon, MB R7A 6A9   (204) 728-9520

Administration. Dr. E.J. Tyler, President; Dr. P.J.C. Hordern, Dean of Arts; Dr. R.E. Florida, Chairman, Department of Religion.

General Description. The Department of Religion is a nondenominational department of religious studies which emphasizes the academic study of religion using the methods of humanities and the social sciences. Both ancient and modern world religions are studied. Also offered are scriptural languages, both Western and Asian. The Bachelor of Arts with a major in Religion is awarded.

Parent Institution. Brandon University is a coeducational, nondenominational, government-supported institution within the Province of Manitoba. Originally founded as a Baptist college in 1898, Brandon became independent in 1967.

Community Environment. The city of Brandon, with a population of 40,000, is located in the heart of the prairie land of Manitoba, on the Assiniboine River. The Manitoba Provincial Exhibition is held in Brandon every year. There are excellent recreational facilities in the nearby area, including camping, hunting, winter sports, and fishing. Brandon is easily accessible by rail and road.

Religious Denomination. Nondenominational.

Religious Emphasis. Academic study of religion.

Accreditation. Association of Universities and Colleges of Canada.

Enrollment in Degree Programs in Religion 1984–85. Total 11; men 6, women 5.

Degrees in Religion Awarded 1984–85. Bachelor of Arts in Religion 1; women 1.

Faculty for Degree Programs in Religion. Total 4; full-time 3, part-time 1.

Admission Requirements. High school graduation as recognized by the Manitoba Department of Educaton; application for admission on the basis of certificates from out of the province will be considered on their merits.

Students from the United States are expected to have completed a Grade 12 program with a C average or better.

Tuition and Fees. Tuition $89.25 for 3 credit hours (Canadian dollars); student union fee $5.50 per 3 credits; building fund fee $2.50 per 3 credits; athletic fee $1.75 per 3 credits.

Financial Aid. Scholarships, bursaries, prizes, and awards are available.

Housing. The University provides residence for 570 undergraduate students.

Library Facilities. The John E. Robbins Library contains more than 330,000 volumes of print material, 2,500 periodical titles, and 150,000 microfilm and non-print materials.

Religious Services/Activities. Various nearby churches seek out students attending the University.

Degree Programs

A Bachelor of Arts with a Religion major is offered and requires a minimum of 48 credit hours in Religion courses in a four-year program. A three-year major must complete a minimum of 30 credit hours in Religion courses. Specific requirements in both programs must be met.

Winnipeg, University of
Faculty of Theology
515 Portage Avenue
Winnipeg, MB R3B 2E9   (204) 786-9390

Administration. A. McKibbin Watts, Dean.

General Description. The Faculty of Theology of The University of Winnipeg is a continuing education center for clergy and laity. Education for the ministry is available in both degree and non-degree programs. Degree programs are for those clergy who are seminary graduates and wish to continue their education while engaged in ministry. In addition, there is a program for church members; a Certificate may be obtained by those successfully completing a prescribed number of courses in this "Lay Theology" program. The Faculty awards the degrees Master of Divinity, Master of Sacred Theology, and cooperates with St. Stephen's College, Edmonton, in offering courses for the Doctor of Ministry degree of that institution. The Bachelor of Theology degree may be awarded in special circumstances.

Community Environment. The location of the University of Winnipeg in a large metropolitan city on the prairies attracts students from a variety of ministries. The issues which arise from ministering in the urban, town, and rural contexts are themes in the curriculum. Hospitals in Winnipeg, Brandon, and Winkler enrich the clinical settings for supervised pastoral education.

Religious Denomination. United Church, Ecumenical.

Religious Emphasis. Orthodox.

Accreditation. Associate Member of the Association of Theological Schools in the United States and Canada.

Term System. Semester; summer term.

Enrollment in Degree Programs in Religion 1984–85. Total 34; men 29, women 5.

Degrees in Religion Awarded 1984–85. Master of Divinity 1; men 1. Master of Sacred Theology 3; men 2, women 1.

Faculty for Degree Programs in Religion. Total 4.

Admission Requirements. Bachelor of Arts degree; Master of Sacred Theology program requires a Bachelor of Arts and a Master of Divinity degree.

Tuition and Fees. Tuition $345 per academic course plus admission fee $15.

Financial Aid. Bursaries and scholarships available.

Library Facilities. The library contains 29,905 volumes.

Degree Programs

The Master of Divinity degree is the first professional degree for ministry. The Faculty does not have a full program to prepare for this degree. However, under the following conditions a candidate will be accepted: completion of work at a recognized theological school equivalent to at least 10 out of 15 courses toward the degree, in which case the candidate will be required to complete five full courses with the Faculty.

The Master of Sacred Theology degree is awarded upon the completion of a total of six courses plus a minor thesis/project. A minimum of three courses must be taken in the area of specialization (Biblical Studies, Historical and Contemporary Theology, Pastoral Care and Counseling, Applied Theology).

Special Programs

The Lay Theological Education Program is designed for all who seek educational opportunities at a more advanced level but who do not wish to take regular University courses. Courses are offered in Biblical Studies, Theology and Church History, Worship, Christian Education, the Helping Arts, Ethics, and Leadership Development.

For those who wish to pursue a course of studies and have recognition of their work at the end, the Certificate of Theology is awarded. Ten 14-hour courses and one

28-week, 180 hour program are required. Candidates specialize in one of four core areas: Christian in Society, Pastoral Care, Christian Leadership, and Church Leadership.

NOVA SCOTIA

Acadia Divinity College
Acadia University
Highland Avenue
Wolfville, NS B0P 1X0   (902) 542-2285

Administration. Dr. Andrew D. MacRae, Principal and Dean.

General Description. Acadia Divinity College exists primarily to train men and women for a wide range of professional Christian ministries. The College was founded in 1968 as a successor to the Acadia University School of Theology. In its affiliate relationship to Acadia University, it has grown rapidly. Its training equips students for pastoral ministry, religious education, prison chaplaincy, hospital chaplaincy, overseas missions, and other service related to the Church.

Parent Institution. Acadia University was founded by the Atlantic Baptist Convention in 1838 and since 1966 has functioned as a secular university in the provinical setting of Nova Scotia. It offers baccalaureate programs in Arts, Science, Business Administration, Education, Engineering, Nutrition and Home Economics, Music, Recreation and Physical Education, and Secretarial Science. It offers graduate studies in the Arts, Science, Education, and Theology.

Community Environment. The campus is located in the Annapolis Valley town of Wolfville, 100 kilometers northwest of Halifax.

Religious Denomination. Baptist.

Religious Emphasis. Evangelical.

Accreditation. Association of Theological Schools of the United States and Canada.

Term System. Semester system.

Enrollment in Degree Programs in Religion 1984–85. Total 95; men 75, women 20.

Degrees in Religion Awarded 1984–85. Master of Arts in Theology 3; men 3. Master of Theology 4; men 4. Master of Divinity 77; men 65, women 12. Master of Religious Education 8; men 2, women 6.

Faculty for Degree Programs in Religion. Total 10; full-time 7, part-time 3.

Admission Requirements. Bachelor of Arts or equivalent (except for the Bachelor of Theology undergraduate program for persons over 30 years of age).

Tuition and Fees. Tuition $1,540; room and board $3,-000; student fees $20.

Financial Aid. Some bursary support based on need.

Housing. Dormitories are available on campus; apartment housing off campus.

Library Facilities. The library contains over 200,000 volumes.

Religious Services/Activities. Chapel is held twice weekly in Divinity College and 4 times weekly in the University Chapel.

Degree Programs

Degree programs offered include Master of Arts in Theology, Master of Theology, Master of Divinity, and Master of Religious Education.

Atlantic School of Theology
640 Francklyn Street
Halifax, NS B3H 3B5   (902) 423-6801

General Description. The Atlantic School of Theology is an ecumenical school of Theology and Christian Ministry. It was founded in 1971 by Holy Heart Theological Institute (Roman Catholic), Pine Hill Divinity Hall (United Church of Canada), and University of King's College (Anglican Church of Canada) to provide for training for Christian ministries and opportunities for theological study within the context of a community of faith. The basic degrees offered are the Master of Divinity and the Master of Theological Studies.

Community Environment. The metropolitan area of Halifax has a population of 300,000. It is Canada's major commercial and naval port on the Atlantic and is recognized as an important educational and cultural location in the nation.

Religious Denomination. Roman Catholic; United Church of Canada; Anglican Church of Canada.

Accreditation. American Association of Theological

Schools in the United States and Canada.

Term System. Semester.

Admission Requirements. Bachelor's degree from a recognized college or university.

Tuition and Fees. Tuition $1,540; room and board $3,000; student fees $20.

Financial Aid. Financial assistance is available in the form of funds from the Churches for which the student is a candidate for ministry as well as government loans and grants.

Housing. Dormitory facilities are available.

Library Facilities. The combined libraries of the founding colleges have holdings of over 60,000 volumes. The libraries of Holy Heart and Pine Hill were merged at Pine Hill in 1972; King's retains its own library. Resources are shared among the member Colleges.

Religious Services/Activities. Various services of the member Colleges are held.

Dalhousie University
Department of Comparative Religion
Dunn Science Building, Room 313
Halifax, NS B3H 3J5   (902) 424-3579

General Description. The Department of Comparative Religion places emphasis on a comparative study of religion. Beginning in the fall of 1986, both a three-year and a four-year major degree program will be available.

Parent Institution. Dalhousie University offers both undergraduate and graduate programs in many fields of study. The overall emphasis in the Faculty of Arts and Science is on a broad liberal arts program with a major in one of the disciplines chosen by the student, usually in the second year of study. Although founded by the Earl of Dalhousie in 1818, the University did not function fully until 1863. Dalhousie University is a private institution administered by a board of governors and a senate. The University is closely associated with the University of King's College, with which a joint Faculty of Arts and Science is maintained.

Community Environment. The University is located on a 60-acre campus in southwest Halifax.

Religious Denomination. Nondenominational.

Term System. Two terms.

Enrollment in Degree Programs in Religion 1984–85. Total 2; men 2.

Degrees in Religion Awarded 1984–85. Bachelor of Arts 1; men 1.

Faculty for Degree Programs in Religion. Total 2.

Admission Requirements. High school graduation; applicants from the United States must have completed 30 credit hours at a recognized American university.

Tuition and Fees. Tuition C$1,400 for the full year (September-April). A differential may be added for foreign students.

Financial Aid. Scholarships, bursaries, and loans are available to students on a competitive and need basis.

Housing. Dormitories on campus are available.

Library Facilities. The library houses approximately 1 million volumes.

Religious Services/Activities. There are chaplains from the major Christian denominations on campus, as well as a Jewish Rabbi.

ONTARIO

Dominican College of Philosophy and Theology
Faculty of Theology (Ottawa) and Institute of Pastoral Studies (Montreal)
96, Avenue Empress
Ottawa, ON K1R 7G3   (613) 233-5696

Administration. Dr. Michel Gourgues, Dean of the Faculty of Theology.

General Description. In 1909 the Order of Friars Preachers (Rome) recognized the College as a "stadium generale" of the order, or a public center for higher studies in philosophy and theology, empowered to grant degrees to the future teachers of those subjects in the Order. In 1965, the Holy See established the Department of Theology as a pontifical university faculty with the power to grant to students of the Dominican Order the canonical degrees of Bachelor, Master, and Doctor in Theology.

Parent Institution. Dominican College is a private university institution, owned by a board of governors and incorporated in the province of Ontario since 1909. In 1967 it took its present name, Dominican College of Philosophy and Theology.

Community Environment. Selected by Queen Victoria as the Canadian capital in 1854, Ottawa today has a population of 300,000 with a metropolitan population of close to 500,000. The national performing arts center is located in Ottawa, providing numerous opportunities for cultural enrichment.

Religious Denomination. Roman Catholic.

Accreditation. Association of Universities and Colleges of Canada; F.I.U.C.

Term System. Semester; summer term in July.

Enrollment in Degree Programs in Religion 1984–85. Total 715; men 228, women 487.

Degrees in Religion Awarded 1984–85. Master of Theology 4; men 2, women 2. Bachelor of Theology 11; men 9, women 2. Bachelor of Pastoral Theology 2; men 1, women 1. Bachelor of Pastoral Education 8; men 7, women 1. Certificate of Theology 4; men 2, women 2. Certificate in Pastoral Studies 46; men 2, women 44.

Faculty for Degree Programs in Religion. Total 24; full-time 14, part-time 10.

Admission Requirements. To first degree courses: applicants who have spent 1 year in a Faculty of Arts of a recognized university will be considered. Bachelor of Pastoral Theology: DEC plus 60 credits in theological studies or equivalent. Bachelor of Pastoral Education: DEC plus 2 certificates in pastoral studies. Higher degrees: Applicant must normally hold a Bachelor of Arts degree or have completed equivalent studies. Mature age entry: Those without normal requirements may be considered for mature matriculation. Applicants must normally have been away from full-time study for at least two years and must be at lest 21 years old.

Tuition and Fees. Tuition $468 per semester; $35 per credit.

Financial Aid. Students may apply for Ontario or Quebec financial aid to students.

Housing. The College does not provide any accommodation but the Convent of Friars Preachers offers room and board to 25 male students.

Library Facilities. The library houses over 85,000 volumes and subscribes to 500 periodicals.

Religious Services/Activities. Students are free to participate in the religious activities of the adjoining chapel of the Friars Preachers in Ottawa.

Degree Programs

Requirements for the various degrees are as follows: Bachelor of Theology, 3 years from the first year of arts - 90 credits. Bachelor of Pastoral Theology, 1 year DEC plus 2 certificates in Pastoral Studies. Bachelor of Pastoral Education, 2 years from the first year of arts. Master of Theology, 1 year full-time after the B.Th.; by course of instruction, examination, and thesis after residence. Master of Pastoral Theology, 1 year full-time after the B.Th.Past. or equivalent, by course of thesis in approved topic. Master of Arts in Theology, 2 years full-time after B.Th.; by course of instruction, examination, and thesis after residence topic. Licentiate in Sacred Theology, 2 years after B.Th.; by course of instruction, examination, and dissertation after residence in approved topic. Ph.D.

in Theology, 2 years full-time after M.Th.; by course of instruction, examination, and thesis after residence in approved topic.

Special Programs

In order to grant access to the regular lectures of the Faculty by a wider public, some courses are given in the evening and Saturdays and during the month of July. They are the "optional" portion of the 90 credits required for the Bachelor of Theology (the basic program being 72 credits).

Emmanuel College of Victoria University
75 Queen's Park Crescent, East
Toronto, ON M5S 1K7   (416) 978-3811

Administration. C. Douglas Jay, Principal.

General Description. Emmanuel College is the faculty of theology of Victoria University and is a founding member of the federation of seven theological colleges at the University of Toronto which came together in 1969 to form the Toronto School of Theology. Emmanuel College and its parent institution, Victoria University, are federated within the University of Toronto and are related to the United Church of Canada. *See:* Toronto School of Theology.

Parent Institution. Victoria University was founded in 1836 by the Methodist Church of Canada. In the 19th century it had four faculties: arts and science, medicine, law, and theology. When it became federated with the University of Toronto, the faculties of medicine and law were subsumed under those of the University of Toronto, and the faculty of arts and science became a federated member of the Faculty of Arts and Science of the University of Toronto.

Community Environment. Toronto is a major city of inland Canada. It is situated on Lake Ontario and offers a great variety of cultural and historical attractions.

Religious Denomination. United Church of Canada.

Religious Emphasis. Liberal.

Accreditation. Association of Theological Schools in the United States and Canada.

Term System. Semester system.

Enrollment in Degree Programs in Religion 1984–85. Total 217; men 130, women 87.

Degrees in Religion Awarded 1984–85. Master of Divinity 30; men 18, women 12. Master of Religious Education 5; men 3, women 2. Master of Theology 4; men 4.

Faculty for Degree Programs in Religion. Total 18; full-time 11, part-time 7.

Admission Requirements. An appropriate Bachelor's degree is required for the basic degrees (Master of Divinity and Master of Religious Education). The Master of Theology degree requires B-plus standing in a Master of Divinity program. The Doctor of Ministry degree requires B-plus standing in a Master of Divinity degree plus 5 years' satisfactory exercise of ministry. The Doctor of Theology requires first class standing in the Master of Divinity or Master of Theology.

Tuition and Fees. Tuition: Master of Divinity and Master of Religious Education $1,380 (Canadian), visa students $5,265 per year (10-course program); Master of Theology and Doctor of Theology $268 (Canadian), visa students $691 per semester course; Master of Arts and Doctor of Philosophy $343 (Canadian), visa students $735 per semester course; Doctor of Ministry $3,150 (Canadian), visa students $3,605.

Financial Aid. Scholarships and bursaries are available on application.

Housing. Residences with board are available for single men and women students. Married students may be accommodated in apartments under the authority of the University of Toronto.

Library Facilities. The library houses 59,081 volumes. Special collections include a Wesleyana Collection and a collection on Canadian Church History.

Religious Services/Activities. Daily chapel services; weekly communion services; retreats several times a year.

Degree Programs

Degrees available include Master of Divinity, Master of Religious Education, Master of Theology, and Doctor of Ministry.

Huron College
University of Western Ontario
The Faculty of Theology
1349 Western Road
London, ON N6G 1H3   (519) 438-7224

Administration. The Reverend Dr. Donald F. Irvine, Dean of Theology.

General Description. The Faculty of Theology is a community of teachers and students helping to equip men and women for the ministry of the church with particular attention to the Anglican/Episcopal denominational family. Huron College has prepared many candidates now serving in the priesthood within the Anglican Communion throughout the world. Most of the graduates serve in parish ministries, but some find their ministry in hospitals, universities, and correctional institutions. Others see their theological training as preparation for a more effective lay ministry. Community life at the College is enhanced by the ecumenical relationships. Baptist, Presbyterian, and United Church students may complete a portion of their theological training at Huron. Students may elect to take courses at St. Peter's Roman Catholic Seminary or in some other graduate professional faculty. The theological program leads to the Master of Divinity degree.

Parent Institution. Huron College was founded in 1863 and is fully recognized by the General Synod of the Anglican Church of Canada for the training of ordinands. The College is also affiliated with the University of Western Ontario. In 1963, Huron College celebrated its centennial year and continues to serve the Church by the care with which men are prepared for the ministry. The motto of Huron College is carved in oak on the lintel of the main door, *True Religion and Sound Learning.*

Community Environment. The city of London, Ontario has a population of approximately 225,000. It is located on the Thames River, midway between Windsor and Toronto. Although London is an industrial city, there are excellent recreational facilities throughout the surrounding area. The city is known as the "Forest City" because of its 1,500 acres of parkland and shady thoroughfares.

Religious Denomination. Anglican Church of Canada.

Religious Emphasis. Liberal.

Accreditation. Association of Theological Schools in the United States and Canada.

Term System. Semester.

Enrollment in Degree Programs in Religion 1984–85. Total 61; men 38, women 23.

Degrees in Religion Awarded 1984–85. Master of Divinity 10; men 9, women 1.

Faculty for Degree Programs in Religion. Total 16; full-time 6, part-time 10.

Admission Requirements. Bachelor of Arts degree; sponsorship or endorsement by an appropriate church authority is important for those students who are preparing for ordination to the ministry.

Tuition and Fees. Tuition $1,034 full-time; $206.80 per course part-time.

Financial Aid. Financial aid is available for students progressing through the theological program and normally to students who are entering the second year.

Housing. Standard university residences are available for single students applying to the program. A seminary apartment will house approximately 8 single divinity students. Married students and their families can find accommodation in Platt's Lane Estates, a development of student townhouses and apartments located near the College.

Library Facilities. The Silcox Memorial Library is the academic center of the college. It contains 116,000 volumes on two stack levels and maintains a periodical collection of over 250 current titles. The major holdings are in theology with a particularly strong collection in the humanities and social sciences emphasizing English literature, history, philosophy, psycholgy, economics, and French language and literature.

Religious Services/Activities. All students in the Faculty of Theology are full members of the Bishop Hallam Theological Society. The main objectives of the society are to promote dialogue about theological issues, to encourage fellowship within the college and within the wider community, and to be the voice of theological students within the Faculty of Theology. The Chapel of St. John the Evangelist is a spiritual center serving not only Huron College but the wider community of the University of Western Ontario. It is a focus for spiritual growth, Christian witness, ministry, and the celebration of life. The Huron community gathers daily (Monday through Friday) for Morning Prayer and for a corporate eucharist on Thursday mornings. Holy communion is celebrated daily (except Saturday). Most theological students participate in parish worship on Sunday mornings.

Degree Programs

The Master of Divinity program is for prospective ordinands. Students who are not seeking ordination are also admitted. The pattern of study consists of three years of training, including twelve weeks of Supervised Pastoral Education taken in the summer prior to admission to the second year. Students entering their graduating year are urged to participate in a Parish Internship Program if a placement is available. This program provides an effective training and learning experience in a rural or city parish with a supervisory priest. While the internship program is not required for the Master of Divinity degree, it is required by the Diocese of Huron for candidates seeking ordination and is strongly recommended for all students in the theological program.

Knox College
Department of Religion
59 St. George Street
Toronto, ON M5S 2E6   (416) 978-4500

Administration. Dr. Donald J. M. Corbett, Principal.

General Description. Knox College is a member of the Toronto School of Theology, a federation of seven theological colleges in Toronto and one affiliated college in Hamilton. The members are: Emmanuel College of Victoria University (United Church of Canada), Knox College (Presbyterian), Regis College (Roman Catholic - Jesuit), St. Augustine's Seminary (Roman Catholic - Diocesan), University of St. Michael's College (Roman Catholic - Basilian), Trinity College (Anglican), Wycliffe College (Anglican), and McMaster Divinity College (Baptist), the affiliate. The member colleges in Toronto award their degrees cojointly with the University of Toronto. Degrees offered are: Master of Divinity, Master of Arts, Doctor of Theology, Doctor of Ministry, and Doctor of Philosophy (Ph.D.). *See:* Toronto School of Theology.

Religious Denomination. Presbyterian.

Accreditation. Association of Theological Schools in the United States and Canada.

McMaster Divinity College
(McMaster University)
1280 Main Street, West
Hamilton, ON L8S 4K1   (416) 525-9140

Administration. Melvyn R. Hillmer, Principal.

General Description. McMaster Divinity College is affiliated with the Toronto School of Theology, a federation of seven theological colleges in Toronto and one affiliated college in Hamilton (McMaster Divinity College). The members are: Emmanuel College of Victoria University (United Church of Canada), Knox College (Presbyterian), Regis College (Roman Catholic - Jesuit), St. Augustine's Seminary (Roman Catholic - Diocesan), University of St. Michael's College (Roman Catholic - Basilian), Trinity College (Anglican), Wycliffe College (Anglican), McMaster Divinity College (Baptist). The member colleges in Toronto award their degrees cojointly with the University of Toronto. Degrees offered are: Master of Divinity, Master of Arts, Doctor of Theology, Doctor of Ministry, and Doctor of Philosophy (Ph.D.). *See:* Toronto School of Theology.

Parent Institution. McMaster University.

Religious Denomination. Baptist.

Accreditation. Association of Theological Schools in the United States and Canada.

Regis College
Department of Theology
15 St. Mary Street
Toronto, ON M4Y 2R5   (416) 922-5474

Administration. Jacques Monet, President.

General Description. Regis College is a member of the Toronto School of Theology, a federation of seven theological colleges in Toronto and one affiliated college in Hamilton. The members are: Emmanuel College of Victoria University (United Church of Canada), Knox College (Presbyterian), Regis College (Roman Catholic - Jesuit), St. Augustine's Seminary (Roman Catholic - Diocesan), University of St. Michael's College (Roman Catholic - Basilian), Trinity College (Anglican), Wycliffe College (Anglican), and McMaster Divinity College (Baptist), the affiliate. The member colleges in Toronto award their degrees cojointly with the University of Toronto. Degrees offered are: Master of Divinity, Master of Arts, Doctor of Theology, Doctor of Ministry, and Doctor of Philosophy (Ph.D.). *See:* Toronto School of Theology.

Religious Denomination. Roman Catholic.

Religious Emphasis. Jesuit.

Accreditation. Association of Theological Schools in the United States and Canada.

St. Augustine's Seminary of Toronto
Faculty of Theology
2661 Kingston Road
Scarborough, ON M1M 1M3   (416) 261-7207

Administration. Rev. Msgr. Peter C. Somerville, President-Rector; Rev. Attila Mikloshazy, S.J., Dean.

General Description. The specific apostolate of St. Augustine's is to educate men for the diocesan ministry. The program of formation is guided by the official documents of the Roman Catholic Church. St. Augustine's Seminary was established in 1913 as the first major seminary constructed in English-speaking Canada for the training of diocesan priests. The Seminary grants the Master of Divinity degree to those students who fulfill all of the requirements.

In 1964, the Seminary became affiliated with the University of Ottawa which in 1965 began an affiliation with the University of St. Paul in Ottawa, operated by the Oblates of Mary Immaculate. St. Augustine's Seminary is also a founding and charter member of the Toronto School of Theology, a federation of seven theological colleges and faculties established in 1969. The seven colleges are Knox, Emmanuel, Trinity, Wycliffe, Regis, St. Michael's, and St. Augustine's. The Toronto School of Theology entered into an agreement in 1978 with the University of Toronto in order to foster academic excellence and improve the resources available for theological education in Ontario. St. Augustine's Seminary, along with the other members of the federation, was empowered to grant degrees in theology conjointly with the University of Toronto. *See:* Toronto School of Theology.

Community Environment. The Seminary is located in the eastern suburbs of Toronto on a 40-acre site overlooking Lake Ontario. There is easy access to all parts of metropolitan Toronto, a growing area of diverse cultural and community development.

Religious Denomination. Roman Catholic.

Accreditation. Association of Theological Schools in the United States and Canada.

Term System. Semester.

Enrollment in Degree Programs in Religion 1984–85. Total 61; men 59; women 2.

Degrees in Religion Awarded 1984–85. Master of Divinity 21; men 21.

Faculty for Degree Programs in Religion. Total 61; full-time 54, part-time 7.

Admission Requirements. Bachelor of Arts degree with at least 18 credits of Philosophy.

Tuition and Fees. Tuition per course for Canadians and landed immigrants $137; for visa students $509; library fee $40; student records and registration fee $35; St. Augustine's Seminarians Association fee (residents only) $20; room and board $520 per month.

Housing. A residence is available for Seminarians.

Library Facilities. The library at St. Augustine's contains more than 35,000 volumes dealing with Theology, Scripture, Canon Law, Philosophy, and Psychology. Over 200 tapes of leading theologians and scripture scholars have been acquired and coordinated together with a library of cassettes which emphasize marriage counseling and the sacraments. Over 100 current periodicals are available.

Religious Services/Activities. Daily Liturgy of the Hours and Eucharist.

Degree Programs

The Master of Divinity program requires a minimum of seven semesters of full-time study; a minimum of 30 one-semester courses according to the core curriculum of the Seminary (Biblical, New Testament, Historical, Pastoral, Systematic Theology, Ethics); Field Education requirements; and a Pastoral Practicum (for candidates for the priesthood). A simultaneous pontifical degree of Bachelor of Sacred Theology is awarded upon completion of seven semesters (at least 30 courses) of theological studies. The degrees of Master of Divinity and Bachelor of Sacred Theology are available not only to candidates for the priesthood but also to interested lay men and women.

Special Programs

Since 1972, St. Augustine's has provided a training program for candidates to the Permanent Diaconate for the Archdiocese of Toronto. The main focus of the program is to prepare the candidates for the ministry of service towards the dispossessed and disadvantaged. The three-year program requires the candidate's participation in one weekend of study each month at the Seminary and one weekly home study group session. Integrated with this are reading assignments, programs of spiritual formation, and the selection and development of specific ministries.

St. Michael's College, University of
Faculty of Theology
81 St. Mary Street
Toronto, ON M5S 1J4   (416) 926-1300

Administration. Anthony Ceresko, Dean.

General Description. The University of St. Michael's College is a member of the Toronto School of Theology, a federation of seven theological colleges in Toronto and one affiliated college in Hamilton. The members are: Emmanuel College of Victoria University (United Church of Canada), Knox College (Presbyterian), Regis College (Roman Catholic - Jesuit), St. Augustine's Seminary (Roman Catholic - Diocesan), University of St. Michael's College (Roman Catholic - Basilian), Trinity College (Anglican), Wycliffe College (Anglican), and McMaster Divinity College (Baptist), the affiliate. The member colleges in Toronto award their degrees cojointly with the University of Toronto. Degrees offered are: Master of Divinity, Master of Arts, Doctor of Theology, Doctor of

Ministry, and Doctor of Philosophy (Ph.D.). *See:* Toronto School of Theology.

Religious Denomination. Roman Catholic.

Religious Emphasis. Basilian.

Accreditation. Association of Theological Schools in the United States and Canada.

St. Paul University
223 Main Street
Ottawa, ON K1S 1C4   (613) 236-1393

Administration. Achiel Peelman, O.M.I., Dean, Faculty of Theology; Jean Thorn, Dean, Faculty of Canon Law; Marcel Patry, O.M.I., Dean, Faculty of Philosophy; Eugene King, O.M.I., Director, Institute of Pastoral Studies; Marcel Dumais, O.M.I., Director, Institute of Mission Studies; Pierrette Daviau, Interim Director, Institute of Social Communications.

General Description. St. Paul University comprises three faculties (Theology, Canon Law, and Philosophy), three institutes (Pastoral Studies, Mission Studies, and Social Communications), and a research center. It also has a service of creation (edition of liturgical and pastoral publications known as Novalis), and a house of spiritual formation and preparation for candidates to the priesthood (University Seminary). Degrees awarded are Bachelor, Master, Doctorate; also Licentiate, Diploma, Certificate.

Religious Denomination. Roman Catholic.

Accreditation. Association of Universities and Colleges of Canada; A.U.P.E.L.F.; A.C.U.

Term System. Trimester; summer term.

Enrollment in Degree Programs in Religion 1984–85. Total 730; men 390, women 340.

Degrees in Religion Awarded 1984–85. Bachelor of Theology 56; men 48, women 8. Bachelor of Canon Law 43; men 32, women 11. Master of Arts in Theology 15; men 13, women 2. Master of Arts in Pastoral Studies 44; men 23, women 21. Master of Arts in Missiology 10; men 5, women 5. Master of Canon Law and Licentiate in Canon Law 36; men 26, women 10. Licentiate in Theology 2; men 2. Doctor of Philosophy (Ph.D.) in Theology 2; men 1, women 1. Doctor of Philosophy (Ph.D.) in Canon Law 7; men 6, women 1. Diploma in Pastoral Studies 11, men 3, women 8. Certificate in Theology 38; men 10, women 28. Certificate in Missiology 10; men 5, women 5.

Faculty for Degree Programs in Religion. Faculty of: Theology, total 436, full-time 214, part-time 222; Canon Law, total 103, full-time 86, part-time 17; Pastoral Studies, total 169, full-time 115, part-time 54; Mission Studies, total 22, full-time 9, part-time 13. Grand Total 730, full-time 424, part-time 306.

Admission Requirements. Vary according to programs.

Tuition and Fees. Tuition undergraduate $515 per trimester, part-time $42 per credit; graduate full-time $595 per trimester; part-time $68 per credit; non-Canadians full-time $2,085 per trimester.

Financial Aid. Students are eligible for various provincial and federal scholarships and loans. The University has established a number of internal bursaries and every year a certain number of bursaries are available for foreign students.

Housing. The University can accommodate 225 students in its various residences.

Library Facilities. The library contains over 350,000 volumes. It is especially well documented in Theology, Biblical Sciences, Patrology, History, Liturgy, Ecumenism, Missiology, Canon Law, Philosophy, History of Religions, and Medieval Studies.

Religious Services/Activities. Integrated with the academic dimension of the University is the growth and development of the faith life of the members of the University community. The Spiritual Animation Service provides for liturgical celebrations on a daily basis as well as on special occasions.

Degree Programs

Degree programs are offered by the various Faculties of Theology, Canon Law, and Philosophy. The Institute of Pastoral Studies offers an innovative educational program leading to the Master of Arts in Pastoral Studies. Each student chooses a concentration from General Ministry, Counseling Ministry, Pastoral Groupwork in Family and Community, and Pastoral Care in Health Care Services. The Institute of Mission Studies offers a program leading to the Master of Arts in Mission Studies. The Institute of Social Communications offers a course leading to a Certificate.

Special Programs

The Research Centre concentrates upon areas of research most relevant to the aims of the Church. The Centre comprises two sectors: Research Centre in Religious History of Canada and Canadian Research Centre in Anthropology.

Toronto School of Theology
47 Queen's Park Crescent, East
Toronto, ON M5C 2C3   (416) 978-4039

Administration. Dr. Iain G. Nicol, Director. Department Chairmen: Heinz O. Guenther, Biblical; Alan Hayes, Historical; Greer W. Boyce, Pastoral; W. James Farris, Theological.

General Description. The Toronto School of Theology is a federation of seven theological colleges in Toronto and one affiliated college in Hamilton. The members are: Emmanuel College of Victoria University (United Church of Canada), Knox College (Presbyterian), Regis College (Roman Catholic - Jesuit), St. Augustine's Seminary (Roman Catholic - Diocesan), University of St. Michael's College (Roman Catholic - Basilian), Trinity College (An-

glican), Wycliffe College (Anglican), McMaster Divinity College (Baptist), the affiliate. The member colleges in Toronto award their degrees conjointly with the University of Toronto. Degrees offered are: Master of Divinity, Master of Religious Education, Master of Religion, Master of Theology, Master of Arts, Doctor of Theology, Doctor of Ministry, and Doctor of Philosophy (Ph.D.).

Community Environment. Toronto is the financial and industrial capital of Canada as well as the provincial capital of Ontario. It is often compared to New York. The city is one of the great inland ports of North America.

Religious Denomination. Nondenominational.

Accreditation. Association of Theological Schools in the United States and Canada.

Term System. Semester.

Enrollment in Degree Programs in Religion 1984–85. Total 307 in advanced degrees.

Degrees in Religion Awarded 1984–85. Degrees are awarded by the individual colleges and conjointly with the University of Toronto.

Admission Requirements. Students seeking admission to the Toronto School of Theology should seek admission first to one of the member colleges; Bachelor's degree with adequate standing from an accredited college or university.

Tuition and Fees. Tuition Canadian citizens and landed immigrants $1,526; visa students $3,948.

Financial Aid. Assistance is available through the individual Colleges.

Housing. Student should contact individual Colleges regarding residential accommodations.

Library Facilities. Students have graduate student privileges in the University of Toronto Library and the libraries of all the Colleges. Special collections include the Archives of the United Church of Canada (Birge Library, Victoria University), the Library of the Pontifical Institute of Medieval Studies (in the J.M. Kelly Library of St. Michael's College), the Centre for Reformation and Renaissance Studies (in the E.J. Pratt Library of Victoria University), the Archives of the Presbyterian Church in Canada (in the Knox College Library), the Archives of the Jesuits of Upper Canada and the Lonergan Centre (in the Regis College Library), and the Thomas Fisher Rare Book Room which is part of the Robarts Library in the University of Toronto Library.

Religious Services/Activities. Various activities and organizations are provided by the individual Colleges.

Degree Programs

The Master of Divinity degree is a basic professional degree in theology. It is conferred conjointly by the University of Toronto and the graduand's college of registration. The program is designed primarily to prepare men and women for effective ministries in the church. The normal residency period is three years (six semesters).

The Master of Religious Education program is offered by Emmanuel College and the Faculty of Theology of the

University of St. Michael's College. The chief purpose of this program is to equip individuals for competent leadership in educational ministry.

The Master of Religion is a three-year program offered by Wycliffe College. It is a purely academic program taken by persons aiming at ministries such as teaching, social work, public service, etc.

Advanced degree programs leading to the Master of Theology, Master of Arts in Theology, Doctor of Theology, and Doctor of Philosophy in Theology are offered. Deparmental requirements are met through completion of courses offered by the Biblical Department, Historical Department, Theological Department, and Pastoral Department.

Toronto, University of
Centre for Religious Studies
130 St. George Street
14th Floor, Room 14335
Toronto, ON M5S 1A1   (416) 978-3057

Administration. Professor Ronald F.G. Sweet, Acting Director.

General Description. The Centre for Religious Studies is designed to bring together from a broad range of disciplines the University's academic resources bearing upon the study of religion. The list of graduate faculty and the list of courses offered in other departments and centres, indicate the wealth of resources available to the student of religion in the various graduate departments of the University of Toronto. The program of the Centre offers specialization at the Master's and Doctoral levels in the study of major religious traditions and religion conceived of as a social, cultural, conceptual, or behavioral phenomenon.

All students in the Ph.D. program are required to work in more than one religious tradition and with more than one method. Three principal methods for the study of religion are emphasized: the historical (including the textual), the philosophical, and the social scientific. The sources employed are usually written documents but may include any expression of religion including those found in art, music, and dance. In the study of religious tradition, specializations are recognized in the following areas: Ancient Near Eastern Religions, Christianity, East Asian Religions, Islam, Judaism, the Religions of Classical Antiquity, South Asian Religions, and certain Tribal Religions.

Parent Institution. The University of Toronto is a publicly funded university of the Province of Ontario. It was founded in 1827 as King's College of York. It offers comprehensive courses of study, continuing studies, and special programs. It has a student population of over 32,000.

Community Environment. Toronto is located on the shore of Lake Ontario and is the largest city of inland Canada. It has an abundance of cultural and historical attractions. Many parks are found throughout the city.

Religious Denomination. Nondenominational.

Accreditation. Provincial accreditation.

Term System. Semester system.

Enrollment in Degree Programs in Religion 1984–85. Total 41; men 26, women 15.

Degrees in Religion Awarded 1984–85. Master's degree 5; men 1, women 4. Ph.D. degree 2; women 2.

Faculty for Degree Programs in Religion. Total 63.

Admission Requirements. Candidates are accepted under the general regulations of the School of Graduate Studies, with the further requirements that each applicant arrange for three confidential letters of recommendation to be sent to the Director of the Centre by teachers familiar with the applicant's recent work in religion or related fields, and submit to the Director a statement (about 200 words in length) indicating the applicant's aims in graduate study and the proposed focus of work.

Tuition and Fees. Tuition full-time Canadian students $1,416.25; medium visa fee $3,049.25; high visa fee $6,353.25.

Financial Aid. All students accepted for admission will be automatically considered for University of Toronto fellowship support, provided the application for admission is received by February 1. The province of Ontario offers Ontario Graduate Scholarships to Canadian citizens and residents. Canadian citizens and landed immigrants are eligible for Social Sciences and Humanities Research Council of Canada doctoral fellowships.

Housing. Accommodation is provided for the fellows, tutors, and dons appointed in the undergraduate and divinity residences of colleges within or affiliated to the University, such as New College, Trinity College, University College, Victoria College, St. Michael's College, and Knox College. Single students interested in such appointments should address the principals of the individual colleges.

Library Facilities. The University of Toronto library has holdings of over 5 million volumes.

Religious Services/Activities. There are several church-affiliated colleges within the Federation of the University of Toronto.

Degree Programs

A Master of Arts program extends over one or two academic years, depending on how well the student is prepared for graduate studies in the field. The student is expected to become conversant with the range of religious traditions and the methods employed in their study, and to choose one specific tradition for concentration and for a major research paper. An appropriate language for primary sources, such as Sanskrit, Arabic, or Greek, may be required and competence must be shown in a language of modern scholarship, generally German or French.

A Doctor of Philosophy program normally requires two years of work beyond the Toronto Master of Arts. It assumes the breadth integral to the Master of Arts program, plus additional work in the tradition and method of the student's specialization. The requirements for "first minor" and "second minor" subjects are met by the study of a second religious tradition and the exploration of a second method of study with reference to the religion of specialization. The student writes general examinations at the end of whatever coursework is required. A dissertation completes the degree requirements.

Trinity College
Faculty of Divinity
Hoskin Avenue
Toronto, ON M5S 1H8   (416) 978-3609

Administration. Peter Slater, Dean.

General Description. The University of Trinity College, Faculty of Divinity, is a member of the Toronto School of Theology, a federation of seven theological colleges in Toronto and one affiliated college in Hamilton. The members are: Emmanuel College of Victoria University (United Church of Canada), Knox College (Presbyterian), Regis College (Roman Catholic - Jesuit), St. Augustine's Seminary (Roman Catholic - Diocesan), University of St. Michael's College (Roman Catholic - Basilian), Trinity College (Anglican), Wycliffe College (Anglican), and McMaster Divinity College (Baptist), the affiliate. The member colleges in Toronto award their degrees cojointly with the University of Toronto. Degrees offered are: Master of Divinity, Master of Arts, Doctor of Theology, Doctor of Ministry, and Doctor of Philosophy (Ph.D.). *See:* Toronto School of Theology.

Religious Denomination. Anglican.

Accreditation. Association of Theological Schools in the United States and Canada.

Waterloo Lutheran Seminary
Wilfred Laurier University
75 University Avenue West
Waterloo, ON N2L 3C5   (519) 884-1970

Administration. Dr. Richard C. Crossman, Principal-Dean.

General Description. Founded in 1911, Waterloo Lutheran Seminary is an institution for the scholarly study of the Christian faith, especially in its Lutheran understanding, and for the education of persons in and for the Christian ministry, especially in the Lutheran Church and the Canadian context. The Seminary believes interdisciplinary study to be essential to sound theological education. As a federated college of Wilfred Laurier University and a member of the University Graduate Council, the Seminary maintains close ties especially with the School of Religion and the Faculty of Social Work on the same campus, thus facilitating interdisciplinary work. As of January 1, 1986, Waterloo Lutheran Seminary became an institution of the Evangelical Lutheran Church in Canada sponsored by the Eastern Synod. The Seminary grants the degrees Master of Divinity, Master of Divinity-Master of Arts, Master of Divinity-Master of Social Work, Master of Theology in Pastoral Counseling, and Master of Theological Studies.

Community Environment. The Seminary is located in the city of Waterloo in the province of Ontario. The twin cities of Kitchener-Waterloo, with a combined population of 200,000, lie in the prosperous rural and urban area known as the Regional Municipality of Waterloo. Waterloo is some 70 miles west of Toronto, 65 miles northeast of London, 30 miles northwest of Hamilton, and 80 miles northwest of Niagara Falls. The Seminary shares campus and resources with Wilfred Laurier University. The University of Waterloo is located less than a mile from the Laurier campus.

Religious Denomination. Lutheran.

Religious Emphasis. Liberal/Ecumenical.

Accreditation. Association of Theological Schools in the United States and Canada.

Term System. Trimester; Spring Term May-August.

Enrollment in Degree Programs in Religion 1984–85. Total 125; men 84, women 41.

Degrees in Religion Awarded 1984–85. Master of Divinity 7; men 7. Master of Theological Studies 5; men 4, women 1.

Faculty for Degree Programs in Religion. Total 20; full-time 8, part-time 12.

Admission Requirements. Master of Divinity or Master of Theological Studies: Bachelor's degree from an accredited university or college. Master of Theology: Bachelor's degree and Master of Divinity degree (or equivalent) from an accredited university of college plus two basic quarters of Supervised Pastoral Education/Clinical Pastoral Education. Diploma in Theology: Five full-year university courses plus church endorsement.

Tuition and Fees. Tuition for Master of Divinity, Master of Theological Studies, Diploma in Theology: $1,114 for a full academic year; new visa student $4,168 for a full academic year; incidental fees $94 per year; Master of Theology students pay a clinical tuition of $1,250 in addition to the above costs; room $1,520-$1,665 per academic year; board $775-$1,725 per academic year depending on plan selected.

Financial Aid. All full-time students are eligible to apply for seminary bursaries which are disbursed on the basis of need. Established residents of Ontario and Canadian citizens may apply for provincial and federal grants/loans.

Housing. Single students may apply for residence accommodation (two to a room) on campus. The Seminary will pay the room cost for Master of Divinity or Diploma students in campus residence but the student is obligated to purchase a meal card for the academic year. There are a limited number of married student apartments on campus for couples without children. Seminary students with children are eligible to rent an apartment at the married student apartments owned by the neighboring University of Waterloo.

Library Facilities. The University library has a total collection of 976,252 items which include 425,584 volumes and 378,138 microforms. The Seminary's holdings, including 36,811 volumes, are housed in the University library. These holdings are complemented by a similar-sized collection in the School of Religion and Culture.

Religious Services/Activities. Daily chapel services are held in the Seminary's Chapel.

Degree Programs

The Master of Divinity program prepares candidates for the professional ministry. In addition to the six terms of academic study, all students must take and successfully complete twelve weeks of supervised (clinical) pastoral education; must meet the internship and/or field education requirements of the church of which they are a member; must be involved in the life of a congregation; and must complete the Comprehensive Seminar.

The Master of Theological Studies program is designed to help persons engage more fully in lay ministry leadership and lay participation in Christian ministry in the church and the world. The degree program normally involves three years of full-time studies.

The Master of Theology degree in Pastoral Counseling is a program aimed at further developing the counseling skills of persons already in the ordained ministry. The program involves two years of full-time studies. In each term of both years the work is divided between studies at the Seminary and at the Interfaith Pastoral Counseling Centre in Kitchener, Ontario. Students are expected to prepare a research study project in the field of pastoral counseling which reflects an integration of theological and counseling skills.

Special Programs

The Diploma in Theology is designed only for students who for reason of age and by special faculty action are exempted from some of the entrance and other requirements of the Seminary. In addition to six terms of academic study, each student must take twelve weeks of supervised pastoral education, an internship and/or field education requirement, and be involved in the life of a congregation.

The Seminary participates regularly in the continuing and lay education programs of the Synod.

Waterloo, University of
Department of Religious Studies
Waterloo, ON N2L 3G1   (519) 885-1211

Administration. Dr. J.P.R. Wadsworth, Chancellor; Dr. D.T. Wright, President and Vice Chancellor; Dr. John

Miller, Chair, Department of Religious Studies.

General Description. The Department of Religious Studies includes course offerings in five distinct areas: World Religions, History of the Christian Tradition, Biblical Studies, Theology-Philosophy-Ethics, and Religion and Culture. While the concentration of courses is in Christian studies, students are also exposed to all the major religious traditions of East and West. The Department sees itself as contributing to a truly liberal education by examining the varied roles religion has played throughout human history and continues to play in people's lives today. The Bachelor of Arts degree is awarded.

Parent Institution. The University of Waterloo is a provincially-funded university with strong faculties in mathematics, engineering, science, environmental studies, and arts.

Community Environment. The University is situated on a 1,000-acre campus in the northwest section of the city of Waterloo. Waterloo and its twin city of Kitchener are steadily growing industrial centers in mid-western Ontario with a combined population of 200,000.

Religious Denomination. Nondenominational.

Term System. Semester; summer term.

Enrollment in Degree Programs in Religion 1984–85. Total 60; men 25, women 35.

Degrees in Religion Awarded 1984–85. Bachelor of Arts General 9; men 5, women 4. Bachelor of Arts Honours 1; women 1.

Faculty for Degree Programs in Religion. Total 14; full-time 10, part-time 4.

Admission Requirements. High school diploma; Ontario Grade 13; minimum average of 60 percent.

Tuition and Fees. Tuition fall and winter terms $1,315.15.

Financial Aid. Numerous scholarships and bursaries are available.

Housing. Housing is available both in University student residences as well as in the residences of the four affiliate church Colleges (St. Jerome's, Conrad Grebel, St. Paul's, and Renison).

Library Facilities. The Dana Porter Library collection numbers over 1,900,000 items including books, pamphlets, theses, microforms, documents, reports, sound recordings, and other materials.

Religious Services/Activities. Numerous religious services and activities are sponsored by the four affiliated Colleges (Roman Catholic, Anglican, United Church, Mennonite).

Degree Programs

The Department of Religious Studies offers a program in General Religious Studies leading to the Bachelor of Arts degree. A four-year program requires the successful completion of a minimum of 40 term courses including Faculty of Arts Group requirements with an overall cumulative average of 60 percent and a cumulative major average of at least 65 percent. An Honours Religous Studies program is also offered.

Special Programs

The University of Waterloo offers numerous Religious Studies courses to Canadians by correspondence.

Wilfred Laurier University
Department of Religion and Culture
75 University Avenue West
Waterloo, ON N2L 3C5   (519) 884-1970

Administration. Dr. Lawrence E. Toombs, Chairman.

General Description. The Department of Religion offers a program leading to the Master of Arts degree. A distinctive feature of the program is its thematic emphasis, intended to assist students in the integration of their work and to bring them into a dialogue with students and faculty in other areas of religioius studies. A student may follow one of three streams to the Master of Arts in Religion and Culture: the thesis stream, an eight course stream, or a humanities stream.

Parent Institution. The University was formerly known as Waterloo Lutheran University. In 1973, it became a provinically assisted institution and adopted its present name. It offers university courses off-campus in centers such as Orangeville, Barrie, and Brampton. Telecollege courses bring instructors into the homes of viewers throughout southwestern Ontario.

Community Environment. The University is located in the city of Waterloo in the province of Ontario. The twin cities of Kitchener-Waterloo, with a combined population of 200,000, lie in the prosperous rural and urban area known as the Regional Municipality of Waterloo. Waterloo is some 70 miles west of Toronto, 65 miles northeast of London, 30 miles northwest of Hamilton, and 80 miles northwest of Niagara Falls. The University of Waterloo is located less than a mile from the Laurier campus.

Religious Denomination. Nondenominational.

Accreditation. Provincial accreditation

Term System. Trimester; Spring Term May-August.

Degrees in Religion Awarded 1984-85. Master of Arts.

Faculty for Degree Programs in Religion. Total 8.

Admission Requirements. Baccalaureate degree from an approved university with a minimum of second class honors or "B" standing.

Tuition and Fees. Tuition $500 per term; visa student full-time $2,407; room $1,520-$1,665 per academic year; board $775-$1,725 per academic year depending on plan selected.

Financial Aid. Established residents of Ontario and Canadian citizens may apply for provincial and federal grants/loans.

Housing. Single students may apply for residence accommodation (two to a room) on campus. There are a limited number of married student apartments on campus for couples without children.

Library Facilities. The University library has a total collection of 976,252 items which include 425,584 volumes and 378,138 microforms. The School of Religion and Culture has a collection of over 36,000 volumes.

Religious Services/Activities. Daily chapel services are held in the Waterloo Lutheran Seminary's Chapel.

Degree Programs

The Master of Arts in Religion and Culture is a program of flexibility. Upon commencing the program, the student works out with an advisor a sequence of courses which best meet the interests of the student and the requirements of the program. Thematic courses are offered in addition to those in Ancient Near Eastern and Mediterranean Religions, Western Religions: Early to Modern, and Research Courses.

Windsor, University of
Department of Religious Studies
Sunset Avenue
Windsor, ON N9B 3P4   (519) 253-4232

Administration. Major-General Richard Rohmer, Chancellor; Dr. Ronald Ianni, President and Vice Chancellor; Dr. Jerome V. Brown, Dean, Faculty of Arts; Dr. John C. Hoffman, Head, Department of Religious Studies.

General Description. The Department of Religious Studies of the University of Windsor is a nondenominational department in the Faculty of Arts, focusing primarily on Western religious history, with a second focus on the religions of India. The Department grants the Bachelor of Arts and the Master of Arts degrees in Religious Studies.

Parent Institution. The University of Windsor is coeducational and nondenominational operating under a Provincial charter. It embodies one federated university (Assumption) and three affiliated colleges (Holy Redeemer, Canterbury, and Iona) which are legally and financially distinct but subject in academic matters to the university senate. The University has 9 faculties: Arts, Social Science, Science and Mathematics, Business Administration, Education, Engineering, Human Kinetics, Law, and Graduate Studies and Research.

Community Environment. The city of Windsor lies across the Detroit River from Detroit, Michigan, and its cultural, entertainment, and athletic attractions. Yet by itself, Windsor is the hub of Canada's automotive industry.

Religious Denomination. Nondenominational.

Accreditation. Association of Universities and Colleges of Canada.

Term System. Semester; summer term.

Enrollment in Degree Programs in Religion 1984-85. Total 371; men 219, women 152.

Degrees in Religion Awarded 1984-85. Honors Bachelor of Arts in Religious Studies 2; men 1, women 1. General

Bachelor of Arts in Religious Studies 10; men 5, women 5. Master of Arts in Religious Studies 5; men 3, women 2.

Faculty for Degree Programs in Religion. Total 14; full-time 10, part-time 4.

Admission Requirements. Undergraduate: Completion in not more than four years beyond Grade 8 of twenty-seven academic credits in a program oriented toward university studies. Graduate: Baccalaureate degree.

Tuition and Fees. Undergraduate tuition and fees $664.50 per semester; Graduate tuition $488.75 per semester; residence $1,455-$1,770 depending upon year and accommodation; food plan $625-$1,850 depending upon year and plan selected.

Financial Aid. Scholarships, bursaries, graduate assistantships, and research assistantships are available.

Housing. Residence halls are available on campus. The Meal plan is compulsory in all residences except Tecumseh Hall.

Library Facilities. The University of Windsor Library has about 250,000 volumes related to Religious Studies and is a member of the Center for Research Libraries of Chicago. Graduate students have access to Ontario Interlibrary Loan Facilities.

Religious Services/Activities. The Chaplaincy of the three church-related colleges (Assumption, Canterbury, and Iona) is responsible for religious activities.

Degree Programs

The general Bachelor of Arts in Religious Studies requires a total of thirty courses including ten to sixteen in Religious Studies. At least two courses must be taken from each of three of the Departmental groups (Biblical, Ethical, Historical, Theological, World Religions).

The Department offers a personalized program of graduate studies leading to the Master of Arts degree. It provides a sound preparation for those students who will continue toward a Ph.D. in Religious Studies or for the further development of teachers and ministers, or for background to careers in counseling, social work, and other disciplines. In addition to the general requirements and stipulations, the candidate must complete four graduate courses plus a thesis, or completion of six graduate courses plus a major paper upon which there will be an examination, or completion of eight graduate courses. A reading knowledge of either French or German is required.

Wycliffe College
5 Hoskin Avenue
Toronto, ON M5S 1H7   (416) 979-2870

Administration. The Reverend Canon Reginald Stackhouse, Principal.

General Description. The basic degree division of Wycliffe College is dedicated to helping men and women

prepare for full-time Christian service. The program is three-fold. First, as members of an academic community, the College strives to examine Christian revelation and tradition critically. Second, as professionals in a pastoral training center, it aims at developing skills for ministry. Third, as committed Christians in a common fellowship, the College endeavors to grow through worship, personal relationships, and social responsibilities. Degrees are awarded jointly by Wycliffe and the University of Toronto.

Evangelical Anglicans in Toronto in the 1870s perceived a growing clericalism in the Church. Excluded from important offices and committees in the diocesan Synod, they formed an independent organization which collected scholarship money for ordinands and published tracts. In 1877, the 500th anniversary of the traditional date of John Wycliffe's translation of Scripture into English, a College building was erected near the University of Toronto. It was called "Wycliffe College," and the name soon denoted the school itself. In 1885 the College was affiliated to the University of Toronto. In 1891 it moved to its present location. It eventually won full recognition in the Church, received degree-granting authority from the Province, and achieved an international reputation for its commitment to home and foreign missions.

Wycliffe College is a member of the Toronto School of Theology, a consortium of seven theological schools. *See:* Toronto School of Theology.

Community Environment. Metropolitan Toronto is an exceptional context for study and ministry, with over two million people representing every facet of the "Canadian mosaic" of languages, religions, and lifestyles. Geographically, Toronto is located on the north side of Lake Ontario. It is honeycombed by ravines and valleys, and contains seven thousand acres of parkland. Culturally, Toronto offers museums of world standard, bookstores, professional sports, and fine theatre and music.

Religious Denomination. Anglican Church of Canada.

Religious Emphasis. Evangelical.

Accreditation. Association of Theological Schools in the United States and Canada.

Term System. Semester; summer term.

Enrollment in Degree Programs in Religion 1984–85. Total 110; men 80; women 30.

Degrees in Religion Awarded 1984–85. Master of Divinity 7; men 7. Master of Religion 2; men 2.

Faculty for Degree Programs in Religion. Total 11; full-time 6, part-time 5.

Admission Requirements. For the basic degree programs, applicants must have a Bachelor's degree from a recognized university or college with good academic standing; for advanced degree programs, a basic degree from a recognized theological college or equivalent.

Tuition and Fees. Canadian students tuition $1,600 per academic year; non-Canadian students $5,500 per academic year; room and board (12 meals a week) $2,905 per academic year.

Financial Aid. Bursary assistance is available to all students, according to need. Preference is given to Anglican students.

Housing. The College has accommodations for about seventy students in single rooms. University housing for married students is available.

Library Facilities. The Leonard Library contains a fine working collection of about 35,000 books and periodicals, including scores of rare books. Students are entitled and encouraged to use the various libraries in the University of Toronto library system. This system has over two million volumes, of which 300,000 are in theology.

Religious Services/Activities. The student Theological Society sponsors visiting speakers. Typically, small groups emerge informally every year to study the Bible or pray together, and to bring a Christian witness to topical social issues. Services are held twice a day during term in the Founder's Chapel. Holy Communion is celebrated Sundays, Wednesdays, and Feast Days as prescribed in the Anglican Calendar. Classical and contemporary authorized Anglican liturgies are used.

Degree Programs

The Master of Divinity is for students considering ordination and parish-based lay ministries. Thirty-two courses over six semesters of study are required for graduation. Half of the program must be taken in courses involving Wycliffe instructors with others selected from courses offered by the Toronto School of Theology.

The Master of Religion is for students considering vocations in teaching or research. The same number of courses are required as for the Master of Divinity program but with a different emphasis.

The Master of Theology requires one year of study beyond the Master of Divinity or Master of Religion.

A Master of Arts is awarded for at least two years of coursework and thesis past the Bachelor's degree.

The Doctor of Theology requires coursework, comprehensive examinations, research thesis, and proficiency in at least three languages. The degree requires at least three years of study past the Master of Divinity or Master of Religion.

The Doctor of Philosophy program has requirements similar to the Doctor of Theology.

Special Programs

Each year one or two places in a Diploma Program become available for students without university degrees, but with at least a year of university study in the humanities. The graduation requirements are comparable to those for the Master of Divinity degree. (Some bishops do not recognize the diploma as sufficient academic qualification for ordination.) Priority in admission is given to Anglicans with episcopal sponsorship.

QUEBEC

Concordia University
Department of Religion and Department of Theological Studies
7141 Sherbrooke Street West
Montreal, PQ H4B 1R6   (514) 848-2475

Administration. Dr. Patrick J. Kenniff, Rector and Vice Chancellor; Dr. Stanley G. French, Dean, Graduate Studies; Dr. Michael Oppenheim, Chairman, Department of Religion; Dr. John J. Ryan, Chairman, Department of Theological Studies.

General Description. The Department of Religion: The faculty members have been trained in the studies of Christianity, Judaism, Islam, Hinduism, and Buddhism. They offer undergraduate and graduate courses in all these areas. The graduate programs and research of the Department have a special focus on the areas of comparative religious ethics and religion and modernization. There are 5 on-going research projects in these areas, funded by social science and humanities granting agencies based in Ottawa and Quebec.

The Department of Theological Studies: All the main areas of Christian theology are taught: Old Testament, New Testament, Systematics (including Christian Ethics), and History of Christianity. Some courses are also offered in non-Christian religions. The Department attracts students of all kinds of religious convictions who are interested in the academic study of Christian Theology. The main emphasis, however, is on Roman Catholicism.

The two Departments and the Division of Graduate Studies grant the degrees Bachelor of Arts in Religion, Bachelor of Arts in Judaic Studies, Master of Arts in History and Philosophy of Religion, Master of Arts in Judaic Studies, and Doctor of Philosophy (Ph.D.) in Religion. There is also a Diploma in Religious Studies offered.

Parent Institution. Concordia University is a public institution that has a total enrollment of 25,000 students. In addition to undergraduate programs, it has one of the largest graduate programs in Canada. Concordia encourages both full-time and part-time students in both graduate and undergraduate levels. It has Faculties in Arts and Science, Commerce and Administration, Engineering and Computer Science, and Fine Arts. Courses are offered in day and evening classes.

Community Environment. Concordia University has two campuses in the city of Montreal, Quebec: Loyola Campus, at 7141 Sherbrooke Street West; Sir George Williams Campus at 2050 Mackay Avenue. The two campuses are only 7 kilometers apart. Montreal is the second largest French-speaking city in the world, second only to Paris. It is the second largest city in Canada and has a rich history in tradition and culture.

Religious Denomination. Nondenominational.

Religious Emphasis. Christian theology in general, with a special interest in Roman Catholicism.

Accreditation. Full government recognition as a university-level institution.

Term System. Semester; summer term.

Enrollment in Degree Programs in Religion 1984–85. Department of Religion: Total undergraduate 76; men 28, women 48. Total graduate 98; men 40, women 58. Department of Theological Studies: Total 342; men 137, women 205.

Degrees in Religion Awarded 1984–85. Bachelor of Arts in Theological Studies 3; men 2, women 1. Bachelor of Arts in Religion 6; men 2, women 4. Bachelor of Arts in Judaic Studies 3; men 1, women 2. Master of Arts in History and Philosophy of Religion 4; women 4. Master of Arts in Judaic Studies 4; men 1, women 3. Doctor of Philosophy (Ph.D.) in Religion 4; men 2, women 2. Diploma in Theological Studies 3; men 1, women 2.

Faculty for Degree Programs in Religion. Total 25; full-time 17, part-time 8.

Admission Requirements. The policy of Concordia University is that admission is open to any qualified applicant in keeping with the general principles accepted by the Quebec universities.

Tuition and Fees. Undergraduate tuition $15 per credit; Graduate tuition $20 per credit; new international students $195 per credit, former international students $145 per credit; housing $1,240-$1,440.

Financial Aid. The Office of the Dean of Students on the Sir George Williams campus and the Financial Aid Office on the Loyola campus maintain staff who are available to help students solve individual financial problems and to explain existing programs and regulations.

Housing. No special housing; accommodations for single students available.

Library Facilities. The Concordia Library System comprises four libraries containing a collection of over one million items.

Degree Programs

The Bachelor of Arts is offered through several Departments. Majors are available in Theological Studies, Religion, and Judaic Studies.

The Master of Arts degrees in History and Philosophy of Religion and Judaic Studies may be pursued, as well as a Doctor of Philosophy degree in Religion.

Laval University
Faculty of Theology
Pavillon Félix-Antoine-Savard
Quebec, PQ G1K 7P4   (418) 656-3576

Administration. Jean-Guy Paquet, Rector; Andre Dufour, Executive Vice Rector.

General Description. The Faculty of Theology of Laval University offers Bachelor and Master degrees and Certificates in theology.

Parent Institution. The University owes its origin to the Seminary of Quebec, founded by Francois de Montmorency Laval, the first bishop of Quebec, in 1663.

Community Environment. Quebec, on the St. Lawrence River, is the provincial capital and is a French-speaking city. There are many beautiful churches.

Religious Denomination. Roman Catholic.

Accreditation. Civil charter of Quebec, and the pontifical charter (Rome).

Term System. Trimester; summer term.

Enrollment in Degree Programs in Religion 1984–85. Total 522; men 301, women 221.

Degrees in Religion Awarded 1984–85. Bachelor of Theology 246; men 169, women 77. Certificate in Theology 61; men 15, women 46. Master in Theology 104; men 76, women 28. Bachelor in Catechetics 78; men 17, women 61. Master of Science in Religion 14; men 7, women 7. Doctorate in Theology 19; men 17, women 2.

Admission Requirements. Premier cycle: DEC; second cycle: baccalaureate degree; third cycle: Master's degree.

Tuition and Fees. Tuition $273 per trimester for Quebec students; $548 for Canadians from outside Quebec; $2,948 per trimester for international students; housing $118 per month.

Financial Aid. Bursaries, scholarships, and limited research positions are available.

Housing. Housing is available.

Library Facilities. The library contains over 1,500,000 volumes.

Religious Services/Activities. Various pastoral services are available on campus.

Degree Programs

The Bachelor of Theology, Master of Arts in Theology, and the Doctor of Philosophy are offered through the Faculty of Theology.

Special Programs

Some courses are offered via television. An extension program is also offered. There is a Certificate in Theology.

McGill University
Faculty of Religious Studies
Birks Building
3520 University Street
Montreal, PQ H3A 2A7   (514) 392-4826

Administration. Dr. David L. Johnston, Principal and Vice Chancellor; Dr. Robert C. Culley, Acting Dean.

General Description. The Faculty of Religious Studies of McGill University offers a variety of programs, both graduate and undergraduate. The Faculty offers Bachelor of Arts Honours and Major programs in the Faculty of Arts. The Faculty participates with its affiliated theological colleges (United, Anglican, and Presbyterian) in a theological program leading to ordination. It consists of two years at McGill (Bachelor of Theology) and one year in the Montreal Institute for Ministry, all leading to a Master of Divinity awarded by the affiliated colleges. Graduate programs are offered for the McGill degrees of Master of Arts, Master of Sacred Theology, and Doctor of Philosophy (Ph.D.) in the areas of Biblical Studies, History and Theology, Religion and Culture, and Comparative Studies. The Institute of Islamic Studies is a graduate research unit within the Faculty.

Parent Institution. McGill University is an internationally known institution located in the center of Montreal. It has 22 Faculties and Schools and 15,000 students, over a third of whom are in Graduate Studies.

Community Environment. Montreal is the second largest French-speaking city in the world, second only to Paris. It is the second largest city in Canada and has a history rich in tradition and culture.

Religious Denomination. Nondenominational, but affiliated colleges are Anglican, United, and Presbyterian.

Accreditation. Association of Theological Schools in the United States and Canada.

Term System. There are two terms of 13 weeks each and two summer sessions.

Enrollment in Degree Programs in Religion 1984–85. Total 188; men 112, women 76.

Degrees in Religion Awarded 1984–85. Bachelor of Arts in Religious Studies (Major) 2; women 2. Bachelor of Arts in Religious Studies (Honours) 3; women 3. Bachelor of

Theology 17; men 13, women 4. Master of Sacred Theology 2; men 1, women 1. Master of Arts in Religious Studies 4; men 3, women 1. Doctor of Philosophy (Ph.D.) in Religious Studies 1; men 1.

Faculty for Degree Programs in Religion. Total 20; full-time 12, part-time 8.

Admission Requirements. The Bachelor of Arts and the Bachelor of Theology programs require the Diploma of Collegial Studies of Quebec or equivalent. The Master of Divinity of the affiliated colleges requires a Bachelor of Arts for entrance into the second year of the Bachelor of Theology. The Master of Arts and Master of Sacred Theology require a Bachelor of Arts or equivalent, normally with second class standing in a Major or Honours program. The Ph.D. requires a Master of Arts with high second class standing in Religion or theology in order to enter Ph.D. 2. Entrance into Ph.D. 1 requires at least a Bachelor of Arts with a major in Religion or Theology and a high standing.

Tuition and Fees. Tuition for B.A. and B.Th. Canadian full-time (30 credits) $764; international full-time $6,940 or $7,928.

Financial Aid. Some scholarships, fellowships, and awards are available from the University. Teaching assistanships are also available.

Housing. Dormitories and off-campus housing are available with very limited possibilities for married students.

Library Facilities. The Faculty of Religious Studies has a collection of over 70,000 volumes. Students also have use of McGill's McLennan Library.

Religious Services/Activities. Most religious services and activities are conducted by the affiliated theological colleges where well developed programs exist.

Degree Programs

The Bachelor of Arts honours and major programs in Religious Studies are administered by the Faculty of Arts. The major consists of 54 credits. The Bachelor of Theology program extends for three academic sessions for those admitted with a Diploma of Collegial Studies and two academic sessions for those admitted with a Bachelor's degree. The normal load consists of five half courses (15 credits each term).

The Master of Arts in Religious Studies requires completion of a minimum of six half-courses and a thesis embodying the results of research which may be undertaken in the areas of: Old Testament (including early Judaism), New Testament, Christian Theology, Church History, Ethics, Philosophy of Religion (including Religion and the Arts), and Comparative Study (Hindu, Buddhist, and Muslim traditions).

The Master of Sacred Theology degree requires completion of 12 half-courses and passing 4 comprehensive examinations. Areas of study are the same as listed above for the Master of Arts in Religious Studies.

The Doctor of Philosophy in Religious Studies is of-

ered and candidates admitted to Ph.D. 1 must reside for three consecutive sessions of full-time study and research. French and German are normally required of all candidates. Comprehensive examinations, a doctoral colloquium, and a thesis are prescribed.

Montreal Diocesan Theological College
3473 University Street
Montreal, PQ H3A 2A8   (514) 849-3004

Administration. The Reverend Anthony C. Capon, Principal.

General Description. Montreal Diocesan Theological College is an Anglican theological college affiliated with McGill University. Its principal objective is the training of men and women for the various ministries of the Anglican Church, especially the ordained ministry. It seeks to achieve this goal through academic studies in a university setting, through a largely field-based experience of learning in ministry, and through personal spiritual growth in a supportive College community. As a diocesan institution, the College has within its faculty and student body, people who represent many different expressions of the one Christian faith, and many different convictions within the general compass of Anglican tradition and liturgy. Although autonomous, the College operates in an ecumenical setting together with the Presbyterian College, the United Theological College, the Faculty of Religious Studies of McGill University, and the Montreal Institute for Ministry.

The College was founded in 1873 by the Most Reverend Ashton Oxenden, second Bishop of Montreal. It became affiliated with McGill University in 1880. Cooperation with the other theological colleges affiliated with McGill began at an early date. In 1912 a "Joint Board of the Theological Colleges affiliated with McGill University" was set up and incorporated.

Community Environment. The College's location in the Province of Quebec, and specifically in the heart of the city of Montreal, has played a significant role in the College's self-understanding and program. Here the College has a unique opportunity to undertake theological and ministerial training in the context of a rich culture and at the same time of profound social and political change. Montreal is the second largest French-speaking city in the world, second only to Paris. It is the second largest city in Canada. Cultural attractions include Musee des Beaux-Arts, McCord Museum at McGill University, Musee des Arts Contemporain, Place des Arts (home of the Montreal Symphony, the Canadian Grand Ballet, and the Quebec Opera), along with many art galleries, museums, cathedrals and historic sights. The city has many recreational areas and the Laurentian Mountain regions just 35 miles north of the city provide all-year outdoor sports facilities.

Religious Denomination. Anglican Church of Canada.
Religious Emphasis. Pluralistic.

Accreditation. Association of Theological Schools in the United States and Canada.

Term System. Semester; limited summer term.

Enrollment in Degree Programs in Religion 1984–85. Total 30; men 23, women 7.

Degrees in Religion Awarded 1984–85. Diploma in Ministry 2; men 2. Licentiate in Theology 3; men 2, women 1. Master of Divinity 1; men 1; Master of Sacred Theology 1; men 1.

Faculty for Degree Programs in Religion. Total 19; full-time 15, part-time 4. (Represents the amalgamated faculty of this College, Presbyterian College, the United Theological College, and the Faculty of Religious Studies of McGill University.)

Admission Requirements. Bachelor of Arts degree or equivalent.

Tuition and Fees. Canadian students tuition $570 per year; non-Canadian students $5,800 per year. Fees are determined by the Government of the Province of Quebec.

Financial Aid. A number of bursaries are available for ordination candidates who are officially sponsored by a diocesan bishop. These are awarded according to need. Several prizes are awarded each year and are granted according to merit.

Housing. Residence rooms for men and women are available under a plan that includes three meals daily, Monday through Friday. Unfurnished accommodation for married students is available under yearly lease from the College.

Library Facilities. The library of the McGill University Faculty of Religious Studies is available to students.

Religious Services/Activities. Daily morning and evening services, also Wednesday noon; annual weekend retreat in September; annual quiet day in January.

Degree Programs

The Bachelor of Theology and Diploma in Ministry is designed for certain candidates who (for reasons such as age) are unable to fulfill the prerequisite of a B.A. degree for the Master of Divinity program. Applicants may, with the permission of their bishop, apply to proceed directly to the Bachelor of Theology degree and the Diploma in Ministry. This will normally require four years. The Diploma in Ministry is awarded by the College on completion of the final year.

The Master of Divinity is offered jointly with the Presbyterian College, United Theological College, and McGill University. The primary goal is the preparation of ordinands for ministry in and through the Christian churches, including parish ministry, teaching, and missionary work in Canada and abroad. It is normally a three-year program with the following main components: (1) a two-year concentration on the classical theological disciplines, leading to the Bachelor of Theology degree of the McGill University Faculty of Religious Studies; (2) a one-year field-based learning process through the "In-Ministry Year" of the Montreal Institute for Ministry; and (3) a College-based

experience spread over all three years in which the student is encouraged to make progress in the areas of spiritual growth, community living, personal maturity, and understanding of the theology, liturgy, and tradition of the Anglican Church.

The Master of Sacred Theology is awarded to students who achieve at least good second class standing in the Bachelor of Theology component of their Master of Divinity work and who complete a one-year further program at McGill University.

Special Programs

Older candidates who are unable to devote more than one academic year to full-time study may, with the approval of their bishop, prepare for the ordained ministry by means of the Reading and Tutorial Course. This course consists of twelve units of study and is undertaken under the supervision of a selected tutor in the student's own home area. It may be completed in two to three years. The student must then take the full-time In-Ministry Year at the College. The Licentiate in Theology diploma is awarded upon successful completion of all requirements.

The Licentiate in Theology diploma may be awarded to students who undertake, with the approval of the candidate's bishop, two years of basic theological studies as a non-degree student at McGill, followed by the In-Ministry Year of the Montreal Institute for Ministry.

Montreal, University of
Faculty of Theology
Case Postale 6128, Succursale "A"
Montreal, PQ H3C 3J7   (514) 343-7080

Administration. Dr. A. Herve Hebert, President; Dr. M. Gilles G. Cloutier, Rector; Dr. Leonard Audet, Dean, Faculty of Theology.

General Description. The Faculty of Theology prepares candidates for the priesthood of the Roman Catholic Church.

Parent Institution. The University of Montreal was established in 1878 as a branch of Laval University. In the 1960's it became an independent institution of the Roman Catholic Church, and is now a provincial university.

Community Environment. Montreal is the second largest French-speaking city in the world, second only to Paris. It is the second largest city in Canada.

Religious Denomination. Roman Catholic.

Religious Emphasis. Specifically Roman Catholic, but open to other approaches of truth.

Term System. Trimester; summer term.

Degrees in Religion Awarded 1984–85. Bachelor of Arts 19; men 9, women 10. Bachelor of Theology 29; men 20, women 9. Master of Theology 19; men 10, women 9. Doctor of Philosophy (Ph.D.) 1; men 1.

Tuition and Fees. Tuition $270 per trimester for full-time students; part-time $64.50 per course.

Library Facilities. The library houses over 90,000 volumes.

Religious Services/Activities. A pastoral service is offered by the University for all students.

Quebec, University of, at Trois-Rivières
Department of Theology
3351 Boul Des Forges, C.P. 500
Trois-Rivières, PQ G9A 5H7   (819) 376-5506

Administration. Raymond Anctil, Director, Department of Theology; Jacques Chenevert, Director, Graduate Studies in Theology.

General Description. The main purpose of the Department of Theology is to prepare specialists for the service of the Church and of Society. Studies are conceived and organized so as to help the student progressively initiate himself or herself to the whole of theology and to develop his or her capacity of reflection and personal study. Students can find in the Department the preparation for an academic career, the instruction required for the reception of Orders, and the theological formation needed for serious apostolic involvement. Admission is granted to all qualified persons, whatever their religious affiliation. All the courses are given in French.

Parent Institution. Established in 1968 by an act of the National Assembly in the Province of Quebec, the University of Quebec is the province's first public university. It is a general body which groups constituent universities, research institutes, and "superior schools."

Community Environment. Trois-Rivières is situated approximately midway between Montreal and Quebec City, near the St. Lawrence River.

Religious Denomination. Nondenominational in principle.

Religious Emphasis. Roman Catholic Theology.

Accreditation. Assembly of Quebec's Catholic Bishops.

Term System. Three sessions of 15 weeks each.

Enrollment in Degree Programs in Religion 1984–85. Total 514; men 172, women 342.

Degrees in Religion Awarded 1984–85. Master of Arts in Theology 4; men 3, women 1. Master of Theology 2; men 1, women 1. Bachelor of Theology 15; men 10, women 5. Certificate in Religious Sciences 39; men 5, women 34.

Admission Requirements. Certificate in Religious Sciences or Bachelor of Theology: Diploma of Collegial Studies of a Quebec CEGEP or an equivalent Diploma. Mature students admission policy: be 22 years of age or older and possess appropriate knowledge and have relevant experience. Master of Theology and Master of Arts: have obtained a Bachelor of Theology with a minimum of 2.5 points.

Tuition and Fees. Individuals interested in being considered for entrance should contact the University Admissions Office for tuition and fee requirements.

Financial Aid. The Student Financial Assistance office is responsible for all aid programs.

Housing. Apartments to let are available in the neighborhood of the University.

Library Facilities. The library of the University contains over 75,000 items in the fields of Theology, Philosophy, Church History, and related subjects.

Religious Services/Activities. Catholic Mass is celebrated daily on the campus.

Degree Programs

Degrees offered are: Bachelor of Religious Sciences, Bachelor of Theology, Master of Arts in Theology, Master of Theology, and Bachelor of Theology.

Special Programs

The Certificate in Religious Studies is offered.

SASKATCHEWAN

Briercrest Bible College
Bachelor of Religious Education Department
Caronport, SK S0H 0S0   (306) 756-2351

Administration. Henry H. Budd, President; Paul Magnus, Vice President - Education.

General Description. The Bachelor of Religious Education program is designed to prepare students for service in the church and para-church organizations in both North America and overseas. The program also offers a solid foundation for continuing education. Degrees offered are Bachelor of Religious Education, Bachelor of Biblical Studies, Bachelor of Sacred Music, and Bachelor of Theology.

Parent Institution. Briercrest College exists to be a servant and ally of evangelical churches, both independent and of various denominations. It is a training school for pastors, Christian education ministers or directors, missionaries, music directors, youth pastors, and Christian lay workers.

Community Environment. The Briercrest College campus of 300 acres is located at Caronport, Saskatchewan, approximately 24 kilometers west of the city of Moose Jaw, and 100 kilometers west of Regina. Situated on the Trans-Canada Highway, it is midway between Calgary and Winnipeg. Briercrest enjoys the seclusion of a country campus, free from distractions, and ideal for study and the development of a Christian atmosphere.

Religious Denomination. Nondenominational (Christian).

Religious Emphasis. Evangelical.

Accreditation. American Association of Bible Colleges; Association of Canadian Bible Colleges; Canadian Association of Independent Universities, Colleges, and Institutes.

Term System. Semester; summer term.

Enrollment in Degree Programs in Religion 1984–85. Total 339; men 216, women 123.

Degrees in Religion Awarded 1984–85. Bachelor of Religious Education 64; men 46, women 18. Bachelor of Biblical Studies 38; men 12, women 26. Bachelor of Sacred Music 1; women 1.

Faculty for Degree Programs in Religion. Total 59; full-time 44, part-time 15.

Admission Requirements. Christian men and women who have a desire to study God's Word and to know Christ more deeply; character and conduct must be compatible with the standards of the College and the student must be willing to submit to regulations; references from the applicant's home church and at least two other adult acquaintances. Applicants should generally be high school graduates.

Tuition and Fees. Tuition $50 per credit hour; room and board $883 to $957 per semester; library fee $50 per semester; student activity fee $45; registration fee $16; parking fee $5; accident insurance $16 per year.

Financial Aid. Some financial assistance is available through the College in the form of grants and scholarships. Briercrest is recognized by the governments of both Canada and the United States for student loans.

Housing. All single students are housed on campus. Most married students are accommodated on campus either in rental suites (200-$275 per month) or in mobile homes, many of which are owned by these students. Lot rental is approximately $40-$45 per month.

Library Facilities. The library contains 35,500 volumes. Special collections include ERIC microfiche, pre-1900 Canadiana, Religious Curriculum Collection, and a music score collection.

Religious Services/Activities. Two Sunday services; prayer meeting; Sunday School; Graduation retreat; Barkman Lecture Series; Pastors' Conference; YouthQuake; Fall and Spring Conferences.

Degree Programs

The Bachelor of Religious Education programs are offered with majors in Pastoral Studies, Christian Education, World Evangelism, Biblical, Theology, and Music and Church Ministries. The student must complete all required courses and elective hours of the prescribed program chosen. The programs are of four-year duration and required 130 credit hours.

The Bachelor of Sacred Music is intended to prepare students to serve as Music Directors in churches, mission organizations, or para-church organizations. It requires 130 credit hours in a specified curriculum.

The Bachelor of Biblical Studies is a three-year program requiring completion of 110 credit hours. It is designed to equip students to serve as lay leaders or to go on to study further toward a secular vocation. There is no specific professional specialization within the program.

The Bachelor of Theology is designed to prepare men and women to apply their Biblical and theological training in a ministry opportunity. It requires 32 credit hours beyond the Bachelor of Religious Education degree or a total of 162 credit hours. The program has a balance between theory and practice, with one half of the study being taken in theoretical preparation for the ministry and the other half in technical and practical experience within the ministry. A field experience segment of the program will include a minimum of six months of ministry in a chosen field.

Special Programs

Special External Educational Development (SEED) correspondence courses are offered by the College.

A Certificate for Advanced Students is designed for graduates of undergraduate degree programs who want to engage in in-depth Bible study. It is a one-year program of two semesters plus one summer and requires the completion of 48 credit hours.

Emmanuel/St. Chad, College of
1337 College Drive
Saskatoon, SK S7N 0W6   (306) 343-1353

Administration. The Rev. Canon J. Russell Brown, Principal; The Rev. Canon Eric Bays, Vice Principal; June Roberts, Administrator.

General Description. The primary aim of the College is to train people for ministry, primarily for ordained ministry. The training course is designed to be a combination of thoughtful understanding, practical experience, and spiritual formation. The combination is expressed in the study of theology, the use of several methods of field education, and the daily life of corporate prayer both at the College and in local parishes.

Parent Institution. The parent institution of the College of Emmanuel/St. Chad is the Anglican Church of Canada. The College is also affiliated with the University of Saskatchewan.

Community Environment. Saskatoon is located on the banks of the South Saskatchewan River in the midst of a gently rolling plain known as the Parklands Region. It is a growing modern city of about 155,000 people, and a distribution point for a rich agricultural and mining area.

Religious Denomination. Anglican.

Term System. Semester.

Enrollment in Degree Programs in Religion 1984–85. Total 32; men 22, women 10.

Degrees in Religion Awarded 1984–85. Bachelor of Theology 1; women 1. Master of Divinity 3; men 3. Master of Sacred Theology 1; men 1.

Faculty for Degree Programs in Religion. Total 18; full-time 6, part-time 12.

Admission Requirements. Bachelor of Theology: Candidates must have completed at least one year of the Arts, including five subjects chosen in consultation with the College, or equivalent preparation. Master of Divinity: Candidates must have a Bachelor's degree from a recognized university.

Tuition and Fees. Tuition $950 per year; student fees $20; room $575 per term; board $1,780 per year.

Financial Aid. The College has a limited number of bursaries available. Bursaries are also available through the Anglican Church of Canada. A few foundations also make bursary money available.

Housing. A small residence is operated by the college providing room and board. Off-campus accommodation is the responsibility of the student.

Library Facilities. The library contains over 80,000 volumes with a special Scandinavian Collection of 5,000 volumes.

Religious Services/Activities. Anglican services of evensong and morning prayer are held eight times per week; two retreats are scheduled per year. The Theological Society provides for particular interests of the theological students. The Society arranges discussions and debates and enables students and staff to meet together on an informal level to talk about issues of general concern.

Degree Programs

Candidates for the Bachelor of Theology degree must complete all of the requirements of the theological program with an overall average of 3.0. A thesis is not required. Courses are offered in Old Testament, New Testament, Church History, Theology and Ethics, and Liturgy and Pastoral Education. The student is required to complete twenty-seven semester courses plus the supervised experiences and other aspects of field education over a period of three years.

Two paths are open toward completion of the Master of Divinity degree. Students may choose, in the final semester, to do either three required courses plus a short thesis or to do three required courses plus two electives.

The Master of Sacred Theology degree may be taken through the Graduate Theological Union at Saskatoon, an interseminary program of the College, the Lutheran Theological Seminary, and St. Andrews's College.

Special Programs

A Lay School of Theology is sponsored by the College for the continuing education of lay persons.

Lutheran Theological Seminary
114 Seminary Crescent
Saskatoon, SK S7N 0X3   (306) 343-8204

Administration. Dr. Roger Wesley Nostbakken, President; Gertrude D. Buck, Registrar.

General Description. Lutheran Theological Seminary was established to prepare candidates for the Christian ministry, especially for the Lutheran Churches in Canada. The Seminary also serves qualified students who wish to pursue the study of theology for its own sake, or solely out of academic interest. The school seeks to be of assistance to pastors in the area of continuing education and as an institution of advanced study and research. The Lutheran Theological Seminary is owned and supported by the Evangelical Lutheran Church of Canada and by the Lutheran Church in America synods in western Canada. In January 1985, the new Evangelical Lutheran Church in Canada came into being and it is now supported by the four western synods of that church - the Manitoba, Saskatchewan, Alberta, and British Columbia synods.

The Seminary is the successor of Lutheran College and Seminary founded in 1913 and of Luther Theological Seminary established in 1939. The merger took place in 1965. A newly constructed school was dedicated in 1968. The Seminary is an affiliate college of the University of Saskatchewan. It participates in a graduate program of theology in cooperation with the College of Emmanuel and St. Chad and with St. Andrew's College. The faculty also is involved in the Department of Near Eastern Studies and in the Department of Religious Studies of the University.

Community Environment. Saskatoon, on the banks of the South Saskatchewan River, is known as the "City of Bridges" with its riverfront and many parks. It is the home of the Western Development Museum, museums of Ukrainian arts and culture, the Mendel Art Gallery, and the Forestry Farm Park.

Religious Denomination. Evangelical Lutheran Church of Canada.

Religious Emphasis. Neo-orthodox Lutheran.

Accreditation. Association of Theological Schools in the United States and Canada.

Term System. Semester; spring term.

Enrollment in Degree Programs in Religion 1984–85. Total 120; men 92, women 28.

Degrees in Religion Awarded 1984–85. Bachelor of Theology 2; men 2. Master of Theological Studies 1; women 1. Master of Divinity 22; men 17, women 5. Master of Sacred Theology 4; men 4.

Faculty for Degree Programs in Religion. Total 12; full-time 8, part-time 4.

Admission Requirements. Master of Theological Studies and Master of Divinity students must have a Bachelor of Arts or equivalent; Bachelor of Theology students must be over 30 years of age and have completed one year with satisfactory grades at a recognized college or university;

Master of Sacred Theology students must have a Master of Divinity degree or the equivalent.

Tuition and Fees. Tuition full-time $900 per year; part-time students $100 per course; student body fee $40 per year; housing approximately $1,300 per semester.

Financial Aid. There are bursary and scholarship funds available to seminary students preparing for ordination or full-time service in the Evangelical Lutheran Church of Canada. The seminary has some student aid funds.

Housing. The Seminary Residence has spaces for 49 men and 35 women, single and double rooms. Off-campus apartments and houses are available in the city of Saskatoon at varying prices.

Library Facilities. The Otto Olson Memorial Library contains 38,000 volumes including several photostats of ancient biblical manuscripts, a sizable collection of source materials relating to Near Eastern Christianity and the Reformation, and Luther's Works in the original languages and in several editions. The library subscribes to 150 learned and professional journals. Close liaison is maintained with the theological libraries of St. Andrew's College and the College of Emmanuel and St. Chad. A union catalogue for these three collections is constantly updated.

Religious Services/Activities. The Seminary confronts students with historic Christianity, and at the same time, points them to their future as servants in the Christian Church. While no attempt is made to impose a particular life-style, the claims of Christ are expressed in the communal life of the Seminary, in both classroom and chapel. Daily worship services are held in the chapel, and at special times during the school year. Students are expected to involve themselves in the life and worship of congregations in Saskatoon. *The Podium* is published periodically and serves as a vehicle for disseminating information, for the airing of theological viewpoints, and for the publication of scholarly articles.

Degree Programs

The Bachelor of Theology program is designed for candidates for ordination who are over thirty years of age and for whom completion of a first university degree would constitute a severe hardship. The candidate needs the approval or certification of the church body into which the candidate is seeking ordination.

The Master of Divinity program is the standard program that prepares a candidate for ordination. The student must gain competence in at least one Biblical language and complete the thirty-three courses required.

The Master of Theological Studies program is designed for lay persons who desire to pursue the study of theology or wish to prepare for a church vocation which does not involve ordination. The degree requires the completion of twenty-two courses. The courses to be included are arranged in consultation with a faculty advisor.

The Master of Sacred Theology program is offered through the facilities of the Graduate Theological Union at Saskatoon and is designed to provide an opportunity for qualified candidates to take part in continuing education programs or to advance their studies toward the doctoral level.

Special Programs

The Certificate in Ministry program is designed for certain selected individuals in consultation with the church body into which they desire to be ordained. The Certificate is granted to students upon fulfillment of all requirements including at least one year of study (11 courses) in a program planned in consultation between the church body and the Seminary.

St. Thomas More College
Department of Religious Studies
1437 College Drive
Saskatoon, SK S7N 0W6   (306) 966-8900

Administration. C. M. Foley, Head, Department of Religious Studies.

General Description. St. Thomas More College is a Roman Catholic liberal arts college offering classes in the humanities and social sciences. It is open to people of all backgrounds providing they meet the admission standards of the University of Saskatchewan with which the College is federated. The Department of Religious Studies is part of the Humanities Program and is academically integrated with the main Religious Studies Department in the College of Arts and Science of the University.

Parent Institution. The University of Saskatchewan was begun in 1909. Coeducational and nondenominational, the University offers many comprehensive programs. It enrolls more than 14,000 students.

Community Environment. The College is located on the campus of the University in Saskatoon. The town is situated on the banks of the South Saskatchewan River and is known as the "City of Bridges."

Religious Denomination. Roman Catholic.

Accreditation. Provincial accreditation.

Term System. Semester system.

Faculty for Degree Programs in Religion. Total 5; full-time 3, part-time 2.

Admission Requirements. High school graduation with 21 academic credits.

Tuition and Fees. Tuition $940; room and board $1,892; student fees $71.50.

Housing. University housing is available to students of the College.

Library Facilities. The Shannon Library has holdings of 36,000 volumes. Special collections are in Canadian Church History and Christian Social Sciences.

Religious Services/Activities. Daily Roman Catholic liturgies are celebrated.

Degree Programs

The Bachelor of Arts degree is awarded.

Saskatchewan, University of
Department of Religious Studies
Saskatoon, SK S7N 0W0   (306) 966-6771

Administration. C.M. Foley, Acting Head, Department of Religious Studies.

General Description. The Department of Religious Studies is within the University's College of Arts and Science. It offers academic/non-confessional courses under three general headings: Religious Tradition - History and Content; Religion and Literature; and Religion and Society. The Department draws on the faculty and appropriate course offerings of other Colleges and Departments to round out its program.

Parent Institution. The University is government funded and offers programs covering most of the standard areas of academic inquiry. There is a strong emphasis on agricultural and veterinary science as well as medicine, law, and commerce.

Community Environment. The University has a main campus of 350 acres in Saskatoon. The town is situated on the banks of the South Saskatchewan River.

Religious Denomination. Nondenominational.

Accreditation. Provincial accreditation.

Term System. Semester system.

Enrollment in Degree Programs in Religion 1984–85. 17 Majors.

Faculty for Degree Programs in Religion. Total 12; full-time 2, part-time 10.

Admission Requirements. High school graduation with 21 academic credits.

Tuition and Fees. Tuition $815-$1,200; room and board $3,500; student fees $135.

Financial Aid. Some scholarships and bursaries are available.

Housing. Dormitories are available on campus.

Library Facilities. The library contains over 850,000 volumes.

Religious Services/Activities. Various denominations hold weekly services.

Degree Programs

Both the 3-year (general) and 4-year (advanced) Bachelor of Arts degrees are awarded. The major (general) in Religious Studies requires completion of 30 credit units including at least 24 in senior courses. The major (advanced) requires the completion of 36 credits, including at least 30 in senior courses. It is recommended that courses be selected from at least two of the three major areas of the program.

DENOMINATION INDEX

ADVENTIST

Maryland
Columbia Union College *Takoma Park*

Massachusetts
Atlantic Union College, Religion Department *South Lancaster*

Berkshire Christian College, Division of Christian Ministries *Lenox*

Michigan
Andrews University, Seventh-day Adventist Theological Seminary *Berrien Springs*

Nebraska
Union College *Lincoln*

Puerto Rico
Antillian College *Mayaguez*

Tennessee
Southern College of Seventh-day Adventists, Division of Religion *Collegedale*

Texas
Southwestern Adventist College, Department of Religion *Keene*

Alberta
Canadian Union College, Department of Religious Studies *College Heights*

ANGLICAN

British Columbia
Vancouver School of Theology *Vancouver*

Nova Scotia
Atlantic School of Theology *Halifax*

Ontario
Huron College, University of Western Ontario *London*

Trinity College, Faculty of Divinity *Toronto*

Wycliffe College *Toronto*

Quebec
Montreal Diocesan Theological College *Montreal*

Saskatchewan
Emmanuel/St. Chad, College of *Saskatoon*

ANGLICAN ORTHODOX

North Carolina
Cranmer Seminary *Statesville*

ASSEMBLIES OF GOD

Missouri
Central Bible College *Springfield*

Texas
Southwestern Assemblies of God College *Waxahachie*

BAPTIST

Arizona
Grand Canyon College, Department of Religion *Phoenix*

Arkansas
Central Baptist College *Conway*

Ouachita Baptist University, Division of Religion and Philosophy *Arkadelphia*

California
American Baptist Seminary of the West *Berkeley*

California Baptist College, Division of Religion *Riverside*

Christian Heritage College, Department of Ministerial Training *El Cajon*

Golden Gate Baptist Theological Seminary *Mill Valley*

Los Angeles Baptist College *Newhall*

Colorado
Denver Baptist Bible College and Theological Seminary *Broomfield*

Denver Conservative Baptist Seminary *Denver*

Florida
Baptist Bible Institute *Graceville*

Georgia
Brewton-Parker College, Division of Christianity *Mount Vernon*

Mercer University, The Roberts Department of Christianity *Macon*

Shorter College, Department of Religion and Philosophy *Rome*

of Theology *Fort Worth*

Wayland Baptist University, Division of Christian Studies *Plainview*

Virginia

Liberty University, (Formerly Liberty Baptist College) *Lynchburg*

Virginia Union University, School of Theology *Richmond*

West Virginia

Alderson-Broaddus College *Philippi*

British Columbia

Carey Hall Baptist College *Vancouver*

Nova Scotia

Acadia Divinity College, Acadia University *Wolfville*

Ontario

McMaster Divinity College, (McMaster University) *Hamilton*

BRETHREN

Illinois

Bethany Theological Seminary *Oak Brook*

Indiana

Grace College, Division of Religion and Philosophy *Winona Lake*

Grace Theological Seminary *Winona Lake*

Ohio

Ashland Theological Seminary *Ashland*

Pennsylvania

Elizabethtown College, Department of Religion and Philosophy *Elizabethtown*

Messiah College, Department of Religion and Philosophy *Grantham*

Virginia

Bridgewater College, Department of Philosophy and Religion *Bridgewater*

BUDDHIST

California

Buddhist Studies, Institute of *Berkeley*

Colorado

Naropa Institute, Buddhist Studies Department *Boulder*

CHRISTIAN AND MISSIONARY ALLIANCE

Minnesota

St. Paul Bible College *Bible College*

CHRISTIAN CHURCH (DISCIPLES OF CHRIST)

California

Chapman College, Department of Religion *Orange*

Indiana

Christian Theological Seminary *Indianapolis*

Kentucky

Lexington Theological Seminary *Lexington*

Transylvania University, Religion Program, Humanities Division *Lexington*

Missouri

Drury College, Department of Philosophy and Religion *Springfield*

North Carolina

Atlantic Christian College, Department of Religion and Philosophy *Wilson*

Oklahoma

Phillips University, The Graduate Seminary *Enid*

Oregon

Northwest Christian College *Eugene*

Texas

Jarvis Christian College, Division of Humanities and Social Science *Hawkins*

Texas Christian University, Brite Divinity School *Forth Worth*

Virginia

Lynchburg College, Department of Religious Studies *Lynchburg*

West Virginia

Bethany College, Department of Religious Studies *Bethany*

CHRISTIAN CHURCHES AND CHURCHES OF CHRIST

California

Pacific Christian College *Fullerton*

Georgia

Atlanta Christian College *East Point*

Illinois

Lincoln Christian College and Seminary *Lincoln*

Kentucky

Kentucky Christian College *Grayson*

Maryland

Eastern Christian College *Bel Air*

Michigan

Great Lakes Bible College *Lansing*

Minnesota

Minnesota Bible College *Rochester*

Nebraska

Nebraska Christian College *Norfolk*

Ohio

Cincinnati Bible College, Cincinnati Bible Seminary: Undergraduate Division *Cincinnati*

Cincinnati Christian Seminary, Graduate Division of Cincinnati Bible Seminary *Cincinnati*

Oregon

Northwest Christian College *Eugene*

Tennessee

Emmanuel School of Religion *Johnson City*

Johnson Bible College *Knoxville*

Milligan College, Area of Biblical Learning *Milligan*

Washington

Puget Sound Christian College *Edmonds*

CHURCH OF CHRIST

Oklahoma

Oklahoma Christian College, Division of Bible *Oklahoma City*

Oregon

Columbia Christian College, Division of Bible and Religion *Portland*

Texas

Abilene Christian University, College of Biblical Studies *Abilene*

CHURCH OF CHRIST, SCIENTIST

Illinois

Principia College, Humanities Department *Elsah*

CHURCH OF GOD

California

West Coast Christian College *Fresno*

Indiana

Anderson School of Theology, Anderson College *Anderson*

North Dakota

Northwest Bible College *Minot*

Oklahoma

Mid-America Bible College *Oklahoma City*

Oregon

Warner Pacific College, Department of Religion and Christian Ministries *Portland*

Tennessee

Lee College, Department of Bible and Christian Ministries *Cleveland*

CHURCH OF THE NAZARENE

Colorado

Nazarene Bible College *Colorado Springs*

Illinois

Olivet Nazarene College, Division of Religion and Philosophy *Kankakee*

Massachusetts

Eastern Nazarene College, Division of Religion and Philosophy *Wollaston*

Missouri

Nazarene Theological Seminary *Kansas City*

Ohio

Mount Vernon Nazarene College, Division of Religion and Philosophy *Mount Vernon*

Oklahoma

Bethany Nazarene College, Division of Philosophy and Religion *Bethany*

CHURCHES OF CHRIST

Arkansas

Harding University, Department of Bible, Religion, and Philosophy. *Searcy*

California

Pepperdine University, Seaver College, Religion Division *Malibu*

Michigan

Michigan Christian College *Rochester*

Tennessee

David Lipscomb College, Department of Bible *Nashville*

Freed-Hardeman College, Department of Bible *Henderson*

Harding Graduate School of Religion *Memphis*

Texas

Lubbock Christian College, Biblical Studies Division *Lubbock*

West Virginia

Ohio Valley College *Parkersburg*

CHURCHES OF CHRIST IN CHRISTIAN UNION

Ohio

Circleville Bible College *Circleville*

CHURCHES OF GOD, GENERAL CONFERENCE

Ohio

Winebrenner Theological Seminary *Findlay*

Winebrenner Theological Seminary - Institute for Biblical Studies *Findlay*

CONGREGATIONAL CHRISTIAN CHURCHES

Michigan

Olivet College *Olivet*

EPISCOPAL

California

Church Divinity School of the Pacific *Berkeley*

Illinois

Seabury-Western Theological Seminary *Evanston*

Massachusetts

Episcopal Divinity School *Cambridge*

New York

Bexley Hall, Colgate Rochester Divinity School *Rochester*

Colgate Rochester Divinity School *Rochester*

Crozer Theological Seminary, Colgate Rochester Divinity School *Rochester*

General Theological Seminary *New York*

Pennsylvania

Theological Seminary of the Reformed Episcopal Church *Philadelphia*

Tennessee

South, University of the, The School of Theology *Sewanee*

Texas

Episcopal Theological Seminary of the Southwest *Austin*

Virginia

Protestant Episcopal Theological Seminary in Virginia *Alexandria*

Wisconsin

Nashotah House Theological Seminary *Nashotah*

EVANGELICAL CONGREGATIONAL CHURCH

Pennsylvania

Evangelical School of Theology *Myerstown*

EVANGELICAL COVENANT CHURCH

Illinois

North Park College and Theological Seminary, North Park Theological Seminary *Chicago*

EVANGELICAL FREE CHURCH OF AMERICA

Illinois

Trinity Evangelical Divinity School *Deerfield*

FOURSQUARE GOSPEL

California

L.I.F.E. Bible College *Los Angeles*

Ohio

Mount Vernon Bible College *Mount Vernon*

FRIENDS (QUAKER)

California

Whittier College, Department of Religion *Whittier*

Indiana

Earlham School of Religion *Richmond*

Kansas

Friends Bible College *Haviland*

Friends University, Division of Religion and Philosophy *Wichita*

Ohio

Malone College, Department of Religion and Philosophy *Canton*

Pennsylvania

Haverford College, Department of Religion *Haverford*

Swarthmore College, Department of Religion *Swarthmore*

JEWISH

California

Hebrew Union College - Jewish Institute of Religion, Los Angeles *Los Angeles*

Judaism, University of, Graduate School of Judaica *Los Angeles*

Illinois

Hebrew Theological College/Jewish University of America *Skokie*

Spertus College of Judaica *Chicago*

Maryland

Baltimore Hebrew College, School of Undergraduate Studies *Baltimore*

Massachusetts

Hebrew College *Brookline*

New Jersey

Rabbinical College of America *Morristown*

New York

Hebrew Union College - Jewish Institute of Religion, New York *New York*

Jewish Theological Seminary of America *New York*

Rabbi Isaac Elchanan Theological Seminary *New*

York

Ohio

Hebrew Union College - Jewish Institute of Religion, Cincinnati *Cincinnati*

Hebrew Union College - Jewish Institute of Religion, Jerusalem, American Headquarters *Cincinnati*

LATTER DAY SAINTS (MORMON)

Hawaii

Brigham Young University - Hawaii Campus *Laie*

Missouri

Park College, Graduate School of Religion *Independence*

Utah

Brigham Young University, Department of Religious Education *Provo*

LUTHERAN

California

California Lutheran College, Department of Religion *Thousand Oaks*

Christ College Irvine, Religion Division *Irvine*

Pacific Lutheran Theological Seminary *Berkeley*

Illinois

Augustana College, Department of Religion *Rock Island*

Lutheran School of Theology at Chicago *Chicago*

Indiana

Concordia Theological Seminary *Fort Wayne*

Valparaiso University, Department of Theology *Valparaiso*

Iowa

Luther College, Department of Religion and Philosophy *Decorah*

Wartburg Theological Seminary *Dubuque*

Michigan

Concordia College *Ann Arbor*

Minnesota

Augsburg College, Department of Religion *Minneapolis*

Concordia College, Religion Department *Moorhead*

Concordia College - St. Paul, Division of Religion *St. Paul*

Dr. Martin Luther College *New Ulm*

Gustavus Adolphus College, Department of Religion *St. Peter*

Luther Northwestern Theological Seminary *St. Paul*

Lutheran Brethren Schools, Junior Bible College and Seminary *Fergus Falls*

St. Olaf College, Department of Religion *Northfield*

Missouri

Concordia Seminary *St. Louis*

Nebraska

Dana College *Blair*

Midland Lutheran College, Department of Philosophy/Religion *Fremont*

New Jersey

Upsala College *East Orange*

New York

Concordia College *Bronxville*

North Carolina

Lenoir-Rhyne College, Department of Religion and Philosophy *Hickory*

Ohio

Capital University, Department of Religion and Philosophy *Columbus*

Trinity Lutheran Seminary *Columbus*

Wittenberg University, Department of Religion *Springfield*

Oregon

Concordia College *Portland*

Pennsylvania

Lutheran Theological Seminary *Gettysburg*

Lutheran Theological Seminary at Philadelphia *Philadelphia*

Muhlenberg College, Religion Department *Allentown*

Susquehanna University, Department of Philosophy and Religion *Selinsgrove*

Thiel College, Religion Department *Greenville*

South Carolina

Lutheran Theological Southern Seminary *Columbia*

Newberry College *Newberry*

South Dakota

Augustana College, Department of Religion *Sioux Falls*

Texas

Texas Lutheran College, Department of Theology and Philosophy *Seguin*

Washington

Pacific Lutheran University, Department of Religion *Tacoma*

Wisconsin

Carthage College, Department of Religion *Kenosha*

Concordia College, Division of Theology and Social Science *Mequon*

Immanuel Lutheran College, Immanuel Lutheran College and Immanuel Lutheran Seminary *Eau Claire*

Northwestern College *Watertown*

Alberta

Camrose Lutheran College, Department of Religious Studies *Camrose*

Concordia Lutheran Seminary *Edmonton*

Ontario

Waterloo Lutheran Seminary, Wilfred Laurier University *Waterloo*

Saskatchewan

Lutheran Theological Seminary *Saskatoon*

MENNONITE

California

Mennonite Brethren Biblical Seminary *Fresno*

Indiana

Goshen Biblical Seminary, (Associated Mennonite Biblical Seminaries) *Elkhart*

Mennonite Biblical Seminary, (Associated Mennonite Biblical Seminaries) *Elkhart*

Kansas

Tabor College, Department of Biblical and Religious Studies *Hillsboro*

Virginia

Eastern Mennonite College, Bible and Religion Department *Harrisonburg*

METHODIST

Alaska

Alaska Pacific University, Value and Religious Service Concentration *Anchorage*

California

Claremont, School of Theology at *Claremont*

Colorado

Iliff School of Theology *Denver*

District of Columbia

American University, Department of Philosophy and Religion *Washington*

Wesley Theological Seminary *Washington*

Florida

Bethune-Cookman College, Area of Religion and Philosophy *Daytona Beach*

Georgia

Emory University, Candler School of Theology *Atlanta*

Wesleyan College *Macon*

Illinois

Garrett-Evangelical Theological Seminary *Evanston*

Indiana

Indiana Central University, Philosophy and Religion Department *Indianapolis*

Iowa

Iowa Wesleyan College, Department of Religion and Philosophy *Mount Pleasant*

Kansas

Kansas Wesleyan College, Religion Department *Salina*

Kentucky

Kentucky Wesleyan College, Department of Religion and Philosophy *Owensboro*

Louisiana

Centenary College of Louisiana, Department of Religion *Shreveport*

Massachusetts

Boston University, School of Theology *Boston*

Michigan

Adrian College, Department of Philosophy and Religion *Adrian*

Albion College, Department of Religious Studies *Albion*

Spring Arbor College, Division of Philosophy and Religion *Spring Arbor*

Minnesota

Hamline University, Department of Religion *St. Paul*

Mississippi

Millsaps College, Preparation for Ministry Program *Jackson*

Wesley College *Florence*

Missouri

Central Methodist College, Department of Philosophy and Religion *Fayette*

St. Paul School of Theology *Kansas City*

Montana

Rocky Mountain College *Billings*

Nebraska

Nebraska Wesleyan University, Religion Department *Lincoln*

New Jersey

Drew University, Theological School *Madison*

North Carolina

Duke University, Trinity College of Arts and Sciences *Durham*

Duke University - Divinity School *Durham*

Greensboro College, Department of Religion and Philosophy *Greensboro*

High Point College *High Point*

Methodist College, Department of Philosophy and Religion *Fayetteville*

North Carolina Wesleyan College *Rocky Mount*

Pfeiffer College *Misenheimer*

Ohio

Allegheny Wesleyan College *Salem*

Baldwin-Wallace College, Department of Religion *Berea*

Methodist Theological School in Ohio *Delaware*

Ohio Wesleyan University, Department of Religion *Delaware*

Otterbein College, Department of Religion and Philosophy *Westerville*

Payne Theological Seminary *Wilberforce*

United Theological Seminary *Dayton*

Wilberforce University, Philosophy and Religion Department *Wilberforce*

Oklahoma

Oklahoma City University, School of Religion and Church Vocations *Oklahoma City*

Pennsylvania

Albright College, Department of Religion *Reading*

Allegheny College, Department of Religious Studies *Meadville*

South Carolina

Claflin College, Department of Religion and Philosophy *Orangeburg*

Southern Methodist College *Orangeburg*

Wofford College, Department of Religion *Spartanburg*

South Dakota

Dakota Wesleyan University, Religion/Philosophy Department *Mitchell*

Tennessee

Lambuth College, Department of Religion *Jackson*

Scarritt College *Nashville*

Tennessee Wesleyan College, Department of Religion *Athens*

Texas

McMurry College, Department of Religion *Abilene*

Southern Methodist University, Dedman College *Dallas*

Southern Methodist University - Perkins School of Theology *Dallas*

Southwestern University, Religion and Philosophy Department *Georgetown*

Texas Wesleyan College, Department of Religion and Philosophy *Fort Worth*

Virginia

Emory and Henry College, Department of Religion *Emory*

Ferrum College, Department of Religion and Philosophy *Ferrum*

Randolph-Macon College, Religious Studies Department *Ashland*

Washington

Puget Sound, University of, Department of Religion *Tacoma*

Seattle Pacific University, School of Religion *Seattle*

West Virginia

West Virginia Wesleyan College, Department of Religion *Buckhannon*

MISSIONARY CHURCH

Indiana

Bethel College, Division of Religion and Philosophy *Mishawaka*

Fort Wayne Bible College, Biblical Studies Division *Fort Wayne*

MORAVIAN

Pennsylvania

Moravian College, Moravian Theological Seminary *Bethlehem*

NAZARENE

Kansas

Mid-America Nazarene College, Division of Religion and Philosophy *Olathe*

Tennessee

Trevecca Nazarene College, Department of Religion and Philosophy *Nashville*

NONDENOMINATIONAL

Alabama

Southeastern Bible College *Birmingham*

Alaska

Alaska Bible College *Glennallen*

Arkansas

John Brown University, Division of Biblical Studies *Siloam Springs*

California

Biola University, Talbot Theological Seminary and School of Theology *La Mirada*

California Institute of Integral Studies, Philosophy and Religion Department *San Francisco*

California, University of - Berkeley, Religious Studies *Berkeley*

California, University of - Los Angeles *Los Angeles*

California, University of - Riverside, Department of Religious Studies *Riverside*

Claremont Graduate School, Department of Religion *Claremont*

Fuller Theological Seminary *Pasadena*

Graduate Theological Union *Berkeley*

Pacific School of Religion *Berkeley*

Patten College, College of Christian Ministries *Oakland*

Pomona College, Department of Religion *Claremont*

San Jose Bible College *San Jose*

Southern California, University of, School of Religion *Los Angeles*

Westmont College, Religious Studies Department *Santa Barbara*

Colorado

Colorado Christian College *Lakewood*

Connecticut

Hartford Seminary *Hartford*

Trinity College, Department of Religion *Hartford*

Yale Divinity School, Yale University *New Haven*

Yale University, Department of Religious Studies *New Haven*

District of Columbia

George Washington University *Washington*

Howard University, The Divinity School *Washington*

Florida

Clearwater Christian College, Division of Biblical Studies *Clearwater*

Florida Beacon Bible College *Largo*

Miami Christian College *Miami*

New College, Humanities Division *Sarasota*

Rollins College, Department of Philosophy and Religion *Winter Park*

Georgia

Carver Bible Institute and College *Atlanta*

Interdenominational Theological Center *Atlanta*

Hawaii

Hawaii, University of - Manoa, Department of Religion *Honolulu*

Illinois

Chicago, University of, Humanities Collegiate Division *Chicago*

Chicago, University of, Divinity School *Chicago*

Illinois, University of - Urbana-Champaign, Program in Religious Studies *Urbana*

Moody Bible Institute *Chicago*

Southern Illinois University, Religious Studies Department *Carbondale*

Indiana

Butler University, Department of Philosophy and Religious Studies *Indianapolis*

Taylor University, Department of Religion, Philosophy, and Biblical Languages *Upland*

Kentucky

Asbury Theological Seminary *Wilmore*

Maine

Bowdoin College, Department of Religion *Brunswick*

Maryland

Washington Bible College, The Bible College and The Capital Bible Seminary *Lanham*

Massachusetts

Amherst College, Department of Religion *Amherst*

Andover Newton Theological School *Newton Centre*

Brandeis University, Lown School of Near Eastern and Judaic Studies *Waltham*

Gordon College *Wenham*

Gordon-Conwell Theological Seminary *South Hamilton*

Harvard Divinity School, Harvard University *Cambridge*

Harvard University, Faculty of Arts and Sciences *Cambridge*

Tufts University, Department of Religion *Medford*

Wheaton College, Department of Religion *Norton*

Michigan

Central Michigan University, Department of Religion *Mt. Pleasant*

Hillsdale College *Hillsdale*

Institute for Advanced Pastoral Studies *Detroit*

Michigan State University, Department of Religious Studies *East Lansing*

Reformed Bible College *Grand Rapids*

Western Michigan University, Department of Religion *Kalamazoo*

William Tyndale College, Department of Bible/Theology *Farmington Hills*

Minnesota

Northwestern College, Division of Bible and Ministries *St. Paul*

Missouri

Calvary Bible College, Division of Biblical Education *Kansas City*

Missouri, University of - Columbia, Department of Religious Studies *Columbia*

St. Louis Christian College *Florissant*

Nebraska

Grace College of the Bible *Omaha*

New Jersey

Northeastern Bible College *Essex Fells*

Rutgers, The State University, Department of Religion *New Brunswick*

New Mexico

Eastern New Mexico University, Department of Religion *Portales*

New York

Barnard College, Department of Religion *New York*

Colgate University, Department of Philosophy and Religion *Hamilton*

Columbia University, Department of Religion *New York*

Hartwick College, Department of Philosophy and Religion *Oneonta*

King's College, Department of Religion *Briarcliff Manor*

New York University *New York*

Roberts Wesleyan College, Department of Religion and Philosophy *Rochester*

Rochester, University of, Department of Religious and Classical Studies *Rochester*

Syracuse University, Department of Religion *Syracuse*

Union Theological Seminary *New York*

Yeshiva University, Bernard Revel Graduate School *New York*

North Carolina

John Wesley College, Division of Biblical Studies *High Point*

North Carolina, University of - Charlotte, Department of Religious Studies *Charlotte*

Ohio

Case Western Reserve University, Department of Religion *Cleveland*

Cleveland State University, Department of Religious Studies *Cleveland*

God's Bible School and College, God's Bible School, College, and Missionary Training Home *Cincinnati*

Marietta College, Department of Religion *Marietta*

Oklahoma

Oral Roberts University, School of Christian Theology and Ministry *Tulsa*

Oregon

Multnomah School of the Bible *Portland*

Oregon State University, Department of Religious Studies *Corvallis*

Oregon, University of, Religious Studies Department *Eugene*

Western Evangelical Seminary *Portland*

Pennsylvania

Bucknell University, Department of Religion *Lewisburg*

Lancaster Bible College *Lancaster*

Lincoln University, Department of Religion *Lincoln University*

Pennsylvania, University of, Department of Religious Studies *Philadelphia*

Philadelphia College of Bible *Langhorne*

Pittsburgh, University of, Department of Religious Studies *Pittsburgh*

Temple University, Department of Religion *Philadelphia*

Puerto Rico

Evangelical Seminary of Puerto Rico *Hato Rey*

Rhode Island

Brown University, Department of Religion *Providence*

South Carolina

Bob Jones University, School of Religion *Greenville*

Columbia Bible College *Columbia*

Limestone College, Department of Religion *Gaffney*

South Carolina, University of, Department of Religious Studies *Columbia*

Tennessee

Bryan College, Division of Biblical Studies and Philosophy *Dayton*

Mid-South Bible College *Memphis*

Vanderbilt University, The Divinity School *Nashville*

Texas

Dallas Christian College *Dallas*

Dallas Theological Seminary *Dallas*

LeTourneau College, Division of Biblical Studies and Missions *Longview*

Rice University, Department of Religious Studies *Houston*

Rio Grande Bible Institute and Language School, Rio Grande Bible Institute *Edinburg*

Trinity University, Department of Religion *San Antonio*

Woodcrest College, (Formerly Dallas Bible College) *Lindale*

Utah

Westminster College of Salt Lake City, Philosophy/Religion Program *Salt Lake City*

Vermont

Vermont, University of, College of Arts and Sciences *Burlington*

Virginia

Sweet Briar College, Department of Religion *Sweet Briar*

Washington

Central Washington University, Religious Studies Program *Ellensburg*

West Virginia

Appalachian Bible College *Bradley*

Alberta

Alberta, University of, Department of Religious Studies *Edmonton*

Calgary, University of, Department of Religious Studies *Calgary*

Manitoba

Brandon University, Department of Religion *Brandon*

Nova Scotia

Dalhousie University, Department of Comparative Religion *Halifax*

Ontario

Toronto School of Theology *Toronto*

Toronto, University of, Centre for Religious Studies *Toronto*

Waterloo, University of, Department of Religious Studies *Waterloo*

Wilfred Laurier University, Department of Religion

South Carolina

Erskine College, Erskine Theological Seminary *Due West*

Presbyterian College, Department of Religion *Clinton*

Tennessee

Bethel College, Department of Religion *McKenzie*

Covenant College, Biblical Studies Department *Lookout Mountain*

King College *Bristol*

Maryville College, Department of Religion and Philosophy *Maryville*

Memphis Theological Seminary *Memphis*

Texas

Austin College, Department of Religion and Philosophy *Sherman*

Austin Presbyterian Theological Seminary *Austin*

Virginia

Hampden-Sydney College, Department of Religion *Hampden-Sydney*

Presbyterian School of Christian Education *Richmond*

Union Theological Seminary in Virginia *Richmond*

West Virginia

Davis and Elkins College, Department of Religion and Philosophy *Elkins*

Wisconsin

Carroll College, Department of Religion *Waukesha*

British Columbia

Vancouver School of Theology *Vancouver*

Ontario

Knox College, Department of Religion *Toronto*

REFORMED

Illinois

Trinity Christian College, Theology Department *Palos Heights*

Iowa

Central College, Department of Philosophy and Religion *Pella*

Michigan

Calvin Theological Seminary *Grand Rapids*

Hope College, Department of Religion *Holland*

Western Theological Seminary *Holland*

New Jersey

New Brunswick Theological Seminary *New Brunswick*

ROMAN CATHOLIC

Alabama

Spring Hill College, Theology Department *Mobile*

California

Applied Theology, School of *Oakland*

Dominican School of Philosophy and Theology *Berkeley*

Franciscan School of Theology *Berkeley*

Jesuit School of Theology at Berkeley *Berkeley*

Loyola Marymount University, Department of Theology *Los Angeles*

Mount St. Mary's College, Graduate Program in Religious Studies *Los Angeles*

St. John's Seminary *Camarillo*

St. John's Seminary College, Program of Theology and Religious Studies *Camarillo*

St. Patrick's Seminary *Menlo Park*

San Diego, University of, Religious Studies Department *San Diego*

San Francisco, University of, Department of Theology and Religious Studies *San Francisco*

Santa Clara, University of, Department of Religious Studies *Santa Clara*

Thomas Aquinas College *Santa Paula*

Colorado

Regis College, Department of Religious Studies *Denver*

St. Thomas Seminary *Denver*

Connecticut

Albertus Magnus College, Department of Religious Studies *New Haven*

Holy Apostles College *Cromwell*

Sacred Heart University, Department of Religious Studies *Bridgeport*

St. Alphonsus College *Suffield*

St. Thomas Seminary, College Formation Program *Bloomfield*

District of Columbia

Catholic University of America, School of Religious Studies *Washington*

Cluster of Independent Theological Schools, c/o De Sales School of Theology *Washington*

De Sales School of Theology *Washington*

Dominican House of Studies *Washington*

Georgetown University, Department of Theology *Washington*

Oblate College *Washington*

Trinity College, Department of Theology *Washington*

Florida

St. John Vianney College Seminary *Miami*

St. Leo College, Division of Philosophy and Theology *St. Leo*

St. Vincent de Paul Regional Seminary, School of Theology *Boynton Beach*

Hawaii

Chaminade University of Honolulu, Department of Religious Studies *Honolulu*

Illinois

Catholic Theological Union *Chicago*

De Paul University, Department of Religious Studies *Chicago*

Illinois Benedictine College, Department of Religious Studies *Lisle*

Lewis University, Religious Studies Department *Romeoville*

St. Mary of the Lake Seminary *Mundelein*

Indiana

Marian College, Theology/Philosophy Department *Indianapolis*

Notre Dame, University of, Department of Theology *Notre Dame*

St. Mary's College, Department of Religious Studies *Notre Dame*

St. Meinrad School of Theology *Saint Meinrad*

Iowa

Divine Word College *Epworth*

Mount Mercy College, Religious Studies Department *Cedar Rapids*

St. Ambrose College, Theology Department *Davenport*

Kansas

Marymount College of Kansas, Department of Religious Studies *Salina*

Kentucky

Spalding University, Programs In Religious Studies - Humanities Department *Louisville*

Louisiana

Loyola University - New Orleans, Department of Religious Studies *New Orleans*

Notre Dame Seminary *New Orleans*

St. Joseph Seminary College *St. Benedict*

Maryland

Loyola College, Department of Theology *Baltimore*

Mount Saint Mary's College, Department of Theology *Emmitsburg*

Notre Dame of Maryland, College of, Religious Studies Department *Baltimore*

St. Mary's Seminary and University *Baltimore*

Washington Theological Union *Silver Spring*

Massachusetts

Boston College, College of Arts and Sciences *Chestnut Hill*

Emmanuel College, Theological Studies Department *Boston*

Merrimack College, Department of Religious Studies *North Andover*

St. Hyacinth College and Seminary *Granby*

St. John's Seminary College *Brighton*

Weston School of Theology *Cambridge*

Michigan

Aquinas College, Department of Religious Studies *Grand Rapids*

Detroit, University of, College of Liberal Arts *Detroit*

Marygrove College, Graduate Studies, Pastoral Ministry *Detroit*

Mercy College of Detroit *Detroit*

Sacred Heart Seminary College *Detroit*

St. John's Provincial Seminary *Plymouth*

St. Mary's College *Orchard Lake*

Siena Heights College *Adrian*

Minnesota

Crosier Seminary Junior College *Onamia*

St. Benedict, College of, Department of Theology *St. Joseph*

St. Catherine, College of, Department of Theology *St. Paul*

St. John's University, School of Theology *Collegeville*

St. Mary's College *Winona*

St. Paul Seminary *St. Paul*

St. Scholastica, College of, Department of Religious Studies *Duluth*

St. Thomas, College of, Graduate Programs in Pastoral Studies *St. Paul*

Missouri

Aquinas Institute of Theology *St. Louis*

Avila College, Department of Religious Studies *Kansas City*

Cardinal Glennon College *St. Louis*

Conception Seminary College, Department of Religion *Conception*

Kenrick Seminary, St. Louis Roman Catholic Theological Seminary *St. Louis*

St. Louis University, Department of Theological Studies *St. Louis*

Montana

Carroll College, Borromeo Pre-Seminary Program *Helena*

New Hampshire

St. Anselm College, Department of Theology *Manchester*

New Jersey

Immaculate Conception Seminary, School of Theology and Pastoral Ministry of Seton Hall University *South Orange*

St. Peter's College, Department of Theology *Jersey City*

Seton Hall University, Department of Religious Studies *South Orange*

New York

Canisius College, Religious Studies Department *Buffalo*

Cathedral College of the Immaculate Conception *Douglaston*

Christ the King Seminary, Graduate School of Theology *East Aurora*

Dominican College *Orangeburg*

Fordham University, Graduate School of Religion and Religious Education *Bronx*

Immaculate Conception, Seminary of the *Huntington*

Manhattan College, Department of Religious Studies *Riverdale*

Maryknoll School of Theology *Maryknoll*

Nazareth College of Rochester *Rochester*

St. Bernard's Institute, Colgate Rochester Divinity School *Rochester*

St. Bonaventure University, Theology Department *St. Bonaventure*

St. Francis College, Religious Studies Department *Brooklyn*

St. John Fisher College, Department of Religious Studies *Rochester*

St. John's University, St. John's College of Liberal Arts and Sciences *Jamaica*

St. Joseph's Seminary, School of Theology *Yonkers*
Wadhams Hall Seminary-College *Ogdensburg*

North Carolina
Belmont Abbey College *Belmont*

Ohio
Athenaeum of Ohio, Mt. St. Mary's Seminary of the West *Cincinnati*
Borromeo College of Ohio *Cleveland*
Dayton, University of, Department of Religious Studies *Dayton*
John Carroll University, Department of Religious Studies *University Heights*
Pontifical College Josephinum, Josephinum School of Theology *Columbus*
St. Mary Seminary *Cleveland*

Oregon
Mount Angel Seminary *St. Benedict*

Pennsylvania
Allentown College of St. Francis de Sales, Department of Theology *Center Valley*
Alvernia College, Theology/Philosophy Department *Reading*
Cabrini College, Department of Religion *Radnor*
Duquesne University, Department of Theology *Pittsburgh*
La Salle University, Graduate Religion Department *Philadelphia*
Mary Immaculate Seminary *Northampton*
Neumann College *Aston*
St. Charles Borromeo Seminary *Philadelphia*
St. Francis College of Pennsylvania, Philosophical and Religious Studies Department *Loretto*
St. Joseph's University, Department of Theology *Philadelphia*
St. Vincent Seminary *Latrobe*

Puerto Rico
Catholic University of Puerto Rico, Theology and Philosophy Department *Ponce*

Rhode Island
Providence College, Department of Religious Studies *Providence*

Texas
Dallas, University of, Department of Theology/Holy Trinity Seminary *Irving*
Oblate School of Theology *San Antonio*
St. Mary's University, Department of Graduate Theology *San Antonio*
St. Thomas, University of, St. Mary's Seminary - School of Theology *Houston*

Vermont
St. Michael's College, Department of Religious Studies *Winooski*
Trinity College, Department of Religious Studies *Burlington*

Washington
Gonzaga University, Department of Religious Studies *Spokane*
St. Michael's Institute, Gonzaga University *Spokane*
Seattle University, Department of Theology and Religious Studies *Seattle*
Seattle University - Institute for Theological Studies *Seattle*

West Virginia
Wheeling College, Department of Theology/Religious Studies *Wheeling*

Wisconsin
Alverno College, Department of Religious Studies *Milwaukee*
Cardinal Stritch College, Religious Studies Department *Milwaukee*
Holy Redeemer College *Waterford*
Marian College, Theology/Philosophy Department *Fond du Lac*
Marquette University, Theology Department *Milwaukee*
Sacred Heart School of Theology *Hales Corners*
St. Francis Seminary, School of Pastoral Ministry *Milwaukee*
Silver Lake College of the Holy Family, Religious Studies Department *Manitowoc*

Nova Scotia
Atlantic School of Theology *Halifax*

Ontario
Dominican College of Philosophy and Theology, Faculty of Theology (Ottawa) and Institute of Pastoral Studies (Montreal) *Ottawa*
Regis College, Department of Theology *Toronto*
St. Augustine's Seminary of Toronto, Faculty of Theology *Scarborough*
St. Michael's College, University of, Faculty of Theology *Toronto*
St. Paul University *Ottawa*

Quebec
Laval University, Faculty of Theology *Quebec*
Montreal, University of, Faculty of Theology *Montreal*

Saskatchewan
St. Thomas More College, Department of Religious Studies *Saskatoon*

SWEDENBORGIAN
Massachusetts
Swedenborg School of Religion *Newton*
Pennsylvania
Academy of the New Church *Bryn Athyn*

UKRAINIAN CATHOLIC
Connecticut
St. Basil College *Stamford*

UNITARIAN UNIVERSALIST ASSOCIATION
California
Starr King School for the Ministry *Berkeley*
Illinois
Meadville/Lombard Theological School *Chicago*

UNITED CHURCH

Manitoba

Winnipeg, University of, Faculty of Theology *Winnipeg*

UNITED CHURCH OF CANADA

Alberta

St. Stephen's College *Edmonton*

British Columbia

Vancouver School of Theology *Vancouver*

Nova Scotia

Atlantic School of Theology *Halifax*

Ontario

Emmanuel College of Victoria University *Toronto*

UNITED CHURCH OF CHRIST

Illinois

Chicago Theological Seminary *Chicago*

Elmhurst College, Department of Theology and Religion *Elmhurst*

Maine

Bangor Theological Seminary *Bangor*

Maryland

Hood College, Department of Philosophy and Religion *Frederick*

Michigan

Olivet College *Olivet*

Minnesota

Carleton College, Department of Religion *Northfield*

United Theological Seminary of the Twin Cities *New Brighton*

Missouri

Drury College, Department of Philosophy and Religion *Springfield*

Eden Theological Seminary *St. Louis*

Montana

Rocky Mountain College *Billings*

Nebraska

Doane College, Philosophy - Religion Department *Crete*

North Carolina

Catawba College *Salisbury*

Elon College, Department of Religion *Elon College*

Ohio

Defiance College, Department of Philosophy, Religion and Christian Education *Defiance*

Pennsylvania

Lancaster Theological Seminary *Lancaster*

Ursinus College, Department of Religion *Collegeville*

Wisconsin

Lakeland College, Humanities Division - Philosophy and Religion Department *Sheboygan*

Ripon College, Department of Religion *Ripon*

WESLEYAN

Indiana

Marion College, Department of Religion/Philosophy *Marion*

New York

Houghton College, Division of **Religion** and Philosophy *Houghton*

Oklahoma

Bartlesville Wesleyan **College,** Division of Religion and Philosophy *Bartlesville*

Pennsylvania

United Wesleyan **College** *Allentown*

South Carolina

Central Wesleyan College, Division of Religion *Central*

WORLDWIDE CHURCH OF GOD

California

Ambassador College *Pasadena*

INSTITUTION INDEX

Belmont Abbey College *Belmont, NC*
Berkeley Divinity School *New Haven, CT*
Berkshire Christian College, Division of Christian Ministries *Lenox, MA*
Bethany Bible College, Division of Biblical Studies and Philosophy *Santa Cruz, CA*
Bethany College, Department of Religious Studies *Bethany, WV*
Bethany Nazarene College, Division of Philosophy and Religion *Bethany, OK*
Bethany Theological Seminary *Oak Brook, IL*
Bethel College, Department of Religion *McKenzie, TN*
Bethel College, Division of Religion and Philosophy *Mishawaka, IN*
Bethel College, Biblical and Theological Studies *St. Paul, MN*
Bethel Theological Seminary *St. Paul, MN*
Bethune-Cookman College, Area of Religion and Philosophy *Daytona Beach, FL*
Beulah Heights Bible College *Atlanta, GA*
Bexley Hall, Colgate Rochester Divinity School *Rochester, NY*
Biola University, Talbot Theological Seminary and School of Theology *La Mirada, CA*
Bishop College *Dallas, TX*
Blue Mountain College, Biblical and Associated Studies *Blue Mountain, MS*
Bob Jones University, School of Religion *Greenville, SC*
Borromeo College of Ohio *Cleveland, OH*
Boston College, College of Arts and Sciences *Chestnut Hill, MA*
Boston Theological Institute *Cambridge, MA*
Boston University, School of Theology *Boston, MA*
Bowdoin College, Department of Religion *Brunswick, ME*
Brandeis University, Lown School of Near Eastern and Judaic Studies *Waltham, MA*
Brandon University, Department of Religion *Brandon, MB*
Brewton-Parker College, Division of Christianity *Mount Vernon, GA*
Bridgewater College, Department of Philosophy and Religion *Bridgewater, VA*
Briercrest Bible College, Bachelor of Religious Education Department *Caronport, SK*
Brigham Young University, Department of Religious Education *Provo, UT*
Brigham Young University - Hawaii Campus *Laie, HI*
Brown University, Department of Religion *Providence, RI*
Bryan College, Division of Biblical Studies and Philosophy *Dayton, TN*
Bucknell University, Department of Religion *Lewisburg, PA*
Buddhist Studies, Institute of *Berkeley, CA*
Butler University, Department of Philosophy and Religious Studies *Indianapolis, IN*
Cabrini College, Department of Religion *Radnor, PA*
Calgary, University of, Department of Religious Studies *Calgary, AB*
California Baptist College, Division of Religion *Riverside, CA*
California Institute of Integral Studies, Philosophy and Religion Department *San Francisco, CA*
California Lutheran College, Department of Religion *Thousand Oaks, CA*
California, University of - Berkeley, Religious Studies *Berkeley, CA*

California, University of - Los Angeles *Los Angeles, CA*
California, University of - Riverside, Department of Religious Studies *Riverside, CA*
Calvary Bible College, Division of Biblical Education *Kansas City, MO*
Calvin Theological Seminary *Grand Rapids, MI*
Campbell University *Buie's Creek, NC*
Camrose Lutheran College, Department of Religious Studies *Camrose, AB*
Canadian Union College, Department of Religious Studies *College Heights, AB*
Canisius College, Religious Studies Department *Buffalo, NY*
Capital Bible Seminary *Lanham, MD*
Capital University, Department of Religion and Philosophy *Columbus, OH*
Cardinal Glennon College *St. Louis, MO*
Cardinal Stritch College, Religious Studies Department *Milwaukee, WI*
Carey Hall Baptist College *Vancouver, BC*
Carleton College, Department of Religion *Northfield, MN*
Carroll College, Borromeo Pre-Seminary Program *Helena, MT*
Carroll College, Department of Religion *Waukesha, WI*
Carson-Newman College, Division of Religious Studies *Jefferson City, TN*
Carthage College, Department of Religion *Kenosha, WI*
Carver Bible Institute and College *Atlanta, GA*
Case Western Reserve University, Department of Religion *Cleveland, OH*
Catawba College *Salisbury, NC*
Cathedral College of the Immaculate Conception *Douglaston, NY*
Catholic Theological Union *Chicago, IL*
Catholic University of America, School of Religious Studies *Washington, DC*
Catholic University of Puerto Rico, Theology and Philosophy Department *Ponce, PR*
Cedarville College, Department of Biblical Education *Cedarville, OH*
Centenary College of Louisiana, Department of Religion *Shreveport, LA*
Central Baptist College *Conway, AR*
Central Baptist Theological Seminary *Kansas City, KS*
Central Bible College *Springfield, MO*
Central College, Department of Philosophy and Religion *Pella, IA*
Central Methodist College, Department of Philosophy and Religion *Fayette, MO*
Central Michigan University, Department of Religion *Mt. Pleasant, MI*
Central Washington University, Religious Studies Program *Ellensburg, WA*
Central Wesleyan College, Division of Religion *Central, SC*
Chaminade University of Honolulu, Department of Religious Studies *Honolulu, HI*
Chapman College, Department of Religion *Orange, CA*
Chicago Cluster of Theological Schools, Jesuit House *Chicago, IL*
Chicago Theological Institute, c/o North Park Theological Seminary *Chicago, IL*
Chicago Theological Seminary *Chicago, IL*
Chicago, University of, Humanities Collegiate Division *Chicago, IL*
Chicago, University of, Divinity School *Chicago, IL*

Christ College Irvine, Religion Division *Irvine, CA*
Christ the King Seminary, Graduate School of Theology *East Aurora, NY*
Christian Heritage College, Department of Ministerial Training *El Cajon, CA*
Christian Theological Seminary *Indianapolis, IN*
Church Divinity School of the Pacific *Berkeley, CA*
Cincinnati Bible College, Cincinnati Bible Seminary: Undergraduate Division *Cincinnati, OH*
Cincinnati Christian Seminary, Graduate Division of Cincinnati Bible Seminary *Cincinnati, OH*
Circleville Bible College *Circleville, OH*
Claflin College, Department of Religion and Philosophy *Orangeburg, SC*
Claremont Graduate School, Department of Religion *Claremont, CA*
Claremont, School of Theology at *Claremont, CA*
Clearwater Christian College, Division of Biblical Studies *Clearwater, FL*
Cleveland State University, Department of Religious Studies *Cleveland, OH*
Cluster of Independent Theological Schools, c/o De Sales School of Theology *Washington, DC*
Colgate Rochester Divinity School *Rochester, NY*
Colgate University, Department of Philosophy and Religion *Hamilton, NY*
Colorado Christian College *Lakewood, CO*
Columbia Bible College *Columbia, SC*
Columbia Christian College, Division of Bible and Religion *Portland, OR*
Columbia Theological Seminary *Decatur, GA*
Columbia Union College *Takoma Park, MD*
Columbia University, Department of Religion *New York, NY*
Conception Seminary College, Department of Religion *Conception, MO*
Concordia College *Ann Arbor, MI*
Concordia College *Bronxville, NY*
Concordia College, Division of Theology and Social Science *Mequon, WI*
Concordia College, Religion Department *Moorhead, MN*
Concordia College *Portland, OR*
Concordia College - St. Paul, Division of Religion *St. Paul, MN*
Concordia Lutheran Seminary *Edmonton, AB*
Concordia Seminary *St. Louis, MO*
Concordia Theological Seminary *Fort Wayne, IN*
Concordia University, Department of Religion and Department of Theological Studies *Montreal, PQ*
Covenant College, Biblical Studies Department *Lookout Mountain, TN*
Covenant Theological Seminary *St. Louis, MO*
Cranmer Seminary *Statesville, NC*
Crosier Seminary Junior College *Onamia, MN*
Crozer Theological Seminary, Colgate Rochester Divinity School *Rochester, NY*
Cumberland College, Department of Religion and Biblical Languages *Williamsburg, KY*
Dakota Wesleyan University, Religion/Philosophy Department *Mitchell, SD*
Dalhousie University, Department of Comparative Religion *Halifax, NS*
Dallas Baptist University, College of Christian Faith and Living *Dallas, TX*
Dallas Christian College *Dallas, TX*
Dallas Theological Seminary *Dallas, TX*

Dallas, University of, Department of Theology/Holy Trinity Seminary *Irving, TX*
Dana College *Blair, NE*
David Lipscomb College, Department of Bible *Nashville, TN*
Davis and Elkins College, Department of Religion and Philosophy *Elkins, WV*
Dayton, University of, Department of Religious Studies *Dayton, OH*
De Paul University, Department of Religious Studies *Chicago, IL*
De Sales School of Theology *Washington, DC*
Defiance College, Department of Philosophy, Religion and Christian Education *Defiance, OH*
Denver Baptist Bible College and Theological Seminary *Broomfield, CO*
Denver Conservative Baptist Seminary *Denver, CO*
Detroit, University of, College of Liberal Arts *Detroit, MI*
Divine Word College *Epworth, IA*
Doane College, Philosophy - Religion Department *Crete, NE*
Dominican College *Orangeburg, NY*
Dominican College of Philosophy and Theology, Faculty of Theology (Ottawa) and Institute of Pastoral Studies (Montreal) *Ottawa, ON*
Dominican House of Studies *Washington, DC*
Dominican School of Philosophy and Theology *Berkeley, CA*
Dr. Martin Luther College *New Ulm, MN*
Drew University, Theological School *Madison, NJ*
Drury College, Department of Philosophy and Religion *Springfield, MO*
Dubuque, University of, Theological Seminary *Dubuque, IA*
Duke University, Trinity College of Arts and Sciences *Durham, NC*
Duke University - Divinity School *Durham, NC*
Duquesne University, Department of Theology *Pittsburgh, PA*
Earlham School of Religion *Richmond, IN*
East Texas Baptist University, Department of Religion *Marshall, TX*
Eastern Baptist Theological Seminary *Philadelphia, PA*
Eastern Christian College *Bel Air, MD*
Eastern College, Religion/Philosophy Department *St. Davids, PA*
Eastern Mennonite College, Bible and Religion Department *Harrisonburg, VA*
Eastern Nazarene College, Division of Religion and Philosophy *Wollaston, MA*
Eastern New Mexico University, Department of Religion *Portales, NM*
Ecumenical Theological Center *Detroit, MI*
Eden Theological Seminary *St. Louis, MO*
Elizabethtown College, Department of Religion and Philosophy *Elizabethtown, PA*
Elmhurst College, Department of Theology and Religion *Elmhurst, IL*
Elon College, Department of Religion *Elon College, NC*
Emmanuel College, Theological Studies Department *Boston, MA*
Emmanuel College, School of Christian Ministries *Franklin Springs, GA*
Emmanuel College of Victoria University *Toronto, ON*
Emmanuel School of Religion *Johnson City, TN*
Emmanuel/St. Chad, College of *Saskatoon, SK*

Institute for Advanced Pastoral Studies *Detroit, MI*

Interdenominational Theological Center *Atlanta, GA*

Iowa Wesleyan College, Department of Religion and Philosophy *Mount Pleasant, IA*

Jackson College of Ministries *Jackson, MS*

Jamestown College, Department of Religion *Jamestown, ND*

Jarvis Christian College, Division of Humanities and Social Science *Hawkins, TX*

Jesuit School of Theology at Berkeley *Berkeley, CA*

Jewish Theological Seminary of America *New York, NY*

John Brown University, Division of Biblical Studies *Siloam Springs, AR*

John Carroll University, Department of Religious Studies *University Heights, OH*

John Wesley College, Division of Biblical Studies *High Point, NC*

Johnson Bible College *Knoxville, TN*

Johnson C. Smith University *Charlotte, NC*

Judaism, University of, Graduate School of Judaica *Los Angeles, CA*

Kalamazoo College *Kalamazoo, MI*

Kansas Wesleyan College, Religion Department *Salina, KS*

Kenrick Seminary, St. Louis Roman Catholic Theological Seminary *St. Louis, MO*

Kentucky Christian College *Grayson, KY*

Kentucky Wesleyan College, Department of Religion and Philosophy *Owensboro, KY*

King College *Bristol, TN*

King's College, Department of Religion *Briarcliff Manor, NY*

Knox College, Department of Religion *Toronto, ON*

La Salle University, Graduate Religion Department *Philadelphia, PA*

Lafayette College, Religion Department *Easton, PA*

Lakeland College, Humanities Division - Philosophy and Religion Department *Sheboygan, WI*

Lambuth College, Department of Religion *Jackson, TN*

Lancaster Bible College *Lancaster, PA*

Lancaster Theological Seminary *Lancaster, PA*

Laval University, Faculty of Theology *Quebec, PQ*

Lee College, Department of Bible and Christian Ministries *Cleveland, TN*

Lenoir-Rhyne College, Department of Religion and Philosophy *Hickory, NC*

LeTourneau College, Division of Biblical Studies and Missions *Longview, TX*

Lewis and Clark College, Religious Studies Department *Portland, OR*

Lewis University, Religious Studies Department *Romeoville, IL*

Lexington Baptist College *Lexington, KY*

Lexington Theological Seminary *Lexington, KY*

Liberty University, (Formerly Liberty Baptist College) *Lynchburg, VA*

L.I.F.E. Bible College *Los Angeles, CA*

Limestone College, Department of Religion *Gaffney, SC*

Lincoln Christian College and Seminary *Lincoln, IL*

Lincoln University, Department of Religion *Lincoln University, PA*

Los Angeles Baptist College *Newhall, CA*

Louisville Presbyterian Theological Seminary *Louisville, KY*

Loyola College, Department of Theology *Baltimore, MD*

Loyola Marymount University, Department of Theology *Los Angeles, CA*

Loyola University - New Orleans, Department of Religious Studies *New Orleans, LA*

Lubbock Christian College, Biblical Studies Division *Lubbock, TX*

Luther College, Department of Religion and Philosophy *Decorah, IA*

Luther Northwestern Theological Seminary *St. Paul, MN*

Lutheran Brethren Schools, Junior Bible College and Seminary *Fergus Falls, MN*

Lutheran School of Theology at Chicago *Chicago, IL*

Lutheran Theological Seminary *Gettysburg, PA*

Lutheran Theological Seminary *Saskatoon, SK*

Lutheran Theological Seminary at Philadelphia *Philadelphia, PA*

Lutheran Theological Southern Seminary *Columbia, SC*

Lynchburg College, Department of Religious Studies *Lynchburg, VA*

Macalester College, Department of Religion *St. Paul, MN*

Malone College, Department of Religion and Philosophy *Canton, OH*

Manhattan College, Department of Religious Studies *Riverdale, NY*

Marian College, Theology/Philosophy Department *Fond du Lac, WI*

Marian College, Theology/Philosophy Department *Indianapolis, IN*

Marietta College, Department of Religion *Marietta, OH*

Marion College, Department of Religion/Philosophy *Marion, IN*

Marquette University, Theology Department *Milwaukee, WI*

Mars Hill College, Department of Religion and Philosophy *Mars Hill, NC*

Mary Hardin-Baylor, University of, Department of Religion *Belton, TX*

Mary Immaculate Seminary *Northampton, PA*

Marygrove College, Graduate Studies, Pastoral Ministry *Detroit, MI*

Maryknoll School of Theology *Maryknoll, NY*

Marymount College of Kansas, Department of Religious Studies *Salina, KS*

Maryville College, Department of Religion and Philosophy *Maryville, TN*

McCormick Theological Seminary *Chicago, IL*

McGill University, Faculty of Religious Studies *Montreal, PQ*

McMaster Divinity College, (McMaster University) *Hamilton, ON*

McMurry College, Department of Religion *Abilene, TX*

Meadville/Lombard Theological School *Chicago, IL*

Memphis Theological Seminary *Memphis, TN*

Mennonite Biblical Seminary, (Associated Mennonite Biblical Seminaries) *Elkhart, IN*

Mennonite Brethren Biblical Seminary *Fresno, CA*

Mercer University, The Roberts Department of Christianity *Macon, GA*

Mercy College of Detroit *Detroit, MI*

Meredith College, Department of Religion and Philosophy *Raleigh, NC*

Merrimack College, Department of Religious Studies *North Andover, MA*

Messiah College, Department of Religion and Philosophy *Grantham, PA*

Piedmont Bible College *Winston-Salem, NC*
Pittsburgh Theological Seminary *Pittsburgh, PA*
Pittsburgh, University of, Department of Religious Studies *Pittsburgh, PA*
Pomona College, Department of Religion *Claremont, CA*
Pontifical College Josephinum, Josephinum School of Theology *Columbus, OH*
Presbyterian College, Department of Religion *Clinton, SC*
Presbyterian School of Christian Education *Richmond, VA*
Princeton Theological Seminary *Princeton, NJ*
Principia College, Humanities Department *Elsah, IL*
Protestant Episcopal Theological Seminary in Virginia *Alexandria, VA*
Providence College, Department of Religious Studies *Providence, RI*
Puget Sound Christian College *Edmonds, WA*
Puget Sound, University of, Department of Religion *Tacoma, WA*
Quebec, University of, at Trois-Rivières, Department of Theology *Trois-Rivières, PQ*
Rabbi Isaac Elchanan Theological Seminary *New York, NY*
Rabbinical College of America *Morristown, NJ*
Randolph-Macon College, Religious Studies Department *Ashland, VA*
Reformed Bible College *Grand Rapids, MI*
Reformed Presbyterian Theological Seminary *Pittsburgh, PA*
Reformed Theological Seminary *Jackson, MS*
Regis College, Department of Religious Studies *Denver, CO*
Regis College, Department of Theology *Toronto, ON*
Rice University, Department of Religious Studies *Houston, TX*
Rio Grande Bible Institute and Language School, Rio Grande Bible Institute *Edinburg, TX*
Ripon College, Department of Religion *Ripon, WI*
Roberts Wesleyan College, Department of Religion and Philosophy *Rochester, NY*
Rochester, University of, Department of Religious and Classical Studies *Rochester, NY*
Rocky Mountain College *Billings, MT*
Rollins College, Department of Philosophy and Religion *Winter Park, FL*
Rutgers, The State University, Department of Religion *New Brunswick, NJ*
Sacred Heart School of Theology *Hales Corners, WI*
Sacred Heart Seminary College *Detroit, MI*
Sacred Heart University, Department of Religious Studies *Bridgeport, CT*
St. Alphonsus College *Suffield, CT*
St. Ambrose College, Theology Department *Davenport, IA*
St. Andrews Presbyterian College *Laurinburg, NC*
St. Anselm College, Department of Theology *Manchester, NH*
St. Augustine's Seminary of Toronto, Faculty of Theology *Scarborough, ON*
St. Basil College *Stamford, CT*
St. Benedict, College of, Department of Theology *St. Joseph, MN*
St. Bernard's Institute, Colgate Rochester Divinity School *Rochester, NY*
St. Bonaventure University, Theology Department *St. Bonaventure, NY*

St. Catherine, College of, Department of Theology *St. Paul, MN*
St. Charles Borromeo Seminary *Philadelphia, PA*
St. Francis College, Religious Studies Department *Brooklyn, NY*
St. Francis College of Pennsylvania, Philosophical and Religious Studies Department *Loretto, PA*
St. Francis Seminary, School of Pastoral Ministry *Milwaukee, WI*
St. Hyacinth College and Seminary *Granby, MA*
St. John Fisher College, Department of Religious Studies *Rochester, NY*
St. John Vianney College Seminary *Miami, FL*
St. John's Provincial Seminary *Plymouth, MI*
St. John's Seminary *Camarillo, CA*
St. John's Seminary College *Brighton, MA*
St. John's Seminary College, Program of Theology and Religious Studies *Camarillo, CA*
St. John's University, School of Theology *Collegeville, MN*
St. John's University, St. John's College of Liberal Arts and Sciences *Jamaica, NY*
St. Joseph Seminary College *St. Benedict, LA*
St. Joseph's Seminary, School of Theology *Yonkers, NY*
St. Joseph's University, Department of Theology *Philadelphia, PA*
St. Leo College, Division of Philosophy and Theology *St. Leo, FL*
St. Louis Christian College *Florissant, MO*
St. Louis University, Department of Theological Studies *St. Louis, MO*
St. Mary of the Lake Seminary *Mundelein, IL*
St. Mary Seminary *Cleveland, OH*
St. Mary's College, Department of Religious Studies *Notre Dame, IN*
St. Mary's College *Orchard Lake, MI*
St. Mary's College *Winona, MN*
St. Mary's Seminary and University *Baltimore, MD*
St. Mary's University, Department of Graduate Theology *San Antonio, TX*
St. Meinrad School of Theology *Saint Meinrad, IN*
St. Michael's College, Department of Religious Studies *Winooski, VT*
St. Michael's College, University of, Faculty of Theology *Toronto, ON*
St. Michael's Institute, Gonzaga University *Spokane, WA*
St. Olaf College, Department of Religion *Northfield, MN*
St. Patrick's Seminary *Menlo Park, CA*
St. Paul Bible College *Bible College, MN*
St. Paul School of Theology *Kansas City, MO*
St. Paul Seminary *St. Paul, MN*
St. Paul University *Ottawa, ON*
St. Peter's College, Department of Theology *Jersey City, NJ*
St. Scholastica, College of, Department of Religious Studies *Duluth, MN*
St. Stephen's College *Edmonton, AB*
St. Thomas, College of, Graduate Programs in Pastoral Studies *St. Paul, MN*
St. Thomas More College, Department of Religious Studies *Saskatoon, SK*
St. Thomas Seminary, College Formation Program *Bloomfield, CT*
St. Thomas Seminary *Denver, CO*
St. Thomas, University of, St. Mary's Seminary -

Upsala College *East Orange, NJ*

Ursinus College, Department of Religion *Collegeville, PA*

Valley Forge Christian College *Phoenixville, PA*

Valparaiso University, Department of Theology *Valparaiso, IN*

Vancouver School of Theology *Vancouver, BC*

Vanderbilt University, The Divinity School *Nashville, TN*

Vermont, University of, College of Arts and Sciences *Burlington, VT*

Virginia Union University, School of Theology *Richmond, VA*

Wadhams Hall Seminary-College *Ogdensburg, NY*

Wake Forest University, Department of Religion *Winston-Salem, NC*

Warner Pacific College, Department of Religion and Christian Ministries *Portland, OR*

Wartburg Theological Seminary *Dubuque, IA*

Washington Bible College, The Bible College and The Capital Bible Seminary *Lanham, MD*

Washington Theological Consortium *Washington, DC*

Washington Theological Union *Silver Spring, MD*

Waterloo Lutheran Seminary, Wilfred Laurier University *Waterloo, ON*

Waterloo, University of, Department of Religious Studies *Waterloo, ON*

Wayland Baptist University, Division of Christian Studies *Plainview, TX*

Wesley College *Florence, MS*

Wesley Theological Seminary *Washington, DC*

Wesleyan College *Macon, GA*

West Coast Christian College *Fresno, CA*

West Virginia Wesleyan College, Department of Religion *Buckhannon, WV*

Western Baptist College, Biblical Studies Division; Christian Ministries Division *Salem, OR*

Western Conservative Baptist Seminary *Portland, OR*

Western Evangelical Seminary *Portland, OR*

Western Michigan University, Department of Religion *Kalamazoo, MI*

Western Theological Seminary *Holland, MI*

Westminster College *Fulton, MO*

Westminster College of Salt Lake City, Philosophy/Religion Program *Salt Lake City, UT*

Westminster Theological Seminary *Philadelphia, PA*

Westmont College, Religious Studies Department *Santa Barbara, CA*

Weston School of Theology *Cambridge, MA*

Wheaton College, Department of Religion *Norton, MA*

Wheeling College, Department of Theology/Religious Studies *Wheeling, WV*

Whittier College, Department of Religion *Whittier, CA*

Wilberforce University, Philosophy and Religion Department *Wilberforce, OH*

Wilfred Laurier University, Department of Religion and Culture *Waterloo, ON*

William Carey College, Department of Biblical Studies and Church Vocations *Hattiesburg, MS*

William Tyndale College, Department of Bible/Theology *Farmington Hills, MI*

Windsor, University of, Department of Religious Studies *Windsor, ON*

Winebrenner Theological Seminary *Findlay, OH*

Winebrenner Theological Seminary - Institute for Biblical Studies *Findlay, OH*

Wingate College, Division of Humanities *Wingate, NC*

Winnipeg, University of, Faculty of Theology *Winnipeg, MB*

Wittenberg University, Department of Religion *Springfield, OH*

Wofford College, Department of Religion *Spartanburg, SC*

Woodcrest College, (Formerly Dallas Bible College) *Lindale, TX*

Wooster, College of, Department of Religious Studies *Wooster, OH*

Wycliffe College *Toronto, ON*

Yale Divinity School, Yale University *New Haven, CT*

Yale University, Department of Religious Studies *New Haven, CT*

Yeshiva University, Bernard Revel Graduate School *New York, NY*